PRINCIPLES OF MEDICA

PRINCIPLES OF MEDICAL LAW

Second Edition

Edited by

ANDREW GRUBB

Training Adjudicator, Immigration Appellate Authority and Visiting Professor, Cardiff Law School; Formerly Professor of Medical Law and Head of Cardiff Law School, Cardiff University

Assisted by

JUDITH LAING

Senior Lecturer, Cardiff Law School
Cardiff University

OXFORD

UNIVERSITY PRESS

OXFORD

UNIVERSITY PRESS

Great Clarendon Street, Oxford OX2 6DP

Oxford University Press is a department of the University of Oxford.
It furthers the University's objective of excellence in research, scholarship,
and education by publishing worldwide in

Oxford New York

Auckland Bangkok Buenos Aires Cape Town Chennai
Dar es Salaam Delhi Hong Kong Istanbul Karachi Kolkata
Kuala Lumpur Madrid Melbourne Mexico City Mumbai Nairobi
São Paulo Shanghai Taipei Tokyo Toronto

Oxford is a registered trade mark of Oxford University Press
in the UK and in certain other countries

Published in the United States
by Oxford University Press Inc., New York

British Library Cataloguing in Publication Data
Data available

Library of Congress Cataloging in Publication Data
Data applied for

ISBN 0–19–926358–2

3 5 7 9 10 8 6 4 2

Typeset in Garamond by
Cambrian Typesetters, Frimley, Surrey

Printed in Great Britain
on acid-free paper by
Antony Rowe Ltd., Chippenham, Wiltshire

EDITOR

Andrew Grubb
Training Adjudicator, Immigration Appellate Authority and
Visiting Professor, Cardiff Law School, Cardiff University

Assisted by
Judith Laing
Senior Lecturer, Cardiff Law School
Cardiff University

CONTRIBUTORS

Bernard Dickens
Professor of Law,
University of Toronto

Michael Freeman
Professor of English Law,
University College London

Christopher Hodges
Partner,
CMS Cameron McKenna

Jonathan Holl-Allen
Barrister,
3 Serjeants' Inn, London

Michael A Jones
Professor of Common Law,
University of Liverpool

Judith Laing
Senior Lecturer, Cardiff Law School,
Cardiff University

Graeme Laurie
Senior Lecturer,
University of Edinburgh

Robert M. Lynn
Cardiff Law School

Jean V. McHale
Professor of Law,
University of Leicester

Sir James Munby
A Judge of the High Court,
Family Division

Christopher Newdick
Reader in Health Law,
Reading University

Mary O'Rourke
Barrister,
3 Serjeants' Inn, London

Harvey Teff
Professor of Law,
University of Durham

Adrian Whitfield QC
Barrister,
3 Serjeants' Inn, London

PREFACE TO THE SECOND EDITION

Over the last twenty years the courts have identified and expounded the common law principles of medical law. Whilst there is always a need to 'tidy up' the law as new problems emerge, the basic structure is probably now settled. The same cannot be said of the regulatory frameworks that apply to health care practitioners, the NHS, and many specific areas of medical practice. Even as I write this preface, Parliament is considering a radical restructuring of the law relating to the removal, retention, and disposal of human tissue in the Human Tissue Bill. Staying ahead of the primary and secondary legislation in the last few years has not just been about 'surfing the net' for the latest offering from Parliament but sometimes has felt more like surfing a tsunami such has been the outpouring! Since the last edition, medical lawyers have had to come to terms with the complexities of the Health Act 1999, the Health and Social Care Act 2001 and, most recently, the Health and Social Care (Health and Community Standards) Act 2003. There is also a growing divide between the configurations of the NHS within the UK as the National Assembly for Wales seeks to shape the structure to meet Welsh needs through NHS Cymru.

This new edition of *Principles* seeks to provide a thoughtful and comprehensive analysis of the common law and statutory provisions pertaining to health care provision in England and Wales. Each of the chapters has been fully updated to take account of judicial and legislative developments since the last edition. Some chapters have been re-written, for example, dealing with the regulation of health care professionals, confidentiality and data protection, and research. New chapters have been added dealing with the regulation of medicinal products and devices and patenting and the human body. The impact of the Human Rights Act 1998 on medical law has not (yet) been as pervasive as some had anticipated, apart from the field of mental health. Nevertheless, important human rights issues do arise and these have been addressed in the context of each chapter's subject matter as relevant, rather than in an artificial way in a discrete 'human rights' chapter. For the present, there is no chapter on mental health law. Even with the Government's 'on–off' attitude to new mental health and incapacity legislation, it was felt prudent to await such developments which do seem likely in the near future.

There are a number of new contributors to this edition and a few who contributed to the first edition who were not able to be involved in this edition. I welcome the former and express my gratitude to the latter for their earlier work. Most prominent

amongst the latter is my long time friend and colleague, Professor Sir Ian Kennedy. His new career as Chair of the Commission for Healthcare Audit and Inspection prevented him contributing to this edition. We have worked together on many writing projects over more than twenty years. I know of no-one with a sharper intellect or quickness of mind and the ability to strip down the most complex legal issue to bare principle. I have learnt so much from him over the years. In this edition, I have taken over editing the bulk of his material and, without in any way being able to emulate him, my familiarity with the way he thinks and his writing style, has, I hope, allowed me at least to imitate him when adding the new material. His absence from this edition remains, however, a considerable loss.

In preparing the new edition I have been immeasurably helped by my colleague, Judy Laing, who, in addition to writing a new chapter with me, has thrown herself into the work of assisting me in the organisation and editing of this edition. I thank her for the substantial contribution that she has made and for her support when the strain of preparing the new edition began to tell. I would also like to thank Jess Gardiner and Ryan Morgan, two former research assistants who helped collate material for the new edition.

The law is stated at 1 September 2003, although one or two later developments have been incorporated where possible.

Andrew Grubb
New Year's Day 2004

CONTENTS—SUMMARY

CONTENTS

I THE HEALTH CARE SYSTEM

1. The Organisation of Health Care

2. Regulating Health Care Professions

II CONSENT TO TREATMENT

3. Consent to Treatment: The Competent Patient

4. Consent to Treatment: Children and the Incompetent Patient

III MEDICAL NEGLIGENCE

5. Duties in Contract and Tort

6. Breach of Duty

IV SPECIFIC ISSUES

9. Confidentiality and Data Protection

10. Medically Assisted Reproduction

11. Abortion

15. Products Liability

Contents

TABLE OF CASES

TABLE OF LEGISLATION

TABLE OF STATUTORY INSTRUMENTS

TABLE OF LEGISLATION FROM OTHER JURISDICTIONS

PART I

THE HEALTH CARE SYSTEM

1

THE ORGANISATION OF HEALTH CARE

Chapter 1 considers the organisation of the National Health Service (NHS) by examining (A) the structure of the NHS, (B) judicial review of matters of NHS resource allocation, and (C) the new NHS governance which has been so influenced by Professor Sir Ian Kennedy's report, *Learning from Bristol*.[1]   **1.01**

A. Structure of the NHS

Section A of Chapter 1 describes the major institutions of the NHS and their relationship with one another. It considers: (1) its macro-structure and the duties of the Secretary of State and Special Health Authorities, (2) its meso-structure and the duties of strategic health authorities, primary care trusts, and care trusts, and (3) its micro-structure and the duties of general practitioners (GPs), NHS Trust hospitals and private providers.[2]   **1.02**

---

[1] *Learning from Bristol—The Report of the Public Inquiry into Childrens' Heart Surgery at the Bristol Royal Infirmary 1984–1995* (Cm 5207, 2001). See also *The Department of Health's Response to the Bristol Inquiry* (Cm 5363, 2002) which accepts much of the Inquiry's analysis.

[2] This chapter considers the structure of the NHS in England. Structures in Scotland and Wales are based on the same model, although specific functions may be performed by different statutory authorities, which will be noted in brief.

1.03   The modern structure and organisation of the NHS has been profoundly affected by *Learning from Bristol* and the conviction for murder of Harold Shipman. Until recently, government was content to delegate discretion to local health authorities. In practice, particularly before the introduction of the 'internal market' for health care in 1992, this meant that managerial power in the NHS was dominated by the medical profession. Supervision of clinical standards was available to the General Medical Council[3] and clinical audits undertaken locally in hospitals, but the system tended to be reactive, in the sense that it was motivated by concerns as to the performance of individuals after the event. There was no supervision of standards in the system as a whole, and no means by which performance in one place could be reliably compared with that of another. *Learning from Bristol* says: 'We cannot say that the external system for assuring and monitoring the quality of care was inadequate. There was, in truth, no such system.'[4] The report remarks:

> In the decades after the establishment of the NHS (in fact right up until the late 1980s) central government, through the Department of Health . . . interpreted its responsibility for the NHS largely in terms of planning and allocating resources. It did not see itself as being responsible for, and thus accountable for, the quality of clinical care, either in terms of setting standards or of monitoring clinical perform-ance. Quality was regarded by government as a matter for individual health care professionals. For their part, health care professionals, particularly hospital doctors, had deeply embedded in their culture the notion of professional autonomy, often expressed in the form of 'clinical freedom'.[5]

1.04   With the benefit of hindsight, such regulatory and managerial passivity through-out the NHS is striking. The Labour government of 1997 committed itself to cre-ating new systems of NHS governance in health care,[6] both in respect of the clinical care given to patients and the *corporate* regulation of the NHS as an insti-tution. This is the background against which the discussion in this chapter should be understood and it explains the creation of a large number of new regulatory bodies with powers to audit and supervise the NHS and the medical profession.

We now examine the rights and obligations arising within the structure of the NHS. Before doing so, however, note that the NHS has been subjected to 18 rounds of reorganisation and reform since 1982.[7] Fund-holding GPs have come

---

[3] Allsop, J and Mulcahy, L, *Regulating Medical Work, Formal and Informal Controls* (Open University Press, 1996). The Medical (Professional Performance) Act 1995 amends the Medical Act 1983 to provide for the retraining of doctors.

[4] *Learning from Bristol* (n 1 above), 6, para 30 and 192, para 21. The report also says of the Department of Health: 'it [had] a role in which the factors which were set out and monitored were focused on finance and the volume of patients treated. The quality and performance of clinical ser-vices were regarded as matter for the local hospital or health service, not the DoH' (186–87).

[5] *Learning from Bristol* (n 1 above), 303, para 2.

[6] Walshe, K, 'The Rise of Regulation in the NHS' (2002) 324 BMJ 967.

[7] Walshe, K, 'Foundation Hospitals—a New Direction for NHS Reform?' (2003) 96 Journal of the Royal Society of Medicine 106.

and gone. The internal market has come, gone and returned again under a different cloak. Personal Medical Services and the Private Finance Initiative are becoming established. District Health Authorities and Family Health Service Authorities were replaced by Health Authorities, which have themselves been replaced by Primary Care Trusts (PCTs). (The term 'health authority' is used to refer generically to this intermediate body). With such rapid pace of change, it is remarkable that, other than via expensive on-line data retrieval systems, the regulations governing the NHS have not been consolidated since 1977. Successive NHS Acts have deleted, inserted, amended and substituted large tracts of the 1977 Act, and, indeed, almost every amendment Act that has followed it. Consequently, for practical purposes, other than via on-line services paid for by large subscriptions, the rights and duties which arise in connection with the NHS are simply inaccessible.

In an area of such sensitivity, which occupies such a high political profile, this is a very poor reflection on the commitment of government claiming to support an open and transparent system of regulation.[8] **1.05**

1. Macro-Structure—Duties of Secretary of State and Special Health Authorities

A number of general statutory duties are imposed on the Secretary of State, the most broad-ranging of which is contained in ss 1 and 3 of the National Health Service Act 1977.[9] Section 1 provides: **1.06**

> (1) It is the Secretary of State's duty to continue the promotion in England and Wales of a comprehensive health service designed to secure improvement (a) in the physical and mental health of the people of those countries, and (b) in the prevention, diagnosis and treatment of illness, and for that purpose to provide or secure the effective provision of services in accordance with this Act.
> (2) The services so provided shall be free of charge except in so far as the making and recovery of charges is expressly provided for by or under any enactment, whenever passed.

In addition, s 3 provides that **1.07**

> it is the Secretary of State's duty to provide . . . to such extent as he considers necessary to meet all reasonable requirements:
>
> (a) hospital accommodation;
> (b) other accommodation for the purpose of any service specified under this Act;
> (c) medical, dental, nursing and ambulance services;
> (d) such other facilities for the care of expectant and nursing mothers and young children as he considers are appropriate as part of the health service;

---

[8] The benefit to the patient of these changes has been doubted. Indeed, some say that they tend to destabilise and interrupt the provision of services in the system. Warner, M, *Re-designing health services; reducing the zone of delusion* (Nuffield Trusts, 1997).

[9] And see the National Health Service (Scotland) Act 1978, s 1.

(e) such facilities for the prevention of illness, the care of persons suffering from illness and the after-care of persons who have suffered from illness as he considers appropriate as part of the health service; [and]

(f) such other services as are required for the diagnosis and treatment of illness.

1.08 It is the duty of the Secretary of State to pay to each Strategic Health Authority 'sums not exceeding the amount allotted [to it] by the Secretary of State',[10] and to pay to each PCT sums equivalent to their general 'Pt 2' expenditure (generally connected with the provision of primary care), and sums not exceeding the amount allotted to it toward meeting its 'main' (or Pt 1) expenditure in that year (generally connected with the provision of hospital and community health services).[11] Primary care expenditure arising under 'Pt 2' of the National Health Service Act 1977 Act is not cash-limited.[12] Until recently, the distribution of NHS resources to health authorities was calculated with reference to a weighted capitation formula[13] which assessed health needs according to: (i) the projected size of the population concerned, (ii) the numbers of elderly people in the population, (iii) the health needs of the population, distinguishing between general, acute and psychiatric care and morbidity and mortality ratios, and (iv) an allowance to allow for local market forces with respect to the cost of labour and the higher costs of the Thames Regions. Now, however, an element of 'performance funding' has been included in the resource allocation mechanism so that additional sums of money may be allocated dependent on the achievement of projects, objectives and targets.[14]

1.09 Under the National Health Service Reform and Health Care Professions Act 2002, one of the factors that may be taken into account in assessing overall annual allocations to PCTs is the trust's Pt 2 expenditure.[15] Thus, the incentive to meet

---

[10] National Health Service Act 1977, s 97 amended by National Health Service Reform and Health Care Professions Act 2002, s 7.

[11] National Health Service Act 1977, s 97C(1) substituted by National Health Service Reform and Health Care Professions Act 2002, s 8.

[12] See eg *Explanatory Notes to Health and Social Care Act 2002* (TSO, 2001), para 23. By contrast, secondary (hospital) care and NHS care provided in the community ('hospital and community health services') are governed by Pt 1 of the 1977 Act. These services are usually provided by NHS Trust hospitals. The funding of this aspect of the NHS is subject to the constraints of the sums available to NHS 'commissioners' of hospital care. Within a fixed PCT budget, any unplanned expansion of GP expenditure under Pt 2 of the Act will necessarily be at the expense of hospital expenditure under Pt 1. For this reason, GPs occupy a sensitive position in the structure of the NHS.

[13] See *Hospital and Community Health Services Resource Allocation: Weighted Capitation Formula* (NHS Executive, 1994).

[14] See para 1.34 below in connection with NHS Trust hospitals. The use of 'incentive payments' is one of the perennial problems of the NHS, in particular, for their potential to divert clinical attention away from patient need and toward the rewards available for not providing treatment. See Orentlicher, D, 'Paying Physicians More to do Less: Financial Incentives to Limit Care' (1996) 30 U of Richmond L Rev 155.

[15] National Health Service Act 1977, s 97C substituted by National Health Service Reform and Health Care Professions Act 2002, s 8.

the objective is that overall allocations to the PCT will be increased if it does so. Similar incentives to improve performance in NHS Trust hospitals have been created by use of the 'star-rating' system, in which additional funds and freedoms are accorded to hospitals with three star ratings. Thus:

> Where the Secretary of State has made an initial determination of the amount ('the initial amount') to be allotted for any year to a Primary Care Trust . . . he may increase the initial amount by a further sum if it appears to him that over a period notified to the Trust (a) it satisfied any objectives notified to it as objectives to be met in performing its functions; or (b) it performed well against any criteria notified to it as criteria relevant to the satisfactory performance of its functions (whether or not the method of measuring its performance against those criteria was also notified to it).[16]

The circumstances in which the formula for allocating funds to health authorities could be successfully challenged are limited. An analogous issue arose concerning expenditure guidance issued by the Secretary of State for the Environment to local authorities, which was challenged for being *Wednesbury* unreasonable, ie so unreasonable that no reasonable person addressing himself to the issue in question could have come to such a decision. Lord Scarman dealt with the claim as follows:

1.10

> We are in the field of public financial administration and we are being asked to review the exercise by the Secretary of State of an administrative discretion which inevitably requires political judgment on his part . . . I cannot accept that it is constitutionally appropriate, save in very exceptional circumstances, for the courts to intervene on the ground of 'unreasonableness' to quash guidance framed by the Secretary of State and by necessary implication approved by the House of Commons, the guidance being concerned with the limits of public expenditure by local authorities and the incidence of the tax burden as between taxpayers and ratepayers . . . these are matters of political judgment for him and for the House of Commons. They are not matters for the judges . . .[17]

In the circumstances of the case, His Lordship refused to examine the detail of the guidance or to assess the impact of its consequences. Equally, the Audit Commission has suggested that performance rating systems are far from perfect and are capable of concentrating on some indicia at the expense of others and giving an inaccurate picture of overall quality. Thus, some 'three star' trusts were judged by auditors to be performing poorly and as having management shortcomings, while others rated weak under the star system performed well.[18] An incentive system which systematically rewarded trusts which were performing

---

[16] National Health Service Act 1977, s 97C(3) inserted by National Health Service Reform and Health Care Professions Act 2002, s 8. And the sum may be reduced again subsequently by an amount not exceeding 'the initial amount', see s 97C(6).

[17] *R v Secretary of State for the Environment, ex p Nottinghamshire County Council* [1986] AC 240, 247. And see the consideration of the case in *R v Secretary of State for the Environment, ex p Hammersmith and Fulham London Borough Council* [1991] 1 AC 521.

[18] *Achieving the NHS Plan* (Audit Commission, 2003), paras 41 and 42.

poorly by failing to measure meaningful criteria would be amenable to challenge by way of judicial review for unreasonableness.

(i) To Whom is the Duty Owed?

1.11 The duty to promote a comprehensive health service is owed to the people of England and Wales who are 'ordinarily resident' in Great Britain, their spouse and children.[19] What is the position with respect to overseas visitors to the United Kingdom? Subject to exceptions, 'where an Authority provides an overseas visitor with services forming part of the health service, that Authority . . . shall make and recover from the person liable . . . charges for the provision of those services'.[20] This responsibility to recover the costs of the care provided is expressed as a duty, rather than a discretion. However, there are a number of exemptions. First, a number of specified services are exempted from charge, for example, accident and emergency care, treatment for notifiable diseases, sexually transmitted diseases and treatment under the Mental Health Act 1983.[21] Also, a number of categories of overseas visitor is exempted, for example, persons who have been ordinarily resident in the United Kingdom for not less than one year immediately preceding the time when the service is provided, those applying for, or who have refugee status, those engaged in employment, those detained in prison under the Prison Act 1952, or those whose services are provided under reciprocal arrangements between the United Kingdom and an overseas country.[22]

1.12 Patients treated as overseas visitors are not to be confused with private patients. The responsible doctor may not charge a fee for treatment unless the patient wishes to be treated under a private contract (say a contract of insurance). Those treated as overseas visitors may be asked to sign an undertaking to pay and should be treated with the same urgency and priority as NHS patients. Guidance suggests that if clinical attention is required without delay, then treatment must always take priority over enquiries into the patient's ability to pay NHS charges. The sum charged is subject to local discretion and should be assessed on a suitable commercial basis. Hospitals should provide a detailed overseas visitor tariff and may consider requiring payment in full prior to treatment where appropriate. Where the patient requires immediate treatment and prior payment is not possible, it is suggested that 'the NHS hospital should provide such treatment as is clinically required to stabilise the patient sufficiently to allow them to return safely to their

---

[19] National Health Service Act 1977, s 121, as amended by the Health and Medicines Act 1988, s 7.
[20] National Health Service (Charges to Overseas Visitors) Regulations 1989, SI 1989/306, as amended, reg 2(1).
[21] ibid, reg 3.
[22] ibid, reg 4.

country of residence for continuing care'.[23] Thereafter, efforts should be made to recover the costs of the urgent treatment provided. However, the difficult question as to what is to become of those with life-threatening conditions who have no overseas insurance cover, or who come from countries with health care systems that cannot respond to their needs, is not considered.

The matter was considered by the European Court of Human Rights in *D v UK*,[24] **1.13** in which the applicant had obtained a visitor's visa but was detained on arrival in England on suspicion of smuggling drugs. He was convicted to a term of imprisonment. During that time, he was discovered to be suffering from AIDS and was treated, in accordance with the regulations, as an NHS patient. On the completion of his sentence, the Secretary of State ordered his deportation from the United Kingdom The applicant resisted under the provisions of Article 3 of the European Convention on Human Rights. His country of residence was St Kitts in the West Indies which could not provide him with the care that he needed. In finding for the applicant, the Court confirmed that, as a general rule, nation states had no obligation to provide care for 'aliens' who had no right to receive such treatment under domestic law. Nevertheless, in the extreme circumstances of this case, in which care had commenced within the United Kingdom, it would have been inhuman and degrading to return a man in the terminal stages of an illness to a country which had no facilities to provide adequate medical and palliative care. Is it crucial that treatment for the illness had commenced within the United Kingdom when the applicant was an 'NHS patient'? If not, will it apply, for example, to those in the process of seeking asylum and illegal immigrants pending their hearing, or deportation?[25]

The government is consulting on reforming Overseas Visitors regulations, which, **1.14** it believes, are inconsistently implemented and used in ways that were not contemplated when they were originally introduced.[26]

2. Meso-Structure—Managing the NHS

In the middle-tier of the NHS, lying between the Secretary of State and the doc- **1.15** tor–patient relationship, we consider (i) the delegation of the Secretary of State's duties, (ii) Strategic Health Authorities, (iii) Primary Care Trusts, and (iv) Care Trusts.[27]

---

[23] See *NHSiS Manual of Guidance: Overseas Visitors* (The Scottish Office), ch 3, para 8.

[24] (1998) 42 EHRR 149.

[25] See, eg, *Anufrijeva (as personal representative of the estate of Kujeva) v Southwark London Borough Council* [2002] All ER (D) 37.

[26] *Proposed Amendments to the National Health Services (Charges to Overseas Visitors) Regulations 1989—a Consultation* (Department of Health, 2003).

[27] Note the general duty imposed on strategic health authorities, PCTs and NHS Trusts to co-operate with one another in exercising their functions: Health Act 1999, s 26.

(i) Delegation of Secretary of State's duties

1.16   Performance of the duties imposed upon the Secretary of State[28] under the 1977
Act is delegated to strategic health authorities, special health authorities and PCTs
by regulations,[29] directions and circulars.[30] Regulations clearly have statutory
effect, but the NHS is also heavily influenced by Secretary of State's 'directions' and
Departmental 'circulars'. What is the distinction between directions and circulars?

1.17   Directions have mandatory effect. By contrast, circulars remain at the discretion
of those to whom they are addressed. Section 17 of the National Health Service
Act 1977 empowers the Secretary of State to give directions to health authorities,
special health authorities, PCTs and NHS Trusts, and '[a]ny person or body to
whom directions are given in pursuance of any provision of this Act or Pt 1 of
the National Health Service and Community Care Act 1990 shall comply with the
directions'.[31] Of course, any such ministerial direction must remain within the
statutory and common law framework which surrounds the NHS.[32] Such directions are often published in a form which resembles a statutory instrument.
However, directions 'do not have to be given in any particular form. It must be
made clear that funds have to be used in a particular manner. There is no magic
form of words that is required and I do not think that the use of the word "direct"
is necessary in order to constitute a "direction".'[33] Thus, directions may appear in
the form of an NHS circular. The difference between statutory directions and
mere guidance was considered in *R v North Derbyshire HA, ex p Fisher*[34] with respect to *New Drugs for Multiple Sclerosis* EL (95)97. The Secretary of State issued
an executive letter (an NHS circular) concerning the availability of the drug beta
interferon to treat multiple sclerosis. It included the following statements:

---

[28] In Wales, much of the authority of the Secretary of State in England is delegated to the
National Assembly for Wales, see National Health Service Reform and Health Care Professions Act
2002, ss 6 and 9.

[29]   Primary Care Trusts (Functions) (England) Regulations 2000, SI 2000/695.

[30]   National Health Service Act 1977, ss 16D–18 (inserted by Health Act 1999, s 12 as amended
by National Health Service Reform and Health Care Professions Act 2002, Sch 1) and Primary Care
Trusts (Functions) Directions 2000.

[31]   National Health Service Act 1977, s 126(3C) (inserted by Health Act 1999, s 65 and Sch 4,
para 37(5)).

[32]   Any contradiction between the two must be resolved in favour of the statute. In reviewing this
matter, the court must 'begin by examining the nature of the statutory power which the administrative authority . . . has purported to exercise and asking, in the light of that examination, what
were, and were not, relevant considerations for the authority to take into account in deciding to exercise its power', *per* Lord Bridge in *Gillick v West Norfolk and Wisbech AHA* [1985] 3 All ER 402,
426. The question may be far from straightforward, as the disagreement between the Court of
Appeal and House of Lords in *Gillick* demonstrates.

[33]   *R v Secretary of State for Health, ex p Manchester Local Medical Committee* 25 BMLR 77, 89, *per*
Collins J.

[34]   [1997] 8 Med LR 327. See also *R. v Secretary of State for Health, ex p Manchester Local Medical
Committee* 25 BMLR 77, 89, *per* Collins J.

7. Key aims . . . are to: target the drug appropriately at patients who are most likely to benefit from treatment . . . 9. Purchasing authorities and providers are asked . . . to develop and implement a prescribing approach for Beta Interferon through hospitals . . . 10 . . . providers are asked to give sympathetic consideration to such GP referrals, taking into account local priorities.[35]

The question arose as to the duty of the health authority to comply with the executive letter and as to whether it constituted a direction, or mere guidance in the form of an NHS circular. Dyson J considered the distinction as follows. He said:

The difference between a policy which provides mere guidance and one in which the health authority is obliged to implement is crucial. Policy which is in the form of guidance can be expressed in strong terms and yet fall short of amounting to direction. There is no reference in the circular to the word 'directions' and read as a whole there is no indication that the circular is intended to trigger the statutory duty of compliance to be found in . . . the 1977 Act. The circular includes words such as 'asks', 'suggested', 'taking into account', it does not include the word 'shall' or any of the other badges of mandatory requirement.

. . . If the circular provided no more than guidance, albeit in strong terms, then the only duty placed upon the health authority was to take it into account in the discharge of their functions. That would be susceptible to challenge only on *Wednesbury* principles if they failed to consider the circular, or they misconstrued or misapplied it whether deliberately or negligently.[36]

Thus, His Lordship rejected the claim that the circular mandated any action on behalf of the health authority, which was at liberty to depart from it in the circumstances described. (Note however, that the application was successful on the ground that the authority had failed to give proper consideration to the circular, which we discuss at para 1.87 below.)[37]

(ii) Strategic Health Authorities

In England, the 2002 round of NHS reorganisation created about 30 Strategic Health Authorities to replace around 100 'health authorities'.[38] Strategic Health   **1.18**

---

[35] ibid, 330 (col 2)–331 (col 1).

[36] ibid, 331 (col 2).

[37] Generally, duties of this nature do not create rights enforceable by individuals. Note, however, that if such measures create a legitimate expectation that certain rights will be conferred, they may succeed in doing so. Rights arising in this way have been explained as follows: 'If a public body has made a representation to a specific individual or group of individuals that a particular policy will be followed, or that they will be informed before such a change of policy takes place, then the individual will be entitled to insist that the policy is pursued in relation to the instant case, provided the implementation of the policy does not conflict with the authority's statutory duty.' See Craig P, *Administrative Law* (3rd edn, Sweet & Maxwell, 1994) 395 and *Council for Civil Service Unions v Minister for the Civil Service* [1985] 1 AC 374, 408 *per* Lord Diplock. See also *R v Devon County Council, ex p Barker* [1995] 1 All ER 73, 91 *per* Simon Brown LJ.

[38] National Health Service Act 1977, s 8 substituted by National Health Service Reform and Health Care Professions Act 2002, s 8. Equivalent functions are performed by Health Boards in

Authorities are accountable to the Secretary of State, will agree performance targets with the Department of Health, and monitor and guide PCTs and NHS Trusts. In doing so, they should create a strategy for improving quality through clinical governance and support mechanisms for involving patients, the public and other interested parties in developing and implementing plans. They will also monitor the extent to which PCTs and NHS Trusts comply with the recommendations and guidance of the Commission for Health Improvement, the National Clinical Assessment Authority, and other statutory authorities.[39] This policy, announced in *Shifting the Balance of Power*, purports to devolve decision-making power to local communities because 'improvements to services can only be delivered by front line staff working with patients and the public . . .'.[40] At the same time, however, following the deaths of children in the Bristol Royal Infirmary, government has established a large number of regulatory and supervisory bodies to set standards, monitor, supervise and hold accountable local decision-makers in matters of clinical and corporate governance. In reality, therefore, the phrase 'shifting the balance of power' is misleading. The balance of power has shifted to intermediate regulators with ultimate powers to refer matters to the Secretary of State. Some say there is a danger that so much regulation and control will generate passive, unimaginative, entirely reactive, and defensive management styles more concerned to achieve a handful of pre-selected targets than to improve standards generally in the local health community.[41]

(iii) Primary Care Trusts

1.19 The NHS imposes a duty on the Secretary of State to create PCTs[42] and over 300 such bodies have been established to assume many of the responsibilities previously performed by the old 'health authorities'. They are the 'purchasers', or 'commissioners' of medical, dental, pharmaceutical, and optical NHS care for their local communities. Thus, they must assess local health needs and develop plans for improving standards whilst meeting national targets. In doing so, they will consult with clinical staff, patients and local people. PCTs will also co-operate with the responsible Strategic Health Authority and (with respect to long-term

---

Scotland and in Wales by Local Health Boards, see National Health Service Reform and Health Care Professions Act 2002, s 6.

[39] See generally, *Shifting the Balance of Power within the NHS—Securing Delivery* (Department of Health, 2002), para 26-35 and annex A.

[40] ibid, para 10.

[41] See Hunter, D. *Things Can Only Get Better—A Commentary on Implementing the NHS Plan* (Durham Business School, 2001).

[42] National Health Service Act 1977, s 16A(1) (substituted by National Health Service Reform and Health Care Professions Act 2002, s 3). These functions are performed by Health Boards in Scotland. In Wales, Local Health Boards are responsible at this 'meso-level', see National Health Service Reform and Health Care Professions Act 2002, s 6 and McCann, S, 'Permissive Powers are Good for the Health: The Health Reforms in Wales' (2002) Wales LJ 176.

care) local authorities and are responsible to the Secretary of State through the Strategic Health Authority. PCTs are responsible for managing and regulating the services provided by GPs, dentists, pharmacists and opticians under their Terms of Service.[43] The duty to make arrangements for primary care is imposed on PCTs. Primary care is provided by GPs who are normally engaged as independent contractors to the NHS and are regulated principally under statutory regulations, the General Medical Services Regulations (separate regulations exist for dentists, pharmacists and opticians), or Personal Medical Services directions.

PCTs are subject to strict financial regulation. In particular: 'It is the duty of every **1.20** Primary Care Trust, in respect of each financial year, to perform its functions so as to secure that the expenditure of the trust which is attributable to the performance by the trust of its functions in that year do not exceed [its income].'[44] A variety of pressures may be imposed upon chief executive officers and directors of PCTs to encourage adherence to this duty. The ultimate sanction is for PCT officers to be suspended, or removed from their posts, or to be made subject to directions.[45] Given the increased role of the Department of Health, the National Institute for Clinical Excellence (NICE), National Service Frameworks and other guidance, achieving local and national objectives and remaining within a fixed financial allocation becomes increasingly difficult.

The creation of 300 PCTs tends to intensify the problems associated with 'post- **1.21** code rationing' in which access to health services throughout the country varies according to the policy and practice of each PCT. If this was a matter of concern in respect of 100 health authorities (which preceded PCTs), how much more pressing is it now? In addition, the sub-division of management of the NHS into relatively small groups of patients (around 100,000 patients per PCT) creates difficulties in connection with the planning of specialist services. This problem was raised in relation to cystic fibrosis patients and neonatal intensive care in 1993.[46] These illnesses present the NHS with a demand for high-cost, low-volume specialist care. Unless it is already provided, many PCTs may decide not to make special arrangements in this area of care because significant investment in facilities is not justified given the unpredictable nature of the demand. Instead, PCTs will be expected to form consortia of specialist centres within a region of the country to which patients should be sent. With the increased number of PCTs, the attention being devoted to new systems of NHS governance, and the vast number of relatively uncommon illnesses for which consortia would need to be arranged, one

---

[43] See generally, *Shifting the Balance of Power within the NHS—Securing Delivery* (Department of Health, 2002), para 13-22 and annex A.

[44] National Health Service Act 1977, s 97D inserted by Health Act 1999, s 3.

[45] National Health Service Act 1977, s 84. New 'intervention orders' were added to the powers by Health and Social Care Act 2001, s 13.

[46] See *Cystic Fibrosis* and *Neonatal Intensive Care* (Clinical Standards Advisory Group, 1993).

would not be surprised to find some areas of care, in some parts of the country, in which some categories of illness were offered inadequate treatment.

1.22   The exact nature of the relationship between Strategic Health Authorities and PCTs is unclear. Strategic Health Authorities are likely to be heavily influenced by central forces and will seek to promote the Department of Health's agenda. By contrast, PCTs are created with independent discretion and should seek to promote the interests of the local community. As we have seen, PCTs are bound to adhere to 'directions' issued by the Secretary of State. On the other hand, the various other guidance, circulars, targets, benchmarks, performance indicators and so on are generally discretionary, not mandatory.

(iv) Care Trusts

1.23   Care trusts have been created as a means of co-ordinating the functions of the various components of the welfare state. They are intended to enable a single organisation to undertake functions that would otherwise be the responsibility of agencies within the NHS and local authority social services departments, eg care of the elderly, those suffering mental health problems, and those needing a variety of services crossing acute, intermediate and social care. Care trusts are formed from NHS Trusts or PCTs and local government either by their mutual agreement,[47] or by the direction of the Secretary of State where he is of the opinion that either the NHS body or the local authority is failing to provide adequate services.[48] The model on which co-operation should take place is not prescribed and may involve the commissioning of specific services, or their management. Approval of care trusts will depend on a persuasive case supporting their need, and the manner in which they will perform and be held accountable for their responsibilities. This will involve details of the level of resources to be transferred to them, their targets and objectives, and the way in which they will deal with overspends and underspends.

1.24   This approach expands upon previous encouragement given to local authorities and health bodies to enter 'pooled funding' agreements contained in s 31 of the Health Act 1999. However, any arrangements whereby the functions of NHS bodies are performed by local authorities, and vice versa, do not disturb the statutory responsibility on whomever the function is originally imposed.[49] This principle of delegation, rather than transfer of authority, is also retained in relation to care trusts.[50]

---

[47] Health and Social Care Act 2001, s 45. See also the Care Trusts (Application and Consultation) Regulations 2001, SI 2001/3788.
[48] Health and Social Care Act 2001, s 46.
[49] See Health Act 1999, s 31(5).
[50] See Health and Social Care Act 2001, ss 45(11) and 46(5).

3. Micro-Structure—Providing NHS Services

We now turn to the organisation of the NHS in so far as it concerns contact be- **1.25**
tween doctors and their patients. The *micro*-structure of the NHS, involving
arrangements involving doctor and patient concerns (i) GP services, (ii) NHS
Trust hospitals, (iii) NHS 'Contracts' between NHS Trust Hospitals and PCTs,
and (iv) the provision of NHS care by non-NHS providers.

(i) GP Services

The statutory relationship between GPs and the NHS will, subject to parliamen- **1.26**
tary approval, be reformed in 2004. Under the present arrangements, a specific
duty is imposed on PCTs by the National Health Service Act 1977 to provide general medical services, as follows:

(1) It is the duty of every Primary Care Trust and every Health Authority, in accordance with regulations, . . . to arrange as respects their area with medical practitioners to provide personal medical services for all persons in the area who
wish to take advantage of the arrangements;

. . .

(2) . . . the arrangements will be such that all persons availing themselves of those
services will receive adequate personal care and attendance, and the regulations
shall include provision—

(a) for the preparation and publication of lists of medical practitioners who
undertake to provide general medical services;

(b) for conferring a right on any person to choose, in accordance with the prescribed procedure, the medical practitioner by whom he is to be attended,
subject to the consent of the practitioner and to any prescribed limit on the
number of patients to be accepted by any practitioner;

(c) for the distribution among medical practitioners whose names are on the
list of any persons who have indicated a wish to obtain general medical services but who have not made any choice of general practitioner or have
been refused by the practitioner chosen.[51]

The 'personal medical services' which it is the duty of PCTs to provide must in- **1.27**
clude:

(a) all necessary and appropriate personal medical services of the type usually provided by general medical practitioners

(b) child health services;

(c) contraceptive services, that is to say—

(i) the giving of advice to women on contraception,

(ii) the medical examination of women seeking such advice,

(iii) the contraceptive treatment of such women, and

---

[51] National Health Service Act 1977 s 29 as amended by the National Health Service and
Community Care Act 1990, s 2(1) and the National Health Service Reform and Health Care
Professions Act 2002, Sch 2, Pt 1, paras 1, 3(1) and (2).

      (iv) the supply to such women of contraceptive substances and appliances;

    (d) maternity medical services; and

    (e) minor surgery services.[52]

GPs may apply to be included on a health authority's Medical List[53] in order to provide general medical services to patients under an agreement known as the Terms of Service.[54] The Medical List contains, inter alia, the names of the doctors who have agreed to provide general medical services, the nature of the services they have agreed to provide, their practice address and the times during which they will be available to see patients. In addition, each health authority must prepare and keep up to date a list of the patients for whom doctors on the Medical List are responsible.[55] Doctors may withdraw their names from the Medical List,[56] and will have their names removed if they have died, ceased to be doctors, or had their names struck off, or suspended from, the Medical Register by the General Medical Council.[57] Under new powers, a doctor may also be removed by the PCT from the Medical List for reasons of efficiency, fraud, or unsuitability.[58]

1.28   The remuneration of GPs is provided by the health authority and they may not receive fees from their patients.[59] Nevertheless, the use of the law of contract to describe the relationship between GP and health authority has been doubted. The matter was considered in a dispute concerning the remuneration due to a GP from his Family Practitioner Committee (the authority formerly responsible for these functions). The preliminary question arose whether the dispute should be dealt with as if it were a matter of private law between private bodies, or as one of public law involving individuals and government departments. Lord Bridge dealt with the question as follows:[60]

---

[52] See the National Health Service (General Medical Services) Regulations 1992 (SI 1992/635), reg 3, as amended by the National Health Service Reform and Health Care Professions Act 2002, Sch 2, Pt 1, paras 1, 3(1) and (2)·

[53] National Health Service (General Medical Services) Regulations 1992, regs 4–7. Doctors whose application to join the list is refused may appeal to the Secretary of State, see ibid, reg 17.

[54] Contained in ibid Sch 2.

[55] ibid, reg 19.

[56] ibid, reg 6. Unless it is impracticable to do so, the doctor shall give the authority three months' notice of his intention to leave the Medical List and the authority shall make the necessary adjustment to it, see ibid, reg 6(2) and (3).

[57] ibid, reg 7. The power of the General Medical Council to remove doctors from the Medical Register is contained in ss 36 and 38 of the Medical Act 1983. Regulation 7 permits the doctor to appeal against such a removal to the Secretary of State.

[58] National Health Service Act 1977, s 49F inserted by Health and Social Care Act 2001, s 25 and see the discussion below in connection with the NCAA at paras 1.143–1.144.

[59] See National Health Service Act 1977, s 29(4). Under s 2 of the National Health Service (Primary Care) Act 1997, GPs may be employed by NHS Trusts, other GPs on the medical list, or other GPs providing services under a pilot scheme. Such an arrangement has yet to be approved. It remains to be seen whether the dual obligations owed to patient and employer will affect the traditional view of the doctor–patient relationship.

[60] National Health Service Act 1977, Sch 2, para 38.

I do not think the issue in the appeal turns on whether the doctor provides services pursuant to a contract with the family practitioner committee. I doubt if he does and am content to assume that there is no contract. Nevertheless, the terms which govern the obligations of the doctor on the one hand, as to the services he is to provide, and of the family practitioner committee on the other hand, as to the payments which it is required to make to the doctor, are all prescribed in the relevant legislation and it seems to me that the statutory terms are just as effective as they would be if they were contractual to confer upon the doctor an enforceable right in private law to receive the remuneration to which the terms entitle him.[61]

The question has also arisen in a case in which a doctor was unavailable to patients **1.29** during a time in which he had agreed to be on duty. On the recommendation of the Family Practitioner Committee, the Secretary of State exercised his discretion to withhold £2,000 from the doctor's remuneration.[62] The doctor appealed on the ground that, since the nature of the relationship between him and the Family Practitioner Committee was analogous to contract, the powers of the Secretary of State should be confined to a right to recover a proper sum of compensation for the loss caused by the breach. He should not, it was argued, be entitled to impose a penalty on the GP far in excess of the damage actually suffered. Having examined the Terms of Service and the provisions regulating the power to discipline GPs, Potts J said:

the terms of the relevant statutes and regulations are such as to indicate unequivocally that the power to withhold money extends beyond, and is different from, any power to recover money as compensation for the lost value of services not performed. It forms part of a clear disciplinary scheme to ensure control of the service . . .[63]

Thus, he refused to interfere with the sanction. This suggests that the relationship between doctors and health authorities has to be considered in its regulatory context and that the law of contract cannot be used as a framework for analysis.

GP services may be provided by means of the GP's Terms of Service, and Personal **1.30** Medical Services.

(a) The GP's Terms of Service

The relationship between GP and PCT is set down in the General Medical **1.31** Services Regulations.[64] The government has obtained the consent of GPs to introduce new General Medical Services Regulations in April 2004 which will be considered in supplements to this volume.

---

[61] *Roy v Kensington and Chelsea Family Practitioner Committee* [1992] 1 All ER 705, 709.
[62] See generally the powers provided in the National Health Service (Service Committees and Tribunal) Regulations 1992 (SI 1992/664), as amended by SI 1994/634.
[63] *R v Secretary of Health, ex p Hickey* (1993) 10 BMLR 126, 137.
[64] See the National Health Service (General Medical Services) Regulations 1992, considered in Kennedy, I and Grubb, A (eds), *Principles of Medical Law* (Oxford University Press, 1998), paras 1.127–71.

(b) Personal Medical Services

1.32   An alternative mechanism by which GPs may provide primary care to patients is under Personal Medical Services which was introduced by the National Health Service (Primary Care) Act 1997. The major difference in organisation is as follows. Under Pt II of the National Health Service Act 1977 (and before that, the National Health Service Act 1946), 'general medical services' were provided by health authorities (and their various predecessors) under agreements entered with individual GPs in accordance with 'terms of service' contained in the General Medical Services Regulations. Following the National Health Service (Primary Care) Act 1997, services may now be provided other than by health authorities (presently, PCTs) and other than by agreement with individual GPs. Thus, any one of the following may provide 'personal medical services': '(a) an NHS Trust, (b) a suitably qualified medical practitioner, (c) an NHS employee, or a pilot scheme employee, (d) a qualifying body, (e) an individual who is providing personal medical services under that or another pilot scheme.'[65] In particular, a 'qualifying body means a company which is limited by shares all of which are legally and beneficially owned by persons falling within paragraph (a), (b), (c) or (e) . . .'.[66] Personal Medical Services are provided 'as if those services were provided as a result of the delegation by the Secretary of State (by directions given under section 17) . . .'.[67] In this way, agreements may be approved by the Secretary of State in which groups of individuals, or a body, agree to provide services which focus on particular issues or difficulties, for example, within areas less well-served by general practices, by clinicians who may be engaged as employees, rather than independent contractors. Nevertheless, Personal Medical Services are 'medical services of a kind that may be provided by a general medical practitioner in accordance with arrangements made under Part II of the [NHS Act 1977]'.[68] Thus, so far as patients are concerned, the difference in the range and quality of the services provided should be insignificant. The nature of those services are set down in directions[69] and closely match those provided in the 1992 General Medical Services Regulations.

(ii) NHS Trust hospitals

1.33   NHS Trust hospitals obtain their income from capital allocations from the Department of Health and by entering into 'NHS contracts' with PCTs as

---

[65] National Health Service (Primary Care) Act 1997, s 2(2).
[66] ibid, s 2(3).
[67] National Health Service Act 1977, s 28C(4) inserted by National Health Service (Primary Care) Act 1997, s 21.
[68] National Health Service (Primary Care) Act 1997, s 1(8).
[69] The Health Authorities and Primary Care Trusts Implementation of Pilot Schemes (Personal Medical Services) Directions 2002.

purchasers of health care. Section 5(1) of the National Health Service and Community Care Act 1990 provides that the Secretary of State may by order establish bodies, to be known as NHS Trusts

(a) to assume responsibility, in accordance with this Act, for the ownership and management of hospitals or other establishments or facilities which were previously managed or provided by Health Authorities or Special Health Authorities, or

(b) to provide and manage hospitals or other establishments or facilities.

The order shall be made by statutory instrument and may be amended or revoked.[70] The NHS Trust shall carry out 'effectively, efficiently and economically the functions for the time being conferred on it by [such] an order'[71] so that its annual revenue is sufficient to meet its outgoings.[72] NHS Trust Hospitals are funded from the revenue generated by contracting with NHS purchasers and others. The nature and function of NHS Trust hospitals is set down in the regulations by which they have been created which generally provide as follows:

(1) The trust is established for the purposes specified in s 5(1)(a) of the [1990] Act.

(2) The trust's functions (which include the functions which the Secretary of State considers appropriate in relation to the provision of services by the trust for one or more health authorities) shall be—

(a) to own and manage hospital accommodation and services provided at [name and address];

(b) to manage community health services provided from [name and address].

Subject to specific financial provisions,[73]

. . . an NHS Trust shall have power to do anything which appears to it to be necessary or expedient for the purposes of or in connection with the discharge of its functions, including in particular power—

(a) to acquire and dispose of land or other property;

(b) to enter into such contracts as seem to the trust to be appropriate;

(c) to accept gifts of money, land or other property, including money, land or other property to be held on trust, either in general or any specific purposes of the NHS Trust or for all or any purposes relating to the health service; and

(d) to employ staff on such terms as the trust think fit.[74]

Over the past decade, NHS hospitals have been required to submit information **1.34** to the Department of Health for the compilation of comparative performance

---

[70] The requirements of such an order are specified in the National Health Service and Community Care Act 1990, Sch 2, Pt I, as amended by Health Authorities Act 1995, s 2(1), Sch 1, para 69(2).

[71] National Health Service and Community Care Act 1990, Sch 2, para 6(1).

[72] ibid, s 10. See also the restrictions imposed in the powers to borrow money in ibid, Sch 7B.

[73] Detailed in ibid, Sch 3.

[74] ibid, Sch 2, para 16(1).

data. The present arrangements confer 'star ratings' on NHS Trusts and PCTs. NHS trusts are assessed against a limited number of key targets and indicators, the most important of which include the number of patients waiting more than 18 months for in-patient treatment, the number of patients waiting more than 26 weeks for outpatient treatment, the numbers waiting on hospital trolleys for more than 12 hours, whether less than 1 per cent of operations are cancelled on the day, whether patients with suspected cancer wait more than two weeks to be seen in hospital, hospital cleanliness and a satisfactory financial position.[75] 'Where a Trust has a low rating based on poor performance on a number of key targets and indicators, this does not necessarily mean that a hospital is unsafe, does not contain some very good clinical services or that the staff are not working hard in often difficult circumstances. It does mean that performance must be improved in a number of key areas.' By contrast, three-star trusts 'will get earned autonomy freedoms to help them even better. They will receive an additional capital allocation of up to £1 million to support service development' and a number of additional freedoms, notable amongst which are less frequent monitoring from the centre.[76] Hospitals with zero rating will be required to develop immediate recovery plans and, if this fails to improve performance, the management of the hospital may be put out to tender. The franchising arrangement seeks to replace the management team with those capable of bringing about change. Franchise arrangements will be subject to tender from three-star-rated NHS Trust hospitals and from non-NHS individuals and organisations.

1.35   An additional form of hospital, known as a Foundation Hospital was created in 2004.[76a] Foundation status will be available to selected three-star hospitals which will be given the freedom to sell assets, borrow money from private institutions, reward staff according to their own discretion, and not be subject to Secretary of State's directions (although they will be subject to the authority of a new 'independent regulator'). The policy behind the creation of this greater independence is that local communities will respond to their own needs in the most sensitive and appropriate manner and well-managed hospitals should be entitled to contribute to this process. There are, however, a number of questions that will need to be addressed in the regulations which govern Foundation hospitals. For example, to what extent will they remain subject to *national* targets? Foundation trusts will be governed by a board and a membership committee representing the local community and PCTs. How will the differences of policy between them be resolved? If a three-star Foundation hospital loses its star-rating, will it lose its autonomy unless it restores itself to the highest quality? Will restrictions be imposed on

---

[75] See *NHS Performance Ratings—Acute Trusts, Specialists Trusts, Ambulance Trusts, Mental Health Trusts 2001/02* (*www.doh.gov.uk/performanceratings/2002/national.html*).

[76] ibid.

[76a] See the Health and Social Care (Community Health and Standards) Act 2003, Pt 1 and Sch 1.

wealthy Foundation hospitals not to 'poach' staff from less pecunious neighbouring hospitals with offers of more attractive salaries, or benefits?[77] Will foundation hospitals enter into 'NHS', or private contracts with PCTs and other commissioners of NHS services?

(iii) NHS 'Contracts' between PCTs and NHS Trust Hospitals

Following the model of the internal market introduced in 1991, PCTs arrange for appropriate care to be provided to patients by entering into NHS contracts with NHS Trusts. In theory, this arrangement permits PCTs to promote public health policies under their own initiative. In practice, however, 'purchasers [have] very little discretion to pursue local concerns in their contracts, because their actions [are] so heavily influenced by central priorities'.[78] As a result, few of the benefits of delegation, such as greater responsiveness to local needs, have been achieved. Although, the notion of 'purchaser' and 'provider', introduced by the Conservatives in the National Health Service and Community Care Act 1990, has been retained, the language surrounding their role has changed: NHS 'contracts' have become 'service agreements', and the purchasing function of health authorities is now referred to as 'commissioning'. Within the NHS, of course, there is a very limited 'market' for health care. Neither 'purchaser', nor 'provider' can abandon a contract and move their business elsewhere because NHS services have to be provided to patients locally and PCT purchasers often have a very limited number of local NHS Trust hospitals with whom to contract. In other words, there is often insufficient competition in the market to provide meaningful incentives. **1.36**

(a) The Nature of NHS Contracts

The change of language is intended to introduce a change of attitude toward greater harmony in the NHS. To what extent will it do so? The process of pre-contractual negotiation, co-operation during contractual performance and resolving disputes when things go wrong may be conducted in a number of ways. A 'hard' approach would be characterised by low levels of trust between the parties in which negotiations were conducted in a competitive environment. The contract would be framed in a way that sought to achieve minimum levels of flexibility, it would be monitored closely and regularly and there would be a real threat of withdrawal by dissatisfied parties and a claim for compensation. By contrast, a 'soft' approach would be based on trust and confidence between the parties in which matters could be developed *during* performance of the contract on the basis of collaboration. **1.37**

---

[77] See generally the report of the House of Commons Health Committee: *Foundation Trusts* (Second Report of Session 2002–3, HC 395-I). Note the duty to co-operate with other NHS organisations in Health Act 1999, s 26.

[78] Davies, A, *Accountability—A Public Law Analysis of Government by Contract* (OUP, 2001), 116–17.

Matters could be left undefined in the contract in the knowledge that the matter would be resolved by negotiation, without the need for conflict, because the parties have a shared purpose. Labour's emphasis on 'service level agreements' is intended to foster a co-operative, 'softer' approach to the process between parties to NHS contracts.[79]

1.38 On the other hand, when the NHS is subject to continuous reorganisation and upheaval, both personnel and institutions become transient and trust between parties who are unfamiliar with one another may be more difficult to achieve. Clearly, there is a need for balance. An unduly 'hard', commercial, approach to the process is normally inappropriate because pursuit of one-sided remedies could frustrate the *common* objectives of the parties. Equally, the raison d'être of NHS contracts as a means of measuring performance and holding parties to account is defeated if parties become too 'soft' and fail to develop a constructive working relationship. Ultimately, therefore, a 'hard sanction' may be desirable. With this in mind, the system of contract funding continues to require hospitals to be sensitive to their performance by comparison to other providers (now called 'contestability'). In addition, emphasis has been placed on the need to enter longer-term agreements which take full account of public health strategies formulated by health authorities and PCTs.[80] Guidance suggests that:

> PCTs should feel free to commission care from wherever they can obtain the best services for patients. Commissioning decisions should be judged against the twin tests of high clinical standards and good value for money. PCTs will have freedom to decide where NHS resources are best spent . . . PCTs will want to use their local commissioning discretion to reshape how local services are delivered to reduce waiting times, increase responsiveness and improve clinical outcomes. They will want to ensure a focus on prevention services as well as treatment, to forge local partnerships to more effectively address health inequalities and ensure an appropriate balance between investment in primary and community services as well as acute services.[81]

This process of commissioning is achieved by entering 'NHS contracts': 'the phrase "NHS contract" means an agreement under which one health service body ("the acquirer") arranges for the provision to it by another health service body ("the provider") of goods and services which it reasonably requires for the purposes of its functions.'[82] And 'health service body' means any of the following, namely:

---

[79] However, even under the Conservative government, market forces were only briefly the primary driving force in the NHS. See, the discussion by the Conservative administration in *Changing the Internal Market* EL(97)33 (National Health Service Executive, 1997).

[80] See *Commissioning in the new NHS* (HSC 1998/198, NHS Executive, Leeds).

[81] *Securing Service Delivery: Commissioning Freedoms of Primary Care Trusts* (HSC 2002/007, NHS Executive, Leeds), para 3-5.

[82] National Health Service and Community Care Act 1990, s 4(1).

(az)   a Strategic Health Authority;
(a)   a Health Authority;
(aa)   a Special Health Authority
(b)   a health board . . . ;
(bb)   a Primary Care Trust
(c)   the Common Services Agency for the Scottish Health Service;
(e)   an NHS Trust;
(ff)   the Commission for Health Improvement;
(g)   the Dental Practice Board or the Scottish Dental Practice Board;
(h)   the Public Health Laboratory Service Board; and
(i)   the Secretary of State . . .[83]

NHS contracts are intended to enable the parties to agree matters of quality, quantity, and cost. Parties to NHS contracts may undertake such obligations as they see
fit. Since 1997, NHS contracts are generally expected to last for 'at least three
years, but could extend in some circumstances for five to ten years . . . Renewal of
agreements will be dependent on satisfactory progress against local objectives,
including both cost and quality targets.'[84] Guidance published during the
Conservative administration of the NHS suggested three basic models of contract
as means of managing the process, ie 'block contracts', 'cost and volume contracts'
and 'cost per case contracts'.[85] Block contracts are agreements in which hospital
units undertake to provide an unlimited number of facilities, or a maximum
number, expressed, for example in terms of beds, over a specified period of time.[86]
Under these arrangements PCTs may commit resources to a hospital provider irrespective of the actual usage of the facilities and, in so doing, will have difficulty
being precise with respect to quantity and quality.[87]

1.39

This model of contracting for services, however, is to be phased out. Health
Related Groups are to be introduced as a mechanism for paying hospitals for the
services they provide. These resemble the old cost and volume contracts and offer
the opportunity for the parties to agree a particular service, or range of services, for
a specific price. The emphasis is on output in the sense that the parties agree to
specific requirements for an exact price. Under Health Related Groups, however,
prices will be set according to a central tariff, adjusted to accommodate local cost
differentials. This has the advantage of reducing the transaction costs which arose
previously during negotiations around price. And it will reward those who can

1.40

---

[83] ibid, s 4(2) as amended by the National Health Service Reform and Health Care Professions
Act 2002, Sch 5, para 31. (Sub-para (d) referred to Family Health Service Authorities and is deleted.)
[84] *The New NHS—Modern, Dependable* (Cm 3807, 1997), paras 9.19–9.20.
[85] See Appleby, J, *Developing Contracting: A National Survey of District Health Authorities, Boards
and NHS Trusts* (NAHAT, 1995), 8. Non-NHS and private work made up the majority of the remainder.
[86] Hospitals generally worked with around 30 NHS contracts.
[87] See Appleby, J, Smith, P, et al, 'Monitoring Managed Competition' in Robinson, R and Le
Grand, J (eds), *Evaluating the NHS Reforms* (King's Fund Institute, 1994), ch 2.

perform their procedures at levels below their cost as set by the tariff. In this case, more revenue will be available to treat more patients and generate more income. By contrast, severe pressure will be imposed on hospitals which cannot achieve similar levels of efficiency, who will lose patients to the more cost-effective hospitals. In this way a new form of internal market for NHS services has been introduced with less time and money spent on the contracting process, but more vigorous competition between hospitals.

1.41 Lastly, cost per case contracts, or individually agreed contracts inevitably carry larger transaction costs. They may be most appropriate where existing agreements fail to accommodate the special needs of a particular patient, say because they have an uncommon condition. In this event, an out of area transfer (OAT) may be suitable on a one-off basis. Purchasers may be reluctant to enter cost per case contracts based on a day-per-day basis, for fear of losing control over their resources. The alternative is to use the contract as a means of negotiating entire episodes of care, with the emphasis on the provider to assess the average cost of each episode, allowing for occasional complications, or to refine cost and volume contracts after specified threshold targets have been achieved.

(b) Disputes Resolution

1.42 PCTs will monitor the performance of the hospitals to which patients have been sent with a view to encouraging improvements in standards, or a change of hospital-provider, if performance is unsatisfactory. And hospitals themselves may make 'tertiary referrals' of patients who need specialist treatment to other hospitals with particular expertise. They too will want to safeguard quality. Each will want to know that it has received the goods and services paid for in the right quantity, quality and at the right time. In cases of dispute what action may be taken where an amicable settlement between the parties is impossible? The 1990 Act removes the possibility of disputes over NHS contracts from proceeding to the courts on grounds of breach of contract. It provides:

> Whether or not an arrangement which constitutes an NHS contract would, apart from this subsection, be a contract in law, it shall not be regarded for any purposes as giving rise to contractual rights and liabilities, but if any dispute arises with respect to such an arrangement, either party may refer the matter to the Secretary of State for determination.[88]

An adjudication may:

> contain such directions (including directions as to payment) as the Secretary of State or, as the case may be, the person appointed under subsection (5) . . . con-

---

[88] National Health Service and Community Care Act 1990, s 4(3). The matter may be determined either by the Secretary of State, or by his appointee. See ibid, s 4(5).

siders appropriate to resolve the matter in dispute; and it shall be the duty of the parties to the NHS contract in question to comply with any such directions.[89]

The adjudicator also has authority to vary the terms of an NHS contract, or bring it to an end.[90] In addition to these rules which assume the existence of an NHS contract, a procedure is available to negotiators who consider that:

(a) the terms proposed by another health service body are unfair by reason that the other party is seeking to take advantage of its position as the only, or the only practicable, provider of the goods and services concerned or by reason of any other unequal bargaining position as between the prospective parties to the proposed arrangement, or

(b) that for any other reason arising out of the relative bargaining position of the prospective parties any of the terms of the proposed arrangement cannot be agreed . . .[91]

The procedure by which such disputes should be resolved is set down in regula- **1.43** tions,[92] but no substantive guidelines have been suggested as a means of settlement. The explanatory notes state, rather ambiguously, that the adjudicator's decisions 'will not constitute precedents for the determination of other disputes, but they will be useful learning tools for all parties in reaching a shared understanding of the ways contracts might develop'.[93] Generally, statutes do not exclude the right to natural justice and judicial review would be available to parties who considered they had been dealt with unfairly by an informal adjudicatory body. Both parties must be heard in order for the adjudicator to have a balanced view of the dispute;[94] and the adjudication must be fair, in the sense that it must be truly independent of the parties.[95] There is a 'presumption . . . that the outcome will give effect to the agreement which was originally reached, rather than a new agreement which the parties should have reached'.[96] Some measure of consistency ought to exist between adjudications so that if similar cases were to be treated inconsistently, the matter could be amenable to judicial review.[97]

This adjudication machinery has been little used. Occasionally, an informal concili- **1.44** ation and arbitration system has been employed to avoid the statutory mechanisms.

---

[89] ibid, s 4(7).
[90] ibid, s 4(8).
[91] ibid, s 4(4).
[92] See the National Health Service Contracts (Dispute Resolution) Regulations 1996 SI 1996/623.
[93] See *NHS Contracts: Arrangements for Resolving Disputes,* HO 302/6 and EL (91)11 (NHSME, 1991).
[94] *Ridge v Baldwin* [1964] AC 40; *Schmidt v Secretary of State for Home Affairs* [1969] 2 Ch 149.
[95] *R v Kent Police Authority, ex p Gooden* [1971] 2 QB 662; *Metropolitan Properties Co (FGC) Ltd v Lannon* [1969] 1 QB 577.
[96] *NHS Contracts: Arrangements for Resolving Disputes,* HO 302/4 (NHSME. 1991).
[97] See *Metropolitan Properties Co (FGC) Ltd v Lannon* [1969] 1 QB 577, which concerned consistency between levels of rent established by rent assessment committees.

But, 'contracting parties were firmly discouraged even from using this informal system. Health authorities and providers were told that invoking it would be a sign of management failure.'[98] Within the 'NHS family', therefore, agreements between purchasers and providers are both legally and (often) practically un-enforceable. In the absence of market incentives to encourage competition, an informal adjudicatory procedure might have provided an alternative means of encouraging parties to adhere to their contracts. 'But the absence of such a pro-cedure created problems for purchasers seeking to set standards of their choice . . . it seemed to render the contractual accountability process *less* effective.'[99] As in the area of resource allocation and clinical governance, the government prefers to leave matters of this nature to the discretion of local parties. The ostensible reason is to permit local forces to shape the service in the light of their own needs. Yet, in reality, government retains such a firm grip over the choices that are available to local decision-makers that many of the benefits that flow from the devolution of power are not realised.

(iv) Private and Other Non-NHS Hospitals

1.45 In what circumstances may NHS treatment be provided to patients in private and non-NHS hospitals? We consider (a) treatment in private hospitals, (b) the pri-vate finance initiative and local improvement finance trusts, (c) treatment in the European Union, and (d) the liability of non-NHS providers of care.

(a) Treatment in Private Hospitals

1.46 The previous Secretary of State, Mr Alan Milburn, said 'the NHS is short of capacity . . . right now we have what is an under-doctored, under-nursed and arguably under-bedded system. Certainly in the short-term we have very clear capacity constraints. Clearly, it takes time to put these right, it takes three or four years to train a nurse, it takes double that to train a hospital doctor or a GP . . . It seems slightly anomalous to me that, if there is spare capacity that is available within private sector hospitals, for example, that we should not be taking advantage of that for the benefit of NHS patients.'[100] One solution to the shortage of skilled staff is for NHS services to be provided by private hospitals and suppliers, as follows:

> The Secretary of State may, where he considers it appropriate, arrange with any per-son or body (including a voluntary organisation) for that person or body to provide, or assist in providing, any service under [the 1977] Act.[101]

---

[98] Davies (n 78 above) 33. See also Flynn, R and Williams, G (eds), *Contracting for Health: Quasi-Markets and the National Health Service* (OUP, 1997).

[99] Davies (n 78 above) 169.

[100] Evidence to the House of Commons Health Committee, 8 November 2000, para 190. See also Finlanson, B, Dixon, J, et al, 'Mind the Gap: the Extent of the NHS Nursing Shortage' (2002) 325 BMJ 538.

[101] See National Health Service Act 1977, s 23(1).

Facilities, including goods, materials, plant, apparatus and premises may be made available for this purpose on such terms as may be agreed, including the making of payments by, or to, the Secretary of State.[102] As the use of private facilities becomes more common, the traditional split between public and private providers will be more difficult to recognise. NHS patients may receive treatment in private hospitals, and staff engaged by private health companies may provide NHS care.

Private hospitals are not 'health service bodies',[103] and cannot, therefore, enter into NHS contracts. Nevertheless, they make a significant contribution to the work of the NHS. In the past, its main contribution has been in the field of nursing homes for elderly people and care for those in hospices. Elsewhere, arrangements made with private hospitals have often been short term, in the sense that they have been designed to relieve occasional pressure on NHS institutions.[104] After some hesitation, the Labour government has committed itself to long-term 'concordat' with the private sector because 'there should be no organisational, or ideological barriers to the delivery of high quality health care free at the point of delivery to those who need it'.[105] The precise nature of such partnership agreements is subject to local discretion, but the concordat suggests a number of models on which agreement might be based. For example, for elective care, a PCT could pay for and use private sector operating and nursing wards while using NHS personnel; or the provision of a specific service could be contracted-out to a private hospital; or the NHS provider could commission the whole service from the private sector over a longer period of time.[106] Similar agreements are encouraged with respect to the intermediate care of those leaving hospital and in need of rehabilitative care. **1.47**

Care in private hospitals may present different issues and risks to that provided in NHS hospitals. For example, doctors more commonly operate alone, not in a 'firm', and may be less amenable to the help and guidance of their colleagues if their performance gives cause for concern. Also, the general facilities available in a private hospital will often not include emergency equipment, nor experienced 'crash' teams available to respond to emergencies. In addition, doctors may not be regarded as employees of a private hospital, but rather licensees of staff and facilities. Against whom should action be taken in cases giving rise to complaint? Governance of private providers of services to the public (be they NHS, or private patients) is regulated by the Care Standards Act 2000 and the National Care Standards Commission and will become the responsibility of the Commission for **1.48**

---

[102] See ibid, s 23(2) and (3).
[103] Under National Health Service and Community Care Act 1990, s 4.
[104] See *The NHS and Independent Hospitals* (National Audit Office, HC 106, 1989).
[105] See *For the Benefit of Patients* (Department of Health and Independent Healthcare Association, 2001), para 1.1.
[106] ibid, para 2.6.

Health Audit and Inspection (CHAI) (see paras 1.138 *et seq* below). Regulations provide a detailed code of conduct for private hospitals. It includes a duty to provide a patient's guide setting out the basis on which the patient will be treated, to offer complaints procedures, provide proper premises and standards of care, devise clinical governance policies designed to monitor and improve standards of care, identify suitable people as registered providers and managers, and introduce and review resuscitation policies.[107] In addition, the Commission for Health Improvement (CHI) has access to the private hospital in respect of NHS patients.[108]

(b) Private Finance Initiative (PFI) and Local Improvement Finance Trusts

1.49   The need to attract private finance into the NHS arises from a number of factors. Much of the capital infrastructure of the NHS needs replacing or improving. At the same time, the political environment of low taxation means that capital funds are much more tightly controlled by the Treasury. Part of the finance required to achieve the government's targets for improving standards in the NHS, therefore, will be raised from the private sector. A number of initiatives have been taken to encourage private finance into the provision of NHS services. Although NHS Trusts have power 'to enter into such contracts as seem to the trust to be appropriate',[109] for the avoidance of doubt[110] the National Health Service (Private Finance) Act 1997 confirms that 'the powers of a National Health Service trust include power to enter into externally financed development agreements', ie those certified as such by the Secretary of State on the grounds that:

(a) in his opinion the purpose or main purpose of the agreement is the provision of facilities in connection with the discharge by the trust of any of its functions; and

(b) a person proposes to make a loan to, or provide any form of finance for, another party in connection with the agreement.[111]

The words 'another party' exclude reference to the trust itself[112] so that any such scheme would usually involve a private 'loan to (say) a consortium which would propose to finance the development of 'facilities' for an NHS Trust and, perhaps, to own and manage it also over a period of time. This could serve to shield the trust from exposure to the same degree of risk as that undertaken by the consortium. The word 'facilities' includes (i) works, buildings, plant, equipment or other

---

[107] See the Private and Voluntary Health Care (England) Regulations 2001, SI 2001/3968. Infringement of some, but not all, of these duties carries criminal sanctions, see reg 51.

[108] See Health Act 1999, s 20(1)(db) inserted by National Health Service Reform and Health Care Professions Act 2002, s 13(1).

[109] National Health Service and Community Care Act 1990, Sch 2, para 16(1)(b).

[110] The doubt was raised in *Credit Suisse v Allerdale BC* [1996] 4 All ER 129 in which the Court of Appeal considered similar arrangements in relation to a local authority to be ultra vires.

[111] s 1.

[112] s 1(5).

property; and (ii) services.[113] In addition, under Local Improvement Finance Trust arrangements, 'the Secretary of State may form, or participate in forming, companies to provide facilities for (a) persons or bodies exercising functions, or otherwise providing services, under this Act; or (b) NHS Trusts'.[114] A Local Improvement Finance Trust is intended to assist the refurbishment of GP premises and the development of health centres.

The manner in which such private interests should be regulated is a cause of much difficulty. The supervision of the NHS, which is generally available in respect of public authorities under judicial review, is not generally available as regards the activities of private companies. PFI arrangements will be negotiated within the private law of contract and, although those terms will certainly include measures by which successful performance of the contract may be assessed, it is not clear how patients will be able to enforce their individual rights.[115] We ought also to be sensitive to the fact that private contractors generally have a 'right' to breach their contracts and to withdraw from further performance. Of course, they may incur liability in damages (assuming they remain solvent), but there may be circumstances in which the 'cost-effective' breach is commercially attractive. Indeed, with duties owed primarily to shareholders rather than the public interest, such a course of action may be inevitable.[116] If such a circumstance were to arise in connection with a PFI hospital responsible for large numbers of patients, the pressure on government to resume responsibility for the hospital would probably be irresistible. To this extent, the policy underlying the PFI is always subject to government re-insurance. **1.50**

(c) *Treatment in the European Union*

The policy supporting the treatment of NHS patients in private hospitals also accommodates the possibility of patients being sent abroad for their treatment. We discuss the practical arrangements for obtaining treatment in the European Union and jurisprudence on the right to obtain treatment. **1.51**

Practical Arrangements   Treatment elsewhere in Europe for *individual* patients with special health needs has long been available within the NHS under reciprocal arrangements with EU Member States. However, longer-term contracts with overseas hospitals are entirely new. Of course, patients most likely to take advantage of **1.52**

---

[113] ibid.

[114] Health and Social Care Act 2001, ss 4 and 5 (amending s 96C, 1977, National Health Service Act 1977, s 96C).

[115] See generally, Newdick, C, 'The NHS in Private Hands—Regulating Private Providers of NHS Services' in Freeman, M and Lewis, A (eds), *Law and Medicine* (OUP, 2000), ch 1.

[116] A similar point was made by Collins J in *R v Northumbrian Water Ltd, ex p Newcastle and North Tyneside HA* (1999), refusing to impose a duty on a private water company to fluoridate its water supply in the public interest as requested by the local health authority.

such arrangements will tend to be reasonably fit and certainly able to withstand the strain of travelling and will often live close to convenient air and sea-ports.[117] Contracts are arranged with overseas treatment in London (where Guy's and St Thomas's hospital is responsible for arrangements with northern European hospitals and Kent Strategic Health Authority (which is responsible for contracts with southern European hospitals). The arrangements have the status of ordinary contracts in law (and not 'NHS contracts' which, as noted, have no status in private law) and are entered into between the relevant PCT and the overseas hospital. They are often governed by the law of the overseas provider. The additional costs of such treatment, including the costs of travel, have to be met from existing PCT resources.[118] Of course, patients are free to decline the option to travel abroad for treatment if they wish.

1.53   Commissioning of overseas care requires assessments of the quality standards of hospitals. This is achieved through analysis of the hospital's own record of clinical standards, further review from national inspectorates, visits by UK commissioning teams, and within the terms of the contract itself in which specific standards can be identified. The Department of Health recommends that all such contracts specify a number of minimum requirements, namely: the professional expertise required of responsible doctors, adequate standards of infection control, good standards of clinical governance and adherence to evidence-based practice, availability of bilingual staff, medical notes are to be translated into English, there should be complaints procedures and adverse incidents protocols, patients should be discharged with sufficient medication for the journey home, and procedures should exist for NHS commissioners to review compliance of the overseas hospital with the terms of the contract, including visits by the CHAI.[119] Special care will also be required to ensure that the flow of care is not disturbed when the patient is returned to the supervision of the UK doctor.

1.54   Travel costs are subject to regulations which permit the patient reimbursement on an income-related sliding-scale of the costs of travel from their home.[120] Travelling companions will not generally have their travelling costs met unless it is medically necessary. Clearly, if a patient is to spend a number of weeks abroad, a travelling companion might be necessary. In this case, the companion's costs are to be assessed on the scale as if they were those of the patient's.[121]

---

[117] *Evaluation of Treating Patients Overseas* (Department of Health and York Health Economics Consortium, 2002). Cataracts and orthopaedic care abroad is common.

[118] *Treating More Patients and Extending Choice—Overseas Treatment for NHS Patients* (Department of Health, 2002) para 2.18.

[119] ibid, para 3.5 and *Evaluation of Treating Patients Overseas* (Department of Health and York Health Economics Consortium, 2002), ch 4.

[120] National Health Service (Travelling Expenses and Remission of Charges) Regulations 1988, SI 1998/551.

[121] ibid, reg 3(3).

The Right to Obtain Treatment in Europe   Until relatively recently, the juris-   **1.55**
prudence of the European Court of Justice suggested that public services were not
'services' within the provisions concerning free movement under Article 49 of the
EU Treaty. Thus, in *Humbel* national education services were not provided as part
of a private, commercial activity for profit, but as public services for which no payment was made. As a consequence, the principle of the free movement of services
did not apply to the public education services in question.[122] Such an approach
clearly defers to Member States in matters of social planning and welfare. More
recently, however, a number of cases have challenged the restriction on rights to
obtain health care elsewhere in the European Union. *Smits and Peerbooms*[123]
challenged the right of Member States to impose restrictions on patients who
wished to obtain health services in other member countries. The European Court
of Justice affirmed the right of patients to obtain health care services under the
terms of the EU Treaty. It reasoned that the element of remuneration, which is
necessary for the provision of services, was present in health systems which
provided benefits in kind because hospital providers were always remunerated by
a health fund, albeit at a fixed rate and that payments for services do not have to
be made by the persons for whom they are performed.[124] The Court added that no
distinction could be drawn between (i) health care systems in which patients paid
for services under a private contract and reclaimed their expenses from an
insurance fund, and (ii) those which provided health care without direct charges
to patients by supplying benefits in kind; a view it confirmed in *Muller-Faure and
Van Riet.*[125]

Clearly, this access to care in the European Union has the potential to destabilise   **1.56**
the central, financial and operational planning of governments, and health insurers. When, therefore, may a Member State insist on prior authorisation as a precondition to a patient obtaining treatment abroad? Any such obstacle should be
justified within the recognised exceptions to Article 49. One such exception to the
right to free movement is the stability of national health care systems. Clearly, the
instability that would arise from an unrestricted right of access to treatment in
Europe would make future planning and the forecasting of demand very difficult
and be likely to lead to the mis-application of scarce resources. Thus, the Court
acknowledged in *Muller Faure and Van Riet* the right of Member States to cir-
cumscribe the benefits to be made available under their health care systems:

> . . . it is for the Member States alone to determine the extent of the sickness cover
> available to insured persons, so that . . . they can claim reimbursement of the costs

---

[122] Case C-263/86 *Belgium v Rene Humbel and Marie-Therese Edel* [1988] ECR 5365, at
[16]–[18].
[123] Case C-157/99 [2001] ECR I-5473.
[124] ibid, at [56]–[58].
[125] Case C-385/99, at [39].

of the treatment given to them only within the limits of the cover provided by the sickness insurance scheme . . .[126]

It said: 'Treaty provision permits Member States to restrict the freedom to provide medical and hospital services in so far as the maintenance of treatment capacity . . . is essential for public health . . . However, . . . it is necessary . . . to ensure that the measures taken . . . do not exceed what is objectively necessary for that purpose and that the same cannot be achieved by less restrictive rules.'[127] Thus, in the United Kingdom, the General Medical Services Regulations include a 'black' and 'grey' list of drugs and treatments which are excluded from use within the NHS, or whose use is restricted.[128] And elsewhere in Europe, health care systems may require patients to pay a contribution to the costs of their care. Reasonable, proportionate and transparent restrictions of this nature are acceptable.[129] Although purely economic aims cannot justify a barrier to the fundamental principle of freedom to provide services, 'the risk of seriously undermining the financial balance of the social security system may . . . constitute *per se* an overriding general interest reason capable of justifying a barrier of that kind'.[130]

1.57   In affirming the right to obtain treatment in other Member States within the ambit of the national health services made available, the Court distinguished between hospital, and non-hospital care. With respect to hospital care, the Court requires two conditions to be satisfied: (i) the treatment is regarded as '*normal* in the professional circles concerned', in the sense that it is 'sufficiently tried and tested by international medical science', and (ii) the treatment cannot be obtained at home 'without *undue delay*'.[131]

1.58   Neither criterion is helpful. The first condition, that the treatment be 'normal', is impossible to define because there are many areas of care in which we do not possess a common understanding of illness and treatment. For example, thalassotherapy is common treatment in France, but largely unknown within the NHS. NICE did not recommend the use of beta interferon for the treatment of multiple

---

[126] Case C-385/99, at [98].

[127] ibid, at [67]–[68].

[128] National Health Service (General Medical Services) Regulations 1992, Schs 10 and 11, which, subject to parliamentary approval, will be replaced in 2004.

[129] In *R v Secretary of State for Health, ex p Pfizer* [1999] Lloyd's Rep Med 289, the Divisional Court confirmed that such exclusions and restrictions should be transparent in the sense that they do not tend to favour national goods and services. However, the court determined that the decision to restrict access to treatment for sexual dysfunction was a political decision not amenable to more detailed economic, or ethical analysis.

[130] *Muller-Faure and Van Riet* (n 125 above) at [72]–[73] and Case C-158/96, *Kohll v Union des Caisses de Maladie* [1998] ECR I-1931 at [41]. Note, however, that it is notoriously difficult to exclude, or restrict health services in this way and most health systems simply promise a 'comprehensive' package, or one based on 'medical necessity'. To this extent, the Court's concession is likely to have limited impact.

[131] *Smits and Peerbooms* (n 123 above) at [108].

sclerosis, but it is more widely used elsewhere in Europe. The word 'normal' appears to assume that there is a generally recognised 'international medical science' throughout Europe, whereas, in truth, there is such a diversity of medical opinion that exists locally, nationally and internationally, that the word is unhelpful.

Secondly, the phrase 'undue delay' is problematic. The Court insists that 'the na-   **1.59**
tional authorities are required to have regard to all the circumstances of each specific case and to take account not only of the patient's medical condition at the time
when authorisation is sought and, where appropriate, of the degree of pain or the
nature of the patient's disability . . ., but also his medical history'.[132] Clearly, therefore, the issue of delay should be considered from the perspective of the individual
patient and not the customary length of waiting lists. When, however, will delay be
'undue' and who is to judge? Doctors will disagree, as will patients. Orthopaedic
doctors will have a very good understanding of their patients' suffering and needs.
Is a nine-month wait an 'undue delay' for an artificial hip when the patient is
otherwise strong, healthy and fit?[133] And how should such needs be compared to
patients suffering cancer, heart-disease, multiple sclerosis, dementia, or
schizophrenia? There is no objective yard-stick on which the measurements of
'undue delay' can be made. The impact of this approach will depend on whether
the Court defers to local (and probably managerial) judgments in this matter. Also,
national policy may *prioritise* certain areas of care (say on the advice of the NICE).
This is not to *exclude*, or *restrict* access to other areas of care. Nevertheless, such a
policy tends to reduce the resources available elsewhere and to increase delay. If the
Court ignores these priority 'preferences', it risks undermining national policy-
making. More seriously, it may encourage reactive, random and chaotic health care
expenditure dependent on the pressures of litigation. Such a development would
do considerable harm to the interests of the community as a whole.

With respect to non-hospital care, as we have observed, Member States may ex-   **1.60**
clude, or restrict some services from the health care menu (as in the United
Kingdom in relation to 'black' and 'grey' lists), or require co-payments from patients. However, within these limitations, patients have access to non-hospital services in other Member States and to recover the costs of their care from the health
care 'system' of the Member State in which they are insured. For those with easy
access to ports and who are willing to travel to obtain access to medicines that may
be less commonly prescribed at home, this may be attractive.

---

[132] ibid, at [103]; *Muller-Faure and Van Riet* (n 125 above) at [90] and [92].
[133] In *Watts v Bedford PCT* [2003] All ER (D) 20, the first case in which an NHS patient sought
to recover the costs of treatment abroad, Munby J said that a 12-month wait for a prosthetic hip for
a patient suffering serious disability was too long. But a wait of four months was not. Applying *Smits
and Peerbooms* (n 123 above) and *Muller-Faure and Van Riet* (n 125 above), his Lordship said that
the treatment was 'normal' and that ordinary NHS waiting times (of 12 months) were of little relevance to the question of 'undue delay' which should be considered essentially from the perspective
of the patient's individual needs.

1.61 For both hospital and non-hospital care, contemporary pressures to obtain treatment abroad are limited and will impose little immediate expenditure on European health systems. Equally, once a patient achieves the right to care in another Member State, patients in the same category, supported by their doctors and pressure groups, may also be inclined to organise themselves to obtain the same right. In addition, the development of 'tele-medicine' makes possible the provision of treatment from remote locations which will serve to encourage cross-border care.[134] In the longer-term, the Court's emphasis on the rights of the individual is likely to have a significant, but not necessarily beneficial, impact on national policy-making.

(d) Liability of Non-NHS Providers of NHS Care[135]

1.62 Should NHS patients treated in private hospitals in the United Kingdom, or abroad, be considered 'NHS patients' and have the same rights against NHS institutions in case of medical negligence? As a general rule, negligence is slow to impose liability on one party for damage caused by another[136] unless there is an especially close relationship between the parties,[137] or the first is under a duty to exercise control over the second.[138] However, there has been an occasional willingness to extend the boundary of non-delegable duties to relations between employer and employee, so that the employer retains responsibility for the safety of employees who have been borrowed by others. Thus, even though the employer has no reason to suspect that the 'borrower' will expose the employee to danger, he will retain responsibility if the employee is injured by unsafe working practices.[139] The same approach was adopted in relation to an agency responsible for providing a taxi service to the public, even though it engaged its drivers as independent contractors and not employees. In this case a person who was injured by the negligence of the taxi-driver was held to have an action against the booking agency.[140] But recent cases suggest that the non-delegable duty is simply one of reasonable care of employees and that, short of negligence, the employer will not be liable unless he ought to have known that the employee would be exposed to unreasonable risk.[141]

---

[134] See McGauran, A, 'Straight to Video', *Health Service Journal*, 31 July 2003, 26.

[135] See also Chapter 8 below.

[136] See, eg, *Perl Exporters Ltd v Camden London Borough Council* [1984] QB 342; *Lamb v Camden London Borough Council* [1981] QB 625.

[137] See *Smith v Littlewoods Organisation* [1988] AC 241, 272 *per* Lord Goff.

[138] *Home Office v Dorset Yacht Company* [1970] AC 1004; *Vicar of Writtle v Essex County Council* (1979) 77 LGR 656.

[139] *McDermid v Nash Dredging Ltd* [1987] 2 All ER 878. Lord Hailsham said (at 887): 'The essential characteristic of the [non-delegable] duty is that, if it is not performed, it is no defence for the employer to show that he delegated its performance to a person, whether his servant or not his servant, whom he reasonably believed to be competent to perform it. Despite such delegation the employer is liable for the non-performance of the duty.'

[140] See *Rogers v Night Riders (A Firm)* [1983] RTR 324.

[141] See *Square D Ltd v Cook* [1992] IRLR 34, in which the Court of Appeal considered *McDermid*

On the other hand, the NHS is committed to a policy of engaging non-NHS **1.63** providers to provide treatment for NHS patients. It may seem anomalous if those treated within the NHS have different, and perhaps less favourable rights of redress than those treated within it. The Department of Health appears to sympathise with this observation and has stated that:

> should a patient sent abroad for treatment wish to raise an issue of medical negligence, the courts may regard NHS bodies as having a non-delegable duty of care despite the fact that the treatment was being provided by a non-UK provider. Patients would then be able to sue in the English courts rather than have to take the case through the foreign courts. This approach is in line with the Government's policy preferences that patients travelling abroad for treatment should have the same rights and remedies as patients being treated in the UK.[142]

Accordingly, contracts governing the provision of care abroad should contain indemnities covering rights of recovery by NHS bodies which have assumed responsibility for the negligence of overseas institutions.[143] To what extent does the common law endorse this policy?

There are two ways in which a claim might arise against a non-NHS provider in **1.64** these circumstances. The first is where the NHS provider has made arrangements for their NHS patients to be dealt with, but has done so carelessly by using services that it should have known would be sub-standard. Perhaps, the hospital, or laboratory, had a poor safety record, or had received poor reviews from safety inspectors. In this case, an action would be available against the non-NHS provider itself in negligence. In addition, action would lie against the NHS provider for negligence for failing to take proper care to ensure that the private provider was competent to provide a reasonably safe service.

What happens, however, if the referral from the NHS has been undertaken com- **1.65** petently in the sense that reasonable steps were taken to ensure that the provider was well-equipped and competent to perform the procedures? Yet, the patient is damaged through the private provider's negligence. Exactly the same question could arise in connection with a private caterer who failed to maintain proper standards of hygiene in his kitchens so that patients were poisoned, or a private clinical screening service that failed to alert a hospital that a blood sample had tested positive for a disease, or a privately run hospital unit that was so badly managed that patients were given inadequate care. Would a patient who suffered damage by the negligence of a private contractor retain a right of action against the

---

v Nash Dredging to be binding on the issue of vicarious liability only. See also *R v Swan Hunter Ship Builders Ltd* [1982] 1 All ER 264.

[142] *Treating More Patients and Extending Choice: Overseas Treatment for NHS patients* (Department of Health, 2002), para 6.1.

[143] ibid, para 6.3.

NHS hospital by whom it was engaged? Or would the action be limited to the private contractor responsible for providing the service concerned? Such a situation is also common *within* the NHS in relation to 'tertiary referrals'. Say a baby is transferred from a general hospital to a special care baby unit in another hospital. The 'tertiary' hospital fails to take proper care of the baby who suffers damage. Which of the two hospitals should be held responsible? Ought the referring hospital to be held directly liable to the patient under a non-delegable duty for the negligence of the tertiary provider? The same problem arises for GPs. If they engage a consultant from a local hospital on a private basis to take out-patient clinics in the surgery, who is liable if the consultant is negligent through no fault of the GP?

1.66   The common law puts the question as follows: do hospitals and GPs bear a non-delegable responsibility for independent contractors engaged to perform functions on their behalf, so that they will be held liable for the negligence of the contractor even without themselves being negligent? Or is the duty limited to taking reasonable care in appointing and retaining the contractor, ie to ensure that they are competent to perform their duties? In general, the rule as between employer and employee does not apply to those who engage independent contractors.[144] Is the position between NHS Trust (or health authority) and patient governed by the same rule? A number of influential cases have said that hospitals do owe a non-delegable duty to those treated in the hospital and it is irrelevant whether the consultant is the hospital's employee or not. Thus, in 1951, Lord Denning said that:

> the hospital authorities accepted the plaintiff as a patient for treatment, and it was their duty to treat him with reasonable care. They selected, employed and paid all the surgeons and nurses who looked after him. He had no say in their selection at all. If those surgeons and nurses did not treat him with proper care and skill, then the hospital authorities must answer for it, for it means that they themselves did not perform their duty to him. I decline to enter into the question whether any of the surgeons were employed only under a contract for services [ie independent consultants], as distinct from a contract of service [ie employees] . . . the liability of the hospital authorities should not, and does not, depend on nice considerations of that sort. The plaintiff knew nothing of the terms on which they employed staff: all he knew was that he was treated in the hospital by people whom the hospital had appointed; and that the hospital must be answerable for the way in which he was treated.[145]

---

[144] *Rivers v Cutting* [1982] 1 WLR 1146. Liability may be imposed in exceptional circumstances, eg if the contractor was authorised or condoned the tort, see *Ellis v Sheffield Gas Consumers Co* (1853) 2 E & E 767; *D & F Estates Ltd v Church Commissioners for England* [1988] 2 All ER 992.

[145] *Cassidy v Ministry of Health* [1951] 2 KB 343 at 365. His Lordship excluded from this rule cases in which the patient had chosen and engaged his own private doctor, at 362. See also *Gold v Essex County Council* [1942] 2 KB 293, 394, *per* Lord Greene MR.

Although his Lordship repeated this view,[146] in both cases, all the doctors con-   **1.67**
cerned appear to have been employees for whom the defendants were vicariously
liable. In the hospital context, therefore, the point has not arisen in this country
on its own merits.[147] In addition, the issue today may be more complicated than
that envisaged by Lord Denning because the negligence of the private contractor
may have been committed elsewhere, away from the hospital premises. The matter is likely to become more pressing as the NHS enters agreements with non-
NHS providers to provide services for NHS patients. Thus, in *M v Calderdale and
Kirklees HA*[148] it was suggested that the 'non-delegable' duty theory applied even
when the NHS body had referred the patient to a separate private hospital over
which it had no control. A 17-year-old girl was referred as an NHS patient to have
an abortion to a private clinic. The arrangement was made between the health authority and the private clinic under a private contract. The procedure was unsuccessful and she gave birth to a boy. She obtained judgment against both the private
clinic and the doctor responsible for the procedure. Neither, however, had obtained insurance cover and the action was recommended against the NHS hospital from which the referral had been made. The health authority conceded that the
clinic had behaved negligently. However, it said that there had been no negligence
in the choice of the clinic, which was accredited by the appropriate authorities.
Therefore, in the absence of any fault on its part, it should not be held directly
liable for the negligence of the private clinic over whom it had no control as regards
the matter of training, supervising, or monitoring staff. Sitting in the County
Court, HH Judge Garner found for the claimant on the ground that the patient
was the responsibility of the health authority who owed her a non-delegable duty
to provide her with reasonable care. His Honour observed that if this were not the
case, those treated outside NHS institutions could be in a less favourable position
by comparison to those treated within the NHS and this would not be acceptable.

This approach was disapproved, however, in *A v Ministry of Defence and Guys and*   **1.68**
St Thomas' Hospital.[149] The claimant and his mother were the family of a British
serviceman living in Germany. Agreement had been made between the Ministry
of Defence and Guys and St Thomas' Hospital under which the latter would
arrange for hospital services for service personnel and their families to be provided
in designated German hospitals. Under these arrangements, the claimant was
admitted to Gilead Hospital. Her pregnancy was managed negligently (as the

---

[146] In *Jones v Manchester Corporation* [1952] 2 All ER 125, 132 and *Roe v Ministry of Health* [1954]
2 QB 66, 82.
[147] Authorities abroad are divided on the point. Compare *Yepremian v Scarborough General
Hospital* (1980) 110 DLR (3d) 513 (Canada) and *Ellis v Wallsend District Hospital* [1989] Med LR
567 (Australia).
[148] [1998] Lloyd's Rep Med 157 in Huddersfield County Court. The case has no binding authority, therefore, on other courts.
[149] [2003] EWHC 849; [2003] Lloyd's Rep Med 339.

English and German parties accepted) as a result of which her child suffered serious brain-damage. The question arose as to her right of action in the English courts. Bell J considered that the authorities supported the principle that there is a special relationship between a hospital and its patient under which the hospital has a personal, non-delegable duty to use reasonable care and skill in the treatment (including advice) of the patient, not simply a duty to provide an appropriate regime of care. However, the 'wider personal, non-delegable duty still depends upon the hospital's acceptance of the patient for treatment, or advice'.[150] In the circumstances of the case, however, neither the Ministry of Defence, nor Guys and St Thomas' Hospital had assumed clinical responsibility for either claimant. The duty of the defendants was to select appropriate hospital providers in Germany and there was no evidence that the choice of German hospital had been made negligently (its record of obstetric safety was comparable to that in the United Kingdom). As a result, it was held that negligence could not be shown against the defendants, that no right of action existed in the United Kingdom and that the matter should be heard in the German courts.

1.69   This distinguishes between the location at which patients are treated and may make the government's policy of extending patient choice to overseas providers less attractive to patients. Rights of recovery for negligence that are more difficult to ascertain, less well-understood and, perhaps, more restricted, are likely to discourage patients from seeking care abroad. If the government wishes patients to take advantage of the policy, it may have to direct that NHS bodies retain legal responsibility for those treated abroad even in the absence of clinical responsibility for the patients' care. The recovery of an indemnity for damages paid to patients can be accommodated within the terms of the contract with the overseas hospital.

B. Policy-Making, Priority Setting and Judicial Review

1.70   Successive governments have consistently refused to confront the dilemma of the hard choices that routinely have to be made throughout the NHS. Instead, government encourages the contrary belief that NHS care should always be available to those who need it and blame for systematic shortcomings within the NHS has been deflected onto managerial and clinical staff. A welcome criticism of this approach was voiced in *Learning from Bristol.*

> Governments of the day have made claims for the NHS which were not capable of being met on the resources available. The public has been led to believe that the NHS could meet their legitimate needs, whereas it is patently clear that it could not. Healthcare professionals, doctors, nurses, managers, and others, have been caught between the growing disillusion of the public on the one hand and the tendency of

---

[150] ibid, at 68.

governments to point to them as scapegoats for a failing service on the other . . . The NHS was represented as a comprehensive service which met all the needs of the public. Patently it did not do so . . .[151]

In the light of these observations, it would be helpful for the government to clarify the basic objectives of the NHS and explain the principles on which its resources should be allocated. In the present circumstances, other than through the piecemeal objectives described by Secretary of State's directions, NICE, or in National Service Frameworks, local resource-allocators have to make these hard choices themselves. The task is performed in England, by PCTs, by health authorities in Wales and health boards in Scotland.

We consider the extent to which the rights and duties arising under the National **1.71** Health Service Act 1977 are capable of being enforced by means of judicial review. Bear in mind that the court has no jurisdiction to take the decision on the authority's behalf. A successful application will result in the matter being referred back to the decision-maker for reconsideration in the light of the court's guidance. The question is especially important in relation to PCTs which work under the dual duty (i) to promote a comprehensive health service on behalf of the Secretary of State and (ii) not to exceed their annual financial allocations. This requires choices to be made with respect to health service priorities. The manner in which this is done varies between PCTs, but the strong recommendation of the recent authorities is that the process should be robust, fair and consistent and always admit the possibility of individual patients presenting exceptional circumstances which merit access to care notwithstanding a policy guideline to the contrary.

We consider claims for judicial review arising under (1) illegality, (2) irrationality, **1.72** (3) procedural impropriety and (4) under the Human Rights Act 1998. We also discuss (5) the distinction between 'health' care and 'social' care.

1. Illegality

Lord Diplock has described the principle of illegality as a ground for judicial re- **1.73** view as requiring decision-makers to understand correctly the law that regulates their decision-making power and to give effect to it.[152] The matter was put another way by Sedley LJ: 'It is axiomatic that a public authority which derives its existence and its powers from statute cannot validly act outside those powers. This is the familiar ultra vires doctrine . . .'.[153] Thus, health authorities are bound by the statutory framework that surrounds them. The difficulty is to define the precise limits of those powers.

---

[151] *Learning from Bristol,* (n 1 above) 57, para 31. The report urges we should 'make explicit that which has been implicit', 261, para 27.
[152] *Council of Civil Service Unions v Minister for the Civil Service* [1985] AC 374, 410.
[153] *R v North and East Devon HA, ex p Coughlan* [1999] Lloyd's Rep Med 306, 323, col 1.

1.74 The first claim to arise in relation to the issue of NHS resources was in *R v Secretary of State for Social Services, ex p Hincks*.[154] Plans for a new orthopaedic unit in Birmingham had been approved by the Secretary of State in 1971, postponed in 1973 and eventually abandoned in 1978. It was alleged that the Secretary of State had failed in his duty to promote a 'comprehensive health service' under s 3 of the National Health Service Act 1977. The Court of Appeal decided, however, that s 3 cannot be interpreted to impose an absolute duty to provide services, irrespective of economic decisions taken at national level. The provision has to be read subject to the implied qualification that the Secretary of State's duty was 'to meet all reasonable requirements such as can be provided within the resources available',[155] which 'must be determined in the light of current Government economic policy'.[156] The Court of Appeal has confirmed its view that the 'duty' imposed by s 3 is not absolute. In *R v North and East Devon HA, ex p Coughlan*[157] it said:

> First it will be observed that the Secretary of State's section 3 duty is subject to two different qualifications. First of all there is the initial qualification that his obligation is limited to providing the services identified to the extent that he considers that they are *necessary* to meet *all reasonable requirements*. In addition there is a qualification in that he has to consider whether they are appropriate to be provided as part of the health service . . .

> The first qualification placed on the duty contained in section 3 makes it clear that there is scope for the Secretary of State to exercise a degree of judgment as to the circumstances in which he will provide the services . . . When exercising his judgment he has to bear in mind the comprehensive service which he is under a duty to promote as set out in section 1. However as long as he pays due regard to that duty, the fact that the service will not be comprehensive does not mean that he is necessarily contravening either section 1 or section 3 . . . a comprehensive health service may never, for human, financial and other resource reasons, be achievable . . .

> In exercising his judgment the Secretary of State is entitled to take into account the resources available to him and the demands on those resources . . . The [NHS] Act does not impose an absolute duty to provide the specified services. The Secretary of State is entitled to have regard to the resources made available to him under current government economic policy.

1.75 We noted above the refusal of the House of Lords to involve itself with a dispute concerning the manner in which local authorities were funded and it is unlikely that the courts will criticise the level at which government funds the NHS. On the other hand, different considerations arise if funds which have been allocated for particular purposes are misapplied. Thus, funds paid to a health authority for the specific purposes of reimbursing GPs for the costs of employing suitable staff at

---

[154] (1992) 1 BMLR 93 (decided in 1980).
[155] ibid, 95 *per* Lord Denning MR.
[156] ibid, 97, *per* Bridge LJ.
[157] [1999] Lloyd's Rep Med 306, 314.

their practices, the cost rent scheme, and premises improvement grants, could not be diverted to other uses, notwithstanding that those uses were intended to promote 'general medical services' which were otherwise the health authority's responsibility.[158]

2. *Irrationality*

The courts have reserved for themselves the right to review the decisions of managers and administrators if they are *Wednesbury* unreasonable, ie so unreasonable that no reasonable person addressing himself to the issue in question could have come to such a decision. Obviously, discretion must be exercised fairly, impartially and in the light of all the relevant evidence. Lord Diplock has described the power of review as follows: **1.76**

> It applies to a decision which is so outrageous in its defiance of logic or of accepted moral standards that no sensible person who had applied his mind to the question to be decided could have arrived at it. Whether a decision falls within this category is a question that judges by their training and experience should be well equipped to answer, or else there would be something badly wrong with our system.[159]

More recently, however, the notion of 'unreasonableness' was explained by Lord Woolf MR. He said: 'Rationality . . . has two faces: one is the barely known decision which simply defies comprehension; the other is a decision which can be seen to have proceeded by flawed logic.'[160] It is the second of these two notions which has become more prominent recently. Clearly, it gives the courts power to question the internal logic of the decision. The changed attitude of the courts in this matter is striking and has led the courts to quash decisions which, previously, might have escaped scrutiny. Part of the reason for the change is explained by the recent interest of the courts in obtaining satisfactory reasons for the decision under review. There has been 'a perceptible trend towards an insistence on greater openness, or . . . transparency in the making of administrative decisions'.[161] As authoritative commentators have said, there are many advantages to such a duty. **1.77**

> To have to provide an explanation of the basis for their decision is a salutary discipline for those who have to decide anything that adversely affects others . . . it encourages a careful examination of the relevant issues, the elimination of extraneous issues, and consistency in decision-making. Moreover . . . [it may] deter applications which would be unsuccessful. In addition, basic fairness and respect for the individual often requires that those in authority over others should tell them why they are subject to some liability or have been refused some benefit.[162]

---

[158] *R v Secretary of State for Health, ex p Manchester Local Medical Committee* 25 BMLR 77.
[159] In *Council of Civil Service Unions v Minister for the Civil Service* [1985] AC 374, 410.
[160] *R v North and East Devon HA, ex p Coughlan* [1999] Lloyd's Rep Med 306, 323, col 2.
[161] *Doody v Secretary of State for the Home Department* [1993] 3 All ER 92, 107.
[162] de Smith, Woolf and Jowell, *Judicial Review of Administrative Action* (Sweet and Maxwell, 1995), para 9-042.

Inevitably, there are also disadvantages, for example that such a duty places further burdens and expenses on decision-makers which may encourage 'anodyne, uninformative and standard reasons'. On balance, however, 'the advantages of providing reasons so clearly outweigh the costs that fairness requires that the individual be informed of the basis for the decision'.[163]

1.78 The following traces this evolution of judicial passivity, and the trend after 1995 in which the courts have adopted a more critical, or 'hard-look', approach to cases of this nature.

(i) Judicial Passivity

1.79 During the 1980s, two cases gave the impression that the courts would generally defer to the decisions of local decision-makers in the resource-allocation process and the prospects of success in action for judicial review were small. Thus, in *R v Secretary of State, ex p Walker*[164] the health authority was satisfied that a premature baby required an operation to his heart. The authority was unable to perform the procedure as a result of a decision not to staff all the intensive care units in its neonatal ward. The plaintiff alleged that her baby had been denied the surgical care the hospital acknowledged he needed. Rejecting the application for an order that the operation be performed, Sir John Donaldson MR, said:

> It is not for this court, or indeed any court, to substitute its own judgment for the judgment of those who are responsible for the allocation of resources. This court could only intervene where it was satisfied that there was a prima facie case, not only of failing to allocate resources in the way in which others would think that resources should be allocated, but of a failure to allocate resources to an extent which was *Wednesbury* . . . unreasonable.[165]

1.80 In *ex p Walker*, there was no immediate danger to the baby and, had an emergency arisen, the operation would have been performed.[166] In *R v Central Birmingham HA, ex p Collier*,[167] however, a four-year-old boy was suffering from a hole in the heart. In September 1987 his consultant said that 'he desperately needed open heart surgery' and placed the boy at the top of the waiting list, expecting that intensive care facilities would be made available by the hospital within a month. By January 1988, the operation had been arranged and then cancelled on a number of occasions because no intensive care bed could be made available. The Court of Appeal was invited to order that, given that the boy would probably die unless the operation was performed, the operation should be carried out. It said, however, that:

---

[163] ibid, para 9-045.
[164] (1992) 3 BMLR 32 (decided in 1987).
[165] ibid, 35.
[166] ibid, 34.
[167] 1988. Discussed in Christopher Newdick, *Who Should We Treat?—Law, Patients and Resources in the N.H.S.* (OUP, 1995), 124–35.

even assuming that [the evidence] does establish that there is immediate danger to health, it seems to me that the legal principles to be applied do not differ from the case of *Re Walker*. This court is in no position to judge the allocation of resources by this particular health authority . . . there is no suggestion here that the hospital authority have behaved in a way which is deserving of condemnation or criticism. What is suggested is that somehow more resources should be made available to enable the hospital authorities to ensure that the treatment is immediately given.

Understandably, the courts must be extremely careful before becoming involved in telling hospital managers which cases should take priority over others. During litigation on behalf of an individual patient, who will speak for the large numbers of patients who are not party to the dispute but who may be affected by its outcome, and for those particular patients whose operations will have to be cancelled if someone else is treated first?[168] Nevertheless, the case of *Collier* concerned a child, as everyone agreed, in need of common, life-saving cardiac surgery who had been placed top of the waiting list by his responsible doctor, yet the hospital was unable to make facilities available. How could this have happened? On what system of priorities was such an apparently meritorious patient considered so much less urgent than the other cases demanding care and attention? Were the nursing staff attending to other patients in greater need of care? Could the operation not have been performed in another hospital? Were managers using the notoriety being attracted by the case as a cynical means of bargaining for additional funding? The most troubling aspect of the case is that no-one seemed to know exactly why intensive care facilities could not be made available to the patient. Counsel for the boy accepted that he simply did not know why the surgery had been cancelled; as he said, 'it may be good reason or bad reason'. **1.81**

Subsequent NHS guidelines issued by the Department of Health specified that, for patients with recognised clinical needs, 'it is not acceptable for a purchaser to refuse authorisation [for treatment] solely on the grounds of the proposed cost of the treatment in relation to the contracted services'.[169] In another context, there has been discussion of a type of decision which 'cries out for reasons'[170] and, it is **1.82**

---

[168] The point was made subsequently in the Court of Appeal, by Balcombe LJ, who said: 'I would stress the absolute undesirability of the court making an order which may have the effect of compelling a doctor or health authority to make available scarce resources (both human and material) to a particular child, without knowing whether or not there are other patients to whom those resources might more advantageously be devoted': *Re J* [1992] 4 All ER 614, 625. But Lord Mustill in *Airedale NHS Trust v Bland* [1993] 1 All ER 821, 879 has taken the opposite view: '. . . it is not legitimate for a judge in reaching a view as to what is for the benefit of the one individual whose life is in issue to take into account the wider practical issues as to allocation of limited financial resources . . .'

[169] *Guidance on Extra Contractual Referrals* (NHSME, 1993), para 51.

[170] *R v Higher Education Funding Council, ex p Institute of Dental Surgery* [1994] 1 All ER 651, 661. And see generally on the emerging duty on decision-makers to give reasons for their decisions in some circumstances (none of which concern access to health care), *R v Civil Service Appeal Board, ex p Cunningham* [1991] 4 All ER 310 and *Doody v Secretary of State for the Home Department* [1993] 3 All ER 92.

suggested, in the light of the more recent cases, *ex p Collier* should now be regarded as wrongly decided for failing to assess the reasons for the decision to refuse treatment.

(ii) The 'Hard-look'

1.83 Subsequent cases suggest the courts may examine two factors in connection with claims that decisions on access to care are irrational, or disproportionate: (a) matters relating to the process of priority setting, and (b) decisions as to the efficacy and necessity of the treatment in question.

(a) The Process of Priority Setting

1.84 *R v North Derbyshire HA, ex p Fisher*[171] was the first rationing case in which judicial review succeeded against a health authority. It arose following the refusal of the health authority to purchase beta interferon for patients suffering from multiple sclerosis. The case was complicated by a number of explanations for the refusal which the judge described as 'disingenuous'. One explanation was that £50,000 had notionally been allocated to fund its purchase, but it was insufficient to provide treatment to everyone who needed it. Therefore, some deserving cases referred at the end of the year would have been denied treatment simply by virtue of the accident of the date of their referral. This, the authority suggested, was so unfair that it would be better to provide no such treatment at all. The court rejected this approach.

> The reason given by [the Director of Public Health] is that the money could only be allocated on a first come, first served basis, which was unfair. I regard this as an irrational reason. If correct it would be a reason for refusing to make any expensive treatment available in almost all circumstances. When deciding whether to prescribe treatment to a patient a clinician has to have regard to many factors including the resources available for that treatment and the needs of and likely benefit to that patient as compared with other patients who are likely to be suitable . . .
>
> It is absurd to suppose that before any patient is prescribed any expensive treatment a survey must be made of all patients who are, or might be, in need of the same treatment in the area. I do not accept that this was a rational justification for not releasing additional funds.[172]

Thus, the refusal was overturned by the court, by an order of certiorari, and referred back to the health authority for reconsideration in the light of the court's observations. Similarly, in *R v NW Lancashire HA, ex p A, D and G*[173] the applicants suffered from 'gender identity dysphoria'. The authority accepted that the condition was an illness, but it adopted a policy which allocated low priority to procedures it considered to be clinically ineffective. The applicants sought judicial review of the refusal of the health authority to pay for transsexual surgery. The

---

[171] (1997) 8 Med LR 327.
[172] ibid, 337, col 1.
[173] [1999] Lloyd's Rep Med 399.

authority identified a number of procedures as falling within the lowest 10 per cent in terms of priority which would not be provided 'except in cases of overriding clinical need': gender reassignment, cosmetic plastic surgery, reversal of sterilisation, correction of shortsightedness, all forms of alternative medicine undertaken outside the NHS and homeopathy 'except when the effectiveness of the treatment has been scientifically proven and accepted by a substantial and appropriate body of medical opinion'. The policy was explained to the court by the authority's consultant in Public Health Medicine. He said that the authority had limited financial resources and could not afford to fund all services of proven clinical effectiveness. In order to serve all those for whom the authority was responsible, it had to make difficult decisions. He said, however, that the case of each of the applicants was considered on its merits, although he conceded that it would be difficult to imagine what an exceptional clinical need for transsexual surgery might be other than evidence of serious psychiatric pathology.

In principle, Auld LJ approved the process of priority setting. His Lordship's observations deserve close attention. Recommending the use of a general policy within which individual cases should be assessed, he said: **1.85**

> It is natural that each authority, in establishing its own priorities, will give greater priority to life threatening and other grave illnesses than to others obviously less demanding of medical intervention. The precise allocation and weighting of priorities is clearly a matter of judgment for each authority, keeping well in mind its statutory obligations to meet the reasonable requirements of all those within its area for which it is responsible. It makes sense to have a policy for the purpose—indeed, it might well be irrational not to have one—and it makes sense too that, in settling on such a policy, an Authority would normally place treatment of transsexualism lower in its scale of priorities than, say, cancer or heart disease or kidney failure. Authorities might reasonably differ as to precisely where in the scale transsexualism should be placed and as to the criteria for determining the appropriateness and need for treatment.

> It is proper for an authority to adopt a general policy for the exercise of such an administrative discretion, and to allow for exceptions from it in 'exceptional circumstances' and to leave those circumstances undefined . . . In my view, a policy to place transsexualism low in an order of priorities of illnesses for treatment and to deny it treatment save in exceptional circumstances such as overriding clinical need is not in principle irrational, provided that the policy genuinely recognises the possibility of there being an overriding clinical need and requires each request for treatment to be considered on its individual merits.

> However, in establishing priorities—comparing the respective needs of patients suffering from different illnesses and determining the respective strengths of their claims to treatment—it is vital: for (1) an authority accurately to assess the nature and seriousness of each type of illness, (2) to determine the effectiveness of various forms of treatment for it and (3) to give proper effect to that assessment and that determination in the application of its policy.[174]

---

[174] ibid, 408.

However, Auld LJ also held that the authority had, in reality, closed its mind to the possibility of making transsexual surgery available in any circumstances. It had, in reality, adopted a blanket ban.

> That basic error, one of failure properly to evaluate such a condition as an illness suitable and appropriate for treatment, is not mitigated by the allowance in both policies for the possibility of an exceptional case of overriding clinical need or other exceptional circumstances. As I have said, such a provision is not objectionable, but it is important that the starting point against which exceptional circumstances have to be rated is properly evaluated and that each case is considered on its individual merits . . . The Authority's relegation of what was notionally regarded as an illness to something less, in respect of which an applicant for treatment had to demonstrate an overriding clinical need for treatment, confronted each [applicant] with a very high and uncertain threshold.[175]

Similarly, Buxton LJ acknowledged that health authorities are obliged to make hard choices between deserving claims to their budgets and, in doing so, may legitimately take into account a wide range of considerations, including the proven success or otherwise of the proposed treatment; the seriousness of the condition and its cost.[176] However, His Lordship emphasised the patient's interests in having the merits of their case properly assessed. He said:

> the more important the interests of the citizen that the decision effects, the greater will be the degree of consideration that is required of the decision-maker. A decision that, as is the evidence in this case, seriously affects the citizen's health will require substantial consideration, and be subject to careful scrutiny by the court as to its rationality. That will particularly be the case in respect of decisions . . . which involve the refusing of any, or any significant, treatment . . .[177]

1.86 There may be cases where the patient and the health authority have very different perceptions of the illness, or condition in question. Note that in this case, the application was made by transsexuals, a condition which some would explain in *psychological*, rather *physiological* terms. Such an explanation might consider surgery to be an inappropriate treatment. Nevertheless, the authority should have paid greater regard to the applicants' perception of their condition. When compared to *ex p Collier*, these cases illustrate a marked increase in the willingness of the courts to scrutinise the reasonableness of rationing decisions.

(b) Assessment of Clinical Efficacy and the Need for Treatment

1.87 How should health authorities consider the evidence surrounding the treatment?

---

[175] ibid.

[176] ibid, 411.

[177] ibid, 412. Note too that in matters involving the liberty of the person, a more intensive review of discretion will be justified, especially if the decision-maker has departed from central guidelines on the matter. See, in the case of a mental health patient held in seclusion under a policy which contradicted such 'guidance': *R (on the application of Munjaz) v Mersey Care NHS Trust, R (on the application of S) v Airedale NHS Trust* [2003] EWCA Civ 1036.

Good evidence of clinical effectiveness requires the treatment receiving fair and equal consideration in the priorities process. Equally, good evidence that the treatment offers only marginal benefits might justify a position low on the priorities list. Good evidence of ineffectiveness would generally lead to exclusion from NHS provision. What if there is *equivocal* evidence of effectiveness, or a minority of clinicians reasonably believe the patient to be an exceptional case? Here, the relative cost of the treatment probably deserves greater attention and it might be reasonable not to devote disproportionate funding to treatments that might not be effective. Thus, in *R v Cambridge District HA ex p B*[178] a 10-year-old girl with leukaemia was refused the resources required to provide her with remedial (as opposed to palliative) treatment that might have prolonged her life. An application to secure resources on her behalf was denied on the grounds that: (i) the doctors responsible for treatment considered it to be so untested that it was 'experimental', (ii) its prospects of success were very small, ie between 1 and 4 per cent overall, (iii) it would have debilitating side-effects which, given her prospects, were not in her best interests, and (iv) given her prospects, the total cost of the two stages of procedures (some £75,000) could not be justified. The unanimous clinical view of the doctors advising the health authority was that the procedure should not be carried out and the health authority accepted that view, confirming at the same time that the decision had been taken in the light of 'all the clinical and other relevant matters . . . and not on financial grounds'.[179]

Overturning the more demanding approach of Laws J,[180] the Court of Appeal **1.88** took a relatively passive and non-interventionist different view. It said: 'Difficult and agonizing judgments have to be made as to how a limited budget is best allocated to the maximum advantage of the maximum number of patients. That is not a judgment the court can make. In my judgment, it is not something that a health authority . . . can be fairly criticised for not advancing before the court.'[181] Thus, although there was the possibility of some benefit, it was insufficient to justify treatment; given her poor prospects, it was not in the patient's best interests and it would have been wasteful in the circumstances of the case.

However, a more refined approach to the question of equivocal evidence was **1.89** adopted in *ex p A, D & G* as to the clinical evidence that transsexual surgery is an effective treatment for gender dysphoria. The Deputy Director of Public Health said that there was uncertainty about the medical evidence supporting surgery in the treatment of the illness. He said (i) that he would require good evidence of

---

[178] [1995] 2 All ER 129.
[179] See ibid, 138. The patient died of her illness about a year later. In the US, see also *McLaughlin v Williams* 801 F Supp 633 (SD Florida, 1992) for a comparable application concerning a liver/bowel transplant for a baby, but offering greater prospects of a successful outcome.
[180] See (1995) 25 BMLR 5, discussed at para 1.99 below.
[181] [1995] 2 All ER 129, 133.

clinical effectiveness as a general rule in all cases and (ii) that the evidence in this case had not been subjected to randomised controlled trials, and that, to the extent that some research had been conducted, it was likely to be biased, and did not indicate what the long-term results of surgery might be. Experts for the defendants took the contrary view of clinical effectiveness. How should such a difference of professional opinion be resolved? Auld LJ said:

> It may be that there is medical support for such scepticism . . . I say nothing about the scope for debate between doctors on the matter. I do not need to do so because the authority accepts in these proceedings that [transsexualism] is an illness. It follows that its policies should, but do not, properly reflect that medical judgment and accord the condition a place somewhere in the scale of its priorities for illnesses instead of relegating it to the outer regions of conditions which it plainly does not so regard.[182]

Similarly, Buxton LJ said that, given the existence of a respectable body of opinion in favour of surgery for transsexualism, 'it is unreal to submit that body of opinion to research trials of the type envisaged in the health authority's paper' (ie randomised control trials). After all, time may not have permitted proper advances in medical opinion to have been endorsed by large-scale randomised controlled trials. His Lordship said:

> I emphasise that the mere fact that a body of medical opinion supports the procedure does not put the health authority under any legal obligation to provide the procedure: the standard here is far removed from the *Bolam* approach in cases of medical negligence. However, where such a body of opinion exists, it is . . . not open to a rational health authority simply to determine that the procedure has no proven clinical benefit while giving no indication of why it considers that is so.[183]

Thus 'blanket bans' will not generally be acceptable. As a general rule, rationing policies should admit the possibility of exceptional circumstances. A policy which purports to allow for exceptional circumstances will be scrutinised to see that it does so in fact. The mistaken logic in this case was the acceptance of the condition as an illness, but treating it in practice as if it was not an illness.[184]

3. Procedural Impropriety

1.90 Until recently, the only statutory duty to consult arose under the various Community Health Council Regulations. Community Health Councils will be abolished and replaced by more extensive duties of consultation which are discussed below in connection with Local Authority Oversight and Scrutiny Committees. However, quite apart from the statutory duty of consultation,

---

[182] [1999] Lloyd's Rep Med 399, 408.
[183] ibid, 412.
[184] Note, however, that a blanket ban may be acceptable on purely *clinical* grounds, ie that IVF treatment is unlikely to be effective in patients over a certain age, as in *R v Sheffield HA, ex p Seale* (1995) 25 BMLR 1.

claims for procedural impropriety may arise in relation to individuals who have been refused access to treatment. Take the example of a health authority which denies treatment because it is too low on its priorities list, or excludes it altogether, other than in *exceptional circumstances*. How should those exceptional circumstances be recognised? Often, exceptional circumstances will be identified in discussion with the patient and the GP. Although it may not be possible to identify precisely, it might cover, for example, the patient being exposed to a significant risk of an *additional* and *severe* illness. If such a process results in a denial of treatment, what procedures should be available to review the decision? Such a review must comply with the rules of natural justice.

Natural justice requires that: (i) the patient must know of the reasons for the **1.91** adverse decision; (ii) the patient must have the opportunity to explain why they believe the adverse decision is mistaken; and (iii) the matter should be given independent consideration by a panel which was not connected with the original decision to refuse treatment. Arguably, the review can be limited to confirming that the procedures were applied properly and consistently, that all the relevant matters were properly considered and irrelevant matters were excluded. It would help to keep a record of the number of successful reviews to show that the system is effective. Procedure in matters of this nature are in no way intended to be formal. In *R (on the application of F) v Oxfordshire Mental Healthcare NHS Trust*,[185] the Trust refused to discharge the applicant to accommodation in Manchester on an extra contractual basis costing £100,000. Instead, it proposed to discharge her locally to a unit with which it had an existing contract. This was not ideal for the applicant, but it was adequate from a clinical perspective. The court considered the priorities committee hearing and whether more formal representation should have been available. Rejecting the application for judicial review, the court said:

> The health authority had to act fairly, but such decisions involving the allocation of scarce resources, where granting one request will inevitably mean refusing others should not be judicialised . . . Fairness requires that the claimant should have the opportunity to tell the Forum in writing why it was contended that resources should be allocated to her . . . Fairness did not require that she should see the material that went before the Forum, . . . since these documents raised no new point. A meeting of the forum is essentially a discussion between medical experts. It is not to be equated with a contested hearing, and rules of disclosure which might be appropriate for such a hearing should not be imposed upon the Forum's deliberations . . . Decisions on funding affect lives, not just liberty. That is not a good reason to judicialise them. They are agonisingly difficult decisions, and they will not be made any easier or better if they are encumbered with legalistic procedures.

---

[185] [2001] EWHC Admin 535 at [77] and [80].

4. The Human Rights Act 1998 and Proportionality

1.92   Does the Human Rights Act 1998 change the way in which judicial review applies
to matters of this sort? Of course, it will carry significant weight in issues concerning, for example, patients' rights to information about treatment, the sterilising of mentally handicapped patients, confidentiality, rights to self-determination
and the status of living wills. To what extent, however, will the Human Rights Act
become involved in applications to obtain access to health care, for example, to
treatment for a life-threatening condition, particularly if such a decision will tend
to divert resources earmarked for other patients? In a claim concerning policing
levels in the community, the European Court of Human Rights has sounded a
note of caution as to the extent to which it can become involved in allocating
funds within the public services. It said:

> Bearing in mind the difficulties involved in policing modern societies, the unpre-
> dictability of human conduct and operational choices which must be made in terms
> of priorities and resources, such an obligation must be interpreted in a way which
> does not impose an impossible or disproportionate burden on the authorities.
> Accordingly, not every claimed risk to life can entail for the authorities a
> Convention requirement to take operational measures to prevent that risk from
> materialising[186]

1.93   A similar point has arisen in connection with application by a person for housing.
The European Court of Human Rights said: 'Whilst it is clearly desirable that
every human being has a place where he or she can live in . . . and which to call a
home there are unfortunately in the Contracting States many persons who have
no home. Whether the state provides funds to enable everyone to have a home is
a matter for political, not judicial decision.'[187] The Court may be sensitive to the
view that human rights must create universal, minimum standards that cannot be
dependent on the wealth available to individual countries. The standards imposed
on relatively affluent countries in northern Europe must be equally achievable in
countries with smaller gross domestic product. If this is correct, the European
Court will be sensitive to the danger of insisting upon standards of public services
which, within present resource constraints, could not be made available throughout the signatories of the European Convention.

1.94   Note too that the European Court preserves for the Member States certain latitude with respect to many of the rights protected by the Convention under the
'margin of appreciation' and the doctrine of proportionality. This margin of discretion is especially significant in relation to the competing claims that arise between private and public interests. Thus, the Court has considered the balance
between the private rights of those living beneath flight paths approaching

---

186   *Osman v UK* (1998) 29 EHRR 245 at [116].
187   *Chapman v UK* (2001) 33 EHRR 18 at [99].

Heathrow airport and whose sleep is regularly disturbed (under the Article 8 right to 'private and family life'), with the national and commercial interests of preserving a thriving international airport. Like the issues considered here, there is no 'right' answer, nor any objective means of identifying which factors are relevant to the decision, or the weight to be accorded to them. Certainly, the government had adopted policies to reduce and discourage night-time noise, but the weight of air traffic continued to increase. Nevertheless, a majority of the Court determined that although the state is required to give due consideration to the rights arising under Article 8, 'it must in principle be left a choice between different ways and means of meeting the obligation. The Court's supervisory jurisdiction . . . is limited to reviewing whether or not the particular solution adopted can be regarded as striking a fair balance.'[188] This too suggests that differing domestic responses to claims in this area of health care resource allocation would be accorded a wide measure of discretion.

Traditionally, courts have been reluctant to engage themselves in disputes of this **1.95** nature. One reason for their caution is the fear that a decision to grant an application by A will simply tend to divert resources away from B, who is unrepresented and about whom the court knows nothing.[189] One mechanism for restricting the duty of the state to provide positive access to health resources is to say that mere *inactivity* is unlikely to expose authorities to liability under the Convention. In the absence of some unwarranted action on their part, there is no wrong which can be the subject of challenge. Thus, in the transsexuals' case of *ex p A, D & G*, Buxton LJ said, denying the relevance of Article 8 to the application, 'in this case there has occurred no *interference* with either the applicants' private life or with their sexuality. The ECHR jurisprudence demonstrates that a state can be guilty of such interference simply by inaction . . . [but] such an interference could hardly be founded on a refusal to fund medical treatment.'[190] Clearly, this would provide a powerful defence to administrative authorities in respect of failure to provide a range of NHS services.[191] Arguably, however, this is too stark a view of the rights available under the Convention. There are a number of ways in which the Human Rights Act might assist applicants for access to NHS care. We consider (i) proportionality and the intensity of judicial review, and (ii) review of mental health cases.

---

[188] *Hatton v UK* (2001) 34 EHRR 1 at [123].

[189] See n 168 above.

[190] *R v NW Lancashire HA, ex p A, D and G* (2000) 53 BMLR 148, 173.

[191] See also *R v Sheffield HA, ex p Seal*, (1995) 25 BMLR 1, decided before the introduction of the 1998 Act, where the applicant sought judicial review of a decision to deny her IVF treatment. The application was refused. Auld J held that 'if the Secretary of State has not limited or given directions as to the way in which such a service, once undertaken, should be provided, the authority providing it is entitled to form a view as to those circumstances and when they justify provision and when they do not'.

(i) Proportionality and the Intensity of Review

1.96 Particularly if one takes the view that there are reciprocal rights and duties which flow between the state and its citizens,[192] analysis of applications for access to health resources requires consideration of the doctrine of proportionality. The introduction of the Convention requires a balance to be made between competing public and private rights. As Lord Steyn has said:

> from time to time the fundamental right of one individual may conflict with the human right of another . . . a single minded concentration of the pursuit of fundamental rights of individuals to the exclusion of the interests of the wider public might be subversive of the ideal of tolerant liberal democracies. The fundamental rights of individuals are of supreme importance but those rights are not unlimited: we live in communities of individuals who also have rights . . . The European Convention requires that where difficult questions arise a balance must be struck.[193]

1.97 The origin of the concept of proportionality in the European Convention stems from the qualifications placed on a number of rights that they be interfered with only when it is 'necessary in a democratic society'. This concept of *necessity* implies a 'pressing social need' in which 'the interference is proportionate to the legitimate aim pursued . . .'.[194] (Indeed, under the right to life provisions of Article 2, the test is more emphatic: 'no more than *absolutely* necessary'.) It has been persuasively suggested that this requires the court to have regard to specific considerations in balancing the competing interests, namely, that (i) the measure contains a legitimate aim, (ii) the interference must be a suitable response to a pressing social need, (iii) it is necessary in a democratic society, and (iv) it is proportionate to the legitimate aim pursued.[195] The Strasbourg Court recognises the need for a 'fair balance between the demands of the general interests of the community and the requirements of the protection of the individual's human rights'[196] and recognises that Member States possess a margin of appreciation in the precise balancing of those interests.[197]

1.98 Until relatively recently, the English courts were very reluctant to embrace the notion of proportionality in English law. As Lord Lowry explained in *ex p Brind*, the courts should be slow to usurp the jurisdiction of public officers, many of whom

---

[192] See the comment of the Supreme Court of India in *Paschim Banga Khet Maxdoor Samity v State of West Bengal* 1996 AIR 2426, 2429: 'The Constitution envisages the establishment of a welfare state [in which] the primary duty of government is to secure the welfare of the people. Providing adequate medical facilities for the people is an essential part of the obligations undertaken by the Government in a welfare state.'

[193] *Brown v Stott* [2001] 2 All ER 97, 118.

[194] *Sunday Times v UK* (1979) 2 EHRR 245 at [62].

[195] See Fordham, M and de la Mere, T, 'Identifying the Principles of Proportionality' in Jowell, J and Cooper, L (eds), *Understanding Human Rights Principles* (Hart, 2001), 53 and generally.

[196] See *Soering v UK* (1989) 11 EHRR 439 at [89].

[197] See *Handyside v UK* (1976) 1 EHRR 737 at [48].

are elected to their posts, especially given the lack of expertise and training of judges in many of the areas concerned. 'The losers in this respect will be members of the public...'[198] This represents a relatively passive view of the role of the court in assessing the propriety of public decision-making; it presumes that provided the decision-maker remains within the confines of his statutory powers, his discretion is immune from review. More recently, however, this approach has been modified. Laws J has explained how the court should seek to balance competing administrative and constitutional rights. His Lordship said:

> *Wednesbury*... is not, at least any longer, a monolithic standard of review. Where an administrative decision abrogates or diminishes a constitutional or fundamental right, *Wednesbury* requires that the decision-maker provide a substantial justification in the public interest for doing so... reasonableness itself requires in such cases that in ordering the priorities which will drive his decision, the decision-maker must give a high place to the right in question. He cannot treat it merely as something to be taken into account, akin to any other relevant consideration; he must recognise it as a value to be kept, unless in his judgment there is a greater value which justifies its loss.[199]

This approach has been endorsed in the House of Lords.[200] In *R v Lord Saville, ex p A*, the Court of Appeal confirmed that a court may not interfere with the exercise of a administrative discretion on substantive grounds unless it is satisfied that it was beyond the range of responses open to a reasonable decision-maker. Significantly, however, it added, 'in judging whether the decision maker has exceeded this margin of appreciation the human rights context is important. The more substantial the interference with human rights, the more the court will require by way of justification before it is satisfied that the decision is reasonable.'[201] This difference with respect to the intensity of the court's scrutiny in cases involving human rights issues is illustrated in *ex p B*, discussed at para. 1.87 above. Recall that the Court of Appeal refused to rule on the merits of the case (although it certainly heard the relevant evidence). It appeared to adopt a passive and essentially deferential role to the difficulties faced by the health authority. Contrast, therefore, the approach of Laws J, who understood the case to give rise to a claim to the right to life. His Lordship subjected the decision to refuse access to treatment to the closest scrutiny. Having heard substantial evidence as to the clinical merits of the proposed treatment, he said:

1.99

---

[198] *Ex p Brind* [1991] 1 AC 696, 767. Nevertheless, a 'total lack of proportionality' would offend the *Wednesbury* test, see ibid, 762.

[199] *Chesterfield Properties plc v Secretary of State for the Environment* [1998] JPL 568, 579.

[200] '[T]he time has come to recognise that this principle [of proportionality] is part of English administrative law, not only when the judges are dealing with community acts but also when they are dealing with acts subject to domestic law': *R (on the application of Alconbury) v Secretary of State for the Environment, Transport and the Regions* [2001] 2 All ER 929, 976 *per* Lord Nolan.

[201] [1999] 4 All ER 860, 871, in which Lord Woolf MR agreed with the submissions of Mr David Pannick QC in *R v Ministry of Defence, ex p Smith* [1996] 1 All ER 257, 263.

Funds for health care are not limitless . . . But merely to point to the fact that resources are finite tells one nothing about the wisdom or, what is relevant for my purpose, the legality of a decision to withhold funding in a particular case. I have no
evidence as to what kinds of case, if any, might be prejudiced if the respondents were
to fund B's treatment. I have no idea where in the order of things the respondent's
place a modest chance of saving the life of a 10-year-old girl. I have no evidence
about the respondent's budget, either generally, or in relation to 'extra contractual
referrals'. The [Director of Public Health's] evidence about money consists only in
grave and well-rounded generalities . . . [W]here the question is whether the life of
a 10-year-old child might be saved, by however slim a chance, the responsible
Authority must . . . do more than toll the bell of tight resources. They must explain
the priorities that have led them to decline to fund the treatment.[202]

1.100 Will this more demanding approach gain favour in the light of the Human Rights
Act?[203] Will every exercise of discretion to allocate resources to one patient, or
group of patients, rather than another require detailed explanation? Clearly, such
a requirement has resources implications of its own. On the one hand, *operational*
decisions (in the sense discussed by Lord Wilberforce in *Anns v Merton London
Borough Council*[204]) taken in respect of individual patients may be amenable to
scrutiny. On the other hand, more generalised matters of 'policy' in which health
authorities seek to allocate resources to optimum effect are arguably less amenable
to judicial review. Thus, the court must remain sensitive to the factors taken into
account by the authority in exercising discretion, in particular, 'social policy, the
allocation of finite financial resources between the different calls made upon them
or (as in the *Dorset Yacht* case) the balance between pursuing desirable social aims
as against the risk to the public inherent in so doing. It is established that the
courts cannot enter upon the assessment of such "policy" matters.'[205]

1.101 The matter is one of balance, but there can surely be no doubt that the old
Wednesbury deference will be modified in cases of this nature. Lord Steyn in *ex p
Daly* has suggested a number of differences between the doctrine of proportionality and the traditional 'unreasonableness' test. For example the doctrine of proportionality may require the reviewing court 'to assess the balance which the
decision maker has struck, not merely whether it is within a range of reasonable
decisions. Secondly, the proportionality test may go further than the traditional

---

[202] *R v Cambridge District HA, ex p B* (1995) 25 BMLR 5, 16–17.
[203] For a similar approach see *B v Minister of Correctional Services* (decided in 1997) (1999) 50
BMLR 206, in which prisoners suffering HIV detained in the Western Cape successfully applied for
access to anti-viral medicines. Brand J accepted that, 'if a proper case were to be made by the
respondents that, due to the constraints of its own budget, the Department of Correctional Services
could not afford the medical treatment claimed by the applicants, I might have . . . have found that
adequate medical treatment for the applicants is dictated by such budgetary constraints' (at 221).
[204] [1978] AC 728.
[205] *X v Bedfordshire County Council* [1995] 3 All ER 353, 369–370, *per* Lord Browne-Wilkinson.
See also Newdick, C, 'Damages for Public Authority Negligence—Public Interests and the Human
Rights Act' (2002) 10 Tort L Rev 127.

grounds of review in as much as it may require attention to be directed to the relative weight accorded to interests and considerations. Thirdly, . . . the intensity of the review . . . is guaranteed by the twin requirements that the limitation of the right was necessary in a democratic society, in the sense of meeting a pressing social need, and the question whether the interference was really proportionate to the legitimate aim being pursued.'[206] Thus, in *ex p Mellor*, a prisoner sought judicial review of the refusal of the Home Office to permit him IVF facilities to artificially inseminate his wife. Although the Court of Appeal dismissed the application, it said: 'It did not follow that it would always be justifiable to prevent a prisoner from inseminating his wife artificially, or indeed naturally. The interference with fundamental human rights permitted by article 8.2 involved an exercise in proportionality. Exceptional circumstances could require the normal consequences of imprisonment to yield because its interference with a particular human right was disproportionate.'[207]

(ii) Review of Mental Health Cases

One respect in which the scope of judicial review in medical cases has been significantly extended is in relation to the court's duties to review the lawfulness of those detained and subject to compulsory treatment under the Mental Health Act. The matter arose in respect of the power available in s 58(3)(b) of the Act to treat a patient without obtaining his consent under the authority of a doctor authorised to give an independent second opinion. In *Wilkinson*, the question arose as to the test by which such a second opinion should be scrutinised in judicial review. The appellant contended that a number of his human rights were raised by the case and that the court could not be satisfied of the need for him to be treated without his consent unless the doctors were available for cross-examination. The respondents argued that the court's responsibility was simply to review the lawfulness of the matter on the papers and not to require the doctors to present themselves in court. **1.102**

The Court of Appeal held that in a case of such gravity, it had to be satisfied of the precedent fact of the patient's need for treatment in these circumstances. A *Wednesbury* review would not be sufficient. Hale LJ said, 'the court has power to make an independent determination of what is the patient's best interests in the broadest sense, not limiting itself to applying the *Bolam/Bolitho* test of medical negligence . . . The wishes and feelings of the incapacitated person will be an **1.103**

---

[206] *R v Secretary of State for the Home Department, ex p Daly* [2001] 3 All ER 433, 446. Lord Cooke added: 'I think the day will come when it will be more widely recognised that the *Wednesbury* case was an unfortunately retrogressive decision in English Administrative law, in so far as it is suggested that there are degrees of unreasonableness and that only a very extreme degree can bring an administrative decision within the legitimate scope of judicial review' (at 447).

[207] *R (on the application of Mellor) v Secretary of State for the Home Department* [2002] QB 13, 29.

important element in determining what is, or is not, in his best interests. Where he is actively opposed to a course of action, the benefits which it holds for him will have to be carefully weighed against the disadvantages of going against his wishes, especially if force is required to do this.'[208] As to the manner in which the court should satisfy itself of this matter, Her Lordship said:

> Whatever the position before the Human Rights Act, the decision to impose treatment without consent upon a protesting patient is a potential invasion of his rights under art 3 or art 8. Super-*Wednesbury* is not enough. The Appellant is entitled to a proper hearing, on the merits, of whether the statutory grounds for imposing this treatment upon him against his will are made out, ie whether it is treatment for the mental disorder from which he is suffering and whether it should be given to him without his consent.[209]

Clearly, this has significant implications for individuals. In doing so, however, it also requires adjustments to the resources needed to support the institutions in which they are detained. The same logic has driven a successful application to review the resources made available to Mental Health Review Tribunals and their capacity to engage sufficient panel members to provide a suitably speedy review of patients' detention to satisfy Article 5(4) of the Convention. In *R (on the application of KB) v Mental Health Review Tribunal,* Sir Stanley Burnton J was satisfied that the applicants should be awarded 'modest' awards of damages for not having had their cases reviewed owing to the unavailability of panel members, and to being detained for longer periods of time than might otherwise have been the case. Clearly, the training and recruitment of suitably qualified personnel is closely linked to the availability of resources and to decisions made by the NHS as a whole. Nevertheless, His Lordship rejected the argument that damages should not be awarded because such an award would tend to divert scarce resources away from the wider community: 'Parliament requires the court to make an award of damages under art 5(5) where that is required by the Convention. It must be taken to have provided the resources to meet such awards.'[210]

---

[208] *R (on the application of Wilkinson) v Responsible Medical Officer, Broadmoor Hospital* (2001) 65 BMLR 15 at [64].

[209] ibid, at [83]. The content of the merits of treatment were discussed in *R v Doctor M* [2003] Lloyd's Rep Med 81 at [19] as follows: '(a) how certain is it that the patient does suffer from a treatable mental disorder, (b) how serious a disorder is it, (c) how serious a risk is presented to others, (d) how likely is it that, if the patient does suffer from such a disorder, the proposed treatment will alleviate the condition, (e) how likely is it that the treatment will have adverse consequences for the patient and (g) how severe may they be.' Inevitably, the court remains heavily dependent on expert evidence in respect of each of these matters.

[210] [2003] EWHC 193; [2003] 3 WLR 185 at [50]. The issue of the appropriate measure of damages also arose in *R (on the application of Bernard) v Enfield London Borough Council* [2002] EWHC 2282; [2003] HRLR 4 as regards the failure of a housing authority to provide suitable housing for a severely disabled person.

5. *Distinction Between NHS and Social Care*

In 1942, the Beveridge Report recommended that our welfare system should sep-   **1.104**
arate responsibility for providing health care on the one hand, from social services
on the other.[211] His proposal was given effect by distinguishing the functions of
the NHS and social services in (respectively) the National Health Service Act
1946 (now the 1977 Act) and the National Assistance Act 1948. The former is the
responsibility of the Secretary of State and is available to patients without charge
(except as is provided in regulations), whereas the latter is the responsibility of
local authority social services departments and is means tested.[212] Clearly therefore, patients, NHS Trust hospitals and local authorities need to know upon
whom the expense of funding care falls. The distinction becomes the more important as we grow older and become more dependent on others, especially as
people often have to sell their homes in order to meet costs of social services care.
Oddly, however, the distinction between the two responsibilities has never been
clear. As long ago as 1953, the Minister of State for Health, Mr Iain Macleod described it as perhaps the most baffling . . . in the whole of the National Health
Service'.[213]

The matter was brought to prominence by the Health Service Ombudsman, Mr   **1.105**
William Reid, in 1993 in connection with the refusal by a health authority to support the costs of providing chronic care. The applicant's 55-year-old husband had
suffered a serious stroke, serious neurological damage and a heart attack which
had left him totally dependent on nursing care. Leeds Health Authority provided
acute care until satisfied that his condition had stabilised and that he was no
longer likely to improve. At that stage it described his condition as 'chronic' and
stated that it 'did not provide for any long stay medical beds in hospital or have any
contractual arrangements for such beds in private nursing homes'.[214] Accordingly,
the patient was discharged to a private nursing home which incurred costs to his
family of £6,000 a year over two years before the case was heard. The application
challenged the right of the health authority to refuse to provide NHS care to a
patient in this condition. Sir William found in favour of the applicant. He said:

---

[211] *Social Insurance and Allied Services* (Cmnd 6404, 1942), paras 426 *et seq.*

[212] Thus, nursing home residents' assets must be assessed to test the level of contribution they
should make, if any, toward the cost of their care. See the National Assistance (Assessment of
Resources) Regulations 1992, SI 1992/2977 as amended, in particular, by the National Assistance
(Assessment of Resources) (Amendment) (England) Regulations 2002, SI 2002/ 410 on capital lim-
its. In Scotland, both nursing and 'personal' care are provided without charge. See the Community
Care and Health (Scotland) Act 2002.

[213] Parliamentary Debates, vol 522, col 167 (14 December 1953). See generally Newdick, C,
'Patients, or Residents?: Long-Term Care in the Welfare State' (1996) 4 Med L Rev 144.

[214] *Failure to Provide Long term NHS Care for a Brain-damaged Patient* (Health Service
Commissioner, HC 197, Session 1993–4) para 18.

The patient was a highly dependent patient in hospital . . . and yet, when he no longer needed care in an acute ward but manifestly needed what the National Health Service is there to provide, they regarded themselves as having no scope for continuing to discharge their responsibilities to him because their policy was to make no provision for continuing care . . . In my opinion the failure to make available long-term care within the NHS for this patient was unreasonable and constitutes a failure in the service provided by the Health Authority.[215]

The authority agreed to compensate the applicant for her expenses and to undertake the costs of her husband's future care. The difficult question remains, however, what is 'the National Health Service . . . there to provide'? The question becomes the more important when hospitals are encouraged to maintain beds for new admissions, but local authorities may be reluctant to accept financial responsibility for additional 'clients' within their social services departments.[216]

1.106 The Health Service Ombudsman's adjudication led to the introduction of new NHS guidelines, but these too came under scrutiny when the matter was considered again in *R v North and East Devon HA, ex p Coughlan*.[217] The applicant had been involved in a serious car accident and was grievously damaged. She was a resident in a nursing home and her condition was described as 'tetraplegic, doubly incontinent requiring regular catheterisation, partially paralysed in the respiratory tract, with consequent difficulty in breathing, and subject not only to the attendant problems of immobility but to recurrent headaches caused by an associated neurological condition'.[218] The guidance introduced after the Health Service Ombudsman's case had suggested that 'specialist or intensive medical or nursing support for people in nursing homes'[219] should be the responsibility of the NHS, but not other care of a more general nature. In the Divisional Court, Hidden J decided that any nursing care provided in a nursing home was the responsibility of, and should be paid for by, the health authority. The implications of the decision were profound and would have necessitated a very substantial diversion of additional funds to health authorities.

1.107 The matter was taken to the Court of Appeal. Lord Woolf MR, as we have seen, described ss 1 and 3 of the National Health Service Act 1977 in terms which did not impose an absolute duty on the Secretary of State to provide the specified services. The associated responsibilities of local authorities are described in s 21 of the National Assistance Act 1948, as amended, as follows, inter alia:

---

[215] ibid, para 22. For a similar Health Service Ombudsman case, see *Health Service Commissioner's Report* (HC 11, Session 1995–96), 121.

[216] Local authorities may now suffer financial penalties for failing to accommodate those ready for discharge from hospital. See the Community Care (Delayed Discharge etc) Act 2003.

[217] [1999] Lloyds Rep Med 306.

[218] ibid, 310, col 1.

[219] Health Service Guidance (95)45, para 4.1.

(1) a local authority may with the approval of the Secretary of State, and to such extent as he may direct, shall, make arrangements for providing (a) residential accommodation for persons aged eighteen or over who by reason of age, illness,
disability or any other circumstances are in need of care and attention which is
not otherwise available to them . . .

(5) References in this Act to accommodation provided under this Part thereof shall
be construed . . . as including references to board and other services, amenities
and requisites provided in connection with the accommodation except where
in the opinion of the authority managing the premises their provision is unnecessary . . .

(8) Nothing in this section shall authorise or require a local authority to make any
provision authorised or required to be made . . . by or under any enactment not
contained in this Part of this Act or authorised or required to be provided under
the National Health Service Act 1977.

His Lordship reversed the decision of Hidden J that all nursing services are prop- **1.108**
erly the responsibility of health authorities. Of s 21(1), he said, 'the express reference to age, illness and disability as being among the characteristics of the person
who is seeking accommodation . . . indicate that in many cases there is likely to
be a need for nursing services as part of the care provided'. Similarly, in relation to
s 21(5), His Lordship said the words 'board and other accommodation' also appear to include nursing services subject to the qualification that they are 'provided
in connection with the accommodation'. Consistent with this view, His Lordship
said of s 21(8) that the powers of the local authority 'are not excluded *by* the existence of a power in the [National Health Service Act 1977] to provide some service, but they are excluded where the provision is authorised or required to be
made *under* the [1977 Act]'.[220] In other words:

> The subsection's prohibitive effect is limited to those health services which, in fact,
> have been authorised or required to be provided under the [1977 Act]. Such services
> would not therefore include services which the Secretary of State legitimately de-
> cided under section 3(1) of the [1977 Act] it was not necessary for the NHS to pro-
> vide . . . The Secretary can exclude some nursing services from the services provided
> by the NHS. Such services can then be provided as a social or care service rather than
> as a health service . . .

> The distinction between those services which can and cannot be so provided is one
> of degree which in borderline cases will depend on a careful appraisal of the facts of
> the individual case. However, as a very general indication as to where the line is to
> be drawn, it can be said that if the nursing services are (i) merely incidental or an-
> cillary to the provision of the accommodation which a local authority is under a
> duty to provide to the category of persons to whom section 21 refers and (ii) of a na-
> ture which it can be expected that an authority whose primary responsibility is to
> provide social services can be expected to provide, then they can be provided under
> section 21. It will be appreciated that the first part of the test is focusing on the over-

---

[220] [1999] Lloyd's Rep Med 306.

all quantity of the services and the second part on the quality of the services provided.[221]

On the facts of this case, the Court of Appeal considered that the applicant's disabilities were of a scale which were beyond the scope of local authority responsibility. The question of how it applies to the vast range of other social services provided to residents suffering varying degrees of dementia is unclear. Nevertheless, the judgment indicates that some nursing care provided in nursing homes, provided it is sufficient in nature or duration, should be considered the responsibility of the NHS.

1.109 The duty to assess need, and to determine whether care should be provided within the NHS, is conferred on the NHS and social services departments.[222] The framework within which they do so is subject to revised Secretary of State's directions[223] but local authorities must develop their own 'eligibility criteria' in order to do so fairly and consistently.[224] (Of course, nursing home residents responsible for paying nursing home fees remain entitled to NHS care, such as the services of their GP, or admission to hospital, without charge.) These developments notwithstanding, however, the manner in which these powers have been delegated to local health authorities has not resolved the problem of improper charging for nursing services. The Health Service Ombudsman, Ms Anne Abrahams, further considered local eligibility criteria in 2003. Adjudicating in favour of four applicants, she said:

> Some of the local criteria I have seen appeared to be significantly more restrictive than the guidance permitted. For instance: some explicitly say that only patients requiring continued consultant supervision, or on site medical expertise, are eligible for NHS-funded care: others seem to suggest that in explanatory text, or to imply that people requiring hospital care are eligible. Yet it is clear from the 1995 guidance, and reinforced by the additional [1996] guidance that some other patients should be eligible.[225]

The Ombudsman continued that, the *Coughlan* ruling notwithstanding, 'any review of the criteria following the judgment seems to have been very limited and criteria remained unchanged even when it is very hard to see that they were in line

---

[221] ibid, 316, col 2-317, col 1.

[222] National Health Service and Community Care Act 1990, s 47.

[223] See the directions in *Guidance on Free Nursing Care in Nursing Homes* (HSC 2001/17, LAC (2001)26, Department of Health, 2001). See also *Ex parte Coughlan: Follow Up Action* (HSC 1999/180, LAC(99) 30, Department of Health, 1999).

[224] The criteria are described in *Fair Access to Care Services—Guidance on Eligibility Criteria for Adult Social Care* (Department of Health, 2002) and LAC(2002)13. Note too that carers also have a right to be assessed as to their own needs, see Carers (Recognition and Services) Act 1995 and the Carers and Disabled Children Act 2000.

[225] *NHS Funding for Long-term Care of Older and Disabled People* (HC 399, 2nd Report, Session 2002–3), para 19.

with the judgment. I would have expected the Department of Health, when reviewing the performance of health authorities, to have picked this up. But I have seen some evidence to suggest that the Department provided little real encouragement to authorities to review their criteria [and] one letter . . . could justifiably have been read as a mandate to do the bare minimum.'[226] Accordingly, the Ombudsman considered that all those who had been wrongly required to pay for medical care should receive compensation. The Health and Social Care Act 2001 has now defined 'nursing care' as 'any services provided by a registered nurse and involving (a) the provision of care, or (b) the planning, supervision or delegation of the provision of care, other than any services which, having regard to their nature and the circumstances in which they are provided, do not need to be provided by a registered nurse'. And nothing in the regulations governing community care services shall authorise or require local authorities to provide nursing care by a registered nurse.[227] This further clarifies the duty of health authorities in relation to nursing care, but, given the cost pressures we impose on the NHS as we become dependent, it is unlikely to remove the problem altogether.

C. The New NHS 'Governance'

NHS governance is concerned to focus attention on systems to monitor, assess and improve quality in the NHS. There is a considerable range of opinion as to the theory on which such a system of regulation should be based. Should it pursue a 'light-touch' based on mutual trust and confidence between regulator and regulated, or a more aggressive 'arm's length' approach in which nothing is left to trust? How should the costs and burden of regulation be assessed so that the service is not deflected from its core duty? Should the regulator be independent of government and, if so, to whom should it be accountable? What range of sanctions should exist to encourage improvement and how should success and failure be measured, and by whom?[228] The new 'governance' of the NHS is at a relatively immature state of development and will certainly provoke differences of view on these and many other questions.

1.110

A new 'duty of quality' is imposed on health authorities, PCTs and NHS Trusts 'to put and keep in place arrangements for the purpose of monitoring and improving the quality of health care provided by and for that Body'; and the term 'health care' means 'services provided to individuals for or in connection with the prevention,

1.111

---

[226] ibid, para 21.
[227] Health and Social Care Act 2001, s 49.
[228] See generally Walshe, K, *Regulating Healthcare—A Prescription for Improvement* (Open University Press, 2003).

diagnosis or treatment of illness, the promotion and protection of public health.[229] This is intended to require NHS bodies to establish clear lines of accountability for clinical care, comprehensive quality improvement programmes and systems, and clear risk-management policies that are understood and implemented by clinicians.[230] The mechanisms each introduce is left to local discretion, although compliance with the duty will inevitably be assessed in the light of the assessment of their general performance by the regulatory bodies discussed in this section. Thus, we examine (1) NHS priority setting, (2) public and patient involvement in the NHS, and (3) oversight of NHS performance.

1. NHS Priority Setting

1.112 Government has traditionally played a very limited role in directing how and where NHS resources should be spent. One of the causes of concern for the system that developed within the 'internal market' prior to 1998 was the tendency for there to be unequal access to care depending on the efficiency and success of individual doctors. The Labour government announced its intention to promote equality of care between patients by creating NICE, a special health authority with responsibility for reviewing different types of treatment and recommending whether they should be provided within the NHS, or not. In addition, it established National Service Frameworks, with the status of persuasive guidance to create standards to which PCTs should aspire throughout the NHS, and against which they would be assessed. Clearly, both will affect the way in which decision-making occurs.

(i) National Institute for Clinical Excellence

1.113 NICE is intended to 'ensure a faster, more uniform uptake of treatments which work best for patients' by creating 'a limited number of ambitious but achievable national targets'.[231] One of the reasons for its creation was concern over 'postcode' rationing in the NHS in which differences in spending plans between the various health authorities throughout the United Kingdom led to unequal access to patient care. The purpose of NICE is to manage investment in new treatments and to ensure greater evenness of uptake amongst PCTs.[232] Thus:

> Subject to and in accordance with such directions as the Secretary of State may give, the Institute shall perform such functions in connection with the promotion of clinical excellence and of the effective use of available resources in the health service as the Secretary of State may direct.[233]

---

[229] Health and Social Care (Community Health and Standards) Act 2003, s 45.
[230] See *Health Act, Explanatory Notes,* para 173.
[231] *The NHS Plan—A plan for investment. A plan for reform* (Cm 4818-I, 2000), para 6.10.
[232] See *A First Class Service—Quality in the New NHS* (Department of Health, 1998), ch 2.
[233] National Institute for Clinical Excellence (Establishment and Constitution) Order 1991, SI 1999/220, reg 3, as amended by SI 1999/2219.

Prior to 2002, NICE's recommendations were persuasive, but not binding on health authorities. Since 1 January 2002, NICE guidance has had the status of 'Directions'. Now, therefore, every health authority, PCT and NHS Trust in England (the directions do not apply in Scotland and Wales):

> Shall, unless directed otherwise by the Secretary of State, apply such amounts as may be required so as to ensure that [NICE Technology Appraisal Guidance] is, from a date not later than three months from the date of Guidance, normally available [to be prescribed, or supplied to patients].[234]

This creates a clear presumption that the treatments recommended by NICE will be available to patients within three months. The funding implications of the new directions are considerable. Inevitably, PCTs may have to *disinvest* from some areas in order to accommodate the extra costs imposed by NICE. A 'blanket' duty to pay for NICE guidance is questionable. NICE makes recommendations as to clinical *effectiveness*. But evidence of efficacy is entirely different to the question whether it should take automatic *priority* over everything else. For example, NICE has recommended use of a drug capable of reducing the duration of influenza by one day.[235] Should a recommendation of this nature *automatically* command greater access to NHS resources than an effective treatment for cancer that has yet to receive NICE approval?

NICE is likely to assist applicants for judicial review who have been refused access **1.114** to treatment recommended by the Institute.[236] Especially in the light of the directions which mandate adoption of its guidance, PCTs will be required to have very good explanations as to why they are unable to purchase treatment recommended by NICE. Equally, recall they are duty-bound not to exceed their budgets. Where a PCT can demonstrate that it is responding reasonably to the pressures imposed upon it and providing an acceptable service to the community, courts ought not to be over-zealous by, in effect, ordering the PCT to *disinvest* funds from other reasonable uses in order to re-apply them to the purchase of treatment recommended by NICE. In these circumstances, the courts will be required to interpret the ambit of the phrase of the directions requiring PCTs to make the treatment 'normally available' within three months. This issue of meaning was raised before the House of Commons Health Committee. In their response to the question, the government said:

---

[234] Directions to Health Authorities, PCTs and NHS Trusts in England, para 2 as amended by amendment directions dated 19 July 2002. NICE has no statutory authority in Scotland (although its guidance is referred to by the Health Technology Board for Scotland) and it has *persuasive* force only in Wales. Note that NICE also publishes more generic 'Guidelines' (not 'Technology Appraisal Guidance') which are not binding on NHS institutions.

[235] *Guidance on zanamivir (Relenza)* (National Institute for Clinical Excellence, 1999).

[236] It may also assist claims in negligence that PCTs are in breach of a statutory duty sounding in damages. See generally Newdick, C, 'Damages for Public Authority Negligence—Public Interests and the Human Rights Act' (2002) 10 Tort L Rev 127.

> The word 'normally' was included . . . to cover unusual circumstances outside the control of PCTs such as disruption to the supply of a medicine . . . Scarce resources is not a good reason for failure to implement NICE guidance . . . PCTs are expected to manage their budgets so that patients can be *guaranteed* that if a treatment recommended by NICE is appropriate for them, they will receive it.[237]

This is a very narrow view of the meaning of 'normally' which suggests that implementation is not mandatory when it is practically *impossible* to do so. With respect, the word is capable of a wider interpretation than that that suggested here and may extend to circumstances where it is practically possible, but very difficult to do so without distorting existing arrangements. For example, NICE may recommend treatment which requires further investment in additional specialist staff. It may be that despite the reasonable efforts of the PCT to recruit suitable staff, it is very difficult to do so within existing salary scales because of shortages of available expertise. Surely, in these circumstances, the treatment could not 'normally' be made available.

1.115 Equally, NICE guidance may require further investment in infrastructure which cannot be accommodated within a three-month period without causing serious dislocation to existing services, or withdrawing services from those presently receiving them. Provided a PCT could demonstrate the existence of such circumstances, it could reasonably argue that the funding could not 'normally' be made available. More contentious, what if circumstances arose in which PCTs reasonably believed that the guidance of NICE was wrong because it had misunderstood, or misinterpreted evidence (including the evidence of its own assessors)? Given the expertise available to NICE such an event ought to be unusual. Nevertheless, provided PCTs could present suitable evidence to support their misgivings, these circumstances too could support the argument of 'abnormal' circumstances in which NICE guidance would not have to be funded within three months. Thus, a reasonable response might be to postpone the introduction of the guidance to (say) six months, or with the PCT's good will, as soon as reasonably practicable.

1.116 What happens while PCTs await publication of NICE guidance? Can they refuse to fund the treatment until NICE has spoken? As we have seen, PCTs are entitled to have policies which promote some treatments over others. However, such a process of priority setting must be fair, consistent and transparent. It cannot introduce 'blanket bans' on treatment because it must recognise that exceptional patients may have exceptional needs which are entitled to special consideration. This applies equally to treatments awaiting NICE guidance. Unless the guidance is expected imminently, PCTs should allocate resources according to the best

---

[237] *Government's Response to the Health Committee's Second Report of Session 2001–02 on the National Institute for Clinical Excellence* (Cm 5611, 2002), 8. Emphasis added.

information available to them in the present—and accept that if that information changes, policies may have to be adjusted in the future.

Finally, NICE guidance is binding on NHS *institutions*. But it is not binding on individual doctors. The decision whether to use the treatment remains entirely a matter for their reasonable clinical discretion. As NICE says, its guidance will be good for a large proportion of patients. But there will always be a significant minority for whom the treatment is inappropriate.[238] Doctors must consider the impact of the guidance and bear it well in mind in deciding what treatment is best for each patient. Although doctors would be expected to be familiar with NICE guidance and to have good reasons for not following it, it could be equally negligent to use it inappropriately just because it emanates from NICE.

1.117

(ii) National Service Frameworks

National Service Frameworks set down more general objectives for the NHS and occupy the status of *influential* guidance and are, therefore, distinct from the NICE guidance. The extent of such guidance was discussed in *R v North Derbyshire HA, ex p Fisher* (see para 1.17 above). The legal status of such guidance, however, should not obscure the political reality that the performance of senior managers will be assessed with reference to their compliance with national service frameworks (and other guidance). Although in law there is discretion as to the local response to guidance, managers will tend to comply with them so far as possible.

1.118

2. Public and Patient Involvement in the NHS

Encouraged by *Learning from Bristol*, the Secretary of State has stated that the NHS needs to do more to engage the public and that the previous arrangements were insufficient to perform the three essential new roles of inspecting NHS facilities, providing mediation and advocacy services to patients, and monitoring and advising on its overall performance.[239] We consider (i) the duty to consult, (ii) PCT forums and Patient Liaison Services, (iii) the Commission for Patient and Public Involvement in Health, and (iv) local authority Overview and Scrutiny Committees.

1.119

---

[238] 'The Institute has always indicated that health professionals, when exercising their clinical judgement, should take its guidance fully into account; but that it does not override their responsibility for making appropriate decisions in the circumstances of the individual patient. This principle is important because even the best clinical guideline is unlikely to be able to accommodate more than around 80 per cent of patients for whom it has been developed.' *Response to the Report of the Bristol Royal Infirmary Inquiry* (National Institute for Clinical Excellence, 2001), 8.

[239] See Evidence to the House of Commons Health Committee, 8 November 2000, para 317.

(i) Duty to Consult

1.120   With the abolition in England of Community Health Councils,[240] a variety of alternative means have been introduced for monitoring the NHS, increasing public involvement in the NHS and assisting patients to bring matters of complaint.
The Health Act 2001 imposes a duty on Strategic Health Authorities, PCTs and
NHS Trusts:

> To make arrangements . . . that persons to whom . . . services are provided are
> directly or through representatives involved and consulted on
>
> (a) the planning of the provision of those services,
> (b) the development and consideration of proposals for changes in the way those
>   services are provided, and
> (c) decisions to be made by that body affecting the operation of those services.[241]

Indeed, whether or not consultation of interested parties and the public is a statutory requirement, if it is embarked upon it must be carried out properly.

> To be proper, consultation [1] must be undertaken at a time when proposals are still
> at a formative stage; [2] must include sufficient reasons for particular proposals to
> allow those consulted to give intelligent consideration and an intelligent response;
> [3] adequate time must be given for this purpose; [4] the product of consultation
> must be conscientiously taken into account when the ultimate decision is taken.[242]

1.121   Exactly how the health service body should respond to the product of the consultation is a matter for local discretion. A decision to close an old and well-liked hospital is likely to generate hostility, yet the need to do so may be irrefutable, for
example, because standards of safety can no longer be maintained given the numbers and cross-section of patients admitted for care. Nevertheless, the decision
must remain open for reconsideration or modification. A number of means have
been developed for consulting the public, including health forums, citizens' (or
patient/carer) panels, focus groups and newsletters. Care must be given to the
need to balance the views of articulate pressure groups with those who are unlikely
to express themselves clearly or at all.[243] The Scottish Executive has said:

> It is also very important to consider the make up of the local community and to
> avoid the risk of token consultation or involvement . . . Care should therefore be
> taken to ensure that . . . every effort is made to obtain the views of as wide a range

---

[240] See National Health Service Reform and Health Care Professions Act 2002, s 22. Community
Health Councils have been retained in Wales, see National Health Service Reform and Health Care
Professions Act 2002, s 22 and their new powers to enter and inspect NHS premises, in Sch 1, para
3.
[241] Health and Social Care Act 2001. s 11. Guidance on the procedures to be considered in giving
effect to this requirement are discussed in *Strengthening Accountability—Involving Patients and the
Public, Policy Guidance on s 11 of the Health and Social Care Act 2001* (Department of Health, 2003).
[242] *R v North and East Devon HA, ex p Coughlan* [1999] Lloyd's Rep Med 306, 332, col 1.
[243] For many of the difficulties associated with extending democracy in the NHS, see Klein, R and
New, B, *Two Cheers?—Reflections on the Health of NHS Democracy* (King's Fund, 1998).

of people as possible. Questions might be worded in a way that seeks to draw out the various perceptions and perspectives of a diverse target group. In addition, special efforts should be made to reach excluded groups such as young and old people, gypsy travellers etc.[244]

Ultimately, however, it is the health body, and not a democratic expression of opinion, which must make the difficult decisions that confront the health service.

(ii) PCT Forums and Patient Advocacy Liaison Services

The Secretary of State shall create for each NHS Trust in England and each PCT a Patients' Forum whose members are appointed by the Commission for Patient and Public Involvement in Health. The duty of Forums is to: **1.122**

(a) monitor and review the range and operation of services provided by, or under arrangements made by, the trust for which it is established,

(b) obtain the views of patients and their carers about those matters and report on those views to the trust, provide advice, and make reports and recommendations about matters relating to the range and operation of those services to the trust,

(c) make available to patients and their carers advice and information about those services,

(d) in prescribed circumstances, perform any prescribed function of the trust with respect to the provision of a service affording assistance to patients and their families and carers,

(f) carry out such other functions as may be prescribed.[245]

In addition, the PCT Forum is responsible for providing independent advocacy services to persons to whom the Trust has provided services, to assist those who wish to bring complaints about services that have been provided. The Secretary of State must arrange for independent advocacy services to such extent as he considers necessary to meet all reasonable requirements to enable patients to make:

(a) a complaint under a procedure operated by a health service body or independent provider, (b) a complaint to the Health Service Commissioner . . . (c) [complaints to be prescribed].[246]

The Forum should seek to involve and advise the public about consultations and processes surrounding decisions and policies of public authorities.[247] Strategic Health Authorities, PCTs, local authorities, NHS Trusts and GPs may, by regulations, be required to allow members of a Patients' Forum to enter and inspect their premises. Patients' Forums may make such representations as they think fit to **1.123**

---

[244] See *Consultation and Public Involvement in Service Change—Draft Interim Guidance* (HDL (2002) 42, Scottish Executive, 2002), annex C, para 9.

[245] National Health Service Reform and Health Care Professions Act 2002, s 15(3).

[246] National Health Service Act 1977, s 19A inserted by Health and Social Care Act 2001, s 12.

[247] National Health Service Reform and Health Care Professions Act 2002, s 16.

such bodies as they think fit arising from the exercise of its functions. In particular, however, they may refer a matter to an Overview and Scrutiny Committee, or the Commission for Patient and Public Involvement in Health.[248] In addition, Patients' Forums are responsible for performing the Secretary of State's duty to arrange for independent advocacy services to assist and, if needs be, represent, individuals intending to make a complaint to an NHS body, an independent provider of NHS services, or the Health Service Ombudsman.[249] The duty is to provide independent advocacy services for persons in the Trust's area, or who have been provided with services within the Trust. Patients' Forums provide advice and information about the making of complaints. They may make representations to those who exercise functions (including overview and scrutiny committees) concerning the views of members of the public about matters affecting their health. Patients' Forums also promote public involvement in consultation processes and advise public health bodies on how to encourage further public involvement in their activities.[250]

1.124   These arrangements are complimented by Patient Advocacy Liaison Services (PALS) which are non-statutory bodies designed to assist and support the process. Misleadingly, PALS are not limited to patients, nor do they provide advocacy services. Guidance says: 'PALS . . . are not advocates. Advocates are wholly on the side of the person they represent . . . As well as representing the interests of users, staff will also be clients of the PALS team. As employees of the Trust, PALS will be in a better position . . . to represent the interests of staff . . .'[251] PALS, then, are more in the nature of a conciliation service which seeks to enable parties to settle complaints and concerns without the need for more lengthy and formal internal procedures, or litigation. Their purpose is to provide complainants with an identifiable person to turn to if they have a problem, or they need information. 'Patient advocates will act as an independent facilitator to handle patient and family concerns, with direct access to the chief executive and the power to negotiate immediate solutions.'[252] There is no prescribed model on which PALS should operate because the Department of Health accepts the need for each system to respond to the particular needs of the patient group. However, direct access to senior staff would, presumably, be a central function of PALS.[253] The service is managed through Strategic Health Authorities.[254] The purpose of the service is

---

[248] National Health Service Reform and Health Care Professions Act 2002, s 15(5)–(6).

[249] See Health and Social Care Act 2002, s 12 inserting s 19A into National Health Service Act 1977.

[250] National Health Service Reform and Health Care Professions Act 2002, s 16.

[251] *Supporting the Implementation of Patient Advice and Liaison Services* (Department of Health, 2002), para 11.6.

[252] See *The NHS Plan—A Plan for Investment, A Plan for Reform* (Cm 4818-I, 2000), para 10.18.

[253] *Supporting the Implementation of Patient Advice and Liaison Services* (Department of Health, 2002), paras 1.7 and 1.8.

[254] ibid, para 1.13.

primarily to provide an effective, speedy and informal mechanism for resolving specific problems, if needs be by taking pro-active steps on behalf of patients.

PALS are not intended as an additional arm of the consultation process. Guidance **1.125** insists that there should be no requirement that patients should use PALS before engaging a formal NHS complaint. On the other hand, it advises that it is not appropriate to use both PALS and the formal procedure at the same time.[255] Equally, if the formal route is chosen, PALS should be available to advise and guide the complainant through the process. Internal governance of PALS is at local discretion. On the other hand, PALS may have very clear insights into clinical and managerial failings in trusts. In this respect they will play an important role in the governance of the NHS as a whole. Sometimes contact with other regulatory bodies within the NHS may be required (such as the National Patient Safety Agency). Given the diversity of problems that will be dealt with informally by PALS, it is essential that NHS bodies share experience and co-operate in developing a reasonably coherent and consistent system for responding to complaints.

PALS have no formal status and trusts might consider limiting the time and re- **1.126** sources committed to the scheme. However, each trust will be subject to review and assessment by, for example, the Strategic Health Authority, the Commission for Health Improvement, the Commission for Public and Patient Involvement in Health and Patients' Forums. There will, therefore, be an imperative at managerial level to introduce and manage PALS effectively.

(iii) Commission for Patient and Public Involvement in Health

The purpose of the Commission for Patient and Public Involvement in Health is **1.127** both national and local. At national level, it will set standards, provide training and monitor the effectiveness of PALS, Patient's Forums and Independent Complaints and Advocacy Services. Locally, it will assist the development and engagement of local groups to enable local communities to take greater control of the local health services, and help existing networks develop their effectiveness. It will monitor the manner in which complaints are handled and work with Patient's Forums to provide a means of sharing and learning from local experiences. The expertise gained at local level will also be available to other parts of the NHS and may serve to influence health policy via strategic health authorities and local authority Oversight and Scrutiny Committees.[256] The Commission's statutory duties are described as follows:

---

[255] ibid, paras 4.1 and 4.5.
[256] See generally, *Involving Patients and the Public in Healthcare: Responding to the Listening Exercise* (Department of Health, 2001), 3.29–42.

(a) advising the Secretary of State, and such bodies as may be prescribed, about arrangements for public involvement in, and consultation on, matters relating to the health service in England,

(b) advising the Secretary of State, and such bodies as may be prescribed, about arrangements for the provision in England of independent advocacy services,

(c) representing to the Secretary of State and such bodies as may be prescribed, and advising him and them on, the views, as respects the arrangements referred to in paragraphs (a) and (b), of Patients' Forums and those voluntary organisations and other bodies appearing to the Commission to represent the interests of patients of the health service in England and their carers,

(d) providing staff to Patients' Forums established for Primary Care Trusts, and advice and assistance to Patients' Forums and facilitating the co-operation of their activities,

(e) advising and assisting providers of independent advocacy services in England,

(f) setting quality standards relating to any aspect of (i) the way Patients' Forums exercise their functions and (ii) the services provided by independent advocacy services in England.[257]

It should report to the Commission for Health Improvement (or other professional regulatory body) any matter which gives rise to concerns about the safety or welfare of patients.[258]

(iv) Local Authority Overview and Scrutiny Committees (OSCs)

1.128 Further 'public' oversight of the NHS is exercised by local authority overview committees.[259] The logic of OSCs may be to encourage greater understanding by NHS bodies of the views and concerns of local people. For example, local authorities in rural areas may be able to offer constructive advice and information to NHS decision-makers as to the difficulties being faced in the local community, for example in respect of areas affected by redundancy. The role of OSCs is comparable to that performed by parliamentary select committees in which members of the committee do not have executive functions and may be more detached from particular party and political issues. Scrutiny may take place before decisions have been made, or after the event. They may concern generic issues such as expenditure plans and performance statistics, or they may scrutinise specific issues, such as the care of a particular category of patients, including matters raised by patients themselves.[260] They may concern, for example, the substantive impact of decisions, the procedures by which they have been reached, or the location in which consultation took place. To foster a constructive relationship between them, NHS

---

[257] National Health Service Reform and Health Care Professions Act 2002, s 20(2).

[258] ibid, s 20(3)–(7).

[259] Created under Local Government Act 2000, s 21 as amended by Health and Social Care Act 2001, s 7.

[260] Corrigan, P, *Overview and Scrutiny: a practitioners guide* (Improvement and Development Agency, 2000).

bodies should routinely disclose reports of critical incidents, performance management reports, inspection findings and the results of consultations with patients. In response, OSCs will need to plan how their responsibilities should be organised and discharged, being careful not to duplicate the 'review' functions performed by other regulatory agencies.

The exact nature of the local authority scrutiny to be performed is not specified. **1.129** What is the function of scrutiny and how should such scrutiny be conducted to most productive effect? Regulations create a duty on local NHS bodies to provide such information about the planning, provision and operation of health services in its area as an OSC may reasonably require.[261] The duty is imposed on Strategic Health Authorities, PCTs and NHS Trusts which provide services to people living in the area of the OSC's local authority.[262] The OSC has the right to require 'an officer' of a local NHS body to appear before it to answer 'such questions as appear to the committee to be necessary for the discharge of its functions'[263] relating to the planning, provision and operation of health services in the area of its local authority. The procedure governing its review and scrutiny is for the committee to determine, other than that it shall have regard to any guidance issued by the Secretary of State, to the views of interested parties who should be invited to comment on the matter, and any relevant information provided to it by a Patients' Forum.[264] The OSC may make recommendations to local NHS bodies and where it does so it shall include an explanation of the matter reviewed, or scrutinised, and a summary of the evidence considered. When a recommendation is made the local NHS body to whom it is made must respond in writing to the committee within 28 days of the request.[265]

In particular, OSCs assume some of the responsibilities previously carried out by **1.130** Community Health Councils. Thus, 'where a local NHS body has under consideration any proposal for a substantial development of the heath service in the area of the local authority, or for a *substantial* variation in the provision of such a service, it shall consult the overview and scrutiny committee of that authority'.[266] Complaints have arisen that proper consultation was not carried out with

---

[261] The Local Authority (Overview and Scrutiny Committees Health Scrutiny Functions) Regulations 2002, SI 2002/3048, reg 5(1), subject to exceptions created for confidential and other sensitive information, unless the information can be 'anonymised' by the NHS body. The regulations are made under the authority of the Health and Social Care Act 2002.

[262] ibid, reg 1(3). Clearly, many hospitals provide services to people living in a number of surrounding local authorities. For this reason, joint committees may be appointed by two or more authorities to perform functions on behalf of each local authority on such terms as they agree. See reg 7. Similarly, a local authority may agree to delegate its powers to another OSC if the other is better able to perform its functions. See reg 8.

[263] ibid, reg 6, again there is no duty to answer questions of a confidential nature.

[264] ibid, reg 2.

[265] ibid, reg 3.

[266] ibid, reg 4(1), emphasis added.

Community Health Councils. How sensitive is the trigger that creates the duty? In *R v North West Thames RHA, ex p Daniels*[267] the authority was responsible for a bone marrow transplant unit at Westminster Children's Hospital, in which Rhys Daniels, aged two and a half, was a patient. Without consultation, the authority closed the unit and Rhys was offered treatment in Bristol instead. The Court of Appeal accepted without hesitation that, notwithstanding the small size of the unit concerned, its closure without the required consultation with the Community Health Council was unlawful for failing to comply with the Community Health Council Regulations.

1.131 The need for prior consultation is waived if 'a decision has to be taken without allowing time for consultation because of a risk to safety or welfare of patients or staff' but in such a case, the NHS body must inform the OSC immediately of the decision and the reason why no consultation has taken place.[268] A comparable matter arose in *R v North and East Devon HA, ex p Pow*.[269] The health authority, conscious of its duty to balance its books under s 97A of the National Health Service Act 1977, published a Health Action Plan as a response to a proposed shortfall in resources. From around September 1996 a number of proposals to make savings were canvassed, including the closure of (or rather the cessation of the purchase of services from) the Lynton Community Hospital, but no final decision was arrived at. Eventually, on 28 May 1997, the decision to close the hospital was taken without consultation, on the ground that there was insufficient time to consult 'in the interests of the health service'. The failure contradicted the regulations. Consultation should have taken place at an earlier stage. Moses J said:

> the process envisaged by the regulation is a process whereby the community health council and the health authority jointly seek to reach a solution to the problem with which the health authority is presented. The health authorities are under a duty, once they are considering a proposal, to consult the community health council before that proposal has evolved into a definite decision . . . [I]t would seriously undermine the purpose of the regulation if a health authority could allow time to pass to the point where matters were so urgent that there was no time left for consultation.[270]

> I well understand the frustration that the respondents must feel, faced as it is with its duty to make savings which are bound to disappoint . . . A period of consultation of six weeks may only confirm the authority in its original view, although it may reveal the opportunity for savings from other sources. [Nevertheless] such a process will have inspired the confidence in its decision which that regulation is designed to achieve.[271]

---

[267] (1994) 19 BMLR 67.
[268] See SI 2002/3048 (n 261 above), reg 4(2).
[269] (1998) 39 BMLR 77.
[270] ibid, 87–8.
[271] ibid, 90.

Clearly, the very process of consultation may suggest alternative solutions to a   **1.132**
problem. During, or following consultation, the NHS body may be attracted by
a proposal which was not included in the consultation process. In these circumstances, is it bound to enter into another period of consultation in respect of the
new proposal? The question arose in *R (on the application of Smith) v East Kent
Hospital NHS Trust*,[272] in which consultation proposed four models as bases on
which the reorganisation of local services could take place. However, the model
finally adopted contained elements of a number of the proposals without being
identical to any one of them. The court endorsed the view that there was a need to
balance the risk that if the trigger for the need for further consultation became too
sensitive, the system would become very resistant to change, either because health
authorities will be disinclined to embark on the process of change, or that decision-making becomes impossible because consultation never comes to an end.[273]
The matter was put as follows:

> [The authority] had a strong obligation to consult with all parts of the local com-
> munity. The concept of fairness should determine whether there is a need to re-con-
> sult if the decision-maker wishes to accept a fresh proposal but the court should not
> be too liberal in the use of its power of judicial review to compel further consulta-
> tion on any change . . . a proper balance has to be struck between the strong obli-
> gation to consult on the part of the health authority and the need for decisions to be
> taken that affect the running of the Health Service. This means that there should
> only be re-consultation if there is a fundamental difference between the proposals
> consulted on and those which the consulting party subsequently wishes to adopt.[274]

Thus if the decision-maker arrives at a conclusion which emerges from the con-   **1.133**
sultation in the sense that it reflects the process, further consultation is not required. This question whether there is a 'fundamental difference' is ultimately a
matter for the court to determine. It is not within the *Wednesbury* reasonable discretion of the public authority.[275] In any event, where an OSC is not satisfied with
the reasons for a decision, or the process of consultation had been inadequate, it
may report the matter to the Secretary of State who may require the NHS body to
carry out such further consultation with the OSC as he considers appropriate.
Ultimately, the Secretary of State 'may make a final decision on the proposal and
require the local NHS body to take such action, or desist from taking such action,
as he may direct' by issuing directions.[276] Clearly, these powers give local authorities the opportunity both to help and hinder NHS bodies. For example, a proposal to close a hospital may attract local opposition and elected councillors may
be under pressure to represent local opinion in objecting to it. On the other hand,

---

[272] [2002] EWHC 2640 (Admin).
[273] See also *R v Shropshire HA and Secretary of State, ex p Duffus* [1990] 1 Med LR 119.
[274] [2002] EWHC 2640 (Admin), at [45].
[275] ibid, at [51].
[276] See SI 2002/3048 (n 261 above) reg 4(5)–(7) and 10.

the decision may be supported within the NHS on grounds of safety. For example, if the numbers of patients being referred to the hospital is insufficient to maintain minimum standards of clinical competence, the NHS may prefer to sell the hospital and divert the resources to expanding another hospital where larger numbers of patients can be treated to a higher standard of care. How should these differing perspectives be managed?

1.134 The NHS body is not bound by the recommendations of the OSC; on the contrary, it is duty-bound to decide matters for itself in the light of its recommendations. NHS and local authority officers will need to invest considerable time and resources in understanding one another's views and aspirations. A failure to do so is unlikely to lead to a constructive relationship. In something of an under-statement, the Audit Commission remarked:

> OSCs may . . . recognise that the most difficult problems facing the NHS have no simple, or universally popular solution. Local NHS bodies have to make complex trade-offs between competing service demands, and have only limited room for manoeuvre within a national framework of policies and standards. And there will sometimes be tensions between the wishes of local people and what is affordable and/or clinically effective.[277]

3. Governance of Clinical Standards

1.135 To the extent that patients elect to litigate in respect of poor standards of care, the law of negligence may have an influence in improving standards, although only after the accident has occurred. However, the new duty of quality is not limited to those who bring complaints; indeed, it extends to matters about which there has been no complaint. It requires authorities to introduce systems of clinical governance capable of identifying short-comings and responding to them appropriately. The Commission for Health Improvement (and its successor the Commission for Health Audit and Inspection), the National Patient Safety Agency and the National Clinical Assessments Authority will each be concerned to see that the duty is complied with. We discuss each in turn.

(i) Commission for Health Improvement (CHI)[278]

1.136 CHI has a broad range of duties conferred upon it connected with monitoring and improving the quality of care provided by PCTs and NHS Trusts as follows:

---

[277] *A Healthy Outlook—Local Authority Overview and Scrutiny of Health* (Audit Commission, 2002), para 25.
[278] In Wales, note the creation of the Wales Centre for Health by the Health (Wales) Act 2003, s 2 and its functions in s 3 and Sch 2. Note that, after submission of the manuscript, CHI was replaced by the Commission for Health Care Audit and Inspection by the Health and Social Care (Community Health and Standards) Act 2003. See para 139 below.

(a) the function of providing advice or information with respect to arrangements by Primary Care Trusts or NHS Trusts for the purpose of monitoring and improving the quality of health care for which they have responsibility,

(b) the function of conducting reviews of, and making reports on, arrangements by Primary Care Trusts or NHS Trusts for the purpose of monitoring and improving the quality of care for which they have responsibility,

(c) the function of carrying out investigations into, and making reports on, the management, provision or quality of care for which Health Authorities, Primary Care Trusts, or NHS Trusts have responsibility,

(d) the function of conducting reviews of, and making reports on, the management, provision or quality of, or access to or availability of, health care for which NHS bodies or service providers have responsibility,

(da) the function of conducting reviews of, and making reports on, the quality of data obtained by others relating to the management, provision or quality of, or access to or availability of, health care for which NHS bodies or service providers have responsibility, the validity of conclusions drawn from such data, and the methods used in their collection and analysis,

(db) the function of carrying out inspections of NHS bodies and service providers, and persons who provide or are to provide health care for which NHS bodies or service providers have responsibility, and making reports on the inspections, and

(e) such functions as may be prescribed relating to the management, provision or quality of, or access to or availability of, health care for which prescribed NHS bodies or prescribed service providers have responsibility.[279]

Notice that the powers extend to private providers of NHS services under para **1.137** (db). The Commission shall conduct reviews and carry out investigations which shall include the collection and analysis of data and the assessment of performance against criteria (such as 'star ratings'), and the Commission must publish at least a summary of each report it makes in the exercise of its functions.[280] These functions are to be discharged by a committee of CHI known as the Office for Information on Health Care Performance.[281] If the Commission is of the view that the body or service in question is of 'unacceptably poor quality (whether generally or in particular areas), or there are significant failings in the way the body or service is being run', the Commission shall report to the Secretary of State and may recommend that he take 'special measures' to improve the health care for which it is responsible.[282] It may enter premises to inspect them, take documents, or require individuals to provide explanations to the Commission.[283]

---

[279] Health Act 1999, s 20 as amended by National Health Service Reform and Health Care Professions Act 2002, ss 12 and 13.

[280] Health Act 1999, s 20(1A) and (1B) inserted by National Health Service Reform and Health Care Professions Act 2002, s 12(3).

[281] Health Act 1999, Sch 2, para 5A(2) inserted by National Health Service Reform and Health Care Professions Act 2002, s 14.

[282] Health Act 1999, s 20(ID)–(1G) inserted by s 13(1), National Health Service Reform and Health Care Professions Act 2002, s 13(1).

[283] S 23, Health Act 1999, s 23. See also the Commission for Health Improvement (Functions) Regulations 2000, SI 2000/662.

1.138 CHI has a short life-expectancy. Subject to Parliamentary approval it will be re-placed by the Commission for Healthcare Audit and Inspection (CHAI, still pro-nounced 'CHI'!) and commence work in April 2004. It will be chaired by Professor Sir Ian Kennedy and combine the functions of CHI, the Audit Commission, the National Care Standards Commission (which is responsible for the inspection of private and voluntary health care provision) and the Mental Health Act Commission. The purpose of CHAI will be to strengthen and co-ordinate accountability in the NHS, conscious of the burden governance can impose on the service. CHAI will be responsible for the inspection of public (including foundation) and privately owned hospitals, and encourage improve-ment in the quality and 'in the economy and efficiency of health . . . care provi-sion as well as the promotion of public health'.

1.139 CHAI will conduct investigations, both into individual institutions and into the NHS in general, and publish reports when it has serious concerns and be duty-bound to report serious matters to the Secretary of State and to recommend the remedial measures that should be taken. It will produce annual performance rat-ings for NHS organisations and an annual report to Parliament. Significantly, CHAI will remain at arm's length from government as a non-departmental pub-lic body whose chair and commissioners will be appointed by an independent process and not by the Secretary of State.[284] It will publish annual performance ratings which, according the chairman of CHAI, will not be based on 'a telephone book of standards' or a 'tick-box' mentality.[285] Nevertheless, it will have the power to take enforcement action (and to remove registration from private and volun-tary providers). CHAI will work closely with the Commission for Social Care Inspection in monitoring, advising and reporting on the provision of social care and care providers in the independent sector. If needs, be they will be empowered to take enforcement action where the safety or welfare of users is at risk. It will also seek to maximise the benefit of regulation and reduce its burden by concentrating scrutiny in organisations and services at greatest risk and rewarding high-quality performance with an appropriately light touch.[286]

(ii) National Clinical Assessments Authority (NCAA)

1.140 The NCAA will enhance the ability of the NHS to address concerns about the performance of doctors. Its functions are described as follows:

---

[284] *Statement of Purpose: Commission for Health Care Audit and Inspection, Commission for Social Care Inspection* (Department of Health, 2003), para 2.4 and Health and Social Care (Community Health and Standards) Act 2003, ss 48–69.

[285] Donnelly, L, 'Kennedy pushes for "intelligent" scrutiny', *Health Service Journal*, 26 June 2003, 5.

[286] See CHAI *Statement of Purpose* (*www.doh.gov.uk/csci/whatsnew.htm*). See also Dewar, S and Finlayson, B, 'The I in the new CHAI' (2002) 325 BMJ 848.

(a) to develop and disseminate . . . good practice guidance for the handling of poor performance cases by trusts, health authorities and [PCTs];

(b) to identify, designate, oversee and set out the responsibilities of local perform-ance assessment service provision and to invite proposals from potential providers;

(c) to identify and agree methodologies for assessment and reporting, seeking advice from those with expertise in this field;

(d) to work closely with the Royal Colleges, specialist societies, those with general practice interests and lay members representatives of the general public, to establish and maintain a list of lay assessors and medically qualified assessors in each specialty;

(e) to undertake and approve the appointment of key staff to organise the assess-ment of performance at local level,

(f) to quality control activities at local level to ensure consistency of advice and ap-proach to performance assessment;

(g) to quality assure assessment activity and reporting at local level, ensuring com-pliance with EC requirements, employment law and natural justice;

(h) to work in partnership with and to liaise with the GMC and CHI in develop-ing policies to ensure that activity overlap is kept to a minimum and that effec-tive channels of communication exist at both national and local levels . . . to look into and consider possible improvements in the assessment of clinical per-formance and the effective use of available resources, and such other matters as may be notified by the Secretary of State.[287]

NCAA assessment may consider doctors' occupational and psychological health, **1.141** their basic clinical knowledge, their practice equipment and medical records. It may also consider the views of patients and other colleagues.[288] The Authority is not primarily concerned with the issue of a doctor's fitness to practise, which is the concern of the General Medical Council. Instead, it provides expert advice to PCTs and hospital managers as to concerns raised about clinical performance. The NCAA will not take over the disciplinary role of the employer, nor will it function as a regulator. Rather, it will help the employer or health authority by carry-ing out an objective assessment, following which, it will advise referring organisa-tions on appropriate action. Exactly what form such an 'objective assessment' will take is not yet clear. What criteria will be used and how? Would frequent staff turnover or the fact that patients were leaving the practice in above average num-bers be relevant? Would excessive, or irregular prescribing be considered in the same way as a failure to meet immunisation targets, or poor clinical record keep-ing? As independent contractors, doctors may organise themselves in very differ-ent ways and it is difficult to see how all can be assessed against the same standard. The particular standards chosen are likely to be the subject of disagreement and complaint. In any event: 'The Authority's recommendations will be advisory and

[287] Directions to the National Clinical Assessments Authority (undated) Annex A, para 2(1).
[288] *NCAA Handbook—General Practice in England* (NCAA, 2002) para 5.11. See also *NCAA Handbook—Hospital and Community Health Services* (NHS, 2002).

the creation of the NCAA does not in any way affect the rights and responsibilities of trusts, health authorities and doctors.'[289]

1.142 Whenever a doctor is being assessed in this way, natural justice and NCAA guidance require that a distinction be made between the *investigation* and *adjudication* of the merits of the case. No central guidance has been offered to PCTs as to how this process should work. Clearly, in the absence of such guidance it is absurd for over 300 PCTs to re-invent separate processes individually and collaboration between regions is sensible. The NCAA recommends:

> a structure that separates [i] decision-making about the seriousness of concerns and the need for onward referral from [ii] performance assessment and educational support. This can be achieved by means of groups this document describes by the terms *Performance Decision-making Group* and a *Performance Advisory Group*. Local groups will want to find their own names, but distinguishing their functions is likely to be important. The performance Advisory Group . . . will usually be external to the contracting organisation.[290]

The NCAA expects that in the majority of cases, concerns should be resolved satisfactorily by means of local procedures, if needs be, with the assistance of its advice but without the need for formal NCAA assessment. When such an assessment is required, however, it will undertake a formal assessment of the doctor in question and propose solutions. In such a case 'a doctor shall co-operate with an assessment by the NCAA when requested to do so by the Health Authority'.[291] The NCAA has no direct power to regulate doctors.

> Rather, it will help the employer or health authority by carrying out an objective assessment. Following such an assessment, it will advise referring organisations on appropriate action . . . The Authority's recommendations will be advisory and the creation of the NCAA does not in any way affect the rights and responsibilities of trusts, health authorities and doctors.[292]

1.143 Nevertheless, the NCAA will have an indirect influence by providing advice to referring organisations with regard to what action could be taken if concern persists about the doctor's performance. Also, the duty of quality imposed on the NHS will create a strong presumption that appropriate action will follow the NCAA's recommendations, and Strategic Health Authorities and CHI will want to see evidence of implementation of NCAA action plans within their review.[293] NHS Trust employers have power to deal with the doctors within the terms of the contract of employment. PCTs have new powers to suspend, or disqualify doctors on

---

[289] *About the Authority* (NCAA, 2002).
[290] *NCAA Handbook for General Practice* (NCAA, 2002) 6.50 and 6.52.
[291] National Health Service (General Medical Services) Regulations 1992, Sch, para 50 (inserted by National Health Service (General Medical Services) Amendment (No 4) Regulations 2001, SI 2001/3742, reg 16(7)).
[292] *About the Authority* (NCAA 2002).
[293] *NCAA Handbook—General Practice in England*, para 5.27.

grounds of 'efficiency', 'fraud', and 'unsuitability'.[294] Suspension is available only if the authority is satisfied 'that it is necessary to do so for the protection of members of the public or is otherwise in the public interests'.[295] Advice surrounding the meaning of these words is imprecise.

'Efficiency' was the criteria used by the former NHS Tribunal to the effect that the inclusion of the person on the list is prejudicial to the efficiency of the particular service they are providing. It was never felt appropriate to define or restrict the term 'efficiency' and this stance has been carried forward in the new provisions . . .

There is no definition of 'fraud' in law, although most people will have a common understanding of what the term means—that someone has obtained resources to which he is not entitled. Under the provisions of 49F(3) of the NHS Act 1977 Act, there does not have to be a proven criminal conviction so long as there are sufficient substantiated facts to satisfy the Health Authority, that a doctor has secured, or tried to secure financial benefit for himself or another to which he knew there was no entitlement.

'Unsuitability' as a concept was considered in the aftermath of the Harold Shipman trial to capture matters such as the effect on a doctor's suitability of a criminal record. However, a decision was taken that we did not wish to provide a restrictive definition within legislation, a decision debated at some length in Parliament before being accepted. Consequently the term can be ascribed its everyday meaning and provides a broad area of discretion for Health Authorities. The overlap with 'efficiency' is marked and in many cases a Health Authority would be able to take action under either heading against a doctor.[296]

In connection with the meaning of 'efficiency' and 'unsuitability', the GP's terms **1.144** of service have always insisted that GPs prescribe the medicines and appliances which are needed by their patients.[297] The threat of disciplinary action against GPs on these grounds merely for expensive, *but appropriate* prescribing would appear, therefore, to be unlawful. In any event, whenever an authority is considering action of this gravity, it must be careful to observe the rules of natural justice and to act proportionately. The nature of the procedures used to adjudicate in matters of this nature are at the discretion of health authorities, but it would be sensible for authorities to co-operate with one another in creating them. Clearly, it is crucial that those responsible for examining and reporting on the matters about which concerns have been raised are not also on the panel which assesses the sanction to be imposed on the doctor. In addition the NCAA recommends that the doctor who is the subject of the assessment have the help and support of a 'friend' of his or her own choice prior to the assessment.[298]

---

[294] See National Health Service Act 1977, s 49F inserted by Health and Social Care Act 2001, s 25. These provisions also apply to dentists and opticians.

[295] National Health Service Act 1977, s 49I(1).

[296] *Delivering Quality in Primary Care* (Primary Care Division, Department of Health, 2001), paras 6.2.5–8.

[297] See *R v Secretary of State for Health, ex p Pfizer* [1999] Lloyd's Rep Med 289.

[298] *NCAA Handbook—General Practice in England,* paras 5.06–5.07.

(iii) Council for Regulation of Health Care Professions

1.145 Following the recommendation of the Bristol Inquiry of the need to align and co-ordinate the activities of regulatory bodies,[299] there was created the Council for the Regulation of Health Care Professionals. Membership of the Council is at the discretion of the Secretary of State and, to promote its independence, the government intends the power to be exercised by the NHS Appointments Commission. It is proposed that a small number will be appointed who will speak for the interests of health care providers, and a larger number who will speak for the interests of patients and the wider public.[300] Its function is:

(a) to promote the interests of patients and other members of the public in relation to the performance of their functions [by specified regulatory bodies[301]] and by their committees and officers,

(b) to promote best practice in the performance of those functions,

(c) to formulate principles relating to good professional self-regulation, and to encourage regulatory bodies to conform to them, and,

(d) to promote co-operation between regulatory bodies; and between them, or any of them, and other bodies performing corresponding functions.[302]

1.146 The Council may investigate and report on the performance by each regulatory authority of its functions and recommend changes to the way it performs its functions.[303] Each such body must, in the exercise of its functions, co-operate with the Council which may issue directions requiring a regulatory body to change its rules to achieve a particular result,[304] for example, to promote consistency between different regulators. Failure to adhere to such a direction would render the body amenable to judicial review. The Council may not intervene in the determination of 'fitness to practise' cases against individuals.[305] However, if it considers that a regulatory body has been unduly lenient with respect to its adjudication in a matter of professional discipline, it may refer the case to be reconsidered by the High Court where the case is to be treated as an appeal by the Council against the

---

[299] *Learning from Bristol* (n 1 above) 25, para 75.

[300] National Health Service Reform and Health Care Professions Act 2002, Sch 7, paras 4 and 5 and *Explanatory Notes to National Health Reform and Health Care Professions Act 2002*, paras 134 *et seq*.

[301] The regulatory bodies include the General Medical Council, the General Dental Council, the General Optical Council, the General Osteopathic Council, the General Chiropractic Council, the Royal Pharmaceutical Society of Great Britain and Nursing and Midwifery Council and the Health Professions Council; see National Health Service Reform and Health Care Professions Act 2002, s 25(3).

[302] National Health Service Reform and Health Care Professions Act 2002, s 25(2).

[303] ibid, s 26. The power to modify the regulation governing specified regulatory bodies 'for the purpose of securing or improving the regulation of the profession, or the services which the profession provides' exists by Order in Council under Health Act 1999, s 60 and Sch 3. The power does not permit the abolition, or replacement of the regulatory body.

[304] ibid, s 27. Such directions must be laid before both Houses of Parliament.

[305] ibid, s 26(3) and (4).

relevant decision.[306] In these extreme circumstances, the respondent clinician would have the right to be represented and the court has the power to dismiss the appeal, allow the appeal and quash the relevant decision, substitute its own decision for the one referred to it, or refer the case back to the regulatory body for rehearing in the light of the court's directions.[307]

(iv) National Patient Safety Agency (NPSA)

It is estimated that around 5 per cent of the 8.5 million patients (ie 425,000) who are admitted to hospital in England and Wales each year experience an adverse event which may have been preventable with the exercise of ordinary standards of care. How many of these events lead to death is not known but it may be as high as 25,000 people a year.[308] *An Organisation with a Memory*[309] observes how little we understand about these accidents and how much can be learned from a systematic analysis of how they occur and why. What is more, the NHS as a single health care system should take advantage of its experience and knowledge.[310] The NPSA has been introduced to promote this objective and will maintain a database of adverse events so as to secure improvements in the quality and treatment of patients.[311] The NPSA has a vitally important and perhaps unique role to play in improving systems of NHS governance. The functions of the NPSA are: **1.147**

(a) to devise, implement and monitor a reporting system based on relevant national standards issued by the Department regarding the promotion of patient safety, (b) to collect and appraise information on reported adverse incidents and other material useful for any purpose connected with the promotion of patient safety, (c) to provide advice and guidance in the maintenance and promotion of patient safety and to monitor the effectiveness of such advice and guidance, (d) to promote research which the Agency considers will contribute to improvements in patient safety, (e) to report to and advise Ministers on matters affecting patient safety.[312]

The NPSA's purpose is to assess the organisational and institutional factors bearing upon medical accidents by identifying and eliminating dysfunctional systems. Towards this objective, the NPSA recommends a number of local duties in relation to the management of the risk of accidents. Thus: **1.148**

(i)   Individuals involved directly or indirectly in patient care should be aware of what constitutes an adverse patient incident.

---

[306] ibid, s 29(4) and (5).
[307] ibid, s 29(8).
[308] Vincent, A, Neale, G, et al, 'Adverse Events in British Hospitals' (2000) 322 BMJ 517.
[309] Department of Health, 2000.
[310] See also *Building a safer NHS for Patients: implementing an organisation with a memory,* para 52.
[311] National Patient Safety Agency (Establishment and Constitution) Order 2001, SI 2001/1743, reg 3 and the National Patient Safety Agency Regulations 2001, SI 2001/1742.
[312] *Directions to the National Patient Safety Agency* (Department of Health, July 2001).

(ii) Incidents should be managed and reported to a designated person, or persons, in accordance with local arrangements.

(iii) All serious incidents should be reported immediately to a locally designated authority and, where appropriate, information on these incidents is 'fast-tracked' to relevant external stakeholders.

(iv) All reported incidents should be assessed and graded according to their severity in terms of their actual impact on the patient(s), and the potential future risk to patients and to the organisation, and reviewed to establish stakeholder reporting requirements.

(v) Adverse patient incidents should be investigated at an appropriate level, subjected to a causal analysis and, where relevant, an improvement strategy is prepared.

(vi) Incidents graded as red, should be reported to the NPSA within three working days of the date of occurrence. For category red adverse events only (ie where serious actual harm has resulted), this information is also reported within three working days to the relevant Regional Office of the Department of Health.

(vii) For all category red incidents, a causal analysis is undertaken by the local organisation and reported to the NPSA and the relevant Regional Office of the Department of Health within 45 working days of occurrence of the incident.

(viii) Where appropriate, there is co-operation between the health body and the Department of Health (and other stakeholders) to establish an independent investigation or enquiry into the circumstances surrounding a particular adverse patient incident.

(ix) Reviews of local incident data/information should be carried out on an on-going basis by the organisation and the significant results communicated to local stakeholders and sent to the NPSA on a quarterly basis.

(x) Lessons are learned from individual adverse patient incidents, from local aggregate reviews and from wider experiences, including feedback from the NPSA, other agencies/bodies, and benchmarking. Improvement strategies are developed and implemented to reduce risk to future patients.[313]

1.149 In *Making Amends*,[314] the Chief Medical Officer proposes to introduce a broad-ranging duty to report medical accidents on NHS staff in return for greater insulation from claims for medical negligence. Such a duty would illuminate many of the shortcomings inherent in the NHS, many of which may not be widely recognised or clearly visible. It would contribute to the work of the NPSA and enhance our understanding of the systemic and institutional risks inherent within the NHS.

---

[313] *www.npsa.nhs.uk/static/reporting.asp.*
[314] Department of Health, 2003.

2

REGULATING HEALTH CARE PROFESSIONS

A. Regulation and the Health Care Professions

Self-regulation has often been seen as the hallmark of professional status. As a **2.01** result of some of the major health care 'scandals' of the late 1990s—specifically *Shipman*, *Ledward*, *Allitt* and the *Bristol heart babies cases*—and the public perception that the medical and related professions failed to take appropriate steps to prevent them, the concept has increasingly come under attack to the extent of increased government scrutiny and intervention by legislation.

The Bristol Royal Infirmary Enquiry Report noted that:[1]   **2.02**

> Regulation is a broad term. It is not merely concerned with discipline and poor performance. To be effective in the service of patients, professional regulation should be understood as encapsulating all the systems which combine to assure the competence of healthcare professionals: education, registration, training, continuing professional development and revalidation, as well as disciplinary matters. It should be concerned to promote good practice at all stages of a professional's career . . . If appropriate efforts are made to assure good performance in the course of a professional's working life, the incidence of poor performance requiring some form of disciplinary action should be significantly reduced.

---

[1] 2001.

2.03   Whilst the main medically related professions (medicine, dentistry, pharmacy and optical) have long enjoyed legally protected status and specifically protection of title (and with it the legal right to self-regulation), before the 1990s professions such as osteopaths and chiropractors had no protection of title and indeed no unified professional body or unified register for the public to consult with the effect that the public seeking such services would have had little basis for knowing whether a practitioner was legitimate or appropriately qualified. Legislation was introduced to correct that position (such as the Osteopaths Act 1993 and the Chiropractors Act 1994). However, other significant health care professions (such as physiotherapists) still await such protection of title.

2.04   Where the right to self-regulation had been recognised by statute with protection of title as a recognised adjunct, concern arose as to those professions 'looking after their own' to the detriment of the public interest. The 'scandals' of the late 1990s (and specifically concerns that the General Medical Council ('GMC') had failed to take appropriate action to prevent such 'scandals') led to increased calls for government involvement. The National Health Service Reform and Health Care Professions Act 2002 resulted and represents a major shift in the self-regulation of medical and allied health care professions by establishing a body known as the Council for the Regulation of Health Care Professions whose functions are stated to be the promotion of the interests of patients and members of the public in relation to the performance of the regulatory and disciplinary functions of the various health care regulatory bodies such as the GMC (doctors), the General Dental Council (dentists), the General Optical Council (opticians), the General Osteopathic Council (osteopaths), the General Chiropractic Council (chiropractors), the Royal Pharmaceutical Societies (pharmacists), the Nursing and Midwifery Council (nurses, midwives and health visitors) and the Health Professions Council (dieticians, physiotherapists, chiropodists/podiatrists, occupational therapists, speech therapists, radiographers, paramedics, etc).

2.05   The principal function of each of the regulatory bodies (Councils) for the individual health care professions was and remains the maintenance of a professional register controlling admission to (and continued presence on) that register—based on the satisfaction of educational and training requirements (and in many cases now continuing professional education/development requirements) and of good character. After admission to an appropriate register issues which are thereafter controlled by the regulatory bodies are issues of conduct (specifically misconduct) and, in the case of certain regulatory bodies (such as the GMC) issues relating to competence and health—being considered to be issues fundamental to the professional's 'fitness to practise' his or her profession.

2.06   There are many similarities in the regulatory schemes governing the different health care professions. In all cases the aim of the regulation is said to be protection of the public against incompetent or inadequate practitioners—thereby maintaining the good reputation or standing of that profession. Maintenance of such good standing is usually by means of a power to remove from the relevant register the 'offending' professional which will have two consequences—in the majority of cases (given protection of title and requirements within the National Health Service (NHS) for professional registration to secure particular employment) inability to practise a profession for which the individual is otherwise qualified, and additionally the preservation of a valuable monopoly for those who do maintain appropriate registration.

Since October 2000 and the coming into force of the Human Rights Act 1998   **2.07** (introducing as part of English Law the 1948 European Convention on Human Rights) the right to practise a profession for which an individual is qualified and has been practising has been subject to additional protections (recognised by the Strasbourg European Court of Human Rights[1a]) which have had significant impact on the manner in which health care regulatory bodies (and public body health care employers) discipline their registered professionals. The impact of human rights law is also responsible for a number of changes now being proposed (and consulted on) in respect of the conduct of disciplinary proceedings against professionals and specifically the problems of self-regulation (where the same regulatory body acts both as 'prosecutor' and 'adjudicator' in the disciplinary case).

Given the monopoly employment position of the (NHS) and consequently the   **2.08** (relative) lack of choice of individual treating health care professionals by members of the public (patients), and the fact that unlike with many other professional services (such as legal, architectural, or accountancy) the entire population at some time during their lifetime will have cause to consult a health care professional (and often repeatedly) the issues of regulation for protection of the public are of huge legal (and political) importance. They are considered in this chapter under three different aspects:

(i)   basis of regulation of health care professionals and efficacy of the aim of protection of the public;

(ii) NHS control (as employer/contractor for services) of its professionals delivering health care services on its behalf;

(iii) complaints' procedures and clinical governance measures as aids to ensuring quality health care provision.

1. The Medical Profession

Since 1858 regulation of the medical profession in the United Kingdom has been   **2.09** primarily governed by statute (the Medical Act 1858 created the GMC). The

---

[1a] *Albert & Le Compte v Belgium* (1983) 5 EHRR 533; *Stefan v UK* (1998) 25 EHRR CD 130.

current Act is the Medical Act 1983. Under this Act and various pieces of delegated legislation (statutory instruments and Orders) the GMC has had delegated to it the regulation of medical education and control of the medical profession.

2.10 Similar primary or delegated legislation exists for other health care professions for example, the Dentists Act 1984, the Pharmacy Act 1954, the Osteopaths Act 1993, the Chiropractors Act 1994, the Opticians Act 1989, the Nurses, Midwives and Health Visitors Act 1997 and the Nursing and Midwifery Order 2001.

2. Who Can Practise Medicine?

2.11 Contrary to what may be the public perception or expectation there is no legislative restriction on who can treat patients or provide medical or health related services (ie, it is not a criminal offence to provide what would be considered medical assistance or treatment to another person). This is in contrast with the position in respect of animals where it is a criminal offence under the Veterinary Surgeons Act 1966[2] for someone who is not a registered veterinary surgeon to provide treatment (save in an emergency) to an animal. The only exceptions for health care professionals are in dentistry[3] and optical care.[4]

2.12 Therefore the public/patients can receive medical treatment—without restriction—from all types of alternative practitioners or unqualified persons or those with training from non-state approved or registered bodies. With the increasing popularity of alternative therapies and homeopathic 'cures' in the 1990s and the increased accessibility to information and treatments through the internet, and most specifically the commercial significance (and market for) such treatments and information, real problems have arisen in terms of controlling the provision of medical treatment in the interests of protection of the public.

2.13 What is controlled or restricted is the right to use certain protected titles. Under s 49 of the Medical Act 1983 it is a criminal offence for any person to wilfully and falsely pretend to be or take and use the name or title of physician, doctor of medicine, licentiate in medicine or surgery, bachelor of medicine, surgeon, general practitioner or equivalent title or description implying legal recognition of a medical qualification or a legal right to practise medicine. Therefore the public have a basis when considering internet based medicinal treatment offers or services offered by alternative practitioners or therapists of knowing whether the practitioners are medically qualified.

2.14 The scope for accessing medical treatment and medicines via the internet and from the increasing number of therapists and practitioners in the High Street and

---

[2] s 19.
[3] Dentists Act 1984, s 38.
[4] Opticians Act 1989, ss 24–26.

advertising in glossy magazines dealing with health care and lifestyle issues, has served to highlight the importance of protection of title for health care professionals—such now existing for doctors, dentists, osteopaths, chiropractors and pharmacists with proposals that it should also apply to physiotherapists and chiropodists/podiatrists.

Apart from statutory protection of title the criminal law will intervene by use of the Theft Act 1968 where an individual dishonestly represents in order to obtain money[5] or a job ('pecuniary advantage')[6] that he holds particular qualifications or is on a professional register either of which entitle him or her to provide the services or obtain the employment or are dishonestly represented to secure the opportunity to provide the services or undertake the employment. **2.15**

If a patient is caused to consent to treatment by a negligent or dishonest misrepresentation by any individual as to the holding of recognised medical or other qualifications then the consent will be vitiated and the practitioner would be at risk of prosecution for assault and battery and in any event would be liable in damages under the civil law for the equivalent torts. **2.16**

Further statutory protection is provided by the fact that certain procedures or types of medical attendance cannot as a matter of law be charged for unless the practitioner is a registered medical practitioner[7] or (save where there is an urgent necessity) a registered midwife or medical practitioner (attendance on a woman in childbirth[8]). **2.17**

3. Registration and Qualifications

The legislation governing the different health care professions has a common approach—establishment of a central council which maintains the professional register and is responsible for issuing guidance on standards and continuing education. As part of the maintenance of that register the council controls issues of competence and conduct. In this era of increasing technology, access to the relevant registers and registration information is often via the websites of the respective councils. **2.18**

The most prominent of the relevant councils is the GMC which controls the register of medical practitioners. As a result of a number of high profile cases concerning the alleged misdeeds of doctors in recent years there has been an increased public awareness of the GMC and the right to make complaint to it about a doctor. This has resulted in a huge increase in the number of cases considered by the **2.19**

---

[5] s 15.
[6] s 16.
[7] Medical Act 1983, s 46.
[8] Nurses, Midwives and Health Visitors Act 1997, s 16.

GMC under its Fitness to Practise Procedures in the last decade and serial increases and changes in the nature of its jurisdictions.

2.20 Entry to the medical register is based on primary qualifications set out in legislation.[9] The commonest route to entry is a medical degree from a medical school at a UK university. This entitles the holder to provisional registration for a year (the pre-registration House Officer/internship training year) which is converted into full registration following completion of 12 months' internship as a hospital-based practitioner with periods of training in surgery and general medicine. A doctor holding provisional registration is entitled to work only in resident junior house officer posts in hospitals or institutions that are approved for the purpose of pre-registration house officer service.

2.21 As a result of the United Kingdom's membership of the European Union and the requirements of European law as to free movement of workers and freedom to provide services across national boundaries there has been secondary EU legislation providing for the mutual recognition of the EU medical qualifications and a consequent entitlement to entry onto the GMC's Medical Register. A medical school qualification from a European Economic Area (EEA) medical school or from Switzerland held by a national of an EEA state or Switzerland (or a non-EEA national with EU rights—based on marriage to an EU national with free movement rights) will entitle the individual to provisional registration if postgraduate internship has not been completed and full registration if it has.

2.22 Different and separate regimes exist for recognition of non-EU qualifications and for entry onto the UK Medical Register of overseas qualified doctors. Those with qualifications from medical schools in Australia, New Zealand, Hong Kong, Singapore, South Africa and the West Indies until December 2003 were entitled to provisional registration if they had not completed internship training and full registration if they have.

2.23 All other overseas qualified practitioners must apply for limited registration. To be entitled to apply an individual must hold a primary medical qualification that is recognised by the GMC (currently some 1,600 overseas primary medical qualifications are so recognised, including all those listed in the World Directory of Medical Schools published by the World Health Organisation). Applicants for limited registration are required to provide the GMC with evidence of capability for practice in the United Kingdom which includes for those whose native language is not English either passing a Professional Linguistic Assessment Board (PLAB) test or providing other objective evidence of linguistic competence. Such requirements have previously led to complaints of racial discrimination by those who have failed the PLAB when EEA practitioners obtain registration without

---

[9] Medical Act 1983; Medical Qualifications (Amendment) Act 1991.

having to satisfy such a requirement. The claims have all failed on the basis of the statutory exceptions in the Race Relations Act 1976 allowing discrimination in favour of EU nationals as a consequence of UK membership of the European Union.[10]

Limited registration is granted only for supervised employment in training posts   **2.24** in the NHS. The maximum period for which a practitioner can hold limited registration is five years in total (and some overseas doctors have only the possibility of lesser periods due to their immigration status—normally full registration will be required by the Home Office to confirm indefinite leave to remain and an unrestricted work permit).

Moving from limited registration to full registration is dependent upon satisfying   **2.25** the GMC's Registration Committee's specific guidelines which generally require demonstration of knowledge, skills and attitudes equal to those expected of a competent senior house officer and satisfactory evidence of 'good character'. In recent years these GMC-imposed guidelines have been perceived as more onerous with the consequence of a shift in balance of non-UK qualified medical practitioners away from those from the Indian subcontinent towards EU practitioners (who often only come to the United Kingdom for shorter periods rather than as part of a permanent move).

The decision as to the grant of full registration to an overseas practitioner before   **2.26** the conclusion of his time-limited period of limited registration is made by application to the GMC which considers the application against the 'experience' guidelines set by the Registration Committee (specifically satisfactory completion of one year's UK experience as a senior house officer or specialist registrar in the previous two years in substantive posts or locum posts of a duration in excess of three months with satisfactory consultant reports covering the experience, or having been appointed to a Type 1 specialist registrar post and having completed satisfactorily 12 months' UK experience at senior house office grade in the previous two years).

Where the GMC is of the opinion that the practitioner has not met the guidelines   **2.27** (and often the stumbling block can be the supervising consultants' reports which express views that the practitioner has not been satisfactory in the post or that his/her performance has raised an issue of 'good character' as a result of complaints made during the post), the application is referred to the Registration Committee of the GMC for a decision.

A practitioner who is refused full registration, without which after the expiry of   **2.28** his/her period of limited registration practice in the United Kingdom as a registered

---

[10] *GMC v Goba* [1988] ICR 885 (EAT); *Ravenska v GMC* [1997] IRLR 367 CA.

medical practitioner is no longer possible—(and which may also result in loss of immigration rights to remain in the United Kingdom) can apply to the Review Board for Overseas Qualified Practitioners for a review of the decision.[11] The decision of this Board does not give rise to any appeal but as the GMC is a statutory body and a public authority the decision is susceptible to judicial review by the Administrative Court on normal judicial review grounds. The difficulty is that the GMC has a discretion on both the experience guidelines and the issue of what constitutes 'good character' such that successful challenge will be difficult with the courts traditionally reluctant to interfere with discretionary decisions of specialist professional bodies.[12] Prior to the Human Rights Act 1998 coming into force in October 2000 the Registration Committee and Review Board received the supervising consultants' reports on a confidential basis and the practitioner faced a huge hurdle in trying to argue satisfactory completion and good character without knowing the case against him/her. As a result of the GMC's acceptance of the application of Article 6 of the European Convention (the entitlement to a fair hearing and specifically 'equality of arms'), consultants' reports cannot be relied upon unless disclosed to the practitioner.

2.29   In the past decisions of the GMC to refuse registration to overseas qualified practitioners on the basis of failing to meet criteria as to training/experience or language competence have been challenged under the race relations legislation in employment tribunals—but without success. However, recent changes in the burden of proof in race cases together with the change in the test of what constitutes 'indirect discrimination'[13] may lead to renewed challenges under this legislation with greater prospects of success.

2.30   In addition to its functions in respect of overseas qualified practitioners holding limited registration, the Registration Committee has jurisdiction in respect of issues concerning the specialist register. As well as the medical register (which currently contains about 200,000 doctors holding full, limited, provisional or temporary registration), since 1996 the GMC has also maintained a specialist register (those included on this must be on the main register). The creation of the specialist register was partly a response to the 1993 Calman review and report of medical training in the United Kingdom and specifically of postgraduate training and specialisation and partly in response to the position in the European Union and recognition of higher training qualifications in EU Member States. The specialist register is subdivided into different medical sub-specialties and the practitioner's name is entered under the appropriate sub-specialty and his/her registration certificate contains details of the appropriate specialisation.

---

[11] Medical Act 1983, s 29.
[12] See *R v GMC, ex p Virik* [1996] ICR 433.
[13] Race Relations Act 1976 (Amendment) Regulations 2003, SI 2003/1626.

Since 1 January 1997 a practitioner cannot be appointed to a substantive (as **2.31** opposed to locum) NHS consultant post in a medical or surgical specialty unless included in the specialist register. It is also extremely difficult for a practitioner to work unsupervised in private practice in a medical or surgical specialisation without being included on the specialist register as the major private health insurers only recognise for payment purposes those so included and the majority of the private hospital groups only grant admitting rights to those on the specialist register.

Entry onto the specialist register (for those other than practitioners who benefited **2.32** from transitional provisions at the time of creation of the specialist register and made application for inclusion before 1 January 1998) is as a result of completion of postgraduate higher specialist training in a unified training grade (specialist registrar) and obtaining a Certificate of Completion of Specialist Training (CCST) from the Specialist Training Authority (STA) of the medical and surgical Royal Colleges, or by the GMC accepting mutual recognition of specialisation certificates obtained on similar bases in other EU Member States or the EEA.

4. The General Medical Council

As a result of the Medical Act (Amendment) Order 2002 the constitution of the **2.33** GMC has undergone significant change with effect from 1 July 2003. The Council has been reduced from 104 members to 35 members—19 of whom are elected by doctors registered in the United Kingdom and must themselves be so registered, 14 of whom are lay members nominated by the Privy Council, and two of whom are medical members appointed by the Academy of Medical Royal Colleges and the Council of Heads of Medical Schools respectively.

Where previously Council members were included in the constitution of various **2.34** GMC adjudicatory committees (for example, the Professional Conduct Committee (PCC), Interim Orders Committee (IOC), Committee for Professional Performance (CPP)) since 1 July 2003 and as a response to concerns as to 'separation of powers' and the role of the GMC as both prosecutor and adjudicator, Council members no longer populate such committees.

Apart from control of entry onto the medical register and maintenance of the **2.35** medical register and the specialist register, the main function of the GMC—now seen by the public as its predominant function—is the control of fitness to practise through its various committees (Preliminary Proceedings Committee (PPC), PCC, Assessment Referral Committee (ARC), CPP, IOC and Health Committee).

The GMC is, however, proposing from the end of 2004 to change its system for **2.36** the registration of doctors by introduction of a new system of a 'licence to practise' supported by periodic revalidation. The aim of the system is to increase public confidence in doctors being up to date and fit to practise medicine throughout their medical careers.

2.37 From 1 January 2005, by law, if a doctor wishes to continue to practise medicine he/she will need a 'licence to practise'. The GMC will grant such a licence by the end of 2004 to all doctors on the register (regardless of type of registration) unless they indicate they do not want one. Any practitioner newly registered after 2004 will get a licence automatically when registered.

2.38 However, to maintain a licence a practitioner must take part in a 'revalidation' process when asked by the GMC. The commencement of invitations for revalidation will be spring 2005 and every doctor will be asked to undergo revalidation normally once every five years. Revalidation is anticipated to work by way of appraisal or what is termed the 'independent route' (involving demonstration by a practitioner that he/she is adopting the standards of the GMC's issued guidance, *Good Medical Practice*, within his/her professional practice and has been undertaking appropriate continuing medical education and professional development).

2.39 The outcome of revalidation will be maintenance of a licence to practise, reconsideration on provision of further information or withdrawal. Given the implications for his/her civil rights and obligations (right to practise a profession), a doctor will have a right to appeal against any decision to withdraw or refuse to restore a licence to practise (which will of course have been automatically withdrawn not just as part of a revalidation process but in any case where medical registration has been suspended or erased as a result of fitness to practise issues).

2.40 In addition a failed appeal against withdrawal of a licence to practise being a decision of a public body will be susceptible to judicial review procedures on normal judicial review grounds.

B. Disciplinary and Fitness to Practise Procedures

2.41 As a result of the increased (and increasing) public awareness since the beginning of the 1990s of the right to complain against health care professionals, the health care professional bodies generally consider their primary responsibilities in protecting the public and maintaining professional and ethical standards to be their powers of restricting a professional's right to practise. In a work such as this it is impossible to encompass all the relevant professions, so the focus is placed on the work of the GMC—being the most prominent (and the busiest) of the professional bodies in the field. Its current procedures have echoes in the procedures of a number of the other health care professional bodies—although more advanced in its range of committees and jurisdictions. The GMC is currently reviewing all of its procedures and at the time of writing is in the midst of a consultation procedure on fairly major changes which are being proposed. In this chapter the current position together with a summary of the major proposals for change will be addressed. The GMC intends that the new changes will be introduced in the summer of 2004 although this seems somewhat optimistic given the consultation period continued until November 2003.

1. Conduct Procedures

The powers of the GMC to discipline registered medical practitioners are set out in s 36 of the Medical Act 1983. Such disciplinary powers are exercisable only on a finding against the practitioner by the PCC of the GMC of 'serious professional misconduct' or on a finding that the practitioner has been convicted of a criminal offence within the British Isles or elsewhere of an offence which if committed in England and Wales would constitute a criminal offence.   **2.42**

The jurisdiction of the PCC is set out in the GMC Preliminary Proceedings Committee and Professional Conduct Committee (Procedure) Rules Order of Council 1988 (as amended).[14] The issues are dealt with by the GMC under what is called its Fitness to Practise Directorate.   **2.43**

(i) Screening

On receipt of a complaint or information in writing[15] where it appears that a question arises whether the conduct of the practitioner constitutes serious professional misconduct, the matter is referred to a medical screener. The medical screener[16] considers the complaint or information and can either refer the matter to the PPC,[17] if satisfied that 'it is properly arguable that the practitioner's conduct constitutes serious professional misconduct' or direct that no further action be taken in the case[18]—although such a direction can only be made provided the medical screener has sought the advice of the lay member appointed under r 4(5) for screening purposes and if the lay member consulted agrees.   **2.44**

Doctors are often (but not always) informed of a complaint in writing prior to it being submitted to the medical screener and invited to comment, although informed that they are not obliged to do so but that any comments made will be relayed to the patient complainant (if there is one) or other complainant (if an NHS employer or public body).   **2.45**

Since 1 November 2002 the screener cannot refer a misconduct allegation to the PPC if at the time the complaint was first made to the GMC more than five years   **2.46**

---

[14] SI 1988/2255.
[15] r 6(1).
[16] r 4.
[17] r 6(3).
[18] r 6(3A).

had elapsed since the events giving rise to the allegation of misconduct[19] unless the medical screener directs that the case be referred because in his opinion 'the public interest requires this in the exceptional circumstances' of the case.[20] Considerable concern had been expressed over a number of years as to the GMC accepting and investigating 'stale' complaints and since October 2000—and as a consequence of the coming into force of the Human Rights Act 1988—the PCC has had to adjudicate by way of preliminary issue on a number of applications for stay of proceedings based on abuse of process due to delay or breach of Article 6 of the European Convention on Human Rights which guarantees a fair trial within a reasonable period. Rules 6(7) and 6(8)—introduced by amendment—are the response.

2.47 The issue of the exercise of the medical screener's judgment under r 6(8) as to what constitute 'exceptional circumstances' (the Rules providing no definition) and what is in the 'public interest' has not yet been tested in the courts, though it is likely that this will happen at some stage as a refusal to direct referral will be a final determination of the matter as far as a complainant is concerned—with only the remedy of judicial review available—and also a final determination on the issue for a practitioner as there is no appeal against the direction to refer under r 6(8) and no basis for submitting before the PPC that a referral should not have been made (although abuse of process and Article 6 arguments would still be open to the practitioner at this stage and before the PCC).

2.48 To succeed on an abuse of process argument the practitioner would have to demonstrate actual prejudice as a result of a delay in the prosecution of the complaint. Reliance on Article 6 does not require proof of prejudice but it has been held by the Administrative Court[21] that in judging whether there has been a hearing within a reasonable time the starting point of computation of 'reasonable time' is not the date of the events which gave rise to the complaint but rather the time when the practitioner is 'charged' (consistent with the jurisprudence of the European Court of Human Rights under the Convention) which has always been said by the GMC to be the date of the r 6(3) referral by the medical screener to the PPC. If this remains a statement of the legal position Article 6 will be of no avail to a practitioner where the complaint is made just less than five years after the events or, as a result of r 6(8), more than five years after the event, if the period after referral to the PPC until hearing of the case by the PCC is a reasonable one.

2.49 The Administrative Court case[22] which appeared to confirm the position always taken by the GMC as to a r 6(3) referral being the trigger for calculation of

---

[19] r 6(7).
[20] r 6(8).
[21] *GMC v Pembrey* [2002] Lloyd's Rep Med 434.
[22] ibid.

'reasonable time' under Article 6 has been the subject of criticism, given that in that case the practitioner had been subjected to GMC (IOC) imposed conditions on his medical registration (and therefore a restriction on his right to practise his profession which is what Article 6 is said to provide protection for) prior to the r 6(3) referral. Moreover, it has been recognised that proceedings before the IOC to which he had been subjected are themselves governed by Article 6.[23]

Decisions of the medical or medical and lay screeners to refer or not to refer a case **2.50** to the PPC are susceptible to judicial review at the behest of a complainant (normally patient) or a practitioner. Judicial review at this stage by a practitioner is rare given that there is still scope to have the case screened out at the PPC when a fuller investigation is conducted and the test for referral onwards is more demanding than just whether '*it is properly arguable*' that the conduct constitutes serious professional misconduct. Judicial review by a complainant at this stage is much more common. The defendant in such proceedings is the GMC itself but the practitioner will have a right to participate in the proceedings as an interested party. In the case of *R v GMC, ex p Toth* [24] the Administrative Court gave guidance as to the approach of the screener (and the PPC) on conduct complaints (although the test to be applied by the screener at that time differed slightly from that applicable today). The guidance has been endorsed and adopted in a number of subsequent cases (*R v GMC, ex p Richards*[25]) including by the Court of Appeal (*R (on the application of Holmes) v GMC* [26]).

In *ex p Toth* Lightman J held that the general principles were that public confi- **2.51** dence in the GMC and the medical profession required, and complainants had a legitimate expectation, that such complaints—in the absence of some special and sufficient reason—would be publicly investigated by the Professional Conduct Committee, with justice in such cases being seen to be done.

(ii) Preliminary Proceedings Committee

Once a case has been referred to the PPC the practitioner is formally invited to re- **2.52** spond in writing within a time limited period (which may be extended by the GMC or on a decision of the Chairman of the PPC or the PPC itself). The PPC sits in private[27] and is composed of medical and lay members. It sits with a legal assessor who is not a voting member of the Committee but is obliged under the GMC (Legal Assessors) Rules 1980[28] to provide guidance on the law and correct

---

[23] *Madan v GMC (No 2)* [2001] Lloyd's Rep Med 539.
[24] [2000] Lloyd's Rep Med 363.
[25] [2001] Lloyd's Rep Med 47.
[26] [2001] Lloyd's Rep Med 366.
[27] r 15.
[28] SI 1980/941.

any errors made by the Committee. The consideration of cases is on the papers only and neither the practitioner nor the complainant has any right to appear before the PPC.

2.53 The PPC may decide to cause further investigations to be made and/or to obtain advice or assistance from the GMC solicitor as it considers requisite (r 13(1)).[29] In recent times the PPC has been interpreting this rule as entitling it to obtain expert (medical or other) evidence on its own motion. Whilst it is debatable whether the rule envisaged such a course of action and whether, strictly speaking, 'further investigations' would stretch to that as opposed to investigation of the factual matrix, the practitioner often benefits from such 'independent' (of the complainant) expert evidence and would not therefore complain.

2.54 The PPC, after consideration of the case, can[30] (r 11(1)) refer the case to the PCC for enquiry, or to the Health Committee or can determine that the case shall not be referred to either committee. The Procedure Rules themselves do not set out any test to be applied as to the circumstances when a referral ought to be made. The GMC publishes its own guidance and failures to refer have been the subject of challenges by patients in the Administrative Court by way of judicial review—resulting in judicial guidance on the issue and approbation of the GMC guidance.[31] The guidance is to the effect that cases should be referred unless there is no real prospect of success, namely a finding of serious professional misconduct. The judicial guidance has suggested that where there are substantial conflicts of fact then the PPC should proceed cautiously given its limited powers of investigation and should not seek to determine them in private and in the absence of the parties and consequently in such cases there should be a referral to the PCC given the function of the PCC to resolve conflicts of evidence. The decision of the PPC (like the decision of the screener) is susceptible to judicial review which more commonly arises at the behest of the patient where the decision is not to refer (and is therefore determinative of the complaint) than by the practitioner who still (arguably) has a remedy available to him in a hearing before the PCC. The practitioner may however seek judicial review and argue that he has exhausted his remedies despite the availability of a PCC hearing because the complaint he makes cannot be remedied by a PCC hearing and he will have to face the hardship of a full public inquiry which should not have been the case.

2.55 The public awareness of the existence and role of the GMC together with the changed emphasis as to cases being referred forward for public hearing since the case of *Toth* in 2000, has resulted in a 500 per cent increase in complaints to

---

[29] r 13(1).
[30] r 11(1).
[31] *R v GMC, ex p Richards* (n 25 above); *R (on the application of Holmes) v GMC* (n 26 above); *Woods (R on the application of) v GMC* [2002] EWHC 1484 (Admin).

the GMC since the beginning of the 1990s and an 800 per cent increase since 1995 in the number of sitting days for the PCC (this figure also being explained by a change in the type of cases considered—leading to longer duration of individual cases—and being accounted for by lengthy hearings in some of the high profile cases—*Ledward, Neale, Bristol*). In 1990 the GMC received 700 complaints. By 1995 this figure had increased to 1,503. By 2000 the figure was 4,470 and for 2001 4,504 with a slight drop for 2002 to 3,943. The number of PCC sitting days in 1995 was 83, by 1998 it had increased only slightly to 91 but by 2000 it was 242. In 2001 it was 479 and in 2002 had reached an all time high of 651. Whereas in the early 1990s the PCC sat only in London at the GMC headquarters and there was only one PCC sitting at any given time and for only a limited number of sessions during the year, by 2003 the GMC had PCCs sitting all year round in both London and Manchester and had six separate PCC panels with the possibility of all six sitting at one time.

The increase in the work has caused a considerable change in the size and compo-**2.56** sition of the panels. Whereas in the mid-1990s a PCC would comprise nine members—the majority medical (and with a medical chairman) with a requirement for one lay member but often two lay members—the position since November 2002 is that a quorum for a PCC is three with at least one lay member. In 2003 the normal panel was five and often the majority of members were lay. In 2001 52 per cent of the membership of PCCs was lay and 47 per cent of panels were chaired by non-medical members (some of these being legally qualified).

Since 2000 approximately half of the complaints received by the GMC have been **2.57** referred to the screener as cases which appear to give rise to a question whether the conduct of the practitioner constitutes serious professional misconduct. Around 30 per cent of these have been referred by the medical screener to the PPC and approximately 40 per cent of those considered by the PPC have been referred on for enquiry by the PCC. Approximately 75 per cent of those cases have resulted in findings of serious professional misconduct.

(iii) Referral to Professional Conduct Committee

If the PPC decide to refer a case to the PCC it will—absent successful judicial re-**2.58** view proceedings by the doctor—proceed to a full and public hearing by the PCC unless the inquiry is cancelled under r 19 on the basis that it appears to the Chairman of the PPC that the inquiry should not be held such that after consulting the members of the PPC he directs that an inquiry not be held. Prior to 2001 this rule was very rarely used but the increased number of cases referred to the PCC has seen an increase in reliance on this rule—usually by the GMC on its own motion but sometimes in response to a request made on behalf of the practitioner (although the rule itself does not necessarily provide for such a request). It appears that cases are being referred back to the PPC under r 19 either as a result of investigations of factual and expert evidence suggesting to the GMC lawyers that there is no reasonable prospect of successfully proving serious professional misconduct or because complainants indicate an unwillingness to pursue the complaint and attend an inquiry.

(iv) 'Serious Professional Misconduct'

2.59 One of the main problems is the lack of statutory definition of 'serious professional misconduct'. The attitude of the courts was always that it was a matter for the profession to determine given that the system was one of peer review.[32] The phrase was first used in the Medical Act 1969 (prior to that the legislation provided for disciplinary action in respect of '*infamous conduct in a professional respect*').

2.60 The difficulty now is with increased lay representation on PCCs and with the various sub-specialities in medicine such that the medical members present may know nothing of the area of practice of the respondent doctor, it is rather more difficult to justify the lack of some statutory or clear judicial definition.

2.61 Historically (before the mid-1990s) the profile of conduct cases was cases of criminal convictions, of fraud, of sexual or inappropriate emotional relationships with patients, advertising and serious dereliction of duty (or repeat offences). These cases provided less problems in judging what might be considered serious professional misconduct—with the major issue being whether the conduct was confined to conduct in the practice of the profession as opposed to 'extra-mural'.[33] They also fitted in with a timetable under the Procedure Rules[34] which provided perhaps only 28 days from the notice of inquiry until the public hearing and only six weeks between the PPC and the PCC hearing. Usually they were cases where not much further investigation or evidence gathering was required and the notice of inquiry was a short document.

2.62 In 1983 the GMC's Blue Book (its Guidance on Professional Conduct for practitioners) expressly stated that the GMC was 'not ordinarily concerned with errors in diagnosis or treatment, or with the kind of matters which give rise to action in the civil courts for negligence, unless the doctor's conduct in the case has involved a disregard of his professional responsibilities to his patients or such a neglect of his professional duties as to raise a question of serious professional misconduct'.

---

[32] In *Evans v GMC (1984)* the Privy Council noted that it had been said time and again that disciplinary committees are the best possible people for weighing the seriousness of professional misconduct and therefore the Board would be very slow to interfere with the exercise of the discretion of such a committee.

[33] In *Roylance v GMC (No 2)* [1999] Lloyd's Rep Med 139 the Privy Council held that serious professional misconduct extended beyond clinical misconduct to misconduct in carrying out medical work but that there must be a link between the conduct and the profession of medicine.

[34] r 17.

During the late 1990s, as a result of high profile 'treatment' scandals (*Bristol,* **2.63**
Ledward, Neale), the GMC underwent a sea change and started to consider cases
of treatment and diagnosis errors. Such a change has had serious implications for
matters such as duration of cases, need for specialised expert evidence, timing and
listing of cases and earlier service of the notices of inquiry than envisaged under
r 17 to enable proper preparation. In addition doctors have found themselves
facing a degree of 'double jeopardy'—concurrent GMC investigation and civil
proceedings with no consistency as to which are considered first.

Hearings before the PCC are in public—although an application can be made to **2.64**
hear some or all of the evidence *in camera*[35]—usually for reasons relating to medical confidentiality. Like the PPC the PCC sits with a legal assessor (who also re-
tires with the Committee when they go into camera to consider any decision[36])
and who is obliged (since 2000 and by virtue of Article 6 ECHR and the GMC
(Legal Assessors) (Amendment) Rules 2000[37]) to communicate in public (or in
the presence of the parties and their legal representatives) any legal advice ten-
dered to the PCC and offering the parties the right to make representations upon
such advice—such representations being matters which the PCC are obliged to
take into account.

The burden of proving the case against the practitioner is on the GMC as pros- **2.65**
ecutor and the standard is to the criminal standard (beyond a reasonable doubt).
The GMC as prosecutor has a duty to disclose unused material or material weakening its case and strengthening the case for the doctor.[38]

(v) Professional Conduct Committee determinations/sanctions

After a finding of serious professional misconduct[39] the PCC can postpone its de- **2.66**
termination[40] or decide that there is no need to make any direction[41] or may make a
direction as to attaching conditions to a practitioner's registration for a period of up
to three years or whether to suspend his registration for a period not exceeding 12
months or whether to erase his name from the medical register.[42] The GMC now
publishes Indicative Sanctions Guidance (available on its website[43]) as to the circumstances which might give rise to each of the sanctions. Erasure is now for a minimum period of five years (where previously after only 10 months an application for

---

[35] r 48.
[36] *Nwabueze v GMC* [2000] 1 WLR 1760.
[37] SI 2000/1881.
[38] *Rajan v GMC* [2000] Lloyd's Rep Med 153.
[39] r 28.
[40] r 30(1).
[41] r 30(2).
[42] r 31.
[43] *www.gmc-uk.org.*

restoration could be made[44]) and, given the introduction of revalidation procedures and the risks of deskilling, can in many cases prove in practice to be erasure
for life (particularly for any practitioner aged over 50 at the time of erasure).

2.67 The PCC must give reasons for any finding of serious professional misconduct
and for the imposition of any penalty, although the requirement is only for a general explanation rather than detailed reasons.[45]

(vi) Statutory appeals

2.68 By s 40 of the Medical Act 1983 a practitioner has a right of appeal against a
direction under r 31 affecting his registration (there is no appeal against a finding
of serious professional misconduct alone which does not result in a direction despite
the potentially serious consequences for a doctor's career of such a finding[46]). In
addition the decisions of the PCC are also susceptible to judicial review and can
be challenged by practitioners who are the subject of an adverse finding on serious
professional misconduct but do not have a s 40 appeal.[47] A complainant has no
right of statutory appeal against a decision of the GMC either on serious professional misconduct or on sanction. Challenge by way of judicial review is in theory
open to a dissatisfied complainant but is likely only to be possible on a matter such
as determination of a preliminary issue on a matter of law (abuse of process or
Article 6) or application of a particular procedural rule (such as use of r 51 to refer
a case to the Health Committee[48]).

2.69 Until 1 April 2003 the s 40 statutory appeal was to the Privy Council (amended
by s 30 of the NHS Reform and Health Care Professions Act 2002). Since 1 April
the appeal has been to the Queen's Bench Division of the High Court to be heard
by a single judge (heard by Administrative Court judges). The period for appeal
is 28 days from the date of the direction and during that period any direction
made does not take effect (subject only to r 32 having been applied). If an appeal
is lodged within the 28 day period the appeal has the effect of suspending the
direction from taking effect until after the determination (or withdrawal) of the
appeal.

2.70 However, in cases where the direction is to suspend or erase, the PCC is required
under r 32 to consider and determine whether 'it is necessary for the protection of
members of the public or would be in the best interest of the practitioner to order
that his registration shall be suspended forthwith'. In such a case an appeal has no
effect on the forthwith suspension.

---

[44] Medical Act 1983, s 41(2)(a) (as amended).
[45] *Selvanathan v GMC* [2001] Lloyd's Rep Med 1.
[46] *R v GMC, ex p Nicolaides* [2001] Lloyd's Rep Med 525.
[47] See *R (on the application of Cream) v GMC* [2002] Lloyd's Rep Med 292.
[48] See *R (on the application of Toth) v GMC (No 2)* (27 June 2003, Admin Ct, Elias J).

The Privy Council was until 2000 very reluctant to interfere with decisions of the **2.71** PCC of the GMC—again respecting the right of self-regulation and peer review and deferring to a specialist committee.[49] Between 1950 and 2000 the number of successful appeals could be counted on the fingers of one hand and, as a consequence and because of the Privy Council's stated restricted approach,[50] appeals were not common. The coming into force of the Human Rights Act 1998 led to a complete revision of approach by the Privy Council and an increase in the number of appeals and (initially) the number of successful appeals. The increased number of appeals was the main factor precipitating the shift of appeals to the High Court. The relevance of the Human Rights Act was the concern as to whether the Article 6 requirements of a fair hearing before an independent and impartial tribunal could be satisfied by a PCC hearing and the limited Privy Council appeal. The problem was that of separation (or lack of separation) of powers within the GMC—which brings the prosecution (in its name) and also determines/adjudicates it through its PCC which (at least until July 2003) included Council members—and whether this meant that the requirements of 'independent' and 'impartial' might not be met.

The Convention jurisprudence of the European Court of Human Rights makes it **2.72** clear that what is in issue is perception or appearance of real danger and that where the same body prosecutes and adjudicates there may be such a real danger and that the requirement of Article 6 can only be satisfied by what is termed a 'full jurisdiction' appeal—ie a right to reconsider and rehear every aspect of the case (and reach a different conclusion) rather than a more limited review of the decision. As a consequence in the cases of *Ghosh v GMC*[51] and *Preiss v General Dental Council*[52] in the summer of 2001, the Privy Council indicated a new approach (and abandonment of the *Libman* approach) and the provision of a full jurisdiction appeal so that the totality of the procedure would be Article 6 compliant.

This led initially to a flurry of successful appeals—if not on the issue of serious **2.73** professional misconduct, or the facts found, then at least in respect of sanction imposed (and significantly so in several erasure cases).[53] In *Bijl* the Privy Council held that public confidence in the self-regulation of the profession did not mean the sacrifice of the career of an otherwise competent and useful doctor who presents no danger to the public in order to satisfy a demand for blame and punishment. In *Hossain* the Privy Council, whilst recognising the experience and knowledge of the PCC members, indicated that the Privy Council would interfere if satisfied it was right to do so and that the penalty was not justified taking

---

[49] *Evans v GMC* (1984, PC).
[50] See *Libman v GMC* [1972] AC 217.
[51] [2001] Lloyd's Rep Med 443.
[52] [2001] Lloyd's Rep Med 491.
[53] See *Bijl v GMC* [2002] Lloyd's Rep Med 60; and *Hossain v GMC* [2002] Lloyd's Rep Med 64.

into account, for example, the long years of service by a doctor in a particular area and the views of his patients and colleagues.

(vii) Referral to court if 'unduly lenient'

2.74   There has remained public discontent, however, at the perception that the GMC 'lets doctors off' and does not impose appropriate sanctions and it was this perception and discontent which led to the establishment of the Council for the Regulation of Health Care Professionals under the NHS Reform and Health Care Professions Act 2002. Under s 29(1)(c) the Council has the power to refer to court a direction of a GMC PCC on professional misconduct (and also under s 29(1)(d) and (e) a similar power in respect of directions in performance and health cases). The power under s 29(2) includes the power to refer a final decision of the PCC (or in performance cases of the CPP) not to take any disciplinary measure and/or a decision to restore a practitioner to the register.

2.75   The basis for referral will be consideration by the Council[54] that the relevant decision 'has been unduly lenient', whether as to a finding of professional misconduct or fitness to practise on the part of the practitioner concerned (or lack of such finding) or as to any penalty imposed or both, and that 'it would be desirable for the protection of members of the public for the Council to take action' by referral to the relevant court, which for practitioners with registered addresses in Scotland is the Court of Session, for those with registered addresses in Northern Ireland, the High Court of Northern Ireland and for those with registered addresses in England and Wales the High Court in England and Wales.

2.76   This particular section is only just in force and there have not yet been any determined referrals and therefore no jurisprudence to assess the impact of the provisions. It is believed that the approach of the courts may mirror that taken in Attorney-General's referrals in criminal cases of lenient sentences for reconsideration by the Court of Appeal Criminal Division. The public pressure for the power and the logic behind its introduction were similar.

2. Health Procedures

2.77   The GMC through its Fitness to Practise Directorate also regulates the performance of doctors where there may be an issue of physical or mental health. The relevant test is whether the practitioner's fitness to practise is 'seriously impaired' by reason of any physical or mental condition. The procedures governing health matters are set out in the General Medical Council Health Committee (Procedure) Rules Order of Council 1987.[55] Originally cases which progressed

---

[54] NHS Reform and Health Care Professions Act 2002, s 29(4).
[55] SI 1987/2174.

down the 'health route' ended up before the Health Committee which had the power to impose conditions upon a practitioner's registration or to suspend him.

Given that in many of the cases that were coming before the Health Committee there was no dispute as to the practitioner's health problems or the consequential impairment of his fitness to practise, the GMC introduced and has moved towards greater use of its voluntary health procedures. **2.78**

The GMC acts on receipt of written complaints or information (often from employers and sometimes self-referral by practitioners) about a practitioner which raise a question whether the individual's fitness to practise is seriously impaired by reason of a physical or mental condition. Sometimes such information can arise in the context of what might otherwise be construed as a conduct complaint. **2.79**

A health screener considers the information and will write to the practitioner inviting him or her to agree to submit to medical examination by two medical examiners appointed by the GMC and to agree that such examiners shall provide the GMC with reports on fitness to practise. The practitioner is also offered the opportunity to nominate other medical practitioners to examine him and report to the GMC (and this can include someone already involved in the treatment of the practitioner). The practitioner is further entitled to submit his own observations or evidence on his fitness to practise at this stage. **2.80**

The practitioner is provided with a summary of the information received by the GMC and copies of any medical reports already held. He is informed[56] that if he refuses to be medically examined or having agreed fails to actually submit then his case may be forthwith referred to the Health Committee. **2.81**

If the practitioner agrees to submit to medical examination and is examined and the examiners report unanimously that he is not fit to practise or not fit to practise except on a limited basis or under medical supervision or both or suffers from a recurring or episodic physical or mental condition which, though in remission at the time of the examination, may be expected in future to render him unfit to practise or unfit to practise except on a limited basis or under medical supervision or both, then the GMC will write to the practitioner inviting him to state within 28 days whether he is prepared to undertake voluntarily to comply with the recommendations in the reports as to the management of his case, including any limitations on his practice which they recommend.[57] If the reports are not unanimous then the practitioner is invited to agree voluntarily to comply with the health screener's recommendations in the light of the balance of the opinions in the reports. **2.82**

---

[56] r 6.
[57] r 8(3).

2.83 If the practitioner undertakes to comply voluntarily with the recommendations for the management of his case[58] and the GMC is satisfied that the undertakings are being observed, further action on the case will be postponed and the practitioner remains under health procedures in so far as there is merely a postponement under the rules.

2.84 If the practitioner does not undertake to accept the management recommendations voluntarily or does not reply to the invitation, or has refused to submit to medical examination his case can be referred to the Health Committee.

2.85 Cases can also be referred to the Health Committee by the Preliminary Proceedings Committee and (in limited circumstances)[59] by the Professional Conduct Committee under r 51 of the Conduct Procedure Rules. In those cases the procedure is the same as the invitation to submit to medical examination by medical examiners and as to the test being considered.[60]

2.86 The Health Committee sits in private.[61] As with other GMC committees it is made up of medical and lay members sitting with a legal assessor. In addition the Committee will have the benefit of one or more (though usually only one) specialist medical assessor sitting with the Committee suitably qualified to give advice on the practitioner's particular medical impairment. The overwhelming majority of cases which come before the Health Committee concern psychiatric impairment and therefore the medical assessor is usually a consultant psychiatrist.

2.87 The Health Committee under r 24 is obliged to consider and determine whether they judge the fitness to practise of the practitioner to be seriously impaired by reason of his physical or mental condition. Significantly in such consideration[62] they are entitled (but interestingly not obliged) to regard as current serious impairment a continuing and episodic condition which although in remission at the time of the proceedings may be expected to cause a recurrence. It is this provision which can cause a practitioner who is an alcoholic or suffers from certain depressive conditions to remain for years under GMC Health procedures although in good health every time examined. It can be a source of concern to the practitioner that, although well, he continues to have restrictions imposed on his right to practise and often restrictions which impinge on his ability to find work or secure employment. The Privy Council has held that the words 'may be expected to cause recurrence' do not impose a need to show that this recurrence is likely but only that it is a possibility.[63]

---

[58] r 8(4).
[59] See *R (on the application of Toth) v GMC (No 2)* (27 June 2003, Admin Ct, Elias J).
[60] Health Procedure Rules, r 11.
[61] r 17.
[62] r 24(2).
[63] *GMC v Brocklebank* [2003] UKPC 57.

The Health Committee, if it determines the fitness to practise impaired, can **2.88** direct that the practitioner's registration is conditional upon his compliance for a period not exceeding three years with such requirements 'as the Committee may think fit to impose for the protection of members of the public or in his interests'.[64] Often such conditions restrict the areas in which the practitioner might work and provide for more supervised work. Usually the conditions will include requirements as to medical supervision and compliance with the instructions of a medical supervisor who is obliged to approve any job taken or post applied for.

The Health Committee additionally has a power under r 25 to suspend a practi- **2.89** tioner's registration for a period not exceeding 12 months if it decides that it is not sufficient to impose conditions, and where it decides to suspend must also consider whether it is necessary for that suspension to be a forthwith suspension for the protection of the public or in the best interests of the practitioner.

Decisions of the Health Committee to impose conditions or suspend are subject **2.90** to statutory appeal—previously to the Privy Council and now to the High Court—but only on a point of law. Human rights issues can arise with respect to some of the conditions imposed (if these restrict guaranteed Convention freedoms such as the right to privacy or family life),[65] but the approach of the courts has been that the Health Committee is a specialist committee with the assistance of expert advice and the courts will be slow to interfere with decisions of such a committee unless there has been an obvious error of law or procedure.

The period for appeal is 28 days with the order not taking effect until the expiry **2.91** of that period or the determination or withdrawal of the appeal (unless there has been an order for forthwith suspension).

If there is no appeal the Health Committee resumes consideration of the case be- **2.92** fore expiry of the relevant period of suspension or period during which conditions have been imposed.[66] At such resumed hearings updated medical evidence is considered and the Health Committee can exercise any of the powers it had at the original hearing except that it cannot extend any period of conditional registration for more than 12 months and may revoke any previous direction or vary any of the conditions.[67]

After a period of suspension lasting two years, if the Health Committee deter- **2.93** mines that it is not sufficient to extend for another 12 months it may direct indefinite extension of the suspension.[68] Such an indefinite suspension in effect is

---

[64] r 24.
[65] *Whitefield v GMC* [2002] UKPC 62; [2003] IRLR 39.
[66] r 27.
[67] r 33.
[68] r 33A.

tantamount to an erasure. The Health Committee currently does not have any power to erase registration.

2.94   Health Committee decisions are also subject to referral by the Health Professions Council to the High Court if considered 'unduly lenient', although given that Health Committee hearings are held in private and generally do not involve individual patient complainants it seems unlikely that there will be significant use of this referral in Health Committee cases.

3. Performance Procedures

2.95   As a result of growing concerns in the late 1980s and early 1990s that cases of medical incompetence or poor performance were not being properly addressed under the conduct procedures, a second jurisdiction (known as Performance Procedures) was introduced by the Medical (Professional Performance) Act 1995. From 1 July 1997 the GMC has had jurisdiction to consider and investigate whether a doctor's standard of professional performance has been or is 'seriously deficient'.[69]

2.96   Only allegations of incompetence or deficient performance post 1 July 1997 can be considered. Normally referral of performance issues to the GMC comes from NHS employers and often is coincident with the employer suspending (since January 2004 'excluding'—see para 2.161 below) the doctor and commencing disciplinary action under NHS disciplinary procedures. The complaint or information is considered under the General Medical Council (Professional Performance) Rules Order of Council 1997[70] and, if judged by a medical screener[71] to raise an issue as to seriously deficient performance, the practitioner is written to and invited to consent to assessment under the GMC's performance procedures.

2.97   If the practitioner refuses to consent the case may be referred to the Assessment Referral Committee (ARC) which then considers whether there may be seriously deficient performance and whether it is necessary to refer the practitioner for assessment.[72] There may be good reason why a referral is not necessary although there is evidence of deficient performance, such as the practitioner in the interim having undergone retraining and/or having retired from practice or having changed specialisation or discipline/area of practice and undergone training in a new field.

2.98   Decisions of the ARC cannot be appealed but are susceptible to judicial review. Whilst the GMC considers that the decisions of the ARC only commence the

---

[69] Medical Act 1983, s 36A.
[70] SI 1997/1529.
[71] rr 5 and 6.
[72] r 6.

investigative (assessment) process which does not of itself bring a detriment to the practitioner, the refusal or inability to undergo assessment (for example for reasons of illness) can lead to referral to the CPP and suspension.

If the ARC does refer or the practitioner has consented to an assessment he is first **2.99** required to complete a portfolio for the assessment panel. Thereafter he will be invited to participate in a two-stage assessment process conducted by a three or four person assessment panel with the lead assessor from his own discipline of medicine, at least one other doctor and one lay assessor.[73] The assessment process will comprise written examinations, oral interviews with the practitioner (including selected case notes reviews) and witnesses nominated by him and with 'third parties' (usually work colleagues or patients who have been involved in the origins of the referral), and a practical skills phase (involving assessment of performance of tasks normal to his field of practice—mock patient consultations or examinations or basic medical or surgical procedures as appropriate).[74]

At the conclusion of the assessment the lead assessor will prepare a report and con- **2.100** clude whether there is evidence of seriously deficient performance.[75] If so the panel will make recommendations as to whether professional performance can be improved by a period of retraining or remedial action and whether in the interim the practitioner should limit his professional practice or cease practice or comply with certain conditions. If remedial action is recommended, the practitioner may be invited by the case co-ordinator to comply with a statement of requirements[76] which can include requirements as to retraining and conditions restricting practice during a period of retraining.

If the case co-ordinator after an assessment is of the view that 'it is necessary for the **2.101** protection of members of the public or would be in the best interests of the practitioner for a direction for suspension or for conditional registration to be made', or the practitioner has failed to comply with requirements set out in the statement of requirements,[77] the case shall be referred to the CPP.

The CPP sits in private with a legal assessor and a specialist adviser (from the same **2.102** discipline as the practitioner). By r 29 of the Professional Performance Rules it has power under s 36A of the Medical Act 1983 to suspend the practitioner's registration (initially for a period of 12 months) or to attach conditions to the practitioner's registration (on finding the standard of the practitioner's performance to have been seriously deficient.[78] The conditions imposed are time-limited (three

---

[73] r 8(1).
[74] r 11.
[75] r 13(2).
[76] r 18.
[77] r 25.
[78] Medical Act 1983, Sch 3, para 10.

years maximum) and at any resumed hearing before the end of the relevant period of conditions or suspension the CPP has the power to revoke or vary the conditions or lift a suspension. It can also make the suspension indefinite.

2.103   An appeal from the CPP lies to the High Court (since April 2003—previously the appeal was to the Privy Council) within 28 days of the order and has the effect of suspending the order coming into effect. However, the CPP also has the power to impose a forthwith suspension which is not affected by lodging an appeal.[79] An appeal lies only on a point of law.[80]

2.104   A resumed hearing may take place before the end of any period of conditions[81] if the case co-ordinator becomes concerned from information received that any requirement or condition is not being complied with or there is some other reason for an early resumption of consideration (and the Privy Council has held that this can be at the request of the practitioner—perhaps on the basis of impossibility of compliance with conditions or changed circumstances requiring changes in conditions[81a]).

2.105   The CPP has a power of indefinite suspension[82] but even such an indefinite suspension must be reviewed[83] and decisions of such review hearings are susceptible to appeal.

2.106   In the case of *Krippendorf v GMC*[84] the Privy Council held that the CPP, in judging seriously deficient performance and in deciding what action to take in respect of registration, must judge the standard of past professional performance based on the matters which had been the subject of the initial complaint and not 'professional competence' as a result of matters which had arisen out of skills performance tests.

2.107   In *Sadler v GMC*[85] the Privy Council qualified the distinction made in *Krippendorf* between competence and performance and said it should not be taken too far as there is an obvious correlation between the two and an assessment panel in assessing past professional performance must not be restricted from considering what could be done to improve standards and to this end should not be restricted from considering professional competence.

2.108   Decisions of the CPP are also susceptible to judicial review—although normally only if the remedy of statutory appeal is for some reason not sufficient. The decision of the CPP if 'unduly lenient' is also susceptible to review by the High Court on

---

[79] Medical Act 1983, Sch 3, paras 10 and 13.
[80] ibid, s 40(1) and (5).
[81] r 12.
[81a] *GMC v Carruthers* [2003] UKPC 58.
[82] Medical Act 1983, s 36A(4).
[83] ibid, Sch 3, para 14.
[84] [2001] Lloyd's Rep Med 9.
[85] The Times, 29 September 2003 (PC).

referral by the Health Professions Council—although it is unlikely that there will be many such referrals as cases before the CPP usually result from referrals by NHS Trust employers who will usually have taken action under NHS disciplinary procedures and will not press for a High Court referral.

4. Interim Orders Committee

Prior to August 2000 the GMC had power to suspend a practitioner for an interim period through the PPC[86]—but the power was rarely exercised. The PPC sat in private and the practitioner had no right to attend save in cases where suspension was in issue and he was invited to attend to be suspended. As a result of adverse publicity surrounding the possibilities for the GMC to take swift action should a Harold Shipman situation recur, the GMC was given power to suspend for periods of up to 18 months[87] (and longer based on an application to the High Court for an extension of up to 12 months[88]). The power is contained in s 41A of the Medical Act 1983 and since 1 August 2000 has been exercised by a new committee known as the Interim Orders Committee (IOC). It has jurisdiction in cases of conduct, performance and health and can accept referrals from screeners, the ARC, CPP, PPC, PCC and Health Committee.

2.109

By s 41A, where the IOC is satisfied that it is necessary for the protection of members of the public or is otherwise in the public interest or in the interests of the practitioner, the IOC can suspend his registration or make it conditional on compliance with requirements which the IOC thinks fit to impose for a period of up to 18 months. The doctor is entitled to an oral hearing and to be legally represented before an order can be made.[89]

2.110

If the IOC makes an order, whether for suspension or conditions, it must review that within a period of six months and thereafter review again at further intervals of three months (now since April 2003 also at six month intervals). The constitution and procedures of the IOC are set out in the GMC (Constitution of Interim Orders Committee) Rules Order of Council 2000[90] and the GMC (Interim Orders Committee) (Procedure) Rules Order of Council 2000.[91]

2.111

In considering whether to make an order and specifically whether to suspend, the IOC must consider the question of proportionality. Article 6 of the European Convention applies to IOC proceedings because of the effect of suspension or restrictive conditions on the right to practise medicine.[92]

2.112

---

[86] s 42(3)–s.42(8) Medical Act 1983, s 42(3)–(8).
[87] ibid, s 41A.
[88] ibid, s 41A(6) and (7).
[89] ibid, s 41A(4).
[90] SI 2000/2052.
[91] SI 2000/2053.
[92] *Madan v GMC (No 2)* (n 23 above); *GMC v Pembrey* (n 21 above).

2.113 Decisions of the IOC can be appealed to the High Court which can terminate, revoke or vary any order[93] and also are susceptible to judicial review. Initially after August 2000 a number of orders of suspension were made. Since *Madan* and the clear application of the doctrine of proportionality the perception has been that fewer orders are made. The IOC essentially deals with the matter on the papers alone—the GMC presents its evidence in written form, although the practitioner may give evidence and can produce written evidence. The IOC sits in private and as with other GMC committees has the benefit of assistance from a legal assessor.

5. Proposals for Reform

2.114 In July 2003 the GMC issued a consultation paper and draft rules and guidance for fitness to practise issues. The consultation period closed at the end of October 2003 and the intention is to have new Fitness to Practise Rules in force by Summer 2004.

2.115 If the consultation process leads to new rules in accordance with the draft rules accompanying the Consultation Paper then the GMC will adopt a more unified approach to issues of fitness to practise and instead of having three different processes to deal with conduct, performance and health issues will have one process where the initial question will be 'Is the practitioner's fitness to practise impaired to a degree requiring action on registration?'

2.116 Fitness to practise may be impaired by reason of misconduct, deficient professional performance, criminal conviction, adverse physical or mental health or as a result of a determination by some other regulatory body.

2.117 The GMC would (where it has no such power at present) have the right to issue a warning to a doctor even where no fitness to practise issue arises (ie where the matter referred is not such as could possibly affect the practitioner's registration).

2.118 Under the proposed changes there would be a common first stage. The case would be considered by the Registrar who has the power to refer the case to the Investigation Committee but may before doing so have the case investigated further. The test for the Registrar would merely be whether the matters raised constitute an allegation of impairment of fitness to practise—the Registrar would not be required to test the allegation as such.

2.119 The Registrar would not be able to refer a case forward if outside the five-year rule (as at present) unless it was considered in the 'public interest' to do so.

2.120 The next stage in all cases would be the Investigation Committee which would have the power to make further enquiries or to decide that the allegation should not proceed further, or that a warning should be issued, or that the case should be

---

[93] Medical Act 1983, s 41A(10).

referred to an Interim Orders Panel (replacing the IOC) and/or to direct an assessment of professional performance or health or to refer to a fitness to practise panel.

It can be seen that the intention is for the Investigation Committee to replace the health screeners, the ARC and the PPC as they exist under the present rules and to provide one common set of rules rather than the different ones presently applying.   2.121

The test for the Investigation Committee for referral of the case to a Fitness to Practise Panel is proposed to be whether there is a realistic prospect of finding fitness to practise impaired. It is also proposed that the Committee may have a power to delegate the matter to Case Examiners.   2.122

One new proposal is the power to issue warnings outside of fitness to practise issues. It is proposed this would arise where it is considered that the behaviour or performance is below acceptable standards to the extent of warranting formal censure but not action on registration. This is a controversial proposal as it appears from the draft rules that the practitioner will not be provided with a right to an oral hearing before such a warning is issued. Given that the Investigation Committee will consider the case on paper alone, it is unclear what standard of proof will be applicable when the evidence against the practitioner has not been tested and there may be a conflict of evidence.   2.123

In place of the Health Committee, PCC and CPP, there will be a Fitness to Practise Panel applying one test only: 'is fitness to practise impaired'. Sanctions will include erasure in all cases except health.   2.124

New powers of case management are proposed with a Case Manager empowered to give directions to the parties as to service of a statement of case and disclosure of documents, witness evidence and expert evidence. One proposal is that witness statements as in civil litigation post the Civil Procedure Rules should stand as evidence in chief.   2.125

It is these proposals which appear to be the most controversial. Until now the criminal rules of procedure have applied to all matters before the PCC (and the other GMC committees) with no requirement on the practitioner to disclose his hand and the right to put the prosecution to proof in any case. Given that what is in issue is disciplinary proceedings with sanctions applicable to one side only many consider it inappropriate to require the 'defendant' to disclose his witness evidence before closure of the prosecution case. There were proposals (endorsed by the previous President of the GMC) that the standard of proof be altered from the criminal standard to the civil. That was rejected and, given the retention of the criminal burden and standard, the introduction of civil case management directions seems somewhat illogical. Given the application of Article 6 and the right to a fair hearing there may also be issues arising as to witness statements standing as   2.126

evidence in chief. At present before the PCC evidence is given orally by prosecution witnesses and the PCC never see the witness statements which have been served on the practitioner. A relatively common feature in PCC cases is witnesses (often patients) not 'coming up to proof' when left to recount their own story (rather than with the assistance of a lawyer-drafted witness statement). The introduction of witness statements will change all that.

6. Disciplinary Powers of the Employer

2.127 At the time of writing both GPs and NHS consultants are awaiting new 'contracts' which have been negotiated with their professional representatives (the British Medical Association) by the Department of Health after wide consultation (including with medical defence organisations, patient organisations and NHS Trusts and Primary Care Trusts (PCTs)). The new 'contracts' (which will have statutory/regulatory elements to them) have been agreed/approved in principle and are at the final drafting stages. Both the GP and NHS Consultant contracts will effect changes in the present systems as to discipline (though in the case of GPs these will be relatively minor given the significant changes introduced in 2001/2). In the case of NHS hospital practitioners the changes are likely to be major and amount to an overhaul of the system and it is therefore proposed to deal with the present systems only in outline.

2.128 GPs are independent (primarily self-employed) practitioners. They are said to be 'in contract' with their local PCTs but the contract takes the form of a regulatory framework set out in the National Health Service (General Medical Services) Regulations 1992[94] (as amended) and the Amendment Regulations 1996[95] with the 'contract' being the GP's 'Terms of Service' as set out in the Schedule to the Regulations.

2.129 Control of GP contracts has been the subject of much change in the 1990s with the contracts initially held by Family Practitioner Committees and then by Family Health Service Authorities, then by Health Authorities and since 1 April 2002 by PCTs. A GP had to have his name included on the medical list of the relevant contracting body and removal of his name from the medical list (and indeed disqualification from being on any NHS list nationally) only resulted from resignation or removal by the NHS Tribunal (as a disciplinary measure).

2.130 The Health and Social Care Act 2001, s 19 abolished the NHS Tribunal and ss 20, 21 and 25 introduced new powers for Health Authorities (now delegated to PCTs) to suspend, remove from and refuse to admit to the list of practitioners providing general medical services.

---

[94] SI 1992/635.
[95] SI 1996/702.

In addition to a PCT having a power to suspend a GP or remove him from the list, **2.131** a local disciplinary process also exists whereby patients can make complaint against their GP of breach of his terms of service (normally failure to provide all appropriate personal medical services) and such complaints are investigated and dealt with under the National Health Service (Service Committees and Tribunal) Regulations 1992[96] (as amended) and the 1996 Amendment Regulations[97] which replaced service committees with Discipline Committees. Such complaints can result in investigation by a Discipline Committee (usually that of a neighbouring Health Authority) and a finding (after an oral hearing) of breach of terms of service resulting in a warning to comply more closely with terms of service or a financial penalty ('withholding' from remuneration). An appeal to the Family Health Services Appeal Authority lies from an adverse decision of a Discipline Committee which has been adopted by the relevant Health Authority.

Section 25 of the Health and Social Care Act 2001 deals with the power of a PCT **2.132** to suspend a GP and to remove him from the NHS medical list. The Health Authority is required by Pt II of the National Health Service Act 1977 to maintain a medical list containing the names and other prescribed details of doctors with whom they have made arrangements for the delivery of general medical services in their area, and since April 2002 this function has been delegated in England by Health Authorities to PCTs. The Regulations governing the medical list and procedures to be followed prior to removal and/or suspension are the National Health Service (General Medical Services) Amendment (No 4) Regulations 2001.[98]

A PCT must remove a doctor from its medical list where he is convicted of murder **2.133** in the United Kingdom or after 14 December 2001 is convicted in the United Kingdom of a criminal offence for which he has been sentenced to a term of imprisonment of more than six months or where he has been the subject of a national disqualification by the NHS Tribunal or Family Health Services Appeal Authority.

In addition a PCT may remove a doctor from its medical list if it becomes aware **2.134** of information from the doctor or another source (often the police or a regulatory body such as the GMC) that provides evidence on which to make a decision that:

(i)   the doctor's continued presence on the list would be prejudicial to the efficiency of general medical services;[99]

(ii)   the doctor has been involved in an incident of fraud;[100]

(iii) the doctor is unsuitable to remain on the medical list.[101]

---

[96] SI 1992/664.
[97] SI 1996/703.
[98] SI 2001/3742.
[99] National Health Service Act 1977, s 49F(2).
[100] ibid, ss 49F(3) and 49H.
[101] ibid, s 49F(4).

2.135   As an alternative to removal from the list the PCT has a power under s 49G of the National Health Service Act 1977 for 'contingent removal' which involves the imposition of conditions on the doctor's retention on the medical list. If the conditions are subsequently breached the doctor can be removed from the list. The conditions can be free standing or can be such as to vary the doctor's formal terms of service. An example of appropriate conditions would be in cases of poor performance or clinical issues conditions as to additional training or supervision.

2.136   Any conditions imposed are subject to review by the PCT where it considers it appropriate and there must be a review of a written request if made by or on behalf of the doctor at any time after three months since the decision to impose conditions or six months after the decision on any previous review.[102] On any review the conditions can be maintained, removed, varied or some fresh conditions can be imposed.

2.137   Breach of conditions can lead to removal of the doctor subject to procedures as to notification and a hearing (given that Article 6 of the European Convention will apply as the PCT is a public body and the practitioner will effectively lose his right to practise as a GP by removal given the role of the NHS as a monopoly employer of those providing general medical services).

2.138   Before it can make a contingent or discretionary removal from its medical list a PCT must give the doctor 28 days notice of its intention and state why it proposes such action. The doctor must be provided with the opportunity to make representations against such action and these representations include the right to make oral representations. Given the applicability of both Article 6 and the rules of natural justice the doctor must be provided with reasons and evidence relied upon by the PCT in reaching its decision such that he can have an effective right to be heard upon the issue.

2.139   A decision (after relevant representations) to remove from the list or impose or vary or review conditions takes effect only 28 days after it is made when there is no appeal (28 days being the relevant time-limit for appeal) or after the Family Health Services Appeal Authority finally disposes of the appeal where an appeal has been lodged. An appeal is a matter of right and is made in writing to the Authority within 28 days of the decision appealed from.[103]

2.140   A PCT has the power to suspend a doctor from its medical list when necessary to do so for the protection of the public or in the public interest (effectively similar grounds to those on which the IOC of the GMC can suspend a doctor under s 41A of the Medical Act 1983).

---

[102] N 98 above, reg 7G.
[103] Health and Social Care Act 2001, s 27 and National Health Service Act 1977, s 495 and Sch 9A.

The power of a PCT to suspend is restricted to certain situations:　　　　　**2.141**

(i)　whilst the PCT considers whether or not to remove or contingently remove the doctor;[104]

(ii)　whilst it awaits the decision of a court or body which regulates the doctor's profession anywhere in the world affecting the doctor (such as the GMC) [s 49I(1)(b) NHS Act 1977];[105]

(iii)　where it has decided to remove the doctor but the decision cannot yet legally take effect (for example, appeal to the Family Health Services Appeal Authority is pending) [s 49I(1)(c) NHS Act 1977];[106]

(iv)　during the period when an appeal by the doctor is being considered but has not yet been lodged.

The effect of suspension is that although the doctor's name remains on the med- **2.142** ical list he is not entitled to provide any general medical services. He is entitled to be paid his normal remuneration and arrangements for the maintenance of his practice and provision of medical services to his patients are undertaken by the PCT which must fund them.

If the suspension is for the purposes of considering removal or contingent removal **2.143** the maximum period of suspension is six months unless extended by application by the PCT to the Family Health Services Appeal Authority.[107]

If the suspension is whilst awaiting the decision of a court or regulatory body, the **2.144** maximum period of suspension is until six months after the relevant decision and the doctor, when suspended, must be informed of the additional period beyond the court or regulatory body decision.[108]

The PCT can revoke a suspension at any time. It can also review it and must do so **2.145** where a written request is made on behalf of the doctor after three months and thereafter after six months after any previous review. At a review the suspension can be revoked, maintained or the period can be revised.

There is no right of appeal from a suspension but as the decision to suspend is by **2.146** a public body the decision is susceptible to judicial review by the High Court (Administrative Court) on normal judicial review grounds. Given the time delay in achieving judicial review a more appropriate way forward may be early review.

Where the outcome of a criminal or regulatory process is no finding against the **2.147** doctor the PCT must lift the suspension (regardless of the specified additional

---

[104]　National Health Service Act 1977, s 49I(1)(2).
[105]　ibid, s 49I(1)(b).
[106]　ibid, s 49I(1)(c).
[107]　ibid, s 49I(1)(a).
[108]　ibid, s 49I(1)(b).

period). If it continues to have concerns despite the lack of an adverse finding it does have open to it the power to re-suspend on the basis of investigating contingent removal or removal.

2.148 A doctor must be given notice of a decision to suspend and must be given reasons for it and evidence supporting it.[109] As suspension is intended to be an urgent measure the minimum notice is 24 hours and the doctor must be provided with an opportunity to make oral representations (should he wish to do so).

2.149 The Family Health Services Appeal Authority, as well as being an appellate body for decisions to remove from the medical list is the only body with the power to make a national disqualification order which, by s 49N of the National Health Service Act 1977, it can do if required by a Health Authority/PCT or as part of any appeal process on its own motion.

7. NHS Practitioners

2.150 Most NHS doctors have incorporated into their individual contracts of employment with their employing Trusts the Terms and Conditions of Service for Hospital Medical and Dental Practitioners and it is these Terms which provide the basis of the unified NHS contract for doctors.

2.151 These Terms include provisions as to disciplinary action in respect of professional and personal misconduct and professional competence issues. The current basis for such action is Department of Health Circular HC(90)9. Under the Circular provision is made for investigation of complaints of personal misconduct under the Trust's own local disciplinary procedures as applied to all its staff (medical and non-medical). Issues of professional competence and conduct are considered under two different procedures under the Circular—under the Intermediate Procedure (set out in Annex E of the Circular) for matters requiring action short of dismissal and under Annex B for more serious matters which might result in dismissal.

2.152 Many NHS Trusts have provided medical staff in recent years with individual contracts which incorporate disciplinary procedures modelled on those provided in HC(90)9 but with localised variations. Others simply incorporate into their own contracts the provisions of the Circular. The format in Trust contracts has been the same in the sense that issues of personal misconduct are dealt with on the same basis as against non-medical staff and matters of professional misconduct are dealt with in procedures which have a much greater independent adjudication element to them with greater legal formality and rights to legal representation.

2.153 The result is that procedures for professional competence and conduct are more protracted and more expensive for Trusts to operate and the decision-making is

---

[109] N 98 above, reg 7F.

not within their own control. Hence the preference for dealing with matters if possible under their own internal disciplinary procedures as for other staff where usually the decision-makers are Trust line managers or directors and where there is no provision for legal representation.

The courts have consequently on a number of occasions been asked to consider **2.154** the question of classification of matters as 'professional' as opposed to personal conduct—with the employer usually seeking to argue a classification of personal (and use of the quick, less costly internal procedures) and the doctor arguing for the greater legal protections of the professional procedures. In the case of *Skidmore v Dartford and Gravesham NHS Trust*[110] the House of Lords finally determined the matter following inconsistent lines of authority as to the application of administrative law and contract principles, holding that the question was one of contract, to be determined by the employer in accordance with normal contractual principles and that if issues of both personal and professional conduct were involved then the matters should be determined in accordance with the procedure for professional conduct, as a purposive construction and common sense approach pointed to a broad interpretation of professional misconduct.

Annex E and Trust procedures based on it provide for investigation by two inde- **2.155** pendent assessors from the same discipline as the clinician (usually nominated by the relevant Royal College or Joint Consultants Committee) and the provision of a report after interviewing the doctor and relevant witnesses and after consideration of the documentation. This procedure is specifically for cases where it is considered that any action taken will be short of dismissal and often the recommendations in the report relate to issues of dysfunction in the relevant department or the need for retraining for the clinician and/or for restriction of his work. Essentially Annex E provides for an investigatory (as opposed to adversarial) process and does not involve the participation of lawyers or formal disciplinary action. In such circumstances there is usually no right of appeal from any determination under Annex E.

Annex B and its equivalents provide for a much more legally based framework and **2.156** essentially an adversarial process. The Medical Director or Chief Executive determines whether on the information provided there is a prima facie case and the clinician is asked to comment to this effect (but is not obliged to do so) having been provided with some detail of the case against him.

If the decision is that there is a prima facie case and that the facts are in issue such **2.157** that an oral hearing is required a panel is then established by the Trust which is independent of the Trust and comprises a legally qualified chairman (usually a practising barrister or solicitor of some standing) and (in cases of competence) two

---

[110] [2003] Lloyd's Rep Med 369.

practitioners from the same discipline as the clinician and independent of the Trust, and in cases of misconduct one such clinician and one other person independent of the Trust.

2.158 The doctor is entitled to legal representation at any panel hearing and, if legally represented, the Trust will normally do the same. The procedure to be adopted is largely a matter for the legal chairman but usually mirrors adversarial court proceedings with the criminal rules of evidence being applied (although the standard of proof is generally accepted as the high balance of probabilities test). Given that the case is a disciplinary one it is unusual for the defence to reveal its witness evidence in advance although increasingly in competence cases it may be beneficial to do so, particularly if expert witnesses are being instructed on both sides, and the legal chairman after argument may so direct.

2.159 Although the timetable in HC(90)9 envisages investigation and completion of the process in less than six months, the normal time-frame for such proceedings is more usually 18 months and in some instances has been two to three years (or more). Often the doctor is suspended during the process (on full pay) and the cost to the Trust of this and employing a locum and meeting the costs of its own legal team and experts and the panel—not to mention management time and time lost for its own employee witnesses—can be huge.

2.160 Disciplinary action (of which Annex B proceedings form part) can only be taken under the contract of employment and arise out of the employer–employee relationship. Termination of the contract of employment, for example by retirement or resignation, will bring such proceedings to an end. In such circumstances if the employer is concerned that serious allegations of misconduct and/or incompetence have been left uninvestigated, the matter can be referred by the employer to the GMC under conduct or performance procedures.

2.161 Until January 2004 suspension by an employer pending disciplinary investigation was unfortunately quite common and could be prolonged. With effect from 5 January 2004 a new framework for all NHS bodies in England exists to deal with the initial handling of concerns about doctors in the NHS and addressing new rules for what is now to be termed 'exclusion from work'.[111]

2.162 Increasingly the Annex B or equivalent procedure has been used for trial of competence issues and is not really suited for such an investigation (where perhaps the doctor's work over a two year period is being scrutinised). Adversarial proceedings do not really facilitate a review of clinical issues and as a consequence proceedings conducted under the procedure have become complex and delayed (for example, conducting 12 or more clinial negligence cases in one hearing).

---

[111] HSC 2003/012 published 29 December 2003.

The panel reports to the Trust as to facts found and fault. The Trust then deter- **2.163** mines what action to take. Annex B itself provides that the Panel can be invited to make recommendations as to disciplinary action—although these do not bind the Trust but may be significant in any subsequent employment tribunal proceedings.

If the Trust institutes disciplinary proceedings and determines to dismiss, the doc- **2.164** tor may have an appeal in accordance with Trust disciplinary procedures. If employed prior to 1991 he may have a preserved appeal under para 190 of the Terms and Conditions of Service for Hospital Medical and Dental Practitioners—provided not summarily dismissed[112]—and an appeal to the Secretary of State for Health is lodged during the notice period. Such an appeal has the effect of suspending the dismissal. The appeal is heard by a specialist panel appointed by and reporting to the Secretary of State.

Due to huge delays and costs involved in such proceedings in September 2003 the **2.165** Department of Health and British Medical Association (on behalf of doctors) published the 'Agreed Principles on Discipline and Suspension' which is to form the basis for discussions in 2004 on procedures to replace HC(90)9 and para 190 appeals to the Secretary of State. The framework under discussion proposes disciplining doctors on misconduct issues under the same procedures as other hospital workers and without rights to legal representation. This is a matter of concern for the medical profession as loss of NHS employment without the protection of legal process and representation given the position of the NHS as a monopoly employer is tantamount to loss of the right to practice in the United Kingdom—rather different to the position for the porter or canteen assistant or even the business manager.

C. Complaints and Inquiries

1. NHS Complaints Procedures

(i) The current system

The elements of the current system have been in place since 1 April 1996. Prior to **2.166** that date NHS complaints procedures were fragmented, with different procedures for primary care practitioners and for clinical and non-clinical complaints. A comprehensive review of NHS complaints procedures had been undertaken by the Wilson Committee, which reported in May 1994.[113] The reforms of April 1996 were designed to implement the recommendations of that Committee. Procedures for the providers of primary and secondary care were to follow the same pattern, and complaints procedures were to be separated from disciplinary action.

---

[112] *R v Secretary of State for Health, ex p Guirguis* [1990] IRLR 30.
[113] *Being heard* (Department of Health, 1994).

2.167   Section 17 of the National Health Service Act 1977 grants to the Secretary of State for Health the power to give directions to health service bodies about the exercise of their functions. Under the Hospital Complaints Procedure Act 1985 the Secretary of State is under a duty to give to Health Authorities, NHS Trusts and PCTs such directions as appear to him to be necessary to ensure that arrangements are in place to deal with complaints by patients at hospitals for which they are responsible, and for publicising those arrangements. The National Health Service (Functions of Health Authorities)(Complaints) Regulations 1996[114] make it a prescribed function under s 15 of the 1977 Act for PCTs to establish and operate in accordance with directions procedures for dealing with complaints about family health service practitioners.

2.168   The detail of the procedure for dealing with NHS complaints is therefore set out in a series of sets of directions given by the Secretary of State to various health bodies but likely changes are imminent: see para 2.186. The directions under which the current system operates were issued in 1996 and in 1998. In 2002 a new set of directions was issued dealing with complaints about PCTs themselves and services commissioned by them, together with a series of amendment directions to reflect the changes in the structure of the NHS brought about by the National Health Service Reform and Health Care Professions Act 2002, in particular the transfer on 1 October 2002 of responsibility for the independent review element of complaints about family health services practitioners from Health Authorities to PCTs. The amendment directions do not alter the detail of the complaints procedure, but essentially ensure that PCTs operate the existing system where responsibility for it has been transferred to them.

2.169   The various procedures have, in accordance with the recommendations of the Wilson Committee, the common elements of local resolution and independent review, with the option of recourse to the Health Service Commissioner or Ombudsman if independent review does not resolve the complaint to the complainant's satisfaction. In the case of GPs, whether providing general or personal medical services, there is a formal requirement to have in place by way of local resolution a practice-based complaints procedure and to co-operate with the investigation of a complaint at the independent review stage by a Health Authority (now PCT).[115]

---

[114] SI 1996/669.

[115] In the case of general medical services provided under Pt II of the National Health Service Act 1977, see paras 47A and B of the Terms of Service in Sch 2 to the National Health Service (General Medical Services) Regulations 1992 (n 94 above). In the case of personal medical services under pilot schemes constituted under the National Health Service (Primary Care) Act 1997, see Directions to Health Authorities Concerning the Implementation of Pilot Schemes (Personal Medical Services) 1998, para 25 and Sch 3.

Investigation of a complaint must cease if a complainant intimates an intention to   **2.170**
bring legal proceedings, or if disciplinary proceedings are considered, although
under certain circumstances investigation may be resumed if, for example, the relevant proceedings are not pursued or do not deal with the subject matter of the
complaint. The complaint must ordinarily be brought within six months of the
events to which it gives rise, or within six months of its subject matter coming to
the complainant's notice, although in the latter case there is a 'long stop' of one
year from the occurrence of the subject matter of the complaint. There is a discretion effectively to extend this time limit in some cases.

If a complainant is dissatisfied with the results of the initial investigation (local   **2.171**
resolution) he may request a convener to consider whether a panel should be
appointed to hear the complaint further. Instead of appointing a panel, the
convenor may ask the service provider to consider disciplinary action or to investigate the matter further under the local resolution procedures, but in the latter
case if the complainant remains dissatisfied he may make a further request for a
panel. If the convener decides not to appoint a panel, the complainant may refer
that decision to the Ombudsman, who may recommend that the decision is reconsidered. A panel consists of three persons, with a lay chairman and a majority
of members who are independent of the provider of the service. Clinical assessors
are appointed to advise the panel where the complaint concerns the exercise of
clinical judgment. Participants have the opportunity to present their case orally
or, if they wish, in writing and are entitled to be accompanied by an adviser (and,
in the case of a complainant, by a relative or friend). The function of the panel is
to investigate the complaint and to provide a report, which may include suggestions as to ways in which the provision of services might be improved. The complainant is entitled to see the report and to know of any action taken by the service
provider on any suggestion made in the report. He must be informed of his right
to complain to the Ombudsman.

(ii) The Health Service Commissioner

The office of the Health Service Commissioner or Ombudsman is regulated by   **2.172**
the Health Service Commissioners Act 1993, as amended by the Health Service
Commissioners (Amendment) Acts of 1996 and 2000. The 1996 Act extended
the jurisdiction of the Ombudsman to cover general medical and dental practitioners, those providing general ophthalmic or pharmaceutical services under Pt
II of the National Health Service Act 1977 and independent providers of health
services.[116] It also[117] removed what had previously been the greatest restriction on
his powers, that is his inability to investigate complaints about clinical judgment.

---

[116] Health Service Commissioners Act 1993, ss 2A and 2B.
[117] ibid, s 3(7).

The Act of 2000 extended the Ombudsman's powers of investigation to retired practitioners.

2.173 The general scope of the Ombudsman's powers is set out in s 3 of the Act. He may investigate a failure in a service provided by a health service body, a failure to provide a service which it was that body's function to provide, or maladministration connected with any other action taken by or on behalf of that body. In the case of family health service providers the Ombudsman may investigate action taken in connection with the provision of family health services, but as with health services bodies he cannot question the merits of a decision taken without maladministration, unless as previously mentioned that decision was taken in consequence of the exercise of clinical judgment.

2.174 In each case the basis for the investigation is alleged injustice or hardship to the complainant or a person whom the complainant is representing. The complaint must be made by the person aggrieved unless that person has died or is unable to act for himself. There is a time limit of one year from the date on which the person aggrieved first had notice of the matters alleged in the complaint. This time limit may be extended by the Ombudsman if he considers it reasonable to do so, but in the case of retired practitioners there is a long stop time limit of three years from the date of retirement.[118] A health service body may itself refer to the Ombudsman a complaint alleging injustice or hardship as a result of a failure or maladministration by that body.[119]

2.175 The Ombudsman cannot conduct an investigation in circumstances in which the NHS complaints procedure is available to the complainant unless that procedure has been invoked and exhausted or he is satisfied that it is not reasonable for the procedure to be invoked or exhausted. A similar provision applies where the person aggrieved has a right to bring the matter before the tribunal or a remedy in a court of law. The Ombudsman might consider it reasonable not to pursue such a remedy where, for example, the damages awarded are likely to be very small. There is an absolute bar to investigation by the Ombudsman where the action in question is or has been the subject of an Inquiry under s 84 of the National Health Service Act 1977 or s 76 of the National Health Service (Scotland) Act 1978.[120] He cannot conduct investigations into action taken in respect of personnel matters such as appointments and pay or generally into contractual or other commercial transactions.[121]

---

[118] Health Service Commissioners Act 1993, s 9.
[119] ibid, s 10.
[120] ibid, s 6.
[121] ibid, s 7.

In conducting his investigation the Ombudsman may require the provision of rele-   **2.176**
vant documents or information by any person able to supply it. He has the same
powers as a court in respect of the attendance or examination of witnesses and the
production of documents.[122] There is no appeal against the findings of the
Ombudsman who has no power to award damages or any other legal remedy but
may make recommendations as to redress and changes in procedures.

(iii) Support and Advocacy Services for Complainants

Under the current system Community Health Councils have frequently provided   **2.177**
support and advocacy services to those seeking to make complaints, but they are
under no statutory obligation to do so. More recently, this work has been undertaken by the PALS (Patient Advisory Liaison Service) and the ICAS (Independent
Complaints and Advocacy Service), the latter being available throughout England
from 1 September 2003. It is intended that Community Health Councils in
England will be abolished.[123]

Those working for PALS are employed by individual NHS Trusts or PCTs and   **2.178**
therefore are not independent of the body against whom the complaint may be
made. They work on Trust premises and should therefore be immediately available. It is their function to seek to resolve any difficulty quickly and informally
without the need to make a formal complaint. PALS is, however, one means by
which a potential complainant may be put in touch with ICAS.

ICAS has been established (for the present on an interim basis) consistently with   **2.179**
the statutory duty imposed on the Secretary of State for Health by s 12 of the
Health and Social Care Act 2001[124] 'to arrange, to such extent as he considers
necessary to meet all reasonable requirements, for the provision of independent
advocacy services'. On 1 January 2003 the Commission for Patient and Public
Involvement in Health was established by s 20(1) of the National Health Service
Reform and Health Care Professions Act 2002. The functions of the Commission
include[125] advising and assisting the providers of independent advocacy services in
England[126] and setting and monitoring quality standards relating to the provision
of those services. ICAS will be commissioned for their local area by PCT Patients'
Forums,[127] established on 1 December 2003. The level of service provided will
depend upon the needs and wishes of the individual complainant, and will range
from simple self-help information to specialist advocacy.

---

[122] ibid, s 12.
[123] NHS Reform and Health Care Professions Act 2002, s 22(1).
[124] s 12 inserts a new s 19A into the National Health Service Act 1977.
[125] NHS Reform and Health Care Professions Act 2002, s 20(2)(e) and (f).
[126] In Wales, independent advocacy services will continue to be provided by Community Health
Councils.
[127] NHS Reform and Health Care Professions Act 2002, s 15(1)(b).

(iv) Proposals for Reform

2.180 In March 2003 the Department of Health published *NHS complaints reform: Making things right*, setting out proposals for reform. This followed an independent evaluation of the NHS complaints procedure and listening exercise which had taken place over two years up to October 2001 and formed part of the government's express commitment in the *NHS Plan* to reform the procedure in the light of the evaluation.

2.181 The proposals do not seek to change the current basic structure of local resolution, beyond which 98 per cent of complaints do not proceed, and independent review, although there is specific reference to the successful use of conciliation and a commitment to the use of alternative dispute resolution generally. The PALS (described above), together with a system of 'modern matrons' with a specific role in the informal resolution of complaints, are intended to minimise the number of cases which need to go forward to a formal complaint. At the local resolution stage complainants are to be permitted to complain directly to the PCT if they do not wish to raise matters directly with a family health services practitioner. Time limits for local resolution of complaints are to be made consistent across primary and secondary care.

2.182 It is at the independent review stage where the proposed changes are most fundamental. The most significant finding to emerge from the evaluation study was widespread dissatisfaction with this stage of the process, which was not regarded by complainants as being sufficiently independent or impartial. It is proposed to transfer responsibility for the independent review stage to the new Commission for Healthcare Audit and Inspection (CHAI), which will be independent of the NHS and the Department of Health. Primary legislation, in the form of the Health and Social Care (Community Health and Standards) Act 2003, has been required to establish CHAI, which will not be operational before April 2004. If it identifies deficiencies in the local resolution process CHAI will be able to recommend that further action be taken at a local level. It will be able to conduct its own detailed investigation of the complaint or, where it is particularly complex, to refer the complaint to the Ombudsman. The complainant himself will retain the right to refer his complaint to the Ombudsman if dissatisfied with the outcome of its resolution by CHAI.

2.183 There is a general emphasis in the proposals on using the information generated by complaints to improve the quality of future provision of health services. Each Trust will be required to have a nominated Board member responsible for the investigation of, and learning from, complaints and other adverse events, a proposal echoed in the report of the Chief Medical Officer referred to below. CHAI will have a responsibility, as part of its role as a health service inspectorate, to use feedback from complaints to improve standards.

The above proposals do not relate to Wales, where the Welsh Assembly **2.184**
Government has issued separate guidance for the handling of NHS complaints.[128]
In particular, a Review Secretariat independent of the NHS will administer the independent review stage. If a complaint is referred to the Secretariat, two lay
people with access to clinical advice will be appointed to review it and a panel may
be set up. Full investigation of a complaint will take place even if it is clear that the
complainant intends to bring a legal claim. Regional variations in the handling of
complaints are inconsistent with the recommendations of the Wilson
Committee, which stressed the need for uniformity of complaints procedures
throughout the United Kingdom.

On 30 June 2003 the Chief Medical Officer published his report, *Making* **2.185**
Amends, on the system of claims for clinical negligence. He has proposed an
NHS Redress Scheme, designed in certain categories of case to provide a remedy
by way of investigation, explanation, the delivery of a package of care, and if appropriate, financial compensation. Under his proposals the Redress Scheme
would be aligned with the complaints procedure and indeed the latter would
serve as a route to the former in some cases. It is clear that the Chief Medical
Officer regards a strengthened complaints procedure as an integral part of the
proposed reforms. The current rule under which the investigation of a complaint
is halted if legal proceedings are intimated would be abolished. He recommends
that a new standard of care should be set for after-complaint management by
NHS providers, with a 'full and objective investigation of the facts of the case,
commensurate with the severity of the harm, so that patients or their families are
provided with a full explanation of what has happened, an apology where something has gone wrong, and a specification of the action (local and national) being
taken to reduce the risk of a similar event happening to future patients'. NHS
staff should be trained in communication in the context of complaints, and a
duty of candour introduced by legislation 'requiring all health care professionals
and managers to inform patients where they become aware of a possible negligent act or omission'.

Under ss 113 and 115 of the Health and Social Care (Community Health and **2.186**
Standards) Act 2003 the Secretary of State has power to make regulations governing the handling and consideration of complaints. In December 2003 draft
regulations which will apply only in England were published by the Department
of Health. A consultation exercise is taking place and the regulations in their final
form are due to come into force on 1 June 2004. The Regulations will revoke the
Secretary of State's directions under which the current system operates. The draft
Regulations broadly implement the proposals for reform in *Making things right*.

---

[128] *Complaints in the NHS: a Guide to Handling Complaints in Wales.*

2. Private Medicine

2.187 From 1 April 2002 regulation of complaints in the private sector has been dealt with through the regulatory framework of the National Care Standards Commission created under the Care Standards Act 2000. The Health and Social Care (Community Health and Standards)Act[128a] makes provision for the abolition of the National Care Standards Commission and the transfer of this aspect of its functions to CHAI from a date to be appointed.

3. Inquiries

2.188 Disciplinary proceedings may be activated where one or more individuals can be identified as being guilty of misconduct or incompetence. In some cases blame cannot be apportioned until there has been a full investigation of what has occurred. The Health Authority may decide to deal with such cases, particularly if they have attracted media attention, by setting up an independent inquiry with a legally qualified chairman. One difficulty is that no person can be compelled to attend the inquiry or to give evidence to it, so that it may be difficult to ascertain the facts.

2.189 Under s 84 of the National Health Service Act 1977[129] the Secretary of State for Health has power to set up an inquiry into any case in connection with any matter arising under the National Health Service Act 1977[130] where he deems it advisable to do so, and such bodies have similar powers to courts of law, in that they can compel witnesses to give evidence and order the production of documents.

2.190 In addition to the power under s 84, the Secretary of State may set up an inquiry under his general powers in s 2 of the 1977 Act provided its scope is limited to matters falling within the 1977 Act.[131] In *Wagstaff*'s case[132] Kennedy LJ stated (in connection with the Shipman inquiry) that 'where, as here, an inquiry purports to be a public inquiry, as opposed to an internal domestic inquiry, there is now in law what really amounts to a presumption that it will proceed in public unless there are persuasive reasons for taking some other course'. He found the Secretary of State's decision to hold the inquiry in private to be in breach of the applicants' right to freedom of expression under article 10(1) ECHR. Article 10 was not at the time incorporated into English law, but the court proceeded on the basis that the right to receive and impart information contained within it did no more than give expression to the common law. In a more recent decision,[133] however, Scott

---

[128a] ss 44 and 102.

[129] And s 76 of the National Health Service (Scotland) Act 1978.

[130] Or Pt I of the National Health Service and Community Care Act 1990, Pt I of the Health Act 1999 or Pt 1 of the Health and Social Care (Community Health and Standards) Act 2003.

[131] *R (on the application of Wagstaff) v Secretary of State for Health* [2001] 1 WLR 292 (DC).

[132] ibid, 320.

[133] *R (on the application of Howard) v Secretary of State for Health* [2003] QB 830 (Ayling and Neale inquiries).

Baker J held that save where the inquiry was ordered under the Tribunals of Inquiry (Evidence) Act 1921 there was no such presumption, the Secretary of State having to form a judgment as to what best suits the circumstances of each case. There was in his judgment no free-standing right to a public inquiry under Article 10(1). It was significant in *Howard* that (unlike in *Wagstaff*) the media were not parties to the applications, and the Secretary of State had permitted the applicants themselves to be present throughout the inquiries, whether themselves or by a representative.

4. Whistleblowing

The GMCs guidelines *Good Medical Practice*[134] lay down that doctors are under a **2.191** professional obligation to protect patients from the risk of harm which may be created by the conduct, performance or health of other doctors or health care professionals. The guidelines state[135] that:

> (i)f you have grounds to believe that a doctor or other health care professional may be putting patients at risk, you must give an honest explanation of your concerns to an appropriate person from the employing authority, such as the medical director, nursing director or chief executive, or the director of public health, or an officer of your local medical committee, following any procedures set by the employer. If there are no appropriate systems, or local systems cannot resolve the problem, and you remain concerned about the safety of patients, you should inform the relevant regulatory body. If you are not sure what to do, discuss your concerns with an impartial colleague or contact your defence body, a professional organisation or the GMC for advice.

Those with management responsibilities are required by the guidelines to have in place systems under which concerns about the fitness to practise of professional colleagues can be raised.

The Public Interest Disclosure Act 1998 amended[136] the Employment Rights Act **2.192** 1996 so as to confer certain rights on workers making protected disclosures under Pt IVA of the Act. The definition of 'worker' for these purposes was extended beyond the categories of those working under contracts of employment, or to perform personally any work or services for another, to include those performing general medical, dental, ophthalmic or pharmaceutical services in accordance with arrangements made under the National Health Service Act 1977 by a Health Authority or PCT,[137] which are treated in this context as the worker's employer.

In order to qualify for the protection conferred by the Act the worker making the **2.193** disclosure must satisfy certain requirements as to the subject matter of the

---

[134] May 2001 edn.
[135] ibid, para 27.
[136] With effect from 2 July 1999.
[137] Employment Rights Act 1996, s 43K(1)(c).

information disclosed, his state of mind when the disclosure was made, and the recipient of the information. It is of potential relevance in the medical context that disclosures which in the reasonable belief of the worker tend to show breach or likely breach by a person of a legal obligation (which could include a common law duty of care) or a danger to the health or safety of any individual are qualifying disclosures.[138] A worker is protected if he makes the qualifying disclosure in good faith to his employer.[139] With limited exceptions, where the disclosure is made other than to the employer more stringent conditions are imposed, including a reasonable belief on the part of the worker that the information disclosed, and any allegation contained in it, are substantially true.[140] A worker has the right not to be subjected to any detriment by his employer on the ground that he has made a protected disclosure[141] and if the reason or principal reason for his dismissal was a protected disclosure he is treated as having been unfairly dismissed.[142] In either case he is entitled to present a complaint to an employment tribunal.

2.193 A health care professional considering the disclosure of information regarding a colleague's practice to a third party must also have regard to the tort of defamation and the common law duty of confidence. Truth is a complete defence to a claim alleging defamation. It is also a defence to such a claim that the communication is covered by qualified privilege, namely that the communicator had a legal, moral or social duty to pass the information on to the recipient, and the recipient had a corresponding interest or duty to receive it,[143] but the privilege will be lost if the claimant can show that the communicator was motivated by malice.[144] An action for breach of confidence lies against anyone who reveals to a third party information which he knows was given in confidence either to him or to some other person.[145] It is, however, a defence to show that it was necessary in the public interest to make disclosure.[146] It can be seen that both the professional guidance of the GMC and the Public Interest Disclosure Act draw on these common law principles.

---

[138] ibid, s 43B.
[139] ibid, s 43C.
[140] ibid, ss 43F–43H.
[141] ibid, s 47B.
[142] ibid, s 103A.
[143] *Adam v Ward* [1917] AC 309.
[144] *Horrocks v Lowe* [1975] AC 135.
[145] *Attorney-General v Guardian Newspapers* [1987] 1 WLR 1248.
[146] *X v Y* [1988] 2 All ER 415; *W v Edgell* [1990] Ch 359.

PART II

CONSENT TO TREATMENT

3

CONSENT TO TREATMENT: THE COMPETENT PATIENT

A. Consent and Battery

1. Introduction

The law relating to consent is of central importance in medical law. Under the **3.01** common law, the legality of a medical treatment or procedure[1] will largely turn upon whether the patient has given a valid consent to it.[2] Treatment without consent may amount to the tort of battery[3] or the crime of assault.[4] Consent, or more

---

[1] Medical *treatment* involves a procedure carried out by, or on behalf of, a medical or health care practitioner for a therapeutic purpose. By contrast, a medical *procedure* includes interventions where the therapeutic intention may be absent, for example, the taking of blood to test for the benefit of others, organ or tissue donation and non-therapeutic research.

[2] But see below, paras 3.31–3.36.

[3] Battery is the intentional application of physical contact to the person without consent or other lawful justification: see *Faulkner v Talbot* [1981] 3 All ER 468 (DC) *per* Lord Lane CJ at 471

footnote 4 on p. 132

accurately the need for it, is the legal reflection of the ethical principle of respect for autonomy.[5] In this particular context, this notion might be better expressed as respect for a person's bodily integrity stemming from a right of self-determination.[6] It is a 'fundamental principle, now long established, that every person's body is inviolate'.[7]

3.02 Human rights law reinforces the common law's position through the protection of an individual's 'physical integrity' as part of the right to respect for private life protected by Article 8 of the European Convention on Human Rights.[8] In *Pretty v UK*,[9] the European Court of Human Rights stated that:

> In the sphere of medical treatment, the refusal to accept a particular medical treatment might, inevitably, lead to a fatal outcome, yet the imposition of medical treatment, without the consent of a mentally competent adult, would interfere with a person's physical integrity in a manner capable of engaging the rights protected under Article 8.1 of the Convention.

3.03 There is, of course, scope for the state to derogate from the individual's right under Article 8(1). That Convention right may be subject to interference if justified under Article 8(2) to the extent that such interference is 'necessary in a democratic society'. The 'proportionality' requirement means that a balance has to be struck between the right of the individual and the legitimate aims specified in Article 8(2). This process requires a balance to be struck on an individual case by case basis. There seems little doubt that English judges would take the view that the common law adequately took account of the 'fair balancing' exercise required in Article 8(2) so that balance is always struck in favour of the individual's right to refuse treatment which is 'paramount' and absolute.[10] The only likely permissible

---

and *Collins v Wilcock* [1984] 3 All ER 374 (DC) *per* Goff LJ at 379. For a discussion of the elements of the tort, see Trindade, F, 'Intentional Torts: Some Thoughts on Assault and Battery' (1982) 2 OJLS 211.

⁴ The crime of 'common assault' includes an assault *stricto sensu* (ie, where the victim merely apprehends a 'touching') and a 'battery' where the 'touching' actually occurs: *DPP v Little* [1992] 1 All ER 299.

⁵ For an authoritative ethical statement of the requirement for (and of) consent: see *Seeking Patients' Consent: the Ethical Considerations* (General Medical Council, 1998). See also DoH guidance in *Reference Guide to Consent for Examination or Treatment* (DoH, 2001) (*www.doh.gov.uk/consent/index.htm*).

⁶ *Malette v Shulman* (1990) 67 DLR (4th) 321 (Ont CA), *per* Robins JA at 327–328. See also *Airedale NHS Trust v Bland* [1993] AC 789; [1993] 1 All ER 821 (HL), *per* Lord Goff at 866.

⁷ *Re F (Mental Patient: Sterilisation)* [1990] 2 AC 1; [1989] 2 All ER 545 (HL), *per* Lord Goff at 563. See also, *Re T (Adult: Refusal of Treatment)* [1993] Fam 95; [1992] 4 All ER 649 (CA).

⁸ Other Convention rights may be engaged where treatment is contemplated without a patient's consent, in particular the individual's right to freedom from inhuman or degrading treatment under Art 3. For a general discussion see Wicks, E, 'The Right to Refuse Medical Treatment Under the European Convention on Human Rights' (2001) 9 Med L Rev 17.

⁹ Application 2346/02 (2002) 66 BMLR 147 (ECtHR), at [63]. See also, *NHS Trust A v M; NHS Trust B v H* [2001] Lloyd's Rep Med 28 at [41] *per* Butler-Sloss P.

¹⁰ *Re T* (n 7 above), *per* Lord Donaldson MR at 661. See also *Bland* (n 6 above), *per* Lord Keith at 860 and *per* Lord Goff at 866. See also *St George's Healthcare NHS Trust v S* [1998] 3 All ER 673 (CA), *per* Judge LJ at 685–687 (competent adult) and 689–692 (pregnant woman).

derogations—and then only by Parliament—will be based upon compelling public health considerations such as the need for public vaccination programmes[11] or in the mental health context where there may be compelling interests justifying the treatment of the patient for his own medical benefit or the protection of others.[12]

English law may be stated simply as follows: any intentional touching of a person **3.04** is unlawful and amounts to the tort of battery unless it is justified by consent or other lawful authority. In medical law this means that a doctor may only carry out a medical treatment or procedure which involves contact with a patient[13] if there exists a valid consent by the patient (or another person authorised by law to consent on his behalf) or if the touching is permitted notwithstanding the absence of consent.[14] The legal position in England is often stated adopting the famous words of Cardozo J in *Schloendorff v Society of New York Hospital*:[15]

> Every human being of adult years and sound mind has a right to determine what shall be done with his own body; and a surgeon who performs an operation without his patient's consent commits an assault, for which he is liable in damages.

English courts have unreservedly accepted that a patient's bodily integrity is in- **3.05** violable such that any physically invasive medical treatment or procedure, however trivial, is unlawful unless authorised by consent or other lawful authority.[16] In *Re F*, Lord Goff stated that:

> It is well established that, as a general rule, the performance of a medical operation on a person without his or her consent is unlawful . . .[17]

Consequently, the medieval tort of battery—developed to deal with fist and sword fights—is the defining legal framework for determining whether a medical treatment or procedure is lawful. At one time, it was suggested that trespass to the

---

[11] See *Acmanne v Belgium* (1984) 40 DR 251 (tuberculosis screening). See also *X v Austria* (1980) 18 DR 154 (compulsory paternity test).

[12] *R (on the application of Wilkinson) v Broadmoor Special Hospital Authority* [2002] 1 WLR 419 (CA).

[13] It would have no relevance, therefore, where the medical 'intervention' did not involve a touching even where there has been no consent; for example, causing a patient to take a drug where the patient is unaware that he is part of a research project. Contrast the US case of *Mink v University of Chicago* (1978) 460 F Supp 713 (battery action allowed to continue on these facts) which would not be followed, on this point, in England.

[14] For treatment without consent involving an incompetent patient or a child see Ch 4 below.

[15] (1914) 211 NY 125 at 126. Cited with approval in *Re F* (n 7 above), *per* Lord Goff at 564 and in *Airedale NHS Trust v Bland* (n 6 above) *per* Lord Goff at 866.

[16] eg, *Re F* (n 7 above); *Re T* (n 7 above); *Re MB* [1997] 8 Med LR 217 (CA). For other recent cases recognising that a competent patient's right of self-determination entitles him or her to refuse any medical treatment even if life-sustaining: see *St George's Healthcare NHS Trust v S* [1998] 3 All ER 673 (CA); *Re JT (Adult: Refusal of Medical Treatment)* [1998] 1 FLR 48 (Wall J); *Re AK* (2000) 58 BMLR 151 (Hughes J) and *Re B (Adult: Refusal of Treatment)* [2002] EWHC 429 (Fam); (2002) 65 BMLR 149 (Butler-Sloss P).

[17] N 7 above at 562. See also at 563 and *per* Lord Brandon at 550–551.

person (here, battery) was irrelevant in the case of medical treatment because a battery could only be committed if the defendant acted with 'hostility'.[18] If this were so, rarely, if ever, would the medical treatment be caught by battery even if there was no consent because the doctor's motives would usually be bona fide, acting, as he would be, in the best interests of the patient. This view has now been conclusively rejected by the House of Lords in *Re F*.[19] It is, as we have seen, the issues of consent or other lawful authority (if any) which are determinative of the legality of the treatment or procedure.

3.06 It is important to notice the extent of the relevance of consent. First, a valid consent licenses what would otherwise be unlawful. However, to be a valid consent, the law requires:

(i)   that it be given by a competent person;
(ii)   that the person must be adequately informed about the 'nature' of what he is agreeing to; and
(iii) that the person should be acting voluntarily and not under the undue influence of another.

Each of these requirements—competence,[20] information,[21] and voluntariness[22] —will be considered separately in this chapter. In particular, it should be noticed that the first requirement means that adults of sound mind may consent to medical treatment, as may children who are sufficiently mature, but those persons who suffer from mental disorder or disability or are immature such that they are not capable of understanding what is involved in the treatment or procedure, may not give a valid consent in law.[23]

3.07 Secondly, in such instances the law will look to another source of justification for the treatment which may, in the case of children, be the consent of a 'proxy' such as parents or a lawful justification based upon 'necessity' to make, what would otherwise be an unauthorised touching, lawful.[24]

3.08 Thirdly, consent is a 'necessary' but it is not a 'sufficient' condition for a patient to be treated. A patient cannot compel a doctor or NHS Trust to provide treatment that is determined by the doctor's clinical judgment not to be in the patient's 'best interests' or which cannot be provided because of limited resources. The courts

---

[18] *Wilson v Pringle* [1987] QB 237, *per* Croom Johnson LJ at 253. For a criticism see Kennedy, I and Grubb, A, *Medical Law* (1st edn, 1989), 172–3.
[19] N 7 above, *per* Lord Goff at 563–564. No other member of the House of Lords commented on this issue.
[20] See below, paras 3.69–3.92.
[21] See below, paras 3.93–3.108.
[22] See below, paras 3.166–3.170.
[23] See below, paras 3.69–3.70 (competence and adults) and Ch 4 (children).
[24] See Ch 4.

will not force a doctor or NHS Trust to treat a patient in a manner contrary to their wishes.[25] There are three reasons for this. As a matter of policy, the court will not make an order compelling a doctor to treat a patient in a manner contrary to his clinical judgment and professional duty. Also, it would be impracticable and uncertain for the court to enforce a mandatory order in this context. Finally, the courts are most reluctant to enter into investigations about the proper allocation of resources within the health service. The court will, as a consequence, simply decline to adjudicate in disputes between patients, doctors and health service institutions arising out of the denial of treatment where, in fact, the issue is one of lack of resources or the allocation of scarce resources to other patients or other forms of treatment.[26] Where the court disagrees with the views of the responsible doctor, the solution lies in finding another doctor who will act on the court's direction, rather than to coerce the patient's existing doctor.

Fourthly, in England, the courts have concluded that the burden of proving lack **3.09** of consent is upon the patient. The defendant does not have to prove he consented.[27] In other words, intentional touching is not prima facie unlawful unless it is proved to be justified.[28] In Canada[29] and Australia the rule is otherwise: the defendant bears the burden of proving consent. In the Australian High Court, McHugh J rationalised this view as follows:

> The contrary view is inconsistent with a person's right of bodily integrity. Other persons do not have the right to interfere with an individual's body unless he or she proves lack of consent to the interference.[30]

Given the importance the law places on the inviolability of the person and the protection of bodily integrity of the individual, it is suggested that the Commonwealth view is the better one and should be adopted in England.[31]

---

[25] *Re J (A Minor) (Wardship: Medical Treatment)* [1993] Fam 15; [1992] 4 All ER 614 (CA) and *Re R (A Minor) (Wardship: Medical Treatment)* [1992] Fam 11; [1991] 4 All ER 177 (CA), *per* Lord Donaldson MR at 187.

[26] *Re J* (n 25 above), *per* Lord Donaldson MR at 623, *per* Balcombe LJ at 625 and *per* Leggatt LJ at 626.

[27] *Freeman v Home Office (No 2)* [1984] QB 524, *per* McCowan J at 524. The Court of Appeal did not specifically refer to the point.

[28] However, judges frequently refer to consent being a 'defence': see eg, *Collins v Wilcock* [1984] 3 All ER 374, *per* Goff LJ at 378.

[29] *Non-Marine, Underwriters, Lloyd's of London v Scalera* [2000] 1 SCR 551 (Can Sup Ct).

[30] *Secretary, Department of Health and Community Services v JWB* (1992) 66 ALJR 300, 337.

[31] Notice the confusing approach in the criminal case of *R v Brown* [1994] 1 AC 212; [1993] 2 All ER 75 (HL), *per* Lord Jauncey at 92, Lord Slynn at 119 and Lord Mustill at 103. It may be, however, that criminal cases are unhelpful in determining upon whom the onus of proof would be in a civil context given the very limited situations where in the former a defendant bears the onus of proof.

2. Refusal of Consent

(i) The General Principle

3.10   Consent and refusal of consent to treatment are, as expressions of the patient's
right to self-determination, opposite sides of the same coin. Where consent to
treatment is legally necessary, a refusal by a competent patient acts as a veto to the
prohibited treatment.[32] For the doctor to act in the face of such a refusal would be
unlawful amounting to a battery.[33] The refusal may be total: 'I don't want any
treatment'; or it may be partial: 'I don't want a blood transfusion.' In either case,
the refusal is legally effective to prevent the prohibited treatment even if the
patient may, or will certainly, die.[34] In *Re T*, Lord Donaldson MR stated:[35]

> An adult patient who . . . suffers from no mental incapacity has an absolute right to
> choose whether to consent to medical treatment, to refuse it or to choose one rather
> than another of the treatments being offered . . . This right of choice is not limited
> to decisions which others might regard as sensible. It exists notwithstanding that the
> reasons for making the choice are rational, irrational, unknown or even non-
> existent.

In the same case Butler-Sloss LJ said:[36]

> A man or woman of full age and sound understanding may choose to reject medical
> advice and medical or surgical treatment either partially or in its entirety. A decision
> to refuse medical treatment by a patient capable of making the decision does not
> have to be sensible, rational or well-considered.

Staughton LJ also stated:[37]

> An adult whose mental capacity is unimpaired has the right to decide for herself
> whether she will or will not receive medical or surgical treatment, even in circum-
> stances where she is likely or even certain to die in the absence of treatment.

---

[32] *Sidaway v Bethlem Royal Hospital* [1985] AC 871; [1985] 1 All ER 643, *per* Lord Scarman at
649.

[33] eg, *Re T* (n 7 above), *per* Lord Donaldson MR at 653. See also *Re MB* (n 16 above), *per* Butler-
Sloss LJ at 221.

[34] *Airedale NHS Trust v Bland* (n 6 above) *per* Lord Goff at 866 citing *Nancy B v Hôtel-Dieu de
Québec* (1992) 86 DLR (4th) 385 (competent adult patient on ventilator entitled to refuse further
intervention). See also *per* Lord Keith at 860 and *per* Lord Mustill at 889. See also *Re B (Adult:
Refusal of Treatment)* [2002] EWHC 429 (Fam); (2002) 65 BMLR 149 (Butler-Sloss P) (tetraplegic
patient found competent to refuse life-sustaining treatment—artificial ventilation—court made a
declaration that continued treatment was unlawful and made a nominal award of damages for past
battery), discussed in Grubb (2002) 10 Med L Rev 201 (Commentary) and *Re W (Adult: Refusal of
Treatment)* [2002] EWHC 901 (Fam) (Butler-Sloss P) (prisoner with a psychopathic disorder was
competent and entitled to refuse treatment for self-harming injury which might lead to his death).

[35] N 7 above at 652–653.

[36] ibid, 664.

[37] ibid, 668.

Consequently, providing the patient is competent, she may refuse any treatment **3.11** including a life-saving operation such as a blood transfusion,[38] anaesthesia and surgery necessary to prevent harm to her and her unborn child,[39] renal dialysis,[40] artificial ventilation[41] and even artificial feeding.[42]

A refusal of medical treatment may be made contemporaneously or in antici- **3.12** pation of becoming incapacitated in the form[43] of an advance directive or, as it is sometimes known, a 'living will'.[44] The legal conditions for a valid advance directive are clear.[45] It must have been made by a patient who was competent and understood what the treatment-refusal decision entailed and it must have been intended to apply in the circumstances that subsequently arise (ie the patient's current medical condition and the procedure that is required). If the 'advance directive' is 'clearly established',[46] then it is as legally binding upon a doctor as would be a contemporaneous refusal[47] unless it has been effectively revoked.[48]

(ii) The Exceptions

There are a number of exceptions to the competent patient's right to refuse any or **3.13** all medical treatments.[49]

(a) Children

In the case of children, a parent (or other with parental authority) or the court may **3.14** override the patient's refusal if that is in her best interests. In principle, this applies

---

[38] eg, *Re T* (n 7 above) (held to be acting under the undue influence of her mother on facts).

[39] eg, *Re MB* (n 16 above) (held incompetent on facts) and *St George's Healthcare NHS Trust v S* (n 10 above), discussed in Grubb (1998) 6 Med L Rev 356 (Commentary).

[40] eg, *Re JT (Adult: Refusal of Medical Treatment)* (n 16 above).

[41] eg, *Re B (Adult: Refusal of Treatment)* (n 16 above) and *Re AK* (n 16 above).

[42] *Secretary of State for the Home Department v Robb* [1995] 1 All ER 677 and Kennedy (1995) 3 Med L Rev 189 (Commentary).

[43] The advance directive may be oral or in writing. One advantage, however, of the latter is that it is more likely to reduce evidential difficulties.

[44] See *Re AK* (n 16 above); *HE v A Hospital NHS Trust* [2003] EWHC 1017 (Fam) (Munby J). For a discussion see Ch 4.

[45] *Re T* (n 7 above), and *HE v A Hospital NHS Trust* (n 44 above), *per* Munby J at [19]–[46].

[46] If there is doubt about the patient's capacity or the directive's applicability, then it seems that a doctor may act as if the patient were incompetent in his best interests, particularly if this will preserve his life: see *Re T* (n 7 above) *per* Lord Donaldson MR at 661.

[47] *Re T* (n 7 above); *Airedale NHS Trust v Bland* (n 6 above) *per* Lord Keith at 860, *per* Lord Goff at 866, *per* Lord Mustill at 892.

[48] On which see *HE v A Hospital NHS Trust* (n 44 above) *per* Munby J at [36]–[45] and Ch 4.

[49] In *R v Ashworth Hospital Authority, ex p Brady* [2000] Lloyd's Rep Med 355 (Maurice Kay J) the judge left open whether it would be lawful to force-feed a competent prisoner on hunger strike in the public interest, for example, in maintaining institutional discipline. The apparently contrary decision in *Secretary of State for the Home Department v Robb* [1995] 1 All ER 677 (Thorpe J) might be distinguished as only holding that the prison authorities had no *duty* to intervene ([71]–[73]).

to competent, as well as incompetent, children although in the case of competent children it is arguable that the ability to do so is more limited requiring a situation where serious harm or death will ensue if the child's refusal is respected.[50]

(b) Part IV of the Mental Health Act 1983[51]

3.15 There are statutory exceptions to the 'right of refusal' of a competent patient, in particular, in Pt IV of the Mental Health Act 1983 where the treatment is for the 'mental disorder' of a detained patient.[52] Section 63 provides that:

> The consent of a patient shall not be required for any medical treatment given to him for a mental disorder from which he is suffering, not being treatment falling within sections 57[53] or 58[54] above, if the treatment is given by or under the direction of the responsible medical officer.

3.16 It is clear, therefore, that s 63 provides in practice a broad exception to the common law rule that medical treatment may only be given to a competent adult patient with consent.[55] Section 63 licenses what would otherwise be trespassory touchings. It is, however, limited to patients 'detained' under the 1983 Act;[56] applies only to treatment 'for the mental disorder'[57] (and not for other physical unconnected ailments or conditions[58]); and the treatment must be given 'by or under the direction' of the responsible medical officer. Importantly, any treatment

---

[50] See *Re W (A Minor) (Medical Treatment: Court's Jurisdiction)* [1993] Fam 64; [1992] 4 All ER 627 (CA) and *Re R (A Minor) (Wardship: Medical Treatment)* [1991] 4 All ER 177 (CA). See Ch 4.

[51] For a full discussion of Pt IV see Hoggett, B, *Mental Health Law* (4th edn, 1996), ch 6; Gostin, L, *Mental Health Services—Law and Practice* (1986), ch 20; and Jones, R, *Mental Health Act Manual* (8th edn, 2003). See also, Kennedy, I, and Grubb, A, *Medical Law* (3rd edn, 2000) 893–909.

[52] See, especially, ss 63, 58 and 62 (urgent treatment).

[53] s 57 applies to psychosurgery and the surgical implantation of hormones to reduce male sex drive where both consent *and* a second medical opinion are required for treatment: s 57(1)(a) and the Mental Health (Hospital, Guardianship and Consent to Treatment) Regulations 1983 (as amended), SI 1983/893, reg 16(1).

[54] s 58 applies to ECT and medication given for more than three months where consent *or* a second medical opinion is required: s 58(1)(b) and the Mental Health (Hospital, Guardianship and Consent to Treatment) Regulations 1983, ibid, reg 16(2).

[55] But note the 'throw away' remark in *R (on the application of B) v Ashworth Hospital* [2003] EWCA Civ 547; [2003] 1 WLR 1886 (CA) that the common law of necessity could justify treatment not covered by s 63 where the patient 'cannot or *will not* consent' (emphasis added), *per* Dyson LJ at [44]. Contrast, Simon Brown LJ at [78] and Scott-Baker LJ at [69].

[56] Although it does not apply to all: see s 56(1). Pt IV of the 1983 Act does not apply to a patient 'subject to after-care under supervision' pursuant to ss 25A–I introduced by the Mental Health (Patients in the Community) Act 1995.

[57] Indeed, it applies only to the mental disorder which justifies the patient's detention: *R (on the application of B) v Ashworth Hospital* (n 55 above), (s 63 did not justify forcible treatment of patient for a personality disorder when he had been detained on the basis that he was suffering from a mental illness, schizophrenia). It will apply, however, where the non-detained condition is treated as part of, or ancillary to, the treatment for the detained condition: ibid, *per* Dyson LJ at [46] and *per* Scott-Baker LJ at [70].

[58] eg, *Re W (Adult: Refusal of Treatment)*, (n 34 above) (renal dialysis).

must be justified not only as being in the patient's 'best interests' but must also be 'convincingly' shown to be a 'medical necessity'.[59]

A series of cases, culminating in the authoritative decision of the Court of Appeal   **3.17**
in *B v Croydon HA*[60] has extended the scope of s 63 of the 1983 Act beyond the
paradigm of medical treatment falling within it, namely that which directly cures
or alleviates the effects of the *mental disorder itself.* The Court of Appeal accepted
that s 63 applied not only to the treatment of the 'mental disorder' itself but also
to its symptoms, such as a refusal to eat. The Court of Appeal noted that the
'emergency' provisions in s 62 of the 1983 Act clearly contemplate the treatment
of symptoms as well as the condition itself as falling within Pt IV of the 1983 Act.
Also, s 145(1) of the 1983 Act defined 'medical treatment' very widely indeed and
so as to include 'a range of acts ancillary to the core treatment'.[61] As a result, the
courts have included medical treatments which 'treat' the *symptoms of the mental
disorder,* for example, force-feeding an anorectic patient who refused food,[62]
force-feeding a patient with borderline personality disorder whose compulsion to
self-harm led her to refuse food[63] and force-feeding a suicidal depressive who
refused food and water.[64]

In each of the cases, the condition that was to be treated (the need for food and/or   **3.18**
water) was directly related to the patient's mental disorder.[65] It was a manifestation
of the mental disorder itself and thus should not be distinguished from it. The
mental disorder caused the need for treatment in each of the cases. In one case,
however, the court went further. In *Tameside and Glossop NHS Trust v CH,*[66] the
patient was a paranoid schizophrenic detained under the 1983 Act. She was found
to be pregnant. By the thirty-first week of pregnancy, there was evidence of intra-
uterine growth retardation, and her obstetrician was of the opinion that an induced labour might become necessary to safeguard the life of the foetus. However,
as a long-term sufferer of schizophrenia, she was prone to delusions, and had

---

[59] Art 3 of the ECHR and *Herczegfalvy v Austria* (1993) 15 EHRR 437 (ECtHR) applied in *R (on the application of Wilkinson) v Broadmoor Special Hospital Authority* (n 12 above) and *R (on the application of N) v M* [2003] 1 WLR 562 (CA).

[60] [1995] 1 All ER 683 (CA) and Grubb (1995) 3 Med L Rev 192 (Commentary). See also *Riverside Mental Health NHS Trust v Fox* [1994] 1 FLR 614 (Stuart-White J and CA) and Grubb (1994) 2 Med L Rev 96 (Commentary); *Re KB (Adult) (Mental Patient: Medical Treatment)* (1994) 19 BMLR 144 (Ewbank J) and Grubb (1994) 2 Med L Rev 208 (Commentary).

[61] *B v Croydon HA* (n 60 above), *per* Hoffman LJ at 687–688. See also *per* Neill LJ at 689–690.

[62] *Riverside Mental Health NHS Trust v Fox* (n 60 above), and *Re KB (Adult) (Mental Patient: Medical Treatment)* (n 60 above).

[63] *B v Croydon HA* (n 60 above)

[64] *Re VS (Adult: Mental Disorder)* (1995) 3 Med L Rev 292 (Douglas Brown J).

[65] Contrast *Re C (Adult: Refusal of Medical Treatment)* [1994] 1 All ER 819 (Thorpe J) and Grubb (1994) 2 Med L Rev 93 (Commentary) where the mentally disordered patient's physical condition (gangrene) was 'entirely unconnected with the mental disorder', *per* Hoffman LJ in *B v Croydon HA* (n 60 above) at 688.

[66] [1996] 1 FLR 762 and Grubb (1996) 4 Med L Rev 194 (Commentary).

resisted some of the attempts to monitor her pregnancy in the belief that her obstetrician and psychiatrist were intent on harming the baby. Her doctors applied to the court for a declaration that it would be lawful to carry out obstetric intervention, including a caesarian section. The patient's consultant psychiatrist gave evidence first, giving the opinion that stillbirth (the alternative to the procedures) would lead to a profound deterioration in the patient's mental health; and secondly, that the pregnancy had interrupted the patient's treatment with strong anti-psychotic medication because of the dangers to her foetus. Wall J concluded on the basis of this evidence that the treatment of the patient's pregnancy fell within s 63. He said:

> [I]t is not . . . I think stretching language unduly to say that achievement of a successful outcome to her pregnancy is a necessary part of the overall treatment of her mental disorder.

Nevertheless, the decision must be questionable especially on the latter basis that the termination of the woman's pregnancy was treatment 'for [her] mental disorder' because she was unable to receive the appropriate medication until then.[67]

3.19   Consequently, there are a number of situations which could arise where a detained patient is in need of medical treatment (broadly defined in s 145 of the 1983 Act to include 'nursing' and also 'care, habilation and rehabilitation under medical supervision'):

(i)   where the treatment is given to treat directly the mental disorder, for example, psychotropic medication (within s 63);

(ii)   where the treatment is for a physical condition which is causing or contributing to the mental disorder, for example, a brain tumour producing or contributing to psychological effect (within s 63);

(iii)   where the treatment is given to alleviate the symptoms or consequences of (and which are related to) the mental disorder, for example, force-feeding where the patient's mental disorder leads to a refusal of food and/or water or stomach pumping following an attempted suicide (within s 63[68]);

(iv)   where the treatment is for a condition (usually physical) which is unrelated to the mental disorder, for example, an appendectomy (not within s 63). The mental disorder is only relevant to the patient's competence to make the decision to refuse the treatment.[69]

---

[67] See Grubb (1996) 4 Med L Rev 193, 194–8 (Commentary).

[68] After *B v Croydon HA* (n 60 above). See also *R v Ashworth Hospital Authority, ex p Brady* (n 49 above) (forced feeding of a prisoner on hunger strike justified under s 63 as his refusal was a 'manifestation or symptom' of the prisoner's mental disorder).

[69] *Re C (Adult: Refusal of Medical Treatment)* (n 65 above).

(c) Necessity and Unknown Competence

Interventions (including medical treatment) may be justified at common law to **3.20**
the extent that it is reasonable to do so in the circumstances, and providing what is
done is reasonable, where the competence of the individual is unknown. The common law justification of 'necessity' would come to the aid of the doctor. It would
not be illegal, for example, temporarily to restrain a 'jumper' in order to ensure
their intentions and competence. Likewise, an apparent suicide victim may be
treated to save her life unless it is absolutely clear that the patient was both attempting to kill herself and was competent at the time to make that decision.[70]
Even if it subsequently transpired that she was competent and wished to kill herself, the intervention would still be legal.[71] Faced with a patient in a casualty department who has taken a drugs overdose, a doctor would be entitled to entertain
these doubts and so act 'out of necessity' to save her life, albeit on a temporary basis.

(d) Public Policy

Finally, the common law may justify interventions against a competent patient's **3.21**
wishes in wholly exceptional circumstances on the grounds of public policy.[72]
Consequently, a patient could not refuse measures designed to maintain basic hygiene and pain relief. The explanation for this is twofold: the patient may not require
his carers, in effect, to abandon him and also the interests of third parties—such as
nurses and others affected by the consequences of the patient's decision to 'turn his
back to the wall'—outweigh his interests in this singular situation.[73]

3. Withdrawal of Consent

The law's recognition and protection of the inviolability of the patient's bodily **3.22**
integrity includes the right to withdraw consent after it is given. A withdrawal of
consent is indistinguishable, in principle, from an initial refusal of consent. To
continue treatment after a patient has validly withdrawn his consent will be unlawful as a battery. There is no relevant English case. However, the issue was considered by the Canadian Supreme Court in *Ciarlariello v Schacter*[74] and there is no
doubt that the decision reflects English law.[75]

---

[70] For an explanation which would extend further, see Skegg, PDG, *Law, Ethics, and Medicine*
(1984), 110–16. The more recent recognition of a competent patient's right to refuse all treatment
has, probably, superseded Professor Skegg's suggested explanation. But note the reference by Butler-
Sloss LJ in *Re T* to 'preventing suicide' (n 7 above) at 665.

[71] Of course, if the patient was known to be suffering from a mental disorder which rendered her
incompetent, there would be no legal difficulty in treating her under the common law or, if
detained, under s 63 of the Mental Health Act 1983 (latter applying even if she is competent): see
para 3.17 above and *Re VS (Adult: Mental Disorder)* (1995) 3 Med L Rev 292.

[72] See Kennedy and Grubb (n 51 above) 1913.

[73] See Grubb (1993) 1 Med L Rev 84, 85 (Commentary).

[74] (1993) 100 DLR (4th) 609 (SCC) and Kennedy (1994) 2 Med L Rev 117 (Commentary).

[75] Kennedy, ibid, 118.

3.23   The claimant was diagnosed with a suspected aneurism. She underwent a diagnostic cerebral angiogram. During the procedure she experienced discomfort and hyperventilation and she asked the doctor to stop, which he did. When she had calmed down, the claimant told the doctor to continue the procedure. She suffered a rare reaction to the dye which was injected during the course of the procedure. The claimant sued the doctor, inter alia, for battery alleging that she had withdrawn her consent during the procedure and its continuation amounted to a battery. The Supreme Court dismissed her action for battery. The court accepted that a patient had a right to withdraw her consent during a procedure. Cory J stated:[76]

> An individual's right to determine what medical procedures will be accepted must include the right to stop a procedure. It is not beyond the realm of possibility that the patient is better able to gauge the level of pain or discomfort that can be accepted or that the patient's premonitions of tragedy or mortality may have a basis in reality. In any event, the patient's right to bodily integrity provides the basis for the withdrawal of a consent to a medical procedure even while it is underway. Thus, if it is found that the consent is effectively withdrawn during the course of the procedure then it must be terminated.

3.24   The Court noted that a consent could only validly be withdrawn if the patient was, in law, capable of doing so. A patient's capacity to withdraw consent, just as his capacity to consent, might be affected by the circumstances.[77] Cory J stated that:[78]

> If sedatives or other medication were administered to the patient, then it must be determined if the patient was so sedated or so affected by the medication that consent to the procedure could not effectively have been withdrawn. The question whether a patient is capable of withdrawing consent will depend on the circumstances of each case. Expert medical evidence will undoubtedly be relevant, but will not necessarily be determinative of the issue.

3.25   Also, the court must decide whether the patient had, in fact, withdrawn his consent. Cory J said:

> The words used by a patient may be ambiguous. Even if they are apparently clear, the circumstances under which they were spoken may render them ambiguous. On some occasions, the doctors conducting the process may reasonably take the words spoken by the patient to be an expression of pain rather than a withdrawal of consent.[79]

---

[76] *Ciarlariello v Schacter* (n 74 above), 619.
[77] See *Reference Guide to Consent for Examination or Treatment*, DoH, March 2001, p 10 (para 18.1).
[78] N 74 above, 619–20.
[79] ibid, 618.

Cory J referred to two Canadian cases where contrasting views were taken on the 3.26
evidence before the courts. In *Mitchell v McDonald*,[80] the claimant during a corti-
sone injection into a chest muscle cried out 'For God's sake stop'. Cory J regarded
as 'reasonable' the trial judge's view in that case that the claimant's exclamation
was a 'cry of pain' equivalent to 'My God, stop hurting me', rather than an attempt
to withdraw consent.[81] By contrast, in *Nightingale v Kaplovitch*[82] the patient was
undergoing a sigmoidoscopic examination which had become extremely painful
and screamed 'Stop, I can't take this any more'. The doctor continued and was
held liable in battery as this amounted to a valid withdrawal of consent by the
patient.

In the *Ciarlariello* case it was recognized that the patient's right meant that it was 3.27
incumbent upon a doctor, where there was any question that the patient was attempting to withdraw his consent, to enquire whether this was the case, and not
blithely continue.[83] Although the Court did not spell out the implications of not
doing so, they are obvious. Continuation in the face of what is subsequently
interpreted as a withdrawal of consent will be a battery.

The Canadian Supreme Court acknowledged that the 'right' to withdraw consent 3.28
was not absolute where the effect of terminating: 'would be either life threatening
or pose immediate and serious problems to the health of the patient.'[84] In this situation, presumably, the Court took the view that as a matter of public policy the
'refusal' is not valid because of the doctor's overriding duty of care to the patient
which would be breached if such serious harm occurred. However, nowhere in the
judgment is the basis of this limitation on the 'right' spelt out. Clearly, it must be
limited to allowing continued intervention to secure the patient from the immediate peril, and not necessarily completion of the procedure, when the patient's
'right' will again take precedence.[85] In practical terms, of course, the 'right' to
withdraw during a procedure cannot apply to major surgical operations performed under general anaesthetic and is limited to more minor surgery or diagnostic procedures (as in *Ciarlariello* itself) performed, at worst, under a local
anaesthetic, and it may be, therefore, that the limitation will not usually apply.

On the facts, the Court held that the claimant had validly withdrawn her consent 3.29
but this had been complied with by the doctors. The only issue remaining for the
Court was whether the procedure had been lawfully recommenced. For the Court
this meant, first, whether there had been a valid consent, and secondly, whether

---

[80] (1987) 80 AR 16 (Alta QB).
[81] N 74 above, 618 *per* Cory J.
[82] [1989] OJ No 585 (QL) (HC).
[83] N 74 above, *per* Cory J at 618.
[84] ibid, *per* Cory J at 619.
[85] See *Reference Guide to Consent for Examination or Treatment*, DoH, March 2001, p 10 (para
18).

the patient had been sufficiently informed for the purposes of negligence. Cory J concluded both questions in the defendant's favour:[86]

> . . . the patient may still consent to the renewal or continuation of the process. That consent must also be informed. Although it may not be necessary that the doctors review with the patient all the risks involved in the procedure, the patient must be advised of any material change in the risks which has arisen and would be involved in continuing the process. In addition, the patient must be informed of any material change in the circumstances which could alter his or her assessment of the costs or benefits of continuing the procedure. Here, there had been no material change in the circumstances and a valid consent was given to the continuation of the process.

3.30　In England, the law would similarly require that the patient should give a valid consent to continuation and also would impose a duty to provide information relevant to that decision. The content of that duty would be a matter for the law of negligence and an application of the *Sidaway* decision.[87] While medical evidence of actual (or potential) practices would be highly influential, it would not be determinative.

4. Limits to Consent

(i) The General Approach

3.31　Thus far it has been stated that the presence of a patient's consent[88] determines the legality of a medical treatment or intervention. In the context of a *tort* action in battery, the patient's consent (or that of an appropriate proxy) is a sufficient condition for legality. The public policy considerations which apply in criminal law to limit the extent of harm that a person may legitimately consent to have little impact on the civil law, concerned as it is with compensation for, rather than prohibition of, harm.[89] However, a medical intervention may also amount to the crime of assault or an aggravated form of it under ss 47, 20 and 18 of the Offences Against the Person Act 1861. In England, a person may not consent to anything which is intended to, or which does, cause more than actual bodily harm.[90] Of course, many surgical interventions cause serious injury even though the doctor's intention is to benefit the patient—unlike the usual violent offender charged under the 1861 Act. English law could take the view that 'medical treatment' is wholly outside the violence offences of the 1861 Act because the effects of surgery do not amount to 'injury' or 'harm' when viewed in their totality or in the light of the doctor's intention.[91] The law does not, however, adopt that approach.[92]

---

[86]　N 74 above, 624.
[87]　See below, paras 3.109–3.151.
[88]　Or that of a proxy acting in the patient's 'best interests'.
[89]　See Skegg (n 70 above), 39.
[90]　*R v Brown* [1994] 1 AC 212; [1993] 2 All ER 75 (HL).
[91]　See Skegg (n 70 above), 30–2.
[92]　*R v Brown* (n 90 above).

Instead, it assumes the doctor's actions do prima facie fall within the criminal prohibition but then creates a specific exemption from the law's refusal to accept consent as a defence to anything which amounts to more than actual bodily harm.[93] In *Attorney-General's Reference (No 6 of 1980)*,[94] Lord Lane CJ stated that 'reasonable surgical interference' fell outside the criminal law.[95] Subsequently in *Airedale NHS Trust v Bland*, Lord Mustill stated the 'medical exception' as follows:

> . . . proper medical treatment stand[s] completely outside the criminal law. The reason why the consent of the patient is so important is not that it furnishes a defence in itself, but because it is usually essential to the propriety of medical treatment. Thus, if consent is absent, and is not dispensed with in special circumstances by operation of law, the acts of the doctor lose their immunity.[96]

In *R v Brown*,[97] the House of Lords accepted the existence of the 'medical exception' and Lord Mustill remarked that 'proper medical treatment . . . is in a category of its own'.[98] Thus, there is no doubt that the consent of a patient to 'proper medical treatment' is valid notwithstanding that the procedure will cause injury which the patient could not otherwise lawfully consent to.   **3.32**

(ii) Therapeutic Procedures

The scope of the 'medical exception' remains unclear.[99] In large part this is because   **3.33** a wholly satisfactory account of the basis of the 'medical exception' is elusive, although it must lie in public policy. It is suggested that, in general, the legitimising criterion for an invasion of bodily integrity must be the doctor's 'therapeutic purpose' or his 'intention to benefit' the patient.[100] The criterion is that the procedure is *intended* to be therapeutic/beneficial to the patient, not whether it *did* actually benefit the patient. The crucial question, in determining whether an intervention falls within the medical exception, must be the doctor's *purpose* given the patient's decision to consent to the procedure reflecting his judgment about its therapeutic or beneficial character.

---

[93] The exception should extend to any qualified *health care practitioner*, for example, a dentist or nurse who is acting within their area of competence (ie providing they have the appropriate qualification, clinical competence, and professional regulation). Examples arise under the Medicinal Products: Prescription By Nurses etc Act 1992 and the Medicines (Products Other than Veterinary Drugs) (Prescription Only) Order 1983, SI 1983/1212 as amended), Art 9(2) and Sch 3, Pt III creating an exception to s 58(2)(b) of the Medicines Act 1968.

[94] [1981] QB 715; [1981] 2 All ER 1057 (CA).

[95] ibid, 1059.

[96] [1993] 1 All ER 821, 889.

[97] [1993] 2 All ER 75.

[98] ibid, 110.

[99] See Skegg (n 70 above), ch 2 and Williams, G, *Textbook of Criminal Law* (2nd edn, 1983), 589–91.

[100] See Kennedy and Grubb (n 51 above), 768–73.

3.34 Obviously, within this context, the reference to 'benefit' solely relates to a benefit to the patient's *life or physical or mental health*.[101] Consequently, a patient could not consent to serious injury, for example the amputation of a leg, in order to enhance her financial interests.[102] A contrasting case which, though superficially similar, falls clearly on the other side of the line, would be where the patient wishes desperately to be rid of his leg, the presence of which he says is causing him severe distress. If the surgeon performs the amputation, honestly intending to benefit the patient's mental health, while many might disagree with that decision, it is not for the criminal law to second guess the patient's own determination of their health interests.

3.35 Providing the therapeutic purpose exists, a patient may consent to serious injury, for example, gender re-assignment surgery.[103] A patient's consent to a procedure will also be valid even if it exposes him to the risk of death providing the procedure, on balance, is in his best medical interests, for example, heart transplant surgery.[104] Of course, if the patient dies as a result of the surgeon's gross negligence, he might be guilty of manslaughter regardless of the validity of the patient's consent.[105]

(iii) Other Procedures

3.36 This account does not, however, deal with all procedures which appear to fall within the medical exception. A number of procedures, though not necessarily intended for the medical benefit of the individual, are widely regarded as socially acceptable and ones to which the individual may consent:[106] research,[107] donation of organs and tissue,[108] contraceptive sterilisation,[109] abortion,[110] and cosmetic surgery. No doubt the courts would accept—and already do accept—an individual's consent to such

---

[101] See the Prohibition of Female Circumcision Act 1985, s 2(1)(a) drawing the line between legitimate and criminal activity at an operation which is 'necessary for the *physical or mental health* of the person on whom it is performed . . .'.

[102] See the guarded comment of Neill LJ in *Re F (Mental Patient: Sterilisation)* [1990] 2 AC 1, 29.

[103] *Corbett v Corbett (Otherwise Ashley)* [1971] P 83 and *Bellinger v Bellinger* [2003] 2 All ER 593 (HL) (legality of gender re-assignment surgery not doubted).

[104] *R v Hyam* [1975] AC 55 (HL) at 74 and 77–78 *per* Lord Hailsham.

[105] *R v Adomako* [1995] AC 171; [1994] 3 All ER 79 (HL) and Grubb (1994) 2 Med L Rev 362 (Commentary).

[106] See Lewis, P, 'Procedures That Are Against the Medical Interests of Incompetent Adults' (2002) 22 OJLS 575 at 575–6 contrasting the position with incompetent adults.

[107] The propriety of non-therapeutic research in prescribed circumstances is recognised in the European Convention on Human Rights and Biomedicine (1996), Arts 16 and 5.

[108] Human Organ Transplants Act 1989, s 2, and the Human Organ Transplants (Unrelated Persons) Regulations 1989, SI 1989/2480.

[109] Originally the National Health Service (Family Planning) Act 1967; now National Health Service Act 1977, s 5(1)(b). Contrast the comments of Denning LJ in *Bravery v Bravery* [1954] 1 WLR 1169 at 1180–1 which no longer can be taken seriously as representing public policy: *Cataford v Moreau* (1978) 114 DLR (3d) 585.

[110] Abortion Act 1967.

procedures. There would, of course, be limits: the courts would not allow a person to donate his heart if, as it usually would, this would lead to his death.[111] There is no 'golden thread' or commonality which would explain this collection of procedures other than that they are currently socially acceptable and thus, as a matter of public policy, they are, or would be, recognised by the judges as lawful. Without statutory guidance,[112] the courts can do no better than to deal with each procedure, as and when it comes before them, and apply their sense of what are the proper limits of public policy.[113]

B. The Nature of Consent

1. Forms of Consent

Consent is a state of mind personal to the patient whereby he agrees to the violation of his bodily integrity.[114] Not every agreement to undergo treatment is, in law, a valid consent because it may be based upon inadequate information to make a meaningful decision whether to undergo the procedure[115] or it may be the product of circumstances, or others' desires, which render the decision involuntary or one which is not really the patient's because of undue influence.[116] **3.37**

A patient's consent need not be given in writing. The common law does not impose such a requirement, although in analogous circumstances statutory provisions may do so.[117] However, 'consent forms' are routinely used in hospitals when a patient undergoes a surgical intervention.[118] They do not, as is sometimes assumed within the medical profession, in themselves constitute a patient's consent. Their function, in law, is purely evidentiary.[119] In stating that the patient has agreed to a particular procedure which has been explained to him and which he **3.38**

---

[111] Contrast the procedure known as a 'domino transplant' where a person in need of a lung transplant for medical reasons receives both lungs and a new heart, making his heart available for donation.

[112] Sometime ago, the Law Commission provisionally proposed a statutory base, including a statutory list of 'borderline' procedures, for the exception: see *Consent and the Criminal Law*, Consultation Paper No 139 (1995), Pt VIII.

[113] Jurisdictions with Criminal Codes often seek to deal with the 'medical exception' albeit in general terms: see, ss 61 and 61A, Crimes Act 1961 (NZ); ss 45 and 216, Criminal Code (Can); ss 282 and 288, Criminal Code (Qld). For a discussion of the latter, see O'Regan, R S, 'Surgery and Criminal Responsibility under the Queensland Criminal Code' (1990) 14 Crim LJ 73.

[114] *Sidaway v Bethlem Royal Hospital Governors* [1985] 1 All ER 643, 658 *per* Lord Diplock.

[115] See below, paras 3.93–3.108.

[116] See below, paras 3.166–3.170.

[117] Human Fertilisation and Embryology Act 1990, Sch 3. Discussed below, Ch 10.

[118] Model consent forms (4) are recommended by the Department of Health in England: see *Good Practice in Consent Implementation Guide: Consent to Examination or Treatment*, HSC 2001/023, 33–46.

[119] See *Reference Guide to Consent for Examination or Treatment*, DoH, March 2001, 8.

has understood, the 'consent' will not be worth the paper it is written on if these recitations are not, in fact, true. It is the patient's *actual state of mind* which is crucial. Consent expressed 'in form only' is no consent at all.[120] An identical approach is called for in respect of forms which purport to record a patient's refusal of treatment, for example, of a blood transfusion. Speaking of such forms in *Re T*, Lord Donaldson MR stated:[121]

> They will be wholly ineffective . . . if the patient is incapable of understanding them, they are not explained to him and there is no good evidence (apart from the patient's signature) that he had that understanding and fully appreciated the significance of signing it.

(i) Express Consent

(a) Actual Consent

3.39   A patient's consent may be express or implied. Express consent is often treated as synonymous with *expressed* consent, that is where the patient demonstrates orally or in writing that he agrees to the treatment or procedure. While this will often be the case, it is sometimes misleading to regard it in these terms. More accurately, the issue is whether the patient has given *actual* consent to the treatment or procedure whether or not this is demonstrated orally or in writing. Consent is, as was seen earlier, a state of mind of the patient. A valid legal consent is given even where the patient does not demonstrate his agreement providing that the state of his mind was, in fact, that he agreed. In other words, an unexpressed *actual* consent is, in law, a valid consent. Of course, there may be evidential difficulties in establishing the patient's actual consent if it is not *expressed* but this does not detract from the analysis of what consent, in law, really is.

(b) Implied and Inferred Consent

3.40   Any other form of consent—such as *implied* consent—is strictly speaking not a 'consent' given by the patient at all.[122] So, where the patient conducts himself such that it is reasonable to *imply* that he consented to the treatment or procedure, the law merely prohibits the patient because of his conduct from denying that he consented even though, in fact, he did not.[123] This is not to say that consent cannot be *inferred* from the patient's conduct and behaviour: it can be, but it should be distinguished from *implied* consent.[124] The latter is a legal device whereby the legality of a treatment or procedure is recognised even though the patient does not, in fact, consent. A patient who allows a doctor to carry out a procedure in full

---

[120]   *Chatterton v Gerson* [1981] 1 All ER 257, 265 *per* Bristow J.
[121]   [1992] 4 All ER 649, 663.
[122]   See below, para 3.43.
[123]   *Sidaway v Bethlem Royal Hospital Governors* [1985] 1 All ER 643, 658 *per* Lord Diplock.
[124]   Kennedy, I and Grubb, A, *Medical Law* (3rd edn, Butterworths, 2000), 589–92.

knowledge of what is to be done will have given *actual* consent to the procedure. His consent is not implied but rather *inferred*. Evidentially, the fact that the patient did not express his consent is not conclusive. Rather, faced with these facts, what other inference is it proper for the court to make other than that the patient was actually consenting.

(ii) Implied Consent

The outward appearance and conduct of the patient may lead to the conclusion that the patient has consented to the treatment or procedure. In these circumstances, it is said that the patient's consent is *implied* and the doctor has a defence to an action in battery. The classic illustration is found in the US case of *O'Brien v Cunard SS Co*.[125] The claimant was vaccinated against smallpox by a surgeon on board a boat bound for Boston. She joined a line of passengers whom the surgeon was examining and vaccinating if necessary. When the surgeon told her she should be vaccinated she held out her arm and he did so. She sued claiming battery on the basis that she had not consented to the vaccination. The Supreme Judicial Court of Massachusetts dismissed her action. The court held that her consent should be implied from the circumstances and her conduct. Knowlton J said:[126]

> If the claimant's behavior was such as to indicate consent on her part, [the surgeon] was justified in his act, *whatever her unexpressed feelings may have been*. In determining whether she consented, he could be guided only by her overt acts and the manifestations of her feelings.

Properly understood, *O'Brien* is almost certainly a case of *inferred* consent. It might be thought that the claimant's conduct irresistibly led to the inference that she actually had consented to the vaccination. What else was she doing in the line, having spoken to the surgeon, holding her arm out. However, as the emphasised words from Knowlton J's judgment show, the court seems not to have inferred that she actually consented. Rather, he conceded that she did not but nevertheless debarred her from relying upon that because of the circumstances and her behaviour: her consent was *implied*.[127] On the facts, no doubt the court was influenced by the fact that notices had been posted around the ship in various languages that day to indicate the need for vaccination; the claimant had stood in line and seen what was happening to other passengers and she had not offered any objection to the surgeon when he went to vaccinate her.

Thus, it is suggested that implied consent is not a species of consent at all. To describe the situation in the *O'Brien* case as one of consent would be fictional.

3.41

3.42

3.43

---

[125] (1891) 28 NE 266 (Mass Sup Jud Ct).
[126] ibid, 266 (emphasis added).
[127] See also *Allan v New Mount Sinai Hospital* (1980) 109 DLR (3d) 634, 641 *per* Linden J.

Rather, implied consent is more properly understood as a species of estoppel.[128] Where the patient so conducts himself in the circumstances that it is reasonable to conclude that he has consented to a treatment or procedure, the patient will not subsequently be permitted to rely on the fact that he did not actually consent. The doctor will have a defence to what would otherwise be an unlawful touching based upon the patient's implied consent.

3.44   Whether a patient will be taken to have impliedly consented to a particular treatment or procedure will be a question of fact in every case. Where a *reasonable* person looking on to the situation would conclude that the patient had agreed to the intervention, even if the patient has not, the doctor will have a defence based upon implied consent.[129] It would be dangerous for a doctor to conclude that a patient's silence alone constituted agreement. The issue is one of reasonable deduction based upon all the circumstances, in particular, taking account of the patient's conduct and anything known about the patient.

3.45   Implied consent is frequently relied upon by doctors as a justification for carrying out treatments or interventions upon patients. The extent to which consent may be implied is, often, controversial.[130] Given that implied consent, though no consent at all, nevertheless licenses an interference with the patient's right of self-determination, the circumstances necessary to impute it require a clear (perhaps unequivocal) indication that the patient appeared to be giving his consent.[131] Some situations, however, should not be analysed as ones where the patient has impliedly consented: two, in particular, are important. Traditionally, it has been argued that treatment of an unconscious or otherwise incompetent patient may be justified on the basis of implied consent.[132] As regards the former, it has been said that the patient would agree to an intervention which was in their 'best interests' if they were able and so their consent to the intervention may be implied.[133] Clearly, the implication or inference of consent is inappropriate where the patient is unable to consent due to incompetence. It is particularly artificial in the case of patients whose mental disability is permanent to justify, for example, sterilisation of mentally disabled women.[134] The more appropriate legal justification in these

---

[128]   *Sidaway v Bethlem Royal Hospital Governors* (n 114 above) at 658 *per* Lord Diplock.

[129]   See, eg, *Canadian AIDS Society v Ontario* (1995) 25 OR (3d) 388 ('reasonable blood donor test' used).

[130]   eg, in the context of HIV testing, see Grubb, A and Pearl, D, *Blood Testing, AIDS and DNA Profiling—Law and Policy* (Jordans, 1991), 11–13.

[131]   *Schweiser v Central Hospital* (1974) 53 DLR (3d) 494, 508 *per* Thompson J.

[132]   eg, Skegg, PDG, 'A Justification for Medical Procedures Performed Without Consent' (1974) 90 LQR 512. Professor Skegg's more recent views rest more strongly on the doctrine of necessity: see his *Law, Ethics and Medicine* (n 70 above) ch 5.

[133]   See eg *Mohr v Williams* (1905) 104 NW 12 (Minn Sup Ct).

[134]   See *Re F (Mental Patient: Sterilisation)* [1989] 2 All ER 545, 563 *per* Lord Goff.

cases is the principle of necessity as recognised by the House of Lords in *Re F* and not implied consent.[135]

Implied consent is also often utilised by doctors to justify treatment or interventions which are considered to be routine by the medical profession. For example, diagnostic tests are regularly performed during maternity care without the explicit consent of the patient. Other examples[136] might include procedures carried out by students as part of their training.[137] To what extent does the law accept that a patient has impliedly consented to interventions of this kind when, a fortiori, the patient has not given actual consent? The answer will depend upon the circumstances.   **3.46**

It will only be proper to imply consent if the reasonable onlooker would conclude, albeit wrongly, that the patient had agreed to the intervention. As a basic minimum, this should require that the patient be given notice of the possibility of the 'extra' intervention and be given an opportunity to 'opt out' which is not taken. Hence, where information sheets or prominent notices in doctors' surgeries or clinics indicate what may occur, a reasonable onlooker might well conclude that a patient had tacitly agreed if he remains silent and does not exercise his right to 'opt out'.[138] The implication is not, of course, dependent upon the patient having *read* the information sheet or notice providing reasonable steps were taken to bring the information to the patient's attention and the information was presented in a reasonable manner (ie visible and intelligible to the average reader). Merely being in a teaching hospital would not, on this basis, be sufficient to give rise to an implication that students may engage in touchings for their own benefit. That fact would have to be brought to the patient's attention or reasonable steps be taken to do so.[139]   **3.47**

Importantly, consent should not be implied unless the patient has had an opportunity (if the notice, etc is read) to opt out of the 'extra' intervention.[140] Otherwise, it would not, it is suggested, be reasonable to imply the patient's agreement merely as the result of his silence. Also, it may only be proper to imply the patient's agreement   **3.48**

---

[135] See below, Ch 4.

[136] An analogous situation is the use of medical records for research, especially epidemiological research.

[137] This should not, however, be done without the explicit (ie actual/expressed) consent of the patient: *Medical Students in Hospitals* (1991, HC (91)18). See also *The Patient's Charter & You* (DoH, 1995), 6.

[138] Analogous situations may be the use of confidential information (*Confidentiality: NHS Code of Practice* (October 2003) and the use of tissue for research, training and teaching removed without explicit consent (*Human Tissue: Ethical and Legal Issues* (Nuffield Council on Bioethics, 1995)).

[139] Note, *Turner v Royal Bank of Scotland plc* [1999] 2 All ER (Comm) 664 (CA) (no implied consent by bank customer to disclosure of confidential information to another bank based upon banking practice of which he was unaware).

[140] Contrast *Human Tissue* (n 138 above), para 13.12.

or accord with procedures which involve minor interventions and are not controversial in nature. In other situations, the importance the law places upon the inviolability of the patient's bodily integrity strongly points to the law requiring explicit consent. Hence, it would not be proper to imply that a woman in a teaching hospital (even with her knowledge) impliedly consented to intrusive gynaecological investigations by students for the purposes of teaching. Equally, it would be wrong to imply that a patient by agreeing to the taking of blood agrees to it being tested for HIV infection or genetic conditions. The implications of the results of such tests for the patient (and others) is such that the law would only countenance explicit consent as justifying the taking from a competent adult.

2. Scope of Consent

3.49 The law of consent requires that the patient authorise the procedure which is carried out. A procedure may be unauthorised for a number of reasons and, subject to what is said below, in such circumstances the doctor will commit a battery. As one Canadian judge put it:

> It is the patient, not the doctor, who decides *whether* the surgery will be performed, *where* it will be done, *when* it will be done and *by whom* it will be done.[141]

3.50 However, it is important to determine what has, or has not, been authorised by the patient. The following situations illustrate the divide between authorised and unauthorised procedures.

(i) Absence of Real Consent

3.51 A patient may agree to a medical procedure but without understanding the basic 'nature and purpose' of what it involves. It is clear that in this situation a patient's agreement is not a valid consent to the medical touching and a battery action will lie.[142]

(ii) In Face of a Valid Refusal

3.52 As was seen above,[143] a valid refusal of treatment by a competent adult patient acts as a veto to any intervention covered by the refusal. The refusal may relate to all medical interventions or limit the range of interventions which the doctor may perform by, for example, instructing a doctor not to inject an anaesthetic into a particular arm[144] or not to perform a sterilisation.[145] In these circumstances, it will

---

[141] *Allan v New Mount Sinai Hospital* (1980) 109 DLR (3d) 634, 642 *per* Linden J (emphasis added).
[142] *Chatterton v Gerson* [1981] QB 432, 443 *per* Bristow J; approved in *Sidaway v Governors of Bethlem Royal Hospital* [1985] AC 871 (HL) and see below, paras 3.93–3.108.
[143] See above, paras 3.10–3.12.
[144] *Allan v New Mount Sinai Hospital* (1980) 109 DLR (3d) 634 (Ont HCt).
[145] *Cull v Royal Surrey County Hospital* [1932] 1 BMJ 1195.

not be a defence that the doctor considered the procedure to be medically desirable.[146] The doctor's duty to act in the best medical interests of the patient is limited by the patient's right to refuse.[147]

(iii) Conditional Consent/Refusal

A patient may conditionally consent to treatment and thereafter the treatment is **3.53** carried out even though the condition is not satisfied. In such an instance, the procedure will be unauthorised in the prevailing circumstances and a battery will be committed. For example, the patient agrees to a blood transfusion providing the blood is provided by a relative[148] or only if the procedure is performed by a particular doctor.[149] In both cases, when the doctor carried out the surgery he carried out a procedure which, in the circumstances, was unauthorised. Looking at it another way, until the condition upon which consent is dependent is satisfied, the patient, in fact, *refused* consent to the procedure. While, in principle, a patient in England could bring a battery action where a different doctor than was anticipated operated,[150] in practice it is unlikely to arise. This is because within an NHS hospital there is no expectation that a particular procedure will be carried out by a particular doctor. This is made plain in the standard consent form used for surgical procedures.[151]

(iv) 'Further' or 'Additional' Procedures

What is the legal position when the patient consents to procedure 'X' and the doctor carries out procedure 'Y' (instead of, or in addition to, 'X')? This could arise, for example, where the doctor discovers condition 'Y' during surgery for condition 'X'. In principle, a patient would have a claim in battery[152] for the performance of the unauthorised procedure.[153] However, it may be that what on the face of it seems an unauthorised[154] procedure was, in fact, authorised or otherwise justified.

---

[146] *Mulloy v Hop Sang* [1935] 1 WWR. 714 (Alta CA) (prohibited amputation which was necessary amounted to a battery).

[147] See *Airedale NHS Trust v Bland* [1993] 1 All ER 821, 866 *per* Lord Goff and *Mohr v Williams* (n 133 above).

[148] *Ashcraft v King* (1991) 278 Cal Rptr 900.

[149] *Perna v Perozzi* (1983) 457 A 2d 431.

[150] *Michael v Molesworth* [1950] 2 BMJ 171.

[151] See *Good Practice in Consent Implementation Guide* (n 118 above).

[152] See also *Williamson v East London and City HA* [1998] Lloyd's Rep Med 6 (Butterfield J) (action in negligence based upon patient's lack of consent when surgeon exceeded P's authority by removing her breast when P had only agreed to less radical surgery).

[153] eg *Mohr v Williams* (1905) 104 NW 12 (Sup Ct Minn) (no consent to operation on left ear during operation on right ear); *Murray v McMurchy* [1949] 2 DLR 442 (BC Sup Ct); *Hamilton v Birmingham RHA* [1969] 2 BMJ 456 (no consent to sterilisation during caesarian section); and *Devi v West Midlands RHA* (1981) (CA Transcript 491) (no consent to sterilisation performed during operation to repair ruptured uterus).

[154] See eg *Abbass v Kenney* (1995) 31 BMLR 157 (Gage J).

(a) Principle of Necessity[155]

3.55 Taking the last possibility first, the unauthorised procedure may be justified in law if it is *necessary* in the sense that the patient's medical condition is such that it would be unreasonable (and not merely inconvenient) to delay the procedure until the patient regains consciousness and can decide for himself.[156] The distinction is highlighted by the Canadian cases of *Marshall v Curry*[157] and *Murray v McMurchy*.[158]

3.56 In *Marshall v Curry*, the doctor discovered a grossly diseased testicle during a hernia operation being performed on the patient. He removed it, as part of the hernia operation, but also because he considered it to be gangrenous and a threat to the patient's life and health. The patient's battery action was dismissed on the basis that a doctor may act without consent 'in order to save the life or preserve the health of the patient'.[159] However, as *Murray v McMurchy* shows, the scope of this apparently broad statement is more limited than providing a justification for exceeding a patient's consent whenever it is considered in his 'best interests' to do so. In the *Murray* case, the patient underwent a caesarian section during the course of which she was sterilised because the doctor considered that the condition of her uterus—she had fibroid tumours—would make future pregnancies hazardous for her. The court upheld her battery action. There was no evidence of any immediate danger to her life; it was merely convenient to carry out the sterilisation whilst she was unconscious.[160]

3.57 There is no directly relevant English case concerned with the temporarily incapacitated. However, in *Re F* the matter was touched upon both in the House of Lords and the Court of Appeal. Lord Goff, in his speech, stated that the doctor 'should do no more than is reasonably required, in the best interests of the patient, before he recovers consciousness'.[161] While he was prepared to identify the correct legal question he declined to go further and discuss *Marshall* and *Murray*.[162] In the Court of Appeal, having referred to the Canadian cases, Butler-Sloss LJ concluded that where the patient was temporarily incapacitated a procedure which was 'necessary for the preservation of life or for the preservation of health' could be

---

[155] More fully discussed below, Ch 4.
[156] See *Re F* (n 7 above), at 37 *per* Butler-Sloss LJ (CA) and at 76–77 *per* Lord Goff (HL). See also Skegg, *Law, Ethics and Medicine* (n 30 above), 102–4.
[157] [1933] 3 DLR 260 (Sup Ct NS).
[158] [1949] 2 DLR 442 (Sup Ct BC).
[159] N 157 above, *per* Chisholm CJ at 265.
[160] See also *Parmley v Parmley* [1945] 4 DLR 81 (patient undergoing limited tooth extraction and dentist removed all the patient's teeth because he discovered advanced tooth decay and gum disease—held a battery).
[161] [1990] 2 AC 1, 77.
[162] ibid.

lawfully performed.[163] Neill LJ spoke in terms which mirror the essence of the Canadian cases:

> The treatment which can be … given … is, within broad limits, confined to such treatment as is necessary to meet the emergency and as such needs to be carried out at once and before the patient is likely to be in a position to make a decision for himself.[164]

Consequently, English law limits the application of the 'necessity' principle in situations where the patient is temporarily incompetent to permit procedures which it would have been unreasonable to delay because of the imminent danger to the life or health of the patient.

3.58

(b) Within the 'Broad Nature' of the Consent Given

It is important to determine precisely what the patient has agreed to prior to the procedure. It may be that looking at all the circumstances surrounding the patient giving consent that the apparently unauthorised procedure was agreed to even it is not included on the consent form.[165] Two cases illustrate how the patient's agreement may be interpreted as broad enough to encompass the 'additional' procedure. In *Davis v Barking, Havering and Brentwood HA*[166] the claimant underwent an operation for the removal of a cyst. She signed a consent form in which it was stated that she consented to the 'administration of general, local or other anaesthetics'. She was told that a general anaesthetic would be used. During the procedure, in addition to this, a caudal block was given. After the operation the claimant temporarily lost movement over her legs and control of her bladder, but was left with some minor problems. She sued in battery and negligence alleging, in respect of battery, that the anaesthetist had administered the caudal block without her consent and which had caused her injury. McCullough J dismissed her action in battery. He concluded that it would be wrong to sectionalise what the claimant had consented to. There were not two separate operations which had been performed for which consent to each would have been necessary. The correct question was 'Have the defendants shown that the claimant consented to a procedure the nature and effect of which had in broad terms been explained to her?'[167] The judge held that the claimant had understood in 'broad terms' the nature of what was to be done to her, namely that she would receive an anaesthetic. The judge did not rely upon the broadly drafted terms of the consent form.[168] Instead, his conclusion was that, viewed 'in the round' the caudal block was 'part and parcel' of the anaesthetic she had (with knowledge) agreed to.[169]

3.59

---

[163] ibid, 37.
[164] ibid, 30.
[165] See *O'Bonsawin v Paradis* (1993) 15 CCLT (2d) 188.
[166] [1993] 4 Med LR 85; Grubb (1993) 1 Med L Rev 389 (Commentary).
[167] ibid, 91.
[168] See below, paras 3.61–3.67 and *Pridham v Nash* (1986) 33 DLR (4th) 304.
[169] For a criticism of the case, see Grubb (1993) 1 Med L Rev 389 (Commentary).

3.60   A case adopting a similar approach is the Canadian decision of *Brushnett v Cowan*.[170] The claimant agreed to undergo a muscle biopsy and signed a consent form stating that she agreed to such 'further or alternative measures as may be found to be necessary during the course of the operation'. During the operation, the defendant carried out a bone biopsy as well as the muscle biopsy. The claimant subsequently fell and damaged her leg at the site of the bone biopsy. She sued the defendant, inter alia, in battery arguing she had not consented to the bone biopsy. The Newfoundland Court of Appeal dismissed her action in battery. The court held that in order to determine what the patient had consented to, it was necessary to look at all the circumstances leading up to the signing of the consent form and not at that alone. On the facts, the claimant had agreed not merely to a muscle biopsy, but to an investigatory procedure for the persistent problem in her right thigh which was 'the overriding general purpose and intent' of the patient consulting the doctor.[171] The court concluded, in effect, that what the claimant had agreed to was, in 'broad terms', an investigatory procedure which included both a muscle and a bone biopsy. Thus, the procedure complained of fell, as in *Davis*, within the scope of what the patient had understood she had given consent for. In addition, the court referred to the broadly worded consent form covering 'further and alternate measures' to support its conclusion.[172] This, however, is a different and altogether more difficult basis for finding that the patient consented to what was done.

(c) Consent Forms[173]

3.61   Standard surgical consent forms in England have long contained clauses which indicate, variously expressed, that the patient agrees to 'such further or alternative operative measures or treatment as may be found necessary during the course of the operation or the treatment'.[174] There can be no doubt that these clauses were included on behalf of doctors to license and provide a legal basis for 'further' or 'additional' procedures carried out for the benefit of the patient during an operation.

3.62   In 1990 the Department of Health introduced (and recommended for use) a consent form which was somewhat different in its construction although the substance remained much the same.[175] It did not state that the patient 'agrees' to these

---

[170] (1990) 69 DLR (4th) 743; [1991] 2 Med LR 271 (Newfd CA).

[171] ibid, 275.

[172] ibid.

[173] For the 'evidentiary' effect of consent forms, see above, para 3.38.

[174] See eg the (then) DoH standardised consent form agreed with the medical protection organisations: HSC (IS)197 (October 1975). The form is discussed in Farndale, WAJ and Larman, EC, *Legal Liability for Claims arising from Hospital Treatment* (2nd edn, 1976), 19–29.

[175] *A Guide To Consent for Examination or Treatment* (DoH, 1990, HC (90) 22 as amended by HSG (92) 32), Appendix A(1). For the current forms, see *Good Practice in Consent Implementation Guide: Consent to Examination or Treatment* (n 118 above), para 3.67.

procedures but rather that 'I understand' that such a procedure will 'only be carried out if it is necessary and in my best interests and can be justified for medical reasons'.[176] The most recent form, introduced in 2001, is not dissimilar but limits additional procedures to ones 'necessary to save [the patient's] life or to prevent serious harm to [the patient's] health'.[177] What is the legal effect of this kind of clause?

On the face of it, the clause cannot in itself evidence (let alone amount to) express **3.63** consent. For that, the patient must understand the 'nature and purpose' of the additional or further procedure and have agreed to it.[178] By definition, reliance would only be placed upon this clause when the patient has not understood even in broad terms the nature of the additional procedure. At best, these clauses could only give rise to the argument that the patient had waived his right to the basic information—a claim which is highly problematic legally—or that by signing the consent form containing the clause he is taken thereby to have impliedly consented to the additional or further procedure. The latter arises, as we have seen already, where the patient has conducted himself such that it is reasonable to imply that he agreed and, importantly, understood what would or might happen. A prerequisite of implied consent is that the patient has actual or constructive notice of the information which he is thereafter estopped from denying. Obviously, this cannot be applied in the context of vaguely drafted clauses in consent forms.[179] Notwithstanding the logic of these arguments, the case law seems to give these clauses some credence. It was referred to as supporting the court's decision in *Brushnet v Cowan*.[180] More importantly, however, it was the basis for the decision in *Pridham v Nash*.[181]

The claimant underwent a laparoscopic abdominal examination to determine the **3.64** cause of pelvic pain. The claimant had agreed to this and had signed a consent form which stated, inter alia, that she consented to 'additional or alternative procedures

---

[176] In full it stated: 'I understand that any procedure in addition to the investigation or treatment described on this form will only be carried out if it is necessary and in my best interests and can be justified for medical reasons.' For a discussion of the form, see Brazier, M, 'Revised Consent Forms in the NHS' (1991) 7 Professional Negligence 148.

[177] N 118 above, Model Form 1, p 3.

[178] eg, *Abbass v Kenney* (1995) 31 BMLR 157: on facts held patient consented to operation carried out and no reliance placed upon the clause in consent form stating she consented to 'further or alternative operative measures as may be found to be necessary'.

[179] For the same reasons it would not be conclusive that the form stated that 'I have been told about additional procedures which may become necessary during my treatment. I have listed below any procedures *which I do not wish to be carried out* without further discussion' (emphasis in original). Unless the patient has been advised about all the possible further procedures he will not have adequate information for his silence in respect of the particular procedure to amount to an 'implied consent'.

[180] (1990) 69 DLR (4th) 743; [1991] 2 Med LR 271 (Newfd CA).

[181] (1986) 33 DLR (4th) 304.

as may be necessary or medically advisable during the course of the procedure'. During the procedure, the doctor discovered adhesions between her pelvis and abdominal wall. The doctor divided the adhesions using a forceps. Later, the claimant developed complications including peritonitis caused by the procedure. The claimant sued in battery and negligence claiming that she had only consented to the investigation and that she had not consented to the procedure to release the adhesions. Holland J disagreed. He concluded that the additional procedure was simple and minor and fell within the words of the consent form. The claimant had, therefore, expressly consented to it.

3.65   Holland J's reasoning is, for the reasons given earlier, open to doubt. Unless the curative procedure fell within the 'broad terms' of the investigative procedure (as in *Davis* and *Brushnett*), it is difficult to see how the claimant *expressly* consented to something she had not contemplated let alone understood its 'nature and purpose'.

3.66   How far should the reasoning of Holland J be taken? Would it permit *any* additional procedure for the benefit of the patient? If it did, there would be no need in practice to rely upon the principle of necessity (or its limitations) in this context providing that a standard consent form had been signed. It is difficult to imagine that the courts would be prepared to allow doctors a carte blanche based upon the vague terms of such a clause to act without—whatever they say—the express consent of the patient. In fact, Holland J himself restricted the impact of the clause in *Pridham* limiting it to minor, and excluding major, surgery. He said:[182]

> If the laparoscopic examination, an investigative procedure, had revealed a major problem requiring surgery then, in my view, the surgeon would not be entitled to rely on the original consent and the general words of the consent . . . to carry out the major surgery. The surgeon would have been required to consult further with the patient and obtain a further consent to the major operation.

3.67   There is no doubt that the Department of Health's (DoH) current consent form is a far more patient-orientated document than before. This is in keeping with the Department's wider policy of improving what doctors call the 'consenting' process, through an enhancement of the quality of information given to a patient and hence of any consent itself.[183] Specifically both the DoH[184] and the General Medical Council (GMC)[185] advise doctors to discuss additional problems (and their possible treatments) that may arise during the principal procedure. It may be, therefore, that the current wording—limited as it is to procedures to save life

---

[182] (1986) 33 DLR (4th) 308.
[183] See *Reference Guide to Consent for Examination or Treatment*, DoH, March 2001. See also GMC guidance, *Seeking Patients' Consent: the Ethical Considerations* (November 1998).
[184] ibid, 7 (para 6.1).
[185] N 183 above, para 8.

or prevent serious harm—goes no further than the doctrine of 'necessity' at common law.[186] Linked to the edict to doctors that 'it is good to talk', the result may leave the patient better informed than ever before and less at risk of unexpected procedures being performed that could await the patient's decision.

C. Elements of Consent

For a consent to treatment, or a refusal of treatment, to be legally valid it must be: **3.68**

(1) made by a person with *capacity*;

(2) *real*, ie based upon adequate information; and

(3) *voluntary* and not made under the undue influence of another.

1. Capacity

(i) General Approach

Legal capacity or competence to consent to treatment is not based upon a person's **3.69**
status or age.[187] Consequently, being a child or suffering from a mental disability or disorder does not mean, in law, that a person is necessarily incompetent. There is a rebuttable presumption that an adult is competent to consent (or refuse) treatment.[188] Equally, in relation to children[189] who have attained the age of 16 there is a similar presumption created by s 8 of the Family Reform Act 1969 in relation to 'medical, surgical or dental treatment' including diagnostic and ancillary procedures.[190] However, the presumption is otherwise in respect of younger children (ie those below 16) where it must be established following the decision of the House of Lords in *Gillick v Wisbech and Norfolk AHA*[191] that the particular child has the capacity to consent to the particular treatment contemplated.[192]

---

[186] ibid, paras 3.55–3.60. Contrast, *Reference Guide to Consent for Examination or Treatment* (n 118 above), 7 (para 6) stating that 'it may be justified to perform the procedure on the grounds that it is in the patient's best interests'.

[187] *Gillick v West Norfolk and Wisbech AHA* [1986] AC 112; [1985] 3 All ER 402 (HL); *Johnston v Wellesley Hospital* (1970) 17 DLR (3d) 139, 144–145 *per* Addy J. See also Skegg, PDG, *Law, Ethics and Medicine* (n 70 above), at 49–56 (children) and 56–7 (adults).

[188] *Re T (Adult: Refusal of Medical Treatment)* [1992] 4 All ER 649, 661 *per* Lord Donaldson MR; *Re MB* (1997) 38 BMLR 175 at 186 *per* Butler-Sloss LJ; *Re B (Adult; Refusal of Treatment)* (2002) 65 BMLR 149 at [28] *per* Butler-Sloss P. However, the burden of proving the continuing validity of an advance refusal (including non-revocation) is upon the patient: *HE v A Hospital NHS Trust* [2003] EWHC 1017 (Fam); [2003] 2 FLR 408 *per* Munby J at [20]. See also Draft Mental Incapacity Bill (June 2003), cl 3.

[189] ie those who have not reached the age of 18.

[190] See below, Ch 4.

[191] N 187 above.

[192] See below, Ch 4.

3.70 Capacity is a question of fact in every case and requires that the patient is able to understand what is involved in the decision to be taken.[193] In children the issue will frequently be a developmental one, namely whether the patient has *acquired* sufficient maturity and intelligence to understand what is involved.[194] In adults, the issue may be the same but usually it will not be. The law will not question the degree of intelligence or education of an adult.[195] In most instances the issue will be whether the patient's mental disability or disorder is such that he has *lost* the capacity to consent (or refuse) treatment or has never acquired it. A patient may have the capacity to make some but not all treatment decisions.[196] For example, a young child may be sufficiently mature to be able to understand what is involved in a minor form of treatment, such as bandaging a wound, but not a major one, such as a heart by-pass operation. Equally, a patient may be incompetent to understand any decision, for example, where the patient is unconscious or suffers from a severe mental disability. While developmental capacity of a child will be attained once and forever,[197] a competent child or adult's capacity may be lost (or absent) temporarily, for example, through an accident rendering the patient unconscious. It may also be permanently absent, for example, where the patient is born mentally disabled.

(a) Mistake as to Capacity

3.71 A doctor who mistakenly believes that a patient has capacity to consent to (or refuse) medical treatment does not necessarily act unlawfully.[198] For example, in the Scottish legislation dealing with the competence of a child under 16 to consent to medical treatments or procedures, Parliament has merely required that 'in the opinion of the doctor' the patient has capacity.[199] In England, a doctor's conduct cannot be based upon a legally valid consent (or refusal). If the doctor treats the patient, who is subsequently found to have been incompetent, he may be justified in treating the patient under the principle of necessity in his 'best interests'.[200] By contrast, a doctor who respects the patient's refusal in such circumstances will only be liable to the extent that he was negligent in not treating the patient, and injury to the patient resulted.

---

[193] *Gillick v West Norfolk and Wisbech AHA* [1985] 3 All ER 402.

[194] ibid. See below, Ch 4.

[195] *Re T* (n 7 above), 661 *per* Lord Donaldson MR.

[196] *Gillick* (n 193 above), *per* Lord Fraser at 409 and *per* Lord Scarman at 422 and 423–424 (children); *Re T* (n 7 above), *per* Lord Donaldson MR at 661–662 (adults).

[197] See *Re R (A Minor) (Wardship: Medical Treatment)* [1992] Fam 11; [1991] 4 All ER 177 (CA) and *Re W (A Minor) (Medical Treatment)* [1993] Fam 64; [1992] 4 All ER 627 (CA).

[198] See Kennedy and Grubb, *Medical Law* (n 51 above), 764–5.

[199] *Re F* (n 7 above). See below, Ch 4.

[200] *Re T* (n 7 above), *per* Staughton LJ at 670.

(b) Mistake as to Incapacity

More problematic is the doctor who acts notwithstanding a competent patient's **3.72** refusal, believing it to be invalid. At common law, there would appear to be no defence since the patient's refusal is valid and the doctor commits a battery.[201] It is likely that in England the judges would fashion a defence of mistake, probably reasonable mistake, if called upon to do so.[202]

A number of important points arise from this general account of the nature of **3.73** capacity/incapacity in law to make a decision about medical treatment.

(c) Ability to Understand Versus Actual Understanding

Capacity to consent is a question of the person's *ability* to understand that which **3.74** the law requires the patient to understand.[203] The law looks to the person's innate facility or aptitude to understand what is involved in giving consent to (or refusing) the treatment.[204] Of course, it is relevant whether a patient does *actually* understand what is involved and in two ways. It will be necessary if the patient's consent is to be *real*, and thus, valid.[205] An uncomprehending 'consent' (or 'refusal') is no consent at all but it does not mean necessarily, or otherwise, that the patient is incompetent. The patient may have the *ability* to understand but not, perhaps because of the incomplete or inadequate explanation offered by the doctor, *actually* understand the information. The patient is not thereby rendered incompetent and unable to decide for himself. Rather, the law imposes an obligation upon the doctor to disclose the information in a reasonably comprehensible way or the consent will be invalid and the touching arising out of the treatment (of the competent patient) will be unlawful. Also, the patient's actual understanding will, of course, assist the doctor and, ultimately, the court in some cases to determine whether the patient is able to understand what is involved. In other words, the patient's actual understanding will be a useful 'yardstick' by which to assess the patient's capacity. But, for the reasons just given, it is no more than that and it is not conclusive.

---

[201] Age of Legal Capacity (Scotland) Act 1991, s 2(4).

[202] *Re MB (Medical Treatment)* (1997) 38 BMLR 175 (CA) at 188 *per* Butler-Sloss LJ: 'The only situation in which it is lawful for the doctors to intervene is if it is *believed* that the patient lacks the capacity to decide' (emphasis added).

[203] See discussion in Kennedy and Grubb, *Medical Law* (n 51 above), 615–17. For a case in which the court looked to the actual understanding of the patient see *Re L (Medical Treatment: Gillick Competency)* [1998] 2 FLR 810 (Stephen Brown P) (14-year-old girl who was a Jehovah's Witness incompetent to refuse treatment—which might include a blood transfusion—for a life-threatening condition). For criticism see Grubb (1999) 7 Med L Rev 58 (Commentary).

[204] eg, Mental Health Act 1983, ss 57 and 58; Age of Legal Capacity (Scotland) Act 1991, s 2(4). See also Draft Mental Incapacity Bill (June 2003), cls 1–2.

[205] See below, paras 3.93–3.108.

(d) Ability to Understand What?

3.75   If legal capacity requires the patient to be able to understand what is involved in the proposed procedure, the question arises as to precisely what that entails. Does it require the patient to be able to understand only that information which, if understood, will make the patient's consent real and the doctor's touching not a battery? In other words, the patient must be able to understand the 'broad nature and purpose' of the procedure. This would have a certain legal symmetry about it and would be consistent with the current view of the Court of Appeal that consent in medical law simply has the function of licensing that which would otherwise be a battery.[206] At the other extreme, the law could require the patient to have an ability to understand all information which the law requires the patient to have in mind when consenting whether in order to avoid a battery claim or because of the doctor's obligation in negligence to provide information. This would, therefore, encompass much more than the 'broad nature and purpose' of the procedure and include some risks etc. There is a logical basis for this approach since it would be curious if the law required disclosure of information which the patient was simply unable to comprehend. However, as is often the case, the law takes a middle course. The patient must be able to understand more than the 'broad nature and purpose' of the procedure. He must also be able to understand the likely (or possible) effects or consequences of undergoing (or not) the procedure in question.[207] In one case, the court stated that the patient should have the ability to understand the 'nature, purpose and effects' of the procedure which was the amputation of part of a leg.[208] More recently, the Court of Appeal in *Re MB* spoke of the patient having capacity if she was able to understand 'the information which is material to the decision, especially as to the likely consequences of having or not having the treatment in question'.[209]

3.76   In children cases, there is some suggestion in the case law that the patient must have a much greater ability to understand than has been suggested above.[210] In the *Gillick* case, for example, the child had to understand the 'moral and family questions' associated with her decision to engage in sexual intercourse and to seek contraceptive treatment secretly without involving her parents.[211] To require this of a child is indeed to expect a lot: more, quite frankly, than could, or indeed would, be expected of an adult patient. It is better to understand the remarks in *Gillick*, at

---

[206]   See *Re R* (n 197 above), *Re W* (n 50 above), and *Re T* (n 7 above).

[207]   See formulation in Age of Capacity (Scotland) Act 1991, s 2(4) and Draft Mental Incapacity Bill (June 2003), cl 2(5), 'relevant information' includes information 'about the reasonably foreseeable consequences of deciding one way or another or of failing to make the decision'.

[208]   *Re C (Adult: Refusal of Medical Treatment)* [1994] 1 All ER 819 *per* Thorpe J at 824.

[209]   N 202 above, at 187 *per* Butler-Sloss LJ.

[210]   For a discussion of the capacity of children to consent (or refuse) medical treatment, see below, Ch 4.

[211]   N 193 above, especially *per* Lord Scarman at 424.

worst, as restricted to the particular context of contraception and the court's desire to move slowly forward in emancipating children or, at best, as simply wrong, going beyond anything that the law could reasonably expect of anyone.[212]

(ii) Determining a Patient's Capacity

(a) The Re C Three-Stage Test

While it is clear that a patient's capacity to consent to (or refuse) treatment is concerned with his *ability to understand* what is involved, how does the law approach a determination of whether the patient has that ability? The courts have developed a three-stage test to assess a patient's capacity or ability to understand. In *Re C (Adult: Refusal of Medical Treatment)* [213] Thorpe J stated that the patient must be able to (i) *comprehend and retain* the relevant information; (ii) *believe* it; and (iii) *weigh* it in the balance so as to *arrive at a choice*. Subsequent courts have applied the so-called '*Re C* three-stage test'.[214] Indeed, it has been applied not only in adult cases, but also in child cases where the issue of the child's capacity is not a developmental one of maturity but is raised by the child's mental disability.[215] In *Re MB* the Court of Appeal authoritatively approved the test.[216] Speaking for the Court of Appeal, Butler-Sloss LJ stated:[217]

3.77

> A person lacks capacity if some impairment or disturbance of mental functioning renders the person unable to make a decision whether to consent to or refuse treatment: That inability to make a decision will occur when
> (a) the patient is unable to comprehend and retain the information which is material to the decision, especially as to the likely consequences of having or not having the treatment in question.
> (b) the patient is unable to use the information and weigh it in the balance as part of the process of arriving at the decision. If . . . a compulsive disorder or phobia from which the patient suffers stifles belief in the information presented to her, then the decision may not be a true one.

---

[212] See *C v Wren* (1987) 35 DLR (4th) 419 (Alta CA) and *Ney v Attorney-General of Canada* (1993) 102 DLR (4th) 136 (BC Sup Ct).

[213] [1994] 1 All ER 819, 824; and Grubb (1992) 2 Med L Rev 92 (Commentary).

[214] In essence the statutory test of 'incapacity' set out in cl 2 of the Draft Mental Incapacity Bill (June 2003)—inability to 'understand', 'retain' or 'use' the information or communicate the decision.

[215] See *Re C (Detention: Medical Treatment)* [1997] 2 FLR 180; and Grubb (1997) 5 Med L Rev 227 (Commentary). See also *Re B (A Minor) (Treatment and Secure Accommodation)* [1997] 1 FCR 618; and Grubb (1997) 5 Med L Rev 233 (Commentary). For an analysis of the relationship between the *Gillick* and *Re C* tests see Kennedy, I, and Grubb (n 51 above) at 624.

[216] [1997] 2 FLR 426, 433: 'the test to be applied where the issue arose as to capacity . . .' *per* Butler-Sloss LJ. See also *Re B (Adult; Refusal of Treatment)* (2002) 65 BMLR 149 at [33] *per* Butler-Sloss P. For a discussion of 'capacity' after *Re MB*, see Kennedy (1997) 5 Med L Rev 317, 320–4 (Commentary).

[217] ibid, 437.

3.78 The *Re C* test requires that the patient have the ability to 'comprehend' the relevant information in making the decision. It does not require the patient to make a 'mature' or 'wise' decision.[218] Nor does it require the patient to achieve the unattainable such as fully appreciating the consequences of his decision (such as the impact of his death upon his family and others).[219] The law will not impose unreachable expectations about a patient's reasoning powers and experiences. Hence, a patient may satisfy the *Re C* test even where they reject alternative treatment of which they have no personal experience[220] or retain a hope of a cure that 'the cavalry will come over the hill'[221] providing that neither undermines their capacity to 'comprehend', 'retain', believe' and 'weigh' the information to reach a decision.

3.79 A patient may, at times, be ambivalent about their decision to refuse treatment but providing this is not the product of an underlying mental incapacity and is not inconsistent with a settled decision to refuse treatment, then the patient will have the legal capacity to make the decision.[222]

3.80 In addition to requiring the patient to be able to 'believe' and 'weigh' the information, the test requires that the patient be able to 'retain' it. In some exceptional circumstances, the patient's mental disability may preclude the patient from retaining the information long enough to make a decision, for instance, in some cases of degenerative brain disease such as Alzheimer's Disease or where the patient has suffered a specific brain injury that destroys short-term memory capacity. Clearly if a patient cannot retain the relevant information long enough (or at all) in order to make a choice, the patient should not be competent in law to make that (or indeed, any) decision.[223]

(b) Applying the Re C Test

3.81 A patient's capacity to decide may be called into question for a number of reasons: through mental disability or disorder, an inability to communicate a decision or because of external factors such as fatigue, pain, or sedation. In general, where a patient is suffering from a mental disorder or disability, a doctor's assessment of a

---

218 Explicitly stated in Draft Mental Incapacity Bill (June 2003), cl 2(2).

219 See Gunn, M (1994) 2 Med L Rev 8, 18–20. For two decisions involving children wrongly requiring this level of 'appreciation', see *Re E (A Minor)* (1990) 9 BMLR 1 and *Re S (A Minor) (Consent to Medical Treatment)* [1994] 2 FLR 1065. For a criticism, see Grubb (1995) 3 Med L Rev 84, 85–6 (Commentary).

220 *Re B (Adult; Refusal of Treatment)* (2002) 65 BMLR 149 (Butler-Sloss P) (no experience of rehabilitation did not affect a patient's competence to reject life-sustaining ventilation): 'It is not possible to experience before choosing in many medical situations' *per* Butler-Sloss P at [93].

221 *Re JT (Adult: Refusal of Medical Treatment)* [1998] 1 FLR 48 (Wall J).

222 *Re B (Adult; Refusal of Treatment)* (n 16 above). See also *Bartling v Superior Court* (1984) 209 Cal Rptr 220 (Cal CA), especially at 23–24.

223 But retaining the information for a short period *may* be sufficient. See statutory reference in the Draft Mental Incapacity Bill (June 2003), cl 2(4).

patient's capacity should be confirmed by a psychiatrist. Of course, this may not be necessary in the case of children where the issue is one of 'maturity',[224] or in an obvious case, for example, where the patient is unconscious. In cases of doubt about the competence of a patient, a ruling from the court should be obtained[225] either by way of declaratory proceedings (in the case of adults), or under the Children Act 1989 or the court's inherent jurisdiction (in the case of children). A judgment about the application of the *Re C* test should, except in the most exceptional circumstances of urgency, preferably be supported by such evidence where a court is asked to determine a patient's capacity to consent to (or refuse) treatment.[226]

In applying the *Re C* test, the courts have repeatedly stated that the patient's **3.82** capacity must be 'commensurate with the gravity of the decision. . . . The more serious the decision, the greater the capacity required.'[227] Precisely what this means is not clear, but in practice the courts give most careful scrutiny to decisions which may (or will) have deleterious consequences for the patient, such as a decision to refuse treatment, in particular life-sustaining treatment. A useful division of the possible situations that could arise, though not comprehensive, is as follows: (i) a patient's beliefs or value system; (ii) misperception of reality; (iii) compulsive or driven behaviour; (iv) external factors; and (v) inability to communicate a decision.

Beliefs and Value Systems In applying the *Re C* test, the courts are not con- **3.83** cerned with the reasonableness of the patient's decision or his reasoning process.[228] Nor is the law concerned with the rationality of the patient's decision or its basis unless that leads the court to conclude that the patient is suffering from a mental disability which deprives him of the ability to 'comprehend', 'retain', 'believe' or 'weigh' the information.[229] In *Re T (Adult: Refusal of Treatment)*, Lord Donaldson MR stated that a competent adult patient had a right to consent to, or refuse, medical treatment based upon reasons which were 'rational, irrational,

---

[224] Perhaps the evidence of other experts, such as developmental psychologists, may be helpful in such cases.

[225] See *Re MB* (n 202 above), 445 *per* Butler-Sloss LJ. But not if there is no doubt: *Re JT (Adult: Refusal of Medical Treatment)* (n 16 above). Guidance was given by the Court of Appeal in *Re MB* (n 202 above) as subsequently modified in *St George's Healthcare NHS Trust v S* [1998] 3 All ER 673, 702–704.

[226] ibid.

[227] See *Re T* (n 7 above), 661–662 *per* Lord Donaldson and *Re MB* (n 202 above), 437 *per* Butler-Sloss LJ.

[228] *Re T* (n 7 above), 664 *per* Butler-Sloss LJ: 'a decision . . . does not have to be sensible, rational or well considered'. See also *Smith v Auckland Hospital Board* [1965] NZLR 191 (NZCA), 219 *per* Gresson J.

[229] *Re MB* (n 22 above). See also *St George's Healthcare NHS Trust v S* [1998] 3 All ER 673 (CA) and *Re JT (Adult: Refusal of Medical Treatment)* [1998] 1 FLR 48 (Wall J).

unknown or even non-existent'.[230] Consequently, religious beliefs which lead patients to refuse some or all medical treatment do not affect a patient's capacity, however irrational the belief may seem.[231] A Jehovah's Witness who refuses a blood transfusion or a Christian Scientist who refuses all medical intervention is not, by reason of the irrationality or otherwise of their beliefs, incompetent to make decisions about their medical treatment. Providing they are able to understand what is involved—'comprehending', 'believing', and 'weighing' the information—their refusals will be legally binding upon the doctors.[232] There are two explanations of the law's position here. First, the law defers to religiously based decisions made by adults, though not those made on behalf of children,[233] as a matter of social tolerance. Providing the person understands what is entailed in their decision, there is no reason for the law to deprive the individual of decision-making power. It would be an act of unjustified state interference to override decisions made on religious grounds. Secondly, and perhaps of more general importance for medical law, such decisions do not stem from any mental disability or mental malfunctioning on the part of the patient. Apart from situations where the patient is unable to communicate his decision, a necessary condition for depriving an individual of decision-making power, and justifying state intervention in his 'best interests', is that the patient is suffering from a mental malfunctioning having a pathological or psychological etiology. It is the impairment or disturbance in the patient's mental ability to understand which potentially renders him, in law, incompetent.[234]

3.84 **Misperception of Reality**   In order for a patient to have capacity to decide, he must be able to understand the information that is material to making the decision. As part of this, a patient must be able to understand what is wrong with him and which requires treatment, and he must be able to understand the consequences to him of undergoing or declining the treatment. However, an irrational belief, whether long-held or of contemporary origin, which affects or influences a patient's judgment about medical treatment will not lead to a finding of incompetence unless it results in an inference that the patient is suffering from a mental disability. In *Re MB* the Court of Appeal acknowledged that it would not be proper to find a patient incompetent merely because his decision was 'irrational', meaning one 'so outrageous in its defiance of logic or of accepted moral standards' that 'no sensible person who had applied his mind to the question to be decided

---

[230] N 7 above, 653. See also *Re MB* (n 202 above), *per* Butler-Sloss LJ at 432 and 436–437.

[231] *Re W* (n 50 above), 637 *per* Lord Donaldson MR.

[232] *Re T* (n 7 above).

[233] See eg *Re S (A Minor) (Medical Treatment)* [1993] 1 FLR 376; *Re E (A Minor)* (1990) 9 BMLR 1; *Re R (A Minor)* [1993] 2 FLR 5; *Re L (Medical Treatment: Gillick Competency)* [1998] 2 FLR 810. See below, Ch 4.

[234] See the Draft Mental Incapacity Bill (June 2003), cl 1.

could have arrived at it'.[235] The Court of Appeal accepted, however, that if the patient's irrational decision was based upon a misperception of reality stemming from a mental disorder, then the patient might lack the ability to 'comprehend' or 'believe' the information under the *Re C* test.[236]

The general approach can be illustrated by the following examples taken from the case law. A patient who denies that she is ill or diseased and in need of treatment is incompetent if that belief derives from a mental disability because she will not be able to 'comprehend' or 'believe' the information relevant to making a decision.[237] Hence a patient who, due to a mental disability, denies that she has a gangrenous foot in need of amputation is incompetent to make a decision. A patient suffering from anorexia nervosa who is unable, because of her mental disorder, to understand her failing physical condition lacks the capacity to refuse food and nutrition.[238] Likewise a patient suffering from paranoid schizophrenia, who denies during a lucid moment that there is anything wrong with her and that she needs treatment to prevent a deterioration in her mental health, is incompetent because she is unable by reason of her mental illness to 'comprehend' or 'believe' the information about her illness and its prognosis.[239]

3.85

However, it is essential to a finding of incompetence that the patient's 'disbelief' derives from a mental disability. Not every patient who disbelieves their doctor's advice fails the second stage of the *Re C* test and is incompetent: indeed, most will not be incompetent. An important distinction has to be drawn between outright disbelief due to mental disorder where the patient is 'impervious to reason, divorced from reality, or incapable of adjustment after reflection' and 'the tendency which most people have when undergoing medical treatment to self assess and then puzzle over the divergence between medical and self-assessment'.[240] Merely to take a different view of the world from a doctor may result in a patient 'disbelieving' him but it does not render the patient incompetent and thus unable to decide, as a matter of law, for themselves.[241] Even a skewed, and indefensible view of the world, does not have this effect *unless* it has its genesis in what might be termed, mental 'malfunctioning'.[242] Hence, a patient's irrational fear of surgery[243]

3.86

---

[235] N 202 above, 437 *per* Butler-Sloss LJ.
[236] ibid.
[237] See, eg, *State of Tennessee v Northern* (1978) 563 SW 2d 197 (Tenn CA).
[238] *Re W* (n 50 above).
[239] *Re R* (n 197 above).
[240] *B v Croydon HA* (1994) 22 BMLR 13 *per* Thorpe J at 20.
[241] *Re C (Adult: Refusal of Medical Treatment)* [1994] 1 All ER 819.
[242] See, eg, *Tameside and Glossop Acute Services Trust v CH* [1996] 1 FLR 762 where the patient had a deluded belief that her doctors were maliciously trying to hurt her and her unborn child. See Grubb (1996) 4 Med L Rev 193 (Commentary).
[243] See, eg, *Re Maida Yetter* (1973) 96 D & C 2d 619 (Comm Pleas Pa) and *Lane v Candura* (1978) 376 NE 2d 1232 (Mass App Ct).

or a particular medical procedure[244] are not sufficient in themselves to make the patient incompetent in law to make a decision about their treatment. Only if the 'fear' acts on the patient's mind so as to 'paralyse the will and thus destroy the capacity to make a decision' will a finding of incompetence be justified.[245]

3.87 **Compulsive or Driven Behaviour** Certain mental disorders result in a patient being deprived of the ability to make a real or true choice. Examples of these are compulsive eating disorders such as anorexia nervosa and compulsive phobias or personality disorders. A patient who is forced or compelled to reach a particular decision, usually to refuse the treatment, is not in law competent to make that decision. The patient is, under the *Re C* test, unable to 'weigh' the information and 'make a choice'. Consequently, a refusal of treatment by a patient suffering from anorexia nervosa,[246] from a borderline personality disorder resulting in self-harm,[247] or a 'needle phobia' compelling the patient to panic and refuse the procedure,[248] will not be valid in law because the patient will be incapable of 'weighing' the information relevant to the decision.

3.88 In addition, the patient's mental disorder may cause the patient to 'skew' the information given to her such that she distorts the relevant factors in her own mind. A patient whose mental illness leads her to minimize past events and selectively ignore or distort information given about her condition will be 'unable to weigh treatment information, balancing risks and needs', and hence will be incompetent to make a decision about the treatment for her mental disorder.[249] So, for example, in *R v Ashworth Hospital Authority, ex p Brady*[250] a prisoner refused food by going on a hunger strike. The court decided that he was incompetent to make that decision. The prisoner's paranoid personality disorder had resulted in a 'battle of wills' with the prison authorities such that he was unable to weigh and balance information in relation to food refusal and force-feeding under the third stage of the *Re C* test.

3.89 However, caution must be exercised in applying the third stage of the *Re C* test. It is potentially an open invitation to make a finding of incompetence because the doctor (or court) finds the patient's decision difficult to understand. This is not what the courts intend. That a patient must have the ability to 'weigh' information

---

[244] See, eg, *Re MB* (n 202 above), 437 *per* Butler-Sloss LJ.

[245] ibid, 437 *per* Butler-Sloss LJ.

[246] *Re W* (n 50 above).

[247] *B v Croydon HA* [1995] Fam 133; [1995] 1 All ER 683 (CA). See Grubb (1995) 3 Med L Rev 191 (Commentary).

[248] See *Re MB* (n 202 above), and *Re L (Patient: Non-Consensual Treatment)* [1997] 2 FLR 837.

[249] eg, *Re C (Detention: Medical Treatment)* [1997] 2 FLR 180. See also *Re MB* (n 202 above), 437 *per* Butler-Sloss LJ.

[250] [2000] Lloyd's Rep Med 355 (Maurice Kay J). Discussed in Fennell (2000) 8 Med L Rev 251 (Commentary).

does not mean that every incongruous decision is an incompetent one. The court is not entitled simply to re-weigh the factors relevant to the patient's decision and, because it would come to a different decision, treat the patient as incompetent. It is the patient's ability to weigh, rather than the actual weight given to particular factors, which is at the core of the third stage of the *Re C* test. A patient may have the ability to weigh the information but, for reasons particular to him, reach a decision that the doctor (or court) would not. That is the patient's choice and the decision may be based upon the patient's own perception of the world or values providing it is not the product of distorted or deluded perceptions stemming from mental malfunctioning, in particular the very mental disorder for which treatment is needed.[251] To do otherwise, would be to introduce a test of unreasonableness or irrationality which the courts have rejected.[252]

External Factors   A patient's ability to understand may be temporarily affected   **3.90**
by external factors such as confusion, shock, fatigue, pain, or medication.[253] Such factors may render a patient incapable of making a decision because the patient is unable to 'weigh' the information and make a choice.[254] However, the court will require a demonstrable effect of the patient's ability to reason and decide before such a finding will be permissible. It is not sufficient that the patient's capacity is merely reduced. The patient's capacity must be 'completely erode[d] . . . to such a degree that the ability to decide is absent'.[255] In *Re MB* Butler-Sloss LJ illustrated how the patient's panic and fear could make them incompetent:[256]

> Another . . . influence may be panic induced by fear. Again careful scrutiny of the evidence is necessary because fear of an operation may be a rational reason for refusal to undergo it. Fear may also, however, paralyse the will and thus destroy the capacity to make a decision.

The importance of the limited scope of this basis for a finding of incompetence is   **3.91**
illustrated by two cases involving obstetric treatment.[257] In one case,[258] a patient in the late stages of labour was held to be incompetent because, in the words of Johnson J, '[s]he was called upon to make the decision at a time of acute emotional

---

[251] See *B v Croydon HA* (1994) 22 BMLR 13, 20 *per* Thorpe J, and see also *Re MB* (n 202 above), *per* Butler-Sloss LJ at 436–437.

[252] *St George's Healthcare NHS Trust v S* (n 229 above)—pregnant woman competent to refuse treatment even though her thinking was bizarre and irrational.

[253] *Re T* (n 7 above), 661 *per* Lord Donaldson MR. See also *St George's Healthcare NHS Trust v S* (n 209 above), *per* Judge LJ at 693.

[254] An alternative way of determining such cases would be to say that the patient was acting involuntarily or under undue influence: *Beausoleil v Soeur de la Charité de la Providence* (1964) 53 DLR (2d) 65 (patient sedated). See discussion below, paras 3.166–3.170.

[255] *Re MB* (n 202 above), 437 *per* Butler-Sloss LJ.

[256] ibid.

[257] For a thorough and scholarly discussion of the case law: see Scott, R, *Rights, Duties and the Body: Law and Ethics of the Maternal-Fetal Conflict* (2002, Hart), especially at 154–163.

[258] *Norfolk and Norwich Healthcare (NHS) Trust v W* [1997] 1 FCR 269.

stress and physical pain in the ordinary course of labour made even more difficult for her because of her own particular mental history'.[259] The patient denied she was pregnant. Even though the psychiatric evidence was that she was not suffering from a mental disorder within the Mental Health Act 1983, she had a history of psychiatric treatment and it is difficult to believe that her denial of the obvious was based upon a difference of opinion or values rather than having a psychiatric etiology. Johnson J was not, therefore, relying upon the patient's circumstances in reaching his decision that she was incompetent. However, in another case decided on the same day,[260] the same judge did make such a finding where the patient had no psychiatric history. Despite the consultant obstetrician's view that she was competent to decide, Johnson J held:[261]

> The patient was in the throes of labour with all that involved in terms of pain and emotional stress. I concluded that a patient who could, in those circumstances, speak in terms which seemed to accept the inevitability of her own death, was not a patient who was able properly to weigh-up the considerations that arose so as to make any valid decision, about anything of even the most trivial kind, surely less one which involved her life.

In *Re MB*, the Court of Appeal rightly doubted this finding.[262]

3.92 **Inability to Communicate**   The patient's incapacity may arise because he is unable to communicate a decision to the doctor. Here, there is no necessity for the incapacity to arise from a 'mental malfunctioning'. It may result from a purely physical disability impairing the patient's facility to communicate. It will usually arise in practice where the patient is unconscious. The incapacity may be temporary, as where the patient has been injured in an accident, or permanent, for example, where the patient is in a persistent vegetative state. The inability to communicate may arise otherwise, for example, in rare cases where the patient is 'locked in' or the patient is somehow physically disabled from communication. Providing all reasonable steps have been taken to communicate their decision, the law regards patients in this residual category of case as incompetent to make a treatment decision.

2. Information

(i) Battery

3.93 In order to give a valid legal consent (or refusal) to treatment, a patient must understand adequately what is involved in the procedure (or in refusing it). It is

---

[259] *Norfolk and Norwich Healthcare (NHS) Trust v W* [1997] 1 FCR 269, 272.
[260] *Rochdale Healthcare (NHS) Trust v C* [1997] 1 FCR 274.
[261] ibid, 275.
[262] N 202 above. See also, *St George's Healthcare NHS Trust v S* (n 229 above).

sometimes said that the patient's consent must be 'informed'. This is an unfortunate phrase and one prone to mislead.[263] It is an expression used by courts in other countries, particularly in America, to describe the scope of a doctor's duty in the tort of negligence to disclose information.[264] It is better avoided in any discussion in the context of battery or, indeed, in negligence in England. In battery, it is more helpful to say that the patient's consent must be 'real'.

On the face of it, if the patient's consent is not 'real' then the doctor commits battery by touching the patient. However, where the patient does not understand the 'nature' of the procedure, a doctor who mistakenly (and reasonably) believes that he does *may* have a defence in that the patient may be estopped from denying he possessed the information if he has led the doctor 'reasonably to assume the relevant information was known to him'.[265]   **3.94**

(a) 'Nature'

When will a patient's consent be 'real'? The patient must understand in broad terms the 'nature' of the procedure he is agreeing to.[266] Providing the patient does, and he is competent and acting voluntarily, his consent will be 'real' and legally valid. No action in battery will lie. It is another question whether he may have a claim in negligence for non-disclosure of other information and this will be discussed later.[267] It is sometimes erroneously, but understandably, thought that a doctor has a duty to disclose that information relevant to the 'nature' of the procedure in order for the patient's consent to be real.[268] In fact, this is not the case since battery and consent are not concerned with the doctor's duty to disclose but rather with the actual knowledge and understanding of the patient. A patient's consent will be real if he understands the 'nature' of a procedure regardless from where he acquired the information. It need not have been from his doctor or other health carer. Of course, by the very nature of things, usually the information will   **3.95**

---

[263] *Rogers v Whitaker* (1992) 109 ALR 625, 633 (H Ct Aust): *Reibl v Hughes* (1980) 114 DLR (3d) 1, 11.

[264] Most famously in *Canterbury v Spence* (1972) 464 F 2d 772 (DC Cir).

[265] See *Sidaway v Bethlem Royal Hospital Governors* [1985] 1 All ER 643 *per* Lord Diplock at 658. See discussion above, paras 3.71–3.72 (mistake as to capacity). On the related, but distinct point, of whether a patient has to understand information for the purposes of negligence see Kennedy and Grubb, *Medical Law* (n 51 above), 243–5, and *Ciarlariello v Schacter* (1993) 100 DLR (4th) 609, 622–623 *per* Cory J (positive duty to ensure patient understands).

[266] *Chatterton v Gerson* [1981] QB 432, 443 *per* Bristow J; *Sidaway v Governors of Bethlem Royal Hospital* [1984] 1 All ER 1018 (CA), at 1026 *per* Sir John Donaldson MR and at 1029 *per* Dunn LJ; *Rogers v Whitaker* (1992) 109 ALR 624 (H Ct Aust), 633.

[267] See below, paras 3.109 *et seq*.

[268] In *Abbass v Kenney* (1995) 31 BMLR 157, Gage J (at 163) stated that 'a doctor has a duty to explain what he intends to do and the implications of what he is going to do'. However, the claimant case was pleaded solely in *negligence* even though the essence of her claim was that she had not consented to the operation. For another case in which the claim was framed in negligence, see *Williamson v East London and City HA* [1998] Lloyd's Rep Med 6 (Butterfield J).

come from the doctor (or other health carers such as a nurse) because that will be the only source of information for the patient. By contrast, in the tort of negligence the law is concerned with the doctor's duty to volunteer information or answer questions posed by the patient.[269]

3.96 What is meant by the 'nature' of a procedure? The *Oxford English Dictionary*[270] defines, inter alia, 'nature' as

> [t]he essential qualities or properties of a thing; the inherent and inseparable combination of properties essentially pertaining to anything and giving it its fundamental character.

In relation to what constitutes the 'nature' of a medical procedure, no general answer can be given other than to say that it is a relatively narrow notion encompassing by *description* the character of the act(s) to be done by the doctor and, *qualitatively*, the intended effect(s) of the procedure and its purpose. There is no doubt that 'nature' includes an understanding of the purpose or intended effect of the procedure. Indeed, although initially referring only to the 'nature' of the procedure, for clarity it is now commonplace for judges to talk of the 'nature and purpose' of the procedure.[271]

3.97 The information needs to state in 'broad terms' what is to be done to the patient and why.[272] However, this information need not descend into minute, or indeed any, real detail. In practice, judges have considerable leeway in determining what information is relevant to the 'nature and purpose' of a procedure and what is co-lateral to that and, therefore, immaterial to the reality of the patient's consent. For example, it may be enough that the patient knows that a diagnostic procedure of a certain type is to be undertaken, such as a biopsy, and what that involves in terms of contact with the patient and incision. Even if the doctor had been speaking in terms of a particular kind of biopsy such as a muscle biopsy, knowledge of this will be sufficient to amount to a real consent to a bone biopsy carried out at the same time.[273]

3.98 The courts' reluctance to read more into the 'nature and purpose' requirement is linked to their unwillingness to expand the tort of battery in medical cases. Instead, they wish to leave claims by patients who have not been informed of relevant information to their decision to consent to the tort of negligence. The judges have 'deplor[ed] reliance' upon battery in medical cases.[274] They have done

---

[269] See below.
[270] OUP, 1971.
[271] eg, *Sidaway v Bethlem Royal Hospital Governors* [1985] 1 All ER 643, 647 *per* Lord Scarman.
[272] *Chatterton v Gerson* (n 266 above).
[273] See *Brushnett v Cowan* [1991] 2 Med LR 271 and the discussion above, paras 3.61–3.67.
[274] *Hills v Potter* [1983] 3 All ER 716, 728 *per* Hirst J; *Chatterton v Gerson* (n 266 above), 265 *per* Bristow J; *Sidaway v Bethlem Royal Hospital Governors* (n 771 above), 650 *per* Lord Scarman; *Abbass v Kenney* (1995) 31 BMLR 157, 163–4 *per* Gage J.

so for a number of reasons. First, battery is an intentional tort usually involving hostile action by an aggressor. Medical cases rarely, if ever, fit this perception of battery particularly when the issue is non-disclosure of information by the doctor. Secondly, to face a civil claim for battery carries a stigma with it for the doctor given the association that could occur in the public's mind with the crime of assault. Thirdly, a battery action affords the patient certain advantages over a claim in negligence; for example, proving negligence and establishing causation may be difficult in a negligence action.[275] In a battery claim, expert evidence of professional practice—and the *Bolam*[276] test—will not avail a doctor as a defence to an allegation of wrongful non-disclosure. Also, establishing what injury flowed from the procedure which was not consented to will, as a matter of causation, usually be obvious in a battery action whereas establishing in a negligence action what the patient would have done if he had known the information which was not disclosed, may create evidential (and legal) difficulties.[277]

Risks and Alternatives The most obvious limitation imposed by the judges **3.99** upon the information relevant to the 'nature' and 'purpose' of a procedure relates to non-disclosure of risks inherent in, and alternatives to, the procedure. Such information is not considered to affect the reality of the patient's consent. In *Chatterton v Gerson*[278] the claimant was treated for chronic pain around the area of an operation scar following a hernia operation. The patient was given an injection of phenol to relieve the pain. Subsequently, this led to her leg becoming numb and thereby impairing her mobility. Although the doctor had described the procedure to the patient he had not informed her of the risk of numbness. She sued in battery and negligence. The court dismissed both actions. As regards her claim in battery, Bristow J held that she had given a 'real' consent even though she had not known the risk of the side-effect. He said:

> I think that justice requires that in order to vitiate the reality of consent there must be a greater failure of communication between the doctor and patient than that involved in a breach of duty if the claim is based on negligence. . . . In my judgment, once the patient is informed in *broad terms of the nature of the procedure* which is intended, and gives her consent, that consent is real, and the cause of action on which to base a claim for failure to go into risks and implications is negligence, not trespass.[279]

Later cases in England have affirmed this approach, in particular, both the Court **3.100** of Appeal and House of Lords in *Sidaway v Bethlem Royal Hospital Governors*.[280]

---

[275] See Robertson, G, 'Informed Consent to Medical Treatment' (1981) 97 LQR 102, 123–4.
[276] *Bolam v Friern HMC* [1957] 1 WLR 582 as interpreted by the House of Lords in *Bolitho v City & Hackney HA* [1997] 4 All ER 771.
[277] See below, paras 3.152–3.163.
[278] [1981] 1 All ER 257.
[279] ibid, 265 (emphasis added).
[280] [1984] 1 All ER 1018 (CA) and [1985] AC 871 (HL).

In *Sidaway*, the claimant underwent an operation upon her neck to relieve pain. Although she was told about the danger of disturbing a nerve root and the consequences of that, she was not told of the risk of damage to her spinal cord and the catastrophic consequences if, which it did, this happened. She sued unsuccessfully in the tort of negligence.[281] It was not argued that her claim could lie in battery.[282] In the Court of Appeal, the judges observed that the claimant had consented to the 'nature of the act'[283] (that is, the procedure carried out or 'the nature of what [was] to be done'),[284] hence her consent was 'real' for the purposes of battery. Dunn LJ expressly approved *Chatterton v Gerson*.[285] On appeal to the House of Lords, the contrary was simply not suggested and it was accepted that the claimant had given a valid consent.[286] Subsequently, in *Freeman v Home Office (No 2)*,[287] Sir John Donaldson MR stated:

> If there was real consent to the treatment, it matters not whether the doctor was in breach of his duty to give the patient the appropriate information before the consent was given. Real consent provides a complete defence to a claim in the tort of trespass to the person. . . . [S]ubject to the patient having been informed in broad terms of the nature of the treatment, consent in fact amounts to consent in law.

Thus, the law in England is clear and, though arguments can be made that the tort of battery could be extended,[288] there seems no prospect that the courts will do so.[289]

3.101   Other common law jurisdictions have taken the same view. The Canadian Supreme Court in *Reibl v Hughes*[290] and the Australian High Court in *Rogers v Whittaker*[291] have adopted the same demarcation line between battery and negligence.[292]

---

[281] See below, paras 3.122–3.133.

[282] This is clear from the transcript of the trial judgment of Skinner J delivered on 19 February 1982 (1977 S 8348).

[283] N 280 above, *per* Dunn LJ at 1029.

[284] ibid, *per* Sir John Donaldson MR at 1026; see also *per* Browne-Wilkinson LJ at 1032.

[285] N 266 above, 1029.

[286] [1985] 1 All ER 643 at 647 *per* Lord Scarman.

[287] [1984] 1 All ER 1036, 1044.

[288] See Somerville, M, 'Structuring the Issues in Informed Consent' (1981) 26 McGill LJ 740; and Keng Feng, T, 'Failure of Medical Advice: Trespass or Negligence?' (1987) 7 LS 149.

[289] See also *The Creutzfeldt-Jakob Disease Litigation* (1995) 54 BMLR 1 (May J) (no battery where parents not advised of the risk of CJD infection through human growth hormone or that the pituitary glands from which it came had been obtained unlawfully. The parents were aware of the nature of the act done).

[290] (1980) 114 DLR (3d) 1, especially *per* Laskin CJ at 10.

[291] (1992) 109 ALR 625, especially *per* Mason CJ, Brennan, Dawson, Toohey and McHugh JJ at 632–633.

[292] For a curious Australian decision where the court held it to be trespass when a patient underwent 'reduction mammoplasty' without being told of all the breast incisions which would be made, that there would be stitching, that there would be some loss of sensation, and that there would be some permanent scarring, see *D v S* (1981) LS (SA) JS 405.

What is Being Done   The notion of the 'nature' and 'purpose' of a procedure is   **3.102**
not limited to a factual description of the essence of what is being done. In addition to information which describes the act of the doctor, it also includes an account of the intrinsic quality of what is being done and, of course, why it is being
done. Hence, in other contexts for a woman to agree to the act of sexual intercourse (the 'act') is not, in law, for her to consent to it if she is wrongly led to believe that it is a medical treatment or voice training (the 'intrinsic quality').[293] She
has not consented to sexual intercourse even though she fully understood the 'act'
because the intrinsic quality of what she thought was being done was different.
Thus, in the medical context a patient who agrees to a procedure believing it to be
for his benefit (therapeutic) whilst, in fact, it is not because the doctor is conducting non-therapeutic research upon him, has not given a valid consent.[294]
Similarly, a doctor who carries out an unnecessary intimate examination of a
woman wholly for his own sexual gratification would commit a battery.[295]

The only reported English case in which a health care professional has been held   **3.103**
liable for battery where, on the face of it, the patient agreed to what was done is
Appleton v Garrett.[296] The claimants underwent at the hands of the defendant unnecessary dental work. The defendant carried out extensive restorative treatment
on teeth which were healthy for financial gain. Dyson J held that the defendant
had committed a battery on his patients. In respect of those teeth that were
healthy, the judge concluded that the patients' consents were not 'real'. The basis
for his decision is not clear but seems, in some part, to be based upon the defendant's fraud and 'bad faith'.[297] However, it is most certainly correct. The patients
did not consent even if they were aware of the nature of the 'act' performed by the
defendant. They were not aware of its 'intrinsic quality', namely that it was of no
benefit to them, in fact rather the contrary was the case. Agreeing to treatment on
unhealthy teeth is to agree to a fundamentally different act to that which was carried out.[298]

How far the courts will go in atomising the 'quality' of a touching by a doctor will,   **3.104**
ultimately, be a matter of policy and which will give rise to differences of judicial
opinion. In one case,[299] a majority of the Canadian Supreme Court held that a

---

[293] *R v Flattery* (1877) 2 QBD 410 and *R v Williams* [1923] 1 KB 340.
[294] *Halushka v University of Saskatchewan* (1965) 52 WWR 608.
[295] Contrast *R v Mobilio* [1991] 1 VR 339 where it was held that a patient had given a valid consent to unnecessary transvaginal ultrasound examinations by a technician because she knew 'the nature and character of the act which was done' (at 352). In England, the courts should not follow this
decision since the non-therapeutic character of the procedure changed the 'nature' and 'purpose' of
what was done.
[296] [1997] 8 Med LR 75 and Kennedy, (1996) 4 Med L Rev 311 (Commentary).
[297] On these see below, para 3.108.
[298] On this basis an English court would not follow *R v Mobilio* [1991] 1 VR 339 (n 295 above).
[299] *R v Bolduc and Bird* (1967) 63 DLR (2d) 82.

patient had given a valid consent to an intimate examination by a doctor in circumstances where he had done so in the presence of a friend, whom he had told the patient was a medical intern. The judges considered that the patient was aware of the 'nature and quality of the act to be done'. Spence J, however, dissented stating that the patient 'only gave [her] consent to such a serious invasion of her privacy on the basis that [the friend] was a doctor intending to commence practice and who desired practical experience in such matters . . .'.[300] At one level the disagreement can be seen as a semantic one but, in truth, it is over the proper scope of battery and the policy of the law.

3.105 A somewhat similar disagreement could arise in respect of a consent given by a person to the taking of a blood sample which is subsequently used for genetic testing or to determine the individual's HIV status. If the patient is only told about what is descriptively to be done (that is, the taking of blood and the method (the 'act') and that it will be used to 'run some tests'), will the person's consent be valid if they are unaware of the precise purpose that the blood will be put to? Is the person aware of the 'intrinsic quality' of what is being done? On one view, he is because he knows that it will be used for his benefit (the tests). On another view, however, it could be said that the significance of genetic and HIV testing for the person (and indeed others close to him) is such that without knowledge of that, the quality of the act is different.[301] Ultimately, however, the issue is a question of policy but given the potential for stigmatisation, discrimination, and personal anxiety to the person, it is suggested that the law should require explicit agreement in these situations.

3.106 **Who is Carrying Out the Procedure**   In some situations who is carrying out the procedure may affect the 'nature' and 'purpose' of what is being done. It is well recognised elsewhere in the law, for example the criminal law, that the identity of the actor may vitiate an individual's consent. Hence, in the law of rape the identity of the man with whom the woman is having sexual intercourse will be relevant.[302] The 'quality' of what is agreed to when a woman consents to sexual intercourse with a man who is impersonating her husband is affected by her misunderstanding. Even though she understands the nature of the 'act' (sexual intercourse), it is of a different 'quality' (adulterous) from that which she believes it to be (marital).[303] Likewise a patient who consents to be touched by a doctor will not, in law, have given a valid consent when she is touched by that person if he

---

[300] *R v Bolduc and Bird* (1967) 63 DLR (2d) 82, 87.

[301] For different views on this, and other analogous situations, of HIV testing, see Grubb, A and Pearl, D, *Blood Testing, AIDS and DNA Profiling* (Jordans, 1990), ch 1 and Keown, J (1989) 52 MLR 790.

[302] *R v Linekar* [1995] 3 All ER 69 and *R v Elbekkay* [1995] Crim LR 163.

[303] In fact, the criminal law goes further than this and regards any mistake as to identity as vitiating consent: see ibid. Quaere whether the 'quality' of the act changes in these cases?

turns out to be impersonating a doctor even if what is actually done is exactly what she expected.[304] The descriptive nature of the 'act' remains the same but its 'intrinsic quality' changes. So, in *R v Tabassum*[305] the defendant, claiming falsely to be a doctor, touched the breasts of a number of women in order to show them how to carry out breast self-examination. The Court of Appeal held that their consents were invalid. The women had consented to the nature of the act but not its quality since they had (wrongly) been led to believe it was a medical examination.[306]

However, the identity of the person carrying out the procedure will not always change the 'nature' or 'quality' of what has been agreed to by the patient. For example, a patient who agrees to a therapeutic procedure which, unbeknownst to him, is carried out by a student or trainee, will have given a valid consent since the 'quality' of the act will not change.[307] It would be different if the agreement was to a therapeutic procedure but the student carried out an unnecessary procedure *simply* in order to learn how to do it or to gain experience.[308] Then, the 'purpose' of the procedure would be radically changed and the patient's consent would not be valid.[309] A change in doctor would not, at least in England,[310] affect the consent given. Even if the patient expected a particular doctor to carry out the procedure, the consent form is likely to indicate that this is a misplaced expectation.[311] In any event, the nature and purpose of what is being done will not change. The only legal relevance of the change in doctor might be that the patient's consent was conditional on that doctor carrying out the procedure: if he did not then there was no consent by the patient at all.[312]

3.107

(b) Fraud and Misrepresentation

Does fraud or a misrepresentation by the doctor as to information about the procedure to be performed affect the validity of the patient's consent? In Canada, the Supreme Court has held that fraud or misrepresentation (even a negligent one)

3.108

---

[304] *R v Maurantonio* (1967) 65 DLR (2d) 674. See also *De May v Roberts* (1881) 9 NW 146.

[305] [2000] Lloyd's Rep Med 404 (CA).

[306] But a mere change in status or qualifications will not affect the 'nature' or 'quality of what is being done. For example, in *R v Richardson* (1998) 43 BMLR 21 (CA) the Court of Appeal held that a dentist had not committed an assault when she treated a patient even though, unknown to the patient, she had been suspended from practice by the General Dentist Council. The patient's consent to the treatment was valid. The patient's misunderstanding about 'the qualifications or attributes' of the defendant was irrelevant.

[307] Good practice is, however, that explicit consent be obtained: See, *Reference Guide to Consent for Examination or Treatment* (n 77 above), 5 (para 4.1).

[308] Explicitly informing the patient that the procedure is not part of his care is described as a *legal* requirement, ibid 5 (para 4.1).

[309] See above, para 3.102.

[310] But see *Perna v Pirozzi* (1983) 457 A 2d 431.

[311] See DoH, *Good Practice in Consent Implementation Guide* (n 118 above), at 35—Model Form 1.

[312] *Perna v Pirozzi* (n 310 above).

will unravel what would otherwise be a valid consent.[313] It would seem that in Canada there will not be a valid consent in these circumstances even though it is 'real', in other words, even though the patient understands the 'nature' and 'purpose' of the procedure. Fraud or misrepresentation as to collateral matters will suffice.[314] In England, the position is otherwise. Notwithstanding one or two broader statements at first instance,[315] the only issue in England is whether the patient has understood the 'nature' and 'purpose' of the procedure. A misunderstanding of that may, of course, arise through fraud or misrepresentation, but it may arise simply through mistake by the patient. If fraud or misrepresentation has occurred, that may provide good evidence that the patient's consent was not 'real'. But, it is the non-consent to the procedure rather than the fraud which makes an apparent consent not a real one.[316] Fraud or misrepresentation as to a collateral matter, such as an inherent risk in the procedure or an alternative procedure, will not, however, affect the patient's consent. In *Sidaway*,[317] Sir John Donaldson MR stated that:

> [I]t is only if the consent is obtained by fraud or by misrepresentation of the nature of what is to be done that it can be said that an apparent consent is not a true consent.

Of course, the patient may have an action in deceit or negligent misrepresentation in such circumstances but he will not have a claim in battery. In England there is no so-called 'fraud exception' to the 'nature' and 'purpose' rule.[318]

(ii) Negligence

(a) Introduction

3.109 When a doctor or other health care professional has no consent at all to touch someone, it has been seen that an action in battery will lie at the suit of the person touched unless some justifying or excusing circumstance exists.[319] It has also been seen, however, that English law is reluctant to see the law of battery invoked in the

---

[313] *Reibl v Hughes* (1980) 114 DLR (3d) 1, 11 *per* Laskin CJ.

[314] But contrast *Lokay v Kilgour* (1984) 31 CCLT 177 (misrepresentation must go to 'the very nature of the procedure'). See discussion in Picard, E and Robertson, G, *Legal Liability of Doctors and Hospitals in Canada* (3rd edn, 1996), 57–60.

[315] *Chatterton v Gerson* (n 266 above), 265 *per* Bristow J and *Appleton v Garrett* (n 296 above), 77 *per* Dyson J.

[316] See, in the context of rape, *R v Linekar* [1995] 3 All ER 69, 73 *per* Morland J. See also *R v Richardson* (n 306 above) *per* Otton LJ at 26.

[317] [1984] 1 All ER 1018, 1026. See also Dunn LJ at 1029.

[318] Notice, however, the remark of Sir John Donaldson MR in *Freeman v Home Office (No 2)* [1984] 1 All ER 1036 at 1044 apparently recognising a wider 'fraud exception'. *Freeman* was decided two weeks after *Sidaway* in the Court of Appeal and it is most unlikely that the Master of the Rolls intended to recant on his clear statement in *Sidaway*.

[319] See above, paras 3.01 *et seq*.

context of medical care.[320] Thus, provided that the person touched knows 'in broad terms'[321] the general nature and purpose of the touching, this will be regarded as sufficient to constitute a valid consent, so as to defeat a claim in battery.

But this is not the end of the story. Any purported consent must also meet the **3.110** requirements of the tort of negligence. This immediately needs explanation. Negligence is concerned not with the presence or absence of consent, but with the defendant's failure to comply with a legally imposed duty of care. Thus, if the tort of negligence is to have a role, two matters must be established: that a *duty* exists and the *content* of that duty (the *quantum* of care demanded). Clearly, a duty exists to take care not to harm the patient through careless acts. But what is being considered here are not the doctor's acts. Instead, the concern is with what the doctor must do *prior to* acting, so as to ensure that proper consent has been given for those acts. In particular, the concern is with the knowledge or information which the patient is entitled to be given (assuming the patient to be competent), before any purported consent is valid. It is important to recognise that, where any complaint arises, what the patient is complaining of is not that a particular procedure was carried out without proper care and skill (it may have been performed with the utmost skill), but rather, that it was carried out without proper permission.

Expressed in this way, it is immediately apparent that if the patient is entitled to **3.111** be informed, the doctor is under a duty to provide the information.[322] To so assert, however, is to place on the doctor a duty of affirmative action. It is trite law that English law regards such a duty as exceptional. While it is one thing to expect people to refrain from careless behaviour, English law, with its aversion to the 'officious intermeddler',[323] will not ordinarily impose a duty to do something on behalf of another. The first step, therefore, is to examine the legal basis for the doctor's duty to inform a patient, so as to obtain valid consent to treatment.

(b) A Duty to Inform

One well-established ground on which a duty to inform could be based would be **3.112** to find that, as between the doctor and the patient, there exists a 'special relationship', giving rise to a duty to act. The traditional example is the parent–child and, by extension, the teacher–child relationship. In effect, therefore, the duty is

---

[320] See above, para 3.98.

[321] *per* Bristow J in *Chatterton v Gerson* (n 266 above), and see *Hills v Potter* (n 274 above). See further, Kennedy and Grubb, *Medical Law* (n 51 above), 651 *et seq.*

[322] When the patient is a child the duty is discharged by advising the child's parents or whoever has parental responsibility for the child: *Thomson v James* (1997) 41 BMLR 144 (CA) (duty to advise parents so as to put them in a position to make an informed decision whether to consent to immunisation for measles). See also *Poynter v Hillingdon HA* (1997) 37 BMLR 192 (Sir Maurice Drake).

[323] See, eg, the discussion in Birks, P, *Introduction to the Law of Restitution* (OUP, 1989), 102–3.

derived from the status of the parties. The common law has not, however, regarded the doctor–patient relationship as falling into the category of special relationship. Its legal origins lay in the law of contract and thus in an assumption that the parties were at arm's length. The notion of vulnerability which underpins the law's recognition of a special relationship, while clearly a central feature of modern medicine, did not colour the earlier development of the law. Thus, a duty to inform cannot be derived from the existence of a special relationship.

3.113   An alternative ground on which English law could base an affirmative duty to inform can be derived from the law of equity. If the relationship between the doctor and patient were fiduciary in nature, a duty to inform could be readily recognised, as an incidence of the more general duty to seek to maximise the interests of the beneficiary. This was the approach adopted by certain courts in the United States.[324] Since these courts had previously categorised the doctor–patient relationship as fiduciary, they had little difficulty in carving out and developing a duty to inform. English law, however, has never regarded the doctor–patient relationship as fiduciary. Indeed, when asked to do so, the House of Lords expressly refused.[325] Furthermore, despite some academic support for the idea,[326] it is unlikely that there will be a change of mind. Thus, any duty to inform cannot be based on a fiduciary relationship.

3.114   So, where does the duty come from? Curiously, when the English courts very belatedly got round to examining whether a doctor is under a duty to inform a patient, the legal-technical difficulties involved in actually finding some juristic basis for a duty of affirmative action were largely ignored. Instead, the general duty of care owed by a doctor to a patient was interpreted as extending not only to acts but also omissions, in this case the failure properly to inform.[327] As ever, the law of torts displayed the English law's preference for pragmatism over principle. From an analytical point of view, what this appears to mean is that once a doctor's assistance has been sought and the doctor has undertaken to offer treatment (that is, a doctor–patient relationship has come into existence), this undertaking includes a duty to act affirmatively on the patient's behalf. This, in turn, translates into a duty to inform so as to obtain from a patient a valid consent.

3.115   As regards the existence of the duty, the remaining point to notice is the point at which the duty arises and for how long it continues. Clearly, it arises whenever the

---

[324] See, eg, *Canterbury v Spence* (n 264 above), and *Cobbs v Grant* (1972) 502 P 2d 1.

[325] In *Sidaway v Board of Governors of the Bethlem Royal Hospital* (n 265 above), 650–651.

[326] See eg, Bartlett, 'Doctors as Fiduciaries' (1997) 5 Med L Rev 193 and Grubb, 'The Doctor as Fiduciary' [1994] CLP 311.

[327] See, eg, the speech of Lord Scarman in *Sidaway* (n 265 above), 652, '[i]f it be recognised that a doctor's duty of care extends not only to the health and well-being of his patient but also to a proper respect for his patient's rights, the duty to warn [and, generally, to inform] can be seen to be a part of the doctor's duty of care'.

doctor proposes a therapeutic intervention. Valid consent must be obtained prior to embarking on therapy, whether it involves touching the patient or prescribing medicines or other such treatment. Moreover, it is a continuing duty—consent is a process rather than a one-off event.[328] This has two implications. First, the doctor should confirm that any previously given consent continues to be in effect at the time the procedure is to be carried out.[329] The longer the gap, the more likely that circumstances may require a fresh discussion between doctor and patient. Secondly, whenever the doctor engages in any new or additional therapeutic intervention, not covered by the previous consent, there arises a fresh duty to obtain consent and, thus, to inform before proceeding. This is rather easier to stipulate than apply, as cases in the United States demonstrate.[330] The general law may well be that where the doctor intends to embark on a course of conduct which is sufficiently different from that previously agreed to and as regards which the appropriate legal standard would demand that the patient be informed, a new duty to inform arises. This analysis is somewhat delphic because it will be clear that the separation between the existence of a duty and its content breaks down in this situation. If the duty to inform is part of the duty of care, then, depending on who determines the extent of that duty, a new duty will arise when the extent of that duty is exceeded. Whether it is exceeded depends, therefore, on who determines its extent.

(c) Content of the Duty

The first question to ask is what sort of information could a duty to disclose be **3.116** concerned with? Obviously, the range includes information about the proposed procedure, risks which arise from it, their likelihood and the consequences if they eventuate, other therapeutic options which exist, including the option not to receive any treatment at all, and the implications of these options.

The next question, of course, is what, from this range, is the doctor under a duty **3.117** to pass on to the patient? Analytically, this translates into the question, what is the criterion by reference to which the duty is determined in law. Beginning from the first principles, there are at least *three options*.

The *first* is that the doctor should be under a duty to pass on all that information **3.118** which the patient being treated wishes to know. This is a subjective test. The underlying philosophy is rights-based. The patient has a right to know as a necessary feature of the overarching right to self-determination. Even as stated, however,

---

[328] See *Reference Guide to Consent for Examination or Treatment* (n 77 above), at 8 (para 10).
[329] See ibid, at 8 (para 10) and at 10 (para 16.1).
[330] See Kennedy (1995) 3 Med L Rev 209 (Commentary), on the cases of *Rizzo v Schiller* (1994) 445 SE 2d 153 and *Sinclair by Sinclair v Block* (1993) 663 A 2d 1137, both of which involved the question whether a separate and further consent was called for before resort to forceps during childbirth, given the specific and new risks associated therewith.

this criterion is not free from difficulty. Should it be expressed as what the patient wishes to know or what the patient would wish to know (if only he knew)? The former is hard enough to satisfy. The latter verges on the impossible.

3.119 A *second* option is that the doctor should pass on that information which any reasonable patient would wish to know before giving consent. The weakness of this approach is clear. It is a compromise. It purports to take account of the patient's right to be informed but does so at the cost of converting the actual patient into a hypothetical reasonable patient. To that extent, the particular circumstances of the patient are in danger of being ignored. At some point, indeed, the purported subjectivity of the test could evaporate into an objective examination of reasonableness.

3.120 A *third* option is that the doctor's duty should be to inform the patient of that which doctors as a profession think it appropriate for the patient to know. Clearly, this test has no element of subjectivity. It reflects a philosophy of paternalism, according to which the doctor is the better judge of what should inform the medical transaction. Not surprisingly, this option has not been free from criticism in an age in which paternalism has fewer defenders.[331] Quite apart from any ethical attack, the option is vulnerable to at least two further criticisms. First, it assumes that information relevant to making a decision about treatment is a matter of technical medical expertise, properly within the purview of medical expertise. Clearly, diagnosis, treatment and prognosis are uniquely matters of medical expertise. How to respond to these; whether to go ahead and accept (ie consent to) treatment, seems to be of a different order. If anything, it would appear to be uniquely within the competence of the patient (the first option set out earlier). Certainly, it would appear hard to describe it as within the *unique* competence of doctors. This is not to say that doctors should have no role in setting the boundaries of the process of gaining consent. If patients expect them to be sensitive in how they communicate what may sometimes be difficult news, doctors are entitled to make judgments as to how to proceed. But this concerns the 'how' of imparting information, which is undoubtedly a matter of medical expertise. It does not relate to 'whether' to inform, which is what is of concern here. It is hard to see how this is a matter for doctors alone. The second criticism which can be raised is that, if the content of the doctor's duty is to pass on that information which other doctors would, it assumes a degree of professional agreement which is unlikely to be demonstrable in practice. Doctors clearly and quite properly may disagree on diagnosis or treatment. There is, however, some structure of learning about these which all (or virtually all) accept and to which all refer, even though they may derive divergent views from it. There is no such body of learning concerning what information a patient should be told which all doctors accept and draw upon.

---

[331] See eg Brazier, M, *Medicine, Patients and the Law* (3rd edn, Penguin, 2003), 99 *et seq*.

Thus, the idea of a professional standard of disclosure may proceed from a completely false premise.

Whatever the weaknesses of this third option, it represents the current position in English law. The starting point for an examination of the doctor's duty of care must, of course, be *Bolam v Friern Barnet HMC*.[332] As has been suggested, this case established that the criterion against which a doctor's conduct falls to be judged is whether it complies with the views of a responsible body of medical opinion.[333] Put another way, to prove breach of duty a patient would have to show that no responsible doctor would have done what was done. The shortcomings of this approach are well known and set out elsewhere.[334] Equally, a slow reappraisal of *Bolam* by the higher courts has been taking place.[335] Thus, there are two matters of importance here. The first is to notice the effect which *Bolam* had on the duty to inform, culminating in the leading case in the House of Lords, *Sidaway v Governors of Bethlem Royal Hospital*.[336] The second is to enquire what any reappraisal of *Bolam* may mean for the law as currently set out in *Sidaway*. **3.121**

(d) Sidaway v Governors of the Bethlem Royal Hospital[337]

Mrs Sidaway brought an action against the Hospital complaining that she had not been warned, when she consented to surgery on her neck to relieve pain, that it carried a small but acknowledged risk of causing damage to the spinal column and nerve roots. Her surgeon had died before the trial, thus making it impossible to establish what precisely passed between him and Mrs Sidaway. For this reason alone, Mrs Sidaway's case was lost. But the courts, right up to and including the House of Lords, opted to take the opportunity to set out the law on the duty to inform. **3.122**

It may seem remarkable that English law had to wait until 1985 for an authoritative statement of the law. Indeed, prior to the *Sidaway* case, there had been only two first reported instance decisions (other than *Bolam*, which, inter alia, was concerned with the doctor's duty to inform) which had clearly addressed the question and both were in the early 1980s.[338] The explanation is complex but, at bottom, reflects the emerging clash between the traditional reluctance to challenge the **3.123**

---

[332] N 276 above. For a critical appraisal of *Bolam*, see Kennedy and Grubb (n 51 above), 440 *et seq*.

[333] 'A doctor is not guilty of negligence if he has acted in accordance with a practice accepted as proper by a responsible body of medical men skilled in that particular art', ibid, *per* McNair J.

[334] See eg Kennedy and Grubb (n 51 above), 424 *et seq*.

[335] *Bolitho v City and Hackney HA* (n 296 above) represents the current (and less than satisfactory) state of reappraisal. See Rt Hon the Lord Woolf, 'Are the Courts Excessively Deferential to the Medical Profession?' (2001) 9 Med L Rev 1.

[336] N 265 above.

[337] ibid. For a detailed analysis of the case, see Kennedy, *Treat Me Right* (Oxford, 1992), ch 9. See also Brazier (n 331 above); and Kennedy and Grubb (n 51 above), 680 *et seq*.

[338] *Chatterton v Gerson* (n 266 above) and *Hills v Potter* (n 274 above), decided in 1981 and 1984.

long-established acquiescence and a preparedness to hold professionals to account.[339]

3.124 **Lord Diplock** There are *three* distinct strands in the speeches delivered by their Lordships in *Sidaway*.[340] The first is that of Lord Diplock. To him, the duty to inform was not a separate duty but part of the overarching duty of care owed by the doctor to the patient. The doctor's 'normal duty of care . . . has hitherto been treated as a single comprehensive duty covering all the ways in which a doctor is called upon to exercise his skill and judgement . . .'.[341]

3.125 Lord Diplock stated that:

> this general duty is not subject to dissection into a number of component parts to which different criteria of what satisfy the duty of care apply, such as diagnosis, treatment, advice (including warning of any risks of something going wrong however skilfully the treatment advised is carried out).[342]

3.126 The content of this duty was set out in *Bolam*. Thus, *Bolam* in all its deferential glory, applies in failure to warn cases. The doctor's duty in obtaining a patient's consent is to provide the patient with that information which a responsible body of doctors would judge to be appropriate. If, therefore, doctors in their wisdom choose to withhold certain information, out of a concern, as they see it, for the patient's interests, it is not for the courts to gainsay them. The extent and limits of the doctor's duty to disclose are, therefore, *per* Lord Diplock, for doctors to determine, through expert evidence of contemporary professional practice. The third of the options set out in para 3.120 above prevails.

3.127 **Lord Bridge** The second strand is that developed by Lord Bridge and, with some variation, Lord Templeman. Lord Bridge, with whose speech Lord Keith concurred, also relied on *Bolam*. But, he then appeared to add a gloss which suggests that the content of the duty to inform may, for him, be more than just *Bolam* simpliciter. For, in his speech, Lord Bridge insisted that the doctor's duty must '*primarily* be a matter of clinical judgement', and thus to be derived from *Bolam*.[343] Undoubtedly, the reason for his adding this rider was his anxiety not to

---

[339] See further Kennedy (n 337 above).

[340] For a different interpretation, see Jones, *Medical Negligence* (3rd edn, Sweet & Maxwell, 2003), 524 *et seq*. Jones' view, when originally advanced in his first edition in 1991, required what was at the time a heroic reading of *Bolam*, not previously endorsed by the courts. The House of Lords' decision in *Bolitho* (n 276 above) suggests that while the courts may not have realised it, Jones was right all the time.

[341] *Sidaway* (n 265 above), 657.

[342] ibid.

[343] *Sidaway* (n 265 above), 663 (emphasis added). Lord Bridge had previously spent some time analysing North American jurisprudence, particularly the cases of *Canterbury v Spence* (n 264 above), and *Reibl v Hughes* (n 263 above). While he 'appreciate[d] the force of [the] reasoning', he chose not to follow it, for reasons which are less than wholly persuasive, see Kennedy (n 337 above).

be seen to be handing over the content of the duty entirely to the medical profession. In this regard, he can be seen to be echoing the similarly cryptic assertion of Sir John Donaldson MR in the Court of Appeal, when he held that, 'the duty is fulfilled if the doctor acts in accordance with a practice rightly accepted as proper by a body of skilled and experienced medical men'.[344] The difficulty, however, lies in understanding what, if anything, Lord Bridge's gloss amounts to. He did provide some guidance. He intimated that where the circumstances were such as to give rise to a 'substantial risk of grave adverse consequences',[345] the doctor could well be under a duty to inform the patient, whatever the prevailing medical view. The example Lord Bridge chose to illustrate this proposition was the circumstances which arose in the Canadian Supreme Court case of *Reibl v Hughes*.[346] In that case, there was a 10 per cent risk of a stroke following surgery. 'In such a case', Lord Bridge averred, 'in the absence of some cogent clinical reason why the patient should not be informed, a doctor, recognising and respecting his patient's right of decision, could hardly fail to appreciate the necessity for an appropriate warning.'[347]

It is clear that, by his gloss on *Bolam*, Lord Bridge was seeking to articulate the view that doctors ordinarily were entitled to set the legal standard of disclosure, but at some point, where the patient might be expected to want a say in things, the doctor could not merely rely on what fellow professionals did but must take account of what the patient may wish to know, indeed the patient's right to know. Lord Bridge's approach may, therefore, be categorised as a combination of old-fashioned paternalism and, at some ill-defined point, modern consumerism based on patients' rights. Quite apart from the unattractiveness of the former and the difficulty in operating the latter, a further weakness lies in knowing when the latter is supposed to displace *Bolam*. The words 'substantial risk of grave adverse consequences' are particularly unhelpful, not least because the question of who determines 'substantial' or 'grave' is the same question as who sets the content of the duty. Furthermore, it is unhelpful to offer by way of guidance an approach based on percentages. Not only does this purport to reduce what is a matter of values to a mathematical calculation, but it also invites medical experts to shift the argument from whether the profession would have informed the patient, to the probability, in percentage terms, of an occurrence and its comparative gravity. Furthermore, it confuses the likelihood of something happening with its gravity,[348] if it does. It is trite to observe that a 1 per cent risk of catastrophic injury may be less attractive than a 20 per cent risk of minor inconvenience. Thus, while Lord

3.128

---

[344] *Sidaway* [1984] 1 All ER 1018, 1028 (emphasis added) (CA).
[345] *Sidaway v Bethlem Royal Hospital Governors* (n 265 above).
[346] N 313 above.
[347] *Sidaway* (n 265 above), 663.
[348] See further, Kennedy (n 337 above).

Bridge's endorsement of *Bolam* was not wholesale, it is not easy to determine what he seeks to add to it. It is not entirely clear that he has adopted the second of the options set out in para 3.119 above, although not wholly endorsing the third. It may not come as a surprise, therefore, that Lord Bridge's speech, though much pored over by commentators, has not been taken up by later courts.

3.129   **Lord Templeman**   Turning to the speech of Lord Templeman, it too equivocates between an acceptance of *Bolam* and a hint of something more. The difficulty lies in identifying precisely what it is that Lord Templeman adds to *Bolam*. The key appears to lie in the distinction he draws between 'general' dangers (or risks), and 'special' dangers.[349] As regards the former, 'a simple and general explanation . . . should have been sufficient to alert [the patient]'.[350] At least, therefore, there is some duty to inform, albeit vestigial. As regards the latter dangers (or risks), the doctor is under a duty to inform the patient. There is, for Lord Templeman, 'no doubt that a doctor ought to draw the attention of a patient to a danger which may be special in kind or magnitude or special to the patient'.[351] Two objections can immediately be made to Lord Templeman's differentiation of these categories of danger or risk. The first is that it may be wrong as a matter both of fact and policy to assume that all patients are aware of, and, therefore, the doctor has no duty to warn of, 'general' risks, such as the risks arising from anaesthesia.[352] Secondly, the terms 'general' and 'special', are not terms of art and it is fair to say that Lord Templeman's attempt to differentiate them is not wholly clear. Indeed, he ultimately falls back on the flawed idea of percentages, endorsed by Lord Bridge. Moreover, it must be self-evident that what might be 'general' to one patient may be 'special' to another, depending on their different circumstances. Thus, the central issue remains unsolved, namely who it is who defines and operates these criteria, the medical profession or the court. In summary, therefore, if Lord Templeman does regard the doctor's duty as being more than *Bolam* (and it is certainly arguable that he does), his speech, when read as a whole, is at best equivocal and certainly does not offer a clear guide.

3.130   **Lord Scarman**   Lord Scarman took a different track from the rest of the court. To him the argument was ultimately one of rights.[353] In analysing the issue in this way, Lord Scarman distanced himself from the other Law Lords. To that extent, although all of their Lordships concurred in dismissing Mrs Sidaway's appeal, Lord Scarman's speech is often referred to as if he were in dissent. For Lord

---

[349] *Sidaway* (n 265 above), 664–665.
[350] ibid, 664.
[351] ibid, 665.
[352] Compare Lord Scarman's view, ibid, 654.
[353] '[T]he doctor's duty arises from his patient's rights', ibid, 654.

Scarman, a patient has a right to know[354] what treatment entails so as to be able to make a reasoned choice and, thus, give a valid consent. This right, he held, finds its expression in English law in the doctor's duty to inform the patient. Unlike Lord Diplock, Lord Scarman was prepared to see that the duty to provide information is of a different order from the duty to take care in treatment. It is not, for Lord Scarman, a matter to be decided solely on the basis of evidence as to prevailing medical practice. This is not to say that Lord Scarman regarded such evidence as irrelevant.[355] It is, of course, relevant, but, beginning from a premisse of patients' rights, it cannot be determinative.

Lord Scarman chose as his guide the case law which had evolved in both the **3.131** United States and Canada in the previous two decades, particularly *Canterbury v Spence*[356] and *Reibl v Hughes*[357] respectively. Although not prepared analytically to adopt the rights-based approach reflected in the North American doctrine of 'informed consent', preferring the common law's duty approach, he was clearly persuaded of the underlying correctness of these cases. But, if Lord Scarman recognised a duty to inform a patient, how did he respond to the oft-repeated sore that this would put every doctor under a legal obligation to pass on to the patient in, at most, a couple of conversations, what it had taken the doctor years of medical school and experience to acquire? Though such rhetoric may go down well at school reunions, it is, of course, an example of *reductio ad absurdum*. What the law can properly expect of doctors, on Lord Scarman's approach, is that they provide the patient with sufficient, or adequate, information to make a considered decision. It could not require, nor has it ever been suggested, that the doctor pass on to the patient everything there is to know about a condition or its treatment.

How is this general idea of the doctor's duty translated by Lord Scarman into more **3.132** detailed law? He first settles on the concept of 'materiality' found in the North American cases. The doctor is under a duty to inform the patient of that information which is 'material' to making a decision.[358] This, in turn, causes Lord Scarman to have to identify what 'material' means. At this point, it is clear that Lord Scarman must choose whether to prefer the first or the second of the options set out in paras 3.118 and 3.119 above (he obviously rejects the third). Information could be material, and thus the doctor would be under a duty to disclose it to the patient, if it were something which the particular patient would wish to know, or, if it were that which a reasonable patient, in the particular patient's

---

[354] Indeed, Lord Scarman termed it a 'basic human right', ibid, 649, terminology which acquires added significance as English law moves gradually to an acceptance of rights-based arguments following the incorporation of the ECHR into English law.

[355] ibid, 654.

[356] N 264 above.

[357] N 313 above.

[358] *Sidaway* (n 265 above), 655.

circumstances, would wish to know. The analytical difficulties associated with adopting the former meaning were referred to in para 3.118. It is also important to notice a pragmatic difficulty. A court hearing a claim in negligence based on a doctor's alleged breach of the duty to inform could be met with evidence from the patient that, had a particular fact been disclosed, he would never have agreed to the procedure which was carried out. If believed, the patient would prevail. However, this may be to cast too onerous a burden on doctors. The law would, in effect, allow them to be judged against the 20/20 vision of hindsight.[359]

3.133   It is not entirely surprising, therefore, that Lord Scarman chose to define 'material' by reference to the reasonable patient, following and endorsing the reasoning in *Reibl* and *Canterbury*. '[T]he duty [to warn] is confined to material risk. The test of materiality is whether in the circumstances of the particular case the court is satisfied that a reasonable person in the patient's position would be likely to attach significance to the risk.'[360] The duty to disclose, therefore, was made subject to the traditional constraint of the tort of negligence—that reasonableness should be a central feature. Lord Scarman then went on to add a further constraint to the duty. To meet the frequent objection (evidence for which is not easily obtained) that it would be better not to inform a patient of certain matters, Lord Scarman added to his analysis a further element: what is called in North America the 'therapeutic privilege'. By this, a doctor is absolved from the duty to inform if, by complying with it the patient would suffer more harm than good. A commonly cited example is the patient who needs an operation but has an abiding fear of anaesthesia, such that, if advised of the risks involved, he might refuse the operation. In such a case, it is argued that the doctor should have a discretion not to inform that patient, out of a concern for the wider interests of the patient. Expressed in this way, the potential drawbacks of the doctrine are immediately apparent. It marks a reversion to the paternalism of *Bolam*, which, if not carefully controlled, could have the effect of reintroducing the professional standard of whether to inform through the back door. Nonetheless, Lord Scarman recognised the validity, in principle, of the doctrine and with suitable words of warning[361] made it part of his overall design for the duty to inform.

3.134   **Breach of Duty**   A final question which should be asked relates to breach of duty. What must the doctor do so as to comply with the duty to inform? Must the

---

[359] See Lord Scarman's remarks: 'Ideally, the court should ask itself whether in the particular circumstances the risk was such that this particular patient would think it significant if he was told it existed. I would think that, as a matter of ethics, this is the test of the doctor's duty. The law, however, operates not in Utopia but in the world as it is: and such an enquiry would prove in practice to be frustrated by the subjectivity of its aim and purpose', ibid, 654.

[360] ibid. It is important to note that, although Lord Scarman referred only to risks, he accepted that the duty to inform extends also to information about alternatives: '. . . the options of alternative treatment', as he put it, ibid, 645.

[361] '[I]t is a defence available to the doctor which, if he invokes it, he must prove', ibid, 654.

doctor make sure that the patient *has understood* what he has been told or need the doctor only *take reasonable steps* to ensure that this is so? Clearly, the former is a particularly onerous duty and, some might argue, impossible to achieve. The doctor may inform, using the best possible techniques of communication, until the cows come home but the patient may still not understand. The view has prevailed, therefore, that English law only requires the doctor to behave reasonably.[362] The issue arose in *Smith v Tunbridge Wells HA*.[363] In that case, Moreland J took what, on its face, seems a rather surprising view. He stated '. . . the doctor, when warning of the risks, must take reasonable care to ensure that his explanation of the risks is intelligible to his patient'. So far, so good. The doctor must behave reasonably and 'ensure' (strong word) that the explanation is 'intelligible' (weaker word). Intelligible only means that someone is capable of understanding, not, critically, that he does so. But then Moreland J goes on to say that: '[t]he doctor should use language [which] . . . will be understood by the patient.' This, with respect, cannot be right, if it means that the doctor must make the patient understand. It would cast too great a burden on the doctor, as well as threaten to bring into disrepute the very notion of the duty to inform (which, in any event. is not without its detractors).[364]

Summary At the end of this review of the three strands in the *Sidaway* case, it **3.135** may be helpful to draw them together to identify what the case on its face decided. The House of Lords held that the doctor's duty to inform is part of the duty to exercise reasonable care and skill. The content of the duty is governed, wholly or in very large part, by the *Bolam* principle: a doctor must pass on to the patient that information which, according to medical evidence, is thought appropriate by a responsible body of medical opinion. The speeches of Lords Bridge and Templeman add a somewhat indistinct caveat to *Bolam*, in somewhat ill-defined circumstances, suggesting some limit to the operation of *Bolam* in the context of the duty to inform. The North American doctrine of 'informed consent' (always something of a misnomer) is not part of English law. The 'reasonable patient' test, adopted by *Reibl* and espoused by Lord Scarman, is equally not part of English law. As a consequence, the doctrine of the therapeutic privilege, only necessary, if at all, if there were a prima facie right to know, is not part of English law.

(e) Gold v Haringey HA [365]

It is trite law that cases become authority for those propositions which courts later **3.136** identify as the ones which they intend to follow. After *Sidaway*, there was genuine

---

[362] *Lybert v Warrington HA* [1996] 7 Med LR 71 (CA).
[363] [1994] 5 Med LR 334.
[364] See further, on *Smith*, Grubb (1995) 3 Med L Rev 198, 201 (Commentary) and Kennedy and Grubb (n 51 above), 767–8.
[365] [1988] QB 481.

disagreement as to its precise significance. It was recognised that a later court could not follow Lord Scarman, since he was in a minority of one. What was important was whether the doctrine emerging from *Sidaway* was seen as being '*Bolam* simpliciter' or '*Bolam* plus', and if the latter, what the 'plus' element might be. It was not a long wait. Within two years, in *Gold*, the Court of Appeal, in the person of Lloyd LJ (with whom Watkins and Stephen Brown LJJ agreed), came down firmly on the side of *Bolam* simpliciter. In referring to *Sidaway*, Lloyd LJ chose to rely exclusively on the speech of Lord Diplock. The apparent agonising of Lords Bridge and Templeman did not appear to move him. Thus, the doctor's duty to inform was to be measured not by what the patient, or a reasonable patient, would wish to know so as to make an informed choice, but by what a responsible body of medical opinion would regard as proper to tell him.[366]

3.137　The fact that the first law relating to what, in ethical terms, is seen to be a critical aspect of the doctor–patient relationship did not emerge until the early to mid-1980s was remarkable enough. Even more remarkable, perhaps, is the fact that in two years the courts had travelled backwards to *Bolam*, while other jurisdictions scrambled to consign the medical paternalism and lack of concern for patients' rights, which *Bolam* can be said to represent, to the archives. Any attempt to explain the courts' preference for *Bolam* cannot, of course, overlook the traditional tenderness which, despite all claims to the contrary, the law has shown to the medical profession. Nor can it overlook the aversion to the possibility of an increase in malpractice litigation which the courts routinely display. Beyond these and a natural conservatism, it is hard to find an explanation for so significant a dissonance between prevailing ethical analysis and public opinion on the one hand and the judicial response on the other.

(f)　The Duty to Answer Questions

3.138　It is possible, of course, to draw some distinction between an affirmative duty to volunteer information and a duty to respond to questions. The latter seems that much more recognisable as a legal duty, since it assumes an existing relationship between doctor and patient. On reflection, however, both derive from an undertaking of responsibility and, thus, are both aspects of the general duty to exercise due care and skill. To say that there is a duty to respond is not, however, to indicate the content of the duty. Remarkably, in this day and age, it remains an issue whether the duty is to answer truthfully, or to give that answer which a responsible body of the medical profession would regard as appropriate, even if it is only part of the truth or no truth at all. This distinction can only exist, of course, if

---

[366] The view taken in *Gold* has subsequently been followed in a number of cases, eg, *Palmer v Eadie* (CA, 18 May 1987); *Blyth v Bloomsbury HA* [1993] 4 Med LR 151 (CA); *Moyes v Lothian Health Board* [1990] 1 Med LR 463 (CS, OH); and see *Powell v Boldaz* (1997) 39 BMLR 35 (CA). See further, Kennedy and Grubb (n 51 above), 704–6.

there is a view within the medical profession that truth is not always the appropriate option.

That such a view used to exist emerged in the well-known case of *Hatcher v Black*.[367] **3.139**
Moreover, in that case, Lord Denning went so far as to endorse it, remarking that, while not telling the truth to a patient might be ethically wrong, it was not necessarily a breach of the doctor's duty of care in law, if it conformed with professional practice. '[The doctor] told a lie, but he did it because he thought that in the circumstances it was justifiable . . . [T]he law does not condemn the doctor when he only does that which many a wise and good doctor would do.'[368] That was in 1954. By the time *Sidaway* reached the House of Lords, it may be thought that attitudes had changed. The speech of Lord Bridge, with which Lords Diplock and Templeman agreed on this point, suggested that they had. Lord Bridge stated unequivocally that '[w]hen questioned specifically by a patient . . . about risks involved in a particular treatment proposed, the doctor's duty must, in my opinion, be to answer truthfully and as fully as the questioner requires'.[369] Thus, it seemed, at least that part of the duty to inform which involved answering questions was not to be governed by *Bolam*.[370] But this was to reckon without the Court of Appeal. Initially in *Blyth v Bloomsbury HA*,[371] the Court of Appeal stepped back from the more onerous duty postulated in *Sidaway*. A doctor was not under a duty to respond truthfully when asked a question; rather, the duty was as laid down in *Bolam*.[372] Thankfully, the Court of Appeal has now restored the *Sidaway* position. In *Pearce v United Bristol Healthcare NHS Trust*[373] Lord Woolf MR stated that, 'if a patient asks a doctor about the risk, then the doctor is required to give an honest answer'.

This is more in tune with emerging concerns within the judiciary,[374] the medical **3.140**
profession[375] and the Government[376] to respect patients' rights and to be less deferential to evidence of professional practice. Frankly, any retrenchment is likely to fall foul of a challenge under the European Convention which—in both spirit and substance—is likely to orientate the law towards more, rather than less, disclosure of information.[377]

---

[367] The Times, 2 July 1954.
[368] ibid.
[369] *Sidaway* (n 265 above).
[370] Expert evidence would, at least, be relevant in determining the risks and alternatives: for an analysis of the steps involved in answering a question, see Kennedy and Grubb (n 51 above), 723–5.
[371] N 366 above.
[372] See eg the observation of Kerr LJ that 'the *Bolam* test is all-pervasive in this context', *Gold* (n 365 above).
[373] [1999] PIQR P53 (CA) at P54.
[374] See eg the Rt Hon the Lord Woolf (n 335 above), especially 1–5.
[375] See GMC Guidance, *Seeking Patients' Consent: the Ethical Considerations* (November 1998), especially at para 9.
[376] See *Reference Guide to Consent for Examination or Treatment*, DoH, March 2001, 6 (para 5.4)
[377] See the Rt Hon the Lord Irvine of Lairg, 'The Patient, the Doctor, their Lawyers and the Judge: Rights and Duties' (1999) 7 Med L Rev 255 at 267.

(g) Post-Treatment Disclosures

3.141 There is one final element of the duty to inform which warrants mention. It relates not to volunteering information before treatment, nor to answering questions, but to volunteering information *after* treatment, specifically where something has gone wrong and an explanation is called for. It might be thought that if *Bolam* governs the first two of these duties, there is not much likelihood of a different standard applying to the third, if, indeed, it is a duty at all. Sir John Donaldson MR appeared to take a different view on two separate occasions. In *Lee v South West Thames RHA*[378] and again in *Naylor v Preston AHA*,[379] he suggested, albeit in what amounted to judicial asides, that there may well be what he termed a 'duty of candour' or 'duty of candid disclosure', as being 'but one aspect of the duty of general care'.[380] By this, he meant that a doctor who knows or, perhaps has reason to suspect, that something has gone wrong in the treatment of a patient owes a duty to inform the patient. This is a far-reaching observation. It may be ethically appealing,[381] but in the context of the trench warfare of medical negligence, it would not be regarded by those who advise doctors as a duty but rather an act of folly. In the event, although his comments have attracted the attention of commentators, they have not been endorsed by the courts.[382] One reason may be that, quite apart from being obiter, Sir John Donaldson MR relied on the speeches of *Sidaway* regarding the duty to answer questions truthfully which, as has been seen, were subsequently disavowed by the Court of Appeal.[383] That said, however, Stuart-Smith LJ, writing for the Court of Appeal in *Powell v Boldaz*,[384] appears not to have entirely closed the door on Sir John Donaldson MR's newly fashioned duty. He held that it could not avail the claimant, but seemed to avoid disavowing it completely.[385]

(h) The Future

3.142 As has been seen, *Sidaway* and the other cases on the duty to inform, derive their sustenance from *Bolam*. If the link between *Bolam* and *Sidaway*, or the very authority of *Bolam* itself, were to be undermined, the duty to inform could well undergo a significant transformation. It is important to assess the likelihood of this happening, not least so as to be able to plot the law's future course.

---

[378] [1985] 2 All ER 385.
[379] [1987] 1 WLR 958.
[380] See further, the discussion in Kennedy and Grubb (n 51 above), 725 *et seq.*
[381] See, GMC Guidance, *Seeking Patients' Consent: the Ethical Considerations* (n 5 above), para 17.
[382] Contrast the Ontario High Court decision in *Stamos v Davies* (1985) 21 DLR (4th) 507. See also *AB v Tameside and Glossop HA* [1997] 8 Med LR 91 (CA) (conceded that HA had a duty to advise current and former patients of HIV status of health care worker).
[383] A further difficulty will lie in establishing that the failure to warn caused any injury to the claimant.
[384] N 366 above.
[385] ibid, 46.

Lessons from Abroad Perhaps, the first point to notice is the current state of 3.143
common law elsewhere. In the United States, despite the assumption that the doctrine of informed consent as expressed in, for example, *Canterbury v Spence*,[386] is
all pervasive, the truth is that the majority of States still adhere to the professional
practice standard.[387] Thus, the pro- and anti-*Bolam* argument is as alive in the
United States as in the United Kingdom. In Canada, as has been seen, the argument is long over. The Supreme Court in *Reibl*[388] came down firmly in favour of
the 'reasonable patient' test. Indeed, in subsequent decisions, the Court has flirted
with the extent to which the doctor–patient relationship should properly be categorised as fiduciary.[389] Such a categorisation would, of course, fix the doctor with
significantly increased duties. Whatever the fate of this line of reasoning, it is clear,
therefore, that there is unlikely to be any going back in Canada as regards the doctor's duty to inform. If anything, the duty is set to make somewhat greater
demands of the doctor, in an attempt to ensure that the inevitable imbalance in
power between patient and doctor is both recognised and alleviated by law.

Perhaps the most interesting common law development has been in Australia. In 3.144
Rogers v Whitaker,[390] the Australian High Court delivered a blistering criticism of
Sidaway and the approach it represented. While accepting the analytical starting
point in *Sidaway*, that there was a 'single, comprehensive duty' of care which covered diagnosis, treatment, and the provision of information so as to secure consent, the High Court made it clear that the content of the duty varies depending
on which activity the doctor is engaged in. Even as regards diagnosis and treatment, the Court was reluctant to endorse the *Bolam* approach, holding only that
medical evidence 'will have an influential, often decisive, role to play'. As regards
the duty to inform, the Court was in no doubt. Whether a patient has received
sufficient information to allow him to make a reasoned choice whether or not to
consent to treatment 'is not a question the answer to which depends on medical
standards or practices'. The content of this aspect of the doctor's duty was that 'a
doctor has a duty to warn a patient of a material risk inherent in the proposed
treatment; a risk is material if, in the circumstances of the particular case, a reasonable person in the patient's position, if warned of the risk, would be likely to
attach significance to it, or if the medical practitioner is or should reasonably be

---

[386] N 264 above.
[387] See Rosenblatt, Law, and Rosenbaum, *Law and the American Health Care System* (Foundation
Press, 1997), 901.
[388] N 313 above.
[389] See eg *McInerney v McDonald* (1992) 93 DLR (4th) 415 and *Norberg v Wynrib* (1992) 92 DLR
(4th) 449, and the discussion in Kennedy, 'The Fiduciary Relationship and its Application to
Doctors and Patients', in Birks (ed), *Wrongs and Remedies in the Twenty-First Century* (Oxford,
1996).
[390] (1992) 67 ALJR 47. References are to the judgment of the majority, Mason CJ, Brennan,
Dawson, Toohey and McHugh JJ. Gaudron J agreed with the majority but wrote a separate judgment.

aware that the particular patient, if warned of the risk, would be likely to attach significance to it. This duty is subject to the therapeutic privilege.' (It may be added parenthetically that, of course, the case concerned risks but the duty is not limited merely to warnings about risks. It extends to information concerning any alternatives which may exist for the patient.)

3.145   The Australian High Court, therefore, has followed the analysis favoured by the Canadian Supreme Court and by Lord Scarman in *Sidaway*.[391] It has done so by recognising that while doctors must be listened to when questions are raised as to the exercise of their technical expertise, it is patients, or at least the notional reasonable patient, who should decide what they ought to be told before treatment may begin. Thus, the High Court broke the link between *Bolam* and the duty to inform. Perhaps even more significantly, the High Court also cast doubt on the continued validity of the *Bolam* principle itself. 'In Australia . . . [e]ven in the sphere of diagnosis and treatment . . . the *Bolam* principle has not always been applied.' The significance of the Court's judgment here lies in the fact that this potentially opens a second front against the prevailing English law approach. It is clear (and always has been), that the duty to inform can be uncoupled from *Bolam*. This is something the English courts have so far chosen not to do. But, secondly, and independently, *Bolam*'s standing can be cast into doubt. If *Bolam* were to be undermined in English law, *Sidaway*, which is entirely a creature of *Bolam*, would appear ripe for re-evaluation by the courts. Any such re-evaluation would, arguably, involve a movement towards the reasonable patient standard, as articulated in Lord Scarman's speech in *Sidaway*.

3.146   **Bolitho v City and Hackney HA**   The decision of the House of Lords in *Bolitho v City and Hackney HA*[392] has marked the beginning of the undermining of *Bolam*. *Bolitho* was not concerned with the duty to inform but with the quantum of care to be expected of a doctor in caring for a patient, that is to say, it was a straightforward *Bolam* case. The House of Lords redefined the relative roles of the medical profession and the courts in determining the content of the duty owed to the patient. Lord Scarman's assertion in *Sidaway* (when referring to diagnosis and treatment), that 'the law imposes the duty of care; but the standard of care is a matter of medical judgement', must now be seen as representing the high water mark of the law's acquiescence to professional practice. In *Bolitho*, the Law Lords reaffirm the classic legal proposition that (pace Lord Scarman in *Sidaway* and *Maynard*), the content of the duty of care is for the courts. Whilst mindful, of course, that in technical medical matters it must lean heavily on evidence of

---

[391] See also the High Court's subsequent decision in *Rosenberg v Percival* (2001) 75 ALJR 734.
[392] [1998] AC 232, discussed in Grubb (1998) 6 Med L Rev 378 (Commentary). See also, for a similar rethinking of their *Bolam*-like approach, the decision of the Irish Supreme Court in *Dunne v National Maternity Hospital* [1988] IR 91.

professional practice, nonetheless, it was held that the last word lay with the courts. Of course, the big question then becomes; under what circumstances will the court impose its view of the doctor's duty, even in the face of contrary medical evidence.[393]

Lord Browne-Wilkinson, speaking for the House, went back to the words of **3.147** McNair J and fastened specifically on the words 'responsible' in the expression 'responsible body of medical men' and 'reasonable' in the expression 'reasonable body of opinion'. To these he added Lord Scarman's reference to 'a "respectable" body of professional opinion' in *Maynard*. These words, ignored by the courts hitherto, separately and taken together, Lord Browne-Wilkinson reasoned, 'all show that the court has to be satisfied that the exponents of the body of opinion relied on can demonstrate that such opinion has a logical basis'. '[I]f, in a rare case,' he went on, 'it can be demonstrated that the professional opinion is not capable of withstanding logical analysis, the judge is entitled to hold that the body of opinion is not reasonable or respectable.' Later courts will have to make sense of Lord Browne-Wilkinson's rather odd use of the word 'logical', but the message is clear. The defences of *Bolam* have been breached. The court's role as the final arbiter of the quantum of care has been reasserted. Admittedly, no sooner had Lord Browne-Wilkinson let in the anti-*Bolam* marauders than he emphasised that 'it will very seldom be right for a judge to reach the conclusion that views genuinely held by a competent medical expert are unreasonable'. But this can be put down to the caution inherent in taking any new step.

The relevance of this move away from *Bolam* simpliciter is clear. With the loosen- **3.148** ing of the courts' commitment to *Bolam*, it can only be a matter of time (and not much time) before *Sidaway* is also consigned to history. It was never necessary anyway to derive the rule in *Sidaway* from *Bolam*. With *Bolam* itself being refashioned, *Sidaway* (apart from Lord Scarman's speech), becomes even less sustainable. Moreover, it is most significant that in his speech in *Bolitho* refashioning *Bolam*, Lord Browne-Wilkinson made no reference at all to the duty to inform. In discussing those cases which cast doubt on the traditional *Bolam* approach, he specifically referred to them as 'cases of diagnosis and treatment' and went on, 'I am not here considering questions of disclosure of risk'. This can, of course, be interpreted in two ways. First, Lord Browne-Wilkinson could be taken to mean that

---

[393] For a fascinating discussion of precisely the same issue, see the decision of the Canadian Supreme Court in *ter Neuzen v Korn* (1995) 127 DLR (4th) 577, and Kennedy (1997) 5 Med L Rev 130 (Commentary). Sopinka J drew a distinction between matters of technical complexity, as regards which evidence of professional practice would be conclusive, and matters of common sense calling for obvious and reasonable precautions, as regards which the court was entitled to form its own view, regardless of expert medical evidence. '[E]xperts remain witnesses', he reminded the Court. While the distinction which he draws is not entirely satisfactory, the importance of the restatement that the duty of care is always for the court cannot be overstated.

the duty to disclose was unaffected by the developments in *Bolitho* and still remained firmly in the grip of *Bolam*. Alternatively, he could be saying that the duty to disclose was a separate issue, to which *Bolam* and *Bolitho* were not relevant. Only this second interpretation has any plausibility. Speaking extra judicially, Lord Woolf has said that '*Sidaway* will now have to be read in light of *Bolitho*'.[394] What precisely will be the effect of this?

3.149 It follows that the effect of *Bolitho* is to enable, indeed require, the courts to cast aside *Sidaway*, based as it is on a flawed interpretation of *Bolam*, and adopt the view that the content of the duty to inform is a matter for the court to determine, guided by, but not ruled by, the approach(es) to informing patients adopted by the medical profession. A doctor has a duty to inform a patient, prior to any medical procedure, of any material facts relating to risks and alternatives. Material facts are those which a reasonable person in the patient's position would regard it as significant to know. In exceptional circumstances, where the doctor could prove that passing on such information would deleteriously affect the patient's health or well-being, the doctor would, to that extent, be justified in invoking the 'therapeutic privilege'[395] and not informing the patient.

3.150 In his judicial capacity, Lord Woolf has already taken up the mantel in the post-*Bolitho* era of what, elsewhere, has been coined 'new *Bolam*'.[396] In *Pearce v United Bristol Healthcare NHS Trust*,[397] the claimants brought a negligence action following the stillbirth of their daughter. The baby's mother was 14 days beyond full term. She was advised against a caesarian section and the baby being induced. The baby was stillborn some five days later. The parents alleged that they had not been advised of the increased risk of stillbirth inherent in the delay of delivery. The Court of Appeal determined the standard of disclosure of information by synthesising the decisions in *Sidaway* and *Bolitho*. Lord Woolf MR concluded that:[398]

> if there is a significant risk which would affect the judgment of a reasonable patient, then in the normal course it is the responsibility of a doctor to inform the patient of that significant risk, if the information is needed so that the patient can determine for him or herself as to what course he or she should adopt.

3.151 On the facts, the Court held that the 'very, very small additional risk' of stillbirth, somewhere between one and two in 1,000, was not 'significant' particularly bearing in mind the female claimant's distressed condition. This was not a case where it was proper for the court to interfere with the clinical judgment of the doctor.

---

[394] N 335 above at 11.
[395] See further Kennedy and Grubb (n 51 above), 701–4.
[396] See Kennedy and Grubb (n 51 above), 441 *et seq* (originally in (1995) 3 Med L Rev 198).
[397] (1998) 48 BMLR 118 (CA), discussed in Grubb (1999) 7 Med L Rev 61 (Commentary).
[398] ibid.

(i) Causation

The Test for Factual Causation   A patient who complains of a doctor's breach   **3.152**
of the duty to inform must, as in any action in negligence, show, as *a matter of
fact*,[399] that the damage complained of was caused by the defendant doctor. The
damage referred to here, of course, is not that the procedure or operation was
badly carried out. Indeed, it may have been performed with consummate skill. It
is that it was done without proper consent. It is this damage which the patient
must show the doctor caused. The patient must, in other words, show that if he
had been properly informed, he would not have consented. Expressed in this way,
it will be immediately obvious that the crucial question becomes; what test of
proof must the patient satisfy? If the test is subjective, it may merely become a
matter of ex post facto assertion. If, by contrast, it is entirely objective, reflecting
what a 'reasonable patient' would have done, it may be difficult for the patient to
succeed. This is because, except for a procedure which was truly elective, such that
the patient really could take it or leave it, it will be hard to persuade a court that a
reasonable patient would have refused treatment which has been carried out with
due care and skill and which proved beneficial.

The issue of which test of factual causation should be employed has received little   **3.153**
analytic attention from the English courts. This is not, perhaps, surprising given
that English law required the patient to surmount the initial barrier of
Bolam/Sidaway. In *Chatterton v Gerson*[400] however, the issue attracted the observations of Bristow J. He commented that, '[w]hen the claim is based on negligence the claimant must prove not only the breach of duty to inform but had the
duty not been broken she [the patient] would not have chosen to have the operation'. On its face, this appears to adopt a subjective approach. But, on the facts, the
judge rejected what the patient claimed that she would have decided, in favour of
a reasonable inference of what someone 'desperate for pain relief' (as she admittedly was) would choose. The net effect of Bristow J's approach, therefore, appears
to be a *hybrid* test of causation. The starting point is subjective: what the particular patient would have chosen to do, if informed. The patient's expressed view,
then, undergoes an objective appraisal as to whether it is reasonably believable. In
other words, the particular patient is expected to behave as, and will be judged as
if he were, a reasonable patient (unless the contrary can be explicitly proved).

This hybrid approach of Bristow J has found favour in other first instance deci-   **3.154**
sions. In *Smith v Barking, Havering and Brentwood HA*,[401] Hutchison J adopted a
'subjective' test but employed an 'objective' yardstick by which to test the

---

[399] On factual causation generally, see Ch 7.
[400] N 266 above.
[401] [1994] 5 Med LR 285.

claimant's subjective evidence. Moreland J did the same in *Smith v Tunbridge Wells HA*.[402] Notwithstanding this apparent agreement, the law has yet to be tested in an appellate court in England.[403] Thus, it may be helpful to notice the contrasting approaches adopted in Canada and Australia respectively.

3.155 In Canada, the Supreme Court in *Reibl v Hughes*[404] initially opted for the objective approach. Laskin CJC expressed the fear that a subjective test would 'result inevitably in liability', once a breach of duty was established. For this reason, he held that 'the objective standard is the preferable one on the issue of causation'.[405] Subsequently, however, the Canadian Supreme Court in *Arndt v Smith*[406] approved the 'modified objective test'. The court must ask what the *reasonable* person with the particular patient's (reasonable) beliefs, fears, desires and expectations (which may be revealed by the patient's questions) together with any objectively ascertainable circumstances such as age and marital status, would have decided if he had been given the relevant information.

3.156 By contrast in Australia, the High Court in *Rosenberg v Percival*[407] has approved the English model—the 'subjective test' but with the claimant's evidence closely scrutinised by reference to what a reasonable person in her situation might do.

3.157 The effect of the Canadian approach is to give with one hand and take away with the other. The duty to inform is established and then a test of causation adopted which will effectively frustrate most claims based on a breach of the duty. The English/Australian hybrid approach strikes a sensible compromise, consistent with principle but nevertheless tinged with the realities of the forensic process.

3.158 **Postponing the Procedure**   What if, instead of refusing to consent to the procedure for all time, the patient would only have postponed the procedure until a future date? She would then be exposed to the very same risk of injury. Can an

---

[402] [1994] 5 Med LR 334, and Grubb (1995) 3 Med L Rev 198 (Commentary), discussing both *Smith* cases.

[403] In *O'Keefe v Harvey-Kemble* (1998) 45 BMLR 74 (CA) the claimant underwent breast augmentation surgery but was not properly informed of all the risks. The Court of Appeal upheld the trial judge's application of the 'subjective test' of causation in the claimant's favour in the face of expert evidence that 'many women, even when fully advised not to undergo surgery, still insist on doing so' (*per* Swinton Thomas LJ at 86). Likewise in *Chester v Afshar* [2002] EWCA Civ 724; [2002] 3 All ER 552 (CA), the subjective test was accepted without demur: see *per* Sir Dennis Henry at [38].

[404] N 313 above.

[405] On the effect of this ruling on litigation, see Robertson, 'Informed Consent 10 Years Later: The impact of *Reibl v Hughes*' (1991) Canadian Bar Rev 423 (where the objective test was employed, 56 per cent of patients failed to satisfy the test and so failed in their actions, despite proving breach of the duty to inform). See also Dugdale, 'Diverse Reports: Canadian Professional Negligence Cases' (1984) 2 Professional Negligence 108, particularly the discussion of *White v Turner* (1981) 120 DLR (3d) 269.

[406] [1997] 2 SCR 539 discussed in Kennedy (1998) 6 Med L Rev 126 (Commentary).

[407] (2001) 75 ALJR 734.

action succeed and, if so, is her claim restricted to damages for the period until she would/might have had the procedure in the future? This is the point of principle decided by the High Court of Australia in *Chappel v Hart*.[408] The claimant underwent surgery for a degenerative condition of her throat. She was not advised that there was a risk of mediastinitis caused by unavoidable perforation of the oesophagus followed by infection, which could result in damage to her vocal cords. The risk eventuated and the claimant suffered damage to her vocal cords and voice loss. It was accepted that the operation had been performed without negligence. Likewise, it was accepted that the defendant had been negligent in not advising her of the risk following the High Court's earlier decision in *Rogers v Whitaker*. Further, the claimant's evidence was accepted that if she had known of the risk she would not have undergone the operation at that time. The defendant argued, however, that the claimant 's condition was such that she would have had to undergo surgery at some time in the future, albeit that it would have been carried out by a different doctor. The claimant would have been exposed to precisely the same risk, and thus in the instant case her injury was merely the result of a random chance of injury. The defendant's negligence could not, therefore, be a legal cause of her injury.

3.159 The majority of the High Court (Gaudron, Gummow and Kirby JJ) held that the claimant was entitled to recover even though she would have had the procedure in the future. Her injury was as a matter of logical and common sense attributable to the doctor's failure to warn her of the risk. It was not, as the minority (McHugh and Hayne JJ) said a matter of coincidence that the injury occurred because the doctor's negligence had not increased the risk of her being injured.[409] On the contrary, it was the very harm that the doctor had negligently failed to advise her about.

3.160 The same point of principle recently arose in the case of *Chester v Afshar*.[410] The claimant suffered from recurrent back pain and consented to elective neurological surgery. Following the procedure, she suffered extensive motor and sensory impairment. It was accepted that the lumbar micro-disectomy she underwent had certain irreducible risks attaching to it, including a 1–2 per cent chance of serious complications, including nerve damage and paralysis. It was also accepted that it would be in accordance with good medical practice to inform a patient of these risks. The extent to which she had actually been warned of these risks was contested. The claimant further contended that had she been properly advised, she would not have consented rapidly to surgery without further reflection and/or

---

[408] (1998) 72 ALJR 1344. For a discussion see Cane, P (1999) 115 LQR 21 and Stauch, M (2000) 63 MLR 261.

[409] The evidence may even have been that the risk in the future may have been reduced by the superior skill of a specialist: see, Gaudron J at [17]–[19].

[410] [2002] 3 All ER 552, discussed in Grubb (2002) 10 Med L Rev 322 (Commentary).

medical opinion and that this was sufficient to establish a causal link between the doctor's negligence and her injuries. The defendant argued that causation would not be established unless Miss C could demonstrate that alternative advice would have led her to continue to refuse such surgery for all time.

3.161 The Court of Appeal approved and applied the majority view in *Chappel v Hart*.[411] A causal connection was established between the defendant's negligence and the claimant's injury. Delivering the judgment of the Court, Sir Dennis Henry set out the Court's assessment of the policy behind the doctor's duty to inform and how that led the Court to its conclusion. He stated:[412]

> The purpose of the rule requiring doctors to give appropriate information to their patients is to enable the patient to exercise her right to chose whether or not to have the particular operation to which she is asked to give her consent. . . . The object is to enable the patient to decide whether or not to run the risks of having that operation at that time. If the doctor's failure to take that care results in her consenting to an operation to which she would not otherwise have given her consent, the purpose of that rule would be thwarted if he were not to be held responsible when the very risk about which he failed to warn her materialises and causes her an injury which she would not have suffered there and then.

3.162 It is difficult to argue with this reasoning. It would undermine the rule and be unjust for a doctor to require a patient to show that she would never have a particular procedure in the future.[413] It is also counterintuitive to think that because the patient may run the risk in the future—by agreeing to and having the procedure—the negligence is not connected to her injury. At worst, she will be exposed to a small risk of injury which is unlikely *then* to eventuate. She had in a real and immediate sense suffered injury that she would not otherwise have suffered. That should be sufficient to establish a causal link.

3.163 How should damages be quantified in this sort of case? The Court of Appeal held that in quantifying the claimant's future loss, her damages would be reduced to take account of the risk of injury arising from the procedure being carried out at a future point. However, in ordinary circumstances common sense will suggest that the small risk (it was of 1–2 per cent in *Chester*) is most unlikely to eventuate at that future date. Therefore, any reduction in her damages would be small and, on principle, arguably there should be none; the risk is no more than speculative. There is one exception to this. Where, following the procedure, it is discovered that the claimant is *particularly* at risk of the injury such that for her the risk is in fact much greater than for the 'ordinary' patient, then the future deduction will be all the greater.[414] Of course, if the risk becomes substantial enough, the evidence

---

[411] The defendant has appealed to the House of Lords.
[412] ibid, at [47].
[413] See also *Chappel v Hart* (n 408 above), *per* Kirby J, especially at [95]–[96].
[414] N 410 above, at [42] *per* Sir Dennis Henry.

may lead the court to conclude that the claimant would not have the procedure in the future in the light of the now enhanced risk to her and she would fall at the first hurdle of proving a causal link with her injury. Alternatively, the evidence may lead the court to conclude that the claimant would indeed have had the procedure because of the more serious consequences to her of not undergoing it; then the court may take the view that the claimant would, on a balance of probabilities, suffer the injury in any event at a future point in time. The Court of Appeal's view seems to be that the claimant would not, in such circumstances, be entitled to compensation for her loss *after* the injury would probably have occurred; she could only recover for any loss or suffering prior to that time.[415] Arguably, the better rule is that there should be a reduction in damages to reflect this probability: this was the approach in *Chappel v Hart*.[416]

Legal Causation and Remoteness   Satisfying the 'but for' test may not necessarily lead to liability. Legal causation and remoteness rules may exclude liability. These are discussed in Chapter 7. Causation is not merely a mechanistic application of the 'but for' test. Causation questions may, in a particular case, require the court to make a policy judgment of whether to attribute responsibility. In general, they present no particular issues in informed consent cases. One particular problem is that of the 'unrelated risk'. Suppose the doctor fails to warn a patient of a risk 'X', the procedure is carried out but instead of suffering injury 'X', the patient suffers injury 'Y'. Can the patient claim damages for injury 'Y'? Clearly, factual causation is established—'but for' the doctor's negligent failure to warn, the patient would not have consented to the procedure (assume this can be proved) and thus would not have suffered injury 'Y'. However, it is doubtful whether the claimant can recover. The injury falls outside the scope of the risk created by the doctor's negligence and, as a matter of policy, should not be recoverable.[417]

3.164

In *Chester v Afshar*, the Court of Appeal approved the view of Gummow J in *Chappel v Hart*[418] that a doctor would not be liable for an injury resulting from something unrelated to the risk of which the patient is not properly informed, for example arising from an anaesthetic accident.[419]

3.165

---

[415] ibid at [41]–[42].
[416] See, eg, *per* Gaudron J at [19] and Gummow J at [84]–[86] referring to the High Court's earlier decision in *Malec v JC Hutton Pty Lrd* (1990) 169 CLR 638, at 642–643 *per* Deane, Gaudron and McHugh JJ.
[417] For analagous cases not concerned with failure to warn, see *R v Croydon HA* (1997) 40 BMLR 40 (CA) and *Brown v Lewisham and North Southwark HA* (1999) 48 BMLR 96 (CA).
[418] N 408 above, at [66]. See also Hayne J at [118]–[119].
[419] N 410 above, at [43] *per* Sir Dennis Henry. For a contrary case which must be considered wrongly decided: *Moyes v Lothian Health Board* [1990] 1 Med LR 463 (Lord Caplan).

3. Voluntariness

(i) Introduction

3.166 Before any consent is valid in law, there is a third requirement which must be satisfied, in addition to the need to show that the person consenting is competent to do so and is properly informed. The consent must be given voluntarily and freely. In the context of medical care, this requirement may appear to be easily satisfied, since compulsion, force and deception are not features of the medical armamentary.[420]

3.167 It would be wrong, however, to forget that there are certain situations in which coercion may at least hover nearby, such as when medical care may be given in prisons or certain mental hospitals. Further, when voluntariness is defined in such a way as to take account of the more or less subtle pressures to which patients may be exposed, there may be a role for the law in drawing a line between the permissible and the impermissible.

3.168 In drawing any line, it is helpful to notice that there are two contexts in which a claim of lack of voluntariness could arise, the first rather more obvious than the second. In the first, the patient may claim that he was treated after a consent which was, in fact, improperly gained. In the second, it may be alleged that the patient's refusal of consent was the consequence of improper pressure, thereby seeking to justify treatment despite the apparent refusal. It is something of a canard (and, therefore, like all canards, true in part), that it is only when he disagrees that it cannot safely be relied upon.[421] The law, of course, should seek to be even-handed and have no truck with such presumptions.[422]

(ii) The Current Law

3.169 In *Freeman v Home Office (No 2)*,[423] an argument of some importance was advanced on behalf of the claimant, a prisoner serving a life sentence, who had received medical treatment which, he claimed was administered against his will. It was not merely argued that, on the facts, Freeman had not consented voluntarily. A much more challenging argument was advanced. Not only had Freeman not

---

[420] With the exception of the very rare case in which the treatment of a mentally disturbed person may warrant some degree of coercion, limited in law to that which is reasonable in the circumstances.

[421] For such a case in the context of withdrawal of consent to the use of sperm under the Human Fertilisation and Embryology Act 1990, see *Mrs U v Centre for Reproductive Medicine* [2002] EWCA Civ 565; [2002] Lloyd's Med 259 (CA).

[422] Nor should it have any truck with cases such as *Latter v Bradell* (1881) 50 LJQB 448 (in which a servant was required to submit to a medical examination but failed in her action against the doctor) which can safely be consigned to the archives.

[423] [1984] 1 All ER 1036.

consented, but there are certain contexts, not least that of being a prisoner where the doctor was also a prison officer, in which consent could never, by virtue of this context, be voluntary. Plausible as the argument may be, it was roundly rejected by the Court of Appeal. Whether someone had consented voluntarily or not was simply a matter of fact in each case. If the patient were confined, or if his liberty were otherwise limited, this should merely put the court on notice to be vigilant in examining the facts. For Stephen Brown LJ the 'matter is one of fact'. He referred with approval to the trial judge's view that, '. . . a court must be alive to the risk that what may appear, on the face of it, to be real consent is not in fact so'.[424] Thus, whatever the circumstances, the issue of voluntariness is an issue of fact.

The leading English case is *Re T (adult: refusal of medical treatment)*.[425] In that case, **3.170** the Court of Appeal recognised that, for the most part, as has been said, claims of lack of voluntariness do not involve brute force or duress. Instead, the pressure may be more insidious. To respond to this, the Court prayed in aid a well recognised and understood doctrine in English law, that of 'undue influence'. Potentially, the Court, while still insisting that everything turned on the facts, thereby widened the scope of the various factors, the influences or circumstances which could render a patient's consent invalid. This is because 'undue influence' is clearly a more insidious and subtle process than overt pressure and, therefore, calls for a closer examination of the facts to determine what, if anything, may lie beneath those facts. As it happens, the case was concerned with a young woman's *refusal* of consent and whether it was voluntary, in view of the influence exercised over her by her mother. As has been said, a court may be more eager to see lack of voluntariness when the patient is 'defying' rather than agreeing to medical advice. That said, however, the case stands as clear authority that involuntariness can be proved by evidence of undue influence as well as the more obvious examples of circumstances which might overbear the will of the patient.

---

[424] ibid.
[425] N 7 above.

4

CONSENT TO TREATMENT: CHILDREN AND THE INCOMPETENT PATIENT

It is a fundamental principle that a doctor who gives medical treatment or performs surgery[1] without the consent of his patient is prima facie guilty of both a tort and a crime. The adult who is sui juris is recognised as having the fundamental human and personal right to control his own body, the right to self-determination or right **4.01**

---

[1] In this Chapter 'treatment' is used as a generic term covering all forms of examination, assessment, diagnosis, treatment, or care, and all procedures, whether surgical, medical, psychiatric, dental, or nursing, which involve any physical touching or penetration of the patient's body, however trivial. 'Doctor' is similarly used as a generic term covering everyone involved in providing 'treatment'.

of autonomy, the right to decide for oneself to the exclusion of others. Two classes of patient lack the capacity to give a valid consent and are therefore unable to exercise their right to self-determination: children,[2] who by reason of non-age lack the *legal* capacity to give consent, or whose refusal of consent can be overridden by others; and those adults[3] who are incompetent,[4] that is to say who by reason of mental disability, lack the *mental* capacity to give a valid consent to treatment, or who by reason of mental or physical disability are permanently unable to communicate. In addition there are children who, by reason of mental disability, lack both the *legal* and the *mental* capacity to give consent. The unborn child or foetus (in legal terminology the child en ventre sa mère) occupies a special position which requires to be separately considered.

A. Sources of the Law

1. Parens Patriae

Children

4.02 In relation to children the Crown retains a prerogative power as parens patriae exercisable by the judges of the High Court. This power, often though not necessarily exercised by means of wardship, is of considerable importance in relation to the resolution of difficult or disputed questions about the treatment of children.[5]

Incompetent Adults

4.03 In relation to incompetent adults the Crown's prerogative power as parens patriae was abrogated in 1960 upon the coming into force of the Mental Health Act 1959.[6] Despite subsequent expressions of judicial regret it has not been reinstated.

---

[2] The terminology is capable of confusing, for 'child' has very different meanings in the law of succession, in the law of persons and in colloquial usage. In this Chapter it is used in the same sense as in the Children Act 1989, s 105(1), that is, as meaning a person who is under the age of 18. In this sense 'child' is the modern equivalent of the older expressions 'minor' and 'infant'. Both 'child' and 'infant' are also used colloquially, even by judges, to refer to younger, and in the case of 'infant' very young, children.

[3] In this Chapter 'adult' is used to mean a person who has attained the age of 18.

[4] In this Chapter 'incompetent', whether on its own or in the phrase 'adult incompetent', is used to refer to a person who, irrespective of whatever other capacity he may or may not have for other purposes, lacks, by reason of mental disability, the mental capacity to give a valid consent to treatment or who, by reason of mental or physical disability, is permanently unable to communicate.

[5] See further paras 4.42–4.47 below.

[6] *In re F (Mental Patient: Sterilisation)* [1990] 2 AC 1, 51, 54, 57–58, 70, 71, 83. See also *T v T* [1988] Fam 52, *Re C (Mental Patient: Contact)* [1993] 1 FLR 940, *Airedale NHS Trust v Bland* [1993] AC 789; *A v A Health Authority, In re J (A Child), R (on the application of S) v Secretary of State for the Home Department* [2002] EWHC 18 (Fam/Admin), [2002] Fam 213, at [35].

The Court of Protection

The Court of Protection has no jurisdiction (whether in relation to a child or an 4.04
adult incompetent) in respect of treatment or other issues relating to bodily welfare. Its jurisdiction is limited by the Mental Health Act 1983, ss 93(2) and 95(1)(d), to the management of the patient's 'affairs', and that expression is confined to business matters, legal transactions, and other dealings of a similar kind.[7]

2. Statute

Certain miscellaneous and socially controversial procedures are now specifically 4.05
regulated by statute, for example, tattooing,[8] the taking of blood samples,[9] certain forms of treatment for mental disorder,[10] female circumcision,[11] and organ transplants.[12]

There are two provisions of general application which are directly relevant to the 4.06
treatment of children or incompetents.

Children

Section 8 of the Family Law Reform Act 1969 provides: 4.07

(1) The consent of a minor who has attained the age of sixteen years to any surgical, medical or dental treatment which, in the absence of consent, would constitute a trespass to his person, shall be as effective as it would be if he were of full age; and where a minor has by virtue of this section given an effective consent to any treatment it shall not be necessary to obtain any consent for it from his parent or guardian.

(2) In this section ' surgical, medical or dental treatment' includes any procedure undertaken for the purposes of diagnosis, and this section applies to any procedure (including, in particular, the administration of an anaesthetic) which is ancillary to any treatment as it applies to that treatment.

(3) Nothing in this section shall be construed as making ineffective any consent which would have been effective if this section had not been enacted.

---

[7] *In re F (Mental Patient: Sterilisation)* [1990] 2 AC 1, 51, 58–60, 70–71, 83.

[8] The Tattooing of Minors Act 1969.

[9] The Family Law Reform Act 1969, s 21(1) (competent adults), s 21(2) (minors who have attained the age of 16), s 21(3) (minors under the age of 16), s 21(4) (persons suffering from mental disorder within the meaning of the Mental Health Act 1983).

[10] As defined in the Mental Health Act 1983, s 1(2). For the treatments in question see the Mental Health Act 1983, s 57(1)(a) (surgical operations for destroying brain tissue or the functioning of brain tissue), s 57(1)(b) (surgical implantation of hormones for the purpose of reducing male sexual drive), s 58(1)(a) (electro-convulsive therapy), s 58(1)(b) (administration of medicine—as to which see *B v Croydon HA* [1995] Fam 133, 137–138); *R (on the application of N) v M* [2002] EWCA Civ 1789, [2003] 1 WLR 562. See also the Mental Health Act 1983, ss 56, 59–62, 64.

[11] The Prohibition of Female Circumcision Act 1985.

[12] The Human Organ Transplants Act 1989.

Section 8 does not extend to the donation of organs, or of blood or other bodily substances, nor even to the taking of a blood sample (for which separate provision is made in s 21(2)), for none of these procedures constitutes either treatment or diagnosis.[13]

Persons Suffering from Mental Disorder

4.08   Section 63 of the Mental Health Act 1983 (which applies by virtue of s 56 of the Act only to patients liable to be detained under the Act) provides:

> The consent of a patient shall not be required for any medical treatment given to him for the mental disorder[14] from which he is suffering, not being treatment falling within section 57 or 58 above[15] if the treatment is given by or under the direction of the responsible medical officer.

Section 145(1) of the Act provides that

> 'medical treatment' includes nursing, and also includes care, habilitation and re-habilitation under medical supervision.

'Medical treatment' in s 63 means treatment which, taken as a whole, is calculated to alleviate or prevent a deterioration of the mental disorder from which the patient is suffering, and includes a range of acts ancillary to the core treatment, including those which prevent the patient from harming himself or which alleviate the symptoms of the disorder.[16]

[R]elieving symptoms is just as much a part of treatment as relieving the underlying cause.[17]

'Medical treatment' in s 63 thus includes forcible feeding for the treatment of anorexia nervosa[18] or other psychiatric illnesses[19] and inducing labour and performing a caesarian section on a pregnant paranoid schizophrenic where effective

---

[13] *In re W (A Minor) (Medical Treatment: Court's Jurisdiction)* [1993] Fam 64, 78, 83, 92, 94; *In re O (A Minor) (Blood Tests: Constraint), In re J (A Minor)* [2000] Fam 139, 147–148.

[14] As defined in the Mental Health Act 1983, s 1(2). S 63 permits compulsory medical treatment only for the mental disorder from which the patient is classified as suffering and which is the basis for his compulsory admission in the first place: *R (on the application of B) v Ashworth Hospital Authority* [2003] EWCA Civ 547; [2003] 1 WLR 1886.

[15] For which see para 4.05 above.

[16] *B v Croydon HA* [1995] Fam 133, 138–140, affirming [1995] 1 FCR 332.

[17] *Re KB (Adult) (Mental Patient: Medical Treatment)* (1994) 19 BMLR 144, 146 *per* Ewbank J approved *B v Croydon HA* [1995] Fam 133, 139, 141.

[18] *Riverside Mental Health NHS Trust v Fox* [1994] 1 FLR 614; *Re KB (Adult) (Mental Patient: Medical Treatment)* (1994) 19 BMLR 144; *B v Croydon HA* [1995] Fam 133, affirming [1995] 1 FCR 332.

[19] *Re VS (Adult: Mental Disorder)* (1995) Aug 17 (Douglas Brown J), [1995] 3 Med LR 292; *R v Collins and Ashworth Hospital Authority, ex p Brady* [2000] Lloyd's Rep Med 355 (force-feeding of prisoner detained in Special Hospital). Contrast *Secretary of State for the Home Department v Robb* [1995] Fam 127 (force-feeding of competent adult prisoner).

treatment of the schizophrenia required that the patient give birth to a live baby and resume medication necessarily interrupted by her pregnancy,[20] including, if necessary, restraint and the use of reasonable force.[21]

3. The Human Rights Act 1998

Section 6 of the Human Rights Act 1998, which gives further effect to the rights and freedoms guaranteed under the European Convention for the Protection of Human Rights and Fundamental Freedoms, agreed by the Council of Europe at Rome on 4 November 1950, makes it unlawful for a public authority (and the court is for this purpose a public authority) to act, or fail to act, in a way which is incompatible with the rights and fundamental freedoms set out in, inter alia, Articles 2 to 12 and 14 of the Convention.   **4.09**

The provisions of the Convention that are most relevant for the purposes of this Chapter are: Article 2 (which provides that, subject to the exceptions in Article 2(2), 'Everyone's right to life shall be protected by law'), Article 3 (which provides in unqualified terms that 'No one shall be subjected to torture or to inhuman or degrading treatment or punishment'), Article 8 (which provides that, subject to the exceptions in Article 8(2), 'Everyone has the right to respect for his private and family life, his home and his correspondence'), Article 9 (which provides that, subject to the exceptions in Article 9(2), 'Everyone has the right to freedom of thought, conscience and religion . . . and freedom . . . to manifest his religion or belief, in . . . practice and observance') and Article 14 (which provides that the enjoyment of Convention rights 'shall be secured without discrimination on any ground').   **4.10**

It is beyond the province of this Chapter to analyse the reported case law of either the European Court of Human Rights or the European Commission on Human Rights. There is now a growing domestic case law bearing on the topics considered in this Chapter in relation to Article 2,[22] Article 3,[23] Article 8,[24] Article 9[25] and   **4.11**

---

[20] *Tameside and Glossop Acute Services Trust v CH* [1996] 1 FLR 762, 771–774. Contrast *In re C (Adult: Refusal of Treatment)* [1994] 1 WLR 290 (schizophrenic held entitled to refuse consent to amputation of gangrenous leg) where the gangrene was 'entirely unconnected' with the mental disorder: *B v Croydon HA* [1995] Fam 133, 139; *Re JT (Adult: Refusal of Medical Treatment)* [1998] 1 FLR 48 (adult with learning difficulties and extremely severe behavioural disturbance refusing treatment for renal failure: renal dialysis not treatment for the mental disorder); *St George's Healthcare NHS Trust v S, R v Collins ex p S* [1999] Fam 26, 52 (obstetric treatment of pregnant woman not treatment for mental disorder).

[21] *Tameside and Glossop Acute Services Trust v CH* [1996] 1 FLR 762, 771, 774.

[22] *A NHS Trust v D* [2000] 2 FLR 677; *In re A (Children) (Conjoined Twins: Surgical Separation)* [2001] Fam 147, 204, 238–239, 256–257; *NHS Trust A v M, NHS Trust B v H* [2001] Fam 348; *R (on the application of Pretty) v Director of Public Prosecutions (Secretary of State for the Home Department intervening)* [2001] UKHL 61, [2002] 1 AC 800 (for the subsequent proceedings before the European Court of Human Rights see *Pretty v UK* [2002] 2 FLR 45).

[23] *R v North West Lancashire HA, ex p A* [2000] 1 WLR 977; *A NHS Trust v D* [2000] 2 FLR 677;

footnotes 24 and 25 on p. 210

Article 14[26] of the Convention. Thus far the indications are that the Convention does not usually affect the outcome.[27]

4. Common Law

4.12 Save to the limited extent to which particular matters are regulated by statute, or, in the case of children, by the Crown's prerogative power as parens patriae, the treatment of children and incompetent adults, and related issues of consent, are regulated, subject to the Human Rights Act 1998, by the general principles of the common law.

B. Consent

1. Children

The Need for Consent

4.13 The law normally requires a valid consent before any treatment can lawfully be given to a child. In certain circumstances the law recognises as valid the child's own consent.[28] In those cases where the child is unable to give a valid consent,[29]

In re A (Children) (Conjoined Twins: Surgical Separation) [2001] Fam 147, 204, 238–239, 256–257; *NHS Trust A v M, NHS Trust B v H* [2001] Fam 348; *R (on the application of Pretty) v Director of Public Prosecutions (Secretary of State for the Home Department intervening)* [2001] UKHL 61, [2002] 1 AC 800 (for the subsequent proceedings before the European Court of Human Rights see *Pretty v UK* [2002] 2 FLR 45); *R (on the application of N) v M* [2002] EWCA Civ 1789, [2003] 1 WLR 562.

[24] *R v North West Lancashire HA, ex p A* [2000] 1 WLR 977; *In re C (A Child) (HIV Testing)* [2000] Fam 48, 57–58 (affirmed *Re C (HIV Test)* [1999] 2 FLR 1004); *In re A (Children) (Conjoined Twins: Surgical Separation)* [2001] Fam 147, 204, 238–239, 256–257; *NHS Trust A v M, NHS Trust B v H* [2001] Fam 348; *Re T (Paternity: Ordering Blood Tests)* [2001] 2 FLR 1190, 1197–1199; *R (on the application of Pretty) v Director of Public Prosecutions (Secretary of State for the Home Department intervening)* [2001] UKHL 61, [2002] 1 AC 800 (for the subsequent proceedings before the European Court of Human Rights see *Pretty v UK* [2002] 2 FLR 45); *Re S (Adult Patient) (Inherent Jurisdiction: Family Life)* [2002] EWHC 2278 (Fam), [2003] 1 FLR 292.

[25] *Re J (Specific Issue Orders: Muslim Upbringing and Circumcision)* [1999] 2 FLR 678, 695, 700–701 (affirmed *Re J (Specific Issue Orders: Child's Religious Upbringing and Circumcision)* [2000] 1 FLR 571, 575); *R (on the application of Pretty) v Director of Public Prosecutions (Secretary of State for the Home Department intervening)* [2001] UKHL 61, [2002] 1 AC 800 (for the subsequent proceedings before the European Court of Human Rights see *Pretty v UK* [2002] 2 FLR 45).

[26] *R (on the application of Pretty) v Director of Public Prosecutions (Secretary of State for the Home Department intervening)* [2001] UKHL 61, [2002] 1 AC 800 (for the subsequent proceedings before the European Court of Human Rights see *Pretty v UK* [2002] 2 FLR 45).

[27] See, for example, *A NHS Trust v D* [2000] 2 FLR 677; *NHS Trust A v M, NHS Trust B v H* [2001] Fam 348; *Re AK (Medical Treatment: Consent)* [2001] 1 FLR 129; *Re T (Paternity: Ordering Blood Tests)* [2001] 2 FLR 1190, 1197–1199.

[28] See paras 4.65, 4.69 below.

[29] See para 4.56 below.

and in cases where the child is able to give a valid consent but refuses to do so,[30] the law recognises as valid a proxy or substitute consent given on behalf of the child either by a parent (or someone having parental responsibility) or by the court. In cases of emergency a doctor can provide treatment notwithstanding the absence of parental or judicial consent.[31]

The Purpose of Consent

The giving of consent to medical treatment has two main functions.   **4.14**

> There seems to be some confusion in the minds of some as to the purpose of seek-ing consent from a patient (whether adult or child) or from someone with author-ity to give that consent on behalf of the patient. It has two purposes, the one clinical and the other legal. The clinical purpose stems from the fact that in many instances the co-operation of the patient and the patient's faith or at least confidence in the efficacy of the treatment is a major factor contributing to the treatment's success. Failure to obtain such consent will not only deprive the patient and the medical staff of this advantage, but will usually make it much more difficult to administer the treatment. I appreciate that this purpose may not be served if consent is given on be-half of, rather than by, the patient. However, in the case of young children know-ledge of the fact that the parent has consented may help. The legal purpose is quite different. It is to provide those concerned in the treatment with a defence to a crim-inal charge of assault or battery or a civil claim for damages for trespass to the per-son. It does not, however, provide them with any defence to a claim that they negligently advised a particular treatment or negligently carried it out.[32]

In the case of a child the right of self-determination plays no part and the clinical   **4.15** purpose of consent is thus limited. Plainly, except as a legal fiction, a proxy or sub-stitute consent is quite inconsistent with a right of *self*-determination. Moreover, even in those cases where a child is treated as having the capacity in law to *give* a valid consent to treatment, he is not treated as having the capacity effectively to refuse consent to treatment, since such a *refusal* can always be overridden by the giving of consent either by the child's parent (or someone having parental respon-sibility) or by the court.[33] The law thus denies even the competent child any right of autonomy, in the sense of the right to decide for oneself to the exclusion of others. Hence the main purpose of consent in the case of a child is to provide the doctor with a defence to a charge of assault or a claim in trespass.

As with an adult patient, so with a child, the right to consent is merely a power to   **4.16** consent, not a power to compel. In the case of a child neither the parent nor the child can compel an unwilling doctor or health authority to provide treatment,

---

[30] See paras 4.66, 4.68, 4.70, 4.71 below.
[31] See para 4.21 below.
[32] *In re W (A Minor) (Medical Treatment: Court's Jurisdiction)* [1993] Fam 64, 76 *per* Lord Donaldson of Lymington MR.
[33] See further paras 4.66, 4.68, 4.70, 4.71 below.

whether that refusal is based on the doctor's clinical or ethical judgment or on a lack of resources. In such a case the patient's only remedy is to find another doctor, if he can, who is prepared to give the desired treatment.

4.17 Nor is the child any better off by seeking to invoke the assistance of the court. The court, even if it is exercising its inherent parens patriae jurisdiction, will never make an order requiring a particular doctor or health authority to treat a child in a manner contary to their wishes.[34] There are two reasons for this. The first is because, as a matter of policy, the court will never make an order compelling a doctor to treat a patient in a manner contrary to his clinical judgment and professional duty.[35] Where the court disagrees with the views of the attending physician the solution is to find another doctor who shares the court's view, not to coerce the existing doctor. Secondly, because, again as a matter of policy, the court declines to become involved in questions relating to the resource implications of proposed treatment, and refuses to adjudicate in disputes between patients, doctors, and health authorities arising out of the denial of treatment because of a lack of resources or the allocation of scarce resources to other patients or other forms of treatment.[36]

---

[34] *In re J (A Minor) (Wardship: Medical Treatment)* [1991] Fam 33, 41, 48; *In re R (A Minor) (Wardship: Consent to Treatment)* [1992] Fam 11, 22, 26; *In re J (A Minor) (Child in Care: Medical Treatment)* [1993] Fam 15, 27, 29, 31. See further para 4.104 below.

[35] *In re J (A Minor) (Child in Care: Medical Treatment)* [1993] Fam 15, 26–27, 29–31; *Re C (Medical Treatment)* [1998] 1 FLR 384, 390.

[36] *R v Secretary of State for Social Services, West Midlands RHA and Birmingham AHA (Teaching), ex p Hinck* (1980) 1 BMLR 93 (patients on waiting list for orthopaedic surgery); *R v Central Birmingham HA, ex p Walker* (1987) 3 BMLR 32 (premature baby requiring heart surgery); *R v Central Birmingham HA, ex p Collier* [1988] CAT 88/1 (4-year-old child in immediate danger to health requiring heart surgery); *In re J (A Minor) (Wardship: Medical Treatment)* [1991] Fam 33, 41; *In re J (A Minor) (Child in Care: Medical Treatment)* [1993] Fam 15, 28, 30–31; *R v Cambridge HA, ex p B* [1995] 1 WLR 898, reversing [1995] 1 FLR 1055 (experimental treatment of 10-year-old child suffering from leukaemia); *R v North Derbyshire HA, ex p Fisher* (1997) 38 BMLR 76 (refusal to fund treatment with beta–interferon of patient suffering from multiple sclerosis). For the most recent general statements of principle see *R v North and East Devon HA, ex p Coughlan* [2001] QB 213 and (addressing the possible impact of Articles 3 and 8 of the ECHR) *R v North West Lancashire HA, ex p A* [2000] 1 WLR 977 (refusal to fund gender reassignment surgery for gender identity dysphoria) and *R (on the application of Watts) v Bedford PCT* [2003] EWHC 2228 (Admin) (delays in waiting list for surgery). And, in relation to the Convention, see the important observation of Lord Hoffmann in *Matthews v Ministry of Defence* [2003] UKHL 4, [2003] 1 AC 1163, at [26]: 'it is well arguable that human rights include the right to a minimum standard of living, without which many of the other rights would be a mockery. But they certainly do not include the right to a fair distribution of resources or fair treatment in economic terms—in other words, distributive justice. Of course distributive justice is a good thing. But it is not a fundamental human right.' For the distinction in this context between the powers of the Family Division when exercising the inherent parens patriae or declaratory jurisdictions and the Administrative Court when exercising its judicial review jurisdiction see *A v A Health Authority, In re J (A Child), R (on the application of S) v Secretary of State for the Home Department* [2002] EWHC 18 (Fam/Admin), [2002] Fam 213, esp at [51]–[53], [89]–[100]. For the impact of Art 49 of the EC Treaty see *R (on the application of Watts) v Bedford PCT* [2003] EWHC 2228 (Admin).

The Effect of Consent

In the case of a child it would seem that the effect of a consent will be the same as the **4.18** effect of a consent given by an adult who is sui juris in those cases where the consent is given either by the child himself (assuming, that is, that the child in question has the capacity to give a valid consent at all) or by the court on his behalf.

The effect of a proxy or substitute consent given on behalf of a child by a parent **4.19** (or by someone having parental responsibility) is more limited, for such a consent will not necessarily provide the doctor with an absolute defence. The right of the parent to give a valid proxy or substitute consent is subject to a variety of limitations,[37] and a doctor cannot rely upon a 'consent' which he knows, or ought to know, ought not to have been given by the parent.

> [B]ecause parents are given authority to act for the benefit of the child, their authority is limited to those acts which advance or protect the welfare of the child. This criterion is a matter which must be determined objectively and not by reference to the good faith opinions of the parent. A parent has no authority, therefore, to consent to medical treatment unless it can be seen objectively that the treatment is for the welfare of the child. If a parent purports to give consent to treatment which is not for the welfare of the child, the consent is of no effect. A person who acts on such 'consent' is guilty of assaulting the child if the treatment involves any physical interference with the child.[38]

The Role of the Doctor

In practical terms parental decision-making in relation to the medical treatment **4.20** of children is subject to control by the doctor. In the final analysis much, if not most, of the ultimate process of decision-making is necessarily borne by the doctor. The doctor is not bound to do what the parent wants, and even if he has the parent's consent he is not necessarily protected from legal proceedings.

On the other hand, the doctor who wishes to treat a child is not necessarily fet- **4.21** tered by the absence, or even the refusal, of parental consent. Except in an emergency,[39] or where parents have abandoned their parental responsibilities without the child yet having been taken into the care of a local authority or someone else in loco parentis,[40] a doctor should always discuss with the child's parents the treatment he proposes and obtain their consent;[41] indeed it is unlawful for a doctor to

---

[37] See further paras 4.74–4.84 below.

[38] *Secretary, Department of Health and Community Services v JWB and SMB* (1992) 175 CLR 218, 316 per McHugh J. To the same effect *In re F (Mental Patient: Sterilisation)* [1990] 2 AC 1, 20 *per* Lord Donaldson of Lymington MR (child would 'undoubtedly have . . . a very substantial claim for damages').

[39] *Gillick v West Norfolk and Wisbech AHA* [1986] AC 112, 181–182, 194, 200.

[40] ibid, 165, 170, 182, 194.

[41] ibid, 169, 173–174, 189; *In re J (A Minor) (Wardship: Medical Treatment)* [1991] Fam 33, 41; *Re R (A Minor) (Blood Transfusion)* [1993] 2 FLR 757, 760.

act in the face of a parental refusal of consent.[42] If a consent which he believes is necessary is not forthcoming he can invoke the assistance of the court. But in a case of emergency, when there is no time to obtain a decision from the court, a doctor can proceed notwithstanding the absence of parental or judicial consent and, if the parents are acting unreasonably or contrary to the best interests of the child, even despite a parental refusal of consent.[43]

The Role of Parental Consent

4.22 It will be seen, therefore, that consent plays a very much more limited role in the case of the patient who is a child than in the case of a patient who is sui juris. Parental consent is only one factor, and except in the case of routine treatment rarely a determining factor, in the treatment of a child. Not even the approval of the court is determinative.

> The doctors owe the child a duty to care for it in accordance with good medical practice recognised as appropriate by a competent body of professional opinion: . . . This duty is, however, subject to the qualification that, if time permits, they must obtain the consent of the parents before undertaking serious invasive treatment. The parents owe the child a duty to give or to withhold consent in the best interests of the child and without regard to their own interests. The court when exercising the parens patriae jurisdiction takes over the rights and duties of the parents, although this is not to say that the parents will be excluded from the decision-making process. . . . No one can dictate the treatment to be given to the child—neither court, parents nor doctors. There are checks and balances. The doctors can recommend treatment A in preference to treatment B. They can also refuse to adopt treatment C on the grounds that it is medically contra-indicated or for some other reason is a treatment which they could not conscientiously administer. The court or parents for their part can refuse consent to treatment A or B or both, but cannot insist upon treatment C. The inevitable and desirable result is that choice of treatment is in some measure a joint decision of the doctors and the court or parents. This co-operation is reinforced by another consideration. Doctors nowadays recognise that their function is not a limited technical one of repairing or servicing a body. They are treating people in a real life context. This at once enhances the contribution which the court or parents can make towards reaching the best possible decision in all the circumstances. Finally mention should be made of one problem to the solution of which neither court nor parents can make any contribution. In an imperfect world resources will always be limited and on occasion agonising choices will have to be made in allocating those resources to particular patients. It is outwith the scope of this judgment to give any guidance as to the circumstances which should determine such an allocation. . . . neither the court in wardship proceedings, nor, I think, a local authority having care and control of the baby is able to require the [health] authority to follow a particular course of treatment. What the court can do is to

---

[42] *In re A (Children) (Conjoined Twins: Surgical Separation)* [2001] Fam 147, 178.
[43] *Gillick v West Norfolk and Wisbech AHA* [1986] AC 112, 200; *In re J (A Minor) (Wardship: Medical Treatment)* [1991] Fam 33, 41; *In re R (A Minor) (Wardship: Consent to Treatment)* [1992] Fam 11, 26.

withhold consent to treatment of which it disapproves and it can express its approval of other treatment proposed by the authority and its doctors.[44]

No doctor can be required to treat a child, whether by the court in the exercise of its wardship jurisdiction, by the parents, by the child or anyone else. The decision whether to treat is dependent upon an exercise of his own professional judgment, subject only to the threshold requirement that, save in exceptional cases usually of emergency, he has the consent of someone who has authority to give that consent. In forming that judgment the views and wishes of the child are a factor whose importance increases with the increase in the child's intelligence and understanding.[45]

2. The Incompetent Adult

The Role of Consent

Except as specifically provided by statute,[46] consent plays no part in the treatment of the adult incompetent, because the patient himself is, by definition, unable to give a valid consent to treatment and the common law does not recognise anyone else as having the legal capacity to give or refuse consent on his behalf. A spouse or relative does not have any power either to consent or to refuse consent to medical treatment on behalf of an incompetent adult.[47] Nor does the court, for neither the Court of Protection nor the High Court has any parens patriae or other jurisdiction over the person, as opposed to the property, of an adult incompetent.[48] **4.23**

The Role of the Court

However, the High Court, in exercise of its inherent jurisdiction and/or its statutory jurisdiction under RSC Ord 15, r 16, can grant declaratory relief to determine questions relating to the lawfulness or unlawfulness of the proposed treatment or care, including the proposed medical treatment or care, of an **4.24**

---

[44] *In re J (A Minor) (Wardship: Medical Treatment)* [1991] Fam 33, 41, 48 *per* Lord Donaldson of Lymington MR.

[45] *In re R (A Minor) (Wardship: Consent to Treatment)* [1992] Fam 11, 26 *per* Lord Donaldson of Lymington MR.

[46] eg, the Mental Health Act 1983, s 63 (treatment of mental disorder), the Family Law Reform Act 1969, s 21(4) (taking of blood samples).

[47] *In re T (Adult: Refusal of Treatment)* [1993] Fam 95, 103; *A v A Health Authority, In re J (A Child), R (on the application of S) v Secretary of State for the Home Department* [2002] EWHC 18 (Fam/Admin), [2002] Fam 213, at [36]; *Re S (Adult Patient) (Inherent Jurisdiction: Family Life)* [2002] EWHC 2278 (Fam), [2003] 1 FLR 292, at [14]. See also *T v T* [1988] Fam 52; *In re F (Mental Patient: Sterilisation)* [1990] 2 AC 1; *Re C (Mental Patient: Contact)* [1993] 1 FLR 940; *Hospital Authority v C* [2003] Lloyd's Rep Med 130, at [27]–[29].

[48] *T v T* [1988] Fam 52; *In re F (Mental Patient: Sterilisation)* [1990] 2 AC 1; *Re C (Mental Patient: Contact)* [1993] 1 FLR 940; *A v A Health Authority, In re J (A Child), R (on the application of S) v Secretary of State for the Home Department* [2002] EWHC 18 (Fam/Admin), [2002] Fam 213, at [35]–[37]; *Re S (Adult Patient) (Inherent Jurisdiction: Family Life)* [2002] EWHC 2278 (Fam), [2003] 1 FLR 292, at [14].

incompetent adult.[49] Such proceedings should be commenced and heard in the Family Division.[50]

Necessity

4.25   In the case of an adult who is incompetent or permanently unable to communicate,[51] the principle of necessity[52] renders lawful, despite the absence of consent, such treatment which in the absence of consent would otherwise be tortious,[53] as a reasonable doctor would in all the circumstances give, acting in the best interests of the patient.[54]

C. The Unborn Child

4.26   As has been said

> From the earliest times the posthumous child has caused a certain embarrassment to the logic of the law, which is naturally disposed to insist that at any given moment of time a child must either be born or not born, living or not living. This literal realism was felt to bear hardly on the interests of posthumous children and was surmounted in the Civil Law by the invention of the fiction that in all matters affecting its interests the unborn child in utero should be deemed to be already born.[55]

Perhaps not surprisingly, the law is both unclear and confused.[56] Thus it has been said that the law treats the foetus as being 'an integral part of the mother' until it

---

[49]   *In re F (Mental Patient: Sterilisation)* [1990] 2 AC 1; *Airedale NHS Trust v Bland* [1993] AC 789. For detailed surveys of the current scope of the declaratory jurisdiction see *A v A Health Authority, In re J (A Child), R (on the application of S) v Secretary of State for the Home Department* [2002] EWHC 18 (Fam/Admin), [2002] Fam 213, esp at [35]–[46]; *Re S (Adult Patient) (Inherent Jurisdiction: Family Life)* [2002] EWHC 2278 (Fam), [2003] 1 FLR 292, at [3]–[60].

[50]   *President's Direction (Declaratory Proceedings Concerning Incapacitated Adults: Medical and Welfare Decisions)* [2002] 1 FLR 177; *A v A Health Authority, In re J (A Child), R (on the application of S) v Secretary of State for the Home Department* [2002] EWHC 18 (Fam/Admin), [2002] Fam 213, esp at [71]–[81].

[51]   The doctrine of necessity also applies if the patient is competent, 'in cases of emergency where the patient is unconscious, and where it is necessary to operate before consent can be obtained': '*Schloendorff v Society of New York Hospital* (1914) 105 NE 92, 93 *per* Cardozo J. Necessity applies in such a case if (i) it is impossible to communicate with the patient (eg, because the patient is unconscious or under anaesthetic) and (ii) urgent action is imperative in the best interests of the patient but consent cannot be obtained until it is too late and (iii) the doctor or surgeon does no more than is reasonably required in the best interests of the patient in the interim before the patient recovers the ability to communicate: *In re F (Mental Patient: Sterilisation)* [1990] 2 AC 1, 71–77.

[52]   For the doctrine of necessity in this context see generally *In re F (Mental Patient: Sterilisation)* [1990] AC 1 and *R v Bournewood Community and Mental Health NHS Trust, ex p L* [1999] 1 AC 458.

[53]   *In re F (Mental Patient: Sterilisation)* [1990] 2 AC 1, 73–76.

[54]   ibid, 51, 56, 75.

[55]   *Elliot v Lord Joicey* [1935] AC 209, 238 *per* Lord Macmillan.

[56]   For the latest discussion see *St George's Healthcare NHS Trust v S, R v Collins, ex p S* [1999] Fam 26, 45–46.

has a separate existence of its own, so much so that an injury to the foetus is treated as being an injury to a part of the mother in the same way as would be an injury to her arm or leg.[57] That view, however, has since been rejected by the House of Lords in favour of the view that the foetus, although dependent upon the mother for its survival until birth, is, from the moment of conception, an organism separate and distinct from the mother.[58]

> There was, of course, an intimate bond between the foetus and the mother, created by the total dependence of the foetus on the protective physical environment furnished by the mother, and on the supply by the mother through the physical linkage between them of the nutriments, oxygen and other substances essential to foetal life and development. The emotional bond between the mother and her unborn child was also of a very special kind. But the relationship was one of bond, not of identity. The mother and the foetus were two distinct organisms living symbiotically, not a single organism with two aspects. The mother's leg was part of the mother, the foetus was not. . . . [T]he foetus does not (for the purposes of the law of homicide and violent crime) have any relevant type of personality but is an organism sui generis lacking at this stage the entire range of characteristics both of the mother to which it is physically linked and of the complete human being which it will later become.[59]

Be that as it may, the criminal law has long protected the unborn child and the civil law recognises that an unborn child can have an independent and legally enforceable right separate and distinct from any right of its mother.[60]

1. The Status of the Unborn Child

Both at common law[61] and by statute[62] the criminal law protects the unborn child.

4.27

The position of the unborn child in civil law is much less clear.[63] There are in reported cases broad and unqualified statements to the effect that, until it is born, a foetus has no status, that it does not exist as a legal person and has no independent

4.28

---

[57] *Attorney-General's Reference (No 3 of 1994)* [1996] QB 581, 591, 593, 598 *per* Lord Taylor of Gosforth CJ.

[58] *Attorney-General's Reference (No 3 of 1994)* [1997] 3 WLR 421, 429, 440.

[59] ibid, 428–429 *per* Lord Mustill.

[60] *Schofield v Orrell Colliery Company Ltd* [1909] 1 KB 178, 181; *Watt v Rama* [1972] VR 353, 376.

[61] *R v Senior* (1832) 1 Mood 346; *R v West* (1848) 2 Car & K 784; *Attorney-General's Reference (No 3 of 1994)* [1997] 3 WLR 421.

[62] Offences against the Person Act 1861, ss 58, 59, Infant Life (Preservation) Act 1929, s 1 (as to which see *C v S* [1988] QB 135; *In re F (In Utero)* [1988] Fam 122), Road Traffic Act 1972, s 1 (as to which see *McCluskey v HM Advocate* [1989] RTR 182; *Attorney-General's Reference (No 3 of 1994)* [1996] QB 581, 597–598, [1997] 3 WLR 421, 442). The criminal law is of course greatly modified by the Abortion Act 1967 (as amended by the Human Fertilisation and Embryology Act 1990).

[63] For a recent partial survey see *Burton v Islington HA* [1993] QB 204, 226–227. For the position in Scotland see *Kelly v Kelly* [1997] 2 FLR 828.

legal personality, that it lacks the status to have any legal right or to be the subject of any legal duty, and that it cannot have a right of action and cannot be a party to an action.

> [I]n England and Wales the foetus has no right of action, no right at all until birth . . . [It is] undefined in law and without status.[64]

> The human being does not exist as a legal person until after birth. The foetus enjoys no independent legal personality . . . An unborn child lacks the status to be the subject of a legal duty.[65]

> It . . . is established beyond doubt for the criminal law, as for the civil law . . . that the child en ventre sa mere does not have a distinct human personality, whose extinguishment gives rise to any penalties or liabilities at common law.[66]

Two judgments, of Sir George Baker P[67] and of Heilbron J[68] at first instance, have been particularly influential:

> The foetus cannot, in English law, in my view, have a right of its own at least until it is born and has a separate existence from its mother. That permeates the whole of the civil law of this country (I except the criminal law, which is now irrelevant) . . . For a long time there was great controversy whether after birth a child could have a right of action in respect of pre-natal injury . . . but it was universally accepted . . . that in order to have a right the foetus must be born and be a child . . . [T]here can be no doubt, in my view, that in England and Wales the foetus has no right of action, no right at all, until birth. The succession cases have been mentioned. There is no difference. From conception the child may have succession rights by what has been called a 'fictional construction' but the child must be subsequently born alive: see per Lord Russell of Killowen in *Elliot v Lord Joicey* [1935] AC 209, 233.[69]

> The authorities, it seems to me, show that a child, after it has been born, and only then, in certain circumstances, based on he or she having a legal right, may be a party to an action brought with regard to such matters as the right to take, on a will or intestacy, or for damages for injuries suffered before birth. In other words, the claim crystallises upon the birth, at which date, but not before, the child attains the status of a legal persona, and thereupon can then exercise that legal right. . . . In my judgment, there is no basis for the claim that the foetus can be a party, whether or not there is any foundation for the contention with regard to the alleged threatened crime.[70]

---

[64] *B v Islington HA* [1991] 1 QB 638, 644, 647 *per* Potts J, on appeal [1993] QB 204.

[65] *De Martell v Merton and Sutton HA* [1993] QB 204, 213, 218 *per* Phillips J, on appeal [1993] QB 204, 223.

[66] *Attorney-General's Reference (No 3 of 1994)* [1997] 3 WLR 421, 434 *per* Lord Mustill. To similar effect see also Lord Mustill at 429 ('foetus does not . . . have any relevant type of personality', 'foetus does not have the attributes which make it a "person" '), 435–436 (foetus 'not a person').

[67] *Paton v British Pregnancy Advisory Service Trustees* [1979] QB 276.

[68] *C v S* [1988] QB 135.

[69] *Paton v British Pregnancy Advisory Service Trustees* [1979] QB 276, 279 *per* Sir George Baker P, followed *C v S* [1988] QB 135, 140 (Heilbron J), approved *In re F (In Utero)* [1988] Fam 122, 138 (May LJ), see also at 140–141 (Balcombe LJ), applied *B v Islington HA* [1991] 1 QB 638, 644 (Potts J).

[70] *C v S* [1988] QB 135, 140–141 *per* Heilbron J, approved *In re F (In Utero)* [1988] Fam 122, 138 (May LJ), see also at 140–141 (Balcombe LJ).

There seems little doubt that these statements, at least in their general and **4.29**
unqualified form, are wrong. English law adopts, though only for the purpose of
enabling the unborn child to take a benefit which, if born, it would be entitled
to,[71] the fiction of the civil law that

> Qui in utero est, perinde ac si in rebus humanis esset, custoditur, quoties de com-
> modis ipsius partus quaeritur: quanquam alii, antequam nascatur, nequaquam
> prosit . . . Qui in utero sunt in toto paene jure civili intelliguntur in rerum natura
> esse.

> [A child in the womb is protected just as if it had been born whenever the question
> concerns benefits which depend on its existing: but another person cannot be ad-
> vantaged before the child is actually born . . . Children in the womb are regarded as
> having been born for almost all the purposes of the civil law.][72]

The principle is applicable not merely to real and personal property but also to
claims by unborn children under Lord Campbell's Act[73] and the Workmen's
Compensation Acts[74] and even, it seems, to actions in negligence for pre-natal
injuries.[75]

The Unborn Child as Litigant

So also, a child en ventre sa mère can be a party to an action, an action for dam- **4.30**
ages or for an injunction can be brought on its behalf, and an injunction can be
granted in its favour.[76]

> It is certain that a child en ventre sa mère is protected by law, and may even be party
> to an action.[77]

---

[71] *Burnet v Mann* (1748) 1 Ves Sen 156; *Doe d Clarke v Clarke* (1795) 2 H Bl 399, 401; *Blasson v Blasson* (1864) 2 De G J & S 665, 670; *Villar v Gilbey* [1907] AC 139, 145–146, 149, 151–152 *Williams v The Ocean Coal Company Limited* [1907] 2 KB 422, 429; *Schofield v Orrell Colliery Company Ltd* [1909] 1 KB 178, 181–183 *Elliot v Lord Joicey* [1935] AC 209, 215, 222, 226, 231, 233–234, 238–240, 241; *Burton v Islington HA* [1993] QB 204, 226–227, 230.
[72] *Blasson v Blasson* (1864) 2 De G J & S 665, 670; *Elliot v Lord Joicey* [1935] AC 209, 238; *Burton v Islington HA* [1993] QB 204, 226.
[73] *The George and Richard* (1871) LR 3 A & E 466, 480–482; *Manns v Carlon* [1940] VR 280 (as to which see *Watt v Rama* [1972] VR 353, 358, 375–376).
[74] *Williams v The Ocean Coal Company Limited* [1907] 2 KB 422, 429, 432; *Schofield v Orrell Colliery Company Ltd* [1909] 1 KB 178 (as to which see *Watt v Rama* [1972] VR 353, 358, 376).
[75] *Montreal Tramways v Leveille* [1933] 4 DLR 337, 346; *Watt v Rama* [1972] VR 353, 376–377; *Burton v Islington HA* [1993] QB 204, 227. For a contrary view see *B v Islington HA* [1991] 1 QB 638, 649.
[76] Lutterel's case temp Lord Bridgman LC cited *Hale v Hale* (1692) Pre Ch 50 (action on behalf of child en ventre sa mère to stay waste: injunction granted); *Musgrave v Parry* (1715) 2 Vern 710, 711; *Wallis v Hodson* (1740) 2 Atk 114, 117; *Thellusson v Woodford* (1799) 4 Ves 227, 322; *The George and Richard* (1871) LR 3 A & E 466, 468, 473, 474, 480, 481–482 (child en ventre sa mère held entitled to bring claim under Lord Campbell's Act; assessment of damages adjourned until birth of child); *Villar v Gilbey* [1907] AC 139, 144; *Manns v Carlon* [1940] VR 280, 284 (child en ventre sa mère held to have right of action under Victorian equivalent of Lord Campbell's Act; trial of action stayed until birth of child); *Watt v Rama* [1972] VR 353, 358, 375–376.
[77] *Villar v Gilbey* [1907] AC 139, 144 *per* Lord Loreburn LC.

The principal reason I go upon in the question is, that the plaintiff was en ventre sa mère at the time of her brother's death, and consequently a person in rerum natura, so that both by the rules of the common and civil law, she was, to all intents and purposes, a child, as much as if born in the father's life-time. . . . First, As to the common law, there is the trite case of an infant en ventre sa mère being vouched in common recovery; a mother also may justify the detaining of charters on behalf of it; a devise to him is good, by the opinion of Treby and Powell, in Scatterwood and Edge, 1 Salk 229, a bill may be brought in his behalf, and this court will grant an injunction in his favour to stay waste, 2 Vern 710, Musgrave versus Parry et al. . . . Secondly, As to the civil law, nothing is more clear, than that this law considered a child in the mother's womb absolutely born, to all intents and purposes, for the child's benefit.[78]

The next objection is, that, supposing, he meant a child en ventre sa mère, and had expressly said so, yet the limitation is void. Such a child has been considered as a non-entity. Let us see what this non-entity can do. He may be vouched in a recovery, though it is for the purpose of making him answer over in value. He may be an executor. He may take under the Statute of Distributions. (22 & 23 Ch II c 10.) He may take by devise. He may be entitled under a charge for raising portions. He may have an injunction; and he may have a guardian. Some other cases put this beyond all doubt. . . . Why should not children en ventre sa mère be considered generally as in existence? They are entitled to all the privileges of other persons.[79]

2. Medical Treatment and the Unborn Child

(i) General Principles

Consent

4.31 There can be no doubt that, as a general principle, the only consent which is either required or relevant for the medical treatment of either the foetus or its mother is that of the pregnant woman. The giving or refusing of consent by the child's father is legally irrelevant, whether or not he is married to the child's mother. Subject only to the provisions of the criminal law, the consent of a pregnant woman makes any treatment either of her or of the foetus lawful, irrespective of any adverse effects which the foetus may suffer, and whether or not the child's father has consented. Conversely, the refusal of consent by the mother is normally decisive, whatever the adverse implications for the foetus. This reflects the biological fact that, until birth, the foetus lives in a symbiotic relationship with, and is totally dependent for its survival upon, the pregnant woman,[80] the very limited

---

[78] *Wallis v Hodson* (1740) 2 Atk 114, 117–118 *per* Lord Hardwicke LC (as to which see *Thellusson v Woodford* (1799) 4 Ves 227, 322, (1805) 11 Ves 112, 139; *Villar v Gilbey* [1907] AC 139, 141, 142, 149; *Montreal Tramways v Leveille* [1933] 4 DLR 337, 343; *Watt v Rama* [1972] VR 353, 375; *Burton v Islington HA* [1993] QB 204, 229–230).

[79] *Thellusson v Woodford* (1799) 4 Ves 227, 321–322, 323 *per* Buller J, on appeal (1805) 11 Ves 112 (as to which see *Montreal Tramways v Leveille* [1933] 4 DLR 337, 340).

[80] *Attorney-General's Reference (No 3 of 1994)* [1997] 3 WLR 421, 428–429, 440.

rights of the father, whether or not he is married to the child's mother,[81] and the public policy which recognises the extreme undesirability of creating conflict between the mother and her unborn child and the insuperable difficulties of attempting to manage the lifestyle or control the actions of an uncooperative mother.[82]

In the same way the law, as a general principle, treats the interests of the foetus as being so bound up with the interests of its mother that the mother's best interests are treated as being likewise those of the foetus and vice versa.

4.32

Wardship and the Unborn Child

Consistently with this principle, it has been held that the court cannot exercise its inherent *parens patriae* jurisdiction in relation to an unborn child or over the mother of an unborn child, nor can it make such a child a ward of court.[83]

4.33

Abortion

Similarly, although the reasoning in the cases may be criticised insofar as they proceed on the footing of the alleged inability of the unborn child to have legal rights or be a party to litigation, there is no doubt that neither the unborn child,[84] nor its father,[85] nor the husband of its mother,[86] can obtain an injunction to restrain the performance of a lawful abortion to which the mother has consented.[87]

4.34

(ii) Possible Exceptions

Whether, and if so in what circumstances, the law will have regard to the independent medical interests of the unborn child, or allow legal intervention by or on its behalf for the purpose of protecting its bodily interests, are questions the answers to which are both uncertain and controversial. There would appear to be no absolute bar as a matter of principle. The law recognises the foetus as an entity capable of having rights, separate and distinct from the rights of its mother, and capable of suing to vindicate those rights. There is no reason in principle why any distinction should be drawn for this purpose between property interests and bodily welfare.

4.35

---

[81] *Paton v British Pregnancy Advisory Service Trustees* [1979] QB 276, 279–281, 282.

[82] *In re F (In Utero)* [1988] Fam 122, 131–132, 138, 143, 144–145.

[83] ibid.

[84] *Paton v British Pregnancy Advisory Service Trustees* [1979] QB 276, 279, *Dehler v Ottawa Civic Hospital* (1979) 101 DLR (3d) 686, 694–700, appeal dismissed (1980) 117 DLR (3d) 512, *Medhurst v Medhurst* (1984) 9 DLR (4th) 252, 255–257.

[85] *Paton v British Pregnancy Advisory Service Trustees* [1979] QB 276, 279–280; *C v S* [1988] QB 135, 140, 141, 148.

[86] *Paton v British Pregnancy Advisory Service Trustees* [1979] QB 276, 280, 281, 282; *Medhurst v Medhurst* (1984) 9 DLR (4th) 252, 257–259; *C v S* [1988] QB 135, 140, 141.

[87] *Paton v British Pregnancy Advisory Service Trustees* [1979] QB 276, 280–281, 282. The position is the same in Scotland: *Kelly v Kelly* [1997] 2 FLR 828.

> I can find no logical reason for rejecting the notion that the common law would protect a child en ventre sa mère against careless acts causing him or her injury. As its property, real or personal, is protected, so should its physical substance be similarly protected.[88]

Moreover, the law does not eschew the application of restraint and the use of reasonable force for the purpose of compelling a pregnant child[89] or an incompetent pregnant adult woman[90] to submit to a caesarian section.

4.36 Thus it might be thought that a child en ventre sa mère could sue for an injunction to restrain violent assaults upon its mother of a kind likely to put it in peril even if the mother, for some reason, was not willing herself to bring proceedings against the assailant. On the other hand, it has been held that the unborn child[91] cannot obtain an injunction to restrain the performance of an unlawful (and thus necessarily criminal) abortion.[92] Other cases are more difficult. Where the mother if competent is refusing or if incompetent is unable to consent to treatment which is in her unborn child's interests, to what extent are the unborn child's interests to be taken into account, and can proceedings be taken by or on behalf of the unborn child for the purpose of authorising or compelling its mother to undergo treatment——for example, if the child requires minor but life-saving treatment in the womb, or if the child's welfare dictates a caesarian section, or if the question is whether a pregnant woman who is in an irreversible coma should be kept artificially alive for the sole purpose of enabling her viable foetus to be born?

The Unborn Child and the Incompetent Mother

4.37 Such problems are likely to be less acute where the mother is herself incompetent or a child and where there is, accordingly, no question of overriding the decision of a competent patient who is sui juris. In such cases the court will be astute to find that a procedure which is medically in the interests of the child, even if not of its mother, is nevertheless in the mother's best emotional and psychological interests, so that it can authorise (in the case of a child) or declare lawful (in the case of an

---

88 *Watt v Rama* [1972] VR 353, 376 *per* Gillard J.
89 *A Metropolitan Borough Council v AB* [1997] 1 FLR 767.
90 *Tameside and Glossop Acute Services Trust v CH* [1996] 1 FLR 762; *Norfolk and Norwich Healthcare (NHS) Trust v W* [1996] 2 FLR 613; *Rochdale Healthcare (NHS) Trust v C* [1997] 1 FCR 274; *Re L (Patient: Non-consensual Treatment)* [1997] 2 FLR 837; *Re MB (Medical Treatment)* [1997] 2 FLR 426.
91 Whether the father of an unborn child, or the husband of its mother, can obtain an injunction to restrain the performance of an unlawful (and thus necessarily criminal) abortion is uncertain: *Paton v British Pregnancy Advisory Service Trustees* [1979] QB 276, 282 (leaving the question undecided); *Medhurst v Medhurst* (1984) 9 DLR (4th) 252, 259–261 (holding that he could); *C v S* [1988] QB 135, 149, 153 (leaving the question undecided).
92 *Dehler v Ottawa Civic Hospital* (1979) 101 DLR (3d) 686, appeal dismissed (1980) 117 DLR (3d) 512; *C v S* [1988] QB 135, 140–1.

adult incompetent) the necessary treatment.[93] But even in this situation the only interests that can properly be taken into account are the interests of the mother, not those of the foetus.[94]

> In our judgment the court does not have the jurisdiction to take the interests of the foetus into account in a case such as the present appeal [a case involving an incompetent adult mother] and the judicial exercise of balancing those interests does not arise. . . . The foetus up to the moment of birth does not have any separate interests capable of being taken into account when a court has to consider an application for a declaration in respect of a caesarian section operation.[95]

Thus, this approach will not resolve the problem presented by the mother in an irreversible coma who may, in truth, have no interests at all.[96]

The Unborn Child and the Competent Mother

The difficulties are particularly acute where a competent mother is refusing treat-   **4.38**
ment in circumstances gravely prejudicial to the life or welfare of her unborn child. The law, however, is clear: the doctor and the court are powerless to act.[97]

> A competent woman who has the capacity to decide may, for religious reasons, other reasons, for rational or irrational reasons or for no reason at all, choose not to have medical intervention, even though the consequence may be the death or serious handicap of the child she bears, or her own death. In that event the courts do not have the jurisdiction to declare medical intervention lawful and the question of her own best interests objectively considered, does not arise. . . . If therefore the competent mother refuses to have the medical intervention, the doctors may not lawfully do more than attempt to persuade her. If that persuasion is unsuccessful, there are no further steps towards medical intervention to be taken. . . . The only situation in which it is lawful for the doctors to intervene is if it is believed that the adult patient lacks the capacity to decide. . . . The law is, in our judgment, clear that a competent woman who has the capacity to decide may, for religious reasons, other reasons, or for no reasons at all, choose not to have medical intervention, even though . . . the consequence may be the death or serious handicap of the child she bears or her own death. . . . The court does not have the jurisdiction to declare that such medical intervention is lawful to protect the interests of the unborn child even at the point of birth.[98]

---

[93] Consider the analyses in *Tameside and Glossop Acute Services Trust v CH* [1996] 1 FLR 762; *In re Y (Mental Patient: Bone Marrow Donation)* [1997] Fam 110; *Norfolk and Norwich Healthcare (NHS) Trust v W* [1996] 2 FLR 613; *Rochdale Healthcare (NHS) Trust v C* [1997] 1 FCR 274; *A Metropolitan Borough Council v AB* [1997] 1 FLR 767; *Re L (Patient: Non-consensual Treatment)* [1997] 2 FLR 837; *Re MB (Medical Treatment)* [1997] 2 FLR 426.

[94] *Norfolk and Norwich Healthcare (NHS) Trust v W* [1996] 2 FLR 613, 616; *Re MB (Medical Treatment)* [1997] 2 FLR 426, 440.

[95] *Re MB* (n 94 above), 440, 444.

[96] Compare *Airedale NHS Trust v Bland* [1993] AC 789 and see further para 4.222 below.

[97] *Re MB* (n 94 above), 436, 438, 440, 441, 444 overruling the extremely controversial decision in *In re S (Adult: Refusal of Treatment)* [1993] Fam 123; *St George's Healthcare NHS Trust v S, R v Collins, ex p S* [1999] Fam 26, 46–50.

[98] *Re MB* (n 94 above), 436–438, 444 Butler-Sloss LJ.

D. Children

1. Who Can Consent

(i) Common Law

Parents and the State

4.39 The common law imposes responsibility for the care, nurture and protection of children on parents, as their guardians by the law of nature, and on the Crown as parens patriae. The powers of the child's parents are limited by law. The prerogative powers of the Crown as parens patriae are theoretically without limit, though in practice they are exercised only within recognised limits.[99] The Crown normally chooses not to exercise its parens patriae powers in relation to children, being content most of the time to leave responsibility for the care, nurture and protection of a child to its parents.

> The best person to bring up a child is the natural parent. It matters not whether the parent is wise or foolish, rich or poor, educated or illiterate, provided the child's moral and physical health are not endangered. Public authorities cannot improve on nature. Public authorities exercise a supervisory role and interfere to rescue a child when the parental tie is broken by abuse or separation. In terms of the English rule the court decides whether and to what extent the welfare of the child requires that the child shall be protected against harm caused by the parent.[100]

> Parenthood, in most civilised societies, is generally conceived of as conferring upon parents the exclusive privilege of ordering, within the family, the upbringing of children of tender age, with all that that entails. That is a privilege which, if interfered with without authority, would be protected by the courts, but it is a privilege circumscribed by many limitations imposed both by the general law and, where the circumstances demand, by the courts or by the authorities upon whom the legislature has imposed the duty of supervising the welfare of children and young persons.[101] When the jurisdiction of the court is invoked for the protection of the child the parental privileges do not terminate. They do, however, become immediately subservient to the paramount consideration which the court has always in mind, that is to say, the welfare of the child.[102]

---

[99] See further para 4.42 below.

[100] *In re KD (A Minor) (Ward: Termination of Access)* [1988] AC 806, 812 *per* Lord Templeman. Consistently with this approach, the common law gives the child no cause of action against a parent for bad parenting, as opposed to parenting which exposes the child to physical dangers: see the discussion in *Surtees v Kingston-upon-Thames Borough Council* [1991] 2 FLR 559 of *McCallion v Dodd* [1966] NZLR 710, *Hahn v Conley* (1971) 126 CLR 276.

[101] See now the Children Act 1989, s 31(2), as explained by the House of Lords in *In re M (A Minor) (Care Orders: Threshold Conditions)* [1994] 2 AC 424; *In re H (Minors) (Sexual Abuse: Standard of Proof)* [1996] AC 563.

[102] *In re KD (A Minor) (Ward: Termination of Access)* [1988] AC 806, 825 *per* Lord Oliver of Aylmerton.

The first [submission] was that the court should never override the decision of a devoted and responsible parent such as this mother was found to be. I would for my part accept without reservation that the decision of a devoted and responsible parent should be treated with respect. It should certainly not be disregarded or lightly set aside. But the role of the court is to exercise an independent and objective judgment. If that judgment is in accord with that of the devoted and responsible parent, well and good. If it is not, then it is the duty of the court, after giving due weight to the view of the devoted and responsible parent, to give effect to its own judgment. That is what it is there for. Its judgment may of course be wrong. So may that of the parent. But once the jurisdiction of the court is invoked its clear duty is to reach and express the best judgment it can.[103]

In making that decision the court will always act cautiously, 'acting in opposition to the parent only when judicially satisfied that the welfare of the child requires that the parental rights should be suspended or superseded'.[104]

(a) Parental Power

At common law responsibility for the care, nurture and protection of a child (including responsibility for the medical treatment of a child) is an aspect of the parental right of custody, the 'bundle of rights' or 'bundle of powers' which enable a parent to exercise physical control over the person of the child, control over the education, religion and marriage of the child and control over the administration of the child's property.[105] Custody in all its aspects necessarily comes to an end with the child's majority at the age of 18, but that part of custodial power which enables a parent to exercise physical control over the person of the child (which is that aspect of custody which is most relevant in the context of treatment) ceases when the child reaches 'the years of discretion'.[106] Thus, custody **4.40**

is a dwindling right which the courts will hesitate to enforce against the wishes of the child, and the more so the older he is. It starts with a right of control and ends with little more than advice.[107]

It is, in my view, contrary to the ordinary experience of mankind, at least in Western Europe in the present century, to say that a child or a young person remains in fact

---

[103] *In re Z (A Minor) (Identification: Restrictions on Publication)* [1997] Fam 1, 32–33 *per* Sir Thomas Bingham MR, adopted in *In re T (A Minor) (Wardship: Medical Treatment)* [1997] 1 WLR 242, 250 *per* Butler-Sloss LJ, 255 *per* Roch LJ.

[104] *In re Z* (n 103 above), 31 *per* Ward LJ (quoting *In re O'Hara* [1902] 2 IR 232, 240 *per* FitzGibbon LJ, approved in *J v C* [1970] AC 668, 715). The test is, of course, easier to state than to apply: compare the facts and the contrasting decisions in *J v C* [1970] AC 668 and *Re M (Child's Upbringing)* [1996] 2 FLR 441 (further proceedings *Re M (Application for Stay of Order)* [1996] 3 FCR 185 and *Re M (Petition to European Commission of Human Rights)* [1996] 3 FCR 377) and consider the, it might be thought surprising, decision in *In re T (A Minor) (Wardship: Medical Treatment)* [1997] 1 WLR 242. See further paras 4.75, 4.78–4.79, 4.170–4.171 below.

[105] *In re Z (A Minor) (Identification: Restrictions on Publication)* [1997] Fam 1, 25–26.

[106] *Hewer v Bryant* [1970] 1 QB 357, 372–373 (a classic description and analysis of custody by Sachs LJ approved in *Gillick v West Norfolk and Wisbech AHA* [1986] AC 112, 184).

[107] *Hewer v Bryant* [1970] 1 QB 357, 369 per Lord Denning MR approved in *Gillick v West Norfolk and Wisbech AHA* [1986] AC 112, 172, 186.

under the complete control of his parents until he attains the definite age of major-ity, now 18 in the United Kingdom, and that on attaining that age he suddenly ac-quires independence. In practice most wise parents relax their control gradually as the child develops and encourage him or her to become increasingly independent. Moreover, the degree of parental control actually exercised over a particular child does in practice vary considerably according to his understanding and intelligence and it would, in my opinion, be unrealistic for the courts not to recognise these facts. Social customs change, and the law ought to, and does in fact, have regard to such changes when they are of major importance.[108]

4.41 Custody of a legitimate child is vested in both its parents; in the case of an illegit-imate child custody is vested in the mother alone. Rights of custody vested in both parents can be exercised by either and thus either parent can consent to a child's medical treatment.[109]

(b) The Crown as Parens Patriae

Nature and Extent of the Jurisdiction[110]

4.42 The Crown as parens patriae is empowered and obliged 'to protect the person and property of . . . those unable to look after themselves, including infants'.[111] The Sovereign, as parens patriae, has a duty to protect those of his subjects who are unable to protect themselves, particularly children who are the generations of the future.[112] The powers of the Crown as parens patriae, and of the court when

---

[108] *Gillick v West Norfolk and Wisbech AHA* [1986] AC 112, 171 *per* Lord Fraser of Tullybelton.

[109] *In re L (An Infant)* [1968] P 119, 132, 135, 136, 155, 160, 172. Because of the potential diffi-culties that arise where parents do not follow the same cultural tradition the BMA has strongly rec-ommended that the written consent of both parents should be obtained for circumcision: 'Circumcision of Male Infants: Guidance for Doctors' (Sept 1996). The General Medical Council has ruled that a doctor must obtain the permission of both parents whenever possible, but in all cases obtain valid consent in writing from a person with parental responsibility: 'Guidance for Doctors who are asked to Circumcise Male Children' (Sept 1997). This principle has since been adopted by the courts: *Re J (Specific Issue Orders: Child's Religious Upbringing and Circumcision)* [2000] 1 FLR 571, 576, 577, affirming *Re J (Specific Issue Orders: Muslim Upbringing and Circumcision)* [1999] 2 FLR 678, 701–702. See further paras 4.49, 4.83, below.

[110] See generally *In re Z (A Minor) (Identification: Restrictions on Publication)* [1997] Fam 1; *A v A Health Authority, In re J (A Child), R (on the application of S) v Secretary of State for the Home Department* [2002] EWHC 18 (Fam/Admin), [2002] Fam 213, esp at [30]–[58]. For illuminating discussions of the Crown as parens patriae, viewed from the perspectives of Canada, Australia, pre-partition Ireland and Scotland respectively, see *Re Eve* (1986) 31 DLR (4th) 1, 13–22 *per* La Forest J; *Secretary, Department of Health and Community Services v JWB and SMB* (1992) 175 CLR 218, 258–260 *per* Mason CJ, Dawson, Toohey and Gaudron JJ, 279–285 *per* Brennan J, 301–302 *per* Deane J; *In the matter of a Ward of Court (withholding medical treatment) (No 2)* [1996] 2 IR 79, 102–107 *per* Hamilton CJ, 139–40 *per* Blayney J; *Law Hospital NHS Trust v Lord Advocate* [1996] 2 FLR 407, 418–423 *per* Lord Hope of Craighead LP, 427–431 *per* Lord Cullen, 434–436 *per* Lord Clyde.

[111] *In re D (A Minor) (Wardship: Sterilisation)* [1976] Fam 185, 192.

[112] *In re X (A Minor) (Wardship: Jurisdiction)* [1975] Fam 47, 51–52; *In re C (A Minor) (Wardship: Medical Treatment) (No 2)* [1990] Fam 39, 46; *In re J (A Minor) (Wardship: Medical Treatment)* [1991] Fam 33, 50; *In re R (A Minor) (Wardship: Consent to Treatment)* [1992] Fam 11, 25.

exercising the parental power of the Crown as part of its inherent jurisdiction, are theoretically without limit, are more extensive than the custodial powers of a parent, and extend beyond anything that either the child, the child's parents, or even an adult sui juris, could authorise or require, but in practice the court declines to exercise a limitless jurisdiction, even when what is in question is the protection as opposed to the custody of the child.[113]

The powers of the Crown as parens patriae are exercised by the judges of the High **4.43** Court, prior to 1971 by the Judges of the Chancery Division, since then by the Judges of the Family Division, as part of their inherent jurisdiction as the successors of the judges of the High Court of Chancery.

Wardship

The inherent parens patriae jurisdiction is often, though not necessarily, exercised **4.44** by means of wardship. Wardship is merely machinery by which the court exercises parens patriae powers in relation to children: the court can exercise its parens patriae jurisdiction whether or not the child is a ward of court.[114] The substantive powers of the court are the same whether it is exercising the inherent jurisdiction or the wardship jurisdiction, for the court, when exercising the wardship jurisdiction, is in truth exercising the inherent jurisdiction, albeit in a particular manner. The only practical difference between wardship and an exercise of the inherent jurisdiction not involving wardship is that in the former case, but not in the latter, the child acquires the *status* of a ward of court.[115]

The court cannot exercise its inherent parens patriae jurisdiction in relation to an **4.45** unborn child or over the mother of an unborn child, nor can it make such a child a ward of court.[116]

---

[113] *Thomasset v Thomasset* [1894] P 295, 299; *Hewer v Bryant* [1970] 1 QB 357, 372; *In re X (A Minor) (Wardship: Jurisdiction)* [1975] Fam 47, 58, 61; *In re X (A Minor) (Wardship: Injunction)* [1984] 1 WLR 1422; *In re C (A Minor) (Wardship: Medical Treatment) (No 2)* [1990] Fam 39, 46; *In re R (A Minor) (Wardship: Criminal Proceedings)* [1991] Fam 56, 63–64, 66; *Re C (A Minor) (Wardship: Jurisdiction)* [1991] 2 FLR 168, 178–179, 184; *In re R (A Minor) (Wardship: Consent to Treatment)* [1992] Fam 11, 25, 28; *Secretary, Department of Health and Community Services v JWB and SMB* (1992) 175 CLR 218, 259, 302; *In re J (A Minor) (Child in Care: Medical Treatment)* [1993] Fam 15, 29; *In re W (A Minor) (Medical Treatment: Court's Jurisdiction)* [1993] Fam 64, 81, 85, 91; *In re Z (A Minor) (Identification: Restrictions on Publication)* [1997] Fam 1, 14–18, 23.
[114] *In re N (Infants)* [1967] Ch 512, 530–531; *In re L (An Infant)* [1968] P 119, 156–157; *In re C (A Minor) (Wardship: Medical Treatment) (No 2)* [1990] Fam 39, 46; *In re M and N (Minors) (Wardship: Publication of Information)* [1990] Fam 211, 223; *In re W (A Minor) (Medical Treatment: Court's Jurisdiction)* [1993] Fam 64, 73, 85; *In re Z (A Minor) (Identification: Restrictions on Publication)* [1997] Fam 1, 13–14.
[115] *In re W (A Minor) (Medical Treatment: Court's Jurisdiction)* [1993] Fam 64, 73.
[116] *In re F (In Utero)* [1988] Fam 122.

4.46   The court cannot exercise its inherent parens patriae jurisdiction in relation to a child who has died, nor can it make such a child a ward of court: it can, however, grant declaratory relief in relation to such a child.[117]

4.47   No 'important' or 'major' step in the life of a ward of court can be taken without the prior consent of the court.[118] What precisely counts as an 'important' or 'major' step has never been defined,[119] but the principle plainly extends to the more significant forms of medical treatment, for example, a sterilisation,[120] an abortion,[121] and even a psychiatric examination undertaken for forensic purposes.[122] No doubt it extends to other procedures. Moreover, a child who is a ward of court can neither marry nor leave the jurisdiction without the consent of the court. These matters apart, the status of wardship confers neither disadvantage nor privilege: a child who is a ward of court should be treated medically in exactly the same way as one who is not (though the doctor will be looking to the court rather than to the parent for any necessary consent), and the fact that a child either is or is not a ward of court is totally irrelevant when it comes to choosing how to allocate scarce medical resources.[123]

(ii) The Children Act 1989

4.48   The effect of the Children Act 1989 is to alter the law in detail but without affecting its substance to any significant extent.

(a) Parental Power

Parental Responsibility

4.49   The common law concept of custody has been replaced by the statutory concept of parental responsibility, defined in s 3(1) as meaning 'all the rights, duties, powers, responsibilities and authority which by law a parent has in relation to the child and his property'. Parental responsibility thus defined plainly includes power to consent to medical treatment.[124] The Act recognises (s 2(5)) that more

---

[117] *Re A* [1992] 3 Med L Rev 303 (child brain-stem dead: jurisdiction to make declaration that child dead and accordingly lawful to disconnect ventilator).

[118] *In re S (Infants)* [1967] 1 WLR 396, 407; *In re D (A Minor) (Wardship: Sterilisation)* [1976] Fam 185, 196; *Re G-U (A Minor) (Wardship)* [1984] FLR 811; *In re C (A Minor) (Wardship: Medical Treatment)* [1990] Fam 26, 32, 38; *In re J (A Minor) (Wardship: Medical Treatment)* [1991] Fam 33, 49; *In re R (A Minor) (Wardship: Consent to Treatment)* [1992] Fam 11, 25; *In re W (A Minor) (Medical Treatment: Court's Jurisdiction)* [1993] Fam 64, 73.

[119] cf *Kelly v British Broadcasting Corporation* [2001] Fam 59, 75–76.

[120] *In re D (A Minor) (Wardship: Sterilisation)* [1976] Fam 185, 196.

[121] *Re G-U (A Minor) (Wardship)* [1984] FLR 811.

[122] *In re S (Infants)* [1967] 1 WLR 396, 407.

[123] *In re J (A Minor) (Wardship: Medical Treatment)* [1991] Fam 33, 41, 42; *In re R (A Minor) (Wardship: Criminal Proceedings)* [1991] Fam 56, 65–66.

[124] *In re Z (A Minor) (Identification: Restrictions on Publication)* [1997] Fam 1, 25–26.

than one person may have parental responsibility for the same child at the same time and provides (s 2(7)) that where more than one person has parental responsibility each may act alone and without the other.[125] However, notwithstanding the language of s 2(7), in the absence of agreement by all those with parental responsibility the specific approval of the court must be obtained if the case falls within what has been described as 'a small group of important decisions'.[126]

The Act provides that the following have parental responsibility: the child's father **4.50** and mother, where they were married to each other at the time of his birth (s 2(1)); the child's mother, but not the father, where they were not so married (s 2(2)), unless the father acquires parental responsibility either by order of the court under s 4(1)(a) or pursuant to a 'parental responsibility agreement' with the mother under s 4(1)(b); a person appointed as the child's guardian (s 5(6)); a person in whose favour the court makes a residence order with respect to the child (s 12(2)); the local authority designated in a care order made with respect to the child (s 33(3)(b));[127] the local authority or other authorised person who has obtained an emergency protection order with respect to the child (s 44(4)(c)).[128]

Carers

A person who does not have parental responsibility for a particular child but has **4.51** care of the child—for example, a relative, a child-minder, a schoolteacher, or even a doctor, if for instance the child is an in-patient in a hospital—may do what is reasonable in all the circumstances of the case for the purpose of safeguarding or promoting the child's welfare (s 3(5)). In an appropriate case such a person can consent to medical treatment on behalf of the child, though it will presumably only be reasonable to act without first obtaining the consent of the child's parents or whoever else has parental responsibility in an emergency or if the treatment is trivial.

(b) Parens Patriae

Section 100(2) of the Act follows the common law in distinguishing between 'the **4.52** High Court's inherent jurisdiction with respect to children' (that is, the exercise by the High Court of the parens patriae jurisdiction) and 'wardship'. Section 100(2)(c), following the common law, recognises that the High Court can exercise its inherent parens patriae jurisdiction without making the child a ward of court.

---

[125] See n 109 above.
[126] See further para 4.83 below.
[127] For an example of consent by a local authority to the treatment of a child in care (voluntary admission to a mental hospital), see *R v Kirklees Metropolitan Borough Council, ex p C* [1992] 2 FLR 117, [1993] 2 FLR 187.
[128] *Re O (A Minor) (Medical Treatment)* [1993] 2 FLR 149, 151.

4.53   In addition to exercising its parens patriae powers either under the inherent jurisdiction or in wardship the court can in some cases exercise comparable powers
under s 8, by making either a prohibited steps order or a specific issue order.

2. The Three Stages of Childhood

4.54   Upon attaining the age of 18 a child who is not mentally incompetent becomes sui
juris and absolutely entitled to decide whether or not to consent to treatment.
Prior to that the normal developing child will have passed through three successive stages of development recognised by the law.

(i) The Child of Tender Years

4.55   Manifestly a young child who has not yet reached 'the years of discretion' lacks the
capacity to consent to medical treatment, because he lacks the intellectual ability
to understand what is involved and the maturity to form a balanced judgment.

Who Can Consent

4.56   In the case of a child of tender years consent to medical treatment can lawfully be
given by the court, by any person with parental responsibility, and, to the extent
that it is reasonable in all the circumstances for the purpose of safeguarding or
promoting the child's welfare, by any person who, although he does not have
parental responsibility, has care of the child.[129]

(ii) The 'Gillick competent' Child

(a) The Test of Competence

4.57   If and when the child achieves a sufficient understanding and intelligence to enable him to understand fully what is proposed he is treated as having the capacity
to give a valid consent to medical treatment.[130] The conventional shorthand is to
refer to such a child as having 'Gillick capacity' or as being 'Gillick competent'.

The Test of 'Gillick Competence'

4.58   The key to 'Gillick competence' is the child's understanding and intelligence.[131]
'Gillick competence' in relation to a particular child is a question of fact for the
judge (or jury).[132]

4.59   In determining whether or not a particular child is 'Gillick competent' in relation
to a particular proposed treatment what is being looked for is the capacity to reach

---

[129] See paras 4.40, 4.42, 4.49, 4.50, 4.51 above.
[130] *Gillick v West Norfolk and Wisbech AHA* [1986] AC 112, 169, 186, 188–189, 195, 201.
[131] ibid, 171, 186, 189, 201; *In re W (A Minor) (Medical Treatment: Court's Jurisdiction)* [1993]
Fam 64, 81.
[132] *Gillick v West Norfolk and Wisbech AHA* [1986] AC 112, 172, 189.

a mature and balanced judgment, 'the attainment by a child of an age of sufficient discretion to enable him or her to exercise a wise choice in his or her own interests'.[133] The factors to be taken into account are: the child's understanding and intelligence, his chronological, mental and emotional age, intellectual development and maturity, his capacity to make up his own mind, and his ability to understand fully, and to appraise, the medical advice being given, the nature, consequences and implications of the advised treatment, the potential risks to health and the emotional impact of either accepting or rejecting the advised treatment, and any moral and family questions involved.[134]

> I would hold that as a matter of law the parental right to determine whether or not their minor child below the age of 16 will have medical treatment terminates if and when the child achieves a sufficient understanding and intelligence to enable him or her to understand fully what is proposed. It will be a question of fact whether a child seeking advice has sufficient understanding of what is involved to give a consent valid in law. . . . When applying these conclusions to contraceptive advice and treatment it has to be borne in mind that there is much that has to be understood by a girl under the age of 16 if she is to have legal capacity to consent to such treatment. It is not enough that she should understand the nature of the advice which is being given: she must also have a sufficient maturity to understand what is involved. There are moral and family questions, especially her relationship with her parents; long term problems associated with the emotional impact of pregnancy and its termination; and there are the risks to health of sexual intercourse at her age, risks which contraception may diminish but cannot eliminate. It follows that a doctor will have to satisfy himself that she is able to appraise these factors before he can safely proceed upon the basis that she has at law capacity to consent to contraceptive treatment[135]

Youth and the potential for development may make it difficult, or indeed impossible, to make the relevant findings of fact to the necessary standard of proof. It must also be borne in mind that, even with an adult, there may be considerable barriers, conscious and unconscious, intellectual and emotional, to a full understanding of the implications of accepting or refusing the advised treatment.

Gillick competence reflects the staged development of a normal child and the progressive transition of the adolescent from childhood to adulthood. The capacity to understand reflects and is conditioned by the gradual acquisition of maturity and the capacity to consent will vary with the gravity of the treatment proposed. A child who has Gillick capacity to consent to dental treatment, the mending of a broken arm, a tonsillectomy or even an appendectomy, may lack the capacity to consent to more serious treatment.[136]

4.60

---

[133] ibid, 188 *per* Lord Scarman.
[134] ibid, 174, 189, 190, 201; *In re R (A Minor) (Wardship: Consent to Treatment)* [1992] Fam 11, 26.
[135] *Gillick v West Norfolk and Wisbech AHA* [1986] AC 112, 188–189 *per* Lord Scarman.
[136] ibid, 169, 201; *In re R (A Minor) (Wardship: Consent to Treatment)* [1992] Fam 11, 25, 31; *In re W (A Minor) (Medical Treatment: Court's Jurisdiction)* [1993] Fam 64, 81.

[T]he extent of the legal capacity of a young person to make decisions for herself or himself is not susceptible of precise abstract definition. Pending the attainment of full adulthood, legal capacity varies according to the gravity of the particular matter and the maturity and understanding of the particular young person.[137]

Mental disability

4.61 Mental disability is not of itself incompatible with a child having 'Gillick capacity', at least for some purposes.

The age at which intellectually disabled children can consent will be higher than for children within the normal range of abilities. However, terms such as 'mental disability', 'intellectual handicap' or 'retardation' lack precision. There is no essential cause of disability; those who come within these categories form a heterogeneous group. And since most intellectually disabled people are borderline to mildly disabled, there is no reason to assume that all disabled children are incapable of giving consent to treatment. In the case of children with intellectual disabilities, the situation is further complicated by the need for future, as well as present, assessment. . . . It may also be said, in this context, that not only are there widely varying kinds and consequences of intellectual disability but such handicaps, possibly more so than other forms of disability, are often surrounded by misconceptions on the part of others in society, misconceptions often involving an underestimation of a person's ability. . . . [I]t is important to stress that it cannot be presumed that an intellectually disabled child is, by virtue of his or her disability, incapable of giving consent to treatment. The capacity of a child to give informed consent to medical treatment depends on the rate of development of each individual.[138]

Fluctuating Capacity

4.62 Gillick competence is a developmental concept and will not be lost or acquired on a day to day or week to week basis. Mental disability must be taken into account particularly where it is fluctuating in its effect[139] or (as with anorexia nervosa) has as one of its features that it is capable of destroying the ability to make an informed choice and creates a wish not to be cured and a compulsion to refuse treatment or accept only ineffective treatment.[140]

But there is no suggestion that the extent of this competence can fluctuate upon a day to day or week to week basis. What is really being looked at is an assessment of mental and emotional age, as contrasted with chronological age, but even this test needs to be modified in the case of fluctuating mental disability to take account of that misfortune. It should be added that in any event what is involved is not merely an ability to understand the nature of the proposed treatment . . . but a full understanding and appreciation of the consequences both of the treatment in terms of intended and possible side effects and, equally important, the anticipated

---

[137] *Secretary, Department of Health and Community Services v JWB and SMB* (1992) 175 CLR 218, 293 *per* Deane J.

[138] ibid, 238–239 *per* Mason CJ, Dawson, Toohey and Gaudron JJ.

[139] *In re R (A Minor) (Wardship: Consent to Treatment)* [1992] Fam 11, 26, 31–32.

[140] *In re W (A Minor) (Medical Treatment: Court's Jurisdiction)* [1993] Fam 64, 81, 83.

consequences of a failure to treat. On the evidence in the present case . . . even if she was capable on a good day of a sufficient degree of understanding to meet the Gillick criteria, her mental disability, to the cure or amelioration of which the proposed treatment was directed, was such that on other days she was not only 'Gillick incompetent', but actually sectionable. No child in that situation can be regarded as 'Gillick competent'.[141]

The Standard of Proof

The standard of proof must be the more rigorous the more serious the implications for the child of either giving or refusing consent. Where life or serious injury to health is at stake, and the child's decision appears to be unreasonable, the doctor (or the court) can be astute to find a lack of capacity to consent. **4.63**

> I find that A is a boy of sufficient intelligence to be able to take decisions about his own well-being, but I also find that there is a range of decisions of which some are outside his ability fully to grasp their implications. Impressed though I was by his obvious intelligence, by his calm discussion of the implications, by his assertion even that he would refuse well knowing that he may die as a result, in my judgment A does not have a full understanding of the whole implication of what the refusal of that treatment involves. . . . I am quite satisfied that A does not have any sufficient comprehension of the pain he has yet to suffer, of the fear that he will be undergoing, of the distress not only occasioned by that fear but also—and importantly—the distress he will inevitably suffer as he, a loving son, helplessly watches his parents' and his family's distress. They are a close family, and they are a brave family, but I find that he has no realisation of the full implications which lie before him as to the process of dying. He may have some concept of the fact that he will die, but as to the manner of his death and to the extent of his and his family's suffering I find that he has not the ability to turn his mind to it nor the will to do so. Who can blame him for that? If, therefore, this case depended upon my finding of whether or not A is of sufficient understanding and intelligence and maturity to give full and informed consent, I find that he is not.[142]

The doctor (or the court) must be astute to the possibility that conscious or subconscious influence is being exerted on a child either by his parents or, where religious beliefs are involved, by religious advisers.[143] **4.64**

---

[141] *In re R (A Minor) (Wardship: Consent to Treatment)* [1992] Fam 11, 25–26 *per* Lord Donaldson of Lymington MR.

[142] *Re E (A Minor) (Wardship: Medical Treatment)* [1993] 1 FLR 386, 391 *per* Ward J (15-year-old Jehovah's Witness refusing blood transfusion necessary to save his life). Similarly, *Re S (A Minor) (Consent to Medical Treatment)* [1994] 2 FLR 1065; *Re L (Medical Treatment: Gillick Competency)* [1998] 2 FLR 810.

[143] *Re S (A Minor) (Consent to Medical Treatment)* [1994] 2 FLR 1065 (15½-year-old Jehovah's Witness refusing blood transfusion necessary to save her life).

(b) Who Can Consent

The child's consent

4.65 A 'Gillick competent' child's consent to treatment is as valid and effective as the consent of an adult who is sui juris.

Parental Consent

4.66 A parent can lawfully consent to the treatment of a 'Gillick competent' child who is refusing to consent.[144] A parent cannot overrule a 'Gillick competent' child's consent to treatment,[145] but can, in effect, overrule a 'Gillick competent' child's refusal to consent to treatment: the parent and the child have concurrent powers to consent and where more than one person has a power of consent, only a failure to, or refusal of, consent by all creates a veto.[146]

4.67 The law is clear and settled (short of the House of Lords) but the cases in which the law was thus established by the Court of Appeal are controversial and have been heavily criticised by academic writers on a number of grounds.[147] First, it is said that the law as laid down by the Court of Appeal conflicts with Lord Scarman's analysis in *Gillick* when he described what he called the parents' 'right to determine whether or not their minor child . . . will have medical treatment' as terminating when the child becomes 'Gillick competent'. The words 'whether or not' certainly suggest[148] that, in Lord Scarman's opinion, the parent's consent is not effective where a 'Gillick competent' child has refused consent. Lord Scarman clearly viewed the policy of the common law as dictating that, once a child of whatever age has the capacity to give an informed and valid consent, that terminates the parent's right to veto the child's *views one way or the other*. Nothing in Lord Scarman's speech in *Gillick* supports the view that the parent's right to consent and the child's right to consent are ever co-existent or co-terminous. Secondly, it is said to be illogical to accept that a parent cannot veto the competent child's consent to treatment while asserting that the patent can overrule the child's refusal of treatment. Such a view is wholly destructive of the child's right to self-determination and capable of producing some extremely odd results: it is not easy to see what

---

[144] *In re R (A Minor) (Wardship: Consent to Treatment)* [1992] Fam 11, 23–25, 26; *In re W (A Minor) (Medical Treatment: Court's Jurisdiction)* [1993] Fam 64, 84, 86, 87; *Re K, W and H (Minors) (Medical Treatment)* [1993] 1 FLR 854, 859.

[145] *In re R (A Minor) (Wardship: Consent to Treatment)* [1992] Fam 11, 23, 26; *In re W (A Minor) (Medical Treatment: Court's Jurisdiction)* [1993] Fam 64, 83.

[146] *In re R (A Minor) (Wardship: Consent to Treatment)* [1992] Fam 11, 22, 26.

[147] See, for example, Bainham, 'The Judge and the Competent Minor' (1992) 108 LQR 194, 198–9; Thornton, 'Multiple Keyholders' [1992] CLJ 34; Dyer (ed), *Doctors, Patients and the Law* (1992), 58–61 (Kennedy), 75–7 (Gostin), 156–7 (Dodds-Smith); Brazier, *Medicine, Patients and the Law* (2nd edn), 345–6.

[148] As Staughton LJ recognised in *In re R (A Minor) (Wardship: Consent to Treatment)* [1992] Fam 11, 27–28.

social purpose or principle of public policy is served by treating the parent, for example, as powerless to veto an abortion which the child wants but the parent objects to, while treating the parent as competent to authorise an abortion which the child does not want but the parent does. The Court of Appeal sought to meet this objection by dismissing the example as 'hair-raising' but inconceivable in real life.[149] But this does not meet the argument of principle and logic. Moreover, and perhaps more to the point, it is difficult to see what purpose is achieved by conferring on parents a power which in practice cannot be exercised. Thirdly, it is said that the distinction drawn between 'consent' and 'determination' is fallacious and unworkable. The Court of Appeal sought to avoid the difficulties created by Lord Scarman's concept of 'determination' by accepting that there is no parental right to determine, in the sense of a right to nullify or veto the 'Gillick competent' child's consent, and asserting only a 'concurrent' parental right to 'consent'. But the truth is (so it is said) that in a case where the child has refused to consent, and the parent then supplies his own concurrent consent, the parent is 'determining' the matter—so the suggested distinction between 'determination' and 'consent' falls apart. Fourthly, it is said to run counter to the philosophy of the Children Act 1989, which, in the context of certain forms of medical and psychiatric examination, assessment and treatment, recognises and gives effect to the child's right to self-determination and treats his objection as conclusive whenever he has 'sufficient understanding to make an informed decision' (ss 38(6), 43(8), 44(7), Sch 3, paras 4(4)(a), 5(5)(a)).

The court

The court is not bound by the wishes or decision of a 'Gillick competent' child.[150] **4.68**
Thus the court, if only it chooses to exercise its inherent powers,[151] can always outflank what might appear to be the perfectly clear legislative policy laid down in the Children Act 1989 and can do the very things which the Act has said that it shall not do. It is not easy to reconcile this view of the law with the principle that prerogative power yields to inconsistent statutory provisions.[152]

---

[149] *In re W (A Minor) (Medical Treatment: Court's Jurisdiction)* [1993] Fam 64, 79, 89–90.

[150] *In re R (A Minor) (Wardship: Consent to Treatment)* [1992] Fam 11, 25, 26, 28, 31, 32; *In re W (A Minor) (Medical Treatment: Court's Jurisdiction)* [1993] Fam 64, 81, 84, 88, 93; *South Glamorgan County Council v W and B* [1993] 1 FLR 574, 584; *Re L (Medical Treatment: Gillick Competency)* [1998] 2 FLR 810, 813. The previous cases bearing on the point were: *B(BR) v B(J)* [1968] P 466; *Re P (A Minor)* [1986] 1 FLR 272, *Re G-U (A Minor) (Wardship)* [1984] FLR 811; *Re E (A Minor) (Wardship: Medical Treatment)* [1993] 1 FLR 386; *Re B (Wardship: Abortion)* [1991] 2 FLR 426.

[151] As in *South Glamorgan County Council v W and B* [1993] 1 FLR 574 (order under inherent jurisdiction for psychiatric examination and assessment of 'Gillick competent' child who had validly refused consent under s 38(6)). See also *In re W (A Minor) (Medical Treatment: Court's Jurisdiction)* [1993] Fam 64, 82.

[152] *AG v De Keyser's Royal Hotel Ltd* [1920] AC 508; cf also *Richards v Richards* [1984] AC 174.

(iii) The 16 or 17-year-old Child

4.69 Section 8 of the Family Law Reform Act 1969 provides:

(1) The consent of a minor who has attained the age of sixteen years to any surgical, medical or dental treatment which, in the absence of consent, would constitute a trespass to his person, shall be as effective as it would be if he were of full age; and where a minor has by virtue of this section given an effective consent to any treatment it shall not be necessary to obtain any consent for it from his parent or guardian.

(2) In this section 'surgical, medical or dental treatment' includes any procedure undertaken for the purposes of diagnosis, and this section applies to any procedure (including, in particular, the administration of an anaesthetic) which is ancillary to any treatment as it applies to that treatment.

(3) Nothing in this section shall be construed as making ineffective any consent which would have been effective if this section had not been enacted.

Section 8 does not extend to the donation of organs, or of blood or other bodily substances, nor even to the taking of a blood sample (for which separate provision is made in s 21(2)), for none of these procedures constitutes either treatment or diagnosis.[153]

Parental Consent

4.70 As in the case of a 'Gillick competent' child, and for the same reasons, a parent cannot overrule a 16 or 17-year-old child's consent to treatment but can, in effect, overrule such a child's refusal to consent to treatment.[154] This view of the law has, again, been the subject of severe academic criticism, as involving an inappropriately narrow construction of the langauge of s 8, which had previously been considered as conferring 'complete autonomy' on the 16 or 17-year-old child.

The Court

4.71 Notwithstanding s 8 of the 1969 Act, the court in the exercise of its inherent parens patriae jurisdiction is not bound by the wishes of a 16 or 17-year old child.[155]

(iv) The Mentally Incompetent Child

The Mentally Incompetent Child Under the Age of 16

4.72 A mentally incompetent child may, because of its mental disability, never acquire 'Gillick competence'. Alternatively, it may have 'Gillick competence' for some limited purposes but lack the capacity to give a valid consent to a particular form

---

[153] *In re W (A Minor) (Medical Treatment: Court's Jurisdiction)* [1993] Fam 64, 78, 83, 92, 94; *In re O (A Minor) (Blood Tests: Constraint), In re J (A Minor)* [2000] Fam 139, 147–148.

[154] *In re R (A Minor) (Wardship: Consent to Treatment)* [1992] Fam 11, 24, 26; *In re W (A Minor) (Medical Treatment: Court's Jurisdiction)* [1993] Fam 64, 74–79, 83–84, 86–87.

[155] *In re R (A Minor) (Wardship: Consent to Treatment)* [1992] Fam 11; *In re W (A Minor) (Medical Treatment: Court's Jurisdiction)* [1993] Fam 64, 81, 83–84, 91–92.

of medical treatment. In such a case the power to decide whether or not the child should be treated will remain in the parents or the court.

The Mentally-Incompetent 16 or 17-year-old Child

All that s 8(1) of the Family Law Reform Act 1969 does is to deem the 16-year-old **4.73** child to have the same *legal* capacity as he would if he were 18 ('consent . . . shall be as effective as . . . if he were of full age'). The bare fact of age apart, s 8(1) does not deem the child to have any *mental* capacity which in fact he lacks. Thus in the case of a mentally incompetent 16-year-old the power to decide will, notwithstanding s 8, remain in the parents or the court until the child attains the age of 18.[156] Consistently with s 8(1) the mental competence of a 16 or 17-year-old child is judged by reference not to 'Gillick capacity' but to the test applicable in the case of an adult, that is, the test in *In re C (Adult: Refusal of Treatment)*.[157]

3. The Ambit of Parental Consent

Limitations on the Parental Power to Consent

Even where the law recognises the capacity of a parent to give a proxy or substitute **4.74** consent on behalf of a child, the parental right to decide is not absolute. The parental power to give a valid consent is subject to five limitations. In the first place no parent can consent to any procedure which is unlawful. Secondly, where the child is a ward of court parental power is limited by the principle that it is necessary to obtain the prior consent of the court before any 'important' or 'major' step is taken in the life of the child.[158] Thirdly, any parental giving or refusal of consent must be in the best interests of the child. Fourthly, there are certain procedures, not unlawful in themselves, but which are nonetheless considered to be of such a nature as to require the prior sanction of the court. Fifthly, there are limits to the consent which a parent can give in the case of a child old enough to understand what is involved.

Control by the Court

Consistently with the principle that the parental right to decide is not absolute, **4.75** the court is not bound by and can override a parent's decision;[159] the court can overrule parental consent to treatment which is not in the best interests of the

---

[156] *In re R (A Minor) (Wardship: Consent to Treatment)* [1992] Fam 11, 24.
[157] [1994] 1 WLR 290; *A Metropolitan Borough Council v AB* [1997] 1 FLR 767, 773; *Re C (Detention: Medical Treatment)* [1997] 2 FLR 180, 195. See further paras 4.117–4.119 below.
[158] See para 4.47 above.
[159] *Gillick v West Norfolk and Wisbech AHA* [1986] AC 112, 184, 200; *In re C (A Minor) (Wardship: Medical Treatment) (No 2)* [1990] Fam 39, 46; *In re J (A Minor) (Wardship: Medical Treatment)* [1991] Fam 33, 52; *In re R (A Minor) (Wardship: Consent to Treatment)* [1992] Fam 11, 25; *In re W (A Minor) (Medical Treatment: Court's Jurisdiction)* [1993] Fam 64, 93; *In re Z (A Minor) (Identification: Restrictions on Publication)* [1997] Fam 1, 30–31.

child[160] and overrule parental refusal to consent to treatment which is in the best interests of the child.[161] However, the court always acts 'extremely cautiously'[162] and will act in opposition to the parent only when judicially satisfied that the parental rights should be suspended or superseded.[163] The question is not whether the parent is acting reasonably but what is in the best interests of the child.[164] But the law recognises that there is a 'margin of appreciation' within which parental decision-making is unlikely to be superseded by the court:

> The law's insistence that the welfare of a child shall be paramount is easily stated and universally applauded, but the present case[165] illustrates, poignantly and dramatically, the difficulties that are encountered when trying to put it into practice. . . . It is not an occasion—even in an age preoccupied with 'rights'—to talk of the rights of a child, or the rights of a parent, or the rights of the court. The cases . . . are uncompromising in their assertion that the sole yard-stick must be the need to give effect to the demands of paramountcy for the welfare of the child. They establish that there are bound to be occasions when such paramountcy will compel the court,

---

[160] *In re D (A Minor) (Wardship: Sterilisation)* [1976] Fam 185 (sterilisation restrained despite parent's consent: as Heilbron J said, 194, 'in wardship proceedings parents' rights can be superseded'); *Re C (Medical Treatment)* [1998] 1 FLR 384 (Orthodox Jewish parents wishing 16-month-old daughter suffering from terminal spinal muscular atrophy, type 1, to be ventilated in event of respiratory relapse and not willing to agree to only palliative care as recommended by doctors); *Royal Wolverhampton Hospitals NHS Trust v B* [2000] 1 FLR 953.

[161] *In re B (A Minor) (Wardship: Medical Treatment)* [1981] 1 WLR 1421 (order directing life-saving operation on 10-day-old mongol child notwithstanding parents' bona fide decision to let nature take its course); *Re P (A Minor)* [1986] 1 FLR 272 (order directing abortion on 15-year-old girl notwithstanding parents' bona fide objections on religious and other grounds); *Re E (A Minor) (Wardship: Medical Treatment)* [1993] 1 FLR 386 (order directing blood transfusion for 15-year-old leukaemic Jehovah's Witness notwithstanding parents' religious objections); *Re B (Wardship: Abortion)* [1991] 2 FLR 426 (order directing abortion on 12-year-old girl not withstanding parent's bona fide objections); *Re S (A Minor) (Medical Treatment)* [1993] 1 FLR 376 (order directing blood transfusion for 4-year-old leukaemic child of Jehovah's Witnesses); *Re O (A Minor) (Medical Treatment)* [1993] 2 FLR 149 (order directing blood transfusion for 2-month-old child with respiratory problems of Jehovah's Witnesses); *Re R (A Minor) (Blood Transfusion)* [1993] 2 FLR 757 (order directing blood transfusion for 10-month-old leukaemic child of Jehovah's Witnesses); *Re C (Medical Treatment)* [1998] 1 FLR 384 (Orthodox Jewish parents wishing 16-month-old daughter suffering from terminal spinal muscular atrophy, type 1, to be ventilated in event of respiratory relapse and not willing to agree to only palliative care as recommended by doctors: order directing palliative care); *Re L (Medical Treatment: Gillick Competency)* [1998] 2 FLR 810 (order directing blood transfusion for 14-year-old Jehovah's Witness suffering from life-threatening burns); *In re C (A Child) (HIV Testing)* [2000] Fam 48 (affirmed *Re C (HIV Test)* [1999] 2 FLR 1004) (order directing HIV testing of 5-month-old baby daughter of HIV positive mother); *Re MM (Medical Treatment)* [2000] 1 FLR 224 (order for lifetime replacement immunoglobin treatment for primary immuno-deficiency in 7-year-old rather than programme of immunostimulant therapy preferred by parents).

[162] *In re C (A Child) (HIV Testing)* [2000] Fam 48, 58, *per* Wilson J (affirmed *Re C (HIV Test)* [1999] 2 FLR 1004).

[163] *In re Z (A Minor) (Identification: Restrictions on Publication)* [1997] Fam 1, 31. See further para 4.39 above, paras 4.78–4.79, 4.170–4.171 below.

[164] *In re T (A Minor) (Wardship: Medical Treatment)* [1997] 1 WLR 242, 250–251, 253–256. See further paras 4.78–4.79, 4.94, 4.144 below.

[165] For the facts of which see below and para 4.209 below.

acting as a judicial parent, to substitute the judge's own views as to the claims of child welfare over those of natural parents—even in a case where the latter are supported by qualities of devotion, commitment, love and reason. . . . All these cases depend on their own facts and render generalisations—tempting though they may be to the legal or social analyst—wholly out of place. It can only be said safely that there is a scale, at one end of which lies the clear case where parental opposition to medical intervention is prompted by scruple or dogma of a kind which is patently irreconcilable with principles of child health and welfare widely accepted by the generality of mankind; and that at the other end lie highly problematic cases where there is genuine scope for a difference of view between parent and judge. In both situations it is the duty of the judge to allow the court's own opinion to prevail in the perceived paramount interests of the child concerned, but in cases at the latter end of the scale, there must be a likelihood (though never of course a certainty) that the greater the scope for genuine debate between one view and another the stronger will be the inclination of the court to be influenced by a reflection that in the last analysis the best interests of every child include an expectation that difficult decisions affecting the length and quality of its life will be taken for it by the parent to whom its care has been entrusted by nature.[166]

Moreover, even in the case of potentially life-saving treatment, the court may be more willing to overrule parental refusal to consent where the child's life-threatening condition can be cured by a simple 'one-off' operation[167] than where the child requires complicated surgery and the total commitment to the treatment, and many years of special care, by a parent upon whom the child's welfare depends but who has conscientiously come to the conclusion that such treatment, with all that it may entail for the child in terms of risks, discomfort and distress, a lifetime of drugs, and the possibility of further invasive surgery, would not be in the child's best interests.[168]

Control by the Doctor

As has already been seen, parental decision-making is in practical terms subject to considerable control by the doctor.[169] **4.76**

(i) Unlawful Procedures

Some forms of interference with the body are unlawful, in the sense that even a competent adult cannot give a consent which the law recognises as lawful and effective.[170] The general rule, however, is that 'reasonable surgical interference' is **4.77**

---

[166] *In re T (A Minor) (Wardship: Medical Treatment)* [1997] 1 WLR 242, 253–254 *per* Waite LJ.
[167] As in *In re B (A Minor) (Wardship: Medical Treatment)* [1981] 1 WLR 1421. See *In re T (A Minor) (Wardship: Medical Treatment)* [1997] 1 WLR 242, 252 *per* Butler-Sloss LJ.
[168] As in *In re T (A Minor) (Wardship: Medical Treatment)* [1997] 1 WLR 242 (child suffering from life-threatening liver defect requiring liver transplant). See the critical discussion by Professor Grubb in [1996] 4(3) Med L Rev 315. See also *In re A (Children) (Conjoined Twins: Surgical Separation)* [2001] Fam 147, 194–195, 244.
[169] See paras 4.20–4.21 above.
[170] *Attorney-General's Reference (No 6 of 1980)* [1981] QB 715; *R v Brown* [1994] AC 212.

lawful as being in the public interest.[171] Nonetheless, from time to time it has been suggested that certain surgical procedures are unlawful. Thus it has been said that female circumcision for non-therapeutic purposes is unlawful at common law[172] (it has now been made illegal by statute).[173] On the other hand, there is no doubt that male circumcision, for whatever reason it is performed, is not as such unlawful,[174] nor is a 'sex-change' or 'gender reassignment' operation whether from male to 'female' (involving castration and removal of the penis)[175] or from female to 'male',[176] nor is a sterilisation, for whatever reason it is performed.[177]

(ii) Best Interests

4.78 Parental rights exist not for the benefit of the parent or anyone else but for the benefit of the child.[178] The parental power to give a substituted consent to medical treatment for a child must be exercised in the best interests of the child, objectively assessed on a judgment of what is best for the welfare of the particular child.[179]

> Parental rights clearly do exist, and they do not wholly disappear until the age of majority. Parental rights relate to both the persons and the property of the child—custody, care, and control of the person and guardianship of the property of the child. But the common law has never treated such rights as sovereign or beyond review and control. Nor has our law ever treated the child as other than a person with capacities and rights recognised by law. The principle of the law . . . is that parental rights are derived from parental duty and exist only so long as they are needed for the protection of the person and property of the child. . . . [P]arental right must be

---

[171] *Attorney-General's Reference (No 6 of 1980)* [1981] QB 715, 719.

[172] Lord Hailsham of St Marylebone LC, *Hansard*, HL vol 441, cols 676–7, 694–5 (1983); Mackay, 'Is Female Circumcision Unlawful?' [1983] Crim LR 717; Hayter, 'Female Circumcision—Is there a legal solution?' [1984] JSWL 323.

[173] Prohibition of Female Circumcision Act 1985.

[174] *R v Brown* [1994] AC 212, 231; *Re J (Specific Issue Orders: Muslim Upbringing and Circumcision)* [1999] 2 FLR 678 (affirmed *Re J (Specific Issue Orders: Child's Religious Upbringing and Circumcision)* [2000] 1 FLR 571). See also The National Health Service (General Medical Services) Regulations 1992, SI 1992/635, Sch 2, para 38(i) (which permits a doctor to charge a fee for 'circumcising a patient for whom such an operation is requested on religious grounds and is not needed on any medical ground'). See also *Hickey v Croydon AHA* The Times, 6 March 1985 (claim for damages for negligence in circumcising adult who sought operation to 'improve his sex life': Michael Davies J justified the legality of the operation by reference to Gen xvii: vv 10–14).

[175] *Corbett v Corbett* [1971] P 83, 99. See also *R v Tan* [1983] QB 1053.

[176] *In re A* (1993) 16 Fam LR 715 (Fam Ct Aus).

[177] Denning LJ's dicta in *Bravery v Bravery* [1954] 1 WLR 1169, 1180–1181, if they were ever good law (Evershed MR and Hodson LJ expressed the contrary view, 1175–1176), are now universally regarded as no longer representing the law: *In re B (A Minor) (Wardship: Sterilisation)* [1988] AC 199; *In re F (Mental Patient: Sterilisation)* [1990] 2 AC 1; *Secretary, Department of Health and Community Services v JWB and SMB* (1992) 175 CLR 218, 234.

[178] For the suggestion that the parental role is fiduciary, and that a parent with a conflicting interest to that of the child is therefore disqualified from giving consent, see *Secretary, Department of Health and Community Services v JWB and SMB* (1992) 175 CLR 218, 317.

[179] *Gillick v West Norfolk and Wisbech AHA* [1986] AC 112, 170, 173, 183–185, 200; *Secretary, Department of Health and Community Services v JWB and SMB* (1992) 175 CLR 218, 240, 278, 295, 316.

exercised in accordance with the welfare principle and can be challenged, even overridden, if it be not. . . . [P]arental right endures only so long as it is needed for the protection of the child.[180]

Community Standards and Parental Views

In determining what is in the best interests of their children, parents are entitled **4.79** to follow their own moral and social views within the limits set by the general standards of society.

> [O]ne can identify two broad common law propositions relating to the authority of parents to authorise surgery in the case of . . . a child who is, as a matter of fact, completely unable to make a reasoned decision for herself or himself about the desirability of the particular treatment. The first of those propositions is that parental authority exists to authorise such surgery for the purpose, and only for the purpose, of advancing the welfare of the child. It does not extend to authorising surgery because of a perception that it is in the interests of those responsible for the care of the child or in the interests of society in general (eg, for eugenic reasons). That which constitutes the welfare of a child in a particular case falls to be determined by reference to general community standards, but making due allowance for the entitlement of parents, within the limits of what is permissible in accordance with those standards, to entertain divergent views about the moral and secular objectives to be pursued for their children. The second broad proposition is that, at least in relation to a serious matter such as a major medical procedure, parental authority can be validly exercised only after due inquiry about, and adequate consideration of, what truly represents the welfare of the child in all the circumstances of the case.[181]

This approach is reflected in the cases[182] and is mirrored both by commentators[183] who acknowledge that, in bringing up their children, parents have to address the basic moral issue of what sort of child they wish to raise and have a wide range of discretion to pursue goals which society as a whole may find undesirable, but which it will tolerate, and by those commentators[184] who justify infant male circumcision (in contrast to female circumcision) on the basis of immemorial usage and social or religious toleration.[185]

---

[180] *Gillick v West Norfolk and Wisbech AHA* [1986] AC 112, 183–185 *per* Lord Scarman.

[181] *Secretary, Department of Health and Community Services v JWB and SMB* (1992) 175 CLR 218, 295 *per* Deane J.

[182] See *In re T (A Minor) (Wardship: Medical Treatment)* [1997] 1 WLR 242, esp, 254 *per* Waite LJ quoted at para 4.75 above.

[183] McCall Smith, 'Is Anything Left of Parental Rights?' in Sutherland and McCall Smith (eds), *Family Rights: Family Law and Medical Advance* (1990), 4; Bainham, 'Non-Intervention and Judicial Paternalism' in Birks (ed), *The Frontiers of Liability, Volume 1* (1994), 173.

[184] Glanville Williams, 'Consent and Public Policy' [1962] Crim LR 74, 154, 157, Glanville Williams, *Textbook of Criminal Law* (2nd edn), 575, 586; Mackay, 'Is Female Circumcision Unlawful?' [1983] Crim LR 717, 719; Hayter, 'Female Circumcision—Is there a legal solution?' [1984] JSWL 323, 326.

[185] For ritual male circumcision see now *Re J (Specific Issue Orders: Muslim Upbringing and Circumcision)* [1999] 2 FLR 678 (affirmed *Re J (Specific Issue Orders: Child's Religious Upbringing and Circumcision)* [2000] 1 FLR 571); *Re S (Change of Names: Cultural Factors)* [2001] 2 FLR 1005. See further paras 4.170–4.171 below.

Procedures not Contrary to the Child's Interests

4.80   Some commentators have suggested that a parent can lawfully give consent to any procedure to which a 'reasonable parent' would consent and which, even if not positively beneficial to the child, is neither cruel, nor excessive nor clearly against the child's interests. It is on this basis that some commentators justify routine neonatal male circumcision, in contrast to circumcision for religious or ritual purposes,[186] on the footing that the attendant risks are not so great as to be 'contrary to the child's interest'.[187] Such a principle is said to be supported by the decision of the House of Lords that a child can be blood-tested for forensic purposes even if it cannot be shown that a blood-test will be in its best interests.[188]

> It is a legal wrong to use constraint to an adult beyond what is authorised by statute or ancient common law powers connected with crime and the like. But it is not and could not be a legal wrong for a parent or person authorised by him to use constraint to his young child provided it is not cruel or excessive. There are differences of opinion as to the age beyond which it is unwise to use constraint, but that cannot apply to infants or young children. So it seems to me to be impossible to deny that a parent can lawfully require that his young child should submit to a blood test. . . . [S]urely a reasonable parent would have some regard to the general public interest and would not refuse a blood test unless he thought that would clearly be against the interests of the child.[189]

This perhaps reflects a suggested wider principle of the child's civic duty:

> Children, whether wards of court or not, are citizens owing duties to society as a whole (including other children), which are appropriate to their years and understanding. Those duties are defined both by the common law and by statute.[190]

This view of the ambit of parental power, at least if it is to be relied upon as a rule of wide-ranging application, is difficult to reconcile either with basic principle or

---

[186] As to which see now *Re J (Specific Issue Orders: Muslim Upbringing and Circumcision)* [1999] 2 FLR 678 (affirmed *Re J (Specific Issue Orders: Child's Religious Upbringing and Circumcision)* [2000] 1 FLR 571); *Re S (Change of Names: Cultural Factors)* [2001] 2 FLR 1005.

[187] Skegg, *Law, Ethics, and Medicine* (2nd edn), 66; Poulter, *English Law and Ethnic Minority Customs*, para 6.28. This is very questionable given the nature of the attendant risks: see further paras 4.156, 4.158 below.

[188] *S v McC, W v W* [1972] AC 24 discussed in *In re Z (A Minor) (Identification: Restrictions on Publication)* [1997] Fam 1, 20, 28–29. See also the Family Law Reform Act 1969, s 21(3); *In re F (A Minor) (Blood Tests: Parental Rights)* [1993] Fam 314; *Re L (A Minor) (Blood Tests)* [1996] 2 FCR 649; *In re H (A Minor) (Blood Tests: Parental Rights)* [1997] Fam 89; *Re T (Paternity: Ordering Blood Tests)* [2001] 2 FLR 1190; *Re H and A (Paternity: Blood Tests)* [2002] EWCA Civ 383, [2002] 1 FLR 1145. For the impact in this context of Art 8 of the ECHR see *Re T (Paternity: Ordering Blood Tests)* [2001] 2 FLR 1190, 1197–1199.

[189] *S v McC, W v W* [1972] AC 24, 43–44 *per* Lord Reid. See also, 48, 51 *per* Lord MacDermott (blood test will not be ordered if it 'would prejudicially affect the health of the infant'), 58–59 *per* Lord Hodson ('protection may be needed for health reasons').

[190] *In re R (A Minor) (Wardship: Criminal Proceedings)* [1991] Fam 56, 65 *per* Lord Donaldson of Lymington MR.

with more recent cases. It is best treated as confined to procedures which involve no more than 'minimal' or 'negligible' risk and discomfort, eg, the taking of nasal or throat swabs and urine or blood samples (including the taking of a blood sample by venepuncture).

(iii) Procedures Requiring the Sanction of the Court

Concern, in particular at the prospect of parents consenting to the non-therapeutic sterilisation of mentally-handicapped children,[191] has led the courts in a number of jurisdictions to consider whether there are not certain procedures, not unlawful in themselves, but which are nonetheless of such a nature that the prior sanction of the court ought, either as a matter of law or at the very least as a matter of good practice, always to be obtained. Thus at first it was suggested[192] that a court exercising the inherent parens patriae jurisdiction is the only authority empowered to authorise such a drastic step as sterilisation. And the High Court of Australia has since held that, as a matter of law, a parent lacks the capacity to give a valid consent to the non-therapeutic sterilisation of a child.[193] In England, however, it would now seem that, unless the child is already a ward of court, the prior sanction of the court is never required as a matter of law,[194] though 'as a matter of good practice' it should always be obtained[195] in those cases falling within what has been described as a 'special category'.[196] A similar approach has been adopted in relation to adult incompetents.[197] **4.81**

Precisely which cases are to be treated as falling within the special category has deliberately been left undefined, to be considered on a case-by-case basis.[198] Initially, it was suggested that the special category would or might include sterilisation, **4.82**

---

[191] There is no doubt that in this country *In re D (A Minor) (Wardship: Sterilisation)* [1976] Fam 185 (in which a highly qualified medical practitioner supported by a caring mother, who were proposing to sterilise a mentally handicapped 11-year-old girl, were held by Heilbron J not to be acting in her best interests, although no one had challenged their skill, bona fides, or quality of care) had a powerful effect in influencing the development of this branch of the law: see *In re F (Mental Patient: Sterilisation)* [1990] 2 AC 1, 20, 41, 69 ('stark warning of the danger'), 79 ('vivid illustration').

[192] *In re B (A Minor) (Wardship: Sterilisation)* [1987] 2 All ER 206, 210, [1988] AC 199, 206.

[193] *Secretary, Department of Health and Community Services v JWB and SMB* (1992) 175 CLR 218.

[194] But cf *Re E (A Minor) (Medical Treatment)* [1991] 2 FLR 585, 587 which can be read as suggesting that it is because the parents of a mentally retarded child are in a position to give a valid consent to a therapeutic sterilisation that 'accordingly' the consent of the court is not required—from which it might be deduced that the consent of the court is required in those cases in which the parents are not in a position to give a valid consent.

[195] In some cases the court, once it has been able to investigate the matter fully, may be willing to devolve the final decision to the attending doctor subject to suitable safeguards: *Re R (Adult: Medical Treatment)* [1996] 2 FLR 99, 104, 106–110. See further para 4.135 below.

[196] *In re F (Mental Patient: Sterilisation)* [1990] 2 AC 1, 19–20, 33, 42, 51, 56–57, 78–80, 83. See also *Airedale NHS Trust v Bland* [1993] AC 789, 805–806, 815–816, 859, 873–874.

[197] See further para 4.129 below.

[198] *In re F (Mental Patient: Sterilisation)* [1990] 2 AC 1, 57.

abortion, organ donation, and the disconnection of life-support machines.[199] Subsequent decisions indicate that the special category of cases which require the prior sanction of the court includes a non-therapeutic sterilisation,[200] the donation of regenerative tissues (bone marrow),[201] the withdrawal of food from a patient in the permanent (formerly called persistent) vegetative state,[202] cases where the capacity of a pregnant woman to consent to or refuse a caesarian section is in issue,[203] and any case in which the application of restraint or use of force on a non-compliant patient is envisaged,[204] but that it does not include a brain scan,[205] psychiatric treatment,[206] an abortion,[207] or a therapeutic sterilisation.[208] It is clear that the donation of a non-regenerative organ (eg, a kidney) falls within the special category,[209] so also, it is suggested, would a 'sex-change' or 'gender reassignment' operation.[210] Whether, and if so to what extent and in which circumstances, the withholding of life-saving treatment generally falls within the special category is unclear.[211]

4.83 The special category thus far considered relates to those procedures for which, as a matter of good practice, judicial sanction should be obtained even if *all* the persons who have parental responsibility for the child (for example, both parents) are united in support of what is proposed. More recently the courts have identified a

---

[199] *In re F (Mental Patient: Sterilisation)* [1990] 2 AC 1, 19, 33, 40, 42.

[200] ibid.

[201] *In re Y (Mental Patient: Bone Marrow Donation)* [1997] Fam 110, 116: quaere in relation to donations of blood or other regenerative bodily fluids.

[202] This was said to be for 'the protection of patients, the protection of doctors, the reassurance of patients' families and the reassurance of the public': *Airedale NHS Trust v Bland* [1993] AC 789, 815 *per* Sir Thomas Bingham MR, approved, 859 *per* Lord Keith of Kinkel, 874 *per* Lord Goff of Chieveley. See further para 4.124 below.

[203] *Re MB (Medical Treatment)* [1997] 2 FLR 426.

[204] *Re VS (Adult: Mental Disorder)* (1995) Aug 17 (Douglas Brown J), [1995] 3 Med LR 292; *Tameside and Glossop Acute Services Trust v CH* [1996] 1 FLR 762, 774.

[205] *Re H (Mental Patient: Diagnosis)* [1993] 1 FLR 28 (a case involving an adult incompetent).

[206] *Re K, W and H (Minors) (Medical Treatment)* [1993] 1 FLR 854.

[207] *Re SG (Adult Mental Patient: Abortion)* [1991] 2 FLR 329 (adult incompetent).

[208] *Re E (A Minor) (Medical Treatment)* [1991] 2 FLR 585 (consent of court not necessary for therapeutic hysterectomy to relieve serious menorrhagia of severely mentally handicapped 17-year-old girl: parents able to give valid consent, as sterilisation would not be the purpose, although the inevitable and incidental result, of the operation). Similarly in the case of a mentally incompetent adult: *Re GF (Medical Treatment)* [1992] 1 FLR 293 (declaration of court not needed regarding legality of hysterectomy to relieve excessively heavy periods which would have the incidental effect of sterilising a mentally handicapped woman of 29 if two medical practitioners are satisfied that the operation is necessary for therapeutic purposes and in the best interests of the patient and that there is no practicable less intrusive means of treating the condition).

[209] *In re F (Mental Patient: Sterilisation)* [1990] 2 AC 1, 19, 33, 40; *In re W (A Minor) (Medical Treatment: Court's Jurisdiction)* [1993] Fam 64, 79, 94.

[210] So held by the Family Court of Australia: *In re A* (1993) 16 Fam LR 715.

[211] Compare *In re J (A Minor) (Wardship: Medical Treatment)* [1991] Fam 33, 51; *Re C (A Baby)* [1996] 2 FLR 43, 45; *Re R (Adult: Medical Treatment)* [1996] 2 FLR 99.

further category of what has been described[212] as 'a small group of important decisions made on behalf of a child which, in the absence of agreement with those with parental responsibility, ought not to be carried out or arranged by a one-parent carer', even if that parent has parental responsibility under s 2(7) of the Children Act 1989, and where 'a decision ought not to be made without the specific approval of the court'. Thus far this category has been held to include circumcision, other than in a case of medical necessity,[213] and what have been described as 'hotly contested issues of immunisation'.[214]

(iv) The Older Child

There are two further limitations upon the parent's power to consent to treatment **4.84** in the case of an older child. In the first place, the commentators suggest, and it would seem correct in principle (for it corresponds with the principle adopted by the court in the exercise of its jurisdiction),[215] that parental consent will not be sufficient in the case of a non-therapeutic procedure if the child is old enough to understand what is involved and is either left uninformed or actually withholds his or her consent.[216] This principle would apply, for example, to a blood-test[217] or the ritual circumcision of an older boy.[218] Secondly, and even in the case of therapeutic procedures, the jurisdiction of the court should always be invoked where parents are prepared to consent, but a child capable of understanding what is involved, is refusing to consent to some major form of treatment.[219]

4. The Court

(i) When the Court is Involved

The court may be involved in matters relating to the medical treatment of a child **4.85** for a variety of different reasons: if the child is already a ward of court, because the law requires prior judicial consent before any 'important' or 'major' step in the

---

[212] *Re J (Specific Issue Orders: Child's Religious Upbringing and Circumcision)* [2000] 1 FLR 571, 577, *per* Dame Elizabeth Butler-Sloss P.

[213] *Re J (Specific Issue Orders: Child's Religious Upbringing and Circumcision)* [2000] 1 FLR 571, 576, 577, affirming *Re J (Specific Issue Orders: Muslim Upbringing and Circumcision)* [1999] 2 FLR 678, 701–702.

[214] *Re C (Welfare of Child: Immunisation)* [2003] EWCA Civ 1148; [2003] 2 FLR 1095 at [16]–[17] (MMR and other vaccinations and immunisations).

[215] See further paras 4.99, 4.178, 4.189 below.

[216] Glanville Williams, *Textbook of Criminal Law* (2nd edn), 576, Poulter, *English Law and Ethnic Minority Customs*, para 6.28.

[217] *S v McC, W v W* [1972] AC 24, 45.

[218] The point, at least in this form, seems not to have been considered either in *Re J (Specific Issue Orders: Muslim Upbringing and Circumcision)* [1999] 2 FLR 678 (affirmed *Re J (Specific Issue Orders: Child's Religious Upbringing and Circumcision)* [2000] 1 FLR 571) or in *Re S (Change of Names: Cultural Factors)* [2001] 2 FLR 1005.

[219] *In re W (A Minor) (Medical Treatment: Court's Jurisdiction)* [1993] Fam 64, 79, 90, 94.

ward's life is taken;[220] if there are disputes between parents and doctor, or between parents and child or between the parents themselves, so that the court can decide what the best interests of the child require; or in cases falling within the 'special category', so that the court can decide whether or not to give the prior sanction which good practice requires.[221]

The Need to Involve the Court

4.86 It is necessary to involve the court only if the child is already a ward of court or if the case falls within the 'special category'. In cases not falling within the 'special category' there is no need to involve the court unless the child is already a ward of court.

Involving the Court Unnecessarily

4.87 Where there is no disagreement between the child's parents and the doctor, and the proposed treatment is not one which, either because of its nature or because the child is a ward of court, requires the prior sanction of the court, the court will treat the parents' consent as sufficient authority and protection for the doctor and refuse to grant relief.[222] The court may decline to act even though there is a dispute between a 'Gillick competent' child, who is refusing to consent, and its parents, so long as the parents have given the doctor their consent to the proposed treatment.[223]

(ii) The Jurisdiction of the Court

4.88 The court may be involved in the exercise of its inherent parens patriae jurisdiction, the wardship jurisdiction, or its statutory jurisdiction under the Children Act 1989.[224] In relation to the medical treatment of children the substantive powers of the court are the same, and are exercised in accordance with precisely the same principles, whichever jurisdiction is being exercised.[225]

Invoking the Jurisdiction of the Court

4.89 If the child is already a ward of court application is made by summons in the wardship.[226] If the child is not a ward, and there are no other relevant proceedings

---

[220] See para 4.47 above.

[221] See paras 4.81–4.82 above.

[222] *Re SG (Adult Mental Patient: Abortion)* [1991] 2 FLR 329 (abortion—a case involving an adult incompetent); *Re E (A Minor) (Medical Treatment)* [1991] 2 FLR 585 (therapeutic sterilisation); *Re GF (Medical Treatment)* [1992] 1 FLR 293 (therapeutic sterilisation—adult incompetent); *Re H (Mental Patient: Diagnosis)* [1993] 1 FLR 28 (brain scan—adult incompetent).

[223] *Re K, W and H (Minors) (Medical Treatment)* [1993] 1 FLR 854 (psychiatric treatment).

[224] See paras 4.44, 4.52, 4.53 above.

[225] *Re K, W and H (Minors) (Medical Treatment)* [1993] 1 FLR 854, 859.

[226] As in *In re C (A Minor) (Wardship: Medical Treatment)* [1990] Fam 26; *In re J (A Minor) (Wardship: Medical Treatment)* [1991] Fam 33.

pending, the court's assistance can be invoked, unless the applicant is a local authority, either under the inherent jurisdiction[227] or by an ad hoc wardship (that is, by making a child a ward of court for the purpose of resolving a question relating to the child's medical treatment)[228] or by an application for either a prohibited steps order or a specific issue order under the Children Act 1989, s 8.[229] Different views have been expressed as to whether, other things being equal, the preferred course is to invoke the inherent jurisdiction or s 8.[230]

Applications by Local Authorities

Applications by a local authority are governed by the Children Act 1989, s 100(2)(c) (which prevents a child who is in care from being made a ward of court), s 100(3) (which requires a local authority to obtain the leave of the court before invoking the court's inherent jurisdiction), and s 100(4) (which provides that such leave can be granted only if (inter alia) the result which the local authority wishes to achieve cannot be achieved through the making of (inter alia) a prohibited steps order or a specific issue order under s 8). In the case of a child in care a local authority is precluded by s 9(1)[231] from obtaining either a prohibited steps order or a specific issue order. The combined effect of the statutory provisions thus appears to be that an application by a local authority in relation to a child in care

4.90

---

[227] As in *In re J (A Minor) (Child in Care: Medical Treatment)* [1993] Fam 15; *In re W (A Minor) (Medical Treatment: Court's Jurisdiction)* [1993] Fam 64; *South Glamorgan County Council v W and B* [1993] 1 FLR 574; *Re O (A Minor) (Medical Treatment)* [1993] 2 FLR 149; *A Metropolitan Borough Council v AB* [1997] 1 FLR 767; and (arguably incorrectly in the light of *Re R (A Minor) (Blood Transfusion)* [1993] 2 FLR 757) in *Re S (A Minor) (Medical Treatment)* [1993] 1 FLR 376; *Re S (A Minor) (Consent to Medical Treatment)* [1994] 2 FLR 1065; *In re T (A Minor) (Wardship: Medical Treatment)* [1997] 1 WLR 242; *Re C (Detention: Medical Treatment)* [1997] 2 FLR 180; *In re A (Children) (Conjoined Twins: Surgical Separation)* [2001] Fam 147.

[228] As in *In re D (A Minor) (Wardship: Sterilisation)* [1976] Fam 185 (sterilisation); *In re B (A Minor) (Wardship: Medical Treatment)* [1981] 1 WLR 1421 (life-saving surgery); *Re P (A Minor)* [1986] 1 FLR 272 (abortion), *In re B (A Minor) (Wardship: Sterilisation)* [1988] AC 199 (sterilisation); *Re P (A Minor) (Wardship: Sterilisation)* [1989] 1 FLR 182 (sterilisation); *Re E (A Minor) (Wardship: Medical Treatment)* [1993] 1 FLR 386 (blood transfusion); *Re E (A Minor) (Medical Treatment)* [1991] 2 FLR 585 (sterilisation); *Re B (Wardship: Abortion)* [1991] 2 FLR 426 (abortion); *In re R (A Minor) (Wardship: Consent to Treatment)* [1992] Fam 11 (psychiatric treatment with anti-psychotic drugs); *A NHS Trust v D* [2000] 2 FLR 677 (resuscitation of dying child).

[229] As in *Re K, W and H (Minors) (Medical Treatment)* [1993] 1 FLR 854; *Re HG (Specific Issue Order: Sterilisation)* [1993] 1 FLR 587; *Re R (A Minor) (Blood Transfusion)* [1993] 2 FLR 757; *Re J (Specific Issue Orders: Muslim Upbringing and Circumcision)* [1999] 2 FLR 678 (affirmed *Re J (Specific Issue Orders: Child's Religious Upbringing and Circumcision)* [2000] 1 FLR 571).

[230] *Re O (A Minor) (Medical Treatment)* [1993] 2 FLR 149, 155 (inherent jurisdiction preferable); *Re R (A Minor) (Blood Transfusion)* [1993] 2 FLR 757, 760 (s 8 preferable). The Official Solicitor's view was that the procedural and administrative difficulties attaching to applications under s 8 are such that the preferred course is to apply within the inherent jurisdiction: *Practice Note (Official Solicitor: Sterilisation)* [1996] 2 FLR 111, para 2 (now superseded).

[231] cf also ss 9(2), 9(5), 91(1), 91(2) and 100(2).

must be made under the inherent jurisdiction[232] but an application by a local authority in relation to a child who is not in care must be made by way of an application for a s 8 order.[233]

Hearing by High Court Judge

4.91 Whichever form of procedure is invoked the proceedings should be commenced in the High Court, not in the Family Proceedings Court or the County Court, and should be heard by a High Court Judge of the Family Division.[234]

(iii) The Official Solicitor

4.92 As part of his wide-ranging duties and responsibilities the Official Solicitor is involved, either ex officio or as litigation friend or by instructing an advocate to the court (amicus curiae), in virtually all cases relating to the treatment of adult incompetents and was (until his functions in this respect were assumed by Cafcass Legal Services and Special Casework) likewise involved in most cases of any significance relating to the treatment of children. Cases relating to children are now normally handled by Cafcass Legal Services and Special Casework (usually referred to as Cafcass Legal).[235] Members of the staff of Cafcass Legal are prepared to discuss such cases before proceedings have been issued.

4.93 Generally, it was recognised that the Official Solicitor should be invited to act in all cases of any complexity.[236] No doubt the same principle applies now in relation to Cafcass Legal.

---

[232] *South Glamorgan County Council v W and B* [1993] 1 FLR 574 (explaining, 583–584 that the Children Act, s 100(2)(d), is no bar to exercising the inherent jurisdiction); *Re O (A Minor) (Medical Treatment)* [1993] 2 FLR 149.

[233] *Re R (A Minor) (Blood Transfusion)* [1993] 2 FLR 757; *Re J (Specific Issue Order: Leave to Apply)* [1995] 1 FLR 669, 673; *In re C (A Child) (HIV Testing)* [2000] Fam 48 (affirmed *Re C (HIV Test)* [1999] 2 FLR 1004). The point seems to have been overlooked in *Re S (A Minor) (Medical Treatment)* [1993] 1 FLR 376; *Re S (A Minor) (Consent to Medical Treatment)* [1994] 2 FLR 1065; *In re T (A Minor) (Wardship: Medical Treatment)* [1997] 1 WLR 242; and *Re C (Detention: Medical Treatment)* [1997] 2 FLR 180 (but see at 190) where local authorities were given leave under s 100(3) to invoke the inherent jurisdiction even though the child was not in care.

[234] *Re HG (Specific Issue Order: Sterilisation)* [1993] 1 FLR 587, 596; *Re O (A Minor) (Medical Treatment)* [1993] 2 FLR 149, 155; *Re R (A Minor) (Blood Transfusion)* [1993] 2 FLR 757, 760. Proceedings in the Administrative Court by way of an application for judicial review are almost always inappropriate in this type of case: *R v Portsmouth Hospitals NHS Trust, ex p Glass* [1999] 2 FLR 905 (affirming (1999) 50 BMLR 269); *A v A Health Authority, In re J (A Child), R (on the application of S) v Secretary of State for the Home Department* [2002] EWHC 18 (Fam/Admin), [2002] Fam 213, at [71]–[81].

[235] See *Cafcass Practice Note (Officers of CAFCASS Legal Services and Special Casework: Appointment in Family Proceedings)* [2001] 2 FLR 151 and *Practice Note (Official Solicitor: Appointment In Family Proceedings)* [2001] 2 FLR 155.

[236] *Re B (Wardship: Abortion)* [1991] 2 FLR 426, 428; *Re HG (Specific Issue Order: Sterilisation)* [1993] 1 FLR 587, 597. For an unsuccessful attempt to have the Official Solicitor removed as a child's guardian ad litem see *Re A (Conjoined Twins: Medical Treatment) (No 2)* [2001] 1 FLR 267.

D. Children

(iv) Exercise of the Jurisdiction

(a) General Principles

The sole and paramount criterion[237] for the exercise by the court of its jurisdiction, whether it be the inherent parens patriae jurisdiction, the wardship jurisdiction, or its statutory jurisdiction under the Children Act 1989, is the welfare of the child. This was the rule adopted by the High Court of Chancery and is now given statutory force by the Children Act 1989, s 1(1)(a).[238]

> The welfare of this child is the paramount consideration and the court must act in her best interests.[239]

> The first and paramount consideration is the well being, welfare, or interests (each expression occasionally used, but each, for this purpose synonymous) of the human being concerned, that is the ward himself or herself.[240]

Welfare

The courts have traditionally been reluctant to articulate the principles and values to be applied in operating the best interests test,[241] but it is clear that welfare for this purpose must be taken in the widest sense[242] and that it includes the child's ethical, moral, spiritual and religious welfare.[243]

> The dominant matter for the consideration of the Court is the welfare of the child. But the welfare of a child is not to be measured by money only, nor by physical comfort only. The word welfare must be taken in its widest sense. The moral and religious welfare of the child must be considered as well as its physical well-being. Nor can the ties of affection be disregarded.[244]

An Objective Standard[245]

In deciding questions of welfare, the court, acting as 'the judicial reasonable parent', acts by reference to the objective standard of the ordinary reasonable and responsible mother and father,[246] but having regard to the subjective needs of the

4.94

4.95

4.96

---

[237] *In re B (A Minor) (Wardship: Sterilisation)* [1988] AC 199, 212.
[238] *In re Z (A Minor) (Identification: Restrictions on Publication)* [1997] Fam 1, 28–29.
[239] *In re D (A Minor) (Wardship: Sterilisation)* [1976] Fam 185, 194 per Heilbron J.
[240] *In re B (A Minor) (Wardship: Sterilisation)* [1988] AC 199, 202 *per* Lord Hailsham of St Marylebone LC.
[241] See further paras 4.145–4.146 below.
[242] See further paras 4.152–4.175 below.
[243] *In re K (Minors) (Children: Care and Control)* [1977] Fam 179, 187, 191. See further para 4.160 below.
[244] *Re McGrath* [1893] 1 Ch 143, 148 *per* Lindley LJ.
[245] See further para 4.150 below.
[246] *J v C* [1970] AC 668, 723; *In re D (A Minor) (Wardship: Sterilisation)* [1976] Fam 185, 194; *Re E (A Minor) (Wardship: Medical Treatment)* [1993] 1 FLR 386, 392–393; *In re J (A Minor) (Wardship: Medical Treatment)* [1991] Fam 33, 50; *In re R (A Minor) (Wardship: Consent to Treatment)* [1992] Fam 11, 25; *Re O (A Minor) (Medical Treatment)* [1993] 2 FLR 149, 153.

particular child.[247] Thus in deciding whether to authorise or direct medical treatment the court adopts that course which, objectively considered, is in the particular child's best interests.[248]

Prevention of Harm

4.97 'It has always been the principle of this court, not to risk the incurring of damage to children which it cannot repair, but rather to prevent the damage being done.'[249] Moreover, the court is justified in interfering not only where there is a 'likelihood' of damage to the child but even if there is no more than 'an apprehension or suspicion of it'.[250]

(b) The Child's Wishes

4.98 In relation to medical treatment generally, the court is bound (whether or not the case strictly falls within the Children Act 1989, s 1(4))[251] to have regard to the ascertainable wishes and feelings of the child, considered in the light of his age and understanding.[252] However, the court is not bound by the wishes even of a 'Gillick competent' child, or a child who has attained the age of 16, though it will not lightly override the child's decision, particularly if the child's decision is sensible or the treatment is invasive.[253]

> This is not, however, to say that the wishes of 16- and 17-year-olds are to be treated as no different from those of 14- and 15-year-olds. Far from it. Adolescence is a period of progressive transition from childhood to adulthood and as experience of life is acquired and intelligence and understanding grow, so will the scope of decision-making which should be left to the minor, for it is only by making decisions and experiencing the consequences that decision-making skills will be acquired. As I put it in the course of the argument, and as I sincerely believe, 'good parenting involves giving minors as much rope as they can handle without an unacceptable risk that they will hang themselves'. As Lord Hailsham of St Marylebone LC put it in *Re B* [1988] AC 199, 202, the 'first and paramount consideration [of the court] is the well being, welfare or interests [of the minor]' and I regard it as self-evident that this involves giving them the maximum degree of decision-making which is prudent.

---

[247] *Re E (A Minor) (Wardship: Medical Treatment)* [1993] 1 FLR 386, 392.

[248] *In re B (A Minor) (Wardship: Sterilisation)* [1988] AC 199, 210.

[249] *Wellesley v Duke of Beaufort* (1827) 2 Russ 1, 18 *per* Lord Eldon LC (cited in *In re X (A Minor) (Wardship: Jurisdiction)* [1975] Fam 47, 51; *In re D (A Minor) (Wardship: Sterilisation)* [1976] Fam 185, 194).

[250] *In re X (A Minor) (Wardship: Jurisdiction)* [1975] Fam 47, 51 quoting *Chambers on Infants* [ed 1842], 20.

[251] *In re W (A Minor) (Medical Treatment: Court's Jurisdiction)* [1993] Fam 64, 93.

[252] *B(BR) v B(J)* [1968] P 466, 473, 481; *Re P (A Minor)* [1986] 1 FLR 272, 276–279; *Re E (A Minor) (Wardship: Medical Treatment)* [1993] 1 FLR 386, 393; *Re B (Wardship: Abortion)* [1991] 2 FLR 426, 428–429. Cf the Children Act 1989, s 1(3)(a).

[253] *In re W (A Minor) (Medical Treatment: Court's Jurisdiction)* [1993] Fam 64, 81–82, 84, 88, 93.

Prudence does not involve avoiding all risk, but it does involve avoiding risks which, if they eventuate, may have irreparable consequences or which are disproportionate to the benefits which could accrue from taking them.[254]

Thus in practice the court is unlikely to overrule the competent child's decision in the ordinary run of relatively routine surgical, medical or dental treatment, though even then it has the power to do so.[255] Moreover, where the views of a competent child conflict with those of its parents, the court is likely to adopt the views of the child rather than the parents.[256] On the other hand, there will be cases where, having given proper weight to the child's views, it is nonetheless appropriate for the court to overrule either a 'Gillick competent' or even a 16- or 17-year-old child's decision, for example where that is necessary in order either to save the child's life or to prevent really serious and irreparable harm to the child, for as a general principle the protection of the child's welfare implies at least the protection of the child's life and it is generally the duty of the court to preserve life and ensure so far as it can that children survive to attain the age of 18.[257] The court has not hesitated, for example, to override the refusal of teenagers to consent to a life-saving blood transfusion[258] or other essential treatment,[259] and, one imagines, would readily overrule a promiscuous teenager's frivolous decision to be sterilised. Likewise, the court would probably be very slow indeed to allow even a willing and 'Gillick competent' teenager to donate an organ.

Non-Therapeutic Procedures

Where the procedure in question is non-therapeutic, and the child is old enough   **4.99**
to understand, the court should not subject it to the operation against its will, certainly unless to do so is 'clearly' in the child's interests.[260]

---

[254] ibid, 81–82 *per* Lord Donaldson of Lymington MR.

[255] ibid, 94.

[256] As in *Re P (A Minor)* [1986] 1 FLR 272 (where a pregnant 15-year-old girl of strong personality and mature views, and able to understand the implications, wanted an abortion but was opposed by her Seventh Day Adventist parents on bona fide religious and other grounds: the court treated the child's welfare, but not her views and wishes, as paramount and, although giving weight to her parents' feelings and taking into account their deeply and sincerely held religious objections, directed the abortion) and *Re B (Wardship: Abortion)* [1991] 2 FLR 426 (where a pregnant 12-year-old girl's wish to have an abortion was opposed by her mother: the court directed an abortion). See also *In re W (A Minor) (Medical Treatment: Court's Jurisdiction)* [1993] Fam 64, 90, 94.

[257] *In re B (A Minor) (Wardship: Medical Treatment)* [1981] 1 WLR 1421, 1424–1425; *In re W (A Minor) (Medical Treatment: Court's Jurisdiction)* [1993] Fam 64, 88, 94.

[258] *Re E (A Minor) (Wardship: Medical Treatment)* [1993] 1 FLR 386; *Re S (A Minor) (Consent to Medical Treatment)* [1994] 2 FLR 1065; *Re L (Medical Treatment: Gillick Competency)* [1998] 2 FLR 810.

[259] *In re R (A Minor) (Wardship: Consent to Treatment)* [1992] Fam 11; *In re W (A Minor) (Medical Treatment: Court's Jurisdiction)* [1993] Fam 64; *A Metropolitan Borough Council v AB* [1997] 1 FLR 767; *Re C (Detention: Medical Treatment)* [1997] 2 FLR 180 (force-feeding for treatment of anorexia nervosa); *Re M (Medical Treatment: Consent)* [1999] 2 FLR 1097 (heart transplant).

[260] *In re L (An Infant)* [1968] P 119, 140; *B(BR) v B(J)* [1968] P 466, 469, 473–474, 481; *S v McC, W v W* [1972] AC 24, 45. See also *In re D (A Minor) (Wardship: Sterilisation)* [1976] Fam 185, para 4.84 above and paras 4.178, 4.189 below.

(c) The Court's Approach to Religious Issues

Religion[261]

4.100　The court recognises no religious distinctions and passes no judgment on religious beliefs unless they are 'immoral or socially obnoxious' or 'pernicious'.[262] Indeed, the court pays every respect and gives great weight to the family's religious principles.[263]

4.101　But, although the parents' views and wishes as to the child's religious upbringing are of great importance, and will be seriously regarded by the court, they will be given effect to by the court only so far as and in such manner as is in accordance with the best interests of the child's welfare. In matters of religion, as in all other aspects of a child's upbringing, the interests of the child are the paramount consideration.[264]

> Parents may be free to become martyrs themselves. But it does not follow that they are free, in identical circumstances, to make martyrs of their children before they have reached the age of full and legal discretion when they can make the choices for themselves.[265]

4.102　Where a child is old enough to be able to express sensible views on the subject of religion, even if not old enough to take a mature decision, the court will pay great regard to (though it cannot be bound by) the child's wishes, and will be slow to dictate the child's religious upbringing.[266] But, just as the court will not allow a

---

[261] See further paras 4.170–4.171 below.

[262] *Stourton v Stourton* (1857) 8 DeGM&G 760, 771; *Re T (Minors) (Custody: Religious Upbringing)* (1981) 2 FLR 239, 244–245; *Re B and G (Minors) (Custody)* [1985] FLR 134, 157; *Re R (A Minor) (Residence: Religion)* [1993] 2 FLR 163, 171.

[263] *Re P (A Minor)* [1986] 1 FLR 272, 281; *Re E (A Minor) (Wardship: Medical Treatment)* [1993] 1 FLR 386, 394; *Re O (A Minor) (Medical Treatment)* [1993] 2 FLR 149, 153. In addition to the various cases involving Jehovah's Witnesses referred to in para 4.75 above, see also *Re C (Medical Treatment)* [1998] 1 FLR 384 (Orthodox Jewish parents wishing 16-month-old daughter suffering from terminal spinal muscular atrophy, type 1, to be ventilated in event of respiratory relapse and not willing to agree to only palliative care as recommended by doctors); *Re J (Specific Issue Orders: Muslim Upbringing and Circumcision)* [1999] 2 FLR 678 (affirmed *Re J (Specific Issue Orders: Child's Religious Upbringing and Circumcision)* [2000] 1 FLR 571) (dispute between Muslim father and Christian mother as to circumcision of 5-year-old boy).

[264] *Stourton v Stourton* (1857) 8 DeGMG 760, 771; *Re McGrath* [1893] 1 Ch 143, 148, 149; *In re W, W v M* [1907] 2 Ch 557, 566–567; *Ward v Laverty* [1925] AC 101, 108; *Re Aster* [1955] 1 WLR 465, 468; *In re E (An Infant)* [1964] 1 WLR 51, 57–58; *J v C* [1970] AC 668, 713, 715; *Re P (A Minor)* [1986] 1 FLR 272, 281; *Re E (A Minor) (Wardship: Medical Treatment)* [1993] 1 FLR 386, 391–394; *Re S (A Minor) (Medical Treatment)* [1993] 1 FLR 376, 380; *Re S (A Minor) (Consent to Medical Treatment)* [1994] 2 FLR 1065. See para 4.75 above.

[265] *Prince v Massachusetts* (1944) 321 US 158, 170 *per* Rutledge J (cited in *Re E (A Minor) (Wardship: Medical Treatment)* [1993] 1 FLR 386, 394, where the passage, due to an error by counsel, is wrongly attributed to Holmes J).

[266] *Stourton v Stourton* (1857) 8 DeGMG 760 (where the LJJ themselves interviewed a 9-year-old boy); *Re E (A Minor) (Wardship: Medical Treatment)* [1993] 1 FLR 386, 393, 394 (where the judge interviewed a 15-year-old boy); *Re S (Minors) (Access: Religious Upbringing)* [1992] 2 FLR 313, 321; *Re R (A Minor) (Residence: Religion)* [1993] 2 FLR 163, 173–174, 175, 179–180.

parent to make a martyr of his child, so the court will be very slow to allow a child to martyr himself.[267]

(d) The Court and the Doctor

The court will naturally pay great respect to, and will not lightly disregard, the opinion of the doctor treating or proposing to treat the child. However, in the final analysis it is for the court, and not for doctors, however eminent, to reach a decision as to what is in the best interests of the particular child.[268] And where there is a diversity or conflict of medical opinion the court is necessarily obliged to choose which view to adopt. In the case of a child, therefore, the 'Bolam' test plays little part:[269] its only function is to identify the opinion of a particular doctor either as being one which can reasonably be held by a competent practitioner (and is therefore deserving of proper consideration by the court) or as being one which fails to meet that criterion (and is therefore not deserving of consideration by the court).

4.103

The court, depending on the circumstances, can either make an order forbidding something to be done to the child (for example, an order restraining a proposed sterilisation)[270] or make an order 'authorising' or 'authorising and directing' something to be done to the child (for example, an order authorising and directing surgery).[271] But the court will never make a compulsive order requiring a particular doctor or health authority to treat a child in a manner contrary to their wishes.[272] It follows that, even when the court 'authorises and directs' treatment, what it is really doing is to authorise the proposed treatment and to indicate that such authorisation is to be effective notwithstanding the absence or refusal of parental consent.[273] To avoid confusion or misunderstanding the court should avoid the 'authorise and direct' form of order and simply make an order 'authorising' the relevant treatment.[274]

4.104

---

[267] *Re E (A Minor) (Wardship: Medical Treatment)* [1993] 1 FLR 386, 394; *In re W (A Minor) (Medical Treatment: Court's Jurisdiction)* [1993] Fam 64, 88; *Re S (A Minor) (Consent to Medical Treatment)* [1994] 2 FLR 1065; *Re L (Medical Treatment: Gillick Competency)* [1998] 2 FLR 810.

[268] cf *In re F (Mental Patient: Sterilisation)* [1990] 2 AC 1, 80; *Frenchay Healthcare NHS Trust v S* [1994] 1 WLR 601, 609–610.

[269] Contrast where the patient is an adult incompetent: *In re F (Mental Patient: Sterilisation)* [1990] 2 AC 1; *Airedale NHS Trust v Bland* [1993] AC 789. For the position where the patient is an adult incompetent see paras 4.140–4.141 below.

[270] *In re D (A Minor) (Wardship: Sterilisation)* [1976] Fam 185.

[271] *In re B (A Minor) (Wardship: Medical Treatment)* [1981] 1 WLR 1421, 1424–1425.

[272] See para 4.17 above.

[273] cf *Secretary, Department of Health and Community Services v JWB and SMB* (1992) 175 CLR 218, 259, 267–268.

[274] *In re J (A Minor) (Wardship: Medical Treatment)* [1991] Fam 33, 48; *In re J (A Minor) (Child in Care: Medical Treatment)* [1993] Fam 15, 29, 31; *In re W (A Minor) (Medical Treatment: Court's Jurisdiction)* [1993] Fam 64, 81.

E. Incompetent Adults

1. General Principles

The Role of Consent

4.105   Except as specifically provided by statute,[275] consent plays no part in the treatment of the adult incompetent, because the patient himself is, by definition, unable to give a valid consent to treatment and the common law does not recognise anyone else as having the legal capacity to give or refuse consent on his behalf. A spouse or relative does not have any power either to consent or to refuse consent to medical treatment on behalf of an incompetent adult.[276] Nor does the court, for neither the Court of Protection nor the High Court has any parens patriae or other jurisdiction over the person, as opposed to the property, of an adult incompetent.[277]

The Role of the Court and the Official Solicitor

4.106   However, the High Court, in exercise of its inherent jurisdiction and/or its statutory jurisdiction under RSC Ord 15, r 16, can grant declaratory relief to determine questions relating to the lawfulness or unlawfulness of the proposed treatment or care (including the proposed medical treatment or care) of an incompetent adult.[278] Such proceedings should be commenced and heard in the Family Division.[279] The Official Solicitor is involved, either ex officio or as litigation friend or by instructing an advocate to the court (amicus curiae), in virtually

---

[275] eg, the Mental Health Act 1983, s 63 (treatment of mental disorder), the Family Law Reform Act 1969, s 21(4) (taking of blood samples).

[276] *In re T (Adult: Refusal of Treatment)* [1993] Fam 95, 103; *A v A Health Authority, In re J (A Child), R (on the application of S) v Secretary of State for the Home Department* [2002] EWHC 18 (Fam/Admin), [2002] Fam 213, at [36]; *Re S (Adult Patient) (Inherent Jurisdiction: Family Life)* [2002] EWHC 2278 (Fam), [2003] 1 FLR 292, at [14]. See also *T v T* [1988] Fam 52; *In re F (Mental Patient: Sterilisation)* [1990] 2 AC 1; *Re C (Mental Patient: Contact)* [1993] 1 FLR 940; *Hospital Authority v C* [2003] Lloyd's Rep Med 130, at [27]–[29].

[277] *T v T* [1988] Fam 52; *In re F (Mental Patient: Sterilisation)* [1990] 2 AC 1; *Re C (Mental Patient: Contact)* [1993] 1 FLR 940; *A v A Health Authority, In re J (A Child), R (on the application of S) v Secretary of State for the Home Department* [2002] EWHC 18 (Fam/Admin), [2002] Fam 213, at [35]–[37]; *Re S (Adult Patient) (Inherent Jurisdiction: Family Life)* [2002] EWHC 2278 (Fam), [2003] 1 FLR 292, at [14].

[278] *In re F (Mental Patient: Sterilisation)* [1990] 2 AC 1; *Airedale NHS Trust v Bland* [1993] AC 789. For detailed surveys of the current scope of the declaratory jurisdiction see *A v A Health Authority, In re J (A Child), R (on the application of S) v Secretary of State for the Home Department* [2002] EWHC 18 (Fam/Admin), [2002] Fam 213, esp at [35]–[46]; *Re S (Adult Patient) (Inherent Jurisdiction: Family Life)* [2002] EWHC 2278 (Fam), [2003] 1 FLR 292, at [3]–[60].

[279] *President's Direction (Declaratory Proceedings Concerning Incapacitated Adults: Medical and Welfare Decisions)* [2002] 1 FLR 177. Proceedings in the Administrative Court by way of an application for judicial review are almost always inappropriate in this type of case: *R v Portsmouth Hospitals NHS Trust, ex p Glass* [1999] 2 FLR 905 (affirming (1999) 50 BMLR 269); *A v A Health Authority, In re J (A Child), R (on the application of S) v Secretary of State for the Home Department* [2002] EWHC 18 (Fam/Admin), [2002] Fam 213, at [71]–[81].

all cases relating to the treatment of adult incompetents. Members of his staff are prepared to discuss such cases before proceedings have been issued. The Official Solicitor issues Practice Notes (which are revised from time to time) detailing the procedure and the nature of his role in such cases.[280] Generally the Official Solicitor should be invited to act in all cases of any complexity.[281]

Necessity

In the case of an adult who is incompetent or permanently unable to communi-   **4.107**
cate,[282] the principle of necessity[283] renders lawful, despite the absence of consent, such treatment which in the absence of consent would otherwise be tortious[284] as a reasonable doctor would in all the circumstances give, acting in the best interests of the patient.[285] But this principle is qualified by the rule that a doctor is never entitled to give treatment, even in cases of emergency or to an unconscious or incompetent patient, which is contrary to the known, competent, wishes of the patient.

> [T]he basic requirements, applicable in these cases of necessity, [are] that, to fall within the principle, not only (1) must there be a necessity to act when it is not practicable to communicate with the assisted person, but also (2) the action taken must be such as a reasonable person would in all the circumstances take, acting in the best interests of the assisted person. On this statement of principle, I wish to observe that officious intervention cannot be justified by the principle of necessity. So intervention cannot be justified when another more appropriate person is available and willing to act; nor can it be justified when it is contrary to the known wishes of the assisted person, to the extent that he is capable of rationally forming such a wish.[286]

Necessity and surrogate decision-making

The relationship between the doctrine of necessity and the principle that the rel-   **4.108**
ative or spouse of an adult incompetent does not have any surrogate decision-making power has been explained in this way:

> English law may deny to the parent of a mentally incapacitated child on and after his eighteenth birthday (just as it does in relation to his fully competent sibling) the surrogate decision-making powers that the parent was clothed with so long as his child was, in the eyes of the law, an infant (or, as one would now say, a minor or a child) . . . Parents who have been looking after mentally incapacitated children during their minority often continue to do so after those children have attained their

---

[280] See *Practice Note (Official Solicitor: Declaratory Proceedings: Medical and Welfare Decisions for Adults Who Lack Capacity)* [2001] 2 FLR 158.

[281] See further para 4.93 above.

[282] *In re F (Mental Patient: Sterilisation)* [1990] 2 AC 1, 71–77.

[283] For the doctrine of necessity in this context see generally *In re F (Mental Patient: Sterilisation)* [1990] AC 1 and *R v Bournewood Community and Mental Health NHS Trust, ex p L* [1999] 1 AC 458.

[284] ibid, 73–76.

[285] ibid, 51, 56, 75.

[286] ibid, 75–76 per Lord Goff of Chieveley.

majority. But the fact that such parents are no longer clothed with the surrogate decision-making powers they enjoyed during their child's minority, does not leave them legally powerless. The doctrine of necessity as explained by the House of Lords in *Re F (Mental Patient: Sterilisation)* [1990] 2 AC 1 and *R v Bournewood Community and Mental Health NHS Trust ex parte L* [1999] 1 AC 458 gives them ample power to look after their child and to take the decisions on his behalf which he is unable to take for himself. And, save in relation to certain medical procedures falling within the 'special' category referred to in *Re F (Mental Patient: Sterilisation)* and *Airedale NHS Trust v Bland* [1993] AC 789, there is no need for parents in this position to invoke the assistance of the court. The doctrine of necessity enables them not merely to assume the responsibility for the day-to-day care of their child, with all the routine decision-making which that entails, but also to decide, no doubt, where appropriate, in conjunction with suitable professional advisers, more important matters such as where their child should live, who he should see, what services offered by public authorities he should make use of, what medication he should take and what nursing, dental and medical treatment he should receive. Cases in the 'special' category apart, the court typically becomes involved only if disputes erupt between those seeking to care for the patient—for example, the disputes between the wife and the mistress which underlay the litigation in *Re S (Hospital Patient: Court's Jurisdiction)* [1996] Fam 1 and *Re S (Hospital Patient: Foreign Curator)* [1996] Fam 23 or the disputes between the mother and the father which underlay in part the litigation in *A v A Health Authority and Others; Re J and Linked Applications*—or if a public authority, for example a local authority or a health authority, seeks, as here and as in *Re F (Adult: Court's Jurisdiction)*, to intervene and take control out of the hands of family carers.

It may be that, in strict legal theory, these rights, duties, powers, responsibilities and authority . . . are vested in such a parent not qua parent but rather because the parent has, in the eyes of the law, reasonably and appropriately intervened in order to care for, or has assumed responsibility for the care of, someone unable to look after himself: see the discussion of principle by Lord Goff of Chieveley in *Re F (Mental Patient: Sterilisation)*. But that is little more than a technicality. The practical and human reality, of course, is that the parents of a mentally incapacitated adult look after him not as some disinterested act of charity but precisely because they are his parents and because they are motivated by natural feelings of parental love and duty.

In this connection it is important also to bear in mind the point made by Lord Goff of Chieveley in *Re F (Mental Patient: Sterilisation)* at 76A:

'. . . officious intervention cannot be justified by the principle of necessity. So intervention cannot be justified when another more appropriate person is available and willing to act . . .'[287]

Best Interests

4.109   What is meant by a patient's best interests is dealt with below.[288]

---

[287]   *Re S (Adult Patient) (Inherent Jurisdiction: Family Life)* [2002] EWHC 2278 (Fam), [2003] 1 FLR 292, at [19]–[22], *per* Munby J.
[288]   See paras 4.144–4.175 below.

2. Advance Directives and the Incompetent Adult

A competent adult patient has an absolute right (the right of self-determination) **4.110**
to refuse consent to any medical treatment or invasive procedure, whether the
reasons are rational, irrational, unknown or non-existent, and even if the result
of refusal is the certainty of death.[289] Consistently with this, a competent adult
patient's anticipatory refusal of consent (a so-called 'advance directive' or 'living
will') remains binding and effective notwithstanding that the patient has subsequently become and remains incompetent.[290]

(i) Proving an Advance Directive

Burden and Standard of Proof

The burden of proof is on those who seek to establish the existence and continu- **4.111**
ing validity and applicability of an advance directive.[291] If there is doubt 'that
doubt falls to be resolved in favour of the preservation of life'.[292] The evidence
must be scrutinised with 'especial care'. Clear and convincing proof is required.
Where life is at stake the continuing validity and applicability of the advance
directive must be clearly established by convincing and inherently reliable
evidence.[293]

---

[289] For striking applications of this principle see *In re C (Adult: Refusal of Treatment)* [1994] 1
WLR 290 (schizophrenic held entitled to refuse consent to amputation of gangrenous leg); *Secretary
of State for the Home Department v Robb* [1995] Fam 127 (prison authorities not entitled to force-
feed competent adult prisoner); *Re JT (Adult: Refusal of Medical Treatment)* [1998] 1 FLR 48 (adult
with learning difficulties and extremely severe behavioural disturbance refusing treatment for renal
failure); *St George's Healthcare NHS Trust v S, R v Collins, ex p S* [1999] Fam 26 (pregnant woman refusing caesarian section); *Re AK (Medical Treatment: Consent)* [2001] 1 FLR 129 (adult suffering
from motor neurone disease seeking removal of his ventilator); *Re B (Consent to Treatment: Capacity)*
[2002] EWHC 429 (Fam), [2002] 1 FLR 1090 (tetraplegic adult seeking removal of her ventilator:
the judgment of Dame Elizabeth Butler-Sloss P contains at [14]–[35] a valuable survey of the authorities and at [100] an important restatement of the basic principles with additional guidelines).
For the impact in this context of the ECHR see *Re AK (Medical Treatment: Consent)* [2001] 1 FLR
129, 136.

[290] *HE v A Hospital NHS Trust* [2003] EWHC 1017 (Fam), [2003] 2 FLR 408, at [20]. For the
earlier authorities see *In re T (Adult: Refusal of Treatment)* [1993] Fam 95, 102, 115, 116, 120–121;
Airedale NHS Trust v Bland [1993] AC 789, 808–809, 816–817, 828, 857, 864, 891–892, 894; *In
re C (Adult: Refusal of Treatment)* [1994] 1 WLR 290, 294–295, 295–296; *Re MB (Medical
Treatment)* [1997] 2 FLR 426; *St George's Healthcare NHS Trust v S, R v Collins, ex p S* [1999] Fam
26; *Re AK (Medical Treatment: Consent)* [2001] 1 FLR 129; *Re B (Consent to Treatment: Capacity)*
[2002] EWHC 429 (Fam), [2002] 1 FLR 1090. The British Medical Association has published
guidance on advance directives: 'Advance Statements about Medical Treatment: Code of Practice
with explanatory notes' (Apr 1995), 'BMA Views on Advance Statements' (Nov 1992, revised May
1995).

[291] *HE v A Hospital NHS Trust* [2003] EWHC 1017 (Fam), [2003] 2 FLR 408, at [23], [46].

[292] *In re T (Adult: Refusal of Treatment)* [1993] Fam 95, 112 *per* Lord Donaldson of Lymington
MR.

[293] *HE v A Hospital NHS Trust* [2003] EWHC 1017 (Fam), [2003] 2 FLR 408, at [24], [46],
applying *In re T (Adult: Refusal of Treatment)* [1993] Fam 95, 103, 112; *Airedale NHS Trust v Bland*

Formal Validity

4.112 There are no formal requirements for a valid advance directive: there is no legal requirement as to form. An advance directive need not be in, or evidenced by, writing: an advance directive may be oral or in writing[294] and may be proved by a single witness deposing to a conversation with the patient on a single occasion; there is no requirement of corroboration. However, the court will plainly scrutinise with great care the evidence of any witness whose interests conflict with those of the patient,[295] and it may well be easier to establish the existence of an oral advance directive if more than one witness is able to depose to more than one conversation with the patient.

Matters to be Proved

4.113 There are five matters which have to be proved in order to establish an advance directive binding and effective in relation to an adult incompetent:[296]

(1) That at the date of the advance directive the patient was of sound mind, ie, competent.[297]

(2) That the patient knew in broad terms the nature and effect of the procedure to which he was giving or refusing consent.[298]

(3) That the patient's decision was (i) voluntary and unequivocal, (ii) 'real' and not 'expressed in form only' and (iii) free of vitiating influences (eg, coercion or undue influence, the withholding of relevant information, misinformation or mistake).[299]

(4) That the patient's decision was made with reference to and was intended to

---

[1993] AC 789, 864; *Re AK (Medical Treatment: Consent)* [2001] 1 FLR 129, 134. English law thus corresponds to the 'specific-subjective-intent rule' applied in the US by the courts of New York and Missouri, which requires 'clear and convincing, inherently reliable evidence': *Re O'Connor* (1988) 531 NE 2d 607, 608, 611–612, 613–614; *Cruzan v Harmon* (1988) 760 SW 2d 408, 414–415, 424–426, appeal dismissed (1990) 497 US 261.

[294] *HE v A Hospital NHS Trust* [2003] EWHC 1017 (Fam), [2003] 2 FLR 408, at [33], [46]; cf *In re T (Adult: Refusal of Treatment)* [1993] Fam 95, 102.

[295] *Airedale NHS Trust v Bland* [1993] AC 789, 817.

[296] Approved in *HE v A Hospital NHS Trust* [2003] EWHC 1017 (Fam), [2003] 2 FLR 408, at [21] (Munby J).

[297] See paras 4.116–4.119 below.

[298] *Chatterton v Gerson* [1981] QB 432, 442, 442–443; *In re T (Adult: Refusal of Treatment)* [1993] Fam 95, 115. But note that English law does not recognise the doctrines of 'informed consent' or 'informed refusal of consent' in the sense in which those terms are used in North America: *Sidaway v Board of Governors of the Bethlem Royal Hospital and the Maudsley Hospital* [1985] AC 871; cf *Malette v Shulman* (1987) 47 DLR (4th) 18, 47–48, (1990) 67 DLR (4th) 321, 336. Nor is it any part of a doctor's duty to dissuade a patient from a decision made on a non-medical (often religious or quasi-religious) basis.

[299] *Chatterton v Gerson* [1981] QB 432, 443; *In re T (Adult: Refusal of Treatment)* [1993] Fam 95, 113–114, 115, 116, 117, 119–120, 121.

cover the particular (and perhaps changed or unforeseen) circumstances which have in fact subsequently occurred.[300]

(5) That the patient's expressed views represented a 'firm and settled commitment' rather than 'informally expressed reactions to other people's medical condition and treatment' or 'an offhand remark about not wanting to live under certain circumstances made by a person when young and in the peak of health'.[301]

The question for the court is well summarised as follows:

> [T]he 'clear and convincing' evidence standard requires proof sufficient to persuade the trier of fact that the patient held a firm and settled commitment to the termination of life supports under the circumstances like those presented.[302]

(ii) Revocation

There are no formal requirements for the revocation of an advance directive. An **4.114** advance directive, whether oral or in writing, may be revoked either orally or in writing. A written advance directive or an advance directive executed under seal can be revoked orally. An advance directive is inherently revocable. Any condition in an advance directive purporting to make it irrevocable, any even self-imposed fetter on a patient's ability to revoke an advance directive, and any provision in an advance directive purporting to impose formal or other conditions upon its revocation, is contrary to public policy and void. So, a stipulation in an advance directive, even if in writing, that it shall be binding unless and until revoked in writing is void as being contrary to public policy. The existence and continuing validity and applicability of an advance directive is a question of fact. Whether an advance directive has been revoked or has for some other reason ceased to be operative is a question of fact. The burden of proof is on those who seek to establish the existence and continuing validity and applicability of an advance directive.[303]

> No doubt there is a practical—what lawyers would call an evidential—burden on those who assert that an undisputed advance directive is for some reason no longer operative, a burden requiring them to point to something indicating that this is or may be so. It may be words said to have been written or spoken by the patient. It may be the patient's actions—for sometimes actions speak louder than words. It may be some change in circumstances. Thus, it may be alleged that the patient no longer professes the faith which underlay the advance directive; it may be said that the patient executed the advance directive because he was suffering from an illness which has since been cured; it may be said that medical science has now moved on; it may be said that the patient, having since married or had children, now finds himself with more

---

[300] *In re T (Adult: Refusal of Treatment)* [1993] Fam 95, 103, 114, 116, 117, 120, 121–122.
[301] *Re Conroy* (1985) 486 A 2d 1209, 1230, 1232; *Re Jobes* (1987) 529 A 2d 434, 443; *Cruzan v Harmon* (1988) 760 SW 2d 408, 424.
[302] *Re O'Connor* (1988) 531 NE 2d 607, 613 *per* Wachtler CJ.
[303] *HE v A Hospital NHS Trust* [2003] EWHC 1017 (Fam), [2003] 2 FLR 408, at [35]–[39], [46].

compelling reasons to choose to live even a severely disadvantaged life. It may be suggested that the advance directive has been revoked, whether by express words or by conduct on the part of the patient inconsistent with its continued validity. It may be suggested that, even though not revoked, the advance directive has not survived some material change of circumstances. But whatever the reasons may be, once the issue is properly raised, once there is some real reason for doubt, then it is for those who assert the continuing validity and applicability of the advance directive to prove that it is still operative. The burden of proof is on them. And . . . what is required is clear and convincing proof. If there is doubt that doubt falls to be resolved in favour of the preservation of life. So, if there is doubt the advance directive cannot be relied on and the doctor must treat the patient in such way as his best interests require.

Whether there truly is some real reason to doubt, whether the doubt is a real doubt or only some speculative or fanciful doubt, will inevitably depend on the circumstances. Holding the balance involves awesome responsibility. Too ready a submission to speculative or merely fanciful doubts will rob advance directives of their utility and may condemn those who in truth do not want to be treated to what they would see as indignity or worse . . . Too sceptical a reaction to well-founded suggestions that circumstances have changed may turn an advance directive into a death warrant for a patient who in truth wants to be treated.

At the end of the day, and however unhelpful for hard-pressed doctors this seeming platitude may be, it must all depend on the facts. All I would add is that the longer the time which has elapsed since an advance directive was made, and the greater the apparent changes in the patient's circumstances since then, the more doubt there is likely to be as to its continuing validity and applicability. There will be cases in which . . . there will need to be especially close, rigorous and anxious scrutiny.[304]

(iii) Capacity to Make an Advance Directive

4.115 The fact that someone is a 'patient' within the meaning of the Mental Health Act 1983, s 94(2), or RSC Ord 80, r 1, as being 'incapable, by reason of mental disorder, of managing and administering his property and affairs', does not of itself render him incapable of giving a legally effective consent or entering into a legally effective transaction. Subject to the principle that a person who is a 'patient' actually subject to the jurisdiction of the Court of Protection cannot lawfully enter into any transaction which 'raises a conflict with the court's control of his affairs'[305] (and that principle cannot apply in relation to the patient's medical treatment[306]) the question whether a 'patient' can lawfully give his consent depends solely upon whether or not he has capacity to do so at common law.

---

[304] ibid at [43]–[45] *per* Munby J.

[305] *In re Walker (A Lunatic so Found)* [1905] 1 Ch 160, 172, 179; *In re Marshall* [1920] 1 Ch 284; *In re W(EEM)* [1971] Ch 123, 143; *In re Beaney* [1978] 1 WLR 770, 772. Thus a patient subject to the Court of Protection, unless of course he lacks testamentary capacity, can make a will (because a will, taking effect only on death, does not interfere with the court's control of his affairs) but cannot without the consent of the court make a valid inter vivos disposition of his property.

[306] Because the jurisdiction of the Court of Protection, being confined to his 'affairs', does not extend to questions affecting the patient's person or body: *In re F (Mental Patient: Sterilisation)* [1990] 2 AC 1, 59. See further para 4.04 above.

Burden of Proof

An adult is presumed to have capacity.[307] The burden of proof is therefore on those **4.116** who seek to rebut the presumption and who assert a lack of capacity.[308]

The Test of Capacity

Whatever the context in which the question arises, the test of capacity at common **4.117** law is essentially one of the person's 'understanding' of the 'nature', 'character' and 'effect' of the act or transaction in question.[309] The test of capacity is in essence the same in relation to medical treatment: the question is whether the patient is 'competent to appreciate the issues involved'[310] so as to be able to exercise a 'right of choice',[311] and whether he sufficiently 'understand[s] the nature, purpose and effects of the treatment'.[312]

The degree of capacity required varies with the circumstances of the particular **4.118** treatment; it must be commensurate with the gravity of the decision,[313] for 'the more serious the decision, the greater the capacity required'.[314] A high degree of capacity is required to refuse life-saving treatment.[315]

There are three aspects to be considered in any analysis of the patient's capacity.[316] **4.119**

(1) The patient's ability (whether or not actually exercised) to function rationally. This involves three questions:[317] (i) Can the patient take in, comprehend and

---

[307] *R v Sullivan* [1984] AC 156, 170, 171 (approving *M'Naghten's Case* (1843) 10 Cl & F 200, 210); *In re T (Adult: Refusal of Treatment)* [1993] Fam 95, 112, 115; *In re C (Adult: Refusal of Treatment)* [1994] 1 WLR 290, 295; *Cambridgeshire County Council v R (An Adult)* [1995] 1 FLR 50, 54; *Re MB (Medical Treatment)* [1997] 2 FLR 426, 436.

[308] *HE v A Hospital NHS Trust* [2003] EWHC 1017 (Fam), [2003] 2 FLR 408, at [20], [46].

[309] *Boughton v Knight* (1873) LR 3 P & D 64, 71–75; *Cambridgeshire County Council v R (An Adult)* [1995] 1 FLR 50, 53.

[310] *In re F (Mental Patient: Sterilisation)* [1990] 2 AC 1, 12 *per* Lord Donaldson of Lymington MR.

[311] ibid, 31, 34 *per* Neill and Butler-Sloss LJJ.

[312] *In re C (Adult: Refusal of Treatment)* [1994] 1 WLR 290, 295 *per* Thorpe J.

[313] *Re MB (Medical Treatment)* [1997] 2 FLR 426, 437.

[314] *In re T (Adult: Refusal of Treatment)* [1993] Fam 95, 113, 116 *per* Lord Donaldson of Lymington MR.

[315] cf *Re E (A Minor) (Wardship: Medical Treatment)* [1993] 1 FLR 386, 391.

[316] See generally *In re T (Adult: Refusal of Treatment)* [1993] Fam 95; *In re C (Adult: Refusal of Treatment)* [1994] 1 WLR 290; *Re MB (Medical Treatment)* [1997] 2 FLR 426, 433–437. For cases illustrating the application of these principles see, in addition to the authorities referred to in nn 317–320 below, those referred to in n 289 above.

[317] *In re C (Adult: Refusal of Treatment)* [1994] 1 WLR 290, 292, 295, followed in *Cambridgeshire County Council v R (An Adult)* [1995] 1 FLR 50, 53–54; *Tameside and Glossop Acute Services Trust v CH* [1996] 1 FLR 762, 766, 769; *Norfolk and Norwich Healthcare (NHS) Trust v W* [1996] 2 FLR 613; *Rochdale Healthcare (NHS) Trust v C* [1997] 1 FCR 274; *Re L (Patient: Non-consensual Treatment)* [1997] 2 FLR 837 and, in relation to 16- and 17-year-old children, in *A Metropolitan Borough Council v AB* [1997] 1 FLR 767; *Re C (Detention: Medical Treatment)* [1997] 2 FLR 180, and approved by the Court of Appeal in *Re MB (Medical Treatment)* [1997] 2 FLR 426, 433, 437. See further para 4.73 above.

retain treatment information? (ii) Does he believe that information? (iii) Can he weigh the information in the balance so as to arrive at a choice? It is not necessary for the patient to understand everything about a complicated decision, so long as he can understand the essentials if explained to him in broad terms and simple language.[318]

(2) The extent to which the patient's normal capacity may have been temporarily reduced by the effects, for example, of injury, illness, drugs, confusion, shock, pain, anxiety, depression, fatigue or panic induced by fear.[319]

(3) The extent to which the patient had the capacity to make not merely a present but also an anticipatory decision, that is, the capacity to weigh the consequences of future hypothetical circumstances.[320]

(iv) Effect of Valid Advance Directive

4.120 If a competent adult has expressed an unequivocal decision to refuse treatment, it is not for the doctor or the court to speculate as to the strength of the patient's personal or religious convictions or as to his reasons for refusing consent. Nor is it for the doctor or the court to speculate as to what the patient's decision might have been if he had been alive to the current crisis, or if he had been more fully informed, or if he had had more forcibly brought home to him all the implications of his refusal. If it is not possible to say what the patient's decision would have been if he had been given more information, his expressed decision, if he was competent to make it, is decisive, even if it was not made in contemplation of life-threatening circumstances.[321]

3. The Court's Declaratory Jurisdiction

The Role of the Court

4.121 As has been seen,[322] the court has no jurisdiction either to consent or to refuse consent to the medical treatment of an incompetent adult. Its only jurisdictions are (1) to award damages and/or grant an injunction (including, in appropriate cases, a quia timet injunction) in respect of anything tortious[323] and (2) to make a

---

[318] *Cambridgeshire County Council v R (An Adult)* [1995] 1 FLR 50, 54.

[319] *In re T (Adult: Refusal of Treatment)* [1993] Fam 95, 111, 113, 115, 118, 122; *Re MB (Medical Treatment)* [1997] 2 FLR 426, 437. For a case of temporary incapacity see *Bolton Hospitals NHS Trust v O* [2002] EWHC 2871 (Fam), [2003] 1 FLR 824. For the relevance of ambivalence see *Re B (Consent to Treatment: Capacity)* [2002] EWHC 429 (Fam), [2002] 1 FLR 1090, at [34]–[35].

[320] *In re C (Adult: Refusal of Treatment)* [1994] 1 WLR 290, 295.

[321] *Malette v Shulman* (1987) 47 DLR (4th) 18, 42–44, 47–48, (1990) 67 DLR (4th) 321, 331–333, 335–338.

[322] See paras 4.23, 4.105 above.

[323] For an example see *In re C (Adult: Refusal of Treatment)* [1994] 1 WLR 290.

declaration either under the inherent jurisdiction or pursuant to RSC Ord 15, r 16.[324] In practice most applications to the court are for declarations.[325]

(i) The Basis of the Declaratory Jurisdiction

The jurisdiction is based upon the physical presence of the incompetent adult within the jurisdiction, irrespective of his nationality or domicile. Jurisdiction is not displaced by the appointment of a guardian by a foreign court of competent jurisdiction. Although the English court is not bound to accede to the wishes of such a guardian it will place weight upon considerations of comity and the guardian's views.[326]

4.122

(ii) The Scope of the Declaratory Jurisdiction

The Effect of a Declaration[327]

It is axiomatic that a declaration is, as its name indicates, merely declaratory in its effect. A declaration changes nothing; it cannot make lawful that which, absent a declaration, would be unlawful. Conversely, that which is declared lawful by declaration is equally lawful absent a declaration.[328] There is therefore never any legal necessity to obtain a declaration before proceeding either to treat or to stop the treatment of an incompetent adult (though the courts have indicated that, in certain circumstances, good practice requires that a declaration should be sought).[329]

4.123

The Purpose of Obtaining Declaratory Relief

The purpose of proceedings for a declaration is thus primarily one of protection of the patient and doctors and reassurance, both of the patient's family and the public, that what is proposed to be done (or not, as the case may be) is lawful.[330]

4.124

It is also axiomatic that a declaration can be granted only in relation to legal (or equitable) rights and obligations and not in relation to questions, however pressing, which are merely moral, ethical, or social.[331] The efficacy of the declaration as

4.125

---

[324] See paras 4.24, 4.106 above.

[325] For a general analysis of the declaration as a remedy see *St George's Healthcare NHS Trust v S, R v Collins, ex p S* [1999] Fam 26, 58–62.

[326] *In re S (Hospital patient: Foreign Curator)* [1996] Fam 23, 30, 31, 32.

[327] See generally *St George's Healthcare NHS Trust v S, R v Collins, ex p S* [1999] Fam 26, 58–62.

[328] *Airedale NHS Trust v Bland* [1993] AC 789, esp 888–890 *per* Lord Mustill; *A v A Health Authority, In re J (A Child), R (on the application of S) v Secretary of State for the Home Department* [2002] EWHC 18 (Fam/Admin), [2002] Fam 213, at [120].

[329] See paras 4.81–4.82 above, para 4.129 below.

[330] *Airedale NHS Trust v Bland* [1993] AC 789, 805, 815, 859, 874, 875. See further para 4.82 above.

[331] *Malone v Metropolitan Police Commissioner* [1979] Ch 344, 353 (court can make binding declarations only as to legal and equitable rights, and not as to moral, social or political matters). For a neat illustration of the point compare *Re C (Mental Patient: Contact)* [1993] 1 FLR 940 (jurisdiction to grant declaration that adult incompetent had right of access to non-custodial parent) and

a means of determining questions of medical treatment which often involve very complex moral and ethical issues derives from two principles of substantive law that underpin the entire jurisdiction: first, the principle that any touching or other interference with the integrity of the human body is, prima facie, unlawful, being both a tort and a crime;[332] secondly, the principle that a doctor (or layman) who, whether or not under any obligation to do so, assumes the responsibility of caring for or looking after a helpless individual, thereby assumes the legal duty to provide, whether himself or by calling for the assistance of others, for that individual's needs, and will be liable if he wrongfully abandons the person he is caring for.[333]

4.126   The efficacy of the declaration is further enhanced by the willingness of the courts (at least in this context) to grant declaratory relief not merely in relation to future questions for example, in declaring whether or not it will be lawful to administer or withhold treatment in the future, but even in relation to purely contingent questions,[334] for example, in declaring whether or not, in the event of a patient's family assuming the domiciliary care of a patient currently being cared for in hospital, it will be lawful for the family to administer or withhold treatment in the future.[335]

Scope of the Declaratory Jurisdiction: Treatment

4.127   It follows that the declaratory jurisdiction is available whether the question relates to medical treatment in the narrow sense, to professional nursing care (for example in a hospital or nursing home), or to care in the widest sense of the word (for example the domiciliary feeding and care by relatives of a bedridden patient). The declaratory jurisdiction extends to the lawfulness or unlawfulness of all aspects of an incompetent adult's 'treatment' and 'care'. Treatment and care are not confined to medical treatment, but include whatever is 'necessary to preserve . . . life, health

---

Cambridgeshire County Council v R (An Adult) [1995] 1 FLR 50 (no jurisdiction to grant declaration that adult incompetent had 'right' of non-access from non-custodial parent) as explained in *In re S (Hospital Patient: Court's Jurisdiction)* [1995] Fam 26, 32, appeal dismissed [1996] Fam 1, further proceedings *In re S (Hospital patient: Foreign Curator)* [1996] Fam 23. See also *Re V (Declaration against Parents)* [1995] 2 FLR 1003.

[332] *In re F (Mental Patient: Sterilisation)* [1990] 2 AC 1.

[333] Thus the breach of that duty, if it leads to the death of the patient, renders the carer, depending upon his mens rea, liable to prosecution for manslaughter or murder: *R v Gibbins* (1918) 13 Cr App R 134; *R v Stone* [1977] QB 354; *In re F (Mental Patient: Sterilisation)* [1990] 2 AC 1, 55–56, 77; *Airedale NHS Trust v Bland* [1993] AC 789, 858, 866, 881, 893; *Swindon and Marlborough NHS Trust v S* The Guardian, 10 December 1994, [1995] 3 Med LR 84. See further paras 4.201–4.204 below.

[334] *Re R (Adult: Medical Treatment)* [1996] 2 FLR 99. See further para 4.135 below.

[335] *Re C (Mental Patient: Contact)* [1993] 1 FLR 940; *Swindon and Marlborough NHS Trust v S* Guardian, 10 December 1994, [1995] 3 Med LR 84; *In re S (Hospital Patient: Court's Jurisdiction)* [1995] Fam 26, appeal dismissed [1996] Fam 1, subsequent substantive proceedings *In re S (Hospital patient: Foreign Curator)* [1996] Fam 23. See further the cases referred to in n 479 below.

or well-being' or 'carried out in order either to save . . . lives, or to ensure improvement or prevent deterioration in . . . physical or mental health'.[336] In addition to appropriate medical, dental and surgical treatment, treatment includes, in the case of someone who is permanently or semi-permanently incapable, care, as part of daily life, of a basic, simple or humdrum nature, such as dressing, undressing, feeding, looking after, and putting to bed, and including the actions of the relative, friend or neighbour who comes in to look after the patient.[337] Treatment and care extend to 'action . . . such as a reasonable person would in all the circumstances take, acting in the best interests of the assisted person'[338] and thus to everything that conduces to the welfare and happiness of the patient, including companionship and the patient's domestic and social environment.[339]

Scope of the Declaratory Jurisdiction: Future Questions

Likewise, the declaratory jurisdiction is available whether the question relates to the proposed administration of treatment (for example the performance of a sterilisation[340]), or to the proposed withholding or termination of treatment (for example the discontinuance of artificial hydration or nutrition).[341]   **4.128**

(iii) The Need to Involve the Court

Although there is never any legal necessity to obtain a declaration before proceeding either to treat or to stop the treatment of an incompetent adult,[342] the courts have indicated that, as in the case of a child, so in the case of an adult incompetent, 'as a matter of good practice', a declaration should always be obtained in those cases falling within what has been described as a 'special category'. This topic has already been dealt with in relation to children;[343] the same principles apply in relation to incompetent adults. Where the court is involved unnecessarily, it may decline to act.[344]   **4.129**

---

[336] *In re F (Mental Patient: Sterilisation)* [1990] 2 AC 1, 52 *per* Lord Bridge of Harwich, 55 *per* Lord Brandon of Oakbrook.

[337] ibid, 72, 76 *per* Lord Goff of Chieveley.

[338] ibid, 75 *per* Lord Goff of Chieveley.

[339] *Re C (Mental Patient: Contact)* [1993] 1 FLR 940; *A v A Health Authority, In re J (A Child), R (on the application of S) v Secretary of State for the Home Department* [2002] EWHC 18 (Fam/Admin), [2002] Fam 213, at [39].

[340] As in *In re F (Mental Patient: Sterilisation)* [1990] 2 AC 1, esp 81–82.

[341] As in *Airedale NHS Trust v Bland* [1993] AC 789, esp 862–863, 880–881, 888–890 (stressing how intolerable it would be if a carer could not obtain authoritative judicial guidance in advance as to the legality of proposed action or inaction). See further para 4.135 below.

[342] See para 4.123 above.

[343] See paras 4.81–4.82 above.

[344] It is unnecessary to involve the court if a patient is clearly competent and refusing treatment: *Re JT (Adult: Refusal of Medical Treatment)* [1998] 1 FLR 48, 51–52; *St George's Healthcare NHS Trust v S, R v Collins, ex p S* [1999] Fam 26, 63–64. See further para 4.87 above.

(iv) Locus Standi

4.130 Three categories of individual have locus standi to apply for a declaration:[345]

(1) The patient (acting by some suitable individual as his next friend): his own legal rights are, of course, in issue.

(2) Any actual or prospective carer, whether professionally qualified or not: the carer's own (albeit prospective) legal rights and liabilities are in issue and the prospective carer needs to know, for example, if he will be acting lawfully or unlawfully (tortiously and criminally) if he arranges for the patient to be accommodated at a place of the carer's choosing, undertakes the task of caring for the patient, and adopts a particular regime for the medical or other treatment and care of the patient.[346]

(3) Anybody whose past or present relationship with the patient, whether formal or informal (for example as parent, spouse, sibling, mistress,[347] or friend), gives him a genuine and legitimate interest in obtaining a decision, in contrast to being a stranger or an officious busybody.[348]

4.131 A spouse or relative does not, qua spouse or relative, have any status either to consent or to refuse consent to medical treatment[349] and therefore cannot, qua spouse or relative, have locus to seek a declaration. Nor, if the question is whether or not a patient under the care of doctors can lawfully be treated by those doctors, can a spouse or relative have locus qua carer. In such circumstances, a spouse or relative can, and normally will, have locus only as a person with a genuine and legitimate interest in the patient.

4.132 Likewise in the case of a local authority.

4.133 Thus the declaratory jurisdiction has been successfully invoked in cases involving the medical treatment of incompetent or competent but unconscious adults by the patient (acting by a next friend)[350] by a doctor or health

---

[345] *In re S (Hospital Patient: Court's Jurisdiction)* [1995] Fam 26, appeal dismissed [1996] Fam 1, further proceedings *In re S (Hospital patient: Foreign Curator)* [1996] Fam 23.

[346] See, for example, *In re S (Hospital Patient: Court's Jurisdiction)* [1995] Fam 26, 35, appeal dismissed [1996] Fam 1, further proceedings *In re S (Hospital patient: Foreign Curator)* [1996] Fam 23.

[347] For an example see *In re S (Hospital Patient: Court's Jurisdiction)* [1995] Fam 26 (where the relevant factors were listed by Hale J, 35), appeal dismissed [1996] Fam 1. For the subsequent substantive proceedings see *In re S (Hospital patient: Foreign Curator)* [1996] Fam 23.

[348] *In re S (Hospital Patient: Court's Jurisdiction)* [1996] Fam 1, 18, 19, dismissing appeal from [1995] Fam 26; *A v A Health Authority, In re J (A Child), R (on the application of S) v Secretary of State for the Home Department* [2002] EWHC 18 (Fam/Admin), [2002] Fam 213, at [42]. For the earlier cases see, in particular, *Royal College of Nursing of the UK v Department of Health and Social Security* [1981] AC 800; *Gillick v West Norfolk and Wisbech AHA* [1986] AC 112; *In re F (Mental Patient: Sterilisation)* [1990] 2 AC 1, 81–82; *Airedale NHS Trust v Bland* [1993] AC 789, 862.

[349] See paras 4.23, 4.105 above.

[350] *In re F (Mental Patient: Sterilisation)* [1990] 2 AC 1; *Re SG (Adult Mental Patient: Abortion)* [1991] 2 FLR 329; *Re W (Mental patient) (Sterilisation)* [1993] 1 FLR 381; *Re S (Medical Treatment:*

authority,[351] by a relative (applying qua relative),[352] by a local authority,[353] by a mistress,[354] and by the prospective donee from an adult incompetent of bone marrow.[355]

(v) Form of Declaratory Relief

Interim or Final?

Cases in which the court's declaratory jurisdiction is invoked often arise at very short notice and as a matter of extreme urgency; many require to be resolved within a day or two, and some within a matter of a few hours or even minutes. The court can grant an interim declaration[356] following an inter partes hearing

4.134

Adult Sterilisation) [1998] 1 FLR 944; *Re ZM and OS (Sterilisation: Patient's Best Interests)* [2000] 1 FLR 523; *Re A (Male Sterilisation)* [2000] 1 FLR 549; *Re SS (Medical Treatment: Late Termination)* [2002] 1 FLR 445. See also *A v A Health Authority, In re J (A Child), R (on the application of S) v Secretary of State for the Home Department* [2002] EWHC 18 (Fam/Admin), [2002] Fam 213 (residence of adult incompetent).

[351] *Re H (Mental Patient: Diagnosis)* [1993] 1 FLR 28; *Airedale NHS Trust v Bland* [1993] AC 789; *Riverside Mental Health NHS Trust v Fox* [1994] 1 FLR 614; *Frenchay Healthcare National Health Service Trust v S* [1994] 1 WLR 601; *Re KB (Adult) (Mental Patient: Medical Treatment)* (1994) 19 BMLR 144; *Re G (Persistent Vegetative State)* [1995] 2 FCR 46; *Swindon and Marlborough NHS Trust v S* Guardian, 10 December 1994, [1995] 3 Med LR 84; *Re C (Adult Patient: Restriction of Publicity after Death)* [1996] 2 FLR 251; *Tameside and Glossop Acute Services Trust v CH* [1996] 1 FLR 762; *Re R (Adult: Medical Treatment)* [1996] 2 FLR 99; *Norfolk and Norwich Healthcare (NHS) Trust v W* [1996] 2 FLR 613; *Rochdale Healthcare (NHS) Trust v C* [1997] 1 FCR 274; *Re L (Patient: Non-Consensual Treatment)* [1997] 2 FLR 837; *Re D (Medical Treatment)* [1998] 1 FLR 411; *Re MB (Medical Treatment)* [1997] 2 FLR 426; *Re H (A Patient)* [1998] 2 FLR 36; *Re D (Medical Treatment: Mentally Disabled Patient)* [1998] 2 FLR 22; *NHS Trust A v M, NHS Trust B v H* [2001] Fam 348; *NHS Trust A v H* [2001] 2 FLR 501; *Re G (adult incompetent: withdrawal of treatment)* (2001) 65 BMLR 6; *A Hospital NHS Trust v S* [2003] EWHC 365 (Fam), [2003] Lloyd's Rep Med 137.

[352] *Re GF (Medical Treatment)* [1992] 1 FLR 293 (mother—proposed sterilisation); *In re T (Adult: Refusal of Treatment)* [1993] Fam 95 (father—blood transfusion after caesarian). See also *Re C (Mental Patient: Contact)* [1993] 1 FLR 940 (mother—contact with adult incompetent); *Re X (Adult Sterilisation)* [1998] 2 FLR 1124 (mother—proposed sterilisation); *Re D-R (Adult: Contact)* [1999] 1 FLR 1161 (father—contact with adult incompetent); *R v R (Interim Declaration: Adult's Residence)* [2000] 1 FLR 451 (mother—residence of adult incompetent); *In re S (Adult Patient: Sterilisation)* [2001] Fam 15 (reversing *Re S (Sterilisation: Patient's Best Interests)* [2000] 1 FLR 465) (mother—proposed sterilisation).

[353] *Re NK* 28 February 1990 (Ewbank J), 4 April 1990 (Scott Baker J); *Re LC (Medical Treatment: Sterilisation)* [1997] 2 FLR 258 (proposed sterilisation). See also *Cambridgeshire County Council v R (An Adult)* [1995] 1 FLR 50; *In re F (Adult: Court's Jurisdiction)* [2001] Fam 38 (residence of adult incompetent); *A v A Health Authority, In re J (A Child), R (on the application of S) v Secretary of State for the Home Department* [2002] EWHC 18 (Fam/Admin), [2002] Fam 213, at [42] (residence of adult incompetent); *Re S (Adult Patient) (Inherent Jurisdiction: Family Life)* [2002] EWHC 2278 (Fam), [2003] 1 FLR 292 (residence of adult incompetent).

[354] *In re S (Hospital Patient: Court's Jurisdiction)* [1995] Fam 26, appeal dismissed [1996] Fam 1. For the subsequent substantive proceedings see *In re S (Hospital patient: Foreign Curator)* [1996] Fam 23.

[355] *In re Y (Mental Patient: Bone Marrow Donation)* [1997] Fam 110.

[356] CPR Pt 25.1.1(b). But the court cannot grant an interim declaration until the legal foundation for the exercise of the jurisdiction has been established, namely that the patient lacks capacity: *R v R (Interim Declaration: Adult's Residence)* [2000] 1 FLR 451.

arranged, if the circumstances warrant, at extremely short notice and, if need be, out of normal court hours.[357] But the court cannot grant an ex parte declaration.[358] However, even if the only substantive relief sought is a declaration, the court can grant an interlocutory injunction to 'hold the ring' pending trial.[359] Furthermore, the practice of the court, even when making a final declaration, is to confine the declaration to the state of affairs as it exists at the date of the hearing and to grant liberty to all parties to apply for further declaratory relief in the event of any material change in circumstances.[360]

Prospective Relief

4.135   In an appropriate case the court can make a prospective declaration to cover the happening of a future event, and declare that steps taken on the happening of that event will, subject to specified conditions and safeguards, be lawful. Thus in one case[361] a declaration was granted in the following terms, the court in effect devolving the future decision to the attending doctor subject to the twin safeguards of a second medical opinion and parental consent:

> Ordered and declared that notwithstanding (a) that the patient is unable to give a valid consent thereto and (b) if such be the case that no further order of the court shall have been obtained in the meantime it shall be lawful as being in the patient's best interests for the Trust and/or the responsible medical practitioners having the responsibility at the time for the patient's treatment and care . . . to withhold the administration of antibiotics in the event of the patient developing a potentially life-threatening infection which would otherwise call for the administration of antibiotics but only if immediately prior to withholding the same (a) the Trust is so advised both by the general medical practitioner and by the consultant psychiatrist having the responsibility at the time for the patient's treatment and care and (b) one or other or both of the [patient's] parents first give their consent thereto.

---

[357] *In re Y (Mental Patient: Bone Marrow Donation)* [1997] Fam 110, 116. Thus in *Swindon and Marlborough NHS Trust v S* The Guardian, 10 December 1994, [1995] 3 Med LR 84 an inter partes hearing with medical evidence on both sides was arranged late on a Friday afternoon and took place, after the patient had been examined by the Official Solicitor's doctor on Saturday morning, on Saturday afternoon. And see *HE v A Hospital NHS Trust* [2003] EWHC 1017 (Fam), [2003] 2 FLR 408.

[358] *St George's Healthcare NHS Trust v S, R v Collins, ex p S* [1999] Fam 26, 60–61.

[359] *In re S (Hospital Patient: Court's Jurisdiction)* [1995] Fam 26, 35–36, appeal on another point dismissed [1996] Fam 1.

[360] See, eg, the declarations granted in *In re F (Mental Patient: Sterilisation)* [1990] 2 AC 1; *Airedale NHS Trust v Bland* [1993] AC 789, and the precedents in *Practice Note (Official Solicitor: Sterilisation)* [1996] 2 FLR 111; *Practice Note (Official Solicitor: Persistent Vegetative State)* [1996] 2 FLR 375.

[361] *Re R (Adult: Medical Treatment)* [1996] 2 FLR 99, 104, 106, 109, 110, justified by Sir Stephen Brown P for the reasons set out, 106–107, 108–109. The criticism of this decision by Professor Ian Kennedy at [1997] Med L Rev 104, 108, is, with respect, unjustified: see the discussion in *Re S (Adult Patient) (Inherent Jurisdiction: Family Life)* [2002] EWHC 2278 (Fam), [2003] 1 FLR 292, at [55]–[59]. See also *Re D (Medical Treatment: Mentally Disabled Patient)* [1998] 2 FLR 22 where the declaration was in terms that it was lawful not to treat 'in circumstances in which in the opinion of the medical practitioners responsible for such treatment it is not reasonably practicable so to do'.

Subject to being satisfied that this really is in the *best* interests of the mentally in-   **4.136**
capacitated person, the court has power to declare that some specified person is to
be, in relation to specified matters, what is, in effect, a surrogate decision-maker
for the incapable adult.[362]

> The court has jurisdiction to grant whatever relief in declaratory form is necessary
> to safeguard and promote the incapable adult's welfare and interests. If the court
> thinks that his interests will best be served by a judicial identification of some third
> party as the most appropriate person to be responsible not merely for his care but
> also for taking the kind of decisions to which I have already referred[363] then . . .
> there can be no objection whatever to the court so declaring. Indeed, were the court
> not to do so in an appropriate case, it would . . . be failing in its duties under both
> the common law and the Convention. After all, to declare that some specified per-
> son who is, in the eyes of the court, the most appropriate person to assume respon-
> sibility for this aspect of a patient's care is also to be clothed with practical
> decision-making on behalf of the patient, is merely to state explicitly that he has
> those powers and responsibilities which would in any event be reposed in him by
> the doctrine of necessity. Moreover, some such mechanism is essential if those car-
> ing for the incapable are to be allowed to get on with their task without the need for
> endless reference to the court—something which (cases in the 'special' category
> apart) would serve neither the public interest nor the interests of the mentally
> incapacitated.
>
> So, subject always to being satisfied that this really is in the *best* interests of the men-
> tally incapacitated person, the court has, and . . . always has had, power to declare
> that some specified person is to be, in relation to specified matters, what is, in effect,
> a surrogate decision-maker for the incapable adult.
>
> Put so starkly the proposition may seem novel. But there is, I believe, authority[364] to
> support it. Even were there not I would unhesitatingly come to the same conclu-
> sion. The inherent declaratory jurisdiction has developed considerably since the
> House of Lords gave judgment in *Re F (Mental Patient: Sterilisation)* and in ways
> which few might have foreseen in 1989. It will, I do not doubt, continue to develop.
> It is right that it should. It probably must if the court is to meet its obligations under
> the Convention.[365]

Precedents

The forms of declaration granted in a variety of cases can be found in the re-   **4.137**
ports.[366] Precedents for use in cases relating to sterilisation and the withdrawal of

---

[362] *Re S (Adult Patient) (Inherent Jurisdiction: Family Life)* [2002] EWHC 2278 (Fam), [2003] 1
FLR 292, at [51].

[363] In the passage cited in para 4.108 above.

[364] In particular *Re R (Adult: Medical Treatment)* [1996] 2 FLR 99.

[365] *Re S (Adult Patient) (Inherent Jurisdiction: Family Life)* [2002] EWHC 2278 (Fam), [2003] 1
FLR 292, at [50]–[52] *per* Munby J.

[366] See, eg, *In re F (Mental Patient: Sterilisation)* [1990] 2 AC 1; *Airedale NHS Trust v Bland* [1993]
AC 789; *Tameside and Glossop Acute Services Trust v CH* [1996] 1 FLR 762; *Re R (Adult: Medical
Treatment)* [1996] 2 FLR 99; *In re Y (Mental Patient: Bone Marrow Donation)* [1997] Fam 110; *Re
G (adult incompetent: withdrawal of treatment)* (2001) 65 BMLR 6.

artificial nutrition and hydration from patients in a permanent (formerly called persistent) vegetative state are set out in the Official Solicitor's Practice Note[367] and can readily be adapted for use in other cases. Where declaratory relief is being sought against a public authority (for instance, a NHS Hospital) care must be taken to ensure that the declaration does not encroach on the authority's public law functions or, if it does, that it can be justified on public law grounds and applying appropriate principles of substantive public law.[368]

(vi) Injunctions in Support of Declaratory Relief

4.138   Where proceedings are brought to restrain a threatened tort involving an interference with the patient's body, the court can grant an injunction, including, in an appropriate case, a quia timet injunction.[369] Even if the only substantive relief sought is a declaration, the court can grant an interlocutory injunction to 'hold the ring' pending trial.[370]

(vii) Procedure

4.139   Proceedings should be commenced in the Family Division of the High Court.[371] Details of the procedure to be adopted have been laid down by the Court of Appeal and the President.[372] Details of the procedure to be adopted in applications to the court in relation to sterilisation and the withdrawal of artificial nutrition and hydration from patients in a permanent (formerly called persistent) vegetative state are set out in the Official Solicitor's Practice Notes.[373] This reflects views expressed by the House of Lords in the leading cases[374] and, mutatis mutandis, can be taken as applying in other applications for declaratory relief.[375]

---

[367] *Practice Note (Official Solicitor: Declaratory Proceedings: Medical and Welfare Decisions for Adults Who Lack Capacity)* [2001] 2 FLR 158.

[368] *A v A Health Authority, In re J (A Child), R (on the application of S) v Secretary of State for the Home Department* [2002] EWHC 18 (Fam/Admin), [2002] Fam 213, at [123]–[126].

[369] *Egan v Egan* [1975] Ch 218. For an example see *In re C (Adult: Refusal of Treatment)* [1994] 1 WLR 290.

[370] *In re S (Hospital Patient: Court's Jurisdiction)* [1995] Fam 26, 35–36, appeal on another point dismissed [1996] Fam 1; *A v A Health Authority, In re J (A Child), R (on the application of S) v Secretary of State for the Home Department* [2002] EWHC 18 (Fam/Admin), [2002] Fam 213, at [44].

[371] *President's Direction (Declaratory Proceedings Concerning Incapacitated Adults: Medical and Welfare Decisions)* [2002] 1 FLR 177.

[372] *Re MB (Medical Treatment)* [1997] 2 FLR 426, 439, 445; *St George's Healthcare NHS Trust v S, R v Collins, ex p S* [1999] Fam 26, 63–65; *Re B (Consent to Treatment: Capacity)* [2002] EWHC 429 (Fam), [2002] 1 FLR 1090, at [100].

[373] *Practice Note (Official Solicitor: Declaratory Proceedings: Medical and Welfare Decisions for Adults Who Lack Capacity)* [2001] 2 FLR 158.

[374] *In re F (Mental Patient: Sterilisation)* [1990] 2 AC 1; *Airedale NHS Trust v Bland* [1993] AC 789.

[375] For the role and involvement of the Official Solicitor see paras 4.92–4.93 above. Further aspects of the procedure in sterilisation cases were considered in *Practice Note (Mental Patient: Sterilisation)*; *J v C* [1990] 1 WLR 1248. On the question of whether the court should sit in public,

4. *Best Interests and the 'Bolam' Test*

The 'Bolam' test[376]

For a long time the precise relationship between the 'Bolam' test and the 'best in-   **4.140**
terests' test was obscure.[377] The matter has now been clarified by two important
decisions of the Court of Appeal, which make clear that what is in a patient's best
interests is not to be determined solely by reference to the 'Bolam' test; both doctors, in the case of action taken without reference to the court, and the court,
when exercising the inherent jurisdiction, have to adopt that course of treatment
which both satisfies the 'Bolam' test *and* is in the patient's best interests.[378]
Accordingly, whether the proposed treatment satisfies the 'Bolam' test is a necessary, but not a sufficient, condition of treatment in a patient's best interests.[379]

> Doctors charged with the decisions about the future treatment of patients and
> whether such treatment would, in the cases of those lacking capacity to make their
> own decisions, be in their best interests, have to act at all times in accordance with a
> responsible and competent body of relevant professional opinion. That is the pro-
> fessional standard set for those who make such decisions. The doctor, acting to that
> required standard, has . . . a second duty, that is to say, he must act in the best inter-
> ests of a mentally incapacitated patient. I do not consider that the two duties have
> been conflated into one requirement. . . . In any event, in the case of an application
> for approval of a sterilisation operation, it is the judge, not the doctor, who makes
> the decision that it is in the best interests of the patient that the operation be per-
> formed.[380]

> The starting point of any medical decision would be the principles enunciated in
> the *Bolam* test and . . . a doctor ought not to make any decision about a patient that
> does not fall within the broad spectrum of the *Bolam* test. The duty to act in accord-
> ance with responsible and competent professional opinion may give the doctor
> more than one option since there may well be more than one acceptable medical
> opinion. When the doctor moves on to consider the best interests of the patient
> he/she has to choose the best option, often from a range of options . . . the best in-
> terests test ought, logically, to give only one answer.

> In these difficult cases where the medical profession seeks a declaration as to lawful-
> ness of the proposed treatment, the judge, not the doctor, has the duty to decide

---

and attendant questions of protecting the patient's anonymity, see *Re G (Adult Patient: Publicity)*
[1995] 2 FLR 528; *Re C (Adult Patient: Restriction of Publicity after Death)* [1996] 2 FLR 251; *Re R
(Adult: Medical Treatment)* [1996] 2 FLR 99, 110; *In re Y (Mental Patient: Bone Marrow Donation)*
[1997] Fam 110, 116.

[376] See *Bolam v Friern Hospital Management Committee* [1957] 1 WLR 582.
[377] See the first edition, paras 4.133–4.136.
[378] *Re A (Male Sterilisation)* [2000] 1 FLR 549; *In re S (Adult Patient: Sterilisation)* [2001] Fam 15
(reversing *Re S (Sterilisation: Patient's Best Interests)* [2000] 1 FLR 465). For valuable summaries by
Dame Elizabeth Butler-Sloss P see *Simms v Simms, A v A (A Child)* [2002] EWHC 2734 (Fam),
[2003] Fam 83, at [42]–[46]; *A Hospital NHS Trust v S* [2003] EWHC 365 (Fam), [2003] Lloyd's
Rep Med 137, at [42]–[48].
[379] *R (on the application of N) v M* [2002] EWCA Civ 1789, [2003] 1 WLR 562, at [27]–[29].
[380] *Re A (Male Sterilisation)* [2000] 1 FLR 549, 555, *per* Dame Elizabeth Butler-Sloss P.

whether such treatment *is* in the best interests of the patient. The judicial decision ought to provide the best answer not a range of alternative answers. There may, of course, be situations where the answer may not be obvious and alternatives may have to be tried. It is still at any one point the best option of that moment which should be chosen. I recognise that there is distinguished judicial dicta to the contrary in the speech of Lord Browne-Wilkinson in *Airedale NHS Trust v Bland* [1993] AC 789, 884. The passage in his speech was not however followed by the other members of the House. Hale J in *In re S (Hospital Patient: Court's Jurisdiction)* [1995] Fam 26, 32 followed the same approach. She said that, in accordance with the *Bolam* test, it followed that a number of different courses may be lawful in any particular case. That may be so, but I do not read *In re F (Medical Patient: Sterilisation)* [1990] 2 AC 1, upon which she relied, as relieving the judge who is deciding the best interests of the patient from making a choice between the available options. I respectfully disagree with Lord Browne-Wilkinson and Hale J . . . the principle of best interests as applied by the court extends beyond the considerations set out in the *Bolam* case [1957] 1 WLR 582. The judicial decision will incorporate broader ethical, social, moral and welfare considerations.

In my judgment, the judge misapplied the *Bolam* test when he said [2000] 1 FLR 465, 477–478:

> 'I did not understand either Dr K or Professor T to say that to move immediately to surgery was outside the *Bolam* test: in other words that in performing a laparoscopic subtotal hysterectomy operation a doctor would not be operating in accordance with a practice accepted at the time by a responsible body of medical opinion skilled in the particular form of treatment in question.'

The question, however, for the judge was not was the proposed treatment within the range of acceptable opinion among competent and responsible practitioners, but was it in the best interests of S? The *Bolam* test was, in my view, irrelevant to the judicial decision, once the judge was satisfied that the range of options was within the range of acceptable opinion among competent and responsible practitioners.[381]

In determining the welfare of the patient the *Bolam* test is applied only at the outset to ensure that the treatment proposed is recognised as proper by a responsible body of medical opinion skilled in delivering that particular treatment. That may be a necessary check in an exercise where it would be impossible to be over scrupulous. But I find it hard to imagine in practice a disputed trial before a judge of the Division in which a responsible party proposed for an incompetent patient a treatment that did not satisfy the *Bolam* test. In practice the dispute will generally require the court to choose between two or more possible treatments both or all of which comfortably pass the *Bolam* test. As most of us know from experience a patient contemplating treatment for a physical condition or illness is often offered a range of alternatives with counter-balancing advantages and disadvantages. One of the most important services provided by a consultant is to explain the available alternatives to the patient, particularly concentrating on those features of advantage and disadvantage most relevant to his needs and circumstances. In a developing relationship of confidence the consultant then guides the patient to make the choice

---

[381] *In re S (Adult Patient: Sterilisation)* [2001] Fam 15, 27–28, *per* Dame Elizabeth Butler-Sloss P.

that best suits his circumstances and personality. It is precisely because the patient is prevented by disability from that exchange that the judge must in certain circumstances either exercise the choice between alternative available treatments or perhaps refuse any form of treatment. In deciding what is best for the disabled patient the judge must have regard to the patient's welfare as the paramount consideration. That embraces issues far wider than the medical. Indeed it would be undesirable and probably impossible to set bounds to what is relevant to a welfare determination. In my opinion the *Bolam* case has no contribution to make to this second and determinative stage of the judicial decision . . . It is simply not helpful for either the family or the doctors to be presented with a declaration that two or more possible treatments are lawful on the grounds that both or all satisfied the *Bolam* test. It is the judge's function to declare that treatment which is in the best interests of the patient and . . . only one treatment can be best.[382]

The Function of the Court

Thus it is now recognised that the jurisdiction is exercised solely by reference to the incompetent adult's best interests, and that this involves a welfare appraisal in the widest sense, taking into account, where appropriate, a wide range of ethical, social, moral, emotional and welfare considerations.[383]   **4.141**

> Best interests are not limited to best medical interests.[384]
>
> Best interests encompasses medical, emotional and all other welfare issues.[385]
>
> In deciding what is best for the disabled patient the judge must have regard to the patient's welfare as the paramount consideration. That embraces issues far wider than the medical. Indeed it would be undesirable and probably impossible to set bounds to what is relevant to a welfare determination.[386]

Evaluation of the patient's best interests will often be assisted by the preparation of a balance sheet listing the advantages and disadvantages for the patient of what is proposed.   **4.142**

> Pending the enactment of a checklist or other statutory direction it seems to me that the first instance judge with the responsibility to make an evaluation of the best interests of a claimant lacking capacity should draw up a balance sheet. The first entry should be of any factor or factors of actual benefit. In the present case the instance would be the acquisition of foolproof contraception. Then on the other sheet the judge should write any counterbalancing dis-benefits to the applicant. An obvious instance in this case would be the apprehension, the risk and the discomfort inherent in the operation. Then the judge should enter on each sheet the potential gains and losses in each instance making some estimate of the extent of the possibility that the gain or loss might accrue. At the end of that exercise the judge should be better placed to strike a balance between the sum of the certain and possible gains against

---

[382] *In re S (Adult Patient: Sterilisation)* [2001] Fam 15, 30–31, *per* Thorpe LJ.
[383] *A v A Health Authority, In re J (A Child), R (on the application of S) v Secretary of State for the Home Department* [2002] EWHC 18 (Fam/Admin), [2002] Fam 213, at [43].
[384] *Re MB (Medical Treatment)* [1997] 2 FLR 426, 439, *per* Butler-Sloss LJ.
[385] *Re A (Male Sterilisation)* [2000] 1 FLR 549, 555, *per* Dame Elizabeth Butler-Sloss P.
[386] *In re S (Adult Patient: Sterilisation)* [2001] Fam 15, 30, *per* Thorpe LJ.

the sum of the certain and possible losses. Obviously, only if the account is in relatively significant credit will the judge conclude that the application is likely to advance the best interests of the claimant.[387]

4.143 For most practical purposes the declaratory jurisdiction in relation to incompetent adults is the same as that of a court exercising the parens patriae jurisdiction.[388]

> The jurisdiction is not strictly the exercise of a parens patriae jurisdiction but is similar to it . . . it is clear that the result of the decision in *Re F* was that a case of this nature did give to the court a jurisdiction which has been referred to as patrimonial and not strictly 'parens patriae' but similar in all practical respects to it.[389]

> The evaluation of best interests is akin to a welfare appraisal.[390]

> It seems to me to be a distinction without a difference, by which I mean that the parens patriae jurisdiction is only the term of art for the wardship jurisdiction which is alternatively described as the inherent jurisdiction. That which is patrimonial is that which is inherited from the ancestral past. It therefore follows that whilst the decision in *In re F* signposted the inadvertent loss of the parens patriae jurisdiction in relation to incompetent adults, the alternative jurisdiction which it established, the declaratory decree, was to be exercised upon the same basis, namely that relief would be granted if the welfare of the patient required it and equally refused if the welfare of the patient did not.[391]

> This jurisdiction has now developed beyond the simple declaration of what will or will not be lawful into something akin to the wardship jurisdiction relating to children. [392]

F. Best Interests

4.144 As has been seen, the defining criterion for the legality of any invasive procedure proposed to be performed on an incompetent adult is the patient's best interests.[393] Best interests is also the criterion by which, normally,[394] the propriety of performing an invasive procedure on a child is determined, whether the decision is that of the court[395] or of a parent.[396]

---

[387] *In re A (Male Sterilisation)* [2000] 1 FLR 549, 560, *per* Thorpe LJ. For an interesting example of such a balance sheet (in the context of a proposed abortion) see *Re SS (Medical Treatment: Late Termination)* [2002] 1 FLR 445, at [30].

[388] *A v A Health Authority, In re J (A Child), R (on the application of S) v Secretary of State for the Home Department* [2002] EWHC 18 (Fam/Admin), [2002] Fam 213, at [45].

[389] *Re G (Adult Patient: Publicity)* [1995] 2 FLR 528, 530 *per* Sir Stephen Brown P.

[390] *Re A (Male Sterilisation)* [2000] 1 FLR 549, 560, *per* Thorpe LJ.

[391] *In re S (Adult Patient: Sterilisation)* [2001] Fam 15, 29–30, *per* Thorpe LJ, with whom both Dame Elizabeth Butler-Sloss P and Mance LJ agreed.

[392] *R (Wilkinson) v Broadmoor Special Hospital Authority* [2002] 1 WLR 419, at [64] *per* Hale LJ.

[393] See paras 4.25, 4.106, 4.109 above.

[394] But see para 4.80 above.

[395] See para 4.94 above.

[396] See paras 4.78–4.79 above.

What exactly is meant by a patient's best interests is neither self-evident nor alto-   **4.145**
gether clear. The problem is well illustrated by the uncertainties which have long
surrounded, and to an extent still surround, the ambit of the parental power, in
furthering the best interests of the child, to consent or refuse consent[397] to medical treatment.[398] Earlier controversies concerned such questions as the blood-
testing of children for forensic rather than therapeutic purposes and female
circumcision. More recent controversy has focused on the non-therapeutic sterilisation of children and incompetent adults. Difficulties and obscurities currently
surround such issues as the withholding of life-saving treatment from children
(particularly neonates) and incompetent adults and the donation by children and
incompetent adults of regenerative tissue or bodily fluids and, more particularly,
non-regenerative organs.

There are two reasons for this uncertainty. First, the question has been given sur-   **4.146**
prisingly little consideration by the courts.[399] Secondly, and notwithstanding
strong criticism, the courts have traditionally failed,[400] and even on occasions refused,[401] to articulate any principles or values to be applied in operating the best
interests test.

> The 'best interests' approach focusses attention on the child whose interests are in
> question. . . . But, that said, the best interests approach does no more than identify
> the person whose interests are in question: it does not assist in identifying the fac-
> tors which are relevant to the best interests of the child. The summary rejection by
> the House of Lords of the criterion offered by *Re Eve* left their Lordships without
> any guidelines by which to decide *Re B* or, at least, any guidelines that could be ar-
> ticulated for general application. That is because the best interests approach offers
> no hierarchy of values which might guide the exercise of a discretionary power . . .,
> much less any general legal principle which might direct the difficult decisions to be
> made in this area by parents, guardians, the medical profession and the courts. . . .

---

[397] For a recent vivid example see the, it might be thought surprising, decision in *In re T (A Minor)*
(Wardship: Medical Treatment) [1997] 1 WLR 242.

[398] The most recent comprehensive, if inconclusive, judicial consideration of the basis and scope
of the common law power of a parent to consent to medical treatment is in *Secretary, Department of*
Health and Community Services v JWB and SMB (1992) 175 CLR 218, esp, 239–240, 278–279,
291–301, 312–317.

[399] *Secretary, Department of Health and Community Services v JWB and SMB* (1992) 175 CLR 218,
312.

[400] *In re B (A Minor) (Wardship: Sterilisation)* [1988] AC 199 is a well-known and much criticised
example of such failure.

[401] As in *In re J (A Minor) (Wardship: Medical Treatment)* [1991] Fam 33, 52 *per* Balcombe LJ: 'I
would deprecate any attempt by this court to lay down such an all-embracing test . . . I do not know
of any demand by the judges who have to deal with these cases at first instance for this court to assist
them by laying down any test beyond that which is already the law: that the interests of the ward are
the first and paramount consideration, subject to the gloss on that test . . . that in determining where
those interests lie the court adopts the standpoint of the reasonable and responsible parent who has
his or her child's best interests at heart.' See also *In re T (A Minor) (Wardship: Medical Treatment)*
[1997] 1 WLR 242, 254 *per* Waite LJ: 'All these cases depend on their own facts and render generalisations—tempting though they may be to the legal or social analyst—wholly out of place.'

[B]y transforming a 'complex moral and social question' into a question of fact, the best interests approach leaves the court in the hands of 'experts' who assemble a dossier of fact and opinion on matters which they deem relevant 'without reference to any check-list of legal requirements'.[402]

To say that a medical or surgical procedure is in the best interests of a child, however, is merely to record a result. Before the best interests of the child can be determined, some principle, rule or standard must be applied to the facts and circumstances of the case.[403]

1. Best Interests and Substituted Judgment

4.147 The propriety of an invasive medical procedure proposed to be performed on a child or an incompetent adult is judged by reference to the patient's best interests, not by the application of a substituted judgment. The test of best interests is objective, assessed with respect to the particular patient and from the point of view of a person suffering his handicaps.

(i) Best Interests or Substituted Judgment?

(a) The Patient's Property and Affairs

4.148 So far as concerns questions relating to the patient's property and affairs, the court applies,[404] and has always applied, a substituted judgment test.[405] The principle is an old one.[406]

(b) The Patient's Physical and Bodily Welfare

4.149 Some jurisdictions in the United States of America have extended the substituted

---

[402] *Secretary, Department of Health and Community Services v JWB and SMB* (1992) 175 CLR 218, 270, 272–273 *per* Brennan J.

[403] ibid, 320 *per* McHugh J.

[404] Where a true substituted judgment is impossible because the patient has always lacked capacity, the court 'must assume that she would have been a normal decent person, acting in accordance with contemporary standards of morality': *Re C (A Patient)* [1991] 3 All ER 866, 870 *per* Hoffmann J.

[405] In *re D(J)* [1982] Ch 237, 244 *per* Megarry VC ('court must seek to [do that] which the actual patient, acting reasonably, would have [done] if notionally restored to full mental capacity, memory and foresight').

[406] *Ex p Whitbread* (1816) 2 Mer 99, 102 ('looking at what it is likely the Lunatic himself would do, if he were in a capacity to act'); *Re Blair* (1836) 1 My & Cr 300; *Re Earl of Carysfort* (1840) Cr & Ph 76, 77 ('one which the lunatic, if he should ever recover, would approve'); *Re Croft* (1863) 32 LJ(Ch) 481; *In re Frost (A Person of Unsound Mind)* (1870) LR 5 Ch App 699; *In re Evans (A Person of Unsound Mind)* (1882) 21 ChD 297; *In re Darling (A Person of Unsound Mind)* (1888) 39 ChD 208, 211, 212 ('what the lunatic would have done himself if of sound mind'), 213 ('what it is likely the lunatic himself would do if sane'); *In re Alice Pauline Freeman (A Person of Unsound Mind Not so Found)* [1927] 1 Ch 479; *In re DML* [1965] Ch 1133; *In re L(WJG)* [1966] Ch 135; *In re TB* [1967] Ch 247.

judgment test[407] to questions relating to the patient's body.[408] However, English law, in common with a number of other jurisdictions in the United States of America which also apply a best interests test,[409] has rejected the substituted judgment test so far as concerns questions relating to the patient's physical and bodily welfare in favour of a best interests test.[410] The reason for the divergence in English law between the objective test applied in cases affecting the person of the incompetent and the substituted judgment test applied in cases relating to his property has never been explained or explored.

(ii) Objective or Subjective?

The test of best interests is objective.[411] One does not, therefore, attempt to find a speculative answer to the question, 'What would this patient have chosen if he had the capacity to make a choice?'[412] But although the test is objective one is necessarily concerned with the question, 'What is in the best interests of *this* particular patient?' One therefore looks at the case not from the point of view of an ordinary or normal fit person but from the assumed point of view of a person suffering the handicaps of the particular patient.[413] In this sense the standard is subjective.[414]

4.150

(iii) Best Interests and the Patient's Wishes

Regard must be had to the ascertainable wishes and feelings of the patient, considered in the light of his age and understanding.[415] Even if the patient lacks the capacity to decide for himself, and has never made an effective advance directive, the personality of the particular patient and the expressed views, wishes and feelings of the patient, whether past or present, are relevant and must be taken into account as a very material factor in ascertaining his best interests.[416]

4.151

---

[407] Explicitly by adopting the English *property* cases and, in particular, *ex p Whitbread* (1816) 2 Mer 99.

[408] *Strunk v Strunk* (1969) 445 SW 2d 145, 147–148 (Ky); *Hart v Brown* (1972) 289 A 2d 386, 387 (Conn); *Re Quinlan* (1976) 355 A 2d 647, 663, 664, 666 (NJ); *Superintendent of Belchertown State School v Saikewicz* (1977) 370 NE 2d 417, 431 (Mass); *Re Doe* (1992) 583 NE 2d 1263, 1267, 1273 (Mass).

[409] *Re Richardson* (1973) 284 So 2d 185, 187 (La); *Lausier v Pescinski* (1975) 226 NW 2d 180, 181–182, 184 (Wis); *Little v Little* (1979) 576 SW 2d 493, 497–498 (Tex); *Curran v Bosze* (1990) 566 NE 2d 1319, 1326, 1331 (Ill).

[410] *Airedale NHS Trust v Bland* [1993] AC 789, 871–872, 894–895.

[411] See further para 4.96 above.

[412] *In re T (Adult: Refusal of Treatment)* [1993] Fam 95, 103.

[413] *In re J (A Minor) (Wardship: Medical Treatment)* [1991] Fam 33, 44, 46–47, 55.

[414] *Re E (A Minor) (Wardship: Medical Treatment)* [1993] 1 FLR 386, 392.

[415] See further, particularly in relation to children, paras 4.98, 4.99, 4.102 above.

[416] *In re W (A Minor) (Medical Treatment: Court's Jurisdiction)* [1993] Fam 64, 88; *In re T (Adult: Refusal of Treatment)* [1993] Fam 95, 103; *Airedale NHS Trust v Bland* [1993] AC 789, 872; *Hospital Authority v C* [2003] Lloyd's Rep Med 130, at [30]–[33].

2. Applicability of the Best Interests Test

4.152   The best interests test governs all aspects of a child's 'upbringing'[417] and all aspects of an incompetent adult's 'treatment' and 'care'. 'Treatment' and 'care' are not confined to medical treatment.

4.153   Treatment and care include whatever is 'necessary to preserve . . . life, health or well-being' or 'carried out in order either to save . . . lives, or to ensure improvement or prevent deterioration in . . . physical or mental health'.[418] In addition to appropriate medical, dental and surgical treatment, treatment includes, in the case of someone who is permanently or semi-permanently incapable, care, as part of daily life, of a basic, simple or humdrum nature, such as dressing, undressing, feeding, looking after, and putting to bed, and including the actions of the relative, friend or neighbour who comes in to look after the patient.[419]

4.154   Treatment and care extend to 'action . . . such as a reasonable person would in all the circumstances take, acting in the best interests of the assisted person'[420] and thus to everything that conduces to the welfare and happiness of the patient, including companionship and the patient's domestic and social environment.[421]

3. Best Interests and Medical Interests

Best interests or best medical interests?

4.155   An invasive medical procedure can be in a patient's best interests even though

(a) it is not therapeutically required;[422]

(b) it is not, of itself, of any medical benefit at all to the patient;

(c) it is attended with some medical risks or disadvantages;[423] and

---

[417] cf the Children Act 1989, s 1(1)(a); *In re Z (A Minor) (Identification: Restrictions on Publication)* [1997] Fam 1, 28–29.

[418] *In re F (Mental Patient: Sterilisation)* [1990] 2 AC 1, 52 *per* Lord Bridge of Harwich, 55 *per* Lord Brandon of Oakbrook.

[419] ibid, 72, 76 *per* Lord Goff of Chieveley.

[420] ibid, 75 *per* Lord Goff of Chieveley.

[421] *Re C (Mental Patient: Contact)* [1993] 1 FLR 940; *A v A Health Authority, In re J (A Child), R (on the application of S) v Secretary of State for the Home Department* [2002] EWHC 18 (Fam/Admin), [2002] Fam 213, at [39].

[422] *In re B (A Minor) (Wardship: Sterilisation)* [1988] AC 199 (non-therapeutic sterilisation of minor for contraceptive purposes); *In re F (Mental Patient: Sterilisation)* [1990] 2 AC 1 (non-herapeutic sterilisation of incompetent adult for contraceptive purposes).

[423] Thus ritual or other non-therapeutic circumcision of minor male children (eg, the routine non-therapeutic circumcision of neonates for reasons which are social or conventional rather than religious) is permissible even though the preponderance of current medical opinion, at least in the UK, is that circumcision is normally of no medical benefit and devoid of rational justification, and notwithstanding that circumcision is not without risks and that the procedure can lead to complications, serious injury, and even death: see Skegg, *Law, Ethics, and Medicine* (2nd edn), 66; Poulter, *English Law and Ethnic Minority Customs*, para 6.26; *Gray v LaFleche* [1950] 1 DLR 337; *Iqbal v*

(d) the primary purpose of the procedure is to further the interests of a third party.[424]

Factors other than the narrowly therapeutic or medical can therefore properly be taken into account in assessing whether or not an invasive medical procedure is in the patient's best interests.[425]   **4.156**

Best interests are not limited to best medical interests.[426]

Best interests encompasses medical, emotional and all other welfare issues.[427]

It would be undesirable and probably impossible to set bounds to what is relevant to a welfare determination.[428]

Countervailing Advantages

Such a procedure may nonetheless be in the patient's best interests if (i) it is not seriously detrimental to the patient[429] and (ii) it is compensated by sufficient countervailing benefits or advantages to the patient, in other words if, having regard to all relevant factors, the balance of benefit and detriment overall is such that it is in the patient's best interests to subject him to the procedure.   **4.157**

Thus a non-therapeutic sterilisation may be justified as being for the benefit of a child or incompetent adult patient's psychological health and well-being.[430] Likewise the donation of bone-marrow to a sibling may be justified as serving the emotional and psychological welfare of an incompetent adult.[431] So also a blood test for purely forensic purposes may be in a child's best interests if the potential personal or financial benefits to the child of ascertaining his paternity outweigh any possible medical disadvantages,[432] and notwithstanding that its primary   **4.158**

Irfan [1994] CLY 1642; *R v Alam* The Independent, 9 July 1994, 15 November 1994. See now *Re J (Specific Issue Orders: Muslim Upbringing and Circumcision)* [1999] 2 FLR 678 (affirmed *Re J (Specific Issue Orders: Child's Religious Upbringing and Circumcision)* [2000] 1 FLR 571) where some of the medical literature is discussed.

[424] So the blood-testing of a child in order to resolve an issue of adultery in a divorce suit: *B(BR) v B(J)* [1968] P 466. Or the donation of bone-marrow in order to save a sibling's life: *In re Y (Mental Patient: Bone Marrow Donation)* [1997] Fam 110.

[425] See *In re T (A Minor) (Wardship: Medical Treatment)* [1997] 1 WLR 242.

[426] *Re MB (Medical Treatment)* [1991] 2 FLR 426, 439 *per* Butler-Sloss LJ.

[427] *Re A (Male Sterilisation)* [2000] 1 FLR 549, 555, *per* Dame Elizabeth Butler-Sloss P.

[428] *In re S (Adult Patient: Sterilisation)* [2001] Fam 15, 30, *per* Thorpe LJ.

[429] cf *S v McC, W v W* [1972] AC 24, 44 *per* Lord Reid (referring to blood-testing): 'unless . . . clearly . . . against the interests of the child'.

[430] *In re B (A Minor) (Wardship: Sterilisation)* [1988] AC 199; *In re F (Mental Patient: Sterilisation)* [1990] 2 AC 1.

[431] *In re Y (Mental Patient: Bone Marrow Donation)* [1997] Fam 110.

[432] *In re L (An Infant)* [1968] P 119, 141, 158, 160, 161; *B(BR) v B(J)* [1968] P 466, 473, 477; *S v McC (orse S) and M (DS intervener)* [1970] 1 WLR 672, 675–676, 679, 681–682. These cases were decided before *S v McC, W v W* [1972] AC 24, and thus at a time when it was generally held that a child could be blood-tested for forensic purposes only if it was in the child's best interests that it should be. Orders were refused, as not being in the child's best interests, in *M(DK) v M(SV) and G (M intervening)* [1969] 1 WLR 843; *B v B and E* [1969] 1 WLR 1800; *W v W* [1970] 1 WLR 682.

purpose is to further the interests of another, for example, the blood-testing of a child in order to resolve an issue of adultery in a divorce suit.[433] So also the ritual circumcision of male children, on the basis that, on balance, the perceived religious advantages outweigh both the absence of medical benefit and the risk of occasionally serious complications.[434] So also a 'sex-change' or 'gender reassignment' operation.[435]

4.159   There are other applications of the same principle: payment away of trust monies to a third party may be for the 'benefit' of a beneficiary if it enables him thereby to discharge what he recognises to be his moral obligation to the third party.[436] Public exploitation in the media of a child's medical problems may be in the best interests of the child if it enables her father, by sale of the story to a newspaper, to raise money needed to pay for the child's further possibly life-saving medical treatment.[437]

4. Factors in the Best Interests Equation

(i) Personal Factors

4.160   An evaluation of best interests involves a welfare appraisal in the widest sense, taking into account, where appropriate, a wide range of ethical, social, moral, emotional and welfare considerations.[438] In assessing an individual's best interests, relevant factors may, in an appropriate case, include: his psychological health, well-being, amenity and quality of life;[439] his ethical, moral, spiritual and religious

---

[433] *B(BR) v B(J)* [1968] P 466.

[434] *R v Brown* [1994] AC 212, 231; *Re J (Specific Issue Orders: Muslim Upbringing and Circumcision)* [1999] 2 FLR 678 (affirmed *Re J (Specific Issue Orders: Child's Religious Upbringing and Circumcision)* [2000] 1 FLR 571); *Re S (Change of Names: Cultural Factors)* [2001] 2 FLR 1005. See further *Secretary, Department of Health and Community Services v JWB and SMB* (1992) 175 CLR 218, 297 *per* Deane J (parents 'plainly' able to consent to 'male circumcision for perceived hygienic—or even religious—reasons'); Kennedy and Grubb, *Medical Law: Text with Materials* (2nd edn, 1994), 270 ('Regard may, of course, be paid to a religious view . . . when the effect on the child is not significant (eg male circumcision)'). It is not altogether easy to accept these rationalisations given the possible seriousness of the attendant risks and the fact that (at least until recently) routine non-therapeutic circumcision of neonates was widespread for reasons which were social or conventional, rather than religious.

[435] So held by the Family Court of Australia: *In re A* (1993) 16 Fam LR 715.

[436] *In re Clore's Settlement Trusts* [1966] 1 WLR 955.

[437] *R v Cambridge District HA, ex p B (No 2)* [1996] 1 FLR 375. Contrast *In re Z (A Minor) (Identification: Restrictions on Publication)* [1997] Fam 1 (not in best interests of child of prominent public figure to appear in television documentary showing her receiving treatment).

[438] *A v A Health Authority, In re J (A Child), R (S) v Secretary of State for the Home Department* [2002] EWHC 18 (Fam/Admin), [2002] Fam 213, para [43].

[439] *In re B (A Minor) (Wardship: Sterilisation)* [1988] AC 199, 202–203, 206, 208–210; *In re F (Mental Patient: Sterilisation)* [1990] 2 AC 1, 52, 76 ('life, health or well-being'), 55 (steps taken to 'ensure improvement or prevent deterioration in . . . physical or mental health').

welfare;[440] his relationship with his parents or other carers;[441] his financial interests;[442] ties of affection;[443] and moral obligations, whether or not they are yet the object of public or social pressure, but only if he himself recognises and feels the moral obligation.[444]

(ii) Third Party Interests

The best interests in question are those of the child or adult incompetent patient, not those of a third party or of society. Benefits accruing to the third party are material only insofar as they further the interests of the patient.   **4.161**

Third Parties

The interests of a third party can legitimately be taken into account in assessing all   **4.162** the relevant facts, choices and other circumstances which have to be taken into account in determining whether or not what is proposed is in the best interests of the patient.[445] But an invasive medical procedure which is not, of itself, of any medical benefit to the patient cannot be justified as being in his best interests merely because it confers a benefit (even a very substantial benefit indeed) on a third party; what has to be shown is some countervailing benefit or advantage *to the patient himself.*[446]

There is no legal (as opposed to moral, ethical or civic) obligation to provide med-   **4.163** ical assistance to another[447] or to subject oneself to a medical procedure[448] for the benefit of another.[449] This is merely the application in the medical context of the general principle that, in the absence of special relationship or assumption of

---

[440] *In re K (Minors) (Children: Care and Control)* [1977] Fam 179, 187, 191.

[441] *In re T (A Minor) (Wardship: Medical Treatment)* [1997] 1 WLR 242.

[442] *R v Cambridge District HA, ex p B (No 2)* [1996] 1 FLR 375.

[443] *Re McGrath* [1893] 1 Ch 143, 148 *per* Lindley LJ quoted para 4.95 above.

[444] *In re Clore's Settlement Trusts* [1966] 1 WLR 955, 959–960; *In re CL* [1969] 1 Ch 587, 599–600.

[445] *In re Z (A Minor) (Identification: Restrictions on Publication)* [1997] Fam 1, 28.

[446] In *Re A (Male Sterilisation)* [2000] 1 FLR 549, 556, 558, both Dame Elizabeth Butler-Sloss P and Thorpe LJ expressly left open the question whether, in a case concerned with the best interests of a patient, the interests of third parties should be taken into account, other than their effect on the welfare of the patient. This, with respect, is surprising, to say the least, for it is quite clear that the interests of a third party are relevant only to the extent that they impact on the welfare of the patient: see paras 4.163, 4.164 below. As Dame Elizabeth Butler-Sloss P correctly said in *Re A (Male Sterilisation)* [2000] 1 FLR 549, 555; 'The concept of best interests relates to the mentally incapacitated person'.

[447] *In re F (Mental Patient: Sterilisation)* [1990] 2 AC 1, 77; *Capital & Counties PLC v Hampshire County Council* [1997] QB 1004, 1035.

[448] This is so even in the case of a mother with a viable foetus: see further paras 4.37–4.38 above.

[449] *In re T (Adult: Refusal of Treatment)* [1993] Fam 95, 99, 102 and, in the US, *McFall v Shrimp* (1978) 10 Pa D&C 3d 90 (see Kennedy and Grubb, *Medical Law: Text with Materials* (3rd edn, 2000), 1776–1779; *St George's Healthcare NHS Trust v S, R v Collins, ex p S* [1999] Fam 26, 47); *Re AC* (1990) 573 A 2d 1235, 1243–1244, *Re Baby Boy Doe* (1994) 632 NE 2d 326, 333–334.

responsibility, the law imposes no obligation to go to the assistance of someone in peril, however immediate and mortal the peril to the person in danger and how-ever trivial or even non-existent the possible risk to the rescuer.[450]

4.164 Thus an invasive medical procedure cannot be justified merely because it will lighten the burden on those who care for the patient.[451] So also the giving or with-holding of medical treatment is not to be determined by reference to the med-ical[452] or financial[453] implications of the decision for other members of the patient's family. On the other hand, the court can be astute to find that a proce-dure which is in the medical interests of a third party, though not necessarily of the patient, is nevertheless in the patient's best interests inasmuch as it furthers the patient's emotional and psychological welfare.[454]

Conflicting Interests of Child Siblings

4.165 Where both the patient and the third party are children (for example, where what is in question is a transplant between minor siblings) it is still the interests of the patient (donor), and not of the third party (donee), which are paramount, for it is the patient (donor) whose interests are directly involved.[455]

---

[450] *Donoghue v Stevenson* [1932] AC 562, 580; *Home Office v Dorset Yacht Co Ltd* [1970] AC 1004, 1027, 1034, 1042, 1060; *The Ogopogo* [1969] 1 LlR 374, 378, [1970] 1 LlR 257, 261, 265, further appeal [1971] 2 LlR 410.

[451] *In re B (A Minor) (Wardship: Sterilisation)* [1988] AC 199, 204, 212; *Secretary, Department of Health and Community Services v JWB and SMB* (1992) 175 CLR 218, 295–296, 297, 300–301. On the other hand, the easing of that burden may indirectly further the interests of the patient: ibid, 300–301. See further *In re T (A Minor) (Wardship: Medical Treatment)* [1997] 1 WLR 242. The wel-fare of even an insentient patient may be adversely affected if his carers are subjected to pressure or put under emotional or other stress, eg, as a result of massive media intrusion: *In re C (A Minor) (Wardship: Medical Treatment) (No 2)* [1990] Fam 39, 47–48, 51–52, 54–55.

[452] *In re Y (Mental Patient: Bone Marrow Donation)* [1997] Fam 110 (whether adult incompetent should donate bone-marrow to be determined by reference to the best interests of the donor and not of the donee, notwithstanding that the donee would die if the operation did not take place).

[453] *Airedale NHS Trust v Bland* [1993] AC 789, 879–880 (not proper to alter the time of death of patient in permanent vegetative state in order to manipulate third party property rights). See further para 4.203 below.

[454] See the analyses in *Tameside and Glossop Acute Services Trust v CH* [1996] 1 FLR 762 (caesarian section); *In re Y (Mental Patient: Bone Marrow Donation)* [1997] Fam 110 (bone-marrow donation); *Norfolk and Norwich Healthcare (NHS) Trust v W* [1996] 2 FLR 613; *Rochdale Healthcare (NHS) Trust v C* [1997] 1 FCR 274; *A Metropolitan Borough Council v AB* [1997] 1 FLR 767; *Re L (Patient: Non-Consensual Treatment)* [1997] 2 FLR 837; *Re MB (Medical Treatment)* [1997] 2 FLR 258 (cae-sarian section) but note the qualification in para 4.37 above.

[455] *Birmingham City Council v H (A Minor)* [1994] 2 AC 212; *F v Leeds City Council* [1994] 2 FLR 60; *Re F (Contact: Child in Care)* [1995] 1 FLR 510; *Re T and E (Proceedings: Conflicting Interests)* [1995] 1 FLR 581. In the case of conjoined twins, where the interests of both siblings are, in the nature of things, directly involved, their interests have to be balanced: *In re A (Children) (Conjoined Twins: Surgical Separation)* [2001] Fam 147, 190–192, 196–197, 242–243.

(iii) Public Interests

In the same way, the general public interest and the moral and civic obligations of **4.166** the patient can legitimately be taken into account in determining whether or not what is proposed is in the best interests of the patient.[456] But it is still necessary to show some benefit or advantage *to the patient* from what is proposed.[457]

The performance of a moral, social or civic obligation can be of benefit to the **4.167** patient, and his moral, social or civic obligations are therefore relevant, only if the patient is able to recognise, and in fact himself recognises and wishes to give effect to, the obligation.[458]

Thus the sterilisation of a child or mentally incompetent adult cannot be justified **4.168** for eugenic purposes[459] or with a view to population control. So also the public interest in publicising a unique and specialised form of treatment with a view to bringing strength and encouragement to other patients and encouraging the use of the treatment in the United Kingdom did not justify the child of a prominent public figure appearing in a television documentary showing her receiving the treatment, bearing in mind the adverse effects upon her of the publicity which the broadcast would generate.[460]

5. The Best Interests Balancing Exercise

The relevant enquiry is thus whether the procedure is, overall, in the best (though **4.169** not necessarily in the best medical) interests of the child or adult incompetent patient. The balancing exercise may arise in two different ways. A procedure which is medically indicated may be resisted on grounds of religious or other beliefs or principles. On the other hand, an attempt may be made to justify some procedure which is not medically indicated, serves no therapeutic purpose, and

---

[456] *S v McC, W v W* [1972] AC 24, 44; *In re R (A Minor) (Wardship: Criminal Proceedings)* [1991] Fam 56, 65; *In re Z (A Minor) (Identification: Restrictions on Publication)* [1997] Fam 1, 28.

[457] Note the emphatic rejection in English law of the doctrine that the public interests of the state can ever prevail over the competent patient's right of self-determination: *In re T (Adult: Refusal of Treatment)* [1993] Fam 95, 102; *Secretary of State for the Home Department v Robb* [1995] Fam 127.

[458] *In re Clore's Settlement Trusts* [1966] 1 WLR 955 and see paras 4.159–4.160 above. This reveals an important practical difference between the best interests test and a substituted judgment test. The discharge on behalf of an incompetent adult of moral or social obligations (eg, financial obligations to family or former employees) may be justified by reference to a substituted judgment test whether or not the incompetent is in fact able to recognise, and wishes to give effect to, the obligation: see the authorities referred to in para 4.148 above. The discharge of such an obligation will not, however, satisfy the best interests test unless the incompetent is in fact able to recognise, and in fact wishes to give effect to, the obligation.

[459] *In re B (A Minor) (Wardship: Sterilisation)* [1988] AC 199, 202, 204, 207, 212; *Re M (A Minor) (Wardship: Sterilisation)* [1988] 2 FLR 497; *Secretary, Department of Health and Community Services v JWB and SMB* (1992) 175 CLR 218, 295.

[460] *In re Z (A Minor) (Identification: Restrictions on Publication)* [1997] Fam 1, 10, 11, 12, 30–31, 32, 33.

may even be attended with some medical risk or disadvantage, on the basis of some non-medical benefit sufficient (so it is said) to justify a procedure which, if harmless, serves no medical purpose or which (it is said) outweighs any medical risk or disadvantage there may be.

(i) The Balancing Exercise and Community Standards

Community Standards[461]

4.170 Best interests have to be assessed by reference to general community standards, making due allowance for the entitlement of people, within the limits of what is permissible in accordance with those standards, to entertain divergent views about the moral and secular objectives they wish to pursue.[462] Within limits the law will tolerate things which society as a whole may find undesirable. Thus the court passes no judgment on religious beliefs or on the tenets doctrines or rules of any particular section of society so long as they are 'legally and socially acceptable' and not 'immoral or socially obnoxious' or 'pernicious'.[463]

4.171 It follows that an invasive medical procedure which is not of itself of any medical benefit to the patient can never be in the best interests of the patient if, judged by albeit flexible and tolerant general community standards, it is 'cruel or excessive'[464] or involves 'mutilation'.[465] Nor will a religious, cultural or social justification be accepted which, judged by the same standards, is 'immoral or socially obnoxious'[466] or 'pernicious'.[467]

(ii) Application of the Balancing Exercise

(a) Procedures which are Medically Indicated

4.172 It follows that there are limits to the extent to which countervailing interests will be permitted to stand in the way of performing a procedure which is medically indicated, especially if the patient's condition is life-threatening or likely to cause

---

[461] See further paras 4.79, 4.100 above. For a valuable survey of the legal problems presented by a variety of ethnic minority customs see Poulter, *English Law and Ethnic Minority Custom*, esp, paras 6.15–6.33, 10.03, 10.24–10.26.

[462] *Secretary, Department of Health and Community Services v JWB and SMB* (1992) 175 CLR 218, 295, 297, 300, 301. And see *In re T (A Minor) (Wardship: Medical Treatment)* [1997] 1 WLR 242, esp 254 *per* Waite LJ quoted para 4.75 above.

[463] *Re T (Minors) (Custody: Religious Upbringing)* (1981) 2 FLR 239, 244–245; *Re B and G (Minors) (Custody)* [1985] FLR 134, 157; *Re R (A Minor) (Residence: Religion)* [1993] 2 FLR 163, 171.

[464] *S v McC, W v W* [1972] AC 24, 43 *per* Lord Reid.

[465] *Secretary, Department of Health and Community Services v JWB and SMB* (1990) 14 Fam LR 427, 448 *per* Nicholson CJ, on appeal (1992) 175 CLR 218.

[466] *Re T (Minors) (Custody: Religious Upbringing)* (1981) 2 FLR 239, 244 *per* Scarman LJ.

[467] *Re B and G (Minors) (Custody)* [1985] FLR 134, 157 *per* Latey J (referring to scientology).

serious harm.[468] Thus the court will readily order a life-saving blood transfusion for a child notwithstanding the sincere and strong religious convictions of the child and his parents.[469] So also the court will refuse to allow the religious objections of a pregnant child's parents to stand in the way of her abortion.[470]

(b) Procedures which are not Medically Indicated

In the same way there are limits to the extent to which countervailing interests, whether religious, social or financial, will suffice to justify an invasive medical procedure which either has no medical benefit or is attended by possible medical disadvantages. **4.173**

It is suggested that an invasive medical procedure which is not, of itself, of any medical benefit at all to a child or adult incompetent patient will be in the best interests of the patient, if but only if: **4.174**

(i)   the procedure is not seriously detrimental to the patient;

(ii) judged by flexible and tolerant general community standards, the procedure is not cruel or excessive, does not involve mutilation, and would not be considered immoral, socially obnoxious or pernicious;

(iii) it is compensated by countervailing benefits or advantages to the patient which are (a) real or substantial, as opposed to fanciful, insubstantial, hypothetical, speculative, nebulous or illusory and (b) significant and not de minimis;

(iv) those countervailing benefits and advantages clearly (if not necessarily by any very great margin) outweigh both the absence of any medical benefit and any possible medical risks or other disadvantages of the procedure;

so that

(v)   having regard to all relevant factors, the balance of benefit and detriment overall is such that it is in the patient's best interests to subject him to the procedure.

Thus, as has already been seen,[471] a non-therapeutic sterilisation, male circumcision for ritual or other non-therapeutic reasons, a blood-test for forensic purposes, the donation of regenerative tissue (for example, bone-marrow), or a 'sex-change' or 'gender reassignment' operation may all be justified as being, overall, in the patient's best interests. So also ear piercing and cosmetic surgery.[472] On the other **4.175**

---

[468] But see *In re T (A Minor) (Wardship: Medical Treatment)* [1997] 1 WLR 242 considered in para 4.75 above, para 4.209 below.

[469] See paras 4.98, 4.101, 4.102 above.

[470] See para 4.98 above.

[471] See paras 4.79, 4.156, 4.158 above.

[472] *Secretary, Department of Health and Community Services v JWB and SMB* (1992) 175 CLR 218, 297 *per* Deane J (parents 'plainly' able to consent to 'plastic surgery to correct serious disfigurement

hand, female circumcision for religious, cultural or social reasons is not justifiable at common law.[473] Nor is ritual incision of the face.[474] Amputation of a child's hand as a punishment for theft cannot be justified on religious grounds.[475] Nor can amputation of a child's limb so as to exploit it for the purpose of gain, for example, by cutting off its foot so that it can earn a living begging.[476] Likewise the common law would surely not permit the removal from a child or incompetent adult of a non-regenerative organ (for example, a kidney) for the purpose of sale.[477]

G. Particular Cases

4.176 Reported cases cover a wide range of different forms of care and treatment. Thus, in addition to cases dealing with the blood-testing of children[478] and with the general care of the handicapped child or adult (including disputes as to where and

---

for purely cosmetic purposes' even though 'not "therapeutic" within the accepted meaning of that word'). To the same effect *Re a Teenager* (1988) 94 FLR 181, 212 *per* Cook J ('cosmetic surgery to a child with malformed features'); *Re Jane* (1988) 94 FLR 1, 31, but see *Secretary, Department of Health and Community Services v JWB and SMB* (1990) 14 Fam LR 427, 448 *per* Nicholson CJ ('there may well be some limitations upon the power to consent to cosmetic surgery on a child, depending upon its purpose').

[473] *Secretary, Department of Health and Community Services v JWB and SMB* (1990) 14 FamLR 427, 448, (1992) 175 CLR 218, 242–243, 252.

[474] *R v Adesanya*, The Times, 16 July 1974, 17.

[475] *Secretary, Department of Health and Community Services v JWB and SMB* (1992) 175 CLR 218, 297.

[476] *Secretary, Department of Health and Community Services v JWB and SMB* (1990) 14 FamLR 427, 448 ('mutilation'), (1992) 175 CLR 218, 240.

[477] Thus, the common law rule. A number of socially controversial invasive procedures are regulated by statute. The Tattooing of Minors Act 1969 makes it a criminal offence to tattoo a minor 'except when the tattoo is performed for medical reasons'. The Prohibition of Female Circumcision Act 1985 makes female circumcision in all its forms a criminal offence unless it is either 'necessary for the physical or mental health of the person on whom it is performed' or 'performed for purposes connected with . . . labour or birth'. S 2 of the Act draws an interesting distinction between mental health and customary or ritual belief by providing that 'In determining . . . whether an operation is necessary for the mental health of a person, no account shall be taken of the effect on that person of any belief on the part of that or any other person that the operation is required as a matter of custom or ritual'. The Human Organ Transplants Act 1989 makes it a criminal offence to make or receive payment for the supply of an organ (as defined in s 7(2), that is any part of a human body . . . which, if wholly removed, cannot be replicated by the body) or to transplant an organ otherwise than between genetically related persons unless authorised by the Unrelated Life Transplant Regulatory Authority in accordance with the Human Organ Transplants (Unrelated Persons) Regulations 1989, SI 1989/2480).

[478] *S v McC, W v W* [1972] AC 24; *In re F (A Minor) (Blood Tests: Parental Rights)* [1993] Fam 314; *Re L (A Minor) (Blood Tests)* [1996] 2 FCR 649; *In re H (A Minor) (Blood Tests: Parental Rights)* [1997] Fam 89; *Re T (Paternity: Ordering Blood Tests)* [2001] 2 FLR 1190; *Re H and A (Paternity: Blood Tests)* [2002] EWCA Civ 383, [2002] 1 FLR 1145. For the impact in this context of Article 8 of the ECHR see *Re T (Paternity: Ordering Blood Tests)* [2001] 2 FLR 1190, 1197–1199.

with whom an incompetent adult should live and have contact),[479] there are reported cases dealing with: the therapeutic[480] and non-therapeutic sterilisation[481] of children and incompetent adults; the abortion[482] of children[483] and incompetent adults;[484] complications during the labour of children[485] and incompetent adult women;[486] the psychiatric assessment and treatment of children[487] and incompetent adults;[488] the forcefeeding of children[489] and incompetent adults[490] for

---

[479] *Re C (Mental Patient: Contact)* [1993] 1 FLR 940; *Cambridgeshire County Council v R (An Adult)* [1995] 1 FLR 50; *In re S (Hospital Patient: Court's Jurisdiction)* [1995] Fam 26, appeal dismissed [1996] Fam 1, subsequent substantive proceedings *In re S (Hospital patient: Foreign Curator)* [1996] Fam 23; *Re V (Declaration against Parents)* [1995] 2 FLR 1003; *Re D-R (Adult: Contact)* [1999] 1 FLR 1161; *Re F (Mental Health Act: Guardianship)* [2000] 1 FLR 192; *R v R (Interim Declaration: Adult's Residence)* [2000] 1 FLR 451; *In re F (Adult: Court's Jurisdiction)* [2001] Fam 38; *A v A Health Authority, In re J (A Child), R (on the application of S) v Secretary of State for the Home Department* [2002] EWHC 18 (Fam/Admin), [2002] Fam 213; *Re S (Adult Patient) (Inherent Jurisdiction: Family Life)* [2002] EWHC 2278 (Fam), [2003] 1 FLR 292.

[480] *Re E (A Minor) (Medical Treatment)* [1991] 2 FLR 585; *Re GF (Medical Treatment)* [1992] 1 FLR 293; *Re ZM and OS (Sterilisation: Patient's Best Interests)* [2000] 1 FLR 523.

[481] *In re D (A Minor) (Wardship: Sterilisation)* [1976] Fam 185; *In re B (A Minor) (Wardship: Sterilisation)* [1988] AC 199; *T v T* [1988] Fam 52; *Re M (A Minor) (Wardship: Sterilisation)* [1988] 2 FLR 497; *Re P (A Minor) (Wardship: Sterilisation)* [1989] 1 FLR 182; *In re F (Mental Patient: Sterilisation)* [1990] 2 AC 1; *Re NK* 28 February 1990, (Ewbank J), 4 April 1990, (Scott Baker J); *Re W (Mental patient) (Sterilisation)* [1993] 1 FLR 381; *Re HG (Specific Issue Order: Sterilisation)* [1993] 1 FLR 587; *Re LC (Medical Treatment: Sterilisation)* [1997] 2 FLR 258; *Re S (Medical Treatment: Adult Sterilisation)* [1998] 1 FLR 944; *Re X (Adult Sterilisation)* [1998] 2 FLR 1124; *Re ZM and OS (Sterilisation: Patient's Best Interests)* [2000] 1 FLR 523; *Re A (Male Sterilisation)* [2000] 1 FLR 549 (proposed sterilisation of male incompetent); *In re S (Adult Patient: Sterilisation)* [2001] Fam 15 (reversing *Re S (Sterilisation: Patient's Best Interests)* [2000] 1 FLR 465).

[482] See paras 4.31, 4.34, 4.36 above for cases dealing with the interests of the foetus and its father.

[483] *Re P (A Minor)* [1986] 1 FLR 272; *Re B (Wardship: Abortion)* [1991] 2 FLR 426.

[484] *Re SG (Adult Mental Patient: Abortion)* [1991] 2 FLR 329; *Re SS (Medical Treatment: Late Termination)* [2002] 1 FLR 445.

[485] *A Metropolitan Borough Council v AB* [1997] 1 FLR 767.

[486] *In re T (Adult: Refusal of Treatment)* [1993] Fam 95; *Tameside and Glossop Acute Services Trust v CH* [1996] 1 FLR 762; *Norfolk and Norwich Healthcare (NHS) Trust v W* [1996] 2 FLR 613; *Rochdale Healthcare (NHS) Trust v C* [1997] 1 FCR 274; *Re L (Patient: Non-Consensual Treatment)* [1997] 2 FLR 837; *Re MB (Medical Treatment)* [1997] 2 FLR 426; *St George's Healthcare NHS Trust v S, R v Collins, ex p S* [1999] Fam 26; *Bolton Hospitals NHS Trust v O* [2002] EWHC 2871 (Fam), [2003] 1 FLR 824; *Hospital Authority v C* [2003] Lloyd's Rep Med 130 (caesarian section of pregnant woman in coma). For the procedure to be adopted in such cases see *Re MB*, ibid, 439, 445; *St George's Healthcare NHS Trust v S, R v Collins, ex p S* [1999] Fam 26, 63–65. For the proper approach to the issue of capacity in such cases see *Re MB*, ibid, 436–437. For the position where the mother is a competent adult see para 4.38 above.

[487] *In re R (A Minor) (Wardship: Consent to Treatment)* [1992] Fam 11; *Re K, W and H (Minors) (Medical Treatment)* [1993] 1 FLR 854; *South Glamorgan County Council v W and B* [1993] 1 FLR 574; *R v Kirklees Metropolitan Borough Council, ex p C* [1992] 2 FLR 117, [1993] 2 FLR 187; *A Metropolitan Borough Council v AB* [1997] 1 FLR 767.

[488] *Re H (Mental Patient: Diagnosis)* [1993] 1 FLR 28.

[489] *In re W (A Minor) (Medical Treatment: Court's Jurisdiction)* [1993] Fam 64; *Re C (Detention: Medical Treatment)* [1997] 2 FLR 180.

[490] *Riverside Mental Health NHS Trust v Fox* [1994] 1 FLR 614; *Re KB (Adult) (Mental Patient: Medical Treatment)* (1994) 19 BMLR 144; *B v Croydon HA* [1995] Fam 133, affirming [1995] 1 FCR 332; *Re VS (Adult: Mental Disorder)* 17 August 1995, (Douglas Brown J), [1995] 3 Med LR 292; *R v Collins and Ashworth HA, ex p Brady* [2000] Lloyd's Rep Med 355 (force-feeding of pris-

the treatment of anorexia nervosa or other psychiatric illnesses; the administration of blood transfusions to child[491] and incompetent adult[492] Jehovah's Witnesses; immunisation of children;[493] immunoglobin treatment for primary immunodeficiency;[494] experimental drug treatment for variant Creutzfeldt–Jakob disease;[495] a heart transplant;[496] the separation of conjoined twins;[497] the donation of bone-marrow by an incompetent adult;[498] the withholding of life-saving treatment (surgery,[499] a liver transplant,[500] kidney transplant,[501] haemodialysis (kidney dialysis [502]), artificial ventilation,[503] cardio-pulmonary resuscitation,[504] and antibiotics[505]) from a child,[506] the handicapped[507] or the dying,[508] and the withdrawal of

---

oner detained in Special Hospital). For a case involving the force-feeding of a competent adult prisoner see *Secretary of State for the Home Department v Robb* [1995] Fam 127.

[491] *Re E (A Minor) (Wardship: Medical Treatment)* [1993] 1 FLR 386; *Re S (A Minor) (Medical Treatment)* [1993] 1 FLR 376; *Re O (A Minor) (Medical Treatment)* [1993] 2 FLR 149; *Re R (A Minor) (Blood Transfusion)* [1993] 2 FLR 757; *Re S (A Minor) (Consent to Medical Treatment)* [1994] 2 FLR 1065; *Re L (Medical Treatment: Gillick Competency)* [1998] 2 FLR 810.

[492] *In re T (Adult: Refusal of Treatment)* [1993] Fam 95. See also *HE v A Hospital NHS Trust* [2003] EWHC 1017 (Fam), [2003] 2 FLR 408 (blood transfusion to incompetent adult former Jehovah's Witness).

[493] *Re C (Welfare of Child: Immunisation)* [2003] EWCA Civ 1148; [2003] 2 FLR 1095 (MMR and other vaccinations and immunisations).

[494] *Re MM (Medical Treatment)* [2000] 1 FLR 224.

[495] *Simms v Simms, A v A (A Child)* [2002] EWHC 2734 (Fam), [2003] Fam 83.

[496] *Re M (Medical Treatment: Consent)* [1999] 2 FLR 1097.

[497] *In re A (Children) (Conjoined Twins: Surgical Separation)* [2001] Fam 147. For the further proceedings see *Re A (Conjoined Twins: Medical Treatment) (No 2)* [2001] 1 FLR 267.

[498] *In re Y (Mental Patient: Bone Marrow Donation)* [1997] Fam 110.

[499] *In re B (A Minor) (Wardship: Medical Treatment)* [1981] 1 WLR 1421.

[500] *In re T (A Minor) (Wardship: Medical Treatment)* [1997] 1 WLR 242.

[501] *A Hospital NHS Trust v S* [2003] EWHC 365 (Fam), [2003] Lloyd's Rep Med 137.

[502] *Re D (Medical Treatment: Mentally Disabled Patient)* [1998] 2 FLR 22.

[503] *In re J (A Minor) (Wardship: Medical Treatment)* [1991] Fam 33; *In re J (A Minor) (Child in Care: Medical Treatment)* [1993] Fam 15; *Re C (A Baby)* [1996] 2 FLR 43; *Re C (Medical Treatment)* [1998] 1 FLR 384; *Royal Wolverhampton Hospitals NHS Trust v B* [2000] 1 FLR 953; *A NHS Trust v D* [2000] 2 FLR 677.

[504] *Re R (Adult: Medical Treatment)* [1996] 2 FLR 99. The BMA has published guidance on cardio-pulmonary resuscitation: 'Decisions relating to Cardiopulmonary Resuscitation: A Statement from the BMA and RCN in association with the Resuscitation Council (UK)' (Mar 1993).

[505] *Re R (Adult: Medical Treatment)* [1996] 2 FLR 99.

[506] *In re T (A Minor) (Wardship: Medical Treatment)* [1997] 1 WLR 242. The Royal College of Paediatrics and Child Health has published guidance: 'Withholding or Withdrawing Life Saving Treatment in Children: A Framework for Practice' (Sept 1997).

[507] *In re B (A Minor) (Wardship: Medical Treatment)* [1981] 1 WLR 1421, reversing (1982) 3 FLR 117; *R v Arthur* (1981) 12 BMLR 1; *In re J (A Minor) (Wardship: Medical Treatment)* [1991] Fam 33; *In re J (A Minor) (Child in Care: Medical Treatment)* [1993] Fam 15; *Re C (A Baby)* [1996] 2 FLR 43; *Re R (Adult: Medical Treatment)* [1996] 2 FLR 99; *Re D (Medical Treatment: Mentally Disabled Patient)* [1998] 2 FLR 22; *A Hospital NHS Trust v S* [2003] EWHC 365 (Fam), [2003] Lloyd's Rep Med 137.

[508] *R v Bodkin Adams* 8–9 April 1957, (Devlin J), [1957] Crim LR 365; *In re C (A Minor) (Wardship: Medical Treatment)* [1990] Fam 26; *R v Cox* (1992) 12 BMLR 38; *Re C (Medical Treatment)* [1998] 1 FLR 384; *Royal Wolverhampton Hospitals NHS Trust v B* [2000] 1 FLR 953; *A NHS Trust v D* [2000] 2 FLR 677. The BMA has published guidance: 'End of Life Decisions: Views of the BMA' (Sept 1996).

artificial nutrition and hydration from patients in a permanent (formerly called persistent) vegetative state[509] or in a vegetative, but not (on one view) strictly speaking a permanent vegetative, state.[510] There are also reported cases dealing with the circumstances in which detention for the purposes of treatment[511] or the application of restraint or the use of force[512] is permissible in relation to a non-compliant child[513] or incompetent adult[514] patient either under the Mental

---

[509] *Airedale NHS Trust v Bland* [1993] AC 789; *Frenchay Healthcare NHS Trust v S* [1994] 1 WLR 601; *Re G (Persistent Vegetative State)* [1995] 2 FCR 46; *Swindon and Marlborough NHS Trust v S* The Guardian, 10 December 1994, [1995] 3 Med LR 84; *Re C (Adult Patient: Restriction of Publicity after Death)* [1996] 2 FLR 251; *NHS Trust A v M, NHS Trust B v H* [2001] Fam 348; *NHS Trust A v H* [2001] 2 FLR 501; *Re G (adult incompetent: withdrawal of treatment)* (2001) 65 BMLR 6. The BMA has published guidance on PVS: 'BMA guidelines on treatment decisions for patients in persistent vegetative state' (revised June 1996).

[510] *Re D (Medical Treatment)* [1998] 1 FLR 411; *Re H (A Patient)* [1998] 2 FLR 36. See further paras 4.219, 4.223 below.

[511] *In re R (A Minor) (Wardship: Consent to Treatment)* [1992] Fam 11; *In re W (A Minor) (Medical Treatment: Court's Jurisdiction)* [1993] Fam 64; *South Glamorgan County Council v W and B* [1993] 1 FLR 574; *Re C (Detention: Medical Treatment)* [1997] 2 FLR 180. For the inter-relationship between the court's inherent power to order the detention of a child for the purposes of treatment and its limited power to make a secure accommodation order under the Children Act 1989, s 25, see *In re CB (A Minor) (Wardship: Local Authority)* [1981] 1 WLR 379, 387; *Re SW (A Minor) (Wardship: Jurisdiction)* [1986] 1 FLR 24; *South Glamorgan County Council v W and B* [1993] 1 FLR 574; *A Metropolitan Borough Council v AB* [1997] 1 FLR 767; *Re C (Detention: Medical Treatment)* [1997] 2 FLR 180. For the power of a parent, or a local authority having parental responsibility, to authorise the admission of a child to a secure unit or as a voluntary patient under the Mental Health Act 1983 see *Re K, W and H (Minors) (Medical Treatment)* [1993] 1 FLR 854 (parent—secure unit); *R v Kirklees Metropolitan Borough Council, ex p C* [1992] 2 FLR 117, [1993] 2 FLR 187 (local authority—voluntary patient), and, for the explanation of the underlying principle, *R v Rahman* (1985) 81 Cr App R 349, 353, 354; *R v Deputy Governor of Parkhurst Prison, ex p Hague* [1992] 1 AC 58, 162; *In re M (A Minor) (Secure Accommodation Order)* [1995] Fam 108, 117. For the power to detain a mentally disordered patient without recourse to the powers in the Mental Health Act 1983 see *R v Bournewood Community and Mental Health NHS Trust, ex p L* [1999] 1 AC 458. For the older cases dealing with the common law power to restrain and detain, where appropriate for the purposes of treatment, a lunatic who is a danger either to himself or to others, see *Brookshaw v Hopkins* (1772) Lofft 240; *Anderdon v Burrows* (1830) 4 Car & P 210; *In re Shuttleworth* (1846) 9 QB 651; *In re Greenwood* (1855) 24 LJQB 148; *Fletcher v Fletcher* (1859) 1 El & El 420; *Scott v Wakem* (1862) 3 F & F 328; *Symm v Fraser* (1863) 3 F & F 859; *Townley v Rushforth* (1964) 62 LGR 95; *B v Forsey* [1988] SC(HL) 28, 38–39, 44–45, 52, 56, 59–60, 63, 68.

[512] *Riverside Mental Health NHS Trust v Fox* [1994] 1 FLR 614; *Re KB (Adult) (Mental Patient: Medical Treatment)* (1994) 19 BMLR 144; *Re S (A Minor) (Consent to Medical Treatment)* [1994] 2 FLR 1065; *B v Croydon HA* [1995] Fam 133; *Re VS (Adult: Mental Disorder)* 17 August 1995, (Douglas Brown J), [1995] 3 Med LR 292; *Tameside and Glossop Acute Services Trust v CH* [1996] 1 FLR 762; *Norfolk and Norwich Healthcare (NHS) Trust v W* [1996] 2 FLR 613; *Rochdale Healthcare (NHS) Trust v C* [1997] 1 FCR 274; *A Metropolitan Borough Council v AB* [1997] 1 FLR 767; *Re L (Patient: Non-Consensual Treatment)* [1997] 2 FLR 837; *Re C (Detention: Medical Treatment)* [1997] 2 FLR 180; *Re MB (Medical Treatment)* [1997] 2 FLR 426, 439; *Re D (Medical Treatment: Mentally Disabled Patient)* [1998] 2 FLR 22.

[513] *In re R (A Minor) (Wardship: Consent to Treatment)* [1992] Fam 11; *In re W (A Minor) (Medical Treatment: Court's Jurisdiction)* [1993] Fam 64; *South Glamorgan County Council v W and B* [1993] 1 FLR 574; *Re S (A Minor) (Consent to Medical Treatment)* [1994] 2 FLR 1065; *A Metropolitan Borough Council v AB* [1997] 1 FLR 767; *Re C (Detention: Medical Treatment)* [1997] 2 FLR 180.

[514] *Riverside Mental Health NHS Trust v Fox* [1994] 1 FLR 614; *Re KB (Adult) (Mental Patient: Medical Treatment)* (1994) 19 BMLR 144; *B v Croydon HA* [1995] Fam 133; *Re VS (Adult: Mental*

Health Act 1983, s 63,[515] or at common law.[516] Other procedures are considered mainly in the academic literature: male circumcision;[517] female circumcision;[518] 'sex-change' or 'gender reassignment' operations;[519] ear piercing and cosmetic surgery;[520] ritual incision of the face;[521] and tattooing.[522]

4.177   Six topics require more detailed consideration: sterilisation; abortion; the treatment of the mentally disordered; blood-testing; organ and tissue donation; and issues of life and death.

Disorder) 17 August 1995, (Douglas Brown J), [1995] 3 Med LR 292, *Tameside and Glossop Acute Services Trust v CH* [1996] 1 FLR 762; *Norfolk and Norwich Healthcare (NHS) Trust v W* [1996] 2 FLR 613; *Rochdale Healthcare (NHS) Trust v C* [1997] 1 FCR 274; *Re L (Patient: Non-Consensual Treatment)* [1997] 2 FLR 837; *Re MB (Medical Treatment)* [1997] 2 FLR 426,439; *Re D (Medical Treatment: Mentally Disabled Patient)* [1998] 2 FLR 22.

[515] *Riverside Mental Health NHS Trust v Fox* [1994] 1 FLR 614; *Re KB (Adult) (Mental Patient: Medical Treatment)* (1994) 19 BMLR 144; *B v Croydon HA* [1995] Fam 133; *Re VS (Adult: Mental Disorder)* 17 August 1995, (Douglas Brown J), [1995] 3 Med LR 292; *Tameside and Glossop Acute Services Trust v CH* [1996] 1 FLR 762.

[516] *In re R (A Minor) (Wardship: Consent to Treatment)* [1992] Fam 11; *In re W (A Minor) (Medical Treatment: Court's Jurisdiction)* [1993] Fam 64; *South Glamorgan County Council v W and B* [1993] 1 FLR 574; *Re S (A Minor) (Consent to Medical Treatment)* [1994] 2 FLR 1065; *Norfolk and Norwich Healthcare (NHS) Trust v W* [1996] 2 FLR 613; *Rochdale Healthcare (NHS) Trust v C* [1997] 1 FCR 274; *A Metropolitan Borough Council v AB* [1997] 1 FLR 767; *Re L (Patient: Non-Consensual Treatment)* [1997] 2 FLR 837; *Re C (Detention: Medical Treatment)* [1997] 2 FLR 180; *Re MB (Medical Treatment)* [1997] 2 FLR 426, 439. For the court's approach in deciding whether or not to adopt coercive measures, and the safeguards to be applied, see *Re C (Detention: Medical Treatment)* [1997] 2 FLR 180, 196–199 (and see the form of the order at 199–201); *Re MB (Medical Treatment)* [1997] 2 FLR 426, 445. For the problem presented by the incompetent patient who is unwilling to submit to treatment see *Re D (Medical Treatment: Mentally Disabled Patient)* [1998] 2 FLR 22 (49-year-old chronic but fluctuating psychotic suffering from chronic renal failure at near-end stage and high blood pressure requiring haemodialysis for four hours three or four times each week to keep him alive but unable because of his mental condition to understand the need for treatment and strongly objecting to procedure: held lawful in the last resort 'not to impose haemodialysis upon him in circumstances in which in the opinion of the medical practitioners responsible for such treatment it is not reasonably practicable so to do', the judge accepting that in the circumstances dialysis, which requires the co-operation of the patient, could only be performed under general anaesthetic which was neither practicable nor desirable in a patient suffering D's disabilities).

[517] *Re J (Specific Issue Orders: Muslim Upbringing and Circumcision)* [1999] 2 FLR 678 (affirmed *Re J (Specific Issue Orders: Child's Religious Upbringing and Circumcision)* [2000] 1 FLR 571); *Re S (Change of Names: Cultural Factors)* [2001] 2 FLR 1005. See further paras 4.77, 4.79, 4.80, 4.84, 4.156, 4.158, 4.175 above. The BMA has published guidance: 'Circumcision of Male Infants: Guidance for Doctors' (Sept 1996). So too has the GMC: 'Guidance for Doctors who are asked to Circumcise Male Children' (Sept 1997).

[518] See paras 4.05, 4.77, 4.79, 4.145, 4.175 above. The BMA has published guidance: 'Guidance for Doctors Approached by Victims of Female Genital Mutilation' (Jan 1996).

[519] See paras 4.77, 4.82, 4.158, 4.175 above.

[520] See para 4.175 above.

[521] See para 4.175 above.

[522] See paras 4.05, 4.175 above.

1. Sterilisation

Therapeutic and Non-Therapeutic Sterilisation

The House of Lords has dismissed the suggested distinction between therapeutic **4.178** and non-therapeutic sterilisations as being 'meaningless', 'irrelevant', 'not helpful', and giving rise to 'arid semantic debate'.[523] The distinction[524] is, nonetheless, of importance for at least two reasons. In the first place, whereas the prior sanction of the court is not required for a therapeutic sterilisation[525] (unless, that is, the patient is a child who happens to be a ward of court already[526]), it is required for any non-therapeutic sterilisation of a child or adult incompetent.[527] Secondly, although there may be circumstances[528] in which the court would authorise the therapeutic sterilisation of a child who either has, or may in later years have, the capacity to make her own choice (for example if the removal of a cancerous womb was necessary to save the life of a 'Gillick competent' girl who was refusing her consent to a hysterectomy), the court will not subject such a child to a non-therapeutic sterilisation.[529]

Form of Procedure

Details of the procedure to be adopted in applications to the court are set out in **4.179** the Official Solicitor's Practice Note.[530]

---

[523] *In re B (A Minor) (Wardship: Sterilisation)* [1988] AC 199, 204, 205, 211.

[524] For the most recent and comprehensive judicial consideration of the distinction between therapeutic and non-therapeutic sterilisation see *Secretary, Department of Health and Community Services v JWB and SMB* (1992) 175 CLR 218, esp, 243, 250, 253, 269, 274, 296–297, 306. See also *Re E (A Minor) (Medical Treatment)* [1991] 2 FLR 585, 587 where Sir Stephen Brown P referred to the 'clear distinction' between therapeutic and non-therapeutic sterilisations.

[525] *Re E (A Minor) (Medical Treatment)* [1991] 2 FLR 585; *Re GF (Medical Treatment)* [1992] 1 FLR 293.

[526] *In re D (A Minor) (Wardship: Sterilisation)* [1976] Fam 185, 196.

[527] *In re F (Mental Patient: Sterilisation)* [1990] 2 AC 1.

[528] By analogy with *In re R (A Minor) (Wardship: Consent to Treatment)* [1992] Fam 11; *In re W (A Minor) (Medical Treatment: Court's Jurisdiction)* [1993] Fam 64.

[529] *In re D (A Minor) (Wardship: Sterilisation)* [1976] Fam 185, and see further paras 4.84, 4.99 above.

[530] *Practice Note (Official Solicitor: Declaratory Proceedings: Medical and Welfare Decisions for Adults Who Lack Capacity)* [2001] 2 FLR 158, issued May 2001, replacing *Practice Note (Official Solicitor: Sterilisation)* [1996] 2 FLR 111, issued June 1996 following the decision in *Re G (Adult Patient: Publicity)* [1995] 2 FLR 528, and replacing with modifications the earlier Practice Notes: *Practice Note (Official Solicitor: Sterilisation)* [1989] 2 FLR 447 (issued Sept 1989, following the decision in *In re F (Mental Patient: Sterilisation)* [1990] 2 AC 1), *Practice Note (Official Solicitor: Sterilisation)* [1990] 2 FLR 530 (issued Sept 1990, following the decision in *Practice Note (Mental Patient: Sterilisation), J v C* [1990] 1 WLR 1248), *Practice Note (Official Solicitor: Sterilisation)* [1993] 3 All ER 222, [1993] 2 FLR 222 (issued May 1993, following the decision in *Re HG (Specific Issue Order: Sterilisation)* [1993] 1 FLR 587). See further para 4.139 above.

Therapeutic Sterilisations

4.180 In cases where it is appropriate to invoke the court's assistance at all, it will readily authorise, in the case of a child,[531] or declare lawful, in the case of an adult incompetent,[532] an operation (for example, a hysterectomy) required for genuine therapeutic reasons, even if such an operation will inevitably result in the sterilisation of the patient.

Non-Therapeutic Sterilisations

4.181 The court will never sanction a sterilisation for eugenic purposes.[533] In the case of a non-therapeutic sterilisation for contraceptive purposes the court adopts a rigorous approach; the kind of considerations which the court is likely to have in mind are set out in Appendix 1 to the Official Solicitor's Practice Note.[534] The court will not sanction the non-therapeutic sterilisation of a girl[535] who has, or may in later years have, the capacity to make her own choice whether or not to be sterilised.[536] Where the child is severely mentally handicapped, will never have the capacity to decide about sterilisation for herself and is likely to be exposed to the risk of a pregnancy which she would not understand and the consequences of which would be harmful to her, and other contraceptive methods are inappropriate, the court may come to the view that a sterilisation so as to prevent future pregnancy is necessary in her own best interests.[537] So in the case of an incompetent adult.[538]

---

[531] *Re E (A Minor) (Medical Treatment)* [1991] 2 FLR 585.

[532] *Re GF (Medical Treatment)* [1992] 1 FLR 293; *Re ZM and OS (Sterilisation: Patient's Best Interests)* [2000] 1 FLR 523.

[533] *In re B (A Minor) (Wardship: Sterilisation)* [1988] AC 199, 202, 204, 207, 212; *Re M (A Minor) (Wardship: Sterilisation)* [1988] 2 FLR 497.

[534] *Practice Note (Official Solicitor: Declaratory Proceedings: Medical and Welfare Decisions for Adults Who Lack Capacity)* [2001] 2 FLR 158.

[535] It is a matter for comment, and a revealing insight into societal attitudes to gender, sexuality and contraception, that, with one exception, all the known cases of sterilisation relate to girls; the question of male sterilisation appears first to have arisen in *Re A (Male Sterilisation)* [2000] 1 FLR 549.

[536] *In re D (A Minor) (Wardship: Sterilisation)* [1976] Fam 185 (11-year-old girl suffering from Sotos syndrome, of dull normal intelligence, whose future prospects were unpredictable, but with sufficient capacity to marry and likely to be able to make her own choice in later years).

[537] *In re B (A Minor) (Wardship: Sterilisation)* [1988] AC 199 (17-year-old girl with mental age of 5 or 6); *Re M (A Minor) (Wardship: Sterilisation)* [1988] 2 FLR 497 (17-year-old girl suffering from Fragile X Syndrome with an emotional and psychological age of 5 or 6); *Re P (A Minor) (Wardship: Sterilisation)* [1989] 1 FLR 182 (17-year-old girl with mental age of 6); *Re HG (Specific Issue Order: Sterilisation)* [1993] 1 FLR 587 (17-year-old severely epileptic girl with mental age of an infant).

[538] *T v T* [1988] Fam 52; *In re F (Mental Patient: Sterilisation)* [1990] 2 AC 1; *Re W (Mental patient) (Sterilisation)* [1993] 1 FLR 381; *Re X (Adult Sterilisation)* [1998] 2 FLR 1124; *Re ZM and OS (Sterilisation: Patient's Best Interests)* [2000] 1 FLR 523. In the following cases the court refused to make an order: *Re LC (Medical Treatment: Sterilisation)* [1997] 2 FLR 258; *Re S (Medical Treatment: Adult Sterilisation)* [1998] 1 FLR 944; *In re S (Adult Patient: Sterilisation)* [2001] Fam 15 (reversing *Re S (Sterilisation: Patient's Best Interests)* [2000] 1 FLR 465). In *Re A (Male Sterilisation)* [2000] 1 FLR 549 the court refused to make an order in the case of an incompetent adult male.

2. Abortion

Abortion is not a procedure which of its nature requires the sanction of the court,[539] unless the patient is a child who is already a ward of court.[540]   **4.182**

In cases where it is appropriate to invoke the court's assistance at all, it will author-   **4.183**
ise or declare lawful (as the case may be) an abortion if satisfied that the requirements of the Abortion Act 1967, as amended by the Human Fertilisation and
Embryology Act 1990, are met and that an abortion is in the best interests of the
pregnant child[541] or adult incompetent.[542]

As has already been seen,[543] neither the unborn child, nor its father, nor the hus-   **4.184**
band of its mother, can obtain an injunction to restrain the performance of a lawful abortion to which the mother has consented. It makes no difference that the
mother is either a child or an adult incompetent; it is quite clear[544] that the only
questions which arise in such a case are, first, whether the requirements of the
Abortion Act 1967 are met and, secondly, whether an abortion is in the best
interests of the mother.

3. Treatment of the Mentally Disordered

Save to the limited extent to which particular matters are regulated by statute, or,   **4.185**
in the case of children, by the Crown's prerogative power as parens patriae, the
treatment of the mentally disordered, whether for their mental disorder or otherwise, is regulated by the general principles of the common law.

Statutory Exceptions

There are three statutory exceptions. All are confined to persons suffering from   **4.186**
mental disorder as that expression is defined in the Mental Health Act 1983,
s 1(2). Two relate to specific procedures: the taking of blood samples,[545] and certain forms of treatment for mental disorder.[546]

---

[539] *Re SG (Adult Mental Patient: Abortion)* [1991] 2 FLR 329.
[540] *Re G-U (A Minor) (Wardship)* [1984] FLR 811.
[541] *Re P (A Minor)* [1986] 1 FLR 272; *Re B (Wardship: Abortion)* [1991] 2 FLR 426.
[542] *Re SG (Adult Mental Patient: Abortion)* [1991] 2 FLR 329; *Re SS (Medical Treatment: Late Termination)* [2002] 1 FLR 445 (order refused).
[543] See paras 4.31, 4.34 above.
[544] *Re P (A Minor)* [1986] 1 FLR 272; *Re SG (Adult Mental Patient: Abortion)* [1991] 2 FLR 329; *Re B (Wardship: Abortion)* [1991] 2 FLR 426.
[545] The Family Law Reform Act 1969, s 21(4) (persons suffering from mental disorder).
[546] For the treatments in question see the Mental Health Act 1983, s 57(1)(a) (surgical operations for destroying brain tissue or the functioning of brain tissue), s 57(1)(b) (surgical implantation of hormones for the purpose of reducing male sexual drive), s 58(1)(a) (electro-convulsive therapy), s 58(1)(b) (administration of medicine—as to which see *B v Croydon HA* [1995] Fam 133, 137–138); *R (on the application of N) v M* [2002] EWCA Civ 1789, [2003] 1 WLR 562. See also the Mental Health Act 1983, ss 56, 59–62, 64.

General Provision

4.187   There is one provision of general application. Section 63 of the Mental Health Act 1983 (which applies by virtue of s 56 of the Act only to patients liable to be detained under the Act) provides:

> The consent of a patient shall not be required for any medical treatment given to him for the mental disorder[547] from which he is suffering, not being treatment falling within section 57 or 58 above,[548] if the treatment is given by or under the direction of the responsible medical officer.

Section 145(1) of the Act provides that:

> 'medical treatment' includes nursing, and also includes care, habilitation and re-habilitation under medical supervision . . .

'Medical treatment' in s 63 means treatment which, taken as a whole, is calculated to alleviate or prevent a deterioration of the mental disorder from which the patient is suffering, and includes a range of acts ancillary to the core treatment, including those which prevent the patient from harming himself or which alleviate the symptoms of the disorder.[549]

> [R]elieving symptoms is just as much a part of treatment as relieving the underlying cause.[550]

'Medical treatment' in s 63 thus includes forcible feeding for the treatment of anorexia nervosa[551] or other psychiatric illnesses[552] and inducing labour and performing a caesarian section on a pregnant paranoid schizophrenic where effective treatment of the schizophrenia required that the patient give birth to a live baby and resume medication necessarily interrupted by her pregnancy,[553] including, if necessary, restraint and the use of reasonable force.[554]

---

[547] As defined in the Mental Health Act 1983, s 1(2). Section 63 permits compulsory medical treatment only for the mental disorder from which the patient is classified as suffering and which is the basis for his compulsory admission in the first place: *R (on the application of B) v Ashworth Hospital Authority* [2003] EWCA Civ 547, [2003] 1 WLR 1886.

[548] See para 4.186 above.

[549] *B v Croydon HA* [1995] Fam 133, 138–139, 140, affirming [1995] 1 FCR 332.

[550] *Re KB (Adult) (Mental Patient: Medical Treatment)* (1994) 19 BMLR 144, 146 *per* Ewbank J approved *B v Croydon HA* [1995] Fam 133, 139, 141.

[551] *Riverside Mental Health NHS Trust v Fox* [1994] 1 FLR 614; *Re KB (Adult) (Mental Patient: Medical Treatment)* (1994) 19 BMLR 144; *B v Croydon HA* [1995] Fam 133, affirming [1995] 1 FCR 332.

[552] *Re VS (Adult: Mental Disorder)* 19 August 1995, (Douglas Brown J), [1995] 3 Med LR 292; *R v Collins and Ashworth Hospital Authority ex p Brady* [2000] Lloyd's Rep Med 355 (force-feeding of prisoner detained in Special Hospital). Contrast *Secretary of State for the Home Department v Robb* [1995] Fam 127 (force-feeding of competent adult prisoner).

[553] *Tameside and Glossop Acute Services Trust v CH* [1996] 1 FLR 762, 771–774. Contrast *In re C (Adult: Refusal of Treatment)* [1994] 1 WLR 290 (schizophrenic held entitled to refuse consent to amputation of gangrenous leg) where the gangrene was 'entirely unconnected' with the mental disorder: *B v Croydon HA* [1995] Fam 133, 139; *Re JT (Adult: Refusal of Medical Treatment)* [1998] 1

footnote 554 on p. 295

4. *Blood-Testing*

Consent to Blood-Testing

Consent to the taking of blood and other bodily samples[555] is now regulated by **4.188** statute.[556] In addition the court can authorise the taking of a blood sample from a child,[557] though not from a competent adult.[558]

Blood-Testing of Children

The court can authorise the taking of a blood sample from a child even if it can- **4.189** not be shown that a blood-test will be in its best interests, unless it is satisfied that it would be against the child's interests.[559] In the case of an older child, however, the court will not order a blood-test against the child's will unless it would 'clearly' be in the child's interests.[560] Similar principles would appear to apply to the giving of consent[561] by the parent or other person having the care and control of the child.[562]

FLR 48 (adult with learning difficulties and extremely severe behavioural disturbance refusing treatment for renal failure: renal dialysis not treatment for the mental disorder); *St George's Healthcare NHS Trust v S, R v Collins, ex p S* [1999] Fam 26, 52 (obstetric treatment of pregnant woman not treatment for mental disorder).

[554] *Tameside and Glossop Acute Services Trust v CH* [1996] 1 FLR 762, 771, 774. For the common law power to use restraint and reasonable force see para 4.176 above.

[555] See the definition in s 25 of the Family Law Reform Act 1969, as amended by the Family Law Reform Act 1987.

[556] The Family Law Reform Act 1969, as amended by the Family Law Reform Act 1987 and the Child Support, Pensions and Social Security Act 2000, s 21(1) (competent adults), s 21(2) (minors who have attained the age of 16), s 21(3) (minors under the age of 16), s 21(4) (persons suffering from mental disorder within the meaning of the Mental Health Act 1983). S 8 of the Act does not apply to the taking of a blood sample: *In re W (A Minor) (Medical Treatment: Court's Jurisdiction)* [1993] Fam 64, 92; *In re O (A Minor) (Blood Tests: Constraint), In re J (A Minor)* [2000] Fam 139, 147–148.

[557] The Family Law Reform Act 1969, s 21(3)(b), reversing the decision in *In re O (A Minor) (Blood Tests: Constraint), In re J (A Minor)* [2000] Fam 139.

[558] *S v McC, W v W* [1972] AC 24, 43.

[559] *S v McC, W v W* [1972] AC 24; *In re F (A Minor) (Blood Tests: Parental Rights)* [1993] Fam 314, 318; *Re L (A Minor) (Blood Tests)* [1996] 2 FCR 649, 653; *In re H (A Minor) (Blood Tests: Parental Rights)* [1997] Fam 89, 103–104. For the approach adopted by the court see *In re H (A Minor) (Blood Tests: Parental Rights)* [1997] Fam 89, 104–108; *Re T (Paternity: Ordering Blood Tests)* [2001] 2 FLR 1190; *Re H and A (Paternity: Blood Tests)* [2002] EWCA Civ 383, [2002] 1 FLR 1145. For the impact in this context of Art 8 of the ECHR see *Re T (Paternity: Ordering Blood Tests)* [2001] 2 FLR 1190, 1197–1199. For the approach adopted by the court in relation to testing for HIV see *Re O (Minors) (Medical Examination)* [1993] 1 FLR 860 and, in particular, *In re C (A Child) (HIV Testing)* [2000] Fam 48 (affirmed *Re C (HIV Test)* [1999] 2 FLR 1004). The procedure for the hearing of applications for HIV testing as laid down in *Re HIV Tests* [1994] 2 FLR 116 has been revised: see now *President's Direction (HIV Testing of Children)* [2003] 1 FLR 1299.

[560] *In re L (An Infant)* [1968] P 119, 140; *B(BR) v B(J)* [1968] P 466, 469, 473–474, 481; *S v McC, W v W* [1972] AC 24, 45.

[561] Under the Family Law Reform Act 1969, s 21(3). Query whether, in the light of ss 21(1), 21(2) and 21(3), a parent can give a valid consent in the case of a child who has attained the age of 16.

[562] *S v McC, W v W* [1972] AC 24, 44, 45.

5. *Organ and Tissue Donation*

4.190 The donation of organs, tissues or body fluids[563] is not illegal, in the sense of being, as such, either prohibited by law or criminal. Transplants of organs (that is, as defined in s 7(2), 'any part of a human body . . . which, if wholly removed, cannot be replicated by the body') are regulated by the Human Organ Transplants Act 1989.[564]

Non-Regenerative Organs and Regenerative Tissue or Body Fluids

4.191 There is (quite apart from the fact that the distinction is drawn for the purposes of the criminal law by the Human Organ Transplants Act 1989) an important distinction between the donation of a non-regenerative organ (for example, a kidney) and the donation of regenerative tissue or body fluids (for example, bone marrow or blood). The donation of regenerative tissue or body fluids by a child or incompetent adult (for example, bone marrow) can, in appropriate circumstances, satisfy the best interests test. Whether the donation of a non-regenerative organ by a child or incompetent adult can ever satisfy the best interests test, and would therefore ever be sanctioned by the court, is an unresolved and very difficult question, which must be open to considerable doubt.[565]

Donation by Children

4.192 The extent to which a child or its parent can validly consent to the donation of organs, tissues or body fluids is obscure. Section 8 of the Family Law Reform Act 1969 does not extend to the donation of organs, or of blood or other bodily substances, for none of these procedures constitutes either treatment or diagnosis.[566] Whatever may be the position in strict legal theory, it has been said to be

---

[563] Useful general discussions are to be found in Kennedy and Grubb, *Medical Law: Text with Materials* (3rd edn, 2000), 1755–63; Mason and McCall Smith, *Law and Medical Ethics* (5th edn, 1999), 342–51; Brazier *Medicine, Patients and the Law* (3rd edn, 2003), 420–36; Dyer (ed), *Doctors, Patients and the Law* (1992), 120–6; Meyers, *The Human Body and the Law* (2nd edn, 1990), 198–203, 206–8; Skegg, *Law, Ethics, and Medicine* (1990), 60–8. The GMC has published guidance: 'Guidance for Doctors on Transplantation of Organs from Live Donors' (Nov 1992).

[564] The Act makes it a criminal offence to make or receive payment for the supply of an organ or to transplant an organ otherwise than between genetically related persons unless authorised by the Unrelated Life Transplant Regulatory Authority in accordance with the Human Organ Transplants (Unrelated Persons) Regulations 1989.

[565] Consider, for example, the views expressed by Kennedy and Grubb (n 563 above), 1086–7; Mason and McCall Smith (n 563 above), 295–6; Brazier (n 563 above), 422–3 (children), 424–5 (incompetent adults); Dyer (ed) (n 563 above), 124; Meyers (n 563 above), 203, 208; Skegg (n 563 above), 61–2, 68. See also the recommendations of the Law Commission in: Consultation Paper No 129, Mentally Incapacitated Adults and Decision-Making, Medical Treatment and Research, 1993, para 6.9; Report Law Com No 231, Mental Incapacity, 1995, para 6.5. See further para 4.200 below.

[566] *In re W (A Minor) (Medical Treatment: Court's Jurisdiction)* [1993] Fam 64, 78, 83, 92, 94.

'inconceivable' that any doctor should proceed with an organ transplant in the case of a child donor without the consent of both the child and its parents.[567]

Need to Involve the Court

The prior sanction of the court is required for the donation of regenerative tissue   **4.193** (bone marrow) by a child or incompetent adult.[568] Assuming that the court would ever be prepared to sanction such procedure, the prior sanction of the court will also be required for the donation of a non-regenerative organ (for example, a kidney) by a child or incompetent adult.[569]

Best Interests

Consistently with principle, the determining criterion is the best interests of the   **4.194** donor. The interests of the potential recipient, however compelling, are relevant only insofar as they further the interests of the donor.[570]

> The test to be applied in a case such as this is to ask whether the evidence shows that it is in the best interests of the [donor] for such procedures to take place. The fact that such a process would obviously benefit the [potential recipient] is not relevant unless, as a result of the [donor] helping the [recipient] in that way, the best interests of the [donor] are served. The approach is as set out in *In re F (Mental Patient: Sterilisation)* [1990] 2 AC 1 . . . The lawfulness of the action depends upon whether the treatment is in the best interests of the patient . . . This case is different from the case of *In re F (Mental Patient: Sterilisation)* because it involves the concept of donation of bone marrow by a donor who is incapable of giving consent where a significant benefit will flow to another person. There was no other person in *In re F* who would have benefitted directly as a result of the declaration sought, the benefits of sterilisation attaching solely to the mentally incapacitated subject of the application. Nonetheless, I am satisfied that the root question remains the same, namely, whether the procedures here envisaged will benefit the [donor] and accordingly benefits which may flow to the [potential recipient] are relevant only insofar as they have a positive effect upon the best interests of the [donor].[571]

Decisions in the United States of America[572] are important because of the reliance   **4.195**

---

[567] ibid, 78–79 *per* Lord Donaldson of Lymington MR.

[568] *In re Y (Mental Patient: Bone Marrow Donation)* [1997] Fam 110, 116. Query in relation to donations of blood or other regenerative bodily fluids.

[569] *In re F (Mental Patient: Sterilisation)* [1990] 2 AC 1, 19, 33, 40; *In re W (A Minor) (Medical Treatment: Court's Jurisdiction)* [1993] Fam 64, 79, 94.

[570] See paras. 4.161–4.165 above. Thus it would seem that it cannot be lawful to take tissue from a donor who is in an irreversible coma or who is unconscious and dying: compare the problem of the pregnant woman in a coma considered in para 4.37 above.

[571] *In re Y (Mental Patient: Bone Marrow Donation)* [1997] Fam 110, 113 *per* Connell J.

[572] *Strunk v Strunk* (1969) 445 SW 2d 145 (Court of Appeals of Kentucky, donation of kidney by adult incompetent authorised); *Hart v Brown* (1972) 289 A 2d 386 (Superior Court of Connecticut, donation of kidney by child authorised); *Re Richardson* (1973) 284 So 2d 185 (Court of Appeal of Louisiana, donation of kidney by child refused); *Lausier v Pescinski* (1975) 226 NW 2d 180 (Supreme Court of Wisconsin, donation of kidney by adult incompetent refused); *Little v Little*

placed in the only English case which has yet been decided[573] upon the reasoning in a recent decision of the Supreme Court of Illinois.[574]

4.196 The American authorities identify, with varying degrees of enthusiasm or scepticism, five factors potentially relevant to the question of whether or not the donation of an organ or tissue is in the best interests of a child or adult incompetent donor:[575]

(1) If the potential recipient dies as a result of the transplant not taking place:
   (a) The adverse emotional or psychological effect on the donor (where the recipient is a sibling with whom the donor has a strong identification, or upon whom the donor is emotionally or psychologically dependent), whether that adverse effect is caused by (i) the mere fact of the sibling's death or (ii) the fact that the relationship no longer continues.
   (b) The loss of a prospective carer for the donor after the donor's parents are dead.
   (c) Feelings of guilt on the part of the donor.
(2) If the transplant does take place
   (d) The increased happiness and gratification of, and psychological benefit to, the donor from having been able to save another person's life.
   (e) The fact that the donor is better off in a family that is happy (because the recipient is alive) than in a family that is distressed (because the potential recipient has died).

The approach adopted in the American cases accords, broadly speaking, with English law, though, consistently with principle[576] (and, indeed, to an extent recognised in the American cases), factors (a)(i), (c) and (d) cannot be relevant unless the donor has sufficient cognitive and social awareness to be able to understand the abstract concept of death, understands that he is in a position to ameliorate the recipient's condition and in fact wishes to do so.

4.197 The critical task is to evaluate the emotional, psychological and social effects on the donor of what is proposed.[577] In the typical case,[578] the benefits to the donor

---

(1979) 576 SW 2d 493 (Court of Civil Appeals of Texas, donation of kidney by child authorised); *Curran v Bosze* (1990) 566 NE 2d 1319 (Supreme Court of Illinois, donation of bone marrow by children refused).

[573] *In re Y (Mental Patient: Bone Marrow Donation)* [1997] Fam 110, 113–114.

[574] *Curran v Bosze* (1990) 566 NE 2d 1319, containing full discussions, 1322–1326 of whether the relevant test was best interests or substituted judgment (holding, 1331 that the test was best interests), 1326–1332 of the previous American case-law and, 1332–1345 of a substantial body of evidence directed to the risks and benefits to the donor of a bone marrow transplant.

[575] These may usefully be compared with the factors referred to in para 4.160 above identified in English cases.

[576] See paras 4.159, 4.160, 4.167 above.

[577] *In re Y (Mental Patient: Bone Marrow Donation)* [1997] Fam 110, 116.

[578] As in ibid, where, on the evidence, factor (b) was not material, where the patient's low level of

which have to be shown if the best interests test is to be satisfied will be found, if at all, in the pre-existing family relationships between the donor, the potential recipient and other members of their family; the critical factor will be proof that there will be emotional, psychological or social benefits to the donor in maintaining an existing, close family relationship which will be interrupted or lost if the donation does not take place.[579]

The Balancing Exercise

4.198 Those benefits then have to be balanced against the possible disadvantages[580] to the donor. The best interests balancing exercise has to be performed by considering (a) if the transplant takes place, (i) the psychological and other benefits to the donor, including any enhancement of his relationships with the potential recipient and other members of his family, balanced against (ii) the medical risks and other possible disadvantages of the procedure; and (b) if the transplant does not take place, (i) the psychological and other detriments to the donor, including any damage to or loss of his relationships with the potential recipient and other members of his family, balanced against (ii) the avoidance of the medical risks and other possible disadvantages of the procedure.

> I must look therefore at the situation of the [donor] and ask whether the proposals placed before the court would benefit her and, if yes, whether those benefits outweigh any possible detriment to her.[581]

Bone Marrow Transplants

4.199 Applying these principles the court has declared lawful the donation of bone marrow by an adult incompetent.[582]

Other Procedures

4.200 Whether the court would ever be willing to authorise (in the case of a child) or to declare lawful (in the case of an adult incompetent) any procedure more serious than a donation of bone marrow must be open to considerable doubt.[583]

> I should perhaps emphasise that this is a rather unusual case and that the family of the [potential recipient] and the [donor] are a particularly close family. It is doubtful that this case would act as a useful precedent in cases where the surgery involved

---

cognitive and social awareness, and lack of ability to understand both her own plight and that of the potential recipient, meant that factors (a)(i), (c) and (d) could not be relevant and where, for the same reason, there could not be any question of the patient benefitting from the performance by her of any perceived moral, social or civic obligation.

[579] ibid, 114–116, adopting, 113–114 the approach of Calvo J in *Curran v Bosze* (1990) 566 NE 2d 1319, 1331, 1343–1344, 1345.

[580] For example as in *In re Y (Mental Patient: Bone Marrow Donation)* [1997] Fam 110, 115–116.

[581] *In re Y (Mental Patient: Bone Marrow Donation)* [1997] Fam 110, 114 *per* Connell J.

[582] ibid.

[583] See para 4.191 above.

is more intrusive than in this case, where the evidence shows that the bone marrow harvested is speedily regenerated and that a healthy individual can donate as much as two pints with no long term consequences at all. Thus, the bone marrow donated by the [donor] will cause her no loss and she will suffer no real long term risk.[584]

6. Life and Death

(i) General Principles

The Duty to Care

4.201   A doctor (or layman) who has assumed the responsibility of caring for a helpless patient thereby becomes subject to a duty to care for him. The breach of that duty, if it leads to the death of the patient, renders the carer, depending upon his mens rea, liable to prosecution for manslaughter or murder.[585] The critical enquiry is, therefore, as to the duration and extent of the duty, because that determines whether or not there has been a breach of duty.

4.202   The duty to care does not oblige a doctor or other carer to pursue invasive treatment or artificial feeding with a view to prolonging life at all costs and regardless of the circumstances.[586]

The crucial question

4.203   In determining the duration and extent of the duty, the question which has to be asked is not, 'Is it in the best interests of the patient that he should die?' The question which has to be asked is, 'Is it in the best interests of the patient that treatment (feeding) which has the effect of artificially prolonging his life should be continued?' If the answer to that question is that the patient's best interests no longer require that it should be, then the withdrawal of the treatment will be lawful; indeed, the continuation of the treatment will be unlawful.[587] This is so even though

---

[584] *In re Y (Mental Patient: Bone Marrow Donation)* [1997] Fam 110, 116 *per* Connell J.

[585] *R v Gibbins* (1918) 13 Cr App R 134; *R v Stone* [1977] QB 354; *In re F (Mental Patient: Sterilisation)* [1990] 2 AC 1, 55–56, 77; *Airedale NHS Trust v Bland* [1993] AC 789, 858, 866, 881, 893; *Swindon and Marlborough NHS Trust v S* The Guardian, 10 December 1994, [1995] 3 Med LR 84.

[586] *In re J (A Minor) (Wardship: Medical Treatment)* [1991] Fam 33, 52, 54, 55; *Airedale NHS Trust v Bland* [1993] AC 789, 864, 865, 867. The BMA has published guidance on various relevant topics: 'End of Life Decisions: Views of the BMA' (Sept 1996); 'Decisions relating to Cardiopulmonary Resuscitation: A statement from the BMA and RCN in association with the Resuscitation Council (UK)' (Mar 1993); 'BMA guidelines on treatment decisions for patients in persistent vegetative state' (revised June 1996). So also the Royal College of Paediatrics and Child Health: 'Withholding or Withdrawing Life Saving Treatment in Children: A Framework for Practice' (Sept 1997).

[587] *Airedale NHS Trust v Bland* [1993] AC 789, 883–884, 885, 897, 898. It follows that, if the *patient's* best interests no longer require that his life be artificially prolonged, he cannot lawfully be kept alive with a view to benefiting third parties, eg for the purpose of enabling his organs or tissues to be harvested (whether before or after his death) or for the purpose of obtaining a financial or fiscal benefit: see further paras 4.164, 4.194 above. If the patient is pregnant with a viable foetus: see paras 4.36–4.37 above.

it may not be possible to say that it is in the patient's best interests that the treatment should be ended.[588]

> [I]t cannot be too strongly emphasised that the court never sanctions steps to terminate life. That would be unlawful. There is no question of approving, even in the case of the most horrendous disability, a course aimed at terminating life or accelerating death. The court is concerned only with the circumstances in which steps should not be taken to prolong life. . . . [T]he court in these cases has to decide, not whether to end life, but whether to prolong it by treatment without which death would ensue from natural causes. . . . I repeat, because of its importance, the debate here is not about terminating life but solely whether to withhold treatment designed to prevent death from natural causes.[589]

It is crucial for the understanding of this question that the question itself should be correctly formulated. The question is not whether the doctor should take a course which will kill his patient, or even take a course which has the effect of accelerating his death. The question is whether the doctor should or should not continue to provide his patient with medical treatment or care which, if continued, will prolong his patient's life. The question is sometimes put in striking or emotional terms, which can be misleading. For example, in the case of a life support system, it is sometimes asked: should a doctor be entitled to switch it off, or to pull the plug? And then it is asked: can it be in the best interests of the patient that a doctor should be able to switch the life support system off, when this will inevitably result in the patient's death? Such an approach has rightly been criticised as misleading . . . This is because the question is not whether it is in the best interests of the patient that he should die. The question is whether it is in the best interests of the patient that his life should be prolonged by the continuance of this form of medical treatment or care. The correct formulation of the question is of particular importance in a case such as the present, where the patient is totally unconscious and where there is no hope whatsoever of any amelioration of his condition. In circumstances such as these, it may be difficult to say that it is in his best interests that the treatment should be ended. But if the question is asked, as in my opinion it should be, whether it is in his best interests that treatment which has the effect of artificially prolonging his life should be continued, that question can sensibly be answered to the effect that his best interests no longer require that it should be.[590]

The Presumption in Favour of Life

But although the question is, 'Is it in the best interests of the patient that treatment should be continued?' (and not, 'Is it in the best interests of the patient that treatment be discontinued?'), there is a very strong presumption in favour of taking all steps which will prolong life; in the great majority of cases, save in exceptional circumstances or where the patient is dying, the best interests of the patient will **4.204**

---

[588] *Airedale NHS Trust v Bland* [1993] AC 789, 857–858, 868, 873, 883–885, 896–898.
[589] *In re J (A Minor) (Wardship: Medical Treatment)* [1991] Fam 33, 53, 54 *per* Taylor LJ. To the same effect *Re R (Adult: Medical Treatment)* [1996] 2 FLR 99, 107 *per* Sir Stephen Brown P.
[590] *Airedale NHS Trust v Bland* [1993] AC 789, 868 *per* Lord Goff of Chieveley.

require such steps to be taken.[591] The burden of proof is accordingly on those who assert that life-saving treatment or life-sustaining artificial feeding should be discontinued.

(ii) The Dying Patient

Life-Prolonging Treatment

4.205 In the case of life-prolonging treatment—that is treatment the purpose of which is merely to prolong the life of a terminally ill patient who cannot be expected to recover from a condition which is incurable—the court will authorise or declare lawful (as the case may be) such treatment as is appropriate to the patient's condition.

4.206 In such a case the goal should be to ease suffering and, where appropriate, to 'ease the passing' rather than to achieve a short prolongation of life.[592]

> If the first purpose of medicine, the restoration of health, can no longer be achieved . . . a doctor . . . is entitled to do all that is proper and necessary to relieve pain and suffering, even if the measures he takes may incidentally shorten life[593]

Withdrawal of Treatment

4.207 Consistently with this approach there may be circumstances in which it is appropriate to withdraw life-prolonging treatment from a dying patient,[594] but a doctor is never justified in taking active steps in order to kill his patient by the introduction of an external agency (for example, the administration of a fatal drug) with the intention of bringing about the patient's death: 'mercy killing' by active means is murder.[595]

Indirect Consequences

4.208 Also consistent with this approach is the recognition[596] by English law of the theological doctrine of double effect:

> 'Thou shalt not kill' is an absolute commandment in this context. But, to quote the

---

[591] *In re J (A Minor) (Wardship: Medical Treatment)* [1991] Fam 33, 46, 51, 53; *Airedale NHS Trust v Bland* [1993] AC 789, 867.

[592] *In re C (A Minor) (Wardship: Medical Treatment)* [1990] Fam 26, 32, 33, 37, 38; *Re C (Medical Treatment)* [1998] 1 FLR 384; *Royal Wolverhampton Hospitals NHS Trust v B* [2000] 1 FLR 953; *A NHS Trust v D* [2000] 2 FLR 677. For the impact in this context of Arts 2 and 3 of the ECHR see *A NHS Trust v D* [2000] 2 FLR 677, 695. The BMA has published guidance: 'End of Life Decisions: Views of the BMA' (Sept 1996).

[593] *R v Bodkin Adams* 8–9 April 1957, (Devlin J), [1957] Crim LR 365.

[594] cf *Airedale NHS Trust v Bland* [1993] AC 789.

[595] *R v Bodkin Adams* 8–9 April 1957, (Devlin J), [1957] Crim LR 365; *R v Cox* (1992) 12 BMLR 38; *Airedale NHS Trust v Bland* [1993] AC 789, 831, 865–866, 892.

[596] By Devlin J in *R v Bodkin Adams* 8–9 April 1957, [1957] Crim LR 365. See the discussion in *In re A (Children) (Conjoined Twins: Surgical Separation)* [2001] Fam 147, 199, 216–218, 251–252.

well known phrase of Arthur Hugh Clough in 'The Latest Decalogue,' in this context it is permissible to add 'but need'st not strive officiously to keep alive'. The decision on life and death must and does remain in other hands. What doctors and the court have to decide is whether, in the best interests of the child patient, a particular decision as to medical treatment should be taken which *as a side effect* will render death more or less likely. This is not a matter of semantics. It is fundamental. At the other end of the age spectrum, the use of drugs to reduce pain will often be fully justified, notwithstanding that this will hasten the moment of death. What can never be justified is the use of drugs or surgical procedures with the primary purpose of doing so.[597]

(iii) The Normal Patient

4.209

In the case of life-saving treatment that is treatment the purpose of which is to enable the patient to recover from a life-threatening condition which is potentially curable—there is usually no difficulty in arriving at the appropriate decision. For reasons which are obvious the court will normally[598] authorise or declare lawful (as the case may be) such treatment in the case of a child or incompetent adult, irrespective of the views of either the child, the child's parents or the patient's relatives, for generally the duty of the court is to preserve life. Thus where it is necessary to preserve the patient's life the court, notwithstanding religious or other objections, will authorise or declare lawful (as the case may be) the administration of blood transfusions to child[599] and incompetent adult[600] Jehovah's Witnesses, the force-feeding of children[601] and incompetent adults[602] for the treatment of anorexia nervosa or other psychiatric illnesses, and the administration, if need be by force, of

---

[597] *In re J (A Minor) (Wardship: Medical Treatment)* [1991] Fam 33, 46 *per* Lord Donaldson of Lymington MR. The distinction was central to the issue for the jury in *R v Cox* (1992) 12 BMLR 38. For a case turning on double effect which attracted much publicity, though it never proceeded to judgement, see *Lindsell v Holmes* The Guardian, 29 October 1997.

[598] But not always. Thus 'on the most unusual facts' the court in *In re T (A Minor) (Wardship: Medical Treatment)* [1997] 1 WLR 242 refused to overrule the parents' refusal to consent to a liver transplant on a 17-month-old boy suffering from biliary atresia, a life-threatening liver defect, notwithstanding unanimous medical opinion that without a transplant the child would not live beyond the age of 2 to 2¹/₂ and a half whilst the prospects of a successful operation leading to many years of normal life were good. This decision might be thought surprising: see the critical discussion by Professor Grubb in [1996] Med L Rev 315 and see further para 4.75 above. See also *In re A (Children) (Conjoined Twins: Surgical Separation)* [2001] Fam 147, 194–195, 244.

[599] *Re E (A Minor) (Wardship: Medical Treatment)* [1993] 1 FLR 386; *Re S (A Minor) (Medical Treatment)* [1993] 1 FLR 376; *Re O (A Minor) (Medical Treatment)* [1993] 2 FLR 149; *Re R (A Minor) (Blood Transfusion)* [1993] 2 FLR 757; *Re S (A Minor) (Consent to Medical Treatment)* [1994] 2 FLR 1065.

[600] *In re T (Adult: Refusal of Treatment)* [1993] Fam 95.

[601] *In re W (A Minor) (Medical Treatment: Court's Jurisdiction)* [1993] Fam 64; *Re C (Detention: Medical Treatment)* [1997] 2 FLR 180.

[602] *Riverside Mental Health NHS Trust v Fox* [1994] 1 FLR 614; *Re KB (Adult) (Mental Patient: Medical Treatment)* (1994) 19 BMLR 144; *B v Croydon HA* [1995] Fam 133, affirming [1995] 1 FCR 332; *Re VS (Adult: Mental Disorder)* 17 August 1995, (Douglas Brown J), [1995] 3 Med LR 292.

surgical procedures necessary to preserve the life of a child[603] or an incompetent woman[604] suffering complications during labour.

(iv) The Handicapped Patient

4.210 The court does not adopt any different approach merely because a patient is physically or mentally handicapped. The fact that the patient is handicapped cannot of course be ignored, for the question is never what treatment would be appropriate for a non-handicapped patient but always, what is the treatment appropriate for this patient given his condition?[605] Nonetheless,

> where . . . the child is severely handicapped although not intolerably so and treatment for a discrete condition can enable life to continue for an appreciable period, albeit subject to that severe handicap, the treatment should be given.[606]

Thus, in the leading case,[607] parents had refused consent to surgery on their 10-day-old mongol baby to relieve an intestinal blockage, taking the bona fide view that 'God or nature has given the child a way out'. Without surgery the baby would have died; the surgery, if carried out, would enable the baby to live the same life as any other mongol child. The Court of Appeal recognised that the child would have a short life expectancy and would be very severely mentally and physically handicapped and thus not able to have anything like a normal existence,[608] but directed surgery.

> If the operation takes place and is successful then the child may live the normal span of a mongoloid child with the handicaps and defects and life of a mongol child, and it is not for this court to say that life of that description ought to be extinguished.[609]

> The child should be put into the same position as any other mongol child and must be given the chance to live an existence.[610]

The principle has subsequently been explained as being that

> It [is] not for the court to decide that the child should not have the chance of the normal life span of a mongoloid child with the handicaps, defects and life of such a child.[611]

---

[603] *A Metropolitan Borough Council v AB* [1997] 1 FLR 767. See further paras 4.98, 4.176 above.

[604] *In re T (Adult: Refusal of Treatment)* [1993] Fam 95; *Tameside and Glossop Acute Services Trust v CH* [1996] 1 FLR 762; *Norfolk and Norwich Healthcare (NHS) Trust v W* [1996] 2 FLR 613; *Rochdale Healthcare (NHS) Trust v C* [1997] 1 FCR 274; *Re L (Patient: Non-Consensual Treatment)* [1997] 2 FLR 837; *Re MB (Medical Treatment)* [1997] 2 FLR 426.

[605] *In re C (A Minor) (Wardship: Medical Treatment)* [1990] Fam 26, 32.

[606] *In re J (A Minor) (Wardship: Medical Treatment)* [1991] Fam 33, 54 *per* Taylor LJ.

[607] *In re B (A Minor) (Wardship: Medical Treatment)* [1981] 1 WLR 1421, reversing (1982) 3 FLR 117, subsequently considered and explained in *In re C (A Minor) (Wardship: Medical Treatment)* [1990] Fam 26; *In re J (A Minor) (Wardship: Medical Treatment)* [1991] Fam 33.

[608] *In re B (A Minor) (Wardship: Medical Treatment)* [1981] 1 WLR 1421, 1423.

[609] *In re B (A Minor) (Wardship: Medical Treatment)* [1981] 1 WLR 1421, 1424 *per* Templeman LJ.

[610] ibid, 1424 *per* Dunn LJ.

[611] *In re C (A Minor) (Wardship: Medical Treatment)* [1990] Fam 26, 35 *per* Lord Donaldson of

(v) The Gravely Handicapped Patient

On the other hand, there are cases in which the degree of handicap is so great that **4.211** it is not in the best interests of the patient to give or to continue (as the case may be) treatment which if given will artificially prolong life. The law recognises three situations where that is so.[612]

Intolerability

The first is where the nature of the patient's condition and the nature of the pro- **4.212** posed treatment are such that, taking everything into account, the patient's life, even if he survives, will be 'intolerable',[613] as it has been put, so intolerable, so full of pain and suffering and so awful,[614] that life-saving treatment would not be appropriate. It is on this footing that the withholding or withdrawal of treatment can be justified in the case of gravely handicapped but sentient patients.[615]

Futility

The second is where the disability is such that the treatment would be 'futile', 'use- **4.213** less' or 'pointless'. In such a case it is the futility of the treatment which justifies its withholding or withdrawal. It is on this footing that the withdrawal of artificial nutrition and hydration is justified in the case of patients in a permanent (formerly called persistent) vegetative state.[616] Treatment can properly be categorised as futile if it cannot cure or palliate the disease or illness from which the patient is suffering and thus serves no therapeutic purpose of any kind.

Impracticability

The third is where it is simply impracticable to administer the proposed treat- **4.214** ment, for example, where it is impracticable to give the treatment against the wishes of a patient who, though incompetent, strongly objects to and is not prepared to submit to the relevant procedure.[617]

Lymington MR. In the light of the decisions in *In re B (A Minor) (Wardship: Medical Treatment)* [1981] 1 WLR 1421; *In re C (A Minor) (Wardship: Medical Treatment)* [1990] Fam 26 and *In re J (A Minor) (Wardship: Medical Treatment)* [1991] Fam 33 it is doubtful whether any useful principles can be extracted from *R v Arthur* (1981) 12 BMLR 1.

[612] cf *Airedale NHS Trust v Bland* [1993] AC 789, 868–869.

[613] *In re J (A Minor) (Wardship: Medical Treatment)* [1991] Fam 33, 54, 55 *per* Taylor LJ; *Re R (Adult: Medical Treatment)* [1996] 2 FLR 99, 107, 108, 110 *per* Sir Stephen Brown P.

[614] *In re B (A Minor) (Wardship: Medical Treatment)* [1981] 1 WLR 1421, 1424. But note that these words are not to be taken as providing a quasi-statutory yardstick: *In re J (A Minor) (Wardship: Medical Treatment)* [1991] Fam 33, 46.

[615] As in *In re J (A Minor) (Wardship: Medical Treatment)* [1991] Fam 33; *In re J (A Minor) (Child in Care: Medical Treatment)* [1993] Fam 15; *Re C (A Baby)* [1996] 2 FLR 43; *Re R (Adult: Medical Treatment)* [1996] 2 FLR 99.

[616] *Airedale NHS Trust v Bland* [1993] AC 789, 869, 870, 884.

[617] *Re D (Medical Treatment: Mentally Disabled Patient)* [1998] 2 FLR 22 (49-year-old chronic but fluctuating psychotic suffering from chronic renal failure at near-end stage and high blood pressure

(a) The Gravely Handicapped but Sentient Patient

4.215   Thus in the leading case mechanical ventilation was held not to be necessary in the case of a 'gravely damaged' 5-month-old baby who was suffering from an 'appalling catalogue of disabilities'.[618]

> [T]here is a balancing exercise to be performed in assessing the course to be adopted in the best interests of the child. . . . This brings me face to face with the problem of formulating the critical equation. In truth it cannot be done with mathematical or any precision. There is without doubt a very strong presumption in favour of a course of action which will prolong life, but . . . it is not irrebuttable. . . . [A]ccount has to be taken of the pain and suffering and quality of life which the child will experience if life is prolonged. Account has also to be taken of the pain and suffering involved in the proposed treatment itself. . . . But in the end there will be cases in which the answer must be that it is not in the interests of the child to subject it to treatment which will cause increased suffering and produce no commensurate benefit, giving the fullest possible weight to the child's, and mankind's, desire to survive.[619]

> There is only the one test: that the interests of the ward are paramount. Of course the court will approach those interests with a strong predilection in favour of the preservation of life, because of the sanctity of human life. But there neither is, nor should there be, any absolute rule that, save where the ward is already terminally ill, that is dying, neither the court nor any responsible parent can approve the withholding of life-saving treatment on the basis of the quality of the ward's life. . . . [I]t could in certain circumstances be inimical to the interests of the ward that there should be such a requirement: to preserve life at all costs, whatever the quality of the life to be preserved, and however distressing to the ward may be the nature of the treatment necessary to preserve life, may not be in the interests of the ward.[620]

> [T]he court's high respect for the sanctity of human life imposes a strong presumption in favour of taking all steps capable of preserving it, save in exceptional circumstances. . . . Despite the court's inability to compare a life afflicted by the most severe disability with death, the unknown, . . . there must be extreme cases in which the court is entitled to say: 'The life which this treatment would prolong would be so cruel as to be intolerable'. . . . Once the absolute test is rejected, the proper criteria must be a matter of degree. At what point in the scale of disability and suffering ought the court to hold that the best interests of the child do not require further endurance to be imposed by positive treatment to prolong its life? Clearly, to justify withholding treatment, the circumstances would have to be extreme. . . . I consider

requiring haemodialysis for four hours three or four times each week to keep him alive but unable because of his mental condition to understand the need for treatment and strongly objecting to procedure: held lawful in the last resort 'not to impose haemodialysis upon him in circumstances in which in the opinion of the medical practitioners responsible for such treatment it is not reasonably practicable so to do', the judge accepting that in the circumstances dialysis, which requires the co-operation of the patient, could only be performed under general anaesthetic which was neither practicable nor desirable in a patient suffering D's diasabilities).

[618] *In re J (A Minor) (Wardship: Medical Treatment)* [1991] Fam 33, 49, 56.
[619] ibid, 46–47 *per* Lord Donaldson of Lymington MR.
[620] ibid, 51–52 *per* Balcombe LJ.

the correct approach is for the court to judge the quality of life the child would have to endure if given the treatment and decide whether in all the circumstances such a life would be so afflicted as to be intolerable to that child. I say 'to that child' because the test should not be whether the life would be tolerable to the decider. The test must be whether the child in question, if capable of exercising sound judgment, would consider the life tolerable.[621]

In the particular circumstances of that case the reasons for arriving at the decision that life-saving treatment should not necessarily be given were that **4.216**

mechanical ventilation is itself an invasive procedure which, together with its essential accompaniments . . . would cause the child distress. Furthermore the procedures involve taking active measures which carry their own hazards, not only to life but in terms of causing even greater brain damage. This had to be balanced against what could possibly be achieved by the adoption of such active treatment. The chances of preserving the child's life might be improved, although even this was not certain and account had to be taken of the extremely poor quality of life at present enjoyed by the child, the fact that he had already been ventilated for exceptionally long periods, the unfavourable prognosis with or without ventilation and a recognition that if the question of reventilation ever arose, his situation would have deteriorated still further.[622]

There are other reported examples of the application of these principles.[623] **4.217**

Life-Saving Treatment and the Quality of Life

As can be seen, the Court of Appeal[624] has accepted that the quality of life is something that can be taken into account in deciding whether or not a gravely handicapped but sentient patient should receive life-saving treatment. But this does not mean that, in the case of a sentient patient, the withholding or withdrawal of life-saving treatment or artificial feeding can ever be justified solely by reference to an **4.218**

---

[621] ibid, 53, 55 *per* Taylor LJ.

[622] ibid, 47–48 *per* Lord Donaldson of Lymington MR.

[623] In relation to gravely handicapped children see *In re J (A Minor) (Child in Care: Medical Treatment)* [1993] Fam 15 (artificial ventilation); *Re C (A Baby)* [1996] 2 FLR 43 (artificial ventilation). For a case where the decision went the other way, see *Re Superintendent of Family & Child Service and Dawson* (1983) 145 DLR (3d) 610, esp 611, 615, 616, 620–621; *Re SD* [1983] 3 WWR 597 considered in *In re C (A Minor) (Wardship: Medical Treatment)* [1990] Fam 26; *In re J (A Minor) (Wardship: Medical Treatment)* [1991] Fam 33. For a case where the proceedings were dismissed without the court addressing the merits see *R v Portsmouth Hospitals NHS Trust, ex p Glass* [1999] 2 FLR 905 (affirming (1999) 50 BMLR 269). For cases involving gravely handicapped adults see *Re R (Adult: Medical Treatment)* [1996] 2 FLR 99 (cardio-pulmonary resuscitation and antibiotics); *A Hospital NHS Trust v S* [2003] EWHC 365 (Fam), [2003] Lloyd's Rep Med 137 (kidney dialysis and transplant).

[624] In *In re J (A Minor) (Wardship: Medical Treatment)* [1991] Fam 33. For comments by the House of Lords on this case see *Airedale NHS Trust v Bland* [1993] AC 789, 858, 868–869, 872, esp Lord Goff of Chieveley's reservation, 869, and see also, 885, 899. For subsequent comments by the Court of Appeal see *Frenchay Healthcare NHS Trust v S* [1994] 1 WLR 601, 607, 610; *In re A (Children) (Conjoined Twins: Surgical Separation)* [2001] Fam 147, 185–188 (an important analysis by Ward LJ).

assessment of the quality of the patient's life, let alone because of physical or mental handicap, however grave. Withdrawal is justified only in extreme circumstances and if the court is satisfied to a high degree of probability that the patient's quality of life (and any prospects of improvement) are demonstrably so very poor as not to be commensurate with the extreme pain, suffering, or distress (physical or mental) being experienced as a result of the patient's condition (including any pain, suffering, and distress resulting from, and any hazards involved in, the treatment itself). In other words, the determining factor is not the patient's quality of life as such but pain, suffering or distress, whether physical or mental, so extreme that the artificial prolongation of the patient's agony cannot be justified.[625]

(b) The Patient in a Permanent (Formerly Called Persistent) Vegetative State

4.219 The essence of the permanent vegetative state (PVS)[626] is that the patient is alive, is not dying (and, if properly treated may live for many years), but is totally insensate, and therefore can feel neither pain nor distress, has no cognitive functions, requires artificial nutrition and hydration to remain alive, and has no hope of either recovery or improvement.

Need to Involve the Court

4.220 Withdrawal of artificial nutrition and hydration from a patient in a permanent vegetative state requires the prior sanction of the court.[627]

---

[625] *In re J (A Minor) (Wardship: Medical Treatment)* [1991] Fam 33, 46, 47–48, 55, 56; *Airedale NHS Trust v Bland* [1993] AC 789, 858, 868.

[626] PVS was fully described in *Airedale NHS Trust v Bland* [1993] AC 789, 795–796, 797–798, 806–807, 860–861. At that time PVS was called the persistent vegetative state. It has since been renamed the permanent vegetative state, so as better to emphasise the fundamental essence of the condition. As currently understood, PVS is defined, albeit slightly differently, in the 'International Working Party Report on the Vegetative State' (The Royal Hospital for Neuro-Disability, London, Feb 1996) and in 'The permanent vegetative state', a Review by a working group convened by the Royal College of Physicians, endorsed by the Conference of Medical Royal Colleges and their Faculties in the United Kingdom (Royal College of Physicians of London, Apr 1996). A patient may be within the criteria identified by the International Working Party whilst not meeting the more stringent criteria identified by the Royal College: *Re D (Medical Treatment)* [1998] 1 FLR 411; *Re H (A Patient)* [1998] 2 FLR 36; *NHS Trust A v H* [2001] 2 FLR 501. In the latter case Dame Elizabeth Butler-Sloss P said it was 'somewhat unhelpful' that this was so and indicated that the criteria in the Royal College of Physicians report should perhaps be reviewed and that the criteria in the International Working Party's report are 'to be preferred, for the purposes of this case at least'. The Royal College of Physicians has now updated its guidelines and issued a new report: 'The Vegetative State: Guidance on Diagnosis and Management' (RCP Publication, 2003). See further para 4.223 below. The BMA has published guidance on PVS: 'BMA guidelines on treatment decisions for patients in persistent vegetative state' (revised June 1996).

[627] *Airedale NHS Trust v Bland* [1993] AC 789, 805, 815, 824, 833, 859, 873, 875.

Details of the procedure to be adopted in applications to the court are set out in **4.221** the Official Solicitor's Practice Note.[628]

Withdrawal of Treatment

Where a patient is diagnosed as being in a permanent vegetative state the court **4.222** will authorise or declare lawful (as the case may be) the withdrawal of artificial nutrition and hydration.[629] This is essentially on the ground that artificial nutrition and hydration is medical treatment[630] and that in the case of a patient in a permanent vegetative state such treatment is futile: the patient has no further interest in being kept alive, his interest in life being in truth null.[631] The function of the court is to verify the diagnosis of the patient as being in a permanent vegetative state. The views of the patient's relatives or of others close to the patient will be taken into account by the court but cannot act as a veto.[632]

Related Conditions

Given the categorisation by the courts of artificial nutrition and hydration as **4.223** medical treatment, it is suggested that there can be no arbitrary reason for distinguishing in this context between those patients who are in a permanent vegetative state and those who are not: the matter must, in each case, be resolved by applying the two criteria of intolerability[633] or futility. This accords with the view

---

[628] *Practice Note (Official Solicitor: Declaratory Proceedings: Medical and Welfare Decisions for Adults Who Lack Capacity)* [2001] 2 FLR 158, issued May 2001, replacing *Practice Note (Official Solicitor: Persistent Vegetative State)* [1996] 2 FLR 375, issued July 1996 following the decisions in *Re G (Adult Patient: Publicity)* [1995] 2 FLR 528; *Re G (Persistent Vegetative State)* [1995] 2 FCR 46; *In re S (Hospital Patient: Court's Jurisdiction)* [1996] Fam 1; *Re C (Adult Patient: Restriction of Publicity after Death)* [1996] 2 FLR 251 and the issue of *Practice Note (Official Solicitor: Sterilisation)* [1996] 2 FLR 111, and replacing with modifications the earlier Practice Note: *Practice Note (Official Solicitor: Persistent Vegetative State)* [1994] 2 All ER 413, [1994] 1 FLR 654 (issued Mar 1994, following the decisions in *Airedale NHS Trust v Bland* [1993] AC 789; *Frenchay Healthcare NHS Trust v S* [1994] 1 WLR 601). See further para 4.139 above.

[629] *Airedale NHS Trust v Bland* [1993] AC 789; *Frenchay Healthcare NHS Trust v S* [1994] 1 WLR 601; *Re G (Persistent Vegetative State)* [1995] 2 FCR 46; *Swindon and Marlborough NHS Trust v S* The Guardian, 10 December 1994, [1995] 3 Med LR 84; *Re C (Adult Patient: Restriction of Publicity after Death)* [1996] 2 FLR 251; *NHS Trust A v M, NHS Trust B v H* [2001] Fam 348; *NHS Trust A v H* [2001] 2 FLR 501; *Re G (adult incompetent: withdrawal of treatment)* (2001) 65 BMLR 6. For the impact in this context of Arts 2, 3 and 8 of the ECHR see *NHS Trust A v M, NHS Trust B v H* [2001] Fam 348, 355–363.

[630] *Airedale NHS Trust v Bland* [1993] AC 789.

[631] ibid, 858, 859, 868, 869, 884, 885, 897, 899.

[632] ibid, 871; *Re G (Persistent Vegetative State)* [1995] 2 FCR 46, 51. In *NHS Trust A v M, NHS Trust B v H* [2001] Fam 348, 361, Dame Elizabeth Butler-Sloss P left open the question of whether the wishes and feelings of the patient's family forms part of the patient's right to respect for family life under Art 8 of the ECHR.

[633] Consider, for example, the patient 'suffering the mental torture of Guillain-Barre syndrome, rational but trapped and mute in an unresponsive body': *Airedale NHS Trust v Bland* [1993] AC 789, 897 *per* Lord Mustill. For Guillain-Barre syndrome see *Nancy B v Hotel-Dieu de Quebec* (1992) 86 DLR (4th) 385; *Auckland Area Health Board v AG* [1993] 1 NZLR 235.

adopted by those courts, not only in this country[634] but also in New Zealand,[635] Eire,[636] and Jersey,[637] which have authorised the withdrawal of artificial nutrition and hydration from incompetent patients who, although not in a permanent vegetative state, lack all awareness. The question of the withdrawal of artificial nutrition and hydration from a patient whose condition falls significantly short of the permanent vegetative state (for example, because there is some, albeit slight, chance of improvement or the patient has what has been described as 'very slight sensate awareness'[638] or the 'glimmerings of awareness'[639]) has been expressly left open for future decision by the House of Lords,[640] the Court of Appeal,[641] and the President of the Family Division.[642] The courts will probably be very slow indeed to take this further step. As the President of the Family Division has said:

> No declaration to permit or to sanction the taking of so extreme a step could possibly be granted where there was any real possibility of meaningful life continuing to exist.[643]

---

[634] *Re D (Medical Treatment)* [1998] 1 FLR 411 (adult in a vegetative state, 'totally unaware of herself or of her surroundings' and of 'anything which is going on about her', but whose condition did not in all respects meet the Royal College's criteria for PVS); *Re H (A Patient)* [1998] 2 FLR 36 (insentient adult in vegetative state, unable to communicate at all or to appreciate anything taking place around her, whose condition met the International Working Party's criteria but not the Royal College's criteria for PVS).

[635] *Auckland Area Health Board v AG* [1993] 1 NZLR 235 (Guillain-Barre syndrome).

[636] *In the Matter of a Ward of Court (withholding medical treatment) (No 2)* [1996] 2 IR 79 (adult in condition 'nearly, but not quite,' a permanent vegetative state).

[637] *In the Matter of an Infant* [1995] JLR 296, sv *Re Representation Attorney General* [1995] Med LR 316 (child in a non-cognitive but not permanent vegetative state).

[638] *Airedale NHS Trust v Bland* [1993] AC 789, 885 *per* Lord Browne-Wilkinson.

[639] ibid, 898 *per* Lord Mustill.

[640] ibid, 869, 879, 885, 899.

[641] *Frenchay Healthcare NHS Trust v S* [1994] 1 WLR 601, 607, 610.

[642] *Re R (Adult: Medical Treatment)* [1996] 2 FLR 99, 105 (adult in low-awareness state).

[643] *Re D (Medical Treatment)* [1998] 1 FLR 411, 420 *per* Sir Stephen Brown P.

PART III

MEDICAL NEGLIGENCE

5

DUTIES IN CONTRACT AND TORT

A. Introduction

Most litigation against doctors concerns actions for medical negligence or, as it is now **5.01** more commonly known, clinical negligence. It is the principal action by which patients seek compensation for injuries caused within the National Health Service (NHS). The only other action which features to any extent is battery.[1] Actions in battery are however rare, not least because they require the patient to prove the doctor acted without the patient's consent, which is not usually the case. Claims for damages generally arise out of treatment or care to which the patient has consented, but which went wrong or did not produce the desired or expected outcome. The essence of the patient's claim is that the doctor was negligent in that he breached his duty to exercise reasonable care and skill in diagnosing, advising or treating the patient.

The frequency and volume of medical negligence actions has increased consider- **5.02** ably in recent years.[2] Prior to the 1980s these actions were relatively rare in

---

[1] See above, Ch 3.
[2] For a discussion of the problems of the present system and suggestions for reform see Kennedy, I and Grubb, A, *Medical Law* (3rd edn, Butterworths, 2000) 530–74 and the Chief Medical Officer's Report, *Making Amends* (DoH, 2003).

England; reported cases were few and far between. Since that time a significant upsurge in litigation has occurred and led some to argue that claims for medical negligence are now out of control, just as in the United States of America, and that litigation has reached 'crisis proportions'.[3] This trend, it is said, can only have bad consequences for patients because of the transaction and direct costs it imposes upon the limited NHS budget. It is also said that the fear of being sued has, or will, encourage doctors to respond in a defensive and undesirable way and lead them to practise 'defensive medicine' whereby their behaviour towards a patient is modified solely to reduce the risk of legal action.[4] Although it is clear that both the number of claims and their costs are rising,[5] there is no hard evidence of the latter practice. In fact, the introduction of 'risk management' systems—defensive practices of a sort—both in clinical and other services provided within the NHS is more likely to contribute to a higher level of care to patients and others. Awareness of risk and a concern to reduce it will, inevitably, reduce accidents and hence take away the basis for some litigation. It will not, however, contribute to a reduction of claims in some situations, for instance, where a doctor's clinical judgment is at the core of the action. Clinical judgment is notoriously difficult to challenge in court either at the level of showing it was a *mis*judgment or, if it was, that it was a negligent one.[6] However, the development of protocols and guidelines by the National Institute for Clinical Excellence (NICE) may have implications by going some way to standardise medical responses and inform doctors (and others) on the available options to treat a particular patient.[7]

5.03   It is also clear that the NHS has taken clinical negligence litigation altogether more seriously in recent years prompted in part by the volume and cost of litigation but also because of the continuing squeeze upon NHS resources and the discipline of the cost-saving regime of the 'internal market'. The introduction of 'NHS Indemnity' in 1990[8] and the subsequent 'Clinical Negligence Scheme for Trusts' administered by the National Health Service Litigation Authority[9]

---

[3] The litigation boom (actual or perceived) and its implications is discussed in Jones, M, *Medical Negligence* (3rd edn, 2003), ch 1 and Kennedy, I, 'Confidentiality, Competence and Malpractice' in Byrne, P (ed), *Medicine in Contemporary Society* (1987), 40, 51–61. See also, *Making Amends*, ibid.

[4] For a discussion of the issue of 'defensive medicine' see Jones, M, *Medical Negligence*, ibid, 16–19 and 252–8.

[5] For informative accounts of the handling of clinical negligence claims and authoritative data on such claims in England and Wales see: *Handling Clinical Negligence Claims in England* (HC 403 Session 2000–2001), Report by Comptroller and Auditor General (3 May 2001) and *Clinical negligence in the NHS in Wales*, Report of the Auditor General for Wales (Feb. 2001). For the most up-to-date account see CMO's Report, *Making Amends* (n 2 above).

[6] See below, Ch 6.

[7] See below, Ch 6 and further see Hurwitz, B, *Clinical Guidelines and the Law* (1998).

[8] Circular HC (89)34; now updated as HSG (96)48.

[9] National Health Service Litigation Authority (Establishment and Constitution) Order 1995, SI 1995/2800; National Health Service Litigation Authority Regulations 1995, SI 1995/2801.

introduced on 1 March 1996,[10] represent attempts at more centralised control to effect a rationalisation of negligence litigation within the NHS.[11]

Clinical negligence is, in reality, no more than an application of the tort of negli- **5.04** gence to professionals such as doctors, nurses and others involved in the provision of health care services. Hence, the law of negligence is applicable (with some peculiar adaptions) to the medical context and medical negligence is a specific form of negligence liability in the professional context.[12] The general principles of liability in negligence are well known and can be found elsewhere.[13]

There are, however, particular factual and legal problems thrown up in the med- **5.05** ical context which necessitate a separate account from the general principles of negligence (and professional) liability. A patient may have an action for breach of contract, in the tort of negligence[14] or for misrepresentation.[15]

B. Breach of Contract

1. Treatment under the National Health Service

(i) No Contractual Relationship

Historically,[16] the legal obligations of a doctor were derived from his status and **5.06** 'common calling', that is, to exercise the skill and diligence expected of his call-ing.[17] Whilst delictual in nature, it was recognised that an action in assumpsit and later contract lay against a doctor who treated a patient for payment.[18] Until the NHS was created in 1948, treatment was either provided privately or on a chari-able basis. However, even in the latter instance, when the patient provided no tan-

---

[10] Pursuant to the National Health Service and Community Care Act 1990, s 21. See the National Health Service (Clinical Negligence Scheme) Regulations 1996, SI 1996/251 (as amended).

[11] Discussed below, paras 8.88–8.101. The schemes only apply in England. In Wales, a cen-tralised 'risk pool' exists run by Wales Health.

[12] On which, see Powell, J and Stewart, R (eds), *Jackson and Powell on Professional Negligence* (5th edn, 2002); Dugdale, A and Stanton, K, *Professional Negligence* (3rd edn, 1995).

[13] eg, *Clerk & Lindsell on Torts* (18th edn, A Dugdale (ed), 2002); Grubb, A (ed), *The Law of Torts* (Butterworths Common Law Series, 2002).

[14] Other actions may include false imprisonment (where the patient is unlawfully restrained) or battery (where the touching is without consent or lawful justification). These torts are discussed in the context of consent and the competent (Ch 3 above) and the incompetent patient (Ch 4 above).

[15] Under the common law principle in *Hedley Byrne & Co Ltd v Heller & Partners Ltd* [1964] AC 465 or, under the Misrepresentation Act 1967, where the patient has been induced to enter into a contract for the provision of the medical services.

[16] See Teff, H, *Reasonable Care* (1995), 159–60 and 173–80 and references contained therein, and Picard, E and Robertson, G, *Legal Liability of Hospitals and Doctors in Canada* (3rd edn, 1996), 1–3.

[17] The first report case against a doctor is *The Surgeon's Case* (or *Morton's Case*) (1374) 48 Edw 11.

[18] *Everard v Hopkins* (1615) 80 ER 1164 and *Slater v Baker and Stapleton* (1767) 95 ER 860.

gible consideration, the courts held that the patient's submission to treatment was sufficient consideration for a contract.[19] Within the NHS today it is generally accepted that there is no contractual relationship between a doctor (whether general practitioner or hospital doctor) and the patient.[20] Equally, there is no contractual relationship between the patient and the hospital, such as the NHS Trust, where the patient is cared for. Any claim for damages based upon a breach of duty lies only in tort and, in particular, in an action for negligence.[21]

(ii) A Contrary Argument

5.07   The basis for the orthodoxy is twofold. First, medical services within the NHS are provided to the patient pursuant to a statutory obligation. Such compulsion to provide a service is considered to be inconsistent with a contractual arrangement.[22] Secondly, the patient fails to provide the consideration in return for the doctor (or other's) promise to treat which is necessary if a contract is to exist. This position is not, however, beyond challenge. The statutory context, for example within which a GP functions, is not necessarily inconsistent with a contractual arrangement.[23] Also, it could be argued, for example, that in the case of a GP consideration may indirectly be provided by the patient since his inclusion upon the doctor's medical list will result in remuneration being paid by the Health Authority to the doctor. Also, in the case of an NHS Trust, it could be argued again that the patient indirectly provides remuneration in cases where his treatment will generate distinct future (and not past) consideration from the NHS provider whether GP fund-holder or Health Authority. Treatment under an 'extra-contractual' referral most closely fits this description.

5.08   In the Canadian decision of *Pittman Estate v Bain*,[24] an Ontario court went even further and held that a contractual relationship existed between the patient and a hospital on the basis that the hospital received funding from the Government funded health insurance scheme. The patient indirectly contributed to this

---

[19] *Coggs v Bernard* (1703) 92 ER 107.

[20] Relying on *Pfizer Corporation v Ministry of Health* [1965] AC 512 (HL): medicines supplied under prescription not a 'sale' even if some payment is made. See now, *Reynolds v Health First Medical Group* [2000] Lloyd's Rep Med 240 (GP). See also Teff, *Reasonable Care* (n 16 above), 161–2 note 138 and Pearson Commission, *Civil Liability and Compensation for Personal Injury* (Cmnd 7054, 1978) para 1313.

[21] However, a duty may also arise under a contract between a doctor or health institution by virtue of a contractual arrangement if the treatment is provided outside the NHS and the requirements for a legally binding contract are satisfied: namely, (i) there is an intention to create legal relations; (ii) the parties have contractual capacity; (iii) the terms are certain or ascertainable; and (iv) there is consideration. On contractual actions in the medical context, see below.

[22] *Pfizer Corporation v Ministry of Health* (n 20 above).

[23] See *Roy v Kensington & Chelsea FPC* [1992] 1 All ER 705 (HL).

[24] (1994) 112 DLR (4th) 257 (Ont Gen Div); further reasons, (1994) 112 DLR (4th) 482, (1994) 112 DLR (4th) 494, and (1994) 35 CPC (3d) 67.

through taxes and health premiums. Further, the hospital obtained a benefit, both financial and in reputation, when patients chose to receive treatment.

However attractive in principle the arguments may appear, there is in truth no real **5.09** reason for an English court to divine a contract between the parties. A contractual claim would not, in most cases, affect the content of the legal rights and obligations of the parties. Even if the courts did determine that a contractual relationship existed, the scope of the duty owed to the patient is unlikely to be any different from that in the tort of negligence.[25]

Two factors tell against the Canadian approach. First, the structure of health care **5.10** provision within the 'internal market' of the NHS is antithetical to contractual arrangements; for example, the National Health Service and Community Care Act 1990 specifically states that agreements between 'commissioners' and 'providers' are not legally enforceable contracts.[26] While the 1990 Act does not deal with agreements with patients, the ethos of regulation of the NHS is *ex pactum*. Secondly, the statutory and regulatory context in which health services are provided may lead a court to infer that the parties had no intention to create legal relations in the form of a contract. In any event, the argument in *Pittman Estate* is most unlikely to be followed by an English court. It stretches the factual boundaries of what amounts to consideration almost to breaking point: the consideration is probably too remote. A recent case directly addressed these issues in relation to a general practitioner. In *Reynolds v The Health First Medical Group*[27] the claimant sued her GP for failing to advise her that she was pregnant and thereby depriving her of the opportunity to have an abortion. She sued for the costs of raising the child and for general damages arising out of the birth. Seeking to avoid the result in *McFarlane v Tayside Health Board*,[28] she sought to amend her claim to rely upon a contractual basis. The judge held that there was no contract between a GP and his patient.[29] He held that capitation payments to a GP for his NHS patients did not amount to consideration and that the statutory nature of the relationship negated any intention by the parties to enter into legal relations.

In the end, therefore, in England a contractual basis for the legal obligations of a **5.11** doctor or hospital is restricted to treatment which is provided privately. It is important to notice that private treatment is not exclusively provided outside NHS

---

[25] Subject to the express terms, the law will imply a duty to exercise reasonable care and skill identical to that imposed in the tort of negligence: *Thake v Maurice* [1986] QB 644 (CA); *Eyre v Measday* [1986] 1 All ER 488 (CA); Supply of Goods and Services Act 1982, s 13. See below, paras 5.20–5.21.

[26] s 4(3).

[27] [2000] Lloyd's Rep Med 240 (Judge Simmons).

[28] [2000] Lloyd's Rep Med 1 (HL), discussed below, Ch 12.

[29] The judge cited and relied upon paras 5.07 and 5.09–5.10 of the First Edition of this work.

facilities. To the extent that it is provided within the NHS in, for example, 'pay beds' then a contractual basis for the parties legal obligations will apply.[30]

2. Private Treatment

(i) Express Terms

5.12   When treatment or other health care is provided privately, a contractual relationship will arise between the doctor and the patient, and usually the clinic or institution and patient. The nature, scope, and terms of these contracts will depend upon the circumstances. Although there are a variety of ways in which contractual relationships may exist for private health care, commonly the patient will make separate arrangements with the doctor (for the treatment and aftercare) and with the clinic for the provision of facilities (such as the operating theatre) and staff (such as nurses). This will be the usual arrangement where the patient consults a doctor privately who then arranges for the patient to be treated at a clinic with which he (the doctor) has an agreement to admit patients. In other situations the arrangement may be directly with the clinic for the provision of the 'services' sought including the doctors who will carry out the procedure. There may, then, be no separate contractual arrangement with the doctor. Examples of this occur in cases of infertility treatment where the patient seeks treatment at an IVF clinic where particular doctors work.[31]

5.13   The terms of these contracts will primarily be a matter for agreement between the parties and then subsequently included expressly in the written contract, if one exists. Terms as to payment, the provision of facilities and staff will be common depending upon the circumstances. The consent form, if any, signed by the patient will form part of the contract.[32] The contract may also specify who is to be the treating doctor and, in such circumstances, it will be a breach of contract if another doctor treats the patient.[33] The obligations of the parties will, therefore, be a matter of construing the terms in the contract in each case, subject to the constraints of public policy.[34]

5.14   One question which has arisen is whether a doctor contractually guarantees the outcome of the treatment. Hence a patient might be able to claim when the treatment does not effect a cure or produce the intended result. An action would certainly be sustainable if the doctor failed to carry out the procedure at all, through

---

[30] Discussed in relation to 'vicarious liability' and 'primary duty', below, Ch 8.

[31] See, eg, *Thompson v Sheffield Fertility Clinic* (6 March 2001, QBD Hooper J).

[32] eg, *Thake v Maurice* (n 25 above) and *Eyre v Measday* (n 25 above).

[33] See *Morris v Winsbury-White* [1937] 4 All ER 494.

[34] eg, restricting liability: *Tunkl v Regents of the University of California* (1963) 383 P 2d 441 (Cal Sup Ct) and Unfair Contract Terms Act 1977, s 2(1). See also *Thompson v Sheffield Fertility Clinic* (n 31 above), discussed in Grubb (2001) 9 Med L Rev 170 (Commentary).

oversight or whatever.[35] The possibility of a contractual warranty action is important because no such duty arises in negligence: the only obligation of the doctor is to act reasonably. There is no doubt that a doctor may enter into a contractual guarantee.[36] However, in order to do so, he must use explicit and unequivocal words such as 'I guarantee you will be cured', 'I will guarantee to make the hand a 100 per cent perfect hand'[37] or 'I assure you will never have children again—you will be infertile'. Absent words of this nature forming part of the contract, the courts will not usually construe contractual terms as amounting to a guarantee of success.

The US case of *Guilmet v Campbell*[38] illustrates the lengths to which a doctor must go before he warrants an outcome for a patient. The doctor treated the claimant for a bleeding ulcer. Prior to the operation the doctor told the patient: **5.15**

> Once you have an operation it takes care of all your troubles. You can eat as you want to, you can drink as you want to, you can go as you please . . . there is nothing to it at all—it's a very simple operation. You'll be out of work three to four weeks at most. There is no danger at all in this operation. After the operation you can throw away your pill box.[39]

Unfortunately, the claimant suffered serious physical after-effects. The Michigan Supreme Court upheld a jury verdict in the claimant's favour that the defendant had contractually guaranteed to cure his peptic ulcer. The court emphasised that it was not saying that a doctor necessarily contracted to produce a cure in these circumstances[40] but rather that there was sufficient evidence for the jury to conclude:

> that the doctor made a specific, clear and express promise to cure or effect a specific result which was in the reasonable contemplation of [the doctors] and the claimant which was relied upon by the claimant.[41]

The leading English decision concerned with a guarantee of cure or an effect is *Thake v Maurice*.[42] The claimants, a married couple, consulted the defendant, a surgeon, privately in order for the husband to undergo a vasectomy as they did not wish to have any more children. The defendant explained the procedure to the claimants and he pointed out that although it was possible to restore the husband's fertility he could not guarantee it, and that the claimants should regard the   **5.16**

---

[35] See, eg, *Zehr v Haughen* (1994) 871 P 2d 1006 (Ore Sup Ct): action for breach of contract held to be sustainable where doctor had failed to carry out the sterilisation operation he had contracted to undertake.

[36] See *Thompson v Sheffield Fertility Clinic* (n 31 above), where it was accepted that it was a breach of contract to return three embryos to an IVF patient when she had only agreed to the return of two.

[37] *Hawkins v McGhee* (1929) 146 A 641 (NH).

[38] (1971) 188 NW 2d 601 (Mich Sup Ct). For the US cases, see *Annotation*, 99 ALR 3d 303.

[39] ibid, 606.

[40] ibid, *per* Kavanagh J.

[41] ibid, 607 *per* Kavanagh J.

[42] [1986] QB 644; [1986] 1 All ER 479 (CA). See Grubb, A, [1986] CLJ 197.

operation as permanent. The claimants signed a consent form which stated, inter alia, 'I have been told that the object of the operation is to render me sterile and incapable of parenthood. I understand that the effect of the operation is irreversible.' The operation was carried out and appeared successful. However, almost three years later, the wife discovered that she was pregnant. The operation had naturally reversed itself by a process known as late recanalisation and the husband's fertility had been restored. Subsequently, a child was born and the claimants sued the defendant in negligence and for breach of contract.[43] The claimants claimed that they had not been warned of the risk of reversal and that this was negligent. Further they claimed a breach of contract in that the defendant had guaranteed the success of the operation namely, the husband's infertility. Peter Pain J held the defendant had not, in fact, warned the claimants of the small risk of reversal. He was liable in negligence for this. Also, Peter Pain J held that the defendant was liable in contract as he had given a contractual warranty of success. The Court of Appeal unanimously upheld the judge on the negligence ground but, by a majority,[44] reversed him on the contract claim.

5.17 Emphasising the inexact nature of medical science and unpredictability of medical treatment, Nourse and Neill LJJ held that a doctor would only be held to have guaranteed the success of an operation if he expressly said so in clear and unequivocal terms.[45] Neither the circumstances of the case, nor the use of the word 'irreversible' could lead the court to reach the conclusion that the defendant had guaranteed the husband's sterility.[46] The defendant had only contracted to exercise reasonable care and skill, which he breached by failing to warn the claimants of the risk of reversal as was his normal practice. Nourse LJ said:[47]

> a professional man is not usually regarded as warranting that he will achieve the desired result. Indeed, it seems that that would not fit well with the universal warranty of reasonable care and skill, which tends to affirm the inexactness of the science which is professed. I do not intend to go beyond the case of the doctor. Of all sciences medicine is one of the least exact. In my view a doctor cannot be objectively regarded as guaranteeing the success of any operation or treatment unless he says as much in clear and unequivocal terms.

Neill LJ agreed, adding that while both the claimants and the defendant expected that sterility would result, that:[48]

---

[43] For a discussion of the 'failed sterilisation' cases: see below, Ch 12.
[44] Nourse and Neill LJJ, Kerr LJ dissenting.
[45] N 42 above, at 511–512 and 510 respectively.
[46] Likewise, therefore, it cannot amount to a misrepresentation so as to found a claim for negligent misrepresentation on the basis of *Hedley Byrne*: see *Gold v Haringay HA* [1988] QB 481; [1987] 2 All ER 888 (CA) at 895–896 *per* Lloyd LJ. See also *Worster v City & Hackney HA*, The Times, 22 June 1987.
[47] N 42 above, 512.
[48] ibid, 510.

does not mean, however, that a reasonable person would have understood the defendant to be giving a binding promise that the operation would achieve its purpose or that the defendant was going further than to give an assurance that he expected and believed that it would have the desired result.

In the *Thake* case all the judges accepted that in some circumstances a guarantee **5.18** of success might be understood from the words used by a doctor.[49] Nourse LJ postulated that a reasonable person might do this where 'the general experience of mankind' was that a particular outcome would, as a matter of fact, result from a procedure. He instanced a surgical procedure to amputate a limb.[50] Nourse LJ contrasted this situation with one 'where an operation is of modern origin, its effects untried over several generations'.[51] There, a reasonable person, even faced with apparently clear and straightforward assurances would not believe that a guarantee of success was being given. In reality, virtually every medical treatment and procedure will fall into the latter, rather than the former, category. As a result, there is little mileage in couching a claim in contract. It will be a wholly exceptional set of facts where the claimant will be able to persuade a court that the doctor was guaranteeing an outcome.

An example of such a case arose in Canada in respect of cosmetic surgery. In **5.19** *LaFleur v Cornelis*[52] the defendant, a cosmetic surgeon performed a procedure to reduce the size of the claimant's nose. He failed to inform her that there was a 10 per cent risk of scarring. She was, in fact, scarred. Barry J held the defendant liable in negligence and for breach of contract. He distinguished between 'an ordinary physician' and a cosmetic surgeon.[53] The defendant had told the claimant what she needed done, had drawn a diagram of what he would do and how she would look and had said: 'no problem. You will be very happy.'[54] Barry J concluded that this, in the light of his failure to warn of the risk of scarring, amounted to a warranty of success. While other courts have similarly regarded cosmetic surgeons, it is not at all clear that English law would follow them. The uncertainties of such surgery are surely no less, usually, than any other. Not every client can be made to look perfect! Absent an undertaking to make the claimant 'stunningly beautiful', 'handsome beyond words', or 'drop-dead gorgeous', even in this context it is suggested that all the surgeon undertakes (as viewed through the eyes of Nourse LJ's perceptive reasonable person) is to exercise reasonable care and skill.

---

[49] See also, ibid, *per* Kerr LJ at 505.
[50] ibid, 511. Kerr LJ, dissenting, considered the instant case as involving 'something in the nature of an amputation', ibid, 505.
[51] ibid.
[52] (1979) 28 NBR (2d) 569 (QB).
[53] ibid, 577.
[54] ibid.

(ii) Implied Terms

5.20 More important in practical terms are the terms *implied* in the contract between doctor (or hospital) and patient. The law implies terms in respect of services or goods provided to patients. Many of these obligations are statutory and cannot be excluded: such as those implied by the Supply of Goods and Services Act 1982 in relation to 'fitness for purpose' and 'satisfactory quality' where goods alone are supplied or together with services, for example, a prosthesis, vaccine, or medicinal product.[55] Further, the law will imply an obligation to respect a patient's confidences which, of course, would otherwise arise by virtue of an equitable obligation alone.[56]

5.21 In the context of medical negligence, the important term that the law implies into the contract is, in the case of doctors, to exercise reasonable care and skill when diagnosing, advising and treating[57] and, in the case of hospitals, for example, in the provision of staff and facilities.[58] These are the very same obligations implied generally in the contracts of other professions and are indistinguishable from the duty of care in the tort of negligence.[59] Hence, in two cases[60] where the patients underwent a sterilisation operation, the Court of Appeal held that the contract between the doctor and patient had implied into it a duty to exercise reasonable care and skill in carrying out the operation. In *Eyre v Measday*,[61] the Court of Appeal concluded that a warranty of success would not be implied where the doctor had stated that the procedure would be 'irreversible'. No 'intelligent lay bystander' would reasonably infer that the defendant was guaranteeing sterility.[62]

C. Negligence: Duty of Care

5.22 Actions for breach of contract will be the exception in the medical context. Where a patient is injured allegedly as a result of a doctor's negligence by far the most common basis for a claim will be in the tort of negligence. The claimant (patient) must establish:

---

[55] See below, Ch 15.

[56] eg, *W v Egdell* [1990] Ch 359 (CA). For a discussion of 'confidentiality', see below, Ch 9.

[57] *Greaves & Co (Contractors) Ltd v Baynham Meikle & Partners* [1975] 3 All ER 99, 103–104 *per* Lord Denning MR.

[58] There appears to be no English case. For a Canadian case in which a hospital was held to have impliedly contracted to exercise reasonable care in providing a safe system of work, see *Osburn v Mohindra* (1980) 29 NBR (2d) 340 (QB). The obligations would be identical to those imposed in the tort of negligence, on which, see below, Ch 8.

[59] Thus little, if anything, turns upon whether the patient pleads the 'negligence' in tort or contract. Indeed, the patient may sue in both tort and contract: see, eg, *Thake v Maurice* (n 42 above).

[60] *Thake v Maurice* (n 42 above); *Eyre v Measday* [1986] 1 All ER 488.

[61] ibid.

[62] ibid, 495 *per* Slade LJ.

(i)   that a duty of care was owed to him by the defendant (health professional or hospital[63]);
(ii) that the defendant was in breach of that duty by not exercising reasonable care and skill;[64] and
(iii) that the breach of duty caused damage, namely the injuries suffered by the patient and that damage was not too remote.[65]

Beyond these—which constitute the legal elements of a claim for medical negligence—there may arise issues concerned with defences to the action,[66] for example, limitation and also calculations of the quantum of damages.[67]

When will a doctor or other health professional owe a duty of care to another?[68]   **5.23**
Usually, this question will not give rise to any difficulty in a medical negligence case. It will be obvious, and accepted, that a duty was owed to the claimant who is the doctor's patient. The real issues in the case will revolve around, for example, breach and causation. There will, however, be problems where the doctor–patient relationship has not been forged fully or at all, for example, where the doctor is employed by another such as an insurance company or a prospective employer to examine the claimant or is a third party who suffers injury as a result of the doctor's negligence (for example, a total stranger injured by the patient or a relative of the patient). Also, legal problems arise where the injury suffered by the patient (or other) is not personal injury arising out of the treatment but rather financial loss or psychiatric harm.

1. To Patients

It may seem blindingly obvious that a doctor owes a duty of care to his patients.[69]   **5.24**
It is a duty to exercise reasonable care and skill in diagnosing, advising and treating the patient.[70] The duty is the same regardless of the experience of the doctor, being instead, as a matter of public policy, tailored to the task that he undertakes and the specialty he professes.[71] Consequently, inexperience is not a defence to a

---

[63] Discussed in Ch 8.
[64] Discussed in Ch 6.
[65] Discussed in Ch 7.
[66] Discussed in Ch 7.
[67] For quantum of damages in general, see McGregor, H (ed), *McGregor on Damages* (17th edn, 2003); and in respect of medical negligence claims, Jones, *Medical Negligence* (n 3 above), ch 9.
[68] See also Kennedy and Grubb, *Medical Law* (n 2 above), 369–92. For 'institutional liability' see below, Ch 8.
[69] For a discussion of who are a general practitioner's patients, see above, Ch 1.
[70] *Sidaway v Bethlem Royal Hospital Governors* [1985] AC 871; [1985] 1 All 643, 657 *per* Lord Diplock, describing it as a 'single comprehensive duty covering all the ways in which a doctor is called on to exercise his skill and judgment in the improvement of the physical or mental condition of the patient'.
[71] *Maynard v West Midlands RHA* [1984] 1 WLR 634 (HL), 638 *per* Lord Scarman.

medical negligence action.[72] An action in negligence lies for a breach of this duty which causes injury. The basis for this duty is an 'undertaking' of care of the person as a patient.[73] An undertaking of care may be expressly made by the doctor or implied by the law arising out of the circumstances. As long ago as 1957 Nathan[74] put it as follows:

> The medical man's duty of care arises . . . quite independently of any contract with his patient. It is based simply upon the fact that the medical man *undertakes the care and treatment of the patient.*

Later Nathan stated that the doctor's duty arises because he has 'assumed responsibility for the care, treatment or examination of the patient'.[75] The language of 'undertaking' and 'assumption of responsibility' reflects the modern approach of the courts when imposing positive duties of care, particularly upon professionals.[76] In general the duty will stem from the doctor's voluntary agreement to 'care for' or 'treat' the person.[77] This will, in turn, lead the law to characterise the doctor's conduct as amounting to 'an assumption of responsibility' to the person. It is important to notice that for a duty to exist, there need be no reciprocation of agreement by the patient. A doctor will equally owe a duty of care to an incompetent adult, for example, an unconscious patient in an Accident and Emergency (A & E) department, or young child brought to his surgery who is too young to consent and whom he examines.[78]

5.25   The same analysis applies to other health care professionals, such as nurses, who come into contact with a patient: the crucial issue being whether that professional has assumed responsibility by undertaking the 'care' of the person.[79]

---

[72] *Wilsher v Essex AHA* [1987] QB 730 (CA); the point was not raised in the House of Lords. For a discussion, see below, Ch 6.

[73] *Jones v Manchester Corporation* [1952] QB 852, 867 *per* Denning LJ (referring to the liability of the hospital). See also *Cassidy v Ministry of Health* [1951] 2 KB 343, 360 *per* Denning LJ. On the latter, see below, Ch 8. See also, *R v Bateman* (1925) 94 LJKB 791, 794 per Lord Hewart CJ.

[74] Nathan, H, *Medical Negligence* (1957), 8 (emphasis added).

[75] ibid, 10.

[76] See, eg, *White v Jones* [1995] 2 AC 207 (HL); *Henderson v Merrett Syndicates Ltd* [1995] 2 AC 145 (HL); *Capital and Counties plc v Hampshire County Council* [1997] 2 All ER 865 (CA), especially *per* Stuart-Smith LJ at 883 *et seq*; *Kirkham v Chief Constable of Greater Manchester Police* [1990] 2 QB 283 (CA).

[77] See *Capital and Counties plc v Hampshire County Council* (n 76 above), 883 and 884 *per* Stuart-Smith LJ.

[78] *Re F (Mental Patient: Sterilisation)* [1990] 2 AC 1 (HL), 56 *per* Lord Brandon and at 77 *per* Lord Goff.

[79] See *Barnett v Chelsea and Kensington HMC* [1969] 1 QB 428: nurse in casualty department owed duty to claimant when he presented himself complaining of illness. Of course, she was not in breach of her duty because she contacted the duty doctor. See also *Junor v McNicol*, The Times, 11 February 1959 (HL) (house surgeon not negligent acting on instructions of consultant); *Wilsher v Essex AHA* [1987] QB 730 (CA) (house officer not negligent as sought opinion of registrar).

(i) General Practitioners

(a) In General

A general practitioner's patients are determined by the Terms of Service contained **5.26**
in Sch 2 to the National Health Service (General Medical Services) Regulations
1992[80] or under the Directions dealing with pilot schemes.[81] The National Health
Service (Choice of Medical Practitioner) Regulations 1998[82] set out the procedure
whereby an individual may request, and a doctor may accept that person, onto his
'list' of patients.[83] Hence, a GP's patients include individuals recorded by the
Primary Care Trust (PCT) as being on the doctor's 'list', those accepted by the
doctor on his 'list' even if the PCT has not been notified and those assigned to him
by the PCT. In addition, in some circumstances an individual may be a GP's
patient under the Regulations even where he has not been accepted by the doctor
or, even, where he has been removed from the doctor's 'list'. The Regulations set
out a range of duties imposed upon the doctor, including, providing 'personal
medical services', relating to visits, prescribing etc.[84]

Undoubtedly, the obligations imposed by the 1992 Regulations will guide the **5.27**
courts in determining the scope and content of the doctor's duty at common law,
though they will not be determinative or exclusive. They will, for example, be crucial in reaching a view on whether a GP was negligent. However, it does not follow that just because the Regulations impose a duty on a GP, that a duty of care
will arise at common law. The 1992 Regulations set out the situations whereby the
formal relationship of doctor–patient is created. It would be artificial to state that
a GP owes all the patients, for example, on his 'list' a duty of care at all times. Apart
from the initial meeting, the GP may never see or hear from the patient subsequently. A GP, in general, only owes his 'formal' patient a duty of care *at common
law* when he has knowledge (actual or constructive) of the circumstances which
trigger his obligations under the 1992 Regulations. Thus, without a direct or indirect request for 'care' from the patient, the GP does not owe a duty of care.[85] It
will be different where the obligation under the 1992 Regulations is a continuing

---

[80] SI 1992/635, as amended.

[81] Directions to Health Authorities Concerning the Implementation of Pilot Schemes (Personal
Medical Services) 1998.

[82] SI 1998/668, as amended.

[83] For a discussion, see Kennedy and Grubb, *Medical Law* (n 2 above), 77–88.

[84] N 82 above, paras 12 and 13 (general); para 14 (newly registered patients); para 15 (patients
not seen for three years); para 16 (patients aged 75 and over).

[85] An alternative analysis would be that the duty always exists and the doctor's knowledge (actual
or constructive) is relevant only to the issue of breach of duty. Perhaps it makes no difference in practice which analysis is correct. However, it is suggested that the better one is that postulated in the
text. See, eg, analogous situations in relation to a landowner's duty to his neighbours for the state of
his premises: *Goldman v Hargrave* [1967] 1 AC 645 (PC) and *Smith v Littlewoods Organisation*
[1987] AC 241 (HL), 272–273 *per* Lord Goff.

one or one that imposes a responsibility upon the GP to seek out the patient. An example of this arises in relation to patients aged 75 or over who should be offered an annual consultation.[86] A GP who fails to do this could be liable in negligence if it is shown that his failure was negligent and caused injury (or death) to the patient. It is irrelevant that the patient did not request a consultation.

5.28 Also, the Regulations are not determinative of when a duty of care ceases to a particular patient. The Regulations set out the circumstances in which a doctor may terminate the relationship to his patient, in general[87] or because the patient is violent.[88] Merely by complying with this procedure does not necessarily terminate the doctor's duty of care *at common law*. First, the Regulations themselves contemplate a continuing obligation to provide treatment which is 'immediately necessary' when requested by a patient who is not yet on another doctor's 'list'.[89] Secondly, the GP continues to owe his (former) patient a duty at common law until such time as it is reasonable for that treatment to be taken over by another doctor. The common law will not allow a GP to 'abandon' his (former) patient. A duty of care continues until such time as it is reasonable for it to cease although, of course, the content of that duty may be different in the circumstances, for example, where the patient behaves violently towards the doctor.[90]

(b) Deputies and Others

5.29 Sometimes a GP's patients will be treated by another doctor, for example, a locum whilst the GP is away on holidays. More frequently, the workload of GPs is such that they often use deputies to cover for them at night. The Terms of Service allow for this practice where it is reasonable to do so.[91] Will a GP be liable for the acts (or omissions) of a deputy? Under the Terms of Service, a GP is not accountable for a deputy who is on the Medical List of a PCT (whether that of the GP or another): the deputy alone is responsible.[92] By contrast, a GP remains responsible for a deputy who is not on a PCT's Medical List.[93] Of course, the Terms of Service are only explicitly concerned with the GP's obligations *vis à vis* his PCT. What is the extent of the GP's duty of care at common law? Is he liable for the acts and omis-

---

[86] SI 1992/635 (as amended), Sch 2, para 16.

[87] ibid, Sch 2, para 9.

[88] ibid, para 9A, inserted by National Health Service (General Medical Services) Amendment Regulations 1994, SI 1994/633, reg 8(4).

[89] N 86 above, para 4(4) as substituted by SI 1994/633, reg 8(2). The obligation is to do so for 14 days or until the person finds another GP.

[90] That an obligation to continue to provide 'immediately necessary treatment' exists is made explicit: ibid, para 4(4)(c) as inserted by SI 1994/633, reg 8(2).

[91] National Health Service (General Medical Services) Regulations 1992, SI 1992/635 (as amended), Sch 2, paras 18–26.

[92] ibid, combined effect of para 20(1) and (2).

[93] ibid.

sions of his deputy? The position is not free from doubt.[94] If the deputy were his employee, then the GP would be liable on the basis of vicarious liability.[95] However, this is doubtful as the deputy is likely to be an independent contractor.[96] To the extent that the GP has already 'undertaken' the care of the patient—that is, gone beyond the formal relationship under the Regulations—then the GP will be liable for the deputy's conduct to the extent that he (the GP) is personally in breach of his duty of care. Hence, if the GP was at fault in selecting a competent deputy or in providing the deputy with adequate information about the patient, the GP could be liable in negligence.[97] However, providing there was no fault of this kind, the GP could not be liable for the negligence of the deputy unless, as a matter of law, the GP is under a non-delegable duty to ensure that care is taken of his patient. It is rare for the common law to impose such a duty which does not look to the personal fault of the defendant but of another and, rather like the devise of vicarious liability, nevertheless places responsibility on the defendant for the fault of another.[98] While this has never been decided in England, it is arguable that the GP's duty is non-delegable. The statutory context in which care is provided under the NHS by GPs is that patients look to the personal care of that individual. Everyone who is registered with a GP is registered with a particular doctor. The deputy will not be associated with the patient's GP or his practice. While delegation to another doctor within a partnership or practice is reasonable and leaves the patient with some assurance of continuity of care, delegation to outsiders lacks this quality. The law would go some way to redress this imbalance by recognising the non-delegability of the GP's duty of care in such cases.

A somewhat similar set of arguments arise where the GP delegates to another, but not a deputy, the performance of a procedure within his surgery or practice. For example, a nurse carries out an examination or administers an injection on the doctor's behalf. In these circumstances, the GP will be vicariously liable for the negligence of the practice nurse (or whoever) who is his employee.[99] In any event, as the arguments in the preceding paragraph show, the GP may be in breach of *his* duty of care if he is personally at fault, for example, by unreasonably delegating a task to a nurse or other. Equally, it was argued that the law might impose upon a GP a non-delegable duty which would entail liability for the negligent acts and omissions of others acting on his behalf, such as nurses. **5.30**

---

[94] See also below, para 8.12.
[95] See ibid.
[96] See ibid.
[97] ibid.
[98] See discussion below, paras 8.24 *et seq.*
[99] See below, para 8.12.

(c) In Emergencies

5.31 Unlike continental legal systems, English law is chary of imposing positive duties upon individuals.[100] As a consequence, doctors are generally not required to act as 'good Samaritans', going to the aid of others who appear to require medical assistance even in emergency situations.[101] There is no legal duty on a doctor to answer the call 'Is there a doctor in the house?'[102] Doctors who come upon an accident may legally 'pass on the other side', though their conduct if it came to the attention of the General Medical Council might lead to disciplinary action.[103] English law, as ever, looks for an 'undertaking' of care or an express or implied assumption of responsibility by the doctor: what has been described as the 'acceptance of a patient as a patient'.[104] Uniquely, in the case of GPs, the Terms of Service may create a doctor–patient relationship (in the formal sense) between a GP and the victim of an accident.[105] The Regulations contemplate *two* situations.[106]

5.32 First, a GP who is requested to give treatment which is 'immediately required' to a person involved in an accident or other emergency in his practice area, must do so. There are further conditions, such as the GP must be 'available to provide such treatment', but providing these are satisfied failure to provide the treatment will put him in breach of his Terms of Service and liable to disciplinary action by the PCT. Secondly, where the accident or other emergency, though not in his practice area, is in the locality of his PCT, he must provide treatment which is 'immediately required' if requested *and he agrees* to do so. The obligation only arises if the victim does not have a GP to provide the treatment or, if he does, he has been requested to provide it but is 'unable to attend'. Consequently, before the obligation in this latter situation comes into existence, the GP must, in effect, be the only (or only reasonably) available GP and, of course, he must *agree* to provide the treatment.

---

[100] See, eg, *Smith v Littlewoods Organisation* [1987] AC 241, 271 *per* Lord Goff. See generally, Markesinis, B, 'Negligence, Nuisance and Affirmative Duties of Action' (1989) 105 LQR 104.

[101] See *Capital and Counties plc v Hampshire County Council* [1997] 2 All ER 865 (CA), 883 *per* Stuart-Smith LJ.

[102] *Re F (Mental Patient: Sterilisation)* [1990] 2 AC 1, 77–78 per Lord Goff.

[103] As 'serious professional misconduct' under the Medical Act 1983, s 35. See GMC, *Duties of A Doctor (Good Medical Practice)* (2001), para 9: 'In an emergency, wherever it may arise, you must offer anyone at risk the assistance you could reasonably be expected to provide.' Indeed, medical altruism may be alive and well in England, see Williams, K, 'Doctors as Good Samaritans: Some Empirical Evidence Concerning Emergency Medical Treatment in Britain' (2003) JLS 258.

[104] *Watson v British Boxing Board of Control Ltd* [2001] 1 WLR 1256 (CA), 1269 *per* Lord Phillips MR.

[105] National Health Service (General Medical Services) Regulations 1992, SI 1992/635 (as amended), Sch 2, para 4(1)(h).

[106] See Kennedy and Grubb, *Medical Law* (n 2 above), 81.

The Terms of Service are not conclusive of the existence or scope of a duty of care **5.33** at common law. Clearly, the second situation involves an 'undertaking' or 'assumption of responsibility' by the doctor and would, on this basis alone, be sufficient for the doctor to owe a duty of care to the victim. However, the common law may go further and reflect the fact that a GP at a site of an accident or emergency within his practice area has *impliedly* assumed a responsibility towards the victim because of his Terms of Service. By contrast, it is unlikely that a GP owes such a duty if he were elsewhere in the country and happened upon an accident: to impose a duty of care here would be to make the doctor a 'good Samaritan' quite contrary to the general approach of English law.

An important Australian case raises the possibility that the common law in **5.34** England might contemplate a duty arising where a doctor is requested in a professional context to provide advice or treatment.[107] In *Lowns v Woods*,[108] the claimant was an 11-year-old boy with a history of epileptic seizures. Whilst on holiday, one morning his mother returned from a walk to find him undergoing a seizure. She sent another of her sons to get an ambulance and her daughter to get a doctor. About five minutes later she arrived at the defendant's surgery. Although it was disputed, the trial judge[109] (Badgery-Parker J) found that the daughter explained the situation and asked the defendant to come but he refused telling her to bring the claimant to him. By the time she returned to her mother, the ambulance had arrived and the claimant was taken to hospital. Unfortunately, the claimant suffered profound brain damage and was quadriplegic as a result of the uncontrolled seizure. It was claimed, inter alia, by the claimant that the defendant was under a duty of care, which included an obligation to attend him, and if he had the defendant would have administered Valium which would have controlled the seizure and prevented his injuries.

By a majority,[110] the New South Wales Court of Appeal upheld the trial judge's **5.35** ruling that the defendant owed the claimant a duty of care. The essence of the court's ruling is stated by Cole JA:[111]

> Dr Lowns accepted that injury ('damage') to a fitting child was foreseeable if he, once requested, did not attend to treat the child. There was obvious physical proximity, for Joanna [the daughter] had come on foot. There also existed an adequate 'circumstantial proximity' in the sense that Dr Lowns was a medical practitioner to whom a direct request for assistance was made in circumstances where, on the evidence presented, there was no reasonable impediment or circumstance diminishing

---

[107] For a discussion of the case and arguments in favour of a duty to treat, see, Williams, K, 'Medical Samaritans: Is there a Duty to Treat?' (2001) 21 OJLS 393.

[108] [1996] Aust Torts Reports 81-376 (NSW CA). Discussed in Haberfield, L, (1998) 6 Tort L Rev 56 and Mendelson, D (1996) 4 Tort L Rev 242.

[109] (1995) 36 NSWLR 344 (NSW Sup Ct).

[110] Kirby P and Cole JA; Mahoney JA dissenting.

[111] N 108 above.

his capacity or indicating significant or material inconvenience or difficulty in him responding to the request, in circumstances where he knew . . . that serious harm could occur to [the claimant] if he did not respond to the request and provide treatment.

5.36   Cole JA also relied on the terms of s 27(2) of the Medical Practitioners Act 1938 which imposed a professional obligation (enforceable through disciplinary proceedings) upon a doctor to attend when requested to do so a person in need of urgent medical attention. While the wording of s 27(2) differs from a GP's Terms of Service, reliance upon it by the court is significant and there is no reason to doubt that an English court would look to the Terms of Service for guidance. However, the decision is a limited one. The doctor had been requested to provide treatment and had refused. It was accepted (even by him) that in these circumstances he ought to do so and it was not inconvenient or otherwise unreasonable for him to attend. Whether the case can be seen as going much further is not clear.[112] Certainly, Cole JA approved the view of Badgery-Parker J that, in general, a doctor had no duty to rescue another.[113] The trial judge had, nevertheless, been influenced by an argument that a doctor 'in a professional context' should respond to requests for urgent help.[114] The defendant was at his surgery when asked for help. The Court of Appeal did not deal with this point but nothing in the judgment of Cole JA (or of Kirby P) rejected Badgery-Parker J's approach. At least, then, it could be argued that a doctor who is requested to provide help or, even if not, but finds himself 'in a professional context', may have to volunteer help or be liable in negligence. Driving past an accident on the way to the shops with your family is one thing; momentarily stopping at an accident in a car marked 'doctor on call' before driving on, is quite another. English law may well impose a duty of care in the latter situation regardless of the precise requirements of the GP's Terms of Service.

5.37   A related, though distinct, point concerns the scope of the GP's duty if he does render help. Properly understood, this must be a matter of what a 'reasonable doctor' would do (or not do) in the circumstances. It is not a question of whether a duty of care exists but rather a question of whether there has been a breach of duty and, therefore, ultimately a matter for determination in each case. No a priori generally applicable statement of the doctor's obligations can be made. In the particular circumstances, a reasonable doctor might only provide temporary relief, such

---

[112] In particular, it would not, it is suggested, be extended to other doctors who happened upon an accident notwithstanding the wording of the GMC's advice, cited above (n 103). It has been suggested that in Canada the law might go further: see Picard and Robertson, *Legal Liability of Doctors and Hospitals in Canada* (n 16 above), 9–10.

[113] N 108 above, referring to (1995) 36 NSWLR 344, 354.

[114] N 109 above, 357–8. Citing English academic authority, inter alia, Jones, M, *Medical Negligence* (1991), para 2.21 and Kennedy and Grubb, *Medical Law* (2nd edn, 1994), 79.

as stemming the flow of blood. In other circumstances, he might have to go further and provide more treatment for the victim. In a number of cases, however, one Court of Appeal judge has in obiter statements suggested that the doctor's 'only duty as a matter of law is not to make the victim's condition worse'.[115] There is no basis for stating this as matter of law and there is no English authority for so limiting the content of the doctor's duty.[116] A doctor who allows a road accident victim to die by failing to deal with his injuries does not make the victim's condition 'worse'—assuming he would have died without immediate treatment. Yet, there can be no doubt that medical evidence will in many circumstances suggest that the doctor could reasonably have done something to *improve, or prevent a deterioration in,* the victim's condition. Such a doctor is in breach of his duty to act reasonably in preventing foreseeable injury to the victim and should be liable in negligence.[117]

(ii) Hospital Doctors

Hospital doctors working within an NHS Trust are in a different position to GPs. **5.38**
The 1992 Regulations do not apply to them. Their employment structure is different and there is normally an employment relationship. A patient who is admitted to a hospital under the care of a particular consultant will be owed a duty of care by that consultant. He will have 'undertaken' the care of that patient. Equally all those in the consultant's 'team', or 'firm' as it is often known, will owe a duty to the patient as soon as they individually 'undertake' the patient's care. When this happens will depend upon the circumstances but would not necessarily require a 'laying on of hands'. The consultant will, at all times, remain legally responsible for the patient's care. He cannot delegate it to another but given the 'team' nature of hospital care in the modern age, it may well be reasonable for him to leave the

---

[115] *Capital and Counties plc v Hampshire County Council* [1997] 2 All ER 865 (CA) *per* Stuart-Smith LJ at 883. See further, *Powell v Boladz* (1997) 39 BMLR 35 (CA) *per* Stuart-Smith LJ at 45: 'only a duty not to make the condition of the victim worse' and *Phelps v Hillingdon London Borough Council* (1998) 46 BMLR 100 (CA) *per* Stuart-Smith LJ at 122: 'The extent of the duty is not negligently to create further danger or make the claimant's situation worse.'

[116] Reference was made to the Canadian decision of the *Ogopogo* [1970] 1 Lloyd's Rep 257 (Ont CA); [1971] 2 Lloyd's Rep 410 (Can Sup Ct). This case did not involve a rescue by a professional but rather, the private owner of a boat whose guest fell overboard. The decision of the Ontario Court of Appeal (the point being left open in the Supreme Court) may be seen as being concerned with the standard of care expected of a rescuer, in effect, not requiring more than not to make the situation worse. Whilst it is obviously correct that less may be expected in an emergency, perhaps even of professionals, it is not at all clear why professional rescuers such as firemen, police, or doctors are given the benefit of the lower duty. In the US, all but one of the state legislatures have sought to exclude physician liability (or limit it to cases of 'gross negligence') in emergency situations through so-called 'Good Samaritan' statutes: see Furrow, B, Greaney, T, Johnson, S, Jost, T and Schwartz, R, *Health Law* (2nd edn, 2000), Vol 1, 297–9 and *Annotation*, 68 ALR 4th 294. For Canada see Picard and Robertson, *Legal Liability of Doctors and Hospitals in Canada* (n 16 above), 178–80.

[117] See, *Kent v Griffiths (No 2)* [2000] Lloyd's Rep Med 109 (CA) *per* Lord Woolf MR at [19] (ambulance service is not equivalent to a volunteer).

patient, at any one time, in the immediate care of a team member whether doctor or other health care professional. He cannot be liable for their acts of negligence as there is no employment relationship giving rise to vicarious liability.[118] Of course, he may be in breach of his own duty if he has entrusted the care to an in-appropriate 'team' member who, for instance, lacks experience or competence. Equally, he may be in breach of his duty if he unreasonably fails to provide any, or adequate, instructions to his 'team' or supervision of its more junior members.[119] These issues are, however, related to breach of his duty rather than to its existence.

5.39 More problematic is the question of the point at which a hospital doctor comes under a duty of care, if at all, prior to a patient's admission.[120] Could a patient who collapses in the A & E department of a hospital claim in negligence against the doctor on duty? The answer depends upon whether an express or implied under-taking of care has been given by the doctor. The only relevant English authority is *Barnett v Chelsea and Kensington HMC*.[121] The deceased, along with two work-mates, drank some tea and began vomiting. They went to the casualty department of the defendant's hospital. The deceased lay down and looked ill. One of the other men told the nurse on duty what had happened. She telephoned the doctor on duty who, being unwell himself, did not see the deceased but told the nurse to send them home and call their own doctors. Some hours later, the deceased died from arsenic poisoning. Nield J dismissed the action on the basis that even if the doctor had seen them, that would have made no difference because an effective antidote could not have been administered in time. Thus, any negligence had not caused the death. However, on the issue of whether the doctor and nurse owed the deceased a duty of care, Nield J concluded that they did because there was a 'close and direct relationship' between them.[122] Of course, in *Barnett* there is no doubt that both the nurse and doctor assumed a responsibility to the deceased by help-ing and advising him. The latter, but not the former, was patently negligent in not seeing, examining and admitting the deceased to hospital. Thus, on its facts the case is unexceptional.

5.40 What the *Barnett* case does not determine is whether the doctor will be under a duty of care if he simply refuses to have anything to do with the deceased. There will, in these circumstances, be no express assumption of responsibility of the care of the individual. However, as was suggested earlier a GP 'in a professional

---

[118] See below, para 8.05, n 45 (nurses).

[119] eg, *Wilsher* (n 79 above).

[120] For a discussion of the hospital's duty, see below, Ch 8. For a case concerned with the liability of an ambulance authority, see, *Kent v Griffiths (No 2)* (n 117 above).

[121] [1969] 1 QB 428; [1968] 1 All ER 1068.

[122] ibid, 1072. The judgment is not entirely clear and he may have been concerned primarily with the hospital's duty to the deceased. Later he speaks of 'a close and direct relationship between the hospital' and the deceased (ibid). See below, para 8.14.

context' *impliedly* undertakes the care of emergency patients: a fortiori a doctor in an open A & E department. The *Barnett* case does not go this far but in principle the duty exists because of the holding out by the doctor that he is there to deal with emergency cases that present themselves.[123]

(iii) Liability for Financial Loss

Generally speaking an action in negligence against a doctor will be for personal in- **5.41** jury or death caused during a medical procedure or it may arise from the illness or disease for which the patient sought advice or treatment. However, a doctor may also cause his patient financial loss. Whether a doctor owes a duty of care in respect of this type of loss will depend upon an application of the complex case law relating to recovery for negligently inflicted economic loss.[124] If the doctor is consulted by a patient for a particular purpose which the doctor is aware of, then it is likely that, on the basis of *Hedley Byrne*, a duty of care to exercise reasonable care and skill in preparing the report will be owed by the doctor to the patient. More generally, where a doctor advises a patient in circumstances where he knows (or ought to know) that the patient will rely upon it, and the patient thereby suffers economic loss, then under the principle in *Hedley Byrne v Heller & Co*[125] the doctor will owe a duty of care. So, in *Hughes v Lloyds Bank Plc*[126] the claimant suffered injury in a road traffic accident. She was treated by her GP whom she later asked to prepare a report detailing her injuries for the purposes of claiming against the other driver. The report understated the claimant's injuries and, as a result, the claim was settled for less than it should have been. The Court of Appeal held that the doctor owed the claimant a duty to take reasonable care in preparing his report.

However, where the doctor is unaware that the patient intends to rely upon his ad- **5.42** vice or, more likely, the patient relies upon it for an unrelated and unexpected purpose, then a duty of care will probably not exist.[127] The point is illustrated by *Stevens v Bermondsey and Southwark Group HMC*.[128] The claimant was advised by a casualty officer at a hospital, following an accident, that there was nothing wrong with him. In fact, the claimant had suffered an injury and subsequently

---

[123] In *Egedebo v Windermere District Hospital Association* (1993) 78 BCLR (2d) 63 (BC CA), a doctor who happened to be in a hospital emergency department, but not 'on call', owed a duty of care to a patient whom he knew required attention but whom he left for the 'on call' doctor who was, at that time, busy.

[124] See, Grubb (ed), *The Law of Torts* (n 13 above), paras 12.187–12.223. The more recent decisions of the House of Lords are discussed in McBride, N and Hughes, A, '*Hedley Byrne* in the House of Lords: an Interpretation' (1995) 15 LS 376.

[125] [1964] AC 465 (HL).

[126] [1998] PIQR P98 (CA). See further Grubb (1998) 6 Med L Rev 368 (Commentary).

[127] See for the general issue, albeit in a different context, *Caparo Industries plc v Dickman* [1990] 2 AC 605 (HL).

[128] (1963) 107 SJ 478.

developed spondylosis of the spine. However, relying on what he had been told, the claimant had already settled his claim against the local authority which was liable for the accident for a small sum of money. He sued the hospital arguing that the doctor's negligent diagnosis had caused him to suffer economic loss since had he been properly advised he would only have settled his claim for more. Paull J held that the defendant was not liable. The hospital doctor had no duty in respect of the claimant's financial affairs, only his physical condition. The answer would, as the judge acknowledged, have been different if the doctor had been consulted with a view to providing advice about litigation. The case remains good law even in the light of developments since *Hedley Byrne*. The doctor did not know, nor in the circumstances of an A & E department should he have known, that the patient would rely upon his advice in settling his claim. It would have been different if he had known.[129] The doctor had assumed a responsibility to him but only in respect of caring for him qua doctor and not as providing the professional services of an expert witness.[130]

5.43 However, a doctor may not only owe a duty of care not to cause his patients financial loss on the basis of a narrow application of the *Hedley Byrne* case. A broader basis of liability was accepted by the House of Lords in *Henderson v Merritt Syndicates Ltd*[131] and *White v Jones*[132] whereby a duty of care may exist where the defendant assumes a responsibility to the claimant.[133] The assumption may be express—arising from an undertaking by the defendant—or implied by the law—arising from the conduct of the defendant and surrounding circumstances. Hence, an employer has been held to owe a duty to an ex-employee when he carelessly produced a reference for the employee's new employer thereby causing the employee to lose the job and suffer financial loss.[134] Likewise, a doctor who was employed by the claimant's potential employer to examine him prior to confirming his job owed a duty of care to the claimant not carelessly to produce a report resulting in the claimant losing the job and suffering financial loss.[135] The

---

[129] On which, see *McGrath v Keily and Powell* [1965] IR 497 (Ir H Ct).

[130] However, if the medical expert's report is prepared as a witness in a trial (*Evans v London Hospital Medical College* [1981] 1 WLR 184) or at a pre-trial stage so intimately connected with the conduct of the case that it affects the way a case is to be conducted (*Landall v Dennis Faulkner & Alsop* [1994] 5 Med LR 268), then 'witness immunity' applies and no action can arise. See also *Hughes v Lloyds Bank Plc* (n 126 above).

[131] [1995] 2 AC 145 (HL).

[132] [1995] 2 AC 207 (HL).

[133] For a criticism of 'assumption of responsibility' as a basis of liability, see Barker, K, 'Unreliable Assumptions in the Modern Law of Negligence' (1993) 109 LQR 461.

[134] *Spring v Guardian Assurance plc* [1995] 2 AC 296 (HL). Although only Lord Goff relied upon the 'touchstone' of 'assumption of responsibility' to decide the case, the subsequent decisions of the House of Lords in *Henderson v Merit* and *White v Jones* have adopted the approach of Lord Goff.

[135] *Baker v Kaye* [1997] IRLR 219 (Robert Owen QC) (doctor not liable on facts because he was not careless). Disapproved by the Court of Appeal in *Kapfunde v Abbey National* (1998) 46 BMLR 176 (CA).

claimant in this case was not in a conventional doctor–patient relationship with the doctor and, as will be seen, the issue of what duty is owed in such situations is not clear in England.[136] However, if a doctor assumes a responsibility to an examinee in such a case, a fortiori in the case of a patient when he produces a report at the patient's request or otherwise for a particular purpose. *Baker v Kaye* illustrates that a duty of care may arise for negligent advice given by a doctor to a patient who consults him for the purpose of a 'medical reference' which the doctor knows (or ought to know) will be relied upon by the patient or a third party to whom it is to be supplied.

(iv) For Psychiatric Injury[137]

A patient who suffers emotional distress, grief, or anguish arising out of injuries resulting from medical negligence will, in the usual way, be able to recover general damages to reflect this in addition to the other non-pecuniary and pecuniary damages recoverable for his personal injuries.[138] A patient who does not suffer any personal injury may not, however, recover damages for mere distress or mental anguish.[139] An action could only be brought if psychiatric injury is caused, that is, there is a recognised psychiatric illness.[140] The complex and limiting rules in *McLoughlin*[141] and *Alcock*[142] which are applied to 'secondary victims' who suffer psychiatric injury, do not apply. The doctor owes the patient a duty of care not to cause personal injury which, for this purpose, includes psychiatric injury. The pre-existing duty owed to the patient, as the 'primary victim', will suffice to base an action for psychiatric injuries even where no other injury is suffered.[143] The duty would also extend to allow a claim for psychiatric injury caused by the *fear* of being injured by a doctor, for example, on discovering that a doctor who had treated the patient was infected with HIV.[144] Providing there was a foreseeable risk of injury to the patient,[145] the psychiatric injury claim would fall within the approach of the House of Lords in *Page v Smith*.[146]

5.44

---

[136] See below, paras 5.115–5.122.

[137] See the comprehensive study, Mullany, N and Handford, P, *Tort Liability for Psychiatric Damage* (1993) and Grubb (ed), *The Law of Torts* (n 13 above), paras 12.142–12.186.

[138] eg, *Kralj v McGrath* [1986] 1 All ER 54 (contract and negligence actions).

[139] eg, *Reilly v Merseyside RHA* [1995] 6 Med LR 246 (CA).

[140] cf *Grieve v Salford HA* [1991] 2 Med LR 295; *Bagley v North Hertfordshire HA* (1986) 136 NLJ 1014.

[141] *McLoughlin v O'Brien* [1983] AC 410; [1982] 2 All ER 298 (HL).

[142] *Alcock v Chief Constable of South Yorkshire Police* [1992] 1 AC 310; [1991] 4 All ER 907 (HL).

[143] *Alcock*, ibid, 923–924 *per* Lord Oliver; *Page v Smith* [1996] AC 155 (HL); *White v Chief Constable of the South Yorkshire Police* [1999] 1 All ER 1 (HL).

[144] For a discussion of the 'AIDS phobia' cases in an instructive US case, see *Faya and Rossi v Almaraz* (1993) 620 A 2d 327 (My CA), discussed in Grubb (1995) 3 Med L Rev 231 (Commentary).

[145] It may also be necessary for the patient to show a 'shocking' event (cf *Walker v Northumberland County Council* [1995] 1 All ER 737) but this could lie in the manner in which the risk of infection was discovered: *Sion v Hampstead HA* [1994] 5 Med LR 170 (CA) *per* Peter Gibson LJ at 176.

[146] N 143 above. But note *Re the Creutzfeldt-Jakob Disease Litigation–Group B (Human Growth*

5.45 An illustration of the 'primary victim' approach can be found in the case of *Tredgett and Tredgett v Bexley HA*.[147] The claimants, who were married, suffered psychiatric illness as a result of the defendants' negligence during the birth of their child who subsequently died. Judge White awarded both claimants damages for their psychiatric illnesses. He relied on the participants' category identified by Lord Oliver in *Alcock* which obviously covered the mother but also, he held, the father.[148]

5.46 Another situation in which a doctor might cause psychiatric injury to a patient is where he gives false information or communicates accurate information carelessly to the patient after treatment.[149] If a doctor did so deliberately, intending to cause harm to the patient, there would be liability under the rule in *Wilkinson v Downton*.[150] This, of course, will be rare. In principle, however, a duty of care exists between a doctor and patient which would encompass negligent post-operative advice whether in its content or in its method of communication.

5.47 In *AB v Tameside and Glossop HA*,[151] the parties conceded that the defendant[152] owed a duty of care when negligently communicating accurate information to obstetric patients (present and former) about their possible exposure to a health worker infected with HIV. While noting that no previous case seemed to deal with this point, the Court of Appeal accepted the concession and was content to state that 'we do not have to decide this point, or to consider whether such a duty exists, or the parameters of that duty, where there is no pre-existing relationship of care'.[153] By embarking upon communication with the patient, the doctor assumes a duty of care in respect of what he is undertaking whether it be diagnosis, pre-treatment advice, treatment or *post-treatment* advice.[154] Providing it is reasonably

---

Hormone) (1997) 41 BMLR 157 (Morland J) (liability to those negligently given human growth hormone (potentially) affected by Creutzfeldt-Jakob Disease and who suffered psychiatric injury arising out of the fear that they might, in the future, contract CJD).

[147] [1994] 5 Med LR 178. Grubb (1995) 3 Med L Rev 213, 215–16 (Commentary). See also *W v Essex County Council* [2000] 2 All ER 237 (HL) (parents of child who was abused by foster child placed in their home who was a known sexual abuser had arguably claim for psychiatric injury as 'primary victims' and as 'secondary victims' under the 'immediate aftermath' doctrine).

[148] *Alcock* (n 142 above), 923–924 *per* Lord Oliver. Contrast *Tan v East London and City HA* [1999] Lloyd's Rep Med 389 (Judge Ludlow) discussed below at para 5.93.

[149] See Mullany, NJ, 'Liability for Careless Communication of Traumatic Information' (1998) 114 LQR 380.

[150] [1897] 2 QB 57. See also *Powell v Boldaz* (1997) 39 BMLR 35 (CA).

[151] [1997] 8 Med LR 91 (CA). See Kennedy (1997) 5 Med L Rev 338 (Commentary).

[152] The case concerned the duty of the hospital but there is no difference, in principle, if the advice is given by a doctor.

[153] N 151 above, 93 *per* Brooke LJ.

[154] There may be a duty to volunteer information about medical mistakes: *Lee v South Thames RHA* [1985] 2 All ER 385 (CA), 389 *per* Sir John Donaldson MR; *Naylor v Preston AHA* [1987] 2 All ER 353 (CA), 360 *per* Sir John Donaldson MR; *Stamos v Davies* (1986) 21 DLR (4th) 507 (Ont H Ct); *Gerber v Pines* (1934) 79 SJ 13; *Daniels v Heskin* [1954] IR 73 (Ir Sup Ct). For a discussion see Robertson, G, 'Fraudulent Concealment and the Duty to Disclose Medical Mistakes' (1987) 25 Alta LR 215.

foreseeable that this negligent advice could cause psychiatric injury, as it may well be depending upon the nature of the advice, then a duty of care will exist. Hence, at least in the case of existing, and even former, patients the concession was surely properly made.[155]

2. To Third Parties

Although a doctor owes a duty of care to his patients, it is unclear whether a doctor will ever owe a duty of care to third parties who are not his patients.[156] In one case, speaking on behalf of the Court of Appeal, Stuart-Smith LJ went so far as to say that a doctor only owed a duty of care to his patients and never anyone else, including in that case the parents of the deceased patient.[157] The statement of the Court of Appeal should, perhaps, be understood as merely asserting the limited proposition that a doctor only owes a duty *qua* doctor *to treat* his patients. This is not, of course, the same as saying he does not owe a duty of care, the content of which might include warning or advising others, but not requiring him to act as their doctor. In certain circumstances, a doctor may owe a duty of care to someone who is not his patient. It is helpful to consider three situations: (i) the dangerous patient; (ii) financial loss; and (iii) psychiatric injury.

5.48

(i) Dangerous Patients

As a result of his treatment and responsibility for the care of a patient, a doctor may know (or reasonably ought to know) that his patient is a danger to others. A number of examples can be contemplated:

5.49

(i)   a doctor who knows that his patient suffers from an infectious disease which he is likely to transmit to others through sexual contact or otherwise;[158]

(ii) a psychiatrist whose mentally ill patient threatens to injure or kill another person and does so;[159]

(iii) a GP who has an epileptic patient who drives and injures or kills someone during an attack;[160]

(iv) a male patient who is wrongly advised that a vasectomy operation has been successful and need not take any contraceptive precautions with the result that his sexual partner becomes pregnant.[161]

---

[155] The legal basis of the duty will be negligence if injury is suffered as a result of non-disclosure. If no such injury is caused the duty must rest elsewhere, for example, as an aspect of the parties' fiduciary relationship: *Gerula v Flores* (1995) 126 DLR (4th) 506 (Ont CA). See generally, Grubb, A, 'The Doctor as Fiduciary' (1994) 47 CLP 311 especially at 335–8.

[156] See generally, Giesen, D, *International Medical Malpractice Law* (1988), 157–61.

[157] *Powell v Boldaz* (1997), 39 BMLR 35, 45 (CA).

[158] eg, *Pittman Estate v Bain* (1994) 112 DLR (4th) 257 (Ont Gen Div).

[159] eg, *Tarasoff v Regents of the University of California* (1976) 551 P 2d 334 (Cal Sup Ct).

[160] eg, *Toms v Foster* (1994) Ont CA LEXIS 346.

[161] eg, *Goodwill v BPAS* [1996] 2 All ER 161 (CA).

Does a doctor owe a duty to any of these 'injured' third parties?

(a) Some Overseas Authority

5.50   **Infectious Diseases**   In the context of transmission of infectious or contagious diseases by a patient to a third party, US courts have held doctors liable for (i) failing to diagnose the disease; (ii) failing to inform the third party (or others) of the danger; (iii) negligently advising the third party that there is no danger; and (iv) failing to prevent the spread of the disease.[162] Usually, however, the courts have restricted the group of potential victims who are owed a duty by the doctor to, for example, close family[163] or sexual partners.[164]

5.51   A number of recent cases have concerned the transmission of HIV by a patient to another. In *DiMarco v Lynch Homes-Chester County*[165] a blood technician accidentally infected herself with hepatitis through a sharps' injury. Her doctors told her that if she remained symptom free for six weeks, it would mean that she had not been infected. She was not advised to refrain from sexual intercourse although she did for eight weeks. She remained symptom free and, thereafter, she resumed sexual relations with her boyfriend (the claimant) who became infected. The claimant sued the doctors arguing that they should have advised the patient to refrain from sexual relations for six months otherwise she could infect her sexual partner. The Pennsylvania Supreme Court (by a majority of 4–3) held that the doctors owed the claimant a duty of care. The Court was greatly influenced by public health policy concerns to prevent the spread of communicable diseases and to further that policy by placing responsibility, in these circumstances, on the only person who was aware of the danger—the doctor. One passage in the majority judgment of Larsen J is particularly important:[166]

> When a physician treats a patient who has been exposed to or who has contracted a communicable and/or contagious disease, it is imperative that the physician give his or her patient the proper advice about preventing the spread of the disease. Communicable diseases are so named because they are readily spread from person to person. Physicians are the first line of defense against the spread of communicable diseases, because physicians know what measures must be taken to prevent the infection of others. The patient must be advised to take certain sanitary measures, or to remain quarantined for a period of time, or to practice sexual abstinence or what is commonly referred to as 'safe sex'.

---

[162] See *Annotation*, 3 ALR 5th 370.
[163] eg, *Bradshaw v Daniels* (1993) 854 SW 2d 865 (Tenn Sup Ct) ('Rocky Mountain Fever' transmitted by ticks). See Kennedy (1994) 2 Med L Rev 237 (Commentary).
[164] eg, *Gammell v US* (1984) 727 F 2d 950 (10th Circ). See Grubb, A and Pearl, D, *Blood Testing, AIDS and DNA Profiling: Law and Policy* (1990), 49–52.
[165] (1990) 525 Pa 558 (Pa Sup Ct).
[166] ibid, 562-2.

Such precautions are not taken to protect the health of the patient, whose well-being has already been compromised, rather such precautions are taken to safeguard the health of others. Thus, the duty of a physician in such circumstances extends to those 'within the foreseeable orbit of risk of harm' . . . If a third person is in that class of persons whose health is likely to be threatened by the patient, and if erroneous advice is given to that patient to the ultimate detriment of the third person, the third person has a cause of action against the physician, because the physician should recognize that the services rendered to the patient are necessary for the protection of the third person.

The majority emphasised the breadth of their decision. The duty was not owed only to married partners:[167] to so limit it would be 'exalting an unheeded morality over reality'.[168] Also, while it might be thought that in *DiMarco* the claimant was both known and identifiable to the defendants, in fact this played no part in the majority's reasoning.[169] The duty was also not so limited: it was owed to 'anyone who is physically intimate with the patient'.[170]

Unlike the situation where a patient suffers from a contagious or infectious disease,[171] in an HIV case a duty of care would not be owed to the patient's 'extended family' since they would not be at risk of infection.[172] It may, however, extend to future as well as current sexual partners who are subsequently put at risk of infection. In *Reisner v Regents of California*,[173] the California Court of Appeal adopted and applied this reasoning and rejected the argument that to impose a duty on the defendants would not prevent future harm. The patient received a transfusion of blood and blood products infected with HIV antibodies. Her doctor, on discovering this the following day, decided not to tell her or her family. Some years later, she commenced a sexual relationship with the claimant and, unknowingly, infected him with the HIV virus. Shortly before her death, the patient was told she had AIDS and immediately communicated this fact to the claimant, who subsequently learned of his own sero-positive status. In his action in negligence, the California Court of Appeal held that the doctor's duty of care extended to the claimant. Although not readily identifiable, the claimant, as a sexual partner of the patient, was a foreseeable victim even though the injury he complained of occurred some years after the negligent act. The defendant's duty was to warn the patient or her parents, who were likely to have warned the claimant of the risks

5.52

---

[167] See also *Pittman Estate v Bain* (1994) 112 DLR (4th) 257 (Ont Gen Div); additional reasons, (1994) 112 DLR (4th) 482, (1994) 112 DLR (4th) 494 and (1994) 35 CPC (3d) 767 (duty owed to wife of HIV positive patient).

[168] N 165 above, 564 *per* Larson J.

[169] See ibid, 565 *per* Flaherty J (dissenting).

[170] ibid, 563 *per* Larson J.

[171] eg, *Gammell v US* (1984) 727 F 2d 950 (10th Circ).

[172] See *Lemon v Stewart* (1996) 682 A 2d 1177 (Ms Ct Spec App).

[173] (1995) 37 Cal Rptr 2d 518.

and thereby have avoided the risk of transmission by abstaining from sexual contact or practising 'safe sex'. Vogel J said:[174]

> Civil liability for a negligent failure to warn under the circumstances of this case may not hasten the day when AIDS can be cured or prevented but it may, in the meantime, protect one or more persons from unnecessary exposure to this deadly virus.

5.53 **Psychiatric Patients**   Likewise in cases of dangerous psychiatric patients, some US courts have recognised that a psychiatrist owes a duty of care to potential victims of a dangerous patient.[175] Most famously, the California Supreme Court held such a duty existed in *Tarasoff v Regents of University of California*.[176] The Supreme Court held that a psychotherapist owed a duty of care to his patient's victim whom he knew was the patient's intended target. Tobriner J stated:[177]

> Although . . . under the common law, as a general rule, one person owed no duty to control the conduct of another, nor to warn those endangered by such conduct, the courts have carved out an exception to this rule in cases in which the defendant stands in some special relationship to either the person whose conduct needs to be controlled or in a relationship to the foreseeable victim of that conduct.

5.54 The Court balanced the public interest in maintaining the confidentiality of the defendant's client against the public interest in protecting others from assaults and concluded that the defendant had a legal duty to take reasonable steps to avert the danger by warning the victim, the police or others who might appraise her of the danger. Tobriner J said:[178]

> In this risk-infested society we can hardly tolerate the further exposure to danger that would result from a concealed knowledge of the therapist that his patient was lethal.

5.55 In *Tarasoff*, it was important that the victim was known and identified to the defendant by his patient. In other US jurisdictions courts have interpreted *Tarasoff* in different ways. Some have interpreted it widely so as to impose a duty to warn whenever it is foreseeable that a person may be endangered.[179] On the whole, however, courts have taken a more limited view, requiring not only that the victim be foreseeable, but also that the particular victim be identifiable.[180] Some jurisdictions have rejected the duty altogether.[181]

---

[174] (1995) 37 Cal Rptr 2d 518, 522.
[175] *Annotation*, 83 ALR 3d 1201.
[176] (1976) 551 P 2d 334 (Cal Sup Ct).
[177] ibid, 343.
[178] ibid, 347.
[179] eg, *Bardoni v Kim* (1986) 390 NW 2d 218 (Mich CA) (foreseeable individual); *Lipari v Sears, Roebuck & Co* (1980) 497 F Supp 185 (DC) (foreseeable class).
[180] See, eg, *Thomson v County of Alameda* (1980) 614 P 2d 728 (Cal Sup Ct).
[181] eg, *Cole v Taylor* (1981) 301 NW 2d 766 (Iowa Sup Ct).

Dangerous Drivers   A patient may be a danger to others because of his medical   **5.56**
condition, for example, if he were to drive a car or other vehicle. In a number of
US[182] and Canadian cases, courts have held doctors liable to passengers and other
road users who have been injured when a patient lost control of a car or other vehicle when he was unfit to drive[183] and suffered, for example, an epileptic fit,[184] a
diabetic attack,[185] or drowsiness brought on by medication prescribed by the doctor. Liability has been imposed in three sorts of situations: where the doctor (i) created the 'dangerous' condition, for example, by prescribing drugs;[186] (ii) was aware
of the patient's physical condition;[187] and (iii) affirmatively advised the patient
that it was safe to drive.[188] The duty of care is owed to the third party but the negligence consists of failing to warn *the patient* of his dangerous condition.[189] Where
it has been suggested that the doctor should control the patient by stopping him
driving, the courts have been reluctant to impose this onerous (and legally impossible) obligation.[190] The duty is generally held to be owed to all foreseeable road
users even though the injured person's precise identity is not known.[191] However,
recently, some courts have adopted a more restrictive approach derived, by analogy, from the 'dangerous psychiatric patient' cases such as *Tarasoff*. Consequently,
courts have refused to impose a duty of care unless the third party is 'known and
identifiable'[192] or where there is a 'special relationship' between the doctor and the
patient whereby the doctor has control over the patient.[193] In context, the latter
approach virtually eliminates claims against doctors by injured passengers or
other road users.

---

[182] Discussed, *Annotation*, 43 ALR 4th 153.
[183] *Joy v Eastern Main Medical Center* (1987) 529 A 2d 1364 (Me Sup Ct) (failure to warn not to
drive wearing an eye-patch); *Toms v Foster* 1994 Ont CA Lexis 346 (driver suffering from cervical
spondylosis).
[184] eg, *Spillane v Wasserman* (1992) 13 CCLT 267 (Ont H Ct).
[185] eg, *Myers v Quesenberry* (1983) 193 Cal Rptr 733 (Cal CA).
[186] eg, *Gooden v Tips* (1983) 651 SW 2d 364 (Tex CA); *Kaiser v Suburban Transportation System*
(1965) 398 P 2d 14 (Wash Sup Ct); *Schuster v Altenberg* (1988) 424 NW 2d 159 (Wis Sup Ct).
[187] eg, *Myers v Quesenberry* (n 185 above); *Freese v Lemmon* (1973) 210 NW 2d 576 (Iowa Sup Ct),
subsequently, following trial, held no negligence: (1978) 267 NW 2d 680.
[188] eg, *Freese v Lemmon*, ibid.
[189] See *Myers v Quesenberry* (n 185 above), 733.
[190] eg, *Purdy v Estate of Shaw* (1987) 514 NYS 2d 407 (NY App Div) (no duty on health facility to
restrain licensed driver).
[191] See *Myers v Quesenberry* (n 185 above), 733. See also *Duvall v Goldin* (1984) 362 NW 2d 275
(Mich CA); *Freese v Lemmon* (1973) 210 NW 2d 576 (Iowa Sup Ct); *Gooden v Tips* (1983) 651 SW
2d 364 (Tex CA).
[192] See *Werner v Varner, Stafford & Seaman* (1995) 659 So 2d 1308 (Fla CA) (duty not owed to
public at large); applying *Pate v Threlkel* (1995) 661 So 2d 278 (Fla Sup Ct) (duty to children of
patient in respect of the patient's inheritable genetic condition), and see below, para 5.57.
[193] See *Caldwell v Hassan* (1996) 925 P 2d 422 (Kan Sup Ct) (failure to warn patient who suffered
from daytime sleep disorder not to drive). The court left open whether liability might exist if the
doctor 'created a risk of harm' to the claimant (at 431) but, on the facts, there was no evidence that
the medication prescribed by the doctor 'caused or worsened [the patient's] daytime drowsiness
problem' (ibid).

5.57 **Genetic Conditions**   Analogous to the situations of the infectious or dangerous psychiatric patient are those where the patient is not strictly speaking 'dangerous' but because of information gained during the course of the doctor–patient relationship the doctor knows that harm may come to the other. An illustration of this occurs where the doctor discovers genetic information about his patient which has relevance to the genetic health of members of the patient's family. The increasing potential for determining a patient's genetic 'make-up' will, undoubtedly, increase the incidence of such cases in the future. In two US decisions, courts have held that a doctor owed a duty of care to the children of a patient whom he discovered had a serious inheritable genetic condition. In *Pate v Threlkel*,[194] the defendant treated his patient for thyroid cancer which was genetically inheritable. Three years later, the patient's adult daughter discovered that she suffered from the same condition which was, by this time, incurable. She claimed that if her father had been told, she would have been tested and taken preventative steps which would, more likely than not, have resulted in a cure. The Florida Supreme Court held that a doctor could owe a duty of care to someone who was not his patient. The court concluded that a doctor owed a duty only to 'known' and 'identifiable' individuals who were at risk.[195] Thus, he owed the patient's daughter a duty to warn the patient of the danger of his children inheriting the condition. Further, the court held that the doctor's duty was to warn the patient and not to breach the confidentiality of the patient by directly warning the child. Wells J stated:[196]

> . . . the patient ordinarily can be expected to pass on the warning. To require the physician to seek out and warn various members of the patient's family would often be difficult or impractical and would place too heavy a burden upon the physician. Thus, we emphasise that in any circumstances in which the physician has a duty to warn of a genetically transferable disease, that duty will be satisfied by warning the patient.

5.58 The reasoning of the Florida Supreme Court is, however, of limited importance in England. First, the court applied a test for determining a duty of care based, in essence, upon 'foreseeability of risk'.[197] English law would require more to establish a duty of care in this context applying the three-stage test in the *Caparo* case. Secondly, the court relied heavily upon the expert evidence that it was a doctor's professional obligation to warn of the dangers of inheriting the condition.[198] While this may be some evidence supporting the imposition of a legal duty of care, English law would not necessarily adopt the professional standard.[199]

---

[194] (1995) 661 So 2d 278 (Fla Sup Ct).
[195] Relying on an 'infectious disease' case: *Hofmann v Blackmon* (1970) 241 So 2d 752 (Fla CA).
[196] N 194 above, 282.
[197] ibid, 280.
[198] ibid, 281 and 282.
[199] But contrast *Baker v Kaye* [1997] IRLR 219.

In the second US case, *Safer v Pack*,[200] a New Jersey appellate court also imposed **5.59** a duty of care in the context of genetic disease. The defendant treated his patient for a genetically related form of colon cancer from which the patient eventually died. At the time the claimant was aged 10, and 26 years later she was diagnosed as suffering from the same condition. The claimant alleged that the defendant knew of the inheritable nature of the condition and should have warned those at risk so that they might take early preventative measures. The New Jersey court held that the doctor did owe a duty of care to the claimant. Relying on cases concerned with the transmission of infectious disease and physical threats by dangerous patients,[201] the court held that the duty was owed to all 'members of the immediate family of the patient who may be adversely affected'.[202] Kesten J stated[203] that '[t]he individual or group at risk is easily identified, and substantial future harm may be averted or minimized by a timely and effective warning'. The court accepted that the limited duty to warn of an avertible risk those defined by familial connection was 'sufficiently narrow to serve the interests of justice'.[204]

As for the content of the duty, the court concluded that the duty 'require[d] that rea- **5.60** sonable steps be taken to assure that the information reaches those likely to be affected or is made available for their benefit'.[205] This, the court contemplated, might be satisfied by warning the patient in a case like *Safer* where the third party was a young child when the genetic condition was discovered. However, unlike the court in *Pate v Threlkel*, the New Jersey court refused to rule out the possibility that the duty might entail an obligation to warn the family member *directly*. Kestin J said:[206]

> It may be necessary, at some stage, to resolve a conflict between the physician's broader duty to warn and his fidelity to an expressed preference of the patient that nothing be said to family members about the details of the disease.

(b) English Law

We will come shortly to the one English case that has directly addressed the ques- **5.61** tion of a doctor's liability in any of these four situations.[207] The analytical structure of English law is clear: it is the 'three-stage' test propounded by the House of Lords in *Caparo Industries plc v Dickman*.[208] For the doctor to owe the third party a duty of care there must be *'foreseeability'*, *'proximity'* of relationship and the

---

[200] (1996) 677 A 2d 1188 (Super Ct App Div).
[201] *McIntosh v Milano* (1979) 403 A 2d 500; *Tarasoff v Regents of University of California* (1976) 551 P 2d 334.
[202] N 200 above, 1192 citing *Schroeder v Perkel* (1981) 87 NJ 53, 65.
[203] ibid, 1192.
[204] ibid, 1192 *per* Kestin J.
[205] ibid, 1192 *per* Kestin J.
[206] ibid, 1192.
[207] *Palmer v Tees HA* [1999] Lloyd's Rep Med 351 (CA).
[208] [1990] 2 AC 605; [1990] 1 All ER 568 (HL).

imposition of a duty must be '*fair, just, and reasonable*'.[209] In this context 'foreseeability' of injury is unlikely to be a problem, the real 'battle ground' will be 'proximity' and the policy issues under the third limb. It is probably unduly narrow to see these requirements as wholly distinct and hermetically sealed from each other because particular factors may well influence a court in reaching a view on both requirements. The law will develop incrementally by analogy to existing situations of recognised liability. There are a number of formidable difficulties in the way of a claimant establishing such a claim.

5.62 **Omissions and Third Parties** First, the third party's claim will often be that the doctor *failed* to protect him by, for example, warning him or another of the danger. English law is generally reluctant to impose a duty of care where the defendant is alleged to have failed to act (ie, for an omission).[210] Secondly, the claimant may be relying on the doctor's failure to prevent an intermediary voluntarily and intentionally injuring the third party.[211] Generally, this person alone is viewed as responsible for the claimant's injuries.[212] A duty may exist, however, if the defendant could (and should) have controlled that intermediary who was the direct cause of the claimant's harm.[213] This is unlikely unless, for example, the patient is a psychiatric patient who has been detained under the Mental Health Act 1983 and is prematurely released, or should have been but the doctor fails to instigate the procedure for detention under the Act. Another illustration could arise in the area of infectious diseases, but only where the provisions of the Public Health (Control of Diseases) Act 1984 allow for detention. In one case, a hospital[214] was held liable where it released a dangerous patient who assaulted and injured the claimant, having broken into her home.[215] However, the authority of this case is somewhat limited: it was a summing up to a jury and the judge assumed a duty of care arose and was more concerned with the issue of breach. Liability may be restricted to injuries caused to others themselves within the control of the defendant[216] or where, once escaped, the 'dangerous patient' injures those in a close vicinity during his escape.[217] It may, therefore, not be followed in the future.[218]

---

[209] See especially, ibid, *per* Lord Bridge at 574 and *per* Lord Oliver at 585.

[210] See *Smith v Littlewoods Organisation Ltd* [1987] 1 AC 241.

[211] As in the 'dangerous patient' or 'driver' cases or 'infectious disease' cases. Not, however, in the 'genetic' transmission cases.

[212] *Smith* (n 210 above).

[213] *Home Office v Dorset Yacht* [1970] AC 1004; [1970] 2 All ER 294 (HL).

[214] The duty is probably that of the institution rather than any particular doctor.

[215] *Holgate v Lancashire Mental Hospitals Board* [1937] 4 All ER 19.

[216] See *Ellis v Home Office* [1953] 2 QB 135 (CA) (injury caused by one prisoner to another). The same reasoning would apply if the injured party was a visitor or, indeed, himself injured: see eg, *Hay v Grampian Health Board* [1995] 6 Med LR 128 and Grubb, A (1995) 3 Med L Rev 299 (Commentary).

[217] As in *Dorset Yacht* itself (n 213 above). Contrast, *Marti v Smith and Home Office* (1981) 131 NLJ 1028.

[218] In *Home Office v Dorset Yacht* (n 213 above), Lord Diplock reserved his opinion on its correct-

Increased Risk of Injury   Thirdly, the courts are unwilling to shoulder a doctor   **5.63**
with the burden of liability where he has not made the claimant's position worse
and they may well insist that he has *increased the risk* of the intermediary harming
the claimant.[219] Hence, a doctor who, for example, creates a risk of 'injury' by infecting a patient with HIV[220] could be liable whilst one who merely failed to avert
the risk by warning of the danger will not.[221] Consequently, for this reason a failure to advise a third party of their genetic condition will probably not give rise to
an action. Ultimately, of course, this is an unsatisfactory distinction. Being the
agent of the risk creation is only one indicium of culpability—it increases the
moral turpitude of the individual—but there are others. Furthermore, it will
inevitably lead to fine distinctions being drawn in cases as to which particular
category any given set of facts falls into,[222] but it seems to appeal to the English
judiciary as encapsulating a necessary condition for culpability.

Identifiable Victims   Fourthly, liability would not be based upon foreseeability   **5.64**
of injury to another alone; certainly if all that is foreseeable is injury to others in
general. Even if all the other requirements for liability were in place, English law
would seek to limit the range of liability by closely circumscribing the breadth of
liability through other control mechanisms.[223] At the very least, foreseeability of
harm to a particular person or perhaps a small identifiable group is likely to be
essential.[224]

Policy and Confidentiality   Finally, the courts will investigate the policy argu-   **5.65**
ments that might tell against imposing liability upon the defendant, such as the
burdens it would create, the inconveniences that would be generated, and any
deleterious effects such a duty might have upon the medical profession. In particular, the courts will be reluctant to impose a duty upon a doctor which requires him
to disclose information in breach of confidence. This may not be crucial where the
duty only contemplates disclosure to the patient rather than to the third party (or
another). Hence, in the *Reisner* case, no breach of confidence was

---

ness (at 328) explaining it as a case involving a person not responsible for his actions; Lord Reid appears to have considered it correct as a matter of private law (but doubted the public law issue raised,
at 301–302); Lord Morris considered it correct (at 309).

[219] eg, *Hill v Chief Constable of West Yorkshire* [1989] AC 53, explaining *Dorset Yacht.*
[220] *Reisner v Regents of the University of California* (1995) 37 Cal Rptr 2d 518 (Cal CA).
[221] *Goodwill v BPAS* [1996] 2 All ER 161 (CA).
[222] Hence, a doctor who prescribes a medication to a patient 'creates' a risk to other road users
whilst a doctor who only fails to diagnose or inform a patient of an existing condition does not: see
its acceptance in *Calwell v Hassan* (1996) 925 P 2d 422 (Kan Sup Ct). The satisfactory nature of this
distinction is questionable.
[223] *Dorset Yacht* (n 213 above); *Hill* (n 219 above) and *Caparo* (n 208 above).
[224] See, eg, *Osman v Ferguson* [1993] 4 All ER 344 (CA) where it was accepted by two judges in the
Court of Appeal that there was proximity between the police and a specific individual who was
known to them to be at risk: see McCowan LJ at 350; Simon Brown LJ agreed; Beldam LJ at 354 expressing no view.

contemplated.[225] The doctor only has a duty to tell his patient in order for her to act responsibly by desisting from risky behaviour or warning her partners of the risk they might be running. Where a breach of confidence is contemplated (even one which could be justified), however, the better position is to *allow* disclosure (a discretion) where there are exceptional circumstances of danger (or harm) to others, but not to *require* it (a duty).[226] In other words, the law should only provide a justification for a breach of confidence. This is consistent with the ethical guidance issued by the General Medical Council[227] and the Department of Health[228] and, in the genetics context, by other bodies.[229]

5.66   **Palmer v Tees HA**   One English case which does concern the liability of a doctor to a third party is *Palmer v Tees HA*.[230] The claimant was the mother of a 4-year-old girl who was abducted, sexually abused and murdered by a psychiatric patient who had been cared for over time by the defendant. The claimant suffered psychiatric injury as a result of discovering her daughter had been abducted, from what she feared had happened and from what she learned had actually happened to her daughter. She sued the defendant alleging it had negligently failed to discover the killer's propensities and to treat him or otherwise prevent him from killing her daughter. She claimed damages on her own behalf for psychiatric injury[231] and on behalf of her daughter's estate. In relation to the latter action, the court considered whether the defendant owed a duty of care to the victim.

5.67   Gage J at first instance,[232] struck out the claimant's action on the basis that no duty of care was owed. First, the judge held that there was no 'proximity' between the victim and defendant. Liability for the actions of a third party only arose if the victim was someone 'who came into a special or exceptional or distinctive category of risk from the activities of the third party'—which she did not. Second, it was not 'fair, just and reasonable' to impose a duty of care on the defendants. He relied upon a number of factors: the danger that doctors might engage in 'defensive medicine', the burden of increased claims upon the health authority and the diversion of resources that defending and dealing with such claims would entail, the limited control the defendant had over the patient, that the defendant might

---

225   See also *Pate v Threlkel* (n 194 above). This would also be the case in the 'dangerous driver' cases where the duty is to advise the driver/patient himself.

226   See Grubb and Pearl, *Blood Testing, AIDS and DNA Profiling* (n 164 above), 48–55.

227   *Serious Communicable Diseases* (GMC 1998), paras 22–3.

228   *Confidentiality: NHS Code of Practice* (DoH, October 2003).

229   Nuffield Council on Bioethics, *Genetic Screening* (1993), ch 5.

230   [1999] Lloyd's Rep Med 351 (CA). See further Grubb (1999) 7 Med L Rev 331 (Commentary).

231   The Court of Appeal held that the claimant's action did not fall within the 'secondary victim' rule in *Alcock v Chief Constable of South Yorkshire* [1992] 1 AC 310—her psychiatric injury was not caused by the sudden appreciation through sight or sound of a horrific event. See below paras 5.77 *et seq.*

232   [1998] Lloyd's Rep Med 447.

be required to breach the patient's confidence in order to warn others and, finally, the fact that the claimant had a claim for compensation from the Criminal Injuries Compensation Board.

The Court of Appeal dismissed the claimant's appeal. The court held that there was **5.68** no 'proximity' between the defendant and the victim.[233] Stuart-Smith and Pill LJJ[234] couched their conclusion in terms of the absence of a special relationship or nexus between the defendant and the victim relying on the earlier House of Lords cases of *Home Office v Dorset Yacht*[235] and *Hill v Chief Constable of West Yorkshire*.[236]

Stuart-Smith LJ specifically referred to a distinction drawn in *Dorset Yacht* be- **5.69** tween the assailant who *escapes* from detention and causes harm and the one who is simply *released* or *not caught and detained*—the contrast between the facts of *Dorset Yacht* and *Hill.* What, if anything, is the difference between these situations? One might be that where the patient escapes the defendant's negligence creates a risk of injury (or death) to others. By contrast, where the defendant merely fails to catch or detain an individual in the community, no special risk is created. The former may more readily engage the court's sense of corrective justice that as between the claimant and the defendant, the defendant *ought* to bear responsibility for the harm. However, the same reasoning would seem to be applicable to the patient who is negligently released or allowed out on 'leave'. It is not clear that the judges in *Palmer* would have taken a different view if the psychiatric patient had been detained under the Mental Health Act 1983 and had been negligently released. The earlier decision in *Holgate v Lancashire Mental Hospital Board*[237] was just such a case. Both Stuart-Smith and Pill LJJ considered *Holgate* to be wrongly decided.[238] It may be, however, that the time and geographical gap between release and the harm occurring in that case was significant.[239] Likewise in *Palmer*, the patient had been released a year before he killed the child and Pill LJ, in particular, noted as important 'the passage of time and distance between [the psychiatric patient's] release and [the child's] murder'.[240]

What then was the significant factor in *Palmer*? What if the victim had been **5.70** known to the defendant or could reasonably be identified from the psychiatric

---

[233] The Court of Appeal did not rely on the 'just, fair and reasonable' limb of the *Caparo* test because of the (then) prevailing view that this was prohibited at the striking out stage by the ECtHR's decision in *Osman v UK* (1998) 5 BHRC 293: *Barrett v Enfield LBC* [1999] 3 WLR 79. But see now: *Z v UK* (2002) 34 EHRR 3 (ECtHR).

[234] Thorpe LJ agreed with Stuart-Smith LJ's judgment.

[235] [1970] AC 1004 (HL).

[236] [1989] AC 53 (HL).

[237] [1937] 4 All E.R. 19.

[238] N 230 above, 359 and 363 respectively.

[239] Contrast *Dorset Yacht* (n 213 above) with *Martin v Smith and Home Office* (1981) 131 NLJ 1028.

[240] N 230 above, 363.

patient's threats? Pill LJ, while not wholly persuaded of the point, concluded that *an* important aspect would be whether the victim was known to the defendant. He was not persuaded, however, that there should necessarily be a different legal result where the threat was 'I will kill X' and where it was 'I will kill the first bald-headed man I meet'.[241] Although, he acknowledged that it would be relevant 'to the extent of the duty and the measures necessary to discharge it'.[242] Stuart-Smith LJ also considered that an 'identifiable' victim might satisfy the 'proximity' test.[243] The victim in *Palmer*, of course, was neither identified nor identifiable. She was merely a member of a section of the public, as in *Hill*, which was at risk from the psychiatric patient.

5.71   It would not be a fair representation of the judgments in *Palmer* to see this issue—'was the victim identified or identifiable?'—as, itself, being a *sufficient* condition for liability. It was, arguably, only seen as a *necessary* condition at least by Stuart-Smith LJ who, in his judgment, set out a number of other important factors militating against a duty of care—the inability to warn the victim or of the authorities to provide protection and the limited powers of control that the defendant had over the patient.[244] It is difficult to see why difficulties over warning an unidentified victim should a priori exclude a duty of care. Warning the victim is only one method by way the duty could be discharged. It may not be the only, or best, one. Why not warn the police? This was, of course, what happened in the US case of *Tarasoff* discussed earlier. Further, the difficulties of involving the compulsory powers of detention under the Mental Health Act 1983 may also have been overstated.

5.72   There must be more than a sneaking suspicion that the judges would, if the facts were to present themselves, agree with Gage J that liability would arise if 'there existed some distinctive feature or characteristic which demonstrated that [the victim] was at some special risk'.[245] It remains unclear whether a singled out victim would be necessary or one of a small group could sue, for example, children at a school where a known dangerous psychiatric patient or paedophile works. Arguably, there is no distinction that could properly be drawn on the basis of 'proximity'.

5.73   In the end, the English courts may have no choice where the third party's life is at risk. In *Osman*,[246] the European Court of Human Rights held that Article 2 of the ECHR required state authorities to take *positive* action where:

---

[241] N 230 above.

[242] ibid.

[243] He left open whether an assumption of responsibility or undertaking towards the victim would also be necessary, n 230 above, 359.

[244] N 230 above, 359.

[245] ibid, 461.

[246] N 233 above, para 116.

[they] knew or ought to have known at the time of the existence of a real and immediate risk to the life of an identified individual or individuals from the criminal
acts of a third party.

Although *Osman* concerned the obligations of the police, there is no doubt that
other state bodies, such as NHS Trusts, also prima facie have the same general
obligation. The state's obligation is to do 'all that could be reasonably expected' to
avoid the risk. And, of course, the extent of the obligation may depend upon
whom the obligation is placed, for example, because the powers and role in society of the police and NHS institutions are different. Nevertheless, arguably the
latter could quite reasonably provide warnings or, if necessary, invoke their own
powers of detention where the risk presented itself.

(ii) For Financial Loss

A doctor who is requested by his patient to provide a medical report to a third **5.74**
party, for example, an insurance company or potential employer, may owe a duty
of care to that third party to do so carefully so that the third party does not incur
economic loss.[247] Following *Hedley Byrne v Heller*, a doctor, knowing whom the
recipient of the report is to be, the purpose for which it will be used, and that the
third party will (or is likely to) rely upon it, undertakes (or assumes) a responsibility to the third party sufficient to impose a legal duty to exercise reasonable care
and skill in preparing the report.[248]

In the unlikely event that the doctor provides a medical report on the patient **5.75**
without knowing what use it will be put to, or if the report is put to an unexpected
use or one which could not reasonably be anticipated by the doctor, it may well be
that the all important 'assumption of responsibility' is absent. It will not, however,
be necessary for the doctor to know the precise identity of the third party providing he knows the nature of the third party's use, for example, that it is an insurance
company.

The same reasoning would apply if the doctor had no pre-existing relationship **5.76**
with the 'patient' but was specifically engaged directly by the third party to provide the medical report. Here, there would undoubtedly be an undertaking or
assumption of responsibility to the third party who requested the report. And, of
course, there would almost certainly be a contract between the doctor and third
party which would include an implied term which could be the basis for a

---

[247] See, eg, *Wharton Transport Corporation v Bridges* (1980) 606 SW 2d 521 (Tenn Sup Ct) (failure by doctor to report to employer the disabilities of an employee resulting in claim by injured person against employer for negligence of employee). See also *North American Co for Life & Health
Insurance v Berger* (1981) 648 F 2d 305 (5th Cir) (insurance company had action against doctor for
negligent medical assessment of employee entitlement under insurance coverage).

[248] This should follow from the reasoning in *Spring v Guardian Assurance plc* [1995] 2 AC 296;
[1994] 3 All ER 129 (HL), but notice the reservation by Lord Goff at 147.

contractual negligence claim unconstrained by requirements for recovering economic loss in the tort of negligence.[249]

(iii) For Psychiatric Injury

5.77 The circumstances in which damages may be recovered for negligently caused nervous shock (psychiatric injury) are confusing and, often, uncertain.[250] A distinction has to be drawn between 'participants' or 'primary victims' and others who are merely 'secondary victims' of the defendant's negligence.[251] As regards the latter, the House of Lords in the three cases of *McLoughlin v O'Brien*,[252] *Alcock v Chief Constable of South Yorkshire*[253] and *White v Chief Constable of South Yorkshire Police*[254] imposed arbitrary limits upon claims for psychiatric injury not for any logical reason but rather to reflect 'the court's perception of what is the reasonable area for the imposition of liability'.[255]

5.78 The courts have explicitly accepted that they are making policy choices about the scope of liability.[256] In particular, the law requires:

(i)   a close relationship between the victim and the claimant (either presumed, for example, parent and child or established in fact, for example, brother and sister) such that psychiatric injury is foreseeable to the claimant;

(ii)   propinquity in time and space between the victim's 'accident' and the claimant's discovery of the victim's injury (ie at the scene or its 'immediate aftermath');

(iii)   that the claimant discover that injury by sight and sound; and

(iv)   that as a result the claimant suffers psychiatric illness through an affront to her senses.

5.79 By contrast, as regards those who are 'participants' or 'primary victims' of the defendant's negligence, *Page v Smith*[257] has made it clear that the *McLoughlin/Alcock* rules do not apply. It suffices that a duty of care arises because it is reasonably foreseeable that the claimant will suffer personal injury whether or not it is also foreseeable that he will suffer psychiatric injury, and the 'proximity' requirements identified in *McLoughlin/Alcock* need not be satisfied.

---

[249] *Spring* (n 248 above).

[250] For a comprehensive study, see Mullany, N, and Handford, P, *Tort Liability for Psychiatric Damage* (1993) and Grubb (ed), *The Law of Torts* (n 13 above), paras 12.142–12.186.

[251] See also discussion, above, paras 5.44–5.47.

[252] [1983] AC 410; [1982] 2 All ER 298 (HL).

[253] [1992] 1 AC 310; [1991] 4 All ER 907 (HL).

[254] [1999] 2 AC 455; [1999] 1 All ER 1 (HL).

[255] ibid, *per* Lord Oliver at 926.

[256] See *White v Chief Constable of South Yorkshire Police* (n 254 above). In *White*, Lord Hoffman observed that the 'search for principle was called off' in *Alcock* (n 254 above), 551.

[257] [1996] AC 155 (HL).

These, perhaps deceptively, simple rules apply in medical negligence cases where the **5.80** issue is whether a third party, usually a relative of the patient, may recover for the psychiatric injury caused by the doctor's negligence directed towards the patient. Claims for psychiatric injury arising out of negligent medical treatment have not until recently troubled the courts in England.[258] Five reported decisions: *Tredgett and Tredgett v Bexley HA;*[259] *Sion v Hampstead HA,*[260] *Taylor v Somerset HA,*[261] *Tan v East London and City HA*[262] and *North Glamorgan NHS Trust v Walters*[263] illustrate the application of the general rules in the context of medical negligence.

(a) Participant/Primary Victim Cases

We are not, of course, here concerned with the claim by a patient for psychiatric **5.81** injury arising out of her treatment.[264] Rather, the issue is whether a relative, usually a close relative such as a spouse, partner or parent, may claim for their psychiatric injury triggered by the negligent care of their relative. It seems that, in some instances, the courts will regard the relative as so involved in the events of medical negligence that the relative will not be seen as a 'secondary victim' but will be regarded as a 'participant' or 'primary victim'. In *Tredgett and Tredgett v Bexley HA,*[265] the claimants, who were married, suffered psychiatric illness as a result of the defendants' negligence during the birth of their child who died 48 hours later. The course of the birth was horrendous in circumstances described as amounting to 'chaos' and 'pandemonium'. Mr Tredgett who was present throughout and witnessed what was taking place, was shaken and stunned by what he saw. After the birth both claimants witnessed the child in intensive care prior to its life-support being switched off. Judge White awarded both claimants damages. He held that they had each suffered a recognised psychiatric illness—pathological grief reaction. This had been caused by 'shock' resulting from their involvement in the birth process and subsequent events. Judge White held that it would be unrealistic to isolate the birth from the continuing events leading up to the child's death 48 hours later. He applied the 'participant' category identified in *Alcock* which obviously covered the mother but also, he held, the father. As regards the latter, he relied upon 'the degree of involvement in and the immediacy of the parents to the birth of the child'.[266] Hence, in obstetric cases where a father is present and (as will often be the case) is actively encouraging and supporting his partner, a claim for psychiatric illness caused by negligence in the birth could be brought.

---

[258] cf US, see *Annotation,* 77 ALR 3d 436.
[259] [1994] 5 Med LR 178.
[260] [1994] 5 Med LR 170.
[261] (1993) 16 BMLR 63.
[262] [1999] Lloyd's Rep Med 389.
[263] [2003] EWCA Civ 1792; [2003] Lloyd's Rep Med 49 (CA).
[264] See above, paras 5.43–5.46.
[265] N 259 above.
[266] ibid, 184.

5.82 This will not be the only situation in which a relative will be considered a 'participant'; there will be others. It will be a matter of fact determined by the closeness and immediacy of involvement of the relative. At the very least, however, the relative will have to be present at the time of the negligence: merely witnessing the effect of the negligence on the patient will not do. In *Tredgett*, of course, the father was actually involved in his wife's care and it may well be that something of this sort will be necessary for the more restrictive *McLoughlin/Alcock* rules not to apply. It is important to note, however, that relatives who merely conduct a vigil at the bedside of the injured patient or are otherwise present at the hospital where the medical negligence occurs will not be considered 'participants'. Rather, their actions for psychiatric injury must fall within the 'secondary victim' rules of *McLoughlin/Alcock* and, as will be seen shortly, are unlikely to succeed.

(b) Witnessing a Traumatic Event

5.83 Damages for psychiatric illness will be recoverable if the claimant witnessed a traumatising event that compromised the medical negligence: providing always that the other *McLoughlin/Alcock* rules are satisfied, for example, that the claimant has a sufficiently close relationship with the 'primary' victim of the medical negligence. Arguably, in *Tredgett* the husband's claim would still have succeeded even if he had only witnessed what the judge described as the 'chaos' and 'pandemonium' at the time of the birth. Thus, seeing a loved one suffer, if sufficiently traumatic, at the hands of a doctor may do. The decision of the Court of Appeal in *Sion v Hampstead HA*[267] illustrates the application of the 'secondary victim' rules.

5.84 The claimant's son was injured in a motor-cycle accident and was admitted to hospital. The claimant stayed at his son's bedside for 14 days watching him deteriorate in health, suffer a heart attack, fall into a coma, and eventually die. The claimant claimed that the hospital had been negligent in that they had failed to diagnose bleeding from his son's left kidney as a result of which he had fallen into a coma. The claimant alleged that he had suffered psychiatric illness as a result of what he had seen whilst at the hospital. The Court of Appeal struck out his action. The claimant's psychiatric illness had not been caused by 'shock' as required under the *McLoughlin/Alcock* rules. There was no evidence that it had arisen from a 'sudden appreciation by sight or sound of a horrifying event'. Instead, the court held that the claimant's condition had arisen from a continuing exposure to the events beginning with his first arriving at the hospital and concluding with the appreciation at the inquest that there had been negligence by the hospital.

5.85 *Sion* is an important case even though the claimant was unsuccessful because it is clear from the judgments, particularly that of Peter Gibson LJ, that a nervous

---

[267] N 260 above. See Grubb, A (1994) 2 Med L Rev 365 (Commentary).

shock claim could arise out of medical negligence.[268] Apart from the necessary relationship to the patient, as *Sion* makes clear, it is crucial if a claim for psychiatric illness is to have any chance of success that what the claimant sees 'shocks' her. Relatives who suffer recognised psychiatric illness subsequent to the death or illness of their loved one, such as pathological grief disorder (PGD), will be able to recover providing the 'traumatising' or 'shocking' event was, at least, a contributory cause of their psychiatric illness.[269] Likewise, if the subsequent events aggravate or prolong 'shock'-induced psychiatric illness then damages may be recovered even if this is characterised as PGD.[270] It will be otherwise, however, where the PGD is wholly caused by subsequent events which do not fall within the *McLoughlin/Alcock* rules.[271] Much will therefore turn on the expert evidence of what caused the claimant's psychiatric illness and will require a degree of sophistication.

However, the need for a 'shocking' event must not be misunderstood. In *Sion*, it was argued that the defendant's conduct must be 'shocking' in the sense of a sudden and violent incident. The Court of Appeal disagreed. Peter Gibson LJ made this clear, doubting the statement of Auld J in *Taylor v Somerset HA*[272] to the contrary. He said:[273]   **5.86**

> I see no reason in logic why a breach of duty causing an incident involving no violence or suddenness, such as where the wrong medicine is negligently given to a hospital patient, could not lead to a claim for damages for nervous shock, for example where the negligence has fatal results and a visiting close relative, *wholly unprepared for what has occurred*, finds the body and thereby sustains a sudden and unexpected shock to the nervous system.

The crucial factor is the unexpected nature of what the claimant *witnesses* through sight or sound rather than the character of the event in itself. Though, of course, merely to be *told* the unexpected is quite illogically not enough.[274] In *Sion*, the claimant's psychiatric illness arose from the gradual realisation that his son would not survive. Hence, his death was not surprising but expected.[275]   **5.87**

What is not covered by the 'secondary victim' rules is, as *Sion* itself shows, a situation where the relative's psychiatric illness arises from a vigil at the bedside and the   **5.88**

---

[268] N 260 above, especially at 176.
[269] *Vernon v Bosley (No 1)* [1997] 1 All ER 577 (CA).
[270] ibid.
[271] See *Calascione v Dixon* (1993) 19 BMLR 97 (CA) (claim for PGD not allowed) as explained by the majority of the Court of Appeal in *Vernon v Bosley (No 1)* ibid, *per* Evans LJ at 600 and *per* Thorpe LJ at 609–10.
[272] (1993) 16 BMLR 63.
[273] N 261 above, 176 (emphasis added).
[274] See *Ravenscroft v Rederiaktiebolaget Transatlantic* [1992] 2 All ER 470 (CA).
[275] See also *Tan v East London and City HA* [1999] Lloyd's Rep Med 389 (Judge Ludlow) (psychiatric injury not 'shock' induced when arising from planned or expected events).

gradual realisation of the victim's fate.[276] A fortiori a claim would not arise if the claimant's illness arose from the long-term care of the victim of medical negligence at home.[277]

5.89   These points are illustrated in the Court of Appeal's decision in *North Glamorgan NHS Trust v Walters*.[278] The claimant's 10-month-old son was admitted to hospital suspected of suffering from hepatitis A. In fact, the defendant failed negligently to diagnose he was suffering from acute hepatitis. The claimant stayed with her child in the hospital. She was awoken in the early hours of the morning to discover her son having a major epileptic seizure which, it subsequently transpired, had led to coma and irreparable brain damage. She was told that her son had not suffered brain damage but was to be transferred to a hospital in London for a liver transplant. Following a scan there, she was told that he had severe brain damage, was on a life-support machine, had only a 50/50 chance of survival and, if he did, would be severely disabled. The next day, following a scan which showed his brain was so severely damaged that he would have no quality of life, the claimant agreed that his life-support should be switched off. Thirty-six hours after his fit, he died in the claimant's arms. The claimant suffered pathological grief reaction.

5.90   The Court of Appeal held that the facts fell within the *McLoughlin/Alcock* rules. First, the 36-hour period amounted to 'an event' as there was an inexorable progression from the moment the fit occurred to the time of the child's death. Second, the claimant's appreciation of the event was 'sudden' and not an accumulation of gradual assaults on her mind. Each event had its impact immediately. This was not a case where the claimant's psychiatric injury arose from a gradual dawning of the realisation that her child's life was in danger. The court approved *Tredgett* and distinguished *Sion* which had not involved a 'shocking' event but rather by a gradual assault on the claimant over a period of time.[279]

(c) Witnessing the Immediate Aftermath

5.91   In addition to situations where the claimant witnesses the event, the *McLoughlin/Alcock* rules contemplate recovery for psychiatric injury as a result of witnessing the 'immediate aftermath'. In *McLoughlin* itself, the House of Lords accepted a claim where the claimant visited the hospital some two hours after the car accident and saw her family in the state they had been brought in. By contrast, in *Alcock* the House of Lords rejected a claim where relatives had visited a

---

[276]   See also *Anderson v Smith* (1990) 101 FLR 34 (15 months vigil) and *Beecham v Hughes* (1988) 52 DLR (4th) 625 (BCCA): gradual realisation that wife severely injured.

[277]   *Alcock* (n 253 above), *per* Lord Ackner at 917; *Andrewartha v Andrewartha* (1987) 44 SASR 1 (South Aus Sup Ct).

[278]   N 263 above. Discussed in Laing, J (2003) 11 Med L Rev 121 (Commentary).

[279]   ibid, *per* Ward LJ at 57–58. He also distinguished the case of *Taylorson v Shieldness Produce Ltd* [1994] PIQR P329 as involving a gradual dawning of the fate of the relative.

mortuary and saw their dead family members eight or nine hours after their death. The distinction between these two factual applications of the 'immediate aftermath' requirement cannot simply be one of time. One important difference is that in *McLoughlin* the victims were in much the same condition as they were immediately following the accident. In *Alcock*, however, the victims had been cleaned up. A further difference is that in *McLoughlin*, the claimant arrived at the hospital not knowing what to expect. In *Alcock*, the claimants knew their relatives were dead and had come to identify them. Applying the 'suddenness' or 'unexpected' requirement of *Sion*,[280] identifying a body will rarely give rise to an *unexpected* shock, unless perhaps in cases where the body is badly mutilated or has not been cleaned up. In *Calascione v Dixon*,[281] the claimant recovered damages for psychiatric injury (post-traumatic stress disorder, 'PTSD') as a result of seeing her dead son's body in a hospital following a road accident. His body was described as 'barely recognisable'.

Consequently, there will be little scope for applying the 'immediate aftermath' requirement in medical negligence cases. A claimant who arrives at the hospital after the patient has died or been injured will only possibly have a claim if the condition of the claimant creates an unexpected (and immediate) reaction in the claimant. Identifying a dead body is very unlikely to qualify. In *Taylor v Somerset HA*[282] the claimant's husband suffered a heart attack. He was taken to hospital and died. The claimant was informed that he was ill and had been taken to hospital. She was told after a short time that her husband had died. Not believing what she was told and in shock, she asked to see the body and identified him in the hospital mortuary. The sight of his body caused her shock and distress. She sued the defendant alleging that she had suffered psychiatric injury as a result of the death of her husband which the defendant had negligently caused by failing to diagnose and treat his serious heart condition. Auld J rejected her claim. He held that she could not claim for any psychiatric injury arising from being told that her husband was dead. Further, her visit to the mortuary did not fall within the 'immediate aftermath' requirement. She had gone there to identify her husband and apart from the 'obvious shock to her of the sight of his dead body, it bore no marks or signs to her of the sort that would have conjured up for her the circumstances of his fatal attack'.[283] The absence of the latter was crucial and distinguished the case from *McLoughlin*. **5.92**

Likewise, in *Tan v East London and the City HA*,[284] the claimant was the husband of a patient whose baby was stillborn following the alleged negligence of the **5.93**

---

[280] N 260 above. See para 5.79.
[281] N 271 above.
[282] (1993) 16 BMLR 63.
[283] ibid.
[284] N 262 above.

defendant. The claimant comforted his wife overnight following the news that their baby had died in utero, he held the dead baby after it was delivered the next day and witnessed the disposal of its remains in a metal box. He claimed damages for psychiatric injury. The judge held that he could not recover as a 'secondary victim': (i) the relevant event that he had to witness or be present at the immediate aftermath was the baby's death in utero; (ii) it could not be said the claimant had been present at it or its immediate aftermath; (iii) in any event, he had not suffered psychiatric injury by 'shock' since, apart from being told of his baby's death, the events relied upon were planned and expected.

(d) Delivering 'Bad News'[285]

5.94 A final situation which should be considered is where a person is negligently told bad news about a relative and, as a consequence, suffers a shock which causes psychiatric injury.[286] The negligence may lie in the way the information is communicated or in its accuracy. It is clear that an action will not lie against the primary defendant where an intermediary acts as a conduit to tell the claimant of injuries that have been inflicted upon the claimant's relative.[287] Unlike that situation, however, we are concerned with the liability of the *intermediary* himself. Can a doctor[288] be liable for negligently[289] breaking 'bad news' to the relatives? In principle there is no reason why he should not.[290] The three elements required for a duty of care—'foreseeability', 'proximity', and the 'fair, just, and reasonable' requirement—seem satisfied. It is readily foreseeable that carelessness might produce an adverse psychiatric reaction. There is a 'close and direct' relationship between the doctor and relative sufficient to create a proximate relationship. Finally, it is not obvious what policy reasons mitigate against imposing liability in this particular context. It should not matter whether the negligence lies in the falsity of the communication or in the method or nature of a (true) communication. As regards the latter situation, there is certainly some analogy with the duty of a doctor to exercise reasonable care when informing his patients post-operatively.[291] However, the contrary has been suggested at least where the information is true.[292]

---

[285] See Mullany and Handford, *Tort Liability for Psychiatric Injury* (n 250 above), at 183–91.

[286] See above, paras 5.46–5.47, for the related issue of liability to the patient.

[287] See above, para 5.87.

[288] Or other, such as a counsellor.

[289] See *Wilkinson v Downton* [1897] 2 QB 57 for malicious communication.

[290] *Jinks v Cardwell* (1987) 39 CCLT 168 (Ont H Ct) (doctor held liable for psychiatric injury caused to a wife when he told her, falsely, that her husband had committed suicide).

[291] See *AB v Tameside & Glossop Health Authority* [1997] 8 Med LR 91 (CA), and above, para 5.47.

[292] *Mount Isa Mines v Pusey* (1970) 125 CLR 383 (Aust H Ct), *per* Windeyer J at 407. But note *Guay v Sun Publishing Co* [1953] 4 DLR 577 (Can Sup Ct) (no liability for false story published in newspaper).

The decision of the Court of Appeal in *Powell v Boldaz*[293] appears to limit the   **5.95**
scope of a doctor's liability in these circumstances. The claimants, a married
couple, brought an action claiming damages for psychiatric injury arising out of
the death of their son. He suffered from a rare condition known as 'Addison's
Disease'. It was accepted that there had been negligence in failing to diagnose and
treat his condition and that had he been treated in time he would have survived.
Sometime after their son's death, the claimants were told the reason for his death
and were shown his medical records. No complaint was made about this.
However, they alleged that seven months later they discovered that their son's
medical notes had been tampered with by the defendants. They alleged that their
GPs had conspired to 'cover-up' the cause of their son's death and that their realisation of this caused them each to suffer PTSD. The judge struck out their
actions. The Court of Appeal dismissed the appeal on the basis that no duty of care
was owed by the defendants in respect of the post-death allegations. The Court of
Appeal held that a duty of care would only arise if the defendants had been called
upon or undertook to treat the claimants as patients. While the defendants were
the claimants' GPs, the court held that at the relevant time they had not been
counselling or treating the claimants. Stuart-Smith LJ said:[294]

> I do not think that a doctor who has been treating a patient who has died, who tells
> relatives what has happened, thereby undertakes the doctor–patient relationship
> towards the relatives. It is a situation that calls for sensitivity, tact and discretion. But
> the mere fact that the communicator is a doctor, does not, without more, mean that
> he undertakes the doctor–patient relationship.

Later, he stated that the case law did not establish:

> some kind of free-standing duty of candour, irrespective of whether the doctor–
> patient relationship exists in a healing or treating context, breach of which sounds
> in damages, such damages involving personal injury. This would involve a startling
> expansion of the law of tort.[295]

Three observations on this decision are worth making. First, the claimants only   **5.96**
alleged that their discovery of the 'conspiracy' caused them psychiatric injury and
not the communication by the GPs to them of false, inaccurate or insensitively
communicated information. Arguably, the claimants' claim would have been
stronger if this had been the case. Secondly, the almost mesmeric effect on the
Court of Appeal of the label 'doctor–patient relationship' has to be questioned. It
is not a necessary condition for a doctor to owe another a duty of care.[296] It is as if
the court thought that the claimants were alleging that the defendants had negligently failed to treat them. If they had, the existence of the relationship would

---

[293] (1997) 39 BMLR 35.
[294] ibid, 45.
[295] ibid, 46.
[296] See below, paras 5.98 *et seq.*

have been important, though even then not conclusive, to the action. But this was in fact irrelevant in the case because it was not what they alleged. The real question was whether the defendants owed a duty not to harm the claimants, rather than one not to diagnose or treat them negligently. Thirdly, the Court of Appeal's denial of a duty of care in circumstances such as these was not quite categorical. The court accepted that if the doctor realised that the news he had broken had shocked the recipient such as to call for treatment, he might be liable for not carrying on and treating the individual. Stuart-Smith LJ stated that it would be 'a question of fact and degree in each case whether the doctor–patient relationship came into existence by the doctor undertaking to treat and heal the person as a patient'.[297]

5.97 It is suggested that the reasoning of the Court of Appeal is so open to question that it is extremely unlikely to survive scrutiny in a future case where a doctor negligently *advises* a relative of a patient's death or injuries and thereby causes psychiatric injury.[298]

3. Doctors Engaged by Others

5.98 In a number of situations a doctor may be requested and engaged by a third party to examine and provide a report on an individual's health. For example, a doctor may be engaged to provide a medical report by an insurance company prior to writing a policy or by a prospective employer to ensure the individual's fitness for the job.[299] In addition, a police surgeon may be called upon to examine the person at a police station prior to detention, or a doctor may be requested by a local social services authority to determine whether there is evidence of child abuse, or requested to provide a statutory opinion necessary for the detention of the person under the Mental Health Act 1983. What, if any, duty does the doctor owe the individual examined who is not, in conventional terms, his patient? Is the doctor's duty limited to not harming the individual during the examination or does it go further and require the doctor, for example, to appraise the person of anything relevant to his health discovered during the examination? The answer in England is not clear, not least because of the paucity of authority on the issue although it has been suggested that English law only accepts the limited duty.[300] Courts in other jurisdictions, particularly in the United States, have however addressed this question.

---

[297] N 293 above, 45.

[298] In *Farrell v Avon HA* [2001] Lloyd's Rep Med 458 (HHJ Bursell QC), the claimant recovered damages for psychiatric injury after he was handed the body of a dead baby that he was wrongly told was his child. In fact, his own baby was alive.

[299] Other examples might include the preparation of a report for the purposes of litigation or for assessing the individual's entitlement under an insurance policy or a statutory benefits scheme.

[300] *X v Bedfordshire County Council* [1995] 2 AC 633; [1995] 3 All ER 353.

(i) Overseas Authorities

In other jurisdictions, particularly the United States, courts have reached different **5.99**
conclusions.[301] Some courts have dismissed claims brought against doctors engaged by (prospective) employers or insurance companies for failure to diagnose a
medical condition or, having done so, to inform or advise the person of it.[302] The
absence of a doctor–patient relationship is seen as crucial; without it courts have
allowed actions only where the person has been injured during the examination.[303] However, some courts have taken a slightly wider view of liability imposing a duty of care where the doctor undertakes to advise the person of his
condition and misrepresents or conceals the results[304] and the advice is relied upon
to his detriment.[305] Liability in the last two situations, though extending beyond
cases where injury is caused by the doctor, can be premised upon rules of liability
for negligent misrepresentation and assumption of responsibility to the individual and should, it is suggested, be followed in England.[306]

However, increasingly US courts are extending liability to cases involving a pure **5.100**
failure to warn or advise a patient about a known (or knowable) health condition
discovered during the examination. In *Green v Walker*[307] an employee was required to undergo annual health checks. The doctor carried out the tests, found
all the results to be normal and classified the employee as 'employable without restriction'. One year later, the employee was diagnosed with lung cancer. He sued
the doctor in negligence alleging that his failure to diagnose the cancer was careless; the failure to disclose these findings and the consequent delay in treatment
had reduced his chances of survival. The employee subsequently died. The Fifth
Circuit Court of Appeals held that the defendant owed the employee a duty of
care notwithstanding the examination occurred ostensibly for the benefit of the
employer. The duty required the doctor to carry out the tests and diagnosis carefully and to advise the employee of any findings that 'pose an imminent danger to
[his] physical or mental well-being'. Subsequent decisions have approved the
court's decision.[308] There is a strong argument for finding that a doctor impliedly
assumes a responsibility to the individual by examining the patient and refraining

---

[301] Many of the cases are helpfully collected in the judgment of the Supreme Court of Montana in
Webb v TD (1997) 95 P 2d 1008. See also *Annotation*, 10 ALR 3d 1071.
[302] eg, *Beaman v Helton* (1990) 573 So 2d 776 (Miss Sup Ct) (no liability for failing to advise examinee that x-ray disclosed cancer).
[303] *Beadling v Sirotta* (1964) 197 A 2d 857 (NJ Sup Ct).
[304] *Hoover v Williamson* (1964) 203 A 2d 861 (Md CA).
[305] *Heller v Community Hospital* (1993) 603 NYS 2d 548.
[306] *Baker v Kaye* (n 135 above) is an example of a duty of care based upon assumption of responsibility.
[307] (1990) F 2d 291 (5th Cir).
[308] See *Daly v US* (1991) 946 F 2d 1467 (9th Cir); *Cleghorn v Hess* (1993) 853 P 2d 1260 (Nev
Sup Ct); *Baer v Regents of University of California* (1994) 884 P 2d 841 (NM CA); *Webb v TD* (1997)
951 P 2d 1008 (Mont Sup Ct).

from disclosing the results or taking other appropriate action to appraise the individual of the need for further investigation. An individual is as likely to rely upon the silence of the doctor as upon a positive misrepresentation of his good health.[309] One US court persuasively put it as follows:[310]

> When a doctor conducts a physical examination, the examinee generally assumes that 'no news is good news' and relies on the assumption that any serious condition will be revealed.

Similar decisions to *Green v Walker* have been reached in Australia[311] and Canada[312] where the doctor was engaged by a third party.

(ii) English Law

5.101   It is perhaps unfortunate that the issue of whether a professional can be liable to an individual when he has been engaged by a third party has arisen in a series of House of Lords cases concerned with statutory frameworks concerned with child protection and other local authority functions.[313] Thus, the courts have considered, for example, of psychiatrists and social workers engaged in child abuse investigations and of educational psychologists dealing with children with learning difficulties. There is no doubt that, at least at first, the courts' approach was heavily influenced by the statutory context and their (again initial) reluctance to contemplate damages actions against the employers of these professionals. It is only relatively recently that the courts have reverted to a principled approach of professional liability in these (arguably) controversial statutory contexts. Unfortunately, in the meantime, the judges' views have influenced the approach in ordinary and standard professional liability contexts.

(a) X v Bedfordshire County Council

5.102   Whether a doctor engaged by a third party owes a duty to the examinee first arose in the House of Lords' decision in *X v Bedfordshire County Council*.[314] The complex legal and facts issues raised by this case can be found elsewhere.[315] The important issue here, however, is whether a psychiatrist who interviews and

---

[309] See *Webb v TD*, ibid, *per* Trieweiler J (Leaphart and Gray JJ dubitante).

[310] *Betesh v US* (1974) 400 F Supp 238 (DC Dist Ct), *per* Bryant J at 246 (liability for failing to advise examinee during military pre-induction physical examination of abnormality on x-ray indicating cancer).

[311] *Thomsen v Davison* [1975] Qd R 93.

[312] *Parslow v Masters* [1993] 6 WWR 273 (action to obtain medical report).

[313] *X v Bedfordshire County Council* [1995] 2 AC 633; [1995] 3 All ER 353; *Phelps v Hillingdon London Borough Council* [2000] 3 WLR 776; *Barrett v Enfield London Borough Council* [2001] 2 AC 550. See generally, Grubb (ed), *The Law of Tort* (n 13 above), ch 17.

[314] ibid.

[315] See Cane, P, 'Suing Public Authorities in Tort' (1996) 112 LQR 13 and Oliphant, K, 'Tort' (1996) 49 CLP 29, 31–44.

examines a child for suspected sexual abuse at the behest of the local social services can be liable to the child for psychiatric injury caused when it is unnecessarily taken into care. The House of Lords held that the psychiatrist did not owe the child a duty of care in such circumstances. Beyond the duty not to injure the child during the examination, the psychiatrist's duty was owed solely to the local authority: there was no proximity between the child and doctor.[316] Lord Browne-Wilkinson stated that the psychiatrist did not

> by accepting the instructions of the local authority, assume any general professional duty of care to the claimant children. The professionals were employed or retained to advise the local authority in relation to the well-being of the claimants but not to advise or treat the claimants.[317]

5.103

Lord Browne-Wilkinson drew an analogy with the situation where a doctor is retained by an insurance company to examine an applicant for life insurance. He said:[318]

> The doctor does not, by examining the applicant, come under any general duty of medical care to the applicant. He is under a duty not to damage the applicant in the course of the examination: but beyond that his duties are owed to the insurance company and not to the applicant.

5.104

No authority is given for this analysis of the relationship in the insurance context; indeed there could not be, since it does not appear that the issue has ever directly arisen in England. It was, however, crucial to the view taken by at least four of the judges in the House of Lords.[319] A similar analogy was drawn by a majority of the Court of Appeal.[320] Staughton LJ asserted (and it was no more) that the psychiatrist was in precisely the same position as a doctor who examined a person for insurance purposes or takes a blood sample from a suspected drunk driver at a police station. The doctor owed the person a duty not to cause harm during the examination but 'the general duty to perform the task allocated with reasonable skill and care' was owed to the insurance company or police authority only.[321] By contrast Sir Thomas Bingham MR dissented on the issue of the psychiatrist's duty. He concluded that a duty of care was owed to the child because it was for the child alone that the psychiatrist was 'being invited to exercise her professional skill and judgment'.[322]

---

[316] Lord Nolan dissented on this point (n 313 above), at 400.
[317] ibid, 384.
[318] ibid, 383.
[319] Lord Nolan disagreed that an analogy could be drawn between the relationship of the insurance doctor and an examinee and the psychiatrist in *Bedfordshire* (ibid, 400).
[320] [1994] 2 WLR 554.
[321] ibid, 582. See also Peter Gibson LJ at 591.
[322] ibid, 570.

(b) Phelps v Hillingdon LBC *and* D v East Berkshire Community NHS Trust

5.105 The law moved on, however, in *Phelps v Hillingdon LBC*[323] and returned to a more principled approach. The case concerned a number of actions by individuals who claimed to have suffered damage as a result of the failure by educational psychologists employed by local authorities to diagnose conditions (such as dyslexia) in the claimants who were schoolchildren. One of the central issues was whether in such circumstances educational psychologists owed the claimants a duty of care such that their employer, local authorities, could be sued in negligence on the basis of vicarious liability.

5.106 The House of Lords held that a duty of care was owed. The judges specifically referred to the situations of professionals, such as doctors, who are engaged by third parties to individuals. The triangular factual situation was not, in itself, a reason why a duty could not be owed to the examinee. Each case would turn upon its own facts assessing the factors usually relevant to establishing a duty.

5.107 Like a doctor or other professionals, the educational psychologists were exercising their professional skill and care in dealing with the children. They were specifically called in to advise on the child's condition and there was an assumption of responsibility to the children—all parties knew that the advice was crucial to the children's future. The fact that the psychologists owed a duty to their employer was no impediment to them also owing a duty to the children. The judges considered the potential for a conflict of duties as crucial in their decision. Unlike the *Bedfordshire* case, there was no conflict between the two duties. Lord Nicholls described the case as 'an example par excellence of a situation where the law will regard the professional as owing a duty of care to a third party as well as his own employer' and considered that the two duties 'march[ed] hand-in-hand'.[324] Lord Clyde specifically acknowledged that a doctor examining an individual for insurance purposes would owe them a duty of care.[325]

5.108 Most recently, in 2003 the Court of Appeal held that the *Bedfordshire* case—ie specifically in the child protection context—could not stand in the wake of the Human Rights Act 1998 and the intellectual pounding it had taken in subsequent House of Lords decisions.[326] In *D v East Berkshire Community NHS Trust*,[327] the Court of Appeal heard three appeals concerned with the liability of health professionals who had mistakenly diagnosed children as being the victims of child

---

[323] [2000] 4 All ER 504. Discussed in Harris, MC (2001) 117 LQR 25.
[324] ibid, 529.
[325] ibid, 537.
[326] eg, *Barrett v Enfield London Borough Council* [2001] 2 AC 550 and *Phelps v Hillingdon London Borough Council* [2000] 3 WLR 776.
[327] [2003] EWCA Civ 1151; [2003] 4 All ER 769.

abuse. Did the professionals owe the children or their parents/carers a duty of care? The court held 'yes' as regards the former but 'no' as regards the latter.

As regards the children, there was no valid public policy reason why a professional should not owe a duty of care to a child who was the subject of investigation. The common law claim raised the same issues which would now arise in a claim under s 6 of the 1998 Act for breach of the child's human rights, in particular under Articles 3 and 8.

5.109

As regards the parents, the Court of Appeal confirmed that no duty of care was owed because the child's interests would conflict with those of the parents and thus public policy required that no duty was owed to them in the course of the investigation.

5.110

Interestingly, the Court of Appeal's decision is concerned wholly with issues of policy. 'Proximity' seems to have been assumed. The upshot must be that the *Bedfordshire* case no longer presents a real obstacle to the courts recognising that a doctor may owe a duty of care to an individual whom, for example, he examines at the behest of another. As we shall see, *Bedfordshire* has been influential in denying such a duty in the leading case in England.

5.111

(c) Applying General Principle

There is no doubt that the doctor owes the person a duty of care in negligence not to cause injury in the course of the examination.[328] Consequently, the doctor who carelessly carries out a medical procedure during the examination, such as taking a blood sample and puncturing an artery, and injures the person will be liable in negligence. This is not the problematic case. The question is whether the doctor owes the patient a broader duty of care than that. To the extent that a doctor already has a relationship with the person (for example, he is that individual's GP), his pre-existing duty of care would extend to all reasonably foreseeable harm.[329]

5.112

Insurance and Employment Examinations   In the private, commercial context of insurance and employment the statutory framework which initially inhibited the application of a common law duty of care in *X v Bedfordshire County Council* is absent. It is clear from the decisions in *Phelps*, and now *D v East Berkshire Community NHS Trust*, that this was the (erroneous in fact) basis of *Bedfordshire*. Equally, there is really no conflict that would arise between the duty owed to the insurance company or employer and the duty which would be owed to the

5.113

---

[328] See, eg, *Leonard v Knott* [1980] 1 WWR 813 (BC CA) (liability for patient who died during annual check-up from an allergic reaction during a procedure). See also *Greenberg v Perkins* (1993) 845 P 2d 530 (Colo Sup Ct) (liability for injury caused to person undergoing tests during medical examination for purposes of litigation).

[329] The fragmentation of a GP's duty proposed in *Powell v Boldaz* (n 293 above), para 5.95 is unsupportable.

examinee. If there were, then a duty of care should not be imposed.[330] The doctor's duty in relation to both would be to exercise reasonable care in carrying out the examination and in interpreting the results. What is reasonable for the doctor *vis à vis* the insurance company is reasonable *vis à vis* the person examined. The doctor's obligations will be tailored to the tasks he undertakes for the third party and what he could (and should) discover and conclude thereafter. A duty to advise the person on the basis of the examination and assessment of his health is entirely consistent with his legal obligations to the third party.[331]

5.114 However, what case law exists in England, is less sanguine in its acceptance of such a duty. Contrast the following two cases.

5.115 In *Baker v Kaye*[332] the claimant was a television sales executive. He was offered a job with a company subject to a satisfactory medical report from the company's doctor. On the strength of this offer, the claimant resigned his existing job. The defendant, a GP in private practice, was employed by the company to carry out a medical examination on the claimant. The results of blood tests taken during the examination suggested to the defendant that the claimant had an alcohol problem; consuming excessive amounts of alcohol made him unsuitable for the demanding job with the company. Consequently, the defendant told the company that he could not recommend the claimant for the job. The company, as a result, withdrew their offer of employment to the claimant. The claimant sued alleging that the defendant had negligently interpreted the test results and, as a result, he had suffered economic loss, namely his lost salary.

5.116 Robert Owen QC (sitting as a Deputy High Court Judge) held that a duty of care was owed to the claimant by the defendant. There had, obviously, been no reliance by the claimant upon the defendant's advice. It was the company in making its decision to withdraw their offer of employment who had relied upon the defendant. Nevertheless, applying the three-stage test in *Caparo*,[333] the judge held that a duty of care existed. First, he held that economic loss to the claimant was foreseeable.

---

[330] A possible example is where a doctor is requested by an insurance company to consider a person's entitlement under an *existing* policy providing, for example, disability or health coverage. Here, the interests of the company and the individual are, arguably, different. The latter is concerned to minimise exposure (down-playing medical condition) while the individual is concerned to discover the full extent of their condition: see, eg, *Keene v Wiggins* (1977) 138 Cal Rptr 3 (Cal CA), *per* Cologne J at 7. The divergence or conflict of interest does not occur when the policy is only in contemplation.

[331] See Lord Clyde in *Phelps* (n 323 above), 537.

[332] [1997] IRLR 219 (Robert Owen QC). For factually similar cases in the US see *Olson v Western Airlines Inc* (1983) 191 Cal Rptr 502 (liability); *Armstrong v Morgan* (1976) 545 SW 2d 45 (Tex CA) (liability). Contrast *Rand v Miller* (1991) 408 SE 2d 655 (W Va Sup Ct App) (no liability); *Felton v Schaeffer* (1991) 279 Cal Rptr 713 (Cal CA) (no liability); *Keene v Wiggins* (1977) 138 Cal Rptr 3 (Cal CA) (no liability).

[333] *Caparo Industries plc v Dickman* [1990] 2 AC 605 (HL).

Secondly, he concluded that there was a proximate relationship between the parties: (i) the defendant knew the claimant's employment depended upon his medical advice to the company; (ii) the claimant entrusted himself and information to the defendant; and (iii) the defendant regarded himself as under a duty to advise the claimant of anything untoward about his health which he might discover during the examination. Finally, the judge could see no policy reason why it was not 'just, fair and reasonable' to impose a duty of care upon the defendant. In the end, however, he held that the defendant was not liable because he had not been negligent.

The decision in *Baker v Kaye* is, however, arguably only of limited importance.[334] **5.117**
It concerned an (allegedly) negligent report produced by a doctor in the knowledge that it would be relied upon and if false was likely to cause loss to the claimant. Thus, liability fell squarely within the case law of the House of Lords beginning with *Hedley Byrne* and, in particular, the employee reference case of *Spring v Guardian Assurance*.[335] Nevertheless, in principle, applying the well-known *Caparo* test, there is no difficulty in holding a doctor liable for *all* the immediate consequences of a failure to exercise reasonable care and skill in the course of the examination. Consequently, he could be liable for failing (carelessly) to diagnose a medical condition which could have been treated or its symptoms alleviated if it had been diagnosed earlier. Injury to the person would be foreseeable and there would be a proximate relationship based upon an implied assumption of responsibility by the doctor. The expectation of both examinee and doctor will usually be that the doctor will perform his professional obligations to the person which would include alerting the person to anything untoward. In one US case the court succinctly stated:[336]

> In placing oneself in the hands of a person held out to the world as skilled in a medical profession, albeit at the request of one's employer, one justifiably has the reasonable expectation that the expert will warn of any incidental dangers of which he is cognizant due to his peculiar knowledge of his specialization.

Obviously, in this situation the doctor would only be required to exercise *reason-* **5.118**
able care. The doctor's duty would not necessarily, perhaps rarely, be to treat the patient. Rather, it would be sufficient for him to discharge his legal duty if he alerted the patient to the danger and advised him to see his own doctor.

---

[334] In *R v Croydon HA* [1998] Lloyd's Rep Med 44 (CA) it was admitted that the duty of a radiologist engaged by an employer to carry out a chest x-ray included a duty to ensure that she was fit for work and would be protected from personal injury whilst in employment by reason of an existing health condition.

[335] [1995] 2 AC 296. Notwithstanding the doubts of the judge, the two cases are very close indeed.

[336] *Webb v TD* (1997) 95 P 2d 1008 (Mont Sup Ct) *per* Trieweiler J (liability for failing to diagnose back condition resulting in injury at work).

5.119 *Baker v Kaye* was, however, disapproved by the Court of Appeal in *Kapfunde v Abbey National.*[337] In *Kapfunde*, the claimant applied for a job with the first defendant. She completed a confidential medical questionnaire on which she indicated that she had been absent from work for periods of time during the previous two years due to sickle cell anaemia. The first defendant passed on the questionnaire to the second defendant, a GP who worked part time for the first defendant. She informed the first defendant that the claimant was likely to have a higher than average absence level. As a result, the first defendant did not give the claimant the job. She sued in tort arguing that the first defendant was vicariously liable for the second defendant's negligence.

5.120 The Court held that the second defendant did not owe a duty of care to the claimant to carry out the assessment carefully so as not to negligently inflict economic loss on the latter: first, there was no doctor–patient relationship between the parties; they never met and the claimant did not know of the second defendant; second, the claim was for economic loss; third, the claimant had not entrusted the second defendant with the conduct of her affairs; and finally, in any event, the second defendant was not, on the facts, in breach of duty since her assessment of the claimant was reasonable. Both Kennedy and Millett LJJ considered that the judge in *Baker v Kaye* should not have held that a duty of care was owed.

5.121 The basis of the reasoning in *Kapfunde* is questionable. Both judges who delivered judgments (Kennedy and Millett LJJ)[338] relied on the general position advocated (obiter) by Lord Browne-Wilkinson in *X v Bedfordshire County Council* that a doctor engaged by a third party, whether insurance company, prospective employer or whatever, owed only the limited duty not to injure the claimant whilst examining the claimant. This, as we have seen, cannot stand with subsequent pronouncements in *Phelps* and should no longer be considered to be sound law—if it ever was!

5.122 The scope of *Kapfunde* is also not clear. There are indications in the judgments of the Court of Appeal that the law may not be so restricted. Both Kennedy and Millett LJJ were anxious to emphasise, and to analyse, the case as being one about economic loss rather than personal injury. Millett LJ also emphasised that it concerned an alleged negligent misstatement for which restrictive rules applied. It is not clear, therefore, what the judges would have held if an examining doctor had failed to discover and/or advise the individual of a deleterious medical condition. Equally, Kennedy LJ (though not Millett LJ) seems to have considered it important that the second defendant had never actually seen, or examined the

---

[337] (1998) 46 BMLR 176 (CA). Discussed in Grubb (1998) 6 Med L Rev 364 (Commentary).
[338] Hutchinson LJ agreed with both judgments.

defendant. In truth, the Court of Appeal has not in *Kapfunde* examined in depth the situation where a third party engages the doctor but rather has relied upon the general—erroneous—remarks in the *Bedfordshire* case. It is open to a future court to re-examine the decision.

Police Surgeons The same rationale applies to the police surgeon examining a **5.123** detained suspect at a police station, with this proviso: the nature of the examination by a police surgeon may be much more limited than for doctors in the other contexts, for example, if the surgeon is merely engaged to take a blood sample. The person's general health condition does not arise. However, if the doctor is engaged to determine the person's fitness to be detained in a police cell overnight, why should not the doctor owe the person a duty to carry out the examination carefully. If a careless mistake is made which leads to the person suffering harm whilst detained, the doctor should, in principle, be liable to the detained person.

Psychiatric Recommendation Leading to Detention What is the position of a **5.124** psychiatrist who negligently recommends that a person be detained under the Mental Health Act 1983? Usually two doctors must recommend detention,[339] at least, one of which will not have a previous relationship with the 'patient'.[340] There is considerable authority to support the view that a doctor owes the (ultimately) detained patient a duty to exercise reasonable care in certifying the patient.[341] The only remaining issues being proof of breach, causation, and damage.[342] In *X v Bedfordshire County Council*, Lord Browne-Wilkinson[343] doubted the authority of one of the earlier 'negligent certification' cases.[344] However, liability falls within

---

[339] Under ss 2(3) (assessment), 3(3) (treatment) and 7(3) (guardianship); only one in an emergency (s 4(3)). See discussion in Hoggett, B, *Mental Health Law* (4th edn, 1996), 66–71.

[340] s 12(2). One doctor must be 'approved': s 12(2).

[341] See *Harnett v Fisher* [1927] AC 573 (HL); *Hall v Semple* (1862) 3 F & F 337 (Crompton J) and *De Freville v Dill* [1927] All ER Rep 205 (McCardie J) and cases cited therein. More recently, *Winch v Jones* [1986] QB 296 (CA) and *James v Havering LBC* (1992) 15 BMLR 1 (CA). See Hoggett, *Mental Health Law* (n 339 above), 248 and Gostin, L, *Mental Health Services—Law and Practice* (1986), para 21.04.1. The position of the approved social worker, who initiates the admission process, is no different in all probability and does not raise the kind of policy questions associated with negligence actions arising out of the performance of statutory functions exemplified by *X v Bedfordshire County Council* (nn 313, 320 above), and see *Buxton v Jayne* [1960] 1 WLR 783 (CA) and *James v Havering LBC*, above.

[342] On which see *Everett v Griffiths* [1920] 3 KB 163 (CA) *per* Atkin LJ at 219 (Scrutton LJ disagreed at 196–7); [1921] 1 AC 631 (HL) *per* Viscount Finlay at 666–667 and *De Freville v Dill* (n 341 above), *per* McCardie J at 212–213 (certification is a cause).

[343] N 313 above, 384.

[344] *Everett v Griffiths* [1920] 3 KB 163 (CA) and [1921] 1 AC 631 (HL). The House of Lords held the certifying doctor not liable because he had exercised reasonable care. The Law Lords did not resolve the different views expressed in the Court of Appeal on the duty issue. Bankes LJ had concluded that a duty to exercise reasonable care but not skill existed (at 183–184). Scrutton LJ held that no duty of care was owed (at 195–196) and Atkin LJ held that a duty to exercise reasonable care existed (at 218). In the House of Lords, Viscount Haldane thought it probable a duty to exercise reasonable care existed (at 657). Viscounts Finlay and Cave and Lords Moulton and Atkinson assumed the duty existed (at 669, 680–681, 697, and 681 respectively).

the principles already discussed and thus, on balance, a social worker or doctor providing a medical recommendation could be liable in negligence. As Lord Denning put it in his famous dissenting judgment in *Candler v Crane Christmas & Co*,[345] the doctor is liable 'because [he] knows that his certificate is required for the very purpose of deciding whether the man should be detained or not'. In modern terminology, there is an assumption of responsibility by the doctors and social worker.

5.125 Nevertheless, it may be that on public policy grounds the courts may not recognise a duty of care owed to detained patients in respect of *the decision to admit* them under the 1983 Act.[346] The statutory (and discretionary) nature of this action, the potential 'chilling' effect of liability in negligence coupled with the spirit of non-liability of hospital managers and others for false imprisonment contained in s 6(3) of the Mental Health Act 1983, could lead a court to decide that no duty is owed. Indeed, the court might accept the argument that the hospital managers are immune because of the quasi-judicial nature of their function.[347]

---

[345] [1951] 1 All ER 426, 435.
[346] cf, liability for negligence once the patient is detained: Jones, M, *Medical Negligence* (3rd edn, 2003), paras 4.108–4.123.
[347] See *X v A, B and C and the Mental Health Act Commission* (1991) 9 BMLR 91 (Morland J): Mental Health Act Commission and appointees not liable for negligent certification that treatment fell within s 57. But contrast the liability of 'second opinion doctor' under ss 57 and 58, *per* Morland J at 99.

6

BREACH OF DUTY

A. Reasonableness

1. The Reasonable Man

The basic test for negligence is whether the defendant's conduct was reasonable in **6.01** all the circumstances of the case. Reasonable conduct is not negligent; unreasonable conduct is culpable. In *Blyth v Birmingham Waterworks Co*[1] Alderson B said that:

> Negligence is the omission to do something which a reasonable man, guided upon those considerations which ordinarily regulate the conduct of human affairs, would do, or doing something which a prudent and reasonable man would not do.

This is an objective standard which does not take account of the subjective attributes of the particular defendant.[2] It is sometimes said that the standard required is that of the reasonable man, the ordinary man, the average man, or the man on the

---

[1] (1856) 11 Exch 781, 784.
[2] *Glasgow Corporation v Muir* [1943] AC 448, 457.

Clapham omnibus.[3] Despite references to the average man, the standard of care is not necessarily determined by the average conduct of people in general if that conduct is routinely careless. Nor is there any concept of an 'average' standard of care by which a defendant might argue that he has provided an adequate service on average and should not be held liable for the occasions when his performance fell below the norm. No matter how competent the defendant's conduct was on average, he will be responsible for damage caused by even a single lapse below the standard of reasonable care.[4]

2. The Reasonable Doctor

6.02 An individual who professes a special skill is judged, not by the standard of the man on the Clapham omnibus, but by the standards of his peers. For the 'reasonable man' is substituted the 'reasonable professional', be it doctor, lawyer, accountant, architect, etc.[5] The classic statement of the test of professional negligence is the direction to the jury of McNair J in *Bolam v Friern Hospital Management Committee.*[6] Now widely known as the '*Bolam* test', this statement of the law has been approved by the House of Lords on no fewer than four times as the touchstone of liability for medical negligence.[7] McNair J said:

> But where you get a situation which involves the use of some special skill or competence, then the test whether there has been negligence or not is not the test of the man on the Clapham omnibus, because he has not got this special skill. The test is the standard of the ordinary skilled man exercising and professing to have that special skill. A man need not possess the highest expert skill at the risk of being found negligent . . . it is sufficient if he exercises the ordinary skill of an ordinary competent man exercising that particular art.[8]

His Lordship agreed that counsel's statement that 'negligence means failure to act in accordance with the standards of reasonably competent medical men at the time' was an accurate statement of the law, provided that it was remembered that there may be one or more perfectly proper standards:

---

[3] *Hall v Brooklands Auto Racing Club* [1933] 1 KB 205, 217.

[4] *Wilsher v Essex AHA* [1986] 3 All ER 801, 810, *per* Mustill LJ. The English courts have not accepted a distinction between 'ordinary' negligence and 'gross' negligence. In *Wilson v Brett* (1843) 11 M & W 113 Rolfe B said that there was no difference: 'it was the same thing with the addition of a vituperative epithet.'

[5] 'The public profession of an art is a representation and undertaking to all the world that the professor possesses the requisite ability and skill. An express promise or express representation in the particular case is not necessary', *per* Willes J in *Harmer v Cornelius* (1858) 5 CB (NS) 236, 246.

[6] [1957] 2 All ER 118. See more generally, Powers and Harris, *Clinical Negligence* (3rd edn, Butterworths, 2000); and Jones, *Medical Negligence* (3rd edn, Sweet & Maxwell, 2003).

[7] *Whitehouse v Jordan* [1981] 1 All ER 267; *Maynard v West Midlands RHA* [1984] 1 WLR 634; *Sidaway v Bethlem Royal Hospital Governors* [1985] 1 All ER 643; *Bolitho v City and Hackney HA* [1997] 4 All ER 771. See also *Chin Keow v Government of Malaysia* [1967] 1 WLR 813, PC. The *Bolam* test is not restricted to doctors, but is of general application to any profession or calling which requires special skill, knowledge or experience: *Gold v Haringey HA* [1987] 2 All ER 888, 894 (CA).

[8] [1957] 2 All ER 118, 121.

A doctor is not guilty of negligence if he has acted in accordance with a practice accepted as proper by a responsible body of medical men skilled in that particular art. . . . Putting it the other way round, a doctor is not negligent, if he is acting in accordance with such a practice, merely because there is a body of opinion that takes a contrary view.[9]

In *Hunter v Hanley* Lord President Clyde dealt with the question of different pro-   **6.03**
fessional practices in these terms:

In the realm of diagnosis and treatment there is ample scope for genuine difference of opinion and one man clearly is not negligent merely because his conclusion differs from that of other professional men, nor because he has displayed less skill or knowledge than others would have shown. The true test for establishing negligence in diagnosis or treatment on the part of a doctor is whether he has been proved to be guilty of such failure as no doctor of ordinary skill would be guilty of if acting with ordinary care.[10]

There is a distinction, however, between a test of negligence based on the standards of the *ordinary* skilled professional and one based on the *reasonably* competent professional. The former places emphasis on the standards which are in fact adopted by the profession, whereas the latter makes it clear that negligence is concerned with departures from what *ought* to have been done in the circumstances, which is measured by reference to the hypothetical 'reasonable doctor'.[11] Of course, what the profession does in a given situation will be an important indicator of what ought to have been done, but it should not necessarily be determinative. In the final analysis it is for the court to determine what the reasonable doctor would have done, not the profession, drawing upon the evidence presented. The *Bolam* test fails to make this distinction between the ordinary skilled doctor and the reasonably competent doctor. The distinction is potentially significant when the question arises whether compliance with common professional practice can be negligent.

3. Reasonable Care

Reasonable care can only be measured by reference to the defendant's conduct in   **6.04**
the circumstances. It is meaningless to say that the standard required is reasonable care, without knowing the particular situation with which the defendant was

---

[9] ibid, 122. Similar formulations of the standard of care required of the medical profession can be found in other Commonwealth jurisdictions: *Crits v Sylvester* (1956) 1 DLR (2d) 502, 508; aff'd (1956) 5 DLR (2d) 601 (SCC). This standard also allows for differences of view within the medical profession: see *Lapointe v Hôpital Le Gardeur* (1992) 90 DLR (4th) 7, 15 (SCC); *F v R* (1982) 33 SASR 189, 190, *per* King CJ.

[10] 1955 SC 200, 204–5. This statement of the law has also been approved by the House of Lords: *Maynard v West Midlands RHA* [1984] 1 WLR 634, 638; *Sidaway v Bethlem Royal Hospital Governors* [1985] 1 All ER 643, 660, *per* Lord Bridge. See also *Dunne v National Maternity Hospital* [1989] IR 91, 109 (Sup Ct Irl).

[11] See Montrose (1958) 21 MLR 259.

confronted. For example, a defendant faced with an emergency and who has to act on the spur of the moment will not be judged too critically simply because with hindsight a different course of action might have avoided the harm.[12] This clearly applies to medical practitioners.[13] Nonetheless, the test remains reasonable care in all the circumstances. If the error is one which a reasonably competent doctor could have made in the circumstances the defendant was not negligent, but if a reasonably competent doctor would not have made that error, the defendant will be liable, notwithstanding the fact that it occurred in the course of an emergency.[14]

6.05   The obligation is to exercise *reasonable* care, and therefore doctors do not guarantee a favourable outcome to their efforts. The medical practitioner is not an insurer and cannot be blamed every time something goes wrong. Indeed, it is widely acknowledged that in medicine, in particular, things can go wrong in the treatment of a patient even with the very best available care.[15] The practitioner is not judged by the standards of the most experienced, most skilful, or most highly qualified member of the profession, but by reference to the standards of the ordinarily competent practitioner in that particular field.[16] Nor is the doctor to be judged by the standards of the least qualified or least experienced. It is not a defence that he acted in good faith, to the best of his ability, if he has failed to reach the objective standard of the ordinarily competent and careful doctor. Nor is it a defence to say that a doctor has committed an 'error of professional judgment' or a 'mere' error of judgment, since this gives no indication as to whether there has been negligence. Some such errors may be consistent with the due exercise of professional skill, but other acts or omissions in the course of exercising 'clinical judgment' may be so glaringly below proper standards as to make a finding of negligence inevitable.[17] If the error of judgment is one that would not have been made by a reasonably competent professional person professing to have the standard and type of skill that the defendant held himself out as having, and acting with

---

[12] *Parkinson v Liverpool Corporation* [1950] 1 All ER 367; *Ng Chun Pui v Lee Chuen Tat* [1988] RTR 298, 302 (both non-medical cases); *Knight v West Kent HA* [1998] Lloyd's Rep Med 18, 23, *per* Kennedy LJ warning against the dangers of hindsight.

[13] In *Wilsher v Essex AHA* [1986] 3 All ER 801, 812 Mustill LJ said that an emergency may overburden the available resources, and, if an individual is forced by circumstances to do too many things at once, the fact that he does one of them incorrectly should not lightly be taken as negligence.

[14] Where an emergency is foreseeable the hospital authority may be negligent if there is an inadequate system for dealing with the known risks that the emergency is likely to create: *Bull v Devon AHA* (1989), [1993] 4 Med LR 117 (CA); *Meyer v Gordon* (1981) 17 CCLT 1 (BCSC).

[15] *Hancke v Hooper* (1835) 7 C & P 81, 84, *per* Tindal CJ; *Mahon v Osborne* [1939] 2 KB 14, 31, *per* Scott LJ; *Daniels v Heskin* [1954] IR 73, 84.

[16] *Lanphier v Phipos* (1838) 8 C & P 475, 479, *per* Tindal CJ; *R v Bateman* (1925) 94 LJKB 791, 794, *per* Lord Hewart CJ. See also *Greaves & Co (Contractors) Ltd v Baynham Meikle and Partners* [1975] 3 All ER 99 at 103–104, *per* Lord Denning MR.

[17] *Whitehouse v Jordan* [1981] 1 All ER 267, 276 *per* Lord Edmund-Davies.

ordinary care, then it is negligent. If, on the other hand, it is an error that a person, acting with ordinary care, might have made, then it is not negligent.[18]

Within the broad term 'reasonable care' it is possible to identify some general **6.06** principles which the courts have used in the decision-making process about what constitutes negligence. They are, however, no more than guidelines, and competing principles can point to different outcomes. Medical evidence is invariably a vital element in an action for medical negligence, but the importance attached to expert opinion should not obscure the underlying basis for a finding that the defendant has been negligent. This is that, in the light of the expert evidence, the defendant has taken an unjustified risk, for example, or has failed to keep up to date, or has undertaken a task beyond his competence, or conversely that the risk was justified by the potential benefit to the patient, or the harm was unforeseeable, and so on. In other words, expert opinion about the defendant's conduct (whether favourable or unfavourable) should itself be measured against the general principles applied to the question of breach of duty. This point has been emphasised by the House of Lords in *Bolitho v City and Hackney HA*[19] where Lord Browne-Wilkinson made it clear that the court has to weigh expert evidence in a form of risk-benefit analysis:

> the court has to be satisfied that the exponents of the body of opinion relied upon can demonstrate that such opinion has a logical basis. In particular in cases involving, as they so often do, the weighing of risks against benefits, the judge before accepting a body of opinion as being responsible, reasonable or respectable, will need to be satisfied that, in forming their views, the experts have directed their minds to the question of comparative risks and benefits and have reached a defensible conclusion on the matter.

B. The Standard of Care Required

1. Common Professional Practice

As a general rule, the fact that a defendant acted in accordance with the common **6.07** practice of others in a similar situation is strong evidence that he has not been negligent.[20] Following a common practice is only *evidence*, however, it is not conclusive, since the court may find that the practice is itself negligent.[21] There could be

---

[18] ibid, 281, *per* Lord Fraser. See also *per* Lord Diplock in *Saif Ali v Sydney Mitchell & Co* [1980] AC 198, 220.

[19] [1997] 4 All ER 771, 778.

[20] *Morton v William Dixon Ltd* 1909 SC 807, 809; *Morris v West Hartlepool Steam Navigation Co Ltd* [1956] AC 552, 579.

[21] See, eg, *Lloyds Bank Ltd v EB Savory & Co* [1933] AC 201; *Cavanagh v Ulster Weaving Co Ltd* [1960] AC 145; *General Cleaning Contractors v Christmas* [1953] AC 180, 193, *per* Lord Reid; *Roberge v Bolduc* (1991) 78 DLR (4th) 666, 710 (SCC).

many reasons, such as convenience, cost, or habit, why a particular practice is commonly followed, which have nothing to do with exercising reasonable care to avoid harming others.[22] There is no reason in theory why the general approach taken by the courts to compliance with accepted practice should not also apply to actions for medical negligence and it is frequently an issue in such cases.

6.08   In *Vancouver General Hospital v McDaniel*[23] Lord Alness said that a defendant charged with negligence can 'clear his feet' if he shows that he has acted in accordance with general and approved practice, and there are numerous cases in which actions for medical negligence have been dismissed on the basis that the doctor conformed to an accepted practice of the profession.[24] Where there is more than one common practice, as the *Bolam* test contemplates, compliance with one of the practices will normally excuse the defendant. In *Maynard v West Midlands RHA*[25] Lord Scarman said that:

> It is not enough to show that there is a body of competent professional opinion which considers that theirs was a wrong decision, if there also exists a body of professional opinion, equally competent, which supports the decision as reasonable in the circumstances. . . . Differences of opinion and practice exist, and will always exist, in the medical as in other professions. There is seldom any one answer exclusive of all others to problems of professional judgment. A court may prefer one body of opinion to the other: but that is no basis for a conclusion of negligence.[26]

It is ostensibly for the court to decide whether, on the evidence before it, the body of opinion which approved of the defendant's conduct could be said to be responsible. However, there are some judicial statements which suggest that the practice of the medical profession is determinative of the issue, and that it is not open to the court to condemn as negligent a commonly adopted practice. In *Maynard's* case Lord Scarman suggested that the 'seal of approval' of a distinguished body of professional opinion, held in good faith, would acquit the defendant of negligence.[27] His Lordship appeared to equate a *competent* (or 'responsible') body of professional opinion with 'distinguished' or 'respectable' in

---

[22] As Lord Tomlin commented in *Bank of Montreal v Dominion Gresham Guarantee and Casualty Co* [1930] AC 659, 666: 'Neglect of duty does not cease by repetition to be neglect of duty'; *Carpenters' Co v British Mutual Banking Co Ltd* [1937] 3 All ER 811, 820, *per* Slesser LJ.

[23] (1934) 152 LT 56, 57–58; *Marshall v Lindsey County Council* [1935] 1 KB 516, 540, *per* Maugham LJ.

[24] *Vancouver General Hospital v McDaniel* (1934) 152 LT 56; *Whiteford v Hunter* [1950] WN 553; *Bolam v Friern Hospital Management Committee* [1957] 2 All ER 118; *Gold v Haringey HA* [1987] 2 All ER 888.

[25] [1984] 1 WLR 634.

[26] ibid, at 638; *Ratty v Haringey HA* [1994] 5 Med LR 413, 416, CA; *Dunne v National Maternity Hospital* [1989] IR 91, 109 (Sup Ct Irl); *Kaban v Sett* [1994] 1 WWR 476, 479–480 (Man QB). On the other hand, where there has been no considered clinical judgment, but rather 'a catalogue of errors', the approach in *Maynard* to competing bodies of professional opinion will not be relevant: *Le Page v Kingston and Richmond HA* [1997] 8 Med LR 229, 240.

[27] ibid, 639.

fact. This tends to conflate accepted practice with the absence of negligence, and, indeed, a 'responsible body of opinion' with the views of distinguished or respectable expert witnesses. This approach is even more apparent in Lord Scarman's speech in *Sidaway v Bethlem Royal Hospital Governors* where he said:

> The *Bolam* principle may be formulated as a rule that a doctor is not negligent if he acts in accordance with a practice accepted at the time as proper by a responsible body of medical opinion even though other doctors adopt a different practice. *In short, the law imposes the duty of care; but the standard of care is a matter of medical judgment.*[28]

As Lord Scarman himself recognised, 'the implications of this view of the law are disturbing. It leaves the determination of a legal duty to the judgment of doctors.' On the other hand, this interpretation of the *Bolam* test was not accepted by Lord Bridge in *Sidaway* who said:

> . . . the issue whether non-disclosure in a particular case should be condemned as a breach of the doctor's duty of care is an issue to be decided primarily on the basis of expert medical evidence, applying the *Bolam* test. . . . Of course, if there is a conflict of evidence whether a responsible body of medical opinion approves of non-disclosure in a particular case, the judge will have to resolve that conflict. But, even in a case where, as here, no expert witness in the relevant medical field condemns the non-disclosure as being in conflict with accepted and responsible medical practice, I am of opinion that the judge might in certain circumstances come to the conclusion that disclosure of a particular risk was so obviously necessary to an informed choice on the part of the patient that no reasonably prudent medical man would fail to make it.[29]

In other words, the court may condemn even a universally followed practice concerning risk disclosure as negligent on the basis that the hypothetical reasonable doctor would not have adopted it. There is no reason to confine this approach to risk disclosure since the majority of their Lordships in *Sidaway v Bethlem Royal Hospital Governors* said that the *Bolam* test applied to all aspects of the doctor's duty of care: diagnosis, advice and treatment.[30]

---

[28] [1985] 1 All ER 643, 649, emphasis added; cf Sir John Donaldson MR in the Court of Appeal, [1984] 1 All ER 1018, 1028: 'The definition of the duty of care is a matter for the law and the courts. They cannot stand idly by if the profession, by an excess of paternalism, denies its patients a real choice. In a word, the law will not permit the medical profession to play God.'

[29] ibid, 662–663. See also Sir John Donaldson MR in *Sidaway v Bethlem Royal Hospital Governors* [1984] 1 All ER 1018, 1028: '. . . in an appropriate case, a judge would be entitled to reject a unanimous medical view if he were satisfied that it was manifestly wrong and that the doctors must have been misdirecting themselves as to their duty in law.' Thus, a practice must be 'rightly' accepted as proper by the profession. His Lordship drew a specific analogy with the cases in which the courts had held the common practice of employers to be negligent. See further the comment of Farquharson LJ in *Bolitho v City and Hackney HA* [1993] 4 Med LR 381, 386.

[30] See, however, *Gordon v Wilson* [1992] 3 Med LR 401, 426 (Court of Session) where Lord Penrose appeared to suggest that Lord Bridge's comments were confined to the disclosure of information to patients, and that 'nothing in the speech of Lord Bridge was intended to qualify the *Bolam* test'. With respect, though this last observation is accurate, it is clear that the *Bolam* test applies to all aspects of a doctor's duty of care to a patient.

6.09 Outside the context of medical negligence actions, the courts have had no difficulty with the notion that commonly adopted practices may themselves be negligent. This has been most apparent in cases of employers' liability,[31] but it is also
evident in some cases involving professional liability.[32] There is no basis for applying a different rule about the effect of complying with common practice to the
medical profession from that which is applied to all other professions, particularly
since the Court of Appeal has emphasised that the *Bolam* test applies to all professions equally.[33] In other common law jurisdictions the courts have been careful to
ensure that, ultimately, decisions as to what constitutes negligence remain for the
court to determine. In *Anderson v Chasney*[34] Coyne JA commented that if general
practice was a conclusive defence:

> a group of operators by adopting some practice could legislate themselves out
> of liability for negligence to the public by adopting or continuing what was an
> obviously negligent practice, even though a simple precaution, plainly capable
> of obviating danger which sometimes might result in death, was well known.

Thus, expert evidence from doctors as to a general or approved practice could not
be accepted as conclusive on the issue of negligence, especially where the conduct
in question did not involve a matter of technical skill and experience.[35] In *F v R*[36]
King CJ acknowledged that professions may adopt unreasonable practices.
Practices may develop in professions, not because they serve the interests of
clients, but because they protect the interests or convenience of members of the
profession. The court has an obligation to scrutinise professional practices to ensure that they accord with the standard of reasonableness imposed by the law. The
ultimate question was not whether the defendant's conduct was in accord with the
practices of the profession or some part of it, but whether it conformed to the
standard of reasonable care demanded by the law. That was a question for the

---

[31] As, eg, in *Cavanagh v Ulster Weaving Co Ltd* [1960] AC 145; *Morris v West Hartlepool Steam
Navigation Co Ltd* [1956] AC 552; *Stokes v Guest, Keen & Nettlefold (Bolts & Nuts) Ltd* [1968] 1
WLR 1776, 1783.

[32] *Lloyds Bank v Savory & Co* [1933] AC 201, 203; *Edward Wong Finance Co Ltd v Johnson, Stokes
and Masters* [1984] AC 296; *Re The Herald of Free Enterprise: Appeal by Captain Lewry*, Independent,
18 December 1987 (Div Ct); *Roberge v Bolduc* (1991) 78 DLR (4th) 666 (SCC).

[33] *Gold v Haringey HA* [1987] 2 All ER 888, 894, *per* Lloyd LJ; *Whitehouse v Jordan* [1981] 1 All
ER 267, 276 *per* Lord Edmund-Davies.

[34] [1949] 4 DLR 71, 85 (Man CA); aff'd [1950] 4 DLR 223 (SCC). See also *Hajgato v London
Health Association* (1982) 36 OR (2d) 669, 693, *per* Callaghan J.

[35] See also *Crits v Sylvester* (1956) 1 DLR (2d) 502, 514; aff'd (1956) 5 DLR (2d) 601; *Reynard v
Carr* (1983) 30 CCLT 42, 68 (BCSC), *per* Bouck J; *Winrob v Street* (1959) 28 WWR 118, 122
(BCSC); *Hajgato v London Health Association* (1982) 36 OR (2d) 669, 693; *Goode v Nash* (1979) 21
SASR 419, 422 (SC of S Aus); *O'Donovan v Cork County Council* [1967] IR 173, 193, *per* Walsh J;
Albrighton v Royal Prince Alfred Hospital [1980] 2 NSWLR 542, 562–563, *per* Reynolds JA
(NSWCA); *Roberge v Bolduc* (1991) 78 DLR (4th) 666, 710 (SCC), *per* L'Heureux-Dubé J.

[36] (1982) 33 SASR 189, 194 (SC of S Aus), approved by Zelling J in *Battersby v Tottman* (1985)
37 SASR 524, 537; and Lockhart, Sheppard and Pincus JJ in *E v Australian Red Cross Society* (1991)
105 ALR 53, 68, 82–83, 87 (Aus Fed CA).

court and the duty of deciding it could not be delegated to any profession or group in the community.[37]

There are, moreover, some English cases in which, on the facts, compliance with common practice has been said to have been negligent. In *Clarke v Adams*[38] the claimant was being treated for a fibrositic condition of the heel and he was warned by the physiotherapist to say if he felt anything more than a 'comfortable warmth'. He suffered a burning injury resulting in the leg being amputated below the knee. Slade J held the defendant liable for giving an inadequate warning to enable the claimant to be safe, although it was the very warning that the defendant had been taught to give. In *Hucks v Cole*, Sachs LJ said that:

6.10

> When the evidence shows that a lacuna in professional practice exists by which risks of grave danger are knowingly taken, then, however small the risks, the courts must anxiously examine that lacuna—particularly if the risks can be easily and inexpensively avoided. If the court finds, on an analysis of the reasons given for not taking those precautions that, in the light of current professional knowledge, there is no proper basis for the lacuna, and that it is definitely not reasonable that those risks should have been taken, its function is to state that fact and where necessary to state that it constitutes negligence. In such a case the practice will no doubt thereafter be altered to the benefit of patients.[39]

His Lordship added that the fact that other practitioners would have done the same thing as the defendant was a weighty factor to be put in the scales on his behalf, but it was not conclusive. The court had to be vigilant to see whether the

---

[37] This view was approved by the High Court of Australia in *Rogers v Whitaker* (1992) 109 ALR 625; [1993] 4 Med LR 79, where it was accepted that, while evidence of acceptable medical practice might be regarded as a useful guide, it was for the court to determine whether the defendant's conduct conformed to the standard of reasonable care demanded by the law; Trindade (1993) 109 LQR 352; McDonald and Swanton (1993) 67 ALJ 145; Malcolm (1994) 2 Tort L Rev 81. In *Naxakis v Western General Hospital* [1999] HCA 22; (1999) 162 ALR 540 the High Court of Australia confirmed that the *Bolam* test had been rejected in *Rogers v Whitaker*. The test for medical negligence was not what other doctors say they would or would not have done in the same or similar circumstances, *per* Gaudron J at [18] and [19]. See also *Dunne v National Maternity Hospital* [1989] IR 91, 109 (Sup Ct Irl) where it was said that reliance on general and approved practice would not exculpate a defendant if the practice has 'inherent defects which ought to be obvious to any person giving the matter due consideration'. In *Collins v Mid-Western Health Board* [2000] 2 IR 154, 156 (Sup Ct Irl) Keane J said that: '. . . a lay tribunal will be reluctant to condemn as unsafe a practice which has been universally approved in a particular profession. The defects in a practice universally followed by specialists in the field are unlikely to be as obvious as the test requires: if they were, it is a reasonable assumption that it would not be so followed. But . . . ultimately, the courts must reserve the power to find as unsafe practices which have been generally followed in a profession.'
[38] (1950) 94 SJ 599; see also *Jones v Manchester Corporation* [1952] 2 All ER 125, 129, *per* Singleton LJ citing Oliver J, the trial judge. Some commentators consider *Clarke v Adams* to be of questionable authority on the basis that it predates *Bolam v Friern HMC* [1957] 2 All ER 118: see Montgomery (1989) 16 J of Law and Soc 319, 323; Dugdale and Stanton, *Professional Negligence* (3rd edn, 1998) para 15.26, n 6. The *Bolam* test, however, was not new, it simply encapsulated earlier statements of the law. This, at least, was Lord Diplock's interpretation: *Sidaway v Bethlem Royal Hospital Governors* [1985] 1 All ER 643, 657.
[39] (1968), [1993] 4 Med LR 393, 397.

reasons given for putting a patient at risk were valid in the light of any well-known advance in medical knowledge, or whether they stemmed from a residual adherence to out-of-date ideas.[40]

6.11 In *Bolitho v City and Hackney Health Authority*[41] a 2-year-old boy suffered brain damage as a result of cardiac arrest caused by an obstruction of the bronchial air passages. The claimant was in hospital at the time for the treatment of croup. The defendants admitted that there had been negligence, in that a doctor who had been summoned for assistance on more than one occasion had failed to attend. It was also common ground that had the claimant been seen by a doctor and intubated, clearing the obstruction, the brain damage could have been avoided. There were two schools of thought, however, as to whether in the circumstances it was appropriate to intubate. The doctor who failed to attend said that had she attended the claimant she would not have intubated, and therefore the cardiac arrest and subsequent brain damage would have occurred in any event. There was evidence from one expert for the defendants, which the trial judge and the Court of Appeal chose to characterise as a responsible body of professional opinion, that he would not have intubated in the circumstances, although five medical experts for the claimant said that the child should have been intubated, and it was agreed that this was the only course of action that would have prevented the damage in this case. In the House of Lords the claimant submitted that the judge had been wrong in law to treat the *Bolam* test as requiring him to accept the views of one truthful body of expert professional advice, even though he was unpersuaded of its logical force, and that ultimately it was for the court, not for medical opinion, to decide what was the standard of care required of a professional in the circumstances of each particular case.

6.12 Delivering the judgment of the House, Lord Browne-Wilkinson agreed that the court was not bound to conclude that a doctor can escape liability for negligent treatment or diagnosis just because he leads evidence from a number of medical

---

[40] In *Bolitho v City and Hackney HA* [1993] 4 Med LR 381, 392 Dillon LJ suggested that the court could only adopt the approach of Sachs LJ and reject medical opinion on the ground that the reasons of one group of doctors does not really stand up to analysis if the court, fully conscious of its own lack of medical and clinical experience, was nonetheless clearly satisfied that the views of that group of doctors were *Wednesbury* unreasonable, ie views such as no reasonable body of doctors could have held. In *Joyce v Wandsworth HA* [1996] 7 Med LR 1, 20, however, Hobhouse LJ took a different view: 'In my judgment (*pace* Dillon LJ [1993] 4 Med LR at p. 392), it does not assist to introduce concepts from administrative law such as the *Wednesbury* test; such tests are directed to very different problems and their use, even by analogy, in negligence cases can, in my judgment, only serve to confuse.' In *X (minors) v Bedfordshire County Council* [1995] 3 WLR 152, 170, in a slightly different context, Lord Browne-Wilkinson commented that: 'I do not believe that it is either helpful or necessary to introduce public law concepts as to the validity of a decision into the question of liability at common law for negligence.'

[41] [1997] 4 All ER 771. For a more detailed discussion of *Bolitho*, see Teff (1998) 18 OJLS 473; Grubb (1998) 6 Med L Rev 378; Jones (1999) 7 Tort L Rev 226; Brazier and Miola (2000) 8 Med L Rev 85; Maclean (2002) 5 Med Law Int 205.

experts who are genuinely of the opinion that the defendant's treatment or diagnosis accorded with sound medical practice. The court had to be satisfied that the opinion had a logical basis, which would involve the weighing of risks against benefits, in order to reach a defensible conclusion. His Lordship referred to the judgment of Sachs LJ in *Hucks v Cole* and the decision of the Privy Council in *Edward Wong Finance Co Ltd v Johnson Stokes & Master*[42] and commented:

> These decisions demonstrate that in cases of diagnosis and treatment there are cases where, despite a body of professional opinion sanctioning the defendant's conduct, the defendant can properly be held liable for negligence (I am not here considering questions of disclosure of risk). In my judgment that is because, in some cases, it cannot be demonstrated to the judge's satisfaction that the body of opinion relied upon is reasonable or responsible. In the vast majority of cases the fact that distinguished experts in the field are of a particular opinion will demonstrate the reasonableness of that opinion. In particular, where there are questions of assessment of the relative risks and benefits of adopting a particular medical practice, a reasonable view necessarily presupposes that the relative risks and benefits have been weighed by the experts in forming their opinions. But if, in a rare case, it can be demonstrated that the professional opinion is not capable of withstanding logical analysis, the judge is entitled to hold that the body of opinion is not reasonable or responsible.[43]

It is rare for the courts to condemn a commonly accepted practice as negligent. **6.13** Normally, it will only be where the risk was, or should have been, obvious to the defendant so that it would be folly to disregard it that the courts will take this step.[44] The point was stressed by Lord Browne-Wilkinson in *Bolitho v City and Hackney Health Authority*.[45] It would very seldom be right, said his Lordship, for a judge to reach the conclusion that views genuinely held by a competent medical expert were unreasonable. It would be wrong to allow the assessment of medical risks and benefits, which was a matter of clinical judgment, to deteriorate into seeking to persuade the judge to prefer one of two views both of which are capable of being logically supported: 'It is only where a judge can be satisfied that the body of expert opinion cannot be logically supported at all that such opinion will not provide the bench mark by reference to which the defendant's conduct falls to be assessed.'

---

[42] [1984] 1 AC 296.

[43] [1997] 4 All ER 771, 779.

[44] *Paris v Stepney Borough Council* [1951] AC 367, 382, *per* Lord Normand: 'obvious folly'; *General Cleaning Contractors v Christmas* [1953] AC 180, 193, *per* Lord Reid: 'obvious danger'; *Morris v West Hartlepool Steam Navigation Co Ltd* [1956] AC 552, 579, *per* Lord Cohen: 'obvious risk'; *Stokes v Guest, Keen & Nettlefold (Bolts & Nuts) Ltd* [1968] 1 WLR 1776, 1783; see also *O'Donovan v Cork County Council* [1967] IR 173, 193, *per* Walsh J; *Gent v Wilson* (1956) 2 DLR (2d) 160, 165 *per* Schroeder JA (Ont CA).

[45] [1997] 4 All ER 771, 779.

6.14 In *Marriott v West Midlands HA*[46] the claimant sustained a head injury in a fall and was unconscious for about half an hour. He was admitted to hospital, and, after X-rays and neurological observations he was discharged the next day. At home he was lethargic, had headaches and no appetite. He did not improve. Eight days after the fall his GP visited the claimant at home, but the neurological tests he carried out showed no abnormality. The GP advised the claimant's wife to telephone him if the claimant deteriorated and suggested analgesics for the headaches. Four days later the claimant's condition suddenly deteriorated, and following emergency surgery on a skull fracture he was left paralysed and with a speech disorder. The trial judge held that if there was a body of professional opinion which supported the course of leaving a patient at home in these circumstances, then it was not a reasonable body of opinion. The risk might be small, but the consequences if something went wrong would be disastrous for the patient. In the circumstances the only reasonably prudent course where there was a risk of an intracranial lesion, judged from the point of view of the patient, was to re-admit the patient to hospital for further testing and observation. The Court of Appeal held that the trial judge was entitled to reject the defendant's expert evidence, applying *Bolitho*. She had considered the small risk of something going wrong, but had weighed that against the seriousness of the consequences for the claimant if the risk did materialise, and the fact that the facilities available in modern hospitals for carrying out scans and other diagnostic procedures were readily available.[47]

6.15 Where the case does not involve difficult or uncertain questions of medical or surgical treatment, or highly technical scientific issues, but is concerned with whether obvious and simple precautions could have been taken, it will be easier for the court to form its own judgment and the practice of experts, though not irrelevant, may be more readily discounted.[48] Where, however, there are difficult, uncertain, highly technical scientific questions requiring information not ordinarily expected of a practitioner, and where the state of medical knowledge was highly variable between scientists, public health authorities and different medical communities, it is not appropriate for the court to find that a practice which

---

[46] [1999] Lloyd's Rep Med 23; Jones (1999) 15 PN 117.

[47] An expert's views which are based on a mistaken diagnosis are likely to be condemned as illogical: *Drake v Pontefract Health Authority; Wakefield and Pontefract Community NHS Trust* [1998] Lloyd's Rep Med 425, 445, QBD. See also *Hunt v NHS Litigation Authority* (2000), (unreported) QBD, where the defendant's expert's view that the circumstances for the administration of the drug syntocinon to a mother in the course of labour (in order to speed up contractions) had not changed in a 47-minute period during which there were signs of foetal distress on the CTG trace were rejected as 'without logical support', not least because it was inconsistent with other answers that the witness had given in evidence. See further *Reynolds v North Tyneside Health Authority* [2002] Lloyd's Rep Med 459, where the defendants' argument that it was reasonable to ignore a small risk of catastrophic consequences, when the burden of precautions was minimal, was rejected as indefensible.

[48] *Anderson v Chasney* [1949] 4 DLR 71, 86–87 *per* Coyne JA (Man CA); aff'd [1950] 4 DLR 223 (SCC); *Chapman v Rix* (1959) 103 SJ 940 *per* Morris LJ (CA).

conformed to what other similarly situated practitioners were following was negligent.[49] In these circumstances the court should confine itself to the prevailing
standards of practice.

Before any question of complying with accepted practice can arise the court must **6.16**
be satisfied on the evidence presented to it that there is a responsible body of professional opinion which supports the practice. It is always open to the court to
reject expert evidence applying the ordinary principles of credibility that would
be applied in any courtroom.[50] In *Hills v Potter*, Hirst J denied that the *Bolam* test
allows the medical profession to set the standard of care:

> In every case the court must be satisfied that the standard contended for . . . accords
> with that upheld by a substantial body[51] of medical opinion, and that this body of
> medical opinion is both respectable and responsible, and experienced in this par-
> ticular field of medicine.[52]

Similarly, in *Bolitho v City and Hackney HA* Farquharson LJ pointed out that:

> There is of course no inconsistency between the decisions in *Hucks v Cole* and
> *Maynard*'s case. It is not enough for a defendant to call a number of doctors to say
> what he had done or not done was in accord with accepted clinical practice. It is nec-
> essary for the judge to consider that evidence and decide whether that clinical prac-
> tice puts the patient unnecessarily at risk.[53]

---

[49]   *ter Neuzen v Korn* (1993) 103 DLR (4th) 473, 506 (BCCA); aff'd (1995) 127 DLR (4th) 577
(SCC).

[50]   For example, an expert witness should be independent. Evidence which, say, descends into advocacy may well be treated as less credible. See, eg, *Murphy v Wirral HA* [1996] 7 Med LR 99, 104;
El-Morssy v Bristol and District HA [1996] 7 Med LR 232, 240; *Wiszniewski v Central Manchester
HA* [1996] 7 Med LR 248, 254, 262. For discussion of the duties of an independent expert see:
National Justice Compania Naviera SA v Prudential Assurance Company Ltd, 'The Ikarian Reefer'
[1993] 2 Lloyd's Rep 68, 81–82; *Sharpe v Southend HA* [1997] 8 Med LR 299, 303. These principles have been expanded upon in the CPR Pt 35, and in particular the Practice Direction that
supplements CPR Pt 35, and more recently the *Code of Guidance on Expert Evidence*: see *Civil
Procedure* (2003, Sweet & Maxwell), vol 1, 35PD and 35.16. The Code of Guidance is also extracted
at (2002) 8 Clinical Risk 60.

[51]   In *De Freitas v O'Brien* [1995] 6 Med LR 108 it was argued that this reference to a 'substantial
body of medical opinion' meant that the defendant could not rely on a small number of experts in
the field as supporting a particular practice. The Court of Appeal rejected this argument. The test is
whether there is a 'responsible body' of opinion, which cannot be measured in purely quantitative
terms. On the facts, a body of 11 doctors who specialised in spinal surgery, out of a total of well over
1,000 orthopaedic and neurosurgeons in the country, could represent a responsible body of opinion.

[52]   [1983] 3 All ER 716, 728. See also *per* Lord Diplock in *Sidaway v Bethlem Royal Hospital
Governors* [1985] 1 All ER 643, 659, stating that the court must be satisfied by the expert evidence
that a body of opinion qualifies as a 'responsible' body of medical opinion; *Dowdie v Camberwell HA*
[1997] 8 Med LR 368, 375 *per* Kay J: 'The mere fact that two distinguished expert witnesses have
testified that it was within the range of acceptable practice to proceed in that way does not oblige me
to accept their evidence and, on this issue, I accept the evidence of the plaintiff's experts . . .'

[53]   [1993] 4 Med LR 381, 386. In *Chapman v Rix* (1960), [1994] 5 Med LR 239, 247 Lord
Goddard said that a doctor cannot avoid a finding of negligence merely by finding two doctors to
say that they would have acted as he did, provided there was evidence the other way. In *Gascoine v*

Following accepted practice, or one of several such practices, is strong evidence of the exercise of reasonable care, but ultimately it is for the court to determine what constitutes negligence.[54] It will be rare for the court to conclude that a common practice was negligent, but when this does happen it will be through a finding that the practice was not 'responsible'. Once the practice followed by the defendant is acknowledged to be a 'responsible' practice it is not open to the court to hold that it was negligent, even where another body of 'responsible' professional opinion is critical of the practice. The inherent danger in the *Bolam* test, however, is that if the courts defer too readily to expert evidence, medical standards may decline, since where there are competing views within the medical profession the *Bolam* test supports the lowest common denominator.

(i) Decisions Not Involving Professional Skill or Reasoning

6.17 In *JD Williams & Co Ltd v Michael Hyde & Associates Ltd*[55] the Court of Appeal held that the *Bolam* test does not apply where no special skill is required in determining whether there has been negligence (in which case the test would be the usual 'reasonable man' standard of reasonable care in all the circumstances). On the facts of the case (which involved a judgment as to whether further investigation of the risk of discolouration of garments by a particular type of heating system was required or not) it was held that the exercise of judgment required did not involve any architectural skills, and therefore the judge was entitled to conclude that the failure to investigate the risk by the defendant architects was negligent, without reference to the *Bolam* test. The fact that other architects would also have ignored the risk was irrelevant. Sedley LJ commented that the *Bolam* test typically applied where the negligence was said to lie in a conscious choice of available courses made by a trained professional, but it was typically inappropriate where the negligence consisted of an oversight. In many, though not all, cases where there was more than one tenable view of acceptable practice, competence had to be gauged by the lower or lowest of them. But 'to extend the *Bolam* principle to all allegations of professional negligence would be to make the professions, to an extent large enough to accommodate much harm to the public, judges in their own cause'.[56]

Ian Sheridan & Co [1994] 5 Med LR 437, 444 Mitchell J commented that 'as a matter of common sense . . . simply because a number of doctors gave evidence to the same effect, that does not automatically constitute an established and alternative "school of thought" if, for example, the reasons given to substantiate the views expressed do not stand up to sensible analysis: see *Hucks v Cole* [(1968) [1993] 4 Med LR 393] (*per* Sachs LJ)'.

[54] See *Jackson & Powell on Professional Negligence* (5th edn, 2002), para 2.117; Dugdale and Stanton, *Professional Negligence* (3rd edn, 1998), paras 15.25–15.26; Norrie [1985] JR 145.

[55] [2000] Lloyd's Rep PN 823.

[56] ibid, 835.

Although Sedley LJ's view is that the *Bolam* test should have a much more **6.18** restricted ambit, so that it could not be invoked by a professional person where he has not in fact exercised a professional judgment, in *Adams v Rhymney Valley District Council*[57] a majority of the Court of Appeal held that the *Bolam* test applied even where the particular defendant did not have the qualifications of a professional in the relevant field, and even though he did not go through the process of reasoning which a qualified professional would undertake before choosing a particular course of action. Thus, if the defendant had in fact adopted a course of conduct which a responsible body of opinion would have supported, even by accident, he was not to be held negligent. In a dissenting judgment, Sedley LJ said[58] that the purpose of the *Bolam* test was to enable the court to determine whether a person professing and purporting to exercise a particular skill has exercised it with sufficient competence to escape a charge of negligence. A defendant who had failed to set about exercising a professional skill could not expect to be judged by the court as if he had exercised it. The court could not proceed as if an educated choice had been made when it knew that it had not. It was a 'requirement of the *Bolam* test that the defendant should have considered and reflected upon the alternative courses available and made a conscious choice between them'. The question then, was whether the defendant's eventual choice of a course of conduct made any difference to the outcome, but that was a question of causation, not professional competence. Thus, if on the balance of probabilities, the professional who should have been consulted would have acted as the defendant did, the negligence did not have any causal effect. But if the professional would probably have done something different which would have affected the outcome, the defendant could not rely on the argument that other responsible professionals might have acted in a way which would not have avoided the damage. The approach of Sedley LJ is out of step with the traditional analysis of negligence. Negligence measures an objective standard of conduct rather than a subjective process of reasoning. If, objectively, the defendant conformed to a standard of care that would have been adopted by a responsible body of professional opinion, the fact that he did so as a result of a flawed process of reasoning, or indeed without any reasoning, is simply irrelevant.[59] An analysis of the reasoning process, the weighing of foreseeable risks and benefits against the burden of precautions, clearly is important when considering whether a

---

[57] [2000] Lloyd's Rep PN 777. See de Prez (2001) 17 PN 75.

[58] ibid, at [16] to [19].

[59] See the comments of Chadwick LJ in *Green v Hancocks (A Firm)* [2001] Lloyd's Rep PN 212 at [60]: 'I do not think it necessary . . . to consider whether it could ever be right to look at the advice given in isolation from the thought process which led to that advice. If the advice is correct, it may well be irrelevant whether the adviser hit upon it as the result of careful and detailed thought, or as the result of experience which overrode the need for a detailed analysis of the reasoning process, or purely by luck. I would not endorse the view that, in every case, a professional adviser will be held negligent because he does not spell out in detail the reasons which lead him to the advice which he gives.'

particular professional practice constitutes a responsible practice. That, however, is part and parcel of subjecting professional practice to the logical scrutiny required by *Bolitho*.

(ii) Questions of Fact

6.19 The *Bolam* test does not apply to the resolution of disputes about fact. Thus, where there is a difference of opinion between expert witnesses about a question of fact the court is not precluded from choosing between the expert evidence, even if both views could be characterised as reasonable or responsible. Indeed, the court has a duty to resolve disputes of fact and reach a finding about the facts. In *Penney, Palmer and Cannon v East Kent HA*[60] the claimants alleged that there had been negligence in the screening of cervical smear tests, in that some of the smears were falsely reported as negative, resulting in delay in obtaining treatment for cervical cancer. Screening was carried out by biomedical scientists or by qualified cytology screeners. They did not diagnose, they merely reported what they saw on the slides. If there was an abnormality or if there was doubt as to what was seen, the slide was passed on to a senior screener (a checker). If the checker agreed with the categorisation it was passed on to a pathologist. If the pathologist confirmed the abnormality the patient was referred to a gynaecologist for a colposcopy or a biopsy. The expert witnesses (five pathologists) agreed that if a screener was in doubt about what was seen on the slide, it should not be classified as negative. In each case the claimants' smears were reported as normal or negative, but they all developed cervical cancer. The Court of Appeal held that the *Bolam* test applied, subject to the *Bolitho* proviso that expert evidence as to the defendants' conduct had to stand up to logical analysis. The *Bolam* test did not apply, however, to questions of fact, including the question of what could be seen on the individual slides. Thus, the questions that had to be asked were: (i) what could be seen on each slide; (ii) could a reasonably competent cytoscreener have failed to see what was on the slide; (iii) could a reasonably competent cytoscreener, bearing in mind what he or she should have observed, have treated the slide as negative? The answer to the first question required expert evidence, but if there was a dispute amongst the experts as to what was visible on the slides the judge had to make his own finding of fact, on the balance of probabilities, a finding which might inevitably involve the rejection of some of the expert evidence. The judge then had to consider the second and third questions in determining whether there had been a breach of duty. Those issues involved an assessment of the expert evidence. All the experts were agreed, however, that an 'absolute confidence' standard should have applied, whereby if there was any doubt in the cytoscreener's mind as to whether the slide was normal it should not have been classified as negative. To the extent that the

---

[60] [2000] Lloyd's Rep Med 41.

defendants' experts were saying that it was acceptable to classify a slide as negative when the cytoscreener could not say whether the features of the slide were or were not pre-cancerous, their opinion did not withstand logical analysis. Similarly, if the question is which of two possible explanations for an event having occurred is to be accepted, and there are competing theories from the expert witnesses, the court has to resolve that dispute in determining factual causation.[61]

2. *Departures from Common Practice*

A departure from accepted practice may be evidence of negligence,[62] but it is not conclusive.[63] If deviation from a common professional practice was considered proof of negligence then no doctor could introduce a new technique or method of treatment without facing the risk of a negligence action if something went wrong.[64] The fundamental test remains whether the defendant acted with reasonable care in all the circumstances, and the significance of compliance with or deviation from common professional practice lies in its evidential value. Sometimes, a departure from accepted practice may provide overwhelming evidence of a breach of duty, particularly where the practice is followed as a precaution against a known risk and the defendant has no good reason for not following the normal procedure. If the risk should materialise the defendant will have great difficulty in avoiding a finding of negligence.[65]

6.20

Some instances of departure from accepted practice are quite clearly negligent. In *Chin Keow v Government of Malaysia*[66] a doctor gave a patient an injection of penicillin without making any enquiry about the patient's medical history. Had he done so he would have discovered that she was allergic to penicillin. The patient died due to an allergic reaction to the drug. The doctor was aware of the remote possibility of this risk materialising but he carried on with his routine

6.21

---

[61] In *Fallows v Randle* [1997] 8 Med LR 160 an operation to sterilise the claimant failed to achieve sterility. There were competing theories as to how the operation could have failed, one of which involved negligence by the defendant whereas the other did not. The trial judge preferred the claimant's explanation. Stuart-Smith LJ said, at 165, that the *Bolam* principle 'has really no application where what the judge has to decide is, on balance, which of two explanations—for something which has undoubtedly occurred which shows that the operation has been unsuccessful—is to be preferred. That is a question of fact which the judge has to determine on the ordinary basis of a balance of probability. It is not a question of saying whether there was a respectable body of medical opinion here which says that this can happen by chance without any negligence, it is a question for the judge to weigh up the evidence on both sides, and he is, in my judgment, entitled in a situation like this, to prefer the evidence of one expert witness to that of the other.'

[62] *Robinson v Post Office* [1974] 2 All ER 737, 745.

[63] *Holland v Devitt & Moore Nautical College*, The Times, 4 March 1960, QBD, where a slight departure from the standard textbook treatment was held not negligent, since the doctor had to treat a particular patient, whereas the textbooks deal with a subject generally; *Dunne v National Maternity Hospital* [1989] IR 91, 109.

[64] *Hunter v Hanley* 1955 SC 200, 206, *per* Lord President Clyde.

[65] See *Clark v MacLennan* [1983] 1 All ER 416.

[66] [1967] 1 WLR 813.

practice of not enquiring because he had not had any mishaps before. He was held to have been negligent. All the medical evidence was to the effect that enquiries, which would have taken no more than five minutes, were necessary. Similarly, in *Landau v Werner*[67] a psychiatrist who engaged in social contact with a female patient who had developed a strong and obsessive emotional attachment to him was held to have been negligent. His conduct was a departure from recognised standards in the practice of psychiatry and led to a serious deterioration in the patient's mental health. Sellers LJ said that:

> . . . a doctor might not be negligent if he tried a new technique but if he did he must justify it before the court. If his novel or exceptional treatment had failed disastrously he could not complain if it was held that he went beyond the bounds of due care and skill as recognised generally. Success was the best justification for unusual and unestablished treatment.

6.22 One consequence of the *Bolam* test is that where there are two competing responsible bodies of professional opinion and the defendant adheres to one view, but carelessly fails to follow his own normal practice with the result that he complies with the alternative approach, he will not be held negligent because he will have conformed to a practice accepted as proper by a responsible body of professional opinion. Thus, where the doctor fails to give a warning about the risks of treatment which he would usually give, but there is a responsible body of medical opinion which, as a matter of deliberate policy, would not warn the patient of the particular risks, the defendant will not be liable since, though he has departed from his own clinical practice, he has conformed to a practice accepted as proper by a responsible body of professional opinion, albeit by accident.[68] In *Gascoine v Ian Sheridan & Co*[69] a case of alleged negligent overtreatment, Mitchell J commented that: 'If on some hit-and-miss basis [the defendants] treated correctly (or correctly in the opinion of a respected reasonably competent body of thinking in 1978) then liability in negligence could not be established.'

6.23 Codified standards of professional conduct, though not conclusive, may constitute significant evidence of what constitutes reasonable care.[70] In the context of health care, the introduction of medical audit and NHS clinical governance could lead to the development of treatment protocols and best practice guidelines, providing a consensus view of experts in the field as to the proper standards.[71] It might

---

[67] (1961) 105 SJ 257 and 1008 (CA).
[68] *Moyes v Lothian Health Board* [1990] 1 Med LR 463, 470.
[69] [1994] 5 Med LR 437, 458. See also *Lachambre v Nair* [1989] 2 WWR 749 (Sask QB).
[70] *Lloyd Cheyham & Co Ltd v Littlejohn & Co* (1985) 2 PN 154. See Gwilliam (1986) 2 PN 175.
[71] One consequence of the introduction of clinical governance has been a proliferation of agencies of the Department of Health issuing guidance, some of which is directly relevant to patient safety. See, eg, the National Patient Safety Agency (*www.npsa.org.uk*), the National Institute for Clinical Excellence (*www.nice.org.uk*), and the Commission for Health Improvement (*www.chi.nhs.uk*). The General Medical Council publishes extensive Codes of Practice for doctors,

then become increasingly difficult for a doctor to argue that the protocol was rejected in favour of some alternative method, even if there are some doctors prepared to state that they disagree with the protocol produced by the experts.[72] There is already evidence that the courts are prepared to consider, and accept as highly persuasive, guidelines produced by the medical profession on appropriate standards of conduct.[73]

The fact that a practitioner who departs from the accepted methods of treatment will normally have to provide some justification for doing so could have an inhibiting effect on doctors who seek to employ novel or experimental methods in the interests of their patients where traditional techniques have failed. There is a public interest in allowing the medical profession to develop new, and more effective methods of health care, without the fear that they may be sued for negligence simply for trying something different from established practice.[74] On the other hand, patients should not be recklessly subjected to untried and potentially dangerous experimentation.[75] The law has to reach a balance between these competing considerations. One response has been to say that in such circumstances the courts should be careful not to make a finding of negligence simply because the patient has sustained injury.[76] There is likely to be a time-lag between the development of new methods and their acceptance by the profession. Where the new treatment is not yet supported by a responsible body of medical opinion a

6.24

---

ranging from general statements of good practice (eg *Good Medical Practice*, May 2001) to specific advice on how to proceed in particular circumstances. These codes are available from the GMC website (*www.gmc-uk.org/standards/default.htm*).

[72] Harpwood (1994) 1 Med Law Int 241, 250, 251. Instructive here are the CEPOD Reports into perioperative deaths which have identified certain systematic errors which can occur during surgery: see Buck, Devlin and Lunn, *Report of a Confidential Enquiry into Perioperative Deaths* (Nuffield Provincial Hospitals Trust and the King's Fund, 1987); Campling, Devlin, Hoile and Lunn, *Report of the National Confidential Enquiry into Perioperative Deaths* (National Confidential Enquiry into Perioperative Deaths, London, 1990). See also Devlin (1995) 1 Clinical Risk 97. On the other hand, rigid adherence to guidelines can be inappropriate. Guidelines and protocols vary in their validity, and attempts to reach professional 'consensus' can result in inadequate and biased guidelines: Hurwitz (1995) 1 Clinical Risk 142; Hurwitz (1999) 318 BMJ 661.

[73] See *W v Egdell* [1990] 1 All ER 835 in the context of confidentiality; and *Airedale NHS Trust v Bland* [1993] 1 All ER 821 in the context of the treatment for patients in a persistent vegetative state. See also *Pierre v Marshall* [1994] 8 WWR 478 (Alta QB) where the defendant was held to have been negligent for failing to follow the recommendations of the Alberta Medical Association and the Society of Obstetricians and Gynaecologists of Canada that there should be universal screening of pregnant women for gestational diabetes, notwithstanding that there was still controversy about the cost-effectiveness of universal screening.

[74] *Sidaway v Bethlem Royal Hospital Governors* [1985] 1 All ER 643, 657 *per* Lord Diplock.

[75] In *Coughlin v Kuntz* (1987) 42 CCLT 142 (BCSC); aff'd [1990] 2 WWR 737 (BCCA) the defendant was held to have been negligent for adopting a method of performing an operation which was experimental, unsupported by clinical study, and favoured by no other orthopaedic surgeon. The procedure was under investigation by the College of Physicians and Surgeons, which had urged the defendant to undertake a moratorium on the procedure.

[76] *Wilsher v Essex AHA* [1986] 3 All ER 801, 812 *per* Mustill LJ.

defendant will have to justify his decision simply by reference to the 'reasonable doctor'. This will depend on the relative risk of the treatment in comparison to the alternative treatments and the nature of the illness for which it was prescribed. Where the patient's condition is very serious and the standard treatment is ineffective, a doctor will be justified in taking greater risks in an attempt to provide some effective treatment. In *Zimmer v Ringrose* Prowse JA said that:

> A physician is entitled to decide that the situation dictates the adoption of an innovative course of treatment. As long as he discharges his duty of disclosure, and is not otherwise in breach of his duties of skill and care, eg has not negligently adopted the procedure given the circumstances, the doctor will not be held liable for implementing such a course of treatment.[77]

The defendant's method of sterilisation was 'experimental and quite unsupported by clinical study as a method acceptable for human beings'.[78] He was held to have been negligent in failing to inform the claimant that the technique had not been approved by the medical profession.

6.25 It is clear that the patient should not be exposed to excessive risk and there should be some attempt to provide scientific validation for a new technique. In *Hepworth v Kerr*[79] the defendant anaesthetist adopted a new hypotensive anaesthetic technique which he knew had never been attempted routinely before, in order to provide a blood-free field for the operating surgeon. He knew that he was experimenting, but did not embark upon any proper scientific validation of his technique in some 1,500 patients by the time of the claimant's operation. It was not a minor adjustment to well-established techniques, but a step completely outside conventional wisdom which was right at the margins of safety and effectively took patients 'to the very edge of existence'. McKinnon J held the defendant liable for the condition of anterior spinal artery syndrome (spinal stroke) which the claimant was subsequently found to have developed, despite the fact that this amounted to a condemnation of the defendant's 'life-time work'.

6.26 A degree of care is expected which is commensurate with the risk involved, and innovative treatment would be regarded as inherently 'risky' until it has become tried and tested. In *Independent Broadcasting Authority v EMI Electronics Ltd and BICC Construction Ltd*[80] the House of Lords held that a defendant employed to design an experimental television mast had to demonstrate that he had exercised a high degree of care both in assessing the risks of the venture and the possible alternatives. He could not justify his actions simply by saying 'we were taking a step

---

[77] (1981) 124 DLR (3d) 215, 223–224 (Alta CA). See also *Waters v West Sussex HA* [1995] 6 Med LR 362.

[78] (1978) 89 DLR (3d) 646, 652, *per* MacDonald J. See also *Cryderman v Ringrose* [1977] 3 WWR 109; aff'd [1978] 3 WWR 481 (Alta SC, Appellate Division).

[79] [1995] 6 Med LR 139.

[80] (1980) 14 BLR 1.

into the unknown and so the risks were unforeseeable'. There was an obligation to think things through and to assess the dimensions of the 'venture into the unknown'.[81] This would apply to claims arising out of a systematic research project, whether therapeutic or non-therapeutic. An allegation of negligence in conducting research would involve proving that the design, the performance, or the follow-up of the experimental procedure was negligent, or that the disclosure of information concerning risks was inadequate. A researcher has a duty to investigate fully the possible consequences of the research using existing published literature and animal experiments where appropriate, prior to conducting research on human subjects.[82] Medical research must seek to minimise the risks to the research subjects, for example by providing for termination of the project if a serious risk of harm became apparent; provision for emergencies; and careful periodic observation of the subjects.[83]

The Creutzfeldt-Jakob Disease Litigation, Plaintiffs v United Kingdom Medical **6.27**
Research Council[84] concerned the transmission of the 'slow virus' which causes Creutzfeldt-Jakob Disease (CJD) from human growth hormone (HGH) extracted from the pituitaries of cadavers. Between 1959 and 1985 almost 2,000 children were treated with HGH, and the claimants had all been treated with HGH when they were children. Since 1985, 16 of the recipients had died of CJD and a further three were expected to do so. Eleven claimants (the group A claimants) had developed CJD as a consequence of receiving HGH contaminated with the CJD virus. There were a further 87 claimants in Group B who had received HGH who had not, as yet, been diagnosed with CJD. The treatment with HGH had originally been a clinical trial under the auspices of the Medical Research Council, but subsequently became a treatment programme for which the Department of Health was responsible. Morland J found that because of the emerging evidence about the transmission of slow viruses the treatment programme should have been partially suspended from 1 July 1977. The defendants had been negligent in permitting the programme to continue, because information about the

---

[81] ibid, 31, *per* Lord Edmund-Davies.
[82] *Vacwell Engineering Co Ltd v BDH Chemicals* [1971] 1 QB 88, where the defendant was negligent in failing to check all relevant publications dealing with a little-known chemical prior to marketing it.
[83] *Zimmer v Ringrose* (1978) 89 DLR (3d) 646, 656. It is also arguable that a research project which failed to comply with national or international ethical codes on medical experimentation could be found to have been conducted negligently, on the basis that the codes constitute evidence of what is reasonable care, by reference to the accepted practice of the profession: see Dugdale and Stanton, *Professional Negligence* (3rd edn, 1998), para 15.23. Both therapeutic and non-therapeutic medical research are governed by the guidelines of the *Declaration of Helsinki*, extracted in Kennedy and Grubb, *Medical Law* (3rd edn, 2000), 1678. See further the Royal College of Physicians, *Guidelines on the Practice of Ethics Committees in Medical Research Involving Human Subjects* (2nd edn, 1990) and Royal College of Physicians, *Research Involving Patients* (1990). See generally, Giesen (1995) 3 Med L Rev 22.
[84] (1996) 54 BMLR 8; [1996] 7 Med LR 309.

risk of slow virus infection was conveyed in a cursory manner. In concluding that the Department had been negligent on the basis of its lethargy in carrying out enquiries and research into the risk of slow virus transmission, once it had been alerted to that risk, Morland J stated a number of general principles. First, the question of negligence has to be assessed on the basis of the standards and knowledge which could reasonably have been expected at the time of the alleged negligence. Secondly, the risks of the programme had to be weighed against the benefits:

> Many advances in medicine carry with them risk. A risk may be, from a scientific point of view, theoretical and may never become a reality. A risk may be a real risk, but, weighed against the benefit of a drug or treatment, a risk upon careful consideration worth taking, but the risks of a drug or a treatment need constant review in the light of expanding knowledge and experience.[85]

In assessing that risk the courts had to balance the dangers of too readily condemning novel procedures which went wrong as negligent, against the potential progress that research could produce:

> The courts must be very cautious in condemning a clinical trial or therapeutic programme. Too ready a labelling of an act or omission as negligent by the courts could stultify progress in medical and scientific research and render eminent experts reluctant to serve on committees voluntarily. However, during the clinical trial of a new drug or form of treatment, and especially when the clinical trial is becoming a general therapeutic programme, all reasonably practicable steps should be taken to minimise dangers and side-effects. To discharge this duty, constant alert and inquiring evaluation of the trial or programme is required.[86]

Thirdly, the standard of care applied to publicly funded or sponsored research should not be lower than that applied to commercial organisations: 'In my judgment, the same duty with the same standard of care is owed to all patients who are the subjects of clinical trials or new therapeutic programmes, whether the responsibility of a pharmaceutical company, government department or other agency.'[87] Finally, in respect of the standard of care that could be expected of an advisory committee Morland J concluded that:

> The standard of care . . . to be imposed in respect of a committee is that of a reasonably competent and carefully inquiring group of professionals in the relevant disciplines, of sufficient standing to be entrusted with the membership of that committee, bearing in mind it is a committee which is not merely advisory but is carrying out executive and administrative functions.[88]

---

[85] (1996) 54 BMLR 8, 14.
[86] ibid, 23.
[87] ibid.
[88] ibid, 24.

This applied as much to the scientific and technical staff advising the committee. The medical and scientific staff of both the MRC and the Department had a dual role, one administrative, the other in the use of their professional skills. In servicing the committee, they were under a duty to alert the members to current medical and scientific knowledge, and it was the failure to do so which gave rise to negligence.

3. Keeping Up to Date

Professional practice tends to change over time so that what was once accepted as the correct procedure may no longer be considered to be responsible. Doctors have an obligation to keep up to date with new developments in their particular field, although it can be difficult to determine precisely when a new development will render adherence to the old method negligent; there is a tension between the obligation to keep up to date and the obligation not to subject patients to untried methods of treatment unless the traditional approach has proved ineffective and the anticipated benefits are justified by the risks. Once the risks associated with the old procedure become generally known, so that an ordinary and reasonably competent practitioner can be expected to have altered his practice accordingly, it would be negligent to continue using that procedure. The problem is to identify precisely when it can be said that a risk has become generally known.[89] For example, there may be a difference of knowledge and understanding between research scientists and clinicians, since research scientists are usually better informed about new discoveries in discrete areas of their discipline than practitioners, who have to rely on researchers and professional publications to keep them informed.[90]

6.28

The obligation is to make a reasonable effort to keep up to date. A doctor cannot realistically be expected to read every article in every learned medical journal,[91] but where a particular risk has been highlighted on a number of occasions the practitioner will ignore it at his peril.[92] The practices adopted or state of knowledge in

6.29

---

[89] Note that changes in technique or the use of particular instruments may sometimes simply be a matter of fashion, so that the fact that 'new methods become available does not make the continued use of the old negligent unless and until they are shown to be wrong or to carry an unacceptably higher risk to the patient than the new': *Newbury v Bath District HA* (1998) 47 BMLR 138, 162 *per* Ebsworth J.

[90] *ter Neuzen v Korn* (1993) 103 DLR (4th) 473, 497–498 (BCCA); aff'd (1995) 127 DLR (4th) 577 (SCC). Moreover, there may be a lack of effective communication between public health officials and practitioners, again producing a 'time lag' in the knowledge of the profession.

[91] Although it is acknowledged that 'where there is developing knowledge, [the defendant] must keep reasonably abreast of it and not be too slow to apply it': *Stokes v Guest, Keen & Nettlefold (Bolts & Nuts) Ltd* [1968] 1 WLR 1776, 1783, *per* Swanwick J; on the other hand, where the defendant's omission involves an absence of initiative in seeking out knowledge of facts which are not in themselves obvious 'the court must be slow to blame him for not ploughing a lone furrow': *Thompson v Smith Shiprepairers (North Shields) Ltd* [1984] 1 All ER 881, 894, *per* Mustill J.

[92] See, eg, *Roe v Minister of Health* [1954] 2 QB 66; *McLean v Weir* [1977] 5 WWR 609; aff'd [1980] 4 WWR 330; *McCormick v Marcotte* (1971) 20 DLR (3d) 345 (SCC).

other countries are not necessarily evidence of the appropriate standard in the United Kingdom.[93]

6.30 In *Crawford v Charing Cross Hospital*[94] the claimant developed brachial palsy in an arm following a blood transfusion. At first instance the defendants were held liable on the basis that the anaesthetist had failed to read an article published in *The Lancet* six months earlier, concerning the best position of the arm when using a drip. The Court of Appeal reversed this decision, taking the view that it would be too great a burden to require a doctor to read every article appearing in the current medical press.[95] It was wrong to suggest that a practitioner was negligent simply because he did not immediately put into operation the suggestions made by a contributor to a medical journal, although the time might come when a recommendation was so well proved and so well accepted that it should be adopted. In *Gascoine v Ian Sheridan & Co*[96] Mitchell J commented that a 'shop floor gynaecologist' had a responsibility to keep himself generally informed on mainstream changes in diagnosis, treatment and practice through the mainstream literature, such as the leading textbooks and the *Journal of Obstetrics and Gynaecology*. However, it was unreasonable to suppose that he had had an opportunity to acquaint himself with the content of more obscure journals.

4. Assessing Degrees of Risk

6.31 In applying general principles to the assessment of whether a defendant has exercised reasonable care, the courts take into account a number of factors, including the foreseeability of the damage, the magnitude of the risk, the purpose of the defendant's conduct, and the cost or practicability of taking precautions. These issues are just as relevant to an action for medical negligence as any other type of negligence action, despite the heavy reliance which is often placed on expert medical evidence in the former. The decision of the House of Lords in *Bolitho v City and Hackney Health Authority*[97] now makes it clear that medical experts will have to be able to demonstrate that they have addressed the question of assessing the relative risks and benefits of adopting a particular medical practice, and that their opinion stands up to logical analysis.

---

[93] *Whiteford v Hunter* [1950] WN 553; *ter Neuzen v Korn* (1993) 103 DLR (4th) 473 (BCCA); aff'd (1995) 127 DLR (4th) 577 (SCC), where it was held that it was not open to a jury to find the common practice of Canadian practitioners to be negligent on the basis of knowledge available in Australia.

[94] The Times, 8 December 1953.

[95] See also *Dwan v Farquhar* [1988] 1 Qd R 234, where an article in a journal concerning the risks of contracting the AIDS virus from blood transfusions was published in March 1983, and a patient contracted HIV from a blood transfusion performed in May 1983. It was held that there was no negligence.

[96] [1994] 5 Med LR 437, 447.

[97] [1997] 4 All ER 771, 779.

(i) Foreseeability of Risk

If a particular danger could not reasonably have been anticipated because it was **6.32** unforeseeable, the defendant did not act negligently, because the reasonable man is not expected to take precautions against unforeseeable consequences. Whether a consequence was foreseeable is not determined by using hindsight but by reference to knowledge at the date of the alleged negligence. Thus, in *Roe v Minister of Health*,[98] heard in 1954, the defendants were found not to have been liable for the injuries inflicted when contaminated anaesthetic was administered to the claimant in 1947, because the anaesthetic had become contaminated in a way which was unforeseeable at the time. The court 'must not look at the 1947 accident with 1954 spectacles', even though it would have been negligent to adopt the same practice in 1954 when the risk was more widely known.[99]

(ii) Magnitude of Risk

A defendant is not negligent simply because the damage was foreseeable.[100] In some **6.33** circumstances it may be reasonable to ignore a small risk, because the chance of it materialising is remote and the cost of precautions high. By contrast, where the cost of avoiding a risk is minimal it may be negligent to ignore even a remote risk.[101]

A degree of care commensurate with the risk created by the defendant's conduct is **6.34** required, so that the greater the risk of harm the greater the precautions that must be taken.[102] This principle applies just as much to professional liability as it does to any other category of negligence:

> . . . there is a clear relationship between the magnitude of the risk and the duty of care, in particular the standard of care. The greater the risks involved in any proposed course of treatment, the more carefully and anxiously must the medical practitioner weigh and consider the possible alternatives before deciding to resort to the proposed treatment.[103]

---

[98] [1954] 2 QB 66.

[99] ibid, 86; *McLean v Weir* [1977] 5 WWR 609; aff'd [1980] 4 WWR 330 (BCCA). There is some doubt as to whether the contamination of the anaesthetic in *Roe* was in fact caused by the manner in which it was stored: see Hutter (1990) 45 Anaesthesia 859.

[100] *Bolton v Stone* [1951] AC 850, 863, *per* Lord Oaksey.

[101] *Overseas Tankship (UK) Ltd v Miller Steamship Co Pty Ltd, The Wagon Mound (No 2)* [1967] 1 AC 617, 642.

[102] *Read v J Lyons & Co Ltd* [1947] AC 156, 173, *per* Lord Macmillan.

[103] *Battersby v Tottman* (1985) 37 SASR 524, 542 *per* Jacobs J; *Glasgow Corporation v Muir* [1943] AC 448, 456, *per* Lord Macmillan: 'Those who engage in operations inherently dangerous must take precautions which are not required of persons engaged in the ordinary routine of daily life'; *McAllister v Lewisham and North Southwark HA* [1994] 5 Med LR 343, 347, QBD, where Rougier J commented that: 'The decision whether or not to operate is the product of a tripartite equation: 1. The risks of operating. 2. The benefits of operating. 3. The risks of not operating'; see also *O'Donovan v Cork County Council* [1967] IR 173, 190, *per* Walsh J; *Buchan v Ortho Pharmaceuticals (Canada) Ltd* (1986) 25 DLR (4th) 658, 678–679, *per* Robins JA (Ont CA).

Thus, when an anaesthetist was handling a highly inflammable substance and knew of the hazard arising from electrostatic sparks in an operating theatre, the degree of care required was correspondingly high and he was bound to take special precautions to prevent injury to his patient.[104]

6.35 The magnitude of the risk involves two elements. First, the likelihood that the harm will occur. The more remote the chance that any damage to the claimant will arise, the more reasonable it will be to take fewer, or even no, precautions against the eventuality. Secondly, the degree of risk also takes into account the severity of the potential consequences. If the harm is likely to be serious, should it occur, then greater precautions must be taken. For example, a risk that a patient may be accidentally infected with HIV from a contaminated blood transfusion will impose a high standard of care upon the supplier of the blood, given the seriousness of the consequences.[105] In *Reynolds v North Tyneside HA*[106] a mother was admitted to hospital for the birth of her child, in circumstances where there was a foreseeable risk, put at between 1 in 250 and 1 in 500, of a cord prolapse. This was considered to be 'low risk', but the potential consequences from foetal hypoxia extended to death or brain damage. The risk materialised and the child suffered from cerebral palsy due to an acute umbilical cord prolapse. The alleged negligence consisted of an omission by the midwife to carry out an immediate vaginal examination given the foreseeable risk. Such an examination was neither difficult nor costly. The defendants argued that the risk of cord prolapse was so slight that it could be ignored. Gross J held that the defendants were not entitled simply to ignore the risk. Although the risk was low, it was not far-fetched or fanciful. It was not a case where a nice clinical balance had to be struck: 'Set against the low risk of cord prolapse were (i) the gravity of the consequences should the risk materialise and (ii) the ease and economy of undertaking an immediate [vaginal examination].'[107] There was a risk of infection from an immediate examination, but a vaginal examination was likely to be conducted at some point during labour and the risks of infection would have been the same whenever it was performed. In any event, said the judge, the risk of infection was heavily outweighed by the risk of cord prolapse. In terms of the gravity of the consequences they were not 'in the same league'.

---

[104] *Crits v Sylvester* (1956) 1 DLR (2d) 502, 511 (Ont CA); aff'd (1956) 5 DLR (2d) 601 (SCC); *Darley v Shale* [1993] 4 Med LR 161, 168 (NSWSC).

[105] *E v Australian Red Cross Society* (1991) 105 ALR 53, 77 (Aus Fed CA) *per* Sheppard J. Despite the high duty, the defendants were found not to have been negligent in this case because of the very limited options for reasonable precautions against infection with HIV at the time (October 1984). A test specifically for HIV did not become available until March 1985. See also *Pittman Estate v Bain* (1994) 112 DLR (4th) 257, 319 *per* Lang J (Ont Ct, Gen Div). Note, however, that the importance of the blood supply in saving lives may justify the taking of greater risk than would otherwise be acceptable.

[106] [2002] Lloyd's Rep Med 459.

[107] ibid, [43].

Where a doctor has formed an opinion as to the appropriate diagnosis of a **6.36** patient's condition, he should take into account the possibility that an alternative diagnosis would explain the symptoms, especially where the consequences of the alternative diagnosis, if correct, would be very serious.[108] The defendant must also take account of the known characteristics of the particular claimant where those characteristics make the likelihood of harm occurring greater than would be the case with a normal individual,[109] or where the damage is likely to be more severe.[110] In these circumstances greater precautions will be required than for the average individual.

The purpose of the defendant's conduct will also be taken into account in assess- **6.37** ing what is reasonable. If sufficiently important, it may justify the assumption of abnormal risk.[111] Unsurprisingly, the saving of life and limb is likely to justify tak- ing considerable risk[112] but this does not mean that this purpose can justify taking *any* risk. It is a matter of balancing the risk against the consequences of not taking the risk. If, for example, the patient's condition is such that he will almost certainly die without some form of medical intervention, then treatment with a high degree of risk will be justified, unless, of course, there is an equally effective alternative treatment that carries less risk.

(iii) Cost of Precautions

A further matter to be considered in assessing whether the taking of a foreseeable **6.38** risk was justified is the practicability (or cost) of taking precautions. The practica- bility of taking precautions should be measured on an objective basis: the defen- dant's impecuniosity is not a defence if objectively a precaution was reasonably required.[113] If the risk can be avoided at small cost or with a trivial expenditure of

---

[108] *Lankenau v Dutton* (1986) 37 CCLT 213, 232 (BCSC); aff'd (1991) 79 DLR (4th) 707 (BCCA); *Bergen v Sturgeon General Hospital* (1984) 28 CCLT 155 (Alta QB); *Law Estate v Simice* (1994) 21 CCLT (2d) 228, 236 (BCSC).

[109] A 'measure of care appropriate to the inability or disability of those who are immature or feeble in mind or body is due from others, who know of or ought to anticipate the presence of such persons within the scope and hazard of their own operations': *Glasgow Corporation v Taylor* [1922] 1 AC 44, 67, *per* Lord Sumner, approved by Lord Reid in *Haley v London Electricity Board* [1965] AC 778, 793.

[110] *Paris v Stepney Borough Council* [1951] AC 367.

[111] *Daborn v Bath Tramways Motor Co Ltd* [1946] 2 All ER 333, 336, *per* Asquith LJ.

[112] *Watt v Hertfordshire County Council* [1954] 1 WLR 835. See also the comments of Lang J in *Pittman Estate v Bain* (1994) 112 DLR (4th) 257, 313 (Ont Ct, Gen Div): 'In the case of blood, the societal need for the component produces different considerations. This is not a product that should be removed from the market if inherently dangerous. Blood is an essential source of life to many. Although a biologic, and, therefore, dangerous, the need for the product outweighs the risk.'

[113] In *PQ v Australian Red Cross Society* [1992] 1 VR 19, 33 (Vict SC) McGarvie J held that the actual resources of the defendants was not an issue relevant to the practicability of the precautions required to protect the claimant from HIV infection from a transfusion of blood products; cf *Pittman Estate v Bain* (1994) 112 DLR (4th) 257 (Ont Ct, Gen Div) where Lang J held that the

time and effort, it will be unreasonable to run the risk. Conversely, some risks can only be eliminated or reduced at great expense. A reasonable man would only neglect a risk if he had a valid reason for doing so, for example, if 'it would involve considerable expense to eliminate the risk . . . [h]e would weigh the risk against the difficulty of eliminating it'. However, a reasonable man would not ignore even a small risk 'if action to eliminate it presented no difficulty, involved no disadvantage and required no expense'.[114] In *Hucks v Cole*[115] Sachs LJ said that when risks of great danger are knowingly taken as a matter of professional practice then, however small the risks, the court must carefully examine the practice, particularly where the risks can be easily and inexpensively avoided. In *Coles v Reading and District Management Committee*[116] it was held to be negligent not to have given the patient an anti-tetanus injection, since it was a simple precaution, and the consequences of the infection are serious.

6.39 Some risks will be unavoidable. In this situation the risks of proceeding have to be weighed against the disadvantages of not proceeding, taking into account the expected benefits to the patient's health. Where the consequences of not treating the patient are potentially very serious, then the doctor will normally be justified in taking greater risks.[117] Conversely, where the treatment is for a minor ailment even small risks should not be disregarded,[118] a fortiori, where a diagnostic test which

---

conduct of a blood bank should be measured against that of other blood banks, not by reference to commercial organisations, on the basis that it was a 'professional service' not a commercial service. If other 'responsible' blood banks were unable or unwilling through lack of resources to take such precautions, the defendant would probably not be liable for failing to take the same precautions.

[114] *Overseas Tankship (UK) Ltd v Miller Steamship Co Pty Ltd, The Wagon Mound (No 2)* [1967] 1 AC 617, 642; and in the medical context see *Chin Keow v Government of Malaysia* [1967] 1 WLR 813, PC. In *Hardaker v Newcastle HA and the Chief Constable of Northumbria* [2001] Lloyd's Rep Med 512 at [54] Burnton J held that it was not negligent for the defendant to fail to devote resources, from 'its doubtlessly limited resources', to deal with the claimant's comparatively rare condition (decompression illness). This case is an example of the proposition that the *Bolam* test takes account of what is reasonable in the circumstances, including whether, *objectively*, precautions against a small risk are reasonably required given the cost of taking those precautions and the degree of risk. It has been argued, however, that the acknowledged under-funding of the NHS should lead the courts generally to adopt a lower standard of care so as to 'ensure that hospitals and their staff are less vulnerable to findings of negligence for systematic failures in care which cannot reasonably be attributed to them': Witting (2001) 21 OJLS 443, 444. The logic of this argument is that the worse the service provided the less likely it is that a claim for negligence will succeed when a patient is injured by that service. Such an approach would not be considered acceptable in any other sphere of service provision, whether public or private.

[115] (1968), [1993] 4 Med LR 393, 397.

[116] (1963) 107 SJ 115.

[117] *Davidson v Connaught Laboratories* (1980) 14 CCLT 251, 270, where the patient suffered an allergic reaction to a rabies vaccine, having come into contact with a rabid animal. Rabies is almost invariably fatal.

[118] The obvious example would be cosmetic surgery, although there may well be room for disagreement as to the importance to the individual patient of removing certain cosmetic defects. In *La Fleur v Cornelis* (1979) 28 NBR (2d) 569, 573 (NBSC) Barry J commented that cosmetic surgeons do not treat illnesses in the ordinary sense, and accordingly a 'doctor who undertakes to operate on the nose of a healthy person for cosmetic purposes has a very high duty indeed'.

carries a real risk of an adverse reaction is conducted when there are no clinical indications for performing such a test.[119] This balancing exercise must take account of the individual patient. In *Battersby v Tottman*[120] a doctor prescribed a very high dose of a drug to a patient suffering from mental illness. He took the view that the benefits of the drug outweighed the risk of it causing serious and permanent eye damage, since without treatment the patient was 'dangerously suicidal', and other methods of treatment had failed. It was held that in these circumstances the decision to prescribe a dosage that was far in excess of the recommended dosages was not negligent.[121]

5. Specialists and the Inexperienced

A specialist is required to achieve the standard of care of a reasonably competent **6.40** specialist in his field, exercising 'the ordinary skill of his specialty'.[122] Thus, while a general practitioner must be judged by the standards of general practitioners and not specialists,[123] if a general practitioner were to undertake a specialist task, he would be judged by the standards of that specialty. If he is unable to meet those standards, he will be held negligent for undertaking work beyond his competence. A practitioner of 'alternative medicine' will be judged by reference to the standards of fellow practitioners, not by the standards of conventional medicine, since he does not hold himself out as practising orthodox medicine. Thus, a practitioner of traditional Chinese herbal medicine must conform to the standards of a reasonably competent practitioner of that art. He is not to be held to the standards of orthodox medicine, unless the claimant can prove that the prevailing standard of skill in that art was deficient in the UK having regard to the risks which were not, but should have been taken into account.[124]

---

[119] *Leonard v Knott* [1978] 5 WWR 511 (BCSC).

[120] (1985) 37 SASR 524; see also Scott LJ in *Mahon v Osborne* [1939] 2 KB 14, 31 on the surgeon's problem of balancing competing risks and objectives when performing an operation.

[121] See also *Vernon v Bloomsbury HA* (1986), [1995] 6 Med LR 297.

[122] *Maynard v West Midlands RHA* [1984] 1 WLR 634, 638, *per* Lord Scarman; *Sidaway v Bethlem Royal Hospital Governors* [1985] 1 All ER 643, 660, *per* Lord Bridge; *Whitehouse v Jordan* [1981] 1 All ER 267, 280 *per* Lord Fraser. See also *McCaffrey v Hague* [1949] 4 DLR 291; *Crits v Sylvester* (1956) 1 DLR (2d) 502, 508; aff'd (1956) 5 DLR (2d) 601 (SCC); *Wilson v Swanson* (1956) 5 DLR (2d) 113, 119, *per* Rand J (SCC).

[123] *Langley v Campbell* (1975) The Times, 5 November 1975; *Sa'd v Robinson* [1989] 1 Med LR 41; *Thornton v Nicol* [1992] 3 Med LR 41; *Gordon v Wilson* [1992] 3 Med LR 401 (CS); *Stockdale v Nicholls* [1993] 4 Med LR 190; *Durrant v Burke* [1993] 4 Med LR 258; *Stacey v Chiddy* [1993] 4 Med LR 216 (NSWSC); aff'd [1993] 4 Med LR 345 (NSWCA).

[124] *Shakoor v Situ (t/a Eternal Health Co)* [2001] 1 WLR 410. The defendant had an obligation to check that there had not been any adverse report on the remedy he used in an orthodox medical journal, but since a general practitioner would not have been negligent in failing to identify the risk, then the defendant had conformed to a reasonable standard of care.

6.41 The standard of care within a specialist field is that of the ordinary competent specialist, not the most experienced or most highly qualified within the specialty.[125] However, where the defendant has knowledge of some *fact* that makes harm to the claimant more likely than would otherwise be the case, he must take account of that fact as a reasonable man, ie a greater than average knowledge of the risks entails more than the average or standard precautions.[126] This appears to require that a specialist must take greater precautions than an average doctor when undertaking the same task, if the specialist's actual knowledge and experience gives him a greater knowledge of the risks that ought to be guarded against;[127] a clinician's conduct should not be judged by reference to lesser knowledge than in fact he had. On the other hand, he is not expected to use a higher degree of skill than comparable specialists.[128]

6.42 There may come a point where a sub-discipline develops within a specialty such that it can be said that a practitioner undertaking that type of work must achieve the standards of the new 'specialty'.[129] Conversely, where it can be said that a new specialty has developed, the question of whether the defendant has conformed to the practice of a responsible body of professional opinion will be judged by reference to the standards of that specialty rather than the standards of doctors engaged in a more generalised practice. This may make it reasonable, for example, for a specialist surgeon to undertake intricate exploratory surgery, on the basis that this conforms to a practice accepted as proper by a responsible body of surgeons in the specialty, in circumstances where surgeons in other fields might consider the procedure to be too risky.[130]

---

[125] *O'Donovan v Cork County Council* [1967] IR 173, 190, *per* Walsh J (Sup Ct Irl); *Giurelli v Girgis* (1980) 24 SASR 264, 277, *per* White J; *F v R* (1983) 33 SASR 189, 205, *per* Bollen J.

[126] *Stokes v Guest, Keen & Nettlefold (Nuts & Bolts) Ltd* [1968] 1 WLR 1776, 1783, *per* Swanwick J; *Wilson v Brett* (1843) 11 M & W 113, 115, *per* Rolfe B: 'If a person more skilled knows that to be dangerous which another not so skilled as he does not, surely that makes a difference in the liability.'

[127] A point accepted as correct by Webster J in *Wimpey Construction UK Ltd v Poole* [1984] 2 Lloyd's Rep 499, 506–507.

[128] In *Duchess of Argyll v Beuselinck* [1972] 2 Lloyd's Rep 172, 183 Megarry J suggested that a solicitor's client might be able to purchase a higher standard of care in contract, the obligation stemming from a contractual term that the solicitor would use the care and skill that he actually possessed rather than the care and skill of the average solicitor specialising in that field of law. Megarry J distinguished contractual duties from the tort of negligence, where 'the unusually careful and highly skilled are not held liable for falling below their own high standards if they nevertheless do all that a reasonable man would have done'; cf *Wimpey Construction UK Ltd v Poole* [1984] 2 Lloyd's Rep 499, 506 *per* Webster J. See also *Matrix-Securities Ltd v Theodore Goddard* [1998] PNLR 290 where Lloyd J held that the obligation of a 'City' firm of solicitors advising tax matters, was to exercise that standard of care which could be expected from a reasonably competent firm of solicitors with a specialist tax department. The fact that the defendants professed very high levels of skill and experience (and presumably charged fees to reflect that) did not lead to an inference that they had undertaken a higher duty.

[129] See, eg, *Poole v Morgan* [1987] 3 WWR 217.

[130] *De Freitas v O'Brien* [1995] 6 Med LR 108.

The defendant who is inexperienced or who is just learning a particular task or skill must come up to the standards of the reasonably competent and experienced person. His 'incompetent best' is not good enough.[131] This is a consequence of the rule that the standard of care expected of the reasonable man is objective, not subjective. It takes no account of the particular idiosyncrasies or weaknesses of the defendant.[132] This principle applies with as much force to an inexperienced doctor as it does to, say, an inexperienced motorist. In *Jones v Manchester Corporation*[133] a patient died from an excessive dose of anaesthetic administered by an anaesthetist who had only been qualified for five months. In an action which was concerned with the respective responsibilities of the junior doctor and the hospital authority, the Court of Appeal made it clear that it was no defence to an action by a patient to say that the anaesthetist did not have sufficient experience to undertake the task, or to say that the surgeon in charge was also to blame.

6.43

The issue arose in *Wilsher v Essex Area HA*,[134] in which a premature baby in a special care baby unit received excess oxygen due to an error in monitoring its supply of oxygen. An inexperienced doctor had inserted a catheter (by which the blood oxygen pressure was to be measured) into a vein rather than an artery. This in itself was not a negligent error. However, on checking the position of the catheter by means of an X-ray, the doctor had failed to spot that the catheter was mispositioned. He did ask a senior registrar in the unit to check the X-ray but the registrar also failed to notice the mistake. The baby was subsequently discovered to be suffering from retrolental fibroplasia which causes blindness, possibly as a result of the exposure to excess oxygen.[135] There was a marked difference of opinion on the question of the appropriate standard of care to be applied to the junior doctor. Sir Nicolas Browne-Wilkinson V-C, dissenting, said that it was unfair to apply an objective standard to a junior doctor in the first year after qualifying, or to someone who has just started in a specialist field in order to gain the necessary skill in that field. The doctor could not be said to be at fault if he lacked the very skills which he was seeking to acquire. His Lordship would only hold such a doctor liable for acts or omissions which a careful doctor with his qualifications and experience would not have done or omitted.

6.44

However, Mustill LJ said that the notion of a duty tailored to the actor, rather than to the act which he elects to perform, had no place in the law of tort. The effect of applying a subjective test would be that the standard of care that a patient would be entitled to expect would depend upon the level of experience of the particular

6.45

---

[131] *Nettleship v Weston* [1971] 2 QB 691, 698, 710.
[132] *Glasgow Corporation v Muir* [1943] AC 448, 457, *per* Lord Macmillan.
[133] [1952] 2 All ER 125.
[134] [1986] 3 All ER 801.
[135] The decision of the Court of Appeal on the causation issue was reversed by the House of Lords: [1988] 1 All ER 871. There was no appeal on the question of the standard of care.

doctor who happened to treat him. A professional person who assumed to perform a task must bring to it the appropriate care and skill, although his Lordship
did add that the standard of care should be related, not to the individual, but to
the post which he occupies, distinguishing 'post' from 'rank' or 'status'. It followed
that the standard was not just that of the averagely competent and well-informed
junior houseman (or whatever the position of the doctor) but of a person who
held such a post in a unit offering a highly specialised service, while recognising
that different posts made different demands. The very structure of hospital medicine envisaged that the lower ranks would be occupied by those of whom it would
be wrong to expect too much.

6.46   With respect, these comments appear to introduce an inconsistency since, having
rejected a subjective test of negligence, his Lordship seems to reintroduce variable
standards of care by reference to the 'posts' occupied by different doctors.[136]
Glidewell LJ simply applied the *Bolam* test, commenting that this was the standard by which to weigh the conduct of all the doctors in *Wilsher*:

> In my view, the law requires the trainee or learner to be judged by the same standard
> as his more experienced colleagues. If it did not, inexperience would frequently be
> urged as a defence to an action for professional negligence.[137]

6.47   It is submitted that this is the correct and long-established approach. A single
standard of care for patients can only be achieved by relating the reasonableness of
the defendant's conduct to the task that is undertaken, and what is objectively reasonable does not change with the experience of the defendant, or, for that matter,
the post he holds.[138] This is at its most obvious if a doctor in a specialist 'post'

---

[136] In *Djemal v Bexley HA* [1995] 6 Med LR 269 Sir Haydn Tudor Evans held that the standard of
care required of a senior houseman in an Accident and Emergency department was that of a reasonably competent senior houseman acting as a casualty officer, though without any reference to length
of experience, applying the view of Mustill LJ.

[137] [1986] 3 All ER 801, 831; *Dale v Munthali* (1977) 78 DLR (3d) 588, 594; aff'd (1978) 90
DLR (3d) 763; *Wills v Saunders* [1989] 2 WWR 715 (Alta QB).

[138] See Dugdale and Stanton, *Professional Negligence* (3rd edn, 1998), para 15.11 and para 15.12
making the same point in relation to the standard to be applied to specialists. The objective nature
of the standard of care applies to other factors as well as inexperience. If the defendant is unable to
measure up to the objectively required standard for any reason, be it stress, overwork, tiredness, or
ill-health he will nonetheless be found negligent. Thus, old age or infirmity is not a defence for a negligent driver of a motor vehicle: *Roberts v Ramsbottom* [1980] 1 All ER 7, 15; cf *Mansfield v Weetabix
Ltd* [1999] 1 WLR 1263 where the Court of Appeal held that a driver who becomes unable to control a vehicle will not be liable for damage caused by his loss of control if he is unaware of the disabling condition from which he is suffering, whether the disabling event is sudden or gradual.
Roberts v Ramsbottom could be supported on the ground that the defendant continued to drive when
he was unfit to do so, and when he should have been aware of his unfitness. In *Nickolls v Ministry of
Health*, The Times, 4 February 1955, the surgeon who operated on the claimant was suffering from
cancer. The question was whether he was in a fit condition to have undertaken the operation. It was
held that, on the facts, he was and therefore he was not negligent. Clearly, if the conclusion had been
that he was unfit, and he was aware of that, it would have been negligent to operate. In *Barnett v
Chelsea and Kensington HMC* [1968] 1 All ER 1068, 1073 Nield J held that the doctor's failure to

undertakes some procedure which is completely outside the sphere of that specialty. He would be required to achieve the standard of the reasonably competent doctor in performing the procedure, and if it were a specialised procedure he would have to achieve the standards of the relevant specialty. This has nothing to do with his post. The duty arises by virtue of the fact that he has undertaken to perform the act, and by doing so professes that he has the competence to perform it with skill and care, just as an unqualified person would be held to the standard of a reasonably competent surgeon if he undertook surgery.[139] Thus, undertaking work which is beyond one's competence constitutes negligence. As a matter of practice the inexperienced doctor will normally undertake less complex tasks than his experienced colleagues, but if he does perform tasks beyond the level of his competence, the fault lies not so much in not having the skills, which by definition he does not possess, but in him undertaking the task at all.[140] This principle is not limited to actions against newly qualified doctors. It can apply at any stage where a doctor 'gets in above his head'. The doctor who holds himself out as a specialist will be held to the standards of a reasonably competent specialist, 'even if he is a novice specialist',[141] and even where he is performing the procedure for the first time.[142] A doctor must recognise his limitations and where necessary seek the advice or supervision of more experienced colleagues, or refer the patient to a specialist.[143] The inexperienced doctor will discharge his duty of care by seeking the assistance of his superiors to check his work, even though he may himself have made a mistake.[144] Of course, if the more senior, experienced doctor makes a

see and examine the deceased was negligent, commenting that: 'It is unfortunate that Dr. Banerjee was himself at the time a tired and unwell doctor, but there was no-one else to do that which it was his duty to do.'

[139] *R v Bateman* (1925) 94 LJKB 791, 794, *per* Lord Hewart CJ; *Freeman v Marshall & Co* (1966) 200 EG 777.

[140] In any event, it is possible that a health authority would be in breach of a primary duty of care to the patient for allowing inexperienced staff to practise without adequate supervision: *Jones v Manchester Corporation* [1952] 2 All ER 125; *Wilsher v Essex AHA* [1986] 3 All ER 801, 833 *per* Sir Nicolas Browne-Wilkinson V-C.

[141] *Poole v Morgan* [1987] 3 WWR 217, 254 (Alta QB). The defendant ophthalmologist was held to be inadequately qualified to use laser treatment, a procedure normally performed by a retina vitreous specialist, even though ophthalmologists were permitted to use laser treatment by their governing body.

[142] *McKeachie v Alvarez* (1970) 17 DLR (3d) 87 (BCSC).

[143] *Wilsher v Essex AHA* [1986] 3 All ER 801, 833; *Fraser v Vancouver General Hospital* (1951) 3 WWR 337 (BCCA); aff'd [1952] 3 DLR 785 (SCC); *Payne v St Helier Group HMC*, The Times, 12 July 1952; *Dillon v Le Roux* [1994] 6 WWR 280 (BCCA).

[144] It was on this basis that the junior doctor was found not to have been negligent in *Wilsher v Essex AHA*. See also *Junor v McNicol*, The Times, 26 March 1959, where the House of Lords held that a house surgeon who had acted on the instructions of a consultant orthopaedic surgeon was not liable; *Tanswell v Nelson*, The Times, 11 February 1959, where McNair J said that a dentist was entitled to rely on a doctor's opinion about a patient's response to antibiotics, unless that opinion was clearly inconsistent with the observed facts; *Weir v Graham* [2002] EWHC 2291 (QB), where it was held that a GP was entitled to assume that, where a patient had been referred to hospital for tests, the hospital doctors were aware of the results of the tests and would take them into account in

mistake in checking the junior's work this could be a basis for a finding of negligence.[145]

6. Emergencies

6.48 In an emergency it may well be reasonable for a practitioner inexperienced in a particular treatment to intervene, or indeed for someone lacking medical qualifications to undertake some forms of treatment. For example, a bystander who renders assistance at a road accident does not necessarily hold himself out as qualified to do so. He would be expected to achieve only the standard that could reasonably be expected in the circumstances, which would probably be very low.[146] This approach is clearly born of the emergency since if there was no urgency, the unqualified person who undertook treatment beyond his competence would be held to the standard of a reasonably competent and experienced practitioner. For example, a person who holds himself out as trained in first-aid must conform to the standards of 'the ordinary skilled first-aider exercising and professing to have that special skill of a first-aider'.[147]

7. Defensive Medicine

6.49 The increase in medical malpractice litigation over the last 15 or 20 years has been accompanied by claims that, in response to the threat of litigation, doctors now practise defensively. This involves undertaking procedures which are not medically justified but are designed to protect the doctor from a claim for negligence. The most commonly cited examples are unnecessary diagnostic tests, such as X-rays, and unnecessary caesarian section deliveries. However, applying the *Bolam* test, a reasonable doctor would not undertake an *unnecessary* procedure and so a doctor could not avoid a finding of negligence by performing one. In fact, to the extent that the procedure carries some inherent risk, a practitioner acting in this

---

reaching a diagnosis; *Leonard v Knott* [1978] 5 WWR 511 (BCSC), where it was held that a radiologist was entitled to rely on the judgment of the referring physician as to whether a radiological investigation was required, unless there was some obvious problem; cf *Davy-Chiesman v Davy-Chiesman* [1984] 1 All ER 321, 332, 335, stating that solicitors should not rely blindly on the advice of counsel, although in this case the solicitor had failed to detect an 'obvious error'; *Matrix-Securities Ltd v Theodore Goddard* [1998] PNLR 290—a solicitor is entitled to rely on counsel's advice, and would be negligent for failing to do so unless that advice was obviously wrong; *FirstCity Insurance Group Ltd v Orchard* [2002] Lloyd's Rep PN 543 at [82].

[145] Which is what happened in *Wilsher v Essex AHA*. See also *Drake v Pontefract HA; Wakefield and Pontefract Community NHS Trust* [1998] Lloyd's Rep Med 425, where a consultant psychiatrist was found to have been negligent in allowing an inexperienced Senior House Officer to interview and treat the claimant without immediate supervision from a more experienced psychiatrist, when the patient had been expressly referred as a suicide risk.

[146] See, eg, *Ali v Furness Withy* [1988] 2 Lloyd's Rep 379, where the question was the standard applicable to a ship's master diagnosing insanity in crewman.

[147] *Cattley v St John's Ambulance Brigade* (1988, QBD).

way may increase his chances of being sued.[148] Moreover, there is little clear understanding within the medical profession of what the term 'defensive medicine' means. 'Defensive' may mean simply treating patients conservatively or even 'more carefully', and this begs the question whether that treatment option is medically justified in the patient's interests. Nonetheless, the courts have apparently acknowledged the existence of the phenomenon of defensive medicine, despite the fact that there is virtually no empirical, as opposed to anecdotal, evidence of such practices in this country.[149]

In non-medical cases the courts have occasionally relied on the prospect of unduly **6.50** defensive practices developing in response to a potential liability in order to deny the existence of a duty of care.[150] This essentially involves a judgment that imposing liability for negligence will tend to 'over-deter' potential defendants, damaging the service in question, rather than contributing to an improvement in standards of conduct, though this is an intuitive judgment rather than being based on empirical evidence.[151] Logically, the same argument would apply to any defendant who is held accountable in the tort of negligence, but no one suggests that imposing a duty of care on, say, motorists makes them drive *too* carefully. The option of denying the existence of a duty of care is not available in most cases of medical negligence, since the doctor undoubtedly owes a duty of care to his patient. In *Barker v Nugent*[152] counsel for the defendant doctor argued that, as a matter of public policy, the courts should be slower to impute negligence to the medical profession than to others, in order to avoid an escalation of defensive medicine. Rougier J rejected the argument, with the comment that:

> I can think of only one thing more disastrous than the escalation of defensive medicine and that is the engendering of a belief in the medical profession that certain acts or omissions which would otherwise be classed as negligence can, in a sense, be exonerated.

---

[148] If a diagnostic test or procedure is unnecessary by reference to the standards of the medical profession, ie according to the standards of the reasonably competent doctor exercising and professing to have that skill, it will be negligence to perform it, and it will be actionable if the patient suffers injury as a consequence. See, eg, *Leonard v Knott* [1978] 5 WWR 511 (BCSC).

[149] *Wilsher v Essex AHA* [1986] 3 All ER 801, 810 *per* Mustill LJ; *Sidaway v Bethlem Royal Hospital Governors* [1985] 1 All ER 643, 653 *per* Lord Scarman. Lord Denning was particularly concerned about the risks of defensive medicine: *Roe v Minister of Health* [1954] 2 QB 66, 86–87; *Lim v Camden and Islington AHA* [1979] 1 QB 196, 217; *Whitehouse v Jordan* [1980] 1 All ER 650, 658; *Hyde v Tameside AHA* (1981) reported at (1986) 2 PN 26; *Hatcher v Black*, The Times, 2 July 1954. See also *per* Lawton LJ in *Whitehouse v Jordan* [1980] 1 All ER 650, 659; *Sidaway v Bethlem Royal Hospital Governors* [1984] 1 All ER 1018, 1031, 1035, *per* Dunne and Browne-Wilkinson LJJ.

[150] *Saif Ali v Sydney Mitchell & Co* [1980] AC 198; *Yuen Kun-yeu v Attorney-General of Hong Kong* [1987] 2 All ER 705, 715–716; *Hill v Chief Constable of West Yorkshire* [1988] 2 All ER 238; *Rowling v Takaro Properties Ltd* [1988] 1 All ER 163, 173; *Elguzouli-Daf v Commissioner of Police of the Metropolis* [1995] 1 All ER 833; *Marc Rich & Co v Bishop Rock Marine Co Ltd* [1995] 3 All ER 307.

[151] See Hartshorne, Smith and Everton (2000) 63 MLR 502 pointing out that the courts rarely have any empirical evidence to justify assertions about 'defensive' practices.

[152] 1987, QBD.

Similarly, in *Wilsher v Essex AHA* Mustill LJ responded to his own acknowledgement of the risks of defensive practice with the comment that 'the proper response cannot be to temper the wind to the professional man. If he assumes to perform a task, he must bring to it the appropriate care and skill.' Nonetheless, the judicial perception of the risk of defensive practices developing may be reflected in the standard of proof that claimants have to achieve in practice, although the formal standard of proof remains the same.

6.51   In *M (a minor) v Newham LBC*[153] the question of defensive practice arose in circumstances where, unusually, it was open to the court to conclude that a duty of care should be held not to exist. A majority of the Court of Appeal held that a psychiatrist and a social worker did not owe a duty of care to a child or its parents when advising a social services authority whether the child had been physically or sexually abused, and as to the identity of the abuser. The child had been needlessly removed from its home into local authority care, and both the child and her mother claimed that they had suffered psychiatric harm as a result. The defendants argued that imposing a duty of care in these circumstances would have serious adverse consequences, particularly in terms of: (i) the financial implications for local authorities; and (ii) the reaction of social workers and doctors working the field of child protection to the risk of liability. Peter Gibson and Staughton LJJ accepted that it would not be desirable if actions in such circumstances resulted in a major diversion of resources to defending legal actions. Sir Thomas Bingham MR, dissenting, also accepted that, to a greater or lesser extent, the overstretched resources of local authorities would be diverted from the function of looking after children and wasted on litigation but said:

> . . . this is an argument frequently (and not implausibly) advanced on behalf of doctors: it has not prevailed. Other professions resist liability on the ground that it will in the end increase the cost to the paying customer; that resistance has not on the whole been effective either. Save in clear cases, it is not for the courts to decide how public money is best spent nor to balance the risk that money will be wasted on litigation against the hope that the possibility of suit may contribute towards the maintenance of higher standards.[154]

The defendants also argued that imposing a duty of care would lead to defensive practices by social workers and doctors engaged in child protection work. Essentially the question was whether imposing liability in negligence would contribute to a deterioration in standards of conduct or lead to their improvement. It was said that the decisions that have to be taken in the context of child protection are difficult and delicate and involve an exercise of professional judgment. Imposing liability could lead to such decisions being taken in a 'detrimentally

---

[153] [1994] 2 WLR 554.
[154] ibid, 576.

defensive frame of mind'. Staughton LJ very much doubted whether the imposition of a duty of care encouraged people not to be negligent, though it might encourage defensive practices. This appears to be inconsistent, for as Sir Thomas Bingham observed: 'The common belief that the imposition of such a duty may lead to overkill is not easily reconciled with the suggestion that it has no effect.'[155] His Lordship did not accept, as a general proposition, that the imposition of a duty of care makes no contribution to the maintenance of high standards. The task may be difficult, delicate and judgmental in nature, but this simply means that it is difficult for a claimant to prove negligence. There was no reason, in a case such as *M (a minor) v Newham LBC*, why a doctor's performance of his duty to form the best judgment and give the soundest advice that he could, would be inhibited by the knowledge that he might be held liable to the child:

> He might no doubt be anxious to be as sure as possible before expressing any opinion, and would be careful to express no opinion stronger than the facts in his judgment warranted, but both these results are to be encouraged. I do not think he would be deterred from prompt action where the facts appeared to warrant it, since he would be as vulnerable to criticism for failing to advise urgent action when the facts appeared to call for it as for acting precipitately when the facts did not. The doctor's only certain protection would be sound performance of his professional duty, and that is how it should be.[156]

In the House of Lords, however, it was accepted that there was a risk of defensive **6.52** practices developing and that local authorities would adopt a more cautious approach to their duties.[157] In circumstances where a speedy decision to remove a child may be vital there would be a substantial temptation to postpone making the decision until further enquiries had been made in the hope of getting more concrete facts. This was a factor in the conclusion that a duty of care should not be imposed for reasons of policy. Clearly, it is not in the interests of children that they be negligently left at risk of abuse, but by the same token it is not in their interests that they be wrongly taken into local authority care as a result of negligence. In other words, the exercise of reasonable care by all those engaged in child protection, including doctors, is in the interests of all children, whether they are the victims of abuse or not. As long as it is remembered that the obligation in negligence

---

[155] ibid, 572. Staughton LJ's view assumes that people on the one hand do not respond to liability rules by acting more carefully, while on the other it assumes that they do respond to liability rules by being over-careful.

[156] ibid, 571–572. It might be added that the 'frame of mind' with which any professional person approaches the tasks to be carried out is so subjective to the individual as to be almost meaningless. What is 'defensive' for one may well be regarded as good practice by another. What counts is whether *objectively* the professional is exercising reasonable standards of professional conduct; and, moreover, questions of immunity aside, this is the only way in which the professional can be sure of being found not liable.

[157] sub nom *X (minors) v Bedfordshire County Council* [1995] 3 WLR 152, 184, *per* Lord Browne-Wilkinson.

is only to exercise reasonable care, not to achieve perfection, and that difficult de-cisions taken in circumstances of some urgency will not lightly be condemned as careless, a duty to exercise reasonable care should hold no terrors for the profes-sional person. The answer to claims about defensive practice lies in the observa-tion of Lord Clyde in *Phelps v Hillingdon LBC*,[158] a case involving allegations of negligence against an educational psychologist in failing to diagnose dyslexia when making an assessment of a pupil's educational needs:

> I am not persuaded that the recognition of a liability upon employees of the educa-tion authority for damages for negligence in education would lead to a flood of claims, or even vexatious claims, which would overwhelm the school authorities, nor that it would add burdens and distractions to the already intensive life of teach-ers. Nor should it inspire some peculiarly defensive attitude in the performance of their professional responsibilities. On the contrary it may have the healthy effect of securing that high standards are sought and secured.

C. Common Types of Error

6.53 It is possible for any diagnosis or treatment to be performed in a careless fashion, or for some essential step to be negligently omitted. What follows is a considera-tion of some of the most common situations in which an action may arise, although these examples should always be measured against the general test for negligence embodied in *Bolam*.

1. Failure to Attend or Treat

6.54 A doctor who fails to attend his patient or who is dilatory in attending may be guilty of negligence if a reasonable doctor would have appreciated that his attend-ance was necessary in the patient's interests. This will depend upon the precise circumstances of the case: how serious was the patient's condition; what was the doctor told; what commitments to other patients did he have at the time?[159] So it may be negligent to arrange a further appointment to see the patient too long into

---

[158] [2001] 2 AC 619, 672. See also *Reynolds v North Tyneside Health Authority* [2002] Lloyd's Rep Med 459 at [43] where Gross J commented that 'in a fault based system, it is indeed necessary both (i) to exclude hindsight and (ii) to recognise the social costs of inadvertently encouraging "defensive" medicine by setting unrealistic standards'. His Lordship concluded, however, that a finding that it was negligent to ignore a small risk of catastrophic consequences (death or brain damage) was neither unfair nor unrealistic.

[159] *Smith v Rae* (1919) 51 DLR 323, 325–326 (Ont SC App Div); see also *Cavan v Wilcox* (1973) 44 DLR (3d) 42, 53 (NBCA), where the information the doctor received over the telephone was not sufficiently serious to alert him to the emergency; *Barnes v Crabtree*, The Times, 1 and 2 November 1955, discussed in Nathan, *Medical Negligence* (1957) 37; on a GP's 'duty to visit' see also *Kavanagh v Abrahamson* (1964) 108 SJ 320; *Stockdale v Nicholls* [1993] 4 Med LR 190; *Durrant v Burke* [1993] 4 Med LR 258; *Morrison v Forsyth* [1995] 6 Med LR 6 (CS), where the seriousness of the pa-tient's condition was not made clear to the general practitioner.

the future, where the patient's condition is such that an earlier review of the situation is indicated.[160]

The duty to attend also extends to post-operative treatment. Thus, in *Corder v* **6.55**
Banks[161] a plastic surgeon who allowed the claimant to go home after an operation
on the claimant's eye-lids, but failed to make any arrangements for the claimant to
contact him if bleeding occurred during the first 48 hours after the operation, was
found to have been negligent. The duty to provide post-operative attendance does
not require the doctor to supervise routine procedures carried out by nursing
staff.[162] In some circumstances the duty to examine and/or treat the patient may
arise independently of any request by or on behalf of the patient. For example, in
Stokes v Guest, Keen and Nettlefold (Bolts and Nuts) Ltd[163] it was held that a factory
medical officer should have instituted six-monthly medical examinations, given
his knowledge of the risk to employees of contracting cancer from their working
conditions and the fact that early diagnosis gave a significantly better chance of
successful treatment. The employers were held vicariously liable for the medical
officer's negligence in failing to implement a system of screening employees for
the disease.

2. Diagnostic Errors

Diagnostic errors can arise from an inadequate medical history, errors in examin- **6.56**
ing the patient, errors in interpreting the patient's symptoms, a failure to conduct
tests or refer the patient for specialist consultation, or a failure to monitor treatment and revise the diagnosis where a treatment is proving ineffective. The duty
is not necessarily to get the diagnosis right, but a doctor should be aware of the risk
that the initial diagnosis is mistaken and consider the option of referring the
patient on for specialist investigation. Diagnosis should be preceded by the taking
of a full history from the patient.[164]

---

[160] *Lowe v Havering Hospitals NHS Trust* (2001) 62 BMLR 69, where the patient had a dangerously high and unstable blood pressure, but the doctor arranged a further appointment to see him
eight weeks later. The patient suffered a stroke, which could probably have been avoided if the medication had been changed sooner.

[161] The Times, 9 April 1960; *Ocloo v Royal Brompton and Harefield NHS Trust* (2001) 68 BMLR
89, QBD—failure to provide clear advice to the patient about a follow-up appointment held to have
been negligent; see also *Videto v Kennedy* (1980) 107 DLR (3d) 612, 616–617; rev'd on other
grounds (1981) 125 DLR (3d) 127 (Ont CA), where the arrangements made by the defendant doctor for post-operative care in the event of complications were 'just about non-existent'; *Cherewayko
v Grafton* [1993] 3 WWR 604, 626 (Man QB) on the failure to provide for 'follow-up'.

[162] *Morris v Winsbury-White* [1937] 4 All ER 494.

[163] [1968] 1 WLR 1776.

[164] In *Collins v Mid-Western Health Board* [2000] 2 IR 154, 164 (Sup Ct Irl) Barron J commented:
'The second defendant [a GP] was not expected to make the correct diagnosis. But he was expected
to be in a position to know when his patient should be referred to a specialist. . . . if no proper history in the sense of correct questions is taken the chance of an accurate diagnosis or decision to refer
is seriously restricted.'

(i) Duty to Take Medical History

6.57   In *Chin Keow v Government of Malaysia*[165] a doctor was held liable in respect of a patient's allergic reaction to penicillin, having administered the injection without first enquiring into the patient's medical history. In *Leonard v Knott*[166] the defendant physician conducted annual 'executive health examinations' for client corporations. He referred the deceased for a radiological examination of the kidneys and urinary tract by means of an intravenous pyelogram. This was part of the 'package' included in the annual check-up, and at that stage the defendant had never even met the deceased, let alone examined him, taken a medical history, done any routine tests, such as urine analysis, or sought any information from the family doctor. The patient died from an allergic reaction to the contrast medium used in the procedure, a risk which was known and foreseeable to the medical profession. The defendant was held liable for exposing the deceased to such a risk without taking a history, examining him, or consulting the family doctor, given that virtually all of the problems could have been thus determined and the deceased had never had any signs or symptoms relating to the kidneys or urinary tract.

6.58   The patient's medical history may include not only the signs and symptoms of the illness or injury for which the patient is seeking treatment, but also details of any previous treatment either for the same condition or, in appropriate circumstances, a previous injury or disease. In *Coles v Reading and District HMC*[167] a patient was given first aid treatment for a crushing injury to his finger at a cottage hospital but he was not given an anti-tetanus injection. He did not go to another hospital for further treatment, as advised, but saw his own doctor, who did not enquire as to what had happened at the cottage hospital but simply redressed the wound. The patient subsequently died of toxaemia due to tetanus infection. Both the cottage hospital and the GP were held liable for omitting to take the elementary precaution of giving the deceased an anti-tetanus vaccination. The GP was negligent in failing to make enquiries of the hospital or the deceased.[168]

6.59   The duty to take a full history requires the doctor to *listen* to what the patient is saying. Sometimes, particularly if the patient is considered to be 'difficult', a doctor may disregard or discount what the patient says and this can colour the diagnosis. A failure to listen to a patient who is describing symptoms which would

---

[165] [1967] 1 WLR 813.
[166] [1978] 5 WWR 511 (BCSC).
[167] (1963) 107 SJ 115.
[168] In *Meyer v Gordon* (1981) 17 CCLT 1 hospital staff failed to take details of the patient's obstetric history, which would have revealed that her previous labour had been a rapid one and put the staff on notice that the labour must be closely monitored; *Schanczi v Singh* [1988] 2 WWR 465 (Alta QB).

affect diagnosis and treatment will amount to negligence, where harm results.[169] Of course, the patient also bears some responsibility to provide appropriate information when questioned by a doctor. If the information is misleading the doctor will not be held liable for acting upon it, at least where it is reasonable to rely upon the information.[170] But it may not be reasonable to rely on the patient where what the patient says is clearly contradicted by the symptoms, or where it is contradicted by information provided by others, such as a spouse or family member.[171] Although a doctor is entitled to rely on what he is told by the patient, that does not absolve him from asking questions to establish that the patient has left nothing out that is material to a proper diagnosis.[172] There is a tendency on the part of patients to 'rationalise' their problem, ie to ascribe the problem to something which they themselves can identify. Thus, it may be dangerous for a doctor to be too ready to put symptoms down to the cause suggested by a patient;[173] and a psychiatrist should not always take at face value what he is told by a patient about how the patient feels.[174]

(ii) Alternative Diagnoses

Whether an error of diagnosis is negligent depends to a large extent upon the difficulty of making the diagnosis given the symptoms presented, the diagnostic techniques available, and the dangers associated with the alternative diagnoses. Where there are two possible diagnoses, one of which is potentially life-threatening but the less likely of the two alternatives, it will not be negligent to undertake diagnostic procedures intended to rule out or confirm that diagnosis before the results of tests for the other possible diagnosis are available.[175] The seriousness of the

6.60

---

[169] *Giurelli v Girgis* (1980) 24 SASR 264. See also *Cassidy v Ministry of Health* [1951] 2 KB 343, 349 on the question of medical staff ignoring the claimant's complaints of intense and excessive pain; *Reitz v Bruser (No 2)* [1979] 1 WWR 31, where it was held that a doctor should not attribute the claimant's complaints of pain to 'anxiety' until all the possible causes of the symptoms have been explored; *Rhodes v Spokes and Farbridge* [1996] 7 Med LR 135, 145 on the duty to 'keep an open mind' when taking a history. In some cases a judgment that the patient's description of physical symptoms is probably attributable to a psychiatric condition may mislead a doctor into failing to spot a genuine physical problem. See, eg, *Panther v Wharton* (2001, QBD), where both a GP and a consultant physician fell into this trap.

[170] See, eg, *Venner v North East Essex AHA*, The Times, 21 February 1987, where the claimant assured the defendant gynaecologist immediately before a sterilisation operation that she could not be pregnant. The defendant did not perform a dilatation and curettage (D and C) which probably would have terminated any pregnancy. The claimant was in fact pregnant at the time of the sterilisation operation, and subsequently gave birth to a healthy child. Tucker J held that the defendant was not negligent in not performing a D and C as a matter of course.

[171] *Collins v Mid-Western Health Board* [2000] 2 IR 154, 165 (Sup Ct Irl) *per* Barron J.

[172] ibid, 164.

[173] *Bova v Spring* [1994] 5 Med LR 120, 127; *Djemal v Bexley HA* [1995] 6 Med LR 269.

[174] *Drake v Pontefract HA; Wakefield and Pontefract Community NHS Trust* [1998] Lloyd's Rep Med 425, 443.

[175] *Maynard v West Midlands RHA* [1984] 1 WLR 634. See also *Dillon v Le Roux* [1994] 6 WWR 280 (BCCA).

consequences of the condition proving to be life-threatening would justify the risks associated with the procedure. The difficulty of making a diagnosis will often excuse a defendant.[176] The diagnosis must be judged in the light of the facts at the time and a doctor cannot be expected to possess the vision and wisdom of hindsight.[177] Thus, the failure to diagnose cancer is not necessarily negligent,[178] nor is to diagnose cancer mistakenly.[179]

6.61 Even where a particular condition cannot be diagnosed, the symptoms may indicate that the claimant is suffering from something serious which needs further investigation. The very difficulty of making a diagnosis may in itself suggest that the doctor should take additional precautions such as admitting the patient to hospital for observation, conducting further tests, or referring the patient to a specialist who was capable of making the diagnosis.[180] For example, in *Bova v Spring*[181] a GP diagnosed a muscle strain in the chest of a patient who died two days later from pneumonia. The defendant was held to have been negligent for 'failing to recognise the uncertainties attending his diagnosis'. In *Langley v Campbell*[182] the

---

[176] *Pudney v Union-Castle Mail SS Ltd* [1953] 1 Lloyd's Rep 73; *Crivon v Barnet Group HMC*, The Times, 18 November 1958, CA; *Walker v Semple* (1993, CA); *Pilon v Bouaziz* [1994] 1 WWR 700 (BCCA).

[177] *Holmes v Board of Hospital Trustees of the City of London* (1977) 81 DLR (3d) 67, 91 (Ont HC); *Wilkinson Estate (Rogin) v Shannon* (1986) 37 CCLT 181 (Ont HC); *Roe v Minister of Health* [1954] 2 QB 66, 83, *per* Denning LJ.

[178] *Hulse v Wilson* (1953) 2 BMJ 890; *Phillips v Grampian Health Board* [1991] 3 Med LR 16; *Judge v Huntingdon HA* [1995] 6 Med LR 223 (though the defendants were held liable on the facts); cf *Sutton v Population Services Family Planning Programme Ltd*, The Times, 7 November 1981, on the diagnosis of cancer; *Stacey v Chiddy* [1993] 4 Med LR 216 (NSWSC); aff'd [1993] 4 Med LR 345 (NSWCA). Where a doctor suspects cancer he should refer the patient to a specialist or arrange for an immediate biopsy: *Wilson v Vancouver Hockey Club* (1983) 5 DLR (4th) 282, 288; aff'd (1985) 22 DLR (4th) 516 (BCCA). In *Taylor v West Kent HA* [1997] 8 Med LR 251 there was a negligent failure to interpret a cytology report correctly. The doctors should have sought clarification of the report, and should have been alerted to the need for further investigations.

[179] *Whiteford v Hunter* [1950] WN 553; *Crivon v Barnet Group HMC*, The Times, 18 November 1958 (CA); *Graham v Persyko* (1986) 27 DLR (4th) 699, 703–704, where a doctor who mistakenly diagnosed Crohn's disease was held not to have been negligent. On missed fractures see: *McCormack v Redpath Brown & Co Ltd*, The Times, 24 March 1961; *Wood v Thurston*, The Times, 5 May 1951; *Newton v Newton's Model Laundry*, The Times, 3 November 1959; *Saumarez v Medway and Gravesend HMC* (1953) 2 BMJ 1109; *Fraser v Vancouver General Hospital* (1951) 3 WWR 337 (BCCA); aff'd [1952] 3 DLR 785 (SCC); *Walker v Huntingdon HA* [1994] 5 Med LR 356.

[180] *Barnett v Chelsea and Kensington HMC* [1968] 1 All ER 1068, 1073; *Seyfert v Burnaby Hospital Society* (1986) 27 DLR (4th) 96. In *Dale v Munthali* (1976) 78 DLR (3d) 588; aff'd (1978) 90 DLR (3d) 763 (Ont CA) the defendant diagnosed the patient as suffering from influenza, when in fact he had meningitis. There was no negligence in failing to diagnose meningitis, but the patient was so extremely ill that the defendant should have realised that it was more than gastro-intestinal influenza.

[181] [1994] 5 Med LR 120, QBD. See also *Riddett v D'Arcy* (1960) 2 BMJ 1607 where a GP who failed to examine a baby closely enough was held liable for failing to diagnose the early stages of pneumonia. On the failure to diagnose appendicitis see: *Edler v Greenwich & Deptford HMC*, The Times, 7 March 1953; *Bergen v Sturgeon General Hospital* (1984) 28 CCLT 155.

[182] The Times, 5 November 1975; see also *Sa'd v Robinson* [1989] 1 Med LR 41; cf *Stockdale v Nicholls* [1993] 4 Med LR 190. On a GP's 'duty to visit' see *Durrant v Burke* [1993] 4 Med LR 258.

patient presented with symptoms of fever, headache and alternate sweating and shivering. His GP diagnosed influenza, but the patient subsequently died from malaria, having recently returned from Uganda. Although GPs did not normally come across malaria, the deteriorating condition of a patient without the recognised complications of influenza should have been the cause of special concern. The defendant might not have been capable of diagnosing malaria, but should have been alerted to the possibility that the patient's illness might not be indigenous.

(iii) Diagnostic Aids

Where diagnostic aids would assist a doctor in reaching an accurate diagnosis it **6.62** may well be negligent to fail to use them, if available,[183] although this is not necessarily the case.[184] Where a gynaecologist was aware that his patient could be pregnant, he should have conducted tests before subjecting her uterus to X-rays.[185] Doctors who ordered X-rays to be carried out but then delayed for five days before examining them were held negligent for failing to inform themselves of the factual data which they had themselves identified as pertinent and necessary to the claimant's diagnosis, and which they knew or ought to have known was available.[186] In *Pierre v Marshall*[187] a GP who failed to screen a pregnant woman for gestational diabetes, contrary to the recommendations of the Alberta Medical Association and the Society of Obstetricians and Gynaecologists of Canada, was held to have been negligent. The defendant also had failed to do an ultrasound

---

[183] *Bergen v Sturgeon General Hospital* (1984) 28 CCLT 155; *Lankenau v Dutton* (1986) 37 CCLT 213; (1991) 79 DLR (4th) 707 (BCCA); *Smith v Salford HA* [1994] 5 Med LR 321, QBD, where it was held that the defendant should have undertaken a CT scan prior to performing a spinal fusion operation, because this would have been a far more sophisticated and informative piece of radiology than the X-rays upon which he relied in assessing the need for the operation and the technique that would be required. The simplest diagnostic tool may be a physical examination of the patient. See *Stacey v Chiddy* [1993] 4 Med LR 216, 224–225 (NSWSC); aff'd [1993] 4 Med LR 345 (NSWCA).

[184] *Whiteford v Hunter* [1950] WN 553; *Lakey v Merton, Sutton and Wandsworth HA* (1999) 48 BMLR 18, CA—casualty officer not negligent in failing to X-ray a patient who presented with pain in the hip following a fall, when there were no clinical signs of a fracture.

[185] *Zimmer v Ringrose* (1981) 125 DLR (3d) 215, (Alta CA); aff'g (1978) 89 DLR (3d) 646, 656–657; *Gardiner v Mounfield* [1990] 1 Med LR 205, where the defendant dismissed the possibility that the claimant, who was overweight and had a history of amenorrhoea, was pregnant.

[186] *Holmes v Board of Hospital Trustees of the City of London* (1977) 81 DLR (3d) 67 (Ont HC). In *Hutton v East Dyfed HA* [1998] Lloyd's Rep Med 335 a doctor who did not carry out a chest X-ray on a patient with chest pain because she was pregnant and he wrongly thought that it would involve danger to the foetus was held to have been negligent.

[187] [1994] 8 WWR 478 (Alta QB). See also *Tucker v Tees HA* [1995] 6 Med LR 54, where the defendant was held negligent for performing a laparotomy to remove a presumed ovarian cyst without first conducting an ultrasound scan to check whether the claimant was pregnant. On the other hand, a doctor should not be criticised for a refusal to offer a CT scan or any other diagnostic procedure which he considered inappropriate just because the patient was willing to pay and wanted reassurance: *Rhodes v Spokes and Farbridge* [1996] 7 Med LR 135, 146.

scan to confirm the expected size of the baby, despite his suspicion that the foetus was slightly larger than it should have been at 36 weeks. Screening for gestational diabetes is not routine practice in the United Kingdom, however, and a doctor is not necessarily negligent for failing to undertake the standard test for that condition. It is a matter of clinical judgment involving a number of factors.[188] In *X and Y v Pal*[189] it was accepted that an obstetrician who failed to test a patient for syphilis during her pregnancy was negligent.[190]

(iv) Diagnostic Review

6.63 The diagnosis should also be kept under review as the treatment progresses. There is a danger in acquiring 'tunnel vision' about the patient's condition.[191] This is even more important where the consequences of the alternative diagnosis, if it turns out to be correct, are likely to be serious.[192] In *Lankenau v Dutton*[193] the medical evidence was that a surgeon confronted with a patient with paralysis after major surgery should not only attempt to diagnose the cause but also 'should make a differential diagnosis, that is to say that he should consider other likely causes of her condition and test them against her symptoms and be ready with an alternative theory to direct her treatment if his first diagnosis and treatment should fail to produce an improvement in her condition'.[194] The defendant had diagnosed an aortic dissection occurring during surgery, which was a reasonable initial diagnosis. As the patient's symptoms progressed, however, he failed to re-assess the diagnosis, which resulted in the paralysis becoming permanent. The surgeon was held to have been negligent for clinging to the original diagnosis even though the symptoms should have made him question it, for failing to test his theory by X-ray, and for failing to seek the assistance of neurological experts quickly

---

[188] *Hallatt v North West Anglia HA* [1998] Lloyd's Rep Med 197, CA.

[189] (1991) 23 NSWLR 26; [1992] 3 Med LR 195 (NSWCA).

[190] There may also be negligence in failing to interpret test results properly: see, eg, *Fraser v Vancouver General Hospital* (1951) 3 WWR 337 (BCCA); [1952] 3 DLR 785 (SCC), and *Roy v Croydon HA* [1998] PIQR Q26 (CA), on the negligent interpretation of X-rays; *Rance v Mid-Downs Health Authority* [1991] 1 All ER 801, an allegedly negligent failure to interpret an ultrasound scan of a foetus; *Penney, Palmer and Cannon v East Kent HA* [2000] Lloyd's Rep Med 41 (CA)—failure to interpret smear tests for cervical cancer accurately. A failure to read a report will be negligent: *Fredette v Wiebe* [1986] 5 WWR 222 (BCSC). On the other hand, a misleading pathology report may result in a finding that a surgeon was not negligent in embarking on radical surgery in a case of suspected cancer: *Abbas v Kenney* [1996] 7 Med LR 47.

[191] *Layden v Cope* (1984) 28 CCLT 140 (Alta QB); *Reitz v Bruser (No 2)* [1979] 1 WWR 31, 47 *per* Hewak J. Tunnel vision was also in evidence in *Panther v Wharton* (2001, QBD), where a GP had formed the view that the patient's symptoms were largely psychiatric in origin, and referred her for a psychiatric assessment, and a consultant physician at the hospital, asked to advise the psychiatric team, failed to approach his physical examination of the patient with an open mind, and so failed to identify a serious vascular problem.

[192] *Bova v Spring* [1994] 5 Med LR 120, 129 (QBD).

[193] (1986) 37 CCLT 213 (BCSC); aff'd (1991) 79 DLR (4th) 707 (BCCA).

[194] ibid, 231, *per* Spencer J.

enough.[195] In *Hutton v East Dyfed HA*[196] a consultant physician was held negligent in failing to revise an initial diagnosis of myopericarditis in a patient with chest pain, having received normal test results for that condition, and in failing to include in his differential diagnosis the risk of pulmonary embolus, despite the real risk of disastrous consequences if a further pulmonary embolus occurred.

(v) Obligation to Refer

The obligation to refer a patient to a specialist or to seek further advice will arise whenever a doctor is unable to diagnose or treat the patient.[197] Even a consultant in a specialist field may come across a problem that he has never previously encountered and accordingly may have a responsibility to seek advice.[198] In *Poole v Morgan*[199] the defendant ophthalmologist was inadequately trained in the use of a laser, although he had often used it in his practice. The treatment that he gave to the claimant was usually performed by a retina vitreous specialist. Since the defendant was unable to come up to the standard of that specialty, he had a duty to refer the claimant to such a specialist.

6.64

3. Failures of Communication

(i) Between Doctor and Patient

Failures of communication can arise between doctor and patient or between the various health care professionals involved in a patient's treatment, but in either case the consequences for the patient can be serious. The doctor has an obligation to provide information to a patient about the nature, purpose, and consequences of proposed procedures, but in addition to the duty to warn patients in advance of the risks associated with the treatment, it is possible that in some circumstances the practitioner will be under a duty to inform the patient that something has

6.65

---

[195] In *Bergen v Sturgeon General Hospital* (1984) 28 CCLT 155 (Alta QB) a female patient, who was admitted to hospital complaining of pains in her abdomen, died from a ruptured appendix, having been provisionally diagnosed as suffering from acute gastroenteritis, with appendicitis to be checked out. A further diagnosis of pelvic inflammatory disease had been made, but no steps were taken to rule out appendicitis, despite the fact that it explained all the symptoms, the patient's condition was not responding to treatment, and that appendicitis is life-threatening. The defendants were held negligent, not for the initial mistaken diagnosis but for failing to keep the diagnosis under review when the patient's condition did not improve. In *Law Estate v Simice* (1994) 21 CCLT (2d) 228, 236 (BCSC) Spencer J observed that: 'Where a potentially life-threatening condition is included in a differential diagnosis, there is a duty on the physician to take prompt steps to confirm it or rule it out with reasonable dispatch.'

[196] [1998] Lloyd's Rep Med 335.

[197] *MacDonald v York County Hospital* (1973) 41 DLR (3d) 321, 349–350, *per* Dubin JA (Ont CA); aff'd sub nom *Vail v MacDonald* (1976) 66 DLR (3d) 530 (SCC).

[198] *Gascoine v Ian Sheridan & Co* [1994] 5 Med LR 437, 447, *per* Mitchell J.

[199] [1987] 3 WWR 217; *Layden v Cope* (1984) 28 CCLT 140, 148; *Lankenau v Dutton* (1986) 37 CCLT 213; (1991) 79 DLR (4th) 707 (BCCA).

gone wrong with the treatment.[200] In *Stamos v Davies*[201] the defendant punctured the claimant's spleen while performing a lung biopsy, but did not tell the claimant, who was then discharged from hospital. The claimant was readmitted as an emergency three days later, due to bleeding into his abdominal cavity. The spleen was removed surgically and the claimant recovered uneventfully. Krever J held that the defendant was in breach of a duty to inform the claimant that the spleen had been punctured. The difficulty with any case of this nature, however, is proving that the breach of duty caused the claimant damage. The claimant's ignorance that something untoward has occurred will rarely contribute to any further loss, and since the damage has already occurred, the failure to be candid is not a cause of the harm.[202]

6.66 In some cases the failure to inform may cause further injury as if, for example, the patient takes a risk that he would otherwise have avoided, or if the patient's ignorance leads to delay in diagnosis (resulting in additional harm) or an emergency subsequently arises as a result of the injury of which he is unaware. In *Kiley-Nikkel v Danais*[203] the claimant's breast was removed following a mistaken diagnosis of cancer. She was not informed of the error, with the result that she sought follow-up treatment for cancer in another locality and lived with the belief that she had cancer for a considerable time. Part of the award of damages was for the psychiatric harm resulting from non-disclosure of the error in diagnosis, since the consequences of this would have been much less serious had she known immediately that she was not suffering from cancer. In *Pittman Estate v Bain*[204] a patient received a blood transfusion during the course of heart surgery. It was subsequently discovered that the blood he had received was contaminated with HIV. The defendants were found to have been negligent in failing to inform him that there was a risk, which in fact materialised, that the transfusion had infected him with HIV. Although there was no negligence in the administration of the transfusion, the

---

[200] See the comments of Sir John Donaldson MR in *Lee v South West Thames RHA* [1985] 2 All ER 385, and *Naylor v Preston AHA* [1987] 2 All ER 353, 360. In *Gerber v Pines* (1934) 79 SJ 13 Du Parcq J said that as a general rule a patient was entitled to be told at once if the doctor had left some foreign object in his body; cf *Daniels v Heskin* [1954] IR 73, 87, *per* Kingsmill Moore J. But on *Daniels v Heskin* see now *Walsh v Family Planning Services Ltd* [1992] IR 496, 520 (Sup Ct Irl). It has been suggested that there is an obligation to break distressing, though truthful, news to patients in a manner which reduces the risk of patients developing psychiatric illness in response to the news: *AB v Tameside & Glossop HA* [1997] 8 Med LR 91, though the defendants were held not to have been negligent in choosing to inform patients that there was a small risk that they might have contracted HIV from a doctor by letter rather than face-to-face. See Dziobon and Tettenborn, 'When the truth hurts: the incompetent transmission of distressing news' (1997) 13 PN 70. A fortiori if, as a result of the defendants' negligence, the distressing information was *inaccurate* and the claimant suffered psychiatric harm from this distressing 'news', even where the incorrect information was imparted in a sensitive and appropriate manner: *Allin v City & Hackney HA* [1996] 7 Med LR 167; Jones, 'Negligently inflicted psychiatric harm: is the word mightier than the deed?' (1997) 13 PN 111.

[201] (1986) 21 DLR (4th) 507 (Ont HC); Robertson (1987) 25 Alberta L Rev 215.

[202] *Daniels v Heskin* [1954] IR 73, 81, 88.

[203] (1992) 16 CCLT (2d) 290 (Qué SC).

[204] (1994) 112 DLR (4th) 257 (Ont Ct, Gen Div).

failure to inform the patient meant that he did not have an opportunity to take measures which could have extended his life expectancy and, moreover, his wife also contracted the infection from unprotected sexual intercourse with her husband. The defendants were held liable for both of these consequences.

A doctor will often need the patient's co-operation, for example, in performing an **6.67** examination or administering treatment. This may be as simple as requiring the patient to keep still or instructing the patient about taking medication. It may also be necessary to give the patient a warning about any danger signs to look out for, with instructions as to what should be done if they occur, such as stopping the medication or seeking medical assistance immediately.[205] Sometimes this will be absolutely vital. In these circumstances the doctor will be under a duty to take special care in giving the patient instructions, to make sure that the patient understands both the instructions and the importance of strictly adhering to them.[206] In *Joyce v Wandsworth HA*[207] the claimant underwent an operative procedure which resulted in a partially occluded artery, leading three months later to an upper brain stem infarction causing almost total paralysis. The Court of Appeal held that the immediate follow-up care that the claimant had received was negligent because the patient was discharged from hospital without proper instructions and advice. In some instances the risk associated with the treatment may be so great that it will be negligent for a doctor to rely on a patient accurately reporting his symptoms, the obligation being to conduct regular tests.[208] There is also a responsibility to bring home to a patient the importance of obtaining further treatment, if necessary, and the dangers involved in failing to do so.[209] Similarly, where it is unwise for a patient to engage in certain types of activity following treatment, he should be warned of this danger.[210] Indeed, there may be a duty to warn patients to make a lifestyle change. In *Hutchinson v Epson & St Helier NHS Trust*[211] the defendants were held to have been negligent in failing to advise a patient who was a heavy

---

[205] See, eg, *Crossman v Stewart* (1977) 82 DLR (3d) 677 where the defendant doctor was held negligent for failing to identify the indications of side-effects.

[206] *Clarke v Adams* (1950) 94 SJ 599; *Stamos v Davies* (1986) 21 DLR (4th) 507. In *Sheridan v Boots Co Ltd* (1980, QBD), a doctor who prescribed a potent anti-inflammatory drug but failed to give the patient a warning that if he experienced any stomach trouble he should stop taking the drug and consult a doctor immediately, was said to have been negligent, although the action failed on causation.

[207] [1996] 7 Med LR 1.

[208] *Marshall v Rogers* [1943] 4 DLR 68, 77 (BCCA); cf *Battersby v Tottman* (1985) 37 SASR 524 where, in the circumstances, a failure to monitor the known and serious side-effects of a drug was held not negligent.

[209] *Coles v Reading and District HMC* (1963) 107 SJ 115.

[210] *Brushett v Cowan* (1987) 40 DLR (4th) 488; aff'd (1990) 69 DLR (4th) 743 (Newfd CA), where the claimant was given crutches to use following a biopsy on her leg, but she was not warned that she should not bear weight on the leg. While engaging in ordinary activity without the crutches the leg broke at the site of the biopsy. The doctor was held negligent.

[211] [2002] EWHC 2363 (QB).

drinker, and at serious risk of developing fatal cirrhosis of the liver, to stop drinking alcohol. Of course, in such a case it would have to be demonstrated that the deceased would probably have heeded the warning.

(ii) Between Health Professionals

6.68 A breakdown in communication between health care professionals with responsibility for a patient can have dangerous consequences for the patient. These errors may be the result of isolated acts of carelessness (such as failing to read the nursing notes[212]) or they may be the product of some organisational failure (for example, relying too heavily on casual exchanges[213]). The system of communication may be so poor that mistakes are almost inevitable, or the methods adopted may fail to take into account the risks of human error by providing some mechanism for checking. Thus, a hospital must have an adequate system for summoning specialist assistance when needed.[214] If a patient is injured by reason of a negligent breakdown in the systems for communicating material information to the clinicians responsible for her care, she is not to be denied redress merely because no identifiable person or persons are to blame for deficiencies in setting up and monitoring the effectiveness of the relevant communication systems.[215] Thus, there must be a system for dealing with a surgeon's patients when the surgeon goes away for a weekend.[216] It is also to be expected that there will be a system for communication between hospitals, or between a hospital and GPs, about the treatment that a patient has received.[217] On the other hand, a GP who is sent the results of a blood test by the hospital is entitled to assume that the hospital doctors are aware of those results and are taking them into account in their investigation of the patient's symptoms, and it is not for the GP to go through hospital notes to check that the hospital has done what it should have done.[218]

---

[212] *Holmes v Board of Hospital Trustees of the City of London* (1977) 81 DLR (3d) 67, 94 (Ont HC); *Starcevic v West Hertfordshire HA* [2001] EWCA Civ 192; (2001) 60 BMLR 221—the failure of an occupational therapist and a nurse to pass on information about the condition of the patient's leg to the surgeon, which would have alerted the doctor to the risk of deep vein thrombosis, held to constitute negligence (the patient died from a pulmonary embolism during minor surgery on his leg).

[213] *Bergen v Sturgeon General Hospital* (1984) 28 CCLT 155, 175.

[214] *Bull v Devon AHA* (1989), [1993] 4 Med LR 117, CA. Of course, even the best systems may not be foolproof. In *Bolitho v City and Hackney HA* [1997] 4 All ER 771 one doctor failed to attend an emergency call from a nurse because the battery in her bleeper was flat.

[215] *Robertson v Nottingham HA* [1997] 8 Med LR 1, 13 *per* Brooke LJ. This may give rise to a 'non-delegable duty' on the part of the hospital to 'set up a safe system of operation in relation to what are essentially management as opposed to clinical matters', ibid.

[216] *Cassidy v Ministry of Health* [1951] 2 KB 343, 359, *per* Singleton LJ; *Crichton v Hastings* (1972) 29 DLR (3d) 692, 700 (Ont CA).

[217] *Coles v Reading and District HMC* (1963) 107 SJ 115; see also *Schanczi v Singh* [1988] 2 WWR 465 (Alta QB) on a specialist's failure to obtain adequate information about a patient from the referring doctor before proceeding to surgery; cf *Chapman v Rix* (1960), [1994] 5 Med LR 239 (HL).

[218] *Weir v Graham* [2002] EWHC 2291 (QB). Similarly, it is not negligent for a GP to fail to advise parents that there was an alternative means of providing immunisation of a child against

Communication errors can occur from simply mishearing or misreading an in-   **6.69**
struction. This may be the result of a single lapse of concentration, but the further
question will then arise as to whether there was any system for checking for such
errors given that it is known that mistakes do sometimes happen. In *Collins v
Hertfordshire County Council*[219] a patient died after being injected with cocaine
instead of procaine as a local anaesthetic. The surgeon had told a junior, unqualified medical officer over the telephone his requirements for the operation, and the
word 'procaine' was misheard for 'cocaine'. The pharmacist dispensing the drug at
the hospital pharmacy did not question the order for an 'unheard-of dosage' of a
dangerous drug, and the surgeon did not check prior to injecting the solution that
he was in fact injecting what he had ordered. It was held that both the surgeon and
the medical officer were liable, as was the hospital authority for having an unsafe
dispensing system.

A pathologist who has been given specimens for testing or analysis owes a duty to   **6.70**
the patient not only to conduct the tests in a proper manner but also to take reasonable steps to communicate the results to the referring doctor, and it is irrelevant that the doctor also has a corresponding duty to find out the results.[220] A
doctor who prepares a report or medical notes which he is aware may be relied
upon by others for the treatment of the patient has a duty to exercise reasonable
care in writing the report.[221] This also applies to the writing of a prescription,
which should be reasonably legible.[222]

4. Treatment Errors

Errors in treatment can take a multitude of forms. The mere fact that a doctor has   **6.71**
departed from the standard treatment will not necessarily indicate negligence,
bearing in mind that doctors have to treat the individual patient and not the 'standard' patient found in textbooks; a slight departure from the textbook therefore
will not necessarily be a mistake, let alone negligent.[223] On the other hand, a substantial departure from standard practice will place a heavy onus on the defendant

---

measles, when immunisation was not imminent and the GP was aware that the parents would be
being advised by another doctor at another practice in 12 to 18 months about the options for immunisation: *Thompson v Blake-James* [1998] PIQR P286, CA.

[219] [1947] 1 KB 598; see also *Strangeways-Lesmere v Clayton* [1936] 2 KB 11, where a nurse who
misread her instructions and gave an excess dose was held to be negligent.

[220] *Thomsen v Davison* [1975] Qd R 93; see also *McKay v Essex Area HA* [1982] QB 1166 on an
alleged omission to communicate test results; *Gregory v Pembrokeshire HA* [1989] 1 Med LR 81
(CA); *Fredette v Wiebe* [1986] 5 WWR 222.

[221] *Everett v Griffiths* [1920] 3 KB 163, 213; *Price v Milawski* (1977) 82 DLR (3d) 130 (Ont CA).

[222] *Prendergast v Sam and Dee Ltd* [1989] 1 Med LR 36 (CA). For similar cases of negligence by a
pharmacist failing to spot prescription errors see *Collins v Hertfordshire County Council* [1947] 1 KB
598 and *Dwyer v Roderick* (1983) 127 SJ 806; McKevitt (1988) 4 PN 185; Crawford (1995) 2 J Law
and Med 293.

[223] *Holland v The Devitt & Moore Nautical College*, The Times, 4 March 1960.

to justify this decision.[224] If a doctor has made a considered decision about treatment, it may be more difficult to conclude that there has been negligence[225] than if he has made an unintentional or inadvertent 'error', since in the latter case there has been no balancing of risks and benefits.[226]

(i) Operations

6.72   The courts have long recognised that the mere fact that something has gone wrong during the course of an operation is not per se indicative of negligence,[227] although knocking out four of the patient's teeth during a tonsillectomy was held to be negligent.[228] Where a patient sustains burns in an operating theatre, this is usually the result of negligence.[229] Perforation of the uterus during the course of performing a Dilatation and Curettage is relatively common, and not in itself negligent, but damage to the small bowel during the operation is so rare as to be outside the range of normal practice and does indicate a lack of reasonable care.[230]

6.73   In *Hendy v Milton Keynes HA (No 2)*[231] the evidence showed that it was possible for ureteric damage to occur during an abdominal hysterectomy despite the use of a competent surgical technique, but these rare instances of non-culpable ureteric damage were attributable to anatomical variations outside the normal range. Most cases of ureteric damage where the anatomy was normal were due to poor technique, and therefore the most likely explanation of damage to the claimant's ureter, in the absence of any evidence of abnormal anatomy, was that there had been negligence.

6.74   Obstetric errors are frequently the subject of litigation, partly because the consequences for the child can be extremely serious, and partly because the parents'

---

[224]   *Clark v MacLennan* [1983] 1 All ER 416.

[225]   See, eg, *Darley v Shale* [1993] 4 Med LR 161 (NSWSC).

[226]   *Goode v Nash* (1979) 21 SASR 419, 423 (SC of S Aus).

[227]   *White v Westminster Hospital Board of Governors*, The Times, 26 October 1961; *Ashcroft v Merseyside RHA* [1983] 2 All ER 245; aff'd [1985] 2 All ER 96; see also *Chubey v Ahsan* (1977) 71 DLR (3d) 550 (Man CA); *Kapur v Marshall* (1978) 85 DLR (3d) 567, 573, *per* Robins J (Ont HC).

[228]   *Munro v United Oxford Hospitals* (1958) 1 BMJ 167.

[229]   *Crits v Sylvester* (1956) 1 DLR (2d) 502; aff'd (1956) 5 DLR (2d) 601 (SCC); *Paton v Parker* (1942) 65 CLR 187; *Crysler v Pearse* [1943] 4 DLR 738; *Clarke v Warboys*, The Times, 18 March 1952. Burns to the buttocks following surgery are, apparently, a common type of claim: Medical Defence Union, *Annual Report 1990*, 45; (1993) 9 J of the MDU 95. The Department of Health has issued a specific warning to hospitals about the danger of inflammable liquids igniting during surgery: HC (Hazard) (90) 25.

[230]   *Bovenzi v Kettering HA* [1991] 2 Med LR 293, QBD.

[231]   [1992] 3 Med LR 119 (QBD). In *Ratty v Haringey HA* [1994] 5 Med LR 413 the Court of Appeal upheld a finding of negligence where there was damage to the claimant's ureter during the course of colo-rectal surgery. The negligence consisted, not in the initial damage to the ureter, which could occur even with the exercise of reasonable care, but in failing to discover and correct the damage before the end of the operation. See also *Bouchta v Swindon HA* [1996] 7 Med LR 62; cf *Hooper v Young* [1998] Lloyd's Rep Med 61 (CA).

expectation is to have a normal, healthy child. The most recent evidence indicates that birth-related brain damage (including cerebral palsy) in the NHS accounts for just over 5 per cent of all cases of medical litigation in which damages are paid, and 60 per cent of all expenditure on medical litigation.[232] In *Whitehouse v Jordan*[233] an allegation that the defendant had pulled too long and too hard in the course of a forceps delivery, and thus was negligent in failing to proceed to a caesarian section delivery, was ultimately rejected on the facts. In *Parry v North West Surrey HA*[234] on the other hand, the defendant was held liable for attempting to deliver a child by forceps when it was too high in the mother's pelvis, and thus for failing to undertake a caesarian section delivery. Human error is frequently implicated in obstetric accidents, many of which are avoidable,[235] although establishing the causal link between any negligence and the child's injuries can be extremely difficult.

A doctor may be liable for proceeding to surgery too quickly without first considering conservative treatment.[236] Conversely, a delay in recommending surgery

6.75

---

[232] *Making Amends* (June 2003), 47, para 43 (*www.doh.gov.uk/makingamends/cmoreport.htm*).

[233] [1981] 1 All ER 267. See also *Knight v West Kent HA* [1998] Lloyd's Rep Med 18; *Corley v North West Herefordshire HA* [1997] 8 Med LR 45; *Hallatt v North West Anglia HA* [1998] Lloyd's Rep Med 197 (CA); *Hinfey v Salford HA* [1993] 4 Med LR 143, where an allegation that the failure to undertake a caesarian section delivery constituted negligence was rejected on the evidence; *James v Camberwell HA* [1994] 5 Med LR 253, where a delay in proceeding to a caesarian section was held not negligent on the facts.

[234] [1994] 5 Med LR 259. See also *Dowdie v Camberwell HA* [1997] 8 Med LR 368 where the defendant was held to have been negligent in failing to proceed to a caesarian section in a case of shoulder dystocia; *Gaughan v Bedfordshire HA* [1997] 8 Med LR 182—midwife used force for longer than was acceptable in a case of shoulder dystocia; *Sutcliffe v Countess of Chester Hospital NHS Trust* [2002] Lloyd's Rep Med 449—injury to the brachial plexus held to be negligent in a case of undiagnosed shoulder dystocia. See also *Murphy v Wirral HA* [1996] 7 Med LR 99, on the duty of a midwife to monitor the progress of labour by conducting regular vaginal examinations; *Reynolds v North Tyneside HA* [2002] Lloyd's Rep Med 459, midwife failed to undertake a vaginal examination despite the existence of circumstances in which the risk of cord prolapse was foreseeable; *Simms v Birmingham HA* (2000) 58 BMLR 66, SHO failed to report the presence of undiluted meconium to the registrar, and left the midwife to interpret the CTG trace in a high-risk situation; *Briody v St Helen's & Knowsley HA* [1999] Lloyd's Rep Med 185; *Wiszniewski v Central Manchester HA* [1998] PIQR P324; *Hill v West Lancashire HA* [1997] 8 Med LR 196; *Bowers v Harrow HA* [1995] 6 Med LR 16. See also *De Martell v Merton and Sutton HA* [1995] 6 Med LR 234 and *Robertson v Nottingham HA* [1997] 8 Med LR 1 where the actions failed on causation.

[235] Ennis and Vincent (1990) 300 BMJ 1365. This reflects a number of general problems, including inadequate training and supervision of junior and middle ranking staff in the labour ward: ibid. See further the Department of Health's *Report on confidential enquiries into maternal deaths in England and Wales* (1989, HMSO).

[236] *Schanczi v Singh* [1988] 2 WWR 465, 472 (Alta QB); see also *Coughlin v Kuntz* (1987) 42 CCLT 142 (BCSC); aff'd [1990] 2 WWR 737, 744 (BCCA); *Haughian v Paine* (1987) 37 DLR (4th) 625, 629–635 (Sask CA); *Mann v Judgeo* [1993] 4 WWR 760 (Sask QB), on the performance of aggressive surgery when 'first treatment surgery' was appropriate; *Cherewayko v Grafton* [1993] 3 WWR 604, 619 (Man QB), on an 'unnecessary' operation; *Doughty v North Staffordshire HA* [1992] 3 Med LR 81 (QBD); cf *De Freitas v O'Brien* [1995] 6 Med LR 108, where the defendant's decision to resort to spinal surgery, despite the absence of definite clinical and radiological evidence of nerve compression, was held not to have been negligent.

may also be negligent. In *Powell v Guttman*[237] the claimant developed a condition of avascular necrosis following an operation on her leg performed by the defendant orthopaedic surgeon. The defendant failed to advise the claimant to undergo an arthoplasty operation to correct this. A year after the first operation another surgeon performed this operation, and during it the claimant sustained a rotary fracture of the femur. Due to the delay, the condition of the bone had deteriorated as a result of osteoporosis, and this was a 'significant cause' of the fracture that occurred. The defendant was held liable on the basis that the delay in the second operation was attributable to his negligence, and this had caused an increase in the osteoporosis rendering the femur more susceptible to the fracture.

(ii) Team Negligence

6.76 Under modern conditions, most medical treatment is undertaken by a team of health care professionals, and this is invariably true of surgical procedures. In *Wilsher v Essex Area HA*[238] the Court of Appeal rejected the concept of 'team negligence' whereby each of the persons who formed the staff of the unit held themselves out as capable of undertaking the specialised procedures which the unit set out to perform. It would not be right, said Mustill LJ, to attribute to each individual member of the team a duty to live up to the standards demanded of the unit as a whole, because that would expose a student nurse to an action in negligence for a failure to possess the skill and experience of a consultant. Each member of the team will be responsible for his or her own contribution to the joint undertaking. For example, a doctor will not normally be responsible for the negligence of others, such as nurses, in carrying out instructions that have been given with regard to the patient's treatment,[239] and, conversely, nursing staff will not be considered to have acted negligently when faithfully carrying out the instructions of a doctor.[240] Acting under the instructions of a doctor, however, does not excuse a nurse from making any professional judgment. There may be circumstances where a nurse could be negligent when following a doctor's instructions; for example, if a doctor ordered an obviously incorrect and dangerous dosage of a drug and the nurse administered it without obtaining confirmation from the doctor or higher authority.[241] Similarly, a pharmacist has been held to be negligent for failing to check a request for an 'unheard-of dosage' of cocaine.[242] A doctor may be

---

[237] (1978) 89 DLR (3d) 180 (Man CA).

[238] [1986] 3 All ER 801, 812–813.

[239] *Perionowsky v Freeman* (1866) 4 F & F 977; *Morris v Winsbury-White* [1937] 4 All ER 494, 498.

[240] *Gold v Essex County Council* [1942] 2 KB 293, 299, *per* Lord Greene MR.

[241] ibid, at 313, *per* Goddard LJ, although his Lordship added that: 'In the stress of an operation, however, I should suppose that the first thing required of a nurse would be an unhesitating obedience to the orders of the surgeon.' See also the analogous case of *Davy-Chiesman v Davy-Chiesman* [1984] 1 All ER 321, 332, 335, stating that solicitors should not rely blindly on the advice of counsel.

[242] *Collins v Hertfordshire County Council* [1947] 1 KB 598.

negligent if he knows or ought reasonably to have known that another person in the team, whether it be the anaesthetist or a nurse, has done something which puts the patient at risk but fails to take any steps to remedy the error.[243] Moreover, it is negligent for a doctor to rely on information provided by a nurse whom he knows or ought to know is overconfident in her own abilities and not qualified to make the clinical judgment in question.[244]

(iii) 'Swab' Cases

The danger of swabs or surgical instruments being left inside a patient at the end of an operation is clearly something which must be guarded against. But even in this type of case a surgeon is not necessarily liable; he only has to exercise reasonable care to see that it does not happen.[245] However, the consequences can be very serious and accordingly the degree of care required in order to satisfy the requirement of reasonableness will be correspondingly high. It is not negligent for a surgeon to delegate the task of counting swabs to a nurse, but a surgeon will not necessarily avoid liability by relying on that count.[246] In *Urry v Bierer*[247] a surgeon conducting a caesarian section relied almost exclusively on the count by the nurse. He was held to have been negligent in failing to take any additional precautions, such as using swabs with tapes, although it was said that different considerations might apply in an emergency. There was no reason why the surgeon should not have made some mental effort to remember where he had placed the swabs, particularly since he had chosen not to use tapes. In practice swab cases are usually settled as indefensible, and most of the cases that are litigated end in a finding of negligence.[248] Even if, on the facts, the conclusion is that the surgeon was not

6.77

---

[243] *Perionowsky v Freeman* (1866) 4 F & F 977, 982; *Wilsher v Essex Area HA* [1986] 3 All ER 801, where the registrar was held to have been negligent in failing to spot the senior house officer's error. In *Jones v Manchester Corporation* [1952] 2 All ER 125 the Court of Appeal took the view that the inexperienced doctor who administered the fatal injection was not as culpable as the experienced doctor who supervised her. See also *Collins v Hertfordshire County Council* [1947] 1 KB 598 on the question of responsibility for injections.

[244] *Wiszniewski v Central Manchester HA* [1996] 7 Med LR 248, 256, a finding that was not challenged on appeal: [1998] PIQR P324, 328 (CA).

[245] *Mahon v Osborne* [1939] 2 KB 14, 31–32 *per* Scott LJ. Note, however, that Scott LJ dissented on the question of whether *res ipsa loquitur* applied to a swab case.

[246] *Mahon v Osborne* [1939] 2 KB 14, 47, *per* Goddard LJ.

[247] The Times, 15 July 1955 (CA).

[248] See, eg, *James v Dunlop* (1931) 1 BMJ 730 which is considered in *Mahon v Osborne* [1939] 2 KB 14; *Dryden v Surrey County Council* [1936] 2 All ER 535; *Holt v Nesbitt* [1951] 4 DLR 478; *Garner v Morrell*, The Times, 31 October 1953; *Urry v Bierer*, The Times, 15 July 1955; *Fox v Glasgow South Western Hospitals* 1955 SLT 337; *Cooper v Nevill*, The Times, 10 March 1961 (PC); *Anderson v Chasney* 1949] 4 DLR 71 (Man CA); aff'd *sub nom Chasney v Anderson* [1950] 4 DLR 223 (SCC). The position will usually be the same in the case of a surgical instrument inadvertently left inside the patient's body: *Hocking v Bell* [1948] WN 21 (PC); *Gloning v Miller* [1954] 1 DLR 372; cf *McDonald v Pottinger* [1953] NZLR 196.

negligent in leaving the swab inside the patient, the result will almost invariably be that the nurse conducting the count was negligent.[249]

(iv) Infection

(a) In Hospital

6.78 About 9 per cent of patients pick up infections while they are in hospital, and this costs the NHS up to £1 billion a year in additional treatment.[250] Many of these cases are unavoidable, but some are due to medical staff ignoring basic hygiene rules.[251] Cases may arise from cross-infection, where patients acquire a disease from another patient, or they may result from surgical intervention. In the case of post-operative infection, the infection itself cannot be treated as evidence of negligence, because no-one can guarantee that post-operative infection will not occur.[252] However, specialists should be quick to recognise the development of infection following surgery.[253] In *Voller v Portsmouth Corporation*[254] the claimant developed meningitis after the administration of a spinal anaesthetic. It was admitted that the illness must have been caused either by contamination of the anaesthetic or by an infection occurring during its administration. It could not be said precisely how the accident occurred but the court concluded that there must have been some failure to follow the appropriate sterilisation procedure resulting in contamination from the equipment used.

6.79 Unnecessarily exposing a patient to the risk of contracting an infection will be negligent. Thus, bringing a patient into contact with other patients who have an infectious disease can constitute negligence,[255] as can discharging an infectious patient from hospital prematurely, with the result that others who come into contact with him contract the disease.[256] It is not necessarily negligent, however, for a

---

[249] In *Frandle v MacKenzie* (1990) 5 CCLT (2d) 113 (BCCA) liability for not keeping a proper count of the swabs was ascribed 80 per cent to the surgeon and 20 per cent to the nurses.

[250] National Audit Office, *The Management and Control of Hospital Acquired Infection in Acute NHS Trusts in England* (HC 230 Session 1999–2000) (*www.nao.gov.uk*). An earlier report, *Hospital Acquired Infections* (Office of Health Economics, 1997), estimated that hospital acquired infections cause 5,000 deaths a year and contribute to a further 15,000 (more deaths a year in the UK than road deaths or suicides). This report suggested that up to a third of hospital acquired infections could be prevented, whereas the NAO report estimated that up to 15 per cent of infections are avoidable.

[251] The Times, 4 September 1990 (news report). See also Cooke (1989) 5 J of the MDU 62.

[252] *Hajgato v London Health Association* (1982) 36 OR (2d) 669, 681 (Ont HC).

[253] ibid, at 682; *Reitze v Bruser (No 2)* [1979] 1 WWR 31, 49–50, (Man QB); see also *Hucks v Cole* (1968), [1993] 4 Med LR 393 (CA).

[254] (1947) 203 LTJ 264.

[255] *Lindsey County Council v Marshall* [1937] AC 97, where the claimant was admitted to the defendants' maternity home notwithstanding an outbreak of puerperal fever in the home a week earlier. See also *Heafield v Crane*, The Times, 31 July 1937, where, after the birth of her child, the claimant was moved from the maternity ward to a general ward where a patient was suffering from puerperal fever, and the claimant caught the infection.

[256] *Evans v Liverpool Corporation* [1906] 1 KB 160.

hospital to adopt a system for managing infectious smallpox patients by sterilisation rather than isolation, where the defendants conform to a practice accepted as proper by a responsible body of professional opinion.[257]

(b) By Donor Organs or Bodily Fluid

Some cases of infection arise from the transplantation of human organs or the **6.80** transfusion of bodily fluids from a donor who carried the infection.[258] Before a test for HIV was developed in 1985, there were a number of cases in Commonwealth jurisdictions concerning the liability of blood banks and hospitals for the infection of patients with HIV from blood transfusions.[259] When the risk of infection was unknown or unforeseeable, it could not be negligent to fail to take precautions against the risk.[260] Therefore actions involving allegations that defendants failed to adopt adequate screening of donors from groups known to be at high risk of being infected with HIV or failed to adopt 'surrogate testing'[261] were not particularly successful. Surrogate testing, for example, namely testing blood for Hepatitis B core antibodies (the anti-HBc test) on the basis that there was an association between those who tested positive and those in high risk groups for AIDS, was highly controversial. It was also not a particularly effective test as there was a risk that introducing surrogate testing could lead to a reduction of the blood supply as a whole, as well as to an increase in the number of undetected donations of HIV-infected blood.[262] In addition, it was alleged that a blood bank or the

---

[257] *Vancouver General Hospital v McDaniel* (1934) 152 LT 56.

[258] See Norrie (1985) 34 ICLQ 442 for discussion of both the principles of liability in negligence and the question of consent. See further Giesen (1994) 10 PN 2. In *Morgan v Gwent HA*, Independent, 14 December 1987 (CA), a young unmarried woman was negligently given a transfusion of Rhesus positive blood instead of Rhesus negative blood, which raised the level of antibodies in her blood and put at risk any future pregnancy. She was awarded £20,000 in damages.

[259] The one English case which raised this issue was settled before trial of the substantive matters. See *Re HIV Haemophiliac Litigation* (1990), [1996] PIQR P220, in which haemophiliacs treated with imported HIV-infected blood products commenced proceedings against the Department of Health, the Blood Products Laboratory and the National Blood Transfusion Service, alleging inter alia negligence in screening donors, failing to treat the blood products to minimise the risk of infection, failing to warn donors of the risk, and failing to achieve a self-sufficiency in blood products within the NHS. The action raised novel points on the potential liability of the Department of Health and certain government agencies. Without determining the issues, the Court of Appeal accepted that the claimants had made out at least an arguable case of negligence. For a comparable Canadian case see *Brown v Alberta* [1994] 2 WWR 283 (Alta QB).

[260] Thus, in *H v Royal Alexandra Hospital for Children* [1990] 1 Med LR 297 it was not negligent to fail to give a warning of the risk to doctors or patients in 1982, though by 1983 the situation had changed.

[261] *H v Royal Alexandra Hospital for Children* [1990] 1 Med LR 297 (NSWSC); *E v Australian Red Cross Society* (1991) 105 ALR 53 (Aus Fed CA); aff'g (1991) 99 ALR 601; [1991] 2 Med LR 303; *PQ v Australian Red Cross Society* [1992] 1 VR 19 (Vict SC); *Pittman Estate v Bain* (1994) 112 DLR (4th) 257 (Ont Ct, Gen Div). On infection with Hepatitis from blood products see: *Kitchen v McMullen* (1989) 62 DLR (4th) 481 (NBCA).

[262] This was because of the possibility of a 'magnet effect' whereby those who were at high risk of having contracted the AIDS virus donated blood for the specific purpose of having the surrogate test

hospital where a transfusion took place failed to warn doctors and/or patients of the risk of contracting HIV from blood transfusions.[263]

6.81 Between 1982 and 1984 the state of knowledge was in constant flux as scientists and health authorities sought to discover the causes of the newly identified condition of AIDS.[264] However, since the risk of transmission of HIV through blood products has become recognised, the question of negligence turns on whether reasonably practicable steps could have been taken to eliminate or reduce the risk although the standard of care to be expected of a blood bank reflects the fact that it is neither a commercial organisation operating for a profit nor a public health organisation, with a duty to monitor, investigate and control the spread of disease.[265] In *Walker Estate v York-Finch General Hospital*[266] the Canadian Red Cross Society was held to have been negligent in the method of screening blood donors for HIV, in that it had asked potential donors about their general health instead of asking about symptom specific conditions (as the American Red Cross had done in its screening procedures). The Supreme Court of Canada held that the trial judge was entitled to reject expert evidence that the screening procedures were reasonable, because he was not asked to assess complex scientific or highly technical matters. The issue was simply whether the general health question was sufficient to deter an HIV infected donor from donating blood. The issue was not how an expert would have responded to the donor screening questions, but how a lay person would have responded.[267]

6.82 Similar issues have arisen from the possibility of transmitting infection through the donor insemination of semen. In *ter Neuzen v Korn*[268] the claimant contracted

---

performed on them. Given that a positive surrogate test had, at best, a 50 per cent coincidence with HIV infection, the numbers of donations screened out by the surrogate test might be more than offset by the additional donations from high risk donors.

[263] *H v Royal Alexandra Hospital for Children* [1990] 1 Med LR 297 (NSWSC); *PQ v Australian Red Cross Society* [1992] 1 VR 19 (Vict SC).

[264] See, eg, the comments of Sheppard J in *E v Australian Red Cross Society* (1991) 105 ALR 53, 82 (Aus Fed CA).

[265] *Pittman Estate v Bain* (1994) 112 DLR (4th) 257, 313, 318–319. Lang J commented that the social need for a continued supply of blood created different considerations. It was not a product that could simply be removed from the market if inherently dangerous because it is an essential source of life to many. The need for the product outweighs the risk.

[266] (2001) 198 DLR (4th) 193 (SCC).

[267] ibid at [82] *per* Major J. Note that the question of whether any NHS body could owe a duty of care in negligence to patients in respect of infected blood has been rendered largely redundant by the ruling of Burton J in *A v National Blood Authority* [2001] 3 All ER 289 that contaminated blood is a defective product to which the strict liability rules of Pt 1 of the Consumer Protection Act 1987 apply. Liability under the Act is strict, in that it does not depend on the proof of fault. The fact that the risk of infection (with Hepatitis C) was unavoidable, the impracticability and the cost of identifying the potentially harmful virus and taking appropriate precautions, and the fact that blood was supplied by the defendants as a service to society, were all held to be irrelevant to the defendants' liability.

[268] (1993) 103 DLR (4th) 473 (BCCA); aff'd (1995) 127 DLR (4th) 577 (SCC). For discussion of the risks of sexually transmitted disease and HIV infection associated with donor insemination see Barratt and Cooke (1989) 299 BMJ 1178, and 1531.

HIV from artificial insemination in January 1985. In Australia it was known that HIV could be transmitted through blood transfusion by late 1994, and because the Elisa test for HIV being developed in the United States was soon to be available for clinical use, a decision had been taken to impose a moratorium on all bodily fluid and tissue transfers. However, the defendant and North American experts did not learn of the Australian moratorium until after September 1985 and the risk of infection from artificial insemination was not widely known in North America until mid-1985. It was held that this was not a case in which the jury, acting judicially, could find the common practice of competent Canadian doctors to be negligent. The proper test was whether the defendant had conducted himself as a reasonable doctor, and this required the jury to confine itself to prevailing standards of practice in North America.

Surgeons who are infected with HIV or Hepatitis B and who knowingly continue **6.83** to practise surgery, expose their patients to an unacceptable risk of infection, given the seriousness of the consequences, notwithstanding that the risk of passing on the infection is comparatively small. This would almost certainly be deemed to be negligent if a patient were infected in this way.[269]

(v) Miscalculating Drug Reactions

Doctors must take account of manufacturers' instructions and known side-effects **6.84** when prescribing drugs, although they should not rely on the manufacturers' information unthinkingly.[270] Where a doctor ignores the manufacturer's instructions and warnings, it is the doctor who is responsible for any adverse reactions, though a decision to exceed the manufacturers' guidelines or dosages indicated in MIMMS in prescribing a drug is not necessarily negligent.[271] The manufacturer will not be liable since a warning addressed to the doctor will normally discharge the manufacturer's duty of care to the patient in the case of prescription drugs.[272]

---

[269] The General Medical Council guidance, *Serious Communicable Disease* (October 1997) (*www.gmc-uk.org/standards*) advises doctors who have any reason to believe that they have been exposed to a serious communicable disease to seek and follow professional advice on whether they should undergo testing, and whether, and in what ways, they should modify their practice to protect their patients. Doctors should not rely on their own assessment of the risks they pose to patients. One surgeon, a Hepatitis B carrier who had infected 19 patients and put hundreds of others at risk, was convicted of the offence of public nuisance and jailed: The Times, 30 September 1994 (news report); see Mulholland (1995) 11 PN 70. See also *R v Thornton* (1993) 13 OR (3d) 744 (SCC). See further Department of Health, *HIV Infected Health Care Workers: A Consultation Paper on Management and Patient Notification* (June 2002) (*www.doh.gov.uk/aids.htm*).

[270] See, eg, *Buchan v Ortho Pharmaceuticals (Canada) Ltd* (1986) 25 DLR (4th) 658 (Ont CA).

[271] *Vernon v Bloomsbury HA* (1986), [1995] 6 Med LR 297.

[272] *Holmes v Ashford* [1950] 2 All ER 76; *Kubach v Hollands* [1937] 3 All ER 907; *Buchan v Ortho Pharmaceuticals (Canada) Ltd* (1986) 25 DLR (4th) 658, 669 (Ont CA); *Davidson v Connaught Laboratories* (1980) 14 CCLT 251, 276 (Ont HC); Ferguson (1992) 12 OJLS 59; Peppin (1991) 70 Can Bar Rev 473.

6.85   Ignorance of known side-effects is negligent if the defendant ought reasonably to have been aware of them. Some mistakes may be isolated errors,[273] but in other cases the doctor is aware of the risk from side-effects, and yet calculates that it is a reasonable risk to run in the circumstances, given the condition for which the drug is prescribed. If the calculation is correct by reference to the standards of the profession he is not negligent, but if the risk was unreasonable in the circumstances he will be liable. For example, in *Battersby v Tottman*[274] a doctor prescribed a very high dose of melleril to a patient who was suffering from a mental illness. He took the view that the benefits of the drug outweighed the risk that the drug would cause serious and permanent eye damage, since without treatment the patient was suicidal, and other methods of treatment had failed. The patient did sustain permanent eye damage. It was held that the decision to prescribe a dosage far in excess of the recommended dosage was not negligent as it was justified by the potential consequences of not using the drug. By way of contrast, in *Graham v Persyko*[275] the defendant gastroenterologist wrongly, but not negligently, diagnosed that the claimant had Crohn's disease, for which there is no cure, and prescribed prednisone, a very potent drug with a multitude of serious adverse effects, and a low safety margin. This caused avascular necrosis of the patient's femoral heads, a rare but known complication. The decision to prescribe the drug was held to be negligent, because the risk from the side-effects was disproportionate to the anticipated benefit to the patient who was asymptomatic at the time.

6.86   It is also possible for the correct dosage of a drug to be undercalculated. A number of cases have arisen in which patients undergoing surgery have been awake and conscious of pain but unable to communicate with medical staff due to being paralysed by muscle relaxant drugs. This may or may not be due to fault in the administration of the anaesthetic.[276]

(vi) Injections

6.87   Injections may be given in the wrong place, the hypodermic may contain the wrong substance or an excessive dose, or the needle may break.[277] Not all errors,

---

[273] See, eg, *Dwyer v Roderick* (1983) 127 SJ 806; *McCaffrey v Hague* [1949] 4 DLR 291.

[274] (1985) 37 SASR 524 (SC of S Aus).

[275] (1986) 27 DLR (4th) 699 (Ont CA); (1986) 34 DLR (4th) 160 (SCC) leave to appeal refused.

[276] See *Ludlow v Swindon HA* [1989] 1 Med LR 104; *Taylor v Worcester and District HA* [1991] 2 Med LR 215; *Ackers v Wigan HA* [1991] 2 Med LR 232; *Phelan v East Cumbria HA* [1991] 2 Med LR 419; *Early v Newham HA* [1994] 5 Med LR 214; *Jacobs v Great Yarmouth and Waveney HA* [1995] 6 Med LR 192. For discussion see (1995) 1 *Clinical Risk* (No 4).

[277] A broken needle is not necessarily an indication of negligence, since it may be due to a latent defect in the needle: *Brazier v Ministry of Defence* [1965] 1 Lloyd's Rep 26. See also *Gerber v Pines* (1935) 79 SJ 13; *Galloway v Hanley* (1956) 1 BMJ 580; *Daniels v Heskin* [1954] IR 73, 79; cf *Cardin v City of Montreal* (1961) 29 DLR (2d) 492 (SCC) where a doctor who administered a vaccine by hypodermic needle to a child who was struggling against his mother's efforts to keep him still was held to have been negligent in not postponing the injection until the child was in a less agitated state.

however, will give rise to a claim for negligence. An injection into the patient's sur-rounding tissues instead of a vein is not necessarily negligent if the vein is difficult to find.[278] On the other hand, a doctor must take responsibility for what he injects into a patient and administering an excessive dose of a drug having misread the instructions is clearly negligent,[279] as is an excessive dose of anaesthetic given through misjudgment attributable to inexperience.[280] Even when allowing for the fact that the person who provides the hypodermic is skilled in such matters and the solution is made up in the hospital pharmacy, there remains an obligation upon a surgeon carrying out the injection to take reasonable steps to check that he is getting what he ordered.[281] In *Ritchie v Chichester HA*[282] the treatment protocol for the administration of an epidural anaesthetic to a woman in the course of labour required both the midwife and the anaesthetist to check that the correct drug had been selected for injection by reading the name on the ampoule. The defendants were held liable on the basis that the anaesthetist must have injected a neurotoxic substance into the claimant when administering the epidural anaes-thetic, despite the fact that there would have to have been a series of errors on the part of the medical staff involved. In *Caldeira v Gray*[283] damage to the sciatic nerve following an injection in the buttocks was found to have been caused by negli-gence, but in *Wilcox v Cavan*[284] the Supreme Court of Canada held that where gangrene had developed in the claimant's arm following an intra-muscular injec-tion, the nurse who administered the injection was not liable under the principle of *res ipsa loquitur*. Although there was no explanation as to how the injection had

---

Note that the fact that an instrument, such as a needle, has broken may indicate that the instrument itself was defective in which case there may be an action against the manufacturer either in negli-gence or under the Consumer Protection Act 1987: see, eg, *G v Fry Surgical International Ltd* (1992) 3 *AVMA Medical & Legal Journal* (No 4) 12, where the blade of a pair of arthroscopy scissors frac-tured during the course of an operation and a fragment was lost in the claimant's knee. An action under the Consumer Protection Act 1987 against the importers of the scissors, on the basis that the scissors were defective, was settled.

[278] *Williams v North Liverpool HMC*, The Times, 17 January 1959; *Prout v Crowley* (1956) 1 BMJ 580; *Gent v Wilson* (1956) 2 DLR (2d) 160.

[279] *Strangeways-Lesmere v Clayton* [1936] 2 KB 11; *Smith v Brighton and Lewes HMC*, The Times, 2 May 1958; *Sellers v Cooke* [1990] 2 Med LR 16, 19.

[280] *Jones v Manchester Corporation* [1952] 2 All ER 125; *Skelton v Lewisham and North Southwark HA* [1998] Lloyd's Rep Med 324, 332 (QBD).

[281] *Collins v Hertfordshire County Council* [1947] 1 KB 598, 607.

[282] [1994] 5 Med LR 187 (QBD); cf *Muzio v North West Herts HA* [1995] 6 Med LR 184, where an anaesthetist was found not negligent when, in the course of inserting a needle for a spinal anaes-thetic, she penetrated the dura, leading the claimant to develop severe spinal headaches. See also Dr J Lunn, 'The Role of the Anaesthetist', in *Action for the Victims of Medical Accidents, Risk Areas in Medical Practice* (1993), 128–36; and Dr Hannington-Kiff, 'Overview of Obstetric Lumbar Epidural Blocks' (1993) 4 *AVMA Medical & Legal Journal* (No 1) 2.

[283] [1936] 1 All ER 540.

[284] (1974) 50 DLR (3d) 687 (SCC); *Fischer v Waller* [1994] 1 WWR 83 (Alta QB), where it was held that perforation of the globe of the eye during the course of administering a local anaesthetic prior to cataract surgery was a rare but recognised risk of the procedure which could occur in the absence of negligence.

found its way into the claimant's circumflex artery, the defendant's version of events was consistent with the absence of negligence.

(vii) Failure to Monitor Treatment

6.88 A doctor has a duty to monitor treatment given to a patient, particularly where the treatment carries a high risk of an adverse reaction.[285] This duty extends to post-operative conditions which the patient may develop.[286] A patient recovering from a general anaesthetic will require careful monitoring. In *Coyne v Wigan HA*[287] the claimant sustained brain damage caused by hypoxia for a period of four to five minutes when she was in the recovery ward following an operation under general anaesthetic. The defendants accepted that the principle of *res ipsa loquitur* applied, seeking to explain the incident on the basis that the hypoxia was the result of silent regurgitation of gastric content. It was held that the evidence did not support the defendants' explanation, which was implausible because there was no recorded instance of silent aspiration leading to brain damage and only one such case was referred to in evidence. Accordingly, the appropriate inference was that there had been negligence in monitoring the patient.

D. Psychiatric Patients

6.89 The *Bolam* test[288] applies to the relationship between a psychiatrist and a psychiatric patient just as it applies to any other doctor–patient relationship. Thus, it was negligent for a psychiatrist to engage in social contact with a female patient who had developed a strong and obsessive emotional attachment to him, leading to a serious deterioration in the patient's mental health, given that this was a departure from recognised standards of practice which no body of professional opinion supported.[289] In some cases the nature of the mental illness makes the patient dangerous, either to himself or to others, and claims can arise out of an alleged failure to exercise control over the patient. A doctor undoubtedly has a duty to take reasonable steps to protect a psychiatric patient from harming himself, and in an

---

[285] *Marshall v Rogers* [1943] 4 DLR 68; *Male v Hopmans* (1967) 64 DLR (2d) 105, 113–115 (Ont CA); *Wilsher v Essex AHA* [1986] 3 All ER 801.

[286] *Bayliss v Blagg* (1954) 1 BMJ 709; *Ares v Venner* (1970) 14 DLR (3d) 4 (SCC) and *Harrington v Essex AHA*, The Times, 14 November 1984 (QBD), on plaster casts; *Poole v Morgan* [1987] 3 WWR 217; *Cavanagh v Bristol and Weston HA* [1992] 3 Med LR 49 (QBD); *Newbury v Bath District HA* (1998) 47 BMLR 138—defendants negligent in failing to carry out tests for neurological deficit in the immediate post-operative period, in light of the patient's symptoms.

[287] [1991] 2 Med LR 301 (QBD).

[288] The claimant in *Bolam v Friern HMC* [1957] 2 All ER 118 itself was a psychiatric patient who sustained serious physical injuries in the course of electro-convulsive therapy administered to treat depression.

[289] *Landau v Werner* (1961) 105 SJ 257, and 1008 (CA).

institutional setting a hospital authority may be responsible for injuries inflicted on a patient by himself,[290] or by a fellow patient, where the injuries are the result of a failure to provide adequate control and supervision.[291]

1. Self Harm

This duty can include an obligation to make reasonable efforts to prevent suicide attempts.[292] In *Thorne v Northern Group HMC*[293] the nursing staff on a medical ward of a general hospital were aware that a patient, who was a suspected depressive, had threatened suicide. The patient walked out of the hospital, went home and committed suicide while mentally ill but not legally insane. It was held that there had been no negligence, because, on the facts, constant supervision was not appropriate. In *Selfe v Ilford and District HMC*[294] on the other hand, it was accepted that reasonable care required continuous observation of a patient who was known to be a serious suicide risk. He was put in a ground floor ward with 27 patients, four of whom were also suicide risks, and there were insufficient nurses available to cope with all the circumstances that could be expected to arise. The claimant climbed out of a window and jumped off a roof, sustaining serious injuries. Hinchcliffe J held the defendants liable. The degree of care required was proportionate to the degree of risk, and in this case there had been a breakdown in proper nursing supervision. However, the degree of care must also take into account the level of restraint or supervision appropriate in the light of the patient's mental condition. In some cases imposing restraint on a patient may exacerbate the patient's condition, or at least inhibit effective treatment. If it is against the

6.90

---

[290] *Jinks v Cardwell* (1987) 39 CCLT 168 (Ont HC); *Kelly v Board of Governors of St Laurence's Hospital* [1988] IR 402 (Sup Ct Irl).

[291] *Wellesley Hospital v Lawson* (1977) 76 DLR (3d) 688 where the Supreme Court of Canada assumed that such a common law duty existed. In *Ellis v Home Office* [1953] 2 All ER 149 prison authorities were held to owe a duty of care to a prisoner assaulted by another prisoner.

[292] Jones (1990) 6 PN 107. Where, on the other hand, the suicide attempt is unforeseeable there will be no liability on the basis that no duty of care is owed: *Orange v Chief Constable of West Yorkshire Police* [2001] EWCA Civ 611; [2002] QB 347 at [41] to [43]; *Lepine v University Hospital Board* (1966) 57 DLR (2d) 701 (SCC). Note that inadequate medical treatment and a lack of effective monitoring of a prisoner who was known to be mentally ill and an identified suicide risk could, in some circumstances, constitute a breach of Article 3 of the ECHR, which provides that 'No one shall be subjected to torture or to inhuman or degrading treatment or punishment': see also *Keenan v UK* (2001) 10 BHRC 319 (ECtHR).

[293] (1964) 108 SJ 484.

[294] (1970) 114 SJ 935. See also *Hay v Grampian Health Board* [1995] 6 Med LR 128 (CS), where the regime for supervising a known suicide risk broke down; *Mahmood v Siggins* [1996] 7 Med LR 76, where a GP was held liable for failing to refer a known manic depressive to a community mental health team for assessment, treatment and supervision; *Drake v Pontefract HA; Wakefield and Pontefract Community NHS Trust* [1998] Lloyd's Rep Med 425, where an inexperienced psychiatrist was held negligent in failing to diagnose the claimant's condition correctly, failing to assess the risk of suicide, and failing to provide appropriate treatment, though the patient had been referred by the GP as a suicide risk; *Villemure v L'Hôpital Notre Dame* (1972) 31 DLR (3d) 454 (SCC).

patient's wishes, it might undermine the trust between doctor and patient. This judgment has to balance competing risks to the patient's health, including the risk of self-harm resulting in death.[295]

6.91 If a non-psychiatric patient makes a suicide attempt the question will be whether non-specialist (ie non-psychiatric) staff ought to have realised that there was a genuine risk of a suicide attempt. This will not be judged by reference to whether a psychiatrist could have made this diagnosis but whether in the defendant's position a reasonable doctor or nurse would have identified the risk. In *Hyde v Tameside Area HA*[296] the claimant was admitted to hospital with a painful shoulder. Twelve days later he jumped from a third-floor window, having convinced himself, erroneously, that he had cancer. He suffered catastrophic injuries. It was alleged that the medical staff had negligently failed to identify the claimant's mental distress, and had failed to realise the patient needed psychiatric treatment. The Court of Appeal held that on the particular facts there was no negligence, merely a 'forgivable failure to achieve a standard approaching perfection'. The court will make allowance for the fact that a decision to introduce psychiatric treatment for patients who are not being treated for a psychiatric illness or disorder is one that involves competing considerations. Watkins LJ pointed out that many patients in hospital suffer from anxiety and worry about their medical condition. They may need reassurance and sometimes need drugs to ease pain or stress, but to tell a patient who requires surgery that he also needs psychiatric help may be counter-productive.[297]

6.92 It has been argued that, quite apart from the question of breach of duty, claims for negligence based on suicide or attempted suicide should not be permitted, on the grounds of causation, *volenti non fit injuria, ex turpi causa non oritur actio*, or simply for policy reasons.[298] The causation argument states that the defendant's negligence merely provided the opportunity for the deceased's act of suicide, which amounted to a *novus actus interveniens*. In *Kirkham v Chief Constable of Greater Manchester Police*[299] Tudor Evans J rejected this contention on the basis that the suicide was the very thing that the defendants had a duty to take precautions against,[300] and concluded that on the evidence the patient's suicide would

---

[295] *Haines v Bellissimo* (1977) 82 DLR (3d) 215 (Ont HC).

[296] (1981), reported at (1986) 2 PN 26.

[297] ibid, 30.

[298] For consideration of the defences of *volenti non fit injuria* and *ex turpi causa* see paras 7.58–7.62.

[299] [1989] 3 All ER 882; aff'd [1990] 2 WLR 987.

[300] Where the intervening conduct is the very thing that the defendant was under a duty to guard against, he cannot avoid liability by arguing that the conduct constituted an intervening act: *Haynes v Harwood* [1935] 1 KB 146, 156; *Perl (Exporters) Ltd v Camden LBC* [1984] QB 342, 353. See also *per* Farquharson LJ in *Kirkham v Chief Constable of Greater Manchester Police* [1990] 2 WLR 987, 997 in relation to the defence of *volenti non fit injuria*.

probably have been prevented.[301] His Lordship commented that although the act of suicide was a conscious and deliberate act 'the deceased's mental balance was . . . affected at the time'.[302] This left open the question whether, if the deceased's mind was not 'affected', the suicide could be regarded as a *novus actus interveniens*.

In *Reeves v Commissioner of Police for the Metropolis*,[303] a case which also involved **6.93** the suicide of a prisoner who was a known suicide risk, though not found to be mentally ill, the House of Lords held that the suicide did not constitute a *novus actus*. The damage arose from breach of a duty to prevent just such an act and thus did not obliterate the defendants' wrongdoing. It was not a new act, but the very harm that the defendants were under a duty to try to prevent. In cases where the law imposes a duty to guard against loss caused by the free, deliberate and informed act of a human being, 'it would make nonsense of the existence of such a duty if the law were to hold that the occurrence of the very act which ought to have been prevented negatived causal connection between the breach of duty and the loss'.[304] Once it was accepted that a duty to protect a person of full understanding from harming himself was owed, it was self-contradictory to say that the breach could not have been a cause of the harm because the victim caused it to himself.[305] The deceased's mental state was irrelevant to this issue, since the defendant's duty arose out of the fact that the deceased was a known suicide risk, not from any particular mental state. For the same reasons the defence of *volenti non fit injuria* did not apply either.[306]

2. Harm to Third Parties

It is uncertain whether, in this country, a psychiatrist would be held responsible **6.94** for foreseeable harm inflicted by a patient on a third party.[307] Even if it were possible to identify reasonably practicable steps that a doctor could have taken (such as seeking compulsory admission for assessment or treatment under the Mental Health Act 1983), it is not clear that a duty of care would be held to exist. Where the patient is compulsorily detained, however, the greater degree of control

---

[301] In *Hyde v Tameside AHA* (1986) 2 PN 26 O'Connor LJ said that he did not think that 'the fact that a patient commits suicide or attempts suicide will necessarily break the chain of causation if breach of duty is established against the hospital. It all depends on the circumstances of an individual case'.

[302] [1989] 3 All ER 882, 889. In *Wright Estate v Davidson* (1992) 88 DLR (4th) 698 (BCCA) the deceased's suicide was held to constitute a *novus actus interveniens* where there was no evidence of disabling mental illness; cf *Costello v Blakeson* [1993] 2 WWR 562 (BCSC).

[303] [2000] 1 AC 360.

[304] ibid, 367–368, *per* Lord Hoffmann.

[305] ibid, 368.

[306] See para 7.59. The Court of Appeal in *Reeves* had also rejected the defence of *ex turpi causa* on the same grounds: [1999] QB 169, para 7.60.

[307] See *Tarasoff v Regents of the University of California* 551 P 2d 334 (1976); *Thompson v County of Alameda*, 614 P 2d 728 (1980); *Brady v Hopper*, 751 F 2d 329 (1984); cf *Jablonski v US*, 712 F 2d 391 (1983).

exercised over the patient may be sufficient to tip the balance in favour of a duty of care being imposed.[308] In *Clunis v Camden and Islington HA*[309] the Court of Appeal rejected a claim in negligence by a patient who had killed an innocent by-stander. He alleged that had he received proper psychiatric treatment he would not have committed the offence and therefore he would not have been convicted of a criminal offence and sent to prison. The claim was struck out as contrary to public policy, because his plea of manslaughter by reason of diminished responsibility still required some degree of personal responsibility, even though it was accepted that his mental responsibility was substantially impaired. The Court of Appeal did, however, contemplate that there could be liability in negligence in such a case if it could be proved that the claimant did not know the nature and quality of his act or that what he had done was wrong.

6.95 In *Palmer v Tees HA*[310] a young child was abducted and killed by a mental patient who had previously stated, while a hospital in-patient, that he had sexual feelings towards children and that a child would be murdered after his discharge. The Court of Appeal held that no duty of care was owed by the defendant health authority either to the child herself or the child's mother, in respect of an alleged negligent failure to diagnose that the patient constituted a serious risk to children. The threats made by the patient in *Palmer* were of a general nature. It would at least be arguable that, if a psychiatric patient were to make threats against a specific individual or individuals, where there was a real risk of such threats being carried out, then a duty of care on the part of a psychiatrist or psychologist might arise.[311]

3. Negligent Certification

6.96 A doctor who provides a written recommendation supporting the compulsory admission of a patient into hospital under Pt II of the Mental Health Act 1983 must exercise reasonable care.[312] This necessarily requires that the doctor examine the patient,[313] and make such further enquiries as are necessary.[314] On the one

---

[308] *Holgate v Lancashire Mental Hospitals Board* [1937] 4 All ER 19. Note, however, that in *Palmer v Tees HA* [1999] Lloyd's Rep Med 351, 358–359 the Court of Appeal dismissed *Holgate* as a case of unsatisfactory authority where little attention was paid to the question of the defendants' duty of care. The case could not be reconciled with *Hill v Chief Constable of West Yorkshire* [1989] 1 AC 53.

[309] [1998] QB 978. This case is not concerned with a claim *by* a third party against the health authority, though it is clear that had the patient's action against the health authority succeeded the deceased's spouse would have had better prospects of obtaining redress from the claimant.

[310] [2000] PIQR P1; [1999] Lloyd's Rep Med 351; See further Jones (2000) 16 PN 3.

[311] As in *Tarasoff v Regents of the University of California* 551 P 2d 334; Sup, 131 Cal Rptr 14 (1976).

[312] *Hall v Semple* (1862) 3 F & F 337; *De Freville v Dill* (1927) 96 LJKB 1056; *Everett v Griffiths* [1921] 1 AC 631; *Harnett v Fisher* [1927] AC 573; *Buxton v Jayne* [1960] 1 WLR 783; [1962] CLY 1167.

[313] Mental Health Act 1983, s 12(1).

[314] *Hall v Semple* (1862) 3 F & F 337, 354, *per* Crompton J.

hand, the court must make due allowance for the difficulty in making an accurate diagnosis in some cases of mental illness, and on the other hand, they should require 'very considerable care' to be taken where a person is being deprived of his liberty.[315]

4. Procedural Bars

Section 139(1) of the Mental Health Act 1983 provides that no person shall be liable to any civil or criminal proceedings in respect of any act purporting to be done under the mental health legislation unless the act was done in bad faith or without reasonable care.[316] In addition, civil proceedings may not be instituted in respect of such an act without leave of the High Court.[317] Proceedings issued without leave are a nullity,[318] although the requirement for leave applies only to patients who are formally detained under the Act; voluntary patients do not need leave to bring an action.[319] The requirement for leave does not apply to actions against the Secretary of State or a health authority.[320] It had been thought that one consequence of s 139(4) was that, irrespective of the substantive defence provided to an individual doctor by s 139(1), the hospital employing that doctor would be vicariously liable for his actions (for example in the tort of battery) even if the doctor was held not liable because he acted in good faith and with reasonable care.[321] But in *R (on the application of W) v Broadmoor Hospital*[322] Hale LJ suggested that a health authority or NHS Trust could only be held vicariously liable for the

6.97

---

[315] ibid, 355–356.

[316] Jaconelli [1998] JSWFL 151. The section does not apply to an application for judicial review, so that proceedings for judicial review of a decision purportedly taken in the exercise of powers conferred by the Mental Health Act 1983 can be brought even though the applicant does not allege that the decision was made negligently or in bad faith: *Re Waldron* [1986] QB 824. It was conceded in this case that s 139 would not apply to a writ of habeas corpus.

[317] Mental Health Act 1983, s 139(2). It is arguable that a private law action brought under s 7 of the Human Rights Act 1998 would require leave under s 139(2) of the Mental Health Act 1983: *R (on the application of W) v Broadmoor Hospital* [2001] EWCA Civ 1545; [2002] 1 WLR 419 *per* Brooke LJ at [54] and Hale LJ at [61].

[318] *Pountney v Griffiths* [1976] AC 314.

[319] *R v Runighian* (1977) Crim LR 361.

[320] Mental Health Act 1983, s 139(4). Accordingly, it does not apply to the Mental Health Act Commission, which is a special health authority: *X v A, B and C and the Mental Health Act Commission* (1991) 9 BMLR 91, 97 (QBD). See, however, *C v South London and Maudsley Hospital NHS Trust* (2001, QBD), where McCombe J, having refused to grant leave under s 139(2) to bring proceedings against the individual doctors, held that the proceedings against the defendant NHS Trust would be bound to fail, for the same reasons as given under s 139(2), and therefore it was inevitable that they would either be struck out under the court's case management powers or judgment would be given in favour of the defendants on the basis that the claim had no real prospect of succeeding. This would seem to undermine the effect of s 139(4).

[321] See *R (on the application of W) v Broadmoor Hospital* [2001] EWCA Civ 1545; [2002] 1 WLR 419 at [24] *per* Simon Brown LJ and [58] *per* Hale LJ.

[322] ibid, *per* Hale LJ.

actions for which the individual doctors would themselves be liable, which would indirectly confer the benefit of s 139(1) on the employers.[323]

6.98   In *Winch v Jones*[324] the Court of Appeal held that it was not necessary for the claimant to establish a prima facie case of negligence against the defendant in order to obtain leave, because this would lead to a full dress-rehearsal of the action, and at the stage of seeking leave an applicant who has a reasonable suspicion that there has been negligence may be quite unable to put forward a prima facie case before discovery has taken place. The test is whether on the materials immediately available to the court 'the applicant's complaint appears to be such that it deserves the fuller investigation which will be possible if the intended applicant is allowed to proceed'.[325] Parker LJ said that the purpose of the section was to prevent harassment by clearly hopeless actions, not to see that only those actions which would be likely to succeed should go ahead.

6.99   In *James v LBC*[326] however, Farquharson LJ suggested that the court did have to decide whether the applicant had a prima facie case. He distinguished *Winch v Jones* and refused the applicant leave under s 139(2) saying that, because it was 'virtually unarguable' that the doctor and the social worker concerned in an emergency compulsory admission for assessment could have acted without reasonable care, an action by the applicant would be bound to fail. Farquharson LJ disagreed with the approach of Sir John Donaldson MR, on the ground that the object of s 139 was to protect a defendant from the consequences of a wrong decision made in purported compliance with the Mental Health Act, particularly in circumstances where decisions have to be made quickly for the safety of the patient or others. Section 139 was not only protection against frivolous claims; it was also a protection from error in the circumstances set out in the subsection.[327] It is arguable, however, that requiring a claimant to establish a prima facie case before disclosure, and in circumstances where facts are in dispute, sets

---

[323] Brooke LJ even suggested, provisionally, that a hospital may not be vicariously liable at all for the actions of a responsible medical officer (RMO) in making treatment decisions under ss 57 or 58 of the Mental Health Act, on the basis that the Act vests the duty to carry out the specified functions in the RMO personally. It was not the hospital, through the agency of one of its medical staff, in whom was vested the power to direct treatment without consent, but the RMO himself: ibid at [42] and [43].

[324] [1985] 3 All ER 97.

[325] ibid, 102, *per* Sir John Donaldson MR.

[326] (1992) 15 BMLR 1.

[327] ibid, 4. See also *C v South London and Maudsley Hospital NHS Trust* (2001, QBD), where the claimant argued that the doctors had used the procedure for compulsory admission for assessment (under s 2) in bad faith, in order to avoid the statutory requirements associated with compulsory admission for treatment (under s 3) because it was known that the claimant's mother objected. McCombe J refused leave under s 139(2), on the basis that there was no reason why a doctor could not reasonably and in good faith take the view that the grounds for admission under s 2 were met, even if he thought that in the end a s 3 admission for a longer period would almost inevitably follow.

the procedural hurdle for claimants too high, a point that had been accepted in *Winch v Jones*.[328]

E. Evidence and Proof

1. Proof of Negligence

The burden of proving, on the balance of probabilities, that the defendant has been negligent and that the negligence caused damage to the claimant lies with the claimant. If there are two equally possible explanations for an accident, one of which indicates that the accident occurred without negligence by the defendant, the claimant's action will fail,[329] although it will only be in an exceptional case that the issue should be decided on the basis of the burden of proof.[330] The claimant does not have to provide direct evidence that the defendant has fallen below the requisite standard of care. He may rely upon any legitimate inferences that can be drawn from the proved facts, and in the absence of evidence to the contrary, the inference may well be that the defendant has been negligent.

6.100

2. Res Ipsa Loquitur

The principle of *res ipsa loquitur* is an evidential principle which enables a claimant who has no knowledge, or insufficient knowledge, of how a medical accident occurred to rely on the accident itself and its surrounding circumstances as evidence of negligence on the part of the defendant. There is no magic in the phrase; it is simply a submission that the facts establish a prima facie case against the defendant which would be sufficient to impose liability in the absence of evidence in rebuttal.[331] Of course, it does not follow that simply because the claimant is in a position to invoke *res ipsa loquitur*, that his action will necessarily succeed. The inference of negligence may be rebutted by evidence adduced by the defendant which explains how the accident occurred without negligence on his part.[332]

6.101

---

[328] Note that the draft Mental Health Bill 2002 (*www.doh.gov.uk/mentalhealth/draftbill2002*) would reverse the burden of proof in the s 139 defence, ie it would be a defence for the defendant to demonstrate that he acted in good faith and with reasonable care.

[329] *Jones v Great Western Railway Co* (1930) 47 TLR 39, 45, *per* Lord Macmillan; *The Kite* [1933] P 154; *Harrington v Essex AHA*, The Times, 14 November 1984 (QBD), where Beldam J felt unable to select either one of two possible explanations for the claimant's necrosis of the skin, and the claimant's action failed on the burden of proof.

[330] *Morris v London Iron & Steel Co Ltd* [1987] IRLR 182 (CA); *The Popi M* [1985] 2 Lloyd's Rep 1, 6 (HL).

[331] *Roe v Minister of Health* [1954] 2 QB 66, 87–88, *per* Morris LJ; *Ballard v North British Railway Co* 1923 SC 43, 56, *per* Lord Shaw: 'If that phrase had not been in Latin, nobody would have called it a principle.'

[332] See, eg, *Roe v Minister of Health* [1954] 2 QB 66; *Brazier v Minister of Defence* [1965] 1 Lloyd's Rep 26; *Moore v Worthing District HA* [1992] 3 Med LR 431 (QBD); *Lindsay v Mid-Western Health Board* [1993] 2 IR 147 (Sup Ct Irl); *Wilcox v Cavan* (1974) 50 DLR (3d) 687 (SCC); *Hajgato v London Health Association* (1982) 36 OR (2d) 669; aff'd (1983) 44 OR (2d) 264 (Ont CA).

Indeed, it is not incumbent on the defendant to explain how the accident happened at all, provided there is evidence to show that he exercised reasonable care.[333] As Hobhouse LJ commented in *Ratcliffe v Plymouth and Torbay HA*: 'There is no rule that a defendant must be liable for any accident for which he cannot give a complete explanation.'[334] But the maxim prevents a defendant who does know what happened from avoiding responsibility simply by choosing not to give any evidence.[335]

6.102 In some cases it has been suggested that the principle has the effect of reversing the burden of proof, requiring the defendant to show that the harm was not the product of his carelessness.[336] The better view would seem to be that this is incorrect. The burden of proof remains with the claimant, but *res ipsa loquitur* requires the defendant to offer some reasonable explanation as to how the accident could have occurred without negligence by him.[337] On this basis, *res ipsa loquitur* 'is no more than the use of a Latin maxim to describe the state of the evidence from which it is proper to draw an inference of negligence'.[338] Where an inference of negligence does arise, a general denial by way of defence will not be sufficient to rebut it.[339] If the defendant adduces no evidence, the claimant will have proved his case. If the defendant does adduce evidence that is consistent with an absence of negligence on his part, then the inference of negligence is rebutted. The claimant then has to produce positive evidence that the defendant has acted without reasonable care[340] although, in practice, it is unlikely that the claimant will be able to do this, since

---

[333] In *Delaney v Southmead HA* [1995] 6 Med LR 355 the claimant suffered a brachial plexus injury in the course of an operation for which, the claimant argued there was no explanation other than that the arm had been hyper-abducted and/or externally rotated. There was no direct evidence as to what the defendant had actually done during the operation, but the Court of Appeal held that a defendant was entitled to rely on evidence as to his normal practice to rebut an inference of negligence, even though there was evidence in the medical literature from 1942 onwards, backed up by expert evidence for the claimant, which suggested that there were effectively only two possible explanations for the claimant's injury, one of which the trial judge found had not in fact occurred, and the other of which was consistent with negligence. The effect of the Court of Appeal's ruling was that there was *no* explanation for the claimant's injury.

[334] [1998] PIQR P170 at 187.

[335] For example, patients under a general anaesthetic are not aware of what is going on about them, and the facts are peculiarly within the knowledge of the anaesthetist and others attending them: *Crits v Sylvester* (1956) 1 DLR (2d) 502, 510, *per* Schroeder JA (Ont CA); see also *Mahon v Osborne* [1939] 2 KB 14, 50, *per* Goddard LJ.

[336] *Henderson v Henry E Jenkins & Sons* [1970] AC 282; *Ward v Tesco Stores Ltd* [1976] 1 WLR 810; *Moore v R Fox & Sons* [1956] 1 QB 596; *Mahon v Osborne* [1939] 2 KB 14, 50 *per* Goddard LJ.

[337] *Ng Chun Pui v Lee Chuen Tat* [1988] RTR 298 (PC).

[338] ibid, 300, *per* Lord Griffiths. In *Lloyde v West Midlands Gas Board* [1971] 1 WLR 749, 755, Megaw LJ regarded *res ipsa loquitur* as 'no more than an exotic, although convenient, phrase to describe what is in essence no more than a common sense approach, not limited by technical rules, to the assessment of the effect of the evidence'. See also *Lindsay v Mid-Western Health Board* [1993] 2 IR 147, 183–184 (Sup Ct Irl); *Crits v Sylvester* (1956) 1 DLR (2d) 502, 510 (Ont CA).

[339] *Bergin v David Wickes Television* [1994] PIQR P167, 168 (CA).

[340] *Ballard v North British Railway Co* 1923 SC 43, 54, *per* Lord Dunedin.

he would not have relied on *res ipsa loquitur* in the first place if he had such evidence. Where the explanation given by the defendant relates to a remote or unusual eventuality,[341] however, this will not necessarily rebut the presumption of negligence. The claimant does not have to disprove every theoretical explanation, however unlikely, that might be devised to explain what happened in a way which absolves the defendant.[342] Just as the claimant is not entitled to rely on conjecture or speculation to establish his case on the balance of probabilities, so the defendant cannot resort to this when he is called upon for an explanation of events, although on occasions the courts are tempted to accept an explanation of events which relies on the occurrence of extremely remote risks.[343]

6.103 *Res ipsa loquitur* may apply where the defendant, or someone for whom he is responsible, has 'control' of the thing or circumstances that caused the damage,[344] and the accident is such as 'in the ordinary course of things' is one which does not happen in the absence of negligence.[345] However, if all the facts about the cause of the accident are known, the maxim does not apply. The question in such a case is whether, on the known facts, negligence by the defendant can be inferred.[346]

6.104 Despite the occasional suggestion that, since much of medical practice is outside the common experience of life, *res ipsa loquitur* should not be invoked in the context of a medical negligence action,[347] the principle may be relied upon in an

[341] *Holmes v Board of Hospital Trustees of the City of London* (1977) 81 DLR (3d) 67, 82; *Glass v Cambridge Health Authority* [1995] 6 Med LR 91, where the defendant's explanation for the claimant's cardiac arrest under general anaesthetic was rejected as 'at best a highly unlikely possibility'.

[342] *Bull v Devon AHA* (1989), [1993] 4 Med LR 117, 138 (CA), *per* Dillon LJ; *Ballard v North British Railway Co* 1923 SC 43, 54, *per* Lord Dunedin; cf *Lindsay v Mid-Western Health Board* [1993] 2 IR 147, 185 (Sup Ct Irl) where it was said that 'it was legitimate . . . for the defendant to adduce evidence of possibilities, remote though they might be, as an explanation; in contradistinction to saying that it could not offer *any* explanation of any description whatsoever' (original emphasis).

[343] See, eg, *Howard v Wessex RHA* [1994] 5 Med LR 57, QBD.

[344] Where the defendant is vicariously liable for all the staff who played some role in the claimant's treatment, this is sufficient control: *Cassidy v Ministry of Health* [1951] 2 KB 343; cf *Morris v Winsbury-White* [1937] 4 All ER 494, 499 where the patient's post-operative treatment was under the control of several people (nurses, and resident medical officers) as well as the defendant surgeon, and it was held that *res ipsa loquitur* did not apply.

[345] *Scott v London & St Katherine Docks Co* (1865) 3 H & C 596, 601; *Cassidy v Ministry of Health* [1951] 2 KB 343, 353–354 *per* Singleton LJ.

[346] *Barkway v South Wales Transport Co Ltd* [1950] 1 All ER 392; *Johnston v Wellesley Hospital* (1970) 17 DLR (3d) 139, 146 (Ont HC).

[347] See, eg, Scott LJ in *Mahon v Osborne* [1939] 2 KB 14, 23. In *Delaney v Southmead HA* [1995] 6 Med LR 355, 359, Stuart-Smith LJ doubted whether the maxim was of much assistance 'in a case of medical negligence, at any rate when all the evidence in the case has been adduced'. In *Ritchie v Chichester HA* [1994] 5 Med LR 187, 205 (QBD), Judge Thompson QC did not understand Stuart-Smith LJ to be saying that *res ipsa loquitur* could not apply in cases of medical negligence, or that medical negligence was in a special category which put it outside the ordinary English law of negligence. Rather, the maxim may not be of much help where there has been a lot of medical evidence. See also *Nesbitt v Holt* [1953] 1 DLR 671 (SCC).

appropriate case, although the court will be cautious about drawing an inference of negligence simply because something has gone wrong with the treatment.[348] The occurrence of injury is not itself necessarily evidence of a lack of reasonable care, since medical treatment carries inherent risks.[349] Nonetheless, even within medicine, there are some circumstances where the maxim *res ipsa loquitur* will apply.[350] For example, leaving swabs or surgical instruments inside a patient after an operation will normally speak of negligence.[351] Where a patient went into hospital for treatment of two stiff fingers but came out of hospital with four stiff fingers, he was entitled to call on the defendants for an explanation of how the injury could have occurred without negligence.[352] Similarly, the heart of a fit child does not arrest under anaesthesia if proper care is taken in the anaesthetic and surgical processes.[353]

6.105   In *Ratcliffe v Plymouth and Torbay HA*[354] the Court of Appeal made it clear that *res*

---

[348]   *Hucks v Cole* (1968), [1993] 4 Med LR 393, 396 *per* Lord Denning MR.

[349]   *Roe v Minister of Health* [1954] 2 QB 66, 80; *O'Malley-Williams v Board of Governors of the National Hospital for Nervous Diseases* (1975) 1 BMJ 635; *Delaney v Southmead HA* [1995] 6 Med LR 355, 360, *per* Dillon LJ; *Holmes v Board of Hospital Trustees of the City of London* (1977) 81 DLR (3d) 67, 78; *Girard v Royal Columbian Hospital* (1976) 66 DLR (3d) 676, 691 (BCSC).

[350]   *Clarke v Warboys*, The Times, 18 March 1952 (CA), where a patient sustained a burn from a high frequency electrical current used for 'electric coagulation' of the blood; *Bull v Devon AHA* (1989), [1993] 4 Med LR 117, 131 (CA), *per* Slade LJ, where there was a delay of 50 minutes in obtaining expert obstetric assistance at the birth of twins when the medical evidence was that at the most no more than 20 minutes should elapse between the birth of the first and the second twin; *Coyne v Wigan HA* [1991] 2 Med LR 301 (QBD), where, following an operation under general anaesthetic, a patient in the recovery ward sustained brain damage caused by hypoxia for a period of four to five minutes; *Roe v Minister of Health* [1954] 2 QB 66, where a spinal anaesthetic became contaminated with disinfectant as a result of the manner in which it was stored, causing paralysis to the patient; *Brazier v Ministry of Defence* [1965] 1 Lloyd's Rep 26, 30 when a needle broke in the patient's buttock while he was being given an injection; *Crits v Sylvester* (1956) 1 DLR (2d) 502 (Ont CA); aff'd (1956) 5 DLR (2d) 601 (SCC); *Cavan v Wilcox* (1973) 44 DLR (3d) 42 (NBCA); rev'd on the facts (1974) 50 DLR (3d) 687 (SCC); *Eady v Tenderenda* (1974) 51 DLR (3d) 79 (SCC); *Reitze v Bruser (No 2)* [1979] 1 WWR 31 (Man QB).

[351]   *Mahon v Osborne* [1939] 2 KB 14, 50 *per* Goddard LJ; *Cassidy v Ministry of Health* [1951] 2 KB 343, 365–366 *per* Denning LJ; *Garner v Morrell*, The Times, 31 October 1953 (CA); *Nesbitt v Holt* [1953] 1 DLR 671 (SCC).

[352]   *Cassidy v Ministry of Health* [1951] 2 KB 343; see also *Fraser v Vancouver General Hospital* (1951) 3 WWR 337, 343, *per* O'Halloran JA (BCCA). In *Moore v Worthing District HA* [1992] 3 Med LR 431, 434 (QBD) it was said that where a claimant goes into hospital with no impediment to the use of his upper limbs and no obvious risk to them, but comes out crippled, this creates a prima facie case of negligence; though on the facts the injury was found to be attributable to the claimant's abnormal susceptibility.

[353]   *Saunders v Leeds Western HA* (1984), [1993] 4 Med LR 355; *Lindsay v Mid-Western Health Board* [1993] 2 IR 147, 181 (Sup Ct Irl) *per* O'Flaherty J: '. . . it seems to me that if a person goes in for a routine medical procedure, is subject to an anaesthetic without any special features, and there is a failure to return the patient to consciousness, to say that that does not call for an explanation from defendants would be in defiance of reason and justice.' See also *Glass v Cambridge HA* [1995] 6 Med LR 91, where it was held that *res ipsa loquitur* applied to a case where the heart of a healthy man went into cardiac arrest while under general anaesthesia.

[354]   [1998] PIQR P170. For comment on *Ratcliffe* see Jones (1998) 14 PN 174.

ipsa loquitur will rarely be relevant in medical negligence cases because in practice the parties will have obtained relevant evidence from the medical records, and have expert medical opinion available. The issue then is simply what weight should be given to the evidence and whether an inference of negligence is appropriate. Brooke LJ summarised[355] the application of the maxim to medical negligence actions:

(1) In its purest form the maxim applies where the [claimant] relies on the *res* (the thing itself) to raise the inference of negligence, which is supported by ordinary human experience, with no need for expert evidence.

(2) In principle, the maxim can be applied in that form in simple situations in the medical negligence field (surgeon cuts off right foot instead of left; swab left in operation site; patient wakes up in the course of surgical operation despite general anaesthetic).

(3) In practice, in contested medical negligence cases the evidence of the [claimant], which establishes the *res*, is likely to be buttressed by expert evidence to the effect that the matter complained of does not ordinarily occur in the absence of negligence.

(4) The position may then be reached at the close of the [claimant's] case that the judge would be entitled to infer negligence on the defendant's part unless the defendant adduces evidence which discharges this inference.

(5) This evidence may be to the effect that there is a plausible explanation of what may have happened which does not connote any negligence on the defendant's part. The explanation must be a plausible one and not a theoretically or remotely possible one, but the defendant certainly does not have to prove that his explanation is more likely to be correct than any other. If the [claimant] has no other evidence of negligence to rely on his claim will then fail.

(6) Alternatively, the defendant's evidence may satisfy the judge, on the balance of probabilities, that he did exercise proper care. If the untoward outcome is extremely rare, or is impossible to explain in the light of the current state of medical knowledge, the judge will be bound to exercise great care in evaluating the evidence before making such a finding, but if he does so, the prima facie inference of negligence is rebutted and the [claimant's] claim will fail. The reason why the courts are willing to adopt this approach, particularly in very complex cases, is to be found in the judgments of Stuart-Smith and Dillon LJJ in *Delaney*.[356]

(7) It follows from all this that although in very simple situations the *res* may speak for itself at the end of the lay evidence adduced on behalf of the [claimant], in practice the evidence is then buttressed by expert evidence adduced on his behalf, and if the defendant were to call no evidence, the judge would be deciding the case on inferences he was entitled to draw from the whole of the evidence (including the expert evidence), and not on the application of the maxim in its purest form.

---

[355] ibid, 184.
[356] *Delaney v Southmead HA* [1995] 6 Med LR 355.

(i) Inherent Risks of Treatment

6.106   As a general rule, *res ipsa loquitur* will not apply where the injury sustained by the claimant is of a kind recognised as an inherent risk of the treatment, since such accidents obviously can occur without negligence.[357] However, if the risk is known but does not normally occur in the absence of negligence, the maxim can apply.[358] As Robins J said in *Kapur v Marshall*,[359] *res ipsa loquitur* only comes into play when common experience or the evidence in the case indicates that the happening of the injury itself may be considered as evidence that reasonable care had not been used; this will not be the case where the complication is a recognised, even if rare, risk inherent in the operation.[360]

(ii) Standard of Proof

6.107   The standard of proof in cases of medical negligence is the same as for any other case of negligence, namely 'on the balance of probabilities', but in practice the cogency of the evidence that the courts require in order to satisfy the test can vary with the issues at stake.[361] It has been suggested that cases of professional negligence create particular problems, and this may result in what is effectively a higher standard of proof than for 'ordinary' cases of negligence.[362] This is particularly

---

[357] *O'Malley-Williams v Board of Governors of the National Hospital for Nervous Diseases* (1975) 1 BMJ 635; *Guertin v Kester* (1981) 20 CCLT 225; *Considine v Camp Hill Hospital* (1982) 133 DLR (3d) 11 (Nova Scotia SC); *Videto v Kennedy* (1980) 107 DLR (3d) 612, 618; rev'd on other grounds (1981) 125 DLR (3d) 127.

[358] *Holmes v Board of Hospital Trustees of the City of London* (1977) 81 DLR (3d) 67 (Ont HC).

[359] (1978) 85 DLR (3d) 566, 574 (Ont HC).

[360] *Fish v Kapur* [1948] 2 All ER 176, dentist broke the claimant's jaw during an extraction; cf *Lock v Scantlebury*, The Times, 25 July 1963; *Fletcher v Bench* (1973) 4 BMJ 17 (CA); *Keuper v McMullin* (1987) 30 DLR (4th) 408, part of a dental drill was left embedded in the jaw; *Considine v Camp Hill Hospital* (1982) 133 DLR (3d) 11 (Nova Scotia SC), claimant became incontinent following a prostate operation; *Girard v Royal Columbian Hospital* (1976) 66 DLR (3d) 676, 691 (BCSC), patient suffered permanent partial paralysis of the legs following anaesthesia; *Kapur v Marshall* (1978) 85 DLR (3d) 566 (Ont HC), patient died from haemorrhage during the course of spinal disc surgery when the surgeon pierced an artery with a surgical instrument; *Rocha v Harris* (1987) 36 DLR 410 (BCCA), paralysis occurred following a cervical laminectomy; *Ferguson v Hamilton Civic Hospitals* (1983) 144 DLR (3d) 214 paralysis occurred following arteriography; *Whitehouse v Jordan* [1980] 1 All ER 650, 658, 661; *Goguen v Crowe* (1987) 40 CCLT 212 (Nova Scotia SC), a baby suffered cerebral palsy following a forceps delivery; *Grey v Webster* (1984) 14 DLR (4th) 706, sterilisation operation failed to render the claimant sterile; *Hobson v Munkley* (1976) 74 DLR (3d) 408 patient's ureter damaged in the course of a tubal ligation operation.

[361] See Pattenden (1988) 7 CJQ 220. It is more difficult, for example, to establish that the defendant has behaved fraudulently than to prove that he was negligent: *Hornal v Neuberger Products Ltd* [1957] 1 QB 247.

[362] In *Dwyer v Roderick* (1983) 127 SJ 806 May LJ said that it was: 'to shut one's eyes to the obvious if one denies that the burden of achieving something more than that mere balance of probabilities is greater when one is investigating the complicated and sophisticated actions of a qualified and experienced lawyer, doctor, accountant, builder or motor engineer than when one is enquiring into the momentary inattention of the driver of a motor car in a simple running-down action.'

true of the medical profession.[363] This may reflect the concern that has been expressed about the effect that findings of negligence can have on the reputation of individual doctors, and the more general consequences of medical malpractice litigation for the practice of medicine. Thus, in *Hucks v Cole* Lord Denning commented that:

> A charge of negligence against a medical man, a solicitor or any other professional man, stands on a very different footing from a charge of negligence against a motorist or employer. The reason is because the consequences for the professional man are far more grave. A finding of negligence affects his standing and reputation. It impairs the confidence which his clients have in him. The burden of proof is correspondingly greater. The principle applies that: 'In proportion as the charge is grave, so ought the proof to be clear': see *Hornal v Neuberger Products Ltd* [1957] 1 QB 247 . . . A doctor is not to be held negligent simply because something goes wrong. . . . He is not liable for mischance, or misadventure. Nor is he liable for an error of judgment . . . He is only liable if he falls below the standard of a reasonably competent practitioner in his field—so much so that his conduct may fairly be held to be—I will not say deserving of censure, but, at any rate, inexcusable.[364]

More rarely, perhaps, the courts also recognise that doctors are only human, and that even a conclusion that a defendant doctor has made a negligent mistake is not to be taken as a statement that the doctor is incompetent to practise medicine. This approach makes it easier for the court to make a finding of negligence without undermining the doctor's professional reputation.[365]

---

[363] *Jackson & Powell on Professional Negligence* (5th edn, 2002), para 12.086. See also Robertson (1981) 44 MLR 457, 459 commenting on the 'strong pro-defendant policy' evident in many medical negligence cases; Giesen (1993) 1 Med Law Int 3, 5. Lord Woolf has suggested that the courts' excessive deference to the medical profession is in the process of changing: (2001) 9 Med L Rev 1.

[364] (1968), [1993] 4 Med LR 393, 396. See also the comments of Lord Denning in *Roe v Minister of Health* [1954] 2 QB 66, 86–87; *Hatcher v Black*, The Times, 2 July 1954; *Whitehouse v Jordan* [1980] 1 All ER 650, 658; *Hyde v Tameside AHA* (1981) reported at (1986) 2 PN 26. Similarly, in *Whitehouse v Jordan* [1980] 1 All ER 650, 659 Lawton LJ commented that: 'The more serious the allegation the higher the degree of probability that is required. In my opinion allegations of negligence against medical practitioners should be considered as serious.'

[365] In *Whitehouse v Jordan* [1980] 1 All ER 650, 666 Donaldson LJ pointed out that very few professionals can claim never to have been negligent, and that often the only difference between those who are sued and their colleagues is that the error happens to have caused harm to the claimant; see also *Clark v MacLennan* [1983] 1 All ER 416, 433; *Thake v Maurice* [1984] 2 All ER 513, 523.

7

CAUSATION AND DEFENCES

A. Causation

1. Introduction

It is trite law that merely to show that a defendant was in breach of a duty owed to **7.01**
the claimant and that the claimant suffered damage does not suffice to ground an
action in negligence. The defendant's breach must have caused the claimant's
damage and, additionally, the damage must be such that the law regards it proper
to hold the defendant responsible for it. These two requirements jointly constitute causation and are often separately referred to as (i) *cause in fact* and (ii) *cause
in law* and *remoteness*.

The concern here is whether there are considerations specific to medical law **7.02**
which call for a treatment of causation beyond that which can be found in standard works on the law of torts.[1] The answer is that there are.[2] While the principles

---

[1] See Fleming, J, *The Law of Torts* (10th edn, ed P Cane, 2002); Grubb, A (ed), *The Law of Torts*
(Butterworths, 2002), ch 14 and, particularly on clinical negligence, Jones, M, *Medical Negligence*

footnote 2 on p. 444

of causation may ordinarily be relatively straightforward, it is fair to say that causation in the context of medical law is fraught with difficulty.[3] This is due both to the complexity of the factual circumstances themselves and to the (perhaps unnecessarily) complex nature of the law, when the principles come to be applied to the facts. As for the former, the complicated and, to some extent, indeterminate nature of medical science means that the causal nexus between X and Y, while suspected, may be hard to demonstrate. Indeed, it could be said that the more medicine is portrayed as a scientific endeavour, rather than as an art or a combination of both art and science, the more difficult it becomes on occasion to demonstrate to the satisfaction of the law a causative link between breach and damage.[4] As for the latter, the law becomes ever more complex as it seeks to serve the twin aims of justice: fairness to the patient and to the doctor.[5] As Leggatt LJ put it in *Tahir v Haringey HA*,[6] 'when a doctor has been at fault no court wishes to send his patient away empty handed'. This, of course, is the crux. A breach of duty is proved, or even admitted, and yet the doctor or hospital is found not liable and the patient recovers nothing. The patient is left bemused. But, equally, if whatever happened to the patient was not the result of the doctor's conduct, it is hard to see why the doctor should be held liable. Only a system which compensated damaged patients on the basis of need rather than proof of someone else's misconduct could square this particular circle.

2. Factual Causation

(i) The Burden of Proof

7.03 In any examination of causation, the first question to ask is who bears the burden of proving the causative link between breach of duty and damage. The answer is unequivocally that in this, as in all other aspects of civil litigation, it is the claimant who must prove causation and it must be established on a balance of probabilities.[7] There was a brief period of time in which it was thought that, in certain particular circumstances, medical law provided an exception to this principle by

---

3rd edn (Sweet & Maxwell, 2003), ch 5. See also, Goldberg, R, *Causation and Risk in the Law of Torts* (Hart Publishing, 1999).

   [2] For a noteworthy discussion of causation in the medical context see, *Chappel v Hart* (1998) 27 ALJR 1344 (HC Aus), especially the judgment of Kirby J.

   [3] It was Lord Bridge in *Hotson v East Berkshire AHA* [1987] 2 All ER 909 who remarked: 'In some cases, perhaps particularly medical negligence cases, causation may be so shrouded in mystery that the courts can only measure statistical chances.'

   [4] See, eg, *Loveday v Renton* [1990] 1 Med LR 117 (whooping cough vaccine) and *Kay v Ayrshire and Arran Health Board* [1987] 2 All ER 417.

   [5] See, eg, *Fairchild v Glenhaven Funeral Services Ltd* [2002] 3 All ER 305 (seeking to strike a balance between fairness to the claimant and defendant in an industrial context).

   [6] [1998] Lloyd's Rep Med 104 at 111. For a Commentary, see (1996) 4 Med L Rev 92 (A Grubb).

   [7] *Pickford v Imperial Chemical Industries plc* [1998] 1 WLR 1189 (HL).

reversing the burden and placing it on the defendant. As will be discussed more fully below, it was Lord Wilberforce's speech in *McGhee v National Coal Board*[8] that gave rise to this strain of reasoning. The claimant had established a breach of duty, the failure to provide showers so as to be able to wash off the brick dust which pervaded the work-place. The presence of the dust in the work-place was not itself a breach of duty. The result was that the brick dust continued to adhere to his skin while he cycled home. He contracted dermatitis. What he could not definitively demonstrate was that the extra time spent cycling home was causative of his dermatitis. Lord Wilberforce's speech was taken to mean that, in such a case, the burden of proof shifted to the defendant to show that his breach of duty did not cause the dermatitis. Certainly Peter Pain J in *Clark v McLennan*[9] interpreted the speech in this way. In *Wilsher v Essex AHA*,[10] however, the House of Lords categorically reasserted that the burden of proof always remains with the claimant. *McGhee* was distinguished on its facts and Lord Wilberforce's speech was relegated by Lord Bridge to the status of a dissent. That marked the end of that brief period of heresy.

Of course, what *McGhee* and *Wilsher* drew attention to was the well-recognised **7.04** fact of litigation in medical law, that proof of causation is often an extremely difficult hurdle for the claimant. The law appears to contemplate some kind of linear connection between X and Y, whereas in reality what is involved in medicine is often a series of interdependent and interacting events from which it is at best difficult to pluck one (the defendant's breach) and point to it as 'the cause'. The claimant's increased ill health may, for example, be as much the consequence of the natural progression of the disease as the defendant's breach. The defendant's breach may be only one of several independent or interacting causal agents, as was the case in *Wilsher*.[11] Or further, the state of medical science may be such that experts may properly disagree as to the exact aetiology of the claimant's condition, as in *Loveday v Renton*.[12] Obvious examples of this in common knowledge are the effects of passive smoking or radiation.

(ii) The 'But For' Test

The standard approach to causation in the law of torts is represented by the 'but **7.05** for' test: that the damage suffered by the claimant would not have been suffered

---

[8] [1973] 1 WLR 1. Discussed in Weinrib, E, 'A Step Forward in Factual Causation' (1975) 38 MLR 518.

[9] [1983] 1 All ER 416.

[10] [1986] 3 All ER 801.

[11] The House of Lords found that there were at least five possible causes of the retrolental fibroplasia suffered by the claimant.

[12] [1990] 1 Med LR 117, where the issue at stake was the relationship (if any) between the pertussis vaccine and brain damage. See also *Kay v Ayrshire and Arran Health Board* [1987] 2 All ER 417.

but for the defendant's breach of duty. The assumption of the law is that it is possible to show (and, therefore, that the law should demand demonstration) that X would not have happened but for Y. The corollary is that if this cannot be demonstrated, causation is not proved and the defendant, regardless of any breach of duty, is not liable. While represented as a principle concerned with fact, it is, of course, self-evident that what is involved is a matter of policy. A limit is placed on the potential liability of the defendant by demanding that a particular form of nexus be shown. And, as has been said, there are numerous circumstances, particularly in medical law, when this policy defeats the claim of the claimant. The clearest example is when the defendant's breach may have been part of the background leading to the claimant's injury. If the defendant can show that the injury would have occurred in any event, regardless of any breach of duty, then the claimant's action will fail. *Barnett v Kensington and Chelsea HMC*[13] was just such a case. The claimant attended an A & E department of a hospital complaining of feeling ill and vomiting after drinking some tea. On the advice of a doctor, a nurse told the claimant to go home and call his own doctor. The claimant was actually suffering from arsenic poisoning and some hours later died. Had the hospital's breach of duty caused the claimant's death? The court found that the claimant would have died in any event, regardless of the defendant doctor's failure to provide proper medical care, because, by the time arsenic poisoning would have been diagnosed, it would have been too late to take any action to save him.

7.06   The difficulties associated with the 'but for' test in medical law are at their starkest when there are several concurrent or successive causal factors contributing to the claimant's injury and/or the real cause of the injury is indeterminate. The intrinsic complexity of medical evidence means, therefore, that if the law fails to mitigate the strict application of the 'but for' test, injustice may be done.[14] One obvious mitigating device would be to *reverse the burden of proof,* providing certain conditions were met. As has been seen, tentative steps in this direction were firmly retraced by the House of Lords in *Wilsher.*[15] By contrast, a second mitigating device is an established part of the ordinary tort rules on causation. It may be relevant in medical law. It consists in the claimant being able to succeed if it can be shown that the defendant's breach was a *material* and not *de minimis* contribution to the damage suffered, and, thus *a,* if not the only, cause of the damage.[16]

---

[13] [1968] 1 All ER 1068.

[14] This may be true elsewhere also and has led the House of Lords to depart from the 'but for' test in the industrial injury context when the cause of the claimant's injuries was indeterminate but was certainly caused by one or more successive employers who were each at fault: *Fairchild v Glenhaven Funeral Services Ltd* [2002] UKHL 22; [2002] 3 All ER 305. Discussed, in Stapleton, J, 'Lords A'Leaping Evidentiary Gaps' (2003) 10 Tort LJ 276. For a possible third judicial development see also paras 7.21 *et seq* below.

[15] N 10 above.

[16] *Bonnington Castings v Wardlaw* [1956] AC 613.

(a) Material Contribution to the Injury

The House of Lords' decision in *Bonnington Castings v Warlow*[17] makes it clear **7.07** that a defendant could be liable if the breach of duty, while not the sole or even a substantial cause, contributed in a material way to the damage suffered by the claimant. This is of some significance to the mitigation of the 'but for' test in medical law. In that case, there were two sources of the silica dust which the claimant inhaled, and because of which he contracted pneumoconiosis. The claimant could not point to the source of dust which was dubbed 'guilty', that is, arising from a breach of duty, as being the sole or even the more important source. But the claimant was allowed to succeed in his action by persuading the court to make an inference from the facts that the 'guilty' dust had made a material contribution to his illness.[18]

The key factor was the court's preparedness, in the absence of any way of know- **7.08** ing, with any degree of certainty, what actually caused the claimant's illness, to draw an inference of fact favourable to the claimant from all the available evidence. This is clearly, at bottom, a nice issue of judgment for any court. On one level, it can be represented as a matter of extremely technical legal analysis in which certain complex verbal formulae must be applied to the facts and, once applied, the solution to causation will emerge. More realistically, the court is ultimately in the business of seeking to honour what have been suggested as the two conflicting policy objectives, namely controlling liability while being fair to claimants. Such a view—whether more realistic or cynical—would suggest that the verbal formulae are precisely that and little else. What the claimant and defendant must do is pile up as many factual arguments as they can muster in favour of their view of the case. The more facts, the more a court can find something to infer, or to deny that any inference can be drawn. Of course, once the decision is made, it will be expressed in the appropriate formulaic manner. But, while participating in this process, the parties to the litigation would be unwise to be so mesmerised by the complex taxonomy of causation that they overlook what is really going on.

(b) Material Increasing the Risk of Injury

So far, what we have seen is where the material contribution made by the defend- **7.09** ant's breach is to the *damage itself* suffered by the claimant. What if the claimant can establish that the defendant's negligence contributed to the *risk of damage*? In *McGhee*, the House of Lords was prepared to infer that the failure to provide

---

[17] ibid.
[18] The result would be different where the injury is divisible and the defendant's negligence can be shown to have caused or contributed to a part only of that injury: *Holtby v Brigham & Cowan (Hill) Ltd* [2000] 3 All ER 421 (CA). Discussed in Gullifer, L (2001) 117 LQR 403.

showers *materially increased the risk* of contracting dermatitis from the brick dust and that *in itself* established a causal link with the defendant's fault. The reason for doing so was the lack of available evidence, such that the claimant could not meet the 'but for' test and establish that the breach had caused or made a material contribution to the injury.

7.10 In their subsequent 'interpretation' of *McGhee* in *Wilsher*, the House of Lords was anxious, as we saw, to reassert the basic principle that the claimant must show either that the damage would not have occurred 'but for' the defendant's breach, or that the breach made a material contribution to it. For Lord Bridge in *Wilsher*, *McGhee* was merely a 'robust and pragmatic approach' to the undisputed primary facts. Thus, all that the court had done in *McGhee* was to make a common sense inference of fact that increased exposure to the dust must have materially contributed to the claimant's dermatitis itself.

7.11 Of course, it is all very well to describe *McGhee* as common sense but it places the defendant in a well-nigh impossible situation. If the court is moved to draw an inference of fact because of the inherent uncertainty of the facts, the defendant cannot, *ex hypothesi*, disprove the inference (given the uncertainty!). Furthermore, to claim that a material increase in the risk constitutes a material contribution to the damage is not only to make one step in the dark, but two. This is because it must also be assumed that the risk which was increased in fact materialised, since merely to increase a risk is not logically to cause anything. The underlying triumph of policy over logic is again laid bare.

7.12 The difficult question for the medical lawyer, however, is when will a court draw an inference of fact based on pragmatism or common sense? Unfortunately, there are few pointers in the cases which can serve as reliable guides in the uncertain world which is the reality of medical science. One plausible guide is the distinction which may be drawn between uncertainty created by the existence of a range of contributing factors, any or all of which may be judged cumulatively to have made a material contribution, and uncertainty created by the existence of a number of possible contributing factors each of which is separate and distinct.

7.13 Where the factors are cumulative, the court, following *Bonnington Castings*, has the option to find the defendant liable. If the factors taken together led to the claimant's injury, then the defendant's breach, as a contributing factor, may be held to have made a contribution which can be described as material, if it is not de minimis. By contrast, where the injury could have been caused by any one of a number of distinct factors, the material contribution principle will not work in the claimant's favour. This is illustrated by the House of Lords' decision in *Wilsher v Essex AHA*.[19]

---

[19] N 10 above. Discussed in Grubb [1988] CLJ 350 and Boon (1988) 51 MLR 508.

In *Wilsher*, the baby's RLF (retrolental fibroplasia) could have arisen from any of   **7.14**
at least five separate and distinct factors. The defendant's breach was responsible
for only one of these. It was impossible to assert that the breach was the sole cause
of the RLF. It was equally untenable to argue that the breach materially contributed to it. It may have had no effect whatsoever. The House of Lords held that
to show that the defendant's negligence materially increased the risk of the
claimant's injury did nothing to exclude the other causes; therefore, it was impossible for the court to infer that the defendant was the cause of the injuries.

It may be that the reasoning in *McGhee*—moving from increased risk of injury   **7.15**
to material contribution to the injury—is more likely to work where the risks are
cumulative and interact, rather than when they are discrete and separate—
McGhee versus *Wilsher*. However, *McGhee* itself was a case where it could have
been that either/or both causes of the risk actually caused (or contributed to) the
dermatitis.

Where there is a breach of duty, and uncertainty as to what may have led to what,   **7.16**
the court has the choice of favouring the claimant or the defendant. If the court
chooses the latter, it can merely decide that the 'but for' test is not satisfied and the
case is over. If, on the other hand, it is thought proper to assist the claimant in pursuit of a remedy, once a defendant is judged to have breached his duty, the court
in effect has two principal policy options. The most effective option, of course, is
to reverse the burden of proof. But this has been rejected. The alternative is for the
court to use the principle of material contribution, particularly in its *McGhee*
manifestation, to draw appropriate inferences of fact.[20] The drawback for both
parties is the lack of certainty such an obviously policy-led approach represents.[21]
These difficulties were rehearsed in the judgment of the Canadian Supreme Court
in *Snell v Farrell*.[22] In *Snell*, Sopinka J revisited *McGhee* in the light of the House
of Lords' decision in *Wilsher*. Beginning from the point that 'proof of causation in
medical malpractice cases is often difficult for the patient', Sopinka J took the
view that Lord Bridge's endorsement of a 'robust and pragmatic approach to the
. . . facts' was a reminder to the courts not to adopt what he described as a 'too rigid
application' of the traditional approach to causation. He cited with approval Lord

---

[20] It was Nourse LJ in *Fitzgerald v Lane* [1987] QB 781 who described *Wilsher's* robust and pragmatic approach as the 'benevolent principle [which] smiles on . . . factual uncertainties and melts
them all away'. See further *Lybert v Warrington* [1996] 7 Med LR 71 (CA).

[21] For a summary of propositions relating to causation, see Commentary on *Tahir v Haringey HA*
(1996) 4 Med L Rev 92 (A Grubb) where it is suggested that in cases of medical negligence, where
'causation is often difficult to establish', 'the plaintiff must establish one of the following: 1. that "but
for" the negligence he would not have suffered *any* injury (plaintiff recovers for all his injuries); or 2.
that "but for" the negligence he would not have suffered *an identifiable part* (X) or *particular
aggravation* (Y) of the injuries (plaintiff recovers for X and Y respectively); or 3. that the negligence
materially contributed to the whole injury (Z) or an identifiable part (X) or particular aggravation (Y)
of the injuries (plaintiff recovers for Z, X and Y respectively)' (emphasis in original).

[22] (1990) 72 DLR (4th) 289.

Salmon's view in *Alpha-cell Ltd v Woodward*[23] that causation is 'essentially a practical question of fact which can best be answered by ordinary common sense rather than abstract metaphysical theory'. Relying on the crucial notion of drawing inferences, Sopinka J went on to state that:

> [i]n many medical malpractice cases, the facts lie particularly within the knowledge of the defendant. In these circumstances, very little affirmative evidence on the part of the plaintiff will justify the drawing of an inference of causation in the absence of evidence to the contrary.

7.17 This was not, he emphasised, a matter of shifting the burden of proof or even the burden of adducing evidence:

> The legal or ultimate burden remains with the plaintiff, but in the absence of evidence to the contrary adduced by the defendant, an inference of causation may be drawn, although positive or scientific proof of causation has not been adduced. If some evidence to the contrary is adduced by the defendant, the trial judge is entitled to take account of Lord Mansfield's famous precept [referred to earlier, that] '[i]t is certainly a maxim that all evidence is to be weighed according to the proof which it was in the power of one side to have produced, and in the power of the other to have contradicted it'.[24]

7.18 It could be said that English law could greatly benefit if the courts were more ready to adopt Sopinka J's approach to causation in this most troubling area of litigation.

(c) Reinstating McGhee

7.19 In *Fairchild v Glenhaven Funeral Services Ltd*[25] the judges refuted the narrow construction of *McGhee* which had been placed upon it by the House of Lords in *Wilsher*.[26] It was, therefore, not to be seen as an application of the traditional 'but for' test, rather as a departure from it in exceptional (and specific) circumstances. The claimants were exposed to asbestos dust over a long period of time whilst working for successive employers. They developed mesothelioma, a cancer of the lung. Claims were brought against some—but not all—of the employers. The evidence was that mesothelioma was caused by exposure to asbestos dust but it was not known whether it was caused by a single fibre or whether multiple fibres were necessary or made development of the cancer more likely. On the evidence, it could not be said which employer's breach of duty in exposing the claimants to asbestos dust had caused, or materially contributed to, their injuries. There was a 'scientific deficit' in the evidence. The House of Lords unanimously held that each

---

[23] [1972] 2 All ER 475.

[24] *Blatch v Archer* (1774) 1 Cowp 63.

[25] [2002] UKHL 22; [2002] 3 All ER 305. Discussed in Morgan, J, (2003) 66 MLR 277; Weir, T [2002] CLJ 519.

[26] With the exception of Lord Hutton who preferred to see *McGhee* as a case where it was proper to make a factual inference of causation: ibid at [108] and [109].

of the employers was liable to the claimant for their injuries.[27] The Law Lords held, on policy grounds, that the *McGhee* test of 'material increase in risk' applied to fix each employer with responsibility for the claimants' injuries. It was just to depart from the 'but for' test of causation where, as in this case, the injustice of holding an employer responsible for injury that he may not have caused (or contributed to) was outweighed by the injustice of leaving the employees without compensation.

The narrowness of the exception carved out by the judges to the traditional test was emphasised by the Law Lords. Whilst not incapable of further extension, the circumstances were exceptional (if not uncommon) and the judges advised caution in extending the application of the *McGhee* test. Certainly, the context of employment was important and it was arguably crucial such that the court will not see the merits of extension beyond it.[28] The likelihood is, however, that the *McGhee* test will have little impact in medical negligence cases for two principal reasons. First, in cases where there is a 'scientific deficit' in the evidence, it is unlikely that the factual context will work in a claimant's favour. Usually, the claimant will be unable to show that the injury suffered was precisely that which flowed from the doctor (or other's) breach of duty but rather that it was the result of one of a number of possible causative events each (or some) of which lacks the same essential characteristics of the risk created by the doctor as in *Wilsher* itself and the Law Lords cast no doubt on the actual outcome in *Wilsher*.[29] Second, and perhaps more significantly, attempting to apply *McGhee* in the medical context may not invoke the same policy response from the judges because of the impact that extending liability would have on the NHS and its budget.[30] The remarks of Lord Hoffman in *Fairchild* suggest that the *McGhee* approach is unlikely to be imported:[31]

7.20

> It is true that actions for clinical negligence notoriously give rise to difficult questions of causation. But it cannot possibly be that the duty to take care in treating patients would be virtually drained of content unless the creation of a material risk of injury were accepted as sufficient to satisfy the causal requirements of liability. And the political and economic arguments involved in the massive increase in liability of the National Health Service which would have been a consequence of the broad rule favoured by the Court of Appeal in Wilsher's case are far more complicated than the reasons given [in McGhee] for imposing liability upon an employer who has failed to take simple precautions.

---

[27] Subject to the issue of contribution proceedings between the defendants inter se, which was not before the House.

[28] See especially *per* Lord Bingham at [2] and *per* Lord Hoffman at [61]. For a suggestion of an even more limited application of the test see Stapleton, J, 'Cause-in-Fact and the Scope of Liability for Consequences' (2003) 119 LQR 388 at 398. But it is not clear that these limitations would have been accepted by the judges, see especially *per* Lord Hoffman at [72] and *per* Lord Rodger at [170].

[29] *Wilsher* was approved *per* Lord Bingham at [22]; *per* Lord Hoffman at [70]; *per* Lord Hutton at [118]; *per* Lord Rodger at [149] and [170].

[30] But quaere if the claimant was treated in a private hospital or clinic?

[31] ibid, at [69]. But contrast *Snell v Farrell* (1990) 72 DLR (4th) 289 (Can Sup Ct).

(iii) Recovering Damages for Loss of Chance

7.21 We have already seen a number of attempts—some successful, some not—by the judges to mitigate the rigours of the 'but for' test when the justice of the case demands it. A third would be the issue of whether damages may be recovered for 'loss of a chance'. The argument here is that as a consequence of the defendant's breach of duty, the claimant did not receive any, or any proper, treatment and thereby suffered damage. In ordinary circumstances, there is no reason why the claimant should not be compensated for any such damage, even if it takes the form of not having his condition improved or having it become worse, rather than some discrete, identifiable additional damage. If the claimant can show that this change for the worse in his condition was, on the balance of probabilities, the consequence of the defendant's breach, the 'but for' rule will apply and recovery will follow.

7.22 The problems arise when the evidence demonstrates that, even if the defendant had complied with his duty of care, it was more likely than not that the claimant's condition would *not* have improved. The claimant's alleged damage, then, is the loss of a *chance* of improvement, but a chance which was less than a 50 per cent chance. Clearly the 'but for' test cannot be satisfied in that the claimant cannot show that, on the balance of probabilities, but for the defendant's breach he would have recovered or his condition would have improved.

(a) Hotson v East Berkshire AHA

7.23 The question of whether damages could be recovered for 'loss of a chance' of improvement in a patient's health first arose in England in the case of *Hotson v East Berkshire AHA*.[32] It was alleged by the claimant that the delay of five days in diagnosing the fracture of his left femoral epiphysis when he fell from a tree caused him to lose a chance of complete recovery. The chance was put at 25 per cent. The claimant argued that although there was always a 75 per cent chance of permanent injury, the defendant's breach made that a 100 per cent certainty. The defendant's response was straightforward. The claimant's case must be established on a balance of probabilities, that is, that it was at least 51 per cent likely that the defendant's breach caused the damage. The evidence, the defendant argued, failed to meet that criterion. It was the fall from the tree that must have been more likely than not the cause of the claimant's damage. The law treats past facts, established on a balance of probabilities, as certain.[33] Hence, it was certain that the cause of the claimant's damage was not the delay in treatment. Simon Brown J, at first instance, preferred the claimant's argument.[34] He held that the issue before him was

---

[32] [1987] AC 750.
[33] See *Judge v Huntingdon HA* [1995] 6 Med LR 223, citing Lord Diplock in *Mallett v McMonagle* [1970] AC 166; 'Anything that is more probable than not is certain.'
[34] [1985] 3 All ER 167.

not one of causation but of quantification; the proper quantum of damages, given the defendant's breach of duty. Assessing the damages arising from the avascular necrosis caused by the fracture at £46,000, he then awarded the claimant 25 per cent of this amount (£11,500) to compensate for the 25 per cent chance of avoiding permanent injury which had been lost.

On appeal, the Court of Appeal affirmed the High Court's decision.[35] In the House of Lords, however, their Lordships saw the facts as raising an issue of causation relating to the claimant's *injury*. As Lord Bridge put it, 'on a balance of probabilities the injury caused by the claimant's fall left insufficient blood vessels intact to keep the epiphysis alive. This amounts to a finding of fact that the fall was the sole cause of the vascular necrosis.'[36] Thus, the House of Lords held that the appeal must be allowed 'on the narrow ground that the claimant had failed to establish a cause of action'.[37]   **7.24**

As a consequence of their view of the evidence, the judges did not take the opportunity to develop the law in a radical way and recognise 'loss of a chance' as being a head of damage recoverable in its own right. It can be argued that, while the claimant is entitled to more than a fair share of sympathy, his position is no different from lots of other situations in which the defendant's breach is egregious but the claimant cannot establish causation and, therefore, loses. *Barnett*[38] is one such well-known example. The answer may be, of course, that the fact that the claimant cannot establish causation is what is under discussion. And, given the policy 'tweaks' which the courts in *Bonnington Castings* and *McGhee* and *Fairchild* were prepared to contemplate, why should they not go a 'tweak' further? The premise again, it will be recalled, is that justice requires that a way be found to compensate a claimant when the defendant is in breach of duty and the claimant has suffered damage, in this case, through the loss of a chance of treatment which could, perhaps, have been beneficial.   **7.25**

(b) Developing the Law

The judges in *Hotson*, and particularly Lord Mackay, did not rule out the possibility of recovery by the claimant. It remained, therefore, following *Hotson* a matter for further argument whether a claimant may bring an action based clearly and unequivocally on a claim that a chance of recovery or improvement was lost through the defendant's breach of duty. The claimant would be able to point to the evidence of the lost chance, and to quantify it. The court would be able to respond to this factual evidence and indeed encourage it, rather than see the law   **7.26**

---

[35] [1987] 1 All ER 210.
[36] N 32 above at 782.
[37] ibid, 782.
[38] N 9 above.

continue to favour doubt over some sort of certainty. The damages to be awarded to the claimant would not be the 100 per cent recovery of all that flowed from the damage suffered, but merely 100 per cent of the lost chance, that is the proportion of the total damage attributable to the lost chance.

7.27   The first argument in favour of allowing the claimant to recover is based on analogous cases from the law of contract. The most obvious case is *Kitchen v Royal Air Force Association*[39] in which the loss of a chance was clearly held to be recoverable. The solicitor's breach of duty in *Kitchen* had prevented the claimant from pursuing a civil action. The claimant recovered damages based on an estimation of his likely chance of success. Lord Bridge in *Hotson* dismissed the analogy somewhat airily, referring to (without specifying) 'formidable difficulties in the way of accepting the analogy'.[40] It would be odd law, however, if a patient treated privately could maintain an action in contract against his doctor and recover damages for the loss of a chance of recovery or improvement, while a patient treated in the public sector and, therefore, restricted to an action in tort could not.

7.28   A second argument might be that to contribute materially to the claimant's prospects of permanent injury, denying him the chance of treatment, is just another way of materially increasing the risk of damage. Post *McGhee* and *Fairchild*, the latter can be the basis for a successful damages claim. The problem is, however, that in those cases the court infers as a matter of law a causal connection between the breach of duty and the claimant's *injury*. Here, the claimant is arguing that there is a causal connection between the breach and the loss of a chance of recovery or improvement. It is as if in those cases the claimant was seeking to recover for *the risk of injury itself*. Perhaps, as a consequence, the analogy breaks down somewhat. What may not be lost, however, is the justice of the claimant's case. In *Hotson*, the claimant had sought to put some estimate on the risk and thereby lost the case by pre-empting the court's ability to draw any factual inference that his injuries had been caused by the defendant's negligence. It could be said that the only difference between *McGhee* and *Hotson* is that in *McGhee* it was impossible to estimate the extent of the increased risk, thereby allowing the court a free hand to draw inferences. But it would be a strange policy if the law preferred the unknown risk (*McGhee*) to the quantifiable (*Hotson*), in circumstances where nothing can be known for sure.

7.29   There are two matters which may tell against the recognition of 'loss of a chance' claims—one of policy and one of identification. First, Lord Hoffman's strictures against the expansion of liability in the NHS context by utilising the *McGhee* test will be recalled. They are no less significant here. Indeed, subject to the matter of

---

[39] [1958] 1 WLR 563.
[40] N 32 above at 782.

identification, the threat to NHS budgets is probably greater. This may prove an insuperable policy objection. Second, there is the issue of quantification. In the usual clinical negligence case, the risk will have eventuated and the claimant will have suffered an injury. The factual focus will almost inevitably be upon who, or what, caused that injury. That is the commonsense and sensible approach to evaluating the facts and the law may not be able to re-focus elsewhere.[41] To require the claimant to prove this causal connection would not, to borrow Lord Hoffman's words in *Fairchild*, 'empty [the doctor's] duty of content'.[42] There are many other ways in which the doctor may be held accountable. More importantly, to hold otherwise would erroneously suggest that the doctor's legal duty is to exercise reasonable care and skill so as to increase *the chance* of improvement or benefit to the patient's health.

There are, arguably, some situations when these arguments may break down or fall away. For example, the patient's situation may be such that all the doctor is expected to do is to act reasonably in order to improve the patient's chance of survival or deteriorating health. The most obvious is the diagnosis and treatment of cancer. Here, very often, the doctor is at best diagnosing and treating an incurable condition but which, with treatment, may improve the patient's chances of survival. It is no coincidence that it is in these cases that, by and large, US courts have developed recovery for 'loss of a chance'.[43] These were essentially the facts of the recent English case of *Gregg v Scott*[44] which will be discussed shortly. **7.30**

(c) Post-Hotson *Jurisprudence*

Subsequently, however, the courts have not interpreted *Hotson* in a benevolent way, preferring instead to see the judges as having excluded the possibility of recovery for loss of a chance.[45] Likewise, the Supreme Court of Canada[46] rejected recovery. However, elsewhere in the world the judges are divided. An increasing number of US jurisdictions allow recovery[47] but the Australian High Court judges are hopelessly split.[48] **7.31**

---

[41] See *Lawson v Laferriere* (1991) 78 DLR (4th) 609 (Can Sup Ct) especially *per* Gonthier J. See also *Naxakis v Western General Hospital* (1999) 197 CLR 269 *per* Gaudron J at para [36].

[42] N 25 above at [62].

[43] See, eg, *Herskovits v Group Health Cooperative* (1983) 664 P 2d 474 (Wash Sup Ct).

[44] [2002] EWCA Civ 1471; [2003] Lloyd's Rep Med 105.

[45] See *Tahir v Haringey HA* [1998] Lloyd's Rep Med 104 (CA) *per* Otton LJ at 108. See also *Pearman v North Essex HA* [2000] Lloyd's Rep Med 174. Contrast *Smith v NHS Litigation Authority* [2001] Lloyd's Rep Med 90.

[46] *Lawson v Laferriere* (1991) 78 DLR (4th) 609.

[47] eg, see *Perez v Las Vegas Medical Center* (1991) 805 P2d 589 (Nev Sup Ct) (where there was a dissent) and *Wollen v DePaul Health Center* (1992) 828 SW 2d 681 (Missouri Sup Ct) and cases cited at 683–684.

[48] *Naxakis v Western General Hospital* (1999) 197 CLR 269: Gaudron J (not recoverable), Callinan and McHugh JJ (recoverable), (Glesson and Kirby J (expressing no opinion).

7.32   The issue of recovery for a 'loss of a chance' arose in the recent case of *Gregg v Scott*.[49] The claimant's GP negligently failed to diagnose that he suffered from non-Hodgkin's lymphoma. The cancer was subsequently diagnosed. The expert evidence was that the negligent delay in diagnosing the condition reduced the claimant's chance of survival for a five-year period from 42 per cent to 25 per cent. Could he recover damages in these circumstances? Following *Hotson*, the trial judge held that the claimant had failed to prove that the delay had made any difference to the outcome for him. As a result, he had failed to prove that the negligence caused or materially contributed to any injury.

7.33   The Court of Appeal (by a majority)[50] rejected the claimant's action for the 'lost chance' of recovery from cancer. Simon Brown LJ considered the case to be indistinguishable from *Hotson* and the result the same. In both cases, the physical effects of delay were that each claimant's condition worsened and made the likely outcome (75 to 100 per cent)) certain (*Hotson*) or further reduced (42 to 25 per cent) the claimant's chances of survival for five years (*Gregg*). *Hotson* itself made it difficult to understand how a loss of a chance claim could ever succeed. There was nothing in *Fairchild* which should lead the court to relax the causation rules in clinical negligence claims to allow recovery for the loss of a chance of avoiding physical injury. The emphatic rejection of any development in the law is all the more significant when it is remembered that Simon Brown LJ had been the trial judge in *Hotson* who had first propounded the 'loss of a chance' theory in an English case.

7.34   Nevertheless, two of the judges were prepared to contemplate such a claim in English law.[51] Mance LJ distinguished *Hotson* as a case there was no 'loss of a chance' because the trial judge had found that the claimant's injury was inevitable and had already occurred before the defendant's negligence. He distinguished between cases where the evidence was purely statistical (as in *Gregg*) and where it leads to a finding of fact about the claimant's own injury (*Hotson*).[52] He took the view that *Hotson* left open the possibility of a 'loss of a chance' claim in the former case. Should the law, then, recognise such a claim for a pure statistical outcome? Mance LJ noted that the doctor's duty in a case of this sort was to maximise the chances of survival. That purpose militated in favour of liability when the doctor's negligence decreased the chances of the claimant surviving. However, Mance LJ accepted that policy considerations should lead to its rejection in clinical negligence cases and so ultimately agreed with Simon Brown LJ:[53]

---

[49] [2002] EWCA Civ 1471; [2003] Lloyd's Rep Med 105. An appeal to the House of Lords is pending.

[50] Simon Brown and Mance LJJ; Latham LJ dissenting.

[51] Latham and Mance LJJ (yes), Simon Brown LJ (no).

[52] On which see Hill (1991) 45 MLR 511. This was a distinction drawn by Croom-Johnson LJ in the Court of Appeal in *Hotson* [1987] 1 All ER 210 (CA) at 223.

[53] N 49 above, at [85].

[T]he respondent cannot be equated with an employer who is the actual source of a noxious agent; and I think that to accept the appellant's suggested approach in the present (very common) category of medical negligence cases, involving failure to diagnose, would both open a considerable gate to claims based on percentages, and create a new category of case which would be difficult to distinguish in practice from other common cases of medical negligence. . . . If one looks at the matter as one of policy, I have come to the conclusion that the considerations in favour of an approach based on probabilities outweigh the argument that negligence that may in the future be causative of some injury should in cases like the present generally attract an award of damages according to the risk that such injury may emerge and it may have been caused by the negligence.

Latham LJ, like Mance LJ, did not consider that *Hotson* precluded 'loss of chance' **7.35** claims and was prepared, in principle, to apply that to clinical negligence cases. However, Latham LJ saw the dangers of applying this approach to what he called cases of 'loss of chance simpliciter' where the claimant had been exposed to a risk of injury, for example, asbestos dust, but had not yet suffered any injury. Such claims would be 'speculative' being based solely on the risk of future injury. It was different, however, where the claimant had suffered injury that necessarily in-cluded 'the loss of a chance of some benefit'. That was the present case where the defendant's negligence had allowed the claimant's cancer to spread and, in the process, the claimant's chances of survival had been reduced. The two were 'inex-tricably linked' and the harm suffered by the claimant fell squarely within the duty owed by the doctor to him.

In fact, as Latham LJ rationalises it, the claimant succeeded on conventional **7.36** grounds. He had suffered a physical injury (the enlarged tumour) which conse-quentially reduced the claimant's chance of survival.[54] So rationalised, it is indis-tinguishable in principle from a case of physical injury, say to the head, which creates a future risk of epilepsy. The claimant is entitled to recover for the risk of future injury. Here, the claimant is entitled to recover for the risk that his life will be cut shorter than it otherwise would.[55]

Latham LJ's interpretation of the facts in *Gregg* has, it must be said, much to **7.37** commend it—if, but only if, the chance of survival is a head of damage which can properly be claimed as consequential to the physical injury. There remains, then, the question of a 'pure' loss of a chance. Whether the law should allow recovery for a statistical chance of injury or avoiding injury, as we have seen, involves policy arguments on both sides. Courts throughout the world have tried to grapple with this issue but with no unanimity of approach or outcome. In the end, however, the

---

[54] Mance and Simon Brown LJJ did not accept this analysis of the facts: see especially, *per* Mance LJ at [89].

[55] The assumption is, of course, that 'diminution in life expectancy' is an injury which can be valued and compensated for in a personal injury claim.

volume of judicial and academic words[56] devoted to this issue may be misplaced. In reality, Simon Brown LJ in *Gregg v Scott* is probably right that it is impossible to visualise where a claim could arise. Either, the claimant will suffer injury and be able to establish (or not as the case may be) that the defendant's negligence caused that injury or the 'chance' will be conceptualised as a future risk/benefit which can be linked and grounded in actual physical injury suffered by the claimant.

3. The Place of Bolam [57] in Causation

7.38 *Bolam* has traditionally been seen as the locus classicus of the test for the quantum of care required of a doctor by the law, so as to comply with his duty of care.[58] The question arose in the case of *Bolitho v City and Hackney HA*[59] as to whether *Bolam* also had a role to play in determining issues of causation. In *Bolitho*, the responsible doctor failed to attend a child patient, despite two separate requests from the senior nurse. The child suffered total respiratory collapse and a cardiac arrest and subsequently died. It was accepted during the course of the trial that had the child been intubated, the respiratory failure, had it occurred, would not have led to cardiac arrest, and that such intubation would have had to be carried out before the final catastrophic event. The doctor's failure to attend (either in person or through a deputy) was conceded to be a breach of duty. The question then arose whether this breach caused the child's death.

7.39 It will be noticed that the breach of duty relied on by the claimant was the doctor's failure to attend the child, rather than a failure to intubate. This had significant consequences for the approach to causation adopted by the courts at all levels. The evidence given by the doctor was that, even if she had attended, she would not have intubated the child. Intubation of a 2-year-old child was, she said, a major intervention not free from risks. The symptoms of the child did not warrant it. On a straightforward application of the 'but for' test, the claimant fails at that point, provided, of course, that the defendant's evidence is believed, which it was. There is, however, an obvious reservation to be entered. As a precedent, does not such an approach lend itself to self-serving, ex post facto justification? Is it not particularly undesirable to base causation on this approach, when there may be evidence to suggest that the failure to carry out a procedure (on the basis that the defendant states that he would not have carried it out), itself constitutes a further breach of duty? It appears counter-intuitive to allow a defendant to avoid liability by pleading in aid the fact that he would have compounded the original breach of duty with a further breach.

---

[56] Most formidably in Stapleton, J (1988) 104 LQR 389.
[57] *Bolam v Friern HMC* [1957] 2 All ER 118.
[58] But see *Bolitho v City and Hackney HA* [1997] 4 All ER 771.
[59] ibid.

Faced with this apparent difficulty, both the Court of Appeal (with Simon Brown   **7.40**
LJ dissenting) and the House of Lords (with Lord Browne-Wilkinson speaking
for the House), decided that something had to be done. What they decided to do,
having asked the first question—would the doctor have attended the child?—and
received a negative response, was to ask a second question—*should* the doctor
have intubated the child? If the evidence was that she should have, then, their
Lordships held, causation would be established. As it happens, the evidence was
sufficiently equivocal to absolve the defendant.

Lord Browne-Wilkinson referred with approval to the judgment of Hobhouse LJ   **7.41**
in *Joyce v Merton, Sutton and Wandsworth HA*.[60] In that case, Hobhouse LJ, commenting on the Court of Appeal's judgment in *Bolitho*, said, '[the situation which
arose in *Bolitho*] involves the factual situation that the original fault did not itself
cause the injury but that this was because there would have been some further
fault on the part of the defendants'. The response to this line of reasoning must be,
first, that the 'original fault', if relied upon as the breach of duty on which the
claimant's case is based, is the relevant fault for the law of causation. Secondly, the
'further fault' does not exist save as a hypothesis and is unrelated to the conduct of
the particular defendant. While it is understandable that the Court would not
want to be seen to allow a defendant to 'get away with it', it is at least doubtful
whether the law of causation is the appropriate mechanism to achieve this. What
the doctor *should* have done may be evidence of what the doctor *would* have done,
but it is no more than that. As has been said elsewhere: '[i]t is relevant to know
what *should* have been done in deciding what a particular doctor *would* have done,
but it cannot be conclusive . . . The fact that some doctors would have intubated
the claimant while others would not cannot determine what *this doctor* would
have done.'[61]

The House of Lords' approach, therefore, is at best odd. What the doctor should   **7.42**
or should not have done relates to her duty of care to the patient. It has nothing to
do with establishing a causative link between breach (non-attendance in this particular case) and the child's injury and death. Causation purports to be a matter of
fact, or, in cases of omission such as *Bolitho*, a matter of plausible hypothesis based
on evidence of the past practice *of the defendant*. What others would have done
cannot be conclusive.

It may seem that this is a somewhat churlish response to *Bolitho*, given that it   **7.43**
sought to mitigate the difficulties encountered by the claimant in dealing with an
entirely hypothetical situation: did the non-attendance cause the child's injury?
The response must be that the route taken by way of mitigation is incoherent even

---

[60] [1996] 7 Med LR 1.
[61] Commentary (1993) Med L Rev 241. For a sustained assault on Hobhouse LJ's judgment in
Joyce, see, Commentary (1996) Med L Rev 86 (A Grubb).

by the standards of the law of causation. It is no answer that it allowed the House of Lords to endorse the move away from *Bolam* as the basis for establishing a breach of duty, which had been signalled by the Court of Appeal. Although this is particularly welcome, it is irrelevant for current purposes. What is relevant is that, in cases in which the breach of duty alleged is an omission to act, the legal enquiry into causation, which is represented as factual, will be converted into a normative investigation as to what the defendant should have done. Admittedly, it is clear from what has gone before, that the supposedly factual enquiry as to causation is not free from an accretion of policy issues. Nonetheless, it has always ultimately resolved itself into a factual issue, even if the courts have sometimes decided to infer one set of facts rather than another. *Bolitho* represents a significant departure from this approach. By introducing a normative element into causation in this way, it has added to the complexity (and, some would say, incoherence) of the law. It only remains to say that the alternative approach for the claimant in *Bolitho* was to have focused on the failure to intubate as the relevant breach of duty—but this was, of course, difficult to establish on the expert evidence. There was little doubt that factual causation could link *this* breach to the child's subsequent injury and death. Had the case been approached in this way, the law of causation may have avoided the strange flirtation with *Bolam*, even at a time when *Bolam*'s death-knell is being rung.

4. Causation and the Duty to Inform[62]

7.44 Where a doctor has breached his duty to obtain a properly informed consent, the patient, if he is to succeed in an action in negligence, must still show that the breach caused the damage complained of. The damage, of course, is the fact that a procedure was carried out without consent. It is immaterial that it may have been carried out with all due skill. The proposition that the breach must cause the damage translates here into the assertion by the claimant that, if he had been properly informed, he would not have gone ahead with the procedure. Obviously, it is open to the claimant, with the benefit of '20:20 vision' to assert that he would not have consented. Provided he is believable, this would clinch the case. Causation would be established on the basis of his say-so. Such a subjective approach to causation, however, may appear to tip the scales too heavily in favour of the claimant. One option is to insist on an objective test: what would the reasonable person in the claimant's position have done? The difficulty with this alternative is obvious. It rests the test of causation on a fiction, the decision of the reasonable person, rather than on the evidence of the particular patient. A further option is to cleave to the subjective approach, but require that the evidence adduced by the claimant be judged against some test of reasonableness, so as to inject some sort of check on

---

[62] Fully discussed at paras 3.109–3.142 above.

the resort to hindsight. This last, hybrid position most closely reflects the current position in English law.[63]

5. *Legal Causation*

(i) Intervening Acts

There is little to be said about legal causation for causation and the impact of in-   **7.45**
tervening acts on the defendant's possible liability in medical law.[64] The ordinary rules of tort law apply. The question for the court, where it is alleged that the intervening act of a third party has broken the chain of causation, is clearly a mixed question of law and fact. If the evidence demonstrates that there was some act of a third party which intervened between the defendant's breach of duty and the claimant's injury, the court must decide what degree of responsibility should still reside with the defendant. The word 'responsibility' is used to seek to demonstrate that the court, as ever, has a choice and that, essentially, the choice is a matter of policy. The policy at issue is, of course, that a defendant should only be held liable if his conduct is sufficiently blameworthy. This translates, in any particular case involving allegations of third-party intervention, into whether the defendant's breach of duty is sufficiently blameworthy that he should continue to attract condemnation through an award of damages.

Although there is little in the cases in medical law which can add to these general   **7.46**
propositions, there are a number of matters which warrant comment. The first is the case of *Knightley v Johns*,[65] in which it was made clear that a subsequent breach of duty by a third party may not break the chain of causation, and thereby absolve the defendant of his breach of duty, if the later breach was reasonably foreseeable. In *Knightley*, Stephenson LJ sought to prescribe some kind of hierarchy of third-party interventions, each of which might have a different effect on the defendant's liability: '[n]egligent conduct is more likely to break the chain of causation than conduct which is not; positive acts will more easily constitute new causes than inactions.' The difficulty with this type of 'analysis by list' is that it omits to identify and analyse the underlying criteria which might give rise to these various conclusions. Given that the criterion is ultimately accepted by Stephenson LJ as being 'common sense rather than logic on the facts and circumstances of each case', it may be wiser to avoid the formulaic approach and concentrate on the complex array of factors which persuade a court to shift responsibility away from a doctor in breach of his duty onto someone else.

---

[63] See *Smith v Barking, Havering and Brentwood HA* [1994] 5 Med LR 285 and *Smith v Tunbridge Wells HA* [1994] 5 Med LR 334.

[64] For a discussion of legal causation and remoteness in the context of medical law see *Chappel v Hart* (1998) 27 ALJR 1344 (HC Aus).

[65] [1982] 1 WLR 349.

7.47   A further matter warranting consideration is what is the status of an intervention by a third party which takes the form of a failure to act—that is, there is no actus interveniens. There is some authority in the general law of torts for the proposition that an omission to act by a third party cannot intervene to break the chain of causation. This was the view expressed by Goff LJ in *Muirhead v Industrial Tank Specialities*.[66] In medical law, in the context of a doctor–patient relationship, it is difficult to sustain this approach. Arguably, it gives too much force to a literal interpretation of actus, rather than seeing it as conduct, a more neutral term embracing both commission and omission. Furthermore, given that doctors are liable for omissions once a doctor–patient relationship can be shown to exist, a failure to act, in breach of duty, which causes damage, should be eligible to be regarded as a cause, and in appropriate circumstances, an intervening cause.

7.48   A third issue relates to the claimant's conduct. It will be recalled that what is under discussion here is conduct of another which may break the chain of causation between the defendant's breach of duty and the claimant's damage. So, here, it must be assumed that the doctor is in breach of his duty. It is submitted that, in appropriate circumstances, the unreasonable behaviour of the claimant could be judged to be contributory negligence.[67] Equally, in appropriate circumstances, there seems no reason in principle why it should not be regarded as an intervening cause, absolving the defendant. In such a case, the claimant would become the author of his own misfortune. That said, it is further submitted that, before a claimant would be held in medical law to have brought his own damage on himself, the court would probably demand a high degree of knowledge by the claimant of what he was doing, its implications and that it was not appropriate and would expose him to a risk of harm, and that he acted voluntarily and not under any duress or other factor reducing the capacity to choose. An example can be found in *Sabri-Tabrizi v Lothian Health Board*[68] where an action for damages for a failed sterilisation failed because the decision of the claimant to have sexual intercourse knowing that the operation had been unsuccessful was a novus actus interveniens.

7.49   A final issue, in the context of intervening cause, is the situation in which the claimant refuses further treatment. Again, the beginning point of analysis is a breach of duty by the defendant doctor. Can the claimant's refusal constitute an intervening cause? Arguing from first principles, it would appear that it should not be so regarded. A patient who is competent is entitled in law to refuse treatment. It is hard to see, therefore, how a refusal to undergo further treatment, so as to rectify a previous breach of duty by the doctor, can be judged adversely. The law may, however, be less simple. The proposition that a competent patient has the

---

[66] [1985] 3 All ER 705.
[67] See below, paras 7.53–7.57.
[68] (1997) 43 BMLR 190 (CS, IH).

right to refuse is, of course, relevant to circumstances in which the patient's personal integrity and inviolability is at stake. Here, it could be argued that the law is concerned with something slightly different. The claimant has had treatment. All that is asked is that the doctor (or another) have the opportunity to take remedial action (for example, intervene surgically to ensure that an operation on the knee which was not done properly does not leave the patient with a permanent limp). Any difference, however, is at best superficial. The integrity of the patient is as much at stake here as in other situations. It would follow that the patient's refusal of further treatment, even if unreasonable or irrational, should not and does not serve as an intervening cause to break the chain of causation. An extreme example in support of this proposition can be found in the case of *Emeh v Chelsea and Kensington AHA*.[69] A doctor was found to be in breach of duty in not performing properly an operation to sterilise the claimant. She became pregnant and brought an action to recover, inter alia, the increased costs associated with the pregnancy and birth of a further child. The trial judge found that her failure subsequently to obtain an abortion was unreasonable and thereby broke the chain of causation. The Court of Appeal in three strongly worded judgments rejected this view. The Court went out of its way to make it plain that a woman's choice not to undergo an abortion should not be regarded as a reason for absolving the defendant doctor, whose breach of duty had confronted her with the very dilemma she sought to avoid.

(ii) Remoteness

Again, the question here is whether there are any issues of remoteness of damage **7.50** which are peculiar to medical law. The answer is that the general rules of remoteness in the law of torts and the need to prove that the injury is reasonably foreseeable apply. A number of illustrative examples can be found in the case law: a doctor who negligently fails to discover that his mountaineer patient has a weak knee is not liable for the subsequent injury suffered by the mountaineer as a result of something not related to the knee because the injury is outside the scope of the doctor's duty of care;[70] a patient's injuries suffered when an operating theatre is struck by lightning would not be attributable to any negligence by the doctor or hospital;[71] a doctor would not be liable for an injury resulting from something unrelated to the risk of which the patient is not properly informed, for example, an injury arising from an anaesthetic accident.[72]

---

[69] [1984] 3 All ER 1044.

[70] *South Australia Asset Management Corporation v York Montague Ltd* [1996] 3 All ER 365 at 371–372 *per* Lord Hoffmann.

[71] *Chester v Ashfar* [2002] 3 All ER 552 (CA), at [43] *per* Sir Dennis Henry. See also, *Hogan v Bentinick Colleries* [1949] 1 All ER 588 *per* Lord MacDermott at 601—employer not liable where worker injured in employment is burned in hospital fire or in accident whilst in ambulance.

[72] *Chappel v Hart* (1998) 72 ALJR 1344 (HC Aus), *per* Gummow J at [66] and *Chester v Ashfar*, ibid, *per* Sir Dennis Henry at [43].

7.51   A rare illustration in the case law of remoteness in the medical context can be found in *R v Croydon HA*.[73] The claimant underwent a pre-employment chest X-ray. The radiographer negligently failed to report a significant abnormality, namely primary pulmonary hypertension (PPH), a potentially fatal condition. The claimant became pregnant and was later admitted to hospital suffering from PPH. The plaintiff gave birth to a healthy child by caesarian section. She sued in negligence for damages for the birth of the child, the complications arising from the pregnancy and loss of earnings. She argued that had she known about the PPH she would not have become pregnant and incurred the loss and damage. The Court of Appeal held, as regards damages arising out of the birth, the loss was too remote from the radiologist's breach of duty. The latter's duty did not extend to the claimant's private life.

B. Defences

7.52   There are several potential defences available to a defendant in a medical negligence action but in practice, with the exception of limitation, they are rarely relevant, given the nature of the relationship between doctor and patient. The defences that will be considered here are contributory negligence, *volenti non fit injuria, ex turpi causa non oritur actio* and limitation of action.

1. Contributory Negligence

7.53   A doctor frequently needs the patient's co-operation, for example, to make an accurate diagnosis or for the purpose of administering treatment. Sometimes this will be absolutely vital. The doctor requires accurate information regarding the patient's symptoms, and medical history. Similarly, the co-operation of the patient may be essential in implementing a treatment regime, for example, with regard to taking medication correctly, or returning for further treatment or tests. If the patient fails to follow proper instructions and this is a cause of his injuries, then it will be possible to argue that the patient has been contributorily negligent, or in an extreme case that his conduct is the sole cause of the damage.[74] Alternatively, where a patient has failed to communicate the nature of the symptoms from which she is suffering, the conclusion may simply be that the doctor was not negligent in failing to make a correct diagnosis on the basis of the available information.[75]

---

[73] [1998] Lloyd's Rep Med 44 (CA). See also *Brown v Lewisham and North Southwark HA* [1999] Lloyd's Rep Med 110 (CA).

[74] *Venner v North East Essex Area HA*, The Times, 21 February 1987; *Murrin v Janes* [1949] 4 DLR 403, 406 (Newfd SC).

[75] *Morrison v Forsyth* [1995] 6 Med LR 6 (CS OH), where a GP was found not liable for failing to visit a patient because the seriousness of the patient's condition was not made clear in the course of a telephone conversation; *Gordon v Wilson* [1992] 3 Med LR 401 (CS, OH); *Friedsam v Ng* [1994] 3 WWR 294 (BCCA).

(i) Law Reform (Contributory Negligence) Act 1945

Section 1 of the Law Reform (Contributory Negligence) Act 1945 provides that **7.54** where damage is attributable partly to the fault of the defendant and partly to the fault of the claimant, then the award of damages may be reduced by reason of the claimant's contributory negligence.[76] The reduction will be to such extent as the court thinks just and equitable having regard to the claimant's share in responsibility for the damage. The Act applies to actions in contract where the defendant's negligent breach of contract would have given rise to liability in the tort of negligence independently of the existence of the contract.[77] Accordingly, the defence will be available in virtually all actions arising out of private medical treatment, since the obligations imposed by the contract are normally the same as the duty to exercise reasonable care in the tort of negligence. On the other hand, where:

(a) liability does not depend on negligence but arises from breach of a strict contractual duty; or

(b) liability arises from breach of a contractual obligation which is expressed in terms of exercising reasonable care, but does not correspond to a common law duty of care which would exist independently of the contract,

apportionment under the legislation is not available.[78] Thus, in the rare circumstances where a patient was able to establish that the doctor had given a contractual warranty to achieve a specific result, this would fall into category (a) and the damages could not be apportioned for contributory negligence. It is unlikely that there are circumstances where category (b) could be relevant to the doctor–patient relationship.

Although, in theory, there is no reason why contributory negligence should not **7.55** apply in a claim for medical negligence, in practice the defence is rarely invoked successfully, and this is reflected in a comparative dearth of cases. It may be that the plea is considered to be inappropriate, given the inequality between the respective positions of doctor and patient. Patients do not generally question the advice or conduct of their doctors, even when they are aware that their condition is deteriorating or not improving. If the patient has ignored the doctor's advice (for example, by discharging himself from hospital or failing to return for further treatment) it may be easier to establish the defence. It would have to be shown that a reasonable person would have been aware of the significance of the advice, which

---

[76] s 4 provides that fault means 'negligence, breach of statutory duty or other act or omission which gives rise to a liability in tort or would, apart from this Act, give rise to the defence of contributory negligence'. The Act probably applies to actions in trespass to the person: *Barnes v Nayer*, The Times, 19 December 1986 (CA); *Wasson v Chief Constable of the Royal Ulster Constabulary* [1987] 8 NIJB 34; *Murphy v Culhane* [1977] QB 94; cf *Lane v Holloway* [1968] 1 QB 379.

[77] *Forsikringsaktieselskapet Vesta v Butcher* [1988] 2 All ER 43 (CA), approving the analysis of Hobhouse J at [1986] 2 All ER 488, 508.

[78] ibid; *Barclays Bank plc v Fairclough Building Ltd* [1994] 3 WLR 1057 (CA).

will depend upon the nature of the advice and whether it was clear to the patient. Moreover, in some circumstances there may well be a responsibility upon the doctor to adopt a system for following up patients who do not comply with advice to re-attend for further treatment or tests. In fact, by raising a plea of contributory negligence, a defendant may highlight the extent of the doctor's duty to take special care in giving the patient instructions, and making sure that the patient understands both the instructions and the importance of strictly adhering to them. In *Marshall v Rogers*,[79] for example, the defendant alleged that the claimant's injury was caused by his own negligence in failing to follow the instructions that he had been given and to report his symptoms. It was held, however, that where a dangerous remedy was being attempted, the doctor was negligent in delegating his own professional duty to decide the true meaning of the patient's progressive symptoms to the patient himself, especially given that the patient was only able to make a subjective assessment. The defendant should have conducted daily tests.

7.56 Some Canadian courts have made findings of contributory negligence against careless patients. In *Brushett v Cowan*[80] the claimant was contributorily negligent in engaging in ordinary activities without crutches following a bone biopsy on her leg, because she had failed to ask for clear instructions regarding the use of the crutches. A failure to have a post-operative check-up, as suggested by the doctor, has been held to be negligent,[81] and in *Crossman v Stewart*[82] a patient who obtained prescription drugs from an unorthodox source, and continued to use the drugs on a prolonged basis without obtaining prescription renewals or consulting the 'prescribing' physician, was described as 'foolhardy in the extreme'. She was held to be responsible for two-thirds of the damage to her eyesight caused by the side-effects of the drug.

7.57 The one English reported case in which the claimant's conduct was held to have been negligent is *Pidgeon v Doncaster HA*[83] where a claimant who developed cervical cancer, having been told that the results of a smear test were negative, was held to have been two-thirds contributorily negligent in failing to have a further smear test despite frequent reminders. It would also be possible for a plea of contributory negligence to apply in cases where the claimant attempts suicide and a claim is brought against medical staff on the basis of a negligent failure to prevent

---

[79] [1943] 4 DLR 68, 77.

[80] (1987) 40 DLR (4th) 488; aff'd (1990) 69 DLR (4th) 743 (Newfd CA).

[81] *Fredette v Wiebe* [1986] 5 WWR 222 (BCSC).

[82] (1977) 82 DLR (3d) 677, 686 (BCSC). It is also possible that unreasonable behaviour by a patient after the defendant's negligent conduct could be characterised as a failure to mitigate his loss. In *Brain v Mador* (1985) 32 CCLT 157 (Ont CA) a patient who failed to take steps to seek further medical advice following a vasectomy which had developed complications was held to have acted unreasonably, and his damages were reduced by 50 per cent for failing to mitigate the loss.

[83] [2002] Lloyd's Rep Med 130 (Doncaster County Ct).

the suicide attempt. In *Reeves v Commissioner of Police for the Metropolis*,[84] a similar type of claim brought against the police, the deceased was held 50 per cent contributorily negligent because he was partially responsible for his death, which was the result of the combination of the failure of the police to protect a prisoner who was a known suicide risk from harming himself and his own deliberate decision to end his life. Possibly, where the deceased was of unsound mind his suicide would not give rise to the defence of contributory negligence, by analogy with the position of young children who are not of full understanding.[85]

2. Volenti Non Fit Injuria

Volenti non fit injuria consists of a voluntary agreement by the claimant to absolve **7.58**
the defendant from the legal consequences of an unreasonable risk of harm created by the defendant, where the claimant has full knowledge of both the nature and extent of the risk. This should not be confused with *consent* to medical treatment which provides a defence to what would otherwise be the tort of battery. The patient who consents to medical treatment does not thereby consent to run the risk of negligence by the doctor.[86]

The one situation where the *volenti* defence could plausibly apply to a medical **7.59**
negligence action is in the case of suicide by a patient in circumstances where the doctor was under a duty to take reasonable precautions to prevent a suicide attempt. The point had been touched upon by the Court of Appeal in *Kirkham v Chief Constable of Greater Manchester Police*,[87] though it was said that the defence would only arise where the person was 'of sound mind'. But in *Reeves v Commissioner of Police for the Metropolis*[88] the House of Lords held that *volenti* does not apply where the claimant's act was the very thing that the defendant was under a duty to take reasonable care to prevent, irrespective of the suicide's mental state. If the defendant owed a duty of care to prevent a suicide attempt he cannot argue that the act which he was under a duty to prevent gave rise to the defence of *volenti*, because that would undermine the point of imposing a duty of care.

3. Ex Turpi Causa Non Oritur Actio *and Other Policy Factors*

(i) Ex Turpi Causa

The fact that the claimant was involved in committing a criminal offence at the **7.60**
time of sustaining damage may, in some instances, constitute a defence. This is usually expressed in the Latin maxim *ex turpi causa non oritur actio*. It will be

---

[84] [2000] 1 AC 360.
[85] ibid, 372 *per* Lord Hoffmann.
[86] See *Freeman v Home Office* [1984] 1 All ER 1036, 1044, *per* Sir John Donaldson MR.
[87] [1990] 2 QB 283.
[88] [2000] 1 AC 360.

extremely rare for a claimant in a medical negligence action to be involved in illegality which is directly linked to the treatment, although in *Kirkham v Chief Constable of Greater Manchester Police* the Court of Appeal accepted that the *ex turpi causa* defence is not confined to criminal conduct, but could apply to illegal or immoral conduct by the claimant if in all the circumstances an award of damages would be an affront to the public conscience.[89] But, awarding damages following a suicide would not affront the public conscience, at least where there was medical evidence that the suicide was 'not in full possession of his mind'.[90] Farquharson LJ said that an action could hardly be said to be grounded in immorality where 'grave mental instability' on the part of the victim has been proved, although 'the position may well be different where the victim is wholly sane'.[91] In the context of a claim following a suicide attempt it would appear that there is considerable overlap between the *ex turpi causa* defence and the volenti defence.[92] But in *Reeves v Commissioner of Police of the Metropolis*[93] the Court of Appeal held that *ex turpi causa* does not apply in a case where the claimant's conduct was the very act that the defendant was under a duty of care to prevent, whether or not the claimant was of sound mind.[94]

7.61   In *Clunis v Camden and Islington HA*[95] the claimant was convicted of manslaughter on the basis of diminished responsibility. He sued the health authority in negligence for failing to treat his mental condition and thereby failing to prevent him from committing the offence, claiming that had he received care he would not have committed the crime and would not therefore have been detained in a special hospital, or at least would not have been detained for as long. The Court of Appeal struck out the claim as contrary to public policy, on the basis that the court would not lend its aid to a litigant who relied on his own criminal or immoral act.

---

[89]   [1990] 2 QB 283, 291, *per* Lloyd LJ. There is controversy about the conceptual basis of the *ex turpi causa* defence, which is sometimes said to rest on the affront to the 'public conscience' if the court is effectively seen to be assisting a criminal, but in other cases depends on whether the claimant has to *rely* on his own criminal act as the basis of the claim. See *Clerk & Lindsell on Torts* (18th edn, 2000), paras 3-02 to 3-19.

[90]   ibid, 291, *per* Lloyd LJ; see also *Funk Estate v Clapp* (1986), reported at 68 DLR (4th) 229, and (1988) 54 DLR (4th) 512.

[91]   The meaning of the phrases 'grave mental instability' and 'wholly sane' is a matter of some conjecture. Query whether a person who is not insane, but whose judgment is impaired by an emotional, as opposed to a psychological, disturbance falls into the category of 'not wholly sane'.

[92]   In *Hyde v Tameside AHA* (1981), reported at (1986) 2 PN 26, 29–30 Lord Denning MR was opposed to allowing actions based on suicide or attempted suicide, a view that was clearly based on considerations of policy. In *Kirkham v Chief Constable of Greater Manchester Police* [1990] 2 QB 283, 292–293 Lloyd LJ did not share this view.

[93]   [1999] QB 169.

[94]   ibid, 185, *per* Buxton LJ. There was no appeal on the issue of *ex turpi causa* in the House of Lords, but the reasoning of their Lordships in relation to the argument that the deceased's suicide constituted a *novus actus interveniens* or that the deceased was *volenti* is entirely consistent with the Court of Appeal's approach to *ex turpi causa*.

[95]   [1998] QB 978. See also *Wilson v Coulson* [2002] PIQR P300.

A plea of diminished responsibility accepted that the accused's mental responsibility was substantially impaired, but it did not remove liability for his criminal act. There could be no liability in negligence unless it could be shown that he did not know the nature and quality of his act or that what he had done was wrong.

Similarly, where a mother had negligently been denied the opportunity to have an abortion, an action for negligence was denied on policy grounds in circumstances where the abortion would not have been lawful under the Abortion Act 1967, since the claimant could not have put the lost opportunity to benefit without breaking the law.[96] For the same reason, a claim for damages in respect of rendering the claimant infertile cannot include the cost of procedures connected with surrogate motherhood if those procedures would be in breach of the Surrogacy Arrangements Act 1985.[97] Accordingly, where potential claims arise out of the negligent performance of procedures which are unlawful, the likelihood is that they will be barred on the grounds of policy, whether or not this is referred to as *ex turpi causa*.[98]

7.62

(ii) Other Policy Factors

Policy factors may also play a role, though rarely, at other points in a medical negligence action, usually in the form of denying the existence of a duty of care. For example, 'wrongful life' claims on the part of a child whose congenital disabilities the defendant negligently failed to diagnose are not actionable.[99] In *M (a minor) v Newham London Borough Council*[100] a majority of the Court of Appeal held that neither a psychiatrist nor a social worker owed a duty of care in negligence to a child and her mother in respect of the manner in which they conducted an interview with the child for the purpose of identifying whether, and if so by whom, the child had been sexually abused. This was partly on the basis that the child was not

7.63

---

[96] *Rance v Mid-Downs HA* [1991] 1 All ER 801, where the period of gestation was such that a termination of the pregnancy would probably have been unlawful. Following amendment of the Abortion Act 1967 by the Human Fertilisation and Embryology Act 1990, s 37, there is no time limit where the termination is necessary to prevent grave permanent injury to the health of the woman, where the pregnancy involves risk to her life, or where there is a substantial risk that the foetus would be seriously handicapped. Where any of these grounds applied the causation issue in *Rance* would be irrelevant. The time limit under s 1(1)(*a*) of the Abortion Act 1967 is 24 weeks.

[97] *Briody v St Helens and Knowsley AHA* [2001] EWCA Civ 1010; [2002] QB 856.

[98] Another possible example would be an unlawful organ transplant operation contrary to the Human Organ Transplants Act 1989. In *Norberg v Wynrib* (1992) 92 DLR (4th) 449 the Supreme Court of Canada held that *ex turpi causa* did not apply to an action where the defendant doctor had supplied drugs to a patient who was addicted to pain-killers and tranquillisers in exchange for sexual contact. The patient had also been obtaining drugs from other doctors, and was convicted of the offence of 'double-doctoring'. The illegality was not causally linked to the harm suffered by the claimant.

[99] *McKay v Essex AHA* [1982] QB 1166; Congenital Disabilities (Civil Liability) Act 1976, s 1(1), (2).

[100] [1994] 2 WLR 554.

the psychiatrist's patient, and therefore the requisite degree of proximity was not established, and partly on the policy grounds first, that such a duty would lead to 'defensive' practices by the professionals involved in child protection, and secondly that actions against local authorities would have an adverse impact on the resources available for the purpose of child protection. This was accepted to be a proper basis for rejecting a duty of care in such circumstances by the House of Lords.[101]

7.64   Another ground of immunity stems from the fact that a witness in legal proceedings has immunity from suit with respect to evidence given in those proceedings,[102] and this immunity applies to a proof or report prepared for trial by a witness.[103] The immunity applies to an expert witness who prepares a joint statement with an expert instructed by the opposing party to the litigation for the purpose of identifying what issues are in dispute between the experts, and this is the case notwithstanding that the expert does not give evidence at the trial.[104] This is based on public policy in protecting the proper administration of justice so that witnesses are able to be frank when giving evidence free from the threat of civil proceedings, and to avoid a multiplicity of actions in which the truth of their evidence would be tried over again.[105] In the case of an expert witness, the immunity extends only to what can fairly be said to be preliminary to giving evidence in court. Thus, the production of a report for disclosure to the other side in litigation is immune, but work done for the principal purpose of advising the client, as to the merits of the claim, for example, is not.[106] In *Landall v Dennis Faulkner & Alsop*[107] the claimant was suing, inter alia, a medical expert who had provided a number of reports on the condition and prognosis of his back for the purpose of a claim being brought by him against a negligent motorist. He alleged that the expert's report and/or advice was negligent in that his opinion relating to the prospects of further successful treatment for the claimant's back condition was unduly optimistic, with the result that the claimant settled his action against the motorist for much less than it was worth. The claimant argued that the reports provided by the expert were not simply for the purposes of the litigation, but also constituted advice to the claimant as to the potential benefits of a spinal fusion operation. This argument was rejected, however. The report constituted:

---

[101] sub nom *X (minors) v Bedfordshire County Council* [1995] 3 WLR 152, 184. Though see now *D v East Berkshire Community Health NHS Trust* [2003] EWCA Civ 1151; [2003] 4 All ER 796, CA, in respect of the duty owed to the child.

[102] *Rondel v Worsley* [1969] 1 AC 191, 268; *Saif Ali v Sydney Mitchell & Co* [1980] AC 198.

[103] *Evans v London Hospital Medical College* [1981] 1 WLR 184.

[104] *Stanton v Callaghan* [2000] QB 75 (CA).

[105] *Watson v M'Ewan* [1905] AC 480; *Saif Ali v Sydney Mitchell & Co* [1980] AC 198; *Evans v London Hospital Medical College (University of London)* [1981] 1 WLR 184.

[106] *Palmer v Durnford Ford* [1992] 1 QB 483, 488.

[107] [1994] 5 Med LR 268 (QBD).

pre-trial work . . . so intimately connected with the conduct of the case in court that it could fairly be said to be a preliminary decision affecting the way that the case was to be conducted when it came to a hearing.[108]

Accordingly, the claim was struck out as disclosing no reasonable cause of action.[109]

4. *Limitation Act 1980*

Where an action is commenced outside the statutory limitation period the defend-   **7.65**
ant can rely on the defence of limitation.[110] An action in tort cannot normally be brought more than six years from the date on which the cause of action accrued,[111] which in the case of an action for negligence is when damage occurs, but in torts actionable per se, such as trespass to the person, the cause of action accrues at the date of the defendant's wrong. In contract the limitation period is also six years from the accrual of the action.[112] These rules are modified, however, in cases of personal injuries and death and claimants under a disability. Medical negligence actions are usually, though not exclusively, concerned with claims for personal injuries or death, which are governed, as a general rule,[113] by the provisions of the Limitation Act 1980, ss 11–14 and 33. The scheme provides for a three-year limitation period running from either (i) the date on which the cause of action

---

[108] *per* Holland J, applying *Saif Ali v Sydney Mitchell & Co* [1980] AC 198 and *Palmer v Durnford Ford* [1992] 1 QB 483, 488; cf *Hughes v Lloyds Bank plc* [1998] PIQR P98 (CA), where no proceedings had been issued and evidence from the defendant GP had been supplied at the patient's request in the context of negotiations between the patient and a third party's insurers. That advice could not be regarded as preliminary to giving evidence as an expert. The documents supplied by the GP were not for disclosure to the other side in the context of proceedings but purely in the context of negotiation.

[109] In *X (minors) v Bedfordshire County Council* [1995] 3 WLR 152, 188 the House of Lords held that a psychiatrist who, in the course of interviewing a child, was negligent in ascertaining the identity of the person who had sexually abused the child was protected by witness immunity (reversing the decision of the Court of Appeal in *M (a minor) v Newham London Borough Council* [1994] 2 WLR 554). The policy considerations which applied to witnesses in criminal proceedings were equally applicable to a local authority's investigation, in the performance of a public duty, of whether or not there is evidence on which to bring proceedings for the protection of children from child abuse. The psychiatrist knew that if abuse was discovered, proceedings for the protection of the child would ensue and that her findings would be the evidence on which those proceedings would be based. The investigations had an immediate link with possible proceedings in pursuance of a statutory duty, and therefore could not be made the basis of a subsequent action in negligence. Note that subsequently the European Court of Human Rights found that, on these facts, the local authority was in breach of Art 8 of the ECHR, the right to respect for family life, in failing to involve the mother in the decision-making process concerning the care of her daughter: *TP and KM v UK* [2001] 2 FLR 549. See further *D v East Berkshire Community Health NHS Trust* [2003] EWCA Civ 1151; [2003] 4 All ER 796, CA on the question of witness immunity.

[110] For a more detailed discussion see Jones, Michael A, *Limitation Periods in Personal Injury Actions* (Blackstone Press, 1995).

[111] Limitation Act 1980, s 2.

[112] ibid, s 5. The action in contract will accrue at the date of the breach of contract.

[113] The Limitation Act 1980 does not apply where a period of limitation is prescribed by other legislation: s 39.

accrued, or (ii) if later, the claimant's date of knowledge of certain facts about the cause of action.[114] Additionally, even if this fixed period has expired, the court has a wide discretion to override the time limit and permit the action to proceed.[115] The Law Commission has recommended reform of the law on limitation periods to introduce a single, core limitation regime, applying, as far as possible, to all claims for a remedy for a wrong, claims for the enforcement of a right and claims for restitution.[116]

(i) Limitation Periods

7.66 Section 11(1) provides that the three-year period applies to 'any action for damages for negligence, nuisance or breach of duty' where the damages claimed by the claimant consist of or include damages in respect of personal injuries. This expressly includes breach of a contractual duty. In *Letang v Cooper*[117] the Court of Appeal held that the wording also applied to an action for trespass to the person, but in *Stubbings v Webb*[118] the House of Lords concluded that s 11(1) was limited to personal injury resulting from accidents caused by negligence, nuisance or breach of a duty of care.[119] The consequence of this is that actions for trespass against the person against a doctor, for example, in respect of a failure to obtain a valid consent to treatment, are not governed by s 11, but by s 2 of the Limitation Act 1980. This means the claimant must bring the action within six years, without any possibility of the court's discretion under s 33 being available.[120] The

---

[114] Limitation Act 1980, s 11(3) and (4). New claims which are outside a relevant limitation period cannot be brought by addition to or amendment of existing proceedings since this would have the effect of depriving a defendant of an otherwise valid limitation defence. The Limitation Act 1980, s 35, in combination with CPR 17.4 and 19.5 allows for limited exceptions to this rule.

[115] ibid, s 33. Similar rules apply to claims brought under the Consumer Protection Act 1987 in respect of defective products, except that there is an overall longstop which expires ten years after the product was put into circulation by the defendant. The longstop is an absolute bar, and the court has no discretion to override this limit in personal injuries cases. See Limitation Act 1980, ss. 11A, 14(1A), 28(7), 32(4A) and 33(1A).

[116] *Limitation of Actions* (Law Com 270, July 2001). Under the Commission's proposals the law would not change significantly in cases of personal injuries or death, except that the basic three-year period plus a discretion to extend the period would apply to all personal injury actions, reversing the effect of *Stubbings v Webb* [1993] AC 498, below.

[117] [1965] 1 QB 232; *Long v Hepworth* [1968] 1 WLR 1299.

[118] [1993] AC 498.

[119] On the other hand, a daughter's allegation that her mother had been negligent in failing to protect her from sexual abuse by her father during her minority falls within s 11 rather than s 2: *Seymour v Williams* [1995] PIQR P470 (CA).

[120] See *Dobbie v Medway HA* [1994] 4 All ER 450, 458–459 (CA). This would not be the case, however, where the patient died and an action was brought by the dependants under the Fatal Accidents Act 1976, since this action is governed by s 12 of the Limitation Act 1980, not s 11. But, a claim under the Law Reform (Miscellaneous Provisions) Act 1934 is governed by s 11(5) of the Limitation Act, with the result that *Stubbings v Webb* applies s 2, and the limitation period will be six years from the date of the battery. A claim against an employer, as vicariously liable for the deliberate abuse by an employee of children in the care of the employer, is subject to a six-year limitation

omission to obtain the patient's consent may be the product of carelessness, but nonetheless the cause of action is in battery because, although battery is an intentional tort, the doctor has the relevant intention (the direct application of force to the patient's body) and is simply careless as to whether he has the *defence* of consent. On the other hand, a psychiatrist/psychologist who enters into an improper relationship with a patient commits a breach of a duty of care in negligence, not 'wilful conduct calculated to cause the claimant injury', and therefore the three-year limitation period specified by s 11 applies, not the six-year period created by s 2 (which would be the case following *Stubbings v Webb* if the conduct was intentional).[121]

'Personal injuries' includes any disease and any impairment of a person's physical **7.67** or mental condition.[122] Where the breach of duty does not itself cause the personal injuries, but deprives the claimant of a chance of receiving compensation for the injuries the three-year period does not apply.[123] So where a patient suffers purely financial loss due to a doctor's negligence (for example as a result of giving up work following a negligent misdiagnosis[124]), the six-year, rather than three-year, period will apply. In *Walkin v South Manchester HA*[125] the Court of Appeal held that a claim for the economic loss attributable to the birth of a child following a failed sterilisation operation fell within s 11, as a claim for 'damages in respect of personal injuries'. The unwanted conception was a personal injury because the physical change to the claimant's body was an unwanted condition which she had sought to avoid by being sterilised.[126] This issue was complicated by the ruling of the House of Lords in *McFarlane v Tayside Health Board*[127] that no duty of care is owed to the parents in respect of the financial cost of bringing up a healthy child following negligent advice about, or the negligent performance of, a sterilisation operation. Subsequently, in *Parkinson v St James and Seacroft University Hospital*

---

period: *KR v Bryn Alyn Community (Holdings) Ltd (in liquidation)* [2003] EWCA Civ 85; [2003] 1 FCR 385. The European Court of Human Rights has held that the operation of the Limitation Act 1980 in this manner does not contravene the ECHR: *Stubbings v UK* [1997] 1 FLR 105.

[121] *Bowler v Walker* [1996] PIQR P22 (CA).
[122] Limitation Act 1980, s 38(1).
[123] *Ackbar v Green & Co Ltd* [1975] 1 QB 582.
[124] See *Hedley Byrne & Co Ltd v Heller & Partners Ltd* [1964] AC 465, 517, *per* Lord Devlin.
[125] [1996] 7 Med LR 211.
[126] cf *Pattison v Hobbs*, The Times, 11 November 1985, where the Court of Appeal had held that such an action was subject to s 2, as a claim in respect of financial loss. In *Walkin* Auld LJ said that *Pattison v Hobbs* was a decision of a two-judge Court of Appeal which turned on a point of pleading, whereas the question whether an action was for damages in respect of personal injuries was a matter of substance, not pleading. See also *Bennett v Greenland Houchen & Co (a firm)* [1998] PNLR 458 where the Court of Appeal applied *Walkin* to an action against a firm of solicitors in respect of financial loss alleged to have been caused by the defendants' negligence, where the claimant also alleged that he suffered clinical depression arising out of the defendants' negligent handling of his case against his former employers.
[127] [2000] 2 AC 59.

NHS Trust[128] the Court of Appeal held that the parents of a disabled child born following a negligently performed sterilisation operation were entitled to the additional costs of raising that child, ie the additional costs attributable to the disability itself. Thus, such claims are in any event limited to cases involving a disabled child. But in *McFarlane* their Lordships categorised the parents' claim for the cost of raising the child as a claim for pure economic loss, a view adopted by the Court of Appeal in *Greenfield v Irwin*.[129] This led Laws LJ to comment that if the Court of Appeal's reasoning in *Walkin* was at variance with *McFarlane* then it was impliedly disapproved by *McFarlane*.[130] But in *Godfrey v Gloucestershire Royal Infirmary NHS Trust*[131] Leveson J applied *Walkin* to a failed sterilisation case where the child had been born disabled. The question was not whether the claim for child-rearing costs was a claim in respect of economic loss, but rather whether it was an action for damages 'consisting of or including damages in respect of personal injuries. That is or at least could be different from the question whether the claim for the cost of upbringing of a child is pure or consequential economic loss.'[132] It followed that s 11 of the Act applied, so that the limitation period was three years from the date of the claimant's knowledge, but with the discretionary power to disapply the limitation period.

7.68   Once the limitation period prescribed by s 2 of the Limitation Act 1980 expires there is no discretion to permit the action to proceed, though the commencement of the limitation period may be postponed in the case of deliberate concealment[133] or latent damage.[134]

---

[128] [2001] EWCA Civ 530; [2002] QB 266.

[129] [2001] EWCA Civ 113; [2001] 1 WLR 1279.

[130] ibid at [53].

[131] [2003] EWHC 549 (QB).

[132] ibid at [35].

[133] Where any fact relevant to the claimant's right of action has been deliberately concealed from him by the defendant, the limitation period does not begin to run until the claimant has discovered the concealment or could with reasonable diligence have discovered it: Limitation Act 1980, s 32(1). This includes the deliberate commission of a breach of duty in circumstances in which it is unlikely to be discovered for some time: s 32(2). This covers the commission of a wrong knowingly or recklessly, but mere negligence is not sufficient: *Cave v Robinson Jarvis & Rolf (a firm)* [2002] UKHL 18; [2003] 1 AC 384. Lord Millett observed, at [25], that s 32 'does not deprive a defendant of a limitation defence where he is charged with negligence if, being unaware of his error or that he has failed to take proper care, there has been nothing for him to disclose'. In *Sheldon v RHM Outhwaite (Underwriting Agencies) Ltd* [1996] 1 AC 102 the House of Lords held that s 32(1)(b) operated to postpone the running of the limitation period in every case where there is deliberate concealment by the defendant of facts relevant to the claimant's cause of action, regardless of whether the concealment was contemporaneous with or subsequent to the accrual of the cause of action. Thus, subsequent concealment has the effect of bringing s 32 into play, thereby excluding ss 2 and 5, and the claimant has a full six years from the date of discovery of the concealment in which to bring the action, or alternatively, the defendant would be estopped from raising the limitation defence. But if the claimant is aware of the relevant *facts* during the period preceding the concealment, the subsequent acts of the defendant cannot conceal those facts from the claimant: *Sheldon v RHM Outhwaite (Underwriting Agencies) Ltd* [1996] 1 AC 102, 144; *Ezekiel v Lehrer* [2002] EWCA Civ 16; [2002] Lloyd's Rep PN 260.

[134] In cases of latent damage (other than personal injuries) the claimant has three years from the

(ii) The Running of the Limitation Period

Time begins to run from either the date on which the cause of action accrued or **7.69** the date of the claimant's knowledge, if later.[135] Once the period has started to run it cannot be suspended; only the issue of the claim form stops time running. The parties may agree, expressly or impliedly, to extend the time, but the mere fact that negotiations towards a settlement were in progress when the three-year period expired will not constitute such an agreement, unless the defendant's conduct is such that he is estopped from relying on the defence.[136]

In negligence the action accrues when damage occurs, whether or not the damage **7.70** is discoverable.[137] In the case of minor or trivial harm it will be a question of fact whether the claimant has sustained 'damage' sufficient for the cause of action to accrue. Damage will only be ignored if it falls within the principle *de minimis non curat lex*.[138] In an action for personal injuries, even if more than three years have elapsed since the action accrued, the primary limitation period will not have expired if the claim form is issued within three years of the claimant's 'knowledge'. By s 14(1), references to a person's date of knowledge are references to the date on which he first had knowledge of the following facts:

(a) that the injury in question was significant; and
(b) that the injury was attributable in whole or in part to the act or omission which is alleged to constitute negligence, nuisance or breach of duty; and
(c) the identity of the defendant; and
(d) if it is alleged that the act or omission was that of a person other than the defendant, the identity of that person and the additional facts supporting the bringing of an action against the defendant . . .

---

date on which he discovered or ought reasonably to have discovered significant damage, subject to an overall longstop which bars all claims brought more than 15 years from the date of the defendant's negligence: Limitation Act 1980, ss. 14A and 14B. Section 14A is expressed in very similar terms to s 14 (see para 7.70 below) and the courts' approach to s 14A closely mirrors that taken to s 14: see *Spencer-Ward v Humberts* [1995] 06 EG 148 (CA); *Hallam-Eames v Merrett Syndicates Ltd* [1996] 7 Med LR 122 (CA); *Oakes v Hopcroft* [2000] Lloyd's Rep Med 394. The latent damage provisions do not apply to claims in contract: *Iron Trade Mutual Insurance Co Ltd v JK Buckenham Ltd* [1990] 1 All ER 808; *Société Commerciale de Réassurance v ERAS (International) Ltd (Note)* [1992] 2 All ER 82. Where, however, the defendant owes concurrent duties in contract and tort the claimant is entitled to pursue the action which will give him a practical advantage on the question of limitation: *Henderson v Merrett Syndicates Ltd* [1994] 3 All ER 506, 525 *per* Lord Goff.

[135] For consideration of who has the burden of proof in respect of the limitation defence see *Fowell v National Coal Board*, The Times, 28 May 1986 (CA); *Nash v Eli Lilly & Co* [1993] 1 WLR 782, 796 (CA); *Driscoll-Varley v Parkside HA* [1991] 2 Med LR 346, 357.

[136] *Deerness v John Keeble & Son Ltd* [1983] 2 Lloyd's Rep 260; *K Lokumal & Sons (London) Ltd v Lotte Shipping Co Pte Ltd* [1985] 2 Lloyd's Rep 28.

[137] *Cartledge v Jopling & Sons Ltd* [1963] AC 758.

[138] ibid.

The word 'knowledge' does not mean 'know for certain and beyond possibility of contradiction'.[139] Suspicion, particularly if it is vague and unsupported, will not be enough, but reasonable belief will normally suffice.[140] The court must assess the intelligence of the claimant, consider his assertions as to how he regarded the information that he had, and determine whether he had knowledge of the facts by reason of his understanding of the information.[141]

7.71   In *North Essex District HA v Spargo*[142] Brooke LJ set out a number of propositions, taken from previous authorities, about the meaning of the word 'knowledge' for the purpose of s 14:

(1) The knowledge required to satisfy s 14(1)(b) is a broad knowledge of the essence of the causally relevant act or omission to which the injury is attributable;

(2) 'Attributable' in this context means 'capable of being attributed to' in the sense of being a real possibility;

(3) A plaintiff has requisite knowledge when she knows enough to make it reasonable for her to begin to investigate whether or not she has a case against the defendant. Another way of putting this is to say that she will have such knowledge if she so firmly believes that her condition is capable of being attributed to an act or omission which she can identify (in broad terms) that she goes to a solicitor to seek advice about making a claim for compensation;

(4) On the other hand she will not have the requisite knowledge if she thinks she knows the acts or omissions she should investigate but in fact is barking up the wrong tree; or if her knowledge of what the defendant did or did not do is so vague or general that she cannot fairly be expected to know what she should investigate; or if her state of mind is such that she thinks her condition is capable of being attributed to the act or omission alleged to constitute negligence, but she is not sure about this, and would need to check it with an expert before she could be properly said to know that it was.[143]

---

[139] *Halford v Brookes* [1991] 3 All ER 559, 573–574 *per* Lord Donaldson MR.

[140] For consideration of the degree of 'certainty' required to constitute knowledge see *Nash v Eli Lilly & Co* [1993] 1 WLR 782, 792 (CA); *Skitt v Khan and Wakefield HA* [1997] 8 Med LR 105; cf *Wilkinson v Ancliff (BLT) Ltd* [1986] 3 All ER 427, 438, and *Stephen v Riverside HA* [1990] 1 Med LR 261, where it was said that reasonable belief is not sufficient to constitute knowledge.

[141] *Nash v Eli Lilly & Co* [1993] 1 WLR 782, 792.

[142] [1997] PIQR P235, 242.

[143] In *Ali v Courtaulds Textiles Ltd* [1999] Lloyd's Rep Med 301, the evidence was that the claimant knew he was deaf, knew that exposure to noise could cause deafness, and also knew that the ageing process could cause deafness. The Court of Appeal held that knowledge as to whether his deafness was noise-induced or age-induced was ascertainable only with the help of expert medical advice, and therefore the case fell within the third category of the fourth *Spargo* principle, ie he thought that his condition was capable of being attributed to the act or omission alleged to constitute negligence, but he was not sure, and needed to check it with an expert before he could properly be said to know that it was. See also *Harrild v Ministry of Defence* [2001] Lloyd's Rep Med 117 (QBD).

It has been said that these principles were intended not simply as guidelines, but as binding rules.[144] In *O'Driscoll v Dudley HA*[145] the Court of Appeal said that the fourth *Spargo* principle has to be read as 'postulating a situation antithetical to that covered by the third principle; ie the fourth principle postulates a state of mind short of a firm belief which takes a potential claimant to a solicitor'. The reference to 'the need to check with an expert' was a reference to the need for an expert's opinion before even the claimant can be said to know that the attributability of her condition to a particular 'act or omission' was a real possibility. That was not the same investigation as was referred to in the first limb of the third principle, which is an investigation into whether the claimant 'has a case against the defendant', an investigation that has to be carried out whilst the limitation clock is ticking.

7.72

(a) Significant Injury

An injury is significant if the person whose date of knowledge is in question would reasonably have considered it sufficiently serious to justify his instituting proceedings for damages against a defendant who did not dispute liability and was able to satisfy a judgment.[146] This is a combined subjective/objective test.[147] It is a question of what a reasonable man of the claimant's age, with his background, intelligence and disabilities would reasonably have known.[148] Other personal reasons that the claimant may have had for not commencing proceedings are irrelevant, even if they are objectively reasonable.[149] The third *Spargo* principle appears to treat any claimant who goes to a solicitor as having the requisite degree of knowledge. But it cannot be the case that simply by going to a solicitor the claimant necessarily has knowledge of all the relevant *facts*. The claimant may be unsure about the position. In *Sniezek v Bundy (Letchworth) Ltd*[150] the Court of Appeal said that, under the third *Spargo* principle there was a distinction to be drawn between a claimant who has a firm belief that he has a significant injury, attributable to his working conditions (especially a belief that takes him to a solicitor for advice about a claim), a belief that he retains whatever contrary advice he receives, and a claimant who believes that he may have, or even probably has, a

7.73

---

[144] *Griffin, Lawson and Williams v Clwyd HA* [2001] EWCA Civ 818, [2001] PIQR P420; *Corbin v Penfold Metallising Company Ltd* [2000] Lloyd's Rep Med 247, 249 (CA): the Court 'intended to lay down, not merely guidelines, but authoritative statements of how s 14 should be interpreted'.

[145] [1998] Lloyd's Rep Med 210, 221–222. See also *Roberts v Winbow* [1999] PIQR P77 (CA) for discussion of the distinction between the *Spargo* principles (3) and (4).

[146] Limitation Act 1980, s 14(2).

[147] *McCafferty v Metropolitan Police District Receiver* [1977] 1 WLR 1073, 1081, *per* Geoffrey Lane LJ; *Denman v Essex AHA* (1984) 134 NLJ 264.

[148] *Davis v City and Hackney HA* [1991] 2 Med LR 366.

[149] *Miller v London Electrical Manufacturing Co Ltd* [1976] 2 Lloyd's Rep 284; *Buck v English Electric Co Ltd* [1977] 1 WLR 806; *McCafferty v Metropolitan Police District Receiver* [1977] 1 WLR 1073.

[150] [2000] PIQR P213, 224.

significant injury which is attributable to his working conditions, but is not sure and feels it necessary to have expert advice on those questions. The former has knowledge of significant injury and attribution for the purposes of s 14, but the latter does not.

7.74 'Significant injury' refers to the gravity of the damage and its monetary value, not to the claimant's evaluation of its cause, nature or usualness.[151] Section 14(2) makes most injuries significant in monetary terms, since it will not take much to justify instituting proceedings against a solvent defendant who admits liability. Where the injury, though minor, is sufficiently serious to institute proceedings, and the claimant subsequently discovers a far more serious injury caused by the same accident, time will run from the date of the first injury.[152] In *Nash v Eli Lilly & Co*[153] the claimants alleged that they had suffered side-effects from the use of the prescription drug Opren. The Court of Appeal accepted that there was a valid distinction between an expected, or accepted, side-effect, which would not constitute significant injury, and an injurious or unacceptable consequence. Time would not begin to run until the claimants had knowledge that the side effects were injurious or unacceptable.[154] Where the claimant's damage consists of psychological harm, there could be some difficulty in determining when a claimant first knew that his injury was significant, particularly where the claimant put the relevant events to the back of his mind, or tried to block or suppress the events. This is a highly fact-sensitive question.[155]

(b) Causation

7.75 The claimant must have knowledge that the injury was attributable in whole or in part to the 'act or omission which is alleged to constitute negligence'. This refers to the claimant's knowledge of factual causation.[156] Ignorance of causation in law is irrelevant. Once the claimant has the broad knowledge that his injuries are attributable to the defendant's acts or omissions, he has sufficient knowledge for the purpose of s 14(1)(b), even if he does not know the specific acts or omissions and

---

[151] *Dobbie v Medway HA* [1994] 4 All ER 450, 457, *per* Sir Thomas Bingham MR, though his Lordship added that time does not run if the claimant would reasonably have accepted it as a fact of life or not worth bothering about.

[152] *Bristow v Grout*, The Times, 3 November 1986; *Roberts v Winbow* [1999] PIQR P77 (CA). The claimant's appreciation of the seriousness of an injury may depend upon the medical advice which he receives: *Harding v People's Dispensary for Sick Animals* [1994] PIQR P270 (CA).

[153] [1993] 1 WLR 782 (CA).

[154] cf *Briggs v Pitt-Payne & Lias* [1999] Lloyd's Rep Med 1 where the Court of Appeal held that the question of balancing side-effects against the overall beneficial effects of a drug was 'simply not relevant' to the question of whether the claimant is aware that he is suffering from 'significant injury'.

[155] *KR v Bryn Alyn Community (Holdings) Ltd (in liquidation)* [2003] EWCA Civ 85, [2003] 1 FCR 385.

[156] *Dobbie v Medway HA* [1994] 4 All ER 450, 462, *per* Steyn LJ. See, eg, *Marston v British Railways Board* [1976] ICR 124.

is not in a position to draft a fully particularised statement of claim.[157] Moreover, a claimant will be taken to know that his injury was 'attributable' to the defendant's act or omission if he knew that it was 'capable of being so attributed'.[158]

Where the claimant has a firm belief that his injuries are due to the acts or omissions of the defendant, but on making enquiries is informed by expert opinion that he is mistaken, the question of whether he had sufficient knowledge to start the limitation period running will be one of degree. If the claimant realised that his belief required further confirmation, then he will not acquire knowledge until he receives that confirmation.[159] On the other hand, if the claimant is convinced in her own mind that there is a causal link, even though objectively that belief is not reasonable in the absence of confirmation from an expert, she nonetheless has the requisite knowledge and it is not open to argue that her knowledge runs from the date of confirmation of that belief by an expert.[160] Moreover, if the claimant has acquired 'knowledge' sufficient to start the limitation period running, he cannot subsequently lose it simply because he receives expert advice which tends to undermine the belief.[161] Everything turns upon the degree of conviction with which the claimant holds his belief, and whether he realised that expert confirmation was required. The Court of Appeal has suggested that where a claimant has sought advice and taken proceedings there would be some difficulty in saying that he did not then have the relevant knowledge.[162] This would mean that where a protective claim form had been issued the claimant would be deemed to have knowledge even where he then received negative expert advice leading him to discontinue the action.[163] In *Nash v Eli Lilly & Co*[164] the Court even went so far as to state that a person who embarks upon the preliminaries to the making of a claim for compensation by taking legal or other advice may be deemed to satisfy the level of 'certainty' required for acquiring 'knowledge' under s 14. It is arguable, however, that even issuing a claim form should not be treated as *conclusive* evidence

7.76

---

[157] *Wilkinson v Ancliff (BLT) Ltd* [1986] 3 All ER 427, 438 (CA); *Hayward v Sharrard* (1998) 56 BMLR 155, 165 (CA).

[158] ibid. 'To "attribute" means "to reckon as a consequence of" ': *Halford v Brookes* [1991] 3 All ER 559, 573, *per* Lord Donaldson MR.

[159] See *Davis v Ministry of Defence*, The Times, 7 August 1985; *Sniezek v Bundy (Letchworth) Ltd* [2000] PIQR P213, 224.

[160] *Spargo v North Essex District HA* [1997] PIQR P235, 244 (CA). Brooke LJ said: 'The test is a subjective one: what did the plaintiff herself know? It is not an objective one: what would have been the reasonable layman's state of mind in the absence of expert confirmation?'

[161] *Nash v Eli Lilly & Co* [1993] 1 WLR 782, 795 (CA).

[162] ibid, 795.

[163] This occurred in *Stephen v Riverside HA* [1990] 1 Med LR 261 and *Davis v Ministry of Defence* The Times, 7 August 1985, but it was held that the claimants did not acquire knowledge until they received further expert advice confirming their original belief that there was a causal connection.

[164] [1993] 1 WLR 782, 792. In *Spargo v North Essex District HA* [1997] PIQR P235, 242 Brooke LJ said that 'attributable in this context means "capable of being attributed to" in the sense of being a real possibility'. See the quotation at n 142 above.

that the claimant had the relevant knowledge. In *Whitfield v North Durham HA*[165] the Court of Appeal held that it was wrong to treat the issue of a protective claim form as determinative, by itself, of the question of knowledge. The claimant may have a firm belief, even a conviction, that his injuries were caused in a particular way, but it subsequently turns out that he was mistaken and his injuries were caused by other acts or omissions of the defendant. In these circumstances he was 'barking up the wrong tree'[166] and on the wording of s 14(1)(b) he does not have the required knowledge until he discovers his mistake, notwithstanding the possibility that a claim form has already been issued. In *Sniezek v Bundy (Letchworth) Ltd*[167] Judge LJ said that *Nash* was not authority for the proposition that time automatically starts to run against a claimant who has taken legal advice. There was nothing in the Limitation Act to suggest that any special consequences must or should be deemed to arise from his doing so. The question remains the individual's state of knowledge of the relevant facts, rather than his adviser's opinion about the prospects of success in legal proceedings. But once time starts to run, it is not postponed even if the claimant sensibly thinks, on the basis of legal and medical advice, that he should not proceed to litigation.[168]

7.77   A particular problem which has arisen in the context of medical negligence actions is the degree of 'specificity' of knowledge required about the causal connection between treatment and the injury. Can it be said that a claimant's knowledge that the injury was attributable to 'medical treatment' is knowledge in 'broad terms' that it was attributable to an act or omission which is alleged to constitute negligence, where the claimant cannot identify the relevant acts or omissions? The difficulty arises because unlike, say, the typical road traffic accident or work accident, the claimant cannot regard the occurrence of injury itself as indicating that there must be a causal connection between the injury and 'act or omission which is alleged to constitute negligence'. Injury following an operation may arise without negligence or without even an error, as an unavoidable complication of the procedure. Alternatively, the operation may simply have been unsuccessful in preventing the claimant's medical condition from deteriorating as a consequence of the original disease or injury which was being treated.[169] Moreover, most people would not regard *successful* medical treatment as constituting an *injury*, so that if a patient is informed that surgery was successful, she would not even consider that she had been injured, let alone address her mind to the question of which acts or omissions had caused the 'injury'.

---

[165]   [1995] 6 Med LR 32, 37.
[166]   See the cases cited at n 173, below.
[167]   [2000] PIQR P213 at 229.
[168]   ibid, 230, *per* Judge LJ.
[169]   See, eg, *Harrington v Essex AHA*, The Times, 14 November 1984, where it was held that knowledge by the claimant that he had contracted an infection in the operating theatre, was not knowledge that the infection was attributable to an act or omission constituting negligence, since an infection can be contracted without negligence on the part of anyone.

In order to distinguish those injuries which were unavoidable consequences of the **7.78** procedure and those which are attributable to an 'act or omission which is alleged to constitute negligence', it is strongly arguable that the minimum knowledge a claimant would require is knowledge that 'something has gone wrong' with the treatment. This has been the approach taken in a number of cases.[170] Conversely, s 14(1) makes it clear that the claimant's ignorance that the defendant's acts or omissions would give rise to a cause of action in law is irrelevant to the running of the limitation period, and it might be argued that requiring knowledge that 'something has gone wrong' would import an element of knowledge about the defendant's negligence.

In *Broadley v Guy Clapham & Co*[171] the claimant underwent an operation to re- **7.79** move a foreign body from her knee and for at least seven months after the operation she needed two sticks in order to walk. It was held that by this time she had constructive knowledge of a potential cause of action because a reasonable person in her position would have sought further medical assistance or made further enquiries of the doctor. The claimant argued that she did not have knowledge until she knew of:

> some act or omission which could adversely affect the safety of the operation or proper recovery from the operation, such as unreasonable interference with the nerve or failure reasonably to safeguard it from damage, or failure properly to investigate and/or repair the nerve lesion in time.

Leggatt LJ said that the use of the words 'unreasonable', 'reasonably' and 'properly' **7.80** could not be justified because s 14(1) provided that 'knowledge that any acts or omissions did or did not, as a matter of law, involve negligence' was irrelevant. The words 'which is alleged to constitute negligence' simply pointed to the relevant act or omission to which the injury was attributable.[172] The situation would be different, said Hoffmann LJ, if the claimant was 'barking up the wrong tree', ie where the claimant thought that the complications from which she suffered had been caused in one way (for example, during the operation) but she later discovered

---

[170] *Bentley v Bristol and Western HA* [1991] 2 Med LR 359, 364, *per* Hirst J: '. . . the performance of a surgical operation . . . is not the act or omission which is itself alleged to constitute negligence. The act or omission which *is* alleged to constitute negligence in operation cases is some conduct or failure which can affect the safety of the operation' (original emphasis); *Nash v Eli Lilly & Co* [1991] 2 Med LR 169 where Hidden J said that there must be a degree of specificity about the act or omission which is alleged to constitute negligence, which in *Nash* consisted of exposing the claimants to a drug which was unsafe in that it was capable of causing persistent photosensitivity and/or in failing to take reasonable steps to protect the claimants from such a condition. The Court of Appeal accepted that this was the appropriate degree of specificity: *Nash v Eli Lilly & Co* [1993] 1 WLR 782, 799 (CA); see also *Driscoll-Varley v Parkside HA* [1991] 2 Med LR 346.

[171] [1994] 4 All ER 439 (CA).

[172] ibid, 447. See also *per* Hoffmann LJ at 448. It followed that the decision in *Bentley v Bristol and Western HA* [1991] 2 Med LR 359 was wrong, since it required knowledge on the claimant's part of all matters necessary to establish negligence or breach of duty, and this was too high a test.

that the real cause was not the operation but the subsequent premature removal of her leg from traction.[173] In these circumstances the issue is the identification of the act which caused the injury and not the appreciation of whether the act was capable of being attributable to negligence or fault. Balcombe LJ said that detailed knowledge (ie sufficient knowledge to enable the claimant's advisers to draft a statement of claim) or qualitative knowledge (ie knowledge that the operation had been performed in such a way as unreasonably to cause injury to a nerve) were not required for the purpose of s 14(1). On the other hand, his Lordship accepted that 'broad knowledge' was required, which consisted of knowledge that the operation had been carried out in such a way that something went wrong.[174]

7.81   In *Dobbie v Medway HA*[175] the claimant issued a claim form in 1989 in respect of the removal of her breast during the course of a breast biopsy operation performed in 1973. Although the surgeon believed a lump to be malignant, subsequent pathological examination revealed that it was benign. The claimant was told by medical staff that the breast had been removed to be safe rather than sorry; that the hospital did not have facilities for testing breast lumps while the patient was under anaesthetic; and that she should be grateful that she did not have cancer. She subsequently suffered psychological problems attributable to the loss of her breast. It was argued that since the claimant had been told at the time that she had received the appropriate treatment, she did not know that she should not have had her breast removed until either she received an expert's report to this effect in 1990, or at the earliest in 1988 when she heard about a successful claim in a similar case. The Court of Appeal held that the claimant had sufficient knowledge to start the limitation period running in 1973. Sir Thomas Bingham MR said that knowledge that the breast had been 'unnecessarily' removed, or that something had gone wrong was irrelevant under s 14, because this would conflict with the closing words of s 14(1) that 'knowledge that any acts or omissions did or did not, as a matter of law, involve negligence, nuisance or breach of duty is irrelevant'. Though it was customary in discussing tortious liability to refer to acts and

---

[173] See, eg, *Driscoll-Varley v Parkside HA* [1991] 2 Med LR 346, and the comments of Hoffmann LJ on this case in *Broadley v Guy Clapham & Co* [1994] 4 All ER 439, 449; *Khan v Ainslie* [1993] 4 Med LR 319; *Spargo v North Essex District HA* [1997] PIQR P235, 242 *per* Brooke LJ (see the quotation at n 142 above). In *Baig v City and Hackney HA* [1994] 5 Med LR 221, 224, Rougier J commented that: 'It seems to me to be a travesty of language to hold that somebody who approaches his case in a wholly erroneous belief—however strong—as to the cause of his injury could ever have the requisite knowledge. On the contrary, he has the reverse.' In *Rowbottom v Royal Masonic Hospital* [2002] EWCA Civ 87; [2002] Lloyd's Rep Med 173, the claimant believed that complications arising from a wound infection following surgery for a hip replacement, leading eventually to amputation of his leg, were due to the failure of a drain inserted into his leg. He did not acquire knowledge that he had not been given prophylactic antibiotics until he received confirmation of this from a medical expert.

[174] [1994] 4 All ER 439, 446–447.

[175] [1994] 4 All ER 450 (CA). Leave to appeal refused: [1994] 1 WLR 1553.

omissions, his Lordship did not believe that the meaning of s 14(1)(*b*) would be any different had the reference been to 'conduct'.[176]

The claimant argued that the word 'injury' should be interpreted in a way which **7.82** distinguished between the normal or expected consequences of successful medical treatment and the consequences of faulty treatment. The man in the street would not regard himself as 'injured' by a successful operation. He would only regard himself as injured if he suffered consequences other than those normally attributed to the treatment. Beldam LJ rejected this argument because the definition of personal injuries in s 38(1), though not exhaustive, indicated that 'injury' could not be qualified by the addition of words implying its source or aetiology. Nor was there any need to import the perception of the reasonable patient.[177] However, the implication of refusing to draw a distinction between successful and unsuccessful surgery appears to be that any patient who undergoes a surgical operation is, by definition, 'injured' and knows that she has suffered injury immediately. The fact that she does not know that the surgery has gone wrong would be irrelevant to the running of the limitation period.

This conclusion is open to question. Consider, for example, a patient who has an **7.83** appendix removed. She would not consider, and reasonably so, that she had suffered any injury at the hands of the doctor. Appendectomy is a potentially life-saving procedure. The pain and suffering involved in the surgery, and the resultant scar, though clearly 'caused' by the surgeon's knife would not normally be thought of as an 'injury' when the operation is undertaken on reasonable grounds. If, however, the operation was totally unnecessary on the clinical signs, then a patient would reasonably consider that she had been damaged by having to undergo a needless operation. If the fact that the operation was unnecessary only became apparent much later, the patient only acquired knowledge that she had suffered an *injury* at that time. It is the decision to undertake the operation itself, rather than the performance of the operation (which may have been technically perfect) that is the gist or the 'essence' of her complaint.[178] However, the decision to perform the operation can only be characterised as an 'injury' if the decision was mistaken, and therefore the claimant can only acquire knowledge that she has suffered an injury when she learns that the decision was mistaken. She need not know that it was a careless or negligent mistake, but she has to know that there *was* a mistake, ie that there was an error or that 'something had gone wrong', before she can have knowledge that she has even suffered an injury.

---

[176] ibid, 456.

[177] ibid, 461. The Limitation Act 1980, s 38(1) provides that ' "personal injuries" includes any disease and any impairment of a person's physical or mental condition, and "injury" and cognate expressions shall be construed accordingly'.

[178] See, eg, *Gascoine v Ian Sheridan & Co* [1994] 5 Med LR 437, 442, where Mitchell J considered that the validity of the decision to treat was an 'act' quite independent from the 'act' constituting the conduct of the treatment.

7.84   While it is correct to say that ignorance of the law does not affect the running of the limitation period, the question of whether the claimant knew that the facts would give her a cause of action in law should not be confused with the question of the claimant being able to identify the relevant act or omission of the defendant as a cause of her injuries. Knowledge that the defendant's acts or omissions have or have not caused the claimant's injuries is knowledge about a fact, not about the law. The question is *which facts* must the claimant have knowledge of, given that s 14(1)(*b*) clearly does *not* state that it is sufficient to know that the injury was attributable merely to the defendant's *conduct*? The subsection directs attention to the specific conduct of the defendant which it is subsequently alleged by the claimant constitutes negligence, nuisance or breach of duty. The claimant need not be aware that this conduct would in law give rise to an action for damages, but she must have *some* knowledge of the relevant acts or omissions.[179] In a medical negligence action the claimant needs more than simply knowledge that the 'injury' was attributable to the treatment or operation.

7.85   This point has been made clear by the Court of Appeal in *Hallam-Eames v Merrett*[180] which was concerned with the interpretation of the analogous provision in s 14A of the Limitation Act 1980 in respect of claims for economic loss. Hoffmann LJ said that:

> If all that was necessary was that a plaintiff should have known that the damage was attributable to an act or omission of the defendant, the statute would have said so. Instead, it speaks of the damage being attributable to 'the act or omission which is alleged to constitute negligence.' In other words, the act or omission of which the plaintiff must have knowledge must be that which is causally relevant for the purposes of an allegation of negligence.

7.86   The words 'which is alleged to constitute negligence' served to identify the facts of which the claimant must have knowledge. It was not sufficient for the claimant to know merely that the relevant damage had been caused by *an* act or omission of the defendant. Commenting on *Dobbie*, Hoffmann LJ said that Mrs Dobbie had to know more than that her breast had been removed. She had to know that a healthy breast had been removed. That was the essence of what she was complaining about. Nor did this require knowledge of fault or negligence:

> The plaintiff does not have to know that he has a cause of action or that the defendant's acts can be characterised in law as negligent or as falling short of some standard of professional or other behaviour . . . He must have known the facts which can fairly be described as constituting the negligence of which he complains. It may be

---

[179]   See, eg, *Baig v City and Hackney HA* [1994] 5 Med LR 221, 224, where Rougier J commented that the words of s 14(1)(b) admitted of no interpretation other than that the knowledge required is 'knowledge, at any rate in general outline, of just what it was that the defendant had either done or failed to do which had caused the damage'.

[180]   [1996] 7 Med LR 122, 125.

that knowledge of such facts will also serve to bring home to him the fact that the defendant has been negligent or at fault. But that in itself is not a reason for saying that he need not have known them.[181]

Many of the cases, including several Court of Appeal decisions, refer to a require- **7.87** ment of knowledge of some error relating to safety by the defendant before s 14(1)(b) is satisfied.[182] In *Nash v Eli Lilly & Co*[183] the Court of Appeal accepted that the relevant acts or omissions of the defendants consisted of exposing the claimants to a drug which was *unsafe*. Knowledge that their symptoms were simply attributable to taking a drug could not constitute knowledge by the claimants of any relevant act or omission on the part of the defendant manufacturers. The reference to 'safety' clearly requires that the claimant know more than simply that the defendant's *conduct* caused the injury. It is submitted that she must either know, or have constructive knowledge, that 'something has gone wrong' sufficiently to consider investigating the circumstances.[184]

In any event, where the claimant is informed at the time by the medical staff in- **7.88** volved that nothing has gone wrong, and that her treatment was consistent with good medical practice, she does not know that she has suffered an injury because there is no basis for challenging either the performance of the treatment itself or the decision to proceed with the treatment. When Mrs Dobbie was informed that she was lucky to be alive, she was not simply being advised that the surgery to remove her breast had been technically competent, she was being advised that the decision to remove her breast was not an error or a mistake. On that information, she did not know that she had suffered an injury.[185]

Where the alleged negligence consists of an omission to treat, the claimant must **7.89** know more than mere fact that he has not been treated. In *Smith v West Lancashire*

---

[181] ibid, 126. See also *Ostick v Wandsworth HA* [1995] 6 Med LR 338 where it was held that it was not sufficient that the claimant knew she had received an injury that had not healed. It was necessary to know that there was a causal link between the treatment or lack of treatment and the subsequent physical disability, ie the fact that the injury had not healed.

[182] *Davis v Ministry of Defence* The Times, 7 August 1985 (CA); *Wilkinson v Ancliff (BLT) Ltd* [1986] 3 All ER 427, 438 (CA); *Farmer v National Coal Board*, The Times, 27 April 1985 (CA).

[183] [1993] 1 WLR 782, 799.

[184] In *Broadley v Guy Clapham & Co* [1994] 4 All ER 439, 446, for example, Balcombe LJ accepted that 'broad knowledge' was required, and that this involved knowledge 'that something went wrong'.

[185] cf *Scuriaga v Powell* (1979) 123 SJ 406; aff'd (1980, CA), where following an unsuccessful abortion on the claimant, the defendant lied to the claimant, telling her that the operation had failed because she had a physical defect. Time did not begin to run until the claimant discovered that the failure was due to the doctor's conduct of the operation. It is apparent that in many of these cases claimants have been given reassurances ranging from statements that nothing further could have been done, implying that the claimant's problem is attributable to the underlying medical condition rather than anything done or omitted by the medical staff, to outright lies. It is unfortunate that claimants should then be caught by the limitation period, having placed reliance on the professional advice of the very defendants that they are now seeking to sue.

HA[186] the claimant had been told that the initial treatment had not worked and that there was nothing further that could be done. He presumed that he had received proper treatment, but in fact the operation had been performed too late to achieve full recovery. Russell LJ said that the alleged negligence consisted of the omission to operate promptly, together with the failure properly to diagnose his condition. The reality was that the claimant did not know that there had been an omission to operate at all until he received advice to that effect from his own expert witness:

> True, he knew that he had not had an operation on or about November 12, 1981, but that knowledge cannot, in my judgment, be knowledge of an omission 'which is alleged to constitute negligence'. One cannot know of an omission without knowing what it is that is omitted. In this case, that was an operation to reduce the fracture dislocations, as opposed to conservative treatment. Simply to tell the plaintiff that the first course of treatment had not worked, is not the same as imbuing the plaintiff with the knowledge of an omission to operate.[187]

7.90   Similarly, in *Bates v Leicester HA*[188] it was held that the claimant's knowledge that his disability was caused by the duration of his mother's labour when he was born was not sufficient to give him knowledge of the omission alleged to constitute negligence, ie the doctors' failure to intervene in a protracted labour. The claimant had to know that the failure to intervene was avoidable, as opposed to knowing that the failure to intervene was negligent, which is irrelevant. Moreover, in determining a claimant's knowledge the court must take into account any advice she has received, because 'until someone or some incident directly challenges the advice, you continue reasonably to assume it was correct'.[189]

7.91   It is also clear that in cases where the claimant mistakenly believed that her injuries were attributable to a particular aspect of her treatment but she subsequently discovered that the injuries were caused by a different aspect of treatment, the claimant does not have knowledge as long as she is 'barking up the wrong tree'.[190] These cases indicate that knowledge that an injury was attributable simply to 'the treatment' or 'the defendant's conduct' is not sufficient.

---

[186]   [1995] PIQR P514.

[187]   ibid, 517. See also *Parry v Clwyd HA* [1997] 8 Med LR 243; *Hind v York HA* [1997] 8 Med LR 377. In *James v East Dorset HA* (1999) 59 BMLR 196 the Court of Appeal held that a patient whose condition had deteriorated following an operation and who inferred that it had not been a success, nonetheless did not acquire knowledge within s 14 when there was nothing to alert him to the fact that he had suffered an injury during the operation. A claimant must know that he has suffered an injury before he can have knowledge that it was a significant injury. Sedley LJ commented, at 201, that: 'I do not believe that in enacting s 14 Parliament intended to reward those alert to assume that every misfortune is someone else's fault and to place at a disadvantage those who do not assume the worst when there is nothing to alert them to it.'

[188]   [1998] Lloyd's Rep Med 93.

[189]   *Oakes v Hopcroft* [2000] Lloyd's Rep Med 394, at [33] *per* Lord Woolf CJ. Clarke LJ commented, at [49]: 'It is not easy to identify what a claimant must know about an omission in order to have knowledge that her loss is capable of being attributed to it.'

[190]   See the cases cited in n 173 above.

(c) Defendant's Identity

Identifying the defendant is not normally a problem in actions for medical negli- **7.92**
gence, although the claimant may not know which individual in a team caused the
injury. However, where the claimant knows that the injuries were caused by one
or other of two defendants, but not both, and does not know which defendant is
responsible, the claimant would be expected to sue both in the alternative.[191] This
will only be relevant in cases of private medical treatment or in actions against
GPs, since in cases of hospital treatment in the NHS, the claimant will sue the
NHS Trust or the health authority which will be vicariously liable for the conduct
of all of its staff.

(d) Vicarious Liability

Section 14(1)(d) refers to the circumstances required to establish an employer's **7.93**
vicarious liability for the torts of employees committed in the course of employment, though the wording is wide enough to cover liability for the conduct of
independent contractors where the defendant is under a relevant 'non-delegable'
duty. The precise identity of the employee is irrelevant if the claimant is aware that
the damage was caused by one or more of the defendant's employees acting in the
course of employment.[192] The claimant's ignorance that on the facts the defendant
would be held vicariously liable in law is irrelevant.

(iii) Constructive Knowledge

A person's knowledge includes constructive knowledge, which by virtue of s 14(3) **7.94**
means:

> knowledge which he might reasonably have been expected to acquire—
> (a) from facts observable or ascertainable by him; or
> (b) from facts ascertainable by him with the help of medical or other appropriate
> expert advice which it is reasonable for him to seek;
> but a person shall not be fixed under this subsection with knowledge of a fact ascer-
> tainable only with the help of expert advice so long as he has taken all reasonable
> steps to obtain (and, where appropriate, to act on) that advice.

This is a combined subjective/objective test. In *Nash v Eli Lilly & Co*[193] the Court
of Appeal said that the claimant is fixed with knowledge which *he* might reasonably have been expected to acquire from facts observable or ascertainable by *him*,

---

[191] *Halford v Brookes* [1991] 3 All ER 559, 574, *per* Lord Donaldson MR.
[192] Where the defendant is responsible in law for all the staff who played some role in the
claimant's treatment, it is unnecessary for the claimant to identify the particular employee who was
at fault: *Cassidy v Ministry of Health* [1951] 2 KB 343.
[193] [1993] 1 WLR 782, 799 (CA); *Colegrove v Smyth* [1994] 5 Med LR 111, 114.

but in *Forbes v Wandsworth HA*[194] the Court of Appeal had some difficulty in seeing how the individual character and intelligence of the claimant could be relevant to the question of constructive knowledge (doubting the view expressed by Purchas LJ in *Nash*). Stuart-Smith LJ said that two alternative courses of conduct may both be perfectly reasonable. Accepting the situation, and saying 'It was just one of those things. The doctors probably did their best' may be reasonable, just as taking a second opinion as to whether there was any lack of care may be reasonable. But a claimant who takes the first option is making a choice. A reasonable man in the claimant's position, who knew that the operation had been unsuccessful, and that he had suffered a major injury which would seriously affect his enjoyment of life in the future (claimant had had his leg amputated following heart bypass surgery) would take advice reasonably promptly (within 12 to 18 months after he came out of hospital). The fact that a claimant was more trusting, incurious, indolent, resigned or uncomplaining by nature was not a relevant characteristic, since this undermined an objective approach. The problem with this is that it may be very difficult for even a reasonable person to know whether he is being 'too trusting', particularly if there is nothing to put him on notice that he should make enquiry. For example, if a patient is informed after surgery that the injury he sustained in the course of the operation was an inherent risk of the treatment, is he entitled to accept that statement at face value? At what point must the patient question what he is told in order to verify whether his trust is misplaced?[195]

7.95 In *O'Driscoll v Dudley HA*[196] Otton LJ commented that it was not easy to reconcile *Nash* and *Forbes* on the question of the subjective/objective approach, and in *Smith v Leicester HA*[197] the Court of Appeal regarded *Nash* and *Forbes* as conflicting decisions, concluding that the claimant's individual characteristics, which might distinguish her from the reasonable woman, should be disregarded. Constructive knowledge involved an objective test which does not take account of the claimant's individual characteristics (such as her forbearance, or unwillingness to criticise) but does take account of her individual circumstances, such as what she has been told by medical staff. The claimant in *Smith* was told and accepted that the cyst which rendered her tetraplegic was congenital, and that the operation in question had saved her life. She had no reason to suppose that the earlier diagnoses were wrong. In the case of an omission what the claimant has to know is that there was a lost opportunity to prevent the injury. It was not correct to treat *Forbes* as suggesting that every time a patient has an operation and, following the

---

[194] [1996] 4 All ER 881. See also *Slevin v Southampton and South West Hampshire HA* [1997] 8 Med LR 175, following *Forbes*.
[195] See the comment of Lord Woolf CJ in *Oakes v Hopcroft* [2000] Lloyd's Rep Med 394 at [33]: 'until someone or some incident directly challenges the advice, you continue reasonably to assume it was correct.'
[196] [1998] Lloyd's Rep Med 210, 217.
[197] [1998] Lloyd's Rep Med 77.

operation is significantly disabled, the patient has some 12 to 18 months to decide consciously or unconsciously whether to investigate a possible claim against those who operated. The question was simply whether it was reasonable for the claimant to seek advice, and whether it was reasonable depended on the facts and circumstances of each case, but excluding the character traits of the individual claimant.[198] Thus, although the apparent conflict between *Forbes* and *Nash* on the subjective/objective test for constructive knowledge has not been expressly resolved, the compromise position is that 'the claimant's situation is obviously relevant but other more personal characteristics are not'.[199]

A failure to seek legal advice will give rise to constructive knowledge of the facts **7.96** which would have been discovered after the date at which it would have been reasonable to seek such advice;[200] but where the question is whether it was reasonable for the claimant to seek expert advice, his personal circumstances should be taken into account. Thus, it may well be reasonable for a claimant who is seriously ill or dying not to seek legal advice,[201] though this is a question of degree.[202] Similarly, it may be reasonable for a claimant to delay seeking legal advice where she was still receiving treatment and did not wish to sour relations with the doctors who were treating her.[203] Some account will be taken of the limited resources available to the claimant by way of advice, where, for example, his solicitors could only seek expert advice to the extent that they were authorised to do so by the Legal Aid Board.[204] Constructive knowledge does not include the knowledge of a child's

---

[198] ibid, 87.

[199] *Adams v Bracknell Forest Borough Council* [2003] EWCA Civ 706 at [27] *per* Tuckey LJ. In *Fenech v East London and City HA* [2000] Lloyd's Rep Med 35 (CA), Simon Brown LJ said, at 38, that, without resolving the difference of view as to whether s 14(3) is objective or subjective, in taking into account the circumstances and character of the claimant 'some degree of objectivity at least must be required in determining when it is reasonable for someone to seek advice—otherwise the provision could never apply save only where a person acts out of character'.

[200] *Hills v Potter* [1983] 3 All ER 716, 728.

[201] *Newton v Cammell Laird & Co (Shipbuilders and Engineers) Ltd* [1969] 1 All ER 708; *Davis v City and Hackney HA* [1991] 2 Med LR 366; *Driscoll-Varley v Parkside HA* [1991] 2 Med LR 346, 357; *Bates v Leicester HA* [1998] Lloyd's Rep Med 93 where the claimant had significant communication difficulties and relied heavily on his mother who was forcefully dismissive of his chances of a claim and therefore he acted reasonably in not pursuing the matter sooner.

[202] In *Forbes v Wandsworth HA* [1996] 4 All ER 881 the Court of Appeal took the view that where the claimant had had his leg amputated following heart bypass surgery he should have sought expert medical advice some 12 to 18 months after he came out of hospital, by which time he would have had time to overcome his shock at losing his leg and take stock of his disability and its consequences.

[203] *Ostick v Wandsworth HA* [1995] 6 Med LR 338.

[204] *Khan v Ainslie* [1993] 4 Med LR 319. On the other hand, in *Skitt v Khan and Wakefield HA* [1997] 8 Med LR 105 the Court of Appeal held that though lack of funds to obtain an expert's report could be a factor, that has to be weighed against the seriousness of the injury and its consequences for the claimant in deciding whether objectively it was reasonable to seek expert medical advice. On the facts it was understandable that the claimant did not seek such advice, but it was not reasonable.

parents during the child's minority.[205] Moreover, an ordinary person of average intelligence and average understanding of medical matters is not expected to infer from the fact that a child is born with cerebral palsy that there was a real possibility that an act or omission of the medical staff was the cause of the injury.[206]

7.97 The proviso to s 14(3) prevents a claimant from being fixed with constructive knowledge where an expert has failed to discover or disclose a relevant fact that ought to have been revealed,[207] but it applies only to facts which are 'ascertainable only with the help of expert advice'. Where the claimant himself could have discovered the information, then he is fixed with any knowledge that the expert acting on his behalf ought to have acquired.[208] Erroneous advice about the law is irrelevant and does not prevent time running.[209] Where the legal advice consists of a failure to discover relevant facts, or a failure to suggest a line of enquiry that would have revealed the facts, then in theory the proviso to s 14(3) applies, although in *Leadbitter v Hodge Finance Ltd*[210] a very narrow view was taken of the facts which are ascertainable only with the help of expert advice. It is also possible that s 14(3)(b) does not apply to *any* form of legal advice, since it has been doubted whether a party's solicitor is an 'expert' within the meaning of the subsection, which is directed to experts in the sense of expert witnesses.[211] This would mean that a claimant is not constructively fixed with the knowledge of his solicitor by virtue of s 14(3), but under the general law of agency it may be that a

---

[205] *Parry v Clwyd HA* [1997] 8 Med LR 243; *Appleby v Walsall HA* [1999] Lloyd's Rep Med 154; cf *O'Driscoll v Dudley HA* [1998] Lloyd's Rep Med 210, 220, where Sir Christopher Slade treated the parents' actual knowledge as imputed to the child, so that her actual knowledge commenced at age 18.

[206] ibid.

[207] See, eg, *Marston v British Railways Board* [1976] ICR 124; *Stephen v Riverside HA* [1990] 1 Med LR 261; *Davis v Ministry of Defence*, The Times, 7 August 1985 (CA).

[208] *Leadbitter v Hodge Finance Ltd* [1982] 2 All ER 167, 174–175; *Halford v Brookes* [1991] 3 All ER 559, 565; including any knowledge about the facts that his solicitors ought to have acquired: *Henderson v Temple Pier Co Ltd* [1998] 1 WLR 1540.

[209] Limitation Act 1980, s 14(1); *Farmer v National Coal Board*, The Times, 27 April 1985 (CA). See also *Jones v Liverpool HA* [1996] PIQR P251, 266 where Glidewell LJ said that: 'if a person has been advised by one consultant, who considers on the information put before him that the plaintiff probably does not have a cause of action, and years later the plaintiff is advised by another consultant that, upon precisely the same facts, he has a possible cause of action, he cannot thereafter claim that he did not gain knowledge for the purposes of ss 11 and 14 . . . until he received the later opinion.' With respect, this rather assumes that it is the function of medical experts to advise about the law, which, clearly, it is not. If the first expert advised that in his opinion there was no causal connection between the relevant acts or omissions and the claimant's injury, then the advice concerns a fact, notwithstanding that the conclusion would also be that no claim in law would be sustainable because the injury could not be attributed to the defendant's acts or omissions. If this was the only information that the claimant had then he would only acquire the relevant knowledge when informed by the second expert that there was a causal connection.

[210] [1982] 2 All ER 167, 174–175.

[211] *Fowell v National Coal Board*, The Times, 28 May 1986 (CA); *Khan v Ainslie* [1993] 4 Med LR 319, 325.

claimant is fixed with the actual, and even the constructive, knowledge of his so-licitor.[212] Of course, it must be reasonable to attribute knowledge to the solicitor. In *Hepworth v Kerr*[213] the claimant suffered paraplegia following an operation under general anaesthetic and, despite a suggestion in the medical notes that his condition might have been attributable to the operation, he was assured on several occasions by the neurosurgeon who subsequently treated him for the paralysis that the operation had not caused his condition. A report by the neurosurgeon to the claimant's solicitors came to the same conclusion. The defendants argued that the claimant had constructive knowledge because a competent solicitor should have realised that the neurosurgeon was the wrong expert and that he had not in-dicated that he had read the hospital medical notes. This argument was rejected by Latham J. To require the claimant or his solicitor to question whether the ex-pert had obtained sufficient information from the medical notes or to question whether or not he was the appropriate expert was 'asking for a startling degree of scepticism'. Some solicitors might have been sceptical, but that did not mean that it was something that any reasonably competent solicitor would have done.

(iv) Section 33 Discretion

Where the primary three-year limitation period has expired, the claimant may seek to persuade the court to exercise its discretion under s 33.[214] The court's dis-cretion is unfettered,[215] except that a claimant who issued a claim form within the primary limitation period but did not proceed with the action and then issued a second claim form outside the limitation period, cannot rely on this section. In *Walkley v Precision Forgings Ltd*[216] the House of Lords held that s 33(1) directs the court to have regard to the degree to which the operation of the primary limita-tion period has prejudiced the claimant, but where the claimant has issued a claim form in time and then for some reason the action has not been pursued, he has not been prejudiced by the effect of ss 11 or 12 but by his own dilatoriness. This rule

7.98

---

[212] *Simpson v Norwest Holst Southern Ltd* [1980] 2 All ER 471, 476. See *Fowell v National Coal Board*, The Times, 28 May 1986, where Parker LJ specifically left this point open. See further the discussion by Hidden J in *Nash v Eli Lilly & Co* [1991] 2 Med LR 169; *Colegrove v Smyth* [1994] 5 Med L Rev 111; *Khan v Ainslie* [1993] 4 Med LR 319, 325. The Court of Appeal in *Nash v Eli Lilly & Co* [1993] 1 WLR 782, 800 could see no reason to depart from Hidden J's general approach to this issue. Cf the position under s 33, when exercising the discretion there is no rule that anything done by the lawyers must be visited on the client: *Das v Ganju* [1999] PIQR P260, 268 (CA); *Corbin v Penfold Metallising Company Ltd* [2000] Lloyd's Rep Med 247, 251 (CA); *Steeds v Peverel Management Services Ltd* [2001] EWCA Civ 419; The Times, 16 May 2001 (CA).
[213] [1995] 6 Med LR 135.
[214] The burden of proving that it is equitable to allow the action to proceed is the claimant's: *Thompson v Brown Construction (Ebbw Vale) Ltd* [1981] 2 All ER 296, 303.
[215] *Firman v Ellis* [1978] QB 886; *Thompson v Brown Construction (Ebbw Vale) Ltd* [1981] 2 All ER 296; *Donovan v Gwentoys Ltd* [1990] 1 All ER 1018, 1023, *per* Lord Griffiths.
[216] [1979] 1 WLR 606.

applies whatever the reason for the claimant not proceeding with the first action: whether it is because he or his solicitors failed to serve the claim form in time; or because the action was dismissed for want of prosecution; or, for good or bad reasons, the action was discontinued by the claimant.[217] On the other hand, *Walkley* will not apply where the claimant has been induced to discontinue the action by a misrepresentation or other improper conduct by the defendant. The defendant is then estopped from relying on ss 11 or 12. This exception will be construed narrowly, however, and does not arise merely from an admission of liability and the making of an interim payment by the defendant.[218]

7.99 Where the first claim form, although issued in time, is technically invalid, a second claim form issued outside the three-year period is not caught by *Walkley* and the claimant can invoke the court's discretion;[219] nor does *Walkley* apply where the second claim is against a different defendant in respect of a different cause of action, even if based on essentially the same facts.[220] Finally, if it can be said that the claimant did not have sufficient knowledge to start the limitation period under s 14, even though an earlier protective claim form has been issued, then *Walkley* is irrelevant, since the 'second' claim form will be within the *primary* limitation period.[221]

7.100 Under s 33(1) the court may direct that the primary limitation period shall not apply if it would be equitable to allow the action to proceed, having regard to the degree to which (i) ss 11, 11A or 12 prejudice the claimant, and (ii) the decision to allow the action to proceed would prejudice the defendant.[222] The court has to balance the degree of prejudice to the claimant caused by the operation of the primary limitation period against the prejudice to the defendant if the action were to

---

[217] *Chappell v Cooper* [1980] 2 All ER 463; *Forward v Hendricks* [1997] 2 All ER 397.

[218] *Deerness v John Keeble & Son Ltd* [1983] 2 Lloyd's Rep 260; *Forward v Hendricks* [1997] 2 All ER 397.

[219] *White v Glass,* The Times, 18 February 1989 (CA); *Wilson v Banner Scaffolding Ltd,* The Times, 22 June 1982; *Re Workvale Ltd (No 2)* [1992] 2 All ER 627 (CA); *McEvoy v AA Welding and Fabrication Ltd* [1998] PIQR P226 (CA)—defendants were in liquidation and the claimant had not obtained the appropriate leave to proceed against a party in liquidation; *Piggott v Aulton* [2003] EWCA Civ 24; [2003] PIQR P371—service of proceedings on the estate of a deceased person where no personal representative had been appointed, without the leave of the court, was invalid.

[220] *Shapland v Palmer* [1999] 1 WLR 2068 (CA)—first action against D's employers, as vicariously liable for D's negligence; second action against D personally.

[221] This occurred in both *Davis v Ministry of Defence,* The Times, 7 August 1985, and *Stephen v Riverside HA* [1990] 1 Med LR 261. In *Nash v Eli Lilly & Co* [1993] 1 WLR 782, 795–796, however, the Court of Appeal queried whether it could be said that a claimant who has previously taken proceedings did not have relevant knowledge.

[222] The word 'equitable' is not a term of art, it is simply another way of saying 'fair and just' as between the parties: *Ward v Foss,* The Times, 29 November 1993 (CA), *per* Hobhouse LJ. Where the claimant has been untruthful and sought to mislead the court on key issues, it is unlikely that the court will consider it equitable to disapply the limitation period: *Long v Tolchard* [2001] PIQR P18 (CA).

be allowed to proceed. The stronger the claimant's case is on the merits, the greater the prejudice to him, and conversely, the weaker his case, the less he is prejudiced.[223] On the other hand, if the defendant has a good case on the merits, there is probably less prejudice to him in allowing the action to proceed, although in *Thompson v Brown Construction (Ebbw Vale) Ltd*[224] Lord Diplock said that it was still highly prejudicial to a defendant to allow the action to proceed even where he has a good defence on the merits. The loss of the limitation defence *as such* is not the prejudice to the defendant that has to be taken into account, but rather the effect of the delay on the defendant's ability to defend.[225] This must be balanced against the prejudice to the claimant of being barred from pursuing the action.[226]

When considering the degree of prejudice to the parties the court is required by s 33(3) to have regard to all the circumstances of the case, and in particular to: **7.101**

(a) the length of and reasons for the delay on the part of the claimant;
(b) the extent to which, having regard to the delay, the evidence . . . is likely to be less cogent . . .;
(c) the conduct of the defendant after the cause of action arose, including the extent (if any) to which he responded to requests reasonably made by the claimant for information or inspection for the purpose of ascertaining facts which were or might be relevant to the claimant's cause of action against the defendant;
(d) the duration of any disability of the claimant arising after the date of the accrual of the cause of action;
(e) the extent to which the claimant acted promptly and reasonably once he knew whether or not the act or omission of the defendant, to which the injury was attributable, might be capable at that time of giving rise to an action for damages;
(f) the steps, if any, taken by the claimant to obtain medical, legal or other expert advice and the nature of any such advice he may have received.

---

[223] *Dale v British Coal Corporation* [1992] PIQR 373, 380, *per* Stuart-Smith LJ (CA); *Forbes v Wandsworth HA* [1996] 4 All ER 881, 894–895.
[224] [1981] 2 All ER 296, 301.
[225] *Hartley v Birmingham City District Council* [1992] 2 All ER 213, 224 *per* Parker LJ; *Ward v Foss*, The Times, 29 November 1993 (CA) *per* Hobhouse LJ. See also *McEvoy v AA Welding and Fabrication Ltd* [1998] PIQR P226, 273 where Pill LJ commented that: 'An important feature of the present case is *the lack of prejudice to the defendants* by reason of the fact that they have, subject to their limitation defence, admitted liability' (emphasis added). In *Shapland v Palmer* [1999] 1 WLR 2068 (CA), the only prejudice to the defendant was being deprived of the limitation defence, and accordingly the Court exercised the discretion in the claimant's favour. It cannot always be said that where the ability of a defendant to defend on the merits has not been affected by the delay the defendant suffers no prejudice in having to defend a weak case, since disapplying the primary limitation period will put the defendants to the expense of defending the action. Allowing the action to proceed may simply enable a dilatory claimant to claim from the defendants a sum in settlement which reflects the risk in costs to the defendants rather than the fair value of the claim: *Nash v Eli Lilly & Co* [1993] 1 WLR 782, 804, 808 (CA).
[226] *Ward v Foss*, The Times, 29 November 1993 (CA) *per* Hobhouse LJ.

The court should consider *all* the circumstances of the case, not simply the issues identified by s 33(3).[227] Provided this has been done, the Court of Appeal will be reluctant to interfere with the trial judge's exercise of discretion.[228]

(a) Length of and Reasons for Delay

7.102 'Delay' in s 33(3)(a) and (b) refers to the period between the expiry of the primary limitation period and the issue of the claim form, not the period between the accrual of the action or the claimant's 'knowledge' and the issue of the claim form.[229] However, in weighing the degree of prejudice to the defendant, the court is entitled to take into account the whole period of delay, including that within the primary limitation period, as part of all the circumstances of the case.[230] In these circumstances it is the delay between the commencement of the limitation period and notification to the defendant of the claim, rather than the issue of the claim form, that is significant, the object being to bar 'thoroughly stale claims'. Therefore, there is a distinction between cases where the defendant was notified of the claim fairly promptly, and so had an opportunity to give it full consideration, but the limitation period has expired through an oversight by the claimant's solicitors,[231] and cases where the defendant first heard of the claim some years after the accident.[232]

7.103 A short delay probably causes little prejudice to the defendant,[233] indeed, a very short delay causes no prejudice at all, particularly where the defendant was notified about the claim at an early stage,[234] whereas a delay of five or six years raises a rebuttable presumption of prejudice.[235] The length of the delay is probably of less significance than the reasons for the delay and the effect on the evidence. Reasons

---

[227] *Taylor v Taylor*, The Times, 14 April 1984 (CA); *Donovan v Gwentoys Ltd* [1990] 1 All ER 1018 (HL).

[228] *Conry v Simpson* [1983] 3 All ER 369; *Bradley v Hanseatic Shipping Co Ltd* [1986] 2 Lloyd's Rep 34, 38. The prejudice to each side may be 'obvious' and may not have to be expressly considered: *Yates v Thakeham Tiles Ltd* [1995] PIQR P135, 139, *per* Nourse LJ (CA).

[229] *Thompson v Brown Construction (Ebbw Vale) Ltd* [1981] 2 All ER 296, 301; *Eastman v London Country Bus Services Ltd*, The Times, 23 November 1985 (CA).

[230] *Donovan v Gwentoys Ltd* [1990] 1 All ER 1018, 1024.

[231] *Thompson v Brown Construction (Ebbw Vale) Ltd* [1981] 2 All ER 296; see also *Simpson v Norwest Holst Southern Ltd* [1980] 2 All ER 471, 478.

[232] *Donovan v Gwentoys Ltd* [1990] 1 All ER 1018, 1024, *per* Lord Griffiths; *Dale v British Coal Corporation* [1992] PIQR P373, 385 (CA).

[233] *Firman v Ellis* [1978] QB 886; *Simpson v Norwest Holst Southern Ltd* [1980] 2 All ER 471, 478.

[234] *Hartley v Birmingham City District Council* [1992] 2 All ER 213; *Hendy v Milton Keynes HA* [1992] 3 Med LR 114.

[235] *Buck v English Electric Co Ltd* [1977] 1 WLR 806; *Pilmore v Northern Trawlers Ltd* [1986] 1 Lloyd's Rep 552. Though note that the Court of Appeal has stated that a *presumption* of prejudice is not justified because it would cut down the wide discretion of s 33: *KR v Bryn Alyn Community (Holdings) Ltd (in liquidation)* [2003] EWCA Civ 85, [2003] 1 FCR 385 at [79]. But as a general proposition, the longer the delay the more likely it is that the balance of prejudice will swing against disapplying the primary limitation period: ibid at [80].

for the delay will vary considerably, and the claimant's subjective beliefs are taken into account.[236] The claimant may have been unaware of his legal rights,[237] or the injury may not have appeared so serious at first,[238] or he may have felt that he was 'sponging' if he sued and may have wanted to maintain good relations with the defendant,[239] or the claimant may have been in a debilitated physical and mental state throughout the relevant period,[240] or the defendant may have contributed to the delay by withholding information from the claimant.[241] Generally, where the claimant's conduct has not been personally blameworthy, this will carry considerable weight in persuading the court to exercise the discretion in his favour.[242]

(b) Cogency of the Evidence

The effect of the delay on the cogency of the evidence will be very significant. If documents have been destroyed or witnesses have disappeared, this is a different situation from cases where there is little real dispute about the facts, since the defendant's ability to defend the case has clearly been prejudiced.[243] Cases which are based on allegations about failures in systems of work are likely to be better documented than one-off accidents.[244] Cases of medical negligence should, in theory, be reasonably well documented in the medical records,[245] although this is not always the case.[246]

7.104

---

[236] *Buck v English Electric Co Ltd* [1977] 1 WLR 806; *McCafferty v Metropolitan Police District Receiver* [1977] 1 WLR 1073; *Coad v Cornwall and Isles of Scilly HA* [1997] 8 Med LR 154.

[237] *Brooks v Coates (UK) Ltd* [1984] 1 All ER 702, 713; *Coad v Cornwall and Isles of Scilly HA* [1997] 8 Med LR 154.

[238] *McCafferty v Metropolitan Police District Receiver* [1977] 1 WLR 1073.

[239] *Buck v English Electric Co Ltd* [1977] 1 WLR 806; *McCafferty v Metropolitan Police District Receiver* [1977] 1 WLR 1073. A patient's natural reluctance to upset the doctor–patient relationship by engaging in litigation is relevant here.

[240] *Mills v Dyer-Fare* (1987, QBD); *Birnie v Oxfordshire HA* (1982) 2 *The Lancet* 281 (QBD); *Pearse v Barnet HA* [1998] PIQR P39.

[241] *Drury v Grimsby HA* [1997] 8 Med LR 38.

[242] *Brooks v Coates (UK) Ltd* [1984] 1 All ER 702; *Bates v Leicester HA* [1998] Lloyd's Rep Med 93, 102.

[243] *Dale v British Coal Corporation* [1992] PIQR P373, 385 (CA); *Hattam v National Coal Board* (1978) 122 SJ 777; cf *Brooks v Coates (UK) Ltd* [1984] 1 All ER 702, 713–714.

[244] *Cotton v General Electric Co Ltd* (1979) 129 NLJ 73; *Pilmore v Northern Trawlers Ltd* [1986] 1 Lloyd's Rep 552; *Buck v English Electric Co Ltd* [1977] 1 WLR 806.

[245] *Bentley v Bristol and Western HA* [1991] 2 Med LR 359; *Farthing v North East Essex HA* [1998] Lloyd's Rep Med 37 (CA); *Smith v Leicester HA* [1998] Lloyd's Rep Med 77 (CA), where the case on liability turned almost entirely on X-rays taken in 1954 and 1955 which did not come to light until 1995. In *Pearse v Barnet HA* [1998] PIQR P39 it was held that there was no prejudice to the defendants from a delay between 1991 and 1994, in dealing with a case based on events in 1970 which would inevitably turn on the medical records (which were virtually complete). Where the defendants have had to investigate and prepare to meet another case on liability arising out of the same facts the cogency of the evidence may not be affected by the delay: *Bowers v Harrow HA* [1995] 6 Med LR 16.

[246] In *Forbes v Wandsworth HA* [1996] 4 All ER 881 the Court of Appeal declined to exercise the discretion under s 33 in the claimant's favour having regard to the prejudice to the defendants after

(c) Conduct of the Defendant

7.105 Section 33(3)(*c*) refers to the extent to which the defendant responded to reasonable requests for information or inspection for the purpose of ascertaining facts which were or might be relevant to the claimant's cause of action. A potential defendant does not have a duty to volunteer information but he should not obstruct the claimant in obtaining information.[247] This includes the conduct of the defendant's solicitors and his insurers. The defendant's conduct is relevant even where he has made an honest mistake in giving misleading information.[248]

(d) Duration of the Disability

7.106 If the claimant is under a disability at the date at which the cause of action accrued, the commencement of the limitation period is postponed until he ceases to be under a disability,[249] but supervening disability does not stop time running. It will be taken into account, however, in the exercise of the discretion. Since minority can never supervene, s 33(3)(d) applies to supervening mental incapacity. The claimant's physical disabilities can be considered under s 33(3)(a), as part of the reasons for the delay, or as part of 'all the circumstances of the case'.[250]

(e) Extent to Which Claimant Acted Promptly

7.107 If the claimant has acted promptly and reasonably once he became aware of the cause of action, it is not to be counted against him that his lawyers have been dilatory and allowed the primary limitation period to expire.[251] In *Yates v Thakeham*

---

a long delay, caused by an inability now to locate medical records and witnesses, fading memories, the difficulty that experts would have in dealing with the appropriate standards of practice of 14 years earlier, and the fact that the claimant's case was supported by scanty evidence and had only modest prospects of success; cf *Hammond v West Lancashire HA* [1998] Lloyd's Rep Med 146 where the defendants had destroyed the claimant's X-rays because they did not consider them to be part of the patient's medical record, and claimed that they suffered prejudice as a result. The Court of Appeal considered that in these circumstances the prejudice, if anything, was to the claimant and upheld the judge's decision to disapply the limitation period.

[247] *Thompson v Brown Construction (Ebbw Vale) Ltd* [1981] 2 All ER 296, 302. A serious delay in providing the claimant's medical records may be a relevant consideration: *Mills v Dyer-Fare* (1987, QBD); *Atkinson v Oxfordshire HA* [1993] 4 Med LR 18 (QBD), where a failure to tell the claimant or his mother what had happened during the course of an operation meant that to a large extent the delay was of the defendants' own making.

[248] *Marston v British Railways Board* [1976] ICR 124.

[249] Limitation Act 1980, s 28. The word 'disability' in s 33 has the same meaning as in s 28, ie as defined in s 38 (see para 7.112 below). It does not include physical disability: *Yates v Thakeham Tiles Ltd* [1995] PIQR P135 (CA); *Thomas v Plaistow* [1997] PIQR P540 (CA).

[250] *Yates v Thakeham Tiles Ltd* [1995] PIQR P135 (CA); *Pearse v Barnet HA* [1998] PIQR P39.

[251] *Thompson v Brown Construction (Ebbw Vale) Ltd* [1981] 2 All ER 296, 303; *Das v Ganju* [1999] PIQR P260 (CA); *Corbin v Penfold Metallising Company Ltd* [2000] Lloyd's Rep Med 247, 251 (CA); *Steeds v Peverel Management Services Ltd* [2001] EWCA Civ 419, The Times, 16 May 2001 (CA); s 33(3)(e) is concerned only with the conduct of the claimant, not his advisers: *Davis v Jacobs and Camden and Islington HA and Novartis Pharmaceuticals (UK) Ltd* [1999] Lloyd's Rep Med 72, 86, *per* Brooke LJ.

Tiles Ltd[252] the claimant consulted solicitors after the expiry of the primary limitation period, and the solicitors did not notify the defendants of a potential claim until a year later. The Court of Appeal held that this was proper where the solicitors were obtaining all the relevant information to support the claim, such as advice from counsel, and obtaining legal aid.

(f) Steps Taken to Obtain Expert Advice

This includes legal advice and whether it was favourable or unfavourable.[253] Thus, **7.108** while erroneous legal advice will not prevent time running under the three-year limitation period, it is relevant under s 33.

(g) Other Factors

The availability of an alternative remedy (for example against the claimant's neg- **7.109** ligent solicitors) is a 'highly relevant consideration', but it is not conclusive. Even where the claimant would have a cast-iron case against his solicitors, he will suffer some prejudice in having to find and instruct new solicitors, additional delay, and a possible personal liability for costs up to the date of the court's refusal of the application.[254] Where there is any real dispute about the solicitors' liability in negligence, then the chances of the claimant having an alternative remedy should be largely disregarded.[255] It is legitimate to take into account the insurance position of both defendant and claimant, as part of all the circumstances of the case,[256] but the court will not apply different principles to multi-party litigation from the principles applied to ordinary, single claimant actions when exercising the discretion. The merits of each case must be considered individually.[257] The financial consequences to the defendant of the delay itself are a relevant consideration (as opposed to the mere fact that removal of the limitation defence may result in the defendant being required to pay damages), but this has to be balanced against the

---

[252] [1995] PIQR P135 (CA).

[253] *Jones v GD Searle & Co Ltd* [1978] 3 All ER 654.

[254] *Thompson v Brown Construction (Ebbw Vale) Ltd* [1981] 2 All ER 296, 301–302. The fact that the claimant would have a cast-iron case against his solicitors is not necessarily a reason to use the occasion to teach the solicitors a lesson, particularly where the delay after the expiry of the limitation period was short and had caused the defendants no material prejudice: *Steeds v Peverel Management Services Ltd* [2001] EWCA Civ 419, The Times, 16 May 2001 (CA).

[255] *Firman v Ellis* [1978] QB 886, 916, *per* Geoffrey Lane LJ; *Das v Ganju* [1999] PIQR P260 270 (CA). See further *Conry v Simpson* [1983] 3 All ER 369; *Ramsden v Lee* [1992] 2 All ER 204; *Donovan v Gwentoys Ltd* [1990] 1 All ER 1018.

[256] *Firman v Ellis* [1978] QB 886, 916; *Liff v Peasley* [1980] 1 WLR 781, 789; *Hartley v Birmingham City District Council* [1992] 2 All ER 213, 224 (CA). In *Kelly v Bastible* [1997] 8 Med LR 15 the Court of Appeal held that the fact that the defendant was insured was one of the factors that could be placed in the scales when weighing prejudice to the parties under s 33, but if, treating the defendant and insurer as a composite unit, the delay had seriously prejudiced their ability to defend the action, and if the court would not have allowed the action to proceed had the defendant not been insured, the weight to be given to the mere fact that the defendant was insured should be nil.

[257] *Nash v Eli Lilly & Co* [1991] 2 Med LR 169; aff'd [1993] 1 WLR 782, 810 (CA).

financial loss that the claimant would suffer if s 11 is not disapplied.[258] The court should also consider the question of proportionality in the exercise of the discretion under s 33, and should be slow to exercise their discretion in favour of a claimant in the absence of cogent medical evidence showing a serious effect on the claimant's health or enjoyment of life or employability, particularly taking into account the amount of damages likely to be awarded.[259] The fact that a medical negligence action is a claim for professional negligence may be a factor in the defendant's favour, because such actions have more serious consequences for defendants and should be prosecuted without delay.[260] This can only be relevant, however, where the defendant has had a claim intimated, but there has been a long delay in issuing the claim form.[261]

(v) Death

(a) Fatal Accidents Act 1976

7.110   In an action for loss of dependency under the Fatal Accidents Act 1976, if the death occurred before the expiry of the deceased's three-year limitation period, then a new three-year period commences in favour of the dependants. This period runs from the date of death or the date of the dependants' 'knowledge', whichever is later.[262] If the action is not commenced within three years of the death or the date of knowledge of the dependants, the action is barred,[263] although the court may disapply the primary limitation period under s 33. If the deceased's three-year limitation period had expired before he died, then in theory he could not have maintained an action at the date of his death and the dependants' action is barred. The court can exercise its discretion under s 33, however, having regard to the

---

[258]   *Smith v Leicester HA* [1998] Lloyd's Rep Med 77 (CA)—where the loss to the claimant would probably have been ten times greater than the additional financial prejudice to the defendants.

[259]   *Robinson v St Helens MBC* [2002] EWCA Civ 1099; [2003] PIQR P128 at [33].

[260]   *Jackson & Powell on Professional Negligence* (5th edn, 2002), para 5.069. In the analogous context of an application to strike out an action for want of prosecution under the old rules of the Supreme Court, prejudice in the form of the worry that professional staff would suffer with the action hanging over them like the 'sword of Damocles', could be taken into account: *Biss v Lambeth HA* [1978] 1 WLR 382 (CA), thought it exceptional to treat the 'mere sword of Damocles' as a sufficient reason in itself to strike out: *Department of Transport v Chris Smaller (Transport) Ltd* [1989] 1 All ER 897, 905, *per* Lord Griffiths. Under the Civil Procedure Rules 'prejudice' is not a requirement on an application to strike out an action for want of prosecution: *Biguzzi v Rank Leisure plc* [1999] 1 WLR 1926, 1934 (CA); *Axa Insurance Co Ltd v Swire Fraser Ltd* [2001] CP Rep 17 (CA) at [20]. See further *Slevin v Southampton and South West Hampshire HA* [1997] 8 Med LR 175, 181 on the question of distress to the defendant as a factor in the exercise of the discretion under s 33 in medical negligence cases; and *Sims v Dartford and Gravesham HA* [1996] 7 Med LR 381.

[261]   *Dobbie v Medway HA* [1994] 4 All ER 451, 462, *per* Beldam LJ. See *Birnie v Oxfordshire AHA* (1982) 2 *The Lancet* 281 (QBD), Glidewell J.

[262]   Limitation Act 1980, s 12. 'Knowledge' is defined in s 14. If dependants have different dates of knowledge, time runs separately against each of them: s 13(1).

[263]   ibid, s 12(2).

length of and reasons for the delay on the part of the deceased.[264] The court may disapply s 12 only where the reason why the deceased could no longer maintain an action was because of the time limit in s 11.[265] If he could no longer maintain an action for any other reason, there is no discretion to allow the dependants' action to proceed.

(b) Law Reform (Miscellaneous Provisions) Act 1934

The position in the case of an action on behalf of the estate of a deceased person **7.111** under the Law Reform (Miscellaneous Provisions) Act 1934 is similar to that which applies to Fatal Accident Act claims. If the deceased died before the expiry of his three-year limitation period, a new three-year period commences which runs from either the date of death or the date of the personal representative's knowledge, whichever is later.[266] If this period expires the personal representative may request the court to exercise its discretion under s 33. Where the deceased died after the expiry of his three-year limitation period, an action by the personal representative is barred by s 11(3), but again the court can exercise its discretion under s 33, having regard to the length of and the reasons for the delay by the deceased.

(vi) Persons Under a Disability

A person is under a disability while he is an infant or of unsound mind.[267] An in- **7.112** fant is a person under the age of 18,[268] and a person is of unsound mind if, by reason of mental disorder within the meaning of the Mental Health Act 1983, he is incapable of managing and administering his property and affairs.[269] If a person to whom a right of action accrues is under a disability at the date when the action accrued, time does not run until he ceases to be under a disability or dies, whichever occurs first.[270] Thus, an infant has an indefeasible right to bring an action for personal injuries at any time before the age of 18,[271] and a person of unsound mind

---

[264] ibid, s 33(4).

[265] ibid, s 33(2).

[266] ibid, s 11(5). If there is more than one personal representative and their dates of knowledge are different, time runs from the earliest date: s 11(7).

[267] ibid, s 38(2).

[268] Family Law Reform Act 1969, s 1.

[269] Limitation Act 1980, s 38(3). Under the Mental Health Act 1983, s 1(2) mental disorder is defined as 'mental illness, arrested or incomplete development of the mind, psychopathic disorder, and any other disorder or disability of mind'. See also Limitation Act 1980, s 38(4) which identifies circumstances in which for the purposes of s 38(2) a person shall be conclusively presumed to be of unsound mind. For discussion of the circumstances in which a person is incapable of managing and administering his property and affairs see *Masterman-Lister v Jewell and Home Counties Dairies* [2002] EWHC 417 (QB); [2002] Lloyd's Rep Med 239; aff'd [2002] EWCA Civ 1889; [2003] PIQR P310.

[270] Limitation Act 1980, s 28(1) and (6). If the person under a disability dies the primary limitation period starts to run, and there can be no further extension under s 28: s 28(3).

[271] *Tolley v Morris* [1979] 2 All ER 561.

has three years from the date he ceases to be of unsound mind. If the accident itself caused immediate unsoundness of mind time will not begin to run.[272] The fact that a defendant may suffer prejudice from a long delay is immaterial.[273] If the claimant was not under a disability when the action accrued, supervening unsoundness of mind will not prevent time running,[274] though the discretion under s 33 is available.

---

[272] *Kirby v Leather* [1965] 2 QB 367 (CA). This applies if the unsoundness of mind arises at any time before the end of the day on which the accident occurred; *Boot v Boot* (1991, CA); *Turner v WH Malcolm Ltd* (1992) 15 BMLR 40 (CA).
[273] *Headford v Bristol and District HA* [1995] 6 Med LR 1, 4 (CA), *per* Rose LJ.
[274] *Purnell v Roche* [1927] 2 Ch 142.

8

INSTITUTIONAL LIABILITY

8.01 Doctors and other health professionals working within the NHS function within an institutional framework.[1] Hospital doctors and nurses perform their professional duties for an institution which is usually an NHS Trust or a Primary Care Trust (PCT) providing community or some hospital services. General practitioners provide general medical services in a relationship[2] with a PCT (in England) or

---

[1] Discussed in Ch 1.

[2] Under the National Health Service (General Medical Services) Regulations 1992, SI 1992/635 (as amended), the legal nature of the relationship remains unclear: see *Roy v Kensington and Chelsea and Westminster FPC* [1992] 1 AC 624 (HL). However, even if there is a contractual element, the relationship is not one of employment. See Kennedy, I, and Grubb A, *Medical Law* (3rd edn, Butterworths, 2000), 60–5.

a Local Health Board (in Wales).[3] They may also provide 'personal medical services' by virtue of s 28C of the National Health Service (Primary Care) Act 1997.[4] Nurses and others may work for the GP practice in which they are based. In addition to the personal liability of an individual for negligence,[5] the law also imposes liability in some circumstances upon the institution. First, the institution will be vicariously liable for the negligence of its employees committed in the course of their employment.[6] Secondly, the institution may owe a primary or direct duty owed to the patient which is breached by the failure to provide a safe 'health environment'[7] or, more controversially, by an act of negligence by any individual working within, and as part of, the institution.[8] The same questions arise in respect of the liability of a clinic or doctor in the context of private medical services.

8.02 The importance of liability being imposed upon the institution is that practically (and legally) it shifts financial responsibility to the organisation providing the medical service. While, in the case of vicarious liability, the employee will in theory remain legally liable to the patient and the employer will have an indemnity[9] claim against the employee,[10] in practice it is the institution who is sued and who pays the damages award.[11] Indeed, as will be seen later in this chapter,[12] since 1 January 1990 within the NHS this practical position has been enshrined in the litigation arrangements following the introduction of the NHS Indemnity Scheme[13] and, since 1 March 1996, the Clinical Negligence Scheme for Trusts.[14] The only contexts in which a doctor remains personally liable in practice is where he is a GP[15] or in private practice. Even in these situations, the doctor will almost

---

[3] From 1 April 2003. Previously, a GP's legal relationship was with a Health Authority and before that with a Family Health Services Authority.

[4] Initially known as 'pilot schemes': see Ch 1, above. The legal relationship between a doctor and PCT may be contractual under a 1997 Act scheme, or if the 'pilot scheme' provider has acquired the status of a 'health service body' (under s 16 of the National Health Service (Primary Care) Act 1997 for the purposes of s 4 of the National Health Service and Community Care Act 1990), then the relationship will constitute an 'NHS contract' governed by the 1990 Act.

[5] Discussed in Chs 5–7.

[6] See below, paras 8.03 *et seq.*

[7] See below, paras 8.18 *et seq.*

[8] See below, paras 8.24 *et seq.*

[9] Or for contribution if the employer is also in breach of an independent duty of care owed to the patient: *Jones v Manchester Corporation* [1952] 2 QB 852 (CA).

[10] *Lister v Romford Ice and Cold Storage Co Ltd* [1957] AC 555 (HL).

[11] Until 1 January 1990, an agreement dating back to 1954 between the medical protection organisations and the Department of Health meant that contribution or indemnity claims were settled privately and not in court: HM (54)32.

[12] See below, paras 8.88–8.107.

[13] HC (89)34; and now updated as HSG (96)48. Discussed by Brazier, M (1990) 6 Professional Negligence 88.

[14] See National Health Service (Clinical Negligence Scheme) Regulations 1996, SI 1996/251 as amended, made pursuant to the National Health Service and Community Care Act 1990, s 21.

[15] The NHS schemes do not apply to negligence actions against GPs arising out of the provision of general or personal medical services and, as will be seen, the relationship with a PCT is not (usually) one of employment giving rise to vicarious liability.

certainly have what is, in effect, insurance cover for his liability from one of the medical defence organisations.[16] As a consequence, he will be liable for his negligence but, in practice, any award of damages will be paid by the defence organisation.

A. Vicarious Liability[17]

Under the common law an employer is vicariously liable for the torts of his employees committed in the course of their employment.[18] The general statement applies within the NHS and private health care facilities.[19] The three relevant issues in determining the institution's liability are: (i) has the individual committed a tort?; (ii) is he an employee of the defendant?; and (iii) did he commit the tort in the course of his employment? The first question does not call for any further comment here.[20] As regards the third, if the negligence occurs on the premises of the institution, it is most unlikely that any question will arise of whether the employee is acting 'in the course of his employment'. He will be so acting, for example, where an employee (such as a doctor) injures a patient in the course of diagnosis or treatment, or an employee (such as a porter) drops the patient whilst lifting them onto a trolley. A doctor will be 'acting in the course of his employment' even if he commits a battery (or false imprisonment) when treating a patient, for example, where force[21] or restraint[22] is used upon an incompetent patient in their best interests but it is excessive and unreasonable. Only the most outrageous displays of individualistic behaviour by the employee, such as a porter who punches a patient, could isolate the institution from liability.[23] The second question is the crucial one: is the negligent person an employee of the hospital?[24]

8.03

---

[16] The Medical Defence Union, Medical and Dental Defence Union of Scotland, and the Medical Protection Society.

[17] For a definitive account of the modern law, see Atiyah, P, *Vicarious Liability in Tort* (Butterworths, 1967).

[18] The modern doctrine dates back to the seventeenth century and, perhaps, to the case of *Tuberville v Stamp* (1697) 1 Ld Raym 264. See generally Williams, G, 'Vicarious Liability and the Master's Indemnity' (1957) 20 MLR 220. For a general discussion, see, eg, Grubb, A (ed), *The Law of Torts* (Butterworths, 2002), ch 3.

[19] For discussion of the 'hospital' cases see Atiyah, P, *Vicarious Liability in Tort* (n 17 above) and Jones, M, *Medical Negligence* (2nd edn, 1996), 392–9.

[20] Vicarious liability extends not only to the tort of negligence but also to other torts such as battery committed in the course of employment.

[21] *Re MB (Medical Treatment)* [1997] 2 FLR 426 (CA).

[22] *Re C (Detention: Medical Treatment)* [1997] 2 FLR 180 (Wall J).

[23] eg, *Keppel Bus Co v Ahmad* [1974] 1 WLR 1082. Contrast situations of authorised force (nn 21 and 22 above) and see generally, Rose, F (1977) 40 MLR 420. For a modern and authoritative discussion of the 'scope of employment' requirement see *Lister v Hesley Hall Ltd* [2001] UKHL 22, [2001] 2 All ER 769 (HL) (school vicariously liable for acts of sexual abuse carried out by warden of a residential boys' school).

[24] For the remainder of this chapter the term 'hospital' will be used to encompass all institutions within the NHS unless the context otherwise requires.

1. Staff in NHS Trusts

(i) *Hillyer*: Vicarious Liability Excluded

8.04   At one time, English law held to the view that hospitals could not be liable for the negligence of their staff exercising their professional skills. In 1909 in *Hillyer v Governors of St Bartholomews Hospital*,[25] the Court of Appeal held that liability could only arise for 'purely ministerial or administrative duties' which, in essence, meant failures that did not involve judgment or the exercise of professional or clinical discretion. The decision was based on a view, now no longer tenable, that a person could not be an employee (for whom an institution could be vicariously liable) unless the institution has 'control' over the performance of the individual's duties.[26] The reasoning in the case is, and indeed was, flawed.[27] First, 'control' is not a satisfactory indicator of who is an employee.[28] It reflects a bygone era when workers carried out the tasks of their employer who was himself skilled in that work.[29] Today, as indeed in 1909, employees in many work-contexts possess skills far beyond their employer's abilities and work not for 'X' but for an institution in a management structure where those above occupy that position because they possess their own skills rather than of those they manage. Secondly, it is difficult to understand the reasoning in *Hillyer*. How could a particular individual have been an employee when carrying out some functions ('purely ministerial or administrative') but not when performing others ('professional skills')? Perhaps, as regards doctors, their functions were thought always to fall into the latter category: a very big assumption. But even if they did, other staff such as nurses carry out functions falling under both classifications. In principle, however, they either were, or were not, employees of the institution. As a result, until the 1950s, hospitals were not liable for medical negligence of their staff. Apart from the preserved category of functions in *Hillyer*, their liability depended upon a breach of a primary or direct duty owed to the patient.

(ii) *Cassidy* and *Roe*: Vicarious Liability Introduced

8.05   The untenable basis of the *Hillyer* decision led to its eventual rejection in other countries such as Canada,[30] Australia[31] and Ireland.[32] English law gradually

---

[25] [1909] 2 KB 820. See also *Evans v Liverpool Corporation* [1906] 1 KB 160.
[26] The modern 'composite' approach is set out in the Privy Council decision of *Lee Ting Sang v Chung Chi-Keung* [1990] 2 AC 374.
[27] See a criticism as far back as 1936 in *Lindsey County Council v Marshall* [1936] 2 All ER 1076, 1094 *per* Lord Wright.
[28] See Atiyah, *Vicarious Liability in Tort* (n 17 above), ch 5.
[29] See Kahn-Freund, O, 'Servants and Independent Contractors' (1951) 14 MLR 504.
[30] *Sisters of St Joseph of the Diocese of London v Fleming* [1938] SCR 172 (Can Sup Ct). See Picard, E and Robertson, G, *Legal Liability of Doctors and Hospitals in Canada* (3rd edn, 1996), 381–97.
[31] *Henson v Perth Hospital* (1939) 41 WALR 15.
[32] *O'Donovan v Cork County Council* [1967] IR 173.

moved away from the 'control test'.[33] But, in the particular context of hospitals, it survived for over 30 years[34] until the Court of Appeal's decision in *Gold v Essex County Council*.[35] In that case, a majority of the Court of Appeal[36] rejected *Hillyer* and held that a hospital was vicariously liable for the negligence of a radiographer. Whilst the case law developed cautiously, the judges came to accept that both permanent and temporary full-time members of a hospital's staff worked under contracts of service (as employees) rather than under contracts for services (as independent contractors).[37] The position of visiting staff remained unclear.[38] In the 1950s the Court of Appeal in *Cassidy v Ministry of Health*[39] and *Roe v Minister of Health*[40] effectively consigned *Hillyer* to the historical dustbin.[41] In *Cassidy*, Denning LJ remarked that the *Hillyer* rule was motivated by a desire 'to relieve the charitable hospitals from liabilities which they could not afford'.[42] The structure of health provision had markedly changed making this rationale no longer applicable and, of course, in particular the introduction of the National Health Service in 1948.[43] Thus, the negligence of all those who form part of the 'organisation'[44] such as doctors, nurses, porters and other staff are, in practice, caught by the doctrine of vicarious liability.[45] It has never been expressly decided that a consultant—the highest employment grade within the NHS—is an employee of a hospital[46] although in one case, Denning LJ asserted it.[47] There is no doubt today,

---

[33] See generally *Kahn-Freud, O*, (1951) 14 MLR 504.

[34] It survived in the US until 1957 and the New York case of *Bing v Thunig* (1957) 143 NE 2d 3. The exclusion of liability was based upon an immunity for the charitable status of hospitals. This is now rejected by the majority of jurisdictions in the US: see Furrow, B, Greaney, T, Johnson, S, Jost, T and Schwartz, R, *Health Law* (2nd edn, 2000), vol 1, ch 7.

[35] [1942] 2 KB 293.

[36] MacKinnon and Goddard LJ, ibid, at 308–309 and 312–313 respectively. Lord Greene MR decided the case on the basis of the hospital's non-delegable duty to the patient, ibid at 301–302. Reliance was placed upon Goodhart, A (1938) 54 LQR 553.

[37] eg, *Collins v Hertfordshire County Council* [1947] 1 KB 598 (junior house surgeon employed on a temporary but full-time basis).

[38] ibid at 619 *per* Hilbery J. See also *Gold* (n 35 above), 310 *per* Goddard LJ and *Cassidy* (n 39 below), 351 *per* Somervell LJ (no vicarious liability).

[39] [1951] 2 KB 343 (vicariously liable for all permanent staff, including assistant medical officer).

[40] [1954] 2 QB 66 (vicariously liable for part-time staff, including anaesthetist).

[41] The Scottish courts followed suit in *MacDonald v Glasgow Western Hospitals* 1954 SC 453 (CS, IH).

[42] N 39 above, 361.

[43] The potential for charitable and non-profit bodies to be liable has been clear in England since 1866: *Mersey Docks and Harbour Board Trustees v Gibbs* (1866) LR 1 HL 93.

[44] *Roe* (n 40 above), *per* Morris LJ at 91.

[45] The view expressed in *Hillyer* (n 25 above) 826 *per* Farwell LJ, that nurses in an operating theatre are employees of the surgeon and not the hospital should no longer be relied upon: see, *Cassidy* (n 39 above), *per* Denning LJ at 361–362. See also *Morris v Winsbury-White* [1937] 4 All ER 494 (rejecting vicarious liability of surgeon for nurse in operating theatre) and *Gold v Essex County Council* (n 35 above), 312–313 *per* Goddard LJ.

[46] The position of a consultant was distinguished by the judges in *Cassidy* (n 39 above), *per* Somervell LJ at 351 and Singleton LJ at 358. See also *Roe* (n 40 above), *per* Denning LJ at 82 ('consultants or anaesthetists selected and employed by the patient himself'); *Collins* (n 37 above), *per* Hilbery J at 619–620.

[47] *Razzel v Snowball* [1954] 1 WLR 1382, 1386.

however, that consultants within the NHS are properly seen as employees of NHS Trusts. Their higher employment status than 'junior doctors' is irrelevant for this purpose. They are as much employees of the institution as anyone else.

8.06   The correct question in determining whether a hospital is vicariously liable for an individual is whether *in the particular case* that member of staff is, or is not, working under a contract of service as an employee. The issue is a factual one turning on the nature of the contractual relationship between the parties having regard to all the circumstances.[48] The court will look for 'indicia' of the employer–employee relationship without regarding any one factor as necessarily conclusive.[49] In practice, however, a hospital will be liable for the negligence of all its full-time and part-time staff,[50] whether permanently or temporarily engaged, on the basis that they are employees of the hospital.[51]

(iii)   Paying Patients within the NHS

8.07   NHS Trusts[52] have statutory powers to provide accommodation and services on a private basis to patients: so-called powers of 'income generation'.[53] What is the position of a patient treated privately within an NHS hospital in a so-called 'pay-bed'? Will the hospital be vicariously liable for the negligence of the doctors or nurses? The staff, both nurses and doctors, will usually be employees of the hospital in which the patient is being treated. The crucial legal issue, therefore, in determining the vicarious liability of the hospital will be whether the staff were acting 'in the course of their employment' or in a purely private capacity when treating the patient. The patient may be entitled to assume that he is an 'NHS patient', given the circumstances, and the hospital may, apart from payment and the level of services, deal with the patient as a NHS patient albeit a 'paying guest'. It may well be that the staff carry out their care of the patient on 'NHS time'.[54] It is possible, therefore, that this combination of factors will lead a court to distinguish this patient from one treated in a wholly private context,[55] and impose vicarious liability on the hospital.[56]

---

[48] *Ready Mixed Concrete (South East) Ltd v Minister of Pensions* [1968] 2 QB 497 and *Lee Ting Sang v Chung Chi-Keung* [1990] 2 AC 374.

[49] See Atiyah, *Vicarious Liability in Tort* (n 17 above), chs 3–6.

[50] Including occupational physicians: see *Stokes v Guest, Keen and Nettlefold (Bolts and Nuts) Ltd* [1968] 1 WLR 1776.

[51] For a masterly survey of the law in common law and civilian jurisdictions see Giesen, D, *International Medical Malpractice Law* (1988), 38–59.

[52] See Ch1 above.

[53] Discussed in Newdick, C, *Who Should We Treat?* (OUP, 1995), 73–5.

[54] The Clinical Negligence Scheme for Trusts applies: National Health Service (Clinical Negligence Scheme) Regulations 1996 SI 1996/251 as amended, reg 2.

[55] On which see below, para 8.13.

[56] This should be distinguished from situations where the patient is treated in a private clinic or hospital pursuant to an agreement with the PCT. While such patients remain 'NHS patients', the only possible liability of an NHS body would be for breach of a direct or primary duty; the doctors and nurses will not be employed within the NHS but by the private provider.

(iv) 'Borrowed' Doctors and Other Staff

While it will generally be beyond doubt that, as a matter of fact, a member of the **8.08** hospital staff is an employee, there are a few situations that call for comment: 'borrowed' or 'visiting' staff and agency staff. A doctor who is loaned by his employer, Trust 'X', to work in a hospital operated by Trust 'Y' probably, in law, remains an employee of Trust 'X'.[57] However, the usual practice in this situation is for the doctor to enter into a temporary contract of service with Trust 'Y'. There is, in effect, a temporary transfer of his duties to another employer. In which case, it is Trust 'Y' who will be vicariously liable for his negligence; an outcome which more accurately places the responsibility on the appropriate party. To the outside world, and particularly to patients of Trust 'Y', he will be seen as working for his 'new' employer, Trust 'Y'. It would simply be incongruous if, whilst being paid by and performing the functions of Trust 'Y', Trust 'X' remained liable for his negligence. It will be Trust 'Y' that possesses all the trappings of his *current* employer. It would be otherwise, of course, if a doctor working for Trust 'X' were on a visit to a doctor-friend at Trust 'Y' who asked him to examine a patient in the course of which he negligently injured them. Here, neither Trust will be liable for him. While he is an employee of Trust 'X', he will not in these circumstances be acting 'in the course of his employment' with Trust 'X'. As regards Trust 'Y', he is simply not an employee. The doctor would, of course, be personally liable but Trust 'Y's liability, if at all, would depend upon a breach of a primary or direct duty owed to the patient.[58]

(v) Agency Staff

In the case of agency staff such as nurses, a hospital is unlikely to be vicariously **8.09** liable for their negligence as their sole contractual relationship is likely to be with the agency (or independent contractors)[59] unless a contract of service is also entered into with the hospital.[60] Again, the hospital's liability, if any, will be for breach of a primary or direct duty owed to the patient.[61]

---

[57] *Mersey Docks and Harbour Board v Coggins and Griffith (Liverpool) Ltd* [1947] AC 1. There is a heavy burden on the permanent employer to shift his prima facie responsibility to the temporary employer, for example, by showing that the entire and absolute control over the employee has been transferred: see, *Bhoomidas v Port of Singapore Authority* [1978] 1 All ER 956 (PC)—no transfer on facts. It is not, therefore, beyond doubt in the hospital context.

[58] See below, paras 8.14 *et seq.*

[59] But note, *Clark v Oxfordshire HA* (1997) 41 BMLR 18 (CA) (a nurse who worked for a health authority 'nurse bank' and whose services were supplied to various hospitals within its area was not employed under a contract of service by the health authority for the purposes of unfair dismissal).

[60] Quaere whether the Clinical Negligence Scheme for Trusts applies as it covers, inter alia, a breach of duty by a person 'employed' by a Trust member or who is '*engaged*' by a Trust member or is an 'employee or agent' of a person so engaged (see National Health Service (Clinical Negligence Scheme) Regulations 1996 (n 54 above), reg 4 (emphasis added)).

[61] See below.

2. General Practitioners

(i) Liability of Primary Care Trusts[62]

8.10 General practitioners provide primary care to their patients on behalf of PCTs who have a statutory duty to make provision for 'personal medical services' to those for whom they are responsible.[63] In doing so, GPs are not employees of the PCTs. As such, they are in an entirely different position to their hospital counterparts. It is doubtful whether the relationship created under the Terms of Service in Sch 2 to the National Health Service (General Medical Services) Regulations 1992[64] even amounts to a contractual relationship.[65] It is clear, however, that even if contractual, the relationship is not one of employment. General practitioners are independent contractors and, consequently, a PCT is not vicariously liable for the negligence of a GP.[66] By contrast, a GP *may* be employed as a salaried individual under a 'pilot scheme'.[67] It will depend upon the particular legal arrangement the GP has with the NHS Trust or PCT. In these circumstances, the employer could be vicariously liable for the torts of the GP employee.

(ii) Liability of a GP's Partners[68]

8.11 General practitioners ordinarily work in partnerships with other GPs. By virtue of the Partnership Act 1890, the partnership will itself be liable for the negligence of a GP in treating a patient.[69] Equally, each of the GP partners will be jointly and severally liable for the negligence of the other partners.[70]

(iii) Liability of GP for Practice Staff

8.12 A GP (and the partnership) will be vicariously liable for the negligence of his own

---

[62] In Wales, the relevant NHS body will be a local health board.

[63] National Health Service Act 1977, s 29. But note, the National Health Service (Primary Care) Act 1997, s 9(2).

[64] SI 1992/635 (as amended).

[65] See the differing views expressed in the Court of Appeal and House of Lords in *Roy v Kensington and Chelsea FPC* [1992] 1 AC 624 (HL) and [1990] 1 Med LR 328 (CA).

[66] This does not mean that a PCT could not in any circumstance be liable to an injured patient. It is conceivable that the courts would hold that a PCT owed a primary or direct duty to patients to exercise reasonable care in selecting and placing practitioners on the Medical List such that liability might flow for selecting (negligently) an incompetent GP. This would not assist a patient who was injured by a competent GP but whose negligence caused the injury. For primary liability see below, paras 8.14 *et seq*.

[67] Or its permanent manifestation under s 28C of the National Health Service (Primary Care) Act 1997.

[68] See Atiyah, *Vicarious Liability in Tort* (n 17 above), ch 11.

[69] s 10.

[70] s 12.

professional or office staff such as practice nurses or receptionists[71] working within his surgery under contracts of service.[72] He will not, however, be vicariously liable for the negligence of his deputy or locum.[73] The latter is an independent contractor.[74] The GP's liability will, again, stand or fall on the basis of whether the GP himself owes a primary or direct duty of care to his patient which is breached. Providing the selection of the deputy was not negligent,[75] it follows that the GP's liability would only arise if he were as a matter of law under a non-delegable duty to ensure that his patient is treated carefully.[76] Notwithstanding the phrasing of the Terms of Service which limit the GP's obligations where the deputy is himself a doctor on the Medical List of a PCT,[77] it is arguable that such a duty could exist.[78]

3. Doctors in Private Practice

A doctor in private practice will usually be a sole practitioner. He will not be employed by anyone and hence no question of vicarious liability will arise for his negligence.[79] Even in situations where the doctor treats a patient in a private clinic or hospital, it is unlikely that the relationship between the doctor and the clinic or hospital will be one of employment. More likely, there will be a contractual arrangement whereby the doctor has 'admission privileges', the private clinic providing the facilities and, perhaps, nursing staff for the patient's treatment. The doctor's position is likely to be somewhat analogous to the position in other countries where the doctors often are not employees, but are in private practice, and have 'admissions privileges' at the hospital under an agreement with that hospital.[80] The legal position is illustrated by one case where an Australian court[81] held

8.13

---

[71] *Lobley (A Minor) v Nunn* 9 December 1985, CA—no breach of duty by receptionist on facts.

[72] For a useful discussion in the Canadian context, see Picard and Robertson (n 30 above), 356–64.

[73] Acting on the GP's behalf under the National Health Service (General Medical Services) Regulations 1992, SI 1992/635, Sch 2, para 19(2).

[74] See *Rothwell v Raes* (1988) 54 DLR (4th) 193 (Ont H Ct). Discussed in Picard, E, and Robertson, G (n 30 above), 361.

[75] On obligation imposed upon a GP by his 'Terms of Service', see National Health Service (General Medical Services) Regulations 1992, SI 1992/635, Sch 2, para 28.

[76] On which, see below, paras 8.24 *et seq* and above, paras 5.29–5.30.

[77] National Health Service (General Medical Services) Regulations 1992 (n 73 above), Sch 2, para 20(2) (as amended by SI 1994/633, reg 8(5)).

[78] See above, para 5.29

[79] In *Kapfunde v Abbey National* (1998) 45 BMLR 176 (CA) a GP who worked part-time for a company as an occupational health adviser and was paid an annual retainer was not an employee working under a contract of service. The Court of Appeal held that he was an independent contractor and, consequently, the company could not be vicariously liable for any negligence on his part in making a medical report on a prospective employee.

[80] Of course, the doctor may be employed by the clinic. Whether or not he is will, in each case, be a question of fact. Even if there is no employment relationship, the clinic may be liable for breach of a direct or primary duty owed to the patient.

[81] *Ellis v Wallsend District Hospital* (1989) 17 NSWLR 553; [1990] 2 Med LR 103 (NSW CA).

that a doctor with 'admission privileges' was not an employee of the hospital. Whilst he was subject to some regulation under the hospitals rules, he was essentially in private practice 'borrowing' hospital space.[82] The clinic will, of course, be liable for the negligence of any of its staff such as the nurses. There may also be a claim for breach of contract, depending upon whether there is a contract between the patient and the clinic and what are its terms, for example, if there is fault by the clinic in providing adequate staff or facilities.[83] Otherwise, its liability in tort will depend upon a breach of a primary or direct duty owed to the patient. This may be co-extensive with its contractual terms or, it might be argued, the clinic owes a non-delegable duty to care for the patient and hence it can even be liable for the negligence by the (non-employee) doctor. It is to these possibilities which we now turn.

B. Primary or Direct Liability

1. *Within the National Health Service*

8.14 In addition to being vicariously liable for the negligence of its employees, a NHS hospital[84] may be liable for a breach of a duty owed directly to the patient.[85] The duty of care will arise when the patient is admitted to the hospital[86] or presents himself at the casualty department seeking medical attention.[87] It is doubtful whether a duty will arise prior to this, for example, merely on receipt of a referral letter by a consultant from a GP or on the making of an appointment at the hospital.[88] There is, in these situations, no assumption of responsibility as yet for the health of the patient.[89]

---

[82] See similarly, *Yepremian v Scarborough General Hospital* (1980) 110 DLR (3d) 513 (Ont CA).

[83] To the extent that 'goods' or 'services' are provided by the clinic under contract, there may be liability under the Sale of Goods Act 1979 or, more likely, the Supply of Goods and Services Act 1982. There may also be liability in tort for injury caused by a 'defective product', either under common law or the Consumer Protection Act 1987, Pt I. See Ch 15 below.

[84] Or, indeed, a private clinic.

[85] As with all negligence action 'breach', 'causation' and 'damage' must be proved: on these, see Chs 6 and 7 and below, paras 8.59–8.87.

[86] *Jones v Manchester Corporation* [1952] QB 852, 867 *per* Denning LJ and *Cassidy v Ministry of Health* [1951] 2 KB 343, 360 *per* Denning LJ.

[87] *Barnett v Chelsea and Kensington HMC* [1969] 1 QB 428; [1968] 1 All ER 1068. Nield J distinguished the situation where the person presents themself and the A & E department is closed when no duty would arise; ibid, 1072. See also, *Capital and Counties plc v Hampshire County Council* [1997] 2 All ER 865 (CA), especially *per* Stuart-Smith LJ at 883. It is arguable that a hospital does owe a duty of care in these circumstances as it will have held itself out as being 'willing and able' to receive emergency patients and, thus, must give reasonable notice (or provide reasonable alternative facilities) to the public before closing: see Picard and Robertson, *Legal Liability of Doctors and Hospitals in Canada* (n 30 above), 10 and 371 citing *Baynham v Robertson* (1993) 18 CCLT (2d) 15 (Ont Gen Div).

[88] *Clunis v Camden and Islington HA* (CA) (1997) 40 BMLR 181 (no duty of care owed to mentally disordered patient referred to hospital and for whom an appointment had been made).

[89] See above, paras 5.24 *et seq* for a discussion in the context of a doctor's duty.

Of course, there may be others who have assumed a duty to the patient at an earlier stage for example, the ambulance service. This duty will clearly exist when the ambulance crew 'assume a responsibility' on collecting the patient, but it may arise even earlier.

In *Kent v Griffiths*[90] the Court of Appeal held that a duty of care was owed by the **8.15** ambulance service where it accepted a call requesting an ambulance but had failed to respond promptly to the call and, as a result of the delay, the claimant had suffered injury. The court distinguished the case law concerned with other public services such as the police and fire service. Unlike them, the ambulance service, in this particular case, owed a duty only to the claimant rather than the public at large, and hence no conflict could arise between the claimant's interests and those of the public at large. The court held that the ambulance service was, in effect, in the same position as other parts of the NHS in providing a health service and the duty arose when the ambulance service accepted the call, by which the court seems to mean 'agreed to send an ambulance'.

The court left open (but really doubted) whether an action could be brought **8.16** where there were insufficient resources to provide enough vehicles or manpower.[91] Likewise the court doubted whether a claim would be successful if an ambulance was provided for a serious accident but due to an error of judgement a less seriously injured patient was transported to hospital first, leaving the more seriously injured to suffer.[92] The basis of this seems to be, not that no duty of care will be owed, but rather that it will be difficult to prove breach, perhaps based upon the need to make a 'snap decision' in an emergency.

It is, perhaps, ironic that primary liability within the NHS was largely all that was **8.17** left in the post-*Hillyer* era, but was all but forgotten by the courts until the 1980s. There were probably two reasons for this. First, after the courts applied the doctrine of vicarious liability to hospital staff in the 1950s for all intents and purposes it became unnecessary in practice for injured patients to rely upon a breach of a duty of care owed by a hospital directly to the patient.[93] Secondly, the agreement reached in 1954[94] between the Government and the medical defence organisations on how to apportion damages between the doctors' 'insurers' and the institution, served to obscure the fact that there might, in a particular case, be joint liability based upon breaches of different duties.[95] Hence, the fact that the

---

[90] [2000] 2 All ER 474 (CA). For earlier proceedings in the case see [1999] Lloyd's Rep Med 58 (CA). Discussed Grubb (2000) 8 Med L Rev 349 (Commentary).

[91] ibid, at [47].

[92] ibid, at [46].

[93] See, *A v Ministry of Defence and Guy's and St Thomas' Hospital NHS Trust* [2003] EWHC 849 (QB) *per* Bell J at [68].

[94] Circular HM (54)32.

[95] *Robertson v Nottingham HA* [1997] 8 Med LR 1, 13 *per* Brooke LJ.

patient's injuries might be attributable to a combination of a doctor's negligence and a hospital's breach of duty to provide, for example, sufficient staff or adequate facilities was hardly ever litigated.[96] Not, that is, until 1986 when it was referred to by the Court of Appeal in *Wilsher v Essex AHA*.[97] Indeed, Mustill LJ commented that counsel for the defendant had asserted that no health authority had, or could, ever be liable on the basis of breach of a primary duty.[98] Both assertions are incorrect. The former simply ignores the pre-1950s law.[99] As regards the latter, there are a number of subsequent Court of Appeal decisions in which the direct duty of an institution has been acknowledged.[100] Consequently, there is no doubt that an NHS institution such as an NHS Trust or Health Authority owes a direct duty to its patients: the real question is what is the nature of that duty.

(i) The Duty to Provide a Safe 'Health Care Environment'

8.18   What then is the scope of the hospital's direct or primary duty? In essence, the hospital's duty could be summed up as one 'to provide . . . a reasonable regime of care at its hospital'.[101] An analogy might be drawn with the employment context and the House of Lords' decision in *Wilsons & Clyde Coal Co Ltd v English*.[102] The duty owed to an employee is to provide a reasonably safe work place, including, equipment, facilities, fellow workers, systems of work, and the like.[103] In the health care context, the hospital's duty includes providing sufficient and competent staff. In *Wilsher v Essex AHA*,[104] Browne-Wilkinson V-C stated that a hospital had a duty 'to provide doctors of sufficient skill and experience to give the treatment offered at the hospital'.[105] This, however, could not have been intended to be a complete description of the institution's duty, and it is not. The duty is broader and extends to providing adequate facilities, including equipment, and safe systems of care, including adequate supervision of junior doctors and others by experienced staff.[106]

---

[96] For a rare instance, see *Jones v Manchester Corporation* [1952] 2 QB 852.

[97] [1987] QB 730; [1986] 3 All ER 801.

[98] ibid, 817.

[99] eg, *Vancouver General Hospital v McDaniel* (1934) 152 LT 56 (PC); *Lindsey County Council v Marshall* [1937] AC 820 (HL); and, of course, *Hillyer* (n 25 above).

[100] eg, *Bull v Devon AHA* [1993] 4 Med L Rev 117 (CA); *Blyth v Bloomsbury HA* [1993] 4 Med LR 151 (CA) and *Robertson v Nottingham HA* (n 95 above).

[101] *Per* Brooke LJ in *Robertson* (n 95 above), 13 citing *Gold v Essex County Council* (n 35 above), *per* Lord Greene MR at 302 and 304; *per* Goddard LJ at 309 and *Roe v Ministry of Health* (n 40 above), *per* Denning LJ at 72.

[102] [1938] AC 57.

[103] See Grubb, A (ed), *The Law of Torts* (Butterworths, 2002), ch 20.

[104] [1986] 3 All ER 803 (CA).

[105] ibid, 833. See also *per* Glidewell LJ at 831.

[106] For a useful discussion of the factual situations in the Canadian context see Picard and Robertson, *Legal Liability of Hospitals and Doctors in Canada* (n 30 above), 367–80.

The duty is concerned with the *fault of the organisation* rather than the negligence of an individual member of staff. It is important to bear in mind that the duty is one of *reasonableness* and not an absolute one. The hospital will not be in breach of its duty simply because a doctor or nurse is negligent. A breach of its primary duty will only occur if that doctor or nurse is incompetent (in general or to carry out the particular task) and the hospital has been negligent in employing him or allowing him to carry out that task. Hence, an inexperienced doctor who is not up to a particular task will be negligent[107] when he carries it out and the institution will be vicariously liable for his tort.[108] However, the hospital will also be liable for its own failure if it either should not have put him in the position of performing a task beyond his abilities[109] or it has allowed him to carry out the task without adequate supervision by a more experienced practitioner.[110]

8.19

Organisational or systems failures are at the heart of the institution's direct liability to a patient. In *Robertson v Nottingham HA*[111] Brooke LJ emphasised the distinction between the institution's liability based upon vicarious liability and breach of its primary duty. The alleged failure concerned a breakdown in communications between the medical and nursing staff during the confinement of a pregnant woman as a result of which, it was alleged, the plaintiff was born with severe physical and mental disabilities. Brooke LJ stated:[112]

8.20

> If effective systems had been in place at this hospital for ensuring that so far as reasonably practicable communications breakdowns did not occur in connection with such a significant area of a patient's treatment then the health authority would be vicariously liable for any negligence of those of its servants or agents who did not take proper care to ensure, so far as was reasonably practicable, that the communications systems worked efficiently. If, on the other hand, no effective systems were in place at all . . . then the authority would be directly liable in negligence for this lacuna.

This basis of liability is of increasing importance within the NHS as working and clinical protocols[113] become more common.[114] Failure to introduce a protocol or failure in setting the content of the protocol may give rise to a breach of the

8.21

---

[107] Inexperience is not relevant in setting the standard of care: *Wilsher* (n 104 above). See for discussion, Ch 6 above.

[108] As would have been the case in *Wilsher* (n 104 above), except for the fact that the inexperienced doctor sought the advice of a more experienced doctor and thereby acted reasonably: see *per* Glidewell LJ at 831.

[109] See, eg, *Hinfey v Salford HA* [1993] 4 Med LR 143 (no breach on facts).

[110] *Hinfey*, ibid, and *Wilsher* (n 104 above).

[111] [1997] 8 Med LR 1, 13.

[112] ibid.

[113] Though there may be differences, these may variously be termed protocols, clinical guidelines, guidance, or advice.

[114] See Newdick, C, *Who Shall We Treat?* (n 53 above), 174–8. See also the impact of the National Institute of Clinical Excellence (NICE) discussed in Chs 1 and 6 above.

hospital's primary duty to the patient. But, a failure to follow or implement such a protocol in a particular instance will, if anything, be a question of breach of duty by a member of staff and vicarious liability for that breach of duty.[115] Of course, this is not to say that the hospital might not be liable itself if it negligently allowed, for example, a culture of non-compliance with a protocol by 'turning a blind eye' to its non-implementation.

8.22   The operation of an institution's primary duty can be seen in the case of *Bull v Devon AHA*.[116] The plaintiff was born with severe brain damage. He was the second of twins to be born and, it was alleged, the delay in delivering him had caused his injuries. The hospital was based on two sites. Unfortunately, a suitably qualified doctor was not available on the site where the plaintiff's mother was in labour. Although attempts were made to summon a doctor from the other site, one did not arrive for some time. The Court of Appeal held that the defendant was liable for breach of its primary duty to the plaintiff.

8.23   Slade LJ held that the defendant had a duty to provide adequate staff, facilities, and equipment for the provision of maternity services.[117] On the evidence he held there had not been a breach of this duty.[118] Looking at the issue on the basis of professional evidence, at the time the staffing arrangements were not inadequate, let alone, negligently inadequate. It was not necessary, in order for the hospital to comply with its duty, to have a doctor immediately available.[119] However, Slade LJ determined that the defendant also had a duty to provide an adequate system for summoning an appropriate doctor to deal with maternity emergencies. On the facts, he concluded that the system for summoning the doctor must either have broken down or a member of staff must have negligently operated it.[120] Consequently, the defendant was liable either for breach of its primary duty[121] or on the basis of vicarious liability. Dillon LJ agreed that the defendant had a duty to provide adequate staff for its maternity services and the system in place was only acceptable if it worked 'with supreme efficiency'[122] which, on the facts, he held it had not: it had been operated negligently.[123] Mustill LJ agreed that the defendant was in breach of its primary duty because the system for summoning a doctor had

---

[115] See, eg, *Thomson v James* (1996) 31 BMLR 1 (no liability for failure to follow DoH guidelines). See also *AB v Tameside and Glossop HA* [1997] 8 Med LR 91 (CA). Though it may reflect on fault by the hospital: *Blyth v Bloomsbury HA* [1993] 4 Med LR 151 (hospital not liable for failing to apply warning system to plaintiff); discussed, Montgomery, J (1990) 140 NLJ 1349.

[116] [1993] 4 Med LR 117 (CA) (decided 1989). See Kennedy (1993) 1 Med L Rev 384 (Commentary).

[117] ibid, 130.

[118] On the issue of institutional breach of duty, see below, paras 8.59 *et seq*.

[119] N 116 above, 131.

[120] ibid, 132.

[121] Applying the maxim *res ipsa loquitur*.

[122] N 116 above, 137.

[123] ibid, 137 and 138.

broken down in its operation.[124] However, he went further and concluded that the system itself was inadequate: the defendant's duty was to provide immediately a doctor who could have delivered the plaintiff. Alternatively, the system was too sensitive to hitches.[125] In either case, the defendant was negligent and in breach of its primary duty to the patient.

(ii) Non-Delegable Duty

More controversially, it has been suggested that a hospital within the NHS owes a non-delegable duty to *ensure* that reasonable care (or skill) is taken of its patients.[126] The legal duty is that of the hospital which is performed on its behalf by its staff or, possibly, independent contractors within the hospital. Where reasonable care (or skill) is not taken of a patient, the institution is, through the breach of the staff member or independent contractor, in breach of its own non-delegable duty.[127] Significantly, if such a non-delegable duty did exist, the hospital would be liable for the negligence[128] not only of its employee but also of independent contractors acting on its behalf.[129]   **8.24**

(a) *The English Cases*

In the hospital context, the duty was first proposed in *Gold v Essex County Council*[130] by Lord Greene MR to impose liability on a hospital for the negligence of a radiographer.[131] MacKinnon and Goddard LJJ relied on vicarious liability.[132] Lord Greene MR stated that the correct question in determining the defendant's duty to patients was to ask what obligation had it 'assumed' or 'undertaken'?[133] He concluded that the hospital assumed an obligation to treat the patient rather than merely provide staff and facilities for his treatment. The hospital was in breach of its duty to treat the patient when he was treated *negligently*.[134] In the subsequent cases of *Cassidy v Ministry of Health*[135] and *Roe v Minister of Health*,[136] Denning LJ (as he then was) applied a hospital's non-delegable duty to fix it with liability for the negligence of all hospital staff. In *Cassidy* Denning LJ stated:[137]   **8.25**

---

[124] ibid, 142. He declined to apply the maxim *res ipsa loquitur*.

[125] ibid, 141–2.

[126] See Jones, M, *Medical Negligence* (3rd edn, 2003), 611–19.

[127] See *McDermid v Nash Dredging and Reclamation Co Ltd* [1987] AC 906 (HL).

[128] Providing it was not 'co-lateral', ie unrelated to the delegated task. See Atiyah, *Vicarious Liability in Tort* (n 17 above), ch 33, especially 376–8.

[129] ibid. See generally, McKendrick, E, 'Vicarious Liability and Independent Contractors—A Re-examination' (1990) 53 MLR 770.

[130] [1942] 2 KB 293.

[131] ibid, 301.

[132] ibid, 308–309 and 312–313 respectively; but notice Goddard LJ at 309. See above, para 8.05.

[133] ibid, 301–302.

[134] ibid, 304.

[135] [1951] 2 KB 343.

[136] [1954] 2 QB 66.

[137] N 135 above, 365.

> . . . the hospital authorities accepted the plaintiff as a patient for treatment, and it was their duty to treat him with reasonable care. They selected, employed, and paid all the surgeons and nurses who looked after him. He had no say in their selection at all. If those surgeons and nurses did not treat him with proper care and skill, then the hospital authorities must answer for it, for it means that they themselves did not perform their duty to him.

8.26   The other judges in *Cassidy* and *Roe* rested the defendants' liability on vicarious liability.[138] No subsequent English case has directly faced up to whether a hospital is under this more onerous duty. Curiously, in *X (minors) v Bedfordshire County Council*,[139] Lord Browne-Wilkinson, relying upon the earlier 'hospital' cases, stated:[140]

> even where there is no allegation of a separate duty of care owed by a servant of the [local social services and health authority] to the plaintiff, the negligent acts of that servant are capable of constituting a breach of the duty of care (if any) owed directly by the authority to the plaintiff.

8.27   What is to be made of this statement is unclear.[141] On the face of it, Lord Browne-Wilkinson is accepting the non-delegable duty in the hospital cases: there is no other plausible explanation of what he said. He is only correct if the non-delegable duty does exist; and, he does, after all, cite the judgments of Lord Greene MR in *Gold* and of Denning LJ in *Cassidy* and *Roe*. His reservation—'the duty of care (if any)'—is not a reservation about the hospital cases but rather about the duty owed in the child abuse context which he is considering in the *Bedfordshire* case and which the House of Lords went on to decide did not exist. Yet, a few sentences earlier he specifically said that he expressed 'no view on the extent of [the hospital's] duty'![142] Finally, in *Robertson v Nottingham HA*, Brooke LJ declined to address the question of whether a hospital owed a non-delegable duty to ensure care is taken of a patient.[143] Thus, the issue remains open in the modern case law.

(b) Yepremian *and* Ellis

8.28   By contrast, two Commonwealth decisions have considered in depth whether an institution has a non-delegable duty of care to its patients. In *Yepremian v Scarborough General Hospital*[144] the plaintiff attended the emergency department of the defendant's hospital. He was hyperventilating and had been vomiting, and also had an increased frequency of urinating and drinking. He was seen by the

---

[138] See above, para 8.05.
[139] [1995] 2 AC 633; [1995] 3 All ER 353 (HL).
[140] ibid, 372.
[141] See Cane, P, 'Suing Public Authorities in Tort' (1996) 112 LQR 13, 20–1.
[142] Notice his later reference to *Gold* (n 139 above, 392–3) as authority for the hospital being 'under a duty to those whom it admits to exercise reasonable care in the way it runs it'. This is a statement of the accepted, and less onerous, primary duty of a hospital.
[143] N 111 above, 13.
[144] (1980) 110 DLR (3d) 513 (Ont CA).

doctor on duty. The doctor failed to diagnose that the patient was suffering from diabetes and although he was subsequently admitted to the hospital he suffered a cardiac arrest and resultant brain damage. He sued the defendant for the negligence of the doctor. The doctor was not an employee of the hospital but had admission privileges. By a majority[145] the Ontario Court of Appeal held that the defendant was not liable since it did not owe the plaintiff a non-delegable duty to exercise reasonable care.[146] The court concluded that the only duty owed was to exercise reasonable care in picking its staff and there was no suggesting that this had been negligent or that the doctor was unqualified or incompetent.[147] The court distinguished the English cases of *Gold, Cassidy,* and *Roe* as simply reflecting the statutory framework of the NHS, namely the existence of a statutory duty to provide services and staff, which did not exist in Ontario. For good measure, the judges also concluded that any change in the status quo should come from the legislature and not the courts. The dissenting judges[148] held that a hospital could owe a non-delegable duty to patients: whether it did depended upon 'whether and to what extent a hospital assumes a direct duty' which 'depends upon the circumstances of the particular case'.[149] The other dissenting judge, Houlden JA, distinguished between two situations in applying this approach:[150]

> First, a general hospital may function as a place where medical care facilities are provided for the use of the physician and his patient. The patient comes to the hospital because his physician has decided that the hospital's facilities are needed for the proper care and treatment of the patient. . . . Where a hospital functions as merely the provider of medical care facilities then . . . a hospital is not responsible for the negligence of the physician. . . . Second, a general hospital may function as a place where a person in need of treatment goes to obtain treatment. Here the role of the hospital is that of an institution where medical treatment is made available to those who require it. . . . Does a hospital in these circumstances have a duty to provide proper medical care to a patient? In my judgment, it does.

On the facts, the minority concluded that the case fell into the second category. **8.29** The approach of the minority is attractive. It reflects the general approach of English law of asking what duty has the defendant 'assumed' or 'undertaken', expressly or impliedly? Not only the approach, but also the conclusion of the minority in *Yepremian,* seems preferable.[151]

---

[145] McKinnon ACJO, Arrup and Morden JJA.
[146] A subsequent appeal to the Canadian Supreme Court was settled. See Picard and Robertson (n 30 above), 390.
[147] See, eg, at 532 *per* Arrup JA (n 144 above).
[148] Blair and Houlden JJA.
[149] N 144 above, 579 *per* Blair JA.
[150] ibid, 581.
[151] In Picard and Robertson (n 30 above), 391, it is stated that the subsequent case law in Canada has followed the majority's approach with the exception of *Lachambre v Nair* [1989] 2 WWR 749 where a Saskatchewan court stated that a hospital had a non-delegable duty to ensure that the patient had given an informed consent. For a different approach in England, see *Blyth v Bloomsbury HA* [1993] 4 Med LR 151 (CA).

8.30   In the other Commonwealth decision of *Ellis v Wallsend District Hospital*,[152] the
New South Wales Court of Appeal essentially applied the approach of the minority in *Yepremian*, although the judges differed in its application. The plaintiff suffered from severe neck pain. She consulted a neuro-surgeon. He advised her that
she should undergo surgery and arranged for her to be admitted at the defendant's
hospital where he had admission privileges. The doctor informed her that there
was a slight risk of numbness but he did not tell her that there was a risk of paralysis or that the operation might not relieve her pain. Following the operation,
the plaintiff developed quadriplegia. She sued the doctor and hospital alleging,
inter alia, that it had been negligent not to warn her of the risk of paralysis and of
failure. Had she known, she would not have agreed to the procedure. Her action
against the hospital was based upon vicarious liability for the negligence of the
doctor and for breach of its non-delegable duty of care to her. A majority of the
Court of Appeal[153] held that the doctor was not an employee of the hospital. He
was an 'honorary medical officer' with admission privileges, but was in private
practice. Hence the hospital could not be vicariously liable.

8.31   As regard the hospital's direct duty to the patient, all the judges accepted that a
hospital did owe such a duty. However, the extent of the duty was dependent upon
the particular circumstances of each case. Samuels JA[154] stated that it was 'a question of what medical services the hospital has undertaken to supply'.[155] Samuels
JA concluded, that in the circumstances of the case, the hospital was not under a
non-delegable duty to ensure that care was taken of the plaintiff. Adopting an approach reminiscent of the minority in *Yepremian*, Samuels JA distinguished between the situation where the patient approached the hospital for treatment and
where the patient approached a doctor who arranged for the patient to be admitted to hospital.[156] In the first situation, which was not that in *Ellis*, Samuels JA
stated that the hospital by accepting the patient 'remains responsible to ensure
that whatever treatment or advice [is given] is given with proper care; its duty cannot be divested by delegation'.[157] By contrast, in the second situation, which was
Ellis, the patient looks to the doctor rather than the hospital for medical care. The
hospital is merely the place where the medical treatment is performed. The hospital's duty is limited to the services it provides, such as nurses and possibly any other
medical treatment following the operation. Kirby P dissented, holding that the
doctor was an integral part of the hospital, and for reasons of policy and practice
it was appropriate to impose a non-delegable duty upon the hospital; it was not a

---

[152] (1989) 17 NSWLR 553; [1990] 2 Med LR 103 (NSW CA).
[153] Samuels and Meagher JJA. Kirby P dissenting.
[154] With whom Meagher JA agreed.
[155] N 155 above, 130.
[156] See also *Gold* (n 130 above), *per* Lord Greene MR at 302.
[157] N 152 above, 130.

'mere custodial institution designed to provide a place where medical personnel could meet and treat persons lodged there'.[158] The patient looked to the hospital to provide care and compensation when something went wrong.

(c) *England Again*

What duty is owed by a NHS institution such as a Trust to a patient? As was noted earlier, the underlying approach of the minority in *Yepremian* and of the New South Wales Court of Appeal in *Ellis*, reflects English law.[159] The difficulty, as *Ellis* well illustrates, is applying the approach.[160] Certainly when a patient is seen at an accident and emergency department (A & E), it is likely that the law imposes a non-delegable duty on the institution to take care of the patient. In *Barnett v Chelsea and Kensington HMC*[161] Nield J, in part, placed the 'duty' in that case upon the defendant directly. It was a duty to ensure that care was taken which was breached by the negligence of the doctor in failing to examine the patient in the A & E department. However, this certainty in the legal position goes no further than situations *within* the A & E department. Once the patient is admitted, then that patient will be in a somewhat similar position to other patients who have been referred to the hospital by their GP. What is their position? Of course, this is the very situation contemplated by Denning LJ in *Cassidy* and *Roe* as giving rise to the non-delegable duty. Is he correct? **8.32**

The usual situation within the NHS is quite different from that in *Ellis*. A doctor does not 'borrow' the hospital bed for his patient through an arrangement between himself and the hospital. The doctor will usually be an integral part of the hospital. The referral by the patient's GP is altogether different and irrelevant. Certainly, the patient would not look to the GP for his care *whilst in hospital*. He will, of course, look to his doctor—the consultant under whose care he is admitted to the hospital—and, to that extent, it might be doubted whether the patient looks to the hospital rather than the doctor for care. But, it would normally be reasonable to say that notwithstanding this, an NHS patient looks to the hospital rather than the particular doctor. That, after all, is part of the ethos of the NHS. The patient is most unlikely to have chosen the doctor. The PCT will have chosen the NHS Trust through the 'commissioning' process, but no one will usually select the *particular* doctor. Consequently, it is suggested that Denning LJ may **8.33**

---

[158] ibid, 112 quoting Reynolds JA in *Albrighton v Royal Prince Alfred Hospital* [1980] 2 NSWLR 542 (NSW CA) at 562.

[159] The essence of the issue is 'undertaking' and what responsibility has the hospital 'assumed', or is deemed to have assumed, to the patient: see *Kondis v State Transport Authority* (1984) 154 CLR 672 (Aust HCt), 687 *per* Mason J.

[160] See McKendrick (n 129 above), 774–6. See also, *Rogers v Night Riders* [1983] RTR 324 (CA) where it was held that a minicab service owed a non-delegable duty of care to a passenger who was injured by the negligence of an independent contractor-driver.

[161] [1969] 1 QB 428; [1968] 1 All ER 1068.

have been correct and that, within the NHS, a hospital does owe a non-delegable duty to its patients to ensure that reasonable care is taken of them during their time in hospital. Even where a particular specialist doctor has been chosen by the patient's GP, *the patient* will still look to the hospital for his overall care.[162]

8.34 In practical terms what, if any, is the effect of recognising this non-delegable duty? The answer is almost none. A hospital will be liable for the negligence of any one acting on its behalf whether employee or independent contractor.[163] Rarely, however, will the negligent individual not be an employee for whom the hospital would be liable in any event on the basis of vicarious liability. In that rare case, perhaps of a visiting doctor or agency nurse who is not employed by the hospital but who negligently injures the patient, the non-delegable duty will impose liability where otherwise there would be none. Otherwise, however, in the NHS context this more onerous duty, novel in modern times, adds little.

8.35 It may, however, have important consequences in cases of treatment in a private hospital or clinic as a NHS patient.[164] With the increase in 'contracted out' services within the NHS, the issue of primary liability will become more significant. Where the care or treatment is provided by a third party, perhaps a private clinic, on behalf of the NHS, can the NHS be liable for the private clinic's negligence because it has a duty to ensure reasonable care is provided to the NHS patient?

(d) Two Recent English Cases

8.36 In *M v Calderdale and Kirklees HA*[165] an English court answered this question in the affirmative. The claimant, who was pregnant, was referred by a doctor employed by the first defendant to the second defendant, a private clinic, for an abortion. The doctor told the claimant that arrangements would be made for the abortion. Thereafter, the claimant was treated at the second defendant's clinic but subsequently it was discovered that the procedure had failed and she was still pregnant. She gave birth to a child and brought an action against both defendants alleging negligence. Judgment was obtained against the second defendant but they were subject to a winding-up order. On the liability of the first defendant, Judge Garner held that the first defendant owed a duty to bring about for the claimant the effective provision of services either *by itself or by arranging for others to do so*. This was a non-delegable duty owed by the first defendant. The claimant

---

[162] Recently, Bell J described Lord Greene MR's view as having 'great force' where a hospital had accepted a patient for treatment or advice: *A v Ministry of Defence and Guy's and St Thomas' Hospital NHS Trust* [2003] EWHC 849 (QB) at [68]. For a discussion of this case, see below paras 8.37–8.41.

[163] For contracted-out services, see the Deregulation and Contracting Out Act 1994, s 72(2).

[164] The primary duty issue may also be important where the patient is being treated as a private patient in a clinic: see below.

[165] [1998] Lloyd's Rep Med 157 (Huddersfield County Ct). See further Grubb (1998) 6 Med L Rev 375 (Commentary).

was always in its care and should be in the same position as a patient treated 'in house'. In any event, the judge held that the first defendant was itself negligent because reasonable care had not been taken in its dealings with the second defendant: (i) it had no idea whether or not indemnity insurance was carried by the second defendant; (ii) it had no up-to-date information about the competence of the second defendant or its staff; and (iii) the first defendant seemed to have relied upon enquiries assumed to be ongoing by others and an apparent absence of complaints.

In the more recent case of *A v Ministry of Defence and Guy's and St Thomas' Hospital NHS Trust*[166] a more restrictive view was taken on the facts. In order to provide medical services to military personnel and their families in Germany, the Ministry of Defence (MoD) entered into an arrangement with Guy's and St Thomas' Hospital NHS Trust (the Trust) to procure certain secondary healthcare with German providers. The Trust duly did so with designated German hospitals. The claimant 'A' and her mother were the child and wife respectively of a British soldier serving in Germany. A was born in a designated hospital and, it was alleged, suffered from serious and permanent brain damage as a result of negligence in the course of delivery. The issue for the English court was whether A's claim could be brought in England—as A's mother, her litigation friend wished or in Germany. The answer would only be 'yes' if the MoD or the Trust owed 'A' a non-delegable duty of care.   **8.37**

Bell J reviewed the authorities relating to employers and hospitals non-delegable duties. He concluded that the scope and extent of any duty depended upon what obligation the MoD or Trust had assumed to service personnel.   **8.38**

As regards the MoD, Bell J held that since 1996, when the MoD ceased to provide its own hospitals, the MoD only undertook to 'arrange' for treatment rather than 'provide it'.[167] The Trust undertook to procure and manage the contractual obligations with the designated hospitals: there was therefore 'no obvious policy reason' for the MoD 'to retain direct personal responsibility' for treating soldiers and their families.[168] Bell J concluded:[169]   **8.39**

> The MoD did not [service personnel and their dependents] as patients for the purposes of hospital care. What it assumed, and put into effect by various contractual arrangements with [the Trust] was the obligation to provide access to an appropriate system or regime of secondary, hospital care provided by another.

---

[166] [2003] EWHC 849 (QB) (Bell J).
[167] ibid, at [97].
[168] ibid, at [100].
[169] ibid, at [101].

The MoD's obligations were limited to exercising reasonable care in selecting and putting in place appropriate providers of hospital care. It discharged that obligation by contracting with the Trust to procure and manage the arrangements with German hospitals.[170]

8.40 As regards the Trust, Bell J applied the 'three stage' approach in *Caparo Industries plc v Dickman*.[171] He concluded that the Trust must have known that if it carelessly selected a hospital or mismanaged a contract with them, this might result in an unsafe hospital regime and injury might result. Thus, the 'foreseeability' and 'proximity' stages of the *Caparo* test were satisfied. However, Bell J held that it was not 'fair, just and reasonable' to impose a duty upon the Trust to 'ensure that reasonable care and skill' was used in a German hospital.[172] The Trust's duty had to be seen in the context of what it had contracted with the MoD to do. It had not contracted to treat British patients nor had it contracted to manage the German hospitals. It had merely contracted to select them and then manage the contracts. Its duty was limited to exercise reasonable care in these respects.[173]

8.41 There is no necessary inconsistency between *M v Calderdale and Kirklees HA* and *A v Ministry of Defence*. Although Bell J was less than complementary about the reasoning in the former case, in essence the difference between the cases lies in the assumption of responsibility by the defendant. In *M*, the claimant was and remained an NHS patient. In *A*, the claimant was never an MoD or Trust patient. Reading Bell J's judgment carefully might lead the reader to conclude that he actually agreed with the non-delegable duty proposed in *Gold* and thus, at least, the result in *M*.[174]

2. In Private Practice

8.42 To what extent will a private clinic or hospital be liable for injuries caused to patients? The answer must principally depend upon the contract, if any, between the clinic and the patient. An action for breach of contract may lie against the clinic either for breach of an express or an implied term. In tort, it is likely the law will impose a direct duty upon the clinic. Depending upon the contractual arrangement, the duty is likely to encompass the exercise of reasonable care in the provision of the services and staff supplied under the contract with the patient.[175] What, however, of the negligence of a doctor? In some (perhaps unusual) situations the doctor will be an employee of the clinic; in which case the clinic will be vicariously liable for his negligence. Where he is not an employee, however, the

---

[170] [2003] EWHC 849 at [107].
[171] [1990] 2 AC 605, especially *per* Lord Bridge at 617–618.
[172] N 166 above, at [110].
[173] ibid, at [110].
[174] N 165 above.
[175] If not an express term, it will certainly be implied.

clinic's liability will turn upon whether it has assumed a non-delegable duty to the patient. This must ultimately be a factual matter depending upon the particular situation. In principle, the legal approach must be the same as that discussed earlier in relation to NHS institutions. A patient who receives treatment in a clinic where the doctor only has admission privileges will not be owed a non-delegable duty of care by the clinic.[176] The patient must look solely to the doctor for compensation for his negligence. In the private context, however, reliance on a particular doctor or particular hospital's reputation is more likely, for instance in the context of infertility treatment. In the former case, the clinic probably does not undertake a non-delegable duty to the patient. It will be the doctor alone who will be liable for his negligence. In the latter case, it will be otherwise.

3. 'Commissioners'

Within the NHS the services which a 'provider' institution, such as a NHS Trust, must provide are set out in 'NHS contracts' made under the National Health Service and Community Care Act 1990.[177] Civil actions based upon the negligent *non-provision* of care through an 'NHS contract' are most unlikely to succeed.[178] The courts will leave the patient to what remedies, if any, that may lie in public law.[179] Could a patient sue a PCT[180] who had commissioned inadequate care which resulted in injury to the patient? Would the PCT owe a duty to exercise reasonable care in placing and providing for care under 'NHS contracts'? Further, could an action lie if negligent care was provided and the PCT had failed properly to monitor the provider in the performance of the 'NHS contract'? To the extent that such actions involve the direct exercise of delegated statutory powers by the PCT and raise questions of policy, it is most unlikely that the law would entertain any private, as opposed to public, law remedies against the PCT.[181] However, if the failure stems from a clinical judgment about the proper 'care package' needed, or from oversights or mistakes in monitoring, then in principle, a direct duty to exercise reasonable care would be owed to an injured patient even if there will be obvious difficulties of proving causation and, in the case of clinical judgments, of establishing a breach of duty.[182]

8.43

---

[176] See *Ellis* (n 81 above) and *Cassidy* (n 135 above), *per* Denning LJ at 362 (referring to 'the patient [who] himself selects and employs the doctor').

[177] s 4.

[178] For a discussion of tort liability within the NHS 'internal market', see Barker, K, 'NHS Contracting: Shadows in the Law of Tort?' (1995) 3 Med L Rev 161.

[179] See Jacob, J, 'Lawyers Go To Hospital' [1991] PL 255 and Longley, D, 'Diagnostic Dilemmas: Accountability in the National Health Service' [1990] PL 527.

[180] Or local health board in Wales.

[181] See below, paras 8.49–8.58.

[182] See by analogy the approach of Bell J in *A v Ministry of Defence and Guy's and St Thomas' Hospital NHS Trust* [2003] EWHC 849 (QB).

4. The Secretary of State

8.44 The National Health Service Act 1977 places a duty upon the Secretary of State to provide a 'comprehensive health service' in England.[183] The Act further imposes a duty upon the Secretary of State to provide certain services such as hospital accommodation and medical, dental, nursing, and ambulance services.[184] The duty is not an absolute one but rather the more limited one to provide them 'to such extent as he considers necessary to meet all reasonable requirements'.[185] In practice, the vast majority of the Secretary of State's functions are delegated by statutory instrument to PCTs in England,[186] although some functions are retained centrally or delegated to Strategic Health Authorities in England. It may be, as a matter of theory, that the duties under the 1977 Act are non-delegable in the sense that the Secretary of State (or National Assembly for Wales) remains responsible for failures to comply with the Act. However, the 1977 Act states that the body to whom the power or function has been delegated should be sued and not the Secretary of State.[187] Hence, a claim against the Secretary of State directly could only lie where the action arises out of (i) the exercise (or non-exercise) of a retained function; or (ii) an ancillary function of the Secretary of State, such as providing advice to doctors or NHS Trusts which are alleged to be negligent.

8.45 Could a civil action for damages be brought by a patient who suffered injury as a result of an alleged breach of the statutory duties contained in the 1977 Act? Almost certainly not; because there will be immense difficulties, first in establishing a breach of the duty[188] and, secondly in fixing the Secretary of State with liability in private, rather than public, law.

8.46 Crucial, however, will be the difficulty faced by a litigant in showing that any civil claim for damages can be established. The two possibilities are (i) civil liability for breach of statutory duty; and (ii) negligence.

(i) Breach of Statutory Duty

8.47 A private cause of action for damages will arise for breach of a statutory duty only in exceptional circumstances. Usually, the only remedy for such breach will lie in public law. If, as a matter of construction, it can be shown that the statutory duty

---

[183] s 1. For Wales, the duty is placed upon the National Assembly for Wales.

[184] s 3(1).

[185] ibid. See also *R v Secretary of State for Social Services, ex p Hincks* (1980) 1 BMLR 93 (CA).

[186] In Wales, most of the functions are delegated by the National Assembly for Wales to local health boards.

[187] National Health Service Act 1977, Sch 5, para 15(1).

[188] See below, paras 8.59–8.87 and see for the difficulties of establishing a breach at the public law level: *R v Secretary of State for Social Services, ex p Hincks* (1980) 1 BMLR 93 (CA); *R v Central Birmingham HA, ex p Walker* (1987) 3 BMLR 32 (CA); and *R v Central Birmingham HA, ex p Collier* (6 January 1988, CA).

was imposed for the protection of a limited class of the public and that Parliament intended to confer on members of that class a private right of action, then a damages action can be brought.[189] What of the 1977 Act? It is almost inconceivable that the courts will construe the duties under the 1977 Act as giving rise to an action for damages. In *X (Minors) v Bedfordshire County Council*, Lord Browne-Wilkinson observed that no case had been cited to the court where such an action had been recognised for breach of 'statutory provisions establishing a regulatory system or scheme of social welfare for the benefit of the public at large'.[190] He concluded that:[191]

> Although regulatory welfare legislation affecting a particular area of activity does in fact provide protection to those individuals particularly affected by that activity, the legislation is not to be treated as being passed for the benefit of those individuals but for the benefit of society in general.

This account wholly covers the NHS legislation. Lord Browne-Wilkinson may **8.48** even have had the NHS in mind since it is the most obvious, and expansive, example of such a welfare scheme as he describes. In *Re HIV Litigation*,[192] the Court of Appeal held that ss 1 and 3(1) of the 1977 Act did not give rise to an action for breach of statutory duty. Referring to the nature of the duties imposed by the 1977 Act, Ralph Gibson LJ said that '[they] do not clearly demonstrate the intention of Parliament to impose a duty which is to be enforced by individual civil action'.[193] It is most unlikely that breach of any duty relating to the health service will be construed as giving rise to a claim for damages.[194]

(ii) Negligence

No less problematic will be a claim by a patient framed in negligence against the **8.49** Secretary of State (or his delegate) arising out of the exercise (or non-exercise) of the statutory powers under the 1977 Act. The reluctance of the courts to spell out a cause of action in negligence when the defendant is exercising statutory powers

---

[189] *X (Minors) v Bedfordshire County Council* [1995] 3 All ER 353 (HL) *per* Lord Browne-Wilkinson at 364.

[190] ibid, 364.

[191] ibid.

[192] [1996] PNLR 290 (CA).

[193] ibid, 310. Contrast the divergent view of Judge Garner in *M v Calderdale and Kirklees HA* [1998] Lloyd's Rep Med 157 at 161 that a 'non-delegable' duty was imposed upon the NHS under s 1 of the National Health Service Act 1977 which could give rise to a claim in damages. Note the criticism: *A v Ministry of Defence and Guy's and St Thomas' Hospital NHS Trust* [2003] EWHC 849 (QB), *per* Bell J at [53].

[194] See *Danns v Department of Health* (1995) 25 BMLR 121 (Wright J); on appeal [1998] PIQR P226 (CA)—where the claim was abandoned and it was 'right to do so' *per* Leggatt LJ at P228. See also *Ross v Secretary of State for Scotland* 1990 SLT 13 (Lord Milligan). When *Danns* reached the Court of Appeal ([1998] PIQR P226), the claimants abandoned their claim for breach of statutory duty under s 2 of the Ministry of Health Act 1919 and Leggatt LJ stated (at P228) that they were 'right to do so'.

is well recognised.[195] The courts will require that the duty requirements applicable against a private defendant are satisfied, namely foreseeability, proximity, and public policy which may be difficult enough in this context for an injured patient.[196] Also, the courts will require that the patient establish that the defendant acted outside his statutory powers under public law principles, namely illegality and irrationality. As a consequence, a decision made under the 1977 Act which is discretionary must be shown to be ultra vires. Importantly, the courts will be unable to do this where the exercise (or non-exercise) of the discretion involved policy considerations which the court is unable to adjudicate upon on the basis that they are non-justiciable.[197] A negligence action which is based upon such a decision will, as a consequence, fail.

8.50   In some cases, the distinction is drawn between 'policy' decisions (non-justiciable) and 'operational' decisions (which may be justiciable). It is illustrated by the case of *Department of Health and Social Security v Kinnear*.[198] The claimant suffered injury allegedly caused by the pertussis or whooping cough vaccine. He sued the Department of Health on the basis first, that it had been negligent to promote immunisation with the vaccine and secondly, that its advice to doctors on the circumstances when it should or should not be administered was negligent. The defendant sought to strike out the action. As regards the Department's policy on immunisation, Stuart-Smith J struck out the claim on the basis that it was a policy within the powers of the Secretary of State. By contrast, he allowed that part of the action relying on the negligent advice to proceed because it fell within the 'operational' area of the statutory power and it was arguable that this could be the basis for a duty of care in negligence.

8.51   It is arguable that Stuart-Smith J misunderstood the 'policy'/'operational' distinction as it would be perceived after the decisions of the House of Lords in *X (Minors) v Bedfordshire County Council*[199] and *Stovin v Wise*.[200] It is not at all clear why the DoH policy was non-justiciable when it was argued that its basis was *factually* flawed due to negligence in the process leading up to the formulation of the policy.[201]

---

[195] eg, *X (Minors) v Bedfordshire County Council* [1995] 3 All ER 353 (HL).

[196] eg, *Danns* (n 194 above). See *X (Minors) v Bedfordshire County Council*, ibid, *per* Lord Browne-Wilkinson at 371.

[197] *X (Minors) v Bedfordshire County Council* (n 195 above) and *Stovin v Wise (Norfolk County Council, third party)* [1996] AC 923 (HL).

[198] (1984) 134 NLJ 886.

[199] N 195 above.

[200] N 197 above.

[201] See, eg, the approach of the Court of Appeal in *R v North West Lancashire HA, ex p A, D and G* [2000] 1 WLR 977 (CA).

Two subsequent Scottish cases have, however, taken a similar view in respect of **8.52** government policies to promote the triple vaccine for whooping cough, diphtheria, and tetanus[202] and the vaccine for smallpox.[203] Indeed, in these cases it was also held that allegations of negligence in the promotional information and guidance sent to the medical profession could not found actions. In *Ross*, Lord Milligan stated that the pursuer's action in negligence related to 'decisions as to what information was to be issued to whom and how it was to be issued'.[204] As such, he concluded these were matters of 'policy and discretion'.[205] Even here, where Stuart-Smith J, in *Kinnear*, regarded the decision as justiciable because it was within the 'operational' area of the discretion, the courts will not impose a duty of care if the discretion is exercised bona fide. In *Bonthrone*, Lord Grieve would have imposed a duty of care if the negligence did not relate to the *decision* of what information to disseminate or to whom it was to be given, but rather to the *actual act of dissemination* by, for example, negligently sending the information out so that not all doctors received it.[206]

Thus, the scope for imposing a duty of care when the Secretary of State (or his dele- **8.53** gate) is engaged in the direct exercise of his statutory powers is extremely limited. Operational activities of the sort contemplated in *Kinnear* and *Bonthrone* will, by and large, be restricted to the actual provision of care by the delegate or on his behalf by a Trust within the NHS. Decisions about local or national policy of what care to provide, and to whom, within the NHS will not give rise to private law actions. A patient's remedy will lie, if at all, in public law.[207]

In *Re HIV Haemophiliac Litigation*,[208] the Court of Appeal went a little further **8.54** than this would suggest the law to be. The plaintiffs were haemophiliacs and their families who had been infected with HIV as a result of using the contaminated blood clotting agent, Factor VIII, imported from the United States. The plaintiffs sued, inter alia, the Secretary of State, alleging he had negligently failed to make the United Kingdom self-sufficient in blood products and thereby remove the greater risk of infection posed by blood products derived from the United States. As a preliminary matter the plaintiffs sought discovery of documents which was resisted on the basis that the plaintiffs did not have a cause of action against the

---

[202] *Bonthrone v Secretary of State for Scotland* 1987 SLT 34 (Lord Grieve).

[203] *Ross v Secretary of State for Scotland* 1990 SLT 13 (Lord Milligan).

[204] ibid, 17.

[205] ibid. See also *Smith v Secretary of State for Health* [2002] EWHC 200 (QB) and (2002) 67 BMLR 34 (Morland J)—no liability in negligence where Committee on Safety of Medicines took a decision not to issue an interim warning of the risk to children of Reye's Syndrome from aspirin as it was a non-justiciable decision within its discretionary power.

[206] N 202 above, 41.

[207] eg, *R v Cambridge HA, ex p B* [1995] 1 WLR 898 (CA); cf *R v North Derbyshire HA, ex p Fisher* [1997] 8 Med LR 327 (Dyson J).

[208] [1996] PNLR 290 (CA).

Secretary of State. The Court of Appeal held that it was arguable that a duty of care was owed. While recognising the rarity of such a duty in this context, the Court of Appeal held that merely because the attack on the government's policy involved questions of resource allocation did not, ipso facto, prevent a duty arising. The judges identified the difficulties facing the plaintiffs in making good their case but they were not prepared to rule out the claim in negligence as unarguable.

8.55 Too much should not be made of this case.[209] First, it was an interlocutory appeal relating to discovery of documents. The Court of Appeal only concluded that a negligence action *might* exist on the facts if established. Bingham LJ, in particular, was circumspect about the plaintiffs' prospects for success at trial.[210] The nature of the decisions that were being taken by the government about the provision of health care for haemophiliacs was a stereotypical one of discretion, laced with more than a tinge of policy and resource allocation which is outside the court's competence to enquire into. Had their actions come to court, they would surely have lost.[211] Secondly, even if the plaintiffs overcame these obstacles, like all other plaintiffs suing the Secretary of State, they would have had insuperable difficulties in establishing 'proximity'. It was, so it would seem from Bingham LJ's judgment, conceded in *Re HIV Haemophiliac Litigation* that such a relationship existed.[212] Why is not clear. There arguably was not a sufficiently close relationship between the parties to found a duty of care.[213]

8.56 The issue is similar to the one which arose more recently in *Danns v Department of Health*.[214] The husband of a couple underwent a vasectomy. Later his wife became pregnant and gave birth to a healthy child. At no time was the husband told the risk of natural reversal by a process known as 'late recanalisation' although the risk was known from research published in the professional press. They sued the Department of Health in negligence[215] alleging that in breach of the duty under s 2 of the Ministry of Health Act 1919, the Secretary of State had negligently failed to disseminate information concerning the risks to the public through 'Dear Doctor' letters. Section 2 provides that the Secretary of State must take all such steps as are desirable, inter alia, to publish and disseminate information relating to the prevention and cure of diseases and the treatment of physical and mental defects. Wright J dismissed the claimants' actions.[216] The Court of Appeal robustly dismissed the claimants' appeal.

---

[209] For a discussion of the action, see Grubb, A and Pearl, D, *Blood Testing, AIDS and DNA Profiling* (1990), 103–7.

[210] N 208 above, 323 and 324.

[211] See Grubb and Pearl (n 209 above), 105.

[212] N 208 above, 324.

[213] See Grubb and Pearl (n 209 above), 106–7.

[214] [1998] PIQR P226 (CA) and Grubb (1998) 6 Med L Rev 371 (Commentary).

[215] And for breach of statutory duty: on which, see above, paras 8.47–8.48.

[216] (1995) 25 BMLR 121 (Wright J) and Kennedy, (1996) 4 Med L Rev 324 (Commentary).

The Court of Appeal held that the judge had been correct to conclude that the **8.57** Department had considered the research and its decision not to disseminate the information further was within its statutory discretion under s 2 of the 1919 Act. Thus, the claimants had failed to establish that the Department had gone outside its statutory power. Leggatt LJ stated that even if the Department had not considered whether to disseminate the research, it would have been rational not to distribute it more widely. The judges went on to consider the claimants' action applying the *Caparo* tests. The claimants argued that there was a 'proximate relationship' between the parties because the general public placed general reliance upon the Department in performing its statutory functions. The court rejected the argument: the relationship was too 'remote' (*per* Leggatt LJ) and they were not 'neighbours' (*per* Roch LJ). Roch LJ also agreed with the trial judge that it was not 'fair, just and reasonable' to impose a duty of care. It would be too onerous an obligation for the Department given that this information was already available to doctors in other publications.

The decision is obviously correct. Absent specific reliance by the claimants and **8.58** knowledge of that by the Department, there was not the necessary 'assumption of responsibility' towards the claimants. Also, looking at the reality of the situation, the Department was surely entitled to rely upon doctors as 'learned intermediaries' to provide such information as was reasonable to their patients.

C. Breach of Duty by Institution

The question asked here is what quantum of care is expected of an institutional **8.59** defendant, such as a NHS Trust (any differences in the law when the defendant is a privately funded institution will be noted as they arise). Two different duties have been identified as being owed by an institution: a non-delegable duty and the duty to maintain a safe system of working. As regards the former, the issues of duty and breach are considered above. It is the latter which will be examined here.

Clearly, whether an institution is in breach of its duty to provide a safe system of **8.60** working is ultimately always a question of fact. But, while this is true, it leaves open certain issues of legal analysis. These are: the *quantum of care* which the law may properly expect of an institution; the *process of establishing breach*, most particularly the relevance, if any, of the *Bolam* case;[217] and the vexed question of the *relevance of resources*. These will be considered in turn.

---

[217] *Bolam v Friern Hospital Management Committee* [1957] 2 All ER 118, and see now *Bolitho v City and Hackney HA* [1997] 4 All ER 771.

1. Degrees of Care

8.61   Is the quantum of care the same for all institutions, or does it vary as between, for example, a general hospital and a centre of excellence? Resort to first principles would suggest two propositions. One proposition is that there must be an irreducible minimum of care which is demanded of any and all institutions. This is reflected in the general law of torts in the well-known case of *Nettleship v Weston*.[218] The case did not involve institutional liability but, mutatis mutandis, would appear to apply with equal force here. Indeed, all of the judgments of the Court of Appeal in *Wilsher v Essex AHA*[219] seem to suggest, while not deciding the point, that an institution may be liable *primarily* if its services do not measure up to that which may properly be expected.[220] As Browne-Wilkinson LJ put it in *Wilsher*, the hospital may be directly liable if it 'so conducts its hospital that it fails to provide doctors of sufficient skill and experience *to give the treatment offered* at the hospital' (emphasis added). The reference to 'the treatment offered' is crucial. It means that the NHS Trust will be judged on what it represented as being available by way of treatment services. But, it also means that whatever treatment is offered must measure up to some basic level of care. This proposition is well illustrated by the decision of the Court of Appeal in *Bull v Devon AHA*.[221] In that case, the court found unanimously that the system for providing obstetric care was deficient. As Brooke LJ put it, in discussing *Bull* in the later case of *Robertson v Nottingham HA*,[222] the defendant did not operate 'a system whereby, except in unforeseen contingencies, a responsible doctor would have attended reasonably quickly in relation to such an emergency [as arose]'. The circumstances which a court is entitled to take account of in deciding what level of care can be expected of an institution are explored more fully below.[223]

8.62   Browne-Wilkinson LJ's reference to 'the treatment offered' also provides the second general principle by reference to which an institution's duty can be judged. While every institution must meet a minimum standard of care, if an institution offers more than the minimum, it will be held to whatever is judged to be the proper level of service for what it offers.[224] Thus, an institution which claims to have a specialist unit in, for example, child care will be expected to have available

---

[218] [1971] 2 QB 691.

[219] [1987] QB 730.

[220] Thus, the standard of care expected of the prison service in respect of ante-natal care provided to a pregnant remand prisoner was the same as if she were at liberty: *Brooks v Home Office* (1999) 48 BMLR 109 (Garland J), distinguishing *Knight v Home Office* (1989) 4 BMLR 85 (Pill J) (psychiatric care for a prisoner detained in prison hospital).

[221] N 116 above.

[222] N 111 above.

[223] At paras 8.66 *et seq*.

[224] As was said earlier, it is a separate question, discussed at para 8.64 below, how the criteria of the appropriate level of care are determined.

an appropriate range of skilled staff and equipment to meet the needs of such a unit. This proposition is no more than an application of the principle that a defendant will be held to the standard of care which he professes to offer.[225] This is confirmed by Mustill LJ's comment in *Wilsher* that, had the case been argued on the basis of *primary* rather than vicarious liability, the plaintiff would have asserted that 'the defendants owed a duty to ensure that the special baby care unit functioned according to the standard reasonably to be expected of such a unit'. Thus, in conclusion, while a general hospital is held to a standard of care commensurate with the services it offers, a centre of excellence breaches its duty when it fails to meet appropriate levels of excellence.

2. Level of Care

As has been noted, to assert that an institution must meet the quantum of care expected of it or claimed by it, is not to determine how that level of care is arrived at, or, put another way, how breach of duty is established. To go to the heart of the question, what weight does the law assign to expert evidence and, even more critically, what role, if any, is played by *Bolam*? Browne-Wilkinson LJ observed in *Wilsher* that to hold an institution primarily liable would 'raise awkward questions'. He expressed the first of these awkward questions as follows: '[t]o what extent should the [health] authority by held liable if . . . it is only adopting a practice hallowed by tradition?' Although Browne-Wilkinson LJ merged this question into a further enquiry about resources,[226] it is a question which must be addressed in its own right. Can an institution claim that it has complied with its duty because it has done that which other institutions of a like nature have done? It is important to state the question in this way to make it clear that what is under discussion is not any alleged breach of duty by the doctors or other staff, for which the hospital would be vicariously liable, but the quantum of care expected of an institution itself in meeting its obligation to patients.

8.63

What evidence is relevant in determining this quantum of care? A starting point may be compliance with relevant Guidelines, Codes of Practice issued within the NHS or, perhaps most importantly, guidelines from NICE that lay down 'best practice'. A court will ordinarily regard failure to observe these as evidence of breach of duty, unless non-compliance can be justified on the facts.[227] Thereafter, expert evidence of those involved in the management and operation of institutions would appear to be the most relevant. Such a view, of course, would suggest that the expert views of doctors and other health care professionals, unless they were managers rather than, or as well as, providing care for patients, would not be particularly relevant. But this must be right if it is institutional liability, the

8.64

---

[225] *R v Bateman* (1925) 94 LJKB 791 (CCA).
[226] Discussed below at paras 8.66 *et seq*.
[227] See, eg, *R v North Derbyshire HA, ex p Fisher* [1997] 8 Med LR 327. See Ch 6 above.

liability of those managing the institution, which is under discussion. The views of doctors and others will, of course, be a critical element in establishing and monitoring any system of medical care. However, there may be other factors which managers must also take account of. Leaving aside the issue of allocating scarce resources,[228] the extent to which the manager may depart from the considered opinion of medical and other staff may still depend on the facts. Clearly, if there is a divergence of opinion among the health care professionals as to which of the various systems of care should prevail, the manager is entitled, indeed obliged, to make his own decision which will ordinarily involve opting for one of the systems proposed. He will not be judged to be in breach of duty if some harm later ensues, if he can show that the choice he made was reasonable and justified based on all the available evidence. This is not an application of *Bolam*. Instead, it is an application of the more general principle of tort law that the defendant's conduct is to be measured against what a reasonable person in the defendant's position and circumstances would have done. It also follows from this conclusion that it is more likely that the expert evidence of other managers of institutions, whether PCTs or hospitals, may be of greater relevance here than that of health care professionals. Of course, by contrast, where medical evidence all points in the same way as to the requirements for any particular system of care, and the manager has chosen to ignore it, a court will find it hard to avoid the conclusion that the institution is in breach of duty, whatever other managers may claim concerning the common practice of institutions.

8.65 What this proposed analysis makes abundantly clear is that, in the case of an alleged breach of duty by an institution, it must be for the *court*, as in the mainstream of tort law, to determine whether *on all the facts*, the defendant is in breach. *Bolam* can be seen to be only tangentially relevant, and even then, must be understood in the light of Lord Browne-Wilkinson's speech in *Bolitho v City and Hackney HA*.[229] As is too well known, *Bolam* came to be regarded as authority for the proposition that in cases of medical negligence, the evidence of medical professionals that the defendant complied with a practice regarded as reasonable by a responsible body of medical opinion was enough to absolve him of liability. *Bolitho* represents an attempt (perhaps less than whole-hearted) to drag medical negligence back into the mainstream of negligence (and into line with other common law jurisdictions), by reserving to the court the final say on breach of duty. *Bolitho* does so by drawing on cases both within and outside medical negligence. A fortiori since institutional liability is not a form of medical negligence (although it involves the practice of medicine), after *Bolitho*, it is the cases outside medical negligence which will guide the court.

---

[228] Discussed below at paras 8.66 *et seq.*
[229] N 217 above.

3. *Relevance of Resources*[230]

One factor which a manager will inevitably have taken account of in establishing   **8.66**
the system of working in any particular institution is the resources, both human
and material, available. If, notwithstanding discussions about resources, the manager is none the less able to provide and maintain a system which complies with
what the law may properly expect of the institution, no further questions arise.
But circumstances may be, and usually are, otherwise. This is where Browne-
Wilkinson LJ's second 'awkward question' in *Wilsher* comes in. 'Should the authority', he asks rhetorically, 'be liable if it demonstrates that due to the financial
stringency under which it operates, it cannot afford to fill the posts with those possessing the necessary experience' (or, fill them at all, it could be added).

It is helpful in answering the 'awkward question' about resources to separate out   **8.67**
two strands of enquiry. The first relates to the factual circumstances: what response has the institution made to the fact that it has insufficient resources to provide all the services that it would otherwise wish to provide? The second relates to
the legal basis of any liability: is any legal remedy founded in public law, through
judicial review, or private law through the tort of negligence? In what follows,
these two strands will be interwoven, but their importance should not be overlooked. Equally, a further, larger question should not be overlooked and will be
discussed as part of the analysis. The question is to what extent, if at all, should
matters of resource allocation be adjudicated upon by the courts when the distribution of scarce public resources is ordinarily perceived of as being a matter first
for politicians and then for managers. The issue is one of justiciability, which itself
is an issue ultimately of the perception by the courts of the proper reach of their
authority and the limits of their competence.

(i) Non-provision of Service

The first response of an institution to scarce resources which calls for analysis is   **8.68**
when the institution simply decides not to provide a particular service or range of
services. An example would be a decision not to offer accident and emergency services or a comprehensive orthopaedic service. This latter circumstance arose in the
well-known case of *R v Secretary of State for Social Services, ex p Hincks*[231] (the defendant was the Secretary of State but would now almost always be the Health
Authority). The Court of Appeal was in no doubt that the four plaintiffs, two
elderly women, an elderly man, and a girl, who had been waiting for orthopaedic
services for a number of years, had no case. The Secretary of State had, in the
event, decided not to fund the proposed scheme to establish such services,

---

[230] See generally, Witting, C, 'National Health Service rationing: Implications for the Standard of
Care in Negligence' (2001) 21 OJLS 443, esp 458–71.
[231] (1980) 1 BMLR 93.

preferring instead to allocate resources elsewhere. This non-provision of services did not, the Court held, give rise to a cause of action. Referring to the Secretary of State's duty, Lord Denning MR expressed himself in his usual pithy way as follows: 'It cannot be that the Secretary of State has a duty to provide everything that is asked for . . . [including] the numerous pills that people take nowadays: it cannot be said that he has to provide all these free for everybody.' Citing with approval Wien J's decision at first instance, that the Secretary of State was not under any absolute duty, but had a discretion as to how to allocate resources, he continued, '[t]he Secretary of State says that he is doing the best he can within the financial resources available to him: and I do not think he can be faulted in the matter'. Bridge LJ, in a concurring judgment, explained that if there are not unlimited resources, the Secretary of State 'must plan to provide a service within the ambit of some limitation upon the resources which are going to be available . . . If there is to be some limitation . . . the limitation must be determined *in the light of current government economic policy*' (emphasis added).

8.69 The action in *Hincks* was an action in public law for judicial review. The Court of Appeal held that the Secretary of State was not acting unreasonably. Put into the context of the current analysis, the Court of Appeal was in reality deciding that the exercise of discretion about resources was a matter for government, not for the courts. The rationale for this judicial self-denial is not hard to find. Most important, government is elected by and answerable to the public as regards the raising and distribution of public funds. Courts are not. In addition, as Lord Denning MR made clear in *Hincks*, financial decisions about particular services are not made in isolation. They are made in the context of the totality of the services offered. An expenditure here is a saving (or cut) there, where the financial cake to be cut is of a constant (or diminishing) size. Courts lack the relevant information, the expertise and the experience to make such decisions. Indeed, the moment they were to presume to enter the field of resource allocation to remedy some particular non-provision of services, they would in effect be taking over the management and running of the Health Service. This is clearly not to be contemplated as long as the Health Service is organised in its current form, with politicians ultimately answerable for its operation.

(a) R v Cambridge HA, ex p B (A Minor)

8.70 Two further cases in which an action for judicial review was brought against Health Authorities challenging the lawfulness of their non-provision of service warrant mention here. The first is *R v Cambridge HA, ex p B (A Minor)*.[232] This case achieved a certain notoriety because of the poignant nature of the facts. B, aged 10, having been diagnosed as suffering from common acute lymphoblastic

---

[232] (1995) 23 BMLR 1 (CA).

leukaemia, received two courses of chemotherapy and then a bone marrow transplant. Sadly, less than a year later, she fell ill with acute myeloid leukaemia. On the basis of expert advice, the Health Authority declined to authorise payment for B to be treated outside the Health Authority (an extra-contractual referral, in the language of the then purchaser–provider split). The case became something of a cause célèbre, with B's father claiming that his daughter had been denied treatment because of resources, while the Health Authority responded by saying that it was the pointlessness of the proposed further therapeutic interventions, in terms of effecting any cure, together with the discomfort which would accompany them, which formed the basis of their decision. They also pointed to the experimental and unproven nature of the therapy proposed. Interestingly, however, while the letter to B's father from the Health Authority's responsible officer sought to make it clear that the non-provision of treatment was *not* based on financial grounds, when it came time to put in an affidavit, this same officer was moved to assert that, 'I also had to consider whether it [the proposed treatment of B] would be an effective use of the [Authority's] limited resources, bearing in mind the present and future needs of other patients'. Thus, the case must be regarded as one raising, inter alia, the issue of the amenability to judicial review of resource allocation discussions.

At first instance,[233] Laws J (as he then was) made a cautious but significant foray **8.71** into the role of the court on the resources issue. While accepting that judges should not make orders about resource allocation which would inevitably have implications for the wider health services when they are ignorant of the consequences for others, Laws J stated that, '[w]here the question is whether the life of a 10 year old might be saved by however slim a chance, the responsible Authority . . . must do more than toll the bell of tight resources . . . they must explain the priorities that have led them to decline to fund the treatment'.[234]

Laws J was, therefore, making two separate points. The first is that the court will **8.72** not seek to interfere with any particular funding decision on its merits. This repeats the conventional approach. The second point is equally important, however. Judicial review is a remedy in public law which, while not addressing the merits of any particular decision by a public authority, is most anxious to ensure that the *process* by which the decision was reached was lawful, that is, that it took account of relevant factors and did not take account of irrelevant factors. This is what Laws J was seeking to establish in *B*. He was anxious to state that it was within the jurisdiction of the court, indeed it was the court's obligation, to insist that any Health Authority should demonstrate that it has asked itself the appropriate questions prior to its deciding not to fund a range of services or a particular

---

[233] (1995) 25 BMLR 5. Discussed, Parkin, A (1995) 58 MLR 867.
[234] ibid, 17.

treatment for a particular patient. For this reason, Laws J was concerned that the Health Authority explain its priorities. It could be objected that in calling on the Health Authority to do so, Laws J was crossing the line into an examination of the merits: the exercise by the Authority of its discretion. This objection can, however, be rebutted. What Laws J was in fact asserting was that English law recognises certain fundamental rights (as being part of the common law and by virtue of the European Convention on Human Rights). This being so, any exercise of discretion must be made in the light of a prior process, whereby the relative values to be ascribed to the various rights at play are determined. Given the very high priority attached to the right to life, which, for Laws J, was at stake in the case, Laws J insisted that the Health Authority demonstrate the process by which this very important right had been made subservient to others.

8.73   This is a legitimate public law approach, concerned with the process of decision making. Its implications are, however, far reaching, in that they would, in effect, have meant that Health Authorities do something which they (and central government) have been scrupulous in avoiding. It would have required the Health Authority to make *explicit* the principles by reference to which resource allocation (or rationing) was determined. This would have been an enormously significant development. While avoiding involvement in the details of health service management, the courts would have found for themselves a crucial role. By insisting, in good public law tradition, on the transparency of decisions about resources, they would have become the agent for a development many consider long overdue, a proper, political discussion about rationing.

8.74   It will come as no surprise, therefore, that the Court of Appeal, in the form of Sir Thomas Bingham MR, took one look at what Laws J had decided, realised its implications and quickly rejected it. In Laws J's telling phrase, they tolled the bell of resources. 'Difficult and agonising judgements have to be made', Sir Thomas Bingham MR held, 'as to how a limited budget is best allocated to the maximum advantage of the maximum number of patients. This is not a judgement which the court can make.'[235] Thus, at a philosophical level, British utilitarianism triumphed over any European notion of rights. At a legal level, the law was dragged back into its non-interventionist mode. Non-allocation of resources was once again non-justiciable in public law.

(b) R v North Derbyshire HA, ex p Fisher

8.75   The second case warranting attention here is *R v North Derbyshire HA, ex p Fisher.*[236] This again was a case in public law seeking judicial review of the decision by the Health Authority not to allocate resources for the prescription of beta-interferon for

---

[235] N 232 above, 9.
[236] [1997] 8 Med LR 327.

a patient suffering from relapsing remitting multiple sclerosis. Superficially *Fisher* could be regarded as a departure from the traditional approach of the courts to the non-provision of services. Dyson J declared the Health Authority's decision not to provide the drug to be unlawful and ordered it to 'formulate and implement a policy which took full and proper account of national policy', which was that the drug should be introduced in a carefully managed way. Is this not an example of a court taking to itself a resource allocation decision? The simple answer is, that it is not. On proper examination, *Fisher* is entirely in accordance with the approach taken by all the previous courts. [237] In *Fisher*, there was a national policy, set out in a Circular, that beta-interferon be introduced. The Health Authority refused to do so, and thereby denied Fisher his treatment. The reason was not entirely clear, but Dyson J concluded that it was basically because the Authority did not approve of the policy set out in the Circular. In taking this view, without good reason, Dyson J held that the Authority behaved unlawfully.[238] But, as will be recalled, he did not order the Authority to see to it that the drug was prescribed. He only ordered that it should introduce a policy which took 'full and proper account of national policy'. This is crucial. This is as far as the Court was prepared to go. Indeed, Dyson J accepted 'unreservedly' the proposition advanced by counsel for the Health Authority that 'clinical decisions must always be taken with due regard to the resources available', relying on *R v Cambridge HA*. Moreover, at the conclusion of his judgment Dyson J repeated his view that the applicant should receive treatment, 'subject to clinical judgement *and the availability of resources*' (emphasis added). Thus *Fisher* does not break new ground. It affirms the existing view of the role of the courts in public law in matters of non-provision of resources: that such matters are non-justiciable and, thus, that it has no role.

For the sake of completeness it may be mentioned that the avenue of complaint in law for non-provision of services is through the public law remedy of judicial review. No private law remedy would appear to exist.[239]   **8.76**

(ii) Curtailed Provision of Service

If the courts regard the non-provision of services as non-justiciable, is this also true when services are provided but in a curtailed manner? An example would be when A & E services are announced to be available only during the week and not on Saturdays and Sundays. Does a person seeking such services have any remedy because of the curtailed nature of their provision? Any remedy again would be in public law, through judicial review. No private law remedy would appear to be   **8.77**

---

[237] See also, *R v North West Lancashire HA, ex p A, D and G* [2000] 1 WLR 977 (CA), discussed in Fennell, P (2000) 8 Med L Rev 129 (Commentary).
[238] See, for a similar analysis, *R v NW Thames RHA, ex p Daniels* [1993] 4 Med LR 364.
[239] See *Re HIV Haemophiliac Litigation* (n 192 above) and Kennedy and Grubb, *Medical Law* (n 2 above), 333–41.

available. What a court is being asked is to declare unlawful the decision of the PCT (or NHS Trust) to allocate resources in this way. Expressed as such, it will be clear that if the courts will not get involved in non-provision, they are equally unlikely to get involved where only a curtailed provision is made.[240] The reason is that the same element of discretion, which the court recognises as properly belonging to the Authority, is involved. The approach of the courts is exemplified in two cases.

8.78   In *R v Central Birmingham HA, ex p Walker*,[241] Macpherson J had to consider the decision of the Health Authority. It chose not to expand the existing intensive care unit, because of a shortage of resources to hire specialist nurses. This meant that it could not extend its services to treat a baby needing surgery, given the existing immediately urgent calls on the unit. To this extent, the Authority chose to curtail, or put limits on, the service offered. Macpherson J held that 'this decision of the health authority is not justiciable, that is to say that it is not a matter in which the court should intervene'. Sir John Donaldson MR affirmed the lower court's decision, declaring, in a sentence which could serve as the vade mecum for this area of law, '[i]t is not for this court, or indeed any court, to substitute its own judgement for the judgement of those who are responsible for the allocation of resources'.

8.79   In a second case, *R v Central Birmingham HA, ex p Collier*,[242] Stephen Brown LJ delivered a similar judgment. The complaint was that not all the beds in a hospital were being used and that this was unlawful, as posing, inter alia, an immediate threat to health. 'This court', Stephen Brown LJ held, 'is in no position to judge the allocation of resources by this particular Health Authority.' Citing and relying on *Walker*, Stephen Brown LJ went on to remark that the 'courts of this country cannot arrange the lists in the hospital'.

8.80   The cases on non-provision and curtailed provision of services suggest that no remedy lies in public law, by way of judicial review, to challenge the exercise of discretion by a PCT (or NHS Trust) as to how resources should be used. A remedy will still lie, of course, if the decision is *Wednesbury* unreasonable.[243] But what the cases make clear is that it is not, of itself, *Wednesbury* unreasonable to make decisions about resources which lead to curtailed, or the non-provision of, services. That said, the cases leave open the question what a court would do if the non-provision of services was so profound as to throw into doubt whether the NHS Trust was actually complying with the statutory duty, imposed on the Secretary of State

---

[240] See also *Kent v Griffiths* [2000] 2 All ER 474 (CA), especially *per* Lord Woolf MR at [47] referring to the failure to provide sufficient ambulances or drivers: 'there then could be issues which are not suited for resolution by the court.'

[241] (1987) 3 BMLR 32.

[242] 6 January 1988. See Kennedy and Grubb (n 2 above), 340.

[243] *Associated Provincial Picture Houses Limited v Wednesbury Corporation* [1947] 2 All ER 680.

and delegated to PCTs, to 'provide a *comprehensive* health service' (emphasis added), pursuant to s 1(1) of the National Health Service Act 1977. An example could be the failure of a PCT covering a large and populous urban area to provide any obstetrical and maternity care services. A court could well hold, in such an admittedly unlikely situation, that this exercise of discretion went beyond a mere decision not to provide certain services, and became a decision to fail to provide a health service.

It would, of course, be different if, rather than offering a curtailed service or no **8.81** service at all, a Health Authority decided to spread its resources as widely as possible, offering some level of service but a level below that which, by common agreement and indeed by their own admission, was appropriate. This is what must now be considered.

(iii) Inadequate Provision of Service

The complaint here is that the services(s) provided by the service provider (NHS **8.82** Trust or PCT) are inadequate. By contrast with what has gone before, any action will be in private law. The action will be in negligence, alleging harm caused through failure to provide an adequate or proper service. An example could be a hospital ward without sufficient nursing staff or staff of a sufficient level of skill and training, such that a patient suffers harm. In such an action, the first step will be for the plaintiff to prove a breach of duty by the NHS Trust. This will be done through the use of relevant evidence, as was discussed earlier.[244] If it is found that the NHS Trust has failed to meet what the evidence indicates is a proper level of service, then the Authority will prima facie be in breach of its duty. All things being equal, liability will follow.[245] However, it is at this point that the issue of resources may be raised. The NHS Trust may say that while admittedly their service did not measure up to the standard required, they have done their best *in the light of available resources*. In other words, the NHS Trust is asking that lack of resources either be regarded as a defence, or that the quantum of care demanded by the law should be relaxed to the point at which it takes account of scarce resources.

The claim that lack of resources should be used as an excusing circumstance places **8.83** the courts in great difficulties. To accept the argument would be to go against the grain of the general law of torts. As a matter of first principles, if a defendant cannot afford to do something properly, that is, to a standard regarded as reasonable, the law's answer is that he should not do it, rather than that he should be excused for doing it badly. It could, of course, be said that a publicly funded institution, such as an NHS hospital, should be regarded differently. But the logic of the law

---

[244] Above para 8.64.
[245] See, eg, *Kent v Griffiths* [2000] 2 All ER 474 (CA), ambulance service negligent where arrival of ambulance was delayed for no good reason.

of torts and the thrust of good public policy would suggest that it is not open to a defendant to concede that the law requires a certain level of care, to admit that this level has not been met, and then to ask nonetheless not to be judged to have been in breach of duty. However, as in all things, there is a counter-argument, which the courts are equally well aware of. To ignore the reference to resources, and to find that a NHS Trust is liable in negligence, inevitably means that the court is drawn into decisions about resource allocation. It will be recalled that Stephen Brown LJ said in *Collier* that 'courts . . . cannot arrange the lists in the hospital'. Equally, the courts have been anxious not to challenge the exercise of discretion by health service bodies as to how they allocate limited resources. A court may point to the inadequacy of a particular service, but a NHS Trust may reply that, from its position, the provision of some, albeit substandard, service is a better option than no service at all, that, in other words, the logic of the law must give way to the realities of an imperfect world. Furthermore, the Authority could well go on to point out that the effect of holding it liable in negligence for inadequate service would be that they would simply take the advice of their risk manager and withdraw the service. It would be a matter of fine judgment, and one that courts are singularly ill-equipped to make, unaware as they are of most of the relevant facts that condition the judgment to be made and insulated as they are from political pressure.

8.84   Clearly, the arguments are finely balanced.[246] In the cases in which the courts have expressed a view, the complexity of the situation has been well recognised. In *Wilsher*, Browne-Wilkinson LJ adverted to the issue, only to take refuge in the view that issues of resource allocation are 'social questions' which are for Parliament, not the courts. While this is, of course, true as far as it goes, does it go far enough? Once Parliament has set the broad parameters, NHS Trusts and PCTs have to set their budgets. Resource allocation at this level can also be described as a 'social question'. But does this description adequately fit a decision to provide inadequate care, whereby a patient is harmed? Perhaps it does in so far as the patient injured is a member of a larger group of actual or potential patients whose interests must also be weighed by the responsible NHS body.

8.85   In *Bull v Devon AHA*,[247] Mustill LJ was less prepared to regard this particular aspect of resource allocation as non-justiciable. While concluding that it did not need to be resolved in the particular case, he warned that issues were raised 'which the courts may one day have to address'. He adverted first to the issue of legal logic. 'Is there not a contradiction', he asked, 'in asserting at the same time that the system put the foetus at risk and that it was good enough?' As for the argument that

---

[246] See Witting, above n 230, arguing for a 'variable' or modified standard of care.
[247] N 116 above.

as a public service, the Health Authority was doing its best on limited resources, Mustill LJ remarked that while hospital medicine was a public service:[248]

> there are other public services in respect of which it is not necessarily an answer to allegations of unsafety that there were insufficient resources to enable the administrators to do everything which they would like to do. I do not for a moment suggest that public medicine is precisely analogous to other public services, but there is perhaps a danger in assuming that it is completely *sui generis*, and that it is necessarily a complete answer to say that even if the system in any hospital was unsatisfactory, it was no more unsatisfactory than those in force elsewhere [or was the best that could be done].

In *Knight v Home Office*,[249] Pill J (as he then was) repeated Mustill LJ's warning, although he found for the defendant (effectively Brixton Prison) on the facts. 'It is not a complete defence', he stated, 'for a Government department any more than it would be for a private individual or organisation to say that no funds are available for additional [but deemed necessary] safety measures.'[250] Taking up the same point made by Mustill LJ, Pill J went on to state that:[251] **8.86**

> [i]n a different context [from the provision of medical services by a public body] lack of funds would not excuse a public body which operated its vehicles on the public roads without any system of maintenance for the vehicle [or, it may be added, an inadequate system of maintenance] if an accident occurred because of lack of maintenance. The law would require a higher standard of care towards other road users.

It can be said that both Mustill LJ and later Pill J were firing a shot across the bows of the NHS. Without having to find the provider liable on the grounds of allocating resources in such a way as to lead to inadequate provision of services, the courts were warning that the day may come when liability will be imposed. But will it? It may be that the court's threat, as represented by these two cases, is somewhat empty. The courts know, as Browne-Wilkinson LJ saw, that resource allocation, even where it produces inadequate service, is an area they enter at their peril, for the reasons already advanced. They cannot know all the facts and are not charged with, nor answerable for, the wide range of services which make up the National Health Service. In fact, what the cases may indicate more than anything else is an impasse. The courts threaten, but find a way to avoid taking action: the health authorities cut the cake dangerously thin, but know that this is what they are there for and will be judged by. The occasional judicial skirmish may serve to remind those who need reminding that resource allocation involves hard choices. It is doubtful that it will lead to judicial intervention. Browne-Wilkinson LJ's counsel **8.87**

---

[248] ibid, 141.
[249] [1990] 3 All ER 237.
[250] ibid, 243.
[251] ibid.

in *Wilsher* that resource allocation was for Parliament will be seen for the pragmatic recognition of reality which it is.

D. Paying Awards of Damages

8.88 The mechanisms for securing payment of awards of damages have undergone considerable changes in recent years. The National Health Service was unusual as an employer, in that prior to 1990 it required doctors employed in NHS hospitals to subscribe to a medical defence organisation as part of the term of the contract of employment.[252] In the event of a malpractice claim arising out of a doctor's professional duties, the defence organisation would meet the cost of the claim. Where there had been negligence on the part of other staff for whom the hospital was vicariously liable, such as nurses, or an organisational error in respect of which the hospital was under a primary duty, the relevant district health authority would be responsible for meeting the claim. If there had been negligence by both nurses and doctor(s), then, in theory, liability could be apportioned amongst the defendants relying on the contribution legislation,[253] but Health Circular HM (54)32 reduced the importance of this legislation in the context of actions against NHS hospital doctors. The Circular established a private arrangement between the defence organisations and the Department of Health by which payment to the claimant was apportioned between the defendants by agreement amongst themselves in each case, or in the absence of agreement in equal shares. The purpose of the Circular was to provide a formal, though not legally binding, mechanism which would reduce defendants' costs and at the same time present a united front to the claimant in the conduct of the litigation.

1. NHS Indemnity

(i) NHS Patients

8.89 The arrangement was replaced from 1 January 1990 with the introduction of 'NHS Indemnity' under which health authorities assumed responsibility for new and existing claims of medical negligence and no longer required their medical and dental staff to subscribe to a defence organisation.[254] The scheme was introduced as a result of substantial increases in the subscription rates of the medical defence organisations in the 1980s, and the growing pressure to relate subscription rates to

---

[252] The principal defence organisations are the Medical Defence Union, the Medical Protection Society, and the Medical and Dental Defence Union of Scotland.

[253] Civil Liability (Contribution) Act 1978. See, eg, *Jones v Manchester Corporation* [1952] 2 All ER 125; *Collins v Hertfordshire County Council* [1947] 1 KB 598, 623–625.

[254] See *Claims of Medical Negligence Against NHS Hospital and Community Doctors and Dentists*, HC(89)34, HC(89)(FP)22; Brazier (1990) 6 PN 88.

the doctor's specialty, with high-risk specialties paying a higher rate. It was considered that this could lead to distortion in pay and recruitment to the medical profession.

Since NHS Indemnity was first introduced the administrative structure of the **8.90** NHS has changed considerably. Health authorities no longer manage NHS hospitals (all NHS hospitals are now NHS Trusts) and Primary Care Trusts are in the process of replacing health authorities as the bodies responsible for commissioning (and in some instances providing) general medical services in primary care. Moreover, a special health authority, the NHS Litigation Authority, now manages all claims for clinical negligence against NHS employees, and administers risk pooling schemes for clinical negligence, the first of which was established in 1995 (the Clinical Negligence Scheme for Trusts (CNST)). Thus, today, the question of who is covered by NHS indemnity tends to resolve into the issue of who is covered by CNST.

NHS indemnity covers only NHS responsibilities, namely the vicarious liability **8.91** of an NHS body for the negligence of staff acting in the course of their employment. There is no attempt to seek contribution from the employee. Although there were no NHS Trusts constituted when NHS indemnity was introduced, the intention of Health Circular (89)34 was that NHS Trusts should be responsible for claims for negligence against their own medical and dental staff. This was consistent with the objective of giving NHS Trusts financial autonomy and it is the basis upon which the scheme has operated since its inception. Health Circular (89)34 stated that NHS indemnity covered consultants and staff provided by external agencies, irrespective of the precise legal relationship between these individuals and the NHS hospital (ie whether or not they are in law employees or independent contractors). Strictly speaking, the Circular did not determine the question whether a health authority was in law vicariously liable for the negligence of, say, agency staff, but simply specified how health authorities were to deal with this in practice. If visiting consultants and agency staff are not in law employees of the NHS Trust, the Circular could not deem them to be employees. So, for example, if a NHS Trust hospital were to take a vicarious liability point in a particular case involving agency staff, the Circular could not change the position in law. Health authorities did not, in any event, take this point for agency staff and consultants before 1990. HSG(96)48 and the accompanying documentation[255] updated the guidance given in HC(89)34 and takes the view that in addition to staff acting in the course of their NHS employment, NHS indemnity also covers locum doctors (in hospitals), medical academic staff with honorary contracts, students,

---

[255] *NHS Indemnity—Arrangements for Clinical Negligence Claims in the NHS* (NHS Executive, 1996). See now *The NHSLA's Risk Pooling Schemes: Who is indemnified?* (November 2002) (available at *www.nhsla.com* under 'Events').

researchers conducting clinical trials, charitable volunteers and people undergoing professional education, training and examinations, 'whenever a NHS body owes a duty of care to the person harmed'. A 'Good Samaritan' act of assisting at an accident, although apparently excluded from coverage under the original guidance, appears now to fall within the coverage of CNST.[256]

General practitioners

8.92 General practitioners are not usually employees,[257] and so a claim for negligence against a GP (or a general dental practitioner) would have to be pursued against the individual doctor. General practitioners will be vicariously liable for the negligence of their employees, such as nurses or receptionists.[258] The position of a locum is unclear. It seems likely that a deputising doctor would not be considered to be an employee, but would be categorised as an independent contractor.[259] If a hospital is essentially providing only hotel services and the patient remains in the GP's care, the hospital authority will not be responsible, and the claim will be dealt with by the GP's defence organisation. Where a case involves a claim against both a NHS Trust and a GP the possibility of a contribution claim exists, but the guidance emphasises that, as previously, NHS defendants should seek to reach agreement out of court as to the proportion of their respective liabilities, and to co-operate fully in the formulation of the defence.

8.93 PCTs are now eligible to participate in CNST, but guidance from the NHS Litigation Authority makes it clear that the scheme only covers employees. Indemnity does not apply to independent contractors, whether providing NHS care or private treatment, unless the contractor is working as a direct agent of the PCT.[260] Thus, NHS indemnity generally does not apply to GPs except where the

---

[256] See *The NHSLA's Risk Pooling Schemes: Who is indemnified?* (November 2002), which states that: ' "Good Samaritan" acts are covered unless prohibited by the employer, notwithstanding the statement implying the contrary in the CNST guideline.'

[257] *Wadi v Cornwall and Isles of Scilly Family Practitioner Committee* [1985] ICR 492; *Roy v Kensington and Chelsea and Westminster Family Practitioner Committee* [1992] 1 AC 624. Nonetheless, a GP has private law rights against the health authority or PCT, arising from the legislation (the National Health Service Act 1977 and the National Health Service (General Medical Services) Regulations 1992, SI 1992/ 635, Sch 2).

[258] See, eg, *Lobley v Nunn* (1985, CA).

[259] This was the conclusion of Osler J in *Rothwell v Raes* (1988) 54 DLR (4th) 193, 262 (Ont HC). The National Health Service (General Medical Services) Regulations 1992, SI 1992/635 Sch 2, para 20, provide that under a GPs terms of service a doctor is responsible for the acts and omissions of a deputy, except where the deputy is included in the medical list of a PCT, in which case the deputy alone is responsible for his own acts and omissions and the acts and omissions of any person employed by the deputy or acting on his behalf. Although this regulates the GP's position under the terms of service with a health authority or PCT, it is not necessarily conclusive in law vis-à-vis the patient.

[260] See *The NHSLA's Risk Pooling Schemes: Who is indemnified?* (November 2002): 'GPs or dentists who are directly employed [by Health Authorities], eg as Public Health doctors (including port medical officers and medical inspectors of immigrants at UK air/sea ports), are covered.' The term 'employment' also includes formal secondment to a PCT from a partner organisation.

GP has a contract of employment (for example as a clinical assistant at a hospital or as a public health doctor) with a PCT or NHS Trust and the treatment is being given under that contract. Staff directly employed by a health authority or PCT clearly are employees for whose negligence the employer is vicariously liable.

(ii) Private Patients

NHS indemnity does not apply to private hospitals or private work performed by a consultant in a NHS hospital. Private hospitals have to take commercial insurance cover, and doctors engaging in private practice will normally be members of a defence organisation providing indemnity against professional negligence claims. It is accepted that, for the purposes of NHS indemnity, where junior medical staff are involved in the care of private patients in NHS hospitals, they would normally be doing so as part of their NHS contract. To the extent that NHS employees participate in the treatment, the hospital will be vicariously liable for their negligence. Work which is outside the scope of a junior doctor's employment (such as reports for insurance companies or locum work for a GP) is not covered by the scheme, and the doctor will have to rely on a defence organisation for indemnity.

8.94

2. *Funding Claims for Clinical Negligence*

In November 1995 the NHS Litigation Authority, a special health authority, was established with the responsibility for administering schemes set up under s 21 of the NHS and Community Care Act 1990 permitting NHS bodies to pool the costs of injury, loss or damage to property and liabilities to third parties arising out of their NHS activities.[261] The NHS Litigation Authority is also responsible for determining standards of risk management and claims handling for members of the scheme (and NHS bodies generally) and managing the handling of claims. The Authority administers two principal[262] schemes: the Clinical Negligence Scheme for Trusts (CNST); and the Existing Liabilities Scheme.

8.95

---

[261] *NHS Litigation Authority Framework Document* (NHS Executive, 1996, amended December 2002) (*www.nhsla.com/docs/framework.doc*).

[262] The NHS Litigation Authority also has responsibility for miscellaneous residual medical negligence liabilities of certain special health authorities and the Regional Health Authorities (which were abolished from 1 April 1996). The Ex-Regional Health Authorities Scheme covers the liabilities of the hospitals and other services formerly managed at a regional level, prior to the abolition of Regional Health Authorities. The Authority also administers two other risk pooling schemes in respect of non-clinical claims.

8.96   CNST covers liabilities for clinical negligence where the adverse event occurred on or after 1 April 1995.[263] The scheme applies to England only.[264] Clinical negligence liability is defined as:

> any liability in tort owed by a member to a third party in respect of or consequent upon personal injury or loss arising out of or in connection with any breach of a duty of care owed by that body to any person in connection with the diagnosis of any illness, or the care or treatment of any patient, in consequence of any act or omission to act on the part of a person employed or engaged by a member in connection with any relevant function of that member.[265]

The scheme is funded by contributions from the NHS Trusts and PCTs who are members of the scheme. It is not an insurance fund, but a 'pay as you go' scheme which only collects enough money each year in contributions to cover the actual costs which fall into that year, plus a small margin to form a contingency reserve and cover administrative expenses. There are discounts on the Trust's contributions for putting into place appropriate risk management standards. CNST operates on a 'claims paid' basis, which means that it will cover a NHS Trust if the Trust is a member of the scheme continuously at the date of the adverse event which subsequently gives rise to the claim and the date of settlement. The object is to permit NHS Trusts and PCTs to spread the cost of claims. From April 2002 the NHS Litigation Authority took over from NHS Trusts the handling and management of all clinical negligence claims against NHS Trusts in England, although the NHS Trust remains the legally responsible defendant.[266]

---

[263] See the NHS (Clinical Negligence Scheme) Regulations 1996, SI 1996/251 which came into force on 1 March 1996; as amended by NHS (Clinical Negligence Scheme) (Amendment) Regulations 1997, SI 1997/527; NHS (Clinical Negligence Scheme) (Amendment) Regulations 1999, SI 1999/1274; NHS (Clinical Negligence Scheme) (Amendment) Regulations 2000, SI 2000/2341; NHS (Clinical Negligence Scheme) Amendment Regulations 2002, SI 2002/1073. See further Hickey (1995) 1 Clinical Risk 43; Pincombe (1995) 1 Clinical Risk 132; Fenn and Dingwall (1995) 310 BMJ 756.

[264] The functions of the Secretary of State under s 126(4) of the National Health Service Act 1977 and s 21 of the National Health Service and Community Care Act 1990 were transferred to the National Assembly for Wales under the National Assembly for Wales (Transfer of Functions) Order 1999, SI 1999/672, art 2 and Sch 1, as amended by s 66(5) of the Health Act 1999.

[265] NHS (Clinical Negligence Scheme) Regulations 1996, SI 1996/251, reg 4. Similar wording, with appropriate amendments, applies to the Existing Liabilities Scheme: NHS (Existing Liabilities Scheme) Regulations 1996, SI 1996/686, regs 4 and 3. There is no reference to claims arising from failures to obtain consent, which give rise to actions in trespass to the person rather than negligence, which technically do not involve breach of a duty of care. This is probably an oversight and the NHS Litigation Authority will not take the point.

[266] Prior to this change there were complicated rules about the levels of 'excess', which ranged from £10,000 to £500,000, that had to be met by the individual NHS Trust before it could claim indemnity from CNST. These excess levels were abolished from 1 April 2002, so that the whole cost of indemnity is now met from the CNST.

The Existing Liabilities Scheme covers incidents of clinical negligence which oc- **8.97**
curred before 1 April 1995.[267] It is funded by the Secretary of State, through the
NHS Litigation Authority. From 1 April 2000, the NHS Litigation Authority
assumed responsibility for recording, handling and accounting for payments
under the scheme, although legal responsibility remained with the NHS Trusts
and health authorities. From the same date, health organisations no longer make,
or account for, any part of the payment, and the NHS Litigation Authority now
undertakes all the administration arrangements.

3. Structured Settlements

A structured settlement allows the claimant to take the award of damages in the **8.98**
form of periodic payments. The possibility that awards of damages in medical
negligence actions can be dealt with as a structured settlement creates certain options for health authorities and NHS Trusts. A structured settlement normally
takes the form of a private arrangement between the claimant and the defendant's
liability insurer under which the usual lump sum damages award can be varied or
'structured' over a period of time.[268] The settlement may include a lump sum element, plus periodic payments intended to meet the claimant's future losses. The
payments can be for a fixed period or until the claimant's death, and they can be
index-linked. The payments are normally financed by the purchase of an annuity by the liability insurer with the money, or part of it, that would have been
paid to the claimant as a lump sum. The annuity is held by the insurer on behalf
of the claimant and the payments are not taxable as income in the claimant's
hands.[269] The insurer is not liable to tax on the annuity either. The result is that
for large awards, where the tax liability on the income generated by investment
of the lump sum damages would be high, the value of the arrangement to both
claimant and insurer is substantially greater than the traditional lump sum
award.[270] This has obvious advantages for both claimants and defendants. The

---

[267] NHS (Existing Liabilities Scheme) Regulations 1996, SI 1996/686; as amended by NHS
(Existing Liabilities Scheme) (Amendment) Regulations 1997, SI 1997/526; NHS (Existing
Liabilities Scheme) (Amendment) Regulations 1999, SI 1999/1275.

[268] For a statutory definition of a structured settlement see the Damages Act 1996, s 5; on the
Damages Act 1996 see Lewis (1997) 60 MLR 230, 235. See further Law Commission Report,
Structured Settlements and Interim and Provisional Damages (Law Com No 224, 1994); Ashcroft
[1995] JPIL 3; Redmond-Cooper [1995] JPIL 12. For a detailed analysis of this subject see
Lewis, R, *Structured Settlements: The Law and Practice* (Sweet & Maxwell, 1993) and the Report of
the Master of the Rolls' Working Party, *Structured Settlements* (August 2002).

[269] See the Income and Corporation Taxes Act 1988, ss. 329AA, 329AB, added by the Finance Act
1996, s 150.

[270] The sum awarded under a structured settlement should be smaller than the normal lump sum
payment, since there are tax savings which result in the same benefits accruing to the claimant: *Kelly
v Dawes*, The Times, 27 September 1990. The discount tends to range between 8 and 15 per cent,
though it can be higher or lower than this: see *Grimsley v Grimsley and Meade* (1991) discussed by
Lewis (1993) 143 NLJ 772.

possibility of index-linking also addresses the problem of inflation eroding the value of the award, though it cannot eliminate this problem entirely when certain costs (such as the cost of care) may increase at a higher rate than the chosen index.

8.99   There are significant differences in structured settlements in the context of NHS medical negligence claims, because there is no liability insurer involved, and it is possible to structure a settlement without purchasing an annuity from a life insurer.[271] This creates cash-flow advantages for the NHS, since the defendant does not have to find a large lump sum to fund the structure, but can spread the cost over a long period, in effect 'mortgaging' future income. It was for this reason that the defendants in *R (on the application of Hopley) v Liverpool HA*[272] refused to agree to a 'with profits' structured settlement, as opposed to an RPI linked structure, since the 'with profits' option would have involved providing an up-front lump sum with which to purchase the 'with profits' annuity. Pitchford J held that the Health Authority, though a public body, was exercising a private law function when settling a claim for medical negligence. The process did not involve any public law duty owed to the claimant, and therefore the refusal to agree to a structured settlement was not amenable to judicial review. Moreover, the decision was not *Wednesbury* unreasonable, having regard to the potential financial implications for the NHS.

8.100   This case also illustrates another drawback of structured settlements, namely that they depend upon agreement between the parties; the court currently has no power to order a defendant to accept this form of settlement.[273] Following positive responses to the Lord Chancellor's consultation paper on the question of whether the courts should be given the power to order periodical payments for future loss and care costs in personal injury cases, the government stated that it would introduce legislation on the matter.[274] Section 100 of the Courts Act 2003 amends the Damages Act 1996 to provide that a court awarding damages for future pecuniary loss in respect of personal injury may order that the damages are wholly or partly to take the form of periodical payments, and that a court awarding other damages in respect of personal injury may, if the parties consent, order that the damages are wholly or partly to take the form of periodical payments.

8.101   An even more radical change in the payment of compensation for medical negligence will occur if the Chief Medical Officer's proposals for amendments to the

---

[271] See Lewis (1993) 56 MLR 844; and Lewis (n 268 above), ch 16. There are disincentives to the medical defence organisations structuring settlements: ibid, 251.

[272] [2002] EWHC 1723; [2002] Lloyd's Rep Med 494; [2003] PIQR P143. See Lewis (2003) 19 PN 297.

[273] *Burke v Tower Hamlets HA*, The Times, 10 August 1989; Damages Act 1996, s 2.

[274] See the LCD's original consultation paper, *Damages for Future Loss* (CP 01/02, March 2002) and LCD, *Responses to Consultation on Damages for Future Loss* (CP (R) 01/02, November 2002).

litigation system are ever introduced.[275] This would effectively take out of the litigation process low value claims (ie claims below £30,000) and claims involving brain damaged babies, which are generally the highest value claims and constitute 60 per cent of all expenditure on medical litigation.[276] The proposals are currently at the consultation stage.

---

[275] See *Making Amends* (June 2003) (*www.doh.gov.uk/makingamends/cmoreport.htm*). The proposals are discussed in Jones, *Medical Negligence* (3rd edn, Sweet & Maxwell (2003), paras 1-054–1-074.

[276] Though representing only 5 per cent of all cases of medical litigation in which damages are paid: *Making Amends* (June 2003), 47, para 43.

PART IV

SPECIFIC ISSUES

9

CONFIDENTIALITY AND MEDICAL RECORDS

9.01   In the course of any consultation with a patient, a doctor collects information personal to the patient. That information will form the basis of the doctor's diagnosis and treatment plan, and it is essential that the patient makes full and frank disclosure to the doctor in order to ensure that the doctor is able to make recommendations taking into account all relevant matters. The situation inevitably arises that the doctor is privy to much that the plaintiff would regard as personal, and has come upon that information in circumstances in which it is appropriate that the doctor is under an obligation of confidence to the patient. This chapter considers first the manner in which the law regulates the use which the doctor may make of confidential information disclosed by the patient, and the circumstances in which the doctor is lawfully entitled to disclose that information to anyone other than the patient.

9.02   A second issue concerns the extent to which a doctor can control information which he collects and records in the course of his relationship with the patient. A patient's medical record will almost always include information over and above that which the patient himself has disclosed to the doctor. Much of this information is sensitive and the doctor or doctors who have contributed to the medical record over the years may be unwilling to disclose the contents of the record to the patient or his advisers. Although there is little dispute that the medical record is regarded at law as the property of the hospital or other health care institution, it is generally believed that patients ought to be entitled to require that they are given access to their medical records, other than when this might in fact be prejudicial to their interests.

9.03   This chapter therefore investigates two separate questions:

(i)   When does the law allow a doctor to disclose information which is personal to the patient? and

(ii)   When does the law require a doctor to disclose information which has been recorded in the course of the patient's medical treatment?

A. The Obligation of Confidence

1. Common Law

(i) Legal Basis

There has been some uncertainty as to the jurisdictional basis for the obligation of confidence, as the courts have tended to apply different principles in different cases. In *Morrison v Moat*[1] Turner VC said: **9.04**

> Different grounds have indeed been assigned for the exercise of that jurisdiction . . . but, upon whatever grounds the jurisdiction is founded, the authorities leave no doubt as to the exercise of it.

It is now generally thought that the action for breach of confidence is a *sui generis* action, the basis of which lies in the law of equity. There is support for this view in the speeches of the Law Lords in *Attorney-General v Guardian Newspapers (No 2)* (the *Spycatcher* case) where Lord Griffiths noted that the jurisdiction in confidence is based 'on the moral principles of loyalty and fair dealing'[2] and Lord Bingham explicitly stated that the law of confidence rests on an obligation of conscience: **9.05**

> The cases show that the duty of confidence does not depend on any contract, express or implied, between the parties. If it did, it would follow on ordinary principles that strangers to the contract would not be bound. But the duty 'depends on the broad principle of equity that he who has received information in confidence shall not take unfair advantage of it'. . . . Like most heads of equitable jurisdiction, its rational basis does not lie in proprietary right. It lies in the notion of an obligation of conscience arising from the circumstances in or through which the information was communicated or obtained.[3]

The action for breach of confidence enables one party who imparts information in confidence to another to obtain relief against the recipient of that information if the latter, without permission, discloses that information directly or indirectly to a third party. In *Hunter v Mann* Boreham J considered the question of whether a doctor owed an obligation of confidence to his patients and concluded that: **9.06**

> [I]n common with other professional men, . . . the doctor is under a duty not to disclose [voluntarily], without the consent of his patient, information which he, the doctor, has gained in his professional capacity.[4]

---

[1] (1851) 9 Hare 241, 255, 68 ER 492, 498.
[2] [1990] 1 AC 109, 269.
[3] ibid, 215–216. See also *R v Department of Health, ex p Source Informatics* [2001] QB 424 (CA) at [24]–[31]; *Douglas v Hello! Ltd* [2003] EWHC 786; [2003] 3 All ER 996 (Ch D) at [181] and *A v B (a company)* [2002] 2 All ER 545 (CA) at 549 *per* Lord Woolf CJ.
[4] [1974] QB 767, 772. Noted by Boyle, C (1975) 38 MLR 69.

9.07   The cases of *X v Y*[5] and *W v Egdell*[6] affirmed this position and there can now be no question but that an obligation of confidence might arise out of the doctor–patient relationship, notwithstanding that the patient may have no contractual or proprietary rights over the information. As noted by Lord Keith in the *Spycatcher* case:[7]

> [T]he law has long recognised that an obligation of confidence can arise out of particular relationships. Examples are the relationships of doctor and patient, priest and penitent, solicitor and client, banker and customer.

9.08   Aside from the legal duty to maintain confidences in the doctor–patient relationship, the obligation to keep patients' secrets has a long-standing ethical basis and is regarded as one of the most fundamental ethical principles of medical practice.[8] The Hippocratic Oath states:

> Whatsoever things I see or hear concerning the life of men, in my attendance on the sick or even apart from therefrom, which ought not to be noised abroad, I will keep silence thereon counting such things to be as sacred as secrets.

And this has recently been restated and reaffirmed in the Declaration of Geneva:

> I will respect the secrets which are confided in me, even after the patient has died.

Furthermore, the duty is expressly recognised in the professional codes of conduct and official guidance which are provided to all members of the health care professions and NHS staff.[9]

9.09   Where the parties are in a contractual relationship, the terms of the contract may modify the nature and scope of the obligation of confidence which might otherwise have been owed. A contract which is silent on the matter of confidence is, however, no bar to the recognition of an obligation of confidence.

9.10   The conventional view is that the obligation of confidence is owed exclusively to the patient and that the right to enforce the confidence is that of the patient rather than the doctor. However, in *Ashworth Hospital Authority v Mirror Group Newspapers Ltd*[10] the court held that an obligation of confidence was owed to a hospital as well as a patient where the patient's medical records contained

---

[5] [1988] 2 All ER 648.

[6] [1990] 1 All ER 835. First instance decision noted by McHale, J (1988) 52 MLR 715.

[7] [1990] AC 109, 255.

[8] For discussion of the relationship between the legal and ethical duty and a critique of current practice see Lesser, H, and Pickup, Z, 'Law, Ethics and Confidentiality' (1990) 17(1) *Journal of Law & Society* 17–28.

[9] See GMC, *Confidentiality: Protecting and Providing Information* (2000); Department of Health, *Confidentiality: NHS Code of Practice* (2003); NMC, *Code of Professional Conduct* (2002) para 5; General Dental Council, *Maintaining Standards: Guidance to Dentists on Professional and Personal Conduct* (1997) para 3.5.

[10] [2001] 1 All ER 991 (CA).

information and opinions on the patient supplied by other hospital staff. An action for breach of confidence could, therefore, be brought by the hospital against a newspaper which had obtained the records unlawfully from another member of staff.

(ii) Scope

(a) General

English courts have retained great flexibility in interpreting the scope of the doctor's obligation of confidence. First, the obligation is one which is focused upon 'confidential information'. Only where the subject of the disclosure is confidential will the law restrain a doctor from disclosing information.   **9.11**

Secondly, in *W v Egdell*, a case which arose out of the proposed disclosure to the Home Office of a report about the mental condition of a psychiatric patient in a secure hospital, the Court of Appeal accepted that the obligation of confidence was not absolute. Bingham LJ described the cases as establishing: **9.12**

(1) that the law recognises an important public interest in maintaining professional duties of confidence; but
(2) that the law treats such duties not as absolute but as liable to be overridden where there is held to be a stronger public interest in disclosure.[11]

(b) Confidential Information

There is no precise definition of confidential information but English courts include within its scope all information which has 'the necessary quality of confidence about it, namely, it must not be something which is public property and public knowledge'.[12] Almost any kind of information can therefore be confidential, as long as it is not in the public domain and as long as it is not 'trivial tittle tattle'.[13] English courts have given a broad scope to the kinds of information that can be protected under the doctrine of confidence.   **9.13**

In the *Spycatcher* case in the Court of Appeal, Bingham LJ suggested that the issue is whether the information has 'the basic attribute of inaccessibility'.[14] In *R v Chief Constable of the North Wales Police, ex p AB*[15] Buxton J in the Divisional Court   **9.14**

---

[11] *W v Egdell* [1990] 1 All ER 835, 848.

[12] *Saltman Engineering Co v Campbell Engineering Co Ltd* (1948) 65 RPC 203, 215.

[13] *Coco v AN Clark (Engineers)* [1969] RPC 41 *per* Megarry J at 48. See Fenwick, H and Phillipson, G, 'Confidence and Privacy: A Re-Examination' (1996) 55 CLJ 447–455 and Phillipson, G, 'Transforming Breach of Confidence? Towards a Common Law Right of Privacy under the Human Rights Act' (2003) 66 MLR 726–758, 732–740 for a discussion of the kinds of personal information that can be protected under the doctrine of confidence.

[14] N 2 above, 215. See also *Ashworth Hospital Authority v Mirror Group Newspapers Ltd* [2001] 1 All ER 991 (CA).

[15] [1997] 4 All ER 691 (DC) at 703–4.

considered this issue in the context of police disclosure of information about paedophiles in their area and, in particular, of the police's decision in the case to inform a caravan site owner of the presence of former convicted paedophiles on that
site. Buxton J considered that the *conjunction* of the information imparted to the
site owner could be argued to have 'the basic attribute of inaccessibility'. Whilst
the fact of the convictions had been publicised and the site owner already knew
the identity and presence of the applicants on the caravan site, it was that conjunction that the police deliberately brought to the attention of the site owner,
when otherwise he probably would not have connected the applicants with their
previous history. On the facts, however, Buxton J found that the subject of that
conjunction of information was not confidential, because none of the information came into the possession of its holder in circumstances that impart an obligation of confidence.

9.15   There are no fixed rules to determine what suffices to confer confidentiality on
any particular item of information. Rather, the courts approach the question in a
pragmatic way, asking whether disclosure in the circumstances would be 'within
the mischief which the law as its policy seeks to avoid . . .'.[16] This would clearly
cover information which the doctor receives from the patient in the course of a
professional relationship. Both information which is directly communicated by
the patient, and information to which the doctor is privy by reason of his position,
for example diagnostic test results, would be regarded as confidential. Similarly,
information which is communicated to the doctor by a third party who is aware
of the doctor's professional relationship with the patient might be subject to an
obligation of confidence.

9.16   The position is less clear where the doctor receives information other than in connection with a professional relationship. This situation could arise either where
the patient discusses matters with the doctor for purely social purposes, or where
a third party discusses the patient with the doctor but is unaware of the professional relationship between the doctor and that patient. The difficulty here is in
determining whether or not the information has the 'necessary quality of confidence', although there is a strong argument that any information about a patient
which the doctor receives should be subject to an obligation of confidence in order
to maintain the essential relationship of trust upon which the effective provision
of medical treatment depends. That is certainly the view reflected in the
Hippocratic Oath, noted at para 9.08 above.

9.17   Once information is in the public domain it will usually cease to be confidential.
This would only pertain to information communicated in the doctor–

---

[16] *Argyll v Argyll* [1967] 1 Ch 312, 330 *per* Ungoed-Thomas J. See also Gurry, F, *Breach of
Confidence* (Clarendon Press, 1984) 70.

patient relationship where any possible disclosure by the doctor would not add anything to that which was already in the public domain. Thus, for example, the fact that the patient had known about her condition for a particular length of time might be confidential notwithstanding that she has disclosed to the public at large that she has the condition. Moreover, it will always be a question of degree whether the information is sufficiently broadly disseminated that it can be said to have lost its confidential character.

Further, it is possible that a court might recognise a continuing obligation of con- **9.18**
fidence in respect of information in the public domain where it would be uncon-
scionable to allow the party to make use of the information in the circumstances.
For example, if English courts were prepared to hold that a doctor owed a fiduciary obligation to his patient,[17] it might be held on analogy with the Californian
case of *Moore v Regents of the University of California*[18] to be a breach of that obligation to allow the doctor to use information which was disclosed in circumstances
of confidence for his own financial gain.

(c) Circumstances of Confidence

English law clearly provides that information is only subject to an obligation of **9.19**
confidence when it is communicated in circumstances of confidence.[19] In the
context of the doctor–patient relationship this will almost always be assumed to
be the case since, according to Megarry J in *Coco v AN Clark* (a case not concerned
with doctors) the test should be whether or not any:

> reasonable man in the shoes of the recipient of the information would have realised
> that upon reasonable grounds the information was being given to him in confi-
> dence . . .[20]

The imposition of the obligation does not depend as such on a pre-existing rela- **9.20**
tionship between the parties. All this is required is the transmission of the information from one party to another.[21] However, one remaining question is whether
or not the description of information as confidential depends upon some expectation of secrecy in the mind of the person communicating the information. Two
views are possible here. First, information could objectively be described as confidential where it possesses the basic attribute of inaccessibility to others,[22] and

---

[17] Although this is unlikely and was rejected in *R v Mid Glamorgan Family Health Services Authority, ex p Martin* [1993] 16 BMLR 81, 94. See further Grubb, A, 'The doctors as fiduciary' (1994) CLP 311.

[18] (1990) 793 P 2d 479.

[19] *Coco v AN Clark (Engineering) Ltd* [1969] RPC 41, 47–8 *per* Megarry J. See further Phillipson (n 13 above) for discussion of this requirement.

[20] ibid.

[21] *A v B (a company)* [2002] 2 All ER 545, 554 *per* Lord Woolf CJ; *Venables v News Group Newspapers* [2001] 1 All ER 908, 933.

[22] Gurry (n 16 above) discusses the characteristics of confidentiality at 70–85.

where the reasonable man in the shoes of the confidant knew or ought to have known that the information has been disclosed for a limited purpose only. Gurry, in his seminal work on breach of confidence, would appear to support this view when he states that the relevant circumstances to be taken into account in determining whether or not an obligation of confidence arises include both:

> the confider's own attitude to the preservation of the confidentiality of the information . . . [and circumstances] apparent from custom—such as the custom, 'which was believed to be universal' that actors do not disclose the details of the plot of a play before its first performance.[23]

Dicta in *A v B (a company)* and the *Spycatcher*[24] case also support this view. For example, in the former case, Lord Woolf CJ stated that:

> A duty of confidence will arise whenever the party subject to the duty is in a situation where he either knows or ought to know that the other person can reasonably expect his privacy to be protected.

9.21   In *Douglas v Hello! Ltd and others*[25] Lindsay J adopted the same approach when applying confidentiality to photographs taken on a private occasion. The action was brought by two prominent celebrities against *Hello!* magazine, which had obtained from the paparazzi and published unauthorised photographs of their wedding. Lindsay J held that the circumstances in which the photographs had been taken deceitfully were such that there was a clear breach of confidentiality. In his view (at 197) the event was entirely private in character and elaborate steps had been taken to exclude the uninvited and preclude unauthorised photography. The photographs taken were images which were 'radiated by the event . . . imparted to those present, including Mr Thorpe and his camera in circumstances importing an obligation of confidence'. Accordingly:

> Mr Thorpe knew (or at the very least ought to have known) that the Claimants reasonably expected the private character of the event and the photographic representation of it to be protected.

Hello! magazine's consciences were equally tainted as they were not acting in good faith or by way of fair dealing and the surrounding facts were such that a duty of confidence should be inferred from them.

9.22   Alternatively, it is possible to argue that information can only be described as confidential where there is an expectation, actual or inferred, of confidence on the part of the person communicating the information. If that person were not capable of forming such an expectation, therefore, the information could not be said to be confidential. Those cases in which it has been held that the deliberate

---

[23]   ibid, 120.
[24]   *Attorney-General v Guardian Newspapers Ltd (No 2)* [1990] 1 AC 109, 281 *per* Lord Goff.
[25]   [2003] EWHC 786; [2003] 3 All ER 996.

seeking of publicity operated to destroy the confidence of personal information could be argued to support this position.[26] These cases can, however, also be explained on the basis that the information in question was in fact already in the public domain.[27] It would seem, therefore, that the test is an objective one and all that must be shown is that a reasonable person who received the information would have realised that it was confidential.

(d) Anonymised Information

It is now settled that there is no obligation of confidence owed with respect to information in a form which is not capable of identifying the patient, or any other person to whom an obligation of confidence might also be owed. In *R v Department of Health, ex p Source Informatics Ltd* the Court of Appeal held that it was not a breach of confidence to disclose anonymised patient information. The applicant was a data collection company, which wished to collect anonymised data from pharmacists about GPs' prescribing habits. The applicant wished to sell these data commercially. It sought a declaration that the Department's policy to advise health authorities and others that it might be a breach of confidence to disclose anonymised patient information was unlawful.

9.23

At first instance,[28] Latham J concluded that the policy was lawful. It could be a breach of confidence to disclose anonymised information without a patient's consent. There was a public interest that confidences were respected. It was important that patients were not inhibited from seeking medical assistance, and some patients might feel strongly about the use of information obtained from their prescription forms. The mere unauthorised disclosure was itself a sufficient detriment to found an action for breach of confidence. A patient's consent could not be implied where the information was to be used for commercial gain. It was not necessary to decide but consent might be implied if the information was to be used for NHS management purposes or for research.

9.24

On appeal, the decision was reversed. Delivering the judgment of the Court of Appeal, Simon Brown LJ identified the issue for the court as being whether a pharmacist would interfere with the patients' 'personal privacy' in *disclosing* anonymised information to Source Informatics. Simon Brown LJ concluded (at 797) that the proposed scheme did not involve a breach of confidence because the patients' identities would be protected:

9.25

> I would . . . hold simply that the pharmacists' consciences ought not reasonably to be troubled . . . The patient's privacy will have been safeguarded, not invaded. The pharmacist's duty of confidence will not have been breached.

---

[26] See eg *Woodward v Hutchins* [1977] 1 WLR 760 (CA) and *Lennon v News Group Newspapers Ltd* [1978] FSR 573 (CA).
[27] See Gurry (n 16 above) 101.
[28] [1999] 4 All ER 185, rev'd [2001] QB 424 (CA).

The obligation of confidence does not therefore apply to fully anonymised information.

9.26 Whether or not information is or is not sufficiently anonymised to excuse the doctor from any obligation of confidence is a question for the court, to be determined upon all of the evidence. If an initial disclosure presents a risk of identification, for example where it would lead to further media investigation and ultimately to tracing of the identity of the patient, then this may be sufficient to justify imposing an obligation of confidence.[29] Similarly, where information is capable of identifying a particular patient because, for example, the patient's symptoms are very rare or the patient is one of a very small community then an obligation of confidence would be owed in respect of that information. In *H (a health care worker) v Associated Newspapers Limited and H (a health care worker) v N HA*[30] the Court of Appeal considered the risk of identification in the context of disclosing the HIV status of a health care worker. Associated Newspapers wished to publish information about the health care worker, his speciality and the health authority where he had been employed. The court had to consider the extent to which that information should be anonymised in order to preserve the identity of the health care worker. The court held that details of the relevant health authority coupled with information already provided in a national newspaper could lead to those who knew the doctor deducing that the article was written about him. Further, disclosure of the health authority's identity would lead to a process of patient reassurance which, in turn, would probably result in the doctor's identification. Consequently, the court refused to allow details of the health authority and doctor's identity to be published, however it concluded that the risk of identification was minimal in relation to disclosing details of his speciality. Thus, that information should be made available for public debate.

9.27 Anonymised information is used widely within the NHS and it is Department of Health policy that patient information within the NHS should be made non-identifying wherever possible prior to its use. The Caldicott Committee[31] recommended that patient-identifiable information should not be used unless it is absolutely necessary and this guiding principle has been adopted by the Department of Health. The Department of Health has recently published a

---

[29] The question was considered but not resolved by Rose J in *X v Y* [1988] 2 All ER 648, 657.
[30] [2002] EWCA Civ 195; [2002] Lloyd's Rep Med 210, noted by Laing, J (2003) 11(1) Med L Rev 124–128.
[31] Caldicott Committee, *Report on the Review of Patient-Identifiable Information* (December 1997) and subsequent implementation in 'Implementing the Recommendations of the Caldicott Report' (HSC 1998/089) and Caldicott Guardians (HSC 1999/012). See also *For the Record—Managing Records in NHS Trusts and Health Authorities* (HSC 1999/053) and *Preservation, Retention and Destruction of GP General Medical Services Records Relating to Patients* (HSC 1998/217).

detailed Code of Practice for NHS Staff on Confidentiality.[32] The Code serves as a guide to required practice for those who work within or under contract to NHS organisations concerning confidentiality and patients' consent to the use of their health records. It replaces previous guidance contained in 'The Protection and Use of Patient Information'[33] and is a key component of emerging information governance arrangements for the NHS. The Code is a comprehensive document, which describes the concept of confidentiality; provides a detailed account of the main legal requirements; recommends a generic decision support tool for sharing/disclosing information; and lists examples of particular information sharing scenarios. Central to the Code is the premise that unless there is a robust public interest or legal justification for using information in a form that identifies an individual, it should not be used in that form.[34] The Code also makes it clear that once information is *effectively* anonymised, it is no longer confidential and may be used with relatively few constraints.[35] This, of course, reflects what is now the position at common law in the light of the *Source Informatics* case discussed above.

A Special Health Authority constituted under s 11 of the National Health Service **9.28** Act 1977 (the NHS Information Authority) has responsibility for supporting the development and implementation of information and communication services in the NHS, including the development of national clinical information standards.[36] The Information Authority is currently developing a confidentiality management system for use throughout the NHS. In order to inform the design of the system, the Information Authority, in conjunction with the Consumers' Association undertook extensive research with patients and the public. The results of the research were published in 2002[37] and the main findings suggest that there was a high level of trust in the NHS to protect patient confidentiality, but low awareness of how the NHS uses patient information. Overall, respondents were more concerned about who used the information and whether it was anonymous,

---

[32] Department of Health, *Confidentiality: NHS Code of Practice* (October 2003), located at *www.doh.gov.uk/ipu/confiden*.

[33] HSG(96)18/LASSL(96)5.

[34] ibid, 4. The GMC guidance *Confidentiality: Protecting and Providing Information* (2000) also advises doctors to anonymise data where unidentifiable data will serve the purpose. See further paras 9.61–9.73 below.

[35] ibid, my emphasis. The Department of Health advises that effective anonymisation generally requires more than just the removal of name and address. Full postcode can identify individuals, NHS number is a strong identifier and other information, eg date of birth, can also serve as an identifier, particularly if looked at in combination with other data items. See *Information Governance for NHS Organisations: Confidentiality & Consent* for further detail on effective anonymisation techniques.

[36] See the National Health Service Information Authority Regulations 1999, SI 1999/64, and the National Health Service Information Authority (Establishment and Constitution) Order 1999, SI 1999/695.

[37] NHS Information Authority, *Share with Care! People's views on Consent and Confidentiality of Patient Information* (October 2002). For a brief discussion of the Information Authority, the public consultation and anonymisation, see Chalmers, J and Muir, R, 'Patient Privacy and Confidentiality' (2003) 326 BMJ 725–6.

than how the information would be used. Once information was anonymised, a majority in the group were happy not to be asked for consent to share it, although some would like to be informed as a courtesy. The Information Authority has also published a Draft National Patient Information-Sharing Charter, which places clear obligations on health care workers to preserve patient confidentiality when using patient information.[38] Additionally, in March 2000, the Department of Health set up a new body to advise on patient confidentiality. The National Confidential and Security Advisory Body works to improve the way in which confidential information is handled by setting national standards to govern confidentiality; promoting awareness; providing support and guidance; and advising the NHS Executive and the Department of Health on confidentiality issues.[39]

(e) Disclosure with the Patient's Consent

9.29   Consent provides a lawful justification for disclosure and the General Medical Council (GMC) ethical guidance to doctors emphasises the centrality of obtaining patient consent. The guidance notes that:

> . . . seeking patients' consent to disclosure is part of good communication between doctors and patients, and is an essential part of respect for patients' autonomy and privacy. Confidential information about patients must not be given to others unless the patient consents.[40]

This principle is mirrored in the Department of Health Code of Practice on confidentiality.[41]

9.30   The general principle is subject to the requirement that, at the time of giving consent, patients are competent to give a valid consent to disclosure and understand the nature of the disclosure proposed.[42]

9.31   Consent need not be express but might be inferred from conduct. It could be argued, for example, that a patient implicitly consents to information about his medical condition being shared with members of a health care team responsible for his care. For example, according to the GMC:

> Where patients have consented to treatment, express consent is not usually needed before relevant personal information is shared to enable the treatment to be provided. For example, express consent would not be needed before general practitioners disclose relevant personal information so that a medical secretary could type

---

[38] NHS Information Authority (2002), located at *www.nhsia.nhs.uk/confidentiality*. See also Information Policy Unit, *Building the Information Core: Protecting and Using Confidential Patient Information. A Strategy for the NHS* (Department of Health, December 2001).

[39] Department of Health Press Release, March 2000 located at *www.doh.gov.uk/ipu/whatnew/newadvis.htm*.

[40] *Confidentiality: Protecting and Providing Information* (2000) para 13.

[41] *Confidentiality: NHS Code of Practice* (2003) 5.

[42] ibid, Introduction and para 38. For further discussion on competence and what constitutes a valid consent in medical law, see Chs 3 and 4 above.

a referral letter. Similarly, where a patient has agreed to be referred for an X-ray physicians may make relevant information available to radiologists when requesting an X-ray. [43]

In this regard, however, the GMC advises that the doctor:　　　　　　　　　　**9.32**

> should make sure that patients are aware that personal information about them will be shared within the health care team, unless they object, and of the reasons for this.[44]

The Department of Health adopts a similar approach in its guidance to NHS staff　**9.33**
where the purpose of the disclosure is directly concerned with the health care of the patient. Accordingly, the Code on confidentiality provides that:

> Where patients have been informed of (a) the use and sharing of their information associated with their health care; and (b) the choices that they have and the implications of choosing to limit how information may be used or shared, then explicit consent is not usually needed for information disclosures needed to provide that health care. Even so, opportunities to check that patients understand what may happen and are content should be taken.[45]

The first instance comments of Latham J on the issue of implied consent in *R v*　**9.34**
Department of Health, ex p Source Informatics Ltd[46] are worthy of mention here. He suggested that implied consent might justify *anonymous* use by doctors and the health service of patient information 'for the purposes of *research, medical advancement or the proper administration* of the service'.[47] However, on appeal, the Court of Appeal held that anonymous disclosure is not a breach of confidence, as discussed at paras 9.23–9.25 above.

Where a patient has explicitly objected to particular information being shared　**9.35**
with others providing care, the GMC states that doctors involved are advised to respect those wishes.[48] This is echoed by the Department of Health, although the Code of Practice cautions that when patients choose to exercise their right to object, it may mean that the care that can be provided is constrained and that, in extremely rare circumstances, it might not be possible to offer certain treatment options.[49]

Where doctors undertake to write a report about/examine patients, or to disclose　**9.36**
information from existing records for third parties such as employers, insurance companies, or local authorities the GMC advises that doctors must (i) be satisfied

---

[43] ibid, para 7.
[44] ibid, para 8.
[45] ibid, 5.
[46] [1999] 4 All ER 185 (QBD).
[47] Emphasis added.
[48] N 40 above, 5.
[49] N 41 above para 13.

that the patient has been told at the earliest opportunity about the purpose of the examination and/or disclosure, the extent of the information to be disclosed and the fact that relevant information cannot be concealed or withheld; (ii) obtain, or have seen, written consent to the disclosure from the patient or a person properly authorised to act on the patient's behalf; (iii) disclose only information relevant to the request; and (iv) include only factual information which can be substantiated, presented in an unbiased manner.[50]

9.37   Although the GMC guidance stresses that written consent to the disclosure should be obtained in such circumstances, in *Kapadia v Lambeth London Borough Council*[51] the court stated that consent to disclose a medical report may be implied where a person undergoes a medical examination at the request of a third party. The case involved a claim by an employee against an employer for disability discrimination before an Employment Appeal Tribunal. The applicant had called his own expert witnesses and had consented to an examination by an independent medical expert instructed by his employers. The doctor who conducted the examination had refused to disclose the report to the respondent employer without first obtaining the consent of the applicant. The applicant had not been prepared to consent to the disclosure without first seeing the report and the case proceeded with no medical evidence being called on behalf of the respondent. In the opinion of Schiemann LJ (at 177), the report should have been disclosed by the doctor to the employers and no further consent was required from the claimant:

> By consenting to being examined on behalf of the employers the claimant was consenting to the disclosure to the employers of a report resulting from that examination. A practice under which a person who has agreed to be examined in circumstances such as these, but then claims a veto upon disclosure of the report to those who obtained it is not, in my view, a good practice.

9.38   It would seem from this that the law sets a minimum standard which does not always reflect the appropriate ethical standards that the government and regulatory bodies require. In some circumstances, such as these, the GMC guidance is more circumspect and goes further than the legal requirement by suggesting that written consent to the disclosure is required. With the greatest respect to Schiemann LJ, it would obviously be best practice for health care practitioners to obtain written consent to the disclosure in such circumstances.

(f) Disclosure Required by Law

9.39   It is clear that the doctor's duty of confidence may be overridden in circumstances where the doctor is required by law to disclose information which would

---

[50] ibid, para 34.
[51] (2000) 57 BMLR 170 (CA).

otherwise be subject to an obligation of confidence. In 1974 in *Hunter v Mann*,[52] Boreham J considered whether or not a statutory obligation to provide information to the police investigating an allegation of dangerous driving could apply to doctors.[53] Having considered both the clear and unambiguous language of the statute and the nature of the doctor's obligation of confidence to his patients, Boreham J concluded that the doctor could be under no obligation of confidence to his patients in relation to information which he was compelled by law to disclose. Rather, the doctor's obligation is one not 'voluntarily' to disclose, without the consent of his patient, information which he has gained in his professional capacity.

Section 60 of the Health and Social Care Act 2001 provides a power to ensure that patient identifiable information needed to support essential NHS activity can be used without the consent of patients. In effect, this measure sets aside the common law obligation of confidentiality and is intended primarily as a temporary measure until anonymisation measures or appropriate recording of consent can be put in place. The power can only be used to support medical purposes that are in the interests of patients or the wider public, where consent is not a practicable alternative and where anonymised information will not suffice. It is designed to support broader medical purposes such as preventative medicine, medical research and epidemiology and was introduced to cater for situations where informed consent cannot be obtained. For example, important research projects may involve tens of thousands of patients where contact would be impracticable. The Department of Health believes that the essential nature of some of this research means that the public good outweighs issues of privacy. Some patients are not capable of giving consent, but the health service still needs to know about them and their conditions. Moreover, excluding those who refuse consent might bias data collection to the extent that it loses all value.

9.40

Section 60 allows the Secretary of State to make regulations requiring or regulating the processing of patient information for medical purposes as he considers necessary or expedient either (i) in the interests of improving patient care; or (ii) in the public interest.[54] 'Medical purposes' are widely defined to include, for example, diagnosis, treatment, medical research, preventative medicine and management of health and social care services.[55] 'Patient information' is defined to

9.41

---

[52] [1974] 1 QB 767.
[53] The relevant provision was the Road Traffic Act 1972, s l68 (2), which provided that: 'Where the driver of a vehicle is alleged to be guilty of an offence to which this section applies . . . any other person shall if required as aforesaid give any information which it is in his power to give and may lead to the identification of the driver . . .'. The doctor in that case had been charged with the offence of failing to provide the relevant information to the police.
[54] s 60(1).
[55] s 60(10).

include anonymised information.[56] The regulations may provide that compliance with them will be lawful despite what would otherwise be a breach of confidence.[57] The regulations may not, however, authorise or require processing in breach of the Data Protection Act 1998.

9.42   Section 60 contemplates, in particular, two types of regulation: (i) which requires disclosure of specified information to patients or others on their behalf;[58] (ii) which requires or authorises disclosure or other processing of specified information between specified individuals subject to certain conditions.[59] The first is concerned with providing a greater level of information to increase the patient's understanding of their treatment etc. The second is more general and is specifically designed (though it is not so restricted) to facilitate transfer of patient information (whether anonymised or not) for the purposes of medical research, epidemiological purposes and cancer registries where this is in the 'public interest'. Where it would be 'reasonably practicable' to anonymise the information 'having regard to the cost of and the technology available', the regulations must not extend to identifying patient information.[60]

9.43   The Act requires proposals (developed by the Department of Health or others wishing support in law for the processing of information, for example the NHS, Public Health Laboratory, or Health and Safety Executive) to be considered by the Patient Information Advisory Group (PIAG). The PIAG's key responsibilities will be:

(i)   to advise the Secretary of State of regulations which should be made under s 60 of the Act; and

(ii) to advise the Secretary of State as required on the use of patient information and other NHS information.

9.44   The first regulations under s 60 came into force in June 2002. The Health Service (Control of Patient Information) Regulations 2002[61] are of the second type and support the operations of cancer registries and the Public Health Laboratory Services with respect to communicable diseases and other risks to public safety. The regulations override the common law duty of confidentiality:

> Anything done by a person that is necessary for the purpose of processing confidential patient information in accordance with these Regulations shall be taken to be lawfully done despite any obligation of confidence owed by that person in respect of it (Regulation 4).

---

[56] s 60(8) and (9).
[57] s 60(2)(c).
[58] s 60(2)(a).
[59] s 60(2)(b).
[60] s 60(3).
[61] SI 2002/1438.

Accordingly, processing of identifiable personal information without patient consent is permitted for the establishment of cancer registries in order to measure mortality and survival rates and for the recognition, control and prevention of communicable diseases such as new variant CJD, and other risks to public health.

The power under s 60 is a sweeping power and not surprisingly, during the Bill's **9.45** passage through Parliament, widespread concerns were expressed about the breadth of the power and the unacceptable encroachments into personal liberty which it could make:[62]

> We believe that all [these] important changes in the law require the greatest scrutiny and the greatest consultation in advance. They are unacceptable increases in the power of Government, and could bring the medical profession into conflict with the law or the GMC. They place unacceptable burdens on doctors.[63]

The BMA and GMC voiced similar concerns and, in particular, there are fears that the power could be used inappropriately in the context of HIV test results, drug trials and genetic information. Much genetic information is discovered during the course of routine testing for specific conditions. Section 60 regulations could permit that information to be held as part of a national epidemiological database about the incidence of particular damaging genetic traits. Moreover, the use of the power could mean that the NHS has access to information about individuals of which they are completely unaware. There is no doubt that cancer and disease registries do contribute to our understanding and treatment of disease, but in light of these concerns, the PIAG and Secretary of State must act responsibly to ensure that the appropriate balance is struck between the interests of the individual and the broader societal interest.[64]

(g) Disclosure in the Public Interest

The *sui generis* obligation of confidence is largely based upon recognition of im- **9.46** portant public interests favouring confidentiality where personal information is communicated in circumstances in which it is clear that the recipient is expected

---

[62] See the debates in HC Standing Committee E12 and 13 sitting 8 February 2001. For discussion see Samuels, A, 'Patient Confidentiality' (2002) 70(4) *Medico-Legal Journal* 191–3.

[63] *per* Dr Fox MP, Standing Committee E12, 8 February 2001.

[64] For a discussion of the impact of s 60 of the Health and Social Care Act 2001 on autonomy in the context of medical research see Case, P, 'Confidence Matters: The Rise and Fall of Informational Autonomy in Medical Law' (2003) 11(2) Med L Rev 208–236. The PIAG has recently published its *First Annual Report* (October 2003). The report describes how the PIAG oversees the s 60 arrangements and outlines the key principles which have emerged from the group's deliberations. These emerging principles suggest that the PIAG is exercising its functions carefully and, where there is any doubt, patient confidentiality has prevailed. The importance of obtaining patient consent; of anonymising data; and of the fact that s 60 is only an interim measure are, it seems, quite rightly informing the PIAG's decision-making. The PIAG considered 65 applications for support under s 60 between December 2001 and June 2003 and approved 42 of these applications. The report can be located at *www.doh.gov.uk/ipu/confiden.*

to respect the privacy of that information. It follows from this that the obligation of confidence may be modified where countervailing public interests favouring disclosure are overriding. There is judicial dictum supporting the public interest justification for disclosure in the context of the doctor–patient relationship. In *R v Department of Health, ex p Source Informatics Ltd*, Latham J at first instance felt that the 'public interest' justification:

> . . . may be an alternative solution to the problem of the use by doctors and health authorities of information gleaned from patients [at 196].

On appeal, however, Simon Brown LJ seemed to express somewhat contradictory views. Initially he agreed with Latham J by favouring the 'public interest' of disclosure of identifying information, but he then went on (at 801) to favour implied consent over the 'public interest' justification (see paras 9.23–9.25 above).

9.47   This dictum suggests that the status of the 'public interest' justification in a health care context is somewhat unclear and there is no judicial guidance upon the precise circumstances in which the doctor's obligation of confidence can be overridden in the public interest. The courts have tended to articulate the public interest exception in rather broad and inconclusive terms. In both *W v Egdell* and the earlier case of *X v Y* the courts paid great heed to the advice provided by the GMC contained in its ethical guidance to doctors (previously known as 'The Duties of a Doctor' but now contained in 'Confidentiality: Protecting and Providing Information'), but the question remains one for the courts and not for professional bodies or the Department of Health.

9.48   The courts balance the public interests favouring confidentiality against those favouring disclosure in the particular circumstances of each case. The balance of the public interest in the context of an action to restrain what was alleged to be a potential breach of medical confidentiality was first considered by English courts in 1987 in the case of *X v Y*. [65] The defendants in that case intended to publish an article identifying two doctors with AIDS who were carrying on general practice in England after having sought and received appropriate medical advice and counselling. The health authority where the doctors' medical records were held

---

[65] [1988] 2 All ER 648. For discussion of the 'public interest' justification where confidential information is obtained by the police see *Hellewell v Chief Constable of Derbyshire* [1995] 4 All ER 473 (Laws J) (disclosure of suspect's photograph for the purposes of preventing and detecting crime); *R v Chief Constable of the North Wales Police, ex p AB* [1997] 4 All ER 691 (DC) (disclosure of history of convicted paedophiles to prevent crime) discussed at para 9.14 above; *Woolgar v Chief Constable of Sussex Police* [1999] 3 All ER 604 (CA) (confidential information about a registered nurse obtained during an investigation disclosed to the UK Central Council in the interests of public health and safety). For discussion of the expansive nature of the 'public interest' justification generally see Milmo, P, 'Courting the Media' [2003] EHRLR, Special Issue: Privacy, 1–11 and Phillipson, G, 'Judicial Reasoning in Breach of Confidence Cases under the Human Rights Act: Not Taking Privacy Seriously?' [2003] EHRLR, Special Issue: Privacy, 54–72.

sought to restrain publication. The question for the court was whether or not the defendants were justified in the public interest in publishing and using the information about the two doctors.

Rose J emphasised that the concern of the courts was with public and not private **9.49** interests. Thus it was not necessary to show any detriment to the individual plaintiffs. It would be unlawful to disclose the information provided the public interests in maintaining confidence, in this case those in loyalty and confidentiality both generally and particularly in relation to the hospital records of patients with AIDS, outweighed the public interests in disclosure, here having a free press and an informed public debate.[66]

Subsequently the scope of medical confidentiality was considered by the Court **9.50** of Appeal in *W v Egdell*.[67] W had been convicted of manslaughter on the grounds of diminished responsibility after having shot and killed five people in an indiscriminate display of violence. At the time of the action for breach of confidence, he was compulsorily detained in a secure hospital but had taken steps to apply to a mental health tribunal for a conditional discharge. To that end his solicitors instructed Dr Egdell to report on W's mental state. His report conflicted substantially with that of W's own medical advisers and he recommended further investigation of this conflict in opinion. Further he recommended that attention should be given to other information, including W's confession that he had a continuing and long-standing interest in explosives, which apparently had not been noted in other reports. W subsequently withdrew his application for conditional discharge and his solicitors refused to forward Dr Egdell's report to those responsible for his care and for any future recommendations as to his discharge. Dr Egdell nonetheless sent a copy of his report to the hospital and also pressed for a copy to be sent to the Home Office to be considered by those responsible for reviewing W's case.

W's solicitors commenced an action for breach of confidence against Dr Egdell, **9.51** claiming damages and injunctive relief. The Court of Appeal emphasised that in determining whether or not there had been a breach of confidence the court should balance the public interests implicated, and should not focus on the private interests of the doctor or the patient. Bingham LJ quoted with approval from the speech of Lord Goff of Chieveley in the *Spycatcher* case:[68]

> [A]lthough the basis of the law's protection of confidence is that there is a public interest that confidences should be preserved and protected by the law, nevertheless that public interest may be outweighed by some other countervailing public

---

[66] [1988] 2 All ER 648, 661.
[67] [1990] 2 WLR 471.
[68] [1988] 3 WLR 776, 807.

interest which favours disclosure. . . . It is this limiting principle which may require a court to carry out a balancing operation, weighing the public interest in maintaining confidence against a countervailing public interest favouring disclosure.[69]

9.52 The court must reach its own decision on the balance. However, in doing so it is legitimate for the court to give 'such weight to the considered judgment of a professional man as seems in all the circumstances to be appropriate'.[70] On the facts that balance:

> clearly lay in the restricted disclosure of vital information to the director of the hospital and to the Secretary of State who had the onerous duty of safeguarding public safety.

9.53 The disclosure in *W v Egdell* was justified by reference to the public interest in ensuring that a properly informed decision was made by those responsible for considering W's release in order to avert a 'real risk of consequent danger to the public'.[71] This raises the question of what risks of harm might be sufficient to justify disclosure of confidential information in the public interest. It has been suggested that, in order to justify disclosure, the risk of harm must be 'real' and not fanciful, and it must be a risk involving the danger of *physical* harm.[72]

9.54 Even if these qualifications are accepted, it is necessary to decide whether or not a doctor will be justified in disclosing information whenever he reasonably believes that such a risk has arisen, or whether he must prove objectively that a real risk of physical harm does in fact exist. This point was not resolved in *W v Egdell*, since it is possible to read the judgments as saying that either might be in the public interest. The earlier decision of the New Zealand High Court in *Duncan v Medical Practitioners' Disciplinary Committee*[73] similarly left the question open:

> The doctor must then exercise his professional judgment based upon the circumstances, and if he fairly and reasonably believes such a danger exists then he must act unhesitatingly to prevent injury or loss of life even if there is to be a breach of confidentiality. If his actions are later to be scrutinised as to their correctness, he can be confident any official inquiry will be by people sympathetic about the predicament he faced.

Brazier suggests that the test should be based on the reasonableness of the particular doctor's belief:

---

[69] Quoted at [1990] 2 WLR 471, 489.

[70] [1990] 2 WLR 471, 490–1.

[71] ibid, 493 *per* Bingham LJ.

[72] See Kennedy, I and Grubb, A, *Medical Law* (3rd edn, Butterworths, 2000), 1101; Brazier, M, *Medicine, Patients and the Law* (3rd edn, Penguin, 2003), 68. The GMC guidelines state that disclosures in the public interest can only be justified to protect the patient, or someone else, from risk of death or serious harm, (n 40 above) 4.

[73] [1986] 1 NZLR 513, 521.

When the doctor reasonably foresees that nondisclosure poses a real risk of physical harm to a third party he ought to be free to warn that person, especially if that person too is his patient. Courts should not be over-zealous in proving him wrong.[74]

The Department of Health Code of Practice on confidentiality[75] attempts to put some flesh on the bones of the 'public interest' justification by including examples of circumstances when it may outweigh the obligation of confidence. The Code states that NHS staff are permitted to disclose personal information in order to prevent abuse or serious harm to others and/or prevent and support the detection, investigation and punishment of serious crime.[76] The Code recognises that the definition of serious crime is not clear, but murder, manslaughter, rape, treason, kidnapping and child abuse are all listed as crimes which may warrant breaching confidentiality.[77] Serious harm to the security of the state or to public order and crimes that involve substantial financial gain or loss would also generally fall within this category, but theft, fraud or damage to property where loss/damage is less substantial would generally not. Disclosures to prevent serious harm or abuse also warrant breach of confidence and the risk of child abuse or neglect, assault, a traffic accident or the spread of infectious disease are included as perhaps the most common examples that staff might face. However, the Code recognises that considerations of harm should also inform decisions about disclosure in relation to crime as serious fraud or theft involving NHS resources would be likely to harm individuals waiting for treatment.[78]

9.55

The Code reminds NHS staff that it is important not to equate the 'public interest' with what may be of interest to the public and each case must be considered on its merits. Whilst this guidance is reasonably detailed and helpful, it is purely advisory and by no means exhaustive. And as noted above, the precise circumstances in which the health worker's obligation of confidence can be overridden in the public interest remains a question for the courts.

9.56

There are a number of recent statutory examples of lawful disclosure in the public interest with respect to official and regulatory bodies. For example the Health Act 1999 permits disclosure to[79] and[80] by the Commission for Health

9.57

---

[74] N 72 above, 68.

[75] *Confidentiality: NHS Code of Practice* (2003). See also guidance from the BMA, *Confidentiality and disclosure of health information* (October 1999), located at *www.bma.org.uk*.

[76] ibid, 31. The GMC guidance defines a serious crime as 'a crime that puts someone at risk of death or serious harm and would usually be crimes against the person, such as abuse of children' (n 40 above, para 37).

[77] ibid, 32.

[78] ibid.

[79] s 23(2)(d) and see also Commission for Health Improvement (Functions) Regulations 2000, SI 2000/662 reg 20(3)(d). Note however that the CHI's days are numbered as its functions will be taken over by the new Commission for Healthcare Audit and Inspection (CHAI) in April 2004. Whilst CHAI will be an England and Wales body and carry out functions in Wales, the local review and inspection of NHS bodies in Wales will be made by a new Healthcare Inspection Unit for Wales (see paras 1.135–1.139). Similar (and broader) statutory powers will apply to CHAI in relation to

Improvement; the Health Service Commissioners Act 1993 permits disclosures
by the Health Service Commissioner (HSC) generally[81] and to the Information
Commissioner;[82] the Freedom of Information Act 2000 allows disclosure by the
Information Commissioner to the HSC;[83] and the Medical Act 1983 permits disclosure of confidential patient medical records to the GMC.[84]

9.58 One final example of the 'public interest' justification is in the context of genetic
information. The nature of genetic information about one person means that it
may be very relevant to other family members because of their common genetic
heritage. Consequently, there are competing interests at stake. As noted by
Ngwena and Chadwick, a major legal and ethical dilemma is:

> . . . whether to allow a third party access to personal and confidential information
> that is generated by the doctor from the patient in the course of diagnostic care. The
> nature of genetic disease, with its vertical transmission down the family tree from
> one generation to the next, means that at any given point, personal and confiden-
> tial genetic information generated from a specific individual might be regarded as a
> legitimate interest by his/her spouse partner, offspring or other relatives such as sib-
> lings and grandchildren. Such third parties may claim especially in the context of
> genetic counselling, to be entitled to access to what would otherwise be confiden-
> tial information on the ground that knowledge of it is the sine qua non for prevent-
> ing or ameliorating probable or actual harm from genetic disease.[85]

9.59 The establishment of the Human Genome Project in 1992[86] and the development
of sophisticated genetic diagnostic techniques have had a profound impact on
health care and brought this dilemma to the forefront of contemporary medical
practice. To what extent does the public interest exception justify the disclosure of
genetic information about a patient to other members of that patient's family?
The BMA is of the opinion that such disclosure can be justified in exceptional circumstances, where the patient cannot be persuaded to agree.[87] This would be on
the basis of the 'harm to others' justification. Ngwena and Chadwick would agree
with this view:

---

information disclosure under the Health and Social Care (Community Health and Standards) Act
2003. For example, s 68 confers upon CHAI a sweeping power to require documents and information, including personal records (ie patient identifiable data) from an NHS body, local authority or
any person providing health care for the NHS body, in pursuance of its statutory functions.
Understandably, there are concerns about the breadth of this power. See Dyer, C, 'Bill gives government power to breach patient confidentiality' (2001) 322 BMJ 256.

[80] s 24(6).
[81] s 15 (as amended).
[82] s 18A.
[83] s 76.
[84] s 35B(2) as inserted by the Medical Act 1983 (Amendment) Order 2000, SI 2000/1803, art 4.
[85] Ngwena, C and Chadwick, R, 'Genetic Diagnostic Information and the Duty of
Confidentiality: Ethics and Law' (1993) 1 *Medical Law International* 73–95, 74.
[86] See further McLean, S, and Giesen, D, 'Legal and Ethical Considerations of the Human
Genome Project' (1994) 1 *Medical Law International* 159–75.
[87] BMA, *Human Genetics: Choice and Responsibility* (1998), 70–2.

It is apparent from decided cases that the public interest exception can be invoked to protect an open rather than closed category of interests. . . . What is crucial is the establishment of tangible anticipated harm to a third party. In principle, therefore, the interest in preventing the deleterious effects of genetic disease in a genetically related third party prima facie falls within the public interest exception.[88]

It is therefore arguable that disclosure of genetic information can be justified where there is a real risk of harm to genetically related third parties.[89] Although some commentators would contend that the common law on confidentiality cannot adequately deal with all the problems which surround genetic information in the family milieu.[90] In particular, Laurie maintains that the public interest justification applies in order to avert harm to others. But if no cure exists for the condition—that is, the harm cannot be prevented—why should the disclosure be made? The Human Genetics Commission, established to develop policy and advise the government on the regulation of genetics, is also concerned about the inadequacies of the common law and is pressing the government to take further action to protect genetic privacy and confidentiality.[91]

9.60

(iii) Guidance from the General Medical Council

In 'The Duties of Doctor' the GMC provided detailed guidance for doctors on the scope of their obligation of confidence. This guidance was updated and radically revised in 2000 with the publication of 'Confidentiality: Protecting and Providing Information'. According to the GMC, the obligation of confidence is founded upon both a patient's right to expect confidentiality from a doctor, and the danger that otherwise patients may be reluctant to give doctors information which they need in order to provide good care.[92] The guidance adopts three key principles governing the provision of information by doctors about patients to others: (i) seek patient's consent to disclosure of information wherever possible, whether or not the doctor judges that patients can be identified from the disclosure; (ii) anonymise data where unidentifiable data will serve the purpose; (iii) keep disclosures to the minimum necessary.

9.61

---

[88] N 85 above, 81.

[89] See Skene, L, 'Patients' Rights or Family Responsibilities? Two Approaches to Genetic Testing' (1998) 6 Med L Rev 1; 'Genetic Secrets and the Family: A Response to Bell and Bennett' (2001) 9 Med L Rev 162–169 for a discussion of whether a duty to disclose exists in law and for a contrary view see Bell, D and Bennett, B, 'Genetic Secrets and the Family' (2001) 9 Med L Rev 130–161.

[90] Laurie, GT, 'The Most Personal Information of All: An Appraisal of Genetic Privacy in the Shadow of the Human Genome Project' (1996) 10 *International Journal of Law, Policy and the Family* 74–101; *Genetic Privacy: A Challenge to Medico-Legal Norms* (Cambridge University Press, 2002).

[91] *Inside Information: Balancing Interests in the Use of Personal Genetic Data* (2002), 13–14.

[92] N 40 above, 2.

9.62   Although the GMC stresses that confidential information should only be disclosed with the patient's consent, it has recognised that circumstances may arise in
which a doctor may be justified in disclosing such information notwithstanding
that the patient has not consented to the disclosure. It should be remembered,
however, that the courts are not bound to follow the guidance from the GMC in
determining the scope of the legal, as opposed to the professional or ethical, obligation of confidence. The guidelines are purely advisory, although some commentators argue that they may become increasingly significant in the courts as
indicators of good practice.[93]

(a) Sharing information with others providing care

9.63   The GMC recognises a number of circumstances in which concern for a patient's
welfare might necessitate the disclosure of confidential information without consent. First, where patients have consented to treatment, express consent is not usually needed before relevant personal information is shared to enable the treatment
to be provided.[94] For example, express consent would not be needed before general practitioners disclose relevant personal information so that a medical secretary can type a referral letter. The reasons for this are that in order to treat patients
safely and provide continuity of care, all members of the health care team need to
be aware of the patient's condition and medical history.

(b) Children and others patients who may lack competence to give consent

9.64   Secondly, where the patient is mentally incapable of giving a valid consent to disclosure by reason of immaturity, illness or mental incapacity. In such circumstances the GMC suggests that disclosure may be justified to an appropriate
person or authority if it is 'essential, in [the patient's] *medical interests*'.[95] In such
cases, the GMC advises that the patient should be told prior to the disclosure and,
where appropriate, the views of an advocate or carer should be sought and carefully considered.

9.65   Where a patient is unable to give or withhold consent by reason of either neglect
or physical, sexual or emotional abuse the GMC recommends that disclosure to
the appropriate responsible person or statutory agency would be justified if it is in
the patient's *best interests*.[96] There is no definition of best interests provided here,
but presumably, in contrast to the first category, disclosure in these circumstances
is not confined to purely medical interests. A number of cases have confirmed that
'best interests' in a medical context does extend beyond the physical and mental

---

[93] Moodie, P and Wright, M, 'Confidentiality, Codes and Courts: An examination of the significance of professional guidelines on medical ethics in determining the legal limits of confidentiality' (2002) 29(1) *Anglo-American Law Review* 39–66, 40.
[94] N 40 above, 3–4. See paras 9.31–9.33 above.
[95] ibid, 9 (emphasis supplied).
[96] ibid (emphasis supplied).

health of the patient to embrace moral, social and welfare interests.[97] The distinction between this and the first category is not altogether clear. The GMC appears to take the view that patients might be either incapable of giving a valid consent to treatment, in which case they would fall into the first category, or may otherwise be 'unable' to give consent, for example, because they are under undue influence or otherwise precluded from making an appropriate medical treatment decision, in which case they would fall into the latter category. For example, the GMC envisages that such circumstances may arise in relation to children, where concerns about possible abuse need to be shared with other agencies such as social services. If the doctor believes that disclosure is not in the best interests of an abused or neglected patient, she must still be prepared to justify his decision.[98] Consequently, it may be that, from the legal point of view, the second category is better viewed as encompassing those cases where the patient *is capable of giving a valid consent* to disclosure but the circumstances are such that disclosure without the patient's consent is *justified in the public interest.*

(c) Preventing Harm to the Patient or Others

Finally, where necessary to prevent a risk of death or serious harm to the patient the GMC takes the view that disclosure to an appropriate person or authority will not be regarded as professional impropriety.[99] In all such cases, doctor must weigh the possible harm (both to the patient, and the overall trust between doctors and patients) against the benefits which are likely to arise from the release of the information. The situations chosen to illustrate this exception are disclosure to the Driver and Vehicle Licensing Authority where a patient continues to drive against medical advice when unfit to do so; disclosure of the fact that a colleague who is also a patient is placing patients at risk of illness or other medical condition; and disclosure necessary for the prevention or detection of a serious crime. In this context, serious crimes will put someone at risk of death or serious harm, and will usually be crimes against the person, such as abuse of children.[100]

9.66

(d) Teaching, Research and Audit

For the purposes of teaching, research and audit it is advised that, wherever possible, information should be effectively anonymised in order to protect the confidentiality of the patient. In relation to audit and teaching, the GMC takes the view that patients' consent must otherwise be obtained in order to justify disclosure.[101] In relation to medical research, however, the position is slightly different.

9.67

---

[97] See eg *Re SL (Adult Patient: Medical Treatment)* (2000) 55 BMLR 105 and *Re Y (Mental Incapacity: Bone Marrow Transplant)* [1997] 2 FCR 172.

[98] N 40 above.

[99] ibid, 8–9.

[100] *cf* Department of Health guidance discussed at paras 9.55–9.56 above.

[101] N 40 above, 7.

Here, research disclosure is possible in exceptional circumstances without consent as long as it has been sanctioned by the appropriate research ethics committee. The GMC suggests that where research projects depend on using identifiable information or samples, and it is not practicable to contact patients to seek their consent, this fact should be disclosed to a research ethics committee which must then decide whether or not the public interest in the research being carried out outweighs the patients' right to confidentiality.[102] The decision of the research ethics committee would then be taken into account by a court if a claim for breach of confidentiality were made. This assumes that a research ethics committee will always be involved prior to the disclosure of confidential information. The reality is, however, that research ethics committees are not routinely involved in much which may be published or discussed as clinical research, for example procedures carried out on a named patient basis, observations of unusual patient symptoms or responses, or trials of new surgical methods. In such circumstances it may well be the case that information is shared for research purposes without first obtaining the consent either of the patient or of a research ethics committee. This would appear to fall outside of the exception to the obligation of confidence recognised by the GMC and may, indeed, be regarded as professionally improper since according to the GMC: 'Disclosures may otherwise be improper, even if the recipients of the information are registered medical practitioners'.[103]

9.68 In light of the *Source Informatics* case and Department of Health policy that patient information within the NHS should be made non-identifying (see paras 9.23–9.27 above), it would be best practice for researchers to anonymise the information wherever possible and keep disclosures to the minimum required. This view is reaffirmed in the additional guidance provided by the GMC on confidentiality in the context of medical research.[104] As discussed in Chapter 13, the guidance sets out the standards expected of all doctors working in research in the NHS, universities and the private sector. One of the key principles governing research practice is the need to respect participants' right to confidentiality and the guidance stipulates that data should be anonymised where unidentifiable data will serve the purpose.[105] Moreover, the guidance states that when disclosures are contemplated in the public interest, researchers must consider factors such as the nature of the information to be disclosed; how long identifiable data will be preserved; how many people may have access to the data, as well as the potential

---

[102] ibid.
[103] ibid.
[104] *Research: The Role and Responsibilities of Doctors* (February 2002).
[105] ibid, para 30. See also Department of Health, *Confidentiality: NHS Code of Practice* (2003) 38: 'The use of anonymised data is preferable for research purposes'. Moreover, in relation to identifiable information, the Code states that where explicit consent has not been gained and the public interest does not justify breaching patient confidentiality, the research project needs support under s 60 of the Health and Social Care Act 2001 (see paras 9.40–9.45 above).

benefits of the research project. It concludes that participant's wishes about the use of the data can be overridden only in exceptional circumstances and researchers must be prepared to justify their decision to disclose on the basis of 'public interest'.[106]

(e) Publication of photographs and case-histories

The GMC states that express consent must be obtained from patients before publishing personal information about them as individuals in the media to which the public has access, for example in journals or textbooks. This applies irrespective of whether or not the doctor believes that the patient can be identified.

9.69

(f) HIV/AIDS and other communicable diseases

Where a patient is diagnosed as being HIV positive or having AIDS, particular problems might arise from the apparent conflict between the obligation of confidence owed to the patient and the doctor's obligation to safeguard the welfare of other doctors or health care professionals caring for the patient or of the patient's sexual partner. In recognition of that fact, the GMC has issued specific guidance concerning 'serious communicable diseases', including HIV infection, tuberculosis and Hepatitis B and C.[107] In relation to safeguarding the welfare of the health care team, the GMC advises that the patient should be advised about the need for disclosure and the difficulties which a refusal of consent to disclosure may cause for the team providing his medical care. If, however, he does refuse consent to disclosure, his wishes ought to be respected unless the 'failure to disclose the information would put a health care worker or other patient at serious risk of death or serious harm'.[108]

9.70

The GMC clearly regards this as an exceptional situation. Accordingly, it must be necessary to show some particularly serious risk of exposure to the disease/virus, for example, where careful barrier precautions would be unlikely to succeed in guarding against infection.

9.71

Disclosure to a known sexual partner of the patient would, in the view of the GMC, be justified only where there is reason to think that the patient has not informed that person, and cannot be persuaded to do so. Moreover, there must be a need to protect that person from 'risk of death or serious harm'.[109] In such circumstances, the patient should be told before the disclosure is made and the information must only be disclosed to those who are at risk of infection. Kennedy and Grubb have observed that whilst there must be a serious risk of death or

9.72

---

[106] See further Ch 13, esp paras 13.87–13.96.
[107] *Serious Communicable Diseases* (October 1997).
[108] ibid, para 19.
[109] ibid, para 22.

serious harm for disclosure to other health professionals, any risk of these outcomes will suffice for a sexual partner.[110] It is not entirely clear why this distinction has been made.

9.73   The GMC has recognised in its guidance that the infected person may also be a doctor who has treated patients who may, as a result, have been at risk of exposure. This occurred in *X v Y* and *H (a health care worker) v Associated Newspapers Limited and H (a health care worker) v N HA* (see para 9.26 above). The Department of Health has issued guidance on the management of such cases: 'AIDS/HIV Infected Health Care Workers'. The guidance encourages health professionals who believe they may have been infected to act responsibly and seek advice from a specialist occupational health physician. This responsibility is also acknowledged in the GMC specific guidance on 'Serious Communicable Diseases'. Both documents recognise that whilst that person's confidences must be respected, it may be necessary to inform patients or other health professionals for them to determine whether they have been infected.[111] In such cases, a careful balance must be struck between the duty of confidentiality and the need to protect others from harm:

> In balancing the duty to the infected health care worker and the wider duty to the public, complex ethical issues may arise. As in other areas of medical practice, a health care worker disclosing information about another health care worker may be required to justify their decision to do this. The need for disclosure must be carefully weighed.[112]

(iv)   Special Cases

(a)   Children

9.74   No English case has dealt specifically with the question of the doctor's obligation of confidence to a child. Whereas the common law has developed in relation to

---

[110]   Kennedy and Grubb (n 72 above) 1102.

[111]   See further Department of Health, *HIV Infected Health Care Workers: A Consultation Paper on Management and Patient Notification* (July 2002), which contains guidance on the procedure for patient notification in such circumstances. Notification of patients identified as having been exposed to a risk of HIV infection by an infected health care worker is considered necessary (i) to provide the patients with information about the nature of the risk to which they have been exposed; (ii) to detect any HIV infection, provide care and advice on measures to prevent onward HIV infection; and (iii) to collect valid data to augment existing estimates of the risk of HIV transmission from an infected worker to patients. It is not necessary any longer to notify automatically every patient who has undergone any exposure prone procedure by an HIV infected health care worker, because the overall risk of transmission is very low (ibid, paras 8.1 and 8.3).

[112]   *AIDS/HIV Infected Health Care Workers: Guidance on the management of infected health care workers and patient notification* (HSC 1998/226), para 10.4. See now revised draft guidance published in 2002 which is intended to replace the earlier guidance and is currently under consultation (*HIV Infected Health Care Workers: A Consultation Paper on Management and Patient Notification* (July 2002) para 10.4, located at *www.doh.gov.uk/aids.htm.*

the question of a child's ability to consent or refuse consent to medical treatment itself, there is still some doubt about the correct analysis of the doctor's obligation to maintain the confidentiality of information which he obtains in the course of his professional relationship with a child.

There are two possible positions which could be taken here. The first would be to **9.75** suggest that there is nothing unique about the doctor–child patient relationship. According to this view, the obligation of confidence depends not upon the patient's expectation that information will be kept confidential, but upon that information itself 'having the necessary character of confidence about it'.[113] More particularly, that information may be described as confidential where the law would impose an obligation of confidence and not merely where it could be said that the person communicating the information thought of it as confidential to him.

If information disclosed within the doctor–child patient relationship could be so **9.76** described as confidential, in every case a balance would have to be struck between the public interests favouring confidentiality in the circumstances and the public interests favouring disclosure. Where a child is very young and the lawfulness of medical treatment depends upon a parent's consent being given, then there will clearly be a public interest served by disclosure of information about the child's medical condition to the parent. Of course that is not to say that the information should be disclosed to anyone else. As the child grows in maturity and intelligence, the public interest in the disclosure of medical information to his parents will correspondingly decrease since in many cases treatment will lawfully be provided without the need for consent to be given by his parents or anyone else.[114]

The alternative is to regard the doctor's obligation of confidence as being depend- **9.77** ent upon the child being competent to form a relationship of confidence with the doctor. The description of information as confidential is, according to this view, dependent upon some expectation on the part of the person communicating it that it will be kept secret. Thus, no obligation of confidence could be owed to a child unless the child was able to understand what secrecy entails, and to make a decision whether or not to restrict disclosure of medical information. Just as a child cannot consent to treatment unless competent, a child could not be owed an obligation of confidence unless capable of understanding what that entails. As noted by Kennedy and Grubb, the latter approach is analytically preferable and would be more in line with the general law relating to children, as the courts have

---

[113] *Per* Lord Greene MR in *Saltman Engineering Co Ltd v Campbell Engineering Co Ltd* (1948) 65 RPC 203, 215.

[114] Note however that in exceptional circumstances it may be prudent for doctors to involve the parents in the treatment decision even where the child is competent. See eg *Re W (a minor) (medical treatment)* [1992] 4 All ER 627.

tended to move away from status towards a capacity based approach.[115] It would follow that a doctor owes no obligation of confidence at all unless a child patient is competent and the information may then be disclosed to those with parental responsibility. If necessary, however, an order specifically restricting the disclosure of information which relates to child patients could be sought from a court exercising its *parens patriae* jurisdiction, or exercising powers specifically conferred under the Children Act 1989.

9.78   The GMC guidance seems to adopt a status approach towards the obligation of confidentiality owed to children. Accordingly, prima facie the doctor owes a duty of confidence to the child, which may be breached on the basis of the child's medical interests. (see para 9.64 above). In contrast, the Department of Health's Code suggests that the appropriate test is the child's capacity:

> Children under the age of 16 who have the capacity and understanding to take decisions about their own treatment are also entitled to make decisions about the use and disclosure of information they have provided in confidence.[116]

(b) Incompetent Adults

9.79   The analysis described above applies equally to incompetent adults. Thus, according to one view an obligation of confidence is owed by the doctor because information disclosed in the relationship could objectively be described as confidential, although this obligation is liable to be overridden where disclosure can be justified in the public interest. The alternative position is that no obligation of confidence can be owed unless the patient is competent at the time of disclosure. The patient who was once competent but ceases to be so may be owed an obligation of confidence in respect of information communicated at a time when he was competent. But a patient who has never been competent, or who is incompetent at the time of disclosure, is owed no obligation of confidence whatsoever.

9.80   Since English courts have no *parens patriae* power in respect of adults the consequence of the latter view is that there is no legal basis upon which a doctor could be restrained from disclosing information relating to adult incompetent patients.[117] The only relevant legal action which could be brought would be to sue in

---

[115] N 72 above, 1078. For a detailed discussion of how the law of confidentiality operates in relation to children see Loughrey, J, 'Medical Information, Confidentiality and a Child's Right to Privacy' (2003) 23 LS 510–535. She suggests that the law recognises that an obligation of confidentiality is owed by health care professionals to *competent* and *incompetent* children. see eg judicial dictum in *Re C (a minor) (wardship: medical treatment) (No 2)* [1989] 2 All ER 791 and in *Venables v News Group Newspapers Ltd* [2001] 1 All ER 908, 939. But the precise basis and scope of this duty remains unclear.

[116] N 41 above, 28.

[117] Note that the government published a Draft Mental Incapacity Bill in June 2003. If enacted, the proposals would provide a statutory framework for determining capacity and making financial,

the tort of negligence where disclosure caused actual harm to the patient and was judged to be unreasonable in the circumstances.

Again here, the GMC's most recent guidance seems to contemplate an ethical **9.81** obligation of confidence to the incompetent patient which may be breached in the patient's medical interests (see para 9.64 above). This view is supported by Hale LJ in *R (on the application of S) v Plymouth City Council*.[118] The case involved an incompetent 27-year old adult whose mother sought access to his medical records, as his nearest relative under the Mental Health Act 1983. The local authority refused access on the basis that it would be a breach of confidentiality. Hale LJ reviewed the relevant law and concluded that an incompetent person does have a right to confidentiality and to privacy under Article 8 of the European Convention on Human Rights. These rights had to be balanced against the public and private interests in permitting, indeed requiring, the disclosure of confidential information for certain purposes. On the facts of the case, the interference with the son's right to confidentiality was justified by the mother's right to be involved as a nearest relative in the decision-making process concerning her son's welfare.

(c) Deceased Patients

There is no settled law determining whether or not an obligation of confidence **9.82** survives the death of the patient. Since it is a personal obligation owed to the deceased, absent any statutory provision to the contrary, English courts are most likely to find that the obligation of confidence does not survive death.[119] In this regard the analogy with the policy underlying the law of defamation is persuasive, that is that where the deceased's reputation and feelings are at stake the interest should not survive for the benefit of the estate. This analysis is certainly convincing and, in the view of Kennedy and Grubb, the courts would most likely reflect this policy in the case of breach of medical confidence.[120] The position is much the same as that of third parties whose interests might be affected by disclosure of information communicated within the doctor–patient relationship, but to whom the doctor owes no obligation of confidence.

---

welfare and health care decisions on behalf of incapacitated adults. A general authority to act in the 'best interests' (as defined) of the patient would be introduced and a new Court of Protection would have authority over all areas of decision-making for adults who lack capacity. Should the proposals be enacted then, presumably, disclosure could be made as long as it was deemed to be in the incompetent patient's 'best interests'. The draft Bill can be located at *www.lcd.gov.uk*.

[118] [2002] EWCA Civ 388; [2002] 1 FLR 1177.

[119] The Access to Health Records Act 1990 allows the personal representatives of a deceased patient to seek access to his medical records.

[120] N 72 above, 1082.

9.83 Although there is no clear legal obligation of confidentiality which applies to the deceased, ethical guidance from the GMC,[121] the BMA[122] and Department of Health[123] is in agreement that confidentiality obligations must continue to apply beyond death. The GMC expressly advises that doctors still have an obligation to keep personal information confidential after a patient dies. The extent to which confidential information may be disclosed after a patient's death will depend on the circumstances, including the nature and intended use of the information; whether it is already public knowledge or can be anonymised; and whether disclosure may cause distress to, or be of benefit to, the patient's partner or family. This would seem to be another situation where the ethical duty exceeds that required by the law (see also para 9.38 above), but it is obviously advisable and good practice to follow the official and professional guidelines. Otherwise, health care practitioners could find themselves facing disciplinary action.

(d) Express Prohibition

9.84 Difficulties arise where a patient forbids a doctor to disclose information which he has gained in his professional relationship. Although there is no case law directly on the point, it is probably correct to say that disclosure contrary to an express prohibition would generally be a breach of confidence since there must be a strong public interest favouring confidentiality in such circumstances. In light of the *Source Informatics* case (discussed at paras 9.23–9.25 above) this does not now apply to information which is not in a form capable of identifying the patient, as no confidence of the patient has been infringed.

9.85 Since, however, the lawfulness of disclosure even where the patient has expressly forbidden disclosure must depend upon whether or not disclosure could be justified in the public interest, there may be exceptional circumstances in which even an express prohibition on disclosure could be overridden. Clearly where disclosure is required by law or is authorised under s 60 of the Health and Social Care Act 2001, there would be no breach of confidence. Probably also where disclosure is necessary in order to prevent a real risk of serious harm it would also be lawful. A doctor would not, however, be justified in disclosing the confidential information for the patient's own benefit, for example, by informing the patient's GP or other health professionals caring for the patient. Similarly, disclosure contrary to an express prohibition for the purposes of teaching or research would probably not be lawful.

---

[121] N 40 above, para 40.
[122] *Confidentiality and disclosure of health information* (October 1999), located at *www.bma. org.uk*. 'The ethical duty of confidentiality extends beyond the death of the patient'.
[123] N 41 above, 9.

2. Disclosure for the Purpose of Litigation

(i) Actions Against a Health Authority, Trust, or Doctor

Where litigation relating to personal injuries or death is actual or in contempla- **9.86**
tion an individual who is 'likely to be a party to subsequent proceedings' can apply
to the High Court to compel a doctor or hospital to make such disclosures as may
be relevant to an issue arising or likely to arise out of a claim for personal injuries
provided that the doctor or hospital is also likely to be a party to the proceedings.[124] The court must be satisfied that disclosure is necessary either to dispose of
the case fairly or to save costs.[125] It is not, however, necessary for the patient to
show that he is likely to succeed on the merits of his claim, or that he has sufficient
evidence to base a claim at the time of making the application for disclosure.

In the leading case of *Dunning v Board of Governors of the United Liverpool Hospitals*[126] **9.87**
the Court of Appeal held that to hold otherwise would be to frustrate the purpose of
the legislation which is to enable potential litigants to discover whether there is sufficient evidence to bring a claim for compensation before incurring the expense of
commencing proceedings. According to Lord Denning MR, the court:

> . . . should construe 'likely to be made' as meaning 'may' or 'may well be made' de-
> pendent upon the outcome of discovery.[127]

Conversely, it is clear that an application for pre-action discovery cannot be used **9.88**
as a 'fishing expedition' and the plaintiff must show that there is a reasonable
prospect of him making a claim in the circumstances.[128]

Courts considering these applications must balance the public interest in favour **9.89**
of disclosure against the public interest in maintaining the confidentiality of the
information, and the relevant legislation empowering the High Court to make
such orders prohibits the making of an order for discovery where 'compliance
with the order, if made, would be likely to be injurious to the public interest'.[129]

---

[124] Supreme Court Act 1981, s 33, and CPR Pt 31.16. See also County Courts Act 1984, s 52. Pre-
action discovery under these statutes is not limited to the applicant or claimant's own medical
records but may include notes of other patients or accident reports. The restriction to claims for personal injury and death is removed by the Civil Procedure (Modification of Enactments) Order
1998, SI 1998/2940.

[125] See CPR Pt 31.16.

[126] [1973] 2 All ER 454, decided under the Administration of Justice Act 1970, s 31, the wording
of which is identical to the Supreme Court Act 1981, s 33(2).

[127] [1973] 2 All ER 454, 475.

[128] See in particular James LJ in *Dunning* [1973] 2 All ER 454, 460 and *Harris v Newcastle upon
Tyne* [1989] 1 WLR 96. See also the discussion in Cowley, R, *Access to Medical Records and Reports*
(NAHAT, Radcliffe Medical Press, Oxford, 1994), 43.

[129] Gurry (n 16 above) at 326 notes that the public interest here represents a higher interest which
overcomes the interest in confidentiality for certain purposes. See also *Campbell v Tameside
Metropolitan Borough Council* [1982] 1 QB 1065 (CA).

9.90 The burden is on the party seeking to maintain the confidence of the information to establish that the court should refuse to order disclosure, since it is generally the case that the public interest in the administration of justice will be overriding. It is clear that the mere fact of information having been communicated confidentially within the confines of the doctor–patient relationship will not of itself be sufficient to justify the court exercising its discretion. Some further consideration would be required before a court would exercise its discretion to refuse to require medical information to be disclosed in the context of litigation.[130]

(ii) After Proceedings Have Been Commenced

9.91 Once litigation has commenced the High Court has the power to order disclosure between the parties to the litigation of any documents which are relevant to an issue arising out of the claim.[131] It also has the power under s 34 of the Supreme Court Act 1981 to order that a person who is not himself a party to the proceedings must disclose whether or not he possesses certain documents, and if so, to disclose them to the plaintiff or defendant or his advisers.[132] These powers are, once again, dependent upon a finding that it is not against the public interest to order disclosure,[133] and that disclosure is necessary either to dispose of the case fairly or to save costs.[134]

9.92 Even as between parties to the litigation English courts have in the past shown their willingness to exercise their discretion to refuse to order disclosure of information where there is an important public interest in maintaining the confidentiality of the information in the circumstances. Thus, for example, in *D v NSPCC*[135] (an action for breach of duty and negligence against the NSPCC), the House of Lords held that documents disclosing the source of a complaint to the NSPCC should be immune from inspection on discovery since otherwise the society's capacity to perform its public functions may be put at risk.[136] It may be that in particular cases information which would otherwise be confidential, for example information disclosed for purposes of maintaining public health or

---

[130] For a discussion of the court's discretion in relation to medical information see *Re C* (16 January 1991), located on Lexis. Where the claimant is legally aided the court may see it as particularly important that information should be provided at an early stage in order to ascertain the likelihood of the action succeeding; see *Shaw v Vauxhall Motors* [1974] 1 WLR 1935, 1040 *per* Buckley LJ.

[131] The High Court has an inherent power to order disclosure between the parties to proceedings which have been commenced.

[132] See also County Courts Act 1984, s 53.

[133] Supreme Court Act 1981, s 35(1). See also *Science Research Council v Nassé* [1979] 3 All ER 673 (HL).

[134] CPR Pt 31.17(3). The restriction to claims for personal injury and death is removed by the Civil Procedure (Modification of Enactments) Order 1998, SI 1998/2940.

[135] [1977] 1 All ER 589.

[136] See the discussion in Gurry (n 16 above) at 347–8.

containing the spread of infectious diseases, may similarly be immune from disclosure in legal proceedings on the basis that disclosure might jeopardise an important public interest.

(iii) In the Courtroom

It will often be the case that a doctor or other health professional is requested to supply information as evidence orally or in a written statement either as a witness or in order to defend the claim. In such cases, the doctor is entitled to include confidential information in his evidence provided that it can be shown that it is in the public interest that such information is before the court.[137] As discussed above, the presumption in favour of disclosure rests upon the weight of the public interest in the administration of justice. In order to justify non-disclosure therefore, a doctor must be able to establish that the public interest in confidentiality in the circumstances outweighs the public interest in disclosure. If the doctor is not able successfully to justify non-disclosure he may be liable for contempt of court if he refuses to give evidence in court regardless of the fact that the information is confidential to his patient.[138]

9.93

The Canadian Supreme Court in *M(A) v Ryan*[139] held that there is no absolute privilege in communications between a psychiatrist and his patient. The court must be satisfied of four requirements for privilege: (i) communication in confidence; (ii) confidence is essential to the full and satisfactory maintenance of the professional relationship; (iii) fostering the relationship is of public importance; and (iv) the interests served by protecting the communications from disclosure outweigh the interest of pursuing the truth and disposing correctly of the litigation. On the facts, in a claim by a patient against her former psychiatrist for abuse, the records of her communications with a subsequent psychiatrist were not privileged since disclosure could be limited to the lawyers and expert witnesses of the defendant and should not be used for any purpose other than defending the claim.

9.94

The above analysis demonstrates that the patient can stop his doctor from disclosing details of his confidential information in virtually all situations save in the courtroom.[140]

9.95

---

[137] For a consideration of the Crown Court's power to set aside a witness summons which would have required the witness to produce records relating to lawful abortions see *Morrow v DPP* (1993) 14 BMLR 54, noted by Kennedy, I [1994] 2 Med L Rev 99.

[138] See *Duchess of Kingston's Case* (1776) 20 State Trials 355; *Nuttall v Nuttall and Twynan* (1964) 108 Sol J 605. For a discussion of the balancing process see *D v NSPCC* [1977] 1 All ER 589, 597.

[139] [1997] 1 SCR 157 (Can Sup Ct).

[140] McHale, J, *Medical Confidentiality and Legal Privilege* (Routledge, 1993), 12. Pursuant to the Coroners Act 1988, s 2(1) a doctor may be required to provide information to the court. See also the GMC guidance relating to disclosure in connection with judicial or other statutory proceedings contained in *Confidentiality: Protecting and Providing Information* (2003), Section 6.

3. *Confidentiality, Warning and Negligence Liability*

(i) **Negligent Disclosure**

9.96 In New Zealand in the case of *Furniss v Fitchett*[141] it was held that liability in negligence might arise from a disclosure of information in breach of confidence. Barrowclough CJ clearly felt that the obligation to take reasonable care to respect confidences might be owed in any situation in which it was reasonably foreseeable that disclosure might injure the plaintiff's mental health:

> I have not forgotten that the certificate was true and accurate, but I see no reason for limiting the duty to one of care in seeing that it is accurate. The duty must extend also to the exercise of care in deciding whether it should be put in circulation in such a way that it is likely to cause harm to another.

9.97 The English courts have considered this issue in the context of negligent disclosure by the police. In *Swinney v Chief Constable of the Northumbria Police*[142] there was an arguable claim for negligent breach of confidence where police allowed an informer's identity held in confidence to be discovered by leaving documents in a car which were subsequently stolen. There was also an arguable claim in the tort of negligence. Applying the current rules relating to recovery in negligence to the facts, it was possible that a special relationship existed which rendered the plaintiffs particularly at risk; that the police had in fact assumed a responsibility of confidentiality to the plaintiffs; and, considering all relevant public policy factors, that the plaintiffs' claim was not precluded by the principle of immunity. The court confirmed that the police do not have blanket immunity and considerations of public policy, such as the need to preserve the springs of information; to protect informers; and to encourage them to come forward without an undue fear of the risk that their identity will become known to the suspect, carried considerable weight. However, at trial, there was no liability in negligence as there was no breach of duty on the facts.[143]

9.98 No English court has yet considered whether an action in negligence could arise out of a breach of confidence by a doctor. In light of the approach taken by the court in *Swinney*, there is a strong argument that in any case in which it could be shown that a doctor had breached the obligation of confidence which he owed to his patient, in circumstances where it was foreseeable that this could harm the patient or put him at risk, he may also have breached the duty of care which he owed to that patient. Even if other doctors might similarly have disclosed the information, it could hardly be described as 'responsible' medical practice to act

---

[141] [1958] NZLR 396. Noted by Davis, AG (1958) 21 MLR 438.
[142] [1996] 3 All ER 449 (CA).
[143] *Swinney v Chief Constable of Northumbria Police (No 2))* The Times, 25 May 1999.

equitable damages can be awarded.[153] If a doctor's breach of confidence caused financial harm to a patient, as for example if it had adverse implications for his employment or business opportunities, this loss could be compensated in an action for breach of confidence. Where, however, the breach of confidence causes mere mental distress and anxiety, the law governing the recovery of damages is less certain.[154] If the patient were able to frame his claim as one in negligence, then damages could be recovered for any personal injury caused by the disclosure and possibly also for psychiatric injury so caused.

In an action for breach of a contractual obligation of confidence it is possible that damages could be claimed for mental distress and anxiety.[155] If the court took the view that a major/important object of the contractual relationship between the doctor and the patient was to provide relaxation, peace of mind and freedom from distress, it might be possible for damages to be awarded for a breach which compromised that very object. Although Scott J at first instance in *W v Egdell* suggested that recovery would be unlikely,[156] the courts have recently awarded general damages in such circumstances.   **9.106**

In *Cornelius v De Taranto*[157] the High Court awarded the claimant £3,000 as fair and reasonable compensation for the injury to her feelings after a medico-legal expert passed a copy of her psychiatric report to the claimant's GP and a consultant psychiatrist without her agreement, because the expert believed the claimant needed urgent psychiatric treatment. Morland J found that there was a clear contract between both parties and the defendant was in breach of an implied contractual duty of confidence. Having reviewed the relevant case law, Morland J concluded that: **9.107**

> In the present case in my judgement recovery of damages for mental distress caused by breach of confidence, when no other substantial remedy is available, would not be inimical to considerations of policy but indeed to refuse such recovery would illustrate that something was wrong with the law. Although the object of the contract was the provision of a medico-legal report, that object could not be achieved without the defendant's examination and assessment of confidential material relating to

---

[153] Humber, S, 'Patient Confidentiality: Breach of Clinical Confidence' (2001) 4 *Journal of Personal Injury Law* 432–8; Toulson, R and Phipps, C, *Confidentiality* (1996), paras 10.10–10.13.

[154] The *Law Commission Report on Breach of Confidence* (Law Com No 110) at para 4.81 recommended against the recovery of damages for embarrassment or distress caused by a non-contractual breach of confidence.

[155] See *Farley v Skinner* [2001] 4 All ER 801; *Watts v Morrow* [1991] 1 WLR 1421 and *Jarvis v Swan Tours Ltd* [1973] QB 233.

[156] [1989] 1 All ER 1089.

[157] [2001] EMLR 329. Morland J's findings on liability for breach of confidence were upheld on appeal [2001] EWCA Civ 1511; [2002] EMLR 6. For a discussion of this case see Stewart, A, 'Damages for mental distress following breach of confidence: Preventing or compensating tears' (2001) 23(6) EIPR 302–304.

the claimant's private and family life. The duty of confidence was an essential indeed fundamental ingredient of the contractual relationship between the claimant and the defendant which she breached.[158]

Given that an injunction would be of little use to the claimant as the damage had already been done, Morland J was prepared to award fair and reasonable compensation.

9.108   Morland J suggested certain factors which are relevant to the assessment of damages in cases such as this, which provide useful guidance in future cases. The nature and detail of the confidential material disclosed; the character of the recipients of the disclosure; the extent of disclosure and the psychological make-up of the claimant known to the defendant are all material factors in weighing up the true degree of injury to the claimant's feelings.

9.109   In reaching his conclusion, Morland J placed heavy reliance on academic commentary. He felt that the remedy was supported by current legal thinking. Accordingly, he described his decision (at [81]) as 'incremental rather than revolutionary'. Moreover, it was consistent with Article 8 of the European Convention on Human Rights, as any victory would be hollow if confidential information could be disclosed and only nominal damages awarded in respect of distress caused. The judge was obviously influenced by the Convention and was prepared to make an award of damages for breach of the Convention right as a cause of action in its own right in order to provide an appropriate remedy.

9.110   This case has clearly opened the door to the recovery of damages for injured feelings caused by breach of confidence when no other substantial remedy is available. It has subsequently been applied in *Lady Archer v Williams*.[159] In that case the claimant was awarded £2,500 damages for breach of confidence and injury to feelings. The judge accepted that where a breach of confidence causes injury to feelings, the court has power to award general damages. However, he cautioned that such damages should be kept to a modest level and should be proportionate to the injury suffered. Furthermore, such awards should be well below the level of general damages for serious physical or psychiatric injury.

(iv) **Restitutionary Damages**

9.111   If a doctor were to profit financially from a breach of patient confidentiality it is possible that he might be liable to account for those profits to the patient. The situation could arise, for example, where a doctor sells a patient's story to the press, or makes use of confidential information derived from the patient for his own financial gain from scientific research or development.

---

[158] ibid, at [69].
[159] [2003] EWHC 1670, [2003] EMLR 38.

5. *Statutory Modifications to the Obligation of Confidence*

There are three different ways in which statute may modify a doctor's obligation **9.112**
of confidence. First, it might reinforce the common law obligation of confidence
by providing specific penalties for unjustified disclosure, or extend its application
to cover circumstances in which the doctor might have been justified in disclosing
information at common law. Secondly, it might empower the doctor to disclose
information in certain limited circumstances, although not in fact requiring him
to do so. Thirdly, a statute might positively require disclosure provided specified
conditions are satisfied, leaving the doctor no discretion whether or not to disclose.

(i) Abortion

Pursuant to the Abortion Regulations 1991[160] any registered medical practitioner **9.113**
who terminates a pregnancy in England or Wales is required to provide the Chief
Medical Officer with notice of the termination together with any other information specified in the prescribed form of notification.[161] The regulations also prohibit disclosure of the notice or other information provided to the Chief Medical
Officer other than for the purposes set out in the regulations themselves.[162]

(ii) Infectious Diseases

The National Health Service (Venereal Diseases) Regulations 1974[163] prohibit **9.114**
the disclosure by a Health Authority of identifying information which was obtained:

> with respect to persons examined or treated for any sexually transmitted disease . . .
> except—
> (a) for the purpose of communicating that information to a medical practitioner,
> or to a person employed under the direction of a medical practitioner in con-
> nection with the treatment of persons suffering from such disease or the pre-
> vention of the spread thereof, and
> (b) for the purpose of such treatment and prevention.[164]

There is no specific requirement that the patient consent to disclosure under the **9.115**
regulations, but clearly disclosure would only be lawful 'for the purpose of

---

[160] SI 1991/499. Wilful contravention or wilful failure to comply with these requirements is an offence under s 2(3). See *R v Senior* [1981] 1 QB 283 *per* Lord Russell for a discussion of what amounts
to willful in these circumstances. See further Ch 11, esp paras 11.74–11.75.

[161] ibid, reg 4(1). In Wales the 'notice' or 'information' must be proided to the National Assembly
for Wales. See further paras 11.74–11.75 below.

[162] See ibid, reg 5. See further paras 11.74–11.75 below.

[163] SI 1974/29.

[164] ibid, reg 2. See also NHS Trusts and Primary Care Trusts (Sexually Transmitted Diseases)
Directions 2000 (in force 15 September 2000 in England only).

treatment' where the recipient of the information was in fact treating the patient for the sexually transmitted disease itself. The Department of Health's Code of Practice on Confidentiality recognises that many patients would regard information about sexually transmitted diseases as particularly sensitive and private. It should therefore never be assumed by NHS staff that patients are content for this information to be shared unless it has a direct and significant bearing on their health care.[165] Disclosure for the purpose of preventing the spread of disease, however, could be lawful even in the face of the patient's objection if, for example, it was felt necessary to inform a doctor responsible for the medical treatment of the individual's partner in order to prevent transmission. A further limitation on the scope of the regulations is that the disease must have been transmitted to the individual sexually, hence they could not authorise disclosure where, for example, HIV had been transmitted other than by sexual intercourse.[166]

9.116 The Public Health (Control of Disease) Act 1984 (supplemented by the Public Health (Infectious Diseases) Regulations 1988)[167] requires a doctor to notify 'the proper officer of the local authority for that district' of identifying particulars and other relevant information set out in the section if he:

> becomes aware, or suspects, that a patient whom he is attending within the district of a local authority is suffering from a notifiable disease or from food poisoning . . . unless he believes, and has reasonable grounds for believing, that some other registered medical practitioner has complied with this subsection with respect to the patient . . .[168]

9.117 Notifiable disease means any of the following: acute encephalitis, acute meningitis, acute poliomyelitis, anthrax, cholera, diphtheria, dysentery, food poisoning, leprosy, leptospirosis, malaria, measles, meningococcal septicaemia, mumps, opthalmia, neonatorum, paratyphoid fever, plague, rabies, relapsing fever, rubella, scarlet fever, small pox, tetanus, tuberculosis, typhoid fever, typhus, viral haemorrhagic fever, viral hepatitis, whooping cough, and yellow fever.[169]

(iii) Drug Misuse

9.118 Pursuant to the Misuse of Drugs (Notification of and Supply to Addicts) Regulations 1973 doctors are required to notify the Chief Medical Officer at the Home Office of identifying particulars about any person who:

> he considers, or has reasonable grounds to suspect, is addicted to any notifiable drug . . .[170]

---

[165] N 41 above, para 47.
[166] But see the discussion in Kennedy and Grubb (n 72 above) 1127 for a contrary view.
[167] SI 1988/1546.
[168] s 11(1).
[169] s 10, as added to by the Public Health (Infectious Diseases) Regulations 1988, SI 1988/1546.
[170] SI 1973/799, reg 3(1).

This does not, however, apply where the doctor, 'is of the opinion, formed in good **9.119** faith, that the continued administration of the drug or drugs concerned is required for the purpose of treating organic disease' or where the particulars have already been supplied to the Chief Medical Officer (although not necessarily by the doctor) during the period of 12 months ending with the date of the doctor's attendance of the patient.[171]

(iv) Births

Any person in attendance on the mother is obliged to notify the district medical **9.120** officer of the birth of any child born dead or alive after the twenty-eighth week of pregnancy.[172] This obligation may be discharged by instructing another person to notify the birth.

(v) Fertility Treatment

As discussed in Chapter 10, there are specific provisions in the Human **9.121** Fertilisation and Embryology Act 1990 (as modified by the Human Fertilisation and Embryology (Disclosure of Information) Act 1992) which regulate confidentiality. Generally, specific and unambiguous consent is required except; (i) in connection with the provision of treatment services, or any other description of medical, surgical or obstetric services, for the individual giving consent; (ii) in connection with the carrying out of an audit of clinical practice; or (iii) in connection with the auditing of accounts.

(vi) In Connection with the Investigation and Prevention of Crime

Under the Police and Criminal Evidence Act 1984, certain material is excluded **9.122** from the ordinary provisions enabling courts to make special procedure orders for the production of documents required for criminal investigations.[173] This material is described as 'excluded material' and covers both personal records created or acquired for professional purposes and held in confidence, and human tissue or tissue fluid taken for the purposes of diagnosis or medical treatment and held in confidence.[174] Personal records are in turn defined in s 12 to include records from which an individual can be identified and which relate to his physical or mental health.

---

[171] ibid, reg 3(2).

[172] National Health Service Act 1977, s 124(4); and National Health Service (Notification of Births and Deaths) Regulations 1982, SI 1982/286.

[173] Police and Criminal Evidence Act 1984, s 9(1).

[174] If, for example, blood was taken to determine an individual's blood-alcohol level it would not be 'excluded material'. Bullets are not excluded material.

9.123   In *R v Central Criminal Court, ex p Kellam*[175] it was held that hospital records detailing which of a psychiatric hospital's patients were absent from the hospital on a particular day fell within the definition of 'personal records' because they enabled patients to be identified by reference to their state of mental health. The fact that the document was created for the purpose of calculating National Insurance payments was not relevant to this enquiry since the critical question is whether or not the information in the record relates to the physical or mental health of the individual who may be identified therefrom. In the context the phrase 'relating to physical or mental health' is to be construed broadly.

9.124   Police may seize excluded material without a court order if they come upon material whilst lawfully on premises for another purpose, provided they have reasonable grounds for believing that it is relevant evidence in relation to an offence and that it is necessary to seize it to prevent it from being destroyed.[176] A court order to produce excluded material will only be given if there are (i) reasonable grounds to believe that there is material which includes excluded or special procedure material on the premises; (ii) a search warrant for that material might otherwise, ie before PACE, have been given; and (iii) the issue of a warrant would, in the circumstances, have been appropriate. The person who is subject to the order must be given notice and cannot then lawfully destroy material.[177]

9.125   Section 19 of the Terrorism Act 2000 imposes a duty on everyone, including doctors, to inform the police if they believe or suspect certain terrorism offences under the Act have been committed. The police must be notified 'as soon as is reasonably practicable' and a failure to do so will amount to an offence under the Act. In addition, s 20 permits the disclosure of information to the police when there is a suspicion or belief that any money or other property is terrorist property or is derived from terrorist property.

9.126   Section 172(b) of the Road Traffic Act 1988 provides that, where the driver of a vehicle, or rider of a bicycle, is alleged to be guilty of a road traffic offence:

> any other person shall if required . . . give such information which it is in his power to give and may lead to identification of the driver.[178]

9.127   *Hunter v Mann* confirmed that this section applied to doctors who received the information in confidence from a patient, and that doctors have the power to disclose such information if so required by statute, even where they might not be entitled otherwise voluntarily to disclose such information without the patient's consent.[179]

---

[175] (1993) 16 BMLR 76 (Evans LJ and Morland). Noted by Grubb, A, (1994) 2 Med L Rev 370.
[176] Police and Criminal Evidence Act 1984, s 19.
[177] ibid, Sch 1.
[178] s 172(4) makes it an offence to fail to give information in accordance with such a request.
[179] *Hunter v Mann* [1974] 1 QB 767.

(vii) Clinical Governance and CHI[180]

Section 23 of the Health Act 1999 allows for Regulations, which permit the **9.128** Commission for Health Improvement (CHI) to obtain confidential information and documents held by NHS bodies in pursuance of its statutory functions.[181] Section 24 of the Act prevents Commission Members, employees or those assisting them from disclosing that or other confidential information when it relates to, and identifies, an individual during that individual's lifetime without 'lawful authority'.[182] It is a criminal offence punishable by fine or up to two years' imprisonment knowingly or recklessly to contravene the prohibition on disclosure,[183] subject to the defence of reasonable belief that there was lawful authority or that the information had previously been disclosed to the public with lawful authority.[184] It is not an offence to disclose the information in a form which does not identify individuals, for example statistical information or when it has in fact previously been disclosed to the public with lawful authority.[185]

Section 24(6) exhaustively defines 'lawful authority' as the following circum- **9.129** stances:

(a) with the consent of the individual to whom the information relates,
(b) for the purpose of facilitating the exercise of any functions of the Commission,
(c) for the purpose of facilitating the conduct of any investigation under the Health Service Commissioners Act 1993,
(d) in accordance with any enactment or order of a court,
(e) in connection with the investigation of a serious arrestable offence,
(f) for the purpose of criminal proceedings in any part of the United Kingdom,
(g) in a case where the information appears to the Commission to reveal—

   (i) that the performance of a health professional in his capacity as such has or may have fallen substantially below that which is expected,
   (ii) that a health professional has or may have been guilty of serious professional misconduct, or
   (iii) that the fitness of a health professional to practise as such is or may be seriously impaired by reason of his physical or mental condition, and the person to whom the information is disclosed is a person to whom the

---

[180] As discussed in Ch 1 and noted at n 79 above, CHI's functions will soon be taken over by CHAI. The Health and Social Care (Community Health and Standards) Act 2003 accords CHAI a much broader power to require information and documents. Section 68 provides that CHAI may at any time require any information, documents, records (including personal records, ie patient identifiable data) or other items which relate to the provision of health care by or for an NHS body; or the discharge of any of the functions of an NHS body and which the CHAI considers it necessary or expedient to have in order to carry out its functions. Not surprisingly, this provision provoked a great deal of concern and controversy during the Bill's passage through Parliament; see Dyer, C, n 79 above.

[181] See the Commission for Health Improvement (Functions) Regulations 2000, SI 2000/662, Pt VIII.

[182] s 24(1).

[183] s 24(3).

[184] s 24(5).

[185] s 24(4).

Commission considers that it should be disclosed in order for appropriate action to be taken, or

(h) in any case where—

(i) the information reveals that a person is likely to constitute a threat to the health or safety of individuals, and

(ii) the person to whom it is disclosed is a person to whom the Commission considers that the information should be disclosed in the interests of the health and safety of individuals.

9.130 The prohibition on disclosure may be narrower than the common law in one respect. It does not survive the death of the individual to whom it relates. The common law may be otherwise (see para 9.82 above). The exceptions in s 24(6) are largely reflective of the common law—consent, disclosure required by law and disclosure in the public interest. The provisions in s 24(6)(g) relate to disclosure to professional regulatory bodies in respect of professional misconduct, poor performance and ill health. Section 24(6)(g)(ii) is curiously worded in terms of the jurisdiction only of such bodies as the GMC and GDC, but 'serious' misconduct is not required for the UK Central Council (now the Nursing and Midwifery Council).

(viii) Health Service Commissioner

9.131 The Health Service Commissioner sits at the 'apex' of the NHS complaints procedure. Section 15 of the Health Service Commissioners Act 1993[186] provides that information obtained by the Commissioner in the course of or for the purposes of an investigation shall not be disclosed save for specified purposes. They include, inter alia, disclosure for proceedings for an offence of perjury or under the Official Secrets Acts; for the investigation and any report to be made in respect of it; for the purposes of any proceedings under s 13 (offences of obstruction and contempt); and most significantly, where 'any person is likely to constitute a threat to the health or safety of patients'.[187]

6. The Impact of the Human Rights Act 1998

(i) European Convention on Human Rights: Article 8

9.132 There is no doubt that disclosure of personal information such as relates to an individual's health which is held in confidence is protected by Article 8 of the European Convention on Human Rights as an aspect of an individual's 'right to respect for his private and family life'. As such, its disclosure must be justified under Article 8(2) as being (i) in accordance with the law; (ii) necessary in a de-

---

[186] As amended by s 11 of the Health Service Commission (Amendment) Act 1996 and s 43 of the Health Act 1999.
[187] S 15(1)(e).

mocratic society (proportionate); and (iii) for a stated purpose: in the interests of public safety, for the economic well-being of the country, for the prevention of disorder or crime, for the protection of health or morals or for the protection of the rights and freedoms of others.

Under the Human Rights Act 1998, disclosure of confidential patient informa-   **9.133**
tion held within the NHS must comply with Article 8. Section 6(1) of the 1998 Act requires that a public authority must act compatibly with the Convention. A Health Authority, NHS Trust, Primary Care Trust (PCI) or other NHS body would be a 'public authority' for the purposes of the 1998 Act (s 6(3)(b)). This would also apply to disclosure by GPs who may not themselves be 'public authorities', but hold patient records on behalf of the PCT.[188]

Like the common law, Article 8 imposes only a qualified obligation and requires a   **9.134**
balance to be struck between the interests of the individual and the needs of the public. The applicability of Article 8 in the context of confidential information has been recognised both by the English courts and the European Court of Human Rights (ECtHR) on several occasions. In *MS v Sweden*[189] the European Court confirmed that Article 8 applied to personal information. In this case, a clinic disclosed the patient's records to the Social Insurance Office which was considering her claim for compensation under the Industrial Injury Insurance Act for an injury to her back she claimed had occurred at work. The court found that (i) Article 8(1) applied to personal data such as medical information; (ii) the disclosure to the Social Insurance Office was an interference with the right to respect for her private life since it was not connected to her medical treatment; (iii) she had not waived that right by requesting compensation; (iv) nevertheless, the interference was justified under Article 8(2): it was in accordance with the law (having a legal basis) and was 'necessary in a democratic society' in that it was for a legitimate purpose ('economic well-being of the country') and in the light of the safeguards against abuse including the Office's duty of confidentiality, it was not disproportionate to that legitimate purpose.[190]

The European Court of Human Rights specifically considered the applicability of   **9.135**
Article 8 in the context of medical confidentiality in *Z v Finland*.[191] The police seized the hospital medical records of an HIV-positive patient when investigating her husband on charges of sexual assault and attempted manslaughter. At his trial, the patient's doctors were required to give evidence and to produce her medical

---

[188] National Health Service (General Medical Services) Regulations 1992, SI 1992/635 as amended, Sch 2, para 36; See also *R v Mid Glamorgan FHSA, ex p Martin* [1995] 1 All ER 356 (CA) (judicial review, inter alia, of Health Authority for failure to grant a patient access to his medical records).

[189] (1997) 45 BMLR 133.

[190] Noted by Fennell, P (1999) 7 Med L Rev 346.

[191] (1997) 25 EHRR 371.

records. The court held that there was no breach of Article 8 on the facts as interference with the patient's Article 8 right was justified under Article 8(2) as being
'in accordance with the law and necessary in a democratic society' in the light of
the safeguards from abuse, namely that the proceedings were held in camera and
sealed by the court and subject to a requirement that all parties kept the patient's
identity confidential. However, a breach of Article 8 had occurred in that the proceedings were only to be sealed for ten years and the patient's identity had been
disclosed in the court's judgment.[192]

9.136 In both cases the Court balanced the rights to confidentiality against other pressing social interests. In both cases the conditions justifying disclosure were given a
broad scope. Consequently, it has been observed that the justifications under
Article 8(2) may be wider than the 'public interest' justification in breach of confidence. The European Court of Human Rights seems to be prepared to afford
states considerable latitude to order the disclosure of confidential information and
impose significant limitations on the right to confidentiality of medical information.[193]

9.137 The approach of the domestic courts to Article 8 can be seen in a number of
cases.[194] In *W v Egdell* Bingham LJ accepted that Article 8(1) of the Convention
may protect an individual against the disclosure of information protected by the
duty of professional secrecy:

> But art 8(2) envisages that circumstances may arise in which a public authority may
> legitimately interfere with the exercise of that right in accordance with the law and
> where necessary in a democratic society in the interests of public safety or the pre-
> vention of crime.[195]

On the facts of the case Bingham LJ concluded that there was no interference by
a public authority. Dr Egdell acted in accordance with the law and, in the judgment of the court, his conduct was necessary in the interests of public safety and
the prevention of crime.

9.138 In *A HA v X*[196] Munby J considered the applicability of Article 8 and the
Strasbourg jurisprudence in the context of an application by the Health Authority
to the court for disclosure of patient records for disciplinary and regulatory purposes. Munby J held that the disclosure was justified under Article 8 provided that
the records remain confidential and there were express conditions to prevent

---

[192] Noted by Fennell, P, (1999) 7 Med L Rev 339.
[193] ibid. See also Brazier (n 72 above) 80.
[194] See also *R v Chief Constable of the North Wales Police, ex p AB* [1998] 3 All ER 310 (CA) *per* Lord
Woolf MR at 321; *R (on the application of S) v Plymouth City Council (C as interested party)* [2002] 1
FLR 1177 *per* Hale LJ.
[195] [1990] 1 All ER 835, 853.
[196] [2001] 61 BMLR 22.

abuse. Munby J adopted a strict approach to confidentiality, as disclosure should be subject to express conditions. These conditions were comparable to the safeguards accepted by the European Court of Human Rights in *Z v Finland* and *MS v Sweden*:

> If there is to be disclosure of materials which entails an interference with a patient's right to respect for private life, . . . then that interference will be justified only if there are what in Z v Finland.. the court referred to as 'effective and adequate safeguards against abuse'. What those safeguards should be will, no doubt, depend upon the particular circumstances. The court's approach in Z v Finland and MS v Sweden suggests, however, that typically what will be required is: (1) the maintenance of the confidentiality of the documents themselves—the documents should not be read into the public record or otherwise put into the public domain; (2) the minimum public disclosure of any information derived from the documents; and (3) the protection of the patient's anonymity, if not in perpetuity then at any rate for a very long time indeed.[197]

In *Woolgar v Chief Constable of Sussex Police*[198] the Court of Appeal was anxious to ensure that the right to confidentiality is considered by a court when police are seeking access to confidential information. The police were investigating a registered nurse and matron of a nursing home following the death of a patient in her care. The investigation concluded without any charges being brought against Woolgar, but the police referred the matter to the UK Central Council, the regulatory body for the nursing profession. Woolgar sought an injunction to restrain the police from disclosing details of the investigation. Her application was dismissed and she appealed to the Court of Appeal. The Court of Appeal held that where a regulatory body, operating in the field of public health and safety, asked the police for access to confidential material, the police were entitled to release that material if they were reasonably persuaded that it was of some relevance to the subject matter of an enquiry being conducted by the regulatory body. Whilst emphasising that the primary decision as to disclosure was for the police, the Court of Appeal stressed that the court should consider the right to confidentiality. If the police refused to disclose, the regulatory body could make an application to the court. Similarly, if the police were minded to disclose, they should normally inform the person affected as to enable him to seek assistance from the court if necessary. Competing interests should therefore be weighed by a court, where this is possible. As noted by Fennell, the Court of Appeal's approach goes beyond the minimum required for Convention compliance under Article 8 as interpreted in *MS v Sweden*.[199]

9.139

---

[197] ibid, 39.
[198] [1999] 3 All ER 604 (CA).
[199] Fennell, P (1999) 7 Med L Rev 346, 350 (commentary).

9.140   English courts have clearly confirmed that Article 8 embraces medical confidentiality. Since the introduction of the Human Rights Act 1998, however, there has been some debate about whether Article 8 extends beyond the right to confidentiality endorsed at common law. In particular, several commentators have argued that there should be a new and separate cause of action in tort which protects privacy.[200] For the most part, the English judiciary have been reluctant to move in that direction. As noted by Lord Woolf CJ in *A v B*:

> It is most unlikely that any purpose will be served by a judge seeking to decide whether there exists a new cause of action in tort which protects privacy. In the great majority of situations, if not all situations, where the protection of privacy is justified, relating to events after the 1998 [Human Rights] Act came into force, an action for breach of confidence now will, where this is appropriate, provide the necessary protection.[201]

9.141   However, a range of attitudes can be discerned. For example, Dame Elizabeth Butler-Sloss in *Venables v News Group Newspapers Ltd* was prepared to extend the current law to recognise that '[t]he duty of confidence may arise in equity independently of a transaction or relationship between the parties'.[202] Furthermore, judicial dicta in the Court of Appeal in *Douglas v Hello! Ltd* had lent some support to the recognition of a freestanding right of privacy. In that case the Court of Appeal ruled that the Douglas' claim against *Hello!* magazine could proceed and Sedley LJ went a step further than Dame Elizabeth Butler-Sloss by suggesting that:

> . . . [W]e have reached a point where it can be said with confidence that the law recognises and will appropriately protect a right of personal privacy . . . the law has to protect not only those people whose trust has been abused but those who simply find themselves subjected to an unwanted intrusion into their personal lives. The law no longer needs to construct an artificial relationship of confidentiality between intruder and victim: it can recognise privacy itself as a legal principle drawn from the fundamental value of personal autonomy.[203]

9.142   But in the final trial judgment, Lindsay J echoed Lord Woolf CJ's sentiment above and, in his view, any inadequacies in the current law should be made good by Parliament:

> So broad is the subject of privacy and such are the ramifications of any free-standing law in the area that the subject is better left to Parliament, which can, of course, consult interests far more widely than can be taken into account in the course of

---

[200] See eg Eady, D, 'A Statutory right to privacy' [1996] 3 EHRLR 243–253; Singh, R and Strachan, J, 'Privacy Postponed?' [2003] EHRLR, Special Issue: Privacy, 12–24; Hudson, A, 'Privacy: A Right by any other Name' [2003] EHRLR, Special Issue: Privacy, 73–85; Phillipson, G and Fenwick, H, 'Breach of Confidence as a Privacy Remedy in the Human Rights Act Era' (2000) 63 MLR 660–693.

[201] [2002] 2 All ER 545, 552–3.

[202] [2001] 1 All ER 908, 933.

[203] [2001] 2 All ER 289, 320. See also *Campbell v Mirror Group Newspapers Ltd* [2003] 1 All ER 224 (CA) at 240 *per* Lord Phillips MR.

ordinary inter partes litigation. A judge should therefore be chary of doing that which is better done by Parliament.[204]

In any event, Lindsay J felt that the current law of confidence provided sufficient protection and enforcement. On the facts he found that the freedom of the press was subject to, and overborne by, the rights of the claimants under the law of confidence.

The House of Lords has recently affirmed Lindsay J's view. In *Wainwright v Home Office*[205] Lord Hoffmann dismissed an appeal by a mother and her son, who had both complained of suffering emotional distress after being strip-searched whilst visiting a relative in prison. They argued that this infringed their rights under Articles 3 and 8 of the European Convention on Human Rights. One of the issues before the Law Lords was whether the law of tort should give a remedy for distress caused by an infringement of the right of privacy protected by Article 8. Lord Hoffmann countenanced against such a move. English courts have so far refused to formulate a general principle of 'invasion of privacy' and he felt equally reluctant to do so in the instant case. In the words of Lord Hoffmann:

9.143

> Nor is there anything in the jurisprudence of the European Court of Human Rights which suggests that the adoption of some high level principle of privacy is necessary to comply with article 8 of the Convention. The European Court is concerned only with whether English law provides an adequate remedy in a specific case in which it considers that there has been an invasion of privacy contrary to article 8(1) and not justifiable under article 8(2).[206]

In other words, the existing common law of confidentiality is thought to be sufficiently flexible to safeguard our rights under Article 8. We have already witnessed this adaptability, for example in Dame Elizabeth Butler-Sloss' willingness to recognise a duty of confidence in the absence of a pre-existing relationship and to grant an injunction against the whole world in *Venables v News Group Newspapers* (see para 9.147 below). And the current law has been strengthened with respect to Morland J's awarding of damages for mental distress for breach of the contractual obligation of confidence in *Cornelius v De Taranto* (see paras 9.107–9.110 above).[207] Moreover, *per* Lord Hoffmann in *Wainwright v Home Office*:

> . . . the coming into force of the Human Rights Act 1998 weakens the argument for saying that a general tort of invasion of privacy is needed to fill the gaps in the existing remedies. Sections 6 and 7 of the Act are in themselves substantial gap fillers; if

---

[204] N 25 above, 229. See also *Home Office v Wainwright* [2001] EWCA Civ 2081; [2002] 3 WLR 405 *per* Buxton LJ and for discussion Milmo, P, 'Courting the Media' (2003) EHRLR, Special Issue: Privacy, 1–11; Curry, G, 'Confidentiality's Ok' (2003) 14 Entertainment L Rev 148–150.

[205] [2003] UKHL 53 on appeal from CA (n 203 above).

[206] ibid, at [32]. Lord Hoffman cited *Peck v UK* (2003) 36 EHRR 41 as an example of this.

[207] See Fenwick and Phillipson (n 13 above) for further discussion of the transformation of the doctrine of confidence post the Human Rights Act 1998.

it is indeed the case that a person's rights under article 8 have been infringed by a public authority, he will have a statutory remedy.[208]

9.144　The message from the courts is therefore loud and clear. For the time being, they are not inclined to develop a freestanding right to privacy in England and Wales. The common law of confidence will continue to be adapted and strengthened to cover intrusions of privacy. And any future reform to introduce a free-standing privacy right will be left in the hands of Parliament.

(ii) European Convention on Human Rights: Article 10

9.145　In addition to Article 8 the applicability of Article 10 has also been considered by the courts in the context of the obligation to maintain confidences. Article 10 provides that everyone has the right to freedom of expression, including the right to receive and impart information. This right is of particular relevance to the media and their freedom to publish. The courts have acknowledged that 'the existence of a free press is in itself desirable and so any interference with it has to be justified'.[209] When courts are considering publication by the media of confidential information they must balance these two potentially conflicting provisions of the Convention:

> There is a tension between the two articles which requires the court to hold the balance between the conflicting interests they are designed to protect.[210]

9.146　Although the court is required to draw up a 'balance sheet' between the competing rights, it must be remembered that by virtue of s 12 of the Human Rights Act 1998, special provisions are made in relation to applications to restrict freedom of expression. Section 12(4) states that '[t]he court must have particular regard to the importance of the Convention right to freedom of expression'. Consequently, the courts have stated that 'if freedom of expression is to be impeded, . . . it must be on cogent grounds recognised by law'.[211]

9.147　In *Venables v News Group Newspapers Ltd*[212] Dame Elizabeth Butler-Sloss considered the relationship between Articles 8 and 10 with respect to the media's desire to publish the new identities of Jamie Bulger's killers, Jon Venables and Robert Thompson. Butler-Sloss P stated that:

> In the light of s 12 of the 1998 Act and art 10(1) of the convention, which together give an enhanced importance to freedom of expression and consequently to the right of the press to publish. . . . There is no doubt, therefore, that Parliament has placed great emphasis upon the importance of art 10 and the protection of freedom of expression, inter alia for the press and for the media.[213]

---

[208]　ibid, at [34] *per* Lord Hoffman.
[209]　*A v B (a company)* [2002] 2 All ER 545, 552 *per* Woolf CJ.
[210]　ibid, 550.
[211]　*Douglas v Hello! Ltd* [2001] 2 All ER 289 (CA) *per* Sedley LJ at 324.
[212]　[2001] 1 All ER 908.
[213]　ibid, 919.

Despite this emphasis, she was prepared to grant an unprecedented lifelong injunction against the whole world, protecting any information leading to the identity, or future whereabouts, of the claimants. A failure to do so would probably lead to serious physical injury or to the death of the claimants. Consequently, it was necessary to place the right of confidence above the right of the media to publish freely information about the claimants. Although Butler-Sloss did stress that her decision was based on the exceptional circumstances of the case.[214]

There is no doubt that the Human Rights Act was significant in justifying the life-long injunction to protect the identities of Thompson and Venables. In the words of Dame Butler Sloss (at 932): **9.148**

> The common law continues to evolve, as it has done for centuries, and it is being given considerable impetus to do so by the implementation of the convention into our domestic law.

Brooke LJ in *Douglas v Hello Ltd*! neatly summed up the approach which is adopted by the courts in the balancing exercise: **9.149**

> Although the right to freedom of expression is not in every case the ace of trumps, it is a powerful card to which the courts of this country must always pay appropriate respect.[215]

In other words, there is no presumptive priority given to such freedom of expression when it is in conflict with another Convention right. Courts will deal with applications to restrain the media by balancing the facts on a case-by-case basis.[216] The outcome will be determined principally by considerations of proportionality.[217] However, an order to restrain the media from publication requires a 'strong case'[218] and an injunction will only be granted where it can be 'convincingly demonstrated' that it is 'strictly necessary'.[219] **9.150**

In *Campbell v Mirror Group Newspapers*, the Court of Appeal found in favour of the press and allowed the publication of information about Naomi Campbell's drug addiction and therapy as being justified in the public interest. The Master of the Rolls made it clear that the interests of the media will be strong and: **9.151**

---

[214] However, she subsequently granted the same lifelong injunctions to protect the identity of Mary Bell and her daughter. See *X (a woman formerly known as Mary Bell) v SO* [2003] EWHC 1101.

[215] N 209 above, 302. See also *Douglas v Hello! Ltd* [2003] EWHC 786; [2003] 3 All ER 996 (Ch D) *per* Lindsay J at [212].

[216] See also *A v B (a company)* [2002] 2 All ER 545, 557 *per* Lord Woolf CJ; *Cream Holdings Ltd v Bannerjee* [2003] EWCA Civ 103 at [54] *per* Simon Brown J. For further discussion see Rogers, H and Tomlinson, H, 'Privacy and Expression: Convention Rights and Interim Injunctions' [2003] EHRLR, Special Issue: Privacy, 37–53.

[217] *Douglas v Hello!* (n 209 above) *per* Sedley LJ at [136]–[137].

[218] *Venables v News Group Newspapers* (n 210 above) *per* Dame Elizabeth Butler-Sloss at 922.

[219] ibid, 934. For criticism of Butler-Sloss's approach to this issue in *Venables*, see Phillipson (n 13 above), 750–751.

> Provided that publication of particular confidential information is justifiable in the public interest, the journalist must be given reasonable latitude as to the manner in which that information is conveyed to the public or his art 10 right to freedom of expression will be unnecessarily inhibited.[220]

9.152 In conclusion, it would appear that Article 10 considerations will weigh heavily in the balance against Article 8 privacy considerations. However, as the judgments of Dame Elizabeth Butler-Sloss in *Venables v News Group Newspapers* and Lindsay J in *Douglas v Hello! Ltd* demonstrate, the balance is being struck on a case-by-case basis and freedom of expression is not always the trump card.

B. Control of Patient Information

9.153 Beyond the law of confidentiality, the common law provides little or no protection to patients in how or when their personal information may be used, for example, disclosed to others or used for research or other purposes. The common law was signally inept at this in the absence of a law of privacy. The courts closed down all other legal avenues which might have given a patient a right to control the use of their records. For example, the courts were unable to offer any protection through the law of contract and chose not to characterise the doctor–patient relationship as fiduciary in nature or to allow a patient to claim any proprietary interest in their medical records.[221] Two recent legal developments have, however, affected the position.

9.154 The incorporation into English law of the European Convention on Human Rights requires the courts to interrogate the effectiveness of the common law of confidentiality and adapt it to be consistent with an individual's 'right to private life' protected by Article 8 of the Convention.[222] This development is discussed above and, as will be seen, the outcome has been to provide a greater robustness to the law of confidentiality but no more such as the development of a regulatory regime.[223] For that legislative intervention is necessary.

9.155 Parliament has, however, intervened in the shape of the data protection legislation in 1984 and 1998 driven by European harmonisation in the form of the Directive on data protection.[224] It is this development which will be examined here. One of

---

[220] [2002] 1 All ER 224, 239 (CA).
[221] See the discussion in relation to 'access' to medical records in Kennedy and Grubb (n 72 above) 992–1019.
[222] See, *A HA v X* [2001] Lloyd's Rep Med 349 (Munby J) and [2002] Lloyd's Rep Med 139 (CA). See also *Campbell v Mirror Group Newspapers Ltd* [2002] EWCA Civ 1373; [2003] 1 All ER 225 and at a European level: *Z v Finland* (1997) 45 BMLR 107 (ECtHR) and *MS v Sweden* (1997) 45 BMLR 133 (ECtHR).
[223] Paras 9.132–9.152.
[224] European Directive on Personal Data (EC) 95/46 [1995] OJ L281.

the main aims of the legislation is 'the protection of individuals against prejudice as a consequence of the processing of their personal data, including invasion of their privacy'.[225]

The Data Protection Act 1984 provided, for the first time in the United Kingdom, a legal framework for controlling the use of personal data stored in an electronic form. The 1984 Act was not however comprehensive, for example, it did not cover information stored in written or other non-electronic form. It was repealed, and replaced, by the Data Protection Act (DPA) 1998 with effect from 1 March 2000.[226]

9.156

1. *The Scheme of the Data Protection Act 1998*

The DPA 1998 Act is complex piece of legislation, the detail of which can be found elsewhere.[227] The following text provides an outline of the main provisions. The DPA 1998 creates a registration (or notification) system with an Information Commissioner (and an Information Tribunal),[228] and processing personal data unless registered is generally a criminal offence[229] but there are exceptions.[230] The DPA 1998 establishes *eight* 'Data Protection Principles'[231] which 'data controllers' must observe. The Act creates a system of enforcement procedures by the Commissioner which are subject to a right of appeal to the Tribunal[232] and personal remedies for 'data subjects' including rectification,[233] preventing the processing of data likely to cause damage or distress,[234] and compensation for damage caused by non-compliance with the Act.[235] The Act also creates a right of access to personal data by the data subject.[236]

9.157

---

[225] *Campbell v Mirror Group Newspapers Ltd* [2002] EWCA Civ 1373; [2003] 1 All ER 225 *per* Lord Philips MR at [73].

[226] Data Protection Act 1998 (Commencement) Order 2000, SI 2000/183. The DPA 1998 was subsequently subject to minor modifications by the Freedom of Information Act 2000. There are, however, transitional provisions which phase in many of the requirements of the Act for manual records created before 24 October 2001 (the 'first transitional period') and, to a lesser extent, after 23 October 2001 but before 24 October 2007 (the 'second transitional period'). The following discussion assumes the Act is fully in force.

[227] General and specific guidance in relation to health data is provided by the Information Commissioner in *Data Protection Act 1998: Legal Guidance* (Version 1), 1998 (hereafter 'Legal Guidance') and *Use and Disclosure of Health Data: Guidance on the Application of the Data Protection Act 1998*, May 2002 (hereafter 'Use and Disclosure of Health Data').

[228] Prior to the Freedom of Information Act 2000 these were, respectively, known as the Data Protection Commissioner and Data Protection Tribunal.

[229] ss 17(1) and 21(1).

[230] s 17(2)–(4).

[231] Schs 1–4.

[232] Pt V.

[233] s 14.

[234] s 10.

[235] s 13.

[236] s 7.

2. The Scope of the Data Protection Act 1998[237]

9.158   The DPA 1998 is concerned with regulating the 'processing' of 'personal data' of 'data subjects' by 'data controllers' and covers data held electronically or in manual/written form.[238]

(i) Data Controller

9.159   Within the NHS, health service bodies such as NHS Trusts and Primary Care Trusts will be 'data controllers' but individual doctors, especially GPs, may also be such.[239]

(ii) Personal Data

9.160   'Personal data' is given a very wide definition in the DPA 1998. It includes expressions of opinion about the individual or statements of intention in relation to that individual.[240] It includes any data which forms part of a patient's health records.[241] Two principal issues arise in the context of health data. First, the data must relate to a 'living individual'.[242] The upshot is that the Act provides no protection against the use or disclosure of medical information posthumously.[243] In this, the 1998 Act probably mirrors the common law on confidentiality.[244] Secondly, the individual must be 'identifiable' from the data or, at least, from that data and any other information in, or likely to come into, the possession of the data controller.[245] Does this mean that the Act has no application where the information is anonymised? The accepted position is that, provided the data is properly anonymised, then the 1998 Act does not apply.[246] However, this assumption must be treated with caution for a number of reasons.[247]

9.161   First, it may be very difficult in practice effectively to anonymise data.[248] Even if

---

[237] The Act should be interpreted in a manner consistent with the EC Directive: *Campbell v Mirror Group Newspapers Ltd* (n 222 above), *per* Lord Phillips MR at [96].

[238] s 1(1).

[239] See, *Use and Disclosure of Health Data* (n 224 above).

[240] s 1(1).

[241] s 1(1) referring to an 'accessible record' within s 68 which includes a patient's 'health records' as defined in s 68(2). See below, para 9.165.

[242] 'Personal data means data which relates to a living individual': s 1(1).

[243] Hence, the right of access in s 7 of the 1998 Act does not apply to allow a deceased's representatives to obtain his medical records. That is covered by the residue of the Access to Health Records Act 1990 not repealed by the 1998 Act: see below, paras 9.227–9.233.

[244] See above paras 9.82–9.83 And Kennedy and Grubb (n 72 above) 1081–3.

[245] s 1(1).

[246] See, *Legal Guidance* (n 227 above) 2.2.5. See also, *R v Department of Health, ex p Source Informatics Ltd* [2000] 1 All ER 786 (CA), *per* Simon Brown LJ at 798.

[247] See, Beyleveld, D, and Townsend, D, 'When is Personal data Rendered Anonymous? Interpreting Recital 26 of Directive 95/46/EC' (2003) 6 *Medical Law International* (forthcoming).

[248] ibid.

data is anonymised—ie is stripped of personal identifiers—it will remain 'personal data' in the hands of the data controller if the data controller is able to re-link the individuals to whom the data related to that data, for example, because the anonymised data is coded or a complete data set is retained by the data controller. Only if the data is 'unlinked' and is 'unlinkable' back, will the 1998 Act not apply to it. This has important implications for the use of medical data in for example, research, management of the NHS, public health surveillance and cancer registries.

Secondly, the act of anonymising the data is, itself, 'processing' the data and as such the data controller is subject to the requirements of the 1998 Act in rendering the data anonymous.[249]   **9.162**

Thirdly, it could be argued that the 1998 Act does, in fact, apply to anonymised data. In other words, the accepted position can be challenged head on. The principal argument[250] is that s 1(2) of the 1998 Act states that 'using' or 'disclosing' in relation to personal data 'includes using or disclosing the information contained in the data'. Does this mean that the data controller who discloses anonymised data and the receiver of such data are deemed to be 'processing' personal data under the Act? The Act would seem to be amenable to such an interpretation.[251] However, it is suggested that this in not the purpose of this provision which would, in effect, write out of the carefully structured definition of 'personal data' in s 1(1) the 'identifying' requirement. Why would Parliament have limited the concept of 'personal data' only, one subsection later, effectively to remove a core definitional aspect of the concept? It is far from clear what was intended by Parliament in this extension of the concept of 'personal data'. A possible interpretation, it is suggested, is that it was for the avoidance of doubt that the processing activities of 'using' and 'disclosing' covered not only the whole data but parts extracted from it. But, importantly, this processing must be 'in relation to personal data'. Therefore, the extension of 'processing' only applies to information that is extracted which is, itself, 'personal data' under the Act.   **9.163**

---

[249] ibid.

[250] A further possible argument relies on the case of *R v Wakefield Metropolitan Council, ex p Robertson* [2002] QB 1052. There, the court was concerned with s 11 of the Act which provides a data subject with the right to prevent direct marketing. The court held that an elector had a right to prevent a council selling its electoral list with his details to a commercial organisation without giving him the opportunity to object. In doing so, the court held that regard should be had to the use to which that data would be put when sold. Read literally, it could be suggested that the case 'fixes' the data controller—and thus the application of the 1998 Act—with future known uses of the data when it has been disclosed to a third party. It is not, however, of any assistance in the context of otherwise (properly) anonymised health data. First, the decision related to s 11 and direct marketing where different considerations as to future use could apply. Second, and far more importantly, the case 'fixed' the data controller with future uses of 'personal data'. The electoral register undoubtedly contained identifying data relating to the applicant and it was going to be used by the commercial concerns as 'personal data'. The data never ceased to be 'personal data' at any time.

[251] Note the explicit inclusion of 'information extracted from personal data' for the purposes of the offence of selling personal data: s 55(7).

9.164   On final point on health data. Does the Act apply to tissue samples and biological tissues? The answer is not straightforward. On the face of it, they probably do not in themselves fall within the Act as they do not consist of data as defined in s 1(1) of the Act.[252] However, it could be argued that if the tissue is added to a patient's health record then it would form part of an 'accessible record', being 'information relating to the physical . . . health or condition' of the patient.[253] In any event, any analysis of the tissue by extracting genetic data from the tissue of a living person (including then recording or holding it) would be covered by the Act as this would involve 'processing' of personal data. And, it should be added, given the nature of genetic information, it may be impossible to anonymise this data so long as the data controller retains samples of the tissue.

(iii) Electronic and Other Records

9.165   The 1998 Act is broader in its reach than was the 1984 Act, such that all health records whether electronic or written are covered, including such documents as X-rays. The personal data may be information held (i) electronically; or (ii) manually *either* as part of a 'relevant filing system', ie where the information is structured by reference to individuals or criteria relating to individuals such that specific information relating to an individual is readily accessible, *or* as part of an 'accessible record'.[254] The latter is defined in s 68(2) of the Act to include a 'health record' namely:

> any record which—
> (a) consists of information relating to the physical or mental health or condition of an individual, and
> (b) has been made by or on behalf of a health professional in connection with the care of that individual.

'Health professional' is given an extensive definition in s 69 of the Act to include doctors, nurses, dentists, opticians, pharmacists and scientific heads of department of NHS bodies.

9.166   The Freedom of Information Act 2000 extended the DPA 1998 to include 'unstructured personal data'.[255] However, this would seem to have little additional effect in the health context where a patient's health information will already be within the definition of 'personal data' in the DPA 1998. In any event, the FIA

---

[252] ie, data or information which is processed automatically or form part of a relevant filing system. See, Human Genetic Commission, *Inside Information Balancing Interests in the Use of Genetic Information* (2002), para 3.43.
[253] s 68(2).
[254] s 1(1).
[255] s 1(1)(e) inserted by s 68(2), FIA 2000.

2000 does not apply all the provisions of the DPA 1998 to 'unstructured personal data'. In fact, it only applies those provisions related to access and accuracy.[256]

(iv) Processing

'Processing' is given a very wide scope. The Information Commissioner has expressed the view that 'it is difficult to envisage any action involving data' which does not fall within the Act's definition of processing.[257] The Act covers obtaining, storing and using data in any way and includes disclosing, or rendering into an anonymised form,[258] health data. The definition is unlikely to cause any difficulty in the medical context. **9.167**

3. The Data Protection Principles

The Data Protection Principles are set out in Sch 1, Pt I to the Act and are elaborated upon in Sch 1, Pt II and Sch 2–4. They are as follows: **9.168**

1. Personal data shall be processed fairly and lawfully and, in particular, shall not be processed unless—
   (a) at least one of the conditions in Schedule 2 is met, and
   (b) in the case of sensitive personal data, at least one of the conditions in Schedule 3 is also met.
2. Personal data shall be obtained only for one or more specified and lawful purposes, and shall not be further processed in any manner incompatible with that purpose or those purposes.
3. Personal data shall be adequate, relevant and not excessive in relation to the purpose or purposes for which they are processed.
4. Personal data shall be accurate and, where necessary, kept up to date.
5. Personal data processed for any purpose or purposes shall not be kept for longer than is necessary for that purpose or those purposes.
6. Personal data shall be processed in accordance with the rights of data subjects under this Act.
7. Appropriate technical and organisational measures shall be taken against unauthorised or unlawful processing of personal data and against accidental loss or destruction of, or damage to, personal data.
8. Personal data shall not be transferred to a country or territory outside the European Economic Area unless that country or territory ensures an adequate level of protection for the rights and freedoms of data subjects in relation to the processing of personal data.

The concern here is with the 'obtaining', 'storage' and 'use' including 'disclosure' of patient information within the NHS. Each of these activities falls within the

---

[256] s 33A, DPA 1998 inserted by s 70, FIA 2000.
[257] *Legal Guidance* (n 227 above) para 2.3.
[258] See para 9.162 above.

statutory term 'processing'.[259] We should notice a number of important issues that are relevant to 'processing' health information.[260]

(i) First Principle

9.169   The first Data Protection Principle requires that patient data must be processed 'fairly' and 'lawfully'. 'Processing' includes their subsequent *use* including *disclosure*. The requirement that the processing be 'lawful' reads into the 1998 Act, inter alia, the common law of confidentiality and compliance with the requirements of the European Convention on Human Rights, especially the patient's right to respect for his private and family life protected by Article 8. Any disclosure in breach of confidence (unless justified at common law) will mean that the information has not been 'processed' (ie disclosed) 'lawfully' within the First Principle.

9.170   Importantly, the First Principle requires that in order for processing to be 'fair', the data controller must 'so far as practicable' provide the data subject with certain information, such as the former's identity and the purposes for which it is intended to process the information.[261] The information must be provided at the time the data is obtained from the data subject or, if obtained from a third party, before it is first processed or disclosed.[262] This obligation requires, therefore, that the patient be made aware at the time it is first processed (perhaps when it is obtained) the purpose(s) to which it will subsequently be put. Section 33 does not apply to the First Data Protection Principle and so use of data for 'research purposes' is covered by this requirement. The Act provides an exemption to the obligation of fair processing when to do so would involve 'disproportionate effort' and certain conditions are satisfied.[263] The Act gives no further guidance on the scope of this exemption which must, in each case, be a question of fact. The Information Commissioner has suggested that its determination involves a consideration of the 'nature of the data, the length of time and cost involved to the data controller in providing the information' and that these factors have to be seen in the context of any prejudicial effect on the data subject which, in turn, will include consideration of whether the patient knows about the processing of his data.[264] It is

---

[259] s 1(1).

[260] See discussion in *Use and Disclosure of Health Data* (n 227 above) chs 2 and 3.

[261] Sch 1, Pt II, paras 2 and 3.

[262] Sch 1, Pt II, paras 2(1)(a) and 2(1)(b) and (2) respectively.

[263] Sch 1, Pt II, para 3 and the Data Protection (Conditions under Paragraph 3 of Pt II of Schedule 1) Order 2000, SI 2000/185—(i) whilst it need not be volunteered, the information must be provided if requested; and (ii) record the reasons why disclosure would involve a 'disproportionate effort'.

[264] *Legal Guidance* (n 227 above) para 3.1.7.6.

unlikely that this provision will have a wide effect in the NHS.[265] It may have some scope, however, where the patient records were created before the Act, for example, research on existing patient records or archives particularly if the research will have no implications for the individual patients or involves anonymised records.[266]

The need to provide to a patient information about possible uses is further reinforced by the requirement under the First Principle that in deciding whether information has been processed 'fairly', regard is to be had to the method by which it has been obtained, including whether the individual has been deceived or misled as to the purposes for which it will be processed.[267] Thus, whilst a use may be compatible with the purposes notified to the Commissioner (or is covered by s 33 for 'research purposes') and so does not offend the Second Principle, misleading or deceiving the patient about its use may still offend the First Principle. **9.171**

(ii) Second Principle

The Second Data Protection Principle requires that information must be 'obtained only for one or more specified and lawful purposes'. The information must not be 'further processed' incompatibly with those purposes. These purposes may be specified in the registration with the Commissioner (under Pt III of the Act) or in a notice given to the data subject at the time it is obtained.[268] Generally, this will not cause any difficulties within the NHS providing the 'registrable particulars' spell out the treatment, management, audit or research purposes, etc to which patient information may be put and, more particularly, by notice given to the patient directly.[269] **9.172**

Section 33 of the Act, however, exempts from the Second Principle's requirement that data must not be further processed inconsistent with the purposes for which it was obtained, processing of data which are for 'research' purposes, ie 'research', 'statistical or historical purposes'.[270] This will be an important exemption for epidemiological research using existing patient records where the relevant notice was not (or could not have been) given to the patients—the 1998 Act may not apply, of course, if the information has already been anonymised. Three conditions must be met: (i) the data are not processed to 'support measures or decisions with respect to particular individuals'; (ii) the processing is not done in such a way as to **9.173**

---

[265] Note also the provision allowing the Secretary of State by Order to prescribe conditions for 'lawful and fair processing' of data by a 'general identifier', for example, patients' NHS numbers: Sch 1, Pt II, para 4.

[266] *Use and Disclosure of Health Data* (n 227 above) 10–11 and 14.

[267] Sch 1, Pt II, para 1(1).

[268] Sch 1, Pt II, para 5, referring back to paras 2 and 3.

[269] See above paras 9.169–9.171 on the First Data Principle's requirements.

[270] s 33(1).

cause, or be likely to cause, 'substantial damage or substantial distress' to the patient; and (iii) the results of the research are made available in a form that does not identify any patient.

(iii) Fifth Principle

9.174 The Fifth Data Protection Principle requires that information be kept no longer than is necessary for the purposes for which it is processed. Section 33(3), however, allows information that is processed only for 'research purposes' (as defined) to be kept indefinitely.

(iv) Exemptions

9.175 By way of general exemption, disclosures required by law, by statute or court order or which are made in connection with legal proceedings or seeking legal advice are exempt from the non-disclosure provisions of the Act, including the First Data Protection Principle (except for compliance with the conditions in Sch 2 and 3) and also the Second Data Protection Principle.[271]

4. *The Conditions for Lawful Processing*

9.176 In addition to what we have already seen, the First Principle requires, as a condition for compliance, that personal data must be processed in accordance with Sch 2 and, if they are 'sensitive personal data', must also be processed in accordance with Sch 3. Health information is 'sensitive personal data' as defined in the Act to include information about an individual's 'physical or mental health or condition'.[272] Schedules 2 and 3 set out a number of conditions for processing. Any use of health information (including disclosure) must satisfy *one condition in each* of the Schedules. The most relevant are as follows:

(i) Schedule 2

(a) *Consent of the Data Subject*

9.177 Condition 1 of Schedule 2 is that 'the data subject has given his consent to the processing'. No explanation is given of this, although it contrasts with the first condition in Schedule 3, which requires the '*explicit* consent' of the individual. Here, something less than 'explicit' agreement is clearly contemplated. The Directive referred to 'any freely given specific and informed indication of [the data subject's] wishes'.[273] The Act does not go so far and seems to contemplate any consent

---

[271] ss 35 and 27(3) and (4).
[272] s 2(e).
[273] Art 2(h).

accepted by the common law, including implied consent.[274] Implied consent to the use of patient information would exist, for example, where it was to be disclosed within the NHS to other professionals for the individual's treatment. It would also arise where the individual had been given reasonable notice of the purposes for which the information might be used and had not 'opted out' by objecting. Thus, well positioned and prominent notices in a GP's surgery or hospital indicating the possible uses of information, for example, for teaching, research or management purposes within the NHS may well satisfy this condition.[275]

(b) *Compliance with a legal obligation*

Condition 3 of Schedule 2 is that the processing is 'necessary for compliance with **9.178** any legal obligation to which the data controller is subject, other than an obligation imposed by contract'. A NHS Trust (or Primary Care Trust) or GP which was required by a binding Direction from the Secretary of State to provide certain patient information would fall within this condition. This would also cover disclosures required by statute, court order, or other legal duty. This would also seem to cover disclosure or other processing *required* (though not if merely *authorised*) under regulations made pursuant to s 60 of the Health and Social Care Act 2001.

(c) *The vital interests of the data subject*

Condition 4 of Schedule 2 is that the processing is 'necessary in order to protect **9.179** the vital interests of the data subject'. Notice the disclosure must be 'necessary' and not merely convenient. The purpose to be achieved by the processing must, it would seem, not be reasonably possible without the processing and the processing must be proportionate to the aim to be achieved.[276] Also, the disclosure (or use) must relate to the patient's 'vital interests'. This should not be read so narrowly as to be limited to 'life and death' situations. Rather, it should be construed as meaning relevant to his life and health. This condition would justify a doctor disclosing information in an emergency in order to protect the life or health of a patient who needed treatment, for example, where a GP informs a casualty doctor that the patient is on a particular medication that is relevant to his emergency treatment.[277] The condition may also be satisfied where disclosure to other health professionals is required for the treatment of the patient. Although this would also fall within condition 1 (see above), it also might fall within this condition even where the patient refuses. It could be argued that only the 'processing' (ie the disclosure) must

---

[274] Though this is not the view of the Information Commissioner: *Legal Guidance* (n 227 above) para 3.1.5—'cannot infer consent from non-response to a communication'.

[275] Note the comments of Simon Brown LJ in *ex p Source Informatics* [2000] 1 All ER 786 at 800 and 801.

[276] *Use and Disclosure of Health Data* (n 227 above) 4.

[277] But note the Information Commissioner's view that it is restricted to matters of 'life and death': *Legal Guidance* (n 227 above) para 3.1.1.

be 'necessary' for the stated purpose. The better view is, however, that disclosure in these circumstances is not 'necessary' since it countermands the patient's wishes. (It would, of course, be 'unlawful' and therefore fall outside the First Principle unless it was a justified breach of confidence.) For the avoidance of doubt, the condition can have no application to research involving a patient's medical records since it will usually not affect *his* 'vital interests', only others when the outcome of the research is known.

(d) Legitimate Interests of the Data Controller or Others

9.180   Condition 6 of Sch 2 applies to processing that is 'necessary for the purposes of legitimate interests pursued by the data controller or by the third party . . . to whom the data are disclosed'. This condition would prima facie allow an NHS body to disclose patient information for its, or the recipient's, legitimate interests. This could include disclosure for the purposes of research, financial accounting, management, audit, preventing fraud within the NHS, for maintaining professional standards or pursuing appropriate legal action against another or defending an action brought against a NHS body. All of these would fall within the 'legitimate interests' of the NHS body or the third party to whom the information is disclosed. It is not clear whether the 'legitimate interest' pursued must be that of both discloser and disclosee. The wording seems to suggest a disjunctive reading. The latter reading would allow disclosure to an individual or other body in order to protect that individual from danger, for example, by the patient. Importantly, the condition requires that the processing should not be 'unwarranted' by reason of the data subject's rights, freedoms and legitimate interests. This may well prevent disclosure where the disclosure is not 'tailored' in scope and content to the particular interests to be pursued. Hence, if the purpose could be achieved using, for example, anonymised rather than identifying health data, then this condition is unlikely to be satisfied. And, arguably, the disclosure would be 'unwarranted' unless the disclosure was for an 'NHS purpose' rather than some other unconnected purpose of the disclosee such as commercial gain, for example as occurred in the *Source Informatics* case.

(ii) Schedule 3

9.181   As we saw, a further condition in Sch 3 must be satisfied because health information is 'sensitive personal data'. However, the additional requirement will rarely present a problem in the health context since the condition in para 8 provides an all-embracing condition for processing for 'medical purposes' (see below).

(a) Explicit Consent

9.182   The first condition in Sch 3 is that the data subject has given 'explicit consent to the processing of the personal data'. We saw earlier how one condition in Sch 2 required the data subject's 'consent' and contrasted that with the requirement of 'explicit consent' here.[278] Clearly something more than the 'mere' consent required under Sch 2 is contemplated. The Information Commissioner takes the view that this condition is 'not particularly easy to achieve'[279] and that may be correct, requiring active communication between the data controller and patient which leads to an informed, unambiguous and overt agreement. It will not suffice, therefore, to offer the patient an 'opt out' and, in its absence, infer consent to the processing—there would be nothing 'explicit' about this agreement. Whilst the Commissioner notes that the conditions in Sch 3 (and Sch 2 for that matter) are not lexically ordered such that a data controller should look, for example, for consent first,[280] that is an advisable approach given the law and the state of public policy which places considerable emphasis on the use of patient information only with a patient's consent.

(b) Medical and Research Purposes

Paragraph 8(1) of Sch 3 permits processing for 'medical purposes' which are broadly defined. It provides: **9.183**

> The processing is necessary for medical purposes and is undertaken by—
>
> (a) a health professional, or
> (b) a person who in the circumstances owes a duty of confidentiality which is equivalent to that which would arise if that person were a health professional,
>
> (2) In this paragraph 'medical purposes' includes the purposes of preventative medicine, medical diagnosis, medical research, the provision of care and treatment and the management of health care services.

The only real limitation is that the use should be 'necessary' but, in practice, this is not likely to be problematic. Paragraph 8(2) seems to bring within the provision every conceivable use by the NHS of patient information whether for treatment, research or management purposes. In effect, this overcomes the need to establish the first condition in Sch 3, which requires the 'explicit consent' of the data subject to the processing.   **9.184**

One situation may not, however, be covered. Paragraph 8(1) does not, on its face, deal with the archiving of health data, although this *could* be brought within the extended definition of 'medical purposes' under para 8(2) if related, for example, to 'research' or 'management' purposes. There could also be an argument that this kind of 'processing' may not be undertaken by an individual who is contemplated by para 8(1) even though this is very broadly drawn. As a result, inter alia, the Data   **9.185**

---

[278] Para 9.177 above.
[279] *Legal Guidance* (n 227 above) para 3.1.5.
[280] ibid. Indeed, an argument could be mounted that the proper interpretation of Schs 2 and 3 requires a data controller, as a 'first port of call', to seek consent in the light of the patient's right to private life under Art 8 ECHR.

Protection (Processing of Sensitive Personal Data) Order 2000,[281] adds an additional condition to Schedule 3.[282] This covers 'processing' which is 'in the substantial public interest' which is 'necessary for research purposes' (as defined in s 33) providing the processing (i) does not support measures or decisions in respect of a particular individual otherwise than with explicit consent, and (ii) does not cause, nor is likely to cause, substantial damage or distress to the data subject or any other person. Unlike the condition in para 8, this additional condition does not assume that the processing for the purposes of research is in the public interest, but requires proof that it is so and, in addition, goes even further in that it must be 'substantially' in the public interest.

(c) Vital Interests of the Data Subject or Another

9.186 Paragraph 3 of Sch 3 applies where processing is in the vital interests of an individual even where the data subject does not consent. It provides:

> 3. The processing is necessary—
>
> (a) in order to protect the vital interests of the data subject or another person, in a case where—
>
>   (i) consent cannot be given by or on behalf of the data subject, or
>   (ii) the data controller cannot reasonably be expected to obtain the consent of the data subject, or
>
> (b) in order to protect the vital interests of another person, in a case where consent by or on behalf of the data subject had been unreasonably withheld.

9.187 To the extent that the disclosure is to protect the vital interests of the patient, this will usually be covered by the 'medical purposes' condition in para 8. Where, however, it is to protect a third party, this paragraph permits disclosure even where the data subject cannot consent, unreasonably refuses consent or it is not reasonable to seek it. No doubt situations concerned with dangerous psychiatric patients, child (or other sexual) abusers or patients carrying an infectious disease would fall within this provision. For the disclosure to be 'necessary', the manner of disclosure must be tailored to the aim to be achieved, hence it must be to the appropriate person or authority.

(d) Legal and Other Proceedings

9.188 Paragraph 6 of Sch 3 also allows processing where it is necessary in connection with legal proceedings or seeking legal advice.

9.189 The Data Protection (Processing of Sensitive Personal Data) Order 2000[283] also adds a further condition to Sch 3 of the 1998 Act which is of considerable

---

[281] SI 2000/417.
[282] Sch 3, para 10.
[283] SI 2000/417.

relevance in the health context. This condition allows 'processing' which is in the '*substantial* public interest' where it is 'necessary' for the discharge of a stated function: functions which are designed for 'protecting members of the public' against 'dishonesty, malpractice, or other seriously improper conduct by, or the unfitness or incompetence of, any person' or 'mismanagement in the administration of, or failures in services provided by, any body'.[284] The scope of these functions is such that it would encompass disclosure to, or by, a professional regulatory body such as the GMC as well as, of course, processing by the body once it was received.[285] It would also cover processing in the context of clinical governance arrangements within the NHS, including disclosure to (and by) the Commission for Health Improvement (CHI) or the soon to be Commission for Healthcare Audit and Inspection (CHAI).

The only limitations are:[286] (i) the need for the processing to be in the '*substantial* public interest'; (ii) that it be 'necessary' for discharging the stated function; and (iii) it must necessarily be carried out without the explicit consent of the individual so as not to prejudice the discharge of that function. The information that is, of course, likely to be covered by these two conditions is that relating to the *health professional* rather than the patient. Information about the latter could probably be processed, for these purposes, with explicit consent.   **9.190**

5. *Remedies*

The DPA 1998 creates *three* remedies, which are principally of interest in the medical context.[287] The first two complement the common law of breach of confidence and negligence. The third provides an additional remedy beyond the common law's scope.   **9.191**

First, s 10 entitles a data subject to serve a notice upon the data controller requiring him to cease, or not to begin, processing personal data relating to him. The right does not apply if one of the conditions in para 1 to 4 of Sch 2 is satisfied. The basis for such a notice must be that the processing (or the manner of its processing) is causing or is likely to cause substantial damage to the data subject or another and that damage or distress is unwarranted.[288] Within 21 days, the data controller must give written notice to the data subject that he has complied, intends to comply or stating why he considers it unjustified.[289] The data subject may apply to the court which may, to the extent it thinks fit, enforce the notice against   **9.192**

---

[284] Para 2, Sch.
[285] The Order also adds a further purpose, namely 'the prevention or detection of any unlawful act' (para 1, Sch).
[286] Paras 1 and 2, Sch.
[287] See generally, *Legal Guidance* (n 227 above) ch 4.
[288] s 10(1).
[289] s 10(3).

the data controller if he fails to comply. Certainly, as regards improper disclosure of patient information the Act may add little to a common law claim for breach of confidence. It does extend the remedies available where the 'processing' does not entail a breach of confidence, for example, because it is being misused without disclosure.

9.193 Secondly, an individual may seek compensation for damage suffered as a result of the breach of the Act by a data controller.[290] The claimant may be the data subject or another who suffers damage, for example, as a result of disclosure in breach of the Act. Compensation is limited to damage and any consequential distress by a patient or other.[291] It is a defence for the data controller to establish that he took reasonable care in all the circumstances to comply with the Act.[292] Given that the claimant must prove damage (physical, financial or psychiatric) and the data controller has a defence of 'no negligence', the remedy may not add much to the common law.

9.194 Thirdly, the court may order the data controller to 'rectify, block, erase or destroy' inaccurate data including an expression of opinion, which appears to be, based upon inaccurate data'.[293]

C. Access to Medical Records

1. General

9.195 It is generally accepted that good clinical care requires that doctors should keep clear, accurate, and contemporaneous patient records which report the relevant clinical findings, the decisions made, information given to patients and any treatment administered. In order to provide a comprehensive picture of a patient's history and medical prognosis these records will frequently include details of all aspects of patients' past and present medical care, including medical and other opinions about the patient's physical and mental condition, together with other information which may be relevant to any doctor treating the patient.

9.196 Here we consider the circumstances in which a patient may be entitled to claim access to medical records as of right. Two distinctions are important here. First, we are not concerned with situations in which it might be alleged to be negligent for the doctor or hospital to refuse access to the plaintiff's medical records, or not to have disclosed certain information therein to the patient.[294] In such cases the

---

[290] s 13.
[291] s 13(2)(a).
[292] s 13(3).
[293] s 14.
[294] See *Sidaway v Governors of Bethlem Royal Hospital* [1985] 1 All ER 643, [1985] 2 WLR 480 (HL); *Lee v South West Thames RHA* [1985] 2 All ER 385 (CA); *Naylor v Preston AHA* [1987] 2 All ER 353, [1987] 1 WLR 958 (CA).

patient's claim is that the doctor has a duty to avoid causing harm, including harm which is caused by withholding medical information from him or his advisers. The claim is not, however, that the patient has a right of access to his medical records per se. In the words of Kirby P (dissenting) in the New South Wales Court of Appeal in *Breen v Williams*:

> there is a quantum leap from the entitlement of a proper explanation by a medical practitioner about the dangers of medical procedures as incidental to treatment to an affirmative obligation to give access to information in records by a medical practitioner who has not been sued and who has never been said to have failed in his duty of explanation to his patient.[295]

Secondly, we are also not concerned with claims for access to medical records as part of pre-action disclosure under ss 33 or 34 of the Supreme Court Act 1981 and CPR, Pt 31 where litigation has commenced or is in contemplation. Again where a patient claims that he has a right of access to his medical records in such circumstances his claim is founded upon the potential usefulness of those records in anticipated litigation, it is not a claim that he has a right of access to the records as such. **9.197**

2. Data Protection Act 1998

(i) Background

Prior to the DPA 1998, the law relating to a patient's right of access to his medical records was not contained in a single piece of legislation. A right of access was first given to patients in the DPA 1984 for electronic records and in the Access to Health Records Act 1990 for manual health records. The 1990 Act was not retrospective in effect and so existing manual records held at the time it came into force did not fall within the statutory right of access. To supplement this, the courts were asked to create a common law right of access which, as we shall see, to an extent they did. The 1998 Act effectively repeals the Access to Health Records Act 1990 and does repeal in its totality the 1984 Act. In this section, we are concerned with the 'subject information provisions' of the 1998 Act so far as they apply to health records and, given their scope, the common law and any development based upon Article 8 of the European Convention on Human Rights is largely redundant. But, before looking at the 1998 Act, we must first consider its relationship with the Freedom of Information Act 2000. **9.198**

---

[295] *Breen v Williams* [1995] 6 Med LR 385, 418. The judgments of the High Court of Australia in *Breen v Williams* are considered below.

(ii) Relationship between the DPA 1998 and the Freedom of Information Act 2000

9.199 It is important to notice the relationship between the DPA 1998 and the Freedom of Information Act (FIA) 2000. The FIA 2000 creates a right of access to information held by public authorities[296] subject to certain exemptions,[297] for example, information provided in confidence,[298] where disclosure is prohibited by or under any enactment[299] or where disclosure is likely to endanger any individual.[300] The FIA 2000 also amends the DPA 1998 in a number of respects,[301] for example, extending the DPA 1998 to cover 'unstructured personal data'.[302] The latter extension will not have an impact on a patient's right of access to his medical records since these would fall within the DPA 1998 anyway as part of an 'accessible record' under s 68 of that Act.

9.200 The very important point is, however, that the FIA 2000 seeks to create a 'bright line' between access to 'personal information' covered by the DPA 1998 and access to other information covered by the FIA 2000. Hence, an individual who seeks access to 'personal data' about himself, which would include medical or health information, has no right of access under the FIA 2000: it is absolutely exempt from the 2000 Act. The patient's only right of access, if any, is under the DPA 1998.[303]

9.201 Where the information is sought by a third party, it is also exempt under the FIA 2000 if disclosure would contravene the DPA 1998 or the person to whom it relates would not have a right of access to it.[304] Taken with the exemption for confidential information in s 41, the effect is likely to be that third party access will only be possible compatibly with the DPA 1998.

9.202 The principal importance, therefore, of the FIA 2000 in the health context must be that it might provide a right of access to non-personal information held by health bodies, for example, policies on access to treatment etc.[305]

---

296 Pt I.
297 Pt II.
298 s 41.
299 s 44.
300 s 38.
301 Pt VII.
302 ss 68 and 69 adding a new s 1(1)(e) and inserting s 9A into the 1998 Act.
303 s 40(1).
304 s 40(2)–(4).
305 See generally, *Butterworths Health Services Law and Practice* (2001) Division B, paras [183]–[1000].

(iii) Right of Access under the DPA 1998

Section 7 of the DPA 1998 confers a right of access upon an individual (the 'data **9.203**
subject') to certain information from a 'data controller', ie the person or persons
who control the purposes for which, and the manner in which, the personal data
are processed. The data controller is required to supply the information
'promptly' and in any event within 40 days.[306] The court may require the data controller to supply the information if he fails to do so.[307] In order to trigger the data
controller's obligation to supply, (i) there must be a request in writing to supply information;[308] (ii) the data controller must receive a fee not exceeding the prescribed maximum which is generally £10 (but there are transitional provisions for
manual health records);[309] and (iii) the data controller has requested and been
supplied with 'further information in order to satisfy himself as to the identity of
the person making the request and to locate the information which that person
seeks'.[310]

Subject to a number of exemptions and other limitations (see below), the data **9.204**
controller must supply the following information:[311]

(i)   whether personal data of which the individual is the subject is being
         processed by or on behalf of the data controller;
(ii)   a description of the data, the purposes for which it is being processed and
         the recipients (or classes of recipients) to whom it may be disclosed;
(iii)   if required by the data subject, where possible and which would not in-
         volve disproportionate effort, a copy in a permanent and intelligible form
         of the information held including the source of the data—this may in-
         clude an explanation of any terms used;
(iv)   the logic of any process of automated data processing applied to the data.

The court may order a data controller to comply with a request under s 7 if his fail- **9.205**
ure to do so is in contravention of the Act.[312]

(iv) Exemptions and Limitations

Pt IV of the DPA 1998 contains certain exemptions from the subject information **9.206**
access provisions. In relation to medical records the following are relevant.

---

[306] s 7(8) and (10).
[307] s 7(9).
[308] s 7(2)(a).
[309] s 7(2)(b) and the Data Protection (Subject Access) (Fees and Miscellaneous Provisions)
Regulations 2000, SI 2000/191.
[310] s 7(3) as substituted by FIA 2000, Sch 6, para 1.
[311] ss 7(1) and 8.
[312] s 7(9).

(a) *Harm to the Patient or Another*

9.207   Section 30(1) of the Act allows the Secretary of State to exempt (or modify) the subject access provisions where the personal data consist of information about the 'physical or mental health or condition of the data subject'. Pursuant to this, the Secretary of State promulgated the Data Protection (Subject Access Modification) (Health) Order 2000,[313] which does so in a number of ways. The Order applies to 'personal data' within the Act consisting of 'information as to the physical or mental health or condition' of the data subject.[314] It allows a health professional not to disclose information which would be 'likely to cause serious harm to the physical or mental health or condition' of the patient or any other person.[315] Provision is made that where the data controller is not a health professional, he must consult the 'appropriate health professional' and only disclose information or withhold the information in accordance with that professional's opinion.[316] The 'appropriate health professional' is the current or most recent professional responsible for the relevant aspects of the data subject's clinical care.[317]

9.208   The Order exempts from s 7 health information where disclosure would be injurious to the patient *or another*. It is not, therefore, only information of the kind in the *Martin* case which is covered. For example, disclosure of information that might lead the patient (on discovering it) to harm another such as his spouse or child would also fall within the exemption. Indeed, the 'other' might be the doctor himself. There will, here, be some overlap with the exemption, which we shall see shortly, covering information about, or provided by, a third party. Not all information which, if disclosed, is likely to injure another need necessarily be information relating to, or identify as the source, that other and thus fall within the more general exemption.

9.209   For health information covered by the Order, the court's powers under s 7(9) are extended. It allows an individual, who is likely to suffer serious harm to his or her physical or mental health or condition if disclosure takes place, to apply to the court which has the power to prevent the disclosure of information by the data controller.[318]

(b) *Research, Statistical or Historical Purposes*

9.210   Personal data which are processed (including held) only for research, statistical or historical purposes are exempt from the right of access under s 7 providing three

---

[313] SI 2000/413.
[314] Art 3(1).
[315] Art 5(1).
[316] Arts 5(2), 6 and 7.
[317] Art 2.
[318] s 7(9) as substituted by Art 8(b).

conditions are met: (i) the data are not processed to 'support measures or decisions with respect to particular individuals'; (ii) the processing is not done in such a way as to cause, or be likely to cause, 'substantial damage or substantial distress' to the patient; and (iii) the results of the research are made available in a form that does not identify any patient.[319]

(c) Infertility Treatment

Section 38(1) allows the Secretary of State to exempt by Order any personal data whose disclosure is prohibited or restricted by or under any enactment if it is necessary for safeguarding the interests of the data subject or the rights and freedoms of any other individual and the exemption should prevail over the right of access. The Data Protection (Miscellaneous Subject Access Exemptions) Order 2000[320] exempts from the subject access provisions of s 7 information falling within ss 31 and 33 of the Human Fertilisation and Embryology Act 1990 that is 'information about the provision of treatment services, the keeping or use of gametes or embryos and whether identifiable individuals were born in consequence of treatment services'.[321]

9.211

(d) Regulatory Bodies

Section 31 exempts certain regulatory activities from the access provisions to the extent that they would be likely to prejudice the proper discharge of their functions. Section 31(2)(a)(iii) covers a statutory body, which protects members of the public against dishonesty, malpractice, or other seriously improper conduct by, or the fitness or incompetence of, persons carrying on any profession. Hence, professional regulatory bodies such as the GMC or UK Central Council and also the CHI or CHAI[322] will be exempt from the subject information provisions. Likewise, the Health Service Commissioner is exempt.[323]

9.212

(e) Third Party Information

Finally, there are special provisions in respect of so-called 'third party data'. Section 7(4) provides that a data controller need not supply information relating to an identifiable third party unless that person has consented to it or it is reasonable in all the circumstances to do so without his consent. This covers not only information *about* a third party but also information which identifies the third party as the *source* of the information.[324] Notice that the exemption does not apply to

9.213

---

[319] s 33(4).
[320] SI 2000/419, made under s 38(1) of the 1998 Act.
[321] Sch, Pt I. See Ch 10 below.
[322] See additionally, s 31(4)(b).
[323] s 31(4)(a)(iii)).
[324] s 7(5). Identified individual includes someone who could be identified taking account of all the information that is, or is likely to be, in the possession of the data subject: s 8(7)).

the extent that the information can be provided without identifying the individual.[325] Also, notice that the absolute prohibition on disclosure without the third party's consent, which appeared in the 1984 Act, has been replaced by a 'reasonableness' requirement to take account of the European Court of Human Rights' decision in *Gaskin v UK*.[326] Section 7(6) expands upon this, requiring that in deciding whether it is 'reasonable in all the circumstances' to comply with a request without the consent of the third party regard is to be had to: (i) any duty of confidentiality owed to the third party; (ii) any steps taken to obtain the third party's consent; (iii) whether the third party is capable of consenting; and (iv) whether the third party has expressly refused. For health information, the Data Protection (Subject Access Modification) (Health) Order 2000,[327] adds to s 7(4) so that disclosure of data cannot be withheld merely because they relate to, or were provided by, another health professional who has 'complied or contributed' to the patient's records or has 'been involved in the care' of the individual 'as a health professional'.

(v) Children and Incompetent Adult Patients

9.214   There was uncertainty about the application of the DPA 1984 to children and incompetent adults. The DPA 1998 also creates difficulties. There is no express provision concerned with applications by child patients unlike the Access to Health Records Act 1990, which dealt with it specifically. Nor is there provision for applications where the patient is an incompetent adult. The express provision in the 1984 Act in s 21(9) allowing the Secretary of State to make regulations in relation to such applications is not repeated—although it has to be said that the power in the 1984 Act was never exercised. Curiously, however, the Data Protection (Subject Access Modification) (Health) Order 2000 assumes there are procedures when, in setting out exemptions from disclosure, it refers to those who are 'enabled by or under any enactment or rule of law' to make a request.[328] Precisely what was intended is not clear.

9.215   So what is the position under the DPA 1998? It would seem from the absence of specific provisions in the 1998 Act that the Government considered there was no difficulty. Whether there is depends upon the correct interpretation of s 7 of the 1998 Act.

(a) Two Interpretations of Section 7

9.216   *Interpretation 1*: On one view, s 7 permits the 'data subject' only to make a request

---

[325] s 7(5).
[326] [1990] 1 FLR 167.
[327] SI 2000/413, Art 8(a)).
[328] Art 5(3).

for the information spelt out in s 7(1). The individual may be an adult or child patient who is competent to make such a request, ie is able to understand the nature and likely consequences of seeking his or her medical records. Section 7(1) seems to envisage that the 'data subject' is the applicant in that it states that 'an individual' is entitled to the statutory information if 'personal data of which *that* individual is the data subject' are being processed.[329]

Interpretation 2: An alternative interpretation would see this provision as merely indicating who must *receive* the information rather than specifying who may *request* it. The 'requesting' provision in s 7(2) is couched in general terms and is not directly linked to the 'data subject'. Arguably, this interpretation is self-defeating in the case of incompetent children and adults. If only the 'data subject' is entitled to receive the information, even if a parent or relative can make a valid request under s 7, he or she cannot receive the patient's medical records in response to it! The uncertainty is manifest and it is remarkable that these issues were not expressly dealt with in the DPA 1998. It would have been relatively straightforward to have included clear statutory provisions, just as was done in the Access to Health Records Act 1990. **9.217**

If *interpretation 1* is correct, the result would create difficulties where the child was incompetent through age or disability and in respect of an incompetent adult. A parent could not exercise the s 7 right of access. However, that does not mean that disclosure to the parents of a child patient would not be lawful under the 1998 Act where to disclose would be in the child's 'best interests'. The doctor would have to ensure that he did so consistently with the Act. This would require that 'parents' were included as potential recipients as part of the 'registrable particulars' lodged with the Commissioner.[330] Further, the doctor would have to comply with the Data Protection Principles in Sch 1 to 3, in particular the First and Second Principles. For the 'processing', ie disclosure, to be 'fair' he would have to satisfy a condition in Sch 2 and, because the health records comprise 'sensitive personal data' (as defined in s 2), he would in addition have to satisfy a condition in Sch 3 to the Act.[331] As regards Sch 2, he could probably rely upon para 4 that the 'processing is necessary to protect the vital interests of the data subject', ie the child, providing always that disclosure was 'necessary' for the 'vital interests' (ie those connected with, or essential to, the life or health) of the child. Likewise, the condition in para 8 of Sch 3 would be satisfied if the disclosure was 'necessary for medical purposes' which it would be if the disclosure was in the child's best interests for its treatment. **9.218**

---

[329] s 7(1)(a), emphasis added.
[330] ss 17, 18 and 16(1)(e).
[331] s 4(4) and Sch 1, Pt I, para 1.

9.219 As regards incompetent patients, it might be assumed that no difficulty arises if a receiver appointed by the Court of Protection applies on behalf of the patient under s 7 of the 1998 Act. This is probably wrong since the Court of Protection and receiver's powers are restricted to the 'management of property and affairs' of the patient in Pt VII of the Mental Health Act 1983. This is limited to 'business matters, legal transactions and other dealings of a similar kind' and does not include questions relating to the medical treatment of the patient.[332] Nor would it include obtaining access to an incompetent patient's medical records.

9.220 As a result, much the same reasoning that applies to the incompetent child will also apply where the patient is an incompetent adult. However, disclosure to relatives is much less likely to be 'necessary' and for the patient's 'vital interests' or for 'medical purposes' because the relatives have no legal power to make medical treatment decisions in respect of the patient. It is the doctor who has that power following *Re F*. However, the relatives do generally have a real interest in the welfare of the incompetent patient and it might be that disclosure would fall within the Act since consultation with relatives about the medical treatment of an incompetent adult is good/best practice. Disclosure is, consequently, an adjunct to the treatment of the patient.

9.221 If *interpretation 2* is correct, and a request for access can be made by someone other than the 'data subject', parents and relatives would, if sufficiently interested in the patient's treatment, fall within s 7. Since, however, granting access would mean that the doctor would disclose information relating to a third party, ie the child or incompetent adult, he may comply with the request only with the consent of that individual or if 'in all the circumstances' it would be 'reasonable' to do so without that person's consent.[333] It is, of course, the latter which will be important since the patient is, by definition, incompetent. Section 7(6) sets out a number of factors to consider in determining what is 'reasonable' including whether the individual is incompetent to consent. Granting access to parents or relatives may be reasonable where it is in the best interests of the patient and is necessary for his or her medical treatment.

(b) Exemption and Limitations

9.222 The Data Protection (Subject Access Modification) (Health) Order 2000[334] exempts from s 7 health information about a child or incompetent patient, where a request is made by a parent or other, in three situations.

9.223 The first situation is where that information was provided by the data subject in the expectation, which continues to subsist, that it would not be disclosed to the

---

[332] *Re F* [1990] 2 AC 1 (HL) *per* Lord Brandon at 59.
[333] s 7(4).
[334] SI 2000/413.

person making the request.[335] This exemption is broad. It covers the situation where the data subject was competent and where they were incompetent when the information was 'provided', so long as he or she had an expectation it would not be disclosed to the person requesting it.[336] Equally, there is no requirement that the expectation be expressed, it may be implicit in the circumstances of the particular doctor–patient exchange.[337] Whilst the exemption relates the expectation of non-disclosure to the person requesting it, it does not state that this should be a person named or identified by the data subject. It could be, but the exemption would also cover the situation where the data subject had an expectation that the information would not be disclosed to anyone ('never tell anyone about this doctor') or to a group of which the requesting individual is a member ('my family should never know about this doctor').

Secondly, health information is exempt if it was obtained as a result of 'any examination or investigation to which the data subject consented' and, again, in the expectation that the information would not be disclosed to the person requesting it.[338] This exemption is similar to the previous one but it is narrower in two respects. Unlike the first situation, the information must derive from an 'examination or investigation'—but curiously not treatment of—the data subject. Also, expressly, the patient must have been competent at the time that occurred. Thus, it could not apply if the child was too immature to consent, nor could it apply to an adult who was incompetent at the time of examination etc. The first situation could, providing that the patient has sufficient mental capacity to have an 'expectation' of non-disclosure.

9.224

The final situation is where the data subject 'has expressly indicated' that the information should not be disclosed to the person making the request.[339] The contrast here with the others is obvious. There need have been no 'examination or investigation',[340] there is no requirement that the individual was competent[341] and the indicator of non-disclosure is an express indication rather than an 'expectation' of non-disclosure.[342] What precisely this adds to the coverage of the other two exemptions is somewhat limited. Almost everything falling within it would be covered by the first exemption since an 'expectation' must include an 'expressed indication'. The only difference is that the information must be 'provided' by the data subject under the first exemption; no such requirement exists in the wording

9.225

---

[335] Art 5(3)(a).
[336] Contrast Art 5(3)(b) below.
[337] Contrast Art 5(3)(c) below.
[338] Art 5(3)(b).
[339] Art 5(3)(c).
[340] Art 5(3)(b).
[341] Art 5(3)(b).
[342] Art 5(3)(a) and (b).

of the third. So, information 'obtained' by the doctor through examination or investigation (the wording of the second exemption) would not fall within the first exemption but only the second. If the data subject were incompetent, then the second exemption could not apply. Thus, the third exemption is only needed for the data subject who is incompetent at the time of an examination or investigation and the information that is sought was 'obtained' through that rather than 'provided' by the patient themselves.

(vi) Remedies

9.226   If a doctor fails to comply with a request under s 7, the data subject (or other person making the request) may make an application to the court for access under s 7(9). The court can order the data controller to comply with the request. The patient may also recover compensation for any 'damage' suffered as a result of the doctor's failure to comply with the request[343] which may include financial or psychiatric injury. But, compensation for 'distress' alone is not recoverable under s 13 in this instance. On application by the data subject, s 14 also gives a court power to order the data controller to 'rectify, block, erase or destroy' data which is 'inaccurate'.[344]

3. Access to Health Records Act 1990

9.227   The Access to Health Records Act 1990 applied to manual health records created on or after 1 November 1991. The DPA 1998 repeals in large part the provisions of the Access to Health Records Act 1990[345] and the right of access to manual records is now covered by the 1998 Act with one exception. The sole remaining basis for access to manual records by virtue of the 1990 Act is under s 3(1)(f) by the personal representatives of a dead patient or by a person who may have a claim arising out of his death where the health records are relevant to an action arising out of the patient's death. The subject access provisions of the DPA 1998 would not apply to this situation since they only cover the medical records of a *living person* and, in any event, it is not at all clear that anyone other than the data subject may apply for access under s 7 of that Act.

(i) Scope of the Right of Access

9.228   The 1990 Act applies to all records made by or on behalf of a health professional[346]

---

[343] s 13.

[344] s 14. Notice the more limited remedies in s 12A for manual data until 23 October 2007.

[345] See 1998 Act, Sch 16, Pt I.

[346] Defined in s 2. The DPA 1998 substitutes a new s 2 into the Access to Health Records Act 1990 so that the definition of 'health professional' in s 69 of the DPA 1998 applies to the 1990 Act: Sch 15, para 11.

in connection with the care[347] of an individual.[348] The application must be made in writing[349] and contain sufficient information to identify the patient and to establish that the applicant is entitled to make the application.[350] A fee may be charged where access is given to information none of which was recorded during the 40 days immediately preceding the application,[351] or where the applicant is supplied with a copy of the record.[352]

Depending upon the time frame to which the application relates, the holder of the   **9.229**
record has either 21 (if it relates even in part to a record made within 40 days preceding the application) or 40 days to respond to the request either by giving access to the record or part of the record. The applicant must be allowed to inspect the record (or so much of the record as is not excluded) or part of the record to which the application relates, or be supplied with a copy of the record or extract.[353]

(ii) Exemptions and Limitations

There are three exceptions in the Act which are of particular importance here.   **9.230**
First, the Act provides that access shall not be given to any part of the record which:

(a) in the opinion of the holder of the record, would disclose—

   (i) information likely to cause serious harm to the physical or mental health of any individual.[354]

Secondly, access should also be excluded in respect of any part of the record which: **9.231**

(a) in the opinion of the holder of the record, would disclose— . . .

   (ii) information relating to or provided by an individual, other than the patient, who could be identified from that information,[355]

unless the individual concerned has consented to the application, or is a health professional who has been involved in the care of the patient.[356]

Thirdly, where the records contain a note at the deceased's request that the per-   **9.232**
sonal representatives should not be granted access.[357]

---

[347] Defined in s 11 to include 'examination, investigation, diagnosis and treatment'.
[348] s 1(1)(b).
[349] s 11.
[350] s 3(6).
[351] The fee is £10.
[352] The fee may not exceed the cost of making the copy and, where relevant, the cost of postage (s 3(4)(b)).
[353] s 3(2).
[354] s (5)(1)(a)(i).
[355] s (5)(1)(a)(ii).
[356] s 5(2).
[357] s 4(3).

9.233   Where access under the Act is excluded, the record holder is under no obligation to inform the applicant that information exists and has been excluded. All that is required is that the record holder inform the patient that he does not hold any information which he is required by law to disclose.

4. *Access to Medical Reports Act 1988*

9.234   The Access to Medical Reports Act 1988, which came into force on 1 January 1989, gives patients the right to see certain medical reports prepared about them for employment or insurance purposes.[358] The right of access conferred by the Act is a right to inspect or be supplied with a copy of the report.[359]

(i) Scope of the Right of Access

9.235   An important limitation on the scope of the Act comes from the fact that 'medical report' is defined to mean:

> a report relating to the physical or mental health of the individual prepared by a medical practitioner who is or has been responsible for the clinical care of the individual.[360]

9.236   'Care' is in turn defined in the Act to include 'examination, investigation or diagnosis for the purposes of, or in connection with, any form of medical treatment'.[361] Accordingly, reports prepared by an independent medical practitioner who is not, and has not been, involved in a therapeutic doctor–patient relationship with the individual concerned are not covered by the Act.[362] Difficult questions arise in relation to the position of an occupational health doctor who is employed to advise employers and employees about issues involving health and safety at work. Whether or not reports prepared by such a doctor will fall within the scope of the Access to Medical Reports Act 1988 will most likely depend upon the degree of involvement with the employees and, in particular, whether the physician has, or has had, any direct responsibility in relation to the mental or physical well-being of the individual concerned.

9.237   The Act provides that the employer or insurance company must obtain the individual's consent when it seeks the report, and that the individual may at that time make his consent conditional upon being given access to the report prior to the supply to the employer or insurance company.[363] Even if he does not so stipulate

---

[358] s 1, defined in s 2(1).

[359] s 4(4). See also s 5(2) conferring upon the individual the right to request corrections to the report.

[360] s 2(1). The DPA 1998 substitutes in s 2(1) the definition of 'health professional' in s 69 of the DPA 1998: Sch 15, para 8.

[361] ibid.

[362] They may, however, be covered by the DPA 1998.

[363] s 3(1).

at the time of giving his consent, he may nonetheless, by notice to the doctor supplying the report, request access prior to the report being given to the employer or insurance company[364] or, again by notice to the doctor, within six months of the report being so supplied.[365]

(ii) Exemptions and Limitations

The individual's right of access to medical reports under the Act is not absolute. **9.238**
There are three situations in which doctors are justified in refusing to provide access. First, where disclosure would:

> in the opinion of the practitioner be likely to cause serious harm to the physical or mental health of the individual or others . . .[366]

Secondly, where disclosure would 'indicate the intentions of the practitioner in re- **9.239**
spect of the individual'.[367]

Thirdly, where disclosure would: **9.240**

> be likely to reveal information about another person, or to reveal the identity of another person who has supplied information to the practitioner about the individual unless—
>
> (a) that person has consented; or
> (b) that person is a health professional who has been involved in the care of the individual and the information relates to or has been provided by the professional in that capacity.[368]

The doctor is obliged to inform the individual that his request for access has been **9.241**
denied under one of the exceptions.[369] The individual is entitled to apply to the county court for an order that the doctor must provide him access under the Act.[370]

(iii) Relationship with the Data Protection Act 1998

What is the relationship between the DPA 1998 and the Access to Medical **9.242**
Reports Act 1988? While a medical 'report' would be a 'record', it might not be a 'health record' within s 68. Probably, the definition of 'health record' excludes medical reports unless made by the patient's *own doctor*, otherwise it would not have been made 'in connection with the care of that individual'.[371] Thus, the DPA

---

[364] s 4(3).
[365] s 6.
[366] s 7(1).
[367] ibid.
[368] s 7(2).
[369] s 7(3).
[370] s 8.
[371] s 68(2)(b).

1998 does not confer a greater degree of access and control for individuals over their 'medical reports' than does the 1988 Act except to the extent that a report by a patient's own doctor for other than 'insurance or employment' purposes—to which the 1988 Act is restricted—would fall within the DPA 1998. Neither Act covers, it seems, a report made by a doctor who is not the examinee's own doctor.

5. The Common Law

(i) Basis for a Right of Access

9.243   There are essentially four possible legal bases for asserting a common law right of access to medical records.[372] First, the court could recognise an innominate common law right which is general but which may be made subject to exceptions. Since there is no historical precedent for such a right, any such analysis must depend upon judicial assertion and upon the demands of practical justice. Secondly, the common law could recognise such a right under Article 8 of the European Convention on Human Rights. However, the Convention is unlikely to be interpreted as creating legal rights that otherwise do not exist,[373] and so judicial reliance upon Article 8 must be limited to bolstering the current common law position. Thirdly, a common law right of access could have been based upon a patient having a proprietary interest in his or her medical records.[374] There can, however, no longer be any doubt that patients have no proprietary interests in their medical records. Rather these are regarded as the property of the relevant health authority or trust in the public sector, whilst in the private sector ownership may depend upon the precise contractual relationship between the parties. Fourthly, a duty of disclosure and a corresponding right of access may be found to arise as part of a series of fiduciary obligations which could be held to arise in the context of the doctor–patient relationship.

(ii) Judicial Development of a Right of Access

9.244   The first English decision to deal with the question of a common law right of access to medical records was *R v Mid Glamorgan Family Health Services Authority, ex p Martin*.[375] Prior to *Martin*, however, the Supreme Court of Canada in *McInerney v MacDonald* had considered the question and determined that a

---

[372] See, Kennedy and Grubb (n 72 above) 992–1019.

[373] *Wainwright v Home Office* [2003] UKHL 53 and discussion above, paras 9.132–9.144.

[374] This position is reluctantly accepted by the BMA: see *Medical Ethics Today: Its Practice and Philosophy* (BMA, 1993), 44. Acceptance of this position is also clear in the judgments in the Court of Appeal in *Martin*. See also *McInerney v MacDonald* (1992) 93 DLR (4th) 415, 421; *Breen v Williams* (1996) 70 ALJR 772. See also National Health Service (General Medical Services) Regulations 1992, SI 1992/635, Sch 2, para 36.

[375] [1995] 1 All ER 356 (CA), noted by Grubb, A (1994) 2 Med L Rev 353 and Feenan, D (1996) 59 MLR 101.

common law right of action could be found from the general fiduciary nature of the doctor patient relationship.[376] The case arose when a patient sought access to the whole of her prior medical records after discovering that she did not in fact need the thyroid pills which she had been prescribed for a number of years. Her current doctor, Dr McInerney gave the plaintiff copies of all notes, memoranda, and reports which she had prepared herself, but refused to produce copies of reports and records she had received from other physicians on the grounds that, in her view, it would be unethical for her to release them. The Canadian Supreme Court found on these facts that the patient had a common law right of access to her medical records, including those compiled by doctors other than Dr McInerney.

LaForest J, delivering the judgment of the Canadian Supreme Court, accepted   **9.245**
that the medical records were the property of the physician, institution, or clinic which compiled them.[377] Nonetheless, in his view, the critical factor was that the relationship between physician and patient, within which medical records are compiled, is one in which trust and confidence must be placed in the physician. Thus he characterised the relationship as fiduciary and confidential then went on to analyse the precise character of the relationship in this context, since in his view the shape and content of a fiduciary relationship depends upon the demands of the situation.[378] In the case of the doctor–patient relationship LaForest J found that the fiduciary qualities of the relationship created a duty upon the physician to grant access to the information the doctor uses in administering treatment,[379] and that this duty extends to requiring the disclosure of information which has been conveyed to the current holder by another doctor.[380]

In England the Court of Appeal in *R v Mid Glamorgan Family Health Services*   **9.246**
Authority, ex p Martin reached a broadly similar conclusion that a patient might have a limited common law right of access to medical records, but this was based on reasoning far removed in substance from that of the Canadian Supreme Court.[381] The plaintiff sought judicial review of the decision of two health authorities to deny him access to medical records relating to two specific incidents in his past, both of which involved his psychiatric treatment, which he sought in order that he might better come to terms with his own personal development. His

---

[376] (1992) 93 DLR (4th) 415 (CSC). See also *R v Dyment* (1988) 55 DLR (4th) 503 and *Halls v Mitchell* [1928] 2 DLR 97.

[377] 93 DLR (4th) 415, 421. Noted by Kennedy, I (1993) 1 Med L Rev 378. Cf *Re Mitchell and St Michael's Hospital* (1980) 112 DLR 3d 360.

[378] ibid, 423.

[379] ibid, 424. See *Emmett v Eastern Dispensary and Casualty Hospital* 396 F 2d 931 (DC Cir 1967) and *Cannell v Medical and Surgical Clinic* 315 NE 2d 278 (Ill App Ct 1974).

[380] (1992) 93 DLR (4th) 415, 425.

[381] For argument in favour of the view that the doctor–patient relationship is fiduciary see Grubb, A, 'The Doctor as Fiduciary' [1994] CLP 311.

repeated requests for access had been refused, on grounds ranging from possible detriment to his overall best interests to a perceived duty to 'protect retired colleagues'. At one stage access was offered provided that the patient would give an assurance that 'the Authority and/or any of its staff are not implicated in any potential litigation being contemplated by Mr Martin in respect of his South Glamorganshire treatment'. Finally in 1993, after the patient had instituted proceedings for judicial review of the decision not to give him access to his medical records, the respondents agreed to disclose the patient's medical records to his medical advisers, but not to the patient himself.

9.247 At first instance Popplewell J, in the course of a judgment which denied the existence of a common law right of access to medical records, rejected the fiduciary approach in *McInerney* on the basis that Lord Scarman in the House of Lords (and Browne Wilkinson LJ in the Court of Appeal) in *Sidaway*[382] had rejected this characterisation of the doctor–patient relationship.[383] Accordingly his judgment contains little examination of whether or not English courts should recognise fiduciary qualities in the doctor–patient relationship, and the point was not discussed when the case reached the Court of Appeal.

9.248 The Court of Appeal declined to consider whether or not a patient has an unconditional right of access at common law to his medical records, preferring to limit consideration to the question whether or not a doctor or a health authority, as the owner of a patient's medical records, is entitled to deny him access to them on the ground that their disclosure would be detrimental to him.[384]

9.249 In this regard, the Court of Appeal considered that the fact that the holder of the records was a public body was irrelevant to the legal principles which should be applied.[385] Nourse LJ, with whom Evans LJ and Sir Roger Parker agreed, held that access to medical records could be denied where it was in the best interests of the patient to do so, for example where disclosure would be detrimental to the patient's health. Given that the health authorities had offered to disclose the patient's medical records to his medical advisers, there was clearly no ground for granting the patient the relief sought in his action for judicial review of the health authorities' decisions. Unfortunately, the narrow basis of this question considered by the Court of Appeal precluded any helpful guidance being issued on questions such

---

[382] '[T]here is no comparison to be made between the relationship of doctor and patient with that of solicitor and client, trustee and *cestui qui trust* or the other relationships treated in equity as of a fiduciary character', 884.

[383] Moreover, Popplewell J criticised the judgment in *McInerney* for failing to distinguish between information in the medical records which had been collected from the patient, and conclusions which a doctor reaches based on that information but which should remain wholly the property of the doctor.

[384] [1995] 1 All ER 356, 359 *per* Nourse LJ, 365; *per* Evans LJ.

[385] ibid, 363 *per* Nourse LJ.

as who has the onus of proving that disclosure would be harmful to the patient, and upon what other grounds might access lawfully be denied.

Of greater interest is the Court of Appeal's analysis of the possible bases upon which a patient could claim a common law right of access to his medical records. Each of the judges found that a health authority has no absolute right to deal with medical records in any way that it chooses.[386] According to Nourse LJ, this right is limited by a doctor or health authority's general duty to act at all times in the best interests of the patient, a duty which he identifies as resting upon the speech of Lord Templeman in *Sidaway v Bethlem Royal Hospital Governors*.[387] By contrast, Evans LJ based the duty to disclose upon the need not to frustrate the very purposes for which medical records are created in the first place. In his view those purposes were to enable a patient's doctor and his successors best to treat the patient, and to provide a record of diagnosis and treatment in the case of future enquiry or dispute.[388] Sir Roger Parker preferred not to set out the scope of the doctor's duty of disclosure because 'the circumstances in which a patient or former patient is entitled to demand access to his medical history as set out in the records will be infinitely various'.[389] He gave the example of a patient requiring access in order to facilitate his medical treatment if he is about to emigrate and his condition is such that he might need treatment before he can nominate a successor doctor.

9.250

The difficulty with the judgments of the Court of Appeal are that they rest more on assertion of the need to qualify a doctor or health authority's right to deny access to medical records than upon any analysis of the possible basis in the common law for a right of access to medical records.

9.251

The lack of any principled foundation for the right of access to medical records, identified by the Court of Appeal in *Martin*, was recognised by the High Court of Australia in *Breen v Williams*.[390] The case arose after a woman was denied access to her medical records which had been compiled by her doctor after treatment he had provided in the private medical sector in connection with complications from a breast augmentation operation which had been performed by another doctor. She sought access to her medical records in order to participate in settlement of breast implant litigation in the United States, but access was refused by her doctor unless she agreed to release him from any possible claim which might arise in relation to his treatment of her. Unlike in *McInerney* and *Martin*, in *Breen* there was no suggestion that disclosure of the information in the records could have any adverse effect on the plaintiff's physical or mental health.

9.252

---

[386] ibid, 363 *per* Nourse LJ, 365 *per* Evans LJ; 366 *per* Sir Roger Parker.
[387] [1985] 1 All ER 632, 665–6, [1985] AC 871, 904.
[388] [1995] 1 All ER 356, 365.
[389] ibid, 366.
[390] (1996) 70 ALJR 772. See Parkinson, P (1995) 17 Sydney LR 433 and Kennedy, I (1997) 5 Med L Rev 115.

9.253 In *Breen* it was held that, unless a patient had a contractual right of access to her records, or disclosure of the information in the records was in her best interests such that it would be negligent to withhold the information, there was no common law obligation on a doctor or hospital to provide access. Moreover, there was no basis for implying such a term into the contractual relationship between the doctor and the patient. Rejecting the authority of *Martin*, the High Court found that the relationship between a doctor and patient is not such that a patient has a *right* to see her medical records.[391] Also of interest was the High Court's rejection of the argument that the fiduciary qualities of the doctor–patient relationship were such that a doctor would be under a fiduciary obligation to provide a patient with access to her medical records. Whilst accepting that a doctor was a fiduciary in some respects, the High Court held that the fiduciary duty as understood in Australia did not provide any foundation for an obligation to provide access to a patient's medical records, or more generally to act in the patient's best interests.[392]

(iii) Scope of the Common Law Right of Access

9.254 In England, the most that can be said with any certainty is that the courts implicitly accept that the owner of medical records does not have an unfettered discretion to deal with them as he or she chooses. The legal basis for qualifying these ownership rights could be based upon one of three possible grounds. First, that patients have a general 'innominate' right of access to medical records subject to certain exceptions. Secondly, that in certain defined circumstances doctors are obliged to disclose information in the medical records or hand over the records themselves to patients. These circumstances include where it is necessary to do so to avoid liability in negligence and where so required by the rules governing disclosure for the purposes of litigation. Thirdly, it is still possible that either the Court of Appeal or the House of Lords could adopt the reasoning of the Canadian Supreme Court in *McInerney* and of Kirby P in dissent in *Breen v Williams*, and hold that the fiduciary qualities of the doctor–patient relationship impose an obligation upon doctors to provide patients with access to their medical records.

---

[391] (1996) 7 ALJR 772, at 784, 789–90, 804.
[392] (1996) 70 ALJR 772, at 776–7, 781–2, 793.

10

MEDICALLY ASSISTED REPRODUCTION

A. Introduction

10.01   This chapter examines infertility, and the ways in which the law in England and Wales responds to the practices developed by scientists and the medical profession to alleviate the problem.

10.02   Infertility has been defined as 'the involuntary, significant reduction of reproductive capacity'.[1] The standard medical definition of infertility is the failure to conceive after 12 months of regular, unprotected sexual intercourse, or the occurrence of three or more consecutive miscarriages or stillbirths.[2] But this definition is not, and no definition can be, precise. For example, there is evidence that about half of all couples who qualify as infertile on the 12 month standard will conceive naturally during the following year.[3] And it has been suggested that the 'twelve month rule is a recent development, partly inspired by "infertility specialists" marketing experimental and expensive new reproductive technologies'.[4] Treatment services may be sought, of course, by those who are not infertile: examples are persons with genetic disease,[5] homosexual couples, individuals with no sexual partner, long-term prisoners,[6] women who fear sexual intercourse, women who wish to postpone pregnancy and want embryos to be created and frozen for later use when they may be past the height of their fertility.

10.03   Estimates vary as to the incidence of infertility. At the time of the Warnock Inquiry (in the early 1980s), 'a commonly quoted figure [was] that one couple in ten [was] childless'.[7] It, however, conceded that accurate statistics were not available, and noted that the proportion of this figure relating to couples who chose not to have children was not known. Higher estimates have been suggested elsewhere,[8] and it may be that as many as one in six couples will experience infertility at some stage in, what would be, their normal reproductive lives. Even the 10 per cent estimate would mean 50,000 or so new cases of infertility in Britain each year.

---

[1] *Per* Canadian Law Reform Commission, *Medically Assisted Procreation* (Working Paper 65) (1992).

[2] *Black's Medical Dictionary* (38th edn, 1995), 252.

[3] Te Velde, Eijkemans and Habbems, 'Variation In Couple Fecundity and Time to Pregnancy, an essential concept in human reproduction' (2000) 355 *Lancet* 1928–9.

[4] *Per* Susan Faludi, *Backlash: The Undeclared War Against Women* (London: Chatto and Windus, 1992), 47.

[5] See HFEA, *Tenth Annual Report and Accounts* (London: HFEA, 2002), 7.

[6] Though in the leading case involving a long-term prisoner, *R v Secretary of State for the Home Department, ex p Mellor* [2001] EWCA Civ 472, [2002] QB 13 medically assisted reproduction was not in issue.

[7] See *Report of the Committee of Inquiry into Human Fertilisation and Embryology* (Cmnd 9314, 1984), para 2.1.

[8] Other estimates put it as high as one in six. Some evidence of the causes of male infertility is found in Jorgensen, N et al, 'Regional Differences In Semen quality in Europe' (2001) 16 *Human Reproduction* 1012.

Questions might also arise as to whether treatment services should be made avail-   **10.04**
able to all forms of fertility compromise. IVF was originally used for inoperably-
blocked fallopian tubes. In Denmark, Lee and Morgan point out,[9] it is largely
confined to such treatment. In the United Kingdom 'it is also indicated in en-
dometriosis, ovulation disorders, anti-sperm antibodies and male infertilities,
many of which, . . ., are socially or environmentally caused'.[10]

Most infertility treatment fails. Most couples who undergo infertility treatment   **10.05**
remain childless. Success rates of clinics relate to a number of variables: not only
the skill and expertise of the clinicians but also 'political' decisions as to whom to
treat, the types of infertility to be treated, the risks particular clinics are prepared
to take. League tables indicating success rates must thus be viewed cautiously (if
not cynically). Robert Winston has expressed the opinion that the very presence
of such tables encourages 'a few clinics to be "somewhat economical with the
truth" '.[11] According to the data collected by the Human Fertilisation and
Embryology Authority[12] the live birth rate per treatment cycle of IVF in
1998–1999 was 16.9 per cent. For micromanipulation techniques (intra cytoplasmic sperm injection is the most commonly used method), the success rate was
21.8 per cent. For donor insemination (including GIFT) it was only 9.9 per cent.
In more than one quarter of cases where a live birth results from IVF or micromanipulation there is a multiple birth.[13]

There are a large number of techniques which have been developed—and con-   **10.06**
tinue to develop—for treating the infertile. These range from donor insemination
(AID as it was once called) which has existed for over a century[14] to surrogacy,
which has claims (dubious it must be said) to biblical roots.[15] It was with the development of in vitro fertilisation (IVF) in the 1970s[16] that medically assisted reproduction has come to concern policy-makers throughout much of the world.[17]
Other technologies which are used, and which will be discussed in this chapter, are

---

[9] *Per* Robert G Lee and Derek Morgan, *Human Fertilisation and Embryology—Regulating The Reproductive Revolution* (London: Blackstone, 2001), 44.

[10] ibid. On environmental influences see Weber, RFA et al, 'Environmental Influences on Male Reproduction' (2002) 89 *British Journal of Urology International* 143.

[11] *The IVF Revolution: The Definitive Guide to Assisted Reproductive Techniques* (London: Vermillion, 1999), 163.

[12] Human Fertilisation and Embryology Authority, *Ninth Annual Report and Accounts* (London: HFEA, 2000), 12, Table 4.1.

[13] ibid. 27.3 per cent and 26.9 per cent respectively.

[14] There is a claim that the first human donor insemination was in the US in 1884: see Snowden, R and Mitchell, GD, *The Artificial Family* (London: Unwin, 1983), 13.

[15] See Singer, P, and Wells, D, *New Ways of Making Babies: The Reproduction Revolution* (Oxford: OUP, 1984), 107–8, citing Genesis 16 (the story of Abram and Sarai).

[16] Louise Brown, the first 'test-tube' baby was born in 1978.

[17] See McLean, SAM, *Law Reform and Human Reproduction* (Aldershot: Dartmouth, 1992); Bonnicksen, AL, *In Vitro Fertilization: Building Policy from Laboratories to Legislatures* (New York: Columbia University Press, 1989).

cryopreservation, assisted insemination by a husband or partner, oocyte donation, gamete intra-fallopian transfer (GIFT), and micromanipulation (intra-
cytoplasmic sperm injection and sub-zonal insemination). Cloning—the use of
which in infertility treatment has been prohibited—will also be discussed.

1. The Warnock Report

10.07　The Warnock Inquiry had its precursors. There were inquiries into donor insemination shortly after the Second World War (the Fisher report[18] recommended it
be criminalised) and in the late 1950s the Feversham Committee,[19] which reported in 1960, concluded that AID was an undesirable practice to be discouraged. A more positive response was made in the Peel report in 1973:[20] AID
should, it recommended, be available at accredited NHS centres for those for
whom it was appropriate. But this led to nothing and no system of accreditation
was established.

10.08　Modern thinking on assisted reproduction begins with the Warnock report.[21] The
Warnock Inquiry was established in 1982 'to consider recent and potential developments in medicine and science related to human fertilisation and embryology;
to consider what policies and safeguards should be applied, including consideration of he social, ethical and legal implications of these developments; and to
make recommendations'.[22] The committee reported in 1984. It took the view that
'actions taken with the intention of overcoming infertility can, as a rule, be regarded as acceptable substitutes for natural fertilisation'.[23] Infertility was not to be
seen as 'something mysterious, nor a cause of shame, nor necessarily something
that has to be endured without attempted cure'.[24] It is, the Inquiry concluded, 'a
condition meriting treatment',[25] and, in the light of its analysis, it recommended
statutory regulation of medically assisted reproduction. The Warnock report was
predicated upon the assumption that fertility services would be integrated into the
NHS (itself a different creature from what it is now). The commercial potential of
fertility services was not foreseen. The problems engendered by commercialisation

---

[18] *Artificial Human Insemination: the Report of a Committee appointed by his Grace the Archbishop
of Canterbury* (London: SPCK, 1948).
[19] Home Office and Scottish Home Department, *Departmental Committee on Human Artificial
Insemination* (Cmnd 1105, 1960).
[20] British Medical Association, *Annual Report of the Council*, Appendix V: Report of the Panel on
Human Artificial Insemination, British Medical Journal Supplement, 7 April, 1973, vol II, 3–5.
[21] *Report of the Inquiry into Human Fertilisation and Embryology* (Cmnd 9314, 1985), subsequently reprinted with an introduction by the chairwoman as *A Question of Life* (Oxford: Basil
Blackwell, 1985). See also Warnock, M, *Making Babies* (Oxford: OUP, 2002).
[22] ibid, para 1.2.
[23] ibid, para 2.4.
[24] ibid.
[25] ibid.

were barely addressed in the Warnock report.[26] Ironically, within months of publication the 'first' commercial surrogacy created a moral panic[27]—and legislation[28]—and alerted us to issues of commercialisation and commodification which
barely surfaced in the Warnock report.[29]

Although the Warnock report was debated both in the House of Lords and in the
House of Commons in 1984,[30] the Human Fertilisation and Embryology Bill,
largely based on it, was not introduced to Parliament until 1989. In the meanwhile there were two Private Member's Bills,[31] both of which had substantial support (in 1985 and 1986 respectively), which if passed would have put an end not
just to embryo research, their primary target, but also to most IVF treatment. The
relatively liberal 1990 Act might have been derailed had it not been for the
Progress Educational Trust (established in November 1985), which successfully
worked to increase public understanding of the benefits of embryo research and
infertility treatment, and for the fortuitous announcement of successful preimplantation sex diagnosis to prevent the birth of a child suffering from a sex-limited
genetic disorder some five days before the House of Commons voted on the
Human Fertilisation and Embryology Bill.[32]

10.09

2. History of Regulation

One immediate response to the Warnock report was the establishment by the
Medical Research Council and the Royal College of Obstetricians and
Gynaecologists of the Voluntary Licensing Authority in 1985. This was subsequently (in 1989) called the Interim Licensing Authority. This body instituted a
self-regulatory mechanism for licensing infertility treatment and research on
human embryos and gametes. The Voluntary/Interim Licensing Authority operated for six years, approved IVF centres and licensed research projects. It established voluntary guidelines for such research work, including provisions for donor
consent and prior ethical committee approval of the work.[33] It ceased to exist on

10.10

---

[26] Outside the context of surrogacy.

[27] See Dyer, C, 'Baby Cotton and the Birth of a Moral Panic', The Guardian, 15 January 1985,
and Hutchinson, A and Morgan, D, 'A Bill Born from Panic', The Guardian, 12 July 1985.

[28] Surrogacy Arrangements Act 1985.

[29] See Brazier, M, 'Regulating the Reproduction Business' (1999) 7 Med L Rev 166, 191. *Cf*
Duxbury, N, 'Do Markets Degrade?' (1996) 59 MLR 331. See also Annas, G, *Some Choice—Law,
Medicine and the Market* (New York: OUP, 1998).

[30] See *Hansard*, HL vol 456, cols 524–593; HC vol 68, cols 547–90.

[31] See, further, Mulkay, M, *The Embryo Research Debate: Science and the Politics of Reproduction*
(Cambridge University Press, 1997), 24–9.

[32] ibid. See also Franklin, S, 'Making Representations: The Parliamentary Debate on the Human
Fertilisation and Embryology Act and Orphaned Embryos' in Edwards, J, Franklin, S, Hirsch, E,
Price, F and Strathern, M, (eds), *Technologies of Procreation: Kinship in the Age of Assisted Conception*
(London: Routledge, 1999), 127.

[33] On its work see Gunning, J and English, V, *Human In Vitro Fertilization* (Aldershot:
Dartmouth, 1993).

1 August 1991 when the Human Fertilisation and Embryology Act 1990 came into force. This established the Human Fertilisation and Embryology Authority.

10.11   The Human Fertilisation and Embryology Act 1990 (hereafter the 1990 Act) regulates infertility treatments that involve the use of donated genetic material, whether sperm, eggs or embryos, or those that involve the creation of an embryo outside the human body. It does not apply to GIFT[34] (even though this is more likely to result in multiple pregnancy[35] and even though 'stimulation of ovulation *without* IVF is almost certainly the most dangerous of any reproductive treatment').[36] Whether the justification for this omission is clinical freedom, as the then Lord Chancellor Lord Mackay of Clashfern argued,[37] or the desire to limit expense, as Lee and Morgan suggest,[38] or a combination of these two factors, is immaterial. The end result is that a much-admired Act falls short of addressing a major infertility technique. And, concomitantly focuses—some might say overfocuses[39]—on another, namely IVF.

10.12   In addition the 1990 Act regulates the storage of all genetic material, and therefore most obviously cryopreservation. The 1990 Act is not directly concerned with the practice of surrogacy. Only in so far as a surrogate birth is effectuated through the use, in part or whole, of donated genetic material or using IVF techniques is the framework of the 1990 Act applicable. The moral panic fanned by the birth of 'Baby Cotton' in January 1985[40] resulted in an attempt to regulate the practice of surrogacy in legislation passed in 1985 (the Surrogacy Arrangements Act 1985[41]). The 1990 Act effects some amendments to this and makes it clear that surrogacy agreements are unenforceable.[42] But surrogacy is best treated distinctly from other techniques for the relief of infertility, and accordingly is given a separate section in this chapter.

---

[34] No embryo is created or kept outside a woman's body: see the 1990 Act, s 1(3).

[35] As observed by Margaret Brazier, 'Reproductive Rights: Feminism or Patriarchy?' in Harris, J and Holm, S (eds), *The Future of Human Reproduction* (Oxford: Clarendon Press, 1998), 68. Because it is not regulated, more than three eggs can be transferred during a cycle of treatment.

[36] *The IVF Revolution* (n 11 above), 145.

[37] *Hansard*, HL vol 516, col 1089.

[38] Lee and Morgan (n 9 above), 13.

[39] This is Lord Winston's view: *The IVF Revolution* (n 11 above).

[40] Reported as *Re C* (1985) FLR 846. A more personal account is Cotton, K and Winn, D, *Baby Cotton: For Love or Money* (London: Dorling Kindersley, 1985).

[41] On which see Freeman, MDA, 'After *Warnock*: Whither The Law?' (1986) 39 CLP 33, 37–48.

[42] See below para 10.192.

B. The Human Fertilisation and Embryology Authority

1. Establishment of the Authority

The 1990 Act established the Human Fertilisation and Embryology Authority (hereafter HFEA).[43] This is a body corporate, and consists of a chairman and deputy chairman, and such number of the other members as the Secretary of State appoints.[44] In making appointments the Secretary of State is to have regard to the desirability of ensuring that the proceedings of the authority, and the discharge of its functions, are informed by the views of both men and women.[45] S/he must also ensure that there is a majority of members who are neither doctors nor research scientists.[46] Neither the chairman nor deputy chairman may come from either of these professional groups. The first two chairs were both academic lawyers/university heads (Sir Colin Campbell, the Vice-Chancellor of the University of Nottingham, and Ruth Deech, the Principal of St Anne's College, Oxford). The third, appointed in 2002, is Suzi Leather.

10.13

Appointments to HFEA are for renewable periods of three years.[47] A member can resign his or her office at any time by giving notice to the Secretary of State.[48] The Secretary of State may also decide that a member should vacate his or her position.[49] An appointed member may be removed from office if he or she:

10.14

(i)   has been absent from meetings of the Authority for six consecutive months or longer without the permission of the Authority; or

(ii) has become bankrupt or has made an arrangement with creditors; or

(iii) is unable or unfit to discharge the function of a member.[50]

A member of the House of Commons is not eligible to become a member of HFEA.[51] There seems to be no such restriction on members of the House of Lords. Appointments are to be made on merit[52] and not in order that particular groups should be represented.

---

[43] s 5. The Authority has been criticised by the House of Commons Science and Technology Committee in *Developments In Human Genetics and Embryology*, Fourth Report of Session 2001–2002 (HC 791, 2002).

[44] s 5(2).

[45] Sch 1, para 4(2).

[46] Sch 1, para 4(4).

[47] Sch 1, para 5(2).

[48] Sch 1, para 5(3).

[49] Sch 1, para 5(5).

[50] Sch 1, para 5(5).

[51] Sch 1, para 6.

[52] Following Nolan guidelines.

2. Functions of HFEA

10.15   The principal functions of HFEA are:

(i)   to license treatment services, the storage of gametes and embryos and re-search on embryos;[53]

(ii)   to monitor and inspect premises and activities carried out under statutory li-cence;[54]

(iii)   to submit an annual report to the Secretary of State on its activities;[55]

(iv)   to maintain a code of practice as guidance for the proper conduct of activities carried out under a licence (five editions have been published and a sixth is promised during 2003).[56]

In addition, it has the following 'general functions':[57]

(i)   to keep under review information about embryos and any subsequent devel-opment of embryos and about the provision of treatment services and activ-ities governed by the 1990 Act, and advise the Secretary of State, if s/he asks it to do so, about these matters;

(ii)   to publicise the services it provides or which are provided in pursuance of li-cences it grants;

(iii)   to provide advice and information for persons to whom licences apply or who are receiving treatment services or providing gametes or embryos for use for the purposes of activities governed by the 1990 Act, or may wish to do so;

(iv)   to perform such other functions as may be specified in regulations.

10.16   HFEA may be called upon to advise the Secretary of State on any of these func-tions. Note they are widely drafted. For example, 'any subsequent development of embryos' could place a review of abortion services within HFEA's remit, perhaps even the scope of abortion law. Hitherto, however, the 'general functions' have been interpreted narrowly and such 'review' has been limited to embryos pro-duced as a result of reproductive services.

10.17   HFEA has a duty to collect data from licence treatments, and to keep a register of them. The Act provides[58] that the register shall include information relating to

(i)   the provision of treatment services for any identifiable individual;

(ii)   the keeping or use of the gametes of any identifiable individual or of an em-bryo taken from any identifiable woman.

---

[53] s 11.
[54] s 9.
[55] s 7.
[56] s 25.
[57] s 8.
[58] s 31(1), (2).

The purposes of the register are:

(i) to provide information to children born as a result of treatment services; a child who is produced as a result of treatment services may, after reaching the age or 18 (or 16 if wishing to marry) and after receiving appropriate counselling, be given information pertaining to genetic background[59] (and see further at paras 10.147–10.149);

(ii) to monitor the provision of treatments;

(iii) to provide information more generally. It should be emphasised that information contained in the register is confidential[60] and its disclosure is accordingly restricted. But information may be sought by the Registrar General,[61] or used to serve the interests of justice,[62] or to reveal a congenital disability.[63]

C. Licensing

1. Types of Licence

The 1990 Act provides that HFEA may grant any one of three types of licence authorising: **10.18**

(i) activities in the course of providing treatment services;[64]

(ii) the storage of gametes and embryos;[65]

(iii) activities for the purpose of a project of research.[66]

In the course of providing treatment services a licence may authorise any of the following:[67]   **10.19**

(i) bringing about the creation of embryos in vitro;

(ii) keeping embryos;

(iii) using gametes;

(iv) practices designed to secure that embryos are in a suitable condition to be placed in a woman or to determine whether embryos are suitable for that purpose;

(v) placing any embryo in a woman;

(vi) mixing sperm with the egg of a hamster, or other animal specified in directions, for the purpose of testing the fertility or normality of the sperm, but

---

[59] s 31(3), (4).
[60] s 33.
[61] s 33(3)(e).
[62] s 34.
[63] s 35.
[64] s 11(1)(a) and Sch 2, para 2.
[65] s 11.
[66] s 11(1)(c) and Sch 2, para 3.
[67] Sch 2, para 1(1).

only where anything which forms is destroyed when the test is complete and, in any event, not later than the two cell stage; and

(vii) such other practices as may be specified in, or determined in accordance with, regulations.

10.20 A licence may be granted subject to such conditions as may be specified.[68] A licence cannot authorise any activity unless it appears to HFEA to be 'necessary or desirable' for the purpose of providing treatment services.[69] A licence cannot authorise altering the genetic structure of any cell while it forms part of an embryo.[70] A licence cannot be granted for a period of more that five years.[71] In 1995 HFEA advocated than this period should be reduced where the treatment clinic applying for renewal had not radically changed since the last inspection or committee decision.[72]

10.21 There are, of course, developments in reproductive technology that post-date the Act. An example is intra cytoplasmic sperm injection which was first performed successfully in 1992.[73] As a result of growing interest in ICSI, in 1995, HFEA set up a Working Group on New Developments in Reproductive Technology.[74] The Group's role includes advising HFEA on the progress and safety of, and the training standards for, new clinical and scientific techniques. This has led to HFEA adding additional standard conditions to the licences of those clinics carrying out ICSI in clinical practice. The conditions are to enable HFEA to monitor the safety and efficacy of the procedure at individual clinics, and to ensure the training and competence of those carrying out ICSI.[75]

10.22 A licence for the purposes of research may authorise the bringing about of the creation of embryos in vitro and the keeping or using of embryos,[76] but it cannot authorise any activity unless it appears to HFEA 'to be necessary or desirable'[77] for the purpose of:

(i)   promoting advances in the treatment of infertility;

(ii) increasing knowledge about the causes of congenital disease;

---

[68] See generally Sch 2.

[69] Sch 2, para 1(3).

[70] Sch 2, para 1(4).

[71] Sch 2, para 1(5).

[72] See *Fourth Annual Report*.

[73] See Gordts, S, Rombauts, L, Roziers, P, Serneels, A, Gaurois, B, Vereruyssen, M and Campo, R, 'ICSI in the Treatment of Male Subfertility' (1998) 81 *European Journal of Obstetrics, Gynaecology and Reproductive Biology* 207.

[74] Human Fertilisation and Embryology Authority, *Fourth Annual Report* (London: HFEA, 1995), 34 (it is pictured on the cover).

[75] Some of the problems associated with ICSI are described by Jones, S, *Y: The Descent of Men* (London: Little, Brown, 2002), 141.

[76] So long as they have not developed a primitive streak (s 3(3)(a), (4)).

[77] Sch 2, para 1(3).

(iii) increasing knowledge about the causes of miscarriages;

(iv) developing methods for detecting the presence of gene or chromosone abnormalities in embryos before implantation; or for such other purposes as may be specified by regulations, but these are limited to projects which 'increase knowledge about the creation and development of embryos, or about disease, or enable such knowledge to be applied'.[78]

A research licence cannot authorise altering the genetic structure of any cell while it forms part of an embryo, except in such circumstances, if any, as may be specified in or determined in pursuance of regulations.[79] The Code of Practice indicates that it is HFEA's policy not to license research projects involving embryo splitting with the intention of increasing the number of embryos available for transfer.[80]   **10.23**

A research licence can only authorise activities to be carried on in premises specified in the licence, and under the supervision of an individual designated in the licence.[81] No licence can authorise more than one research project: each proposed research project requires a separate licence.[82] No licence can authorise more than one individual who is to be responsible for the licensed activities,[83] nor apply to premises in different places.[84]   **10.24**

A licence which authorises treatment services or a licence which authorises research can also permit the storage of embryos or gametes. However, a treatment licence cannot authorise research. Nor can a research licence authorise treatment. Each of these activities must be considered in a separate licence application.[85] A storage licence may also be issued in its own right.[86]   **10.25**

Licences are granted to an individual, described in the 1990 Act as the 'person responsible'.[87] Treatment licences authorise particular classes of treatment to be carried out under the control of the 'person responsible' at the designated premises. Licences for research are granted for a specific project of research for one or more of the purposes set out in Sch 3, para 2 (and see para 10.22 above).   **10.26**

---

[78] Sch 2, para 3(3).
[79] Sch 2, para 3(4).
[80] *Code of Practice* (4th edn), para 10.5. This is confirmed in HFEA, *Tenth Annual Report and Accounts* (London: HFEA, 2002) 18.
[81] s 12(a).
[82] Sch 2, para 4(2)(b).
[83] Sch 2, para 4(2)(c).
[84] Sch 2, para 4(2)(a).
[85] Sch 2, para 4(2)(a).
[86] See Sch 2, para 4(2)(a) (licences for storage come within para 2).
[87] s 17.

10.27   Licences are subject to a maximum time-limit. This is five years in the case of licences for treatment[88] and for storage,[89] and three years in the case of licences for research.[90] Licences used to be renewable annually, but established clinics are now issued with three-year licences.

2. The Licence Committee

10.28   HFEA is to maintain one or more committees to discharge its functions of granting, varying, suspending and revoking licences.[91] Other functions may be discharged also by members or employees of HFEA.[92] A committee, other than a licence committee, may appoint sub-committees.[93] A licence committee is therefore the only committee that cannot delegate to a sub-committee. Also it cannot co-opt members other than existing members of HFEA. A licence committee consists of five members of HFEA: the required quorum is three. It must include at least one person who is not authorised to carry on or participate in any activity under the authority of a licence and would not be so authorised if any application s/he had made were approved.[94] The committee can run its own procedures in whatever way it sees fit.[95] However, the Secretary of State may make such regulations as appear to be 'necessary or desirable', in particular including provision for requiring persons to give evidence or produce documents and about the admissibility of evidence.[96]

10.29   A member of HFEA who is in any way directly or indirectly interested in a licence granted, or proposed to be granted, must disclose the nature of his/her interest to HFEA,[97] which must record this.[98] The member concerned is not to participate in any deliberation or decision with respect to the licence.[99] If he/she does so, the deliberation or decision will have no effect.[100] There can be no doubt that any breach of these rules would lead to a successful judicial review.

3. Licensing Procedure

10.30   A licence may be granted to any person who makes an application to HFEA in a

---

[88] Sch 2, para 1(5).
[89] Sch 2, para 2(3).
[90] Sch 2, para 3(9).
[91] s 9(1).
[92] s 9(2).
[93] s 9(3).
[94] s 9(5).
[95] Sch 1, para 9(1).
[96] s 10.
[97] Sch 1, para 10(1).
[98] Sch 1, para 10(2).
[99] Sch 1, para 10(3).
[100] Sch 1, para 10(3).

form approved and accompanied by the initial fee.[101] The requirements of s 16(2) must be satisfied. These are:

(a) that the application is for a licence designating an individual (it must be an individual and not a legal person) as the person under whose supervision the activities to be authorised by the licence are to be carried on,

(b) that either the individual is the applicant or—

    (i)   the application is made with the consent of that individual, and

    (ii) the licence committee is satisfied that the applicant is a suitable person to hold a licence,

(c) that the licence committee is satisfied that the character, qualifications and experience of that individual are such as are required for the supervision of the activities and that the individual will discharge the duty under s 17 . . .

(d) that the licence committee is satisfied that the premises in respect of which the licence is to be granted are suitable for the activities, and

(e) that the other requirements of [the] Act in relation to the granting of the licence are satisfied.

10.31 The initial fee is decided by HFEA with the approval of the Secretary of State and the Treasury. This is currently £200 for research-only and storage-only licences, and £500 for treatment licences. Additional fees are permitted, and these are required for treatment licences. HFEA aims to find 70 per cent of its expenditure through fees. Concerns have been raised that this could compromise HFEA's independence. There is no evidence of this. It has also been said that since patients ultimately foot the bill, this is in effect a 'tax on the infertile'.[102]

10.32 When an application is received, there is a site visit by a team of inspectors, consideration of the application and inspection report by a licence committee, and notification of the outcome to the applicant. If the applicant is not content with the decision, representations may be made to the committee before the decision takes effect. This may be followed by an appeal to the full Authority and, finally on a point of law, an applicant may appeal to the High Court.

10.33 There have been few refusals. Where treatment licences have been refused, the reasons for the refusal have been given to the applicants. According to HFEA: 'Generally these have been cases where the centres failed in significant ways to meet the standards required by the Act and the Code of Practice, and where it appeared to the licence committee that the centre would be unable to meet the required standard within a reasonable period of time'.[103] As HFEA acknowledged in its Second Annual Report, 'while much of the licensing procedure is set out in

---

[101] s 16 (1).
[102] See, in relation to so-called 'postcode lottery', The Times, 23 February 1999.
[103] HFEA, *Second Annual Report* (London: HFEA, 1993), 7.

statute [the 1990 Act], the corresponding administrative arrangements are entirely at the discretion of the authority'. It is therefore aware that 'it is important to ensure that the right information is available to centres, to inspectors and to licence committees'. It has accordingly standardised licence conditions 'to maintain consistency',[104] and to show how they relate to particular parts of the Code of Practice.

10.34   The 'person responsible' has a number of duties.[105] S/he must secure:

(i)   that the other persons to whom the licence applies are of suitable character and hold suitable qualifications to participate in the activities authorised by the licence. These people are those specified as any person designated in the Act or to whom the licence applies after notice has been given to HFEA. It includes any person acting under the direction of the person responsible;[106]

(ii)   that proper equipment is used;[107]

(iii)   that proper arrangements are made for the keeping of gametes and embryos and for the disposal of gametes and embryos that have been allowed to perish;[108] and

(iv)   that the conditions of the licence are complied with.[109]

4. Licence Conditions

10.35   Licences may be granted subject to conditions.[110] The 1990 Act lays down both general conditions, and conditions for licences for each of treatment,[111] storage[112] and research.[113]

(i) General Conditions

10.36   The general conditions, which must be imposed, are

(i)   licensed activities can only be carried on in the premises to which the licence relates and under the supervision of the 'person responsible';[114]

(ii)   proper records must be maintained in the form specified by HFEA.[115] Copies of extracts from those records or any other specified information is to be provided to HFEA when and how it specifies;[116]

---

[104] ibid.
[105] s 17.
[106] s 17(2)(c).
[107] s 17(1)(b).
[108] s 17(1)(c).
[109] s 17(1)(e).
[110] See generally Sch 2. The general conditions are in s 12.
[111] s 13.
[112] s 14.
[113] s 15.
[114] s 16, 17, and Sch 2, para 4(1).
[115] s 12(d).
[116] s 12(g).

(iii) the requirements as to written consent (see paras 10.111–10.116 below) must be complied with;[117]

(iv) no money or other benefit is to be given or received in the supply of gametes or embryos other than in accordance with authorisation given by HFEA in directions.[118]

It was suggested[119] that the waiving of charges for private treatment in consideration of the donation of eggs would be waiving a payment for advantage, and not a payment in money or money's worth, and therefore would have fallen outside the precursor of this provision. 'Money's worth' is not an identical concept to 'other benefit'. The latter is wider so that the example used should accordingly fall within the prohibition in s12(e). There is uneasiness surrounding payment but a concern that the entire service might be jeopardised if it were prohibited.[120] At present, expenses may be reimbursed. So long as expenses are allowed, the question needs to be answered as to how far the concept extends.[121] It is suggested that compensation for loss of earnings should be acceptable, but more dubious is recompense for inconvenience and discomfort. Morgan and Lee expressed the view that 'there is a good case for allowing financial benefit to be greater where more invasive procedures are used. However, the medical profession has generally disdained payments calibrated according to use. This would seem to militate against large sums of money being offered for the supply of healthy eggs.'[122] HFEA concluded in 1996 that a donation should be 'a gift, freely and voluntarily given'.[123] It was of the view that donors should not be out of pocket as a result of becoming donors, so that 'reasonable direct expenses', such as for travel and child care should be reimbursed. A Working Party then examined the implementation of this policy in detail. By 1999, however, HFEA concluded that it was not practicable to ban payments and it decided accordingly to allow £15 per donation, plus reasonable expenses, to continue.[124] It should be added that a person to whom a licence applies and who gives or receives any money or any benefit, other than in accordance with HFEA directions, commits an offence.[125] Such persons are liable on

---

[117] s 12(c) and Sch 3.
[118] s 12(e).
[119] By Morgan, D and Lee, R, *Blackstone's Guide To The Human Fertilisation and Embryology Act 1990.* (London: Blackstone Press, 1991), 99.
[120] See Deech, R, 'Payment to Gamete and Embryo Donors' (1999) 6(1) *Journal of Fertility Counselling* 6.
[121] It was reported in 1995 that a treatment centre was using an agency to pay women to donate eggs (The Guardian, 2 November 1995). This led to an amendment of directions in 1996 to cover payments from third parties.
[122] Morgan and Lee (n 119 above), 99.
[123] HFEA, *Fifth Annual Report* (London, HFEA, 1996), 23–4.
[124] HFEA, *Eighth Annual Report* (London, HFEA, 1999), 28. The issue of payment 'could not be considered as an issue of principle in isolation from others'.
[125] s 41(8).

summary conviction to imprisonment for six months or to a fine not exceeding level five on the standard scale or both.

(v) where gametes are supplied by one licence holder to another, the supplier is to give to the recipient such information as HFEA may specify in directions;[126]

(vi) any member or employee of HFEA is to be permitted to enter and inspect premises as well as equipment and records. Such persons may also observe any activity. Inspections are to be carried out at reasonable times. If required to do so, the member or employee must produce identification.[127]

10.37 HFEA may also attach further conditions.[128] These can be specific to the centre, and can relate to a range of issues. Many of the conditions imposed have related to security, counselling and confidentiality, as well as to the welfare to the child and information for patients. HFEA has reported that '[l]icence conditions have been used, when appropriate, as a means of applying pressure on centres to conform quickly in areas where there have been observed deficiencies in their practice'.[129] It is HFEA's view that it is 'reasonable for the Authority to recognise that in some centres it may take a little time to develop adequate procedures'.[130]

(ii) Treatment Licence Conditions

10.38 The 1990 Act prescribes conditions of licences for treatment. These relate to record-keeping. Such information is to be recorded as HFEA may specify in directions which relate to the persons for whom the services are provided in pursuance of the licence; the services provided; the persons whose gametes are kept or used for the purposes of services provided in pursuance of the licence or whose gametes have been used in bringing about the creation of embryos so kept or used; any child appearing to the person responsible to have been born as a result of treatment in pursuance of a licence; any mixing of sperm and eggs and any taking of an embryo from a woman or other acquisition of an embryo; and other matters specified by HFEA in directions.[131] Records are also to record consents required under Sch 3[132] to the 1990 Act.[133] No information may be removed from any records maintained in pursuance of the licence before the expiry of such period as may be

---

[126] s 12(f).
[127] s 12(b). See also the enforcement powers in s 39, which include retaining embryos or gametes (s 39 (3)).
[128] The ones in ss 12–15 are those which must be imposed: others may (and are).
[129] HFEA, *Second Annual Report* (London: HFEA, 1993).
[130] ibid.
[131] s 13(2).
[132] As to which see para 10.111, below.
[133] s 13(3).

specified in directions for records of the class in question.[134] Where a treatment licence holder does not know whether a child has been born following the provision of treatment services, the information held shall be maintained for a period of not less that 50 years from when it was first recorded.[135]

Two other conditions of licences for treatment, dealing with counselling and with the prospective welfare of any born as a result of treatment are considered below (see paras 10.117–10.123 and 10.85).

10.39

(iii) Research Licence Conditions

The conditions of research licences are: that the records maintained in pursuance of the licence shall include such information as the HFEA may specify;[136] that no information shall be removed from any records maintained in pursuance of the licence before the expiry of such period as may be specified in directions for records of the class in question;[137] that no embryo appropriated for the purposes of any project of research shall be kept or used otherwise than for the purposes of such a project.[138] This prohibits another line of research being carried out under the guise of the original research licence.[139]

10.40

(iv) Storage Licence Conditions

The 1990 Act prescribes conditions of storage licences.[140] Every licence must require that 'gametes of a person or an embryo taken from a woman shall be placed in storage only if received from that person or woman or acquired from a person to whom a licence applies', and that 'an embryo the creation of which has been brought about *in vitro* otherwise that in pursuance of that licence shall be placed in storage only if acquired from a person to whom a licence applies'.[141] An embryo may not be placed in storage if it has been created in vitro by an unlicensed person. The words 'a person to whom a licence applies' are ambiguous. Literally interpreted, it would include persons not licensed to bring about the creation of embryos (persons, indeed, who may have committed an offence in so doing). The better interpretation must be that it envisages persons licensed to bring about the creation of embryos.

10.41

In addition, it is a condition of every licence authorising the storage of gametes or embryos that gametes or embryos which are or have been stored shall not be

10.42

---

[134] s 13(4).
[135] s 24(1).
[136] s 15(2).
[137] s 15(3).
[138] s 15(4).
[139] Sch 2, para 4(2)(b).
[140] s 14.
[141] s 14(1)(a).

supplied to a person otherwise than in the course of providing treatment services unless that person is a person to whom a licence applies.[142]

10.43   The statutory storage (and freezing) period for gametes may not exceed ten years.[143] For embryos the period must not exceed five years.[144] If still stored at the end of these respective periods they must be allowed to perish.[145] An embryo created from stored gametes may itself be frozen and stored for five years. Accordingly, an embryo could be used for treatment services, or for the purposes of research, for up to 15 years after the egg or sperm from which it derives was donated. Regulations may, however, provide for a shorter maximum period of storage,[146] and, in circumstances as may be specified, a longer period.[147]

10.44   The Human Fertilisation and Embryology (Statutory Storage Period) Regulations 1991 have extended the storage period for gametes where:

the gametes were provided by a person:

(a)   whose fertility since providing them has or is likely to become, in the written opinion of a registered medical practitioner, significantly impaired,

(b)   who was aged under 45 on the date on which the gametes were provided, and

(c)   who does not consent to the gametes being used for the purpose of providing treatment services to persons other than that person, or that person and another together, and has never so consented while the gametes were ones to which this regulation applied.[148]

Thus the storage period for a 25-year-old, about to undergo radiotherapy for cancer, would be 30 years, that is calculated as the normal ten years maximum for storage of gametes plus 20 further years.

5. Prohibited Activities

10.45   Sections 3 (as amended, see below paras. 10.54–10.56) and 4 of the 1990 Act prohibit certain activities in connection with embryos (s 3) and gametes (s 4).

10.46   No person may bring about the creation of an embryo, or keep or use an embryo, except in pursuance of a licence.[149] 'Embryo' is defined as a 'live human embryo where fertilisation is complete',[150] but it also includes, puzzlingly, 'an egg in the

---

[142] s 14(1)(b).
[143] s 14(3).
[144] s 14(4).
[145] s 14(1)(c).
[146] s 14(5)(a).
[147] s 14(5)(b).
[148] SI 1991/1540, reg 2(2).
[149] s 3(1).
[150] s 1(1)(a).

process of fertilisation',[151] though, for this purpose, 'fertilisation is not complete until the appearance of a two cell zygote'.[152] The intention of Parliament is to require a licence for any activity which results in the creation of an embryo ex utero. But the language used is confusing and clumsy. Nor may it be any longer apt because an embryo may be created by cell nucleus replacement and not from the fusing of egg and sperm. In such a situation fertilisation never takes place. But in *R (on the application of Quintavalle) v Secretary of State for Health*,[153] the House of Lords expressed the opinion that the words 'where fertilisation is complete' were not 'intended to form an integral part of the definition of embryo but were directed to the time at which it should be treated as such'.[154] Lord Millett observed that Parliament had not banned the placing of 'a human embryo in an animal where this was created by cell nucleus replacement, and therefore not by fertilisation, but, as he rightly commented, this would be no 'less abhorrent'[155] than doing so where an embryo was created by fertilisation (and see para 10.50).

The placing in a woman of a live embryo, other than a human embryo, or live gametes, other than human gametes, is prohibited.[156] **10.47**

Research on embryos is permitted provided HFEA has licensed the research project.[157] Licences may only be granted for certain purposes, for example to promote advances in the treatment of infertility and to increase knowledge about the causes of congenital disease.[158] Since January 2001 stem cell research has also been covered.[159] **10.48**

However, a licence cannot authorise keeping or using an embryo after the appearance of the primitive streak.[160] The primitive streak is to be taken to have appeared in an embryo not later than the end of the period of 14 days beginning with the day when the gametes are mixed, not counting any time during which the embryo is stored.[161] Note, however, that treatment licences may authorise practices **10.49**

---

[151] s 1(1)(b). Mary Warnock has written that since, in 1990, it was assumed the only way to produce an embryo was by fertilisation, the four words were 'otiose' (*Making Babies* (Oxford: OUP, 2002), 100).

[152] ibid.

[153] [2003] 2 All ER 113.

[154] ibid, 119.

[155] ibid, 129.

[156] s 3(2).

[157] Sch 2, para 3(1)(b).

[158] s 3(3)(a).

[159] Initially recommended by the HGAC and HFEA in *Cloning Issues In Reproduction, Science and Medicine* (London: Human Genetics Advisory Commission, 1998), and endorsed in *Stem Cell Research: Medical Progress and Responsibility* (London: Department of Health, 2000). The change is in Human Fertilisation and Embryology (Research Purposes) Regulations 2001, SI 2001/188, reg 2(2).

[160] s 3(3)(a).

[161] s 3(4). This endorses the opinion of the majority of the Warnock Committee (n 7 above), para 11.30.

designed to secure that 'embryos are in a suitable condition to be placed in a woman or to determine whether embryos are suitable for that purpose'.[162] This author agrees with Lee and Morgan that this may legitimate practices which in practice look 'uncommonly like research'.[163] Since no embryo 'appropriated for the purposes of any project of research' may be kept or used otherwise, embryos that have been the subject of research may not be returned to the womb of a woman.[164]

10.50 A licence cannot authorise the placing of an embryo in any animal.[165] There is no similar prohibition in the legislation on the placing of human sperm and an egg in an animal. The mixing of gametes with the live gametes of an animal is prohibited, except in pursuance of a licence,[166] but what is here envisaged is different. The placing of human sperm and eggs in an animal would probably require a licence: it would if the gametes were then 'stored' in the animal's uterus.[167] Although this seems a far-fetched argument, it would have the merit of bringing any such experiment within the framework of licensing and presumably, therefore, stopping it.[168]

10.51 A licence cannot authorise the keeping or using an embryo in any circumstances in which regulations prohibit its keeping or use.[169]

10.52 A licence cannot authorise replacing a nucleus of a cell of an embryo with a nucleus taken from the cell of any person, embryo or subsequent development of an embryo.[170] There is no doubt that Parliament intended to prohibit cloning[171] and, where the technique involves replacing the nucleus of a cell of an embryo with a nucleus taken from elsewhere (a person or another embryo), has done so. But cell nucleus substitution and cell fusion do not involve the replacement of the nucleus of the cell of an embryo: rather the replacement of the nucleus of an unfertilised egg. So how is this provision to be interpreted? If interpreted literally it prohibits

---

[162] Sch 2, para 1(1)(d).

[163] Lee and Morgan (n 9 above), 88.

[164] s 15(4)

[165] s 3(3)(b).

[166] s 4(1)(c).

[167] s 4(1)(a). On the meaning of 'stored' see also s 2(2).

[168] Carl Wood and Anne Westmore (see *Test-Tube Conception* (London: Allen and Unwin, 1984)) apparently did try, unsuccessfully, to introduce human eggs and sperm into the fallopian tube of a sheep. They were 'relieved' when it failed, since 'it may have been difficult to convince the community that the sheep was an appropriate place for human fertilisation and early human development'.

[169] s 3(3)(c).

[170] s 3(3)(d).

[171] In the 1990 Act, s 3(3)(d). It was the view of the HGAC and HFEA in their Consultation Paper on cloning and their report *Cloning Issues In Human Reproduction* (1998) and of the Chief Medical Officer (see *Stem Cell Research* (2000)) that nuclear replacement was within the 1990 Act. See *Cloning Issues*, para 3.4. HFEA made it clear that it would not issue a licence for research which has reproductive cloning as its aim (ibid, para 5.4).

only 'embryo nucleus replacement'. 'Cell nucleus substitution' and 'cell fusion' do not involve the replacement of the nucleus of the cell of an embryo.[172] A strict interpretation of the words of the prohibition in s 3(3)(d) suggests that techniques of cloning not contemplated, or at least not possible, in 1990, when the prohibition was formulated, are not caught.[173] Nor is 'embryo splitting'.[174] This occurs naturally at a very early stage of embryonic development in the formation of identical twins and can be done in vitro in some species at the eight-cell stage with the result that 'cloned' embryos may develop. HFEA decided in 1994 to ban embryo splitting as a possible fertility treatment,[175] but it did not similarly prohibit cell nuclear replacement research.

It is a standard principle of statutory construction that penal provisions should be **10.53** interpreted in the defendant's favour.[176] Were the 'Dolly' technique[177] applied to human reproduction it would not involve the creation of an embryo at all because the Act defines an embryo as a 'live human embryo where fertilisation is complete',[178] including 'an egg in the process of fertilisation'.[179] Fertilisation does not take place when a cell is cloned. However, both the HGAC and HFEA in their 1998 Report[180] and the Chief Medical Officer's report *Stem Cell Research* in 2000[181] rejected these arguments, and concluded that cloning was either prohibited or subject to licensing (depending on the method used), and the HGAC and HFEA indicated that no licences for research into reproductive cloning would be issued.[182] The HGAC and HFEA concluded in their joint report that while, 'the nuclear replacement of eggs [was] not expressly prohibited', it involved 'the use or creation of embryos outside the body', and so fell within the Act and the 'jurisdiction of HFEA'.[183] This interpretation is purposive in that it undoubtedly achieves the result that Parliament intended in 1990. Beyleveld and Pattinson are of the opinion that 'in practice, it is very unlikely that the term "fertilisation" will

---

[172] See Klotzko, AJ, *The Cloning Sourcebook* (New York: OUP, 2001).

[173] Because what is prohibited is 'replacement'.

[174] It is thought that this would anyway 'probably not be very effective in the human', even though monozygotic twins and higher multiples do occur naturally (see opinion of the Group of Advisers on The Ethical Implications of Biotechnology of the European Commission in Klotzko (n 168 above), 284, 285–286).

[175] HFEA, *Third Annual Report* (London: HFEA, 1994), 11. And see *Code of Practice* (5th edn, 2001), para 9.11.

[176] See *DPP v Ottewell* [1970] AC 642, 649 *per* Lord Reid. But courts now tend to adopt a purposive approach even to the interpretation of penal statutes.

[177] Wilmut, I, Schnieke, AE, McWhir, J, Kind, AJ, Campbell, KHS, 'Viable Offspring Derived from Fetal and Adult Mammalian Cells' (1997) 385 *Nature* 810.

[178] s 1(1)(a).

[179] s 1(1)(b).

[180] *Cloning Issues in Human Reproduction, Science and Medicine* (London: HGAC, 1998), para 3.4.

[181] *Stem Cell Research*.

[182] *Cloning Issues in Human Reproduction, Science and Medicine* (n 180 above), para 5.4.

[183] ibid, para 3.4.

not be judicially construed to include the nuclear substitution of an egg, especially since HFEA seems to be acting according to the construction of this term'.[184] This prediction has proved to be accurate, as we will see shortly.[185] The All-Parliamentary Pro-Life Group, responding to the HGAC/HFEA report also observe that it was the 'clear intention of Parliament . . . to prohibit the creation of cloned human embryos, both for research and reproductive purposes' but, concerned that the legislation of 1990 might not hit its target, argued for legislation to put the matter beyond doubt.[186] Lee and Morgan took a different approach. They could see no 'difficulty in accepting the view to which the HFEA works, that the creation of embryos by cell nucleus substitution is *already* brought within the scheme of the Act by an extended interpretation of s.1'.[187] But they also draw attention to the fact that s 1(1)(a) states that 'embryo means a live human embryo where fertilisation is complete' except where otherwise stated. Parliament, they point out, 'could have provided for embryos created other than by *in vitro* fertilisation to be included within the statute but evidently did not do so'.[188] That is correct but unrealistic. Parliament could not provide for that which was beyond the realms of science in 1990. It is their view that whether a literal or purposive interpretation is adopted should depend on context.[189] If an embryologist advised of the literal interpretation argument were to be prosecuted for conducting experiments which on their face fall outside the Act, he should, they argue, be able to seek the protection of literalism. If, on the other hand, the case were to be litigated as a judicial review challenging the refusal of HFEA to grant a licence to conduct experiments on cell nucleus replacement embryos, 'the strength of the case for a literal rather than a purposive interpretation of the Act is far less compelling'.[190]

10.54 The legality of cell nucleus replacement embryology was ultimately litigated in neither of the contexts envisaged by Lee and Morgan. *R (on the application of Quintavalle) v Secretary of State for Health*[191] was a challenge on behalf of the Pro-Life Alliance. This succeeded at first instance. Crane J ruled that an 'embryo' created by cell nucleus replacement was not protected by the 1990 Act, so that no licence was required for the creation or use of embryos created by this process. Crane J adopted a literal interpretation of the Act, which so concerned Parliament that within 19 days of the judgment it had enacted the Human Reproductive Cloning Act 2001. The aim of this Act is to prevent human reproductive cloning

---

[184] Beyleveld, D and Pattinson, S, *The Ethics of Genetics in Human Procreation* (Aldershot: Ashgate, 2000), 233.
[185] See the Court of Appeal's decision in *R (on the application of Quintavalle) v Secretary of State for Health*, para 10.55 below.
[186] All Parliamentary Group (1998), para 1. 3. 2–3.
[187] Lee and Morgan (n 9 above), 94.
[188] ibid, 95.
[189] ibid.
[190] ibid.
[191] [2001] 4 All ER 1013.

taking place in the United Kingdom by making it a criminal offence to place in the womb of a woman a human embryo that has been created other than by fertilisation. This Act came into force on 4 December 2001. The offence carries a maximum sentence of ten years or a fine (which is unspecified) or both.[192] A prosecution requires the consent of the Director of Public Prosecutions.[193] The limitations of this legislation are discussed below (para 10.56).

After the 2001 Act came into operation the Court of Appeal allowed the Secretary of State for Health's appeal.[194] It held that an organism created by cell nucleus replacement came within the definition of 'embryo' in s 1(1) of the 1990 Act. It achieved this result by a deliberate invocation of purposive construction. Lord Phillips of Worth Matravers MR said, 'the court has to ask, not what would Parliament have enacted if it had foreseen the creation of embryos by CNR, but, do such embryos plainly fall within the genus covered by the legislation and will the clear purpose of the legislation be defeated if the extension is not made'.[195] In his view:

> The fact that the organism was created by fertilisation was not a factor of particular relevance to the desirability of regulation.
>
> The embryo created by cell nuclear replacement and the embryo created by fertilisation are essentially identical as far as structure is concerned. . . . It is the capacity to develop into a human being that is the significant factor and that it is one that is shared by both types of embryo.[196]

He found 'the most compelling reasons for giving s 1 of the 1990 Act the strained construction for which [counsel for the Secretary of State] contends, and very little that weighs against it'.[197] The House of Lords agreed.[198] Their Lordships accepted that s 3(3)(d) of the 1990 Act did 'not prohibit cloning in general but only cloning when the host is an existing embryo',[199] that it was directed at nucleus substitution and not nucleus replacement. Like the Court of Appeal, the Lords adopted a purposive construction of the legislation.[200] Lord Bingham conceded that there were provisions in the 1990 Act which could not apply in embryos created by cell nucleus replacement, but he thought the 'discrepancies were not significant'.[201] It was the view of the Lords that the 1990 Act should be construed in

10.55

---

[192] s 1(2).
[193] s 1(3).
[194] [2002] 2 FCR 140.
[195] ibid, 150.
[196] ibid, 150–151.
[197] ibid, 154.
[198] [2003] 2 All E R 113.
[199] *Per* Lord Hoffmann, ibid, 127.
[200] Lord Steyn observed that the 'pendulum has swung to purposive construction', ibid, 123.
[201] ibid, 121.

the light of contemporary scientific knowledge.[202] Seen thus, it was straightforward to conclude that Parliament did not intend to distinguish live human embryos produced by fertilisation from those produced without such fertilisation.[203] Lord Steyn summarises the Lords' ruling as follows: 'The long title of the 1990 Act makes clear, and it is in any event self-evident, that Parliament intended the protective regulatory system in connection human embryos to be comprehensive. This proactive purpose was plainly not intended to be tied to the particular way in which an embryo might be created. The overall ethical case for protection was general. Not surprisingly there is not a hint of a rational explanation why an embryo produced otherwise than by fertilisation should not have the same status as an embryo created by fertilisation. It is a classic case where the new scientific development falls within . . . "the same genus of facts" and in any event there is clear legislative purpose which can only be fulfilled if an extensive interpretation is adopted'.[204] He was 'fully satisfied that cell nucleus replacement falls within the scope of the carefully balanced and crafted 1990 Act'.[205]

10.56   On one view this decision is unnecessary, given the new legislation, but it will remain of importance because the 2001 Act has significant limitations.[206] Thus, it makes it an offence to place a human embryo 'in a woman' if this has been created otherwise than by fertilisation. It does not therefore criminalise the incubation (by ectogenesis, for example[207]) and use of a cloned human embryo outside the body of a woman. Nor, it seems, would the time limits in the 1990 Act apply in such a case. The Act also will not prevent human clones being exported—and European legislation may assist this[208]—for implantation into a woman in a country where this is not prohibited (Belgium or the Netherlands for example[209]). In addition, the Act uses, but does not define, the concepts 'embryo' and 'fertilisation'. We must assume, if we can assume anything, that Parliament intended these concepts to have the meanings given to them by the 1990 Act (see para 10.46).

---

[202] See eg Lord Steyn, ibid, at 124.

[203] See eg Lord Bingham, ibid at 118.

[204] ibid.

[205] ibid.

[206] And see Wood, P and Good, J, 'Human Reproductive Cloning—Nipped in the Bud?' (2001) 151 *NLJ* 1760. But *cf* Grubb, A, 'Reproductive Cloning in the UK' (2002) 10 Med L Rev 327–329 who concludes that the 2001 Act is 'very clever' (see at 328).

[207] See Singer and Wells (n 15 above).

[208] EC Treaty, Art 49. And see R *v Human Fertilisation and Embryology Authority, ex p Blood* [1997] 2 All ER 687, and *U v W* [1997] 2 FLR 282.

[209] It is common to use Italy as an example but a decree in 1997 prohibits all forms of experimentation directed at cloning. Nevertheless, the impression is conveyed that assisted reproduction is unregulated and Dr Severino Antinori has claimed to have cloned the first human foetus. See The Observer, 26 May 2002, 4. And see Cibelli, J, Lanza, R, West, M and Ezzell, C, 'The First Human Cloned Embryo', *Scientific American*, January 2002, 42.

The question is thus asked:[210] '. . . would "fertilisation" encompass kick-starting an organism created by CNR [cell nucleus replacement] into growing by using sperm extracts or "artificial sperm"? Such sperm could in the future be engineered to be devoid of genetic material (therefore falling outside the scientific definition of a "gamete") but retain the ability to trigger growth of an organism created by CNR. The result would be a cloned human, genetically identical to the nucleus donor, but arguably "created by fertilisation" and therefore not caught by the new Act'. It may be doubted whether Parliament has understood cloning. It has certainly failed to define it in an Act which purportedly bans human reproductive cloning. If an embryo is created from one individual (there is no mixing of genetic material), it is difficult to see, short of further purposive interpretation, how the 2001 Act impacts upon it. But whatever, it is unlikely that legislation will keep pace with scientific development. And this may suggest that regulation is best left to a standing and professionally-equipped body, namely the Authority.

At first instance Crane J raised a number of other questions which were not dealt with by the Court of Appeal or the House of Lords. His remarks, it should be stressed, are obiter, but since the questions are left open by the amending legislation they cannot be ignored. He considered what the implications would be, were he wrong in his interpretation of the main question, and an organism produced by cell nucleus replacement were held to be an 'embryo'. It would then fall within the licensing framework. Does this mean that experimentation on such an organism would be allowed for only 14 days? (see para 10.49). It would seem that the 14-day time limit should not apply because this is calculated by reference to 'when the gametes are mixed' (s 3(4)). Crane J accepted this, but held that nevertheless the organism could not be kept beyond the appearance of the primitive streak because notwithstanding that the 14-day time limit would not apply, the primitive streak would appear. The 14-day time limit was a 'deeming provision' and as such would bring the organism produced by cell nucleus replacement back within the definition of 'embryo'. If, therefore, a licence were ever issued in relation to an organism produced by cell nucleus replacement, it would have to comply with s 3(3)(a) of the 1990 Act. He added that it would fall to HFEA to decide whether to include in such a licence a 14-day time limit.[211] It is difficult to see why he should have thought that HFEA would have such a discretion, unless real doubts about keeping and experimenting upon embryos after this period of time remain. **10.57**

Crane J also addressed the consent question (and see para 10.111). In particular, he speculated on the following (the supposition being that 'embryo' included an **10.58**

---

[210] Wood and Good (n 206 above), 1762. See also the view of Pattinson, S, *Influencing Traits Before Birth* (Aldershot: Ashgate, 2002) that 'a better approach would have been to modify the definition of an embryo under the 1990 Act so that it covered any human embryo capable of implantation' (at 125).
[211] N 191 above, 1022–3.

organism created by cell nucleus replacement): a woman donates an unfertilised egg, from which a nucleus is then removed before cell nucleus replacement. There is then inserted into her egg a nucleus from *any* cell, not necessarily from an egg, sperm or embryo, of the person to be 'cloned'. Whose consent would be required? Crane J, expressed the view obiter, that the 1990 Act would require consent from the woman donor, but not from the individual whose cell nucleus was used for transplanting into the donor's denucleated egg. It may be thought extraordinary that the individual to be 'cloned' would not have to consent. [212] It is difficult to imagine that this can have been Parliament's intention in 1990. But neither the Court of Appeal, the House of Lords or Parliament in 2001 addresses this question.

10.59   There are other prohibited activities. Gametes (ova or sperm) cannot be stored, and thus frozen, without a licence.[213] A licence is also required for the mixing of gametes with the live gametes of any animal.[214]

10.60   A licence cannot authorise storing or using gametes in any circumstances in which regulations prohibit their storage or use.[215]

10.61   No person is to place sperm and eggs in a woman in any circumstances specified in regulations except in pursuance of a licence.[216] Regulations could bring gamete intra-fallopian transfer (GIFT), using the couple's own gametes, which currently falls outside the 1990 Act, into the regulatory framework of the Act, but this has not been done. Nevertheless HFEA's Code of Practice purports to subject GIFT to the 'welfare of the child' conditions (and see para 10.84).[217] But, as a licence is not needed to carry out GIFT, it is difficult to see whether there could be any sanction for failing to observe this advice.

10.62   No person, in the course of providing treatment services for any woman, is to use the sperm of any man, unless the services are being provided for the woman and the man together.[218] This, as we shall see (para 10.177) was one of the stumbling blocks to the treatment of Mrs Diane Blood after the death of her husband.[219] Nor can the eggs of any other woman be used.[220] It is clear, however, from the wording of s 4(1)(b) that the Act does not apply where the sperm of a living male partner is being used.

---

[212]   ibid, 1023.
[213]   s 4(1)(a) and s 2(2).
[214]   s 4(1)(c).
[215]   s 4(2).
[216]   s 4(3).
[217]   N 175 above, para 3.9.
[218]   s 4(1)(b).
[219]   Thus, not only did the removal of sperm from Mr Blood breach the Act, but so did the insemination of Mrs Blood.
[220]   s 4(1)(b).

Also now prohibited is the use of 'female germ cells taken or derived from an embryo or foetus' or the use of 'embryos created by using such cells', where this is done 'for the purpose of providing fertility services for any woman'.[221] This overcomes the problem that foetal eggs are not gametes, and thus the storage and use of them (or foetal cells) fell outside the 1990 Act. The proposer of the amendment (in 1994)[222] wanted, as she put it, 'to send a message out to scientists that there is no point in spending any more time on research [on aborted foetuses], or in messing about with aborted mouse eggs, rat eggs, or anything similar. The end product from using aborted human eggs for fertilisation purposes will simply not be allowed to be used.'[223] But the new provision does not go as far as this: it prohibits only the use of cells from an aborted foetus to create an embryo 'for the purpose of assisting women to carry children'. As a result, cells or eggs from an aborted foetus may still be used to create an embryo for the purpose of research, provided this complies with the limits on research imposed by the 1990 Act (see para 10.48). It is also possible to do research on the cells themselves. HFEA has 'no objection in principle'[224] to the use of eggs from adult female cadavers: it does not, however, approve their use in infertility treatment, although licences may be granted for research on ovarian tissue from cadavers.

10.63

Although not its primary purpose, the new provision also clarifies the law on the use of foetal eggs for treatment. As the HFEA Report on *Donated Ovarian Tissue in Embryo Research and Assisted Conception* points out, the 1990 Act, as originally formulated, controls only the use of mature eggs (or 'gametes').[225] Foetal eggs are not, as pointed out above (para 10.63), gametes. Thus, for example, under the 1990 Act a licence is required and the donor's consent must be obtained only for the storage or use of gametes (and see para 10.25): the storage and use of foetal eggs were not controlled by the original Act at all. The new s 3A (inserted by the Criminal Justice and Public Order Act 1994, s 156) makes it clear that the statutory prohibition extends to the use of foetal germ cells or eggs for treatment.

10.64

As pointed out above (para 10.63), the use of foetal eggs for research is not banned or controlled by either the 1990 Act or its 1994 amendment. The Polkinghorne report[226] recommended that the use of foetal material for research purposes should be allowed subject to (i) the consent of the mother[227] (though not the

10.65

---

[221] s 3A, inserted by the Criminal Justice and Public Order Act 1994, s 164.
[222] Dame Jill Knight.
[223] *Hansard*, HC vol 241, col 158.
[224] HFEA, *Report on Donated Ovarian Tissue in Embryo Research and Assisted Conception* (London: HFEA, 1994).
[225] ibid, para 20.
[226] *Review of the Guidance on the Research Use of Fetuses and Fetal Material* (Cm 762, 1989).
[227] ibid, paras 3.10 and 6.3.

father);[228] (ii) the consent should be general rather than specific,[229] (iii) there should be no inducements.[230] The Polkinghorne committee rejected the need for legislation, favouring instead regulation through research ethics committees. The European Parliament, however, has said that 'it is not enough to regulate the problems by means of guidelines within the medical profession'.[231] But, although it has prohibited the creation of embryos for research purposes[232]—the 1990 Act is in breach of this and will doubtless lead to a reservation when the United Kingdom adopts the European Convention on Human Rights and Biomedicine—it does nothing to regulate this by other means. It may be thought that the 1994 amendment, as so often hastily drafted and barely debated, has obstructed proper Parliamentary consideration of these issues. Although further legislation is needed, none is anticipated in the foreseeable future.[233]

6. Directions, Regulations and the Code of Practice

10.66   Section 23 of the 1990 Act empowers HFEA to give directions for any purpose for which directions may be given under the Act, or directions varying or revoking such directions. A person to whom any requirement contained in directions is applicable must comply with the requirement.[234] Directions may be general or given to a particular person (or clinic). A licence can be revoked if the 'person responsible' fails to comply with directions given in connection with any licence.[235] Directions may be given for a very wide range of regulatory purposes. These are (in the order they appear in the 1990 Act):

(i)   maintenance of proper records in the form specified;[236]

(ii)   authorising payment or other benefit for gametes or embryos,[237] which would otherwise be unlawful (most reported directions are in relation to this);

---

[228] ibid, para 6.7. His relationship to the foetus was said to be less intimate. HFEA (n 226 above) endorses the Polkinghorne recommendation that the mother's consent should be obtained (see paras 5 and 17).

[229] It was thought undesirable to allow the woman to specify possible uses of foetal tissue since this might influence the timing and techniques used in the abortion procedure.

[230] And see HFEA Report (n 224 above), para 7.

[231] European Parliament, Committee on Legal Affairs and Citizens' Rights, *Ethical and Legal Problems of Genetic Engineering and Human Artificial Insemination* (Luxembourg, 1990), Resolution 31.

[232] European Convention on Human Rights and Biomedicine, Art 18(2). If the UK signs (or ratifies) the Convention, it will doubtless enter a reservation under Art 36.

[233] See, further, Plomer, A and Martin-Clement, N, 'The Limits of Beneficence: Egg Donation under the Human Fertilisation and Embryology Act 1990' (1995) 15 *LS* 434.

[234] s 23(2).

[235] s 18(1)(c).

[236] s 12(d).

[237] s 12(e).

(iii)   information to be supplied to the licensed recipients of gametes or embryos;[238]

(iv)   information to be recorded in pursuance of a treatment licence;[239]

(v)   length of time for which information must be maintained;[240]

(vi)   records dealing with the storage of gametes or embryos to include the consents required for their storage, the terms of those consents and the circumstances of the storage, and any other matters which HFEA specifies;[241]

(vii)   length of time for which information about the storage of gametes or embryos must be preserved;[242]

(viii)   information to be maintained in research licence records, the length of time for which such information must be held;[243]

(ix)   in respect of treatment licences which involve any of

   (a)   bringing about the creation of an embryo in vitro,

   (b)   keeping embryos,

   (c)   using gametes,

   (d)   any therapeutic practice with an embryo to ensure it is in a suitable condition for transfer to a woman,

   (e)   placing an embryo in a woman,

   (f)   using the hamster or other specified test to determine the fertility or normality of sperm, or

   (g)   any other specified practice,[244]

information is to be recorded and given to HFEA in respect of:

   (a)   the persons for whom any of these service have been provided,

   (b)   the services provided,

   (c)   the persons whose gametes are kept or used for those purposes or the bringing about the creation of any embryo,

   (d)   any child appearing to the person responsible to have been born as a result of the licensed treatment service, and

   (e)   any mixing of egg and sperm or taking of an embryo from any woman or other acquisition of an embryo from another licensed person, whether inside or outside the United Kingdom.[245]

(x)   the receiving or sending of embryos or gametes from the United Kingdom (or to it) to be subject to specified conditions, and the provisions dealing with conditions (in ss 12–14) to be modified accordingly;[246]

---

[238]   s 12(f).
[239]   s 13(a)–(f).
[240]   s 13(4).
[241]   s 14(1)(d).
[242]   s 14(2).
[243]   s 15(2), (3).
[244]   Sch 2, para 1.
[245]   s 2(2) and s 13(2)(a)–(e).
[246]   s 24(4).

(xi) licence committees to direct what is to happen where a licence is to be varied or cease to have effect, whether by expiry, suspension, revocation or otherwise;[247]

(xii) the draft code, as approved by the Secretary of State, to come into force in accordance with directions;[248]

(xiii) the egg of an animal other than a hamster not to be used under a treatment or research licence to test the fertility or normality of sperm until proposed directions have been reported by the Secretary of State to each House of Parliament.[249]

10.67 Where there is a breach of directions or one is alleged HFEA may make preliminary enquiries and if these establish evidence of a breach refer its findings to a licence committee (see para 10.28) which will make the decision on further action (if any). Should this lead to a decision to revoke or suspend a licence, there is an appeal to an appeal committee, and to the High Court on a point of law. If enquiries reveal a criminal offence, the matter should be referred to the Director of Public Prosecutions.

10.68 The Secretary of State may make regulations by statutory instrument. Section 45(4) requires regulations in three areas to be submitted for affirmative resolution. These are:

(i) regulations which would permit the keeping or use of an embryo in a way or for a period of time prohibited in the 1990 Act (s 3(3)(c));

(ii) regulations which would relax the law prohibiting the storage or use of gametes (s 4(2));

(iii) regulations which would relax the law prohibiting the alteration of the genetic structure of any cell while it forms part of an embryo (Sch 2, para 1(4)).

10.69 There are other matters which fall within the negative resolution procedure.[250] These are:

(i) additional functions to be undertaken by HFEA (s 8(d));

(ii) composition of HFEA licence committees (s 9(5));

(iii) changes in the licensing procedure (s 10(1), (2));

(iv) changes in permitted periods for the storage of gametes or embryos (s 14(5));

(v) any changes in the information which HFEA must disclose to an applicant under s 31 (s 31(4)(a)) (and see para 10.144).

---

[247] s 24(5)–(7).
[248] s 26(5).
[249] s 24(11), Sch 2, para 1(1)(f), Sch 3, para 2(4).
[250] s 45(5).

HFEA is obliged to maintain a Code of Practice giving guidance about the proper **10.70** conduct of activities carried on in pursuance of a licence under this Act, and the proper discharge of the functions of the person responsible and any other persons to whom the licence applies.[251] In particular, the Code is to include guidance 'for those providing treatment services about the account to be taken of the welfare of children who may be born as a result of treatment services (including a child's need for a father), and of any other children who may be affected by such births'.[252] The Code may also give guidance 'about the use of any technique involving the placing of sperm and eggs in a woman'.[253] HFEA is given the power to revise the Code. It has done this four times: the Code is now in its fifth edition,[254] and a sixth edition is imminent. The object of the Code, as stated in the Introduction to the Fifth Edition:

> . . . is wider than to secure the safety and efficacy of particular clinical or scientific practices which raise fundamental and ethical and social questions. In framing it, we have been guided both by the requirements of the . . . Act and by:
> —the respect which is due to human life at all stage in its development;
> —the right of people who are or may be infertile to the proper consideration of their request for treatment;
> —a concern for the welfare of children, which cannot always be adequately protected by concern for the interests of the adults involved; and
> —a recognition of the benefits, both to individuals and to society which can flow from the responsible pursuit of medical and scientific knowledge.[255]

Each edition of the Code has had broadly the same format. The fifth edition has a **10.71** new structure, with individual chapters divided into a general section applicable to all individuals followed by some more specific sections for people seeking treatment, people providing gametes and embryos for donation, people seeking longer term storage of gametes, and people involved in egg sharing arrangements. The fifth edition contains numerous substantive changes on;

(i)   advertising;
(ii)   annex of guidelines produced by professional organisations;
(iii)   calculating the limit of ten for donors;
(iv)   clinical responsibility;
(v)   Data Protection Act;
(vi)   egg sharing;
(vii)   embryo donation;

---

[251] s 25(1).
[252] s 25(2).
[253] s 25(3).
[254] This was published in 2001. A sixth edition was scheduled to be published in spring 2003 but had not yet been published on 1 December 2003 (see HFEA, *Tenth Annual Report and Accounts* (London: HFEA, 2002), 16).
[255] HFEA, *Code of Practice* (5th edn), 7.

(viii) home insemination;
(ix) long term storage;
(x) payment of expenses to donors;
(xi) production of sperm at home;
(xii) reduction of the upper age limit of sperm donors;
(xiii) research licensing;
(xiv) safe cryopreservation;
(xv) screening for surrogacy arrangements;
(xvi) screening of people considering donation.

10.72 Failing to observe the Code will not of itself give rise to civil or criminal liability.[256] However, a licence committee may, in considering, where it has power to do so, whether or not to vary or revoke a licence, take into account any observance of or failure to observe the provisions of the Code. In addition, a licence committee must, in considering whether there has been any failure to comply with any licence conditions, in particular conditions requiring anything to be 'proper' or 'suitable', take account of any relevant provision of the Code.[257]

10.73 Whether the Code of Practice is effective has been questioned. According to research conducted by Savas and Treece[258] it has not prevented inconsistent decisions. The Code gives scope for different interpretations and leads these researchers to conclude that it is of questionable legal value. But, as Lee and Morgan point out, 'there are local ethics committees and . . . there is a hierarchy of regulatory mechanism, with the Code ranking lowest in terms of its prescription'.[259] The fact that there have been few legal challenges to HFEA must be attributed in part to the success of the Code of Practice.

7. Challenging Decisions

10.74 If a condition is imposed which the applicant does not like, s/he may apply for a variation of that condition.[260] Applications may be made by the 'person responsible' or the nominal licensee. However, the licence can only be varied so far as it relates to the activities authorised by the licence by changing the manner in which the licensed activities are conducted or the conditions of the licence.[261] To the extent that the licence authorises the conduct of activities of licensed premises, the licence can be varied only so far to extend or restrict the premises to which the

---

[256] s 25(6).
[257] s 25(6)(a).
[258] Savas, D, and Treece, S, 'Fertility Clinics: One Code of Practice?' (1998) 3 *Medical Law International* 243.
[259] Lee and Morgan (n 9 above), 112.
[260] s 18(4).
[261] s 18(6)(a).

licence relates.[262] So an application to vary a licence cannot add new premises which were previously unlicensed, nor can it add new services, nor can it authorise the conduct of an activity, not previously authorised, which will need a separate application for a new licence. However, it may, on an application by the nominal licensee, vary the licence so as to designate another individual in place of the 'person responsible' if the committee is satisfied that the character, qualifications and experience of the other individual will discharge the duties stipulated in s 17 of the 1990 Act.[263]

The other avenue open to an aggrieved applicant is recourse to ordinary public law remedies. Thus, the conditions imposed by HFEA must be '*Wednesbury* reasonable'.[264] As formulated by Lord Greene MR, 'a person entrusted with a discretion must . . . direct himself properly in law. He must call his own attention to the matters which he is bound to consider. He must exclude from consideration matters which are irrelevant to what he has to consider.'[265] In *Secretary of State for Education and Science v Tameside Metropolitan Borough Council*, Lord Diplock said that 'the very concept of administrative discretion involves a right to choose between more than one possible course of action upon which there is room for reasonable people to hold differing opinions as to which is to be preferred'.[266] Thus, the conditions that a licence committee may lawfully impose are not without limit. They must be properly related to the aims and scheme of the 1990 Act. **10.75**

HFEA must not fetter its discretion.[267] This does not mean that it may not exercise its discretion by means of a policy or rule. But it must 'be prepared to make an exception to that rule or policy in a deserving case'.[268] Thus, if, for example, a decision were taken that a certain category of research within Sch 2, para 3(2)(a)–(e) could never be pursued, the courts might be prepared to conclude that this offended against legality by fettering discretion. Interested parties (treatment clinics) must be allowed the opportunity to persuade the licensing authority to amend or deviate from the rule or policy, but the rule against fettering does not extend to the point of requiring any particular form or hearing or any particular technique of making or receiving representations.[269] **10.76**

---

[262] s 18(6)(b).

[263] s 18(5)(a). The other individual's consent is also required (see s 18(5)(b)).

[264] See *Associated Provincial Picture Houses v Wednesbury Corporation* [1948] 1 KB 223.

[265] ibid, 229.

[266] [1977] AC 1014, 1064.

[267] De Smith, S, Woolf, Lord, and Jowell, J, *Judicial Review of Administrative Action* (London: Sweet and Maxwell, 1996), 505.

[268] ibid. See also *R v Secretary of State for the Home Department, ex p Venables* [1997] 3 WLR 23, 47.

[269] *R v Secretary of State for the Environment, ex p Brent LBC* [1982] QB 593.

10.77   The recent case of *R v Human Fertilisation and Embryology Authority, ex p Assisted Reproduction and Gynaecology Centre and H*[270] illustrates this. This was an application for judicial review of HFEA's refusal to deviate from guidance in its Code of Practice that 'no more than three eggs or embryos should be placed in a woman in any one cycle, regardless of the procedure used'. The clinic wished to provide treatment for a 46-year-old woman using five eggs. The authority disagreed that the transfer of more than three was medically necessary or essential and considered that there was a significant risk of multiple births in H's case because she produced large numbers of good quality embryos. HFEA relied on an American research paper dealing with the transfer of embryos. It was argued by the claimants that the decision and advice was irrational, that it was fettered by a policy drawn so narrowly as to prevent consideration of individual circumstances or that Articles 8 and 12 of the European Convention on Human Rights were applicable. It was the claimants' submission that it would be for HFEA to show that H's human rights had not been breached. Ouseley J held: (i) it was fundamental to the arguability of the claimants' case that there were demonstrated facts that took the case out of the range of available decisions; (ii) the statistics used by the claimants did not arguably contradict the approach adopted by HFEA, namely that the risk of multiple births from pregnancy was greater with a patient who had good eggs if more than three were transplanted; (iii) applying its policy guidance, HFEA had considered H's medical circumstances and age; (iv) the court could not adjudicate between two views of an academic paper or its relationship to the US Vital Statistics Reports; (v) the claimants' evidence had not answered HFEA's point that any pregnancy would involve overcoming some unknown but adverse factor in the receiving area, which would have been overcome for all the eggs transplanted in one cycle; (vi) the claimants' evidence had not shown that HFEA was irrational but had merely shown that two views were possible (it was not for the court to intervene in a decision on the merits on a level far beyond that necessary for scrutiny of the lawfulness of the decision in which human rights were potentially engaged); (vii) HFEA was entitled to reach the view that two successive cyclical treatments with three eggs as opposed to five eggs in one cycle would achieve better prospects of pregnancy without a greater risk of multiple births; (viii) the decision letter had not shown any fettering of HFEA's views such that the appropriate or proportionate application of the guidelines to H was ignored. The appeal to the Court of Appeal failed.[271] The Court of Appeal noted that this was an area of rapidly developing scientific knowledge and debate in which HFEA, as the licensing body established by Parliament, made decisions and gave advice. It was not the function of the court to enter the scientific debate, nor was it the function of the court to adjudicate on the merits of HFEA's

---

[270] [2002] EWCA Civ 20; [2003] 1 FCR 266.
[271] ibid.

decisions or any advice it gave. Like any public authority, HFEA was open to challenge by way of judicial review but only if it exceeded or abused the powers and responsibilities given to it by Parliament. It was clear in this case that HFEA had considered the request for advice carefully and thoroughly, and it had produced opinions that were plainly rational. The Court had no part to play in the debate, and no power to intervene to strike down any such decision.

10.78 Decisions may be challenged also for procedural ultra vires. This can take two forms: failure to follow the direction of the Act, and failure to observe the principles of natural justice. As regards directions under the Act, there are both mandatory prescriptions (where disobedience will normally render invalid what has been done) and directory ones, in which case disobedience may be treated as an irregularity not affecting the validity of what has been done.[272] It is not always easy to distinguish the two requirements, but it may be said that where statutory words require things to be done as a condition of making a decision, especially when the form of words requires that something *shall* be done, an inference is raised that the requirement is mandatory, so that failure to do the required act renders the decision unlawful.[273] Examples from the Act are a determination by a licence committee which is improperly constituted in breach of the regulations determining the composition of such committees,[274] and the failure by a licence committee to give notice of a determination of a licence application contrary to the requirements of s 19(5). Where the procedures are merely directory,[275] the courts will not normally find committees bound, with the result that failure to meet the procedural requirements will not generally be fatal to the validity of the decision taken. It is important to emphasise that all statutory requirements are prima facie mandatory.[276] In order to decide whether a presumption that a provision is mandatory is in fact rebutted, the whole scope and purpose of the Act must be considered: one must assess 'the importance of provision that has been disregarded, and the relation of that provision to the general object intended to be secured by the Act'.[277]

10.79 A key element of procedural propriety is the duty to observe the principles of nature justice. The Act itself embodies these[278] (there is, for example, a right to be heard in the Act itself), but recourse must still be had to common law principles.

---

[272] N 269 above. See also *Cullimore v Lyme Regis Corporation* [1962] 1 QB 715.

[273] But the decision is presumed valid until set aside or otherwise held to be invalid by a court of competent jurisdiction: *Smith v East Elloe RDC* [1956] AC 736.

[274] s 9(5).

[275] An example is where a licence committee may by notice suspend a licence (s 22(1)).

[276] N 269 above, 267.

[277] *Howard v Bodington* (1877) 2 PD 203, 211. See also *R v Tower Hamlets HA, ex p Tower Combined Trades Association* [1994] COD 325.

[278] See the 'right to be heard' in the Act and Regulations, and protections against bias (eg Sch 1, para 10(1)).

It has been said that rules of natural justice 'mean no more than the duty to act fairly'.[279] The courts have offered some guidance as to which interests should be protected by fair procedures. In *McInnes v Onslow Fane*,[280] three situations were distinguished: 'forfeiture' or 'deprivation' cases, where there is a decision which takes away some existing right or position (in our context, the operation of an existing licensed treatment clinic); 'application cases', for example to run a treatment clinic; and an intermediate category of 'expectation cases', where there is a reasonable expectation of an existing benefit (the renewal of a licence is an example) which falls short of a right. A fair hearing, the court suggested, should be granted in cases involving 'forfeiture' and, normally, 'expectation', but not in those involving a mere 'application'. A strict application of this reasoning could result in injustice, with one clinic securing a licence and another not, and so the courts have held that deciding bodies are under a duty to give an applicant an opportunity to make representations and to be apprised of all information on which the decision may be founded.[281] It has been argued that 'wherever a public function is being performed there is an inference, in the absence of an express requirement to the contrary that the function is required to be performed fairly'.[282] This inference is all the more compelling where a decision may adversely affect a person's rights or interests, or when a person has a legitimate expectation of being treated fairly, as is clearly the case with applications for licences under the Act. 'The court is the arbiter of what is fair':[283] where fairness is required and what is involved to achieve fairness is a decision for the courts as a matter of law.

10.80 The question may arise, given the controversial nature of the decision HFEA may be engaged in, as to who has the standing to challenge such decision. It is not 'a function of the courts to be there for every individual who is interested in having the legality of an administrative action litigated'.[284] The applicant must have 'sufficient interest in the matter to which the application relates'.[285] The courts are increasingly receptive to challenges by public interest groups,[286] even to individual applications. Note Sedley J's remarks that he is 'perfectly entitled as a citizen to be concerned about, and to draw the attention of the court to, what he considers is an illegality'.[287]

---

[279] *Per* Lord Diplock in *O'Reilly v Mackman* [1983] 2 AC 237, 275.

[280] [1978] 1 WLR 1520.

[281] See *R v Huntingdon DC, ex p Cowan* [1984] 1 WLR 501. The obligation may be qualified by a right to refrain from disclosing the source and precise content of highly confidential information: *R v Gaming Board for Great Britain, ex p. Benaim and Khaida* [1970] 2 QB 417, 431.

[282] N 269 above, 405.

[283] *Per* Woolf and Lloyd LJJ in *R v Panel on Takeovers and Mergers, ex p Guinness* [1990] QB 146. The test is not whether no reasonable body would have thought it proper to dispense with a fair hearing.

[284] *R v Secretary of State for the Environment, ex p Rose Theatre Trust Co* [1990] 1 All ER 754, 768.

[285] RSC Ord 53: see CPR 1998, Sch 1.

[286] See eg *R v Secretary of State for the Foreign and Commonwealth Office, ex p World Development Movement* [1995] 1 WLR 386, and *R v Inspectorate of Pollution, ex p Greenpeace* [1994] 4 All ER 348.

[287] In *R v Somerset CC and ARS Southern Ltd, ex p Dixon* [1997] COD 323, 331.

The implications of the Human Rights Act 1998 (operative 2 October 2000) **10.81** must also be considered. HFEA is clearly a public body.[288] It is therefore unlawful for it to 'act in a way which is incompatible with convention rights'.[289] However, 'standing' is more narrowly defined under the Convention and under s 7 of the Human Rights Act. This adopts a 'victim' test.[290] Whether SPUC or LIFE could claim 'victim' status perhaps in an appeal to the 'right to life' provision in Article 2 of the Convention is open to question.[291] But the reality is that such an organisation should have little difficulty finding one of its members to stand as a putative victim. The precedent of *Bowman v United Kingdom*[292]—Mrs Bowman was held to be a victim when the UK government stopped the publication and distribution by an organisation of anti-abortion leaflets which provided the opinions of parliamentary candidates—should offer the support to pressure groups wishing to challenge HFEA decisions on embryo research, for example. The courts, which have adopted a liberal position on 'standing', are likely to take a similar stand on 'victim'.

D. Access to Treatment

1. Introduction

In a legal text it would not normally be necessary, or some would think appropri- **10.82** ate, to spell out the most obvious constraint on access to treatment: namely, that restriction upon NHS funding may confine access to infertility treatment to those with considerable financial resources. But this would be to ignore the European dimension. Those who are denied assisted conception services in the UK may seek treatment abroad: a postmenopausal woman might go to Italy and, conversely a Swedish couple wanting to use anonymously donated sperm might seek treatment in the United Kingdom, which currently guarantees donor anonymity (see para 10.146). Article 59 of the European Treaty only applies to services which are 'normally provided for remuneration'. There is thus no right to publicly-funded assisted conception in another Member State, but those who can pay can go abroad and, as Hervey puts it, ' "buy their way out" of ethical or moral choices given legislative force in their own Member State'.[293] Thus, those wealthy enough to do so can buy into private infertility treatment in this country and buy out of

---

[288] Within s 6 of the Human Rights Act 1998.
[289] See s 6(1).
[290] See s 7(1) (in Art 34 of the ECHR).
[291] cf *F v Switzerland* (1988) 10 EHRR 411.
[292] (1998) 26 EHRR 1.
[293] See Hervey, T, 'Buy Baby: the European Union and Regulation of Human Reproduction' [1998] 18 OJLS 207, 229.

our regulatory framework (which is stricter than many countries in the European Union).[294]

10.83 The Warnock committee was 'not prepared to recommend that access to treatment should be based exclusively on the legal status of marriage'.[295] It did, however, express the view that 'as a general rule it is better for children to be born into a two-parent family, with both father and mother'.[296] It concluded that 'eligibility' raised difficult questions, and that 'hard and fast rules' were not applicable to its solution.[297] Instead, the Warnock committee recommended that where consultants declined to provide treatment 'they should always give the patient a full explanation of the reasons'.[298] During the passage of the 1990 Act through Parliament, an attempt was made to restrict access to infertility treatment to married couples or, at least, to heterosexual couples in a stable relationship but this failed.[299] Four years later France passed legislation limiting assisted conception services to those whose infertility was 'of a pathological character which has been medically diagnosed' and who were heterosexual married couples or at least able to prove that they have lived together for at least two years.[300]

10.84 The 1990 Act 'contains no statutory bars upon the treatment of any competent adult, so single, lesbian or postmenopausal women may all lawfully receive assisted conception services'.[301] The Act only addresses the question of access to treatment in one provision, and then obliquely rather than directly. Section 13(5) provides:

> A woman shall not be provided with treatment services unless account has been taken of the welfare of any child who may be born as a result of treatment (including the need of that child for a father), and of any other child who may affected by the birth.

Kennedy and Grubb point to the significance (indeed, uniqueness) of this provision. 'Parliament has required that the clinical judgement of the doctor must be exercised having regard to others and not just the "best interests" of his patient. In this respect, the 1990 Act departs from what would be the normal understanding of a doctor's duty to his patient.'[302]

---

[294] On France, see Latham, M, *Regulating Reproduction* (Manchester: Manchester University Press, 2002). Most useful on the international response is Lee and Morgan (n 9 above), ch 11.

[295] Warnock report (n 7 above), para 2.5.

[296] ibid, para 2.11.

[297] ibid, para 2.13.

[298] ibid.

[299] An amendment moved in the House of Lords to make it an offence to provide treatment services for an unmarried couple was defeated by a single vote (see *Hansard*, HL vol 515, col 787).

[300] See Law 94-654 of 29 July 1994 (Lee and Morgan (n 9 above), 278–9). On this law see Ball, N, 'The Re-emergence of Enlightenment Ideas in the 1994 French Bioethics Debates' [2000] 50 *Duke LJ* 545.

[301] See Douglas, G, *Law, Fertility and Reproduction* (London: Sweet & Maxwell, 1991), 135.

[302] Kennedy, I and Grubb, A, *Medical Law — Text with Materials* (London: Butterworths, 2000), 1272.

The provision is incoherent. It refers to the welfare of children as yet unconceived   **10.85**
('who are only a twinkle in the doctor's eye'[303]). It asks us to compare the utilities
of not being born to a single mother; surely a nonsense since existence will nearly
always (perhaps always) be preferable to non-existence.[304] Jackson finds it difficult, 'perhaps even impossible', to imagine circumstances in which it would be
preferable not to be born.[305] And literally interpreted that must be right, but only,
this author would suggest, because there are circumstances in which you would remove the child from the parents at birth.[306] If the prospective mother had already
killed or seriously harmed several of her previous babies, would it not be better to
invoke s13(5) and deny her infertility treatment than allow her this service and
then remove the child? But Parliament's concern—and certainly the HFEA's—
goes beyond ensuring that patients reach a minimal level of parental adequacy. It
requires—and here this author agrees with Jackson—that clinicians take into
account 'factors such as the would-be parents' commitment to having and bringing up a child; their ability to provide a stable and supportive environment; their
future ability to look after or provide for a child's needs and the possibility of any
risk of harm to their child'.[307] This list, drawn from the Code of Practice, is modelled on the checklist in the Children Act 1989 (see s 1(3)) but, whilst it is undoubtedly useful there, in resolving a conflict over an existing child, it is difficult
to see how apposite it is where there is yet no child.

Also incoherent is the emphasis in s.13(5) on 'the need of that child for a father'.   **10.86**
It is particularly odd in a statute which, as we shall see (paras 10.179–10.181) creates legally fatherless children. All children have genetic fathers: what the provision requires is a *social* father. Should fertility services therefore be refused if the
prospective father cannot fulfil that role? Because he is in prison? Or is a homosexual, not able to offer the 'appropriate' role model? Or is 'just a City workalco-
holic?'[308] Or is the reality that what the provision is targeting is lesbians and that
'father' is actually a cloak for a 'man'? And, of course, no fertility clinic can guarantee that a man 'on the scene' a the time of conception will still be about in a year
or five years time.

The provision only requires 'account' to be 'taken of the welfare of any child who   **10.87**
may be born as a result of treatment' and 'of any other child who may be affected

---

[303] See Douglas (n 301 above), 121.
[304] And see Parfit, D, *Reasons and Persons* (Oxford: OUP, 1984); Harris, J, *Wonderwoman and Superman* (Oxford: OUP, 1992).
[305] Jackson, E, 'Conception and the Irrelevance of the Welfare Principle' [2002] 65 MLR 176, 181. See also Jackson, E, *Regulating Reproduction—Law, Technology and Autonomy* (Oxford: Hart Publishing, 2001), 190 *et seq*.
[306] By means of an emergency protection order (see Children Act 1989, s 44).
[307] Jackson (n 305 above) [2002] 65 MLR 176, 181.
[308] *Per* Lee and Morgan (n 9 above), 166.

by their birth'. There is no indication as to the weight, if any, to be attached to the welfare of either set of children. An amendment which would have made the welfare of the child paramount (*cf* Children Act 1989, s 1(1)) did not pass.[309] But what is mean by account? On whom exactly does the duty fall?[310] What has to be shown to demonstrate that it has been discharged? Who can challenge a decision taken allegedly in breach of the duty? The 1990 Act is silent on locus standi,[311] either to determine that account has not been taken or to challenge that which has and the resultant conclusion.

10.88   The Act does not define 'welfare' (though the Code of Practice, see para 10.85) attempts to inject some content into this. Conventionally, 'welfare' is given a broad definition.[312] It includes material welfare, so that the poverty of the prospective parents may be taken into account. But stability, security, warmth, compassion and commitment of those parents are of greater significance. The directive to take account also of the welfare of the other children who may be affected by the birth means that such extraneous considerations as that an existing child would stand to inherit less as a result of the birth of a new medically-assisted sibling may also be considered.

10.89   But little if any of this was in the minds of those responsible for s 13(5). This was introduced, and passed, expressly to prevent the creation of one-parent families through assisted reproduction, and, in particular, to prevent lesbian women from receiving treatment service. The provision, say Lee and Morgan, 'has all the hallmarks of a profamilist ideology. Assisted conception is to be, for the most part, for the married, mortgaged middle-class.'[313]

10.90   Section 13(5) makes no reference to the need of the woman for treatment services. What, for example, of the woman who wants a child but who does not wish to have sexual intercourse or genuinely fears sexual relations? Her welfare might dictate the provision of assisted conception to enable her to achieve a 'virgin birth'. The woman's welfare is also an issue where fertility clinics impose age-limitations on the provision of services (and see para 10.100).

10.91   The focus in s 13(5) is on the welfare of the child. One limitation thus imposed is the best interests of the individual born as a result of assisted conception beyond his/her childhood. This is significant in the context of an individual's quest to construct an identity. The 1990 Act, as we shall see (paras 10.145 and 10.149), gives

---

[309] *Hansard*, HL vol 517, col 1097.

[310] Evidence of the way clinics interpreted the welfare provision in the first years of the Act is found in Douglas, G, 'Assisted Reproduction and the Welfare of the Child' (1993) 46 CLP 53.

[311] And see paras 10.80–10.81 above.

[312] Lord Mackay of Clashfern (n 309 above), quoted Hardie Boys J in the New Zealand case of *Walker v Harrison* [1981] 257 New Zealand Recent Law.

[313] Lee and Morgan (n 9 above), 164.

very little scope to the child's search for his/her origins. 'Welfare' does not seem to address positive self-image or 'genealogical bewilderment'.[314]

The width of s 13(5) must also be noted. It extends to any treatment service. This is defined in the Act to mean 'medical, surgical or obstetric services provided to the public or a section of the public for the purpose of assisting women to carry children'.[315] In theory, ante-natal services could be denied to a lesbian woman on the ground that it would be better for the child if she miscarried. No one, one must assume, would put this construction on s 13(5), but, however extraordinary, it is capable of bearing this meaning.

10.92

Section 13(5) clearly also applies to surrogacy (on which see paras 10.184–10.221, below). This means that treatment services to a surrogate mother must take account both of the abilities of the commissioning parents (or parent where the surrogate's own egg is being used) to advance the child's welfare—this is clearly very relevant to Parliament's intention where the commissioning parent is a homosexual man—and the psychological effect that a woman giving birth and then giving the child away may have on her other children.[316] The surrogate's own welfare is not within the ambit of s 13(5) (and see para 10.90).

10.93

HFEA's Code of Practice recognises 'the right of people who are infertile to the proper consideration of their request for treatment'.[317] It goes on to list the 'factors' to be considered by those offering treatment services. The Code states:

10.94

3.11 Centres should take all reasonable steps to ascertain who would be legally responsible for any child born as a result of the procedure and who it is intended will be bringing up the child. When people seeking treatment come from abroad, centres should not assume that the law of that country relating to the parentage of a child born as a result of donated gametes is the same as that of the United Kingdom.

3.12 People seeking treatment are entitled to a fair and unprejudiced assessment of their situation and needs, which should be considered with the skill and sensitivity appropriate to the delicacy of the case and the wishes and feelings of those involved.

3.13 Where people seek licensed treatment, centres should bear in mind the following factors:

a. their commitment to having and bringing up a child or children;

---

[314] See Sants, H, 'Genealogical Bewilderment in Children With Substitute Parents' (1964) 37 *British Journal of Medical Psychology* 133.

[315] s 2(1).

[316] Krimmel, H, 'The Case Against Surrogate Parenting', *Hastings Center Report*, October 1983, 35, quotes a 9-year-old girl who, when told that the child her mother was carrying would be given away to another family, responded: 'All right . . . But if it's a girl, let's keep it and give Jeffrey away' (her 2-year-old brother).

[317] HFEA, *Code of Practice* (5th edn, 2001).

b. their ability to provide a stable and supportive environment for any child produced as a result of treatment;

c. their medical histories and the medical histories of their families;

d. their health and consequent future ability to look after or provide for their child's needs;

e. their ages and likely future ability to look after or provide for a child's needs;

f. their ability to meet the needs of any child or children who may be born as a result of treatment, including the implications of any possible multiple births;

g. any risk of harm to the child or children who may be born, including the risk of inherited disorders or transmissible diseases, problems during pregnancy and of neglect or abuse; and

h. the effect of a new baby or babies upon any existing child of the family.

3.14 Where people seek treatment using donated gametes, centres should also take the following factors into account:

a. a child's potential need to know about their origins and whether or not the prospective parents are prepared for the questions which may arise while the child is growing up;

b. the possible attitudes of other members of the family towards the child, and towards their status in the family;

c. the implications for the welfare of the child if the person providing the gametes for donation is personally known within the child's family and social circle; and

d. any possibility known to the centre of a dispute about the legal fatherhood of the child . . .

3.15 Further factors will require consideration in the following cases:

a. where the child will have no legal father. Centres are required to have regard to the child's need for a father and should pay particular attention to the prospective mother's ability to meet the child's needs throughout their childhood. Where appropriate, centres should consider particularly whether there is anyone else within the prospective mother's family and social circle willing and able to share the responsibility for meeting those needs, and for bringing up, maintaining and caring for the child . . .

10.95 The Code of Practice goes on to list the enquiries to be made. It states:

3.19 Centres should take a medical and social history from each prospective parent. They should be seen together and separately . . .

3.20 Centres should seek to satisfy themselves that the GP of each prospective parent knows of no reason why either of them might not be suitable for the treatment to be offered. This would include anything that might adversely affect the welfare of any resulting child.

3.21 Centres should obtain the client's consent before approaching the GP. However, failure to give consent should be taken into account in considering whether or not to offer treatment.

The Code of Practice also emphasises multi-disciplinary assessment. On this it   **10.96**
states:

> 3.25 The views of all those at the centre who have been involved with the prospect-
> ive parents should be taken into account when deciding whether or not to
> offer treatment. People seeking treatment should be given a fair opportunity
> to state their views before any decision is made and to meet any objections
> raised to providing them with treatment.
>
> 3.26 If a member of the team has a cause for concern as a result of information
> given to them in confidence, they should obtain the consent of the person
> concerned before discussing it with the rest of the team. If a member of the
> team receives information that is of such gravity that confidentiality *cannot* be
> maintained, they should use their own discretion, based on good professional
> practice, in deciding in what circumstances it should be discussed with the
> rest of the team.
>
> 3.27 The decision to provide treatment should be taken in the light of all the avail-
> able information. Treatment may be refused on clinical grounds. Treatment
> should also be refused if the centre believes that it would not be in the inter-
> est of any resulting child, or any child already existing, to provide treatment,
> or is unable to obtain sufficient information or advice to reach a proper con-
> clusion.
>
> 3.28 If treatment is refused for any reason, the Centre should explain to the woman
> and, where appropriate, her husband or partner, the reasons for this and the
> factors, if any, which might persuade the centre to reverse the decision. It
> should also explain the options that remain open and tell clients where they
> can obtain counselling.
>
> 3.29 Centres should record in detail the information that has been taken into ac-
> count when considering the welfare of the child or children. The record
> should reflect the views of all those who were consulted in realising the deci-
> sion, including those of the people seeking treatment.

The Code does not exclude any category of persons as such from access to services   **10.97**
for assisted reproduction. But, as can be seen above, it does emphasise 'the child's
need for a father', and stresses that treatment should be refused if the Centre believes that 'it would not be in the interests of any resulting child, or any children
already existing'. It leaves decisions to rest with individual centre's assessments of
an applicant's suitability.[318] It also emphasises the importance of giving reasons for
decisions. Where these prove inadequate, there may be a challenge by judicial review.

There are as yet few reported challenges. The first case, which antedates both the   **10.98**
Act and the Code is *R v Ethical Committee of St Mary's Hospital (Manchester), ex p
Harriott*.[319] The applicant, who had been turned down as suitable foster or adop-
tive parent because she had a criminal record involving prostitution offences and

---

[318] And see HFEA, *Tenth Annual Report and Accounts* (London: HFEA, 2002).
[319] [1988] 1 FLR 512.

a 'poor understanding' of fostering, was removed from the IVF waiting list after the clinic became aware of her background. At this clinic, the criteria for offering treatment was that couples 'must, in the ordinary course of events, satisfy the general criteria established by adoption societies in assessing suitability for adoption . . .[320] [and there] must be no medical, psychiatric or psychosexual problems which would indicate an increased probability of a couple not being able to provide satisfactory parenting to the offspring or endanger the mother's life or health if she became pregnant'.

10.99 The applicant sought judicial review of the decision to refuse to treat her. She failed because she had been given an opportunity to make representations against the refusal. There was, accordingly, no procedural unfairness (as to which see paras 10.78–10.79 above). However, Schiemann J noted that 'it is not, and could not be, suggested that no reasonable consultant could have come to the decision to refuse treatment to the applicant'.[321] The clinic's criteria were therefore not *Wednesbury* unreasonable. He was prepared to accept obiter that a blanket policy to refuse treatment to 'anyone who was a Jew or Coloured (sic)' might be illegal.[322] Why Schiemann J had any other doubt as to the propriety of a policy which would deny treatment on grounds of race or colour is surprising because such policies are unlawful under the Race Relations Act 1968. Discrimination on grounds of religion is not, however, unlawful under any legislation in operation in England. It may be added that such blanket policies would also fetter discretion and be unlawful for this reason too.

10.100 Upper age limits for publicly-funded treatment are common. This policy was challenged in *R v Sheffield AHA, ex p Seale*.[323] The applicant, who was 37, was outside the age range within which the authority provided treatment (it had an upper age limit of 35). This had been imposed in order to ration treatment, within a limited budget, to women upon whom it was likely to have the greatest benefit. Auld J found the policy to be neither illegal nor irrational 'applying the high test that that word imports under the *Wednesbury* decision'.[324] He also found no fettering of discretion—but his conclusion here is dubious—or procedural impropriety. Although Mrs Seale's challenge failed (she didn't even persuade the judge that she had an arguable case that would justify granting leave to bring an application for judicial review), a future challenge to an inflexible age policy may succeed. The policy may be lawful but it should not be applied blindly but rather flexibly, which, it may be argued, did not happen in Mrs Seale's case.

---

[320] See, generally, Campion, MJ, *Who's Fit To Be A Parent?* (London: Routledge, 1995). On adoption, see ch 2; on assisted reproduction see ch 4.
[321] N 319 above.
[322] ibid.
[323] [1995] 25 BMLR 1.
[324] ibid.

It is common to find other criteria employed by NHS clinics. Examples are evidence of the stability of a non-marital relationship (it seems marital relationships are assumed to be stable), and that the woman is close to her ideal body weight.[325] In addition, most NHS clinics will fund no more than three cycles of treatment.[326] As Jackson states, 'although these eligibility guidelines may seem overly restrictive, it must of course be remembered that funding any infertility treatment is more generous than the norm'.[327] It is unlikely that challenges to any of these criteria will succeed. The latter two (body weight and restriction on the number of courses of treatment) can clearly be medically justified and thus, it would seem, are rational decisions.

10.101

The 1990 Act deals with treatment services only within the UK. However, s 24(4) of the Act does invest HFEA with a discretion to permit a licence-holder to export gametes or embryos. Accordingly, the possibility of using treatment services abroad, most particularly within the European Union, and the legal implications of doing so, has arisen in two cases. In *R v Human Fertilisation and Embryology Authority, ex p Blood*,[328] when Mrs Diane Blood was denied permission to take her dead husband's sperm to Belgium with a view to treatment services being performed in a Brussels clinic, she invoked provisions of the Treaty of Rome.[329] The Court of Appeal held that the prohibition on exporting gametes, imposed by HFEA, was tantamount to a denial of the right of access to medical treatment abroad, and could only be justified if it were absolutely necessary in the public interest. HFEA was entitled to place restrictions on the export of sperm, but such restrictions had to be justified on grounds of public policy. HFEA was accordingly directed to reconsider its position in the light of (what is now) Article 49 of the EC Treaty. Lord Woolf MR said:

10.102

> Parliament has delegated to the Authority the responsibility for making decisions in this difficult and delicate area, and the court should be slow to interfere in its decisions. However, the reasons given by the Authority, while deeply flawed, confirm that the Authority did not take into account two important considerations. The first being the effect of Article [49] of the Treaty. The second being that there should be, after this judgment has been given, no further cases where sperm is preserved without consent. The Authority is not to be criticised for this because, in relation to the law, it was dependent on the guidance it received. However, the fact remains that having not received the appropriate guidance, the Authority did not take into account two matters which Mrs Blood is entitled to have taken into account'.[330]

---

[325] See Jackson, *Regulating Reproduction* (n 305 above), 198.
[326] ibid.
[327] ibid.
[328] [1997] 2 All ER 687.
[329] [1997] 2 All ER 687.
[330] ibid, 702.

10.103 Following the decision of the Court of Appeal, HFEA reconsidered its position. It considered that the case would set no precedent since sperm should never again be taken without consent. It also agreed that it had failed to establish a sufficiently compelling public policy exception to Mrs Blood's rights to transfer her dead husband's sperm across borders. Mrs Blood subsequently had treatment in Belgium, and gave birth to a son. She has since done this a second time.[331] The Court of Appeal's decision was criticised for failing to observe that there was surely a presumption that before sperm was exported it have first been obtained and stored in conformity with national law.[332] The Government commissioned Professor Sheila McLean to report on the implications of the *Blood* decision. She commented:

> It surely cannot have been intended that the discretion to permit export was intended to cover gametes which were unlawfully obtained and/or unlawfully stored. It would be a most unusual piece of legislation which created legislation only to build into itself the power to defeat them by the exercise of discretion.[333]

The Government indicated that as a result of the *Blood* case and the *McLean* report it would amend the Human Fertilisation and Embryology Act.[334] Amongst the changes likely to be effected is one which will enable the posthumously created child to have a legal father (as we will see below at para 10.181 the 1990 Act has created the category of the legally fatherless child and Diane Blood's two children do not have fathers in law). The amendment is likely to be retrospective[335] and will still require written consent prior to the removal of gametes. The only likely exception to this will be where gametes are removed and stored in the person's best interests from an individual who is temporarily incapacitated (for example, a child about to undergo chemotherapy which might affect future fertility).[336]

10.104 The second case is *U v W (Attorney-General Intervening)*.[337] U and W sought treatment in Rome, having previously received infertility treatment in England. U became pregnant and subsequently the mother (in both the genetic and gestational senses) of twins. Neither of the twins was genetically related to W. But by this time U and W, who had never married, had parted. U brought an application under the Child Support Act 1991 for a declaration that W was the father of her twins. W had signed a form in the clinic in Rome acknowledging paternity of any children born as a result of the treatment there. U and W had attended the clinic together

---

[331] A second son was born in July 2002.

[332] See Morgan, D and Lee, R, 'In The Name of the Father? *Ex parte Blood*: Dealing With Novelty and Anomaly' (1997) 60 MLR 840, 851.

[333] *Consent And The Law: Review of the Current Provisions in the Human Fertilisation and Embryology Act 1990 for the UK Health Ministers* (London: HMSO, 1997), para 7.4.

[334] *Government Response to the McLean Review on Consent to Storage and Use of Human Sperm and Eggs* 2000/0486 (25 August 2000).

[335] ibid.

[336] ibid. And see Jackson (n 325 above), 211.

[337] [1997] 2 FLR 282.

(this is important for the purposes of s 28(3), discussed at para 10.177). Wilson J considered that s 28(3) of the 1990 Act represented a restriction on the freedom to provide services under, what is now, Article 49. But he held the restriction to be justified on the grounds that an unmarried man joining with a woman seeking treatment with donor sperm had to be aware of all the consequences and given an opportunity to make an informed choice. A short, clear answer should be available to any question whether treatment had been provided for a woman and a man together. And the issue of paternity could arise long after the birth of a child, when the licence-holder's records would be the best source of evidence as to the identity of the alleged father. Further, on making a provision relating to non-genetic paternity, a Member State had been given considerable discretion under Community law to determine which restriction was proportionate to its legitimate objectives. The licensing system with its code of practice was not out of proportion to the reasons which justified the restriction. It should be noted that the court may well have been influenced by the absence of any regulation of assisted conception in Italy.[338] Were these facts to recur and the treatment to have taken place in a Member State with a regulatory system comparable to that in the UK, it is distinctly possible that the Court might have come to a different conclusion. It would certainly have had to adduce different arguments.

The argument was also put in *U v W (Attorney-General Intervening)* that in deny- **10.105** ing the twins W as a father the provisions of the legislation (s 28(3)) contravened Article 8 of the European Convention on Human Rights. Wilson J held that this was not so.[339] There was no family life between W and the twins: no genetic link and no de facto relationship. He further held that even if Article 8(1) was contravened, as clearly it might have been were the facts different, the challenge would fail under Article 8(2).

E. Conscientious Objection

The 1990 Act contains a conscience clause provision designed to permit individ- **10.106** uals to opt out of participating in any of the activities covered by the Act. It provides: 'No person who has a conscientious objection to participating in any activity governed by this Act shall be under a duty, however arising, to do so'.[340] However, 'in any legal proceedings the burden of conscientious objection rests on the person claiming to rely on it'.[341]

---

[338] When regulation was proposed it met with fierce opposition from clinicians, so much so that mooted legislation has not come to fruition. See Lee and Morgan (n 9 above), 281–2.
[339] N 337 above, 302.
[340] s 38(1). And see Wicclair, M, 'Conscientious Objection in Medicine' (2000) 14 *Bioethics* 205.
[341] s 38(2).

10.107   The provision is modelled on s 4 of the Abortion Act (as to which see chapter 11, para 11.76 *et seq*, but there is an important difference. The 1990 Act does not contain an exception to the right to object where action is necessary to save a patient's life or prevent grave permanent injury.[342] However, it will be noted that s 38 refers to 'any activity governed by this Act', and abortion is in part governed by the 1990 Act.[343] There is thus a conflict between s 4 of the Abortion Act 1967 and s 38 of the 1990 Act. This was created unintentionally but still has to be resolved. The better view must be that the exception does not apply to activities covered by the 1990 Act, except abortion. However, two other points may be noted. First, life-threatening conditions are not likely to arise in the context of infertility treatment. Secondly, were they to do so, there is a common law duty on doctors to intervene to arrest conditions which are life-threatening or are causing grave physical injury.[344] The omission and the conflict are not therefore of overwhelming significance.

10.108   The objection must be 'conscientious'. 'Conscience' is widely interpreted and will include not only religious beliefs but also other principled reasons which impel a person to believe that an activity is inherently wrong.

10.109   The provision states that 'no person' with a conscientious objection is under a duty to participate in any of the Act's activities. This clearly extends to doctors and to nurses,[345] but, in the light of the House of Lords' decision in *Janaway v Salford AHA*,[346] whether it extends any further will depend on how 'participate' is interpreted. There can be no doubt that a research scientist or laboratory technician may invoke the conscience clause. But, whether a secretary, instructed to type letters or forms in connection with, for example, embryo research to which she takes moral objection, would be similarly protected is generally thought unlikely after *Janaway*.[347] However, the language of the abortion provision, interpreted in *Janaway*, and s 38 are not identical. Section 4 of the Abortion Act 1967 refers to participation in *any treatment* authorised by the Act, and s 38 is couched more widely in terms of *any activity* governed by the Act. A secretary does not, so it has been held, participate in treatment, but it is not stretching language too far to hold that she does participate in an activity governed by the 1990 Act. In support of this interpretation it may be noted that Lord Keith in *Janaway* argued that: 'If Parliament had intended the result contended for by the applicant (ie that typing

---

[342] As the Abortion Act 1967 does.

[343] s 37.

[344] See *F v Berkshire HA* [1990] 2 AC 1.

[345] See *Royal College of Nursing of the UK v Department of Health and Social Security* [1981] AC 800.

[346] [1989] AC 537.

[347] Where a secretary was held not to be participating in abortion when she typed a letter referring a patient to a second doctor for a second opinion.

a letter amounted to participating in treatment), it could have procured it very clearly and easily by referring to participation 'in anything authorised by this Act', instead of 'in any treatment [so] authorised'.[348] In effect this is what Parliament has done in the 1990 Act. It is thus arguable that even activities remote from treatment are covered by the conscience clause in s 38. Whether s 38 in addition reverses the ruling in *Janaway* (note the argument in para 10.107 above that abortion is an activity covered by the 1990 Act) must be arguable, although there can be no doubt that Parliament had no such intention.

The conscience clause permits an individual to object to *any* activity governed by the 1990 Act. S/he may thus, for example, object to embryo research on conscientious grounds, without also objecting to assisted reproduction. However, difficult questions arise in relation to this. Most obviously, can an individual who assists assisted reproduction conscientiously object to the use of in vitro fertilisation in the case of, for example, a single woman or a lesbian woman? Does acceptance of an activity entail acceptance of all instances of that activity? It has been argued that the conscience clause could be successfully invoked by those who do not wish to treat lesbians.[349] This is not very convincing for two reasons. First, such an objection would be rooted in prejudice, rather than based on conscience[350] (though it must be conceded that a definitive understanding of what is meant by 'conscience' awaits clarification by the courts). Secondly, it does not seem that the person invoking conscientious objection is objecting to the activity as such, but rather to the sexual orientation and/or lifestyle of the person who is the potential beneficiary of the activity. It would be straining language to hold that the objection is to the activity of creating unconventional families. This is not the natural meaning of the language used, nor was it Parliament's intention. Lee and Morgan[351] and Kennedy and Grubb[352] are more convinced by the second of these arguments. Lee and Morgan are specifically critical of the first of them. They say that 'however misconceived the objection, if it is a genuinely felt objection on grounds of conscience then it must surely be open for the person to demonstrate this and rely on it. To begin to look behind the reasons for the objection would lead into very tricky territory.'[353] With respect this author cannot agree. The courts have been prepared to refuse to recognise 'religions'—Scientology is a notorious example[354]—when it has been clear that they lack the essential incidents. Similarly, the author believes a court would be willing to expose 'conscience' when it is nothing more than a smokescreen for prejudice.

10.110

---

[348] N 346 above, 570.
[349] See Douglas (n 301 above), 122.
[350] And see Dworkin, R, *Taking Rights Seriously* (London: Duckworth, 1977), ch 10.
[351] Lee and Morgan (n 9 above), 170.
[352] Kennedy and Grubb (n 302 above), 1282.
[353] Lee and Morgan (n 9 above), 170.
[354] *R v Registrar General, ex p Segerdal* [1970] 2 QB 697.

F. Consent to the Use of Genetic Material

10.111 The most firmly entrenched principle of medical law requires that a person consent to treatment. There is probably no more commonly quoted dictum in English medical law than Cardozo J's in *Schloendorff v Society of New York Hospital*:

> Every human being of adult years and sound mind has a right to determine what shall be done with his own body; and a surgeon who performs an operation without his patient's consent commits an assault . . . .[355]

10.112 In the case of medically assisted reproduction which is regulated by the 1990 Act—and not all is[356]—the common law (on which see chapter 3) is supplemented by the 1990 Act, and by the Code of Practice (revised in 2001). The common law remains important both because it underpins the legislation and therefore may be prayed in aid in its interpretation, and because it needs must govern procedures and techniques which fall outside the legislative framework. It is also important where a question arises (for example, whether a withdrawal of consent was the result of undue influence) which requires recourse to it.[357] The question therefore needs to be raised as to what infertility treatment which falls outside the remit of the 1990 Act a person may consent to. There is no direct authority on this, but on principle it would seem that one can consent to any 'proper medical treatment'. It may be a matter of some controversy as to what is to be regarded as proper medical treatment. The courts are likely to apply the *Bolam* principle (as to which see Chapter 6) and rely on the views of institutions like the Royal College of Obstetricians and Gynaecologists.[358] The courts have stressed that the *Bolam* principle should not be allowed to inhibit innovative work: this is an especially important ruling in the context of medically assisted reproduction where development of new technologies is an ongoing process.[359]

10.113 The *Blood* litigation in 1996–1997[360] (and see paras 10.102–10.103) re-emphasised the necessity of consent. Sperm was removed from Mr Blood, who was in a coma dying from bacterial meningitis, on the instructions of his wife. According

---

[355] (1914) 211 NJ 125, 126, cited with approval, inter alia in *Re F* (*Mental Patient: Sterilisation*) [1990] 2 AC 1 and in *Airedale NHS Trust v Bland* [1993] AC 789.

[356] eg, GIFT.

[357] Examples of undue influence in medical law include *Re T* [1993] Fam 95.

[358] As courts have done in areas like persistent vegetative state diagnosis. See, eg, *An NHS Trust v M; An NHS Trust v H* [2001] 2 FLR 367; *NHS Trust A v H* [2001] 2 FLR 501. Thus in relation to egg giving, where the 'three embryos' rule does not apply, the question must be raised as to whether consent may be given to more than three embryos being inserted. Dr Ian Craft has admitted to inserting as many as 13 (*Panorama*, BBC 1, 6 July 2003). It is dubious whether the woman concerned could consent to this if the *Bolam* principle were adhered to, which, it is argued, should be the case.

[359] See *JS v An NHS Trust; JA v An NHS Trust* [2003] 1 FLR 879.

[360] *R v Human Fertilisation and Embryology Authority, ex p Blood* [1997] 2 WLR 806.

to Lord Woolf MR, in the Court of Appeal, 'humanity dictated that the sperm was taken and preserved first and the legal argument followed'.[361] There was argument that Mr Blood's consent could be implied from conversations that he and his wife had had about starting a family. The Court of Appeal agreed with the Human Fertilisation and Embryology Authority that consent had to be express and written, as stipulated in the 1990 Act,[362] and could not be constructed in this way. It also agreed with HFEA that the storage of Mr Blood's sperm was 'technically' a criminal offence: it was contrary to s 41(2)(b) of the Act. Although the Court of Appeal did not address the issue, it is also clear that Mrs Blood had no capacity to consent on behalf of her husband. Such capacity would have to be grounded on the need 'to save life or to ensure improvement or prevent deterioration in physical or mental health',[363] and none of these conditions could possibly have applied. Further, if treating Mr Blood in this way was not in his best interests, it is difficult to see how he would have an interest in treatment which was designed to produce offspring whose lives he would never see.

The 1990 Act provides in s 13(6) that: **10.114**

A woman shall not be provided with any treatment services involving—

(a) the use of any gametes of any person, if that person's consent is required under paragraph 5 of Schedule 3 to this Act for the use in question,

(b) the use of any embryo the creation of which was brought about *in vitro*, or

(c) the use of any embryo taken from a woman, if the consent of the woman from whom it was taken is required under paragraph 7 of that Schedule for the use in question,

unless the woman being treated and, where she is being treated together with a man, the man, have been given a suitable opportunity to receive proper counselling about the implications of taking the proposed steps, and have been provided with such relevant information as is proper.

Consent must be in writing. This is not a requirement of common law, so that **10.115** procedures outside the 1990 Act such as GIFT do not require consent to be evidenced. It would be rather foolhardy for a treatment clinic not to insist on written consent to such treatment. The Code of Practice appends consent forms.[364] Consent can be withdrawn: the withdrawal will be effective, even if there has been pressure, provided this does not amount to undue influence.[365]

Section 13(6) confirms and reinforces the common law, and supplements it by re- **10.116** quiring an opportunity for counselling and the provision of relevant information.

---

[361] ibid, 814.
[362] Sch 3, para 8.
[363] *Per* Lord Brandon of Oakbrook in *Re F* [1990] 2 AC 1, 55.
[364] 5th edn, Annex E.
[365] *Centre for Reproductive Medicine v U* [2002] 1 FLR 927.

The need for counselling was recognised in the Warnock report.[366] It envisaged 'non-directional' counselling aimed at 'helping individuals to understand their situation and to make their own decisions about what steps should be taken next'.[367] The 1990 Act does not state what counselling is to consist of, nor when it is to be made available, nor whether a centre can direct or merely encourage the use of counselling services. However, the Code of Practice is very specific on the content of counselling (see para 6 of the Code, below). However, the 1990 Act is expressed in the present continuous tense ('being treated'). This raises the question, not addressed in the Code, as to whether proper counselling must also be offered each time the patient or patients return for treatment. Given resource constraints, the better interpretation would be to limit the obligation to before initial treatment is offered. On the question whether counselling may be directed or merely offered, the Code is clear that what is required is the making available of counselling. There must be concern about the adequacy of counselling, and doubt as to whether the Authority has the ability to police the requirement effectively.

G. Counselling

1. The Provision of Counselling

10.117 Prior to the 1990 Act there was, it seems, very little counselling for those who wanted infertility treatment. The 1990 Act provides that counselling arrangements should be set up within the Code of Practice. This accordingly provides:

General Obligations

8.1 People seeking licensed treatment (ie, *in vitro* fertilisation or treatment using donated gametes) or consenting to the use or storage of embryos, or to the donation or storage of gametes, *must* be given 'a suitable opportunity to receive proper counselling about the implications of taking the proposed steps', before they consent.

8.2 Counselling should be clearly distinguished from:
   a. the information which is given to everyone, in accordance with the guidance in Pt 6 [see below];
   b. the normal relationship between the clinician and the person considering donation or seeking storage or treatment, which includes giving professional advice; and
   c. the process of assessing people in order to decide whether to accept them for treatment or as a donor, or to accept their gametes and embryos for storage, in accordance with the guidance given in parts 3 and 4.

8.3 No one is obliged to accept counselling. However, it is generally recognised as beneficial.

---

[366] N 7 above, paras 3.3–3.4.
[367] ibid, para 3.4.

8.4 Three distinct types of counselling should be made available in appropriate cases:

    i.   implications counselling: this aims to enable the person concerned to understand the implications of the proposed course of action for themselves, for their family, or for any children born as a result. It may include genetic counselling;

    ii. support counselling: this aims to give emotional support at times of particular stress, eg when there is a failure to achieve a pregnancy;

    iii. therapeutic counselling: this aims to help people to cope with the consequences of infertility and treatment, and to help them to resolve the problems which these may cause. It includes helping people to adjust their expectations and to accept their situation. Therapeutic counselling may be an ongoing process and can take place or continue after the course of treatment has ended.

8.5 Centres should present the offer of counselling as part of normal routine, without implying either that the person concerned is in any way deficient or abnormal, or that there is any pressure to accept. Centres should allow them sufficient time to consider the offer.

8.6 Centres should allow sufficient time for counselling to be conducted sensitively, in an atmosphere that is conducive to discussion.

8.7 Centres should offer people the opportunity to be counselled by someone other than the clinician responsible for their treatment, donation or storage. Such counselling should be independent of the clinical decision-making process.

8.8 Centres should offer people the opportunity to be counselled individually and with their partner if they have one. Group counselling sessions may also be offered, but it is not acceptable for a centre to offer only group sessions.

8.9 People should be able to seek counselling at any stage of their investigation or treatment. However, counselling should normally be made available after the person seeking treatment or considering providing gametes or embryos for donation has received the oral and written explanations described in Pt 4, above. Discussion may then focus on the meaning and consequences of the decision, rather than on its practical aspects.

Implications Counselling

8.10 Centres *must* make implications counselling available to everyone. They should also provide access to therapeutic counselling in appropriate cases or refer people to sources of more specialist counselling outside the centre.

8.11 Implications counselling may be given by counsellors and/or other professionals, but for the purposes of this section the term counsellor will be used to describe the person providing implications counselling.

8.12 The counsellor should invite people to consider the following issues:

    a. the social responsibilities that centres and providers of gametes and embryos bear to ensure the best possible outcome for all concerned, including the child;

    b. the implications of the procedure for themselves, their family and social circle, and for any resulting children;

    c. their feelings about the use and possible disposal of any embryos derived from their gametes;

> **d.** the possibility that these implications and feelings may change over time, as personal circumstances change;
>
> **e.** the advantages and disadvantages of openness about the procedures envisaged, and how they might be explained to relatives and friends.
>
> **Genetic Counselling**
>
> **8.13** Centres should have arrangements in place to make genetic counselling available. Centres should ensure that when people are referred for genetic counselling the confidentiality provisions of the HFE Act are taken into account.
>
> **Later Counselling**
>
> **8.14** Centres should take all practicable steps to provide further opportunities for counselling about the implications of treatment, donation or storage after consent has been given, and throughout the period in which the person is providing gametes, or receiving treatment, if this is requested. If someone who has previously been a donor or patient returns to the centre for further counselling, the centre should take all practicable steps to help them obtain it.
>
> **Support Counselling**
>
> **8.15** Centres should also take all practicable steps to offer support to people who are not suitable for treatment, whose treatment has failed and people considering donation who are found to be unsuitable, to help them come to terms with their situation.
>
> **8.16** These steps should include, wherever practicable, reasonable assistance in contacting a support group.
>
> **8.17** Centres should ensure that, as part of their training, all staff are prepared to offer appropriate emotional support at all stages of their investigation, counselling and treatment to people who are suffering distress.
>
> **Therapeutic Counselling**
>
> **8.18** Procedures should be in place to identify people who suffer particular distress and to offer them, as far as is practicable, therapeutic counselling, with the aim of helping them to come to terms with their situation.
>
> **8.19** If a person experiences mental ill-health or a severe psychological problem that may or may not be related to infertility, for which it would be more appropriate to seek help and advice outside the centre, the centre should take all practicable steps to help them to obtain it.
>
> **Records**
>
> **8.20** A record should be kept of all counselling offered and whether or not the offer is accepted.
>
> **8.21** All information obtained in the course of counselling should be kept confidential, subject to paragraph 3.26, above.

10.118 The Code of Practice lists additional information that should be considered, differentiating between people seeking treatment, people providing gametes and embryos for donation, people seeking long term storage of gametes and embryos and people involved in an egg sharing arrangement.

10.119 In relation to people seeking treatment:

8.22 . . . counsellors should invite [them] . . . to consider

    a. their attitude to their own, or partner's infertility;

    b. the possibility that treatment will fail.

8.23 If a woman is undergoing infertility treatment and the possibility of her or her partner becoming a donor also arises, counselling about the implications of donation should be undertaken separately from counselling about the implications of treatment in the first instance (see guidance for people considering donation paragraphs 8.27–8.28). If the possibility of donation arises at a later stage in the treatment, donation should not proceed unless the woman and, where appropriate, her partner have been given a suitable opportunity to receive counselling about it.

8.24 Counselling about the implications of donation may be combined with counselling about the other implications of treatment at a later stage, if this is advisable in the light of the initial counselling sessions and the wishes of the people considering treatment.

8.25 In addition, where treatment using donated gametes or embryos is contemplated, people seeking treatment should also be invited to consider:

    a. their feelings about not being the genetic parents of the child;

    b. their perceptions of the needs of the child throughout their childhood and adolescence.

8.26 If a woman is already undergoing infertility treatment when the question of treatment with donated gametes or embryos derived from them arises, counselling about the implications of receiving donated material should be offered separately from counselling about the other implications of treatment. Treatment with donated material should not proceed unless the woman and, where appropriate her partner have been given a suitable opportunity to receive counselling about it.

In relation to people providing gametes and embryos for donation: **10.120**

8.27 . . . counsellors should invite people considering donation . . . to consider in particular:

    a. their reasons for wanting to provide gametes for donation;

    b. their attitudes to any existing children, and their willingness to forego [*sic*] knowledge of and responsibility for such children in the future;

    c. the possibility of their own childlessness;

    d. their perception of the needs of any children born as result of their donation;

    e. their attitudes to the prospective legal parents of their genetic offspring;

    f. their attitudes to allowing embryos which have been produced from their gametes to be used for research.

8.28 If a person seeking to donate or store gametes and/or embryos is married or has a long-term partner, the centre should counsel them together if they so wish. If a partner wishes to be counselled separately about the implications of donation or storage, centres should take all practicable steps to offer counselling at the centre, or to assist them in contacting an external counselling organisation.

10.121 In relation to people seeking long term storage of gametes and embryos:

> **8.29** . . . centres should ensure that the sources of more specialist counselling outside the centre are available and may be more appropriate for oncology patients or others requiring long term storage of their gametes or embryos.
>
> **8.30** Centres should be aware of the special needs of people seeking long term storage of gametes and embryos and should ensure that counselling is available after storage.

10.122 In relation to people involved in an egg sharing[368] arrangement:

> **8.31** . . . the HFEA strongly recommends that all couples contemplating participation in an egg sharing arrangement receive implications counselling.
>
> **8.32** Independent counsellors should be aware of the medical processes involved as well as the particular legal and social issues relevant to egg sharing arrangements.
>
> **8.33** Counselling equivalent to that provided for people seeking treatment and considering donation should be given to an egg provider and her partner as covered in paragraphs 8.22–8.28.
>
> **8.34** Implications counselling *must* be offered to both egg providers and recipients and should cover the following issues:
>
> > **a.** the implications of not knowing whether the recipient has succeeded or not;
> > **b.** the implications if the provider remains childless;
> > **c.** the implications for the recipient of using a sub-fertile egg provider; and
> > **d.** the implications of there possibly being half-siblings of a similar age resulting from the treatment.

10.123 It will have been observed that, although there is a great emphasis on counselling, no one is under any obligation to accept it. It may also be noted that a distinction is drawn between implications counselling, which must be made available to everyone, and therapeutic and support counselling. In the case of therapeutic counselling, access must be provided: in the case of support counselling 'all practicable steps to offer support' is emphasised. There is, it seems, a low take-up rate on counselling. The Code clearly sees counselling as beneficial but there is nothing in it to strengthen participation. There must be a concern—Lee and Morgan also recognise this[369]—that centres do not promote counselling lest it deter potential patients who are, after all, a source of profit. There is concern also that the Authority's enforcement of the counselling code is weak.

2. The Provision of Information

10.124 As regards the obligation to give information, the Code of Practice lays down the following:

---

[368] The Code omits to offer guidance on 'egg giving'.
[369] Lee and Morgan (n 9 above).

General Obligation

6.1 Before anyone is given licensed treatment . . ., they *must* be given 'such relevant information as is proper'. This should be distinguished from the requirement to offer counselling, which people who are seeking treatment, providing gametes/embryos for donation or wishing to store their gametes/embryos need not accept.

6.2 People seeking treatment, providing gametes/embryos for donation or wishing to store their gametes/embryos should be given oral explanations supported by relevant written material. They should be encouraged to ask for further information and their questions should be answered in a straightforward, comprehensive and open way.

6.3 Centres should devise a system to ensure that:

   a. the right information is given;
   b. the person who is to give the information is clearly identified, and has been given sufficient training and guidance to enable them to do so; and
   c. a record is kept of the information given.

6.4 Information should be given on the following points:

   a. that counselling is available;
   b. that they are free to withdraw or vary the terms of their consent at any time, up to the point that the gametes or embryos have been used in treatment services or in a project of research;
   c. the purposes for which their gametes might be used;
   d. the procedures involved in collecting gametes, including (where relevant) the possible deterioration of gametes or embryos associated with storage; in addition any possible pain, discomfort and risks to that person, eg from the use of superovulatory drugs;
   e. any costs, fees or reimbursements relevant to treatment, donation or storage;
   f. the statutory storage period for gametes and embryos, and the regulation for extension of storage;
   g. the options available to them in the event of their death or mental incapacity and the consent required to ensure their wishes are fulfilled.

In addition the Code of Practice states that information should be given to those seeking treatment on the following: **10.125**

6.5 . . .

   a. the possible disruption of the client's domestic life which treatment will cause, and the length of time he or she will have to wait for treatment;
   b. any other infertility treatments which are available, including those for which a licence is not necessary;
   c. the limitations and possible outcomes of the treatment proposed, and variations of effectiveness over time. Any data given in publicity material should be accompanied by the centre's own live birth rate per treatment cycle as verified by the HFEA and the national live birth rate per treatment cycle;
   d. the centre's statutory duty to take account of the welfare of any resulting or affected child; and (where relevant) the advantages and disadvantages of continued treatment after a certain number of attempts;

e. the possible side effects and risks of the treatment to the woman and any resulting child. This should include: the possible side effects and risks of ovarian stimulation (where relevant) for the woman, including the risks associated with ovarian hyperstimulation syndrome (OHSS) and the putative risk of cancer;

f. the availability of embryo freezing facilities, including the likelihood of success of embryo freezing, thawing, transfer and implications of storage; including (where relevant) the possible deterioration of gametes or embryos associated with storage;

g. the risks to the woman and fetus associated with multiple pregnancy and the possible practical, financial and emotional impact of a multiple birth on the family unit;

h. the importance of telling the treatment centre about any resulting birth.

6.6 In addition, if the treatment involves donated gametes, people seeking treatment should receive information on the following:

a. the genetic and other screening that people providing gametes at that centre undergo. This should include the sensitivity of the tests that are carried out and the likelihood that a screened people [*sic*] providing gametes will be a carrier;

b. the availability of genetic screening, especially if the people providing gametes at the centre are not screened for cystic fibrosis;

c. who will be the child's parent or parents under the HFE Act. Clients who are nationals or residents of other countries, or who have been treated with gametes obtained from a foreign donor should understand that the law in other countries may be different from that of the United Kingdom . . .

d. the information which centres *must* collect and register with the HFEA and the extent to which that information may be disclosed to people born as a result of the donation;

e. a child's potential need to know about their origins;

f. the child's right to see information about their origins on reaching 18 or 16 years if contemplating earlier marriage.

10.126 In addition the Code of Practice states that information should be given to those providing gametes and embryos for donation on the following:

6.7 . . .

a. the screening which will be carried out, and the practical implications of having an HIV antibody test, even if it proves negative;

b. the genetic testing that will be carried out, its scope and limitations and the implications of the result for the person considering donation and their family;

c. whether or not they will be regarded under the HFE Act as the parents of any child born as a result;

d. that donated gametes and embryos created from them will not normally be used for treatment once the number of live birth events believed to have been born as a result of the donation has reached 10, or any lower figure specified by the person considering donation;

  e. that the HFE Act generally permits people providing gametes to preserve their anonymity;

  f. the information which centres *must* collect and register with the HFEA and the extent to which that information may be disclosed to people born as a result of the donation;

  g. the possibility that a child born disabled as a result of a donor's failure to disclose defects, about which they knew or ought reasonably to have known, may be able to sue the donor for damages;

  h. in the case of altruistic egg donation where the woman is not undergoing infertility treatment herself, she will not incur any financial or other penalty if she withdraws her consent after preparation for egg recovery has begun;

6.8 . . . people consenting to the use of gametes or an embryo for the purpose of any project of research may specify conditions subject to which the gametes or embryo may be so used and should be given the following information:

  a. that research is experimental and any gametes or embryos used and created for the purposes of project of research will not be transferred for treatment;

  b. that only those gametes and embryos (fresh or frozen) that are surplus to treatment will be used for research;

  c. that research will not affect the treatment cycle;

  d. that the donation of gametes and embryos to research will not compromise treatment;

  e. that they are under no obligation to donate their gametes and embryos to research;

  f. that they have the right to vary or withdraw their consent from the study at any time up until the gametes and embryos are used for the purposes of any project of research;

  g. that they should have an opportunity to ask questions and discuss the research project;

  h. that after the research has been completed, all donated gametes and embryos will be allowed to perish;

6.9 In addition, if the donated gametes and embryos could be used in secondary research the people giving consent should be informed of this and provided with the following information;

  a. that it is possible that gametes and embryos or embryo cell samples may be fixed for future studies . . . [secondary research];

  b. that secondary research could include genetic research and the implications of this;

  c. that as a means of protecting confidentiality, gametes and embryos for secondary research may be anonymised and this can be reversible or irreversible;

  d. if the gametes and embryos are to be reversibly anonymised and if genetic research is proposed, people considering donation should be told that particular results may be fed back to them and offered counselling about the implications of this;

  e. if the gametes and embryos are to be irreversibly anonymised, people considering donation should be fully informed of the implications of this ie the inability to feed results back.

10.127   As will have been observed, the level of detail required by the Code of Practice far exceeds the requirements of common law. The question therefore arises as to the liability of a clinician who fails to comply with the Code of Practice. Section 25(6) states that: 'A failure on the part of any person to observe any provision of the code shall not of itself render the person liable to any proceedings . . .'. On its face this suggests that failure to observe a provision of the Code will not, without more, be sufficient to render a doctor liable to civil or criminal proceedings. However, a case may be made that the Code of Practice establishes what is regarded as good medical practice, and thus what a responsible doctor would do, with the consequence that failure to comply with it could constitute a breach of duty and expose the doctor concerned to a civil action for negligence.[370] The latter is the better view, and, in the absence of a legal ruling to the contrary, should be followed.

10.128   Where the treatment falls outside the 1990 Act, and thus the Code of Practice, the common law will govern what information must be given. The details of this are found in Chapter 2. Briefly, it is thought that there should at the very least be disclosure of information where the risk would be sufficiently substantial to require disclosure. Note the language of Lord Bridge in *Sidaway v Board of Governors of Bethlem Royal Hospital* that the 'judge might in certain circumstances come to the conclusion that disclosure of a particular risk was so obviously necessary to an informed choice on the part of the patient that no reasonably prudent medical man would fail to make it'.[371] He gave as an example, 'an operation involving a substantial risk of very adverse consequences', and viewed a 10 per cent risk as 'substantial'.[372]

H. Control of Gametes and Embryos

10.129   The 1990 Act in Sch 3 sets out an elaborate framework the purpose of which is to vest control of gametes and embryos in those who provide the genetic material.

10.130   It is a requirement of the 'licence condition' that the consent provisions in Sch 3 are complied with.[373] Failure to observe the provisions will breach the duty upon the 'person responsible' for the licensed activities to ensure that the conditions of the licence are complied with.[374] A breach of such duty, for example, proceeding without an effective consent, is a ground for the revocation of the licence.[375]

---

[370] See *Bolam v Friern HMC* [1957] 1 WLR 582.
[371] [1985] AC 871, 900.
[372] ibid.
[373] s 12(c).
[374] s 17(1)(e).
[375] Under s 18(1)(c).

The Schedule requires that a gamete provider must, at the time the gametes are procured, indicate in a written consent to what use or uses the gametes may be put.[376] The gametes, and any resulting embryos, may only be used in accordance with the consents (this includes those consents as varied).[377]

10.131

A gamete provider must specify the purposes to which the gametes may be put. They may not be used for treatment services unless there is an 'effective consent'[378] by that person to their being so used, and they are used in accordance with the terms of the consent.[379] Nor may they be kept in storage unless there is an effective consent by that person to their storage, and they are stored in accordance with the consent.[380] Nor may they be used to bring about the creation of an embryo in vitro unless there is effective consent by that person to such a creation.[381] In this case , the gamete provider must both consent to the future use and/or storage of the embryo.[382]

10.132

A consent to the use of any embryo may specify conditions subject to which the embryo may be so used.[383] Similarly, a consent to storage of gametes or embryos may specify conditions subject to which they may remain in storage.[384] But may the provider specify any conditions? For example, would a condition which stipulated that the gamete not be used for the treatment of individuals of a particular racial, ethnic or religious group be valid or invalid? The 1990 Act does not provide an answer to this question. But common law does. There can be little doubt that such a condition would be regarded as invalid.[385] A treatment centre should therefore not accept gametes or embryos subject to such conditions. Whether such a condition would invalidate the 'effective consent' is more contentious. There are two views: one which argues that, if the consent could be valid with the unlawful condition removed, it should be upheld; the second would uphold the consent only if it gave effect to the provider's underlying intention.[386] The better view is, this author believes, the first one which would sever the invalid condition. The public interest in making gametes available should prevail over the selfish prejudice of the provider.[387]

10.133

---

[376] Sch 3, para 2(1).
[377] Sch 3, para 4.
[378] 'Effective consent' means consent which has not been withdrawn: see Sch 3, para 1.
[379] Sch 3, para 5.
[380] Sch 3, para 8(1).
[381] Sch 3, para 6(1).
[382] Sch 3, para 6(3).
[383] Sch 3, para 2(1).
[384] Sch 3, para 2(2).
[385] See *Re Dominion Students' Hall Trust* [1947] Ch 183; *Re Lysaght* [1966] Ch 191.
[386] See Kennedy and Grubb (n 302 above).
[387] As happens with charitable trusts. Certainly, this should happen if, once the invalid condition is removed, the public interest in having gametes and embryos preserved could be upheld.

10.134   A consent to the storage of any gametes or embryos must specify the maximum period of storage, if less than the statutory storage period[388] (on which see para 10.43–10.44), and state what is to be done with the gametes or embryos if the person who gave the consent dies or is unable, because of incapacity, to vary the terms of the consent or to revoke it.[389] The 1990 Act does not state what should happen, only that the provider of gametes and embryos should address the issue.

10.135   Consent can be varied and withdrawn[390] by notice. By implication notice must be in writing[391] (though this is not specifically stated in the 1990 Act). Nor does the Act say what notice must be given: the assumption must be that any notice will suffice. The terms of any consent to the use of any embryo cannot be varied, and the consent cannot be withdrawn, once the embryo has been used in providing treatment services or for the purpose of any project of research.[392]

10.136   An embryo taken from a woman[393] must not be used for any purpose unless there is effective consent by her to the use of her embryo for that purpose, and it is in accordance with the consent,[394] or it is used for the purpose of providing that woman with treatment services.[395] Nor must it be kept in storage unless there is effective consent to this by her.[396]

10.137   A person's gametes must not be kept in storage unless there is effective consent by that person to their storage and they are stored in accordance with the consent.[397] An embryo, the creation of which was brought about in vitro must not be kept in storage, unless there is effective consent to the storage by each person whose gametes were used to bring about the creation of the embryo, and the embryo is stored in accordance with those consents.[398] It follows that, upon the valid withdrawal of consent by at least one gamete provider, any gametes or embryo may no longer be lawfully stored. They must then either be used in accordance with any remaining consents to their use or, if no such consent exists, must presumably be 'allowed to perish'.[399] The 1990 Act is silent as to what should happen in these

---

[388] Sch 3, para 2(2)(a).

[389] Sch 3, para 2(2)(b).

[390] Sch 3, para 4(1).

[391] The definition of 'notice' in s 46 does not require notice to be in writing, but the language of s 46(2) ('delivering', 'leaving', 'sending by post') strongly suggests this.

[392] Sch 3, para 4(2). This provision seeks to overcome the problems which arise where there are disputes over frozen embryos, for example over their 'custody', as happened in *Davis v Davis* 842 SW 2d 588 (1992), and see para 10.137, below.

[393] By lavage.

[394] Sch 3, para 7(1), (2).

[395] Sch 3, para 7(3).

[396] Sch 3, para 8(3).

[397] Sch 3, para 8(1).

[398] Sch 3, para 8(2).

[399] *The Code of Practice* (5th edn, 2001) requires the procedure for disposal to be 'sensitively devised', given the special status of the human embryo (see para 9.13).

circumstances but no other consequence seems possible in terms of general scheme of the Act. Of course, it would be possible to prioritise the man's right to be free from unwanted reproduction (as an American court did in *Davis v Davis*[400]), or the woman's right on the grounds that after fertilisation, natural or in vitro, a man has no rights over the reproductive process (a conclusion arrived at by another American court in *Kass v Kass*[401]). In effect the English courts have now taken the *Davis v Davis* route in *Evans v Amicus Healthcare Ltd; Hadley v Midland Fertility Services.*[402] Implanting embryos could not be said to constitute 'treatment together' when couples had separated, and the men opposed treatment. Even if after separation a man agrees to the woman using the embryos, a clinic may refuse treatment because s 13(5) requires it to consider the welfare of any child born, including that child's need for a father. Wall J could find no breach of the European Convention on Human Rights.

10.138 A centre which fails to comply with these provisions would be in breach of a condition of its licence. This could be reviewed by HFEA, and revoked. The 1990 Act is silent on whether gamete or embryo providers have any remedy in law. There would appear to be four possibilities.[403]

10.139 One possible avenue of redress is by way of an application for judicial review, and then to seek a declaration or an order of mandamus. For this to succeed it would be necessary to show that the licence-holder was exercising a public function.[404] Although Kennedy and Grubb characterise it as a private activity[405] and, therefore, not subject to judicial review, there is a strong argument for saying that even a private clinic would be carrying out a public function. It is, after all, licensed by an institution established by the state (HFEA), and is highly regulated.

10.140 A remedy in contract is the second resource. In default of express terms, Kennedy and Grubb argue, rightly, the author of this chapter believes, that Sch 3 'could be said to be implied into the contract such that a claim for breach of contract could be brought against the licence-holder'.[406] Remedies would include, injunction, or specific performance as well as damages (which might extend to any distress[407] caused, given the personal nature of the contract). It may be more difficult to argue in contract where treatment or storage is provided under the aegis of the National Health Service: but, even here, where there is payment, it should be possible to proceed in contract.

---

[400] 842 SW 2d 588 (1992).
[401] 91 NY 2d 554 (1998).
[402] [2003] 4 All ER 903.
[403] And see Kennedy and Grubb (n 302 above).
[404] See *R v Panel on Take-Overs and Mergers, ex p Datafin plc* [1987] QB 815.
[405] Kennedy and Grubb (n 302 above), 1307–8.
[406] ibid, 1308.
[407] See eg *Hayes and Another v Dodd* [1990] 2 All ER 815.

10.141   Although s 25(6) (and see para 10.127, above) states that breach of the Code of
Practice does not render the person concerned liable to any proceedings, it is arguable that a breach of statutory duty, for example, the duty to allow embryos to
perish, could give rise to a private right of action for breach of statutory duty. The
1990 Act imposes a statutory duty upon the licence-holder: 'the conditions of the
licence [must be] complied with'.[408] But it is silent on whether civil liability can
exist for breach of the Act. Kennedy and Grubb, however, argue that the Act is 'so
emphatic'[409] in its commitment to the wishes of the gamete providers that a court
might well take the view that a private right of action should arise. The provisions
of Sch 3 clearly contemplate gamete providers as the beneficiaries of the obligations imposed upon licence-holders.[410] They add that this argument 'gains
force'[411] from the absence of any remedy. However, it is argued that remedies may
well exist in judicial review and in contract.

10.142   Whether or not there is a property claim has not been aired in any English case.[412]
The Tennessee decision of *Davis v Davis*[413] is no support for the gamete provider's
claim to exercise a property right over their embryos where the licence-holder fails
to comply with the 1990 Act. The Warnock report is equivocal, maintaining that
'the concept of ownership of human embryos seems to us to be undesirable',[414]
and that a couple who have stored an embryo should have 'rights to the use and
disposal of the embryo'.[415] If 'use and disposal' are not incidents of ownership,
what are?[416]

10.143   A court might have to decide the property question if gametes or embryos were to
be damaged or destroyed, or, indeed, lost. How would it respond to an action of
conversion? Kennedy and Grubb's response that this is essentially 'a question of
metaphysical proportions' making it 'idle to predict the outcome of such a case
should these . . . circumstances arise' seems apt.[417]

---

[408] s 17(1)(e).

[409] Kennedy and Grubb (n 302 above), 1308.

[410] ibid.

[411] ibid.

[412] But one may be imminent: see The Times, 23 August 2002.

[413] 842 SW 2d 588 (1992). It may be otherwise with sperm or eggs (though not in the view of
Hecht v Superior Court 20 Cal Rptr 275 (1993). Nor is *Moore v Regents of the University of California*
793 P 2d 479 (1990) likely to assist.

[414] N 7 above, para 10.11.

[415] ibid.

[416] And see Kennedy I, *Treat Me Right: Essays in Medical Law and Ethics* (Oxford: OUP, 1991),
134.

[417] Kennedy and Grubb (n 302 above), 1315. And see further Steinbock, B, 'Sperm as Property'
in Harris, J and Holm, S (eds), *The Future of Human Reproduction* (Oxford: OUP, 1998), 150.

I. Access to Information

Section 31 of the 1990 Act imposes upon HFEA a statutory obligation to keep a register of information relating to: **10.144**

(i)   The provision of treatment services for any identifiable individual, or;

(ii) The keeping or use of the gametes of any identifiable individual or of an embryo taken from any identifiable woman; or if it shows that any identifiable individual was, or may have been, born in consequence of treatment services.[418]

The 1990 Act requires licence-holders to collect this information and provide it to HFEA.[419]

Who has access to the statutory information held by HFEA? Section 31(3) gives applicants over the age of 18 access to specified and limited information, or will do when regulations are made.[420] We still await these 13 years after the 1990 Act was passed. The Warnock report's compromise hinged on the 'need to maintain the absolute anonymity of the donor',[421] whilst recognising that a child born following donor insemination 'should have access to basic information about the donor's ethnic origin and genetic health'.[422] Baroness Warnock herself admitted in May 2002 that the report bearing her name had come to the wrong conclusion, and she now advocates removing anonymity from donors.[423] She still couches the debate in terms of sperm donors, which is where it was in 1984 when the Report was published. But it must, of course, to be broadened to cover egg and embryo donation. The issues may not be identical, but are sufficiently similar to warrant no distinction of policy.   **10.145**

A challenge to donor anonymity was expected once the Human Rights Act 1998 came into operation and was mounted in May 2002 by a 29 year-old woman, Joanna Rose, and the parents of a six-year-old girl.[424] 'What the claimants [were] trying to obtain is information about their biological fathers, something that goes to the very heart of their identity, and to their make-up as people'.[425] The challenge was based primarily on Article 8 of the European Convention on Human Rights. The European Court of Human Rights long ago held that this requires that 'everyone should be able to establish details of their identity as individual   **10.146**

---

[418] s 31(2).

[419] s 12(g).

[420] s 31(5).

[421] N 7 above, para 4.22.

[422] ibid, para 4.21.

[423] *Making Babies* (n 151 above), para 21.65; The Independent, 13 May 2002. See also leading article 'An End to Anonymity', The Independent, 14 May 2002. A useful collection of essays is Blyth, E, Crawshaw, M, and Speirs, J, *Truth and the Child Ten Years On* (Birmingham: BASW, 1998).

[424] *Rose v Secretary of State for Health and Human Fertilisation and Embryology Authority* [2002] 2 FLR 962.

[425] ibid, 973 *per* Scott Baker J.

human beings'.[426] However, under Article 8(2) donors have 'rights and freedoms'. Scott Baker J concluded that Article 8 was engaged both with regard to identifying and non-identifying information. But the 'fact that Art 8 is engaged is far from saying that there is a breach of it. That question . . . involves consideration of other matters and may depend on any future action taken by the Secretary of State.'[427] The judge admitted that identifying information was likely to become 'very relevant when one comes to the important balancing exercise of the other considerations in Art 8(2).'[428] The claimants did not seek identifying information. Were they to have done so, it may be predicted that at least as regards this the challenge would fail on para 2 of Article 8. The challenge also used the discrimination provision of the European Convention.[429] Adopted children have the legal right to discover their genetic parents.[430] This argument was not addressed by the judge and he came to no conclusion, not even a provisional one, on it. Whether it should succeed depends upon whether an argument can be sustained that children produced by donation are in a comparable situation to adopted children:[431] but the argument for 'open adoption' largely rests on the fact that most adopted children today are children with histories not babies. The judge went on to conclude that s 6(6)(a) of the Human Rights Act 1998 was an answer to any complaint that the Secretary of State had failed to enact primary legislation or make regulations under s 31(4)(a) of the 1990 Act, but no answer to a failure to make regulations under s 8(d) of the 1990 Act.[432] It was not, he held, possible to rule at this stage whether, if the claimants' arguments succeeded, they would be entitled to a declaration of incompatability.[433]

10.147   The Regulations, when made, will not be able to require HFEA to give any information as to the identity of a person whose gametes have been used or from whom an embryo has been taken, if a person to whom a licence applied was provided with the information at a time when HFEA could not have been required to give information of the kind in question.[434] A donor of gametes (or embryos) will thus always know exactly what information may be given to a resulting child 18 years after that child was born. This means that even if, as must now be virtually certain, regulations expand the amount of information to be made available to children as a result of donation, only children who are the products of post-regulation donations will benefit.

---

[426]   ibid, 976.
[427]   ibid.
[428]   *Gaskin v UK* [1990] 1 FLR 167, 176. See also *Mikulic v Croatia* [2002] 1 FCR 720.
[429]   Art 14.
[430]   Adoption Act 1976, s 51 (though it is not an absolute right: see *R v Registrar General, ex p Smith* [1991] 2 QB 393).
[431]   *Cf* Blyth, E, 'Donor Assisted Conception and Donor Offspring Rights to Genetic Origins Information' (1998) 6 *International Journal of Children's Rights* 237.
[432]   N 423 above, 977.
[433]   ibid, 980.
[434]   s 31(5).

The Code of Practice requires that treatment centres should take into account, **10.148**
amongst other factors, ' a child's potential need to know about their origins'.[435] A
'potential need' is not, of course, a 'right', and the epithet 'potential' in itself suggests that the need to know is only a remote contingency, and not one of overwhelming importance. The way the Code of Practice deals with the counselling of
adults who wish to become recipients of gamete donation (and see also para 8.1 of
the code above) also shows thin understanding of rights issues.[436] Thus, people
seeking licensed treatment are to be invited to consider 'the advantages and disadvantages of openness about the procedures',[437] and 'their perceptions of the needs
of the child throughout their childhood and adolescence'.[438] There must be doubt
as to whether in this respect the Code of Practice complies with the United
Nations Convention on the Rights of the Child.[439] This provides for the recognition of the right to identity,[440] which is stipulated for the first time in any international human rights document. It also stipulates a right to know parents,
though this is hedged with the qualification 'as far as possible'.[441]

The 1990 Act additionally provides that information may be made available to **10.149**
someone between the ages of 16[442] and 18 where that person is concerned that
someone whom he or she proposes to marry may be genetically related.[443] It is provided that the minor must be given a suitable opportunity to receive proper counselling about the implications of compliance with the request.[444] This provision is
targeted at the feared horrible consequence of siblings mating. They can, of
course, do this without marrying. To provide complete (or at least better) protection the legislation would need to be amended to read 'whom he or she proposed
to have sexual intercourse with'. It will be noted that the information to be so provided to minors is less than that envisaged to be vouchsafed to those over the age
of 18. The provision is anyway defective because only on the application of both
intending marriage partners would HFEA be able to disclose whether this is a
genetic relationship.

---

[435] 5th edn , 2001, para 3.14.
[436] And see Blyth, E, *Infertility and Assisted Conception: Practice Issues For Counsellors*
(Birmingham: BASW, 1995).
[437] 5th edn , 2001, para 8.12.e.
[438] ibid, para 8.25.b. See also para 6.5.e.
[439] See Stewart, G, 'Interpreting the Child's Right to Legal Identity in the UN Convention on the
Rights of the Child' (1992) 26 *Family Law Quarterly* 221. See also Van Bueren, G, *The International
Law on the Rights of The Child* (Dordrecht: Martinus Nijhoff, 1995), 126–7 (her argument is
limited to sperm donation).
[440] In Art 8.
[441] Art 9.
[442] But not to someone under 16, who may be able to marry according to his/her personal law (for
an example see *Mohamed v Knott* [1969] 1 QB 1).
[443] s 31(6).
[444] s 31(6)(b).

10.150   The Registrar General[445] may request information from HFEA in fulfilling his statutory functions.[446] HFEA is bound to comply with any request made by the Registrar General by notice[447]—presumably in writing, though the 1990 Act does not so stipulate[448]—to disclose whether any information on the register (which HFEA is obliged by s 31 to keep) tends to show that a particular man may be the father of the child[449] and, if it does, disclose that information.[450] This provision applies where a claim is made before the Registrar General that a man is or is not the father of the child and it is 'necessary or desirable' for the purpose of any function of the Registrar General to determine whether the claim is or may be well-founded.[451]

10.151   A court may require HFEA to disclose information, excluding that relating to any donor,[452] where in any proceedings the question of whether a person is or is not the parent of a child by virtue of the status provisions of the 1990 Act (on which see paras 10.173–10.183, below) falls to be determined. The court cannot do this of its own motion: it requires an application by any party to the proceedings.[453] The court must not comply unless it is satisfied that the interests of justice require it to do so, taking into account any representation by any individual who may be affected by the disclosure and the welfare of the child if a minor and of any other minor who may be affected by the disclosure.[454] If the proceedings are civil proceedings, the court may direct that they (or part of them) be heard in private,[455] and applications for such a direction must themselves be heard in private.[456]

10.152   A court may require HFEA to disclose the identity of a donor when a child wishes to bring a claim for injury caused before birth under s 1 of the Congenital Disabilities (Civil Liability) Act 1976[457] (see further Chapter 12). The 1976 Act provides for civil liability in the case of children born disabled in consequence of the intentional act, negligence or breach of statutory duty of some person prior to the birth of the child. The defendant is answerable to the child if he/she was liable to one or both parents in respect of matters which gave rise to the disability at birth. Such matters could arise either before conception, during pregnancy or in

---

[445] Defined in s 32(3).
[446] s 32(1).
[447] s 32(2).
[448] Though the wording of s 46(2) would make it difficult to give or serve a notice, if it were not in writing.
[449] By virtue of s 28 of the 1990 Act, discussed below at paras 10.174, 10.176–10.181.
[450] s 32(2).
[451] s 32(1).
[452] s 34(1) and s 31(2)(b).
[453] s 34(1).
[454] s 34(2).
[455] s 34(3).
[456] s 34(4).
[457] s 35(1).

the process of childbirth. The 1990 Act contemplates the situation where it is necessary to identify a person who is the genetic, but because of the Act, not the legal parent of the child. The provisions of s 34(2)–(4) (and see para 10.151 above) apply to these applications as well. This provision becomes a resource of importance when a child wishes to sue a donor for the donor's negligence.[458]

The Data Protection Act 1998, which regulates the processing of personal data, **10.153** must be considered here (see also generally Chapter 9). Clinicians are 'data controllers' and 'processing' includes the obtaining, storage and use of personal data produced in the treatment service environment. The 1998 Act entitles a patient to serve notice on a doctor to stop the processing of personal data, allowing the doctor as data controller to rectify or erase inaccurate data. Individuals have the right to seek compensation for damage. The 1998 Act covers all health records, whether held electronically or in written form. Under an order made under the previous legislation (the 1984 Act),[459] permission was given to withhold data which might otherwise have had to be disclosed. The new legislation is similarly accompanied. The Data Protection (Miscellaneous Subject Access Exemptions) Order 2000,[460] made under s 38(1) of the 1998 Act, exempts from the subject access provisions of s 7 of the 1998 Act information falling within ss 31 and 33 of the 1990 Act, that is 'information about the provision of treatment services, the keeping or use of gametes or embryos and whether identifiable individuals were born in consequence of treatment services'. There are two possible interpretations of this exemption provision. First, it could be said to remove from the regime of the 1998 Act any access questions relating to the relevant personal data. Thus, a child or patient or donor seeking access to this information about him/herself from a licensed clinic or HFEA would only be able to do so in accordance with and, importantly, through the processes provided by the 1990 Act. The right of access—for example the right of someone about to marry to find out whether he is genetically related to his intended wife—would remain under the 1990 Act itself since it is exempted from s 7 of the 1998 Act by the Order. A second interpretation is possible, however. The 2000 Order exempts the relevant information covered by ss 31 and 33 of the 1990 Act 'the disclosure of which is prohibited or restricted' (Article 2). It might therefore be said that the exemption from s 7 is more limited: namely, only to the extent that the information covered by the 1990 Act cannot be disclosed under the 1990 Act is it exempt from s 7. Thus, information which can or must be disclosed by a clinic or HFEA under s 31 or 33 remains subject to the right of access by a data subject under s 7 of the 1998 Act. This will be important only when the information is personal data, that is health information about the individual seeking access him/herself. If it relates to others , for example, a donor or a child's

---

[458] s 33 (8), inserting a new s 35A into the Data Protection Act 1984.
[459] Data Protection (Subject Access Modification) (Health) Order 1987, SI 1987/1903.
[460] SI 2000/419.

parents when the applicant is a child, disclosure under the 1998 Act would be modified.

10.154   The 1990 Act imposes a strict secrecy requirement for statutory information held by HFEA and by licence-holders. As regards HFEA, s 33 provides:

(1)   No person who is or has been a member or employee of the Authority shall disclose any information mentioned in sub-section (2) below which he holds or has held as such a member or employee.

(2)   The information referred to in sub-section (1) above is—

(a)   Any information contained or required to be contained in the register kept in pursuance of s 31 of this Act, and

(b)   Any other information obtained by any member or employee of the Authority on terms or in circumstances requiring it to be held in confidence.

10.155   As regards a licence-holder, s 33(5) of the 1990 Act provides:

(5)   No person who is or has been a person to whom a licence applies and no person to whom directions have been given shall disclose any information falling within s 31(2) [as to which see para 10.144 above] of this Act which he holds or has held as such a person.

The requirements of the 1990 Act, which were thought over-harsh, have been relaxed by amending legislation: namely, the Human Fertilisation and Embryology (Disclosure of Information) Act 1992. This permits a greater degree of disclosure by licence-holders than did the 1990 Act. The law on disclosure by HFEA remains as set out in the 1990 Act.

10.156   As regards disclosure by HFEA of *statutory information*, the following is permitted:

(i)   disclosure to a person who is a member or employee of HFEA;[461]

(ii)   disclosure to a person to whom a licence applies for the purposes of his/her functions as such;[462]

(iii) disclosure of such information so that no individual to whom the information relates can be identified;[463]

(iv)   Disclosure in pursuance of a court order[464] or to the Registrar General in pursuance of a statutory request;[465]

(v)   Disclosure in accordance with s 31[466] (on which see paras 10.145 and 10.149);

---

[461] s 33(3)(a).
[462] s 33(3)(b).
[463] s 33(3)(c).
[464] s 33(3)(d).
[465] s 33(3)(e).
[466] s 33(3)(f).

(vi) disclosure to patients or donors which relates exclusively to themselves;[467] where an individual is treated together with another, disclosure is permitted to both of them.[468]

As regards confidential information held by HFEA which is not 'statutory infor-   **10.157**
mation', the 1990 Act imposes a statutory obligation of confidence.[469] But this does not apply to disclosure of information made to members or employees of HFEA acting in that capacity,[470] or where disclosure is made with the consent of the person or persons whose confidence would otherwise be protected[471] or which has been lawfully made available to the public before the disclosure is made.[472]

Licence-holders' duties as regards confidence are governed both by the common   **10.158**
law[473] and by the statute (1990 Act, s 33(6), amended by the 1992 Act). The common law duty of confidentiality, though never in much doubt, was only authoritatively stated in recent years. It is discussed fully in Chapter 9.

The 1990 Act goes further than the common law in limiting disclosure. In addi-   **10.159**
tion, a licence-holder or nominal licensee who gives or receives any money or other benefit, not authorised by directions, in respect of the supply of gametes or embryos, is guilty of a criminal offence.[474]

Disclosure of statutory information is permitted only circumstances listed in s   **10.160**
33(6), (6A), (6B), (6C), (6D), (6E), (6F), (6G), (7), and (9). Disclosure is permitted:

(i)   To a person as a member or employee of the Authority.
(ii) To a person to whom a licence applies for the purposes of his functions as such.
(iii) So far as it identifies a person who, but for the Act (as to which see paras (viii)–(xi) below) would or might be a parent of a person who institutes proceedings under s 1A of the Congenital Disabilities (Civil Liability) Act 1976, but only for the purpose of defending such proceedings, or instituting connected proceedings for compensation against that parent.
(iv) For statistical or other purposes where no individual can be identified.
(v)   In pursuance of directions given by virtue of s 24(5) or (6) of the 1990 Act.[475]

---

[467] s 33(7).
[468] s 33(7)(b).
[469] s 33(2)(b).
[470] s 33(4)(a).
[471] s 33(4)(b).
[472] s 33(4)(c).
[473] See *X v Y* [1988] 2 All ER 648 and *W v Egdell* [1990] Ch 359.
[474] s 41(8).
[475] s 33(6)(e).

(vi) '[N]ecessarily' for any purpose preliminary to proceedings or for the purposes of, or in connection with, any proceedings. The word 'necessarily' imports objectivity into what is otherwise a wide provision. It is insufficient that the clinician thinks it is necessary to disclose information or that he/she is acting in good faith. 'Any proceedings' is defined to include 'any formal procedure for dealing with a complaint',[476] but not any further.[477] The width of (vi) is such that the preliminary proceedings do not , it seems, need to be proceedings in which doctors are involved. But disclosure which identifies a donor is not permitted, at any rate where a child was, or may have been born, as a consequence.[478] However, as Kennedy and Grubb point out, 'the latter information may be important where the medical negligence claim is based on inadequate screening of the donor(s) or testing of the donated material. Here what passed between the doctor and the donor may well be important to the doctor's defence and yet he cannot disclose any identifying information to his legal advisers.'[479] A court has the power to order disclosure of information which identifies a donor (see the discussion of s 35 in para 10.152 above) , but this is only for the purpose of instituting proceedings against the donor.

(vii) For the purpose of establishing for the purposes of a parental order in a surrogacy case[480] (as to which see para10.213 below) whether the conditions as to parentage for such an order are met.

(viii) To support an application for information where there is a right of access to health records, generally by someone other than the patient (for example, a relative of a deceased patient), since the patient would already have a right of access (under s 33(7), discussed above at para 10.160).

(ix) With the consent of the patient.[481]

Where a man and a woman are treated together, disclosure may be made with the consent of both,[482] or if disclosure is made for the purpose of disclosing information about the provision of treatment services for one of them, to disclosure with the consent of that individual.[483] It is provided[484] that consent to disclosure must be to a specific person, except when it is to a person who needs to know in connection with the provision of treatment

---

[476] s 33(9).

[477] Though they would include any proceedings brought against a licensed doctor; a complaint against a GP (licensed to provide DI) under the National Health Service (Service Committee and Tribunal Regulations 1992, SI 1992/664; and a complaint against an NHS hospital doctor under the complaints procedure.

[478] s 33(6A)(a).

[479] Kennedy and Grubb (n 302 above), 1339–40.

[480] s 33(6)(g).

[481] s 33(6B)–(6D).

[482] s 33(6B)(b)(i).

[483] s 33(6B)(b)(ii).

[484] s 33(6C).

services, or any other description of medical, surgical or obstetric services, for the individual giving the consent, or in connection with the carrying out of an audit of clinical practice or in connection with the auditing of accounts.[485]

A patient's consent is not valid,[486] unless reasonable steps have been taken to explain to him/her the implications of the disclosure.[487]

(x)   In an emergency, by a doctor who is 'satisfied that it is necessary to make the disclosure to avert an imminent danger to the health of a patient and 'it is not reasonably practicable to obtain that patient's consent'.[488] If it is reasonably practicable , the patient's consent must be obtained. The doctor must be satisfied that disclosure is necessary: *cf* (vi) above (there is more leeway for subjective judgment here). But danger to health must be 'imminent' and not, for example, likely at some time in the future. Disclosure under this provision is also permitted.[489]

(xi)   In such circumstances as may be specified in Regulations promulgated by the Secretary of State.[490]

J. Pre-implantation Genetic Diagnosis

Pre-implantation genetic diagnosis (PGD) developed post-Warnock. The technique was first successfully used in 1990 to produce two sets of twin girls where families were at high risk of passing on a serious X-linked disorder.[491] PGD is not specifically tackled in the 1990 Act. But, since it involves the creation and use of embryos, it must be licensed by HFEA to be lawful.[492] It has licensed PGD for certain severe or life-threatening disorders at a limited number of clinics,[493] but it has rejected the use of PGD for sex selection for social reasons.[494] Some jurisdictions,

10.161

---

[485] This avoids the circuitous procedure which HFEA formerly advised, whereby a patient was to be given a sealed envelope to deliver to his/her GP. See, further, *Code of Practice* (5th edn, 2001), Annex B.

[486] s 33(6D).

[487] 'Implication' must be interpreted broadly in terms of what the person concerned would understand.

[488] s 33(6E)(a), (b).

[489] s 33(6F).

[490] s 33(6G).

[491] See HFEA/ACGT Consultation Document, *Pre-Implantation Genetic Diagnosis* (1999), para 10.

[492] s 3(1). And see McMillan, J, 'Sex Selection in the United Kingdom' (2002) 32(1) *Hastings Center Report* 28.

[493] This is said to be 'implicit' in the 1990 Act.

[494] For an example see the Louise and Alan Masterston case, The Guardian, 16 October 2000. For the view that it should be legal see McCarthy, D, 'Why Sex Selection should be Legal' (2001) 27 *Journal of Medical Ethics* 302. This has recently been reaffirmed: see The Guardian, 12 November 2003, 13.

for example Victoria, have specifically banned sex selection, in Victoria's case unless 'it is necessary for the child to be of a particular sex so as to avoid the risk of transmission of a genetic abnormality or a disease to the child'.[495] English legislation does not currently ban sex selection where this is carried out for social purposes, and it is known to take place using the technique of sperm sorting. In a report issued in November 2003 HFEA reaffirmed its opposition to sex selection on social grounds.[496]

10.162 HFEA allows for PGD in situations where abortion legislation would permit termination of a pregnancy[497] (in the words of the Abortion Act 1967, as amended by the 1990 Act, where there is 'a substantial risk that, if the child were born, it would suffer from such physical or mental abnormalities as to be seriously handicapped'[498]). In 2001, HFEA allowed for the first time PGD to be employed to produce a child who would be a good tissue match for a sibling who needed a bone marrow transplant.[499] PGD had been already used for this purpose in the United States (the *Nash* case[500]) and had also been used by a British couple in the United States.[501] In allowing PGD in such circumstances HFEA may be thought to have gone beyond its guidelines: certainly the creation of a human being to assist another was controversial.[502] And it has been recently challenged.[503] Did the Authority exceed its remit? A first instance judge ruled that it had, that it was wrong to allow PGD to be used in the 'Hashmi' case to select an embryo which could be tissue-typed to find the best match for an existing child who has beta thalassaemia major. The Court of Appeal, rightly, it is submitted, disagreed, and has given the go-ahead. Lord Phillips of Worth Matravers MR was persuaded that if the Act permitted the licensing of embryo research activities for the purpose of 'developing methods for detecting the presence of gene or chromosome abnormalities in embryos before implantation',[504] the clear inference was that Parliament approved of PGD to avoid implantation of embryos carrying genetic defects. He noted: 'Parliament chose to permit the licensing of research. It makes

---

[495] Infertility Treatment Act 1995, s 50.

[496] Human Fertilisation on and Embryology Authority, *Sex Selection: Options for Regulation* (London: HFEA, 2003).

[497] And therefore not to test for 'any social and psychological characteristics, normal, physical variations, or any other conditions which are not associated with disability or a serious medical condition' (n 490 above, para 22).

[498] Abortion Act 1967, s 1(1)(d), discussed at para 11.53 *et seq.*

[499] Ethics Committee of HFEA, 'Ethics Issues in the Location and Selection of Pre-implantation Embryos To Produce Tissue Donors', 22 November 2001 (*www.hfea.gov.uk/2002*).

[500] See Dobson, R, ' "Designer Baby" Cures Sister' (2000) 321 *British Medical Journal* 1040.

[501] See Gottlieb, S, 'US Doctors Say Selection Acceptable for Non-Medical Reasons' (2001) 323 *British Medical Journal* 828.

[502] See Robertson, JA, Kahn, JP, Wagner, JE, 'Conception To Obtain Hematopoietic Stem Cells' (2002) 32 (3) *Hastings Center Report* 34.

[503] [2003] 2 All ER 105 (Maurice Kay J); [2003] 3 All ER 257 (CA).

[504] Human Fertilisation and Embryology Act 1990, Sch 2, para 3(2)(e).

little sense for Parliament, at the same time, to prohibit reaping the benefit of that research even under licence.'[505] The Court of Appeal also had no doubt that genetic analysis for the purpose of tissue typing was 'necessary or desirable for the purpose of providing treatment services'.[506] Lord Phillips of Worth Matravers conceded that his 'initial reaction'[507] was the same as the first instance judge, that is that the phrase suggests 'treatment designed to assist the physical processes from fertilisation to the birth of a child'.[508] But he now saw that 'if the impediment to bearing a child is concern that it may be born with a hereditary defect, treatment which enables women to become pregnant and to bear children in the confidence that they will not be suffering from such defects can properly be described as 'for the purposes of assisting women to carry children'.[509] He concluded that 'whether the PGD has the purpose of producing a child free from genetic defects, or of producing a child with stem cells matching a sick or dying sibling, the IVF treatment that includes PGD constitutes 'treatment for the purpose of assisting women to bear children'.[510] Mance LJ was influenced by the welfare imperative in s 13(5) of the Act (and see para 10.84, above,). This, he said, 'points towards a wider concern for the future child and siblings, which is better served if the legislation is read as permitting [the] screening'[511] envisaged in the case.

There remain a number of other unanswered questions. First, after PGD who ultimately decides whether the embryo is transferred to the woman's uterus? Suppose doctors decide that the embryo is 'handicap-free' and want it transferred to the woman. Can she refuse? On principle the answer must be that the ultimate decision belongs to the woman.[512] Nor can it be argued that doctors have a legal duty to implant the embryo. This must presumably mean that a woman may refuse to have the embryo implanted for any reason, including a preference for the other sex. Sex selection for social reasons is thus able to creep in through the back door. **10.163**

Secondly, and conversely, if the doctors do not wish to implant the embryo because they perceive there to be a risk (perhaps one below the abortion handicap threshold) but the woman wants the embryo transferred to her uterus, can she insist? Draper and Chadwick argue that once women have parted with their gametes and the resulting embryos have been tested 'it is possible for them to lose control **10.164**

---

[505] N 501 above, 269.
[506] ibid, 276.
[507] ibid, 270.
[508] ibid.
[509] ibid.
[510] ibid, 271.
[511] ibid, 283.
[512] See *St George's Healthcare NHS Trust v S* [1998] 3 WLR 936 and Harris, J, 'Rights and Reproductive Choice' in Harris J, and Holm, S, *The Future of Human Reproduction: Ethics, Choice and Regulation* (Oxford: Clarendon Press), 5,33.

over what happens next . . . she cannot compel him to implant embryos against his wishes'.[513] The embryo is not in her body so that her bodily integrity is not impugned, but her reproductive autonomy is. It seems unlikely that any court would compel a doctor to implant an embryo against his judgement.

10.165   Thirdly, and following on from the last query, the question may be raised as to whether a couple might choose to have a child with a particular disability. The most commonly-cited example is the deaf couple wishing to have a deaf child.[514] Would English law allow them to use PGD to ensure that only a deaf embryo was implanted? There has been considerable discussion of the ethics of making such a decision. Rather less on the law. But the much-maligned s 13(5) of the 1990 Act (see para 10.84 above) may be valuable here if nowhere else. It stipulates that 'a woman shall not be provided with treatment services unless account has been taken of the welfare of any child who may be born as a result of the treatment . . .'. A clinic which knows that a couple is requesting PGD in order to produce a deaf child could thus, it is submitted, refuse them treatment services. But can this be done? Jackson is uncertain, arguing that s 13(5) is assumed to be 'concerned with *access* to infertility treatment, rather than choices made once treatment has begun'.[515] But this author believes the better view is that implantation into a woman's uterus after IVF and PGD is a 'treatment service', and so is governed by the 'welfare principle' in s 13(5). Indeed, there seems to be no better use for s 13(5) than to justify a doctor's refusal to countenance PGD where the intention is to produce a deaf child, or once there has been PGD to refuse the express wishes of a couple to transfer an embryo known to be afflicted by congenital deafness. This is, of course, assuming that it is not in the best interests of a child to be born deaf. The author is aware of the views of proponents of a 'deaf culture'.[516] They give dubious legitimacy to a form of child abuse.

10.166   At present, if PGD discovers genetic abnormality, the embryo can be discarded. Preimplantation gene therapy is not yet possible, though it is thought to be distinctly possible.[517] Clinical trials of gene therapy products require the authority of

---

[513] Draper, H and Chadwick, R, 'Beware! Pre-implantation Genetic Diagnosis May Solve Some Old Problems But It Also Raises New Ones' (1999) 25 *Journal of Medical Ethics* 114, 119. See also Savulescu, J, 'Should Doctors Intentionally Do Less Than the Best?' (1999) 25 *Journal of Medical Ethics* 121.

[514] And see Holm, S, 'Clinical Issues In Pre-Implantation Diagnosis' in Harris, J, and Holm (n 510 above), 176. To allow such a practice is to foreclose the child's right to 'an open future', as Dena Davis strongly argues (see *Genetic Dilemmas* (New York: Routledge, 2001), 49. However preventing deaf parents choosing a deaf child has been described as 'coercive eugenics', by Gregory Stock in *Redesigning Humans* (London: Profile Books, 2002), 181.

[515] *Per* Jackson, E, *Regulating Reproduction* (n 305 above), 245.

[516] eg Sacks, O, *Seeing Voices* (Berkeley: University of California Press, 1989) and Lane, H, *When the Mind Hears* (New York: Random House, 1984).

[517] See Robertson, J, 'Genetic Selection of Offspring Characteristics' (1996) 76 *Boston U L Rev* 421; Robertson, J, 'Liberty, Identity and Human Cloning' (1998) 76 *Texas L Rev* 1371.

the Medicines Control Agency, and must be approved also by the Genetic Therapy Advisory Commission (which was established in 1992). The Commission has issued guidance which advises that there should only be research into gene therapy to target disorders that are 'life threatening or cause serious handicap' and for which treatment is either unavailable or unsatisfactory, and that it should be limited to somatic cells. It also maintains that the use of direct mediated gene therapy in utero is likely to be unacceptable for the foreseeable future because of safety and ethical difficulties. In addition the 1990 Act prohibits germline therapy by a provision[518] which states that a treatment licence cannot 'authorise altering the genetic structure of any cell while it forms part of an embryo', though associated research is permitted if allowed by regulation.[519] But there is currently no such regulation.

K. The Status of Children

Until statutory intervention in 1987,[520] parentage was tied by the common law to genetics: a sperm donor was the father, although in practice a combination of a common law presumption (the husband of a mother is presumed to be the father of her child) and pious perjury (the child was often registered as the husband's child) meant that social fatherhood often prevailed. There was little discussion of egg or embryo donation[521] before the emergence of surrogacy in the mid-1980s: in theory, the genetic should have prevailed here too, though in practice it is thought the gestational mother was regarded as the legal mother.[522]

10.167

In 1987 the Family Law Reform Act[523] tackled the situation of the married couple who had a child through donor insemination. It reversed the common law rule and made the husband of a woman who was artificially inseminated the father of the child, unless it was proved that he did not consent to the procedure. However, this legislation did not deal with egg or embryo donation or with other techniques such as GIFT. This provision has now been repealed and replaced by a more comprehensive set of provisions in the 1990 Act. There is, it has been said, 'a particular need for certainty in provisions affecting status . . .'.[524] As we shall see, this need is not met.

10.168

---

[518] See Sch 2, para 1(4).
[519] See Sch 2, para 3(4).
[520] Family Law Reform Act 1987, s 27.
[521] See Freeman, MDA, 'The Unscrambling of Egg Donation' in McLean, SAM (ed) *Law Reform and Human Reproduction* (Aldershot: Dartmouth, 1992), 273.
[522] As in California: see *Johnson v Calvert* 851 P 2d 776 (1993).
[523] In s 27.
[524] *Per* Wilson J in *U v W (Attorney-General Intervening)* [1997] 2 FLR 282, 303.

2. Statutory Motherhood

10.169 The 1990 Act provides [525] that a woman who is carrying or has carried a child as a result of the placing in her of an embryo or of sperm and eggs, and no other woman, is to be treated as the mother of the child. The gestational woman is thus in law the mother of any child born as a result of IVF procedures or GIFT or ZIFT (zygote intra-fallopian transfer). Where egg donation does not involve IVF, GIFT, or ZIFT, ie where the egg is directly implanted in the woman for natural fertilisation, the Act does not apply and who is the mother is a question that would fall to be determined by the common law, which, as indicated (see para 10.167) can offer no conclusive answer. Where the donation is only sperm (note the wording 'sperm and eggs'), the gestational mother will be the legal mother.

10.170 Where the mother is a surrogate, the legislation does not achieve the objective of tying legal to social motherhood,[526] and the gestational mother becomes the legal mother even though she is not intended by the parties involved to be the social mother. The social mother, who will rear the child, is denied the status of parent even where her egg, fertilised by the sperm of her husband or partner, is used. She can, if married, seek a parental order under s 30 of the 1990 Act (as to which see paras 10.213–10.216 below).

10.171 There is a saving for adoption.[527]

10.172 Section 27 applies whether the woman was in the United Kingdom or not at the time of the placing in her of the embryos or the sperm and eggs.[528]

2. Statutory Fatherhood

(i) The Married Mother

10.173 The 1990 Act provides[529] that if a married woman becomes pregnant following embryo transfer, GIFT, ZIFT or DI, her husband is to be treated as the father of any child who results from such treatment. It has been said to be contrary to Parliament's express wish to treat such a man differently from the father of any other child when considering an application for contact.[530] The court held it would go against the principles of justice to deny rights to a man who had consented to, and participated fully with the mother in, fertility treatment merely because of an absence of a biological link between him and the child. That contact

---

[525] s 27(1).
[526] Hence the need for the parental order established by s 30 and discussed in para 10.213.
[527] s 27(2).
[528] s 27(3).
[529] s 28(1) and (2).
[530] *Re CH* [1996] 1 FLR 768.

may not always be granted is clear from the case of *Re D*,[531] the unusual facts of which are considered below (see para 10.177). It was not in Parliament's mind that mistakes would occur and an embryo would be placed in a woman which used the wrong sperm. That this could happen came to light in 2002 when a white couple who had had ICSI treatment gave birth to mixed-race twins.[532] (and see para 10.175).

If a man can show that he did not consent to the treatment service, he is not be **10.174** treated as the father under s 28(2), although he will remain the presumed father by virtue of s 28(5), which preserves the common law presumption of paternity. This is a rebuttable presumption,[533] which may be most obviously rebutted by DNA evidence showing the contrary.[534] Although it is not clear, it may be supposed that a husband who consented to the treatment service but changed his mind in the nine months between treatment and birth, will also be the presumed father, if he is not treated as the father under s 28(5). It is not a requirement of treatment that a married woman should get her husband's consent. However, the Code of Practice does advise that this be sought as a matter of good practice.[535] Research indicates that clinics are sensibly reluctant to treat without his consent.[536]

It is clear that a mistake as to the identity of the embryo being placed in a man's **10.175** wife vitiates his consent, so that s 28(2) does not apply.[537] It is also clear that s 28(3) does not apply to husbands.[538] Even if it could be construed as applying to married couples as well as unmarried couples, 'a fundamental error resulting in the use of the sperm of another in place of the use of sperm of the man taking part in the treatment must vitiate the whole concept of 'treatment together' for the purposes of the 1990 Act'.[539] In *Leeds Teaching Hospitals NHS Trust v A*, the question arose as to whether the husband could consent retrospectively. The court refused to accept that this was possible.[540] The court accepted that its interpretation of s 28 constituted an interference with the right to respect for private and family life of

---

[531] [2001] 1 FLR 972. Indirect contact was ordered in this case. And see below at para 10.177. On appeal this case is *Re R* [2003] 1 FLR 1183. The Court of Appeal hoped the parties could reach agreement about what contact, if any, would be best for the child (see at 1193).

[532] See *Leeds Teaching Hospitals NHS Trust v A* [2003] 1 FLR 1091, 1101 *per* Dame Elizabeth Butler-Sloss P.

[533] Rebuttable on a balance of probabilities.

[534] As in *Leeds Teaching Hospitals NHS Trust v A* [2003] 1 FLR 1091, 1101.

[535] 5th edn, para 7.28.

[536] See Douglas, G, *Access To Assisted Reproduction—Legal and other Criteria for Eligibility* (Cardiff: Cardiff Law School, 1992).

[537] See *Leeds Teaching Hospitals NHS Trust v A* [2003] 1 FLR 1091, 1102.

[538] *Re R* [2003] 1 FLR 1183, 1190 *per* Hale LJ; *Leeds Teaching Hospitals NHS Trust v A* [2003] 1 FLR 1091, 1103 *per* Dame Elizabeth Butler-Sloss P.

[539] *Leeds Teaching Hospitals NHS Trust v A* [2003] 1 FLR 1091, 1105 *per* Dame Elizabeth Butler-Sloss P.

[540] ibid, 1101–2.

the mother, her husband and the twins (under Article 8 of the European Convention on Human Rights). And it was the human right of the twins that were 'most obviously and seriously infringed'.[541] But it held that no declaration of incompatibility was needed, since there were domestic remedies available to secure and protect those rights. All concerned agreed that the twins should remain with the family into which they were born and a residence order was granted—giving the husband the parental responsibility he otherwise lacked. The application of the genetic father for a declaration of parentage[542] was adjourned. Dame Elizabeth Butler-Sloss P was of the opinion that 'truth . . . is more important to the rights of the twins and their welfare than a fictional certainty . . . To refuse to recognise . . .their biological father is to distort the truth about which some day the twins will have to learn through knowledge of their paternal identity'.[543]

(ii) The Unmarried Mother

10.176 The 1990 Act provides that, if no man is treated as the father of the child by virtue of s 28(2) (in effect because the woman is unmarried), and an embryo is placed in the woman 'in the course of treatment services provided for her and a man together by a person to whom a licence applies, and the creation of the embryo carried by her was not brought about with the sperm of that man, then . . . that man shall be treated as the father of the child'.[544] This is subject to the presumption in s 28(5) (discussed in para 10.174 above). There is, it has been said, 'a conundrum about what the unmarried man must have said and/or intended and/or done before it can be concluded that treatment services not involving the use of his sperm were provided for the woman and him together'.[545] This conundrum concerned Johnson J in *Re Q (Parental Order)*.[546] He needed to look at s 28(3) only in passing because it was patently applicable to the case under consideration. But he remarked: 'it seems plain to me that the subsection envisages a situation in which the man involved himself received medical treatment, although as presently advised I am not sure what treatment is envisaged since the subsection refers to a man whose sperm was not used in the procedure'.[547] The notion of the provision or receipt of treatment services for or by a woman and a man together is found elsewhere in the 1990 Act (see s 4(i)(b) and Sch 3, para 5(3), both of which Bracewell J addressed in *Re B (Parentage)*.[548] In that case the woman's boyfriend had donated sperm under medical supervision with which, five months later, after

---

[541] ibid, 1109.
[542] Under s 55A of the Family Law Act 1986.
[543] N 535 above, 1109.
[544] s 28(3).
[545] *Per* Wilson J in *U v W (Attorney-General Intervening)* [1997] 2 FLR 282, 293.
[546] [1996] 1 FLR 369.
[547] ibid, 371.
[548] [1996] 2 FLR 15.

the breakdown of their relationship, she was inseminated. The judge concluded that the man's gametes had been used, presumably at the time of the insemination, for the purpose of their receiving treatment services together.

In *R v Human Fertilisation and Embryology Authority ex parte Blood*[549] (on the facts see para 10.102 above), the Court of Appeal approved the analysis of *Re B (Parentage)* by Sir Stephen Brown P in the Family Division, that the man '. . . was a willing, consenting party to the treatment which they had commenced together when the sperm sample had been removed and that he had not subsequently withdrawn his deemed consent'.[550] In the *Blood* case, the posthumous use of sperm taken from man in a coma was inevitably held not to be capable of constituting 'treatment . . . together'. It has been said that there is a 'mental element inherent in the notion of "treatment . . . together" '.[551] This is not 'whether the man consented either to be deemed in law to be the father of the prospective child or to become legally responsible for him: it is whether the relevant treatment services were provided for the woman and him together. It stretches the requisite mental element in the man too far to require either form of such consent . . . [w]hat has to be demonstrated is that, in the provision of treatment services with a sperm donor, the doctor was responding to a request for that form of treatment made by the woman and the man as a couple, notwithstanding the absence in the man of any physical role in such treatment'.[552] In this case (*U v W (Attorney-General Intervening)*), it was held that treatment services had been provided for the parties together since they had attended the clinic together, received information together, and had both signed a form permitting the use of donor sperm. However, in the particular case, since the treatment services had been given at a clinic in Rome, and were therefore not licensed treatment, the implications of the subsection did not apply, and the court was unable to give a declaration that he was the father, with the result that the woman was unable to obtain a maintenance assessment under the Child Support Act 1991. Section 28(3) can also lead to the absurd conclusion that a man who is clearly not the father is the legal father, and man who clearly is the genetic father is not the legal father. This is graphically illustrated by the decision in *Re D*,[553] referred to briefly at para 10.173, above. In *Re D* a man and a woman sought fertility treatment, acknowledging that under s 28(3) he would be the father of any resulting child. The treatment failed, the relationship foundered, and she presented herself the following year without telling the clinic that her new partner was not the man who had signed the original forms. The

10.177

---

[549] [1997] 2 WLR 806.
[550] ibid, 816.
[551] *Per* Wilson J in *U v W* (n 541 above), 294.
[552] ibid, 295.
[553] [2001] 1 FLR 972. The first instance decision is reported as *Re R (Contact: Human Fertilisation and Embryology Act 1990)* [2001] 1 FLR 247.

treatment using anonymous sperm donation was successful. The first man sought a parental responsibility order and contact. The judge took it for granted that he was the father, though this is probably not so—these treatment services were not provided for the woman and this man together, as s 28(3) requires.[554] The man's application for a parental responsibility order was deferred and will presumably fail when it is realised that he is not the father and it was suggested an order for direct contact not be made until the child was three years old (some two and a half years hence). As a result of an unchallenged concession the child in this case is assigned a legal father who is neither her genetic nor social father, but merely her mother's ex-partner. Not surprisingly the court thought the concerns it had about this conclusion should be drawn to the attention of the Human Fertilisation and Embryology Authority,[555] but this, as yet, has not addressed the issue.

10.178   Where a man is, by virtue of s 28(2) or (3) treated as the child's father, s 28(4) provides that no other man is to be so regarded. Also, there is a provision in the 1990 Act[556] ensuring that the provisions dealing with the meaning of 'father' apply whether the woman was in the UK or elsewhere at the time of the placing within her of the embryo or the sperm and eggs or her artificial insemination.

(iii) The Legally Fatherless Child

10.179   Section 28(6) is intended to protect a donor whose sperm is used with his consent to establish a pregnancy in a married woman whose husband has not consented. It also protects the donor of sperm when this is given to an unmarried woman. It provides that the donor is not to be treated as the father of the resulting child. The sperm donor is not accordingly at risk of being exposed to the responsibilities of a father. But if neither the mother's husband nor the donor is the father, who is? The answer is, it seems, no one: in law, the child has no father. So an Act, which rather nonsensically insists (in s 13(5)) that all children have fathers, creates legally fatherless children.

10.180   If the sperm is used without the donor's consent, the donor may not be protected by s 28(6)(a), and may, as a result be treated as the child's father without his consent. Although it is unlikely that this could happen, the possibility may arise where a man, for example, agreed to donate sperm for research purposes, but not for treatment services, and it is accidentally used in infertility treatment.

10.181   The 1990 Act creates a further category of the legally fatherless by the way it regulates posthumous births. Section 28(6)(b) provides that where the sperm of a man, or an embryo the creation of which was brought about with his sperm, is used after his death, he is not be treated as the father of the child. This applies

---

[554] ibid, 974, 979, 980–1.
[555] ibid, 974, 980 and 981.
[556] s 27(3).

whether the woman becomes pregnant using her deceased husband's frozen sperm (after the *Blood* case, presumably only when he has give his express consent) or that of an unknown donor. One result is that a child, produced using frozen sperm left in storage by a soldier, who dies in battle after expressly consenting to his wife using it after his death, does not have a legal father, and is also illegitimate, since the marriage ended upon the soldier's death.[557] But, oddly, if the widow remarried before the child's birth, her new husband would be treated as the child's father under s 28(2) (see para 10.174, above).

(iv) Unlicensed Services

If an infertile couple do not use licensed treatment services (for example, if they use DIY insemination), then, if they are married, s 28(2) applies and the husband will be deemed to be the father of the child unless it can be shown that he did not consent, which may be more difficult in a non-regulated environment. The presumption of legitimacy also applies.[558] If, on the other hand, they are not married, the 1990 Act does not apply: s 28(3) is restricted to situations where the woman 'together' with a man *receives treatment services* under the Act. Parentage will be decided according to the common law, and the donor will be legally the father of any child born as a result of the insemination.

10.182

(v) Post-Mortem Inseminations

The 1990 Act does not address paternity or legitimacy in the context of post-mortem inseminations. No presumption of legitimacy can apply because the marriage ended on death. It has been argued by Lee and Morgan[559] that a statutory provision[560] dealing with void marriages may by analogy be used as in interpretational device. A child of a void marriage is legitimate if at the time of insemination resulting in his or her birth, or at the time of child's conception, or at the time of the celebration of the marriage if later, both or either of the parties reasonably believed that the marriage was valid (the so-called 'putative marriage'). If, for the purposes of conception in vitro, conception takes place when the egg is fertilised, and not when the resulting embryo or zygote is replaced in the uterus, then if either of the parties believed the marriage was valid, a child born years later from a frozen embryo, even after the man's death, would be legitimate. But whether this argument can be successfully invoked is dubious: it would seem to place such a child in a better position than one whose parents were married. The courts, it may be supposed, might wish to resist such a conclusion.

10.183

---

[557] Even though her pregnancy is in accordance with his express consent given under Sch 3, para 2(2)(b).
[558] See Family Law Reform Act 1969, s 26.
[559] Lee and Morgan (n 9 above).
[560] Legitimacy Act 1976, s 1(1), as amended by the Family Law Reform Act 1987, s 28(1).

L. Surrogacy

10.184   Surrogacy, as defined in the Warnock report, is 'the practice whereby one woman carries a child for another with the intention that the child should be handed over after birth'.[561] It can take a number of forms: the commissioning mother may be the genetic mother, in that she provides the egg, or she may make no contribution to the establishment of the pregnancy. The surrogate may simply lease her womb. She may also be the genetic mother. The genetic father may be the husband of the commissioning mother (or a partner). He may also be the husband or partner of the gestational mother, or a donor. Surrogacy may involve payment (the Brazier report found typical payments of between £10,000 and £15,000[562]) or the reimbursement of expenses. There is also so-called altruistic surrogacy, where for example, one sister carries the pregnancy for another.

10.185   The practice of surrogacy (or 'contract pregnancy') has proved very controversial.[563] The Warnock report went so far as to describe 'surrogacy for convenience', of which there is no evidence, as 'totally ethically unacceptable'.[564] Even where there are 'compelling medical circumstances', the report castigates the practice of surrogacy using Kantian language: 'That people should treat others as a means to their own ends, however desirable the consequences, must always be liable to moral objection'.[565] Although the committee was more concerned with the commercial exploitation of surrogacy, it recommended the criminalisation of surrogacy agencies, both profit and non-profit making organisations.[566] It also recommended that it be provided by statute that all surrogacy agreements are illegal contracts and unenforceable in the courts.[567] Legislation was passed within a year of the Warnock report,[568] but the speed of response is attributable to the first major surrogacy case in the United Kingdom, the 'Baby Cotton' case.[569] The Surrogacy Agreements Act 1985 (the 1985 Act) did not go as far as Warnock recommended. It distinguished the practice of commercial agencies from those which are non-profit making, and it said nothing about the

---

[561] N 7 above, para 8.1.
[562] *Surrogacy: Review for Health Ministers of Current Arrangements for Payments and Regulation* (Cm 4068, 1998), para 5.4.
[563] See Freeman, M, 'Is Surrogacy Exploitative? in McLean, SAM (ed), *Legal Issues In Human Reproduction* (Aldershot: Gower, 1989), 164. See generally Field, MA, *Surrogate Motherhood* (Cambridge, Mass: Harvard University Press, 1988).
[564] N 7 above, para 8.17.
[565] ibid.
[566] ibid, para 8.18.
[567] ibid, para 8.19.
[568] Surrogacy Arrangements Act 1985.
[569] *Re C (A Minor)* [1985] FLR 846.

status of the surrogacy contract. The latter issue was picked up, after the 1987 White Paper had addressed it, in the 1990 Act.[570]

There is an excellent summary of the law on surrogacy in Hale LJ's judgment in **10.186** *Briody v St Helen's and Knowsley AHA*.[571] On the basis of this she concluded that surrogacy 'as such is [not] contrary to public policy'.[572] But the 'issue is a difficult one, upon which opinions are divided, so that it would be wise to tread with caution'.[573] She expressed the view that 'if there is a trend it is towards acceptance and regulation as a last resort rather than towards prohibition'.[574] That surrogacy can cause distress is manifest (the 'Baby M' saga in the United States is an egregious example[575]). The mess created in *W and B v H*[576] (discussed in para 10.221 below) led Hedley J to caution against 'an imbalance between our scientific and ethical capacities'.[577]

1. Surrogacy Agreements

The status of surrogacy agreements can be examined from the perspectives both **10.187** of the criminal law and the civil law.

(i) The Criminal Law

As far as the criminal law is concerned, there are a number of ways in which sur- **10.188** rogacy may be thought to be sanctioned. Most obviously, an offence may be committed under s 57 of the Adoption Act 1976 if the commissioning couple intend to adopt the child once born. This provides that:

> it shall not be lawful to make or give to any person any payment or reward for or in consideration of (a) the adoption by that person of a child; (b) the grant by that person of any agreement or consent requested in connection with the adoption of a child; (c) the handing over of a child by that person with a view to the adoption of the child; or (d) the making by that person of any arrangements for the adoption of a child.

However, in *Re an Adoption Application (Surrogacy)*,[578] Latey J put a somewhat liberal construction on this statutory provision. He held that whether there is 'any

---

[570] *Human Fertilisation and Embryology. A Framework for Legislation* (Cd 259, 1987), paras 66–75.
[571] [2001] 2 FLR 1094, 1098–1100.
[572] ibid, 1100.
[573] ibid.
[574] ibid.
[575] On which see Gostin, L, *Surrogate Motherhood* (Bloomington: Indiana University Press, 1990), 233 and 243 and Merrick, J in Bartels, D *et al*, (eds) *Beyond Baby M* (Clifton, NJ: Humana Press, 1990), 183.
[576] [2002] 1 FLR 1008.
[577] ibid, 1009.
[578] [1987] Fam 81.

payment or reward' for adoption is 'a question of fact to be decided on the evidence'.[579] He could see 'nothing commercial in what happened',[580] although the couples admitted that sums of £10,000 and £5,000 had changed hands. In his view, it 'was only after the payments had been made and the baby was born that any of them began to turn their minds in any real senses to adoption and the legalities'.[581] 'Legalities' may be a Freudian slip on the judge's part: surely, he meant 'illegalities'. He seems to have been influenced by the absence of a written contract and the fact that lawyers were not consulted until after the baby was born. The arrangement was one of 'trust which was fully honoured on both sides'.[582]

10.189 Even if there is a payment or reward, s 57(3) of the Adoption Act 1976 provides: 'This section does not apply . . . to any payment or reward authorised by the court to which an application for an adoption order in respect of a child is made'. And in *Re an Adoption Application (Surrogacy)*, Latey J held that 'authorised by the court' covers not only authorisation in advance of making a payment but can also cover retrospective authorisation. Otherwise, he held, it would mean, that 'any payment, however modest and however innocently made, would bar an adoption and do so however much the welfare of the child cried loud for adoption . . . and that, be it said, within the framework of legislation whose first concern is promoting the welfare of the children concerned'.[583] He did not believe that Parliament intended to produce such a result: it 'produced a balance by setting its face against trafficking in children . . . but recognising that there may be transactions which are venial and should not prohibit adoption'.[584] An adoption order was made. Latey J cannot fail to have been influenced by the fact that the child was two-and-a-half years old and had spent his entire life with the commissioning couple who were, according to the pre-adoption reports, excellent parents. But whether Latey J was right to construe 'authorisation' to include subsequent ratification by a court may be doubted.[585] In *Re MW (Adoption: Surrogacy)*[586] payments were again retrospectively authorised and an adoption order made. There had been clear breaches of the Adoption Act. This child too had lived with the applicants for two-and-a-half years.

10.190 It is not unlawful under the Adoption Act 1976 for a surrogate mother to receive a payment for handing over her child to another, nor is there a crime of 'baby selling'.

---

[579] ibid, 86.
[580] ibid, 84.
[581] ibid, 86.
[582] ibid, 84.
[583] ibid, 87.
[584] ibid.
[585] ibid.
[586] [1995] 2 FLR 759. Retrospective authorisation was approved in *Briody v St Helen's and Knowsley AHA* (n 567 above), 1099.

The criminal law might also be invoked if the agreement were thought to consti- **10.191**
tute a conspiracy to corrupt public morals or outrage public decency.[587] Although
a body of opinion would support this,[588] it seems unlikely that such a prosecution
would be brought. No English case has addressed this question, and there has
been ample opportunity for Directors of Public Prosecutions to have initiated a
prosecution should they have wished to do so.

(ii) The Civil Law

From the perspective of the civil law it is now clear that a surrogacy arrangement **10.192**
is unenforceable. The 1990 Act inserted a new s 1A into the 1985 Act:

> No surrogacy arrangement is enforceable by or against any of the persons making
> it'.

The commissioning parents thus have no right to the child, and the surrogate no
right to her emolument (expenses, fee, etc).

(iii) Public Policy

Is the agreement also void on grounds of public policy? In *Re P (Minors)* **10.193**
(Wardship: Surrogacy), Sir John Arnold P said obiter that there was a view that an
element of the surrogacy agreement was 'repellent to proper ideas about the procreation of children, so as to make any such agreement one which should be rejected by law as being contrary to public policy'.[589] *In A v C*, Comyn J held that an
agreement made between a prostitute and a man that she would bear his child and
hand it over to him was contrary to public policy as 'a purported contract for the
sale and purchase of a child'.[590] The Court of Appeal described the arrangement as
'most extraordinary and irresponsible, bizarre and unnatural', 'a sordid commercial bargain',[591] and 'a kind of baby-farming operation of a wholly distasteful and
lamentable kind'.[592] Although an Australian court has been less censorious, arguing that it was 'appropriate [to] take account of the intentions and expectations of
the four adults who co-operated to bring about [the] birth',[593] there can be little
doubt that English courts regard surrogacy arrangements as contrary to public
policy.

---

[587] On which see *Shaw v Director of Public Prosecutions* [1962] AC 220, and *Knuller v Director of Public Prosecutions* [1973] AC 435.
[588] See eg Lord Devlin, *The Enforcement of Morals* (Oxford: Clarendon Press, 1965).
[589] [1987] 2 FLR 421, 425.
[590] [1985] FLR 445, 449 (decided in 1978).
[591] ibid, 455, 457 *per* Ormrod LJ.
[592] ibid, 459 *per* Cumming—Bruce LJ.
[593] *Re Evelyn* (1998) FLC 92–807, 29 *per* Jordan J. This is discussed by Otlowski, M, 'Re Evelyn: Reflections on Australia's First Litigated Surrogacy Case' (1999) 7 Med L Rev 38.

10.194 And this question remains of importance despite the insertion of the new provision in the 1985 Act (see para 10.192 above). The new provision applies to 'surrogacy arrangements' as defined in the 1985 Act.[594] These do not include agreements reached after the child is conceived and which are intended to result in the child being handed over by the surrogate mother. Such arrangements would remain governed by the common law and on the basis of the case law considered in para 10.196, would be held to be both contrary to public policy and unenforceable.

(iv) Activities Connected with Surrogacy

10.195 English law does not prohibit surrogacy arrangements, but the 1985 Act prohibits a number of activities in connection with surrogacy. Where IVF or DI techniques are used to achieve pregnancy (and the latter does not employ DIY), the activities will be licensed under the 1990 Act[595] and, as such, HFEA may regulate the use of the techniques to achieve a surrogate pregnancy. Its Code of Practice provides:

> The application of assisted conception techniques to initiate a surrogate pregnancy should only be considered where it is physically impossible or highly undesirable for medical reasons for the commissioning mother to carry the child'.[596]

Clearly, assisting a surrogacy for convenience (see para 10.185) would be contrary to the Code.[597] A licence-holder may have his/her licence withdrawn or varied if he/she assists a surrogate pregnancy for other than compelling medical reasons.

10.196 Attention should also be drawn to the British Medical Association's *Changing Conceptions of Motherhood*, which contains guidelines for practitioners. The attitude to surrogacy is more relaxed than in a previous report published in 1990. No longer are doctors to exercise 'extreme caution' before helping to achieve a surrogate pregnancy: it is still emphasised that they should only do so 'as a last resort'. Surrogacy is now described as 'an acceptable option of last resort in cases where it is impossible or highly undesirable for medical reasons for the intended mother to carry a child herself'.[598] The report stresses that the interests of the potential child must be paramount, and the risks to the surrogate mother must be kept to a minimum.

---

[594] See s 1(2)(a) of the 1985 Act.
[595] s 2(1).
[596] *Code of Practice* (5th edn, 2001), para 3.16.
[597] This follows from ibid, para 3.16, quoted above. See, for agreement, Kennedy and Grubb (n 302 above).
[598] *The Changing Conceptions of Motherhood—The Practice of Surrogacy in Britain* (London: BMA, 1996), 59.

2. Surrogacy Agencies

(i) Statutory Provisions

The 1985 Act, as amended by the 1990 Act,[599] seeks to outlaw commercial surro-   **10.197**
gacy agencies. It provides[600] that:

> No person shall on a commercial basis do any of the following acts in the United
> Kingdom, that is—
>
> (a) initiate or take part in any negotiations with a view to the making of a surrogacy
>   arrangement,
> (b) offer or agree to negotiate the making of a surrogacy arrangement, or
> (c) compile any information with a view to its use in making, or negotiating the
>   making of, surrogacy arrangements, and no person shall in the United
>   Kingdom knowingly cause another to do any of these acts on a commercial
>   basis.

An act is done on a 'commercial basis' if 'any payment is at any time received by
himself or another in respect of it' or 'he does it with a view to any payment being
received by himself or another in respect of making, or negotiating or facilitating
the making of, any surrogacy arrangement'.[601] Contravention of these provisions
is a criminal offence.[602] However, a person is not to be treated as doing an act on a
commercial basis by reason of having received a payment if it is proved that he did
not do the act knowing or having reasonable cause to suspect that any payment
had been received in respect of the act or, where payment was received after he did
the act, that he did not do the act with a view to payment being received.[603]

(ii) Statutory Definition

For this purpose 'payment' does not include payment 'to or for the benefit of a sur-   **10.198**
rogate mother or prospective surrogate mother'.[604] Both she and the commissioning couple are specifically excluded from the provisions of the legislation under s
2(2).

It has been seen (para 10.197 above) that the provision outlawing the negotiation,   **10.199**
etc, of surrogacy arrangements is broadly defined. There have been no reported
prosecutions, and there was reluctance, it seems, on the part of the Director of
Public Prosecutions to get involved in a case where the payment was (supposedly)
for the writing of a pregnancy diary.[605]

---

[599] s 36(2).
[600] s 3(2).
[601] s 2(3).
[602] s 2(2).
[603] s 2(4).
[604] s 2(3).
[605] As reported in The Daily Telegraph, 15 May 1986.

10.200   'Surrogate mother' and 'surrogate arrangement are also broadly defined'.[606] 'Surrogate mother' means 'a woman who carries a child in pursuance of an arrangement made before she began to carry the child' with a view to the child being handed over and parental responsibility being met by another person or persons: it therefore does not cover an arrangement reached after conception. The 1990 Act[607] has extended the meaning of this—and therefore of a surrogacy arrangement—to include not just insemination and embryo transfer but also 'the placing in [the woman] . . . of an egg in the process of fertilisation or of sperm and eggs . . . that results in her carrying the child'.

10.201   In determining whether an arrangement is made with a view to the child being handed over, and parental responsibility being met by another person or persons:

> regard may be had to the circumstances as a whole (and, in particular, where there is a promise or understanding that any payment will or may be made to the woman or for her benefit in respect of the carrying of any child in pursuance of the arrangement, to that promise or understanding).[608]

An arrangement may be regarded as made with such a view although there are conditions relating to the handing over of the child.[609] 'Payment' is defined to include 'money's worth'.[610]

(iii) Advertising

10.202   It is a criminal offence to publish an advertisement seeking a surrogate mother or offering to act as a surrogate mother in a newspaper or periodical.[611] The offence is committed by the proprietor, editor or publisher.[612] The offence is also committed by a person who conveys an advertisement through radio or television[613] or through the internet or otherwise (for example, a shopkeeper who places a notice on his or her window would commit an offence).[614] Whether the potential surrogate mother and the commissioning couple also commit offences is far from clear. It could be argued that they 'cause' an advertisement to be 'conveyed' or 'published' or 'distributed' by placing the advertisement with the publisher.[615]

---

[606] s 1(2) and s 1(3)–(6) respectively.
[607] By substituting in s 1(6) for 'or, as the case may be, embryo insertion', 'or of the placing in her of an embryo, of an egg in the process of fertilisation or of sperm and eggs, as the case may be' (see 1990 Act, s 36(2)).
[608] s 1(4).
[609] s 1(5).
[610] s 1(8).
[611] s 3(4).
[612] s 3(2).
[613] s 3(3).
[614] s 3(5).
[615] s 3(4), and see Kennedy and Grubb (n 302 above).

3. Parentage and Parental Responsibility for the Child

Where a child is born as a result of a surrogacy arrangement who are his/her par- **10.203**
ents and who has parental responsibility?

(i) Maternity

On the question who is the mother, English is clear and unequivocal. The woman **10.204**
who gives birth is the legal mother. It matters not that she is a surrogate or whose
eggs were used.[616] Nor does the law distinguish different types of surrogacy: the
same test applies whether the gestational mother is also the genetic mother or not.
The woman in the commissioning couple is not the mother even if her eggs are
used. As Jackson notes, the consequence of assigning legal status in this way is that
'the presumed interests of the surrogate mother even take priority over the interests of the child'.[617] The surrogate has no interest in bringing up the child, but it is
she who has parental responsibility, not the commissioning parents who intend to
rear the child. The conservatism of the English model is brought strikingly into relief should the commissioning parents reject the child for any reason, perhaps because he/she has special needs or their marriage has broken down.[618]

(ii) Paternity

Where the surrogate is married, her husband is the father of the child, unless he **10.205**
can prove that he did not consent to the procedure. The man of the commissioning couple is not the father even if his sperm is used for DI or IVF.[619] He is treated
in such a case in the same way as an anonymous sperm donor. By providing for an
untruthful conclusion, the law encourages dishonesty.

Where the surrogate is unmarried, the commissioning man will be the father of **10.206**
the child if his sperm is used in DIY insemination or if the child is conceived as a
result of sexual intercourse. This is the common law position, and it is not affected
by the 1990 Act. If there is medical intervention, s 28 of the 1990 Act (on which
see para 10.174) will alter the position if the surrogate and the commissioning
man are being treated 'together'.[620] This seems unlikely. The purpose of infertility
treatment is to produce families: 'together' suggests that the man and woman
being treated together will bring up the child produced as a result of the treatment
as a couple. In coming to this conclusion the history and context of the 1990 Act
should be noted: these suggest that Parliament envisages treatment services for

---

[616] s 27(1), discussed at para 10.169, above.
[617] *Regulating Reproduction* (n 305 above), 266.
[618] See further Shapiro, M, 'How (Not) To Think About Surrogacy and Other Reproductive
Innovations' (1994) 28 U of San Francisco L Rev 647.
[619] s 28(2), (3), (4).
[620] s 4(1)(b).

conventional two-parent families. Section 13(5) (discussed in para 10.84) should not be overlooked in interpreting the meaning of 'together'. The better view is that the surrogate and the commissioning man are not treated 'together'. The consequence of this is that the provision of treatment must be licensed because the commissioning man's gametes will constitute donated material. As a donor his consent to the use of his sperm is then required,[621] and, when it is used with his consent, 'he is not to be treated as the father of the child'.[622] The resulting child will have no legal father.[623]

(iii) Registration of Birth

10.207   A child born to a surrogate must be registered as her child and if applicable, that of her partner or the person treated as the father under the 1990 Act. The Code of Practice confirms this: the surrogate must register the baby to which she has given birth in the normal way: 'her husband or partner should normally be registered as the father'.[624] Of course, this is an implicit admission by HFEA that there are situations which fall outside the norm. Most obviously, where the surrogate is a single woman. If the surrogate and the commissioning father were to attend the Registrar of Births and jointly request that the father should be recorded on the birth certificate of the child as his/her father, it is difficult to find a justification for the Registrar to refuse the request. He is the father and DNA tests will confirm this. It may be wondered whether the advice in the Code of Practice is enforceable, and if so, in what way.

4. Acquiring Legal Parenthood

10.208   In most cases after the birth of the child, he/she will be handed over by the surrogate mother to the commissioning couple. A number of legal avenues are then open to them.[625] They can adopt or acquire a parental order under s 30 of the 1990 Act. Until they do so, neither the commissioning father—even in cases where he is unusually regarded as the legal father—will have parental responsibility for the child (the commissioning father, even if the legal father, will not be married to the surrogate).

(i) Adoption

10.209   For full details of the law of adoption, standard books on child law should be

---

[621] Sch 3, para 5.
[622] s 28(6)(a).
[623] See paras 10.179–10.181, above.
[624] *Code of Practice* (5th edn, 2001), Annex D, 59.
[625] To cement the relationship. Only adoption will imitate nature and confer total parental status. A s 30 order, however, comes sufficiently close to this to make this difference in practice. With wardship only care and control is conferred.

consulted. New legislation on adoption is likely to come into operation in 2004.[626] In short much depends on whether the surrogate is married, whether or not assisted procreation was used, and, if she is married, whether or not her husband consented to her becoming a surrogate.

Where the surrogate is unmarried, or the pregnancy was achieved after sexual intercourse or by DIY, or she is married and her husband did not consent to the assisted procreation procedure, the commissioning father is the 'putative father' and as such a 'relative'.[627] An adoption order can be made, provided the child is at least 19 weeks old and has at all times during the preceding 13 weeks lived with the commissioning parents. A single applicant can adopt,[628] so that a single commissioning father is not barred from applying, though whether an adoption order would be made will depend on whether it is considered to be in the child's best interests. As the law stands,[629] a joint adoption order can only be made in favour of a married couple: a cohabiting couple cannot adopt together, and two homosexual men who commission a child through a surrogate cannot both become the legal parents of any child thus born. It is possible to make an adoption order in favour of one person, together with a joint residence order in favour of two unmarried persons (whether of the same or different sexes). Under the Adoption and Children Act 2002, when this comes into operation, unmarried but cohabiting couples, whether heterosexual or homosexual, will be able jointly to adopt.[630]

10.210

Where the surrogate is married and the child results from assisted procreation procedures *with* her husband's consent, the surrogate's husband, not the commissioning father, is the legal father. As a result, before an adoption order can be made, the child will have to have lived with the commissioning parents for at least 12 months.[631] Unless the child has been placed by an adoption agency, and it is difficult to envisage circumstances where this could have occurred, an offence is committed: independent placements for adoption, other than by relatives, are not allowed, unless sanctioned by an order of the High Court (although this can be done retrospectively).[632] The commissioning parents must notify the local authority, and it will report to the court on their suitability as parents. It will also have to inform the court that the ban on private placements has been broken. A

10.211

---

[626] Adoption and Children Act 2002.
[627] See Adoption Act 1976, s 72(1).
[628] See Adoption Act 1976, s 15 (and *Re W* (*Adoption: Homosexual Adopter*) [1977] 2 FLR 406 (s 15 should not be construed narrowly).
[629] See Adoption Act 1976 ss 14, 15. The possibility exists of an adoption order in favour of one and a joint residence order: see *Re AB* (*Adoption: Joint Residence*) [1996] 1 FLR 27. An adoption order may be made in favour of a separated couple jointly: see *Re WM* (*Adoption: Non-Patrial*) [1997] 1 FLR 132.
[630] ss 49–51.
[631] Adoption Act 1976, s.13(2).
[632] Adoption Act 1976, s 57.

reporting officer will be appointed to ensure that the necessary agreements have been given (for example, the surrogate's husband's agreement is required[633]). In adoption cases generally, a guardian ad litem must also be appointed to safeguard the child's interests, where the child's welfare is thought to require this. Where surrogacy is involved, it is thought that a guardian ad litem should certainly be appointed.[634]

10.212   Adoption is currently governed by a test which requires the court and the adoption agency to give 'first consideration' to the welfare of the child.[635] When the Adoption and Children Act 2002 comes into operation the test will be one of 'paramount consideration',[636] thus placing a greater emphasis on the welfare of the child. The critical case will occur where the surrogate changes her mind and refuses to hand over the child to the commissioning parents. The emphasis is on the child's best interests, and this emphasis is about to increase. But there are other interests to be considered: the surrogate's and those of the commissioning parents (and, arguably, their respective families). What is in a child's best interests is not easily determined. Nor is it easy to avoid reference implicit or explicit, to the decision-maker's values. Questions which will arise include (i) are the circumstances of the child's birth relevant?[637] (ii) is there a presumption that it is in a child's best interests to be reared by the woman who gave birth to him/her?[638] (iii) should the residential status quo be disturbed?[639] (the length of this is important) (iv) should we be looking to short-term interests, particularly significant if the child has bonded, or the long-term?[640] There are questions of identity to consider here.

(ii) The Section 30 Parental Order

10.213   The 1990 Act introduced the parental order as an alternative to adoption.[641] Before a court may make this order (which provides for the child to be treated in law as the child of the commissioning parents[642]) a number of conditions must be satisfied:

>   (i)   the child must have been born to a surrogate as a result of assisted procreative techniques[643] (the s 30 procedure is not applicable where DIY has been used or the commissioning father has had sexual intercourse with the surrogate);

---

[633] If, as is likely, he is the legal father.
[634] See Adoption Act 1976, s 65.
[635] Adoption Act 1976, s 6.
[636] s 1(2).
[637] In the Australian case of *Re Evelyn* (589 above), Jordan J thought they were.
[638] See *Re S* [1991] 2 FLR 388 ('a consideration but not a presumption') *per* Butler-Sloss LJ at 390.
[639] As in *Re B* [1998] 1 FLR 368.
[640] A point made by Mnookin, R, 'Child-Custody Adjudication: Judicial Functions in the Face of Indeterminacy' (1975) 35 *Law and Contemporary Problems* 226.
[641] s 30.
[642] s 30(1).
[643] s 30(1)(a).

(ii)   the gametes of at least one of the commissioning couple have been used to bring about the creation of the embryo[644] (the child must thus be genetically related to at least one of the commissioning couple);

(iii)   the applicants must be husband and wife[645] (cohabitants and gay couples are not permitted to take advantage of the s 30 procedure);

(iv)   the applicants must apply within six months of the birth of the child or for births before the 1990 Act came into force within six months of that[646] (this provision is not entirely clear but it seems Parliament's intention was to allow applications to be made under s 30 for any birth arising before s 30 came into force and made within six months of that date);

(v)   the child must have his or her home with the applicants both at the time of the application and at the time of the order[647] (this may prove difficult to establish in a case where the surrogate refuses to hand over the child. It also means that the Act requires persons who have no parental responsibility to look after the child prior to the order);

(vi)   at least one of the applicants must be domiciled in a part of the United Kingdom or in the Channel Islands or the Isle of Man[648] (the emphasis on domicile means that even where both applicants are living in the UK etc they may not be eligible to apply for a s 30 order);

(vii) both husband and wife must be at least 18 years old[649];

(viii) the court must be satisfied that the child's father, where he is not the husband, and the surrogate mother freely agree to the making of the order. When an unmarried woman, acting as a surrogate for a married couple, carried and gave birth to a child created from the egg of the wife fertilised by sperm donated at a clinic under a licensed arrangement rather than the sperm of the husband, it seems that there is no man who is to be treated as the father and whose consent is therefore required to the making of the parental order.[650] The agreement must be unconditional and with full understanding of what is involved.[651] No agreement is required of a person who cannot be found or is incapable of giving agreement.[652] The surrogate is not permitted to agree until six weeks have elapsed since the child's birth.[653] (In contrast to adoption, there is no provision for dispensing with a surrogate's agreement, or her partner's agreement, where it is being unreasonably withheld. The effect of this is to give the surrogate (which may be understandable) and her partner (which is less easy to defend) a veto over the making of a s 30 order);

(ix)   the court must be satisfied that no money or other benefit (other than for expenses reasonably incurred) has been given or received by the husband or wife for or in consideration of the making of the parental order, any agreement required, the handing over of the child to the applicants or the making of any

---

[644] s 30(1)(b).
[645] s 30(1).
[646] s 30(2).
[647] s 30(3)(a).
[648] s 30(3)(b).
[649] s 30(4).
[650] *Re Q (Parental Order)* [1996] 1 FLR 369.
[651] s 30(5).
[652] s 30(6).
[653] s 30(6).

arrangements with a view to the making of the order.[654] The court can, however, authorise payments. On the clear analogy of the adoption legislation, it may be assumed that courts will do this retrospectively as well as prospectively. And this has happened. Examples of this being done are *Re Q*,[655] where a payment of £8,280 was found to be reasonable and retrospectively authorised, and *Re C*.[656] where £12,000 was held to be not so disproportionately greater than the 'usual' sum. (It will be observed that reasonable expenses can be paid and that, as in *Re Q* and *Re C*, this is interpreted liberally, but, of course, retrospectively. It has been recommended that a list of 'prescribed' expenses be stipulated. Wall J in *Re C* stressed the need for 'transparency in the definition and true extent of expenses reasonably incurred under s.30 (7) of the [1990] Act').[657]

10.214 Applications for a s 30 order may be made to the High Court, a county court or to a Family Proceedings court.[658] In deciding whether to make a s 30 order, the court must 'have regard to all the circumstances, first consideration being given to the need to safeguard and promote the welfare of the child'.[659] Whether the paramountcy principle will replace this must await the implementation of the Adoption and Children Act 2002, and any subsequent regulations. The guardian ad litem[660] must establish whether the s 30 criteria are met and must then determine whether there is any reason why a parental order would not be in the best interests of the child (applying at present at least the 'first consideration' standard).[661] It is thought that guardians will often confront the dilemma that the criteria are not satisfied (most obviously, because the surrogate has been paid) but the child's best interests mandate an order. Courts, it seems, extricate them from this dilemma by retrospectively authorising unlawful payments as reasonable expenses.[662] *Re C*[663] is the clearest of examples of this: it was manifestly in the interests of a 'much loved and cherished child' that she be treated in law as the child of the commissioning couple despite £12,000 having passed to a surrogate (who in addition was claiming income support—a fact not known by the couple). But would the court have come to a different conclusion had they known? I suspect not: the welfare of the child would still have dictated the order.

---

[654] s 30(7).

[655] [1996] 1 FLR 369.

[656] [2002] 1 FLR 909.

[657] ibid, 918.

[658] s 30(8)(a).

[659] Parental Orders (Human Fertilisation and Embryology) Regulations 1994, SI 1994/2767, Sch 9(1)(a).

[660] See Local Authority Circular LAC (94) 25.

[661] The Parental Orders (Human Fertilisation and Embryology) Regulations 1994 (n 655 above); Local Authority Circular LAC (94) 25.

[662] The Brazier report (Cm 4068, 1998) described the reference to expenses reasonably incurred as 'laconic' (para 7.11).

[663] N 651 above, 917.

A parental order gives parental responsibility to the applicants.[664] It also extinguishes **10.215** the parental responsibility which any person has for the child immediately before the making of the order, as well as any order under the Children Act 1989 (for example, a residence order[665]), and any duty arising by virtue of an agreement or the order of a court to make payments, so far as the payments are in respect of the child's maintenance or upbringing for any period after the making of the order.[666] The child is to be treated for all purposes as if she is the child of the marriage of the applicants for the parental order, and not the child of anyone else.[667] There are a number of exceptions to this. One of these is with regard to prohibited degrees of relationship in relation to marriage and incest as against the genetic relations of the child.[668] Part of the reason for this is to allow for a register of parental orders.[669]

The Registrar General is required to maintain a 'Parental Order Register' to record **10.216** the effects of parental orders made under s 30.[670] The child, upon reaching the age of 18, is entitled to obtain details of his/her birth, including the name of the surrogate mother.[671] Prior to being given this information, the person concerned will be offered counselling.[672] The children of surrogacy arrangements are thus the only children born following medically assisted reproduction to be granted this right.[673] Though, as indicated in para 10.145, it is distinctly possible that this will change. Surrogacy is equated for these purposes (and others as we have seen) with adoption. The analogy however breaks down where the surrogate leases her womb but does not provide her egg. In such a case the child will at 18 be able to discover his/her gestational mother, but, unless the egg of a third woman has been used, will already know his/her genetic mother. Where the child is born to a surrogate using egg donation from a third party woman, the child will be able to find out the identity of the genetic mother if the commissioning parents who cannot use the s 30 procedure adopted him/her. In addition, a child under 18 who is subject to a 'parental order' may discover whether a person he/she intends to marry is within the prohibited degrees of relationship.[674] For this purpose both the commissioning couple and the surrogate and her partner, if she has one, will be the child's parents. The child is not allowed to marry the surrogate's son or daughter, who are considered siblings even where the surrogate was the gestational mother only.[675]

---

[664] See *op cit*, n 619, r 2.2.
[665] ibid.
[666] ibid.
[667] ibid, r 2.2.
[668] ibid, r 2.3(e).
[669] ibid, r 2.4.
[670] ibid.
[671] ibid, r 2.4(b).
[672] ibid.
[673] See para 10.145, above.
[674] *Op cit*, n 619, r.w2.4(b)(11).
[675] ibid.

(iii) Children Act 1989

10.217 Proceedings under s 30 are 'family proceedings' within the meaning of the Children Act 1989.[676] This means that the powers available under that Act are also available on an application for a 'parental order', including the power to make s 8 orders.[677] The court could thus grant the applicants a residence order instead of a parental order.[678] It could also make an additional order, for example, a contact order[679] in favour of the surrogate mother, a specific issue order[680] (perhaps relating to the religion in which the child is to be brought up) or a prohibited steps order[681] (for example, relating to the removal of the child from this country).

(iv) Wardship[682]

10.218 If the surrogate mother refuses to hand over the child, the only way the dispute may be resolved is by warding the child. The commissioning parents may involve the inherent jurisdiction of the High Court as parens patriae to decide matters relating to the child's future. In *Re P (Minors) (Wardship: surrogacy)*, Sir John Arnold P said:

> The court's duty is to decide the case, taking into account as the first and paramount consideration [now the paramount consideration], the welfare of the child or children concerned and if that consideration leads the court to override any agreement that there may be in the matter, then that court is fully entitled to do'.[683]

In this case, 'preserving the link with the [surrogate] mother to whom they [there were twins in this case] are bonded and who has exercised over them a satisfactory level of maternal care'[684] tipped the balance in favour of the surrogate and against the commissioning parents. In *Re C (A Minor)* Latey J remarked that 'the moral, ethical and social considerations are for others and not for this court in its wardship jurisdiction'.[685] His only concern was 'what is best for this baby'.[686] He was in no doubt that care and control should be given to the commissioning parents. The surrogate did not disagree: it was the local authority, who had taken a place of safety order, who were obstructing the commissioning parents.

---

[676] s 30(8)(a) and see Children Act 1989, s 8(3), (4).
[677] See Freeman, MDA, *Children, Their Families and the Law* (Basingstoke: Macmillan, 1992), ch 3.
[678] s 8(1).
[679] s 8(1).
[680] s 8(1).
[681] s 8(1).
[682] As to which see Lowe, N and White, RAH, *Wards of Court* (Chichester: Barry Rose, 1986).
[683] [1987] 2 FLR 421, 425.
[684] ibid, 427.
[685] [1985] FLR 445.
[686] ibid.

It is possible for the court to grant commissioning parents contact with the child, whilst leaving him/her in the care of the surrogate mother.[687] In the well-known *Baby M* case[688] in New Jersey, the commissioning parents were awarded custody, but the Supreme Court of New Jersey decided that the surrogate mother should have 'visitation'.[689] The issue has only been considered in one English case (*A v C*), where the Court of Appeal firmly rejected it. To Ormrod LJ, it would lead to 'the whole of this sordid story . . . (be[ing] revived weekly or monthly . . . The mother's position will be handicapped, and the handicapping of her position handicaps the child.'[690] Although the facts were different from almost all surrogacy cases (the 'contract' resulted from a casual encounter with a prostitute), courts are unlikely today to make a 'contact order' in favour of commissioning parents if they decide that the child should continue to reside with the surrogate mother. Nor are they likely to follow the precedent of *Baby M* and award contact to a surrogate mother.

10.219

(v) Informal Transfers

The Brazier report believes that 'a substantial proportion of commissioning couples are failing to apply to the courts to become the legal parents of the child'.[691] The likeliest reason is that informal transfers have taken place and commissioning parents are ignorant of their lack of status or, less likely, indifferent. The consequences of this are that the surrogate retains parental responsibility.[692] If she has a husband he is likely to have this too. They can, as a result, interfere with decisions the commissioning parents take about the child. The potentiality for acrimonious disputes is obvious. Concomitantly, the commissioning parents will not have parental responsibility. Nor will they be 'parents'. They will have 'care' of the child and may, subject to the provisions of the Children Act, 'do what is reasonable . . . for the purpose of safeguarding or promoting the child's welfare'.[693] With the leave of the court,[694] they may apply for a residence order and acquire parental responsibility in this way.[695] It is also possible for a competent child[696] to seek a residence order in favour of his/her social parents,[697] but then he/she could equally well ask it to be in favour of the surrogate or some other person or persons.

10.220

---

[687] Under s 8 of the Children Act 1989.
[688] 537 A 2d 1227 (1988).
[689] 'Contact' in English legal terminology.
[690] *Op cit*, n 643, 458.
[691] *Surrogacy: Review for Health Ministers of Current Arrangements for Payments and Regulations* (Cm 4068, 1998), para 5.7.
[692] Children Act 1989, s 2 (1).
[693] ibid, s 3(5).
[694] ibid, s 10(1)(a)(ii).
[695] ibid s 12(2).
[696] That is a child who has 'sufficient understanding to make the proposed application for the s 8 order' (s 10(8) of the Children Act 1989).
[697] See *Re SC* [1994] 1 FLR 96, 100 *per* Booth J.

(vi) Abductions

10.221 If a child is born in England and Wales to a surrogate, the surrogacy agreement and conception having taken place abroad, will an English court return the child to the foreign country? This issue arose in the complex case of *W and B v H*.[698] The surrogacy agreement was entered into in California, by the law of which it was legally binding,[699] between an English surrogate and a California couple. The egg was from an anonymous donor. This was fertilised by commissioning father's sperm. When it was discovered that the surrogate was carrying twins, there was considerable dispute (talk of 'selective reduction' and alternative parents). The surrogate invoked the jurisdiction of the Californian court to divest herself of custody, and, after achieving this, changed her mind, and came to England where she gave birth. The forum conveniens for this dispute would appear to be California,[700] but the genetic father sought the protection instead of the Hague Convention on International Child Abduction.[701] He had rights of custody under Californian law but the Convention would not bite unless the children were or ever had been habitually resident in California. They clearly were not nor had ever been. Hedley J held that they were not habitually resident in England either.[702] This conclusion is less easy to justify. Would he have come to the same conclusion if the surrogate had been the genetic mother? There is reason to doubt this, within his judgment. He concluded that the children were not habitually resident anywhere (they were presumably domiciled in England[703]—a legal connection that is irrelevant to the problem). Abduction proceedings failed. In effect an English court refused to uphold a surrogacy agreement valid by its applicable law[704] and at the same time undermined the order of a foreign court giving custody to the commissioning parents. And this, ironically, in an area where comity prevails over paramountcy.[705]

---

[698] [2002] 1 FLR 1008.

[699] ibid, 1009.

[700] And so Hedley J held in *W and W v H (Child Abduction: Surrogacy) No 2* [2002] 2 FLR 252.

[701] Brought into English law by the Child Abduction and Custody Act 1985.

[702] A baby was held not to have the habitual residence of his mother (the surrogate). To hold otherwise was to confuse domicile with habitual residence (as had happened, so it was held, in *B v H (Habitual Residence: Wardship)* [2002] 1 FLR 388.)

[703] As illegitimate children they would take the domicile of their mother as a domicile of origin.

[704] There was no express choice of applicable law but it seems this contract was more closely connected with California than England, so that even if the surrogate was the characteristic performer (see Rome Convention, Art 4(2)) the presumption would be rebutted by Art 4(5).

[705] See Freeman, M, 'Images of Child Welfare in Child Abduction Appeals' in Murphy, J, (ed), *Ethnic Minorities, Their Families and the Law* (Oxford: Hart, 2000), 1.

11

ABORTION

A. Abortion and the General Law

Abortion is the termination of a pregnancy by surgical or medical means intended **11.01**
to result in the death of a foetus.[1] As with other medical procedures the general
requirements of medical law apply, in particular, the law of consent and negligence.[2] Consequently, either the patient[3] or another must validly consent to the
abortion or, in the case of an incompetent adult, it must be lawful to carry out the
termination notwithstanding the fact that the patient is unable to consent.[4]

---

[1] It is arguable that Parliament also intended 'late terminations of pregnancy' to be dealt with as
'abortions', where only the pregnancy, but not the child, is unwanted. Hence some intended live
births are brought within the Act: see Kennedy, I and Grubb, A, *Medical Law* (3rd edn,
Butterworths, 2000), 1184–5 and Scowen, E and Grubb, A, 'Is Induction of Labour Unlawful?'
(1991) 1(3) *Dispatches* 4.
[2] See Ch 4 (consent), Chs 5–7 (negligence) and Ch 12 (pre-natal actions).
[3] For the requirements of consent, see Ch 3.
[4] *Re F (A Mental Patient: Sterilisation)* [1990] 2 AC 1.

Consequently, a competent patient, whether child[5] or adult, must consent to the procedure.[6] In the case of an incompetent child the consent of the parents[7] or the court[8] must be obtained acting in the child's best interests.[9] And, if the patient is an incompetent adult, an abortion may only be performed if the principle of necessity permits it in the best interests of the patient.[10] Except in the case of a child who is already a ward of court,[11] there is no requirement to seek the court's consent or a declaration of the procedure's legality.[12]

B. Statutory Regulation of Abortion

1. The Abortion Act 1967

11.02 In addition to the general law, however, the Abortion Act 1967 regulates the availability and delivery of terminations of pregnancy in England, Scotland, and Wales.[13] Unusually, the availability of abortion, unlike other medical procedures, is not left to agreement between the doctor and patient.[14] An abortion or termination of pregnancy must, to be lawful, be covered by the provisions of the 1967 Act. The Abortion Act 1967 operates by creating a defence to what would otherwise amount to the criminal offence of 'procuring a miscarriage' under s 58 of the Offences Against the Person Act 1861[15] or, if the foetus is 'capable of being born alive', of the offence of 'child destruction' contrary to the Infant Life (Preservation) Act 1929.[16]

---

[5] Under the Family Law Reform Act 1969, s 8 (aged 16–18) or the common law if *Gillick*-competent (under 16). See discussion, Ch 4.

[6] It appears that the court may, in some circumstances, consent even if a competent child *refuses* to consent: *Re W (A Minor) (Medical Treatment)* [1992] 4 All ER 627 (CA); but probably the parents cannot override the refusal; ibid *per* Nolan LJ at 648–9. For discussion, see Ch 4, above.

[7] A parent or other with 'parental responsibility' under the Children Act 1989. It is impossible to imagine circumstances where the 'carer' provision in the Children Act 1989, s 3(5), could be applied to abortion.

[8] Under its inherent jurisdiction (requiring leave under the Children Act 1989, s 100), under the Children Act 1989, s 8, or, unusually under the wardship jurisdiction if the child is already a ward of court.

[9] See eg *Re P (A Minor)* [1986] 1 FLR 272; *Re B (Wardship: Abortion)* [1991] 2 FLR 426. See discussion, paras 4.78 *et seq*.

[10] eg *Re SG (Adult Mental Patient: Abortion)* [1991] 2 FLR 329 and *Re SS* [2001] 1 FLR 445.

[11] *Re G-U (A Minor) (Wardship)* [1984] FLR 811.

[12] *Re SG (Adult Mental Patient: Abortion)* [1991] 2 FLR 329.

[13] The Act does not extend to Northern Ireland where the common law still applies: see *Northern Health & Social Services Board v F and G* [1993] NI 268 (Sheil J) and Grubb, (1994) 2 Med L Rev 371 (Commentary); *Re AMNH* (1994) 2 Med LR 374 (MacDermott LJ); *Re SJB (A Minor)* (28 September 1995, Pringle J) 28 Sept 1995, and *Re CH (A Minor)* (18 October 1995 Sheil J).

[14] Another important instance of Parliamentary intervention is in the area of assisted reproduction through the Human Fertilisation and Embryology Act 1990. See Ch 10.

[15] In Scotland, it is a common law crime. For the position in Scotland, see Norrie, K, 'Abortion in Great Britain: One Act, Two Laws' [1985] Crim LR 475, especially 481–6.

[16] Abortion ('procuring a miscarriage') has been a statutory offence since 1803. Whether there

The Abortion Act 1967 regulates the availability of abortion in a number of ways. **11.03** First, it sets out four grounds, one of which must exist, for an abortion to be lawful.[17] Secondly, the Act lays down the time limits within which an abortion may be carried out.[18] Thirdly, it stipulates who may carry out abortions[19] and where they may be performed, providing in the latter case for a system of licensing for private clinics.[20] Finally, it provides for regulatory matters such as reporting, certification, and confidentiality.[21]

2. Background to the 1967 Act

(i) Offences Against the Person Act 1861, s 58

The present legislation dates back to 1967 and began life as a Private Member's **11.04** Bill sponsored by David Steel MP. It came into force on 27 October 1967. It replaced the common law as stated in *Bourne*.[22] In *R v Bourne*[23] it was held that an abortion would not be 'unlawful' under s 58 of the Offences Against the Person Act 1861 if it was 'done in good faith for the purpose only of preserving the [life of the mother]'. Macnaghten J adopted an expansive interpretation of this phrase to include cases where the probable consequence of the continuance of the pregnancy would be to make the woman a physical wreck. Subsequent case law made it quite clear that a doctor could perform an abortion to preserve the mental or physical health as well as the life of the mother.[24]

(ii) The Infant Life (Preservation) Act 1929

However, until 1991, the Abortion Act 1967 had to be read subject to the effect **11.05** of the Infant Life (Preservation) Act 1929. Compliance with the 1967 Act did not

---

was a crime of abortion at common law is uncertain, though the better view is that there probably was. For discussions of the common law and the legislation between 1803 and 1861, see Keown, J, *Abortion, Doctors and the Law* (1988) and Grubb, A, 'Abortion Law in England: The Medicalisation of a Crime' (1990) 18 *Law, Medicine and Health Care* 146.

[17] s 1(1).

[18] ss 1(1)(a) and 5(1).

[19] s 1(1): only 'registered medical practitioners'.

[20] s 1(3) and (3A). Notice the emergency exception in s 1(4).

[21] s 2 and the Abortion Regulations 1991, SI 1991/499 as amended by the Abortion (Amendment) (England) Regulations 2002, SI 2002/887 and the Abortion (Amendment) (Wales) Regulations 2002, SI 2002/2979 (W 275).

[22] s 6.

[23] [1939] 1 KB 687. For a judicial account of the law of abortion prior to the 1967 Act see; *R (on the Application of Smeaton on behalf of SPUC) v Secretary of State for Health* [2002] EWHC 610 (Admin); (2002) 66 BMLR 59 *per* Munby J at [78]–[107].

[24] *R v Bergmann* [1948] 1 BMJ 1008 (Morris J) and *R v Newton and Stungo* [1958] Crim LR 469 (Ashworth J). For a recent discussion in an Australian context, see *CES v Superclinics (Australia) Pty Ltd* (1995) 38 NSWLR 47 (NSW CA) and Grubb, A (1996) 4 Med L Rev 102, 107–9 (Commentary).

provide a defence to the crime of 'child destruction' created by the 1929 Act.[25] In fact, the Infant Life (Preservation) Act 1929 was enacted to close a loophole in the law where a child was killed in the course of being born; which was neither an offence under s 58—it could not be said to be procuring a 'miscarriage'—nor murder or manslaughter because the child would not yet have 'an existence independent of its mother'. However, s 1(1) of the 1929 Act is broader in its scope. It provides that 'any person who, with intent to destroy the life of a child capable of being born alive, by any wilful act causes a child to die before it has an existence independent of its mother' shall be guilty of an offence. Aborting a foetus 'capable of being born alive' could amount to the offence under the 1929 Act.

11.06 As a result, the 1929 Act had the practical effect until 1991 of setting the upper time limit for an abortion when the foetus was 'capable of being born alive'. The meaning of this statutory phrase is not, however, clear and unambiguous.[26] The Act itself gives one indicator: s 1(2) creates a presumption that a 28-week old foetus is 'capable of being born alive'. That, however, is no more than a presumption and the courts have interpreted the Act as applying to less mature foetuses. In *C v S*[27] the Court of Appeal rejected the argument that the 1929 Act prevented the destruction of any foetus which showed 'recognisable signs of life'. The court concluded that the 1929 Act required that the foetus should have the capacity to survive and, hence, did not apply to a foetus of 18- to 21-weeks gestation which could not because its lungs were insufficiently developed.

11.07 In *Rance v Mid-Downs HA*[28] Brooke J held that a 26-week old foetus was 'capable of being born alive' within the terms of the 1929 Act because '. . . after birth, it exists as a live child, that is to say breathing and living by reason of its breathing through its own lungs alone, without deriving any of its living or power of living by or through any connection with its mother'. Brooke J rejected an argument that the foetus must have the capacity to survive for a reasonable period when it is born.

11.08 Thus, prior to 1991,[29] the time limit for a legal abortion was, because of the impact of the 1929 Act, somewhere between 22 and 24 weeks depending upon the development of the particular foetus.[30] Hence, the 1929 Act continued to dictate

---

[25] s 5(1) as originally enacted.

[26] *Per* Heilbron J in *C v S*, and see Keown, J, 'The Scope of the Offence of Child Destruction' (1988) 104 LQR 120.

[27] [1987] 1 All ER 1230 (Heilbron J and CA). Discussed, Grubb, A, and Pearl, D, (1987) 103 LQR 340.

[28] [1991] 1 All ER 801, 817.

[29] When the Abortion Act 1967, s 5(1) was amended so as also to create a defence to the crime of 'child destruction' under the 1929 Act.

[30] This will remain important where the legality (or availability) of an abortion prior to 1 April 1991 is still relevant, for example, in a 'wrongful birth' claim arising before that date: see *Rance v Mid-Downs HA* [1991] 1 All ER 801. See discussion below, Ch 12.

the upper time limit for lawful abortion where the foetus was 'capable of being born alive'.[31]

3. Section 37 of the Human Fertilisation and Embryology Act 1990

Despite numerous back-bench attempts to change its terms, in particular, to lower the upper time limit for abortions and to restrict the grounds upon which an abortion could be carried out, the substance of the 1967 Act remained unaltered until 1991. During the passage of the Human Fertilisation and Embryology Act 1990 through Parliament the Government allocated time in order to allow a full debate upon what should be the law. In the result, s 37 of the Human Fertilisation and Embryology Act 1990, which came into force on 1 April 1991,[32] amended the 1967 Act principally in *four* ways:[33]

11.09

(i) it substituted (and enlarged) the grounds for abortion contained in s 1(1) of the 1967 Act;[34]

(ii) it disengaged the 1967 Act from the Infant Life (Preservation) Act 1929 and the time limit it imposed so that compliance with the 1967 Act created a defence both to the 1861 and 1929 Acts;[35]

(iii) it set an upper time limit of 24 weeks for the most common ground for an abortion under the new s 1(1)(a) of the 1967 Act and removed any time limit for the other grounds;[36]

(iv) it sought to clarify the law, and make legal, the procedures of selective reduction and foeticide.[37]

4. Abortion and Post-Coital Contraception[38]

It is important to determine the scope of the regulation of abortion given the criminal prohibition contained in s 58 of the Offences Against the Person Act 1861. The most important situation, in practice, concerns certain birth control practices which may not be purely contraceptive in their effects.[39] A contraceptive is a medicinal substance or device which prevents fertilisation of the egg by the

11.10

---

[31] Unless the abortion was carried out 'in good faith for the purpose only of preserving the life of the mother': s 1(1). The burden of proof lies on the prosecution.

[32] Human Fertilisation and Embryology Act 1990 (Commencement No 2 and Transitional Provision) Order 1991, SI 1991/480.

[33] For discussions of s 37, see Grubb, A, [1991] Crim LR 659; Montgomery, J, (1991) 45 MLR 524, 531–3; Murphy, J, [1991] JSWFL 375.

[34] See s 1(1)(a)–(d).

[35] See s 5(1).

[36] Combined effect of ss 1(1)(a) and 5(1).

[37] See s 5(2).

[38] See Norrie, K, *Family Planning Practice and the Law* (1991), ch 2.

[39] For a description of modern contraceptive technology: see, *R (on the Application of Smeaton on behalf of SPUC) v Secretary of State for Health* [2002] EWHC 610 (Admin); (2002) 66 BMLR 59, *per* Munby J at [191]–[201].

male sperm. Obvious examples of this are the so-called 'pill' or barrier methods such as condoms. These prevent fertilisation by chemical or physical means. Other methods may not prevent fertilisation but act in such a way that the fertilised egg, if any, does not implant in the woman's uterus. Examples of these are post-coital methods like the so-called 'morning after pill' or intra-uterine devices (IUDs) whether fitted post-coitally or not. In these situations it is better to term the methods as contragestive rather than contraceptive since they act *only* to prevent gestation. Further complications may arise, and will be returned to later, in that the agents may act not to prevent gestation but to end it. In other words, after the developing embryo has implanted they effect its expulsion from the woman's uterus. Are any of these properly subject to the legal regulatory regime for terminations or abortion? The answer depends principally upon one issue: do they effect a 'miscarriage' so as to fall within the criminal prohibition in the 1861 Act?

(i) Miscarriage

11.11   It is clear that a purely contraceptive agent does not produce a 'miscarriage'. A failure to fertilise cannot properly be considered a 'miscarriage'. By contrast it is widely accepted that if the effect is to cause an implanted embryo to be expelled from the mother's uterus that is a 'miscarriage' and the effect is abortifacient rather than contraceptive. The Abortion Act 1967 must be complied with for this to be done legally. What, however, of the contragestive method? Is a failure to implant also a 'miscarriage'? In one sense, the woman has ceased to 'carry' and, hence has 'miscarried'. What was previously within her body will be expelled. However, this does not tally within the ordinary notion of 'miscarriage' which would entail a lost 'pregnancy' (ie which had become established to the woman's knowledge). This, of course, only occurs once a period is missed which itself can only follow the implantation of the developing embryo. Also, a broad notion of 'miscarriage' is not consistent with modern medical usage. While legislation has to be interpreted in the sense intended at the time of its enactment (originally 1803), attempts to show that the broader meaning was intended merely illustrate the ambiguity in the language used or the relative ignorance of the time about the reproductive process.[40] In short, little of any value can be gleaned about the meaning of 'miscarriage' by reliance on early or late nineteenth century medical or legal dicta.

11.12   What then amounts to a 'miscarriage'? The weight of legal writing supports the view that 'carriage' requires the developing embryo to have implanted.[41] This comports most easily with accepted notions of what it is to be pregnant and for it

---

[40] Keown, J, 'Miscarriage': A Medico-Legal Analysis' [1984] Crim LR 604.
[41] Kennedy, I, *Treat Me Right* (1988) ch 3; Williams, G, *Textbook of Criminal Law* (2nd edn, 1983), 294–5 and Kennedy, I and Grubb, A, *Medical Law* (n 1 above) 1410–14. Contrast Keown, J, ibid; and Tunkel, V, [1974] Crim LR 461.

to end by means of an abortion. Further, there is no convincing public policy argument which would bring contragestive measures within the mischief or desirable scope of the law regulating abortions or would justify the court intervening to prevent what is a socially accepted practice relating to 'an intensely personal and private matter'.[42]

In addition, there is strong support for the need for implantation from the (then) **11.13** Attorney-General in a written answer in the House of Commons in 1983[43] and Parliament has, in effect, accepted that the concept of 'carriage' requires implantation in the Human Fertilisation and Embryology Act 1990. Section 2(3) provides, for the purposes of the 1990 Act,[44] that 'a woman is not to be treated as carrying a child until the embryo has become implanted'.[45] Other jurisdictions have made this interpretation explicit in their legislation based upon the 1861 Act.[46]

(ii) The Morning-After Pill Case

The point finally arose for judicial decision in 2002 in *R (on the Application of* **11.14** *Smeaton on behalf of SPUC) v Secretary of State for Health*.[47] The claimant on behalf of the Society for the Protection of Unborn Children (SPUC) sought judicial review of a statutory instrument[48] which allowed pharmacists to dispense 'the morning-after pill' as 'an emergency contraceptive' without the need for a prescription.[49] The claimant argued that in doing so a pharmacist would commit a criminal offence under ss 58 and 59 of the Offences Against the Person Act 1861 as the effect on the woman would be to procure a 'miscarriage'. It was contended that 'miscarriage' covered any interference with a fertilised egg whether before or after implantation.

In a learned and exhaustive judgment, Munby J analysed the case law[50] and the **11.15** medical[51] and legal literature[52] at some length. The judge held that when enacting

---

[42] See Munby J's remarks in *R (on the Application of Smeaton on behalf of SPUC) v Secretary of State for Health* [2002] EWHC 610 (Admin); (2002) 66 BMLR 59, *per* Munby J at [209]–[225] and [393]–[398]. The quotation is from para [398] of the judgment.

[43] 42 Parl Deb HC 238, 239.

[44] Thus, it is not directly applicable to the Offences Against the Person Act 1861, ss 58 and 59.

[45] Contrast, Surrogacy Arrangements Act 1985, s1(6) which defines carrying a child at the point of insemination or embryo transfer.

[46] Crimes Act 1961 (NZ), s 182A.

[47] [2002] EWHC 610 (Admin); (2002) 66 BMLR 59 (Munby J).

[48] The Prescription Only Medicines (Human Use) Amendment (No 3) Order 2000, SI 2000/3231 amending the Prescription Only Medicines (Human Use) Order 1997, SI 1997/1830.

[49] The particular product was marketed as 'Levonelle'. Previously, the 'morning after pill' had only been available on prescription from a doctor.

[50] ibid, at [226]–[255].

[51] ibid, at [125]–[169] including expert evidence submitted at the hearing.

[52] ibid, at [256]–[277].

the nineteenth century legislation, Parliament had not had in mind the issue of contraception and there was nothing to suggest that Parliament had intended to protect life from conception. Further, the word 'miscarriage'—which was left undefined by Parliament—should be interpreted as it would *currently* be understood and in the light of the best current scientific knowledge available.[53] There was no dispute on that evidence: 'miscarriage' was the termination of a post-implantation pregnancy. This, he considered, accorded with a linguistic analysis that there could be no 'true carriage' prior to implantation. It also corresponded to the overwhelming weight of legal writings[54] and was supported by the only English decision directly in point.[55]

11.16   Thus, Munby J dismissed the application and concluded that 'miscarriage' required the fertilised egg to have implanted which would not be the case in the circumstances when the 'morning after pill'[56] was taken by a woman.

(iii) Problem Cases?

11.17   As a result, purely contragestive methods of birth control are not regulated by the 1967 Act. However, where the method may work pre- or post-implantation, the position may be otherwise. This may occur with an IUD. The legal issue is whether the doctor acts 'with *intent*' to procure a miscarriage.

(a) 'Intent to Procure a Miscarriage'

11.18   Certainly, if the doctor believes that the woman is pregnant, in the sense of 'carrying' a foetus in utero, what he is doing falls within the 1861 Act and he must comply with the requirements of the Abortion Act. Hence, where a doctor fitted an IUD to a woman whom the doctor believed to be about 14 weeks pregnant, the Court of Appeal in *R v Price*[57] upheld his conviction under s 58. In that case, of course, there could be no doubt as to his intention given the state of his knowledge.

11.19   Where, however, an IUD is fitted much sooner after sexual intercourse has taken place the doctor's understanding and knowledge is likely to be less certain. Clearly, if the woman has already missed a monthly period following sexual intercourse,

---

[53] Munby J concluded that the 1861 Act was 'always speaking' and in seeking Parliament's intention must, as a matter of construction, be interpreted in the light of advancing knowledge, technology and social standards: see, *R v Ireland, R v Burstow* [1998] AC 147, HL, especially *per* Lord Steyn at 158 and *Birmingham CC v Oakley* [2001] 1 AC 617, HL, especially *per* Lord Hoffmann at 628 and 631.

[54] The judge referred to paras 11.10–11.15 of the 1st edition of this work and, inter alia, the writings cited above, nn 40 and 41.

[55] *R v Dhingra* (24 January 1991, Birmingham CC, Wright J).

[56] Or IUDs, the pill or mini-pill were used.

[57] [1969] 1 QB 541 (CA).

the likely knowledge of the doctor is that implantation has occurred and his intention will be manifest. What, however, if he fits the IUD before that, ie during the 28 days or so since her last period? The woman may, of course, not actually be pregnant (ie 'carrying') since ovulation takes place around 14 days into her cycle and implantation is unlikely to occur for another six to ten days after that. It is not, however, necessary for the offence under s 58 to be committed that the woman be pregnant or, as the s 58 quaintly puts it, 'be with child'. As is clear from the only case where this issue has arisen, the relevant issue is always the doctor's intention. Nevertheless, given that the defendant will be a doctor who can be expected to have some knowledge of the physiology of conception and pregnancy, his knowledge of the woman's particular sexual and menstrual history will be evidentially significant.

(b) R v Dhingra

In *R v Dhingra*[58] the defendant, a doctor inserted an IUD into a patient 11 days **11.20** after they had had sexual intercourse which was 17 days after the start of her last monthly period. He was charged with the offence under s 58 of the Offences Against the Person Act 1861. The judge held that the issue was:

> whether the defendant, at the time he inserted the coil, knew or believed that [the woman] was pregnant, and, accordingly, introduced the instrument with intent to produce a miscarriage; or whether, as is the case for the defence, that he knew or believed that she was not pregnant . . . and that his purpose in inserting the coil was for contraceptive purposes; in other words, to prevent her becoming pregnant thereafter.[59]

Presaging Munby J's decision in 'the morning-after pill' case, Wright J decided **11.21** that 'miscarriage' meant dislodging an implanted fertilised egg.[60] Wright J further held, on the basis of the expert evidence, that the woman could not have been pregnant (ie 'carrying') until at least the 20th day of her cycle so that, at the time the IUD was fitted on the 17th day of her cycle, she probably was not pregnant.[61] However, this was not conclusive of the defendant's knowledge. But, on the evidence, Wright J concluded that the defendant had been fully aware that the woman could not have been pregnant when he inserted the IUD and had, when confronted by her prior to fitting the IUD, told the woman that she could not possibly be pregnant. Thus, the judge held that the defendant could not possibly have intended to procure a miscarriage when he fitted the IUD[62] and withdrew the case from the jury.

---

[58] 24 January 1991, Birmingham CC, Wright J.
[59] Transcript, p1.
[60] Transcript, 9.
[61] Transcript, 9.
[62] Transcript, 9–10.

11.22 Factually *R v Price* and *R v Dhingra* lie at opposite ends of a spectrum of knowledge which establish or refute the intention to procure a miscarriage. Not all cases need be like this. A doctor may fit an IUD at a time during a woman's cycle when he cannot know—one way or another—whether implantation has occurred. And thus, he may lack a determinative belief either way. He may, instead, be unsure and prepared to take the risk on the effect the IUD will have. If the doctor undertakes the procedure prepared if necessary to bring about a 'miscarriage', his conditional state of mind ('Do 'X' if necessary') is an intent to procure a miscarriage. If 'miscarriage' is entailed as an acceptable outcome of what he is doing, then he has the requisite mens rea. If his state of mind is otherwise, he will only be reckless as to procuring a miscarriage which is insufficient for a conviction under s 58. In such circumstances there may be considerable difficulty in establishing beyond a reasonable doubt that the doctor intended to procure a miscarriage.

C. The Abortion Act 1967[63]

11.23 Section 1(1) of the 1967 Act (as amended) states that:

> Subject to the provisions of this section, a person shall not be guilty of an offence under the law relating to abortion when a pregnancy is terminated by a registered medical practitioner if two registered medical practitioners are of the opinion, formed in good faith—
>
> (a) that the pregnancy has not exceeded twenty-four weeks and that the continuance of the pregnancy would involve risk, greater than if the pregnancy were terminated, of injury to the physical or mental health of the pregnant woman or any existing children of her family; or
>
> (b) that the termination is necessary to prevent grave permanent injury to the physical or mental health of the pregnant woman; or
>
> (c) that the continuance of the pregnancy would involve risk to the life of the pregnant woman, greater than if the pregnancy were terminated; or
>
> (d) that there is a substantial risk that if the child were born it would suffer from such physical or mental abnormalities as to be seriously handicapped.

1. The Scope of the Act

11.24 The Abortion Act 1967 creates a defence to the offences of 'procuring a miscarriage' under ss 58 and 59 of the Offences Against the Person Act 1861[64] and of 'child destruction' under the Infant Life (Preservation) Act 1929.[65] The Act contemplates a number of prerequisites to a lawful abortion.[66]

---

[63] Amended by the Human Fertilisation and Embryology Act 1990, s 37, with effect from 1 April 1991.

[64] s 6 defines 'the law relating to abortion' as meaning the Offences Against the Person Act 1861, ss 58 and 59, and, rather mysteriously, 'any rule of law relating to the procurement of abortion'. It is not clear what this latter phrase relates to.

[65] s 5(1).

[66] For a discussion of other procedural requirements under the 1967 Act and Abortion Regulations 1991 (as amended), see below, paras 11.61 *et seq.*

(i) '. . . a pregnancy is terminated . . .'

The wording of s 1(1) of the 1967 Act states that the woman's 'pregnancy' must be **11.25** 'terminated'.[67] This is a curious formulation since it seems to presuppose that the crime—to which the 1967 Act provides a defence—is couched in similar terms. Of course, the 1861 Act is not. It makes no reference to a 'pregnancy' but to a 'miscarriage'[68] and, more importantly, it does not require that a miscarriage actually should occur. Section 58 creates an offence where the person does one of the specified acts[69] 'with intent to procure the miscarriage' of a woman. The crime is committed even if the person is unsuccessful providing that was his intention and, in the case of anyone except the woman herself,[70] even if she is, in fact, not 'carrying' or pregnant. On the face of it, however, the 1967 Act does not apply where the pregnancy is not terminated in these circumstances. This would be a most bizarre outcome. A person would have a defence if the abortion was successful but not where it failed or where the woman was wrongly believed to be pregnant; even though both amount to offences under s 58. In practical terms, the situation could arise where a doctor undertook 'speculative' action in case the woman should be pregnant.[71] It is not clear that the 1967 Act applies to him.[72] His conditional intent to procure a miscarriage if the woman was pregnant would suffice for an offence to be committed under s 58.

When the issue was raised in the case of *Royal College of Nursing v DHSS*,[73] the **11.26** Law Lords, who discussed it, expressed differing views. Lord Diplock considered that the 1967 Act should be interpreted to cover 'the whole treatment undertaken' and not merely, should it occur, the miscarriage.[74] Lord Wilberforce (dissenting) took the opposite view. For him, the 1967 Act did not apply: '[t]ermination is one thing; attempted and unsuccessful termination wholly another'.[75] Lord Edmund-Davies (also dissenting) agreed with Lord Diplock on the effect of the 1967 Act, in these circumstances, but for a different reason. For him, a doctor would not be acting unlawfully because he was attempting to do that which was lawful, namely

---

[67] For difficulties in respect of 'selective reduction', see below, paras 11.89 *et seq.*

[68] For a discussion of the meaning of 'miscarriage', see above, paras 11.11 *et seq.*

[69] The 'act' means administer a poison or other noxious thing or use any instrument or other means to procure the miscarriage.

[70] If the woman is charged she must be 'with child'. She may, however, commit an attempt if she believed she was pregnant, or be charged an accessory to another's crime or with conspiracy: *R v Sockett* (1908) 24 TLR 893 and *R v Whitchurch* (1890) 24 QBD 420.

[71] See Tunkel, V, 'Abortion: How Early, How Late, How Legal?' (1979) BMJ 253 discussing the procedure known as 'menstrual extraction'.

[72] See Lane Committee (Committee on the Working of the Abortion Act, Cmnd 5579, 1974) which recommended an amendment to the Act to make the law clear.

[73] [1981] AC 800; [1981] 1 All ER 545 (HL).

[74] ibid, 828.

[75] ibid, 823.

'terminate' the woman's pregnancy.[76] Whether he was successful did not, there-fore, matter. Even though the issue cannot be said to be free from doubt, it is sug-gested that the approaches of Lord Diplock and Lord Edmund-Davies represent a commonsense interpretation of a Private Member's Bill which would be adopted by a court.

(ii) '. . . by a registered medical practitioner . . . .'

11.27 The 1967 Act also requires that the pregnancy is terminated by a registered med-ical practitioner, that is, a doctor registered with the General Medical Council. To the extent that an abortion is effected by a surgical procedure, there is no difficulty. Later abortions, however, where labour is induced using prostaglandin, involve a team of health care professionals, including both doctors and nurses who carry out composite parts of the woman's treatment. Indeed, it may be more directly the actions of the nurses which bring about the termination. In the *Royal College of Nursing* case, the House of Lords was asked whether the nurses' involvement in such abortions meant that the 1967 Act did not apply as the pregnancy was not being terminated by a doctor. By a majority (3–2), the House of Lords held that the Act did apply. The majority (Lords Diplock, Roskill, and Keith) adopted a broad interpretation of s 1(1) so as to take account of modern medical practice and of the notion of the health care 'team'. The termination was within the Act if the treatment was prescribed or determined by a doctor, carried out in accordance with his directions and he remained in charge throughout. Lord Diplock stated that which acts were performed by a doctor personally and which by others, such as a nurse, did not affect the application of the Act providing what was done was 'in accordance with accepted medical practice'.[77] The case effectively settles the law in respect of the procedures currently, and indeed foreseeably, used to effect an abortion.[78]

11.28 Where a pregnancy is terminated by a doctor, any person who might otherwise be guilty of an offence under s 58 has a defence.[79] This would include nurses carrying out parts of the procedure as contemplated in the *Royal College of Nursing* case. However, if a late abortion is being carried out (ie one where the foetus is 24 weeks or more), it is not clear whether a nurse has a defence to the crime of child destruc-tion under the Infant Life (Preservation) Act 1929. Section 5(1) of the 1967 Act states that the offence will not be committed by 'a registered medical practitioner who terminates a pregnancy' in accordance with the 1967 Act. Clearly, therefore, the doctor has a defence but the nurse would not where her involvement amounts

---

[76] ibid, 832–3.
[77] ibid, 828–9.
[78] For a discussion of the use of RU-486 ('Myfigene' or 'Mifepristone') where the woman herself administers the drug, see Kennedy, I and Grubb, A, *Medical Law* (n 1 above), 1436–8.
[79] s 1(1).

to a wilful act causing the death of a child capable of being born.[80] Parliament plainly overlooked this possibility and has, as a result, left an unfortunate gap in the law.

(iii) '. . . two registered medical practitioners are of the opinion, formed in good faith . . .'

Section 1(1) of the 1967 Act requires that two doctors certify that one or more of the grounds for abortion set out in the Act applies. The 'certificate of opinion' must use the standard form specified in the Abortion Regulations 1991[81] or may be a 'DIY' certificate prepared by the doctors jointly or severally containing the same information.[82] The standard certificate is known as the 'blue form' because of its colour.[83] Except in emergencies, the certificate must be completed prior to commencement of the treatment.[84] In the case of emergencies, it may be signed[85] if it is not practicable to do so before commencing treatment within 24 hours of the termination.[86] The certificate must be retained by the doctor who terminates the pregnancy for at least three years following the termination.[87]

11.29

It may well be that the two doctors who sign the certificate will be the woman's GP and the consultant gynaecologist who carries out the abortion. However, the Act does not require that any particular doctor should sign the form. Indeed, there is no legal requirement that either doctor should have seen, let alone examined, the woman,[88] and the Act would be complied with even, for example, if the doctor carrying out the abortion had not signed the certificate. It also seems consistent with the wording of s 1(1) that the doctor performing the abortion need not himself be one of the certifying doctors. Though in practice this would be unusual, it would be lawful. Section 1(1) only requires that the pregnancy is terminated by a doctor and two doctors certify that a statutory ground exists. Thereafter, a

11.30

---

[80] s 1(1) of the 1929 Act, unless done 'for the purpose only of preserving the life of the mother' which is unlikely.

[81] SI 1991/499, reg 3(1) (as amended), Sch 1: Certificate A (usual case), Certificate B (emergencies).

[82] The latter option was introduced in 2002 in the Abortion Regulations 1991, reg 3(1) as substituted by the Abortion (Amendment) (England) Regulations 2002, SI 2002/887, reg 3 and the Abortion (Amendment) (Wales) Regulations 2002, SI 2002/2979 (W 275), reg 3.

[83] Previously, under the Abortion Regulations 1968, SI 1968/390 it was green and known as the 'green form'.

[84] Abortion Regulations 1991, SI 1991/499, reg 3(2).

[85] In this instance it need only be signed by one doctor: s 1(4) and Sch 1 (Certificate B).

[86] ibid, reg 3(3).

[87] ibid, reg 3(4).

[88] Notice that the standard certificate asks the signing doctor to strike out as appropriate 'Have/have not seen/and examined' the woman and the 'DIY' version must specify whether the doctor has 'seen or examined, or seen and examined the pregnant woman before giving the certificate': Sch 2, Abortion Regulations as substituted by SI 2002/887 (England) and SI 2002/2979 (W 275) (Wales).

'person', who may be a completely different doctor or another such as a nurse involved in the procedure, has a defence under the 1967 Act.

11.31 The 1967 Act does not require that one of the statutory grounds actually exists. Instead, it merely states that two doctors must form the opinion 'in good faith' that the particular ground exists. Both certifying doctors must form an opinion that a ground under the Act is satisfied. It does not appear from the wording of the Act that the doctors need agree on which ground is satisfied; they may take a joint or several view of the basis for the abortion. Also, an abortion will be lawful even if the doctors are mistaken about the woman's condition providing they honestly believe the ground to exist.[89] Even an unreasonable belief will, in law, be sufficient although, of course, the unreasonableness of the doctor's belief will be relevant in determining whether the belief was actually held.

11.32 The upshot of the wording of the 1967 Act is that it will be very difficult to establish that an abortion does not fall within the Act if two doctors conscientiously conclude that a ground, usually under s 1(1)(a), is fulfilled providing always that the required procedures under the 1967 Act and Abortion Regulations 1991 are followed.[90] Remembering also, that in a criminal case, the prosecution has the burden of proving beyond reasonable doubt that the 1967 Act was not complied with. The 1967 Act in effect places a 'great social responsibility' firmly 'on the shoulders of the medical profession'.[91] In *Paton v BPAS*,[92] a case in which a husband sought an injunction to prevent his wife having an abortion, Sir George Baker P stated that it would not only:

> be a bold and brave judge . . . who would seek to interfere with the discretion of doctors acting under the 1967 Act, but I think he would really be a foolish judge who would try to do such a thing, unless possibly, there is clear bad faith and an obvious attempt to perpetrate a criminal offence.

11.33 In extreme circumstances, the conduct of the doctor may call into question the bona fides of his opinion. In the only reported case of a successful prosecution,[93] the doctor concerned carried out a limited examination of the pregnant woman, did not obtain a medical history, but agreed to carry out the procedure a week later for cash. No further investigations or enquiries were carried out and a second opinion was not sought until given by the anaesthetist on her admission. The doctor's conviction under s 58 was upheld by the Court of Appeal. On the facts, the Court of Appeal concluded that the jury had been entitled to take the view that the doctor had not formed his opinion in 'good faith'.

---

[89] *R v Smith* [1974] 1 All ER 376 (CA).

[90] *Paton v BPAS* [1978] 2 All ER 987, 992.

[91] N 89 above, 378 *per* Scarman LJ.

[92] [1978] 2 All ER 987, 992. See also *C v S* [1988] QB 135; [1987] 1 All ER 1230, 1243 *per* Sir John Donaldson MR.

[93] *R v Smith* (n 89 above). For two unreported prosecutions both ending in acquittals, see *R v Dhingra* (n 58 above) and *R v Dixon*, The Times, 22 December 1995 (news report).

2. The Grounds For Abortion

The amended s 1(1) of the 1967 Act does not extend or narrow the substance of **11.34** the grounds for abortion which previously existed. There are four grounds of abortion based upon

(i)   risk to maternal physical and mental health;[94]
(ii) where necessary to prevent grave permanent physical or mental injury;[95]
(iii) risk to maternal life;[96] and
(iv) where there is a substantial risk that the child will suffer from physical or mental abnormalities so as to be seriously handicapped.[97]

Prior to 1991, grounds (i) and (iii) were combined in the old s 1(1)(a) of the Act **11.35** and ground (iv) merely reproduces exactly what was previously in s 1(1)(b). Ground (ii) did not explicitly exist, except as a basis for carrying out emergency abortions not in an NHS hospital or approved clinic.[98] The amended section tidies up the grounds and, importantly, was necessary because only the ground in the new s 1(1)(a)—where there is risk to the mother's physical or mental health— is subject to a time-limit.

(i) 'Risk of Physical or Mental Injury'—s 1(1)(a)

Section 1(1)(a) is, in practice, the most commonly relied upon ground for abor- **11.36** tions. It is also, as we shall see below, limited to cases where the woman's pregnancy has not exceeded its 24th week. There are, in fact, two distinct grounds contained within s 1(1)(a) relating first, to a risk to the *mother's* health and secondly, to that of the *existing children of her family*.[99]

(a) The Comparative Exercise

This ground for abortion[100] requires that the certifying doctors engage in a com- **11.37** parative exercise and decide whether there is a greater risk to the mother's (or existing children's) physical or mental health if the pregnancy continues than if it were terminated. It is not sufficient merely that the pregnancy creates a risk to the mother's (or existing children's) physical or mental health.

---

[94] s 1(1)(a).
[95] s 1(1)(b).
[96] s 1(1)(c).
[97] s 1(1)(d).
[98] s 1(4).
[99] Abortion Regulations 1991, SI 1991/499, Sch 1, distinguishes between these two bases for relying on s 1(1)(a): see Certificate A indication 'C' and 'D' respectively.
[100] As does s 1(1)(c) relating to risk to the mother's life.

(b) 'Risk to Woman's Mental Health'

11.38 As regards the risk to the pregnant woman, the ground is very broad in its scope. It covers any risk of any physical or mental injury providing the comparative exercise is satisfactorily performed. Many of the terminations carried out under it involve what have become known as 'social abortions' performed because the pregnancy is unwanted and an inconvenience to the mother and her family. In truth, of course, the doctors must always be satisfied of the effect on her health. However, distress and pressure generated by the unwanted child are readily seen as creating a risk to the 'mental health' of a pregnant woman. Two doctors are easily able to certify that there is a greater risk to a pregnant woman's mental health if she is forced to have an unwanted child than if an abortion is performed, certainly early on in the pregnancy where the risks inherent in the abortion procedures are very low. The Act is concerned with the 'risk' to the woman's mental health and not the certainty or even probability of its occurring and the notion of 'mental health' under the Act is itself very broad indeed. Mental health is not to be equated with recognised psychiatric injury. It is much broader and less well defined. It means, in effect, 'mental well-being' encompassing all deleterious effects upon a woman's emotional life.

(c) The Statistical Argument

11.39 A further reason why abortions under s 1(1)(a) have come to be seen as being carried out 'on demand' is because of the so-called 'statistical argument'. This is that early in a pregnancy—usually in the first 12 weeks—the risks to a 'normal' mother of continuing the pregnancy are always greater than the risks involved in the techniques used to terminate pregnancy. Therefore, the comparative exercise always falls out in favour of the pregnant woman's decision to seek an abortion. Ultimately, of course, the two doctors must form an opinion that the ground applies to this *individual* and not solely on the basis of abstract statistics though, as we have seen, there is no legal requirement that they examine her. Thus, the argument is logically inescapable, providing there is nothing in the individual woman's circumstances to upset the 'statistical argument'. The only doubt that remains, since the amendments in 1991, is the extent to which it can be based solely on the risk of morbidity rather than mortality. A risk to the 'health' of the woman is all that is left under s 1(1)(b) since the separation out of 'risk to life' is now contained in s 1(1)(c) of the Act. However, it is likely that the statistical argument would, in practice, stand up to expert evidential scrutiny under either ground if tested. Jointly or severally, the risks to the woman's health or life are greater by remaining pregnant in the early stages of the pregnancy.

capable of surviving. At this point the legislative intent was that the foetus should not be aborted except under the further grounds set out in the remainder of s 1(1). If any of the other options for starting time to run were accepted, this premise would be nullified.

By contrast, there are arguments favouring options (B) or (C). First, it is wrong to adopt an interpretation which leads to the absurd conclusion that a woman is pregnant in the 14 days (approximately) between the first day of her last period and the time of conception when this is patently not the case. Secondly, the medical profession's approach exemplified in option (A) could act to the detriment of a defendant since it results in the shortest possible time for the 24-week period to run. A pregnancy calculated on the basis of (A) at 25 weeks is likely, in fact, to be a case where conception and implantation will have occurred less than 24 weeks before the abortion. Ambiguities in criminal statutes should be construed in a defendant's favour and not against him, particularly when interpreting a section providing a defence to a criminal offence.   **11.46**

On balance, however, it is suggested that (C) is legally the most justifiable.[106] As a matter of common sense, the Abortion Act should be interpreted so that the defence to the crime in s 58 operates from the point in time when that crime could first be committed. That offence only applies after an embryo has implanted.[107]   **11.47**

(ii) 'Necessary to prevent Grave Permanent Injury to Physical or Mental Health'—s 1(1)(b)

Section 1(1)(b) introduces a new substantive ground for abortion. Prior to 1991 it had merely justified not carrying out an abortion at an NHS hospital or approved clinic.[108] There is no time limit in s 1(1)(b). As with the remaining grounds under the Act, Parliament did not wish to impose a time limit on abortions where serious dangers to the woman's health existed. Though s 1(1)(b) is still concerned with the pregnant woman's health, it requires injury of a different order to that under s 1(1)(a). Parliament clearly intended manifest proof of the more serious danger specified. The examples given by Lord Mackay LC, in the House of Lords' debates on the provision of when 'grave permanent injury' might arise, were where a woman suffered from severe hypertension and continuation of the pregnancy might result in permanent kidney, brain, or heart damage.[109]   **11.48**

---

[106] There is even indirect Parliamentary support for this interpretation in s 2(3) of the Human Fertilisation and Embryology Act 1990 which states that '[f]or the purposes of [the Act], a woman is not to be treated as *carrying* a child until the embryo has become implanted' (emphasis added).

[107] See above, paras 11.10 *et seq.*

[108] s 1(4).

[109] *Hansard*, HL vol 522, col 1039.

11.49 Where does s 1(1)(b) apply? Unlike s 1(1)(a), the comparative exercise is, on the face of it, abandoned. It requires the certifying doctors to decide that the termination is 'necessary to prevent grave permanent injury to the physical or mental health' of the woman. The termination must be 'necessary' to avoid all or some injury of this kind. On the other hand, a *risk* of 'grave permanent injury', however great, will not fall within s 1(1)(b). Section 1(1)(b) only contemplates preventing what will actually, or is reasonably certain to, occur. In any other case, the doctors would have to rely upon ss 1(1)(a), bearing in mind that there is a 24-week time limit for any abortion. Equally, a termination will only be necessary if there is no other alternative course available to avoid the effect on the woman's health. Section 1(1)(b) not only lays down a very stringent requirement of harm—'grave permanent injury'—it also only applies where termination is effectively a last resort.

(iii) 'Risk to Woman's Life'—s 1(1)(c)

11.50 Prior to 1991, the ground in s 1(1)(c) was lumped in together with what is now s 1(1)(a). Both require the two certifying doctors to engage in the comparative exercise of whether the risk to the pregnant woman—here to her 'life'—is greater if the pregnancy is continued than if it is terminated. The risk must be to *her*; there is no equivalent in this ground to that which we saw earlier of risk to her existing children. The ground only requires that the termination *reduces* the risk to her life. It does not require that the termination eliminate the risk altogether. There may exist a continuing, though lesser, risk to her life but the termination will fall within s 1(1)(c) nevertheless if she stands a better chance of surviving there having been a termination. As we shall see later, this may be important in respect of selective reduction procedures where one or more foetuses are killed in utero when the woman has a multiple pregnancy.[110]

11.51 As we saw in respect of s 1(1)(a), an abortion under this ground may also be justified on the basis of the 'statistical argument' in early pregnancy (ie approximately the first 12 weeks).[111] Beyond this time, however, the risk to the woman increases by undergoing the abortion, and consequently to satisfy s 1(1)(c) there would have to be a greater countervailing risk to her life by remaining pregnant.

11.52 The ground looks to the risk to the woman's life. In *R v Bourne*[112] and subsequent cases,[113] the courts took a broad view at common law of what was meant by a risk to a pregnant woman's life so as to include risks to her health.[114] This broad

---

[110] See below, paras 11.89 *et seq*.
[111] See above, para 11.39.
[112] [1939] 1 KB 687.
[113] *R v Newton and Stungo* [1958] Crim LR 469 and *R v Bergmann* [1948] 1 BMJ 1008.
[114] See above, para 11.04.

interpretation cannot be applied to s 1(1)(c) since it would be inconsistent with the other grounds in the Act, in particular s 1(1)(a) where Parliament intended to restrict to 24 weeks abortions performed solely because of the risk to the woman's health.

(iv) 'Substantial Risk (so as to be) Seriously Handicapped'—s 1(1)(d)

The final ground for abortion is in s 1(1)(d) which states that a pregnancy may be **11.53** terminated if two doctors are of the opinion that there is 'a substantial risk' that if the child is born it will be 'seriously handicapped' due to 'physical or mental abnormalities'. The interpretation of this ground is not without difficulty.[115] Since 1991, there has been no time limit applicable to this ground. In theory at least an abortion on the basis of foetal abnormality could be obtained up to full-term. However, in practice very few abortions are performed after the foetus is 24 weeks old.[116] Although there are a few cases where foetal abnormality is not detected before 24 weeks gestation, more generally the trend is towards earlier rather than later abortions with ever earlier detection of abnormalities. Also, many gynaecologists will not be prepared to perform an abortion late in pregnancy on the ground that the foetus is seriously handicapped unless the handicap is unusually severe as, for example, in the case of anencephaly where most, if not all, of the foetus's higher brain will be missing.

(a) Substantial Risk

It is unclear what is meant by a 'substantial risk' of physical or mental abnormali- **11.54** ties so as to be seriously handicapped. What degree of risk is contemplated? Proof of certainty is clearly not essential. No doubt, a substantial risk exists if there is more than 50 per cent chance that the child will have the disability. But, will a one in four chance of disability suffice? It is simply not clear from the Act. It has been suggested that whether a risk is 'substantial' cannot be viewed in isolation from the nature of the disability.[117] Hence, a relatively low risk of a very serious disability may be 'substantial' whereas a rather higher risk of a less serious disability would be required. However, there is no justification for conflating the magnitude of the risk with the nature of the disability. The Act treats them as distinct and separate. The interpretative difficulty will be exacerbated in 'double risk' cases where there is a risk that the child will inherit a genetic condition but it is not certain, if he does, what effect that will have upon him. There will, however, be an increased risk of him developing a particular disability. There may be a 'substantial' risk of inheriting but this must necessarily be seen in the context of the risk of developing the disability. The

---

[115] Professional guidance can be found in the Royal College of Obstetricians and Gynaecologists, *Termination of Pregnancy for Fetal Abnormality* (1996).

[116] Such late terminations cannot be performed in private abortion clinics and are, therefore, only available in NHS hospitals: see, para 11.66 below.

[117] Williams, G, *Textbook of Criminal Law* (2nd edn, 1983), 298.

latter will statistically dilute the former and it is the overall risk (the risk of suffer-ing physical or mental abnormalities so as to be seriously handicapped) which must be 'substantial'.

11.55   When is a risk 'substantial'? Answering this question may increase in importance as medical science develops better and more sophisticated methods of detecting pre-natal and genetic abnormalities. On the other hand, the answer may decrease in sig-nificance as these tests achieve a greater certainty in the diagnosis of foetal abnormalities. The answer cannot be found by recourse to the 'safe haven' of med-ical evidence and the two doctors' 'good faith' opinions. Of course the courts will look to medical evidence to determine what are the risks in a particular instance, but whether they are 'substantial' requires an interpretation of the statute and, as such, it is a legal issue. Equally, two doctors may, in good faith, conclude that a particular risk is substantial but that will not be conclusive that s 1(1)(d) has been complied with. If their mistake is factual, for example, if they thought the risk was 50 per cent when it was only 25 per cent, their honest beliefs ('good faith') will protect them under the Act. However, if their mistake is not factual but rather whether 25 per cent is a 'substantial' risk, their 'good faith' will not protect them under the Act if a court takes the view that that is a misinterpretation of the Act. They will, simply, have mis-directed themselves in law. No doubt, however, the courts will give doctors consid-erable leeway and perhaps consider any risk which a reasonable parent would consider significant in making an abortion decision to be one which is 'substantial'.

(b) Seriously Handicapped

11.56   A further problem of interpretation arises in relation to the meaning of the phrases 'physical or mental abnormalities' so as to leave a child 'seriously handicapped' under s 1(1)(d). The former phrase will largely be a matter of medical evidence and rarely be problematic. The latter phrase, however, seems to be incapable of precise definition. What counts as a 'serious handicap'? Again, like the meaning of the phrase 'substantial risk', this is a question of law for the court. The courts will be guided by medical evidence of the nature of the condition. Certainly, the child does not have to have a life-threatening condition for it to be 'seriously handi-capped'. Nor is the phrase restricted to children who would be 'grossly abnormal and unable to lead any meaningful life'.[118] There is no basis for taking such a nar-row view of the scope of s 1(1)(d) which, though phrased in terms of the foetus's condition, is really concerned with the parents' ability to cope with a 'seriously' disabled child.[119] Further, the woman's interests implicated in carrying and

---

[118] Report of the Select Committee on the Infant Life (Preservation) Bill (HL Paper (1987–88) No 50), 18.

[119] See Williams, *Textbook of Criminal Law* (n 41 above), 297 and (for qualified acceptance), Sheldon, S, and Wilkinson, S, 'Termination of Pregnancy for Reasons of Foetal Disability: Are There Grounds for a Special Exception in Law?' (2001) 9 Med L Rev 85.

bringing up the child means that it is inappropriate (and unnecessary) to interpret its scope consistently with the limited situations where a severely handicapped newborn child may be allowed to die solely *in its own best interests.*[120]

In practice, and quite properly, much less serious conditions form the basis for **11.57** abortions under s 1(1)(d). Providing the condition is not trivial, easily correctable (such as harelip), or will merely lead to the child being disadvantaged, the law will allow doctors scope for determining the seriousness of a condition.[121] At a minimum, it is suggested, a 'serious handicap' would require the child to have physical or mental disability which would cause significant suffering or long-term impairment of their ability to function in society. The most serious genetic or other conditions which manifest themselves at birth or almost immediately thereafter are, by and large, likely to fall within the scope of s 1(1)(d).

When must the serious handicap exist? Must it exist at birth or immediately there- **11.58** after, or could it be a latent condition which develops later in the child's life. Section 1(1)(d) is concerned with the life of the 'child' 'if born'. Consequently, the condition must exist after birth at some point. However, to require the condition, and its manifestation, to exist at the point of birth or immediately thereafter is too narrow a reading of the Act. The Act is concerned with 'the child'. A reasonable interpretation would allow the doctors to project forward during the child's life, if born, and assess what its condition would be and whether it would suffer 'serious handicap'. An example of such a condition is Tay-Sach's disease. Of course, there must be a 'physical or mental abnormality' during this time. This would not be broad enough to catch a carrier of a defective gene which did not manifest itself in the child, for example, a recessive condition such as sickle-cell anaemia or cystic fibrosis. There is no basis for including physical abnormalities (if that is what these are) of this kind within the Act. In any event, the carrier child would not be 'seriously handicapped'. His only impairment in life would be to make wise reproductive choices in the future in case his partner were also a carrier of the recessive gene.

Some conditions might, however, fall within the Act even though there is no man- **11.59** ifestation at birth. Will, for example, an abortion be justified if a baby is diagnosed as HIV-positive in its mother's womb? It would have to be established that the HIV-antibodies which are detected are the baby's own and not its mother's for it to be established that there be 'a substantial risk' of the child being infected. Even so, would the HIV-positive baby suffer from 'physical abnormalities' given that it would almost certainly be asymptomatic at birth? Pathologically, the baby will

---

[120] Contrast Morgan, D, 'Abortion: The Unexamined Ground' [1990] Crim LR 687.
[121] Abortion Regulations 1991, reg 4 requires the doctor carrying out the termination to notify the Chief Medical Officer of the suspected condition in the foetus and the method by which it was detected.

suffer from a physical abnormality (the infection) even if there are no symptoms; but is the baby 'seriously handicapped'? On one view the baby is not even handicapped because it is asymptomatic and so suffers no appreciable medical detriment. However, this is a very narrow meaning of 'handicap' and, given the social conditions, including the prejudice and discrimination, that the baby will exist in, it is quite plausible to say that the baby will be 'seriously handicapped' because of its infection.

11.60 Some conditions do not, however, manifest themselves and so lead to 'serious handicap' until much later in the child's life after birth, for example, Huntingdon's Disease.[122] Are these within s 1(1)(d)? On one view they are not. The Act speaks of the 'child' if born suffering from 'physical or mental abnormalities as to be seriously handicapped'. Huntingdon's Disease does not usually manifest itself until a person is in his forties. Only a broad construction of 'child' could encompass this situation. And, although it is difficult on the wording of s 1(1)(d) to include adulthood conditions, once it is accepted that the handicap need not manifest itself at birth, it would seem to undermine the purpose of the ground to restrict it narrowly to childhood.

3. Operation of the Abortion Act

11.61 The 1967 Act together with the Abortion Regulations 1991[123] provide a statutory regulatory framework for abortion. Any person who wilfully contravenes or wilfully fails to comply with the requirements of the 1991 regulations commits a summary offence.[124] In particular, they provide for (i) the places where terminations may be performed; (ii) the certification of the grounds for the abortion; (iii) notification to the Chief Medical Officer of information about the abortion performed; and (iv) the restriction on disclosure of information.

(i) Places

11.62 Section 1(3) of the Abortion Act 1967 provides that an abortion ('termination of pregnancy') may only be carried out in a hospital vested in a NHS Trust, (Primary Care Trust)[125] or in a place approved by the Secretary of State. An exception is provided for in cases of emergencies. Section 1(4) states that a termination need not be carried out in such a place where the doctor:

---

[122] Even if HIV infection is not seen in itself as a serious handicap, AIDS-Related-Complex and AIDS which will develop later are undoubtedly serious handicaps.

[123] SI 1991/499 as amended by the Abortion (Amendment) (England) Regulations 2002, SI 2002/887 and the Abortion (Amendment) (Wales) Regulations 2002, SI 2002/2979 (W 275) (made pursuant to s 2).

[124] Abortion Act 1967, s 2(3). Liable to a fine not exceeding level 5 on the standard scale.

[125] Added by the Health Act 1999 (Supplementary, Consequential etc Provisions) Order, SI 2000/90, art 6.

. . . is of the opinion, formed in good faith, that the termination is *immediately nec-essary to save the life or to prevent grave permanent injury to the physical or mental health of the pregnant woman.*

(a) The Private Sector

Private clinics require the approval of the Secretary of State to carry out abortions.[126] The Department of Health, in effect, though not name, operated a licensing procedure.[127] Until recently these clinics also had to be registered as a 'nursing home' under the Registered Homes Act 1984 by the appropriate health authority.   **11.63**

Since 1 April 2002, private clinics and hospitals that provide terminations of pregnancies have been regulated by the National Care Standards Commission (NCSC).[128] Thus, the regulatory regime that now exists for private hospitals and clinics in general applies to private clinics that offer terminations.[129] The NCSC is the registration body and monitors and inspects private clinics. The Department of Health has delegated its inspection function for abortion clinics to the NCSC. The NCSC regulates in accordance with detailed Regulations[130] and national minimum standards set by the Secretary of State under s 23(1) of the Care Standards Act 2000.[131] These standards provide 'core standards' applicable to all clinics and 'service specific standards', including ones for private abortion clinics. The core standards relate to such matters as: provision of information to patients; quality of treatment and care; management and personnel; complaints procedures; premises, facilities and equipment; risk management procedures; and patient records and information management.[132]   **11.64**

The standards which are specific to abortion clinics[133] require compliance with the DoH guidance.[134] In addition, inter alia, these standards relate to pre- and post-procedure information that should be given to patients and the maintenance of patient privacy.[135] Also, the standards require that foetal tissue is treated with dignity and respect and that a patient's wishes in respect of disposal are taken into   **11.65**

---

[126] S 1(3).

[127] See *Procedures for the Approval of Independent Sector Places for the Termination of Pregnancy* (DoH, October 1999).

[128] Care Standards Act 2000, ss 2(3)(b) and (7)(d), defining 'independent hospital' as one which includes amongst its services the provision 'termination of pregnancies'.

[129] From April 2004, the new Commission for Healthcare, Audit and Inspection (CHAI) will take over these functions of the NCSC.

[130] Private and Voluntary Health Care (England) Regulations 2001, SI 2001/3968.

[131] TP1 referring to *Independent Health Care: National Minimum Standards Regulations* (DoH, February 2002).

[132] ibid, chs 1–8.

[133] ibid, ch 13.

[134] *Procedures for the Approval of Independent Sector Places for the Termination of Pregnancy* (DoH, October 1999).

[135] Standards TP2 and TP3.

account. Policies and procedures on these matters must be in place.[136] The supply and use of foetal tissue for research should comply with the Polkinghorne guidance.[137]

11.66 The Regulations applicable to private abortion clinics place some limits on when a termination may be carried out. Terminations after the 24th week of gestation are prohibited.[138] And terminations between 20 and 24 weeks may only be performed by suitably qualified, skilled and experienced staff and providing that appropriate procedures to deal with a medical emergency are in place.[139]

(b) Medicinal Abortions[140]

11.67 The Human Fertilisation and Embryology Act 1990[141] introduced a new s 1(3A) into the 1967 Act. It provides:

> The power under subsection (3) of this section to approve a place includes power, in relation to treatment consisting primarily in the use of such medicines as may be specified in the approval and carried out in such manner as may be specified, to approve a class of places.

11.68 The provision is intended to allow for the use of *medicinal agents* as an abortifacient. In particular, it is intended to allow the use of the drug 'Mifepristone' or RU-486[142] which is widely used, and was developed in, France. Mifepristone is an anti-progesterone which prevents the implantation of a fertilised egg in a woman's uterus and as such it operates as a contragestive and not as an abortifacient. However, the drug also can dislodge any fertilised eggs which have implanted at the time of treatment and so it can also function as an abortifacient. It is the latter use which necessitated amendment to the 1967 Act. In 1991 Mifepristone was licensed under the Medicines Act 1968 for use as an abortifacient.[143]

11.69 The use of Mifepristone does not require the initial hospitalisation of the patient. The drug has been proven to be safe with few side-effects.[144] All that is required is that the woman should be prescribed the drug; that she should take a course of the drug for three days followed by a prostaglandin vaginal pessary which ensures that

---

[136] Standard TP4 and Private and Voluntary Health Care (England) Regulations 2002 (n 130 above), reg 41(10).

[137] HSG(91)19, EL(91)144 and Polkinghorne Committee Report on the *Review of the Guidance on the Research Use of Fetuses and Fetal Material* (Cm 762, 1989).

[138] Private and Voluntary Health Care (England) Regulations 2002 (n 130 above) reg 41(5).

[139] ibid, reg 41(4).

[140] This section is based upon Grubb, A, [1991] Crim LR 659.

[141] s 37(3).

[142] Product name 'Myfigene'.

[143] The Times, 4 July 1991.

[144] Couzinet *et al*, 'Termination of Early Pregnancy by Antiprogesterone RU486 (Mifepristone)' (1986) 315 New Eng J Med 1565 and Cherfas, J and Palca, J, 'The Pill of Choice?' (1989) 245 Science 1319.

the termination is successful and that no products of conception remain in the uterus. While it is essential that the woman should remain under the care of a doctor, apart perhaps from the administration of the prostaglandin pessary, the remainder may be carried out at a GP's surgery or in a hospital clinic as an outpatient. For the rest of the time the woman can go home and carry on her normal life.

Section 1(3) would require the Secretary of State to approve each place (such as an **11.70** individual GP's surgery) separately. Section 1(3A) permits him to approve such places as a *class*. It is not clear whether the Secretary of State has yet approved a class of places under his new power in s 1(3A). In any event, s 1(3A) may fail to achieve its desired goal. It assumes that the 'treatment for the termination of pregnancy' in the 1967 Act is restricted to the prescription of the drug and, perhaps, the administration of the prostaglandin pessary. However, a much broader interpretation of the statutory phrase is possible. Arguably, the 'treatment' begins with the prescription of the drug and continues until the pregnancy is terminated. In *Royal College of Nursing of UK v DHSS*[145] the House of Lords adopted a wide interpretation of 'treatment' under the Abortion Act to include all the activities undertaken by the 'hospital team' designed to bring about the termination of a woman's pregnancy. 'Treatment for the termination of pregnancy' is, in the case of Mifepristone, a process spanning a number of days. A woman will only be at one or more of the classes of places contemplated as falling for approval under s 1(3A) for part of the time that the 'treatment' is taking place. Only if the Secretary of State approves all the places a patient might visit between the prescription of Mifepristone and the eventual abortion will the Act be complied with. It is doubtful whether s 1(3A) allows the approval of places for terminations outside the medical environment. Even if it did permit approval of such places as patients' homes, public transport etc, this is an absurd possibility to contemplate. If this is correct, s 1(3A) requires further amendment to achieve its desired aim.

(ii) Certification

The two doctors' opinions given in 'good faith'[146] and required under s 1(1) of the **11.71** 1967 Act must be given in the prescribed form of the 'certificate of opinion' set out in Sch 1, Pt 1 to the Abortion Regulations 1991[147] or, since 2002, the doctors may jointly or severally prepare a 'DIY' certificate(s) in like terms to the standard certificate.[148] The certificate must be completed 'before the commencement of the

---

[145] [1981] AC 800. See discussion above, paras 11.26 *et seq*.

[146] See also paras 11.29–11.32 above.

[147] Certificate A. Colloquially known as the 'blue form' because of its colour. Under the previous Abortion Regulations 1968, (SI 1968/390) the certificate was known as a 'green form' for a similar reason.

[148] SI 1991/499, ref 3(1) as substituted by SI 2002/887, reg 3 (England) and SI 2002/2979 (W 275), reg 3 (Wales).

treatment for termination of the pregnancy'.[149] Where the termination is to be carried out in an emergency under s 1(4),[150] then a single doctor's opinion will suffice and that opinion must be given in accordance with the certificate set out in Sch 1, Pt II to the 1991 Regulations or in an equivalent 'DIY' form.[151] Unlike the usual case, in this situation the certificate must be completed before the commencement of treatment or, if that is not reasonably practicable, not more than 24 hours after the termination.

11.72 The certificate must be retained by the practitioner who terminates the pregnancy for not less than three years beginning with the date of the termination[152] and, thereafter, if it is no longer to be preserved it must be destroyed by the person having custody of it.[153] Wilful failure to comply with the Regulations is a criminal offence.[154]

(iii) Notification

11.73 The Abortion Regulations 1991 provide that a doctor terminating a pregnancy must within 14 days of the termination[155] provide the relevant Chief Medical Officer[156] with notice of the termination and information relating to it as required by Sch 2 to the Regulations.[157] Until 2002, there was a standard form contained in Sch 2 to the Regulations that had to be sent to the Chief Medical Officer. Schedule 2[158] now only states the information that must be supplied such as the personal and medical history of the woman, the circumstances of the termination, its statutory basis, details of the foetus's gestational age and any foetal abnormality and its method of diagnosis and, in the case of selective reduction, the original number of foetuses and the number remaining after the procedure. The change in the Regulations is largely one of form. However, and perhaps not without significance, no distinction is now drawn between terminations before and after the 24th week of pregnancy when, in the latter case, 'a full statement of the medical condition of the pregnant woman/fetus' was required.

---

[149] ibid, reg 3(2).

[150] ie, where the doctor is of the opinion that it is 'immediately necessary to save the life or to prevent grave permanent injury to the physical or mental health of the pregnant woman'. See above, paras 11.40 *et seq.*

[151] Certificate B and reg 3(1)(b) as substituted.

[152] SI 1991/499 reg 3(4).

[153] ibid, reg 3(5).

[154] Abortion Act 1967, s 2(3) and above, para 11.61.

[155] Increased from seven days in 2002: SI 1991/499, reg 4(1)(ii) as amended by SI 2002/887, reg 4 (England) and SI 2002/2979 (W 275), reg 5 (Wales)

[156] Of England or for Wales: SI 1991/499, reg 4 as amended by SI 2002/887, reg 4 (England) and SI 2002/2979 (W 275), reg 5 (Wales).

[157] The information must be sent in a sealed envelope or electronically through the NHS network and in the latter case, the information may be sent to an authorised individual responsible for the relevant CMO's computer system: SI 1991/499, reg 4(1)(b)(ii) as amended by SI 2002/887, reg 6 and Sch (England) and SI 2002/2979 (W 275), reg 6 and Sch (Wales).

[158] As substituted by SI 2002/887, reg 4 (England) and SI 2002/2979 (W 275), reg 5 (Wales).

(iv) Disclosure of Information

(a) The Restriction

As in other situations of medical treatment, the common law protects the confi-   **11.74**
dentiality of the information provided by, or relating to, the pregnant woman.[159]
However, the 1991 Abortion Regulations go further and give statutory protection
to this information. Regulation 5 imposes a duty not to disclose a 'notice given or
any information' supplied to the relevant Chief Medical Officer in pursuance of
the Regulations except[160] as provided in the Regulations. The Regulations are
widely drawn. They do not merely prohibit disclosure of the notice under
Schedule 2 to the Act but also 'any information' contained in it. However, the
Regulations do not specify upon whom the 'duty' is imposed. They merely state
that the notice or information 'shall not be disclosed'. There can be little doubt
that the Regulation applies to everyone.[161] Of course, the criminal offence created
by the 1967 Act if a breach occurs is only committed if the discloser acts 'wilfully'.[162] Also, the Regulations do not, in themselves, create a civil cause of action
enforceable by a patient. However, given the specificity of their scope and the obvious person whose confidences they are designed to protect, the courts are likely
to construe the Regulations as creating a civil cause of action in the pregnant
woman's favour.[163] She alone[164] could seek an injunction, and perhaps damages,
to prevent disclosure in breach of the Regulations.

(b) The Exceptions

There are *nine* circumstances specified in Regulation 5 in which disclosure of the   **11.75**
'notice' or 'information' supplied to the relevant Chief Medical Officer is permitted:[165]

(i)   to an authorised officer of the Department of Health or National Assembly
        for Wales[166] or to the Registrar General (or an authorised member of staff)
        for the purpose of carrying out their duties;

(ii)   to the Director of Public Prosecutions (or an authorised member of staff)
        for the purposes of carrying out his duties in relation to offences under the
        Abortion Act 1967 or the law relating to abortion;[167]

---

[159] See Ch 9.
[160] See below, para 11.75.
[161] Including the relevant Chief Medical Officer him- or herself.
[162] Abortion Act 1967, s 2(3).
[163] Alternatively, on the basis of *Gouriet v Union of Post Office Workers* [1978] AC 435, as the person suffering 'special damage'.
[164] Leaving aside the Attorney-General who could do so as the guardian of the public interest.
[165] reg 5(a) to (i).
[166] Including an authorised person responsible for the relevant CMO's computer system: reg
5(a)(i) added by SI 2002/887, reg 5(b) (England) and SI 2002/2979 (W 275), reg 5(b) (Wales).
[167] Namely, the Offences Against the Person Act 1861, ss 58, 59. Notice that this does not include
an offence under the Infant Life (Preservation) Act 1929 which might well have been significant
prior to the 1991 amendment of the Abortion Act 1967.

(iii)   to a police officer not below the rank of Superintendent (or a person autho-rised by him) for the purposes of investigating whether an offence has been committed under the Abortion Act 1967 or the law relating to abortion;[168]

(iv)   pursuant to a court order for the purposes of proceedings[169] which have begun;

(v)   for the purposes of bona fide scientific research;

(vi)   to the medical practitioner who terminated the pregnancy;

(vii)   to a medical practitioner,[170] with the consent in writing of the woman whose pregnancy was terminated;

(viii)   to the President of the General Medical Council (or an authorised member of staff) when requested by him for the purpose of investigating whether there has been serious professional misconduct by a[171] medical practitioner;

(ix)   to the woman whose pregnancy was terminated if she supplies the Chief Medical Office with written proof of her identity including a birth certifi-cate and the place and date of the termination.[172]

(v) Conscientious Objection[173]

11.76   The Abortion Act 1967 does not require a doctor to perform an abortion even if the particular circumstances of the pregnant woman fall within one or more grounds in the Act. To this extent, however, the doctor is in no better position and the pregnant woman no worse position than in any other medical consultation. English law will not require a doctor to treat a patient if he considers it inappro-priate in his clinical judgment.[174] The doctor–patient relationship is perceived by the law to be one of partnership requiring joint agreement for treatment to go ahead.[175] The objection will, however, usually be a matter of clinical judgment rather than personal preference or predilection. In the context of abortion, a doc-tor (or other) may have a conscientious objection to be involved in the procedure as a result of their moral or religious beliefs. The Abortion Act 1967 provides specifically for this situation.

11.77   Section 4(1) of the Abortion Act 1967 provides that:

---

[168] See ibid.

[169] Not limited to *court* proceedings providing always that a court has ordered disclosure, for ex-ample, in disciplinary proceedings on the basis of 'fairness' or natural justice.

[170] But not anyone else, even with the woman's consent.

[171] But not necessarily *the* doctor who terminated the pregnancy so, for example, the investigation could relate to another certifying doctor.

[172] reg 5(i) added by SI 2002/887, reg 5(c) (England) and SI 2002/2979 (W 275), reg 5(c) (Wales).

[173] For a general discussion, see Braithwaite, C, *Conscientious Objection To Compulsions Under the Law* (1995).

[174] See *Re J (A Minor) (Wardship: Medical Treatment)* [1992] 4 All ER 615 (CA).

[175] ibid, and *Re R (A Minor) (Wardship: Medical Treatment)* [1991] 4 All ER 177, 184 *per* Lord Donaldson MR.

> no person shall be under any duty, whether by contract or by any statutory or other legal requirement, to participate in any treatment authorised by this Act to which he has a conscientious objection.

The 'conscientious objection' cannot be relied upon in emergencies. Section 4(2) provides that: **11.78**

> [n]othing in subsection (1) . . . shall affect any duty to participate in treatment which is necessary to save the life or to prevent grave permanent injury to the physical or mental health of the pregnant woman.[176]

Subject to the exception, s 4(1) allows a doctor or nurse not to participate in an abortion which they otherwise would be required to by virtue of their legal duty to their employer or to the patient. The burden of proving the conscientious objection lies upon the individual.[177] There are two essential elements to the 'conscientious objection': first, that the person's objection is *conscientious*; and secondly, that they would otherwise be asked to *participate* in an abortion.   **11.79**

(a) Matters of Conscience

Rarely will this be a problem in practice.[178] 'Conscience' is not used here in the sense of a mere thought or state of mind of an individual but rather as a conviction or belief based upon a moral assessment. The *Oxford English Dictionary* refers to: **11.80**

> [t]he internal acknowledgment or recognition of the moral quality of one's motives and actions; the sense of right and wrong as regards things for which one is responsible; the faculty or principle which pronounces upon the moral quality of one's actions or motives, approving the right and condemning the wrong.

A matter of 'conscience' is widely understood to cover, for example, religious, moral, or other principled beliefs which lead the individual to conclude that the activity is wrong. Thus, objections based upon prejudice rather than principle would not be covered. However, a doctor who took a particular view of the sanctity of human life—including foetal life—would have a conscientious objection whether his belief was religious or secular.   **11.81**

It seems also that the Act permits a doctor (or other) to have a conscientious objection to some but not all abortions. Section 4(1) speaks of the person having a conscientious objection to '*any* treatment' covered by the Act. Although it is not free from doubt, this provision would seem to allow a doctor to object to, say, late abortions only, or to terminations on the basis of foetal disability while not objecting to others. Providing the limited nature of his objection is 'conscientiously' based, rather than misguided or 'borne of prejudice', he need not participate in the termination.   **11.82**

---

[176] ie, falling within s 1(1)(b) and in extreme cases under s 1(1)(c).

[177] For proof in Scotland, see s 4(3).

[178] The position may be otherwise under s 38 of the Human Fertilisation and Embryology Act 1990: see Kennedy and Grubb (n 1 above), 1282.

(b) Who is Covered?

11.83 Section 4(1) applies to any 'person', and not just the doctor carrying out the termination, providing that they would be 'participat[ing]' in the 'treatment authorised' under the Act. Undoubtedly, nurses and others who perform acts as part of the 'team' under the direction of the responsible doctor[179] will be covered by s 4(1). But what of others less directly involved?

11.84 The issue arose in *Janaway v Salford HA*.[180] The plaintiff was a receptionist/secretary at a health centre. She was asked by a doctor working there to type a letter referring a patient for an appointment with a consultant with a view to him forming an opinion as to whether the patient's pregnancy should be terminated under the Abortion Act. She refused and was dismissed. She brought judicial review proceedings seeking to quash the decision on the basis that she was entitled to rely on the 'conscientious objection' provision in s 4(1) of the 1967 Act. Nolan J (at first instance) refused her application and her appeal was subsequently dismissed by the Court of Appeal[181] and House of Lords.[182] The House of Lords rejected the approach of a majority of the Court of Appeal[183] that s 4(1) should be interpreted as covering any activity which would be a criminal offence either as a principal or as an accessory under the Offences Against the Person Act 1861.[184] Instead, the Law Lords held that the word 'participate' had to be given its ordinary and natural meaning. The plaintiff was not entitled to rely on s 4(1) because she was not:

> actually taking part in treatment administered in a hospital or other approved place . . . for the purpose of terminating a pregnancy.[185]

11.85 The interpretation of s 4(1) adopted by the House of Lords is a narrow one and would exclude from its ambit all health care professionals and other staff who are not directly taking part at the hospital or clinic in the patient's treatment under the 1967 Act (ie the termination). Also, incidental or unrelated activities carried on within a hospital would not fall under the umbrella of s 4(1). It is doubtful whether nurses involved in the general care of the woman or ancillary staff looking after her, for example, by changing the bed sheets or delivering her meals, could rely on s 4(1) since they are not involved in the 'treatment' authorised by the Act.

---

[179] See *Royal College of Nursing v DHSS* [1981] AC 800 discussed above, paras 11.27–11.28.
[180] [1989] AC 537 and [1988] 3 All ER 1079 (HL).
[181] ibid, noted Grubb, A, [1988] CLJ 162.
[182] Noted Grubb, A [1989] CLJ 17.
[183] N 180 above, Slade and Stocker LJJ.
[184] The majority of the Court of Appeal held that the plaintiff lacked the mens rea of an accessory since her intention was 'merely to carry out the obligations of her employment' (*per* Slade LJ at 452). This narrow view is problematic on the facts (see Grubb, A [1988] CLJ 163) and in the House of Lords, Lords Keith and Lowry probably disagreed (n 180 above, 1083 and 1083–4 respectively).
[185] N 180 above, 570 *per* Lord Keith.

One situation which remains problematic concerns the doctor, usually a GP, who **11.86** refuses to act as one of the statutory 'opinions' and sign the certificate for conscientious reasons. Is he entitled to rely on s 4(1)? In *Janaway*, Lord Keith left the point open. However, this much is clear: on the basis of the House of Lord's interpretation of 'participate' such a doctor could not be said to be participating in the treatment authorised under the Act. Indeed, as Lord Keith acknowledged, the certificate must come into existence 'before the commencement of the treatment'.[186] It is logically impossible to construe signing the certificate as 'participation' in the treatment and at the same time it occur prior to the treatment. Consequently, such a doctor would not be able to rely upon s 4(1) to relieve him of any duty he would otherwise have to sign the certificate or refer the pregnant woman. The crucial question, therefore, is whether he has such a duty under the law assuming that the abortion is medically justified, ie, it falls within the Act.

In the Court of Appeal in *Janaway*, Stocker LJ took the view that a doctor had a **11.87** legal duty to sign the certificate.[187] Whether this view is correct turns upon the GP's obligations under the Terms of Service.[188] Paragraph 12 of the Terms of Service provides:

(1) . . . a doctor shall render to his patients all necessary and appropriate personal medical services of the type usually provided by general practitioners.
(2) The services which a doctor is required by sub-paragraph (1) to render shall include the following . . .
    (d) arranging for referral of patients, as appropriate, for the provision of any other services under the Act . . .

There is no doubt that a termination of pregnancy amounts to 'other services' pro- **11.88** vided under the National Health Service Act 1977. Consequently, at the very least the GP has the legal duty under his Terms of Service[189] to refer the patient to another doctor in respect of her pregnancy. Such would also be the duty of the doctor at common law. In *Barr v Matthews*,[190] a GP was unsuccessfully sued in negligence for failing to offer or arrange a termination of pregnancy. In the course of his judgment, Alliott J stated that 'once a termination of pregnancy is recognised as an option, the doctor invoking the conscientious objection clause should refer the patient to a colleague at once'.[191] It could be argued that it suffices if he refers her to another GP who may act as the first statutory 'opinion' by signing the certificate.[192] However, it is plausible to argue that, in this context, 'referral' within para 12(2)(d) also contemplates referral to a consultant, having himself signed the

---

[186] ibid, 572. See Abortion Regulations 1991, SI 1991/499, reg 3(2) and above, para 11.82.
[187] N 180 above, 556.
[188] National Health Service (General Medical Services) Regulations 1992, SI 1992/635, Sch 2.
[189] Which will reflect his duty to the patient.
[190] (1999) 52 BMLR 217.
[191] ibid, 227.
[192] Grubb, A [1989] CLJ 17, 18.

form, for the purpose of obtaining the second 'opinion' and if so the termination—as occurred in *Janaway* itself.[193]

(vi) Selective Reduction[194]

(a) The Techniques

11.89 Modern technology has developed techniques whereby a multiple pregnancy may
be reduced by killing one or more foetuses in utero. This has become particularly
important in cases where infertility treatment has led to a multiple pregnancy. The
greater the number of foetuses carried by a woman the greater is the risk to her
health during pregnancy and at delivery. Equally, in these circumstances there is
the risk of foetal mortality and of foetal handicap, including cerebral palsy, blindness, and mental retardation. Consequently, it is often desirable out of the interests of the mother and/or the foetuses that the pregnancy should be reduced in
number.[195] This is usually done in the first 14 weeks of the pregnancy by either injecting potassium chloride into the amniotic sac or into the heart of the foetus or
by aspiration. The foetus(es) will die and may be spontaneously expelled or, more
likely, will remain in the mother, wither, and what remains will be expelled at the
time the remaining healthy foetuses are delivered. This procedure is known as 'selective reduction'.

11.90 In addition, a similar procedure may be used later in pregnancy when one of a
number of foetuses (usually twins) is discovered to be seriously handicapped.
Because of the slightly differing circumstances when it is used, it is sometimes distinguished from selective reduction and is sometimes known as selective foeticide.[196]

(b) Legal Position Before 1991

11.91 **Miscarriage**   It was not clear under the law prior to 1 April 1991 whether selective reduction and selective foeticide were covered by the abortion legislation. It
could be argued that, in cases where the 'reduced' foetus(es) is (are) not expelled,
no 'miscarriage' occurs within the terms of s 58 of the Offences Against the Person
Act 1861.[197] The better view is, however, that the term 'miscarriage' does not require expulsion of the contents of the womb but merely that some or all of the

---

[193] Kennedy and Grubb (n 1 above), 1446–7.
[194] This section is based upon Grubb, A [1991] Crim LR 659, 667–9.
[195] See Howie, PW, 'Selective Reduction—Medical Aspects' in Templeton, A and Cuisine, D
(eds), *Reproductive Medicine and the Law* (Churchill Livingstone, 1990), 25.
[196] The procedures are discussed in Berkowitz *et* al, 'Selective Reduction of Multifetal Pregnancies
in the First Trimester' (1988) 318 N Engl J Med 1043 and Howie, PW, 'Selective Reduction in
Multiple Pregnancy' (1988) 297 BMJ 664.
[197] The argument is put and rejected by Keown, J, 'Selective Reduction of Multiple Pregnancy'
(1987) 137 NLJ 1165.

contents cease to be carried alive within it. This would bring both procedures within s 58 of the 1861 Act. In any event, the argument overlooks the fact that, ultimately, the withered and dead products of the foetus will be expelled at the time the remaining foetuses are delivered.

Termination of Pregnancy   A further complication was raised as to whether se-   **11.92**
lective reduction was a 'termination of pregnancy' within the Abortion Act 1967 because the woman is still pregnant in the sense that one or more of the healthy foetuses remains after the procedure. If there was no termination of pregnancy, then the procedure could never be lawful because what was being done would not fall within the wording of the Abortion Act.[198] There would then be a potential crime but no possible defence. It is most likely that a court would have taken the view that the destruction of one or more foetus was a termination of a pregnancy. Hence, providing a doctor complied with the terms of the Abortion Act, he would have acted lawfully in performing a selective reduction. The matter is now entirely academic since Parliament has intervened.

(c) Legal Position After 1991

In an attempt to put the matter beyond doubt, s 5(2) of the 1967 Act was   **11.93**
amended by the Human Fertilisation and Embryology Act 1990[199] to include the following:

> . . . in the case of a woman carrying more than one foetus, anything done with in-
> tent to procure her miscarriage of any foetus is authorised by [section 1] if—
>
> (a) the ground for termination of the pregnancy specified in subsection (1)(d) of
>   that section applies in relation to any foetus and the thing is done for the pur-
>   pose of procuring the miscarriage of that foetus, or
> (b) any of the other grounds for termination of pregnancy specified in that section
>   applies.

The effect of the amended s 5(2) is to bring the two procedures of selective reduc-   **11.94**
tion and selective foeticide within the Abortion Act and to require compliance with its terms if a doctor is to act lawfully. Interestingly, s 5(2) assumes that the procedures do result in a 'miscarriage' for the purposes of the 1861 Act. The first of the difficulties mentioned is now put beyond doubt because a court is very un-likely to reach a contrary conclusion given this assumption by Parliament.

Selective Foeticide   Section 5(2)(a) covers the procedure of selective foeticide   **11.95**
where the particular foetus is identified by pre-natal screening (using, for exam-ple, amniocentesis or chorion villus sampling techniques) as suffering from a physical or mental abnormality which would lead to the child being 'seriously

---

[198] Price, DPT, 'Selective Reduction and Feticide: The Parameters of Abortion' [1988] Crim LR 199.
[199] s 37(4).

handicapped' within s 1(1)(d) of the Act when it is born. As a result of s 5(2)(a), providing the foetus could be aborted on the foetal abnormality ground had it been a singleton (ie the whole pregnancy would be terminated), it alone may be aborted as part of a multiple pregnancy.

11.96 **Selective Reduction**   Section 5(2)(b) covers the procedure of selective reduction. If a doctor would be justified in terminating the whole pregnancy under s 1(1) of the Act because of the risk to the mother's health or life or because of the serious injury she will suffer if the pregnancy continues, he may reduce the number of foetuses in the multiple pregnancy in order to remove (or reduce) the risk of danger to her.

11.97 Unlike s 5(2)(a), which requires the doctor to kill only the handicapped foetus which specifically falls within the ground under the Act, s 5(2)(b) permits the doctor randomly to select which foetus(es) to kill. He may selectively reduce any foetus(es) where a multiple pregnancy creates a risk to the mother's health within one of the grounds in s 1(1). This difference between the two provisions is inevitable because no one foetus can be singled out as a threat to the mother; rather it is the cumulative effect of the presence which creates the risk to her.

11.98 One final point to notice. Selective reduction may be desirable because a multiple pregnancy can risk damage to the foetuses themselves. Section 5(2) does not permit selective reduction in this situation because a risk of injury to a foetus is not a ground for abortion under s 1(1).[200] Only a risk to the mother would satisfy the Act but this will probably exist in the case of quadruplets, quintuplets or sextuplets and even in the case of triplets.

D. The Impact of the Human Rights Act

11.99 To what extent will the Human Rights Act 1998 impact upon the law of abortion? The court is required to read and interpret the Abortion Act 1967 so as to be compatible with Convention rights[201] and, to the extent that it cannot do so, the court may grant a declaration of incompatibility.[202] Is the 1967 Act susceptible to a human rights challenge?

11.100 Two principal Convention issues arise.[203] First, does an unborn child have a 'right to life' under Article 2? And, if so, secondly, how will the court give effect to that right if it conflicts with the human rights of the pregnant woman, for example, her own 'right to life' or her 'right to private life' protected by Article 8?

---

[200] But note the comment by Lord Mackay of Clashfern LC, *Hansard*, HL vol 522, cols 1041–2.
[201] s 3(1).
[202] s 4.
[203] Claims by fathers to be involved in termination decisions by virtue of Art 8 and his 'right to private and family life' are considered below, paras 11.132–11.133.

1. Article 2—the 'Right to Life'

Article 2(1) of the European Convention on Human Rights states that: **11.101**

> *Everyone's* right to life shall be protected by law. No one shall be deprived of his life intentionally . . . [emphasis added].

Does an unborn child fall within the terms 'everyone' and 'no one'? At present, **11.102** there are no UK cases which deal with the application of Article 2 to the unborn child. There are, as has already been seen, a number of cases concerned with the common law or statutory provisions which expressly exclude the unborn child from legal protection.[204] However, there are decisions of the European Commission, but not the European Court, which have considered the issue. In large measure, the Commission has left open the possibility that an unborn child is covered by Article 2(1) but, in each case, the Commission has upheld the compatibility of the particular abortion law it has considered *even if* Article 2 was engaged.[205]

(i) *X v UK*

The leading Commission decision is *X v UK*.[206] There, a father sought an injunc- **11.103** tion to prevent his wife undergoing a termination of her ten-week pregnancy on health grounds. Having been unsuccessful before the English courts,[207] he relied upon Articles 2 and 8 in Strasbourg. The Commission declared his application to be manifestly ill-founded. However, the reasoning of the Commission is not entirely clear.

The Commission noted that the term 'everyone' as used in the Convention ap- **11.104** plied in situations which arose only post-natally. Likewise, the exceptions to the 'right to life' found in Article 2(2) clearly only applied to persons who were already born.[208] Both of these factors tended towards an interpretation which did not include unborn children within the scope of Article 2.

Nevertheless, the Commission chose to leave open the applicability of Article 2 and **11.105** to decide the case on a different basis. If recognised, the 'right to life' of the foetus could not be absolute. The Commission reasoned that the foetus' right would be in conflict with the very same right of the mother where her life was also seriously at risk. The Commission noted that—with one possible exception—abortion on this

---

[204] See Ch 4 above.
[205] *X v UK* [1981] 3 EHRR 408 (also known as *Paton v UK*) and *H v Norway* (1992) 73 DR 155.
[206] ibid.
[207] The English court case is *Paton v BPAS* [1979] QB 276.
[208] Namely, when using force which is no more than absolutely necessary (i) in self-defence, (ii) to effect a lawful arrest or preventing the escape of a detained person, and (iii) in the course of quelling a riot or insurrection.

ground was permitted by the Parties to the Convention in 1950. The conflict would have to be resolved in favour of the mother otherwise the right to life of the unborn would have a higher value than that of a person who was born and that would be contrary to the objects and purpose of the Convention. Hence, the Commission read in an 'implied limitation' to the unborn child's right to life in addition to those express limitations in Article 2(2). The Commission noted that the abortion had been at ten weeks gestation and in order to protect the mother's physical and mental health. It concluded that this also fell within an 'implied limitation' on the unborn child's right and hence was compatible with Article 2(1).

11.106   The Commission's decision—and of course it is not that of the Human Rights Court itself—leaves much unanswered.[209]

11.107   First, the principal issue of the applicability of Article 2 to the unborn child was not resolved. Subsequently, the European Court also left the matter open in *Open Door Counselling and Dublin Well Woman v Ireland*.[210]

11.108   Second, the resolution of the parties' conflicting rights that the Commission was, as a result, forced to make is not without difficulty. The prioritisation of the mother's right over that of the unborn child begs the very question at the heart of the abortion cases. Further, it is far from clear that Article 2 should be construed as having 'implied limitations' beyond those expressed in Article 2(2). When the 'conjoined twins' case of *Re A* was before the Court of Appeal, the judges disagreed over whether this was an appropriate interpretation of the Convention.[211]

11.109   Third, the Commission emphasised that it was concerned with an early abortion (ten weeks gestation) and one justified on the grounds of the mother's health—what the Commission termed the 'medical indication'. It was not concerned, in its own words, with 'ethnic indication, eugenic indication, social indication [or] time limitation'. How the Commission would have played out its 'implied limitation' in these situations—all of which fall to some extent within the Abortion Act 1967—is left unanswered.

(ii) *H v Norway*

11.110   The only subsequent guidance comes from the decision in *H v Norway*.[212] In this case, a father sought an injunction to prevent his (unmarried) partner terminating her 14-week pregnancy on social grounds. Inter alia, the father claimed that this

---

[209] For a discussion of human rights, see Scott, R, *Rights, Duties and the Body* (Hart, 2002), ch 3.
[210] (1992) 15 EHRR 244, at [66]. Contrast dissent of Judge Blayney.
[211] *Re A (Children) (Conjoined Twins: Surgical Separation)* [2000] 4 All ER 961 (CA), 'reluctant' to accept *per* Brooke LJ at 1050. Contrast Ward LJ at 1017.
[212] (1992) 73 DR 155

breached the unborn child's 'right to life' under Article 2. The Commission disagreed. As in *X v UK*, the Commission assumed that Article 2 applied and then went on to conclude that account must be taken of the interests of the woman. The Norwegian legislation required the approval of a board of two doctors where the pregnancy exceeded 12 weeks. They had approved the termination on the ground that the 'pregnancy, birth or care for the child may place the woman in a difficult position in life'.[213] The Commission concluded that the legislative scheme fell within the State's 'discretion . . . in this sensitive area of abortion' and struck a 'fair balance between the legitimate need to protect the foetus and the legitimate interests of the woman in question' and thus was compatible with Article 2. It would seem, therefore, that the Commission considers that terminations—at least ones early in pregnancy—on 'social grounds' to be permissible. But here again, the Commission offers no guidance on late terminations or ones performed because of foetal disability.

(iii) The Way Forward

It is often said that inherent in the Convention is the balancing, or accommodation of, individual's rights with the public or community interest.[214] The Convention explicitly recognises this, for example, in the second paragraphs of Articles 8–11. But, even in other Articles, the need for accommodation between individuals' rights and the rights and interests of others is implied, for example, in the 'right to marry and found a family' in Article 12[215] and the 'right to a fair trial' in Article 6.[216] Other Articles, by the very nature of the individuals' rights that they protect, are absolute in their terms, for example, Article 3 ('freedom from torture and inhuman or degrading treatment') and Article 2 itself, apart from the limited exceptions spelt out in Article 2(2). Reaching an accommodation between an unborn child's 'rights'/'interests' and those of its mother is not well suited to the adjudication process inherent under Article 2. Indeed, it is arguably impossible. The Commission relied on the first sentence of Article 2(1) which, in effect, has been interpreted to require 'respect' for an individual's right to life and is not absolute in the obligation that it places upon the state.[217] By contrast, where life is taken by the state, the second sentence—subject to the stated exceptions—makes intentional deprivation unlawful. At least within the NHS, it is this second, and absolute, obligation under Article 2(1) that is engaged. **11.111**

The problems of seeking within the adjudication process to resolve apparently absolute Convention rights ought to steer an English court away from interpreting **11.112**

---

[213] Termination of Pregnancy Act, No 50 of 13 June 1975 (as amended), s 2.
[214] *Soering v UK* (1989) 11 EHRR 439 at [89].
[215] eg, *R v Secretary of State for the Home Department, ex p Mellor* [2002] QB 13 (CA).
[216] eg, *Brown v Stott* [2001] 2 WLR 817 (PC) and *R v A (No 2)* [2002] 1 AC 45 (HL).
[217] *Osman v UK* (1998) 29 EHRR 245 (ECtHR).

Article 2 as being engaged in the abortion situation. Such a view would also be consistent with the common law tradition.[218] It is, no doubt, the reason why most other jurisdictions[219] such as the United States[220] and Canada[221] do not give constitutional recognition to an unborn child as 'a legal person',[222] choosing instead to take account of the latter's 'interests' elsewhere in their constitutional settlements so that they can be appropriately weighed against the right of the mother. Thus, the US jurisprudence locates the constitutional debate in the 'liberty interest' protected by the 14th Amendment to the Constitution[223] and in similar fashion the Canadian Supreme Court looks to s 7 of the Canadian Charter of Fundamental Rights and Freedoms which recognises the woman's right to 'life, liberty and security of the person'.[224] In England, the court would find the framework of Article 8 ('the right to private and family life') closest to the US and Canadian models. It is suggested that the very real interpretative problems posed under Article 2 should lead the court to consider the compatibility of the Abortion Act 1967 with the Convention under Article 8.

11.113 Shifting the human rights debate to Article 8 has the effect that the rights of the mother become the starting point. Legislative limits upon her right to decide (and indeed to undergo a termination) require justification. Hence, requiring specific grounds, imposing time limits or access must be defensible. Thus, a court may not only be faced with challenges by others (putative fathers etc) to the 'liberal' nature of the Abortion Act but also, though less likely, with challenges by women themselves where the Abortion Act places obstacles in their way to obtaining a termination.[225]

2. Article 8—'the Right to Private and Family Life'

(i) The Right

11.114 Article 8 protects an individual's right to 'private and family life'. The state is both under a positive duty to 'respect' those rights and also a negative obligation not to 'interfere' with the rights except to the extent permitted under Article 8(2).

---

[218] See eg *Christian Lawyers Association of South Africa v Minister of Health* 1998 (4) SA 1113, *per* McCreath J.

[219] An exception is Germany: see, the German Constitutional Court decision, 88BVerfGE203, discussed in Van Zyl Smit, D, 'Reconciling the Irreconcilable? Recent Developments in the German Law on Abortion' (1994) 2 Med L Rev 302

[220] *Roe v Wade* 410 US 113 (1973) (US Sup Ct).

[221] *Borowski v A-G* [1987] 4 WWR 385 (Sask CA); left open by the Canadian Supreme Court in *Tremblay v Daiglé* (1989) 62 DLR (4th) 634.

[222] See also *Christian Lawyers Association of South Africa v Minister of Health* (n 218 above).

[223] *Roe v Wade* 93 S Ct 705 (1973) (recognising a 'right of privacy') as interpreted, most recently, by the Supreme Court in *Planned Parenthood of South-Eastern Pennsylvania v Casey* 112 S Ct 2791 (1992).

[224] *Morgentaler v R* (1988) 44 DLR (4th) 385.

[225] Including the more limited access in the private sector: see above paras 11.63–11.66.

It seems unlikely that a woman's 'right to family life' is engaged in a decision not to have a child since there must be '*existing* family life' for Article 8 to be engaged.[226] Rather, it is her 'right to private life' which will be affected by any decision whether or not to have a termination. The European Court has recognised that 'private life' is a broad term and includes the 'physical and psychological integrity of a person'.[227] The breadth of this right would undoubtedly 'catch' any unwanted intrusive medical intervention[228] or, as here, the decision whether to undergo such a procedure particularly one as sensitive as a termination of pregnancy.[229]

11.115

(ii) The Justification

Both the notion of 'respect' for an individual's right to private life and the justification for interference by the state with that right, entail the court in a balancing exercise of competing rights and interests which must, to be lawful, be weighed to reach a 'proportionate' result.[230] Thus, in determining the compatibility of the Abortion Act with human rights, the crucial battleground will be under Article 8(2) or the equivalent issues inherent in the notion of 'respect'. For the present purposes, it will be helpful to couch the issues in the language of Article 8(2). The interference with the woman's right must be (i) in accordance with the law; (ii) for a legitimate aim; and (iii) 'necessary in a democratic society', ie be a proportionate response to achieve the legitimate aim and which serves a 'pressing social need'.

11.116

(a) 'In Accordance with the Law'

There is no difficulty with the first of these requirements providing the termination is carried out in accordance with the requirements of the Abortion Act 1967. It is the remaining two that present the challenges to the compatibility of the Act with the Convention and, of these, it is principally the requirement of 'proportionality'.

11.117

(b) 'Legitimate Aim'

The legitimate aim of any limitation upon a woman's right to choose may be her own health interests, for example, the requirement[231] about the places where terminations may occur. Most limitations, however, such as the grounds and time limit of

11.118

---

[226] If anything, it may engage Art 12 and her right *not*' to found a family'. Note Lord Bingham's view in *R (on the application of Pretty) v DPP* [2002] 1 AC 800 at [6] that the 'right to marry' under Art 12 includes a right not to marry.

[227] See, eg, *Pretty v UK* (2002) 12 BHRC 141 at [61].

[228] *X v Austria* (1979) 18 DR 154 (blood test).

[229] Indeed, if the physical or psychological effect of refusing a termination were sufficiently severe, Art 3 of the ECHR might also be infringed.

[230] eg, *Stjerna v Finland* (1994) 24 EHRR 194.

[231] Abortion Act 1967, s 1(3).

24 weeks gestation on maternal health and social grounds, are related to a protection of the interests of the foetus and seek to strike a balance between those interests and the mother's right. It can readily be accepted that the state has an interest in protecting all human life, even before birth. And, this is not inconsistent with the law failing to recognise an unborn child as a legal person with all the concomitant rights that flow from that. Both aims can comfortably be accommodated under Article 8(2) as being 'for the protection of health and morals' and possibly also 'for the protection of the rights and freedoms of others'.

(c) 'Proportionality'

11.119 In determining whether the legislative provision is 'necessary in a democratic society', ie 'proportionate', the court must itself strike a 'fair balance' between the competing claims of mother and unborn child. The UK courts are likely to scrutinise closely the compatibility of the Abortion Act with the Convention as human life is involved.

11.120 As we have seen, the Commission's jurisprudence in *X v UK* and *H v Norway* provides little concrete guidance beyond cases of early terminations for health or social reasons. In the latter decision, the Commission does emphasis that abortion is a 'sensitive area' which allows the national legislatures considerable discretion in striking a fair balance between the competing rights/interests of the woman and the unborn child.[232] Likewise when the state acts to protect maternal health by requiring terminations to take place within the NHS or other approved places.

11.121 Some jurisprudence from overseas places considerable emphasis upon the gestational age of the foetus.[233] The older the foetus the greater its interests weigh against a woman's right (here under Article 8). Congruently with this, the decision to have a termination must be based upon increasingly more serious grounds (viewed from the woman's standpoint) as the foetus matures such that, for example, only risks to the mother's life or health would justify a termination of a viable foetus.

11.122 The structure of this thinking was taken to the level of constitutional doctrine by the US Supreme Court in *Roe v Wade* where it developed the trimester system which progressively permitted the US states to limit terminations either on the basis of maternal health (second semester) or the interests of the foetus where it is viable (third trimester).[234] The Supreme Court has now resiled from this analytic framework for constitutional review on the basis that it has no constitutional basis

---

[232] See also, Ewing, KD, and Gearty, CA, 'Terminating Abortion Rights?' (1992) 142 NLJ 1696.
[233] eg, the US case law beginning with *Roe v Wade* (n 220 above) and ending with *Planned Parenthood v Casey* (n 223 above).
[234] Access to first trimester terminations could not be limited.

and also because it is not in keeping with developments in neonatal care. In the *Planned Parenthood* case, a divided Supreme Court abandoned the *Roe v Wade* framework and substituted a test which asked whether the limitation placed an 'undue burden' on the woman's right to choose throughout the pregnancy and thereby presented a substantial obstacle to her seeking a termination.[235] No observer of US abortion law could fail to see that the US courts have embroiled themselves in a constitutional 'mess' over the scope of constitutional intervention with state laws limiting abortion. The discredited trimester framework has nothing—apart from an element of certainty—to commend it. The UK courts should not follow their lead, at least in its detail. However, the underlying approach does have some validity and may provide guidance to the UK courts.

The case law under the Human Rights Act acknowledges that Parliament has an **11.123** 'area of discretion' when seeking to limit a right such as that protected by Article 8.[236] The extent to which the court will defer to a legislative decision depends upon the subject matter and whether the decision raises, for example, 'social, economic and political factors'[237] to which the court must of necessity show due deference.[238] In determining the limits of judicial intervention and its concomitant the extent of judicial deference, 'context is everything'.[239]

Given the controversial nature of the abortion and the moral disagreements that **11.124** it engenders, it is most unlikely that an English court will wish to 'second-guess' Parliament's weighing of the competing interests that finds form in the grounds for abortion in s 1(1) of the Act. That section was most recently amended in 1990 during the passage of the Human Fertilisation and Embryology Act 1990 and it is clear from reading the debates in *Hansard* that Parliament carefully and deliberately chose the blend of grounds that emerged. Both the substance of the grounds and the choice of time-limits were debated, variously voted upon and ultimately decided. There was a collective and conscious weighting of competing interests.

It seems likely that the UK courts will, therefore, respect the legitimacy of **11.125** Parliament's choices in setting the grounds for abortion and permitting terminations beyond the point of viability where the mother's life is at risk[240] or she will suffer serious injury[241] if the pregnancy continues. In these situations, her right should prevail: at least that is a permissible legislative response.

---

[235] *Per* O'Connor, Kennedy and Souter JJ whose judgments were joined by Stevens and Blackman JJ.

[236] *R v Secretary of State for the Home Department, ex p Daly* [2001] 2 AC 532 (HL).

[237] *R (on the application of Samaroo) v Home Secretary* [2002] INLR 55 (CA) *per* Dyson LJ at [35].

[238] For a discussion of the general principles: see, *International Transport Roth GmbH v Secretary of State for the Home Department* [2002] 3 WLR 344 *per* Laws LJ at [81]–[87].

[239] *Ex p Daly* (n 236 above) at [28] *per* Lord Steyn.

[240] Abortion Act 1967, s 1(1)(c).

[241] ibid, s 1(1)(b).

11.126 More problematic is the so-called 'foetal abnormality' ground in s 1(1)(d) of the Act. The argument for Convention compatibility is less clear and even more fragile once the unborn child is viable. A solution may exist if this ground is based, at least in part, on parental health grounds and the effect upon them of bringing up and caring for the disabled child. Perhaps, here, the court would find solace in the Act's requirement that there should be a 'substantial risk' that the child will be 'seriously handicapped'. Read together, these requirements would tailor the ground to foetal conditions which are likely to have significant impact upon the parents' lives and so provide a sufficient justification even after the foetus has reached a stage of 'viability'. Ultimately, the compatibility issue may turn upon the level of deference the court is prepared to show Parliament.

E. Injunctions to Prevent Abortions

11.127 In what, if any, circumstances, will a court grant an injunction to prevent a woman undergoing an abortion? Courts throughout the world have rejected claims by the father of an unborn child for such an injunction: Australia,[242] Canada,[243] Scotland,[244] and England.[245] In America it has been held unconstitutional for a state to require that a husband's consent be sought prior to an abortion[246] or even that he be consulted.[247] English law regards the decision whether or not to terminate a pregnancy as exclusively one for the patient and her doctor subject to the regulatory requirements. Third parties, such as fathers or others, have no legal role to play in that process although, of course, a father might well be involved in practice with the consent of the pregnant woman.

11.128 There are a number of grounds upon which a father has claimed an injunction: (i) as a representative of the foetus in order to prevent a wrong being committed against it; (ii) on his own behalf to enforce his right to agree or be consulted as the foetus's father; and (iii) as a public spirited citizen on the basis that in the particular circumstances the abortion will be a crime.

1. As Litigation Friend of the Foetus

11.129 In order for a father (or other) to act on behalf of the foetus, the law would have to regard the foetus as a legal person possessing rights which could be enforced by a

---

[242] *Attorney-General of Queensland (ex rel Kerr) v T* (1983) 46 ALR 275 (Aust HCt).
[243] *Tremblay v Daiglé* (1989) 62 DLR (4th) 634 (Can Sup Ct).
[244] *Kelly v Kelly* 1997 SLT 896 (CS (IH)).
[245] *Paton v Trustees of BPAS* [1978] 2 All ER 987 (Baker P) and *C v S* [1987] 1 All ER 1230 (Heilbron J and CA).
[246] *Planned Parenthood of Central Missouri v Danforth* 428 US 52 (1976) (US Sup Ct).
[247] *Planned Parenthood of SE Pennsylvania v Casey* 112 S Ct 2791 (1992) (US Sup Ct).

'litigation friend'. In England, as elsewhere,[248] the courts have conclusively rejected the view that an unborn child has legal personality.[249] Hence, for example, an unborn child cannot be made a ward of court,[250] bring an action for pre-natal injury until it is born,[251] and is not protected by the criminal law of murder or manslaughter if killed in utero.[252] In the context of paternal injunctions, in *Paton v BPAS*[253] and in *C v S*,[254] courts denied injunctions based upon an unborn child's right. In the latter case, Heilbron J (at first instance) stated:[255] '. . . there is no basis for the claim that the foetus can be a party, whether or not there is any foundation for the contention with regard to the alleged threatened crime . . . '.

Most recently in the Scottish case of *Kelly v Kelly*[256] a father claimed an interim interdict—the Scottish equivalent of an interlocutory injunction—to prevent his estranged wife from undergoing an abortion. The Inner House of the Court of Session approached his claim by asking whether the foetus had any legal rights at all which could be enforced on its behalf by the father. The court concluded that it did not since it was not a legal (or juridical) person until birth. The court referred to, and adopted, the English, Commonwealth, and American jurisprudence that denies an unborn child legal status. The court accepted in *Kelly* that, therefore, the father had no claim on behalf of the foetus because the foetus could have no legal claim of any kind until it was born alive. **11.130**

2. As a Father

Does a father have any right himself to prevent an abortion? The English courts have dismissed the idea that a husband or partner of a pregnant woman has any right, common law or otherwise, in his unborn child, or which is implicated by her decision to have an abortion. Not least, the courts have reached this conclusion because such involvement would run counter to the structure of the Abortion Act 1967 which contemplates a private decision reached between doctor and **11.131**

---

[248] Recently by the Canadian Supreme Court in *Winnipeg Child and Family Services (Northwest Area) v DFG* (1997) 152 DLR (4th) 193. See also *Tremblay v Daiglé* (1989) 62 DLR (4th) 634 (Can Sup Ct).

[249] We also saw earlier that the foetus was unlikely to fall within the protection of Art 2 ('right to life') of the ECHR, above, paras 11.101–11.113.

[250] *Re F (In Utero)* [1988] 2 All ER 193 (CA).

[251] *Burton v Islington HA* [1992] 2 All ER 833 (CA) and Congenital Disabilities (Civil Liability) Act 1976, s 4(2)(a).

[252] *Attorney-General's Reference (No 3 of 1994)* [1997] 3 All ER 936 (HL). See also, *R v Tait* [1989] 3 All ER 682 (CA): foetus not 'a third party' so that a threat to kill the foetus amounts to a crime of threatening to kill 'a third party' under s 16, Offences Against the Person Act 1861, s 16.

[253] [1978] 2 All ER 987 (Baker P).

[254] [1987] 1 All ER 1230.

[255] ibid, 1235. The Court of Appeal decided the case on the basis that no crime would be committed under the Infant Life (Preservation) Act 1929. However, the judges did not doubt the approach of Heilbron J or that in *Paton*: see, especially, *per* Sir John Donaldson MR at 1243.

[256] 1997 SLT 896. Grubb, A, (1997) 5 Med L Rev 329 (Commentary).

patient.[257] For these reasons, English law does not confer upon a husband (or partner) a right which entails the need for his consent or that he be consulted.

11.132 Could a father claim that his exclusion from the decision to undergo a termination breached his 'right to private and family life' protected by Article 8 of the Convention? The answer is probably 'no'. In *X v UK*,[258] the European Commission accepted that a father's Article 8 right was engaged in this situation but concluded that its infringement was justified under Article 8(2) as being necessary for the protection of her rights, ie her own Article 8 right because the termination was carried out to avert the risk to her physical and mental health. Certainly, any claim by a father that amounted to a veto of a woman's decision would not be a valid basis for a Convention challenge. Excluding the father will be justified under Article 8(2) because of the burden to the pregnant woman of being forced—against her wishes—to carry a child to term and then bring it up. It is difficult to imagine that a pregnant woman's decision not to have a child could ever be overridden by a father's wish to be a parent. To take a contrary position would, in effect, turn the law back to the nineteenth century when wives were under the legal control of their husbands.

11.133 In *X v UK*, the father also claimed a right to be consulted about the proposed abortion. Here, the interference with the woman's right to decide is somewhat less since it does not necessarily entail an interference with her bodily integrity. Nevertheless, the Commission, following its earlier decision,[259] concluded that Article 8 could not be interpreted 'so widely as to embrace such procedural rights'.[260] An equally conclusive argument, it is suggested, lies in the effect such consultation could have on a pregnant woman in some circumstances, for example, where she was estranged from the father, she had been raped or she simply had no continuing relationship with the man. These would justify as 'proportionate' an infringement with the father's right to private life.[261]

3. As Guardian of the Public Interest

11.134 The final basis upon which to claim an injunction might be the criminal nature of the proposed abortion. An 'interested' individual might argue that an injunction should be granted to prevent the commission of an offence under s 58 of the OAPA 1861 (or the Infant Life (Preservation) Act 1929) if the Abortion Act 1967

---

[257] *Paton* (n 253 above). See also *C v S* (n 245 above), 1235 *per* Heilbron J and *Tremblay v Daiglé* (n 248 above), 665.

[258] N 205 above.

[259] *Bruggemann and Scheuten v Federal Republic of Germany* (1977) DR 10 100; [1977] 3 EHRR 244.

[260] N 205 above, at [27].

[261] See the highly persuasive reasoning of the US Supreme Court in *Planned Parenthood of SE Pennsylvania v Casey* 112 S Ct 2791 (1992).

has not been complied with. Leaving aside the difficulty of substantiating such an allegation where two doctors have conscientiously concluded that the Abortion Act 1967 applies, would an individual have locus standi? Common law jurisdictions throughout the world have rejected a father's locus standi to enforce the criminal law through the civil courts following the House of Lords' decision in *Gouriet v Union of Post Office Workers*.[262] Absent a private wrong, a citizen will only in *the most* exceptional circumstances, if ever, be allowed by the courts to claim a civil remedy to prevent a criminal offence.

In practice, only an application by the Attorney- General will be entertained by the courts, and then rarely.[263] The English cases have not yet applied the *Gouriet* reasoning in a paternal injunction case either because there was no suggestion that the abortion was illegal[264] or because the court chose, for whatever reason, to ignore the procedural issue and dismiss the claim on its merits.[265] There can be no doubt, however, that *Gouriet* would be fatal to the standing of a father in this sort of case even if the abortion was outside the terms of the Abortion Act.[266] The matter would be for the Crown Prosecution Service to determine whether a criminal trial was in the public interest after the abortion had been performed. For this reason, a judge's decision in 1996 (reported in the newspapers) to grant an ex parte injunction, albeit temporarily, to a pro-life group to prevent a woman undergoing an abortion on the basis that it did not fall within the Act must seriously be called into question.[267]

11.135

F. Abortion and Homicide[268]

1. Killing In Utero

It is neither murder nor manslaughter to kill a foetus in utero. Homicide requires the death of 'a person in being' (or *in rerum naturae*), namely that the child is fully extruded from the mother's body and is 'breathing and living by reason of its breathing through its own lungs alone, without deriving any of its living or power of living by or through any connection with its mother'.[269] The rule was recently re-affirmed by the House of Lords in *Attorney-General's Reference (No 3 of*

11.136

---

[262] [1978] AC 435. See also *League for Life in Manitoba v Morgentaler* [1985] 4 WWR 633 (Man QB).
[263] See eg, *Attorney-General v Able* [1984] 1 All ER 795 (Woolf J).
[264] *Paton* (n 253 above).
[265] *C v S* (n 253 above).
[266] See *C v S* (n 253 above), *per* Sir John Donaldson MR at 1243.
[267] See 'Selective Abortions Hit the Headlines' (1996) 313 BMJ 380.
[268] See Skegg, PDG, *Law, Ethics and Medicine* (1994), 19–26.
[269] *Rance v Mid-Downs HA* [1991] 1 All ER 801, 817 *per* Brooke J. For a discussion of the historical precedents, see Atkinson, S, 'Life, Birth and Live-Birth' (1904) 20 LQR 134.

1994).[270] The common law rule is widely recognised throughout the world[271] but not universally.[272] Consequently, an abortion which results in the death of the foetus in utero will not amount to homicide.

2. Killing Ex Utero

11.137 What, however, would be the position if the abortion procedure results in the foetus being born and dying ex utero? Could this be murder or manslaughter? It is helpful to consider two situations: first, where the doctor terminates the pregnancy intending to kill the unborn child in utero but for whatever reason the child dies after birth; and secondly, where the intention is to produce a live birth and let the child die. Clearly, in both situations it would have to be proved that the doctor's action in terminating the pregnancy caused or substantially contributed to the child's death after birth. This will be a factual matter turning upon expert evidence. More problematic legally are the questions of whether the doctor has the requisite mens rea for murder or manslaughter and, if he does, whether he has any defence on the basis that what he did was lawful under the Abortion Act 1967.

(i) Death In Utero Intended

(a) Murder and Manslaughter

11.138 Where a doctor intends to terminate the pregnancy by killing the unborn child in utero, he will lack the mens rea of murder, namely an intention to kill or cause serious injury to a legal person since, prior to birth, the unborn child has no legal personality. However, could the doctrine of 'transferred intention' apply?[273] Thus, the intention to kill the foetus is transferred to the child once born.[274] In *Attorney-General's Reference (No 3 of 1994)*[275] the House of Lords decided that for murder the doctrine of 'transferred intention' could not be applied where the only intention was directed against the pregnant woman, because that would require a 'double transfer': first, from the mother to the foetus, and secondly, from the foetus to the child subsequently born. This was a fiction too far for the House of Lords. However, where the intention is directed against the foetus—as it will be in the situation of an abortion—the House of Lords' decision leaves open the possibility of

---

[270] [1997] 3 All ER 936, 948 *per* Lord Mustill.

[271] See eg, *Keeler v Superior Court* (1970) 470 P 2d 617 (Cal Sup Ct): not murder under California Penal Code to kill an unborn child; cf now s 187 amended in 1970 to include killing of a foetus in definition of murder.

[272] *Commonwealth v Lawrence* (1989) 404 Mass 378 (Mass Sup Jud Ct): killing of viable foetus in utero is murder.

[273] For a discussion of the doctrine in this context see Tempkin, J, 'Pre-Natal Injury, Homicide and the Draft Criminal Code' [1986] CLJ 414.

[274] As was held in *R v West* (1848) 2 Cox CC 500 (murder) and *Kwok Chak Ming v R* [1963] HKLR 349 (manslaughter).

[275] [1997] 3 All ER 936 (HL), overruling the Court of Appeal, [1996] 2 All ER 10.

transferring the intention from the foetus to the child subsequently born: a single transfer and 'fiction'. The better view is, however, that the doctor's intention cannot be transferred because he does not intend to kill a 'legal person'. First, as a matter of principle, the House of Lords held that the foetus was not 'the mother' but a 'distinct organism . . . living symbiotically'.[276] Second, the foetus itself is not a legal person. These reasons also prevent the doctor's conduct amounting to manslaughter by an 'unlawful act' even though the House of Lords held that a 'double transfer' of intention was, by contrast to murder, possible. In the situation of abortion, unlike that of a violent attack on the pregnant woman, there will not for the reasons given above be any intention to injure a 'legal person', only the discrete organism that is the foetus.

One possibility of an offence does, however, exist where the doctor in the course **11.139** of a termination inadvertently brings about a live birth and the child dies.[277] The doctor could commit the offence of manslaughter by gross negligence if his negligence in bringing about the live birth and subsequent death was characterised as sufficiently serious by a jury.[278]

(b) A Lawful Justification

In any event, the law would, in all probability recognise that the doctor would **11.140** have a defence to a charge of murder or manslaughter if the child died after birth as the result of a lawful abortion. In *Attorney-General's Reference (No 3 of 1994)*,[279] the Court of Appeal stated that a doctor's action in terminating the pregnancy, unlike that of the violent assailant, would not be unlawful if the terms of the 1967 Act were complied with, and hence he would have a defence to a charge of murder or manslaughter. However, the basis for the defence is not clear.[280] Such a defence is analytically problematic. First, the Abortion Act 1967 does not expressly or impliedly create a defence to a charge of murder or homicide. The legislative intention behind the 1967 Act is clear from its provisions which remove criminal liability for an offence under 'the law relating to abortion' which means under the 1861 Act.[281] Parliament was only concerned with offences prohibiting in utero deaths.[282] Secondly, murder does not require an unlawful act. What murder requires is that *the death be caused unlawfully*: but by this the law means merely not

---

[276] ibid, 943 *per* Lord Mustill. See also Lord Hope at 954. See discussion in Grubb, A, 'Unborn Child (Pre-Natal Injury): Homicide and Abortion' (1995) 4 Med L Rev 302, 306–8 (Commentary).

[277] *R v Senior* (1832) 1 Mood CC 346 (gross negligence by midwife leading to death ex utero).

[278] See *R v Adomako* [1994] 3 All ER 79 (HL).

[279] [1996] 2 All ER 10 (CA). The issue was not addressed by the House of Lords.

[280] See Grubb, A, 'Unborn Child (Pre-Natal Injury): Homicide and Abortion' (1995) 4 Med L Rev 302, 308–10 (Commentary).

[281] ss 1(1) and 6(1) and, since 1990, under the Infant Life (Preservation) Act 1929: s 5(1).

[282] See Skegg, PDG, *Law, Ethics and Medicine* (Clarendon Press, 1984), 23–6.

in circumstances where the defendant has a defence, for example, self-defence, provocation, diminished responsibility, etc. Murder may be committed by a wholly lawful act. The same is true for manslaughter committed by 'gross negligence' but not, of course, for 'unlawful act' manslaughter.

11.141   It is suggested that the answer to the doctor's criminal liability really lies in the mother's ability in law to consent to the harm to herself—which a 'miscarriage' undoubtedly is—and to the foetus which the Abortion Act 1967, as matter of public policy in England, permits a woman to do if the termination falls within the grounds set out in s 1 of the 1967 Act. If the mother's consent is sufficient to exempt the doctor from liability under ss 20 or 18 of the OAPA 1861 (for serious harm caused to her) and under s 58 (for the miscarriage of the foetus), the legality of the abortion procedure is established and there is no good reason why the unintended fact that the child is born should affect that.

(ii) Death Ex Utero Intended

11.142   In the unlikely situation that a doctor carried out an abortion intending the foetus to die after birth, he would commit murder if the child were 'born alive'. More likely in practice would be the situation were the doctor inadvertently brought about a live birth and the child then dies. Here, the doctor would commit the offence of manslaughter by gross negligence if his negligence in bringing about the live birth and subsequent death was characterised as sufficiently serious by a jury.[283] In these situations, it is arguable that the doctor would not have a defence or lawful justification. Certainly, as regards murder, if the true basis of his defence is the woman's consent, she could not lawfully consent to the death of her child once born.

11.143   In addition, the law imposes a duty upon a doctor to act reasonably in trying to save the child's life once born. Of course, this is not an absolute duty. The courts have already recognised that a doctor will not necessarily breach his duty by allowing a severely disabled premature newborn to die.[284] The fact that the child was born following a termination would in itself, however, be irrelevant. The doctor would have to take reasonable steps given the gestational age, the physical and mental condition, and prognosis of the child to save its life. Once born it would be entitled to the same care from the doctor and protection from the law as any premature baby in its circumstances. Undoubtedly the surest way to avoid a charge of murder or manslaughter is to prevent the situation arising altogether by adopting a method of termination which will certainly kill the foetus in utero.

---

[283] *R v Senior* (n 277 above) and para 11.139 above.
[284] See eg, *Re J (A Minor) (Wardship: Medical Treatment)* [1990] 3 All ER 930 (CA) and Ch 4.

12

ACTIONS ARISING FROM BIRTH

A. Introduction

The scope of this chapter[1] is the investigation of the nature of events occurring be-   **12.01**
fore birth, whether or not preceding conception, which give a right of action to
the child who is eventually born or to a member of his family. It will be seen that

---

[1] For academic discussion generally, see: Cane, PF, 'Injuries to Unborn Children' (1977) 51 ALJ
74; Eekelaar, JM and Dingwall, RWJ, 'Some legal issues in Obstetric Practice, (1984) JSWL 258;
Fortin, JES, 'Is the "Wrongful life" Action Really Dead?, (1987) JSWL 306; 'Legal Protection for
the Unborn Child' (1988) 51 MLR 54; Kennedy, I and Grubb, A, *Medical Law* (3rd edn,
Butterworths, 2000), ch 12; Lovell, PH and Griffith Jones, RH, 'The Sins of the Fathers—Tort
Liability for Pre-Natal Injuries' (1974) 90 LQR 531; Mullis, A, 'Wrongful Conception Unravelled'
(1993) 1 Med L Rev 320; Pace, PJ, 'Civil Liability for Pre-Natal Injuries' (1977) 40 MLR 141;
Rogers, WVH, 'Wrongful Life and Wrongful Birth: Medical Malpractice in Genetic Counselling
and Testing' (1982) 33 SCL Rev 713; 'Legal Implications of Ineffective Sterilizations' (1985) LS
296; Sarno, GG, 'Tort Liability for wrongfully causing one to be born' (1978) 83 ALR 3d 15;
Symons, CR, 'Policy Factors in Actions for Wrongful Birth', (1987) 50 MLR 269; Tedeschi, I, 'On
Tort Liability for "Wrongful Life" ' 4 Israel Rev 513; Teff, H, 'The Action for "Wrongful Life", in
England and the United States' (1985) 34 ICLR 423; Whitfield, A, 'Common Law Duties to
Unborn Children' (1993) 1 Med L Rev 28; Scott, R, 'Maternal Duties Towards the Unborn?
Soundings from the Law of Tort' (2000) 8 Med L Rev 1.

claims can only be made by or on behalf of children who are born alive or by parents, and not by other relations.

12.02   Most claims by children in England and Wales will now be brought under the Congenital Disabilities (Civil Liability) Act 1976, which by s 4(5) replaces the common law in respect of all births after its passing on 22 July 1976. However, it is necessary also to discuss the common law rights of children, partly because of their relevance to other jurisdictions and partly because, under the Limitation Act 1980,[2] some children born before the Act came into effect may have claims which are not and may never become statute barred. Furthermore, all claims by a parent will be brought under the common law.

12.03   The general assumption is that, whether at common law or under statute, children can only claim for disabilities which they have suffered as a result of some prenatal event, and not for the mere fact of being born or for so-called 'wrongful life'. A parent, on the other hand, may have a claim for the so called 'wrongful conception' or 'wrongful birth' of a child who is born alive but who would not have been born alive but for negligence. The parent may also have, in addition to a right of action in respect of personal injuries resulting from the circumstances of birth, a strictly limited claim in the case of a miscarriage or stillbirth.

12.04   However, it is unfortunately not possible to keep the categories of claims completely separate, and problems can overlap. For example, where one event is responsible both for the conception of, and for a disability in, a child eventually born, does that child's claim succeed as a prenatal injury claim? Does it fail as a 'wrongful life' claim? How would it dovetail with any claim by a parent arising out of the same event? These, and other problems, await final analysis.

B. Claims by Living Children for Injuries Caused Before Birth

1. Claims for Injuries at Common Law

(i) The Status of the Foetus[3]

12.05   An unborn child has no 'legal personality'. In *Paton v British Pregnancy Advisory Service Trustees*[4] Sir George Baker P considered an application by a husband to

---

[2] The Limitation Act 1980 appears to apply to all causes of action which have not accrued before 4 June 1954; see *Arnold v Central Electricity Generating Board* [1988] 1 AC 228 and *Keenan v Miller Insulation and Engineering Ltd* (1988) PMILL Vol 4, No 3, 11.

[3] The form 'fetus' is preferred by many purists to 'foetus', though, for consistency, the latter spelling is used throughout this volume. Etymologically the word is connected with the obscure Latin verb 'feo', meaning 'bear' or 'produce', as are the words 'fecundus' (fruitful), 'felix' (fortunate) and 'femina' (woman).

[4] [1979] QB 276. The husband later took the case to the European Commission of Human Rights, which rejected his complaint under Art 2 and 8: *Paton v UK* [1980] EHLR 408.

restrain his wife and the British Pregnancy Advisory Service from causing or permitting an abortion, for which she had obtained a certificate under the Abortion Act 1967, from being carried out upon her. The case thus raised the question of the rights of the unborn child. He concluded: 'in England and Wales the unborn child has no right, no right at all, until birth.'[5]

In *C v S*,[6] where a putative father of a foetus also failed in an application for an injunction to restrain an abortion, Heilbron J said: **12.06**

> The authorities, it seems to me, show that a child, after it has been born, and only then in certain circumstances, based on his or her having a legal right, may be a party to an action brought with regard to such matters as the right to take on a will or intestacy, or for damages for injuries suffered before birth. In other words, the claim crystallises upon the birth, at which date, but not before, the child attains the status of a legal persona, and thereupon can exercise that legal right.[7]

These views were endorsed by the Court of Appeal in *Re F (in utero)*[8] when deciding the somewhat different issue of whether it had jurisdiction to ward an unborn child. The answer, that it had not, was primarily based on the fact that the unborn child has no existence independent of the mother. Consistently with that decision the Court of Appeal in *Re MB (an adult, medical treatment)*[9] and in *St George's NHS Trust v S*,[10] held that an unborn child does not have an existence or interest separate from the mother such as would justify a court overriding a competent women's refusal of a caesarian section intended to save the child's life.

In this respect, the law of Scotland appears identical; in *Hamilton v Fife Health Board*[11] Lord McCluskey said:[12]   **12.07**

> An unborn person, a foetus, is not a person in the eyes of the law—at least in relation to the law of civil remedies—and there can be no liability to pay damages to a foetus, even although the foetus sustained injuries resulting from a negligent act or omission constituting a breach of duty owed.

---

[5] ibid, 279.

[6] [1988] QB 135.

[7] ibid, 140.

[8] [1988] Fam 122.

[9] [1997] 2 FLR 426; 38 BMLR 175; [1997] 8 Med L R 217. See commentary, Kennedy (1997) 5 Med L Rev 317.

[10] [1999] Fam 26; [1998] 3 All ER 673. See also *Winnipeg Child and Family Services (North West Area) v DFG* (1997) 152 DLR (4th) 193 (Can Sup Ct) and Commentary, Grubb (1998) 5 Med L Rev 356.

[11] [1993] SC 369, [1993] SLT 624 and [1993] 4 Med LR 201. Generally, the common law world does not confer rights upon children as legal persons. See *Attorney-General (Qld) ex re Kerr v T* [1983] 46 ALR 275 (Aus H Ct); *Trembley v Daigle* [1989] 62 DLR (4th) 634 (Can Sup Ct); *R v Sullivan* [1989] 1 SCR 489 (Can Sup Ct); *Roe v Wade* [1973] 410 US 113 (US Sup Ct). But cf *In the matter of Baby P (an unborn child)* [1995] NZFLR 255, and [1997] Med L Rev 143.

[12] ibid, at 382, 629 and 206.

However, it is important to understand the limits of these propositions. While a foetus has no legal personality, and therefore cannot sue or recover damages, it does not follow that there is no duty to exercise reasonable care not to injure a foetus. It may lack legal capacity when unborn, but it does not follow that it is unprotected by the common law.

(ii) The Civil Law

12.08   By contrast, the civil law very clearly protects the rights of an unborn child. There is a well-established rule of civil law that an unborn child shall be deemed to be born whenever its interests require it.[13] The application of that maxim is typically in the field of succession. For example, a gift to a class of children living on a particular date is held to benefit a child *en ventre sa mère* at that date but later born alive within that class. The rule appears in certain Latin versions, one of which is '*nasciturus pro iam nato habetur quotiens de eius commodo agitur*' ('one about to be born will be held already to have been born whenever that is to his advantage'). It is to be noted that it was under the influence of that principle that Sir Robert Phillimore held in the Admiralty Court in *The George and Richard*[14] that a child born after the death of its father—in that case a ship's carpenter, drowned in a shipwreck—counted as a 'dependent' for the purposes of bringing an action under Lord Campbell's Act, the Fatal Accidents Act 1846. As will be seen, the influence of the civil law upon developments in this branch of the common law has been considerable.

(iii) The Criminal Law

12.09   The criminal law provides sanctions against some, but not all, conduct directed against a foetus. Its destruction by abortion is made unlawful by s 58 of the Offences Against the Person Act 1861, save in the circumstances set out in the Abortion Act 1967 as amended by s 37 of the Human Fertilisation and Embryology Act 1990. The Act of 1861 did not criminalise the taking of a child's life while it was being born and before it was fully born, but that loophole was blocked by the Infant Life (Preservation) Act 1929. However, s 5(1) of the 1967 Act as amended provides that no offence is committed under the Act of 1929 if termination is in accordance with the Act of 1967. It is to be noted that three grounds for termination under the 1967 Act as amended, namely those under Section 1(1) (b), (c) and (d), are not subject to any time limit and so termination on any such ground can lawfully be carried out at any stage of the pregnancy.

---

[13] See *Villar v Gilbey* [1907] AC 139, where the rule is fully discussed.
[14] [1871] LR 3 A and E, 466. See also *Williams v Ocean Coal Ltd* [1907] 2 KB 422, in which reliance was placed on the principle to establish the dependency of a posthumous child under the Workmen's Compensation Act 1897, and *Burton v Islington HA and de Martell v Merton and Sutton HA* [1933] QB 204 per Dillon LJ at 227.

Once the child has 'an existence independent of its mother'[15] its life is protected by the law of homicide.[16]

In *R v Tait*[17] the Court of Appeal decided that the threat 'I am going to kill your **12.10** baby' addressed to a pregnant woman, if meant as a threat to kill the foetus in utero, was not a threat to kill 'a third person' within the meaning of s 16 of the Offences against the Person Act 1861. The reason was that the foetus in utero was not, in the ordinary sense, 'another person' distinct from its mother.

However, if a child is injured *in* utero but is later born alive and dies of that injury, **12.11** then assuming the necessary mens rea the person who inflicted it is guilty of manslaughter or murder. Thus in *R v Senior*[18] an incompetent male midwife broke a child's skull with a knife as he became visible during birth. The child died immediately after he was born: a conviction for manslaughter was upheld. The justification for that result is the 'born alive' rule, namely that the child, having been born alive, then becomes 'a person' independent of the mother and thus is so at the time of death.

A more complex set of facts was considered in *Attorney-General's Reference (No. 3* **12.12** *of 1994).*[19] The respondent stabbed his girlfriend, whom he knew was pregnant, in the abdomen, penetrating the foetus. Two weeks later she gave birth at 26 weeks' gestation, but the child died from the complications of prematurity. He was charged with murder, but acquitted on the judge's direction that the facts adduced by the prosecution could not result in a conviction for murder or manslaughter. The Court of Appeal, on a reference under s 36 of the Criminal Justice Act 1972, did not consider the question of causation but only whether, assuming proof of a causal link between the wound and the death, the facts could justify such a conviction. It held that they could. The reasoning was as follows. In law a foetus was to be treated as an integral part of the mother, so an injury to the foetus was thus as unlawful as an injury to any other part of her, and where, having subsequently been born alive, the child died of that injury, the actus reus of homicide would be proved. As to mens rea the Court invoked the doctrine of

[15] Infant Life (Preservation) Act 1929 s 1(1). For a full discussion see *Rance v Mid-Downs HA* [1991] 1 QB 587, 620 per Brooke J. See also Russell, EJ, 'Abortion Law in Scotland and the Kelly Foetus', 1997, SLT Issue No 24, 187. See generally ch 11 above.

[16] Note the Infanticide Act 1938 in relation to the killing by a mother of her child under the age of 12 months.

[17] [1990] 1 QB 290.

[18] [1832] 1 Mood CC 346. For summaries of the case-law identifying the moment of birth see *Rance v Mid-Downs HA* (n 15 above) and Archbold, *Criminal Pleading, Evidence and Practice.* (2002 edn), 19–17. See also Fovargue S and Miola J, 'Policing Pregnancy: Implications of the Attorney-General's Reference (No 3 of 1994)' (1998) 6 Med L Rev 265.

[19] [1996] QB 581, [1996] 2 All ER 10.

transferred malice[20] (whereby if A intends to kill B but instead kills C he is as guilty as if he had intended to kill C). It held that it was irrelevant that the foetus had no separate existence at the time of the act, and that the respondent's intention in relation to the mother could be transferred to the child after its birth.

12.13 This line of reasoning did not commend itself to the House of Lords.[21] In the event it decided that the doctrine of transferred malice simply could not be stretched far enough to justify a conviction for murder, but that as manslaughter was a crime of 'basic intention' an unlawful and dangerous act directed at a woman who later gave birth to living child which died could give rise to a conviction for manslaughter. However, it roundly rejected the identification of the foetus with the mother, principally on obvious physiological grounds.[22] One can go further. The proposition that an unborn child has no legal status does not imply that it has no interest of any kind. Were that so, the problems which have arisen when a mother declines caesarian section required in the interests of her unborn child would simply not exist.[23] Indeed, the Abortion Act 1967 and the Human Fertilisation and Embryology Act 1990 clearly recognise that a foetus is a separate organism whose interests must be considered. What is more, the whole issue as to whether and how a civil claim can be brought for damages for injury to a child inflicted pre-natally would never arise if there was identity of mother and child for all purposes. It is therefore unsurprising that in *R v Tait*[24] Mustill LJ referred to the 'confused and unsatisfactory state of the law' and to:

> the complex legal issues not yet fully worked out which concern the status of the unborn child in the community and the obligation of the community and its members towards the unborn child.

(iv) The Development of the Common Law

12.14 No English decision dealt with the question of the common law duty of care to an unborn child before *Burton v Islington HA* and *De Martell v Merton & Sutton HA*.[25] The common law, however, had developed in other jurisdictions, gradually moving from denial of claims by those injured in utero to their general acceptance.

---

[20] See eg *R v Mitchell* [1983] QB 741. 76 Cr App R 293, CA. A struck B, who fell against C causing C to fracture her femur; death resulted; and the conviction for manslaughter was upheld. See *R v Latimer* [1886] 17 QBD 359: A aimed a blow at B but hit C; the conviction of unlawful and malicious wounding was upheld. See also Archbold, *Criminal Pleading, Evidence and Practice*, (2002 edn), 19–214.

[21] [1998] AC 245: [1997] 3 All ER 936.

[22] Per Lord Mustill at 255–6, 943 and Lord Hope at 267, 954.

[23] See para 12.06 and nn 9 and 10 above.

[24] [1990] QB 290, 299, 300. See also the discussion in (1995) 3 Med L Rev 302.

[25] [1993] QB 204.

Early objections are illustrated by two American decisions. In *Dietrich v Inhabit-* **12.15**
ants of Northampton[26] Mr Justice Holmes considered a case where, as a result of a
fall by the mother, a child was born at four or five months' gestation and survived
its premature birth only by 10 or 15 minutes. He declined to follow the criminal
and civil law analogies, and rejected a claim based on the infant's loss of life on the
grounds that it was not a 'person' recognised by law at the time of its injury. He
went on to rule that

> as the unborn child was a part of the mother at the time of the injury, any damage
> to it which was not too remote to be recovered for at all was recoverable by her.[27]

Objections to claims at common law were put more succinctly in *Drobner v* **12.16**
Peters.[28] The plaintiff was an infant allegedly injured when, 11 days before his
birth, his mother fell down a coal-hole left uncovered in the sidewalk. Numerous
arguments were raised by the defendant.

> The reasons given to defeat recovery in such a case are: lack of authority; practical in-
> convenience and possible injustice; no separate entity apart from the mother and, there-
> fore, no duty of care; no person or human being in esse at the time of the accident.[29]

In the event the claim was rejected on the ground that the injuries were to the
mother, and the defendant owed a duty of care to her alone.

A further obstacle to the development of such claims was the Irish case of *Walker* **12.17**
v Great Northern Railway Company of Ireland.[30] In that case a mother claimed for
injuries allegedly sustained by her unborn child in a railway accident. On a de-
murrer, a court of the Queen's Bench Division decided that the Statement of
Claim disclosed no cause of action. On any analysis, the decision is unsatisfactory.
The majority view was based principally on the failure to plead a contract of carriage with the unborn child, an approach based on the fallacy that privity of contract is a prerequisite to a duty in tort. The court also drew support from the
plaintiff's failure to plead that the carrier knew of the pregnancy and, further,
from the absence of any case law on the matter. However *Donoghue v Stevenson*[31]
exploded the 'privity of contract' fallacy and, based as it was upon the technical
issue of the pleadings, *Walker* has become irrelevant.

A turning point was the influential decision of the Supreme Court of Canada in **12.18**
Montreal Tramways v Leveille,[32] a decision under the Civil Code of Quebec,
Article 1053 of which provided:

---

[26] [1994] 138 Mass 14 (Mass Sup Jud Ct).
[27] ibid, 17.
[28] [1921] 25 NY 220 (NYCA).
[29] [1921] 25 NY 220, 222 (NYCA).
[30] [1891] 28 LR Ir 69.
[31] [1932] AC 562.
[32] [1933] 4 DLR 337.

every person capable of discerning right from wrong is responsible for the damage caused by his fault to another, whether by positive act, imprudence, neglect or want of skill.

Recognising that judicial opinion in common law courts tended to deny the right of a child when born to maintain an action for prenatal injury, the majority of the court held that the civil law fiction should apply and that 'a child will . . . be deemed to have been born at the time of the accident of the mother'.[33] However, of greater interest to the common lawyer is the judgment of Cannon J. It was delivered in French: the ratio appears in translation in the Australian case of *Watt v Rama*[34] in these terms:

> [T]he cause of action arose when the damage was suffered and not when the wrongful act was committed. The plaintiff's right to compensation came into existence only when she was born with the bodily disability with which she suffered. It was only after birth that she suffered the injury, and it was then that her rights were encroached upon and she commenced to have rights.[35]

This judgment, as will be seen, contains the genesis of the modern analysis of the problem.

12.19   Eventually, the right of a child when born alive to sue for injuries caused by a prenatal event became recognised not only in Canada, in the United States of America (where every jurisdiction now permits such a claim)[36] but also in Australia,[37] South Africa,[38] Scotland,[39] Ireland (by statute),[40] and in England and Wales by virtue of the Court of Appeal decision in *Burton* and *De Martell*.[41]

(v) The Legal Basis of the Right

12.20   A large number of Commonwealth cases depend as much upon assertion as analysis. For at least 50 years it has been generally accepted that denials of claims for prenatal injury are unjust. However, in various ways the courts have been oppressed by the argument that because at the time of the insult the foetus, the child-later-to-be-born, has no legal personality, therefore no duty can be owed to it. In

---

[33] ibid, 346.

[34] [1972] VR 353 (Sup Ct of Victoria).

[35] ibid, 357. For further Canadian decisions see *Duval v Sequin* (1972) 26 DLR (3d) 318 and *Cherry v Borsman* (1991) 75 DLR (4th) 668 (British Columbia Sup Ct), [1991] 2 Med LR 396: on appeal (1992) 94 DLR (4th) 487 (BCCA).

[36] Prosser, WL and Keeton, P, *Torts* (5th edn West Publishing, 1984) 368: see *Second Restatement of the Law of Torts* (1977) para 869.

[37] *Watt v Rama* (n 34 above); *X and Y v Pal* [1991] 23 NSWLR 26, [1992] 3 Med LR 195 (NSWCA): *Lynch v Lynch* [1992] 3 Med LR 62 (NSWCA).

[38] *Pinchin v Santam Insurance Co Ltd* [1963] 2 SA 254.

[39] *Hamilton v Fife Health Board* (n 11 above); for a commentary see (1993) 1 Med L Rev 392.

[40] Civil Liability Act 1961, s 58.

[41] N 25 above.

Burton, it was further argued at first instance[42] that, because all the physical injury occurred to an entity without legal personality, it must follow that any damage sustained by the 'legal person' which first came into being upon birth was purely economic and as such irrecoverable by reason of the House of Lords decisions in *Caparo Industries plc v Dickman*[43] and *Murphy v Brentwood District Council.*[44]

The closest analysis of the law appears in the decision of the Supreme Court of   **12.21**
Victoria in *Watt v Rama*.[45] The claim was brought by the plaintiff allegedly injured in utero by the negligent driving of the defendant, and the defendant took the preliminary point that the allegations disclosed no cause of action on the grounds that at the time of the collision the defendant owed no duty of care to the infant plaintiff who was then unborn; that he owed the infant plaintiff no duty not to injure her mother; and that the damages sought to be recovered by the infant plaintiff were in law too remote. The majority (Winneke CJ and Pape J) defined the issue as:

> not whether an action lies in respect of pre-natal injuries but whether a plaintiff born with injuries caused by the pre-natal neglect of the defendant has a cause of action in negligence against him in respect of such injuries.[46]

The solution was to define the relationship of the defendant to the plaintiff in utero as 'contingent or potential' which would 'crystallize' or 'ripen into a relationship imposing a duty' when the plaintiff's identity as a legal person became defined by birth. At that stage the act of neglect could be treated as a breach of duty, and the inter-uterine damage as 'merely an evidential fact relevant to the issue of causation and damage': the damage consisted of 'injuries as a living person'.[47] Thus, duty, breach, and damage remained potential until at and after birth, at which point they became actual. This line of reasoning was adopted by Potts J at first instance in *Burton*.[48]

In contrast with the majority, the approach of Gillard J in *Watt v Rama* was less   **12.22**
metaphysical. He derived from *Donoghue v Stevenson*[49] and *Grant v Australia Knitting Mills Limited*[50] the proposition that:

> it would be immaterial whether at the time of fault the victim was in existence or not, so long as the victim was a member of a class which might reasonably and probably be affected by the act of carelessness.[51]

---

[42] [1991] 1 QB 638, 651.
[43] [1990] 2 AC 605.
[44] [1991] 1 AC 398.
[45] [1972] VR 353 (Sup Ct of Victoria).
[46] [1972] VR 353, 358 (Sup Ct of Victoria).
[47] ibid, 360–1 and 366.
[48] [1991] 1 QB 638.
[49] [1932] AC 562.
[50] [1936] AC 85.
[51] N 45 above, 373. See also Lovell and Griffith-Jones, *The Sins of the Fathers* (n 1 above), 534, for the argument that unborn children, as a class, are foreseeable in their own right.

He noted that the pleaded and relevant '*damnum*' or damage was 'physical disabilities at and after her birth'. From this he inferred that the only difference made to a plaintiff by the passage of time was that by birth she acquired capacity to sue. He then went on to provide two linked answers to the contention that prior to birth no duty could be owed to an unborn child because it was not a legal person:

> The first depends on the views I have already expressed. The cause of action for negligence only comes into existence when the damage is suffered. The infant plaintiff at that period . . . is, I repeat, a persona juridica, with capacity to institute proceedings and to whom a duty might be owed. The injury while en ventre sa märe was but an evidentiary incident in the causation of damage suffered at birth by the fault of the defendant. . . . As a second answer there is probably at the time of the defendant's fault also damnum contemporaneous with the injuria to a subject which is sufficiently protected by the rules of the common law, so that when it reaches the capacity of a person in being by subsequent birth to institute legal proceedings, it is entitled to bring those proceedings for its own benefit in relation to the damage suffered.[52]

(vi) *Burton* and *de Martell*

12.23　It was the first answer of Gillard J which attracted Phillips J at first instance in *de Martell*:[53]

> To say that the plaintiff suffered his injuries the moment after his birth rather than in the period leading up to his birth involves a legal fiction. But the fiction is that which denies the living creature which became the plaintiff a persona in the period prior to birth. It is that legal fiction which the health authority relies upon in denying liability to the plaintiff. It is not open to the health authority to deny liability on the ground that the organism that they injured was not in law the plaintiff and yet to deny responsibility for the defects with which the plaintiff was born on the ground that they inflicted them before birth. In law and in logic no damage can have been caused to the plaintiff before the plaintiff existed. The damage was suffered by the plaintiff at the moment that, in law, the plaintiff achieved personality and inherited the damaged body for which the health authority (on the assumed facts) was responsible. The events prior to birth were mere links in the chain of causation between the health authority's assumed lack of skill and care and the consequential damage to the plaintiff.

The second answer given by Gillard J effectively identifies a complete cause of action at the time of the initial trauma, with the reservation only that it cannot be enforced until after a live birth. This, it is submitted, raises without resolving the problem of how a being with no legal identity can possess a 'chose in action', and is the less preferable analysis.

---

[52]　N 45 above, 374–5.
[53]　[1993] QB 204, 219.

The Court of Appeal heard the defendants' appeals in *Burton* and *De Martell*[54] **12.24** together and dismissed them without calling on the appellants. The majority followed *Watt v Rama*[55] without analysing its different approaches or expressing preference for either of the two first instance decisions. In a short concurring judgment, however, Leggatt LJ appears to express a preference for the first formulation of Gillard J, stating the issue as follows:

> [T]he plaintiffs claim that each was injured when at birth he or she became a legal person damaged by the prior act of the respective defendants, and that when each such act was done it was reasonably foreseeable that it might result in the plaintiff being born damaged.[56]

(vii) The Scope of the Duty

It is to be observed that the performance of the duty to avoid injury may extend **12.25** beyond a diagnosis and treatment to the provision of advice to the mother. In *Howarth v Adey*[57] Winneke J, permitting an amendment to the case to allow a plaintiff with cerebral palsy secondary to perinatal hypoxia to allege that the mother should have been warned of the risks of continued attempts at vaginal delivery and advised of the alternatives, said:

> Once it is accepted that a medical practitioner in the position of the respondent owes a duty of care both to the other and the child (see *Whitehouse v Jordan* [1981] 1 WLR 246) the scope of that duty must extend to providing advice and information to the mother as to maternal risks affecting the potential well-being of the infant inherent in the proposed management of the delivery. In the circumstances, the mother is the only person in the position to make the relevant decision in the interests of the infant.

(viii) The Common Law Right Defined

The common law of England and Wales, thus analysed, now seems to be clear.   **12.26**

(a) There is a duty not by lack of reasonable care to cause damage to a person;
(b) an act or omission which is in breach of that duty is actionable at the suit of the injured party once the injury occurs;
(c) a human being injured as a result of a prenatal event first sustains injury for the purposes of the law and acquires a right to sue when, at birth, he or she first becomes a person recognised as such by the general law.

---

[54] ibid; for a commentary, see Kennedy (1993) 1 Med L Rev 103.
[55] N 45 above.
[56] N 53 above, 232–3.
[57] [1996] 2 VR 535, 546 (Vic CA).

(ix) Pre-conception Occurrences

12.27 From the premise that a claim can be made by a living child for the effects of an occurrence which preceded its birth, it is but a short step to conclude that a living child can also make a claim for the consequences of an incident which preceded its conception. However, it is probably too simplistic to approach 'pre-conception occurrences' as if they formed one category susceptible of one answer in law. Distinctions may have to be made between:

(a) bringing about an injury to a child not yet conceived at the time of the act complained of but who would have been conceived whatever the defendant did;

(b) bringing about the conception of a child who, having been conceived, is doomed to disability for reasons unconnected with the act of the defendant, and

(c) bringing about both the conception of and the injury to the child.

This section considers only the first of these categories: the other two are discussed later.[58]

12.28 The problem was considered in *X and Y v Pal*.[59] In that case the New South Wales Court of Appeal considered the claim of an infant plaintiff, born with congenital syphilis, that her disabilities were caused by the negligence of her mother's gynaecologists in failing to screen and treat the mother for syphilis before she became pregnant. The defendants argued that the doctors owed no duty to the infant plaintiff: the argument failed. Clarke JA said:[60]

> [I]n principle . . . it should be accepted that a person may be subjected to a duty of care to a child who was neither born nor conceived at the time of his careless act or omission such that he may be found liable in damages to that child. Whether or not that duty will arise depends upon whether there is a relevant relationship between the careless person and the class of persons of whom the child is one.

12.29 A number of pre-conception occurrences may give rise to injuries to a child subsequently conceived. For example, a doctor may perform an operation which negligently weakens the uterus so that some years later it ruptures at the end of pregnancy and injures the child. A further example would be that of pre-conception exposure to chemicals or radiation which caused gene mutation and consequent disability to children later conceived. It may also be the case that some trauma to the mother leads to disability in a child not yet conceived when it occurs. *Burton* and *de Martell*[61] have removed the objection to such claims that the

---

[58] See below, paras 12.59–12.68 and 12.71–12.74.
[59] [1991] 23 NSWLR 26, [1992] 3 Med LR 195.
[60] ibid, 41 and 205.
[61] [1993] QB 204.

child was not alive at the time of the trauma. The extent to which such claims are likely to succeed, however, requires some discussion. There will in many cases be difficulties of proof in showing that, 'but for' the occurrence complained of, the child would have been born and born without the relevant disability. Leaving questions of evidence aside, however, there is also difficulty in predicting which categories of incident are most likely to give rise to successful claims.

Since *Caparo Industries plc v Dickman*[62] it has become clear that in a novel situa- **12.30** tion, such as that of a child claiming for injuries resulting from an incident which preceded his conception, a plaintiff must demonstrate that the damage was not only foreseeable but that a relationship of 'proximity' or 'neighbourhood' existed between him and the defendant. He must also show that it would be fair, just and reasonable for the law to impose a duty in the novel situation, and in general the courts only do so incrementally and by analogy with established categories of duty situations.

In America there has been reluctance to permit such claims to be brought against **12.31** negligent motorists, on the ground that there is no 'special relationship' between the careless driver and the future child or the woman he injures.[63] However, where the child's disabilities are caused by the conduct of a doctor or pharmaceutical manufacturer, a 'special relationship' has been said to exist and such claims have been permitted.[64] Without the 'special relationship', injury to the future (as yet unconceived) child is as a matter of law treated as unforeseeable, and hence no duty of care is owed to the child.[65] It remains to be seen whether English courts would be so reluctant to find the existence of a duty of care. Such common law claims are unlikely to arise in England now, and answers will be theoretical. Child plaintiffs injured in utero by vehicle accidents were successful in *Watt v Rama*[66] and also in *Lynch v Lynch*.[67] While it could be argued that a woman injured prior to conception is less likely to have an injured child than one injured during pregnancy, it cannot really be argued that injury caused to a child by a

---

[62] [1990] 2 AC 398; see in particular 617G–618E *per* Lord Bridge and 633F–635F *per* Lord Oliver. See also para 12.93 below.

[63] *Hegyes v Unjian Enterprises Inc* (1991) 286 Cal Rptr 85 (Cal App 2 Dist) (driver of motor vehicle not liable to child subsequently conceived and suffering disability in utero as a result of mother's injuries sustained in the accident). A majority of the Court of Appeal held that a 'special relationship' only existed between a doctor and a female patient and between a manufacturer of pharmaceuticals and their users. See also *McAuley v Wills* 303 SE 2d 258 (1983) (Ga Sup Ct).

[64] See eg *Bergstresser v Mitchell* 577 F 2d (1978) (8th Cir) (negligent caesarian section leading to weakened uterus); *Renslow v Mennonite Hospital* 367 NE 2d 1250 (1977) (Ill Sup Ct) (negligent blood transfusion leading to injury due to its incompatible Rhesus factor); and see cases cited in *Hegyes* (n 63 above).

[65] See *Hegyes* (n 63 above), 93 and 103 *per* Woods JA (Lillie PJ concurring). Contrast Johnson JA (dissenting at 108. See also *Yeager v Bloomington Obstetrics and Gynaecology Inc* (1992) 585 NE 2d 696 (Ct App Indiana) and the commentary, Grubb (1993) 1 Med L Rev 247.

[66] N 45 above.

[67] (1992) 3 Med LR 62 (NSWCA).

pre-conception event is 'unforeseeable'. It is suggested that as the Congenital Disabilities (Civil Liability) Act 1976[68] allows a claim for injuries to a child resulting from an incident which occurred before its conception, it would not be unfair if the common law did the same. However, the extension of a defendant's duty to such a situation would indeed be great, and the English courts might well find that the 'proximity' test was satisfied and a duty imposed on a defendant only where that defendant, as might a doctor or drug manufacturer, knowingly acted in a way which might affect a parent's health.

(x) The Liability of Parents

12.32   A parent can be liable to a child injured by his or her negligent driving of a car. It is not difficult to imagine other contexts in which parental liability might arise, for example where there is persistent refusal by a parent to take a child to hospital despite specific medical advice in obvious circumstances. This view is reinforced by the dictum of Lord Donaldson MR in *Re J (Wardship: Medical Treatment)* where he stated plainly:[69]

> [T]he parents owe the child a duty to give or withhold consent [to medical treatment] in the best interests of the child and without regard to their own interests.

Furthermore, analysis of the law set out in *Burton* and *de Martell*[70] implies that a parent may owe a duty at common law not to damage the health of a child as yet unborn.

12.33   The Law Commission,[71] however, was much troubled by the idea of a child having an unfettered right to sue his or her mother in respect of injuries arising from some antenatal event. It felt that such a right of action could further stress the already difficult relationship between mother and disabled child, or become a weapon between parents in a matrimonial conflict to its further detriment. It was impressed by the difficulty and unseemliness of possible allegations against mothers, such as those of excessive drinking and smoking, and pointed to the fact that in any event a mother, even if liable, would probably be unsupported by funds. In the end it recommended that a woman should only be liable for causing antenatal injury to her child if she was negligent in driving when she knew or ought reasonably to know herself to be pregnant. However, the Law Commission did not recommend any such special exemption for a father.[72]

12.34   These considerations of policy would be likely to affect any court considering a

---

[68] s 1(2)(a).
[69] [1991] Fam 33, 41.
[70] [1993] QB 204.
[71] Law Commission Report No 60: *Report on Injuries to Unborn Children* (Cmnd 5709, 1974); paras 54–63.
[72] ibid, para 61.

common law claim by a child against a parent for an antenatal occurrence. There may be further difficulties. For example, the interests of the foetus and the parents do not always coincide. Thus a pregnant mother may exercise her individual right to refuse caesarean section and thereby, perhaps knowingly, injure a viable foetus.[73] By parity of reasoning it is not easy to envisage a court actually finding a mother negligent in refusing or delaying other treatment to herself which might benefit her unborn child. Furthermore, if the standard of care to be expected to the mother cannot be identified, then it cannot be imposed upon her, and no claim will succeed.[74] For example, it will be extremely difficult to identify the point at which drinking or smoking in pregnancy becomes negligent.

It would, however, be going too far to say that no child could ever sue a parent at common law for injuries resulting from some antenatal occurrence. Thus, in *Lynch v Lynch*[75] a mother was successfully sued by a child injured in utero in a driving accident. Equally, if a mother failed to follow explicit prenatal advice which involved no assault upon her (eg to stop water skiing or the consumption of damaging drugs)[76] there would be no particular difficulty in judging her conduct. It could be assessed by the same standards as those which would apply, for example, to a teacher who disregarded a school doctor's instructions on how to react to a pupil's sudden illness, or to one who knowingly gave a child damaging substances. It is therefore suggested that where, as in motoring cases, a parent's conduct can be assessed by the same tests as those which can be applied to non-parents, then in the absence of a very good reason it is strongly arguable that lack of care by parents which damages a foetus may be actionable by the child, if and when born alive.[77]

12.35

(xi) Transgenerational Claims

It is possible to envisage something happening to a person as a result of which not (or not only) his or her child but that child's child and indeed succeeding generations may be injured. The establishment of a causal link between the occurrence and the subsequent harm to later generations may be difficult to establish, but at

12.36

---

[73] See *Re MB* and *St George's NHS Trust v S*, nn 9 and 10 above.

[74] See *Jackson v Harrison* [1978] CR 438 (H Ct of Australia), 455–6 per Mason J: *Pitts v Hunt* [1991] 1 QB 24, 50–1 *per* Balcombe LJ, where the principle is discussed in the context of illegal joint enterprises (joy-riding). See also *Gala v Preston* [1991] ALJR 366.

[75] N 67 above. But see *Dobson (Litigation guardian of) v Dobson* (1999) 174 DLR (4th) (Can Sup Ct) rejecting maternal liability at common law for injury to an unborn child caused by negligent driving.

[76] ibid, 71 *per* Clarke JA.

[77] See *Surtees v Royal Borough of Kingston* [1992] 1 PIQR 101, 121: 'the development of duties owed by a parent to his child has tended to result from claims by third parties either for damages or for contribution': *per* Beldam LJ, dissenting in the result. There are dicta in all three judgments on the need for care in imposing duties on a parent in the home context: *per* Stocker LJ at 111–2, Beldam LJ at 121, Browne-Wilkinson V-C at 123–4. For a full discussion see Scott R, 'Maternal Duties to the Unborn? Soundings from the Law of Tort' (2000) 8 Med L Rev 1.

least in logic the claim of successive generations might be thought to be entitled to succeed under the *Burton*[78] principle. It is, however, likely that such claims will be rejected on straightforward policy grounds. The Law Commission[79] was of the view that no duty should be owed to any but the immediate children of the parent affected by the occurrence. The same conclusion has been reached in the litigation of the American DES daughters. Diethylstilbestrol (DES) was a drug which, between 1947 and its banning in 1971, was given to millions of pregnant women to prevent miscarriages. It was alleged that in utero exposure to DES resulted in genital tract abnormalities to daughters later born, who in turn and as a result suffered obstetric problems including premature births. In *Enright v Eli Lilly & Co*[80] the grand-daughter of a woman who had ingested the drug during pregnancy alleged that in consequence her mother had given birth prematurely, as a result of which she suffered from cerebral palsy, and sued the manufacturers of the drug. The New York Court of Appeals rejected the claim, strongly influenced by policy considerations including the unquantifiable extent of the potential liability of drug companies to future generations. It is suggested that English courts would be extremely reluctant to reach a different conclusion.

(xii) Exclusion and Restriction of Liability

12.37 An unborn child is not a 'person' in law,[81] and it is difficult to envisage how any contract term or notice given by a defendant while it is in utero can exclude or restrict a defendant's liability for injuries with which the child is born. Certainly, in strict law the mother can hardly be described as an agent, fixing the foetus as a legally non-existent principal with notice or with the terms of a contract to which she was a party.

12.38 This conclusion, however, did not attract the Law Commission,[82] which concluded on social grounds that it would be unfair on a defendant if he could not limit liability to a child as yet unborn to the same extent as he could limit liability to the mother. In the context of prenatally inflicted injuries, however, the debate has now become of limited practical importance since the Unfair Contract Terms Act 1977.[83] Section 2(1) of the Act provides:

---

[78] See para 12.26 above.
[79] N 71 above, paras 79–80.
[80] (1991) 570 NE 2d 198 (NYCA).
[81] See para 12.05 above.
[82] N 71 above, paras 67–71.
[83] s 31(2) of the 1977 Act provides: 'nothing in this Act applies to contracts made before [1 February 1978]; but subject to this it applies to liability for loss or damage which is suffered on or after that date'.

a person cannot by reference to any contract term or to a notice given to persons generally or to particular persons exclude or restrict his liability for death or personal injury resulting from negligence.

This language is sufficiently broad to refer to injury arising from a prenatal event.

The protection provided by s 2(1) is however not completely all-embracing. **12.39** 'Negligence' is defined[84] so as to include 'contractual' as well as common law negligence, and also an occupier's common duty of care, but it does not include 'any stricter duty' than common law negligence (such as an obligation under *Rylands v Fletcher*)[85] nor breaches of any statutory duty other than those of an occupier. Nevertheless, for the reasons given above[86] it is thought that, even in the absence of the protection conferred by the Act of 1977, a defendant cannot restrict his liability for injuries inflicted before birth.

(xiii) *Volenti Non Fit Injuria*

Should a parent's voluntary assumption of a risk to his or her as yet unborn child **12.40** negative a defendant's liabilities, as a result of his conduct, to the child if later born injured? On strict legal analysis, a parent's assumption of a risk would only absolve a defendant of a duty not to injure an unborn child if he or she was treated as having authority to consent on behalf of the child, which is highly artificial. The Law Commission[87] thought it unfair that a defendant should be liable to the child born of a volens mother, and proposed that legislation should counter this injustice. Nevertheless, the problem remains at common law. One practical solution, it is suggested, is that although the doctrine of *volenti non fit injuria* might not exempt a defendant from his duty to a child as yet unborn, yet the fact of the mother's consent might prevent the defendant's conduct from amounting to a breach of that duty. Theoretically, that might not always be so. If, for example a pregnant woman insisted on a bizarre birth plan that might absolve her medical attendants of liability to her. However, if her child was later born injured as a result he might well wish to argue that it was their duty to him (as opposed to his mother) forcefully to try and persuade her to follow an alternative course which avoided the risk of inter-uterine damage, and that if proper persuasion had been employed it would have changed the mother's mind and avoided the injury. Thus, in highly unusual circumstances it might be arguable that a mother's consent would not protect the defendant against a claim by the child. In practice, however, it is not easy to see such an argument succeeding.

---

[84] Unfair Contract Terms Act 1977, s 1(1).
[85] [1868] LR 3 HL 330 [1861–73] All ER Rep HL.
[86] See para 12.37 above.
[87] N 71 above, paras 67–9.

2. *Claims for Injuries under the Congenital Disabilities (Civil Liability) Act 1976*

(i) The Purpose of the Act

12.41 The 1976 Act has its origins in the Law Commission Report on Injuries to Unborn Children.[88] The proposed legislation was justified on five grounds,[89] namely:

(i)   because in the absence of English authority there was doubt whether a child had a cause of action at all for injuries caused before birth;

(ii) because the basis upon which the cause of action existed in other common law jurisdictions varied;

(iii) to avoid the cost of law reform falling upon one individual;

(iv) because the first factual situation litigated would almost certainly leave a number of ancillary questions unanswered, and

(v)   because it recommended departures on social grounds from the probable results of strict application of legal principles, eg to claims by a child against the mother.[90]

(ii) The Availability of the Act

12.42 The Act applies to a child who is 'born disabled' after 22 July 1976, and in respect of such births it replaces the common law. By 'born'[91] is meant being 'born alive (the moment of a child's birth being when it first has a life separate from its mother)'.[92] To take advantage of the Act however, the child need not be 'disabled' in the ordinary sense of the word because disability denotes: 'any deformity, disease or abnormality, including pre-disposition (whether or not susceptible of immediate prognosis) to physical or mental defect in the future'.[93] In other words, any child born alive with any personal injury has a claim in appropriate circumstances. Social disadvantage, however, does not found a claim under the Act.

(iii) The Scope of the Act

12.43 To succeed, the child must prove that the disability resulted from an occurrence within the meaning of s 1(2) of the Act, namely:

---

[88] N 71 above.

[89] ibid, para 110.

[90] In retrospect it must be asked whether this difficult Act, a reaction to the thalidomide cases (see *S v Distillers Co* [1970] 1 WLR 114), was really necessary, and whether it is an improvement on the common law as now established.

[91] s 1(1), s 4(5).

[92] s 4(2)(a).

[93] s 4(1). Contrast the criteria for 'disabilities' in wrongful conception and birth claims; see para 12.95 below.

one which–

(a)   affected either parent of the child in his or her ability to have a normal, healthy child; or

(b)   affected the mother during her pregnancy, or affected her or the child in the course of its birth, so that the child is born with disabilities which would not otherwise have been present.

Section 1(2) requires two comments. First, although its sub-sections were intended to deal with pre-conception occurrences and post-conception occurrences respectively,[94] they are not mutually exclusive. For example, a badly performed caesarian section may affect the mother's subsequent ability to have a normal healthy child, but also affect her during a later pregnancy. Second, the language of the statute does not make it absolutely clear that s 1(2)(b) covers all post-conception occurrences which might damage the foetus. For example, it might be the case that X-rays and inter-uterine investigations affected the foetus without 'affecting' the mother, at least in the sense of injuring her. However, despite that lack of clarity it is most unlikely that a court would adopt so narrow a construction and thereby deprive the child of a statutory right of action. This is particularly so because a child has a right of action even though the mother has not been injured.[95] It is therefore likely that a court would construe 'affected' as meaning not 'injured' but rather as merely meaning 'involved'.[96]

(iv) Infertility Treatments

Section 1 of the Act has been extended to a child's disabilities which result from certain infertility treatments, namely: **12.44**

> an act or omission in the course of selection, or the keeping or use outside the body, of the embryo . . . or of the gametes used to bring about the creation of the embryo.[97]

(v) The Mother as a Defendant

With one exception, a child born disabled has no claim against its mother.[98] The   **12.45** exceptional case is that of claims arising from the negligent driving of a motor vehicle by a woman when she knows (or ought reasonably to know) herself to be pregnant. In such circumstances the mother owes a direct 'duty to take care for the safety of the unborn child', who may sue her if later born with disabilities. It is to be noted that this right of action extends only to the driving of motor vehicles and not, for example, to the riding of a bicycle or horse. In other words, it extends to

---

[94]   See note 5 to Clause 1 of the Draft Bill, Appendix 1 to the *Report*, n 71 above.
[95]   See s 1(3).
[96]   Note 5 (n 94 above) uses the verb 'involve' as equivalent to 'affect'.
[97]   s 1A, inserted by the Human Fertilisation and Embryology Act 1990, s 44(1).
[98]   The general rule appears in s 1(1), the exception in s 2 of the Act.

claims covered either by insurers or by the Motor Insurance Bureau. In these circumstances the policy arguments for disallowing claims against a mother are much diminished.

(vi) The Father as a Defendant

12.46   It is to be noted that a father does not enjoy the same immunity from action as does the mother. This apparent anomaly was justified by the Law Commission's views that, inter alia, there would be less ways in which congenital disabilities could be caused by a father than by a mother: that a father's responsibility for a child's injuries would be less likely to raise family disputes than a mother's: and that a child born disabled as a result of an assault by a man on the mother (even a rape which caused the conception) should have a cause of action against the man.[99]

(vii) The Derivative Nature of the Claim

12.47   The basis of liability under the Act is unique, because, save in claims against a mother for motoring injuries,[100] a defendant is liable to the child only if the defendant has committed a breach of duty to a parent. He:

> is answerable to the child if he was liable in tort to the parent or would, if sued in due time, have been so: and it is no answer that there could not have been such liability because the parent suffered no actionable injury, if there was a breach of legal duty which, accompanied by injury, would have given rise to the liability.[101]

In other words, a child's claim is derivative from a breach of duty to the parent which gives rise to, or would if accompanied by damage give rise to, liability in tort. This includes not only tortious liability at common law but also cases where such liability is created by statute when the wrong, though commonly called 'breach of statutory duty' is a proper analysis the infringement of a private law right created by statute.[102] However the Act does not apply where the injury to the parent is a breach of a term in a contract, whether express or implied. Thus, a child born injured as a result of breach of a term implied by the Sale of Goods Act 1989 as amended as to the quality of goods bought by her would have no remedy under the 1976 Act.

12.48   It may be thought that this approach seems unnecessarily tortuous. However, it avoids a number of anomalies. For example, an occupier's duty may require a different level of care to be exercised towards lawful visitors from that which is owed

---

[99] N 71 above, paras 92–3. See Cane, PF, 'Injuries to Unborn Children' (n 1 above), 154–5 for criticism of this 'inequality of treatment of parents' liabilities'.
[100] See above, para 12.45.
[101] s 1(3).
[102] See *X (Minors) v Bedfordshire CC* [1995] 2 AC 633, 731C–732B *per* Lord Browne-Wilkinson.

to trespassers;[103] to impose an unrestricted duty of care to unborn children upon an occupier could mean that he owed a higher duty to the unborn child than to its trespassing mother. Thus, by making the child's action derivative on a breach of duty to a parent, the Act avoids the problem which would arise if a defendant owed two levels of duty in respect of one incident. More importantly, this approach enables the child to sue the maker of a negligent misstatement to the mother. This would not otherwise have been possible. For if the only duty upon which an action could be based was one owed directly to a child as yet unborn, it is not easy to see how liability could be imposed for negligent advice given to the mother before the birth.

Nevertheless, this approach is not entirely without disadvantage to the child. **12.49**
First, if the parents' actions would have given rise, had they sued, to a defence, then the child is without remedy; this might arise if the mother perversely refused appropriate treatment such as a caesarian section in appropriate circumstances, or refused to go into hospital despite a warning that the labour was high risk. Here the child will be without remedy either against the medical attendant or against the mother (because she is immune from action save in motoring claims). Furthermore, undue solicitude for the mother, even at risk to the child, might not be a breach of any duty to her, and the child injured by such excess of care would be without remedy.[104] Cane gives an example of another anomaly.[105] A manufacturer of a drug known to create a risk to both mother and foetus warns the mother of the risk to herself but negligently states that the drug is safe for the foetus. The mother consumes the drug: only the foetus is injured. Because the child's claim is derivative only on an assumed breach of duty to the mother, he has no claim against the drug manufacturer. This is clearly unjust. As yet, these problems remain unlitigated.

(viii) Product Liability

Section 6(3) of the Consumer Protection Act 1987 provides that: **12.50**

> Section 1 of the Congenital Disabilities (Civil Liability) Act 1976 shall have effect the purposes of this Part as if–
>
> (a) a person were answerable to a child in respect of an occurrence caused wholly or partly by a defect in a product if he is or has been liable under s 2 above in respect of any effect of the occurrence on a parent of the child, or would be so liable if the occurrence caused a parent of the child to suffer damage;
> (b) the provisions of this Part relating to liability under s 2 above applied in relation to liability by virtue of paragraph (a) above under the said s 1; and
> (c) subsection (6) of the said s 1 (exclusion of liability) were omitted.

---

[103] See *Herrington v British Railways Board* [1972] AC 877: Occupiers' Liability Act 1984: s 1(3).
[104] See Eekelaar JM and Dingwall, RWJ, 'Some legal issues in Obstetric Practice' (n 1 above),102.
[105] See Cane, PF, 'Injuries to Unborn Children' (n 1 above), 707–8, n 42.

In brief, it extends the protection of product liability legislation to the unborn child, while adopting the general scheme of the Act of 1967 in making liability to the child derivative on liability to a parent under the Act of 1987.

(ix) The Statutory Standard of Care

12.51   The special position of the professional attendant is recognised by s 1(5) of the Act which provides

> the defendant is not answerable to the child, for anything he did or omitted to do when responsible in a professional capacity for treating or advising the parent, if he took reasonable care having due regard to then received professional opinion applicable to the particular class of case; but this does not mean that he is answerable only because he departed from received opinion.

This is an attempted codification of the common law, of which the Law Commission said:

> [I]t demands of a professional man that he should exercise such care as accords with the standards of reasonably competent medical men at the time unless he has in fact greater than average knowledge of any risks in which case his duty will be that much greater.[106]

Emphasis is correctly placed by the subsection both on the standards of the day and on the principle that departure from approved practice is not necessarily a breach of duty.[107] No reference is made to responsibility for diagnosis (as opposed to treatment or advice) but this distinction is unlikely to commend itself to a court: no distinction was made between 'diagnosis' and 'treatment' in *Hunter v Hanley*.[108] Finally, the language, it is suggested, gives some comfort to those who seek to argue on policy grounds that the *Bolam*[109] test is unduly favourable to medical defendants. While accepting the relevance of medical opinion to the question of negligence it stops short of making it determinative of the issue.

(x) Transgenerational Claims

12.52   It will be recalled[110] that difficult questions arise at common law in considering whether a child should have a claim for injuries caused by a pre-conception occurrence which affects not the parent but a grandparent or more remote ances-

---

[106] *Report on Injuries to Unborn Children* (n 71 above), para 94. In this connection see *Newell v Newell and Goldenberg* [1995] 6 Med LR 371, 374 per Mantell J: 'The *Bolam* principle provides a defence for those who lag behind the times. It cannot serve those who know better'.

[107] See Kennedy, I and Grubb, A, *Medical Law* (n 1 above), 453–5.

[108] [1955] SLT 213.

[109] *Bolam v Friern HMC* [1957] 1 WLR 582. See also *Maynard v West Midlands RHA* [1984] 1 WLR 634; *Sidaway v Board of Governors of the Bethlem Royal Hospital* [1985] AC 871; and *Bolitho v City and Hackney HA* [1998] AC 232; [1997] 4 All ER 771.

[110] See para 12.36 above.

tor. The Act, in somewhat obscure language, excludes such a claim. Section 1(3) makes a child's claim dependent upon his establishing that a defendant is 'liable in tort' to the parent or would, if sued in time, have been so. However s 4(5) of the Act provides that:

> [I]n section 1(3) of this Act the expression 'liable in tort' does not include any reference to liability by virtue of this Act or to liability by virtue of [any law in force before its passing whereby a person could be liable to a child in respect of disabilities with which it might be born.]

This means that the liability in tort to a parent from which a plaintiff's rights under the Act derive must arise from an event taking place after the parent's birth. Therefore, a defendant would not be under any liability for an occurrence which affects the second or subsequent generation from the victim of the original occurrence.

(xi) Exclusion and Restriction of Liability

The question of the exclusion or restriction of liability to children to whom the Act does not apply has been discussed above.[111] Those to whom it does apply are equally protected, because s 1(6) of the Act provides:

12.53

> [L]iability to the child under this section may be treated as having been excluded or limited by contract made with the parent affected, to the same extent and subject to the same restrictions as liability in the parent's own case; and a contract term which could have been set up by the defendant in an action by the parent, so as to exclude or limit his liability to him or her, operates in the defendant's favour to the same, but no greater, extent in an action under this section by the child.

This confers on a child born disabled the same extensive protection against exclusion clauses in contracts with the parents as they, if injured, would enjoy by virtue of s 2(1) of the Unfair Contract Terms Act 1977. In product liability claims the same effect is achieved even more directly because, although s 6(3)(c) of the Consumer Credit Act 1987 excludes the operation of s 1(6) of the 1967 Act, s 7 provides:

> [T]he liability of a person by virtue of [Part I of the 1987 Act] to a person who has suffered damage caused wholly or partly by a defect in a product, or to a dependant or relative of such a person, shall not be limited or excluded by any contract term, by any notice or by any other provision.

(xii) *Volenti Non Fit Injuria* and Parental Knowledge of Risks

If a claim by a parent arising out of the occurrence which injured the unborn child would have been defeated by the defence of *volenti non fit injuria*, then the child

12.54

---

[111] See, paras 12.37–12.39 above.

will be unable to succeed under the Act. This is because, as has been pointed out,[112] the child's claim is derivative, and presupposes that the defendant would have been liable to the parent.

12.55 However, children born with a disability face another obstacle. Section 1(4) of the Act provides:

> [I]n the case of an occurrence preceding the time of conception, the defendant is not answerable to the child if at that time either or both of the parents knew of the risk of their child being born disabled (that is to say, the particular risk created by the occurrence); but should it be the child's father who is the defendant, this sub-section does not apply if he knew of the risk and the mother did not.

This subsection requires certain comments. First, it is probable that the Law Commission[113] intended this to be a statutory form of *volenti non fit injuria*. However, such a provision would be unnecessary,[114] and in any even knowledge without assumption of that risk does not make a plaintiff *volens*.[115] Perhaps unintentionally, a defence of *scienti non fit injuria* has been introduced. Second, s 1(4) does not apply to a risk attaching to post-conception occurrences, but only to those attaching to occurrences which precede conception. Nor, in cases where the child sues the father, can the father claim that his knowledge of the risk amounted to a defence unless that knowledge was shared by the mother. Were the law otherwise, a man who knew he had syphilis, of which a woman was unaware, and who in raping her infected a child thus conceived with that disease might be able to plead his own knowledge of it as a defence, which would be absurd. Third, a comparable but not identical provision applies to claims arising out of the infertility treatments referred to in s 1A(3)[116] of the Act, providing that

> [T]he defendant is not under this section answerable to the child if at the time the embryo, or the sperm and eggs, are placed in the woman or at the time of her insemination (as the case may be) either or both of the parents knew the risk of their child being born disabled (that is to say, the particular risk created by the act or omission).

In the circumstances contemplated, as neither parent will be responsible for the infertility treatment, and thus neither will be a defendant, there is no reason why either's knowledge of the risk involved should not be a defence available to those who provided it.

---

[112] See para 12.47 above.

[113] N 71 above, paras 71 and 93, and note 10 to the Draft Bill, Appendix 1 to the *Report*, suggesting a defence 'if either or both of the parents knew of the risk of their child being born disabled *and accepted it*'.

[114] See para 12.54 above.

[115] *Smith v Baker* [1891] AC 325, 355 *per* Lord Watson.

[116] N 97 above.

(xiii) Contributory Negligence by Parents

Section 1(7) of the Act provides: **12.56**

> [I]f in the child's action . . . it is shown that the parent affected shared the responsi-
> bility for the child being born disabled, the damages are to be reduced to such ex-
> tent as the court thinks just and equitable having regard to the extent of the parent's
> responsibility.

This in effect gives a partial or complete defence on grounds equivalent to the contributory negligence of a parent. In doing so, the Act recognises the injustice
which would otherwise result to a wrongdoer who is made to pay damages in full
when his fault was slight compared with that of the parent. By implication, it also
recognises the responsibility of a parent for the well-being of a child as yet unborn.
The disadvantage is that (save in motoring claims) a child may have his damages
severely reduced by reason of the mother's responsibility, and yet because of her
exemption from liability have no right to recover the balance of compensation
from her.[117]

(xiv) Radiation Injuries

The Nuclear Installations Act 1965 as amended provides compensation provi-   **12.57**
sions for those injured by a nuclear incident, and the Act of 1967 extends them to
children subsequently born disabled. Section 3(2) of that Act includes as an injury
for the purposes of the compensation provisions of the Act of 1965:

> anything which
> (a) affects a man in his ability to have a normal, healthy child or
> (b) affects a woman in that ability, or so affects her when she is pregnant that her
>   child is born with disabilities which would not otherwise have been present.

Section 3(3) then provides that a child's disabilities resultant on such an injury
caused by a breach of a duty under ss 7 to 11 of the 1965 Act are also compensatable. The child's compensation is however by s 3(4) subject to a reduction caused
by the contributory fault of the parent within the limits of s 13(6) of the 1965 Act,
namely by: 'any act . . . committed with the intention of causing harm to any person or property or with reckless disregard for the consequences of his act;. Finally,
s 3(5) of the 1976 Act provides:

> compensation is not payable in the child's case if the injury to the parent preceded
> the time of the child's conception and at that time either or both of the parents knew
> the risk of their child being born disabled (that is to say, the particular risk created
> by the injury).

---

[117] See Pace, PJ, 'Civil Liability for Pre-Natal Injuries' (n 1 above), 157 for arguments that this provision is unfair and inconsistent with the Law Commission's wish to avoid bitterness in the family.

Detailed discussion of the Act of 1965 is beyond the scope of this work.

(xv) The Nature of the Remedy

12.58   Finally, s 1(1) of the Act confers a remedy in these terms: 'the child's disabilities are to be regarded as damage resulting from the wrongful act . . . and actionable accordingly.' The scope of that remedy is defined by s 4(3): 'liability is to be regarded as liability for personal injuries sustained by the child immediately after its birth.' One purpose of this provision is to exclude a right to compensation for any prenatal suffering, and to provide for damages to be assessed as if the prenatal injury had been inflicted after birth without the disabilities due to the prenatal wrong.[118] Secondly, the intention was to limit the claim to damages for personal injuries. Whether this has been achieved will be discussed below.[119] When the Act was passed there was a right to damages for loss of expectation of life, and therefore (to avoid the apparent absurdity of a child which survives only for a few minutes having such a claim) s 4(4) the Act provided that no damages should be recoverable for loss of expectation of life unless the child lived for at least 48 hours. However, in respect of causes of action accruing after 31 December 1982 damages in respect of any loss of expectation of life were abolished save in respect of claims for damages in respect of loss of income.[120] In most actions under the Act such claims will be worthless, because claims for loss of income during the 'lost years' are not recoverable on behalf of a young child save to the extent that they may be reflected occasionally in 'some small adjustment to the multiplier'.[121] Occasionally, however, claims are made on behalf of those injured as a result of a prenatal occurrence but do not reach court until after the plaintiff's maturity. In those circumstances, there is no reason why a claim should not be made for loss of income during any 'lost years'.

C. Claims by Living Children for 'Wrongful Life'

1. 'Wrongful Life' Claims at Common Law

(i) The 'Wrongful Life' Claim

12.59   In *McKay v Essex AHA*,[122] the Court of Appeal considered claims arising from the birth of a child born disabled as a result of an infection of rubella suffered by the

---

[118] N 71 above, para 100.
[119] See paras 12.76–12.79 below.
[120] Administration of Justice Act 1972, s 1.
[121] *Housecroft v Burnett* [1986] 1 All ER 332, 345. See also *Croke v Wiseman* [1982] 1 WLR 71, [1981] 3 All ER 853.
[122] [1982] QB 1166.

mother during pregnancy. One claim brought by the child was that, but for the negligence of the defendants in managing the pregnancy, the mother would have had a lawful abortion and the child would not, as the Statement of Claim alleged, have 'suffered . . . entry into a life in which her injuries are highly debilitating, and distress and loss and damage'.[123] It was clear that the injuries resulted not from the negligence but from untreated rubella. The claim by the child was therefore analysed as one for negligently allowing her to be born alive in an injured condition: a claim now traditionally described as one for 'wrongful life'.

(ii) Objections to a 'Wrongful Life' Claim

That claim was struck out, essentially on three grounds: first, that it was contrary **12.60** to public policy as being inconsistent with the concept of the sanctity of human life; second, that despite the possible legality of an abortion a doctor was under no obligation to the child to give the mother an opportunity to terminate its life; and third, that as a court could not evaluate non-existence it could not award damages for life, ie for the denial of non-existence. These three arguments require separate discussion.

(iii) Public Policy and the Sanctity of Life

The argument that public policy should not permit a claim for 'wrongful life' re- **12.61** quires some care in its deployment. First, while such policy in general may support life actually in existence, it cannot apply in a case in which an abortion is lawful under the Abortion Act 1967, for in such a case the termination has in effect been approved by Parliament as being consistent with the public interest. Second, the argument cannot be applied to bar claims for 'wrongful life' arising out of pre-conception events such as negligently performed sterilisation or vasectomy or negligently given contraceptive advice or indeed rape, as a result of which the child is in fact conceived. For public policy actively supports the provision of contraceptive services and advice, and condemns rape as a crime. Therefore, generalised appeals to 'the sanctity of life' are of doubtful weight in countering 'wrongful life' claims.

(iv) The Nature of the Doctor's Duty

The second objection to 'wrongful life' claims is more formidable. It is that there **12.62** is an insuperable problem in establishing a duty to a child to bring about, or help to bring about, its non-existence. The legality of contraceptive services or abortion does not imply an obligation on a doctor to provide such services or perform an abortion: and it is difficult to impose on a doctor in this context a duty to do

---

[123] ibid, 1174.

more than advise the parent or parents. On what basis could such a duty be owed to the child? No duty can be owed to the hypothetically non-existent, so any duty would have to be owed to the child in fact born in some way to facilitate his non-existence. But tort law is concerned with defendants who make claimants worse, not with those who merely make claimants exist. Unless existence is to be defined as an injury to the person who exists, or some other damage can be identified, nothing can be identified as the injury to be avoided by reasonable care.

(v) Identifying Damage and Quantifying Damages

12.63   In *McKay* the Court was unable to quantify damages, and therefore unable to identify compensatable damage. It was argued,[124] by analogy with cases in which damages were assessed for loss of expectation of life, that difficulties in computation should not bar the claim. The argument was rejected. Stephenson LJ[125] said:

> [I]n measuring the loss caused by shortened life the courts are dealing with a thing, human life, of which they have some experience; here the court is being asked to deal with the consequences of death for the dead, a thing of which it has none. To measure loss of expectation of death would require a value judgment where a crucial factor lies altogether outside the range of human knowledge.

To the same effect Ackner LJ[126] said:

> [H]ow can a court begin to evaluate non-existence, 'the undiscovered country from whose bourne no traveller returns?' No comparison is possible and therefore no damage can be established which a court can recognise. This goes to the root of the whole cause of action.

The objection is, and will remain, formidable.

(vi) American Authorities

12.64   A number of American cases were considered in *McKay*, and some of the thinking is illustrated by three of them. In *Gleitman v Cosgrove*[127] the Supreme Court of New Jersey by a majority rejected a claim by a child born disabled as a result of intra-uterine rubella on the grounds that the action did not give rise to damages cognisable in law, in that a child could not complain that it would have been better off not being born.

12.65   However, a different approach was taken in *Curlender v Bio-Science Laboratories*.[128] There the Californian Court of Appeal considered a case in which it was alleged that, as a result of negligently conducted genetic tests, a child was born suffering

---

[124] [1982] QB 1166, 1170.
[125] ibid, 1181–2.
[126] ibid, 1189.
[127] 49 NJ 22, 227 A 2d 689 (1967).
[128] (1980) 165 Cal Rptr 477 (Cal CA).

from Tay-Sachs disease, which was defined as 'amaurotic familial idiocy'. The court, accepting that the real crux of the problem was whether the breach of duty was the proximate cause of an injury cognisable at law, was able to identify as such an injury not the physical defect (for which the defendant was not responsible) nor the birth alone, but the composite concept of 'the birth of the plaintiff with such defect'. It therefore ruled that damages could be quantified for: 'the pain and suffering to be endured during the limited lifespan available to such a child and any special pecuniary loss resulting from the impaired condition.'[129]

This development was curtailed by the Supreme Court of California in *Turpin v Sortini*.[130] There, the Court considered the claim by a child Joy that clinicians had been negligent in failing to advise her parents that the deafness of an elder sister Hope was hereditary. The claim was for 'general damages for being deprived of the fundamental right of a child to be born as a whole, functional human being without total deafness',[131] and special damages were also claimed for expenses necessary to treat the hereditary illness. Unlike the *Curlender* court, that in *Turpin* rejected the claim for general damages. Taking into account the benefits of life itself as well as the detriment of the affliction, it ruled: **12.66**

> [B]ecause of the incalculable nature of both elements of this harm–benefit equation, we believe that a reasoned, non arbitrary award of general damage is simply not obtainable.[132]

Special damages were however allowed for the extraordinary expenses of specialized teaching, training, and hearing equipment as there was no benefit or amenity enjoyed by the plaintiff which could fairly be set off against these requirements.

It has been persuasively argued[133] that English courts could follow *Turpin*, as has been done in two other American jurisdictions.[134] It can be said that quantifiable and foreseeable loss occurs as a function of a defect which becomes apparent on birth which itself was caused by negligence. The difficulty here is that, as the defect was not caused by the defendants, and as birth is not an injury to the one who is born,[135] the harm recognisable in law or 'damage' necessary to constitute the tort of negligence must be economic loss alone.   **12.67**

---

[129] ibid, 489.
[130] (1982) 643 P 2d 954 (Sup Ct Cal).
[131] ibid, 956.
[132] ibid, 964.
[133] See Kennedy, I and Grubb, A, *Medical Law* (n 1 above), 1542–7. For a critique of the rule in *McKay*, see Morris, A and Saintier, S, 'To Be or Not to Be: Is That the Question? Wrongful Life and Misconceptions' (2003) 11 Med L Rev 167.
[134] See *Harbeson v Parke-Davis Inc* (1983) 656 P 2d 483 (Wash Sup Ct); *Procanite v Cillo* (1984) 478 A 2d 755 (NJ Sup Ct).
[135] See *P's Curator Bonis v Criminal Injuries Compensation Board* 1997 SLT 1180, 1189 (OH) in which Lord Osborne said that congenital disabilities could not be regarded as injuries because there was no 'pre-injury state which is capable of assesment and comparison with the post-injury state'. But see paras 12.85–12.89 below: unwanted birth may be an injury to the parents.

12.68 It has to be conceded that there is an element of artificiality in compensating for the economic consequences of a non-compensatable defect. There would be social justice in it, because the multiplier used to calculate such a claim would be based only on the child's expectation of life, rather than (as in the case of a parent's 'wrongful birth[136] claim for caring for a disabled child) on the period for which a parent would be expected to survive and provide care. It is, however, to be expected that general 'policy' considerations such as led the Law Commission to recommend[137] the exclusion of 'wrongful life' claims from statutory remedy, however arguable, will prevail and with them the authority of *McKay*.

(vii) Disadvantaged Life

12.69 In *Zepeda v Zepeda*,[138] an illegitimate child sued his father for conferring on him the status of illegitimacy by fraudulently inducing his mother to have sexual relations with a promise of marriage when he was already married. In *Williams v State of New York*[139] a child, conceived as a result of the rape of the mother when she was a patient in a state mental hospital, asserted that the conception resulted from negligence in the hospital and that in consequence she was: 'deprived of property rights; deprived of a normal childhood and home life; deprived of proper parental care, support and rearing; caused to bear the status of illegitimacy.' In *Stills v Gratton*,[140] a child alleged that, as a result of a negligently performed abortion, he was born out of wedlock and 'various reasons' affected him to his detriment.

12.70 All these imaginative claims failed. The courts have refused to recognise the social incidents of existence itself, however depressing, as 'injury' for the purposes of the law of negligence. Moreover, not surprisingly there has been a strong policy element in their approach:

> It is not the suits of illegitimates which give us concern, great in numbers as these may be. What does disturb us is the nature of the new action and the related suits which would be encouraged. Encouragement would extend to all others born into the world under conditions which they might regard as adverse. One might seek damages for being born of a certain colour, another because of race; one for being born with a hereditary disease, another for inheriting unfortunate family circumstances; one for being born into a large and destitute family, another because a parent has an unsavoury reputation.[141]

It can be said with confidence that no such claim will be allowed in England.

---

[136] See paras 12.113–12.114 below.
[137] Report (n 71 above), para 89.
[138] (1963) 190 NE 2d 849 (Ill CA).
[139] (1966) 223 NE 2d 343 (NYCA).
[140] (1976) 127 Cal Rptr 652 (Cal CA).
[141] *Zepeda v Zepeda*, (n 136 above), 858, *per* Dempsey PJ. See also *Cowe v Forum Group Inc* (1991) 575 NE 2d 630 (Sup Ct Indiana), a claim for 'wrongful life' base on rape of plaintiff's intellectually disabled mother and commentary, Grubb (1993) 1 Med L Rev 261.

(viii) Events which cause Injury and Birth

So far we have considered cases at common law where prenatal occurrences cause **12.71**
injury (in which damages claims by children may lie) and where they cause birth
(where *McKay* effectively prevents such claims). Situations may, however, arise,
particularly in a preconception context, in which an occurrence can cause both
the injury and the birth. The Law Commission[142] gave the examples of the negligent supply of damaged sperm for artificial insemination or of a contraceptive pill
which might prove both ineffective and damaging to the child consequently born
because of its ineffectiveness. More dramatically, under the heading 'wrongful life'
it asks the following question: 'if a man suffering from syphilis has intercourse
with a woman without telling her that he is infected, would the child resulting
from the assault have a cause of action against him?' There is justice in the view
that in such a case there should be compensation, not for the fact of being born
but for the disability itself. A further example might be the over-prescription of a
fertility drug, leading to a multiple pregnancy which, by reason of its multiplicity,
resulted in births so premature that the children suffered the disabilities associated
with premature birth. In such a case the drug will have caused both life and injury.

In this context *Cherry (Guardian ad litem of) v Borsman*[143] is instructive. the de- **12.72**
fendant attempted an abortion, but negligently failed and in so doing injured the
foetus. The child subsequently born sued not for wrongful life but for injuries sustained in the procedure. Before trial the surgeon admitted liability to the mother
in failing to conclude that the operation had failed and thus allow her to have a
second operation to terminate the pregnancy. The child's claim went to trial. On
behalf of the surgeon it was argued that he owed no duty to protect the foetus because that was inconsistent with the duty to the mother to terminate. However,
the court said:

> a surgeon on performing an abortion in a case such as this owes a duty of care to the
> mother to perform his task properly but at the same time owes a duty of care to the
> fetus not to harm it if he should fail in meeting the duty of care he owes to the
> mother . . . it is significant that the infant plaintiff relies on the injuries she alleges
> she suffered in the . . . abortion. No reliance is placed by the infant plaintiff on the
> defendant's failure to realise the abortion had failed. The duty of care in that respect,
> say the plaintiffs, is a duty to the mother and the mother only. That, say the plain-
> tiffs, is why it is not a wrongful life case. We agree with that analysis.

What the language of the judgment does not make clear, but what is plain from
the facts, is that the court allowed the claim for injuries which resulted from the
very procedure which, because it was negligently performed, permitted the pregnancy to continue and the infant plaintiff to be born.

---

[142] *Report* (n 71 above), paras 7 and 88.
[143] (1992) 99 DLR (4th) 487 (BCCA).

12.73   A comparable problem has however been considered, and the opposite conclusion arrived at, by the Supreme Judicial Court of Massachusetts in *Payton v Abbott Labs et al*.[144] The plaintiffs were women whose mothers had ingested during pregnancy the drug diethylstilbetrol (DES) which was manufactured by the defendants and designed to prevent them miscarrying, but which could cause abnormalities in their daughters. Thus, the one drug could be responsible both for giving life and for causing injury to the 'DES daughters'. The claims, however, were not for 'wrongful life' but only for injury. The allegation was that the defendants were negligent in marketing without adequate testing or warnings. One question was put:

> [I]f the trier of fact concludes that a plaintiff would probably not have been born except for the mother's ingestion of DES, is that plaintiff barred from recovery because of physical or emotional damage suffered as a result of the mother's ingestion of DES?[145]

The plaintiffs contended that, just as rescuers have a duty to exercise reasonable care in their efforts to save or protect the lives of others, so by analogy the defendants as manufacturers of a drug designed to preserve life were under a duty to exercise reasonable care in connection with their drug. It was however pointed out that the analogy was not exact, because whereas in a 'rescue' case the plaintiff might be better off if no attempt had been made to save her than if an attempt had been made negligently, in a DES case she would simply not have been born but for the drug, and just could not say that in those circumstances she would have been better off than if born, albeit injured, as a result of its use by the mother. In those circumstances the claims were rejected as if they had been claims for wrongful life, the court concluding:

> the provider of the probable means of the plaintiff's very existence should not be liable for unavoidable, collateral consequences of the use of that means.[146]

12.74   It is suggested that this conclusion is not wholly satisfactory, certainly as an authority for the proposition that a plaintiff can never sue for injury caused by an occurrence which gave him life. First, it is not in every case that the collateral injurious consequences are 'unavoidable': might it not be open to a drug manufacturer to eliminate the dangerous side-effects from some life-giving drugs? Second, and more generally, it hardly lies in the mouth of one who has caused a disability to say that it is non-compensatable because he has also caused the life which bears the disability.[147] To allow such an argument would be to permit such

---

[144] (1982) NE 2d 171 (Sup Ct Jud Mass).

[145] ibid, 181.

[146] ibid, 182.

[147] See the remarks of Lord Osborne in *P's Curator Bonis v Criminal Injuries Compensation Board* (n 135 above), 1200. Considering a child born as a result of incestuous rape with disabilities due to consanguinity he said, obiter, 'I consider that (a jury) would accept that the birth of the child and its disabilities were both directly attributable to the same criminal act.'

a defendant to rely on the child's very existence to defeat a claim. It is suggested that since, as we have seen, the courts prevent a plaintiff from relying on that existence to raise a 'wrongful life' claim, they should also in fairness prevent a defendant from seeking to rely upon it to defeat a claim for injury.

To be distinguished from such occurrences, each of which may have the double effect of causing both life and injury, is the case of a set of circumstances one of which causes injury and another of which causes life. Let us suppose that a gynaecologist negligently damages a foetus, and then goes on negligently to fail to warn the parents of what has happened with the result that they are deprived of the opportunity, which would have been accepted, of a lawful abortion: in the result the child is born disabled. It is suggested that in such a case the child would succeed in an action against the gynaecologist by arguing that the dominant event was the intra-uterine injury, and that the gynaecologist could not escape liability for the consequences of that act by relying on a further act of negligence, saying that if he had been more careful the plaintiff would never have been born, and that the action was really only one for 'wrongful life'. **12.75**

2. 'Wrongful Life' Claims Under the Congenital Disabilities (Civil Liability) Act 1976

(i) The Intention of the Statute

The view of the Law Commission,[148] that no claim should lie by statute by 'wrongful life', was influenced by such reasoning as the following: **12.76**

> [S]uch a cause of action, if it existed, could place an almost intolerable burden on medical advisers in their socially and morally exacting role. The danger that doctors would be under subconscious pressures to advise abortions in doubtful cases through fear of an action for damages is, we think, a real one.

It was therefore the clear intention of the legislature that the Congenital Disabilities (Civil Liability) Act 1976 should allow no such cause of action. It attempted to achieve this result by s 1(2) which provides:

> [A]n occurrence to which this section applies is one which–
> (a) affected either parent of the child in his or her ability to have a normal, healthy child; or
> (b) affected the mother during her pregnancy, or affected her or the child in the course of its birth, so that the child is born with disabilities which would not otherwise have been present.

In *McKay*[149] Stephenson LJ and Ackner LJ interpreted s 1(2)(b) as being worded so as:

---

[148] *Report* (n 71 above), para 89.
[149] [1982] QB 1166, 1178 and 1186–7.

to import the assumption that, but for the occurrence giving rise to a disabled birth, the child would have been born normal and healthy, not that it would not have been born at all.

They thus concluded that the Act excluded claims by children for 'wrongful life', and Griffiths LJ agreed.[150]

(ii) Academic Support for 'Wrongful Life' Claims

12.77   It is, however, to be noted that academic writers have raised three reasons for doubting this conclusion. First, it has been suggested by Jane Fortin[151] that the Act does not really abolish any common law right of action for 'wrongful life'. The argument is as follows. Section 4(5) of the Act provides:

> [T]his Act applies in respect of births after (but not before) its passing, and in respect of any such birth it replaces any law in force before its passing, whereby a person could be liable to a child in respect of disabilities with which it might be born.

A 'wrongful life' action is not, so the argument runs, an action 'in respect of disabilities', but rather in respect of life itself: therefore, s 4(5) leaves intact any pre-existing common law right to sue for 'wrongful life'. It has, however, to be said that, even if the English courts could be persuaded that such actions could be brought at common law, which is doubtful, they would probably hesitate long before allowing such an interpretation and bypassing the intention of the statute so as to permit a 'wrongful life' claim by a disabled child. In any event the phrase 'in respect of' is extremely wide. Thus in *Paterson v Chadwick*[152] the phrase 'a claim in respect of personal injuries' was held to include a claim against a solicitor for permitting a medical negligence action to become statute-barred, on the ground that the nature and extent of the plaintiff's personal injuries formed an essential ingredient in the proof of the claim. It is true that *Paterson* was distinguished in *Ackbar v CF Green and Co Ltd*[153] and its principle disapproved, obiter, in *Howe v David Brown Tractors (Retail) Ltd*[154] by Nicholls LJ who said that in such a claim:

> the damages claimed do not consist of or include damages in respect of personal injuries. The damages claimed comprise damages in respect of the solicitor's failure to issue a writ in time.[155]

However, in the *Howe* case the Court held that a firm's claim for financial loss arising from an injury to one of its partners was 'in respect of personal injuries', on the grounds that the same facts gave rise both to the firm's claim and to the partner's

---

[150]   ibid, 1191.
[151]   See Fortin, J E S (1987) (n 1 above).
[152]   [1974] 1 WLR 890.
[153]   [1975] QB 582.
[154]   [1991] 4 All ER 30.
[155]   ibid, 42.

claim for personal injury. It is suggested that, by parity of reasoning, the courts would probably proceed on the basis that, as both the child's life and 'the disabilities with which it might be born' came into existence simultaneously at the moment of birth, it would be artificial to separate the two concepts: that therefore a 'wrongful life' claim by a child born disabled was 'in respect of disabilities', and was therefore excluded by s 4(5).

12.78 Second, it has been pointed out by Kennedy and Grubb[156] that the *McKay* dicta cited above referred to s 1(2)(b), and not to s 1(2)(a), of the 1976 Act. It is suggested that negligence in a pre-conception context, for example in the course of genetic counselling, could amount to an occurrence which affected the parents' opportunity to have a normal healthy child, and therefore his or her 'ability' so to do within the meaning of s 1(2)(a). To give a concrete example: let us assume that a doctor has negligently advised a mother that conception after the age of 45 created no greater risk of Down's Syndrome than conception after the age of 35: that as a result the mother started her family ten years later than she would otherwise have done; that a child is born with Down's Syndrome, and that he or she is able to demonstrate that that syndrome was a function of the delayed conception. There is an argument of reasonable strength that the child was, to summarise s 1 of the Act: 'born disabled as the result of . . . an occurrence . . . which . . . affected [the mother] of the child in . . . her ability to have a normal healthy child.' Under s 1(1): 'the child's disabilities are to be regarded as damage resulting from the wrongful act of that person and actionable accordingly at the suit of the child'. By this reasoning the statute would in fact give the child a remedy in such circumstances, whatever was its intended policy. And indeed there would be some justice in this conclusion, for damages could be computed by reference to the life of the child and not (as in a 'wrongful birth' claim)[157] by reference to the, frequently shorter, life of the caring parent.

12.79 Third, Kennedy and Grubb[158] also draw attention to s 1A of the 1976 Act, which allows a child to claim for negligence in the course of infertility treatment. They point to the fact that the section covers negligence in the 'selection' of the embryo that becomes the child. From this they go on to reason that since (but for the negligence) some other embryo would have been selected and the child claimant himself would never have been born, therefore the claim can truly be classified as one for 'wrongful life'. It is, however, suggested that the courts may approach the section more cautiously. Section 1A provides:

---

[156] *Medical Law,* (n 1 above), 1551–2.
[157] See paras 12.113–12.114 below.
[158] *Medical Law* (n 1 above). 1552.

[I]n any case where–

(a) a child carried by a woman as the result of the placing in her of an embryo or of sperm and eggs or her artificial insemination is born disabled,

(b) the disability results from an act or omission in the course of the selection, or the keeping or use outside the body, of the embryo carried by her or of the gametes used to bring about the creation of the embryo, and

(c) a person is under this section answerable to the child in respect of the act or omission,

the child's disabilities are to be disregarded as damage resulting from the wrongful act of that person and actionable accordingly at the suit of the child.

There is at least a risk that the courts would interpret the whole phrase 'in the course of the selection' so as to restrict claims to those based on acts or omissions during the selection process, rather than on the very act of choice. If they did not, they would have no alternative but to quantify the difference between the condition of the disabled claimant as it was in fact on the one hand and his non-existence on the other hand, a process from which they will continue to shrink. The alternative, to compare the claimant's disabled state with that of a healthy but hypothetical child who might otherwise have been born had the selection process been different, is an even less realistic exercise.

D. Claims by Parents of Children Born Alive

1. Claims by Parents for Wrongful Conception or Birth

(i) Introduction

12.80 Claims by the family of unwanted children born alive are, for reasons to be discussed, available only to the father or the mother and not to siblings or more remote relations. To distinguish them from 'wrongful life' claims, that is those which (if permitted) would be brought by the children themselves, they are usually categorised as claims for 'wrongful conception' or 'wrongful birth'.

(ii) Factual Contexts

12.81 Such claims may arise in various factual contexts, all of which are medical in nature. Where the patient undergoes an operation designed to prevent conception, there may be negligence in pre-operative counselling (eg a failure to warn of the risk of recanalisation of the vas), in the operation itself (eg if the doctor ligates a ligament during an operation for female sterilisation rather than a fallopian tube), in post-operative testing (eg a failure to carry out sperm tests properly after vasectomy), or in post-operative counselling (eg if there is a failure to warn of the need to use contraceptives until sperm tests after vasectomy have proved negative).[159]

---

[159] See Mullis, A, 'Wrongful Conception Unravelled' (n 1 above).

Claims may also be brought if a child is born after an attempt at an abortion has failed.[160] There may also be negligence quite outside the context of an operation, for example in failing to give appropriate contraceptive advice to a young person who needs or requires it, to screen for genetic abnormalities, to warn of the risk to a foetus from maternal rubella or chickenpox or to conduct appropriate tests of foetal health during pregnancy.

(iii) Terminology

There is, however, some variation in the terminology. Some commentators[161] have used the term 'wrongful pregnancy' or 'wrongful conception' to denote claims by parents where a child subsequently born is healthy, confining the term 'wrongful birth' to cases where the child is not only unwanted but born with a disability. The distinction between these two categories of claim, however, is not based on any difference in the legal bases for the claims, but only on different factual bases for quantifying damages. An alternative approach would be, for example, to define 'wrongful conception' claims as those where the wrong consists in responsibility for an unwanted conception, and 'wrongful birth' claims as being those where the fault lies in permitting a pregnancy to continue to birth. This distinction now has the authority in England and Wales of the Court of Appeal in *Parkinson v St James and University Hospital NHS Trust*[162] and in *Groom v Selby*.[163] The approach to compensation appears however to be the same in each case.

12.82

(iv) Problems in 'Wrongful Conception' and 'Wrongful Birth' Claims

The problems may be illustrated in this way. Where an operation is carried out, it may be conducted negligently in a way which causes injury to the patient other than the physiological consequence which the operation was designed to procure. An example already given is of a ligament being damaged by mistake in the course of an ineffective sterilisation. If an unwanted child is born as a result, the true claim by the mother is not just for a damaged ligament (which is clearly a personal injury) but for an unwanted pregnancy, labour, and child and their financial consequences. The legal problem becomes more acute when the operation has produced no unwanted injury but only the desired result, for example a successful vasectomy, yet a child is born because the father was not warned to use contraceptives until sperm tests proved negative. Here, the doctor's patient was the father,

12.83

---

[160] See *Scuriaga v Powell* [1979] 123 SJ 406, aff'd, [1980] CA Transcript 597.

[161] See Kennedy, I and Grubb, A (n 156 above), 1553, 1586. See also Rogers, WVH, Teff, H and Sarno, GG, (n 1 above) for different terminologies and Mason, JK, 'Wrongful Pregnancy, Wrongful Birth and Wrongful Terminology' (2002) 6 Edinburgh L Rev 46.

[162] [2001] EWCA Civ 530, [2002] QB 266, [2001] 3 All ER 97. For a discussion see Grubb (2002) 10 Med L Rev 78.

[163] [2001] EWCA Civ 1522, [2002] Lloyd's Rep Med 1 at [18] *per* Brooke LJ.

whose body was given the treatment he required, no more no less, and whose only injury may be to his pocket. The only person who was physically affected was the mother, who was not the doctor's patient, who was not operated upon, who received no misleading advice, and whose only complaint may be that she has had a baby which she will doubtless come to love and which may result in no financial loss to her but only redistribution of family income, all of which is provided by the father.

12.84   Thus 'wrongful conception' and 'wrongful birth' actions raise at least six questions.

(i)   are pregnancy and birth to be considered 'personal injuries'?
(ii) in what circumstances can the cost of bringing up an unwanted child be recovered?
(iii) what is the application of the Limitation Act 1980?
(iv) what is the nature of a doctor's duty, and to whom is it owed?
(v)   what is the effect of a mother's refusal to terminate an unwanted pregnancy?
(vi) how are damages for 'wrongful conception' or 'wrongful birth' to be quantified?

(a) Pregnancy and Birth as Personal Injury

12.85   Whether or not pregnancy and birth can be treated as 'personal injury' is a question with double significance. First, it is easier to justify an award for 'pain, suffering and loss of amenity' caused by pregnancy and birth if they can be so treated. Second, unless the 'wrongful birth' claim is one where the damages claimed for negligence, nuisance, or breach of duty consist of or include damages in respect of personal injuries to the plaintiff or any other person,[164] the limitation period will be six years and not the three year period appropriate[165] to personal injury cases.

12.86   The phrase 'personal injury' has been defined by s 38 of the Limitation Act 1980 'personal injuries' includes any disease and any impairment of a person's physical or mental condition, and 'injury' and cognate expressions shall be construed accordingly'.[166] Pregnancy and birth, as elements in the natural process of reproduction, are not self-evidently injuries. However, in *Allen v Bloomsbury HA*[167] Brooke J considered a claim by a mother who was negligently deprived of the opportunity to have a pregnancy terminated:

> for the discomfort and pain associated with the continuation of her pregnancy and the delivery of her child [as] a claim for damages for personal injuries . . . comparable to,

---

[164]   Limitation Act 1980, s 11(1): see s 14 for 'date of knowledge'.
[165]   Subject to extension under s 28 in the case of disability and discretionary exclusion under s 33.
[166]   See also CPR 2.3(i) for a similar definition.
[167]   [1993] 1 All ER 651.

though different from, a claim for damages for personal injuries resulting from the infliction of a traumatic injury.[168]

The question was fully considered by the Court of Appeal in *Walkin v South Manchester HA*,[169] where a mother who had given birth following a failed sterilisation tried to avoid the three year limitation period under section 11 of the Limitation Act 1980 by bringing an action only in respect of financial loss. It was held that 'failure of the attempt to sterilise the plaintiff was not of itself a personal injury. It did her no harm; it left her as before'.[170] Equally, it was held that the birth itself was not the injury,[171] but in the event, the court decided that the conception was a personal injury because it was unwanted, and because the consequent physical change in the plaintiff's body was in effect an 'impairment' of her physical condition. There is academic support for this view.[172] The reasoning is that an unwanted pregnancy can very readily be viewed as such an impairment because it 'involves an element of danger, certain discomfort and possibly severe disruption of the woman's employment and pattern of life'.[173]

The question has more recently been variously addressed by the House of Lords **12.87** in *McFarlane v Tayside Health Board*.[174] That case was concerned with wrongful conception resulting from failed vasectomy. Lord Slynn[175] said that as the conception and childbirth were unwanted and known to be so by the health board it was unnecessary to consider whether there was a personal injury. Lord Steyn[176] held that they were a personal injury: Lord Hope[177] that the claim was 'analogous to that which may be made by a pursuer in the case of personal injury', and Lord Clyde[178] that they were 'a clear example of pain and suffering such as could qualify as a potential head of damages'. Lord Millett, however, would have rejected the claim as formulated, but allowed both parents a conventional sum for infringement of their freedom to limit the size of their family.[179] Despite the variety of

---

[168] ibid, 657–8.
[169] [1995] 1 WLR 1543, 4 All ER 132. For a full discussion see (1996) 4 Med L Rev 94. See also para 12.98 below.
[170] ibid, 1550, 139 *per* Auld LJ.
[171] ibid, 1554, 144 *per* Neill LJ.
[172] See Mullis, A (n 159 above), 324–5.
[173] See Rogers, WVH, (n 1 above), 310.
[174] [2002] 2 AC 59: [1999] 4 All ER 961. For academic discussions of this controversial case see Thomson, J, 'Abandoning the Law of Delict?' 2000 SLT (News) 43; Weir, A, 'The Unwanted Child' (2000) CLJ 238;: Norrie, K McK, 'Failed Sterilisation and Economic Loss: Justice Law and Policy in McFarlane v Tayside Health Board' (2000) 16 PN 76; Jones, MA, 'Bringing up Baby', (2001) Tort L Rev 14; Hoyano, LCH, 'Misconception about Wrongful Conception' (2002) MLR 883; Whitfield, A, 'The fallout from McFarlane' (2002) 18 PN 234.
[175] ibid, 74C, 970 d–e.
[176] ibid, 81G, 977 a–b.
[177] ibid, 86C, 981 a.
[178] ibid, 102H, 995 j.
[179] ibid, 114D–E, 1006 d–e. This solution was subsequently adopted by the majority of the House of Lords in *Rees v Darlington Memorial Hospital NHS Trust* [2003] UKHL 52, [2003] 3 WLR 1091; the conventional sum was fixed at £15,000.

approaches, however, it may be possible to conclude that the majority of the House has not overruled *Walkin* on this point.

12.88 Yet the *Walkin* case leaves certain problems unresolved. First, failure in itself of an attempt to sterilise (such as might result, as in that case, from the failure of diathermy to seal the fallopian tubes) may not of itself be an injury, yet it may be the case that sterilisation does not take place because the surgeon inflicts an injury instead, for example by operating not on the tube but on a ligament. If that occurred it would be for consideration whether, following *Walkin*, there would be two injuries, one consisting in the damage to the ligament and the other consisting of the unwanted conception, occurring at different times. Second, the identification of conception as an injury in any one case depends upon whether or not the mother wanted to conceive. This presents the conceptual difficulty of the claimant's right to damages being dependent not upon the defendant's acts but upon the claimant's attitude to the defendant's act. It also presents some practical problems. What should the just solution be if at the time of conception the woman would not wish it, but has changed her mind and wants to become pregnant by the time that she finds out? Roch LJ in *Walkin* identified a further problem:

> I have some difficulty in perceiving a normal conception, pregnancy and the birth of a healthy child as 'any disease or any impairment of a person's physical or mental condition' in cases where the only reasons for the pregnancy and subsequent birth being unwanted are financial.[180]

In such a circumstance it is not the pregnancy which is unwanted but the financial difficulties. The tendency to restrict 'wrongful birth' claims was further illustrated in *R v Croydon AHA*.[181] In that case the Court of Appeal considered a claim by a woman who wanted and indeed had a healthy child, but would not have done so had a radiologist, who misinterpreted an x-ray taken in the course of a pre-employment health check, picked up an abnormality which would have indicated that pregnancy and birth would place her own health at risk. A breach of duty had been conceded. However, the Court of Appeal held that:

> when the mother wants both the pregnancy and a healthy child there is simply no loss which can give rise to a claim in damages in respect of either of the normal expenses and of trauma of pregnancy or the cost of bringing up the child.

It further held that the plaintiff's family life fell outside the scope of the conceded duty and accordingly confined her claim to damages for injury to her own health.

12.89 Third, if the claim against a doctor was for failure to diagnose an unwanted pregnancy in time for termination, then the *Walkin* definition of injury could hardly

---

[180] [1995] 1 WLR 1543, 1553; 4 All ER 132, 142.
[181] [1998] Lloyd's Rep Med 44.

apply: if it did then the injury (unwanted pregnancy) would pre-date the breach of duty (failure to diagnose). In such a case the injury would have to be the unwanted continuation of pregnancy. Fourth, let us suppose that the pregnancy is wanted, but that there is a failure to diagnose a possible foetal abnormality in time for termination. Again, the *Walkin* definition of the injury could hardly apply, because the pregnancy was wanted. The injury would presumably be either the continuation of the pregnancy after the time when it should have been diagnosed and would have been terminated, or the birth itself. Fifth, if the criterion for conception amounting to an injury is that it is unwanted by the woman, then a woman who wants a child but has one by a man who does not but becomes a reluctant father only because his vasectomy has, through negligence, failed, would have no personal injury claim herself. Nor would the man, the failure would have left him as before.[182] His claim, if any, would be for economic loss.[183]

(b) Claims for the Cost of Bringing Up an Unwanted Child

In *McFarlane v Tayside Health Board*[184] the unwanted child was born healthy, and the House of Lords, for a number of reasons, rejected a claim for the costs of bringing her up. The reasons have subsequently been analysed and discussed in a number of cases, notably by Brooke LJ in *Parkinson*.[185]   **12.90**

All their Lordships approaches the case on the basis that the claim for upbringing costs was for 'economic loss or "pure economic loss" '.[186] This second description is not self-evidently correct. There is force in the approach of Hale LJ in *Parkinson*, and in *Groom v Selby*[187] and in the majority speeches in *Rees v Darlington Memorial Hospital NHS Trust*[188] that the real detriment is the unwanted imposition of responsibility to bring up a child, and that the obligation to pay is simply a consequence of that wrong.   **12.91**

Lord Slynn concluded that the doctor had not assumed responsibility for such loss.[189] He stated: **12.92**

> if a client wants to be able to recover such costs he or she must do so by an appropriate contract.

---

[182] *Naylor v Preston AHA* [1987] 1 WLR 938, 971, *per* Sir John Donaldson MR, cited in *Walkin* at 1550 *per* Auld LJ.

[183] *per* Roch LJ in *Walkin* (n 169 above), 1553, 142.

[184] N 174 above. Such a claim was allowed by the majority of the High Court of Australia in *Cattanach v Melchior* [2003] HCA 38, but *McFarlane* was affirmed by the House of Lords in *Rees v Darlington Memorial Hospital NHS Trust* (n 179 above). However the effect of *Cattanach* in New South Wales is being reversed: see Civil Liability Amendment Act 2003.

[185] N 162 above.

[186] N 174 above: see Lord Slynn, 75F-G, 971g; Lord Steyn, 79F, 975b; Lord Hope, 89D-E, 983h; Lord Clyde, 105G, 988e; Lord Millett, 109A: 1001c.

[187] N 163 above, at [31].

[188] N 179 above, at [21].

[189] N 174 above at 76C-D, 972c.

This approach was somewhat unexpected. In *Hedley Byrne & Co Ltd v Heller & Partners Ltd*[190] Lord Devlin had castigated the suggestion that pure financial loss caused by medical negligence could be claimed only in contract but not in tort as:

> nonsense. It is not the sort of nonsense that can arise even in the best system of law out of the need to draw nice distinctions between borderline cases. It arises, if it is the law, simply out of a refusal to make sense.

What matters, it is suggested, is whether responsibility has been assumed for professional services.[191]

12.93 Other members of the House of Lords approached the problem more broadly. Lord Steyn, relying on the principle of distributive justice,[192] held that the claim for upbringing costs did not satisfy the requirement of being fair, just and reasonable. Lord Hope reached a similar conclusion. Lord Clyde held that the relief of financial obligation went beyond what should constitute reasonable restitution for the wrong done and that the potential expense was disproportionate to the doctor's culpability. Lord Millett simply concluded that the birth of a healthy child was a blessing, not a detriment.[193] As Robert Walker LJ said in *Rees v Darlington Memorial Hospital NHS Trust*,[194] 'there is a strong moral element in the basis of the decision'. The majority of the House of Lords had clearly recognised that on normal principles the claim would be allowable but

> at the heart of it all is the feeling that to compensate for the financial costs of bringing up a healthy child is a step too far.[195]

12.94 *McFarlane* left open the question of whether the costs of bringing up a disabled child are recoverable. Initially, a series of first instance decisions decided that they were.[196] The matter has now, subject to any future decision of the House of Lords, been put beyond doubt by the Court of Appeal in *Parkinson v St James & Seacroft*

---

[190] [1964] AC 465 at 517.

[191] See *X & Y v Pal* [1992] 3 Med LR 195 at 206 *per* Clarke JA: *White v Jones* [1995] 2 AC 207 at 273 G-H *per* Lord Browne-Wilkinson: *Henderson v Merrett Syndicates Limited* [1995] 2 AC 146 at 181C-G *per* Lord Goff: *Williams v National Health Foods Limited* [1998] 1 WLR 830 at 834 F *per* Lord Steyn.

[192] See *White v Chief Constable of South Yorkshire Police* [1999] 2 AC 455. Originally this principle had nothing to do with compensation for wrongdoing, but was concerned with the distribution of honours or money among members of society in proportion to their merits as assessed by the standards of that society: Aristotle, *Nicomachean Ethics*, V, 2–3. For a discussion of this principle see Mullender, R, 'Corrective justice, distributive justice and the law of negligence' (2001) 17 PN 35.

[193] For these respective views see n 174 above at 83 D-E, 978 f-g; 97 C-D, 990j; 105 F-H, 998 d-h; 114A, 1005g.

[194] [2002] EWCA Civ 88; [2002] 2 All ER 177 at [29].

[195] Per Hale LJ in *Parkinson*, n 162 above, at [87].

[196] *Taylor v Shropshire HA* [2000] Lloyd's Med Rep 96 (failed sterilisation): *Rand v East Dorset HA* [2000] Lloyd's Med Rep 181 (failure to advise parents of Downs syndrome foetus): *Hardman v Amin* [2000] Lloyd's Med Rep 498 (failure to advise of the risk of foetal deformity due to maternal rubella).

University Hospital NHS Trust.[197] In that case the reasoning of *McFarlane* is carefully analysed, and Brooke LJ identified five techniques, derived from recent House of Lords decisions, for deciding whether a claim for financial loss in cases not involving physical injury or damage should be recoverable, namely consideration of:

(i)   assumption of responsibility for services;

(ii) the purpose of those services;

(iii) analogies with established categories or liability;

(iv) whether, given forseeability and sufficient proximity, compensation would be fair, just and reasonable;

(v)   whether the principles of distributive justice would provide a more just solution than an approach based only on corrective justice.

The court was unanimous in deciding that, subject to two qualifications, the costs attributable to the disabilities of an unwanted child (although not the basic upbringing costs) were recoverable in a case arising out of failed sterilisation.

12.95 The first qualification was that the disabilities had to be 'significant'.[198] For that purpose the Court adopted the definition in s 17(11) of the Children Act 1989:

> a child is disabled if he is blind, deaf or dumb or suffers from mental disorder of any kind or is substantially and permanently handicapped by illness, injury or congenital deformity or such other disability as may be prescribed.

This definition, it should be noted, is significantly more restrictive than the definition of disability for which an injured child may claim under the Congenital Disabilities (Civil Liability) Act 1976.[199]

12.96 The second qualification is that, for the claimant to be successful, the child's disabilities must not result from a new intervening or 'ultroneous' cause. Hale LJ concluded:

> any disabilities resulting from genetic causes or foreseeable events during pregnancy (such as rubella, spina bifida or oxygen deprivation during pregnancy or childbirth) up until the child is born alive, and which are not novus actus interveniens, will suffice to found a claim.[200]

The practical implications of this guidance are not yet clear. An apparent extension of this restriction appears in *Groom v Selby*[201] in which the mother of a

---

[197] N 162 above. See commentary, Grubb (2002) Med L Rev 78. But note that in *Rees v Darlington Memorial Hospital NHS Trust* (n 179 above), Lord Bingham at [9] and Lord Scott at [145] doubted the correctness of *Parkinson*.

[198] N 162 above, *per* Brooke LJ, at [52]; *per* Hale LJ, at [91].

[199] See para 12.42 above.

[200] N 162 above, at [92]: see also *per* Brooke LJ at [63]–[91].

[201] N 163 above.

premature child who appeared healthy at birth but developed salmonella meningitis at three weeks of age was held entitled to recover in a wrongful birth action
because the child had been exposed to bacteria during delivery and was never born
'healthy'. The chain of causation was accordingly not broken. However, it seems
likely that if the disability to the unwanted child arises from an injury caused by
negligence then the parents' claims for the costs attributable to disability will be
secondary to and reduced and perhaps extinguished by that of the child under the
Congenital Disabilities (Civil Liability) Act 1976. This would seem to be fair,
even though not all medical negligence breaks the chain of causation: to do so it
must usually be gross and/or unforeseeable.[202]

12.97 Three unsuccessful attempts have been made to side-step the decision of
McFarlane. In *Greenfield v Irwin*[203] a claim was brought for the loss of a mother's
earnings said to be attributable to her need to bring up an unwanted but healthy
child, born as a result of failure to do a pregnancy test when providing contraception by injection. It was argued that *McFarlane* had not addressed the issue of
earnings loss, and that it was concerned with negligent advice and not, as in the
instant case, with an omission in the course of treatment. Those arguments were,
as was the claim, rejected by the Court of Appeal. In *AD v East Kent Community
NHS Trust*[204] the claimant was a female psychiatric patient sectioned under s 3 of
the Mental Health Act 1983. She had a healthy child, allegedly as the result of negligence on the part of the Trust in failing to protect her from pregnancy. The child
was brought up by the maternal grandmother under a residence order, and the
claimant claimed all the upbringing costs, arguing that the grandmother incurred
them because of her own disability. The courts drew no distinction between physical disability and mental disability. However, the claim was rejected, partly on the
authority of *McFarlane* and partly because the mother could not recover for the
gratuitous services provided by the grandmother to the child. Most recently, in
Rees v Darlington Memorial Hospital NHS Trust[205] the House of Lords, following
McFarlane, by a majority of four to three rejected a claim by a severely visually
handicapped mother of a healthy child, born as the result of a negligently performed operation for sterilisation, for the extra cost of care attributable to her own
disability, but awarded her £15,000 for the denial of her right to live her life as she
had wished and planned.

---

[202] See eg *Webb v Barclays Bank Ltd* [2001] Lloyd's Rep Med 500.
[203] [2001] EWCA Civ 113, [2001] 1 WLR 1279, [2001] 1 FLR 599, and [2001] Lloyd's Rep Med
143 sub nom *Greenfield v Flather*. see commentary, Grubb (2001) 9 Med L Rev 54.
[204] [2002] Lloyd's Rep Med 424, per Cooke J; [2002] EWCA Civ 1872, [2003] 3 All ER 1167.
See, in addition to the commentaries noted at n 174 above, Priaux, N, 'Parental Disability and
Wrongful Conception' [2002] Fam Law 117.
[205] N 179 above. See commentary, Grubb (2002) 10 Med L Rev 206.

(c) Limitation Act Problems

Failed Sterilisation Section 11(1) of the Limitation Act 1980 applies a three year **12.98** limitation period:

> to any action for damages for negligence, nuisance or breach of duty . . . where the damages claimed for the negligence, nuisance or breach of duty consist of or include damages in respect of personal injuries to the plaintiff or any other person.

In *Allen v Bloomsbury HA*[206] Brooke J touched on a problem. He expressed the view, obiter, that a claim by a mother in a 'wrongful birth' action which is not for damages for personal injuries but only for economic loss, such as lost wages or the cost of upkeep of an unwanted child, might well be subject to the different six year limitation period, since it is hard to see how s 11 of the Limitation Act 1980 would apply to a claim limited to the financial costs associated with the upbringing of an unwanted child. However, it is now clear that a claimant actually injured by a tort cannot escape from the three year limitation period merely by abandoning a claim for physical injuries and pursuing a claim for economic loss. The earliest authority was *Ackbar v C F Green & Co Ltd*,[207] in which Croom-Johnson J said that the proper test for deciding whether an action fell within the section was to ask 'what is the action all about?' That case was cited in the Court of Appeal in *Howe v David Brown Tractors (Retail) Limited*[208] in which Nicholls LJ expressed the view that a plaintiff injured by medical negligence could not escape the application of the three year limitation period by abandoning any claim for physical injury and claiming only damages in respect of loss of earnings.[209] The Court of Appeal reached a decision to the same effect in *Walkin v South Manchester HA*.[210] Although there was no claim for pain, suffering, or inconvenience as a result of the failed sterilisation operation, pregnancy, or birth, but only for financial loss, on a preliminary issue it was held that the claim was 'in respect of personal injuries', that time ran from the moment of conception and that the action was therefore statute-barred. Consistently with that approach, the suggestion of Brooke J in the *Allen* case, that different limitation periods might apply to physical injury and economic loss was disapproved. More recently, in *Godfrey v Gloucestershire Royal Infirmary NHS Trust*,[211] Leveson J, in a 'wrongful birth' case, treated *Walkin* as binding authority (despite *McFarlane*) that such claims were to be treated as personal injury claims for the purpose of the Limitation Act 1980.

---

[206] [1993] 1 All ER 651, 658.
[207] N 153 above.
[208] [1991] 4 All ER 30.
[209] ibid, 40–41.
[210] N 169 above.
[211] [2003] EWHC 549; [2003] Lloyd's Rep Med 398.

12.99   **Failed Vasectomy** An apparently inconsistent conclusion had been reached by a two-judge Court of Appeal in *Pattison v Hobbs*.[212] In that case a vasectomy which had been performed by the defendant doctor failed, and in consequence the husband remained fertile and the wife conceived a child. Both sued, neither claiming damages for personal injury as such but only for financial loss. On an application to strike out for want of prosecution the question of limitation was raised, and the Court of Appeal held that the six year limitation period applied as the claim was not for 'damages in respect of personal injuries' within the meaning of s 11 of the Limitation Act 1980. A distinction between the failed sterilisation and the failed vasectomy cases may certainly be made, in that in the former it is the mother who was the patient and who clearly sustained personal injury, whereas in a failed vasectomy case it is the father who was the patient yet sustained no physical injury, being able to complain only that a planned operation was ineffective, but only economic loss.

12.100   However, it does not follow that a male claimant in a failed vasectomy case can thus escape the three year limitation period. His loss may be purely financial, and for that reason Roch LJ in *Walkin*[213] reserved the question of a proper limitation period. Yet it is likely that if the pregnancy was unwanted by the woman the man's claim will be interpreted as 'in respect of personal injuries to . . . any other person' within the meaning of, and thus caught by, s 11 of the Limitation Act 1980.[214] If, on the other hand, the woman wanted a pregnancy which resulted only because, as a result of negligence, a vasectomy had failed, it might well be that, as there was no personal injury, the man would have the benefit of a six year limitation period.[215] One must comment that these paradoxes and anomalies suggest that the time is now right for reconsideration of the law of limitation in this context.

(d) A Doctor's Duty: Contract and Tort

12.101   In *Eyre v Measday*[216] and *Thake v Morris*[217] the Court of Appeal considered cases of failed laparoscopic sterilisation and vasectomy respectively. In each case claims were made in contract. In *Eyre* the mother alone was the plaintiff. In explaining the operation the doctor had emphasised that it was 'irreversible'. She thus argued that he had contracted to render her absolutely sterile, that the use of the word 'irreversible' amounted to an express guarantee that the operation would achieve

---

[212] The Times, 11 November 1985, CA Transcript 85/676. Technically *Pattison* should bind later Courts of Appeal even though only a two-judge court: *Langley v North West Water Authority* [1991] 3 All ER 610 (CA).

[213] [1995] 1 WLR 1543, 1553, 4 All ER 132, 142.

[214] ibid, *per* Auld LJ at 1552, 142. This view is supported by *Howe v D and Brown Tractors (Retail Ltd,* 154 above.

[215] ibid, *per* Neill LJ at 1555, 144.

[216] [1986] 1 All ER 488, (CA).

[217] [1986] QB 644, [1986] 1 All ER 497 (CA).

its object of sterilising her, and that alternatively there was an implied warranty to that effect. All those arguments failed. The Court of Appeal held that the contract was only to carry out the particular type of operation and not to sterilise: that 'irreversible' meant only that the operation could not be reversed and not that it would achieve its object, and that in a contract to operate the court will imply an obligation to exercise reasonable skill and care but would be:

> slow to imply against a medical man an unqualified warranty as to the results of an intended operation, for the very simple reason that, objectively speaking, it is most unlikely that a responsible medical man would intend to give a warranty of this nature.[218]

In *Thake* both parents sued. They too sued in contract but, (Kerr LJ dissenting) **12.102** this claim failed. The possibility of an enforceable warranty was firmly rejected by the majority. Neill LJ said:

> a reasonable man would have expected the defendant to exercise all the proper skill and care of a surgeon in that speciality: he would not have expected the defendant to give a guarantee of 100% success.[219]

More firmly still, Nourse LJ said:

> of all sciences medicine is one of the least exact. In my view, a doctor cannot be objectively regarded as guaranteeing the success of any operation or treatment unless he says as much in clear and unequivocal terms.[220]

However, the courts are unwilling to encourage different rights to compensation as between private and NHS patients. Thus in *Hotson v East Berkshire HA* Sir John Donaldson MR and Croom Johnson LJ respectively stated that such a distinction would have no 'rational basis' or 'sense'.[221] However, the importance of a clear understanding or agreement as to what is to happen during procedures affecting the size of the family was emphasised in *Thompson v Sheffield Fertility Clinic*.[222]

A Doctor's Duty: Relationships with Non-Patients

It therefore follows that 'wrongful birth' claims by parents must in reality be **12.103** founded upon an alleged breach of a duty of care. Now a doctor, of course, owes such a duty to the patient whom he or she is treating or advising. But is such a duty owed to the patient's partner? In *Thake* both parents sued, and it was not submitted that

---

[218] N 216 above at 495 *per* Slade LJ.
[219] N 217 above at 685, 510.
[220] ibid, 688, 512.
[221] [1987] 1 AC 750, 760 A-B, 768F. See also para 12.92 above, and note Lord Steyn's reservations as to what difference might arise as a result of a warranty of an outcome in *McFarlane* n 174 above at 77A, 972j.
[222] 6 March 2001, Hooper J. In that case a mother who had three embryos replaced during IVF treatment was able to establish a breach of an agreement that only two should be replaced. See commentary, Grubb (2001) 9 Med L Rev 170.

the mother (upon whom no operation had been performed) had no right of action. It is probable that the court would have rejected so discriminatory a suggestion, particularly as both had been advised directly about the vasectomy and had signed forms consenting to it. Support for the proposition that a doctor may owe a duty to a person who is not a patient has been sought in cases where the courts have accepted that one person may owe a duty to another to prevent a third person causing him harm.[223] Thus, in *Carmarthenshire County Council v Lewis*[224] an education authority was held responsible to a driver who was killed in avoiding a child who was negligently allowed to wander out of a nursery school onto the road. The parallel, however, seems a little far fetched. It is suggested that the existence or otherwise of a duty owed by a doctor to the partner of a patient can more easily be assessed by reference to more recent formulations of principle than by such analogies.

12.104 As has been pointed out,[225] the criteria for deciding whether a duty is owed are foreseeability, proximity, and an assessment of whether it is fair, just, and reasonable to impose a duty to the plaintiff on the defendant. If this principle is applied, there should be no difficulty in finding that a doctor may owe a duty of care, at least in the abstract, to the known sexual partner of the patient. However, it does not follow that the doctor would owe a duty to every sexual partner of the patient, for example to every woman impregnated by a man whose vasectomy he had negligently performed.

12.105 This problem was addressed by the Court of Appeal in *Goodwill v British Pregnancy Advisory Service*.[226] The plaintiff was a woman who, at about the time of her divorce, had commenced a sexual relationship with a married man who had had a vasectomy and negative semen tests arranged by the defendant about three years earlier. She became pregnant because the vasectomy had undergone spontaneous reversal and brought an action claiming not for personal injury but only for financial loss. The allegations of negligence were of failure to warn the man of the possibility of late spontaneous reversal of the vasectomy and its consequences. Curiously, *Walkin v South Manchester HA*[227] was not cited, and the decision turned on whether the plaintiff's claim fell within the principles either of *Hedley*

---

[223] See the discussion by Mullis, A, 'Wrongful Conception Unravelled' (n 1 above), 326.

[224] [1955] AC 549.

[225] See paras 12.30 and 12.93 above. For a general discussion of duties to non-patients, see Giesen, D, *International Medical Malpractice Law* (JCB Mohr, Paul Siebeck, 1988), 157–61. See also *Tarasoff v Regents of the University of California* (1976) 551 p 2d 334 (Sup Ct Cal) (psychiatrist's duty to inform third party of threats made against her by his patient): cf *Webb v Jarvis* (1991) 575 NE 2nd 992 (Sup Ct of Indiana) (plaintiff shot by patient: defendant physician not in breach of duty to avoid harm to plaintiff in his prescribing of medicine to patient). See Commentary at (1993) 1 Med L Rev 265.

[226] [1996] 2 All ER 161.

[227] N 169 above.

Byrne v Heller and Partners Ltd[228] as explained in *Caparo Industries PLC v Dickman*[229] and *James McNaughton Papers Group Ltd v Hicks Anderson & Co*[230] or of *White v Jones*.[231] The claim was struck out, principally on the basis that it could not be shown that, at the time it was given, the defendant knew that its advice was likely to be acted upon by the plaintiff without independent enquiry, or that it had in fact been so acted upon by the plaintiff to her detriment. But dealing with the question of a doctor's duty to a non-patient Peter Gibson LJ said:[232]

> the doctor is concerned only with the man, his patient, and possibly that man's wife or partner if the doctor intends her to receive and she receives advice from the doctor in relation to the vasectomy and the subsequent tests. Whether the avoidance of pregnancy is a benefit or a disadvantage to a sexual partner of the man will depend on her circumstances. If the existence of that partner is known to the doctor and the doctor is aware that she wishes not to become pregnant by the man and the vasectomy is carried out to meet her wish as well as the man's wish, it may be said that the doctor is employed to confer that benefit on her.

More succinctly Thorpe LJ said:[233]

> the doctor in the circumstances regards himself as advising the patient and, if a married man, the patient's wife. It cannot be said that he knows or ought to know that he also advises any future sexual partners of his patient who chance to receive his advice at second-hand. Presented with such a set of facts a doctor is entitled to scorn the suggestion that he owes a duty of care to such a band so uncertain in nature and extent and over such an indefinite future span.

In short, it would seem that the scope of duty extends only to a patient's spouse or known sexual partner at the time of the advice who is likely to be affected by it.[234]

(e) *Refusal by a Mother to Terminate an Unwanted Pregnancy*

In *Emeh v Kensington & Chelsea & Westminster HA*,[235] where a sterilisation opera-   **12.106**
tion had failed, it was argued, and the judge at first instance accepted, that the mother had behaved unreasonably in failing to have an abortion, and that her refusal was so unreasonable as to amount to a *novus actus interveniens*, or failure to mitigate damage which eclipsed the negligence for which the Health Authority was responsible. The Court of Appeal reversed the first instance decision on the ground that the Health Authority had, by its negligent failure to effect a sterilisation, created the very dilemma which the plaintiff had sought to avoid, and thus

---

[228] N 190 above.
[229] [1990] 2 AC 398.
[230] [1991] 2 QB 113.
[231] [1995] 2 AC 207, 1 All ER 691.
[232] N 226 above at 167.
[233] ibid, 170.
[234] See *Miller v Rivard* (1992) 585 NYS 2d 523 (Sup Ct NY, App Div) on the distinction between known and casual sexual partners. See also Rogers, WVH (1985), n 1 above.
[235] [1985] QB 1012, [1984] 3 All ER 1044.

had no right to expect that she would undergo an abortion with its attendant risks, pain, and discomfort. The child in was in fact born with a disability. There was no evidence that this was or could have been known before the birth, and so there was no discussion of the question of whether the mother would have been held unreasonable had she known of the disability but nevertheless declined the offer of a lawful abortion on the grounds 'that there [was] a substantial risk that if the child were born it would suffer from such physical or mental abnormalities as to be seriously handicapped'.[236] Nevertheless, it is possible that there may be cases in which a mother's refusal to terminate the pregnancy may defeat her claim. In *Emeh* Slade LJ[237] said:

> save in the most exceptional circumstances, I cannot think it right that the court should ever declare it unreasonable for a mother to decline to have an abortion, in a case in which there is no evidence that there were any medical or psychiatric grounds for terminating this particular pregnancy,

and Purchas LJ[238] said:

> if the sole motivation of a plaintiff [for continuing a pregnancy] was in order to promote an action, [that] would be at least a factor to be taken into account in deciding whether, on an objective test of unreasonableness, there had been a break in the chain of causation.

12.107 The question was discussed somewhat elliptically in the wrongful birth case of *Goodwill v British Pregnancy Advisory Service*.[239] The facts are not completely clear from the judgments, but it appears that the plaintiff originally thought that her symptoms meant that she had an ovarian cyst, and was pleased later to discover that she was pregnant. Nevertheless, she was worried because the father was still married and living with his family, and feared the prospect of single parenthood. She:

> spent a couple of weeks in a great state of turmoil and anxiety before deciding to go ahead with the pregnancy. Although it might have been still possible to terminate the pregnancy, the implications were much more serious because the foetus was so well developed and because of her belief that life was sacred. She also knew in her heart of hearts that she could not abort the life that she had previously thought was an omen of death.[240]

Yet despite this emotional ambivalence, in circumstances which can hardly be described as exceptional, the plaintiff's decision to continue with the pregnancy influenced the Court in its view that a claim should be struck out as frivolous, vexatious, and an abuse of process.[241]

---

[236] Abortion Act 1967 s 1(i)(b).
[237] N 235 above, at 1024, 1053.
[238] ibid, 1027, 1055.
[239] N 226 above.
[240] ibid, 165 *per* Peter Gibson LJ.
[241] ibid, 169 *per* Peter Gibson LJ, 170 *per* Thorpe LJ.

However in *McFarlane*[242] all members of the House of Lords firmly rejected the **12.108** idea (not that the submission had been made) that a mother's failure to seek termination of an unwanted pregnancy or to have an unwanted child adopted amounted to a failure to mitigate the loss or broke the chain of causation. Lord Slynn[243] said:

> there was no legal or moral duty to arrange an abortion or an adoption of an unplanned child.

Lord Steyn[244] said:

> I cannot conceive of any circumstances in which the autonomous decision of the parents not to resort to even a legal abortion can be questioned. For similar reasons, the parents' decision lot to have the child adopted was plainly natural and commendable. It is difficult to envisage any circumstances in which it would be right to challenge such a decision of the parent. The starting point is the right of the parents to make decisions on family planning and, if those plans fail, their rights to care for an initially unwanted child. The law does and must respect these decisions of parents which are so clearly tied to their basic freedoms and rights of personal autonomy.

Lord Millet[245] said:

> I agree with Slade LJ in *Emeh* that save in the most exceptional circumstances (which it is very hard to imagine) it can never be unreasonable for parents or prospective parents to decline to terminate pregnancy or to place the child for adoption.

(f) Quantification of Damages in an Action for 'Wrongful Conception' and 'Wrongful Birth'

General Damages The mother will have a claim for the discomfort and suffering **12.109** of pregnancy and childbirth, but in calculating damages there should be taken into account any suffering she may have been spared. For example if (but for the negligence) a pregnancy would have been terminated, the unpleasantness of that avoided procedure must be set against what she in fact suffered.

The next question is whether a claim can be made for the impact of having an un- **12.110** wanted child on the parents' life, for a 'wrongful birth' claim is a claim by the parent for the injury suffered by him or her. It is therefore unlikely that such a claim can be made for any such effect by anyone but the parent. Moreover, a distinction must be made between cases where the child is born healthy and cases where the child is born disabled. In relation to the former type of case, Brooke J summarised the law in *Allen v Bloomsbury HA*[246] summarised the law in the following words:

---

[242] N 174 above.
[243] ibid, 749, 970h.
[244] ibid, 81E–F, 976 h–j.
[245] ibid, 113B, 1004j.
[246] [1993] 1 All ER 651, 657.

> [A]lthough the law recognises that it is foreseeable that if an unwanted child is born following a doctor's negligence a mother may suffer wear and tear and tiredness in bringing up a healthy child, the claim for general damages she might otherwise have had on this account is generally set off against and extinguished by the benefit of bringing a healthy child into the world and seeing one's child grow up to maturity.

This 'set-off' approach is known in America as the 'benefits rule'.[247]

12.111   Where, however, the child is born handicapped, the position is different. In *Allen* Brooke J continued:[248]

> [H]owever, the law is willing to recognise a claim for general damages in respect of the foreseeable additional anxiety, stress and burden involved in bringing up a handicapped child, which is not treated as being extinguished by any countervailing benefit, although this head of damages is different in kind from the typical claim for anxiety and stress associated with and flowing from an injured plaintiff's own personal injuries.

He referred to a 'claim for damages for the loss of amenity associated with bringing up a handicapped child', and stated:

> [I]n a case where the future child is foreseeably born handicapped, for example because the effects of rubella have not been explained to its pregnant mother by a negligent defendant, I can see reasons why a court is willing to award the mother an extraordinary item of general damages for the burden of bringing up a handicapped child.

Such a claim was allowed in *Taylor v Shropshire HA*,[249] *Rand v East Dorset HA*[250] and *Hardman v Amin*.[251] A claim of this nature is not dissimilar to one for breach of a contract to provide peace of mind and freedom from distress.[252] The rule in contract should, as was accepted by Purchas LJ in *Hayes v Dodd*,[253] apply also in tort. Conceptually, such a claim should be treated separately than a claim for psychiatric injury, as was done by Steel J in *Farrell v Merton Sutton and Wandsworth HA*.[254] Unlike a psychiatric injury claim by a parent consequent upon negligently inflicted injury to a child, a claim of this sort can arise even though the injury to the child was not negligently inflicted and in the absence of any element of shock.

---

[247] See 'Wrongful Pregnancy Damages', 89 ALR 4th at 632.

[248] N 246 above at 657–8, 662. See also *Emeh v Kensington AHA* (n 235 above), where the award of general damages included compensation for the 'extra care' of a disabled child, and *Thake v Maurice* (n 217 above).

[249] [2000] Lloyd's Rep Med 96.

[250] [2000] Lloyd's Rep Med 181.

[251] [2000] Lloyd's Rep Med 498.

[252] See *Bliss v South East Thames RHA* [1987] ICR 700 at 718 *per* Dillon LJ: *Watts v Morrow* [1991] 1 WLR 1421 at 1445 *per* Bingham LJ. See also *Hobbs v London and South West Railway* [1875] LR 10 QB 111 and *Johnson v Gore Wood & Co* [2001] 2 WLR 72, [2001] 1 All ER 481.

[253] [1990] 2 All ER 815 at 826j.

[254] See *Farrell v Merton Sutton and Wandsworth HA* (2000) 57 BMLR 158: for psychiatric injury claims see paras 12.120–12.125 below.

In calculating the value of such claim, care must be taken not to duplicate any compensation recoverable for psychiatric shock or for the value of 'family care' provided by the parent of a disabled child. It is however suggested that awards for such claims are different from and should not be subsumed in the new type of award for interference with parental autonomy.[255]

So the law allows an award to the parent, classified as general damages, for caring **12.112** for a child who is foreseeably handicapped. The question of foreseeability will be construed very broadly. It is not necessary that the defendant should have foreseen the precise disability of the unwanted child or even that such a child, more probably than not, would have been born disabled. That this is so emerges from *Emeh v Kensington AHA*, a case of failed sterilisation following which an unwanted child was born with congenital abnormalities requiring constant medical and parental supervision. Waller LJ[256] said:

> [I]n my view it is trite to say that if a woman becomes pregnant, it is certainly foreseeable that she will have a baby, but in my judgment, having regard to the fact that in a proportion of all births—between 1 in 200 and 1 in 400 were the figures given at trial—congenital abnormalities might arise, makes the risk clearly one that is foreseeable, as the law of negligence understands it. There are many cases where even more remote risks have been taken to be 'foreseeable' . . . [T]his child would need to be under constant supervision, both medically and by her mother, and her abnormalities would have to be carefully watched . . . [T]hose conditions which arose by reason of birth were, in my judgment, not too remote to be taken into account when considering what damages should be awarded for the admitted negligence of the defendant's doctors in this case.

Claims for costs attributable to disability It is established by *Parkinson*[257] that **12.113** loss and expense attributable to the disabilities of an unwanted child and reasonable. However in *Hardman v Amin*[258] it was argued that no claim could be brought for the value of care provided by the family of a disabled child. The argument was rejected. Indeed as the economic costs attributable to a child's disability, which can include loss of earnings and the cost of professional care, are recoverable by a parent, it surely follows that the value of care provided by a parent alone is recoverable. The matter has been put beyond doubt by *Hunt v Severs*[259] which decided that while a voluntary carer of an injured claimant has no personal claim for the value of such care, the claimant can recover that value in trust for the carer. If the carer has a beneficial interest in the value of care provided to a claimant, it

---

[255] See *Rees v Darlington Memorial Hospital NHS Trust* (n 179 and para 12.97 above).
[256] N 235 above, 1019–20, 1049–50. But see *per* Lord Scott in *Rees v Darlington Memorial Hospital NHS Trust* (n 179 above) at [147], doubting whether foreseeability of such a risk was enough to impose liability.
[257] N 162 above: but see the comments in *Rees* (n 179 above).
[258] N 251 above.
[259] [1994] 2 AC 350, 2 All ER 385.

surely follows that a claimant who reasonably provides care to another can claim for it.

12.114 The question arises, however, as to whether a claim can be made for such costs after the child becomes 18. There are several American authorities[260] on the point, the gist of whose arguments seems to be that if under the relevant State law the parents remain liable for the support of a disabled child after majority, then they can recover for such expenditure by them attributable to such disabilities (see the New Hampshire case of *Smith v Cote*[261] and the Massachusetts case of *Viccaro v Milunsky*).[262] If, on the other hand, there is no legal obligation on parents to support a disabled child after majority, then they cannot recover the cost of extraordinary expenses for continued support and special care of a disabled child even though they have a moral obligation to provide it; see the New York case of *Bani-Esraili v Lerman*.[263]

The argument that there is no legal obligation on the defendants to compensate for any provision for disability after majority was rejected by Swinton Thomas J in *Fish v Wilcox*.[264] The claim was for wrongful birth of a child who had spina bifida but was likely to survive into adult life. The judge accepted as a matter of general principle the plaintiff's argument that: 'the measure of damages must be a sum of money which will put the party who has been injured in the same position as she would have been in if she had not sustained the wrong', and clearly would have awarded damages for maternal services after the age of 18 had he not found as a fact that the child would not require them. The argument was again rejected in *Rand*[265] and in *Nunnerley v Warrington HA*[266] and an application for permission to appeal the latter case on this point was rejected by the Court of Appeal.[267] It is within the contemplation of the parties that parents of children born with disabilities will wish and indeed feel under a moral obligation to make reasonable provision for them throughout the children's lives, and this sense of obligation is supported by common and statute law.[268]

---

[260] See Louisell, D W and Williams, M, *Medical Malpractice*, Vol 1, para 18.09.
[261] 513 A 2d 341 (1986) (Sup Ct NH).
[262] 551 NE 2d 8 (1990) (Sup Ct Jud Mass).
[263] 505 NE 2d 947 (1987) (NYCA).
[264] 9 April 1992. The point was not pursued on appeal: [1994] 5 Med LR 230, 231.
[265] N 250 above.
[266] [2000] Lloyd's Med Rep 170.
[267] Sub nom *N v Warrington HA* [2003] Lloyd's Rep Med 365.
[268] As to the common law duty to disabled adults see *R v Stone* [1997] 1 QB 354 and *Feinberg v Diamant* (1979) 389 NE 2d 998. See also *Anderson v Forth Valley Health Board* [1997] 44 BMLR 108 (C, IH). For penalties for wilful neglect of legal and moral obligation to mentally disordered patients see Mental Health Act 1983, s 127(2). As to power to make financial provision orders for disabled children see Children Act 1989, Sch I, paras 2(1)(b) and 4(1)(d).

In *Rand*[269] a novel question arose in considering how the costs of providing for **12.115** disability should be calculated. It was submitted, and Newman J held, that as the claim was for economic loss it should be limited to the amount which the parents would have been able to pay for in caring for their child in the absence of compensation. However, to categorise the claim as one for economic loss is to do no more than identify the need for control mechanisms on the imposition of liability: it says nothing about the quantification of damages. Such a principle would simply serve to penalise the impecunious parents, and would seem unjust. For such reasons Henriques J in *Hardman v Amin*[270] concluded that the parents' means were not relevant to the calculation of their claim for costs attributable to their child's disability. This decision has been followed in *Lee v Taunton & Somerset NHS Trust*[271] and in *Roberts v Bro Taf HA*[272] and, it is submitted, will be followed in the future.

A further problem arises on the construction of s 2(4) of the Law Reform **12.116** (Personal Injuries) Act 1948 as amended which provides that:

> In an action for personal injuries (including any such action arising out of a contract) there shall be disregarded, in determining the reasonableness of any expenses, the possibility of avoiding those expenses or part of them by taking advantage of facilities available under the National Health Act 1977 or the National Health Service (Scotland) Act 1978 or of any corresponding facilities in Northern Ireland.

The question arises whether, as a claim for the costs attributable to disability was said in *McFarlane*[273] to be one for economic loss, s 2(4) has any application to that claim. In *Lee v Taunton & Somerset NHS Trust*[274] Toulson J expressed the 'provisional view' that the sub-section did not apply to that part of the claim:

> because although the action is in part of a claim for personal injuries suffered by Mrs Lee, the costs of caring for George are not in truth damages for personal injuries suffered by her.

Formally, however, the question remains undecided. There is a counter-argument of reasonable strength that a wrongful conception or birth action, if by a mother who claims damages for perinatal pain and suffering, is an action for personal injuries even though it is also an action for economic loss. As Hale LJ said in *Groom Selby*:[275]

---

269 N 250 above.
270 N 251 above.
271 [2001] 1 FLR 419 at 433B *per* Toulson J.
272 [2002] Lloyd's Rep Med 163 *per* Turner J.
273 N 174 above.
274 N 271 above, 431 G.
275 N 163 above, at [31]. See *Godfrey v Gloucestershire Royal Infirmary NHS Trust* (n 211 above) for comparable reasoning in the context of the Limitation Act 1980.

they are economic losses consequent upon the invasion of bodily integrity suffered by a woman who becomes or remains pregnant against her will.

12.117 **Claims by Siblings** The question which finally arises is whether the siblings of children born in consequence of negligence can claim damages on the basis that the 'wrongful birth' has prejudiced them, socially, emotionally, or economically. Such claims have been described as 'wholly without merit'.[276] Three points may be made. First, in a normal case it will be difficult to persuade a court that any financial loss was foreseeable, because if the parents have a 'wrongful birth' claim (as ex hypothesi they will) then damages recovered should prevent existing siblings from suffering financial loss, save possibly on inheritance. Second, it is unlikely that a court would find sufficient proximity between a sibling and the parents' doctors to found any duty of care. Third, if a court is reluctant to permit a claim by a child born into a disadvantaged family, as is undoubtedly the case,[277] by parity of reasoning it will hardly find it fair, just or reasonable to allow an action by a sibling claiming to be disadvantaged by an unplanned new arrival in the family.[278]

2. Claims by Parents for Physical and Psychiatric Injuries and Disruption of the Family

(i) Physical Injury

12.118 Circumstances which lead to neonatal injury or death may also injure the mother. The leading English case is *Kralj v McGrath*.[279] In that case the mother was admitted to hospital for the birth of twins. After attempted internal cephalic version of the second twin without any anaesthetic, a procedure described as horrific and completely unacceptable, he was delivered by caesarian section, but died eight weeks later. The mother claimed, inter alia, for aggravated damages and damages for grief arising out of the loss of a child. Woolf J held that the concept of aggravated damages should not be introduced into personal injury actions, although to the extent that the mother's experience of her baby's injuries and death made it more difficult for her to overcome the consequences of her own injuries, the award would correspondingly be increased. He further ruled that while damages cannot be awarded for grief in isolation at common law, the mother could be compensated for the shock she had sustained as a result of being told what had happened and of seeing her son, and, to the extent that grief had made her injuries have a

---

[276] *Sala v Tomlinson* 422 NYS 2d 506 (1979) (Sup Ct App Div): cf *Bowman v Davies* 48 Ohio St 2d 41 (1976). In *Fish v Wilcox*, (n 264 above), Swinton Thomas J considered, obiter, the possibility of the father and brothers of a damaged child being joined in a wrongful birth action brought by the mother so that they might recover damages for the services they had provided to the child. It is doubtful that this is correct.

[277] See paras 12.69–12.70 above.

[278] As to these criteria, see para 12.30 above.

[279] [1986] 1 All ER 54.

more drastic effect on her, that could be taken into account in calculating the personal injury award.

A further, and not unimportant, factor in computing damages was identified by 12.119
Rose J in *Grieve v Salford HA*[280] The facts of that case were that, following a negligent obstetric procedure, a psychiatrically vulnerable unmarried woman had a stillborn child. The stillbirth was held to be particularly damaging because she had been given a variety of inconsistent explanations as to what had been the cause of death. In two cases Sir John Donaldson MR[281] expressed the view, obiter, that a doctor's general duty of care requires him to tell a patient what has gone wrong. One of the difficulties facing claimants who allege that they have suffered from such a breach of duty must be in establishing that they have suffered damage in consequence. The approach of Rose J sidesteps that difficulty by treating a failure to inform a patient of what has gone wrong not as a separate tort but as a factor increasing an award for the original wrong.[282]

(ii) Psychiatric Injury

The law relating to damages for psychiatric injury remains difficult. At the time 12.120
writing the following propositions seems to be accepted.

(i) A person physically injured by negligence can recover for the psychiatric concomitants of that physical injury.

(ii) A person who sustains a psychiatric illness as a result of an incident in which he or she was directly involved as a participant may be described as a 'primary victim' and will be able to recover damages for that illness if the defendant could reasonably foresee that his conduct would expose the primary victim to the risk of some injury, either physical or psychiatric. It is no answer that the primary victim was predisposed to psychiatric injury.[283]

(iii) Where a person sustains a recognised psychiatric injury as a result of the shock of seeing or hearing an event, or the immediate aftermath of such event, which injures one with whom he or she has a close tie of affection he or she may have a claim as a 'secondary victim' of that event.[284]

The application of these principles to medical negligence claims is still being 12.121
worked out. For present purposes the relevant question is whether a parent can claim for psychiatric injury consequent on perinatal injury to a child. In the

---

[280] [1991] 2 Med LR 295 at 296.
[281] *Lee v South West Thames RHA* [1985] 1 WLR 845, 850–1: *Naylor v Preston AHA* (n 182 above), 967.
[282] See the discussion in Kennedy and Grubb, *Medical Law* (n 1 above), 1516.
[283] See *Page v Smith* [1996] 1 AC 155; [1995] 2 All ER 736.
[284] See *McLoughlin v O'Brian* [1983] 1 AC 410; *Alcock v Chief Constable of South Yorkshire Police* [1992] 1 AC 310; *McFarlane v EE Caledonia Ltd* [1994] 2 All ER 1.

important decision of *Jaensch v Coffey* [285] the High Court of Australia, in considering a claim for 'nervous shock' by the wife of a victim of a road traffic accident whom she visited in hospital, gave important general guidance which, inter alia, emphasises the requirement that in a claim by a secondary victim the illness must be caused by 'shock'. Of particular relevance is the passage in a judgment of Brennan J in which he said:[286]

> [T]he spouse who has been worn down by caring for a tortiously injured husband or wife and who suffers psychiatric illness as a result goes without compensation; a parent made distraught by the wayward conduct of a brain-damaged child and who suffers psychiatric illness as a result has no claim against the tortfeasor liable to the child.

12.122   In *Taylor v Somerset HA*,[287] a widow, whose husband's death resulted from medical negligence, unsuccessfully claimed damages for psychiatric shock allegedly resulting from seeing his body in the hospital mortuary. It was successfully submitted to Auld J that, in order to succeed, a plaintiff had to demonstrate that the defendant's breach of duty did not just cause injury or death to the plaintiff's relation, but had actually resulted in 'some external, traumatic event in the nature of an accident or violent happening'. That submission was repeated to the Court of Appeal in *Sion v Hampstead HA*,[288] a case in which a father unsuccessfully claimed for psychiatric shock allegedly caused by witnessing his son's gradual death in hospital as a result of mis-diagnosis. However, Peter Gibson LJ said:[289]

> [I]t is the sudden awareness, violently agitating the mind, of what is occurring or has occurred that is the crucial ingredient of shock. I see no reason in logic why a breach of duty causing an incident involving no violence or suddenness, such as where the wrong medicine is negligently given to a hospital patient, could not lead to a claim for damages for nervous shock, for example where the negligence has fatal results and a visiting close relative, wholly unprepared for what has occurred, finds the body and thereby sustains a sudden and unexpected shock to the nervous system.

12.123   The application of these principles appears in the decision of *Tredget v Bexley HA*.[290] In that case, as a result of admitted negligence in failing to deliver by caesarian section, a child was born severely asphyxiated, and died two days later. The father was present at the birth. The judge found that:[291]

> the actual birth with its 'chaos' or 'pandemonium', the difficulties that the mother had of delivery, the sense in the room that something was wrong, and the arrival of

---

[285] [1984] 155 CLR 549.
[286] ibid, 565.
[287] [1993] 4 Med LR 34, 37.
[288] [1994] 5 Med LR 170 (CA).
[289] ibid, 176.
[290] [1994] 5 Med LR 178.
[291] ibid, 183.

the child in a distressed condition requiring immediate resuscitation was, for those immediately and directly involved as each of the parents was, frightening and horrifying.

He found that the period from onset of labour until the child's death was effectively one event, that there was no need to invoke the 'aftermath' doctrine, and that the parents were victims of an experience sufficient to establish liability even though a full appreciation of the gravity of that child's condition only developed in the 48 hours between birth and death. As that composite event was a powerful factor in contributing to the pathological grief thereafter suffered by the parents, each was entitled to damages for psychiatric injury.

A secondary victim, to recover, must prove that he or she sustained the injury as a **12.124** result of the shock caused by witnessing the horrifying event or its immediate aftermath. This leaves uncompensated the parent whose psychiatric illness develops only as a result of learning of and experiencing the injury to the child (devastating cerebral palsy, for example), a long time after the birth. The question, however, may be asked: if such a mother is, as she must be, the patient of the obstetrician,[292] can she present her claim as if she was a primary victim? If so, would it be possible for her to claim that her psychiatric illness was a foreseeable consequence of the long-term stress caused to her by the negligence of her obstetrician? In *Walker v Northumberland CC*[293] an employee succeeded in a claim against his employer for a severe nervous breakdown caused by stress at work, and in *Johnstone v Bloomsbury HA*,[294] the Court of Appeal refused to strike out a claim by a hospital doctor caused by stress and depression caused by long working hours. Although it may be clear that psychiatric injury caused by stress should be compensatable in an action by a primary victim,[295] the problem is that while a mother traumatized by the circumstances of birth is clearly a primary victim, one injured by developing stress suffers not because of the circumstances of birth but because she later learns of her child's developing disability. It is questionable whether there refinements result in justice.

This problem was recognised by Steel J in *Farrell v Merton Sutton and Wandsworth* **12.125** *HA*.[296] In that case a claimant gave birth by caesarian section to a son who developed cerebral palsy. The operation itself was traumatic, and she was not able to see

---

[292] To whom the duty is owed: see s 1(3) of the Congenital Disabilities (Civil Liability) Act 1976: see also para 12.47 above.

[293] [1995] 1 All ER 737: 'the landmark case', *per* Hale LJ in *Hatton v Sutherland*, [2002] 2 All ER 1, at [39], a case concerned with the general principles relevant to claims of this type.

[294] [1992] QB 333 (Leggatt LJ dissenting).

[295] See the dissenting judgment of Sir Thomas Bingham MR in *X v Bedfordshire CC* [1995] 2 AC 633, 663–4.

[296] (2000) 57 BMLR 158. For recent decisions suggesting judicial sympathy for those suffering psychiatric injury as a result of events in hospital see also *Farrell v Avon HA* [2001] Lloyd's Rep Med 458 and *Walters v North Glamorgan NHS Trust* [2002] EWHC 321.

the child for over 24 hours, at which time he was in intensive care, when she was told he had irreversible brain damage. A claim by the child was settled, and the mother claimed for psychiatric injury. She succeeded as a primary victim, Steel J saying:

> I am satisfied that there is no break in the chain of causation and that the 'trauma of the birth' encompasses not only the events in the operating theatre but also the position up to and including the first sight of her baby and the realization (when told by the paediatric SHO) of his disability.

In the alternative she found that, as the delay was attributable to the defendants, in the circumstances the claimant's first sight of the child was in the immediate aftermath of the birth, and she succeeded as a secondary victim. The claimant was also held to be entitled to damages for loss of amenity consisting in 'loss of a private life far beyond the normal constraints imposed by bringing up a healthy child', but the total award of general damages did not distinguish between the two claims.

(iii) Stillbirths and 'Dashed Hopes'

12.126 It has been held that a stillbirth in itself may give rise to a claim for damages. In *Bagley v North Herts HA*,[297] the negligent failure to carry out a blood analysis in pregnancy deprived the plaintiff of her opportunity of successful delivery by caesarian section, and the child was stillborn. Simon Brown J considered that the mother was entitled to compensation for 'dashed hopes', that is to say the loss of the satisfaction of bringing her pregnancy, confinement and labour to a successful, indeed joyous conclusion. In similar circumstances in *Grieve v Salford HA*,[298] Rose J came to the same conclusion. However, in *Kerby v Redbridge HA*,[299] Ognall J disagreed. He was considering the case not of a stillbirth but of a neonatal death resulting from negligence. He rejected a 'dashed hopes' formulation of the claim partly on the basis that it would duplicate statutory damages for bereavement[300] (which are of course not available in the event of a stillbirth) but also because it amounted to no more than awarding damages for 'the normal emotions by way of grief, sorrow or distress attendant on the loss of a loved one'[301] which are not compensatable in law. It is suggested that he was probably correct in identifying a difficulty in treating 'dashed hopes' as the subject matter of a separate head of damages, rather than as a factor in quantifying a personal injury claim.

---

[297] [1986] NLJ 1014.
[298] N 280 above.
[299] [1993] 4 Med LR 178.
[300] See para 12.127 below.
[301] N 2997 above, 179, quoting *McLoughlin v O'Brian* (n 284 above), 431 *per* Lord Bridge.

(iv) Claims by Parents: Bereavement Awards

Where a child has died after 31 December 1982 the parents (if it was legitimate) **12.127**
or the mother (if it was illegitimate) are entitled to a statutory award of damages
for bereavement.[302] The award is conventional. In relation to death before 1 April
1991 it is £3,500, in relation to later death before 1 April 2002 it is £7,500, and
in relation to subsequent death it is £10,000.[303] Where both parents have an
entitlement the award is to be divided equally between them.

(v) 'Shattered Family Plans'

In *Kralj v McGrath*[304] the parents had always intended to have three children. **12.128**
They already had one when the mother gave birth to twins. One twin died as a result of the defendant's negligence, and the claim included damages for the consequences, including financial loss, of having another child to replace the one who
had died. On the evidence the probability that the mother would become pregnant again was only 66 per cent. However, Woolf J awarded £18,000 under this
head to take account of the financial loss which would arise if a pregnancy occurred and the loss of satisfaction of achieving the planned family if it did not.
Similarly, in *Bagley v North Herts HA*,[305] following the stillbirth, the parents decided not to attempt another pregnancy, because that would have carried a 50 per
cent risk of mortality. Simon Brown J made it plain that he was not able to award
damages for loss of the society of the stillborn child, but that he was able to compensate for loss of the pleasure of bringing up an ordinary healthy child who
would now not be born. Such an entitlement was, however, like the 'dashed hopes'
claim, doubted by Ognall LJ in *Kerby v Redbridge HA*,[306] His views were obiter,
because the plaintiff planned to get pregnant again and indeed was awarded
£1,500 for the prospect of 'the rigours of a further pregnancy'. However, the judge
took the view that the plaintiff, in making a claim for damages for 'shattered family plans', was doing no more than advancing 'the normal facet of a mother or a
mother's emotions when bereaved of a child'. In support of his view it can be
pointed out that in *Kralj v McGrath*[307] no statutory bereavement award was available, as the child's death pre-dated 1 January 1983, nor was one available in *Bagley
v North Herts HA*[308] because the child was stillborn. However, it is suggested that

---

[302] Fatal Accidents Act 1976, s 1A, inserted by Administration of Justice Act 1982, s 3: for commencement see s 73(1).
[303] Damages for Bereavement (Variation of Sum) (England and Wales) Orders 1990, SI
1990/2775 and 2002, SI 2002/644.
[304] [1986] 1 All ER 54.
[305] N 297 above.
[306] N 299 above.
[307] N 304 above.
[308] N 297 above.

the statutory bereavement award does not in fact replace a claim for 'shattered family plans' of the type contemplated in those two cases, which are based not on grief but on interference with the ordered planning of life and the economic and other consequences of such interference.

E. Stillbirths and Neonatal Deaths: Claims on Behalf of the Estate

1. Stillbirths

12.129 In *Burton v Islington HA* and *de Martell v Merton & Sutton HA*[309] Dillon LJ said, obiter:

> I doubt very much whether there are any claims now outstanding which are not statute barred, in respect of children stillborn before 22 July 1976 or any children born before that date, who are locked in litigation with their mothers over whether the mother tasted alcohol or followed a diet other than that recommended by the current phase of medical opinion during pregnancy.

This dictum appears to imply that a claim can be brought on behalf of a stillborn child. If so, it is surprising. At common law, there can be no actionable breach of duty to those born dead: before they are born they are not 'persons',[310] and after they are born, because they never lived, they have no legal rights. Nor is the position different under statute. In a number of American states, recovery by a child who has died in utero as a result of the defendant's negligent conduct has been admitted under Wrongful Death Acts. The Second Re-statement of the Law of Torts, however, states that 'if the child is not born alive, there is no liability unless the applicable wrongful death statute so provides'.[311]

12.130 The English position is that where a child is stillborn there is no liability under statute to anyone, for the following reasons. First, it is a precondition for recovery under the Congenital Disabilities (Civil Liability) Act 1976 that the child is born alive. Secondly, no right either of bereavement or dependency can arise out of the Fatal Accidents Act 1976, because death is a precondition of such rights. A court will inevitably conclude that one who, in the eyes of the law, has never become a 'person',[312] cannot be said to have obtained life, and therefore cannot be said to have suffered death. Third, for the same reason there will be no claim under the Law Report (Miscellaneous Provisions) Act 1934 which applies only simply 'on the death of any person'.[313]

---

[309] [1993] QB 204, 232.
[310] See para 12.05 above. For the definition of a still-birth, see Still-Birth (Definition) Act 1992.
[311] Para 369(2).
[312] See para 12.05 above.
[313] s 1(1).

2. *Neonatal Deaths*

Three types of claim are possible on behalf of the estate of a child dying as a result   **12.131**
of a birth injury. First, there may be a claim for reasonable funeral expenses.[314]
Second, in respect of deaths before 1 January 1983 a claim could be made for loss
of expectation of life; in *Kralj v McGrath*[315] the award was £1,650, less than the
conventional £1,750, as the child survived for only eight weeks. (Such claims,
however, will almost inevitably be statute barred by now.) Finally, a claim for the
pain, suffering and loss of amenity of the child before death will survive for the
benefit of the estate but will be modest. In *Kralj v McGrath*[316] the award was
£2,500; in *Kerby v Redbridge HA*,[317] where the child survived only for three days,
the award was £750.

---

[314] Law Reform (Miscellaneous Provisions) Act 1934, s 1(2)(c).
[315] N 304 above.
[316] ibid.
[317] N 299 above.

13

CLINICAL RESEARCH

A. Introduction[1]

The drive for progress in medicine and science has led to a vast increase in the   **13.01**

---

[1] On the legal regulation of clinical research see generally Kennedy, I and Grubb, A, *Medical Law* (3rd edn, London: Butterworths, 2000), ch 14; Mason, JK, McCall Smith, RA and Laurie, G, *Law*

amount of clinical and scientific research undertaken. Such research may lead to incredible discoveries and 'miracle' cures but at the same time this is an area dogged with controversy. The abuses which occurred in Germany during the Second World War have cast a long shadow. Since that time there has been concern at the international level to ensure that in the future research practices will be ethical and in accordance with legal principles. This led to the Nuremberg Code in 1949 and the Declaration of Helsinki which was initially produced in 1964.[2] In the European context statements which have been influential, at least at a rhetorical level, include the Council of Europe Convention on Human Rights and Biomedicine—although the United Kingdom is still not a signatory to this convention. The Council of Europe has now issued a Draft Additional Protocol to the Convention on Human Rights and Biomedicine.[3] The European Convention on Human Rights is also of undoubted importance and in the UK context is of particular relevance in the light of the Human Rights Act 1998.[4]

13.02   Nonetheless, despite the promulgation of such statements scientific research has still been dogged with controversy. In the notorious Tuskegee experiment, experiments were undertaken on black US males to determine the progression of syphilis despite the fact that there had been accepted treatment forr many years.[5] A further more recent incident was at Johns Hopkins University in 2001.[6] Ellen Roche, a 24-year old technician, died after acting as a volunteer in a non-therapeutic study of asthma. The review into her death led to major criticisms as to the safety of the trial, the review procedures of the project, inadequate consent procedures as well as inadequate failure to report unexpected adverse events and the suspension of all federally funded projects until corrective action plans were produced. In a damning statement the external review committee found that 'many people at Hopkins believe that oversight and regulatory processes are a barrier to research and are to be reduced to the minimum'.[7]

---

and Medical Ethics (6th edn, London: Butterworths, 2002), chs 19 and 20; Montgomery, J, *Health Care Law* (2nd edn), Oxford:OUP, ch 14; Fox, M, in Tingle, J and Cribb, A, *Nursing Law and Ethics* (2nd edn, Oxford: Blackwell Scientific, 2002). For further detailed discussion regarding the interface with the ethical debate see Foster, C, *The ethics of medical research on humans* (Cambridge: CUP, 2001), *Manual for Research Ethics Committees* (London: Kings College, 2002).

   [2] Adopted by the 18th World Medical Assembly, Helsinki, Finland 1964.

   [3] Council of Europe Steering Committee on Bioethics, *Draft Additional Protocol to the Convention on Human Rights and Biomedicine on Biomedical Research*, Strasbourg, 23 June 2003, CDBI/INF(2003) 6.

   [4] Further recent guidance includes the Council for International Organisations of Medical Sciences, *International Ethical Guidelines for Biomedical Research Involving Human Subjects* (Geneva, 2002).

   [5] Jones, J, *Bad Blood: The Tuskeegee syphilis experiment* (New York: The Free Press, 1981).

   [6] 'Death of research volunteer at Johns Hopkins', *Bulletin of Medical Ethics*, September 2001, 3.

   [7] ibid, 7.

In the United Kingdom the main drive towards regulating clinical research prac-   **13.03**
tices began in the 1960s. In 1968 the then Minister of Health, following a report
of the Royal College of Physicians, sent a letter to health authorities requesting
that they establish research ethics committees (RECs). These bodies sat on a part-
time basis and were primarily composed of health professionals. The first major
piece of guidance to research ethics committee members was produced in 1984 by
the Royal College of Physicians. In 1991 the Department of Health itself finally
issued major guidelines to RECs in the form of the so-called 'Red Book'.[8] The
Department of Health guidance was accompanied by a raft of guidance on specific issues produced by health professional bodies. The promulgation of such
guidance at times perhaps obscured the fact that the legal regulation of this area
was exceedingly limited. Research ethics committees themselves were non-statutory bodies, as was the guidance. Explicit statutory regulation of research activities was rare. One example, is that of embryo research regulated under the Human
Fertilisation and Embryology Act. Some statutory regulation did exist in relation
to those trials which were undertaken on medicinal products under the Medicines
Act 1968. Before drugs can be used in a clinical trial a 'clinical trial certificate' is
required from the Department of Health.[9] This is subject to scrutiny by the relevant licensing authority which is able to seek advice from an expert committee.
There is also a special procedure in the Medicines (Exemption from Licences)
Order 1981.[10] Under this Order trials may be undertaken without a clinical trial
certificate for a three year period subject to the proviso that the licensing authority does not object and various undertakings are provided. This is known as the
clinical trial exemption or CTX. There are further specific provisions relating to
doctors and dentists which are known as the DDX provisions and which again enable them to use drugs without a clinical trials exemption having been provided.[11]
But the scope of statutory regulation was limited.

However in the decade since the publication of the 'Red Book' there has been a   **13.04**
movement towards increasingly structuring the work of RECs. REC members are
provided with training programmes. Material on research ethics is increasingly
being made available.[12] Nonetheless the development of legal knowledge in this
area, amongst clinicians at least, appears to have been more limited. A recent study

---

[8] Department of Health, *Local Research Ethics Committees* (1991).
[9] Medicines Act 1968, ss 31–38.
[10] SI 1981/1964.
[11] Medicines (Exemption from Licence) (Special Cases and Miscellaneous Provisions) Order
1972, SI 1972/1200.
[12] See eg the Ethics Research Informations Catalogue (ERIC) which is a resource database currently being developed; (*http://www.eric-on-line.co.uk/index.php*) and there is a mass of guidance, eg
Royal College of Physicians, *Guidelines on the Practice of Ethics Committees in Medical Research
Involving Humans* (3rd edn, 1996); General Medical Council, *Research: The Role and Responsibilities
of Doctors* (London: GMC, 2002).

of health care professionals undertaken by Ferguson indicated that while clinical researchers were concerned with ethical issues in clinical trials, their knowledge of the applicable law in this area was limited.[13] One may express some sympathy with the clinicians as much of the applicable law in this area could only be ascertained through extrapolation from related case and statute law but there was no coherent statutory regulation. While we are still a considerable way from overarching statutory regulation, the conduct of clinical trials is now set to change radically through the implementation into English law of the EU Clinical Trials Directive. The Directive aligns procedures for clinical trials on medicinal products in the European Union and places the establishment of RECs on a statutory basis.[14] It applies to both commercial and non-commercial trials. Clinical trials are defined as 'an investigation to ascertain the efficacy or safety of a medicine in human subjects'.[15] All clinical trials must be undertaken in accordance with the standards of 'good clinical practice'.[16] The impact of the Directive will be raised at the relevant points throughout this chapter. The Directive is being implemented through regulations and consequent amendments are being made to the Medicines Act 1968.[17] The changes which are being introduced are discussed at appropriate points during this chapter. Generally the importance of the Directive impacts upon the issue of consent, upon issues of liability and the role of the 'sponsor'. Its incorporation has been met with a mixed response. Concerns have been expressed that the Directive may raise costs in publicly funded trials and reduce the number of such trials in the future.[18] Cave and Holm have commented that the 'industry led' approach of the Directive which, they have argued, has been followed in the Governance Arrangements,[19] places undue emphasis upon the facilitation of research rather than upon safeguarding participants' interests.

13.05 Despite the emphasis in recent years upon the need for practices in clinical research to be seen as 'ethical', the medical and scientific community in the United Kingdom has also been dogged with controversy. The scandals caused by the widespread unauthorised retention of human material led to the consideration of

---

[13] Ferguson, P, 'Legal and Ethical Aspects of Clinical Trials: The Views of Researchers' [2003] 11 Med L Rev 48–69.

[14] As implemented in the draft Medicines for Human Use (Clinical Trials) Regulations 2003, regs 4–9.

[15] Directive; Draft Regulations, reg 2 and see explanatory notes, para 4.1.4.

[16] Arts 1(4) and 3–5 of the Directive as incorporated in the 2003 Draft Regulations, reg 26 and Sch 1. The statement on good clinical practice is to be found on the Commission website (*http://www.pharmacos/eudra.org*).

[17] See Medicines Control Agency, *Consultation letter on the Medicines for Use (Clinical Trials) Regulations 2003* MLX 287 (referred to as the 'MCA Consultation).

[18] Medical Research Council *Good regulation of clinical trials for patients* (2003).

[19] Cave, E and Holm, S, 'New governance arrangements for research ethics committees: is facilitating research achieved at the cost of participants interest?' (2002) 28 *Journal of Medical Ethics* 318–321.

this issue in the Bristol Interim Inquiry Report [20] and also through the establishment of the enquiry into events at the Royal Liverpool Children's Hospital (better known as the Alder Hey inquiry).[21] In the context of clinical research, the process of obtaining consent in a clinical trial came under critical scrutiny in an enquiry into a study involving children in which it was alleged that adequate parental consent had not been obtained.[22] Part of the revision of the current research governance guidance derives from these scandals and can also be seen through the current major consideration of reform of the law concerning human material. The area of research has been influenced by the rhetoric of clinical governance, standards and accountability. As in other areas standards frameworks have been introduced in relation to research governance. There are Research Governance Frameworks (RGF) for England and currently separately for Wales.[23] However the content of the Welsh Framework is closely modelled on that of the English Framework and it is the case that the new RGF, which is currently in draft form, is intended to apply to both England and to Wales. The RGF applies both to health and to social care. It interestingly makes reference to 'participants' rather than to 'subjects', a discernible shift in emphasis and as regarding consideration of the ethical issues. The RGF now provides that key elements of such a culture include:

> Respect for participants'dignity, rights, safety and well-being
> Valuing the diversity within society
> Personal and scientific integrity
> Leadership
> Honesty
> Accountability
> Openness[24]

The RGF emphasises the need to safeguard consent,[25] and the protection of personal data.[26] In the light of enquiries at Bristol Royal Infirmary and Alder Hey it stresses the need for particular care in relation to research involving tissue and organs.[27] The RGF refers to the need for 'participants or their representatives' to be involved wherever possible in the design.[28] This is an important use of the terminology 'participants' rather than 'research subjects'.

---

[20] Bristol Inquiry Interim Report, *Removal and Retention of Human Material* (2000) (*www.bristol-inquiry.org.uk*).

[21] *Report of the Inquiry into the Royal Liverpool Childrens Hospital*(Alder Hey) (2001) (*www.rclinquiry.org.uk*).

[22] Griffiths, R, *NHS Executive West Midlands Regional Office Report of a Research Framework in North Staffordshire Hospital NHS Trust* (2001).

[23] *Research Governance Framework for Health and Social Care in Wales* (Cardiff: Wales Office of Research and Development for Health and Social Care, November 2001).

[24] RGF England and Wales, para 2.7.2.

[25] ibid, para 2.2.3.

[26] ibid, para 2.2.5.

[27] ibid, para 2.2.4.

[28] ibid, para 2.2.6

13.06 This chapter sets out the regulatory structure for clinical research in this country, focusing in particular upon the operation of research ethics committees. We consider the clinical trials approval process and problematic issues regarding assessment of risk and consent. The different position at common law regarding consent is contrasted with that of the proposed regulations implementing the Clinical Trials Directive (Directive (EC) 2001/20 of the European Parliament and of the Council on the approximation of the laws, regulations and administrative provisions of the Member States relating to the implementation of good clinical practice in the conduct of trials on medicinal products for human use). The provision made today for monitoring clinical trials and the responsibilities of the parties to the clinical trial are outlined. Particular areas which may give rise to difficulty for researchers, namely confidentiality and use of human material, are discussed. Finally, the provisions made for compensation in the event of injury to the research subject are considered. The discussion here centres upon clinical trials. Nonetheless it should be noted that over the years there has been considerable controversy in relation to the pioneering of new experimental therapeutic techniques. These are now the subject of consideration by the National Institute for Clinical Excellence but will not be discussed further in this chapter.[29]

B. Regulation of Clinical Research: Regulatory Structures

1. Central Office for Research Ethics Committees and the UK Ethics Committee Authority

13.07 In the past one of the criticisms of the conduct of RECs was related to the lack of effective co-ordination of their operation at national level.[30] Recent initiatives however are changing the situation. Initially the NHS established the Central Office for Research Ethics Committees (COREC).[31] This has the task of co-ordinating operational systems for local and multi-centre RECs. Its role includes the provision of an overview of the REC system. It is concerned with the management of Multi-centre research ethics committees (MRECs) and training programmes for REC members/administrators. It is also concerned with the development of standards/operating procedures for RECs.

13.08 One impact of the Clinical Trials Directive has been that of the need for comprehensive overview of clinical research activities. As a consequence oversight of the establishment of RECs is now to be undertaken by a new body, the UK Ethics Committee Authority.[32] This body is to be comprised of the Secretary of State for

---

[29] 'Interventional procedures overviews and consultation document' (*www.nice.org. uk/article.asp?a=81853*). See further ch 1, esp paras 1.113–1.117

[30] Warnock, M, 'A National Research Ethics Committee' (1988) 297 BMJ 1626; Gelder, 'A National Committee for the Ethics of Research' (1990) 16 J of Medical Ethics 146.

[31] *www.corec.org.uk*.

[32] Medicines for Human Use (Clinical Trials) Draft Regulations, para 4.

Health, Scottish Ministers, National Assembly for Wales, Department of Health, and also encompasses Social Services and Public Safety for Northern Ireland. It appears that the Authority will have its functions undertaken by other NHS bodies such as strategic health authorities.[33] Its powers are to extend to abolition of an ethics committee or the variation of operating conditions. Moreover it may 'recognise an ethics committee established by another relevant authority as long as it meets the UKECA requirements for the constitution and operation of an ethics committee'.[34]

2. Role of Research Ethics Committees

(i) Remit of Research Ethics Committees

The Governance Arrangements for NHS RECs provides that   **13.09**

> 3.1. Ethical advice from the appropriate NHS REC is required for any research proposal involving;
>
> > a. participants and users of the NHS. This includes all potential research participants recruited by virtue of the patient or users past or present treatment by, or use of, the NHS. It includes NHS patients treated under contracts with private sector institutions.
> > b. Individuals identified as potential research participants because of their status as relatives or carers of patients and users of the NHS, as defined above
> > c. access to data, organs or other bodily material of past and present NHS patients
> > d. fetal material and IVF involving NHS patients
> > e. the recently dead in NHS premises
> > f. the use of, or potential access to, NHS premises or facilities
> > g. NHS staff-recruited as research participants by virtue of their professional role

In addition a REC may, on request, give opinions in relation to other studies.[35]   **13.10**
The Governance Arrangements provide as illustrations private sector companies, the Medical Research Council, etc. The remit of RECs also relates to health services research.[36] In relation to trials involving medicinal products, Article 6 of the Clinical Trials Directive requires an ethics committee to provide an opinion regarding clinical trials. Regulation 14(6) of the draft regulations implementing the Clinical Trials Directive is based upon Article 6 of the Directive. It sets out a number of issues that a committee must consider which are to include the following factors: the relevance and design of the trial; any anticipated risks/benefits; the

---

[33] ibid, and see also MCA consultation, para 5.3.2.
[34] ibid, para 5.3.2.
[35] Para 3.2.
[36] For a critical discussion as to the validity of application of the same ethical approaches to clinical trials and health service research in the context of consent see Cassell, J and Young, A, 'Why we should not seek individual informed consent for participation in health services research' (2002) 28 J of Medical Ethics 313.

trial protocol and investigator's brochure; the suitability of the investigator and of supporting staff and also the quality of the facilities provided; the recruitment of subjects; information which is to be given to subjects and 'informed consent' procedures; in the case of persons lacking capacity, why this trial is justified; availability of indemnity and compensation regarding death/personal injury; any liability insurance/indemnity cover for investigator/sponsors; information regarding rewards/compensation for investigators/trial subjects.

13.11   As the MCA Consultation notes

> As now an ethics committee would have to consider any other matter which is relevant to the ethical approval of the trial in question. Furthermore in accordance with Regulation 14(9) of the draft, an ethics committee would be obliged to consider and give an opinion on any other issue relating to the clinical trial if raised by the applicant and it appears to the committee to be relevant to the ethical considerations of the trial.[37]

While the reconstituted ethics committees under the Regulations enacting the Clinical Trials Directive are to be concerned with 'clinical trials', it is nonetheless envisaged that they will, where appropriate, continue to review other forms of research.[38]

13.12   RECs are expected to operate independently of the NHS Trust R & D structure.[39] The RGF stresses that the role of the REC is not to provide legal advice to researchers.[40] Where there is the prospect that a particular project may give rise to legal issues, it states that the REC should advise both the researcher and the 'appropriate authority' regarding its concerns. In addition, while the RGF notes that research projects should not proceed without REC approval, that by itself is not the only factor and, as the RGF notes , a NHS organisation may need to consider other issues before it sanctions the project.[41] In the past RECs were criticised for the fact that they did not routinely undertake the monitoring of decision making.[42]

13.13   When considering the appropriateness of the REC remit one difficult issue arises as to the extent to which ethically controversial issues, giving rise to a public policy dimension, should be subject to determination by only one committee acting on a localised basis. It is suggested that where there is a proposal to undertake a research project which involves a particularly controversial procedure with public policy dimensions there should be consideration of such issues at national level. An illustration of a situation in which the public policy issues raised may suggest

---

[37] Para 5.3.3.
[38] MCA Consultation, para 5.3.2.
[39] RGF, para 3.12.4.
[40] ibid, para 3.12.7.
[41] ibid, para 3.12.6.
[42] See eg Pickworth, E, 'Should local research ethics committees monitor research they have approved?' (2000) J of Medical Ethics 330.

that a local consideration of such issues may be insufficient was that of the use made of a video-surveillance technique in a Staffordshire hospital to ascertain whether children were victims of Munchausen's syndrome by proxy.[43] This may be an issue which, in the future, is appropriate for consideration by the new UK Ethics Committee authority.

(ii) Relationship of Research Ethics Committeess with Other Bodies; General

A feature of clinical research in the last decade has been that of the proliferation of new regulatory bodies.[44] Thus while REC approval is considered essential before a clinical trial is undertaken, authorisation may also be required from another appropriate body. There are a number of situations in which an application is required to another body in addition to the REC. Examples of such bodies are the Gene Therapy Advisory Committee which is concerned with research concerning gene therapy, the Xenotransplantation Interim Regulatory Authority,[45] and the Human Fertilisation and Embryology Authority's role regarding embryo research.

13.14

A further important body in relation to trials of medicinal products is the Medicines and Healthcare Products Regulatory Agency (this body was formerly the Medicines Control Agency). Applicants must provide the Agency with information which relates to the manufacture and control of medicines under the CTX system. Information must also be given to support the specification of the product. In this regard the Directive will not have a fundamental effect as the level/ nature of information required to be provided will be similar to the current position.[46]

13.15

In addition to ethics committee approval, trials concerning medicinal products need to receive favourable authorisation from the licensing authority.[47] For these purposes the 'Licensing Authority' is defined as the statutory licensing authority established under s 6 of the Medicines Act .[48] To begin a trial without having obtained such authorisation is a criminal offence. The sale or supply of medicinal products for use in a clinical trial is a criminal offence unless the sponsor has been authorised to undertake a trial and the products have been manufactured or

13.16

---

[43] See further Evans, D, 'The Investigation of life-threatening child abuse and munchausen's syndrome by proxy' (1995) 21 J of Medical Ethics 9; Southall, D and Southall, MP, 'Some ethical issues surrounding covert video surveillance—a response' (1995) 21 J of Medical Ethics 104; Gillon, R, Editorial: Covert surveillance by doctors for life threatening Munchausen's syndrome by proxy' (1995) 21 J of Medical Ethics 104; 'Symposium on covert video surveillance' (1996) 22 J of Medical Ethics 16.

[44] See further Montgomery (n 1 above), ch 21.

[45] (*www.doh.gov.uk/ukxira*).

[46] MCA Consultation, para 3.1.7.

[47] Medicines for Human Use (Clinical Trials) Draft Regulations 2003, reg 11.

[48] ibid, reg 2(1).

imported by a person with a marketing authorisation in United Kingdom or the European Economic Area.[49] Application to the licensing authority must be made in writing by the sponsor.[50] Different rules relate to different classes of product.[51] In relation to general medicinal products[52] a licensing authority is required to inform the sponsor of the decision. This may take the form of acceptance, acceptance subject to condition, or rejection. If the sponsor is not informed within 30 days then the trial is regarded as authorised.[53] If the request is not accepted then the sponsor may submit an amended request to the licensing authority within 14 days.[54] However, if this is not submitted then the request for authorisation is deemed rejected and the licensing authority will not consider it further. Where an amended request is submitted the licensing authority must respond within 60 days from the receipt of the original request that there are grounds for rejection.[55] But if there is no such response again the request may be treated as accepted.

13.17   Where the trial concerns products for gene therapy and/or somatic cell therapy,[56] while the procedure is similar to general medicinal products the time periods are longer. In relation to applications these must be dealt with in a period of 30 days,[57] but where a licensing authority refers this to a relevant committee the period is then extended up to 120 days.[58] In a situation in which the request has been rejected, the sponsor has 30 days in which to submit an amended request (or such amended period as allowed by the licensing authority).[59] Where an amended request has been submitted the licensing authority must respond within 90 days or in a situation in which the matter has been referred to the appropriate committee within 180 days (reg 18(7)). Again in such a situation they may alternatively authorise the trial subject to conditions.

13.18   Thirdly, a separate procedure is being established for authorisation of those trials involving products with special characteristics other than set out above.[60] These are those medicinal products which have been developed through the use of biotechnological processes stated to be: recombinant DNA technology;

---

[49] ibid, reg 12.
[50] ibid, reg 16.
[51] The Directive and the 2003 Draft Regulations also consider the issue of the manufacture and importation of investigational medicinal products but these are not considered further in this chapter: see Art 13 and reg 35 respectively.
[52] Draft Regulations, reg 17.
[53] ibid, reg 17(2)–(4).
[54] ibid, reg 17(5).
[55] ibid, regs 17(6)–8.
[56] Including xenogeneic cell therapy and medicinal products containing genetically modified organisms, reg 18(1).
[57] Draft Regulations, reg 18(2).
[58] reg 18(5).
[59] reg 18(6).
[60] This refers to those products set out in Pt A to Annex of Regulation (EEC) 2309/93.

controlled expression of gene coding for biologically active proteins in prokaryotes and eukaryotes included transferred mammalian cells; hybridoma and monoclonal antibody methods. They also have active ingredients which are 'biological products of human or animal origin, or contains biological components or human or animal origin or requires such components in its manufacture' (Draft Regulations, reg 19(1)ii).

While the processes are the same as for medicinal products, here the trial cannot be sanctioned by default because no objection has been expressed by the licensing authority. Instead the licensing authority must provide written authorisation.[61] The Regulations provide procedures enabling the licensing authority compulsorily to amend the clinical trial conditions.[62] In such a situation it is required to give the sponsor at least 14 days' notice to enable the sponsor the opportunity to respond in writing. The licensing authority is required to take those responses into account before making its decision.

(iii) Research Ethics Committee Membership

REC members are to be appointed following Nolan principles after there has been public advertisement of the post.[63] An application form must be completed and the guidance provides that the selection of members is to be subject to standard operating procedures. Appointments are made for fixed periods. The Governance Arrangements suggest that these shall normally be for five years. Although terms are renewable the guidance does not envisage that members should serve more than two consecutive terms on the same REC.[64] Moreover Governance Arrangements state that: **13.19**

> The appointing Authority shall ensure that a rotation system for membership is in place that allows for continuity, the development and maintenance of expertise within the REC, and the regular input of fresh ideas.[65]

Over the last decade steps have been taken to ensure, as far as possible, full and informed participation by REC members. Today members are required as a condition of their appointment to undertake appropriate initial and continuing education.[66]   **13.20**

The maximum overall membership of a REC is 18 (see Governance Arrangements, para 6.11). A quorum for committee meetings is stated in the Governance Arrangements to be seven members and this is to include chair/vice chair, at least one expert member with relevant expertise, one lay member and one other   **13.21**

---

[61] Draft Regulations, reg 19.
[62] ibid, reg 22.
[63] Governance Arrangements, para 5.3.
[64] ibid, para 5.10.
[65] ibid, para 5.11.
[66] ibid, para 5.6.

member who is 'independent of the institution or specific location where the research is to take place'.[67] Members are to be drawn from a 'sufficiently broad range of experience and expertise'.[68] The REC should have a balanced age and gender composition[69] and should also contain a mixture of 'expert' and 'lay' members.[70] The Governance Arrangements state that the expert members are to be selected such that the REC has expertise in four areas.[71] First, in relation to methodological and ethical experience in both clinical and non-clinical research and qualitative or other research methods which are applicable to health services, social science and research in the area of social care. Secondly, in relation to clinical practice, which is stated to include hospital and community staff and general practice. Thirdly, statistics that are relevant to research and, finally, pharmacy. In cases in which 'a member provides unique expertise'[72] there is provision to appoint deputies. These are also to be appointed in accordance with the standard recruiting processes.

13.22 The Governance Arrangements provide that at least one third of the composition of the committee should be made up of 'lay' members.[73] The definition of 'lay' does include non-medical clinical staff in a situation in which they have not been involved in professional practice for a period of five years or more.[74] Nonetheless the Governance Arrangements state that half of the 'lay' group must have never been health or social care professionals and have never been involved in undertaking research which involves human participants, tissue or data.[75] REC members are not representatives of a particular group but are rather to act as appointees in their own right[76]. The RGF provides that RECs must have systems in place regarding the identification of possible conflicts of interest.[77] The Governance Arrangements also make provision for the appointment of specialist referees in situations in which a particular proposal lies outside the expertise of the individual member.[78]

(iv) Research Ethics Committee Chair

13.23 While the Governance Arrangements do provide for the appointment of a chair and a lay chair, they do not state what constituent groups they should be drawn

---

[67] ibid, para 6.11.
[68] ibid, para 6.1.
[69] ibid, para 6.2.
[70] ibid, para 6.3.
[71] ibid, para 6.4.
[72] ibid, para 6.15.
[73] ibid, para 6.5.
[74] ibid, para 6.6.
[75] ibid, para 6.7.
[76] ibid, para 6.8.
[77] RGF,t para 4.5.
[78] Governance Arrangements, para 6.10.

from.[79] In the past there was some debate as to whether such office holders should be 'lay'. The draft of the original 'Red Book' provided that the chair should be a lay member and the final version stated that the chair or lay chair should be a 'lay member'. One advantage of the appointment of a lay chair is that of perceptible detachment and objectivity. Nonetheless Marshall and Moodie have commented that there may be some perceived difficulties in a lay chair,[80] perhaps relating to situations where the proposal submitted was of a very complex technical nature. A lack of specialist knowledge may create difficulties in a situation in which a lay chair is asked to take 'chair's action' between committee meetings, although concerns regarding such lack of expertise may of course be met by thorough consultation by the chair. The Governance Arrangements provide that chairs should be given personal training regarding research ethics reviewing and that they should also be offered 'any necessary supplementary training' before appointment.[81] There is also provision for the appointment of a 'scientific officer' who may liaise with applicants and may, if appropriate, act as the REC representative on scientific management and discussions. Although the Governance Arrangements note that these may be chair/vice-chair or administrator, this is a task which may also be shared with other RECs.[82]

(v) Research Ethics Committee Procedures

The Governance Arrangements provide for standard operating procedures regarding, for example, constitution, appointment and internal procedures, etc.[83] One particular issue raised in the EU Directive Articles 6(5) and (7) was that of time limits, the aim being to ensure the expeditious processing of research applications. In the context of trials on medicinal products the draft Regulations now state that an REC must normally provide an opinion within 60 days of receipt of application.[84] Extensions of 30 days may be allowed in relation to those medicinal products which concern gene therapy, somatic cell therapy or those medicinal products which contain genetically modified organisms. There is also provision for a further 90 day extension in a situation in which ethics committees consult a group/committee (of the type noted in para 13.14 above) regarding such a trial.[85] Ethics committees may also request supplementary information and where this occurs the appropriate time limits are suspended. In the case of trials on medicinal products the Regulations incorporating Article 10(a) of the Directive now

13.24

---

[79] ibid, para 6.12.
[80] Marshall, P and Moodie, P, 'Guidelines for Local Research Ethics Committee' (1992) 304 BMJ 1293.
[81] Governance Arrangements, para 6.12.
[82] ibid, para 6.13.
[83] ibid, para 7.2.
[84] Draft Regulations, reg 14(10).
[85] ibid, reg 14(4).

provide that the ethics committee will have to provide an opinion on amendments which involve changes to the trial protocol or other related documents used in the application.[86] As the MCA consultation notes, decisions should be reached and communicated within 60 days.[87] This is in line with the reforms prompted by the EU Directive.

13.25   The Governance Arrangements provide that proceedings are normally held in private.[88] This approach has, however, been the subject of some critical comment and it can be argued that there is a legitimate public interest in opening up REC deliberations to public scrutiny. Ashcroft and Pfeffer have explored the arguments for maintaining such secrecy.[89] First, it can be argued that this safeguards clinical confidentiality. But, as they note, this is only likely to be an issue in exceedingly rare cases, for example, where a trial involves a rare or serious condition where it is possible for an individual patient to be identified. Secondly, maintaining confidentiality can be seen in terms of maintaining 'commercial or academic confidentiality'. However Ashcroft and Pfeffer suggest that in practice today a vast amount of information regarding drug trials does in any case have to be made public. They question the extent to which other researchers could realistically benefit substantially from disclosure of data and of methods. In their view there is no risk to the commercial confidentiality of researchers and a strong pressure to ensure that the results of research are made widely known in the NHS. While there may be arguments for safeguarding the privacy of a researcher, nonetheless they suggest that if it is the case that decisions about competence are raised these could be dealt with under reserved business with a researcher being given a right of reply. Finally, they consider the argument that confidentiality is required to safeguard the privacy interests of RECs themselves and promote candour, with, for example, analogies being drawn with the operation of the jury system. Ashcroft and Pfeffer persuasively rebut this on the basis that jury secrecy is safeguarded through a raft of policy considerations such as preserving finality of verdicts and protecting them from defendant that are not applicable in the research context. They are sceptical of the secrecy as promoting candour argument, pointing to the growing trend in other public areas towards enhanced disclosure. This concern is now met somewhat by a provision in the Governance Arrangements which enables the summary of application details to be made publicly available after the REC has reached its final decision, although whether this is sufficient may perhaps be questioned.[90]

---

[86] ibid, regs 10, 22, 23.
[87] MCA Consultation, para 7.10.
[88] ibid, para 7.17.
[89] Ashcroft, R and Pfeffer, N, 'Ethics behind closed doors; do research ethics committees need secrecy?' (2001) 322 BMJ 1294–1296.
[90] Governance Arrangements, para 7.18.

(v) Monitoring Research Ethics Committee Performance

The RGF provides that those who establish REC's must create systems for the **13.26** monitoring of their performance. RECs are required to submit annual reports to their reporting authority.[91] This report is to include information regarding committee members, meetings, attendance, proposals made and decisions reached, and the time taken to process such applications. In addition the report should list the projects which were completed or terminated during that year and any training which was undertaken by the 'committee or its members.[92] The increased openness of decision making is to be welcomed. However this reporting procedure is still very much on a localised basis with RECs reporting to their appointing authority. It is thus difficult to achieve an effective overview of RECs as a whole. This position may however change in the future in the light of the work of the new UK Ethics Committee Authority which is currently being established.

3. Multi-centre Research Ethics Committees

In the past where trials were undertaken over a number of areas this created diffi- **13.27** culties because there was no effective overview of the review process. As a consequence researchers had to apply to a multiplicity of RECs. An illustration of the difficulties which may result and the inconsistency of approach which may be found across such committees can be found in a study undertaken in 1995 of the submission of the same proposal to 24 health authorities in nine regions. This study found that there was considerable variation in the approval of the proposal. Fourteen RECs gave approval without requiring modification, six committees asked for some minor modifications, three rejected it.[93] This position was altered when in 1999 the multi-centre research ethics committee (MREC) system was established. Arrangements for MRECs are now included in the Governance Arrangements.[94] Arrangements for approval of protocols through MRECs is now also mandated in the case of trials on medicinal products through the Clinical Trials Directive. The Directive provides in Article 7 that member states should establish procedures in relation to obtaining opinions on multi-centre trials. Consequently reg 13 of the Draft Regulations provides that multi-centre trial applications should be made to an ethics committee which is established/recognised for an area in which the chief investigator is 'professionally based' or for the United Kingdom as a whole. This ethics committee must be responsible for consideration of the particular trial in question.

---

[91] ibid , para 7.19.
[92] ibid, para 7.20.
[93] Redshaw, M, Harris, A, Baum, D, 'Research Ethics Committee Audit; Difference Between Committees'(1996) 22 J of Medical Ethics 78.
[94] Governance arrangements, para 8.

13.28   Currently applications must be made to MRECs in a situation in which a trial is to be undertaken in five or more sites.[95] Research sites are defined as being 'the geographical area covered by one strategic health authority whether the research is based in institution(s) or in the community'. Even when the research may physically take place at several locations within that geographical boundary, a favourable ethical opinion on the research protocol is required from only one NHS REC within that health authority boundary.[96] However the procedures for MREC approval are to change in 2003. There is to be a new definition of multi-centre research: '[r]esearch taking place within the boundaries of two or more research sites'.[97] There are interim arrangements currently in operation such that researchers who are undertaking research within two to four sites are to be able to opt for MREC or REC approval.

13.29   There is now a central allocation system for applications to MRECs.[98] Applications are to be made to the 'Central Allocation Point' based in the COREC office. If a MREC provides a favourable opinion on the trial protocol this is then applicable across the United Kingdom. In a situation in which a MREC has refused approval but has indicated that it may consider it again if amendments are made then an application for a second review to the MREC may be made, again through the Central Allocation Office.[99] Where a MREC has rejected the application there is also now provision for an appeal to a different MREC. Again applicants will have to apply to the Central Allocation Office for their application to be allocated to a MREC. If a proposal has been approved by a MREC it will still require consideration by a REC in relation not to the ethics of the protocol but concerning 'locality' issues.[100] The Governance Arrangements limit 'locality issues' to:

> the suitability of the local researcher
> the appropriateness of the local research environment and facilities
> specific issues relating to the local community including the need for provision of information in languages other than English.[101]

In their determination of such issues the Governance Arrangements state that RECs should work alongside the local NHS 'host' organisation[102] and should establish any necessary administrative arrangements to enable this liaison to be undertaken.[103] It is intended that such consideration should be undertaken

---

[95] ibid, para 8.1.
[96] ibid, para 3.
[97] *www.corec.org.uk/Interim.htm.*
[98] *www.corec.org.uk/centralallocations.htm.*
[99] *www.corec.org.uk/appeals.htm.*
[100] Governance Arrangements, para 8.7.
[101] ibid, para 8.8.
[102] ibid, para 8.9.
[103] ibid, para 8.10.

contemporaneously with the MREC consideration of the protocol.[104] A decision on locality issues should be undertaken and communicated within 60 days after a valid application has been submitted.[105]

C. Evaluating a Research Protocol: Legal and Ethical Issues

The Governance Arrangements require RECs when considering research proto-   **13.30**
cols to examine a number of factors. These include the scientific design and conduct of the trial, confidentiality,[106] informed consent[107] and 'community
considerations'. This last factor concerns the impact and indeed the relevance of
the research upon the local community and/or concerned communities from
which the participants are drawn.[108] In this section we consider in particular the
issues of risk—which relates to the design of the trial, consent and confidentiality.

1. Assessing Risk

The Declaration of Helsinki states that: **13.31**

> Medical research involving human subjects should only be conducted if the impor-
> tance outweighs the inherent risks and burdens to the subject. This is especially im-
> portant where the human subjects are healthy volunteers.

The Governance Arrangements emphasise the need to ensure care and protection
of research participants.[109] The first criteria which RECs are directed to consider
is that of the scientific design and conduct of the trial. As in earlier guidance they
are asked to look at the balance of risks and inconveniences weighed against anticipated benefits for research participants and for other present and future patients and also 'concerned communities'.[110] Prior to consideration by RECs it is
now the practice and indeed the expectation of the guidelines that protocols will
have been subject to prior scientific review by appropriate experts.[111] The risk-
benefit calculation is of course problematic.

English law does not allow the competent adult to consent to the infliction of any   **13.32**
harm, however grave.[112] Unlawful infliction of harm may result in prosecution for
a range of offences including battery or one of the statutory offences contained in
the Offences Against the Person Act 1961. Difficult issues surround inclusion of

---

[104] ibid, para 8.11.
[105] ibid, para 8.12.
[106] ibid, para 9.16.
[107] ibid, para 9.17.
[108] ibid, para 9.18.
[109] ibid at para 9.15.
[110] ibid at para 9.13
[111] RGF, paras 2.3.1–2.3.2 and Governance Arrangements, para 9.8.
[112] See also *R v Brown* [1993] 2 All ER 75.

subjects in 'risky' trial procedures. There has, for example, been considerable discussion regarding the legitimacy and legality of the inclusion of subjects in trials for experimental procedures (such as xenotransplantation) which involve considerable risks.[113] The precise boundaries of what constitutes a legitimate level of risk is unclear.[114] Some guidance has been given in codes of practice issued by health professional bodies. For example, the Royal College of Physicians in its guidance has divided risks into three main categories.[115] First, 'minimal risk' includes such things as headaches and tiredness or where there was a very remote prospect that serious injury or death could result. Secondly, the 'less than minimal risk' category relates to, for example, the situation in which a research subject provides a urine sample. Thirdly, more than minimal risk. In such a situation patients are to be included only if: the risk is still small in comparison with that which patients incur through the disease itself; the disease is serious; the information obtained as a consequence of the research is of 'great practical benefit'; no other means is available by which this information can be obtained; and, finally, fully informed consent is given. In some instances the project may be regarded as comparatively 'risk free' because, for example, it involves questionnaire-based research. However this itself may prove to be an unduly simplistic way of examining such an issue.[116] It has been noted that some 'harms' may be identified even, for example, in the context of postal questionnaires concerning breast disease management, such as worry or anxiety or giving rise to inappropriate expectations.

13.33 One further factor related to the assessment of risk in clinical trials which RECs are invited to consider is that of the inducements which may be offered to participants in the trial, researchers and research hosts.[117] Inducements may be other than financial. An illustration is the inclusion of prisoners in clinical research. There have long been concerns that prisoners are potentially vulnerable participants. Their decision as to whether to be included in a clinical trial could be influenced by the fact that such inclusion may facilitate the parole process. At the same time there are reasons why prisoners may receive considerable benefits from involvement in clinical trials. The draft additional protocol to the Convention on Human Rights and Biomedicine now provides in Article 20 that:

---

[113] See generally discussion in Fox, M, 'Clinical Research and Patients' in Tingle, J and Cribb, A (eds), *Nursing Law and Ethics* (2nd edn, Blackwell Scientific, 2002).

[114] See *Consent in the Criminal Law*, Law Commission Consultation Paper No 139, 1996, paras 8.38–8.52.

[115] Royal College of Physicians, *Guidelines on the Practice of Ethics Committees in Medical Research Involving Human Subjects* (3rd edn, London: Royal College of Physicians, 1996).

[116] Evans, M, Robling, M, Maggs Rapport, F, Houston, H, Kinnersley, P and Wilkinson, C, 'It doesn't cost anything just to ask does it? The ethics of questionnaire-based research' (2002) 21 J of Medical Ethics 41–44.

[117] Governance Arrangements, para 9.16 (k), (m).

Where the law allows research on persons deprived of liberty, such persons may participate in a research project in which the results do not have the potential to produce direct benefit to their health only if the following additional conditions are met;

i) research of comparable effectiveness cannot be carried out without the participation of persons deprived of liberty ;

ii) the research entails only minimal risk and minimal burden.

The potential risks to a particular group which is perceived as vulnerable are obviously a matter which should of concern to REC's. We consider below two further groups which give rise to particular problematic consideration in this context, children and mentally incompetent adults.

2. Consent and the Competent Adult

The Declaration of Helsinki provides that: **13.34**

> In any research on human beings each subject must be adequately informed of the aims, methods, anticipated benefits and potential hazards of the study and the discomfort that it might entail. He or she must be informed that he or she is at liberty to abstain from participation in the study and that he or she is at liberty to withdraw his or her consent to participation at any time. The physician should then obtain the subject's freely given consent preferably in writing.

This emphasis on informed consent is reflected in a whole series of major ethical guidelines. The EU Clinical Trials Directive [118] contains provision for 'informed consent'.[119] It is defined in Article 2(j) as being a decision which is 'taken freely after being duly informed of its nature, significance, implications and risks'. Article 13 of the draft protocol to the Council of Europe's Convention on Human Rights and Biomedicine states that research participants are to be given adequate information regarding the purpose, nature, possible risks and benefits of the project and, separately in Article 14, stresses the fact that no research should be undertaken without free and informed consent. In the future it is possible that the Human Rights Act 1998 may have an impact here. This is particularly the case in relation to Article 3—the prohibition on the imposition of torture and inhuman and degrading treatment—and Article 8—the right to privacy militates in support of providing persons with 'informed' consent.

Of course what precisely constitutes consent may be problematic. In relation to   **13.35**
trials on medicinal products the EU Directive sets very broad parameters which afford considerable discretion to member states. Nonetheless there is the issue as

---

[118] Directive (EC) 2001/20 of the European Parliament and of the Council on the approximation of the laws, regulations and administrative provisions of the Member States relating to the implementation of good clinical practice in the conduct of clinical trials on medicinal products for human use [2001] OJ L121/34.

[119] ibid, Art 3(2)(b).

to what extent enhanced disclosure equates with enhanced comprehension by research participants. Some commentators, such as Thornton, have been sceptical as to the reality of consent and have suggested that the best which may be achieved is partly informed consent.[120] This extent of comprehension by research participants of information which has been given to them by researchers is a relatively undeveloped research area. In a study of patients participating in clinical trials Ferguson found that a very high proportion of participants were happy with the information given to them by researchers. Of the sample, 94 per cent were happy with the information as provided; in terms of patient understanding some 50 per cent stated that they had understood all of the information given, and some 49 per cent were of the view that they comprehended most of the information provided.[121] Interestingly it appeared that patients felt that they were receiving more information because they were involved as participants in a clinical trial. There is of course a question as to the extent to which patients' perceptions regarding their comprehension were realistic and, as Ferguson notes, this is an issue which requires further research.

13.36 One particular difficulty in the consent process relates to the use of randomisation in clinical trials. Randomisation can assist the trial process by reducing the prospects of findings illustrating an improvement whereas this particular improvement may simply be because a new treatment has been given. Provision of information regarding the nature of the trial and that it is a placebo is necessary. The whole notion of randomisation is exceedingly problematic in a situation in which a drug which is under trial represents the only known chance of a cure for a life-threatening condition. A notable illustration of this was the controversy of the randomisation of drugs under test in the case of HIV. In the United States one trial was rendered ineffective when patients who were desperate for treatment pooled the drugs.[122] The draft additional protocol on Biomedical Research to the Convention on Human Rights and Biomedicine now provides in Article 24 that '[t]he use of placebo is permissible where there are no methods of proven effectiveness, or where withdrawal or withholding of such methods does not present unacceptable risk or burden'.

---

[120] See Thornton, H, 'Clinical Trials: A Brave New Partnership?' (1994) 20 J of Medical Ethics 19 and note the response by Baum, M, 'Clinical Trials—a brave new partnership; a response to Mrs Thornton' (1994) 20 J of Medical Ethics 23.

[121] Ferguson, PR, 'Patients' perceptions of information provided in clinical trials' (2002) 28 J of Medical Ethics 45.

[122] See further discussion in Arras, JD, 'Non-compliance in AIDS Research' (1990) Hastings Centre Report 24 and see also Young, A and McHale, JV, 'The Dilemmas of the HIV Positive Prisoner'(1992) Howard J of Criminal Justice 89.

(i) Informed Consent: Liability in Battery

In relation to consent to treatment it is accepted at common law that a health pro- **13.37**
fessional is only required to provide a patient with a general explanation in broad
terms of the nature of a procedure to avoid liability in battery,[123] as far as a therapeutic procedure is concerned. It is possible that the courts may be prepared to
take a more rigorous approach in relation to disclosure in non-therapeutic
research. A notable Canadian case frequently cited for its support of an approach
of broad disclosure to volunteers in clinical trials is *Halushka v University of
Saskatchewan*.[124] In this case Hall J stated that:

> The subject of medical experimentation is entitled to a full and frank disclosure of
> all the facts, probabilities and opinions which a reasonable man might be expected
> to consider before giving his consent. It has been suggested that such an approach
> should be employed in relation to both patients and volunteers.

It is suggested that this approach should be followed in relation to non-therapeutic procedures. If trials can be seen as being undertaken in the public interest then
surely the position of the volunteer in such a trial should be safeguarded through
full and frank disclosure of all applicable risks.

The situation regarding therapeutic procedures is more problematic. To allow ac- **13.38**
tions to be brought in battery on the basis of failure to inform in the context of
therapeutic procedures would require a different approach to be taken between
therapeutic research and therapeutic treatment as the courts have indicated their
unwillingness to extend the boundaries of liability in battery.[125]

(ii) Informed Consent: Liability in Negligence

Where there is a claim that a research participant was provided with insufficient **13.39**
information regarding the risks of involvement in a clinical trial, an action is most
likely to be brought in negligence. The leading case on the test for information
disclosure in relation to treatment is that of the House of Lords in *Sidaway v Royal
Bethlem Hospital Governors*.[126] Although the majority rejected a 'prudent patient'
approach to disclosure, the majority while rooting the test for disclosure in professional practice differed somewhat regarding the scope of disclosure.
Nonetheless in subsequent cases following *Sidaway*, the narrowest approach, that
of *Bolam*, was followed,[127] even in respect of a situation in which patients asked

---

[123] *Chatterson v Gerson* [1981] 1 All ER 257.
[124] [1965] 53 DLR(2d) 436.
[125] See generally Tan Keng Feng, 'Failure of Medical Advice: Trespass or Negligence?' [1987] 1 LS
149 and Brazier, M, 'Patient Autonomy and Consent to Treatment' [1987] 1 LS 169.
[126] [1985] 1 All ER 673.
[127] *Gold v Haringey HA* [1987] 2 All ER 888; *Blyth v Bloomsbury AHA* decided in 1987 but
reported in [1993] 4 Med LR 151.

questions of the health care professional. However more recently in the Court of Appeal in *Pearce v United Bristol NHS Trust*,[128] a more expansive approach was taken. Lord Woolf held that:

> if there is a significant risk which would affect the judgment of a reasonable patient then in the normal course it is the responsibility of a doctor to inform the patient of that significant risk, if the information is needed so that the patient can determine for him or herself as to what course that she should adopt.

Although in this particular case the claimant was unsuccessful, Jones has argued that the effect of the judgments is that of a combination of the 'prudent patient' standard with the reasonable doctor standard and that, in the light of this case, it could be argued that 'no reasonable doctor would fail to disclose a risk regarded as significant by a reasonable patient'.[129] A more critical approach to scrutiny of clinical decision-making may be reflected in the context of any judicial consideration of information provided to participants involved in a therapeutic trial.

13.40   A second and related factor is that even if the test in negligence is rooted in the professional practice standard that standard has itself been subject to reconsideration in the light of developments over the last decade. The impact of the Bristol Royal Infirmary Inquiry report and the Griffiths report cannot be underestimated. Professional practice guidelines are emphasising the need for enhanced openness and better communication. It is submitted that researchers today would be at the very least unwise to withhold information from research subjects. Enhanced disclosure and frankness in spelling out the possibilities are moreover surely the best ways to facilitate enhanced participation in research activities in the future.

(iii) Non-Consensual Inclusion

13.41   One of the elements of consent is that the consent which is given should be voluntary. Coercion implicitly negates the reality of the consent process. Nonetheless in the 1990s there were some indications that in exceptional situations the judiciary may be prepared in some limited situations to sanction involvement in clinical procedures despite a competent patient's refusal.[130] However this approach was subjected to judicial criticism in *Re MB*[131] and *St George's NHS Trust v S*[132] and see also *Re B (Adult) Refusal of Medical Treatment* [2002] 2 All ER 449, which confirmed the right of the competent adult to refuse treatment regardless of the consequences. It is thus exceedingly unlikely that in the future the courts would be prepared to override the refusal of a competent adult to be involved in a research procedure even where this procedure represented that person's only chance of survival.

---

[128] [1999] PIQR P53 (CA).
[129] Jones, M, 'Informed Consent and other fairy stories' [1999] 7 Med L Rev 103.
[130] *Re S (Adult: Refusal of Medical Treatment)* [1992] 3 WLR 806.
[131] [1997] 2 FLR 426.
[132] [1998] 3 WLR 936.

(iv) Pregnancy

13.42 One problematic issue is the extent to which pregnant women should be involved in clinical trials. While research on this subject group may lead to important therapeutic benefits it is nonetheless a potentially vulnerable group. The inclusion of pregnant women in clinical trials is is not an issue directly addressed in the research governance guidelines. In contrast there is some specific reference to this in the form of the additional protocol on Biomedical Research to the Convention on Human Rights and Biomedicine which provides in Article 18 that:

1. Research on a pregnant woman which does not have the potential to produce results of direct benefit to her health or that of the embryo or foetus or child after birth, may only be undertaken if the following conditions are met ;

    i) the research has the aim of contributing to the ultimate attainment of results capable of conferring benefit to other women in relation to reproduction or to other women in relation to reproduction or to embryos, foetuses or children

    ii) research of comparable effectiveness cannot be carried out on women who are not pregnant

    iii) the research entails only minimal risk and minimal burden

2. Where research is undertaken on breast feeding women, particular care shall be taken to avoid any adverse impact on the health of the child

13.43 A further difficulty relates to the fact that involvement of a pregnant woman in a clinical research project may arise unexpectedly, perhaps due to an emergency situation arising. The Royal College of Physicians' guidelines provide that in a situation in which a researcher intended to examine unexpected events during pregnancy, the pregnant woman should be asked whether, should an emergency arise, she would be prepared to be involved.[133] Should the trial concern medicinal products and the woman is found to be incompetent, then the issue of whether she should be included needs to be considered in the light of the EU Clinical Trials Directive and consequent proposed new regulations—see para 13.66 below.

3. Consent and the Child Participant : Common Law[134]

13.44 The involvement of children in clinical trials necessitates careful ethical scrutiny. While the general principle is that wherever possible research should not be undertaken on competent adults, it may be necessary to undertake research on children. It is necessary to undertake certain forms of research using child subjects. This may relate to the fact that the study is to focus on childhood diseases. Alternatively it may be because a particular drug may have differential effects on

---

[133] Royal College of Physicians, *Report of Working Party on Research Involving Patients* (London: RCP, 1991), para 7.51.
[134] See generally on children and clinical research Nicholson, R, *Medical Research and Children* (Oxford: OUP, 1985).

children and adults. Inclusion of children can give rise to particularly difficult issues regarding risk assessment. The Royal College of Paediatricians and Child Health guidelines provided that it would not be appropriate to subject a child to a risk which was more than minimal in the case of a non-therapeutic trial.[135] The Clinical Trials Directive places explicit limitations on the inclusion of children in clinical trials concerning medicinal products. It provides that research should only be undertaken on children where:

> some direct benefit for the group of patients is obtained from the clinical trial and only where such research is essential to validate data obtained in clinical trials on persons able to give informed consent or by other research methods: additionally such research should either relate to a clinical condition from which the minor concerned suffers or be of such a nature that it can only be carried out on minors.[136]

While this, as noted earlier, relates to medicinal products should there be judicial consideration of the common law position it is possible that this statement may be influential in relation to the rest of the clinical trials process. Further consideration is given at p. 881 below to the regulations which are being introduced to bring English law into line with the EU Clinical Trials Directive in this respect. Moreover the Directive provides that the design of the trial must be such that it minimises the discomfort, fear and other risks which are foreseeable.

(i) Children and Consent

13.45   Children over the age of 16 have a statutory right to consent to surgical, medical and dental treatment under s 8 of the Family Law Reform Act 1969. While children under that age may be competent to consent, this is a decision-relative test under the common law, namely, does the child have sufficient maturity to comprehend the information given and to make a choice.[137] It should be noted that ethical guidance suggests that, in relation to research projects, even where a child may be technically competent to consent, that consent should also be obtained from the child's parents. Non-therapeutic trials are more problematic. It is submitted that it would be very difficult for a researcher to justify the conduct of such a trial on a minor without parental consent following the approach taken by the Court of Appeal in *Re W* in 1992.[138] Here the Court of Appeal indicated that s 8(1) referred to 'surgical medical and dental treatment'. This suggests that in a case of non-therapeutic research reference would be required to the position at common law. Thus in such a situation parental consent would, in practice, invariably be required.

---

[135] Royal College of Paediatrics and Child Health, Ethics Advisory Committee *Guidelines for the Ethical Conduct of Medical Research Involving Children* (London: BPA, 1992).

[136] Art 4.

[137] *Gillick v West Norfolk and Wisbech AHA* [1985] 3 All ER 402. See further Ch 4.

[138] *Re W (a minor) (medical treatment)* [1992] 4 All ER 627.

A further difficult issue is the extent to which children should ever be compelled   **13.46**
to be involved in clinical research. In the vast majority of situations it would be
difficult to envisage researchers seeking to continue a project in the face of opposition from a minor. However there may be exceptional cases, for example involving therapeutic research projects, in which compulsion may be sought. In the past
in relation to treatment decisions the Court of Appeal has held that a decision by
a competent minor to refuse treatment may be overridden. In *Re W* Lord
Donaldson memorably stated that:

> No minor of whatever age has power by refusing to consent to treatment to override
> a consent to treatment by someone who has parental responsibility for the minor.
> Nevertheless such a refusal was a very important consideration in making clinical
> judgments and for parents and the court in deciding whether themselves to give
> consent.[139]

Although the judicial willingness to override the refusal of the competent minor
has been subject to trenchant academic criticism this principle still holds. While
circumstances in which a protesting adolescent would be compelled to be included in a clinical research project—albeit therapeutic—are likely to be limited,
one possible exception is when the procedure itself represents a potentially life-
saving therapy and the only chance for a critically ill adolescent.

4. *Consent; Adults Who Lack Capacity: Common Law Principles*

(i) Therapeutic Procedures

As with children the perceived vulnerability of mentally incompetent adults has led   **13.47**
to professed concerns regarding their inclusion in clinical research projects. In *Re F*
in 1990 the House of Lords confirmed that once a person reaches the age of maturity, no one has the power to make clinical decisions on their behalf.[140] While treatment may be give, the basis for this treatment is that of the best interests of the
incompetent adult. The assessment of best interests was judged to be referable to a
test of clinical judgment and thus this meant that the boundaries of best interests
in decision making were circumscribed by the *Bolam* test. However, while this is a
clinically based test, in decisions concerning medical treatment generally the courts
have shown themselves willing to take a more expansive approach to the interpretation of best interests, notably in *Re SL* [2000] 3 WLR 1288. The courts have now
indicated that they are prepared to sanction the performance of experimental therapy upon an incompetent adult. In *Simms v Simms and An NHS Trust*[141] the Court

---

[139] ibid.
[140] *Re F* [1990] 2 AC 1. See further Ch 4.
[141] [2002] EWHC 2734; [2003] Fam 83 and see further Harrington, J, 'Deciding Best Interest:
Medical Progress Clinical Judgment and the "Good Family" ' (2003) 3 Web J of Current Legal
Issues.

of Appeal authorised the administration of experimental therapy upon two patients who were suffering from Creutzfeldt Jakob disease (CJD). The treatment was authorised in the face of opposition expressed regarding this therapy by the UK National CJD Surveillance Unit and the local NHS Trust.

(ii) Non-Therapeutic Trials

13.48 While the application of the test in *Re F* would potentially at least sanction the inclusion of the mentally incompetent adult in the therapeutic trial process, their involvement in non-therapeutic procedures is considerably more problematic. A number of possible alternative bases for the legality of inclusion have been considered by Lewis.[142] One approach may be to consider whether their inclusion has been sanctioned because of a previously exercised advance directive. However this is unlikely to have arisen in most instances. Moreover, in their report on *Mental Incapacity* in 1995 the Law Commission also noted that advance consent to treatment other than 'reasonable treatment which is in a person's best interests' would not be lawful.[143] Alternatively a substituted judgment approach could be taken. However such an approach has been rejected by the English courts and its application is indeed highly problematic in a situation in which the individual had never previously possessed decision making capacity. Moreover even if there had been prior competence nonetheless there are difficulties in making a realistic assessment using a substituted judgment test. As Lewis notes, [a] decision based on the individual's previously competent preferences may be imposed on the incompetent who is no longer the same person'.[144] Alternatively it could be suggested that non-therapeutic research was justified under the 'best interests' test set out in *Re F*. However this may be considered to be unlikely. In their 1995 report the Law Commission were of the view that such research was currently unlawful. They commented that if:

> the participant lacks capacity to consent to his or her participation and the procedure cannot be justified under the doctrine of necessity, then any person who touches or restrains that person is committing an unlawful battery. The simple fact that the researcher is making no claim to be in the best interests of that individual person and does not therefore come within the rules of law set out in *Re F*.[145]

13.49 Lewis however invites reconsideration of this approach and in an extensive review of the area outlines a number of alternative approaches. First, she considers whether there may be some situations in which there may be benefit to the participant and examines a number of alternatives. One is the prospect of an emotional

---

[142] See further Lewis, P, 'Procedures that are against the medical interests of incompetent adults' (2002) 22 OJLS 575, 578.
[143] Law Commission *Mental Incapacity* No. 231 Law Commission HMSO (1995), para 5.13.
[144] Lewis (n 143 above).
[145] Law Commission, *Mental Incapacity* (1995), para 6.29.

tie. She comments upon the difficulties in ascertainment of such a tie and the fact that such benefits may be viewed as being very speculative. Secondly, an alternative approach is the ascertainment of some form of 'caring or social relationship'—one illustration of such an approach being the judicial authorisation of a bone marrow transplant from a mentally incompetent adult in *Re Y*.[146] She notes the difficulties in such a situation, notably evidentiary problems regarding the relationship. Alternatively she raises the prospect of perceptible benefit through altruism, but dismisses this as being inapplicable in a situation in which the incompetent has no capacity to experience altruism. Other possibilities which she explores include benefits unrelated to the procedure such as better medical care or financial compensation. But, as Lewis comments, this is subject to the 'necessity' criteria and if provision for mentally incapacitated adults is inadequate it would be more appropriate to provide for them as a group rather than as individuals. An alternative justification is that a particular procedure is legitimated because it is in the interests of society. Such arguments may be rooted in a presumed consent approach or a utilitarian approach. Presumed consent in turn may be rooted in the individual's sense of social responsibility. However, as Lewis notes, the limitations on this argument include the boundaries of presumed consent—why restrict it to the mentally incapacitated or would it justify compulsion of clinical procedures upon competent adults? Another argument comes from utilitarianism, namely that incompetent adults included in such research may themselves benefit ultimately from such inclusion and also that, as for example in guidelines such as the Council of Europe's Convention on Human Rights and Biomedicine explanatory report, 'recourse to research on persons not able to consent must be scientifically the sole possibility'.[147] As she notes, the prevailing argument today is that such a group may be included where the risk is 'minimal', but again this does give rise to difficult definitional issues. Ultimately the utilitarian justification provides what is the only realistic way in which many of the procedures may be justified. However, Lewis comments, there is an unwillingness to face up to the use of such calculations and the rationales are frequently hidden under justifications which are rooted in respect for the dignity of the individual.

Despite the difficulties in ascertaining an effective and coherent theoretical basis for the decision regarding the inclusion of mentally incompetent adults in clinical trials, nonetheless the Law Commission in their 1995 report noted that a strong argument had been advanced for their inclusion in clinical trials.[148] It proposed the introduction of safeguards regarding the conduct of clinical trials including this group of participants. It proposed that their inclusion should be lawful in a situation in which the research is into an incapacitating condition which is or

13.50

---

[146] *Re Y (Adult patient) (Transplant; Bone marrow)* (1996) 35 BMLR 111.
[147] At 104.
[148] Para 6.31.

which may affect the person and certain statutory criteria are met. Notable amongst these recommendations was a proposal for the establishment of a mental incapacity research committee. The lawfulness of non-therapeutic research upon mentally incapacitated adults was to be dependent upon a clinical trial protocol being referred to this committee.[149] The Law Commission recommended that clinical trials were to be sanctioned by the committee if the following criteria were satisfied:

(1) that it is desirable to promote knowledge of the causes or treatment of, or of the care of people affected by the incapacitating condition with which any participant is or may be affected,

(2) that the object of the research cannot be effectively achieved without the participation of persons who are or may be without capacity to consent and

(3) that the research will not expose a participant to more than negligible isk and will not be unduly invasive or restrictive of a participant and will not unduly interfere with a participant's freedom of action or privacy.[150]

13.51   Secondly, after the committee had considered the proposal the decision to include an individual participant in research was then to be subject to a second stage . At this stage the inclusion of the mentally incapacitated adult should be sanctioned either by a court, the consent of an attorney or manager, or from a certificate of a doctor who was not involved in the research that the participation of this individual was appropriate or that the research had been designated as 'not involving direct contact'.[151] The latter category refers to observational research. This is a controversial recommendation. It can be argued that such research has the potential to be distressing and that it does need appropriate special safeguards.

13.52   The Law Commission's proposals regarding clinical research were however ultimately not included in the LCD document Making Decisions in 1999[152] nor were they included in the draft Mental Incapacity Bill in 2003 (despite the fact that this Bill did include a number of aspects of the Law Commission's report which had been abandoned by the time of the 1999 document).

13.53   Interestingly the draft protocol on Biomedical Research to the Convention on Human Rights and Biomedicine limits research on mentally incapacitated adults under Article 15 primarily to the situation in which the results of the research have a potential to produce real and direct benefit to their health and any necessary authorisation has been given by the appropriate person or authority. It does sanction other research subject to the following conditions. Article 15(2) provides that:

---

149   Para 6.33.
150   Para 6.34.
151   Para 6.37.
152   Cm 4465.

i) the research has the aim of contributing through significant understanding of the individual's condition, disease or disorder to the ultimate attainment of results capable of conferring benefit to the person concerned or to other people in the same age category or afflicted with the same disease or disorder or having the same condition.

ii) the research entails only minimal risk and minimal burden for the individual concerned and any consideration of additional potential benefits of the research shall not be used to justify an increased level of risk or burden.

Importantly the protocol also emphasises that:

3 Objection to participation, refusal to give authorisation or the withdrawal of authorisation to participate in research shall not prejudice the right of the individual concerned to receive medical care.

On the issue of what constitutes 'minimal risk and minimal burden', Article 17 comments that:

it is deemed that it bears a minimal burden if it is to be expected that the discomfort will be, at the most, temporary and very slight. In assessing the burden for an individual a person enjoying the special confidence of the person concerned shall assess the burden where appropriate.

The draft Mental Incapacity Bill 2003 now sets out a proposed statutory framework for decision making concerning mentally incompetent adults. What this does not do as noted above is make specific provision for clinical research. **13.54**

5. Consent and Incapacity: Children and Adults; Clinical Trials Directive

A further consequence of the EU Clinical Trials Directive is the introduction of specific provisions relating to the inclusion in clinical trials of those persons lacking capacity. Article 3(2) of the Directive provides that where a person is unable to consent themselves then consent may be obtained from their 'legal representative'. Consent is also required in an emergency situation. These provisions are to be incorporated into English law through the Medicines for Human Use (Clinical Trials) Regulations 2003. Nonetheless in their Draft Guidance on this provision the Department of Health commented that: **13.55**

the Directive does permit flexibility in implementing the provision so that if necessary different arrangements can apply in different circumstances. Such flexibility is particularly important in the emergency situation, There is no intention that the implementation of the Directive should prevent ethical and necessary research in the emergency situation from continuing; such research is necessary to develop improved treatment and care for those in such situations.[153]

---

[153] Draft Guidance on Consent by a Legal Representative on Behalf of Person Not Able to Consent under the Medicines for Human Use (Clinical Trials) Regulations 2003 (referred to as the 'Draft Guidance), DoH, March 2003, para 2.

13.56 Article 4(a) of the Clinical Trials Directive provides that in the case of minors a clinical trial may only be undertaken if it is with the informed consent of the minor's parent/legal representative. The consent is to be on the basis of the presumed will of the minor and it can be revoked at any time without detriment to the minor. In the case of the incapacitated adult Article 5 is applicable where an equivalent provision applies with the difference that consent must in this situation be obtained from the 'legal representative' of the incapacitated adult. Moreover, the Directive requires information to be given both to the minor/incapacitated adult, in relation to their capacity to comprehend it, regarding the trial and its consequent risks and benefits.[154] Further, there are to be no financial inducements provided to either group in relation to participation.[155] A major difference between the approval of trials relating to these groups concerns the wording of Articles 4(e) and 5(e). In relation to the minor Article 4(e) provides that the trial may only be undertaken if:

> some direct benefit for the group of patients is obtained from the clinical trial and only where such research is essential to validate data obtained in clinical trials on persons able to give informed consent or by other research methods; additionally, such research should either relate directly to a clinical condition from which the minor concerned suffers or be of such nature that it can only be carried out on minors.

13.57 Article 5(e) of the Directive provides in contrast in relation to incapacitated adults that research should only be undertaken it:

> such research is essential to validate data obtained in clinical trials on persons able to give informed consent or by other research methods and relates directly to a life-threatening or debilitating clinical condition from which the incapacitated adult concerned suffers.

Moreover, in the case of incapacitated adults it also states that it must be shown that:

> there are grounds for expecting that administering the medicinal product to be tested will produce a benefit to the patient outweighing the risks or produce no risk at all.[156]

13.58 The Directive goes on to provide in relation to both minors and incapacitated adults that it must be shown that:

> clinical trials have been designed to minimise pain, discomfort, fear and any other foreseeable risk in relation to the disease and developmental stage, both the risk threshold and the degree of distress shall be specially defined and constantly monitored.[157]

---

[154] Arts 4(b) and 5(b).
[155] Arts 4(d) and 5(d).
[156] Art 5(i).
[157] Arts 4(g) and 5(f), the wording in the last line of the former provision being slightly different as it refers to 'the degree of distress has to be specifically defined and monitored'.

The ethics committee in considering such trial protocols is required either to have expertise in the relevant disease or patient population or to take advice regarding clinical, ethical and psychosocial questions regarding the disease and the patient population.[158]

These provisions are now being incorporated into English law in the form of the **13.59** Medicines for Human Use (Clinical Trials) Regulations 2003. Schedule 1 to these Regulations, which are currently in draft form, relates in Pt 4 to a minor and in Pt 5 to an incapacitated adult. In the case of the minor the draft Regulations clearly state that it is the person with parental responsibility who should make that decision save where 'if because of the emergency nature of the treatment provided as part of the trial no such person can be contacted prior to the proposed inclusion of the subject in the trial.[159]

The provisions concerning trials relating to medicinal products will operate **13.60** alongside the existing common law. In the case of the child the personal legal representative is to be the person who has parental responsibility.[160] The provision for the introduction of a legal representative in relation to the incompetent adult could potentially lead to an anomalous position in relation to the adult participant in that at common law no third party has the power to consent on behalf of a mentally incompetent adult—there is no existing parens patriae jurisdiction. These provisions do concern incapacity and, as the Medical Research Council commented in its response to the consultation exercise on the draft regulations, although RECs have in the past considered that mental illness is to be categorised as mental incapacity, the definition of capacity should recognise that this is not necessarily the case.[161]

(i) The Legal Representative

Individuals may be able to act as a legal representative 'by virtue of their relation- **13.61** ship' and if they are available to make the decision and are prepared to do so.[162] As noted above, in the case of a child this is to be the person with parental responsibility. [163] In other situations it should be the person who is closest to the incapacitated adult, but assessing the degree of closeness may prove more problematic. However a degree of priority in choosing an applicable decision maker is not set out in the draft regulations. The Draft Guidance does suggest that, save where the

---

[158] Arts 4(h) and 5(g).
[159] Sch 1, Pt 4, para 1.
[160] ibid.
[161] MRC Response to the MHRA Consultation letter on the Medicines for Human Use (Clinical Trials) Regulations 2003 (MLX 282) and draft legislation London: MRC 2003 at page 15.
[162] Sch 1(2)(a)(i).
[163] Draft Guidance, para 12.

clinician is involved in the research process, they should make the determination. Otherwise a professional 'of appropriate seniority' should be involved.[164] This, it is submitted, may lead to inconsistency in decision making in the future and this process should have been clarified in the regulations.

13.62 Where there is a dispute as to who will be the personal legal representative the Draft Guidance suggests that normally an individual should not be included in the clinical trial.[165] Nonetheless it is suggested that where it may be said to be against the best interests of the individual to be excluded, the Guidance suggests that the clinicians should seek to approach the courts for guidance on this issue. A person must be available to make the decision. This, as the Guidance notes, does not equate to physical presence. It is suggested that consent may be obtained, for example, by telephone although it is regarded as being good practice for such a telephone conversation to be witnessed.

(ii) Professional Legal Representative

13.63 The Draft Guidance provides that while normally the role of the legal representative will be undertaken by a person who is close to the patient, this may not always be the case because:

> there may be no-one who is sufficiently close to the patient who is able and willing to take on this role; or

> in emergency situations, it may be possible to identify and contact a person close to the individual concerned before it is medically necessary to give the intervention.[166]

It is anticipated in the draft regulations that in such a situation the patient's doctor will undertake this role save where the doctor is 'connected with the conduct of the trial'. Persons 'connected with the conduct of the trial' are defined as being

a) The sponsor of the trial
b) A person employed or engaged by or acting under arrangements made with, the sponsor and who undertakes activities in connection with the management of the trial,
c) An investigator for the trial (defined as the authorised health professional responsible for the conduct of the trial at a trial site and if the trial is conducted by a team of authorised health professionals at a trial site, the leader responsible for that team)
d) A health care professional who is a member of the investigator's team for the purposes of the trial, or
e) A person who provides health care under the direction or control of a person referred to in paragraphs c or d whether in the course of the trial or otherwise.[167]

---

[164] ibid, para 16.
[165] ibid, para 18.
[166] ibid, para 2.
[167] Draft Regulations Sch 1(2)b Draft Guidance, para 27.

Where the health professional responsible for the patient's care is involved in the   **13.64**
research it is provided that they should nominate a person to undertake this
role.[168] However while this may be seen as a practical measure facilitating the operation of the trial it may prove to be problematic. In such a situation they may be
regarded as not being totally objective in that decision and thus to ask them to
nominate a person may not be appropriate. The MRC has commented that it will
not always be possible to identify a suitable legal representative in time and that
compliance with the regulations may necessitate a pool of such persons being
available, although:

> For multi-centre trials this would be a costly exercise and probably very inefficient,
> leading to trials not being carried out or being abandoned through lack of pa-
> tients.[169]

(iii) Professional Legal Representative Nominated by Health Professional

In a situation in which the doctor who is concerned with the care of a person   **13.65**
who may potentially be a research subject is involved in the research the draft
guidance notes that it is the responsibility of the health care provider to ensure
that a person is nominated to act as legal representative.[170] The Draft Guidance
emphasisesd that the professional legal representative should have no conflict of
interest. It suggests that persons who may potentially fulfil this role include
chaplains, social workers or members of the Patient Advisory Liaison Service.[171]
The Draft Guidance also emphasises that such persons should receive appropriate training in terms of their role and responsibilities and also in relation to factual information enabling them to understand clinical research principles.[172]
This is in contrast with the lack of training in the context of the personal legal
representative discussed earlier. The emphasis in the Draft Guidance in this situation is very much in terms of the professional legal representative understanding the significance of the trial.[173] Interestingly the Guidance also
contemplates the possibility of the professional legal representative in such a situation acting for more than one person,[174] which may, for example, arise in a situation concerning nursing home residents. While this may be seen as practically
efficacious, at the same time it may lead to the fear of 'block booking' of consent.

---

[168] ibid, para 3.
[169] MRC(2003) supra at p. 15.
[170] Draft Guidance, para 31.
[171] ibid, para 32. See also Ch 1 above.
[172] ibid, para 33.
[173] ibid, para 34.
[174] ibid, para 35.

(iv) Taking the Decision

13.66 As the Guidance notes, the basis for such a decision is that of the individual's 'presumed will'.[175] Any explicit decision made by a person prior to becoming incapacitated must be respected. In making the decision consideration should be given to any objections to the involvement of the individual in the research project, but such objections may not be conclusive. This is because, for example, as the Guidance notes objectors' motivations may not be solely in relation to the welfare of the subject but may relate to the individual's own views regarding research or medical treatment.[176] This issue may give rise to difficult determinations in the future. The Draft Guidance suggests a broader test of best interests rather than clinical interests and this is in line with judicial interpretations of the best interests test in cases such as *Re SL*.[177]

13.67 Where the decision is made by a professional legal representative the doctor may also have knowledge regarding an individual's clinical condition which would suggest that, although the application of the test of presumed will may support an individual's inclusion, it may in fact be clearly against their own interests. In such a situation the Draft Guidance notes that the decisions will require very careful documentation.[178]

13.68 A professional legal representative who is not the clinical carer may consult persons they regard as being appropriate in making a decision in accordance with the 'presumed will' of the potential subject.[179] However they are not under any obligation to make exhaustive enquiries. Again if there is a 'valid and applicable advance refusal' this is to be regarded as conclusive of the presumed will of the subject.[180]

(v) Monitoring Continued Participation

13.69 The legal representative has a right to withdraw the research subject from the trial and this right may be exercised at any time.[181] The Draft Guidance indicates that close contact from a personal legal representative or clinician providing care and acting as legal representative will facilitate the determination as to whether someone should be included in a clinical trial. However this prima facie contact is unlikely in the case of other professional legal representatives.[182] In such a situation

---

[175] ibid, para 5.
[176] ibid, para 23.
[177] ibid, para 24.
[178] ibid, para 30.
[179] ibid, para 36.
[180] ibid, para 38
[181] ibid, para 39.
[182] ibid, para 40. See also Draft Regulations, Sch 1(4)(5)—in the case of the minor—Sch 1(5)(5) in the case of the adult.

the Draft Guidance proposes that there should be specific arrangements to ensure on-going review. What constitutes an 'appropriate interval' for such a review will be determined by the particular circumstances. A maximum period for participation without further review by legal representative is to be established at the start of the trial.[183] Where those with clinical responsibility believe that there should not be continued participation of the subject in the trial, this information should be given to the personal legal representative.[184] Where there is disagreement between clinician and personal legal representative there should be an attempt to resolve this.[185] The Draft Guidance notes that in a situation in which either party believes that continued participation is inappropriate, legal advice should be sought.[186] If evidence emerges during the trial regarding any previous wishes of the subject regarding research participation then this information should be given to the legal representative.[187] A professional legal representative may pass responsibility to another if a personal legal representative emerges.[188] The Draft Guidance notes that this will not affect any decision undertaken by the professional legal representative.

(vi) Emergency Situations

The EU Clinical Trials Directive requires consent from a legal representative in all **13.70** situations including an emergency. This prompted some expressions of concern in the research community that this might lead to such trials having in many instances to be abandoned.[189] However the Draft Guidance from the Department of Health notes that, '[n]evertheless it is our understanding that there was no intention that the Directive should stop ethical and necessary emergency research'.[190] The Guidance states that consideration should be given as to whether a person, close to the potential subject, may be able to act as a legal representative.[191] The Guidance however suggests that in an emergency situation the views of a professional legal representative are the most likely to be sought. The Draft Guidance gives as an example:

> . . . in a trial of a new treatment for myocardial infarction that is designed to be delivered as quickly as possible after the event—for example in an ambulance—the paramedic in charge of the ambulance may be the only person who could feasibly act as a legal representative.[192]

---

[183] ibid, para 41.
[184] ibid, para 43.
[185] ibid, para 44.
[186] ibid, para 45.
[187] ibid, para 46.
[188] ibid, para 47.
[189] Singer, EA and Mullner, M, 'Implications of the EU directive on clinical trials for emergency medicine' (2002) 324 BMJ 1169.
[190] Draft Guidance, para 54.
[191] ibid, para 57.
[192] ibid, para 60.

13.71   The extent to which this necessarily complies with the spirit of the Clinical Trials Directive may be subject to some speculation. It may be seen as problematic in terms of the objectivity of the determination of the patient's presumed will. The Draft Guidance attempts to pre-empt such concerns by suggesting that:

> the health care provider will need to ensure that any paramedic who might be involved in the trial receives both the general and specific training concerning the trial.[193]

13.72   The Guidance suggests that different centres have different arrangements for ensuring the role of the legal representatives and that this is compatible with the Directive and Regulations.[194] This may however prove to be problematic over time and may be seen to be at odds with the heightened trends towards standardisation of clinical procedures.[195] A further statement in para 63 of the Draft Guidance may also lead to difficulties. It provides that:

> In the absence of any information to the contrary, it is justiciable for a professional legal representative to assume that a potential subject would wish to receive an intervention which has the greatest chance of saving his or her life or improving (or minimising detriment to) his or her health. Where there is equipoise between standard treatment and a new treatment and a new trial is being conducted, it may be reasonable to assume (other things being equal) that a potential subject would wish to enter a trial.

Whether this assumption can necessarily be made may, however be questioned.

13.73   Where an emergency has ended the Guidance provides that there should first be a review of whether continued participation is appropriate.[196] In a situation in which the project is intended to continue and the subject is not expected to regain capacity then the Guidance states that those undertaking the trial should ascertain whether someone is capable of acting as a personal legal representative.[197] However if there is not then the clinician who is responsible for the care of the subject may take over as professional legal representative although the Draft Guidance notes that initial authorisation for inclusion in the trial will remain valid until revoked.[198] It may also be the case that although no person suitable to be a personal legal representative exists, relevant information may emerge as to the views of the person involved in the trial and this should be conveyed to the professional legal representative.[199]

---

[193] ibid, para 60.
[194] ibid, para 62.
[195] ibid, para 62.
[196] ibid, para 64.
[197] ibid, para 65.
[198] ibid, para 66.
[199] ibid, para 67.

(vii) Recovery of Competence

The Draft Guidance states that if the research subject gains competence they must be informed regarding their participation in a clinical trial.[200] Their consent must be obtained to any further involvement. In addition their consent must be obtained to use any personal data and/or biological materials. If they refuse consent then those materials and/or data must be disposed of or destroyed respectfully. A further issue relates to participants who decide to withdraw. The Draft Guidance notes that:

> It would be possible to bias results by seeking consent after recovery in a manner that makes it more or less likely that a subject will withdraw. It is important that those responsible for seeking consent are aware of this possibility and minimise the risk of this occurring. As part of the governance procedures for the trial audit of the process of seeking consent from those who have recovered may be helpful.[201]

If a personal legal representative is identified the Draft Guidance states that they should be asked for consent for involvement in research, collection of personal data and/or biological samples for research purposes alone and also to sanction use of personal data or biological materials which have already been collected for research purposes.[202] Where the personal legal representative refuses consent for subsequent use then the guidance indicates that this would depend upon whether the data and/or materials are needed for clinical use. If the latter then the Draft Guidance indicates that any subsequent use and/or disposal must be in accordance with standard practice for clinical records and samples. Where consent is refused and the subject has died and there is no requirement for this material to be used for clinical purposes, the Draft Guidance states that such material should be 'destroyed or respectfully disposed of.[203]

D. Monitoring the Conduct of the Trial: General

The RGF provides that RECs are to require NHS researchers to provide them with information regarding the progress of studies and as a consequence they may review advice which has been given as to the ethical acceptability of the study.[204] If researchers intend to deviate from the protocol the REC must be informed. The Governance Arrangements provide for exceptions where the reason for the deviation concerns immediate hazards to research participants or where changes are

13.74

13.75

13.76

---

[200] ibid, para 75.
[201] ibid, para 76.
[202] ibid, para 69
[203] ibid, para 71.
[204] RGF, para 3.12.8

only envisaged to the 'logistical or administrative aspects of the research'.[205] This can be contrasted with the procedures relating to follow-up regarding trials under the Clinical Trials Directive discussed below. Nonetheless, as the RGF notes, responsibility as to whether a study does follow the protocol and any consequent monitoring on its progress lies with the researchers themselves.[206] Interestingly, in situations in which there are anticipated problems in recruiting subjects, the Governance Arrangements state that the REC may also require that there shall be reports regarding the potential subject's perception of the project's 'accountability'.[207] In addition, in a situation in which a REC member have information that there may hgave been a possible breach of good practice in research, this should be notified to the REC chair and Administrator.[208] The administrator should also inform the appointing authority of this information. When it approves the application the REC shall state whether it requires progress reports. Within three months of the study having ended it will require a final report.[209]

E. Monitoring of Trials Concerning Medicinal Products

13.77 In relation to those trials which concern medicinal products the position is more complex. Currently the Medicines Control Agency has powers for enforcement against researchers. With the implementation of the Directive there is to be a new series of provisions. Regular 'good clinical practice' inspections are to be undertaken. Those sites which are involved in clinical trials (which will include the premises of the investigator/laboratories used for analysis, and the sponsor's premises) are liable to inspection by the competent authority of the Member State.[210] It is intended that there will be consequent penalties relating to non-compliance.[211] In addition there will also be an infringement notice procedure.[212]

1. Reporting Requirements

13.78 The implementation of the Clinical Trials Directive can be seen as a development on the existing provisions under the Medicines Act regarding the reporting of serious adverse reactions to the licensing authority.[213] The new provisions relate to serious adverse events and suspected unexpected serious adverse reactions (SUSARs) (Clinical Trials Directive, Articles 16 and 17). Investigators must

---

[205] Governance Arrangements, para 7.24.
[206] ibid,para 7.33.
[207] ibid, para 7.31.
[208] ibid, para 7.34.
[209] ibid, para 7.26.
[210] Clinical Trials Directive, Art 15.
[211] Draft Regulations, Sch 7, Pt 8.
[212] ibid, reg 47.
[213] ibid, regs 31–34.

report all serious adverse events to the sponsor followed by a detailed report.[214] Additional reporting requirements may also have been imposed by the trial protocol and if so these should also be complied with. SUSARs must be recorded and reported to the licensing authority, to the competent authority and also to the ethics committee. SUSARs which are 'fatal and life-threatening' must be initially reported within seven days and then additional information must be supplied within an eight day period. Trial sponsors are required to inform all investigators who are responsible for conduct of a trial.[215] SUSARs are also to be included in a European database which has been established under Article 11(1) of the Directive. [216] Sponsors are also required to give the licensing authority and ethics committee annual reports of all suspected serious adverse reactions at those sites (whether in the United Kingdom or elsewhere) for which they are sponsors.[217] Failure to comply with these notification provisions will, in a change to the existing provisions, become a criminal offence.[218]

2. Amendments to the Trial Protocol

There are various situations in which researchers may seek to amend the trial protocol. First, an amendment may be required for safety reasons. Appropriate urgent measures may be taken by the sponsor or investigator in order to safeguard subjects from immediate hazard to health and safety.[219] Sponsors may also make amendments to the trial protocol at any time.[220] In the case of a substantial amendment, which is defined as one 'which is likely to affect to a significant degree (a) the safety or physical or mental integrity of the subjects of the trial, (b) the scientific value of the trial, (c) the conduct or management of the trial, or (d) the quality or safety of any investigational medicinal product used in the trial' and involves an amendment of the authorisation including one relating to the terms of request for authorisation of the trial, or its particulars, then a valid notice of amendment is to be sent to the licensing authority.[221] In addition, where the amendment would amount to an amendment to the ethics committee's authorisation, a notice of amendment needs to be submitted to the REC.[222]

13.79

The licensing authority is to respond within 35 days stating why it rejects the amendment or that it accepts it subject to conditions stated in the notice.[223] In the case of the ethics committee it must give an opinion to the sponsor again within 35 days.[224]

13.80

---

[214] Clinical Trials Directive, Art 16, and Draft Medicines (Human Use) Regulations, and, ibid, reg 31.
[215] ibid, reg 32(5).
[216] See further on this database at *www.pharmacos/eudra.org.*
[217] Draft Regulations, reg 34.
[218] Reg 48(g).
[219] ibid, reg 28.
[220] ibid, reg 23(1).
[221] ibid, reg 10.
[222] ibid, reg 23(3).
[223] ibid, reg 23(4).
[224] ibid, reg 24(5).

Where an amendment proposal has been rejected the sponsor may amend this and give at least 14 days' notice in writing to the licensing authority or relevant ethics committee of their intention to make an amendment.[225] The licensing authority or ethics committee may within 14 days of this notice state why they do not accept the amendment (or in the case of the ethics committee why they are giving an unfavourable opinion in relation to the amendment). Where applications for amendments are refused or accepted subject to conditions this can be referred to the Committee on the Safety of Medicines and the Medicines Commission.[226]

3. *Infringements of Clinical Trial Protocol Requirements*

13.81   The licensing authority is to have powers to deal with infringements through the issue of an infringement notice.[227] This will state what steps should be taken to ensure that a breach should not continue or reoccur within a set period of time. Licensing authorities are to have powers to suspend or prohibit a trial. This power is to arise either where authorisation conditions have not been complied with or where information raises doubts as to the safety, scientific validity or conduct of the trial.[228] Save in a situation in which there is an imminent risk to health and safety the licensing authority must give written notice to the sponsor or investigator as to its intention to issue a notice.[229]

4. *Appeal Procedures*

13.82   Sponsors may make representations to the appropriate committee in relation to the rejection of a request for authorisation, or failure to obtain an amendment, or termination of a trial.[230] Notice must be given by the sponsor within 28 days (although there is a discretion for the licensing authority to extend this). After a hearing the committee will advise the licensing authority and the authority must take the committee's decision into account but is not bound by it. An application may be made to the Medicines Commission again within a 28 day period.[231] Again the licensing authority must consider the report and any advice given by the Commission but is not bound by it. There is also a provision by which the sponsor, etc, may ask to appear before the licensing authority itself—or a person whom the licensing authority may nominate to undertake this task. On request this hearing may be held in public. Again while the licensing authority is required to take

---

[225] ibid, reg 24(2).
[226] ibid, reg 25, Sched 3, para 5.13.
[227] ibid, reg 47 implementing Art 12(2).
[228] ibid, reg 29.
[229] ibid, regs 29(5), (6).
[230] ibid, reg 25.
[231] ibid, Sched 3, para 2(1).

into account the report and consider whether to confirm or alter its decision it is not bound by the report.

5. The End of the Trial

Specific provisions relate to trials on medicinal products. Sponsors are required to state in the trial protocol when the trial will end. The sponsor is then required to notify the licensing authority in writing and the ethics committee who had approved the trial that it has come to an end within 90 days.[232] Where the trial has ended early this notification must be within 15 days and reasons should be given for its early termination. Failure to comply with this information is a criminal offence.

13.83

6. Provision of Information

The Clinical Trials Directive contains certain specific provisions regarding the provision of information concerning clinical trials in the European Union. Article 11 provides that information concerning trials conducted in member states is to be entered into a central European database, which is to be accessible only to competent authorities within member states and to the Commission. Detailed guidance on the database has been issued by the European Commission,[233] which notes the purposes of the database including providing an overview of all EU clinical trials, facilitating communication between Member States, EMEA and the Commission on clinical trials, the identification of those trials within the European Union which are on-going, completed and terminated, generation of clinical trial statistics, provision of information concerning GCP, and also notification to the competent authorities where trials are ended for reasons of safety.[234] Member States are to enter extracts from the request that a trial be authorised,[235] amendments which have been made to the trial protocol,[236] the approval of the ethics committee,[237] inspections which have been undertaken to ensure that the conduct of the trial is in accordance with the principles of good clinical practice,[238] and the declaration that the trial has come to an end.[239] In addition the database will include the identification of trials and medicinal products in order to enable links between with clinical trial information and any reports regarding 'suspected unexpected serious adverse reaction'.[240]

13.84

---

[232] ibid, reg 30.
[233] European Commission, *Detailed Guidance on the European clinical trials database EUDRACT database.* ENTR/6421/01 Brussels, July 2002.
[234] ibid, para 5.
[235] Clinical Trials Directive, Art 11(1))(a).
[236] ibid, Art 11(1)(b)(c).
[237] ibid, Art 11(1)(d).
[238] ibid, Art 11(1)(f)
[239] ibid, Art 11(1)(e)
[240] European Commission (n 224 above) para 5.

13.85   The European Commission has also issued guidance on the establishment of a separate database, Eudravigilance–Clinical Trial Module, concerning suspected unexpected serious adverse reactions,[241] which is provided for under Article 17(3)(a) of the Directive. Its role is comparable with that of the EUDRACT database and will include the provision of an overview of the occurrence of SUSARs, the facilitation of communication between competent authorities in member states, the Commission and the EMEA, enable a separate review to be undertaken of SUSARs in individual Member States, review of SUSARs and the generation of statistics and the links between trials and medicinal products to provide links with SUSARs.[242]

7. Specific Criminal Offences

13.86   Several new criminal offences are to be introduced in the Regulations implementing the Directive.[243] These relate to the provision of 'relevant information'[244] which is false or misleading in relation to clinical trial authorisations. It is also an offence for sponsors, investigators, contract research organisations and persons involved in the conduct of a trial, etc, to provide information which is false or misleading to the MCA or to an ethics committee.[245] These are to be strict liability offences. Regulation 50 provides that it is a defence to show that a person undertook all reasonable caution and exercised all due diligence to avoid commission of the offence.

F. Confidentiality, Privacy and Research Participants' Information

13.87   Health care professionals are required to safeguard the confidentiality of their patient information subject to certain exceptions. The obligation of confidentiality is bolstered by other obligations through statute such as the Data Protection Act 1998 and principles such as the right to privacy of home and family life in Article 8 of the European Convention on Human Rights. The draft protocol on Biomedical Research to the Convention on Human Rights and Biomedicine in Article 28 that:

---

[241] European Commission, *Detailed Guidance on the European Database of suspected unexpected serious adverse reactions (Eudravigilance-Clinical trial module)*, Brussels, July 2002, draft 2.8.

[242] ibid, para 5.

[243] 2003 Regulations, reg 49.

[244] This refers to information relevant tog the assessment of the safety, quality or efficacy of an investigational medicinal product; the safety or scientific validity of a clinical trial; or whether the conditions and principles of GCP have been met.

[245] Offences under these provisions would be liable at the magistrates' court for a fine not exceeding £5,000 or term of imprisonment not exceeding three months; in the case of the Crown Court of a fine and/or prison term not exceeding two years.

Any information of a person nature collected during biomedical research shall be considered as confidential and treated according to the rules relating to the protection of private life.

The perceived need to safeguard confidentiality and privacy of research partici-   **13.88**
pants' information is reflected in guidance regarding the use of information for clinical research purposes.[246] The Governance Arrangements provides that research protocols should contain information as to who will have access to the research participant's data and samples, what measures are to be undertaken to maintain the confidentiality and security of the research participant's information, and whether this information will be anonymised. The protocol must address how data and samples will be obtained, kept and used and, if it is intended for this material to be used in other jurisdictions, to which countries data and samples will be sent. The Governance Arrangements also specifically require the REC to consider the 'adequacy of the process for obtaining consent for the above'.[247] Use of information for clinical research purposes must comply with existing legal obligations including the equitable remedy of breach of confidence, the Data Protection Act 1998, and the Human Rights Act 1998. Participant information used in clinical research may be derived from existing clinical information or obtained during the study itself.

1. Consent and Anonymisation

Generally the research participant should consent to their information being used   **13.89**
to avoid the prospect of an action for breach of confidence. The tenor of guidance issued by professional bodies suggests however that in a situation in which the patient information is anonymised then it may legitimately be used without further consent being obtained.[248] Such an approach is in line with that taken in the Court of Appeal in *R v Department of Health, ex p Source Informatics*.[249] In the context of genetic research the Human Genetics Commission found such an approach to be an attractive one.[250] But whether anonymisation can be regarded as a satisfactory solution is dependent upon the precise reasons as to why an individual may want to exercise control over their personal information. They may simply be interested in ensuring that they cannot be linked to their own personal information. However it can be argued that anonymisation is not the answer because that does not obviate an individual's wish to exercise control over whether their information should be subsequently used in a particular clinical research project. While the empirical research in this area is limited it is the case that some

---

[246] eg MRC, *Personal Information in Medical Research*.
[247] Governance Arrangements, para 9.16.
[248] See eg General Medical Council, *Confidentiality: Protecting and Providing Information* (London: GMC, 2000) para 15.
[249] [2000] 1 All ER 786. See further Ch 9.
[250] Human Genetics Commission, *Inside Information* (London: HGC, 2002).

research has indicated that patients have considerable reservations regarding the sanctioning of access to health records for researchers and associated purposes.[251] Particular problems may also arise in a situation in which it is proposed to access and use such material over a much longer period of time. This difficulty can be exacerbated where the research project relates to a longer term use, for example, in relation to a genetic databases used for major population studies—we return to this issue below.

13.90 What of the situation in which information has not been anonymised? Some research guidelines envisage the possibility of disclosing confidential information for research purposes without the participant's consent having been obtained. For example, the Medical Research Council guidelines provide that confidential information may only be disclosed where consent 'is impracticable' if:

> the likely benefits to society outweigh the implications of the loss of confidentiality so that it is clearly in the public interest for the research to be done
>
> there is no intention to feed information back to the individuals involved or take decisions that affect them, and
>
> there are no practicable alternatives of equal effectiveness.[252]

13.91 The guidelines comment that infringement of confidentiality in such situations must be kept to a minimum. In practice the justification for sanctioning disclosure without consent on the basis of a general 'public interest' exception is problematic. What constitutes the 'public interest' in a breach of confidence action is a somewhat fluid concept. In the past the courts have indicated that they are prepared to consider professional guidelines, such as those of the General Medical Council,[253] but whether there would today be unquestioning acceptance of such guidelines is more uncertain . The Medical Research Council suggested that disclosure could only be justified on a case by case basis with reference to a number of criteria. First, the necessity for use of data. Secondly its sensitivity and the information which it revealed about this particular individual. Thirdly, the importance of the proposed research. Fourthly, what safeguards existed, for example, regarding the prospect of unauthorised disclosure. Fifthly, had the research protocol been considered by a REC? Nonetheless, while there are suggestions that disclosure may be justifiable without consent on public interest grounds, the extent to which the courts will be prepared to uphold this in the case of clinical research is uncertain and all such proposed disclosures need to be subject to exceedingly careful consideration.

---

[251] See the discussion in O'Brien, J and Chantler, C, 'Confidentiality and the duties of care' (2003) 29 J of Medical Ethics 36–40.

[252] MRC, *Personal Information in Medical Research* para 2.2.2.

[253] *W v Egdell* [1990] 1 All ER 835.

2. Statutory Exceptions Sanctioning Disclosure for Research Purposes

As noted in Chapter 9 above the disclosure of sensitive personal clinical informa-   **13.92**
tion without consent may conflict not only with the common law safeguards relating to breach of confidence but also with the Data Protection Act 1998 which
concerns personal data held in both computer and manual records. Some regarded this as, effectively, an inhibitor to clinical practice.[254] The impact of the
Data Protection Act 1998, particularly in relation to the legality of holding clinical information in, for example, cancer registries and its use for clinical research
purposes without further consent being obtained for such use, led to the enactment of s 60 of the Health and Social Care Act 2001.[255] This provision enables the
Secretary of State to make regulations which allow the processing of 'prescribed
patient information for medical purposes as he considers necessary or expedient'.
Such regulations may be made in the interests of providing patient care or in the
public interest. The Regulations provide for disclosure of patient information
without consent in relation, for example, to communicable diseases and other
public health purposes.[256] The Health and Social Care Act 2001 also establishes a
'Patient Information Advisory Group' to provide advice to the Secretary of State
in relation to applications under s 60. It appears that the NHS is intending to develop 'class support' which would enable certain proposals which fit within 'standard categories' to proceed.[257] While s 60 is a provision which has been welcomed
by many in the scientific community as facilitating transfer of information for research purposes, in other respects it may be viewed as problematic. It enables the
enactment of broad brush exceptions to the equitable remedy of breach of confidence. There remains the prospect that, in the future, there may be challenges
brought by an individual's objection to automatic use of their information albeit
anonymised with reference to the Human Rights Act 1998 and Article 8.

3. Feedback of Clinical Information to Participants

One further problematic issue concerns the extent to which an individual about   **13.93**
whom information is generated is entitled to any feedback regarding the study
which has been undertaken in a situation in which the study itself may have produced information which may be regarded as relevant to that person's health. The
draft additional protocol on Biomedical Research to the Convention on Human
Rights and Biomedicine provides in Article 27:

---

[254] Strobl, J, Cave, E, and Walley, T, 'Data Protection Legislation: Interpretation and Barriers to
Research' [2000] BMJ 890 and Case, P, 'Confidence Matters: the Rise and Fall of Informal
Autonomy in Medical Law' [2003] 11 Med L Rev 208.
[255] Health Services (Control of Patient Information) Regulations 2002, SI 2002/1438, reg 4.
[256] ibid, clause 3.
[257] Lowrance, WW, *Learning from Experience: Privacy and the Secondary Use of Data in Health
Research* (London: Nuffield Trust, 2002) 40.

> If research gives rise to information of relevance to the current or future health or quality of life of research participants, this information must be offered to them. That shall be done within a framework of health care or counselling. In communication of such information, due care must be taken in order to protect confidentiality and to respect the wish of the participant to receive such information.

13.94 While such an approach can be regarded as providing respect for autonomy it can also be viewed as problematic. It may give rise to particular difficulties in a situation in which a study is undertaken over a very long period of time and where the information in question may relate to a person's genetic susceptibility to develop illness or disability. On the one hand individuals may be interested in such information, particularly if the prediction may enable them to seek treatment. On the other hand they may as a consequence be entrusted with information which they would otherwise not have wanted to receive and indeed may infringe any 'right not to know'. Such information may be regarded as harmful if it is then incorporated into their medical records. The prospect of such feedback inevitably leads to considerations of exactly how the feedback process should be undertaken. It may be the case that in relation to genetic information the feedback relates to risks rather than certainties and the calibration of such risks may be fundamentally problematic.[258] The Medical Research Council is of the view that this is something which must be determined in relation to the individual study.[259] However interestingly it goes on to comment that:

> Research results obtained on anonymised unlinked samples cannot have any impact on the interests of an individual donor.

13.95 There is some suggestion that where results have immediate clinical relevance, a clinician has a duty of care to inform the research participant of this directly or through their doctor.[260] Nonetheless it has been suggested that in such a situation verification of the result should be obtained to obviate the risk of error.

4. Use of Information for Research Purposes After Death

13.96 In its guidance, 'Personal Information in Medical Research', the Medical Research Council has advised that the law does not normally apply to information regarding the deceased person.[261] In fact the law in this area is unclear. It is certainly the case that the Data Protection Act 1998 does not apply in such a situation and that access to the records of deceased persons are governed by the previous legislation in the form of the Access to Health Records Act 1990. The position at common law is the source of some controversy and there is some debate as to the extent to which the equitable remedy of breach of confidence extends to cover information which relates to a deceased person (cf. Chapter 9).

---

[258] See further discussion in Richards, MPM, 'Issues of consent and feedback in a genetic epidemiological study of women with breast cancer' (2003) 29 J of Medical Ethics 93–96.
[259] Para 8.1.
[260] MRC (1991) para 8.3.
[261] ibid.

5. Using Human Material in Clinical Research

(i) General Issues: Consent

After the controversy generated regarding the unauthorised retention of human **13.97** material, in particular children's organs, in enquiries at Bristol Royal Infirmary and Alder Hey, the boundaries of legality for the use of human material which can be used for research purposes is currently the subject of heated debate in the United Kingdom.[262] The law in this area is subject to detailed consideration in another chapter in this volume (see Ch 16). There has also been particular consideration given to the use of material and information in relation to genetic research.[263] Legal regulation is divided between use of material from cadavers and from live subjects. In relation to the cadaver researchers who seek to use samples must comply with the provisions of the Human Tissue Act 1961 and the Anatomy Act 1984. It may be the case that samples have been donated explicitly by the deceased. Alternatively material may be used in a situation in which the person in lawful possession of the body has sanctioned such use after having made such enquiries as are reasonably practicable of the spouse or surviving relatives. The uncertainties around these words have been the subject of extensive consideration and this area is currently being examined by the Department of Health as part of its review of the use of human material.[264]

(ii) Use of 'Spare' Material

In the case of samples from live subjects it is today presumed that consent should **13.98** be obtained. A difficult issue has concerned the legitimacy of use of 'spare' or 'waste' human material.[265] The Medical Research Council as of the view that it was acceptable to use unlinked and anonymised human material where this was

---

[262] *Report of the Inquiry into the Royal Liverpool Childrens Hospital* (Alder Hey) (2001) (*www.rclin-quiry.org.uk*). 'The Removal, Retentiona and Use of Human Organs and Tissue from Post Mortem Examination', Advice from the Chief Medical Officer, Department of Health, Department for Education and Employment, Home Office Summit meeting on Organ Retention, 11 January 2001 (*www.cmosummit.org.uk*). For an earlier review of issues regarding the legality of the use of human tissue for research and other purposes see the *Nuffield Council on Bioethics Human Tissue; Ethical and Legal Issues* (1995); *Bristol Inquiry Interim Report Removal and Retention of Human Material* (2000) (*www.bristol-inquiry.org.uk*); and see also Grubb, A, 'I Me Mine; Bodies, Parts and Property' (1998) *Medical Law International* 247.

[263] Human Genetics Commission, *Inside Information* (2002); House of Lords Select Committee on Science and Technology Fourth Report 2001, *Report on Human Genetic databases: challenges and opportunities* (*www.parliament.thestationeryoffice.co.uk/pa/ldselect/ldsctech/57/5702.htm*).

[264] Department of Health, *Human Bodies: Human Choices* (2002). For further discussion see Price, D, 'From Cosmos and Damien to Van Veltzen: The Human Tissue Saga Continues' [2003] Med L Rev 1–47.

[265] McHale, J, 'Waste, Ownership and Bodily Products' (2000), *Health Care Analysis* 123–35.

surplus to clinical requirements.[266] The Nuffield Council on Bioethics in its earlier report on 'Human Tissue' in 1995 suggested that in such situations the material could be presumed to be subject to the legal doctrines of 'res nullius' or 'abandonment'.[267] However this report has been the subject of considerable powerful academic criticism[268] and the Nuffield Council's application of these terms drawn from property law is exceedingly questionable. More recent guidance such as that of the Medical Research Council indicates that the patient's consent should now normally be obtained in relation to the use of 'spare' material.[269]

(iii) Secondary Uses

13.99 A difficult issue however is that of subsequent use of human material after initial consent for use from live participants has been obtained. Is it necessary for researchers to return to obtain further consent from the participant? This is an issue which has received particular consideration in relation to the use of genetic material. In terms of subsequent use the Medical Research Council in its guidelines in 2001 recommended a two-stage process. First, that consent should be obtained for the initial use and then secondly consent should be given for storage and future use of the material for other research.[270] The guidelines provide that '[u]nless the sample is to be anonymised and unlinked prior to storage (in which case this should be explained to the donors) it is not acceptable to seek unconditional blanket consent, for example using terms such as 'all biological or medical research' '.[271] The guidelines went on to state that if an individual provides consent only for material to be used for one study then the only acceptable reason for further use of the material is to verify the results of that study.

(iv) Databases of Human Material

13.100 In recent years there has been considerable support given to the establishment of large-scale population genetic databases which are seen as being particularly helpful in epidemiological research. A recent notable illustration of one such database is that of UK Biobank,[272] a joint venture by the Medical Research Council, Wellcome Trust and the Department of Health consisting of genetic information involving a population sample of 500,000 persons between the ages of 45 and 69.[273] Constraints of

---

[266] MRC, *Human Tissue and Biological Samples for Use in Research-Operational and Ethical Guidelines*, MRC Ethics Series (2001), para 3.2.
[267] Nuffield Council on Bioethics Working Party, *Human Tissue Ethical and Legal Issues* (1995).
[268] Matthews, P, 'The Man of Property' [1995] Med L Rev 251.
[269] Medical Research Council, *Human Tissue and biological samples for use in research* (2001).
[270] ibid, para 6.2.
[271] ibid, para 6.2.
[272] N 253 above and McHale, JV, 'Regulating Genetic Databases: Some Legal and Ethical Issues' [2004] 12 Med L Rev 70.
[273] *www.wellcome.ac.uk/en/1/biovenpop.html* and see Kaye, J and Martin, P, 'Safeguards for research using large scale DNA collections' [2000] 321 BMJ 1146.

space preclude detailed consideration of this issue in the present chapter 00. However the creation of such databases illustrates some of the difficulties with existing legal regulation. Samples stored in such databases are subject to common law principles regarding use of human material, therefore any information store , which is likely to be derived at least in part from those samples, will be regulated by reference to what is a wholly distinct legal regime of confidentiality and data protection. They also give rise to the same problems indicated above with regard to primary and secondary use of human material and of information, but on a wider scale and for a longer duration than the majority of proposed projects. Determining the boundaries of consent may thus give rise to problematic issues. First, what consent is required? Is one-off generic consent adequate or is specific consent needed for each subsequent use? The latter option may pose difficulties in terms of practicality and cost regarding tracing research participants possibly many years after initial consent has been given. The Human Genetics Commission has supported use of generic consent procedures for genetic material in research databases where the material is anonymised.[274] This interpretation, as noted above, although consistent with the approach in *R v Department of Health, ex p Source Informatics*, may not be sufficiently sensitive to individual choice and the wish to exercise control. It remains to be seen whether such issues will lead to challenge in the courts in the future.

G. Regulating Bad Practice: Fraud in Scientific Research[275]

Scientific research is undertaken in a 'high pressure' competitive environment. **13.101** Researchers are under pressure to show that the money invested in their project was well spent. Career advancement is dependent upon a prolific publication record. Thus there are risks that particular individuals may be tempted to falsify results. Concerns regarding misconduct in scientific research has led to calls over many years for more centralised review,[276] and the Committee on Publication Ethics was established as a means through which medical and scientific journal editors could manage research fraud.[277] Subsequently the Academy of Medical Sciences has been involved in developing a framework to monitor research misconduct, including a database of information, although there is disagreement as

---

[274] *Human Genetics Commission* (n 281 above) para 5.19.
[275] Lock, S (ed), *Fraud and Misconduct in Medical Research* (2nd edn, London: BMJ, 1996).
[276] Smith, R, 'Time to face up to research misconduct' (1996) 312 BMJ 789; Editorial, 'Dealing with Deception' [1996] *Lancet* 843; Rennie, D, 'Education and debate; Dealing with research misconduct in the UK' (1998) 316 BMJ 1726–1733.
[277] *www.publicationethics.org.uk.*

to whether an audit function was appropriate here.[278] While there is the possibility of professional sanctions which will flow from research fraud, for example through disciplinary action from the General Medical Council, there is no explicit legal regulation of this issue.

H. Responsibility and Accountability

13.102   The language of the RGF is cast in terms of 'responsibilities'. Interestingly it begins by raising the issue of the responsibility of the research participant. It notes that:

> All those using health and social care services should give serious consideration to invitations to become involved in the development or undertaking of research.[279]

This statement can be seen as very much reflecting principles such as those of social solidarity and the public interest in participation in the research process.[280] One important issue highlighted in the RGF is that of the need to ensure the coordination of research responsibilities.[281] The guidance notes that clear agreements which are documented particularly need to be in place in relation to studies complex in nature where there may be:

> work on more than one site; and/or
> researchers employed by more than one organisation; and/or
> patients, users and care professionals from more than one care organisation; and/or
> more than one funder.[282]

I. The Researchers

13.103   Secondly the RGF focuses upon the responsibility of the researchers themselves.[283]

> They are responsible for ensuring that any research they undertake follows the agreed protocol, for helping care professionals to ensure that participants receive appropriate care while involved in research, for protecting the integrity and confidentiality of clinical and other records generated by the research and for reporting any failures in these respects, adverse drug reactions and other events or suspected misconduct through the appropriate systems.[284]

---

[278] Mayor, S, 'Proposals for a UK Body to Investigate Research Fraud lack "teeth" ' (2002) BMJ 325.

[279] RGF, para 3.4.1.

[280] See eg O'Neil, and Chadwick, R and Berg, K, 'Solidarity and equity: new ethical frameworks for genetic databases' (2001) 2 *Nature Reviews Genetics* 318.

[281] RGF, para 3.

[282] ibid, para 3.2.3.

[283] ibid, para 3.5.1.

[284] ibid, para 3.5.1.

Again the phrasing used is interesting. Nowhere is there any reference at all to the rights of the participants in the research process.

The focus for the conduct of the trial is now placed upon the 'principal investiga-   **13.104**
tor'.[285] This person's responsibilities include ensuring that, '[t]he dignity, rights safety and well-being of participants are given priority at all times by the research team'. Thus here, finally, there is a reference to the participants' rights, but it is rather anomalous in the light of the fact that such a statement is not included in relation to the responsibilities of the researchers generally. Paragraph 3.6 continues by providing that the principal investigator is to ensure that the research is undertaken within the RGF, that the trials are registered, that the person with organisational responsibility such as the Chief Executive is informed. In a situation in which research participants are included while they are under the care of a health or social care professional then that professional is to be informed as to the research participant's involvement in the study. Where services users, carers, children under the auspices of a local authority are invited to participate, the agency director or their deputy must agree to their inclusion or be made aware of any consequent arrangements regarding disclosure of information. The principal investigator is required to ensure that members of the research team are appropriately qualified to undertake their roles and that where the study involves new researchers or students, appropriate training should be given. Other responsibilities outlined in para 3.63 include ensuring that the research should follow the approved protocol but that any proposed changes should be submitted to the ethics committee, research sponsor and also any appropriate body;[286] that there should be dissemination of funding; and that the researcher accepts a key role in detecting and preventing scientific misconduct.

2. The Sponsor

The RGF also refers directly to the role of the research sponsor. This is an issue   **13.105**
which derives from the Clinical Trials Directive but, as implemented through the RGF, the concept of the sponor is being extrapolated across all health and social care research. As it makes clear, any research which involves the NHS or social care must from April 2004 involve a research sponsor who has confirmed that it accepts its research responsibilities. After this date NHS care organisations are not to approve any new research which concerns human participants, their organs, tissue or data.[287] The definition of the 'sponsor' flows from the Directive. It is to be 'the individual or body who takes on ultimate responsibility for the initiation and management (or arranging the initiation and management) of, and the financing (or arranging the financing) for that trial'.[288] Their role involves the

---

[285] ibid, para 3.6.
[286] ibid, para 3.6.3.
[287] ibid, para 3.8.1.
[288] Draft Regulations, reg 2 and explanatory note 4.1.6. Clinical Trials Directive, art 2(e).

assessment of the quality of the research, of the research environment and the experience and responsibility of the principal investigator and of other key researchers. Sponsors are charged with ensuring that arrangements are in place in relation to the management and the monitoring of research.[289] The RGF provides that in a situation in which there is no external sponsor, a situation termed 'own account research', then care organisations must accept the responsibility (see RGF, para 3.85). The Department of Health already has a list of 'recognised sponsors', though in some instances those outside that list may be able to be sponsors.[290] The RGF gives as an example that of a student's supervisor who may undertake the function of a sponsor in relation to the student's research. It provides that there must be a clear written agreement which identifies the organisation which is responsible for the management and co-ordination of the study.[291] The need to ensure safety and accountability is emphasised. It also provides that agreements should have been reached in relation to provision of compensation where harm arises which is non-negligent. The RGF emphasises that research sponsors require appropriate systems and access to such systems for independent review which may enable them to satisfy themselves regarding the project's standing.[292] The reviews are to be directed at the project's scientific and ethical standing, what 'strategic relevance' it may have, and also its 'value for money'.

13.106 A further set of responsibilities is outlined for research funders.[293] This is in line with the division of responsibility under the EU Clinical Trials Directive. The RGF provides that:

> Organisations that fund research have a responsibility for ensuring that the work is a proper use of the funds they control and provides value for money.[294]

It emphasises that those bodies which want to fund research in collaboration with the NHS or social care must be willing to undertake the responsibilities of research sponsor or to collaborate with another organisation.[295] As the Medical Research Council comments, the sponsor role is one which has followed the model of the pharmaceutical industry. Under such a model 'a single company develops a product, initiates, funds and manages the trials necessary to gain a Marketing authorisation and then recoups its costs and profits directly from its sales. It is in the interests of that company to take responsibility for all aspects of trials undertaken for regulatory purposes.'[296] In contrast the Medical Research Council notes that publicly funded trials are by their very nature a collaborative

---

[289] RGF, para 3.8.3.
[290] ibid, Appendix 1, 8.
[291] ibid, para 3.8.6.
[292] ibid, para 4.2.
[293] ibid, para 3.7.
[294] ibid, para 3.7.1.
[295] ibid, para 3.7.2.
[296] MRC, *Good regulation of clinical trials for patients* (2003) 12.

partnership and in such a situation individuals and organisations have differing levels of sponsorship. While it is the case that the MCA Consultation Document does suggest that a sponsor may delegate part of their responsibilities, nonetheless the Council has criticised this because of the consequent transaction costs which may result. They note that there may be difficulties for example, where normally pilot work would be commissioned from charities, because charities etc would not be interested in taking on the consequent legal responsibilities of what they describe as 'high risk and unprofitable ventures'.[297] The Department of Health comments that there may indeed be situations in which funders feel that they are unable to take on such legal responsibilities and in such a situation it states that the funders should make it a precondition of funding that another body accepts the role of sponsor.[298]

3. Universities/Organisations Employing Researchers

The RGF emphasises that employers, whether private or public sector, of persons undertaking research in health and social care have an obligation to promote and develop a quality research culture.[299] It stresses that employers must support and also, where relevant, hold staff to account in relation to professional conduct of research. This also includes provision regarding training, career planning and development. It also extends to the use of codes of practice and compliance monitoring systems. Employers are also directed to have provision for dealing with non-compliance and misconduct and in relation to learning from complaints. **13.107**

The employing organisations are themselves required to ensure that researchers both understand and are able to discharge their responsibilities under the RGF.[300] There is an interface between the responsibilities of the employer and those of the research sponsor. The RGF notes that the nature of the employers' responsibilities needs to be agreed with the sponsor and care provider. Moreover it notes that ultimate responsibility regarding management and monitoring of the study is in the hands of the sponsor. The employers are charged with ensuring that the appropriate agreements are in place between research funders and care organisations regarding intellectual property issues (see RGF, Appendix one, 10, para 3.93). **13.108**

Universities and other employers are required to ensure compliance with relevant employment and health and safety legislation and codes of practice regarding other issues.[301] It is the employers who are required to ensure that the principal investigator and other staff both understand and comply with the RGF. They are required to have systems in place to detect and address fraud and other scientific or **13.109**

---

[297] ibid.
[298] RGF, Appendix one, 10.
[299] ibid, para 3.9.1.
[300] ibid, para 3.9.2.
[301] ibid, para 3.9.4.

professional misconduct. They are also required to ensure that they are in a position to compensate anyone who is harmed through negligent behaviour of their staff. They must permit and sanction investigations where these flow from complaints in respect of the employer's actions.

4. *Responsibilities of Organisations Providing Care*

13.110 The RGF also sets out the responsibilities of UK health and social care organisations.[302] This requires that such organisations must be aware of the research which is undertaken within their organisation or which involves participants, organs, tissues or data through the organisation. Appropriate information is to be given to patients, users and carers where this may impact upon care, experience of care and their work in the organisation. Interestingly the RGF states that, '[t]hey must ensure that only activity which is being managed formally as research within the provisions of this framework is presented as research' (see RGF, Appendix one, 10, para 3.10.1). It is the organisation providing care which is required to ensure that the research undertaken meets RGF standards and that an identifiable research sponsor is in place.[303] The Chief Executive/Agency Director is required to ensure accountability here. Reference is made to the duty of care of Chief Executives of NHS organisations and it is noted that they are accountable for quality.[304] Where researchers are not employed by the NHS organisation but 'interact with individuals in a way which has a direct bearing on the quality of their care [they] should hold an NHS honorary contract'. The RGF notes that further guidance will be issued on employment and accountability relating to university staff working within the NHS consequent upon a review of this area.

5. *Responsibilities of Care Professionals*

13.111 The RGF emphasises that health and social care professionals retain responsibility for care of patients and users where they are involved in research.[305] Moreover, care professionals are also required to satisfy themselves, before patients or clients are involved, that the research has been subject to approval by scrutinising authorities.[306]

6. *Responsibilities of Research Ethics Committees*

13.112 The RGF also makes reference to the responsibilities of research ethics committees. The RGF provides that RECs must act within their terms of reference and have a clearly defined remit (footnote to para 3.12.1). They must also act in good

---

[302] ibid, para 3.10.1.
[303] ibid, para 3.10.2.
[304] ibid, para 3.10.3.
[305] ibid, para 3.11.1.
[306] ibid at para 3.11.2.

faith providing impartial advice and safeguarding the rights and interests of research subjects (footnote insert para 3.1.12). The position of the REC is considered in more detail in para 13.09 of this chapter above. It should be noted that the RGF states that 'It is not the role or responsibility of the research ethics committees described above to give legal advice, nor are they liable for any of their decisions in this respect'. Nonetheless as we shall see in section 1 below RECs may themselves be the subject of litigation.

I. Accountability to the Research Participant

Where clinical trials go wrong and where injury results to trial participants then it is likely that ay consequent legal proceedings will be brought against those conducting the trial. The applicable principles of civil and criminal liability consequent upon clinical malpractice or product liability are considered elsewhere in this book (see Chapter 00).[307] This section primarily focuses upon the prospect for consequent legal challenges to decisions made by RECs but also considers the prospect for compensation for clinical trials subjects in the light of the Clinical Trials Directive.

13.113

The decisions of RECs may be subject to review in the courts through what is termed 'judicial review'.[308] Their decisions may be viewed on the basis that they have acted *ultra vires*, irrationally or contrary to the rules of natural justice.[309] The decision may, as a result, be struck down or the decision referred back to the ethics committee to re-determine. One problematic issue in relation to the prospect of bringing other legal proceedings against a REC is that of their legal status. This appears at present to be somewhat uncertain. Such committees do not currently have a legal personality which is distinct from that of their members.[310] However it has been suggested that as NHS RECs are now in fact constituted as sub-committees of Strategic Health authorities, that it is the Strategic Health Authorities who will be legally responsible for the decisions of the REC.[311] The current situation is however likely to change somewhat through the implementation of the Clinical Trials Directive into English law. The draft Medicines for Human Use (Clinical Trials) Regulations 2003 which are intended to implement the Directive into UK law now provide for the proposed new UK National Ethics Committee

13.114

---

[307] See eg discussion of *CJD Plaintiffs v UK MRC* (1996) 56 BMLR 8.
[308] See further McHale, JV, 'Guidelines for Medical Research: Some Ethical and Legal Problems' [1993] 1 Med L Rev 160.
[309] *R v St Mary's Hospital, ex p Harriot* [1988] 1 FLR 512.
[310] See Brazier, M, 'Liability of Ethics Committees and their Members' (1990) *Professional Negligence* 186.
[311] See discussion in Brazier, M, *Medicine, Patients and the Law* (3rd edn, London: Penguin, 2003) 399.

to establish or approve ethics committees.[312] Such ethics committees would certainly in the future have a statutory basis. Nonetheless it is the case that REC members may themselves also be individually responsible as Kennedy has noted:

> Principal among these duties is the duty of each member to act with due care. The role of each member is to review proposals for research and make recommendations as to the ethical propriety, or otherwise, of them. In carrying out this role, members must take account of the twin aims, referred to above [para 13.70], of fostering research while safeguarding the welfare of research subjects. Members must, therefore, seek to understand, so as to take an ethical view about, complex issues of, inter alia, biomedical science, statistics and moral philosophy. The members' duty, expressed in this way, may seem somewhat daunting. The standard of care demanded by the law, however, is that of reasonableness.[313]

13.115   Brazier suggested that, in principle, individual REC members owe a duty of care to research subjects.[314] REC members acting in accordance with their duties are covered by NHS indemnity. Nonetheless, while in theory a REC may be held liable where the committee or its members have acted negligently in scrutinising the conduct of a clinical trial, in practice establishing liability would be problematic. As Brazier has commented, to establish the action the research participant would be required to demonstrate that the committee member's negligence in approving the project led to the injury which this participant suffered. This is likely to be particularly difficult regarding the need to establish causation.

13.116   The involvement of those who participate in clinical trials, while they may be acting in their own interests in a therapeutic trial, may fundamentally be seen in terms of the public interest in the furthering of clinical reseach and scientific development.[315] Consequently the view has been expressed that if injury results there should be resultant compensation. So, for example, provision for ex gratia compensation has long been recognised in the guidelines issued by the pharmaceutical industry.[316] The MRC Guidelines provide that while they cannot give guarantees regarding compensation they will give sympathetic consideration to claims of non-negligent harm.[317]

---

[312] Medicines for Human Use (Clinical Trials) Regulations 2003, Pt 2, and see above, paras 13.16.

[313] Kennedy, I, 'Research and Experimentation' in Kennedy, I and Grubb, A, (eds), *Principles of Medical Law* (1st edn, Oxford: OUP, 1998).

[314] Brazier, M, 'Liability of ethics committees and their members' (1990) 6 *Professional Negligence* 186.

[315] *Report of the Royal Commission on Civil Liability and Compensation for Personal Injury* (London: HMSO, 1978) and also Royal College of Physicians, *Research Involving Patients* (London: RCP, 1990) 39–41.

[316] Association of the British Pharmaceutical Industry, *Guidelines for Compensation in Non-Patient Human Volunteers* (1994).

[317] MRC, *Guidelines for Good Clinical Practice in Clinical Trials* (1998) and see generally Jeffs, J and Mayon-White, R, 'Indemnity in Medical Research' in *Manual for Research Ethics Committees* (Kings College London, 1997); and McHale, J and Miola, J, 'Liability for Biomedical Research Concerning Human Subjects: Health Law Issues' and Jones, M, 'Liability for Medical Research

Concerns regarding the prospects for litigation and the need for resultant insur- **13.117**
ance and indemnity feature in the provisions of the Clinical Trials Directive relating to trials on medicinal products. The GMC guidance 'Research: the role and
responsibilities of doctors' also states that doctors should provide participants
with details regarding any compensation available should harm be suffered.[318]

The Clinical Trials Directive has now led to a reconsideration of the procedures **13.118**
for ensuring that research participants can obtain compensation should something go wrong during a clinical trial. Article 6(h) of the Clinical Trials Directive
now requires the REC, when examining a trial protocol, to consider the 'provision
for indemnity or compensation in the event of injury or death attributable to a
clinical trial'. Article 6(i) of the Clinical Trials Directive requires the REC when
making a decision regarding a trial protocol to consider 'any insurance or indemnity to cover the liability of the investigator or sponsor'. The 'sponsor' is defined
in the Directive as being 'an individual, company, institution or organisation
which takes responsibility for the initiation, management and/or financing of a
clinical trial'.[319] This is being incorporated into English law through the
Medicines for Human Use (Clinical Trials) Regulations 2003, currently in draft
form in s 14(6). The role of the research sponsor is now enshrined in the RGF and,
as noted above, RECs in considering the trial protocol should examine the availability of indemnity and compensation. In considering the whole area of compensation in the law of tort the Pearson Commission, while rejecting generally the
introduction of a no-fault compensation system in relation to the United
Kingdom, nonetheless supported the introduction of a specific no-fault compensation system in relation to clinical trials.[320] Interestingly this proposal has not
been taken forward in the most recent recommendations on reforming the law of
clinical negligence in the Chief Medical Officer's report in 2003 although these
recommendations do pave the way for some resolution of clinical negligence actions outside the courtroom.[321]

J. Conclusions

In the early 1990s the operation of RECs came under criticism. Neuberger writing **13.119**
in 1992 commented that '[s]ome ethical committees are very good indeed but

---

Concerning Human Subjects: Tort Law Issues' in Dute, J, (ed.) *Biomedical Research Concerning
Human Subjects* (Springer, forthcoming, 2004).

[318] GMC (1998).

[319] Art 2(e).

[320] *Royal Commission on Civil Liability for Personal Injury*, ch 24 'Medical Injury', para 1341.

[321] 'Clinical Negligence: What are the issues and options for reform?' (*www.doh.gov.uk/clinical
negligencereform*).

others are not. Overall the system is a mess.'[322] It is undoubtedly the case that today the systems in place for review of research protocols are infinitely superior than in the past. However this is an area still notable for the lack of clarity of its legal principles. While the implementation of the Clinical Trials Directive is playing an increasingly important part in structuring this area, there is still much to be done. Lack of trust in clinical researchers has been excerbated by recent controversies. There is urgent need for clarification of many issues—notably the boundaries of the consent process, confidentiality and use of tissue in particular. The Government announced in the Queen's Speech of 2003 that it intends to introduce a new Human Tissue Bill in the forthcoming parliamentary session. It is to be hoped that this will be the case. The role of the new UK Ethics Committee Authority will also be crucial both in terms of guidance and to link with what appears to be an increasing proliferation in regulatory bodies relating to clinical research. Perhaps the time has come for a comprehensive, clear statutory structure setting out the legal principles regarding regulations of all clinical trials.

---

[322] Neuberger, J, *Ethics and Health Care; the Role of Research Ethics Committees in the UK* (London: Kings Fund Institute, 1992).

14

THE REGULATION OF MEDICINAL
PRODUCTS AND MEDICAL DEVICES

A. Common Principles of Product Regulation

1. The Nature of Product Regulation

14.01 Product regulation is the system of administrative control over the marketing of products. It may potentially cover all the activities of producers and distributors, including design, research, manufacture, labelling, distribution, advertising, post-marketing vigilance and recall. It does not currently generally impose regulatory duties on users of products, but imposes regulatory duties on producers or others responsible for placing products on the market, and sometimes distributors. Breach of such duties is enforceable by regulatory authorities, through sanctions applied by administrative authorities or ultimately by the criminal courts.

2. Overview of this Chapter

14.02 There are many detailed legal provisions which regulate the placing on the market and safety of products. The aim of this chapter is to give an overview of the most important features that affect some of the products that are used in the medical context. It does not seek to be an exhaustive discussion but to outline the main points that would be relevant in a medical context. Accordingly, we do not deal with aspects of the legislation that relate to the more commercial aspects of products, such as the data exclusivity provisions for research-based products.

14.03 Many product types are regulated by specific, vertical regulatory provisions. Medicinal products and medical devices are each subject to specific, and different, regimes. These are outlined in separate parts of this chapter. We do not deal with all product regulatory systems, such as those for personal protective equipment or metrology.

Consumer products generally are regulated by horizontal provisions, which are at the time of writing set out in the General Product Safety Regulations 1994, which implement Directive (EEC) 1992/59. Those provisions are due to be significantly expanded with effect from January 2004. An outline of some aspects of these horizontal provisions is given in the fourth part of this chapter. The exact overlap between the horizontal general consumer provisions and the vertical provisions is a complex issue that is not fully clarified. **14.04**

We begin, however, with an outline of some general features of the legal systems that apply to each of the systems that are discussed subsequently. These aspects need to be understood in order to understand the detail which follows, particularly relating to the overarching provisions of EC law. **14.05**

3. Basis in EU law

(i) Competing Objectives of Common Market Trade and Safety

The product regulatory systems that apply in the United Kingdom have their legal basis in EC law, as part of the legal rules that harmonise the laws relating to trade within the Community so as to create a common internal market.[1] There is an inherent conflict in the fact that rules which are in social terms intended to ensure the safety of products' users and bystanders are ultimately primarily justified and construed by the courts in legal terms on criteria of trading issues, albeit that such laws are required to achieve a high level of health and safety of persons.[2] **14.06**

(ii) The Origin of Product Regulation

Historically, regulation arose as a result of safety concerns: regulation of medicinal products began in Europe during the 1960s following concern at phocomelia injuries caused by thalidomide. The first EC legislation[3] was enacted in 1965 (which did not apply to the United Kingdom until it joined the Community in 1972) and the first UK legislation was the Medicines Act 1968, effective from 1971: since then the initial rules have been regularly reformed and extended in scope. There was some confusion between the Community and UK national laws until the mid-1990s from when UK regulations were enacted that essentially applied the Community provisions.[4] **14.07**

---

[1] EC Treaty, Art 95.
[2] ibid: the phrase 'high level of safety' is usually recited in individual product Directives.
[3] Directive (EEC) 65/65.
[4] Such as the Medicines for Human Use (Marketing Authorisations Etc) Regulations SI 1994/3144.

14.08   Regulation of medical devices was introduced during the 1990s, having largely not existed before that time under European national laws, as a result of the desire, which was held jointly by an increasingly multi-national manufacturers' sector and the Community trade authorities, to avoid fragmentation of national systems.

(iii) Relationship Between Community Legal Instruments and National Law

14.09   The Community legal instruments that form the basis of product regulation are nearly always directives:[5] the instrument of a Council regulation is used once but importantly in the pharmaceutical sector.[6] A Council regulation has direct effect in the Member States whereas a directive is binding on each Member State, which is obliged under the EC Treaty to implement the directive into its national law. A Member State has the discretion to choose the manner in which the directive may be implemented so long as the effect of the directive is achieved under its national legal order. Most Member States transpose directives into their national law by enacting domestic legislation which follows the text of the directives closely, if not *verbatim*. However, differences between implementing laws can arise, particularly in relation to enforcement and sanctions for non-compliance, which are aspects only governed by directives in broad terms so are in any event matters for the national authorities. It is the national law which is directly binding on people, companies and operations within a particular state, not the directive. However, since the directive ultimately governs the national law, people often colloquially refer to the directive rather than the national law and this approach will be adopted in this chapter. Nevertheless, in any given situation, one must always check the relevant national law and consider, first, what are its provisions, second, to what extent they differ from the directive and, third, whether any difference constitutes a breach of Community law by the Member State and what consequences might flow, such that the national provision might be unenforceable.

4. *Major Differences Between the Systems of Regulation of Medicinal Products and Medical Devices*

14.10   There are significant differences between the regulatory systems for medicinal products and medical devices. First, there is a fundamental difference in the regulatory methodology between the two systems, in that the system for medicinal products requires companies to apply for and hold authorisations granted by competent authorities (ie, governmental licensing authorities) in order to undertake the activities of placing a product on the market, manufacture, and wholesale

---

[5] Of the Council and the European Parliament: some Commission Directives are sometimes used.

[6] Regulation (EEC) 2309/93.

distribution. In contrast, the onus for certifying regulatory compliance for medical devices[7] falls on the manufacturer, in some cases with the prior and continuing certification of some activities by a notified body (a private organisation with a contractual relationship with the manufacturer but acting in accordance with regulatory powers authorised by a competent authority).

Secondly, the scope of the medicinal products regulatory system is appreciably wider than that for medical devices. The former regulates almost all commercial activity, encompassing pre-market testing, authorisation to market, manufacture, labelling, advertising, distribution, retail supply[8], post-marketing vigilance and recall. In contrast, the law relating to medical devices only currently regulates the activities of placing on the market (encompassing certain aspects of pre-market testing, design, production and labelling) and, in part, post-marketing vigilance. The medical device regulatory system currently has no specific rules on advertising[9] or distribution.[10]   **14.11**

B. Medicinal Products

1. Overview

Both the volume and complexity of the regulatory provisions and control for medicinal products are extensive. The controls extend over the conditions for animal and human research, pre-marketing safety conditions, control of manufacturing quality and distribution, advertising and informational parameters, and post-marketing vigilance requirements. The provisions have grown steadily since their inception in the 1960s[11] and are still being developed. This chapter gives an overview of the scope of the provisions that are of primary importance in relation   **14.12**

---

[7] As with all Directives that are of the type prescribed in Council Resolution of 7 May 1985 on a new approach to technical harmonisation and standards [1985] OJ C136/1.

[8] This is not covered directly by Community legislation but in the UK is subject to control partially under the Medicines Act 1968 (eg, licensing of premises) and partially under professional rules of pharmacists (enforced by the Royal Pharmaceutical Society of Great Britain): see Dale and Applebe, *Pharmacy Law and Ethics* (7th edn, Pharmaceutical Press, 2001).

[9] Directives (EEC) 84/450 and (EC) 97/55 on misleading and comparative advertising; the Control of Misleading Advertisements Regulations 1988, SI 1988/915 as amended by the Control of Misleading Advertisements (Amendment) Regulations 2000, SI 2000/914.

[10] Not at least under Community or UK law: certain other Member States have national provisions on distribution of medical devices. Certain regulatory provisions do, however, apply to distributors of consumer products, as discussed at paras 14.206 *et seq* below.

[11] Regulation followed recognition that the tragic effects of phocomelia in children were caused by thalidomide taken as a prophylactic for symptoms of morning sickness by pregnant women in the early 1960s: see Teff, H and Munro, CR, *Thalidomide: the legal aftermath* (Saxon House, 1976). As a result, the European Community introduced Directive (EEC) 65/65 in 1965 and the UK government introduced a non-statutory Committee on the Safety of Drugs (the 'Dunlop Committee') followed by the Medicines Act 1968. Considerable revision and extension of these provisions has been undertaken on a regular basis.

to medical practice, notably the authorisation and safety issues. This discussion covers the primary legal provisions, but there are in addition extensive supplementary guidelines issued by the authorities.[12]

14.13 The situation is somewhat confused by the existence of two approval systems for marketing authorisations:[13] a *centralised system*, in which a single marketing authorisation valid throughout the Community is granted by the European Commission after advice from the European Agency for the Evaluation of Medicinal Products (EMEA), and a *mutual recognition system*, in which marketing authorisations valid only for individual Member States are granted by national competent authorities[14] for which abbreviated procedures of cross-referencing to the first state's assessment and approval are applied to applications for authorisation by second and subsequent states. This duality of systems gives rise to two sets of legal instruments, albeit with many virtually identical provisions and considerable overlap. The centralised system is set out in Council Regulation (EEC) 2309/93 and the mutual recognition system in Directive (EC) 2001/83 which comprises a comprehensive Community code relating to medicinal products for human use, many provisions applying under the centralised approval system, and which consolidates and repeals 11 previous directives.[15]

14.14 This analysis will focus on medicinal products for human use rather than veterinary use, since this work is concerned primarily with the safety of products for humans. It should, however, be noted that, since the use of veterinary medicines is relevant to the safety of animals in the food chain, particular provisions govern maximum residue limits. The basic structure of the veterinary legislation and much of the detailed provisions are identical to the system governing human products but there are significant differences in matters of detail.

14.15 As discussed in paras 14.01 to 14.11, almost all of the UK law that governs this area is subject to provisions of Community law. For this reason, the following description and references are primarily based on the applicable Community law

---

[12] Guidance documents at Community level comprise a sequence of categories from the less formal Concept Papers and Points to Consider and the more permanent guidelines issued by Working Parties of the European Agency for the Evaluation of Medicinal Products, to the more formal guidelines authorised by that Agency's Committee for Proprietary Medicinal Products in consultation with the competent authorities of the Member States and issued by the European Commission in its series of volumes entitled *The Rules governing Medicinal Products in the European Union*. Reference should be made to *www.europa.eu.int*.

[13] These systems are further described at paras 14.26 *et seq* below.

[14] In the UK the Licensing Authority comprises the Ministers of Health for England and Wales, Scotland and Northern Ireland, whose functions are assisted by the Medicines Control Agency and who may be advised by expert committees such as the Committee on Safety of Medicines: see Medicines Act 1968, ss 1–4.

[15] Directives (EEC) 65/65, (EEC) 75/318, (EEC) 75/319, (EEC) 89/342, (EEC) 89/343, (EEC) 89/381, (EEC) 92/25, (EEC) 92/26, (EEC) 92/27, (EEC) 92/28 and (EEC) 92/73. All the current legislation is accessible at *http://dg3.eudra.org/eudralex/index.html*.

provisions, supplemented where necessary by the national provisions. Naturally, if a particular issue arises under UK law, it will be necessary to consider the national law provisions that apply, but it is always relevant to check that the national provisions conform to the governing Community provisions: if there are differences between the two, it is then necessary to consider whether and what legal consequences may flow, but that is an issue of Community law that is outside the scope of the current work.

The basis of the UK legislation[16] predated this state's entry into the Community, with the result that the original national and Community schemes[17] differed somewhat in conception as well as detail. Although the national scheme has since been aligned as regards the detailed provisions of Community law, there remain differences both in some general aspects and in many details. The Medicines Act 1968, supplemented by a series of statutory instruments, has confusingly been in part disapplied by the Medicines for Human Use (Marketing Authorisations Etc) Regulations 1994.[18] It is impracticable to give here detailed descriptions or references to many detailed matters, such as the extensive provisions of subsidiary legislation[19] or the criminal enforcement provisions,[20] but the objective is to give a clear outline of the main structure.[21]

14.16

2. Products Covered

(i) Definition of Medicinal Product

A medicinal product is defined as:

14.17

> Any substance or combination of substances presented for treating or preventing disease in human beings.
>
> Any substance or combination of substances which may be administered to human beings with a view to making a medical diagnosis or to restoring, correcting or modifying physiological functions in human beings is likewise considered a medicinal product.'[22]

---

[16] Medicines Act 1968.

[17] Which began in 1965 with Directive (EEC) 65/65.

[18] SI 1994/3144. These Regulations were introduced after criticism by the Court of Appeal identified several substantial differences between the national and Community provisions which put the UK in breach of its Treaty obligations: *Organon Laboratories Limited v Department of Health and Social Security* [1990] 2 CMLR 49.

[19] Such as the Medicines (Standard Provisions for Licences and Certificates) Regulations 1971, SI 1971/972.

[20] Such as the Medicines for Human Use (Marketing Authorisations Etc) Regulations 1994, reg 7(4) and Sch 3; the Medicines Act 1968, ss 45, 67, 84, 91, 123, 124 and 125.

[21] For detailed review of the practical requirements relating to pharmaceutical companies see Griffin JP and O'Grady J (eds), *The Textbook of Pharmaceutical Medicine* (4th edn, BMJ Books, 2002) and Shah RS and Griffin, JP, 'Regulation of human medicinal products in the European Union' in Griffin, JP and O'Grady, J (eds), *The Regulation of Medical Products* (BMJ Books, 2003).

[22] Directive (EC) 2001/83, Art 1(2).

14.18   The term 'substance' is defined as any matter, irrespective of origin, which may be human, animal, vegetable or chemical.[23] There are two distinct tests under this definition of medicinal product: presentation and function, although the Court of Justice has commented that the two limbs cannot be regarded as strictly separate from each other, since a substance which is endowed with properties for treating or preventing disease in human beings or animals falls in principle within the scope of the 'function' limb.[24] Nevertheless, satisfaction of either test is sufficient for a substance to be considered a medicinal product.

14.19   It is for the relevant competent authorities and the national courts to determine on a case by case basis, and consistent with the relevant directives, the classification of each product having regard to all its characteristics, in particular to its composition, to its pharmacological properties (as they may be ascertained in the current state of scientific knowledge), to the way in which it is used, to the extent to which it is sold, to consumers' familiarity with it, and even to the risks which its use may entail.[25] The Court of Justice has itself recognised that differences in the classification of identical products may occur as between member states and that this is 'difficult to avoid' under the current system.[26]

14.20   It is clear that if a product satisfies either of the limbs of the definition of medicinal product it will be subject to the medicinal product legislation, to the exclusion of any other rules, such as those for cosmetics,[27] food[28] or medical devices.[29] Thus, a product will be subject to the medicinal product regime even if it otherwise satisfies the definition of a cosmetic in Directive (EEC) 76/768 if, for example, it is presented as possessing properties for the treatment or prevention of illness or disease, or if it is intended to be administered with a view to restoring, correcting or modifying physiological functions.[30]

14.21   The 'presentation' limb of the definition is to be construed broadly.[31] The Court of Justice has held that a product is 'presented for treating or preventing disease' when it is expressly 'indicated' or 'recommended' as such, possibly by means of

---

[23] ibid, Art 1(3); Case C-35/85 *Procureur de la République v Gérard Tissier* [1985] ECR II-1207 (the definition applies not only to substances to be administered as they are but also to substances requiring processing, for example by mixing, such as carrier constituents of radio-pharmaceuticals).

[24] Case C-290/90 *Re Eye Lotions: EC Commission v Germany* [1995] 2 CMLR 65.

[25] Case C-112/89 *Upjohn Co and Upjohn NV v Farzoo Inc and JAWMJ Kortmann* [1991] ECR I-1703; Case C-212/91 *Angelopharm GmbH v Feie und Hansestadt Hamburg* [1994] ECR I-00171; Case C-60/89 *The Republic v Jean Monteil and Daniel Samanni* [1992] 3 CMLR 425; Case C-290/90 (n 24 above).

[26] Case C-290/90 (n 24 above); Case C-369/88 *Delattre* [1991] ECR I-1487.

[27] Case C-60/89 (n 25 above).

[28] Case C-219/91 *Ter Voort* [1995] ECR I-5485.

[29] Directive (EEC) 93/42, Art 1(5)(e).

[30] Case C-60/89 (n 25 above).

[31] Case C-227/82 *Van Bennekom* [1983] ECR I-3883; Case C-60/89 (n 25 above).

labels, leaflets or oral representations: consequently herbal teas which are expressly indicated or recommended as having therapeutic or prophylactic properties are to be regulated as medicines.[32] However, the Court of Justice has also held that it is not necessary that the product be expressly indicated or recommended as suitable for treating or preventing disease, for example by means of labels, leaflets or oral representation: it is sufficient that any averagely well-informed consumer gains the impression, even impliedly (so long as it is definitive) that the product would, having regard to its presentation, have those properties.[33] However, in one case it was decided that the fact that a product is antiseptic and antibacterial is not conclusive of its medicinal function since many non-medicinal products, including soap, also display such properties.[34]

The 'function' limb of the definition 'must be given a sufficiently broad interpretation to cover all substances capable of having an effect on the actual functioning of the body. However, that criterion does not serve to include substances such as certain cosmetics, which while having an effect on the human body, do not significantly affect the metabolism and thus do not, strictly, modify the way in which it functions.'[35] The application of the definition of 'medicinal product' can be far from straightforward and there can, in particular, be room for more than one opinion in relation to the 'function' test, where the result can be very much a question of judgment.[36] Accordingly, the Court of Appeal has said that a competent authority is to be allowed a margin of appreciation in decisions on such questions since, in discharging their initial heavy responsibility of protecting public health, the Agency is an expert body, has accumulated experience in relation to other products and has to develop a consistent policy between similar products.[37]   **14.22**

A Member State may, at its discretion, enforce national legislation prohibiting or restricting the sale, supply or use of medicinal products as contraceptives or abortifacients.[38] A simplified registration procedure applies to homeopathic products.[39] It is intended to introduce a simplified registration procedure for herbal medicinal products, notably where evidence is produced of at least 30 years' traditional use.[40]   **14.23**

---

[32] Case C-219/91 (n 28 above).

[33] Case C-227/82 (n 31 above) (external form and concentration may be relevant, so as to render a vitamin a medicinal product); Case C-60/89 (n 25 above).

[34] Case C-60/89 (n 25 above).

[35] Case C-112/89 (n 25 above), 1742; see also Case C-227/82 (n 31 above).

[36] *R v Medicines Control Agency, ex p Pharma Nord (UK) Ltd* [1998] 3 CMLR 109 (CA).

[37] ibid. The Medicines Control Agency issued revised Guidance Note No 8 on borderline products in December 2000, *A Guide To What Is A Medicinal Product* (amended March 2002).

[38] Directive (EC) 2001/83, Art 4(4) (introduced by Directive (EEC) 93/39, Art 1(5)).

[39] introduced by Directive (EC) 92/73; the Medicines (Homeopathic Medicinal Products for Human Use) Regulations 1994, SI 1994/105.

[40] Proposal for a Directive on herbal medicinal products, COM/2002/00001.

(ii) Products Not Covered

14.24 The regulatory controls do not apply to:[41]

(i) any medicinal product prepared in a pharmacy in accordance with a medical prescription for an individual patient (commonly known as the magistral formula);

(ii) a medicinal product which is prepared in a pharmacy in accordance with the prescriptions of a pharmacopoeia and is intended to be supplied directly to the patients served by the pharmacy in question (commonly known as the official formula);

(iii) medicinal products intended for research and development trials;[42]

(iv) intermediate products intended for further processing by an authorised manufacturer;

(v) any radionuclides in the form of sealed sources;

(vi) whole blood, plasma or blood cells of human origin.

14.25 A Member State may, in accordance with legislation in force and to fulfil special needs, exclude from the provisions of Directive (EC) 2001/83 medicinal products supplied in response to a bona fide unsolicited order, formulated in accordance with the specifications of an authorised health care professional and for use by his individual patients on his direct personal responsibility.[43] Specific provisions apply to homeopathic medicinal products.[44]

3. Requirement for a Marketing Authorisation: Data Requirements

(i) The Primary Criteria of Safety, Efficacy and Quality

14.26 Regulatory decisions in relation to the grant of marketing authorisations are to be based on three criteria, namely safety, efficacy[45] and quality, which are designed to ensure the protection of public health. This is established as a matter of policy in the recitals to the governing legislation:[46]

---

[41] Directive (EC) 2001/83, Art 3.

[42] But as discussed below, certain aspects are now controlled, such as labelling and pharmacovigilance.

[43] Directive (EC) 2001/83, Art 5.

[44] ibid, Arts 13–16.

[45] The concept of the protection of public health means that a medicinal product must not only not be harmful but also must be effective, catching products which are not sufficiently effective or which do not have the effect which their presentation might lead to expect: Case C-219/91 *Ter Voort* [1992] ECR I-5485; Order of the President of the Court in Case C-471/00 *Commission of the European Communities and Cambridge Healthcare Supplies Ltd* (11 April 2001); Joined Cases T-74/00, T-76/00, T-83/00 to T-85/00, T-132/00, T-137/00 and T-141/00 *Artegodan GmbH v European Commission* (26 November 2002).

[46] Regulation (EEC) 2309/93, recital 3; virtually identical wording had been used in Council Directive (EEC) 93/93, third recital, which amended the primary measure, Council Directive

Whereas in the interest of public health it is necessary that decisions on the authorisation of . . . medicinal products should be exclusively based on the objective criteria of the quality, safety and efficacy of the medicinal product concerned to the exclusivity of economic or other considerations; whereas these criteria have been extensively harmonised by Council Directive 65/65/EEC[47] . . .; whereas, however, Member States should exceptionally be able to prohibit the use on their territory of medicinal products which infringe objectively defined concepts of public order or public morality . . .

Subsequent recitals to Council Regulation (EEC) 2309/93 also stress the importance of making decisions on the basis of criteria of safety, efficacy and quality, and of making decisions that are of the highest possible quality:

14.27

Whereas only after a single scientific evaluation of the highest possible standard of the quality, safety or efficacy of technologically advanced medicinal products, to be undertaken within the European Agency for the Evaluation of Medicinal Products should a marketing authorisation be granted by the Community by a rapid procedure ensuring close co-operation between the Commission and Member States;

Whereas . . . in the event of a disagreement between Member States about the quality, safety or efficacy of a medicinal product which is the subject of a decentralised authorisation procedure, the matter should be resolved by a binding Community decision following a scientific evaluation of the issues involved within a European medicinal product evaluation agency; . . .

. . .

Whereas the primary task of the Agency should be to provide scientific advice of the highest possible quality to the Community institutions and the Member States for the exercise of the powers conferred upon them by Community legislation in the field of medicinal products in relation to the authorisation and supervision of medicinal products;

. . .

Whereas, therefore, the exclusive responsibility for preparing the opinions of the Agency on all matters relating to medicinal products for human use should be entrusted to the Committee for Proprietary Medicinal Products created by the Second Council Directive 75/319/EEC . . .

Whereas the establishment of the Agency will make it possible to reinforce the scientific role and independence of these two Committees, in particular through the establishment of a permanent technical and administrative secretariat;

Whereas it is also necessary to make provisions for the supervision of medicinal products which have been authorised by the Community, and in particular for the intensive monitoring of adverse reactions to those medicinal products through Community pharmacovigilance activities in order to ensure the rapid withdrawal

---

(EEC) 65/65, but curiously this wording was omitted from the consolidating measure, Directive (EEC) 2001/83, although it was apparent from the complete text that no change in policy was intended. The three criteria are set out in the Medicines Act 1968, s 19, but the Community provisions are applied to nearly all products by virtue of the Medicines for Human Use (Marketing Authorisations Etc) Regulations 1994.

[47] In Council Regulation (EEC) 2309/93 this wording is in the subsequent recital.

from the market of any medicinal product which presents an unacceptable level of risk under normal conditions of use;

Whereas the Commission, working in close co-operation with the Agency, and after consultation with Member States, should also be entrusted with the task of co-ordinating the discharge of the various supervisory responsibilities of Member States and in particular the provisions of information about medicinal products, monitoring the respect [sic] of good manufacturing practices, good laboratory practices and good clinical practices;

Whereas the Agency should also be responsible for co-ordinating the activities of Member states in the field of the monitoring of adverse reactions to medicinal products (pharmacovigilance).

14.28   In considering whether a product can be safely administered, Mustill LJ has commented:

. . . there is no absolute standard of safety. Very few drugs are entirely free from the risk of inducing adverse side effects in some patients. The question must always be whether the degree of risk is sufficiently low to be acceptable, and this cannot be addressed without an appreciation of the benefits to be gained from taking a risk of that degree.[48]

14.29   The President of the Court of Justice has said that in decisions on grant, variation, suspension or revocation of a marketing authorisation, the requirements of public health unquestionably take precedence over economic considerations, and involve a benefit/risk assessment, in which the degree of harmfulness which the authority may regard as acceptable depends on the benefits which the medicinal product is considered to provide.[49] The means by which the above policy considerations are achieved in practice will now be examined.

(ii) Requirement for a Marketing Authorisation

14.30   No medicinal product may be placed on the market within the Community unless the relevant authority has granted a marketing authorisation.[50] In the case of medicinal products derived from biotechnological processes or other specified categories of new products[51] the relevant authority is the European Agency for the

---

[48] *Organon Laboratories Limited v Department of Health and Social Security* [1990] 2 CMLR 49 (CA), 78.

[49] Order of the President of the Court in Case C-471/00 *Commission of the European Communities and Cambridge Healthcare Supplies Ltd* [2001] ECR I-02865.

[50] Regulation (EEC) 2309/93, Art 3; Directive (EC) 2001/83, Art 6(1); the Medicines for Human Use (Marketing Authorisations Etc) Regulations 1994, regu 3 and Sch 1 (formerly the Medicines Act 1968, s 7) prohibits inter alia the placing on the market of a medicinal product save in accordance with a marketing authorisation (product licence), subject to certain exceptions.

[51] In particular, the centralised approval system, as discussed below, is optional for medicinal products with new active ingredients. It is anticipated that the categories of products subject to the jurisdiction of the EMEA will increase and ultimately leave the national agencies with no formal licensing jurisdiction, although they may retain other functions in relation to manufacturing authorisations, inspections and pharmacovigilance.

Evaluation of Medicinal Products (EMEA), that commenced operations on 1 January 1995, operating the centralised system. Marketing authorisations granted by the EMEA are valid throughout the European Economic Area (EEA). The relevant competent authorities for other medicinal products are those of each Member State,[52] which each has jurisdiction over its national territory.

All decisions to grant, refuse, vary, suspend, withdraw or revoke a marketing au- **14.31** thorisation shall state in detail the reasons on which they are based and be notified to the party concerned.[53] A marketing authorisation shall not be refused, varied, suspended, withdrawn or revoked except on the grounds set out in the legislation.[54] Applications for variations of marketing authorisations must be made in accordance with prescribed procedures.[55]

(iii) Application for a Marketing Authorisation: Particulars and Documents Recording the Results of Tests and Clinical Trials

In order to obtain a marketing authorisation, the person responsible for placing **14.32** the product on the market must submit an application to the relevant authority accompanied by the particulars and documents referred to in Article 8(3) and Annex I of Directive (EC) 2003/63.[56]

The particulars and documents that must accompany an application are: **14.33**

    (a) Name or corporate name and permanent address of the applicant, and, where applicable, of the manufacturer.
    (b) Name of the medicinal product.
    (c) Qualitative and quantitative particulars of all the constituents of the medicinal product in usual terminology, but excluding empirical chemical formulae, with mention of the international non-proprietary name recommended by the World Health Organisation where such name exists.
    (d) Brief description of the manufacturing method.
    (e) Therapeutic indications, contra-indications and adverse reactions.
    (f) Posology, pharmaceutical form, method and route of administration and expected shelf life.
    (g) If applicable, reasons for any precautionary and safety measures to be taken for

---

[52] In the UK, the authority is the Medicines Control Agency.
[53] Regulation (EEC) 2309/93, Art 67 and Directive (EC) 2001/83, Art 125. A relevant authority or advisory committee must be allowed a broad discretion by the courts in judicial review cases in considering how best to approach scientific evidence (such as evidence of a lack of safety in overdose by the elderly) and what weight to give to it: *In the matter of Organon Laboratories Ltd* (CA transcript CO/1738/88, 17 February 1989).
[54] Regulation (EEC) 2309/93, Art 68 and Directive (EC) 2001/83, Art 126.
[55] Commission Regulation (EC) 1084/2003 governs products authorised under the centralised procedure, and Commission Regulation (EC) 1085/2003 governs those authorised under the mutual recognition procedure.
[56] See also Regulation 2309/93, Art 6; Medicines Act 1968, s 18; the Medicines (Applications for Grant of Product Licences—Products for Human Use) Regulations 1993, SI 1993/2538.

the storage of the medicinal product, its administration to patients and for the disposal of waste products, together with an indication of any potential risks presented by the medicinal product for the environment.

(h) Description of the control methods employed by the manufacturer (qualitative and quantitative analysis of the constituents and of the finished product, special tests, eg sterility tests, tests for the presence of pyrogenic substances, the presents of heavy metals, stability tests, biological and toxicity tests, controls carried out at an intermediate stage of the manufacturing process).

(i) Results of:[57]

—physico-chemical, biological or microbiological tests,
—toxicological and pharmacological tests,
—clinical trials.

(j) A summary, in accordance with Article 11, of the product characteristics, one or more specimens or mock-ups of the other packaging and the immediate packaging of the medicinal product, together with a package leaflet.

(k) A document showing that the manufacturer is authorised in his own country to produce proprietary products.

(l) Copies of any authorisation obtained in another Member State or in a third country to place the medicinal product on the market . . .

14.34   In summary, a considerable quantity of data must be produced to the competent authority in support of an application for a marketing authorisation. The data must record that the required tests and clinical trials on the product have been carried out so as to found an opinion that the product affords a sufficient level of safety. Production of this data is time-consuming and expensive.

14.35   The requirements for the results of tests and clinical trials in Article 8(3)(i) are considerably amplified in Annex I to Directive (EC) 2003/63.[58] The main headings covered in the Annex are set out in table 1.[59]

---

[57] There are certain exceptions to the provision of full results, notably where an applicant can demonstrate (i) either that the product is essentially similar to a medicinal product that has been authorised in the Member State for which the holder of the marketing authorisation has consented to the data references being used for reference, or (ii) that the constituents of the product have a well established medicinal use with recognised efficacy and an acceptable level of safety, by means of a detailed scientific bibliography, or (iii) that the product is essentially similar to a medicinal product that has been authorised in the Community for six (or in some cases or states ten) years: Directive (EC) 2001/83, Art 10(1) and Annex I, Pt 3.I and 4.I. In relation to the second exception, under which the scientific literature in the public domain must be complete, see Case C-440/93 *R v Licensing Authority of the Department of Health and Norgine Ltd, ex p Scotia Pharmaceuticals Ltd* [1995] ECR I-2851: 'the abridged procedure in no way relaxes the requirements of safety and efficacy which must be met'. In relation to the third exception, see Case C-368/96 *R v The Licensing Authority established by the Medicines Act 1968 (acting by The Medicines Control Agency), ex p Generics (UK) Limited* [1999] ECR I-7967 which affirmed the same point.

[58] Amended by Directive (EC) 2003/63. First introduced by Directive (EEC) 75/318 and significantly amended by Directive (EEC) 91/507.

[59] The format of the dossier is to change to a Common Technical Document which will standardise the data requirements for the EU, US and Japan: see *http://pharmacos.eudra.org?F2/pharmacos/docs.htm.*

Table 1: **Analytical Pharmacotoxicological and Clinical Standards and Protocols in Respect of the Testing of Medicinal Products**

TABLE OF CONTENTS

Table 1: *continued*

3.2.2.7	Container and closure of the finished medicinal product
3.2.2.8	Stability of the finished medicinal product
4.	Module 4: Non-clinical reports
4.1.	Format and Presentation
4.2.	Content: basic principles and requirements
4.2.1.	Pharmacology
4.2.2.	Pharmaco-kinetics
4.2.3.	Toxicolgy
5.	Module 5: Clinical study reports
5.1.	Format and Presentation
5.2.	Content: basic principles and requirements
5.2.1.	Reports of bio-pharmaceutics studies
5.2.2.	Reports of studies pertinent to pharmaco-kinetics using human bio-materials
5.2.3.	Reports of human pharmaco-kinetic studies
5.2.4.	Reports of human pharmaco-dynamic studies
5.2.5.	Reports of efficacy and safety studies
5.2.5.1.	Study Reports of Controlled Clinical Studies Pertinent to the Claimed Indication
5.2.5.2	Study reports of uncontrolled clinical studies reports of analyses of data from more than one study and other clinical study reports
5.2.6.	Reports of post-marketing experience
5.2.7.	Case reports forms and individual patient listings

Part II: Specific marketing authorisation dossiers and requirements

1.	Well-established medicinal use
2.	Essentially similar medicinal products
3.	Additional data required in specific situations
4.	Similar biological medicinal products
5.	Fixed combination medicinal products
6.	Documentation for applications in exceptional circumstances
7.	Mixed marketing authorisation applications

Part III: Particular medicinal products

1.	Biological medicinal products
1.1.	Plasma-derived medicinal product
1.2.	Vaccines
2.	Radio-pharmaceuticals and precursors
2.1.	Radio-pharmaceuticals
2.2.	Radio-pharmaceutical precursors for radio-labelling purposes
3.	Homeopathic medicinal products
4.	Herbal medicinal products
5.	Orphan Medicinal Products

Part IV: Advanced therapy medicinal products

1.	Gene therapy medicinal products (human and xenogeneic)
1.1.	Diversity of gene therapy medicinal products

Table 1: *continued*

1.2.	Specific requirements regarding Module 3
2.	Somatic cell therapy medicinal products (human and xenogeneic)
3.	Specific requirements for gene therapy and somatic cell therapy (human and xenogeneic) medicinal products regarding Modules 4 and 5
3.1.	Module 4
3.2.	Module 5
3.2.1.	Human pharmacology and efficacy studies
3.2.2.	Safety
4.	Specific Statement on Xeno-transplantation Medicinal Products.

(iv) Expert Reports

Reports from experts in each of three disciplines for which documents are re-   **14.36**
quired (analysis, pharmacology and similar experimental sciences, and clinical trials) are to be submitted with the particulars and documents of the application.[60]
These reports fulfil two main functions: first, verification that the experts have
carried out the relevant tasks and have described the results objectively; secondly,
to describe their observations in accordance with the requirements of Annex I of
Directive (EC) 2003/63 and to state, in particular:[61]

—in the case of the analyst, whether the medicinal product is consistent with the
declared composition, giving any substantiation of the control methods employed by the manufacturer;
—in the case of the pharmacologist or the specialist with similar experimental competence, the toxicity of the medicinal product and the pharmacological properties observed;
—in the case of the clinician, whether he has been able to ascertain effects on persons treated with the medicinal product which correspond to the particulars
given by the applicant in accordance with Articles 4, 8 and 10, whether the patient tolerates the medicinal product well, the posology the clinician advises and
any contra-indications and side-effects.

Where applicable, the experts must also state the grounds for using published ref-   **14.37**
erences rather than the results of clinical studies.[62]

In effect, therefore, there is expert assessment giving an overview of the scientific   **14.38**
aspects. This function effectively constitutes a regulatory verification and assessment prior to that of the competent authority. An expert need not, however, be
independent of the applicant. The competent authority may use its power of assessment to ascertain whether or not the applicant, and consequently the expert

---

[60] Directive (EC) 2001/83, Art 12 (first introduced by Directive (EC) 75/319, Art 2); Regulation
(EEC) 2309/93, Art 6.
[61] Directive (EC) 2001/83, Art 12(2)(b).
[62] ibid, Art 12(2)(c).

who prepared the documentation supporting the application, took account of current technical developments and scientific progress and whether or not he or she was satisfied that the scientific publications were up to date.[63]

(v) Duration of a Marketing Authorisation

14.39 A marketing authorisation is valid for five years and is renewable for five-year periods, on application by the holder at least three months before the expiry date and after consideration by the competent authority of a dossier containing in particular details of the data on pharmacovigilance and other information relevant to the monitoring of the medicinal product.[64] An authorisation may be granted in exceptional circumstances subject to conditions, such as the carrying out of further studies or the notification of adverse reactions.[65]

(vi) Procedures for Assessment

(a) The centralised procedure and the CPMP

14.40 A centralised application is considered by the Committee for Proprietary Medicinal Products (CPMP), which is responsible for formulating the opinions of the (EMEA)[66] on any question concerning the admissibility of the files submitted, the granting, variation, suspension or withdrawal of a marketing authorisation and pharmacovigilance.

14.41 The CPMP consists of representatives of the Member States and of the Commission and draws up its own rules of procedure.[67] The CPMP prepares its opinion on the application.[68] It is required to verify that the particulars and documents submitted are those required by Article 8 of Directive (EC) 2001/83 and Annex I of Directive (EC) 2003/63 and to examine whether the conditions specified in the Regulation for issuing a marketing authorisation for the medicinal product are satisfied. It has power to ask for a test of the medicinal product, its starting materials and, if need be, its intermediate products or other constituent materials to be carried out, in order to ensure that the control methods employed by the manufacturer and described in the application documents are satisfactory. It also has power, where appropriate, to request the applicant to supplement the particulars accompanying the application within a specific time limit.

---

[63] Case C-440/93 *R v Licensing Authority of the Department of Health and Norgine Ltd, ex p Scotia Pharmaceuticals Ltd* [1995] ECR I-2851.

[64] Regulation (EEC) 2309/93, Article 13; Directive (EC) 2001/83, Art 24; Medicines Act 1968, s 24.

[65] Directive (EC) 2001/83, Art 22.

[66] Established under Directive (EEC) 75/319; now see Directive (EC) 2001/83, Art 27.

[67] Directive (EC) 2001/83, Art 27.3

[68] Regulation (EEC) 2309/93, Art 7.

Where the opinion of the CPMP is that the application does not satisfy the criteria for authorisation, or the summary of product characteristics proposed by the applicant should be amended, or the labelling or package leaflet is not in compliance with Title V of Directive (EC) 2001/83, or the authorisation should be granted subject to conditions appropriate for exceptional circumstances and reviewed annually, the EMEA shall forthwith inform the applicant, who may appeal to the EMEA/CPMP. The EMEA forwards the final opinion of the CPMP to the Commission, the Member States and the applicant, together with a report describing the assessment of the product and stating the reasons for its conclusions.[69] Where the opinion is favourable, the opinion annexes a draft summary of the product characteristics, details of any conditions or restrictions, which are recommended to be imposed, the draft text of the labelling and package leaflet proposed by the applicant, and the assessment report.

14.42

A centralised marketing authorisation is issued by the Commission. The Commission issues a draft of the decision and has power to make a decision that is not in accordance with the opinion of the EMEA, in which case its draft decision shall annexe a detailed explanation of the reasons for the differences.[70] The Regulation states that the Commission shall only differ from the EMEA 'occasionally'! The Commission's draft decision is forwarded to the Member States and the applicant. It is also forwarded to the Standing Committee on Medicinal Products for Human Use, whose function is to 'assist' the Commission. This Committee delivers its opinion on the draft decision, based on weighted majority voting in accordance with Article 148(2) of the Treaty.

14.43

The Commission shall adopt the measures envisaged if they are in accordance with the opinion of the Committee. If the measures envisaged are not in accordance with the opinion of the Committee, or if no opinion is delivered, the Commission shall, without delay, submit a proposal to the Council, which shall act by a qualified majority. If, on the expiry of three months from the date of referral to the Council, the Council has not acted, the Commission shall adopt the proposed measures, save where the Council has decided against the measures by a simple majority.[71] Each Member State may forward written observations to the Commission and where, in the opinion of the Commission, these observations raise important new questions of a scientific or technical nature that have not been addressed in the opinion of the EMEA, the matter is referred back to the EMEA for further consideration.

14.44

---

[69] ibid, Art 9(2).
[70] ibid, Art10.
[71] ibid, Art 73.

(b) The mutual recognition procedure

14.45   An application for a marketing authorisation may be made to a national competent authority for a marketing authorisation that is valid solely in that authority's Member State. The procedure which must be followed, including the particulars and documents which must be submitted, and the criteria which apply to the grant of the application are essentially as set out above. The national authority has similar powers to the EMEA in relation to testing the substance and requiring the applicant to supplement the particulars accompanying the application in respect of the items listed in Article 8 of Directive (EC) 2001/83.[72] Similarly, it is authorised to examine the application to verify whether the particulars submitted comply with Article 8 and examine whether the conditions for issuing an authorisation are complied with.

14.46   An application for a marketing authorisation for the medicinal substance which applies in a second or further Member State is subject to the decentralised (mutual recognition) procedure. Under this procedure, the holder of the marketing authorisation in the first Member State may request the competent authority of the first Member State, known as the 'reference Member State',[73] to prepare or update an assessment report, and forward it to the other Member States to whom the authorisation holder has applied.[74] Any one of the other Member States may oppose the application only if it considers that there are grounds for supposing that the medicinal product may present a risk to public health, in which case the Member States are required to reach agreement, failing which the matter is referred to the CPMP for a binding decision.[75]

(vii) The UK Authorities

14.47   The competent authority in the United Kingdom responsible for the grant, renewal, variation, suspension and revocation of authorisations and certificates is the licensing authority, which is a body consisting of the Ministers of health and agriculture.[76] Any function conferred on the licensing authority under the Medicines Act may be performed by one such Minister acting alone, or by two or more of them acting jointly.[77] The Medicines Commission may give advice to the Ministers on relevant matters.[78] Further committees may be established to advise

---

[72]   Directive (EEC) 75/319, Art 4.
[73]   Directive (EC) 2001/83, Art 28.
[74]   ibid, Art 28.
[75]   ibid, Arts 29–34. In practice, the applicant will often withdraw an application in the Member State where an authority raises objections.
[76]   Medicines Act 1968, ss 6 and 1.
[77]   ibid, s 6(2).
[78]   ibid, ss 2 and 3.

Ministers on particular issues:[79] one such is the Committee on Safety of Medicines, which has a particular function in relation to safety issues and appeals on licensing issues.[80]

(viii) Grounds for Refusal

The test for refusal of an application for a marketing authorisation is different under the centralised and mutual recognition procedures. Under the former, the authorisation shall be refused if, after verification of the required information and particulars submitted, 'it appears that the quality, the safety or the efficacy of the product have not been adequately or sufficiently demonstrated by the applicant'.[81] Authorisation shall likewise be refused if the particulars and documents provided by the applicant are incorrect or if the labelling and package leaflets proposed by the applicant are not in accordance with Directive (EC) 2001/83/EC.[82]

14.48

In contrast, the test under the mutual recognition procedure for refusal of an application is if, after verification of the particulars and documents, 'it proves that: (a) the medicinal product is harmful in the normal conditions of use, or (b) that its therapeutic efficacy is lacking or is insufficiently substantiated by the applicant, or (c) that its qualitative and quantitative composition is not as declared'; or if the particulars and documents do not comply with Articles 8 and 10(1).[83]

14.49

No doubt the tests for refusal are intended to be the same under both procedures but it may be argued that there are differences between the two wordings used, in particular that there is a difference between it being proved that the product is *harmful in the normal conditions of use* or that its *safety has not been adequately or sufficiently demonstrated*. The required level of safety under the centralised procedure test is not defined and is, therefore, legally uncertain, whereas the mutual recognition test not only states a supposedly objective standard but is also restricted to the normal conditions of use. No doubt there remains some uncertainty over what level of safety is 'harmful' and what constitutes 'normal' conditions of use,[84] but the existence of different tests for the two systems is curious.

14.50

---

[79] ibid, s 4.

[80] The Medicines for Human Use (Marketing Authorisations Etc) Regulations 1994, Sch 2.

[81] Regulation (EEC) 2309/93, Art 11 and, with slightly different wording, Directive (EEC) 65/65, Art 5.

[82] ibid.

[83] Directive (EC) 2001/83, Art 26.

[84] These are presumably defined by reference to the conditions of use stated in the summary of product characteristics.

4. Authorisation of Research

14.51 It has been said above that an applicant for a marketing authorisation must include in the documents submitted the results of physico-chemical, biological or
microbiological tests, pharmacological tests and clinical trials. The carrying out of
all these tests and trials is subject to regulatory requirements, which have the object of laying down uniform rules for the compilation and presentation of dossiers
to competent authorities, but are also founded, in relation to the conduct of clinical trials, on the protection of human rights and the dignity of the human
being.[85] National provisions may provide sanctions on those involved in research
for breach of the rules,[86] but the primary issue for the purposes of this discussion
is to ensure that reliable data are produced on which sound decisions on the safety
of products can be based: thus the principal result of non-compliance for product
regulatory purposes would be that the data would be wholly or partially invali-
dated.

(i) Research with Animals

14.52 First, the individuals, facilities and performance of animal experiments are regulated.[87] Laboratory experiments must be carried out in accordance with the standard of good laboratory practice (GLP)[88] which is linked to the OECD principles
of GLP. All test procedures shall correspond to the state of scientific progress at the
time and shall be validated procedures, the results of validation studies being provided.[89] GLP[90] also applies to laboratories carrying out tests on chemical products,[91] which are subject to inspection and verification.[92] Provisions also apply
regarding the protection of animals used for experimental and other scientific
purposes.[93] It is prohibited to sell or supply a medicinal product for the purposes
of a medicinal test on animals without an authorisation or unless a specified exemption applies.[94]

(ii) Research with Humans

14.53 A Directive on clinical trials of medicinal products for human use, harmonising
national rules (of which there was a wide variation, with some Member States

---

[85] Directive (EC) 2001/20, recitals 1 and 2.
[86] The extent to which this applies in the UK is discussed in Ch 13.
[87] Directive (EEC) 86/609; the Animals (Scientific Procedures) Act 1986.
[88] Directive (EEC) 87/18.
[89] Directive (EC) 2001/83/EC; Annex, Pt 2, as amended.
[90] Originating from Annex 2 of the Directive of 12 May 1981 of the Council of the OECD on
the mutual acceptance of data for the evaluation of chemical products.
[91] Directive (EEC) 87/18, applying Directive (EEC) 67/548.
[92] Directive (EEC) 88/320, as amended by Directive (EEC) 90/18.
[93] Directive (EEC) 86/609.
[94] Medicines Act 1968, ss 32 and 33.

having no legislation), was only enacted in 2001, to come into effect before 1 May 2004,[95] although previous practice was established from 1987[96] and developed in 1990[97] and 1991.[98] Directive (EC) 2001/20 notes that clinical trials are complex operations, generally lasting one or more years, usually involving numerous participants and several trial sites, often in different Member States.[99] Both Directives (EEC) 75/318 and (EC) 2001/20[100] provide that all phases of clinical investigation, including bioavailability and bioequivalence studies, shall be designed, implemented and reported in accordance with good clinical practice. Guidelines on good clinical practice (GCP) recognised by the EMEA constitute the standard that is applied in the Community; the currently recognised GCP guidelines are those drafted by the International Conference on Harmonisation of Technical Requirements for the Registration of Pharmaceuticals (ICH). The GCP guidelines provide that all clinical trials must be carried out in accordance with the ethical principles laid down in the latest revision of the Declaration of Helsinki.[101]

Directive (EC) 2001/20 requires prior approval of the ethics of a proposed proto-   **14.54** col and its documentation by an independent ethics committee;[102] prior approval by each competent authority of the Member State in which the trial is to be conducted;[103] provision of written and oral information to research subjects and time for consideration before their giving of informed consent, which is documented;[104] labelling[105] and control of manufacture and import of investigational products; including the holding of a manufacturing authorisation and certification by a qualified person;[106] verification of compliance by Community inspectors of investigational medicinal products with good clinical and manufacturing practice;[107] notification of adverse events by investigators and sponsors to competent authorities and ethics committees,[108] backed by competent authority powers

---

[95] Directive (EC) 2001/20, Art 22.
[96] *Recommended basis for the conduct of clinical trials of medicinal products in the European Community,* III/411/87-EN Rev.
[97] *Good Clinical Practice for trials on medicinal products in the European Community.*
[98] Directive (EEC) 91/507. For further analysis and history see Hodges, CJS, 'Harmonisation of European Controls over Research' in Goldberg, A and Dodds-Smith, I (eds), *Pharmaceutical Medicine and the Law* (Royal College of Physicians of London, 1991).
[99] Directive (EC) 2001/20, recital 10.
[100] Art 1.
[101] World Medical Association, *Declaration of Helsinki: Recommendations Guiding Physicians in Biomedical Research Involving Human Subjects,* 1957 as amended, available at *www.wma.net/e/policy/17-c_e.html:* see also (EC) Directive 2001/20, recital 2.
[102] Directive (EC) 2001/20, Art 6.
[103] ibid, Art 9.
[104] ibid, Art 3(2): there are particular restrictions in Arts 4 and 5 in relation to trials involving minors or incapacitated adults not able to give informed legal consent.
[105] ibid, Art 14.
[106] ibid, Art 13.
[107] ibid, Art 15.
[108] ibid, Arts 16 and 17.

of suspension or prohibition of a trial.[109] The GCP guidelines also require complete and timely recording of trial data and results, with verification by a monitor. Member States' surveillance and knowledge are assisted by information on the content, commencement and termination of clinical trials which is to be available to them on a confidential database.[110]

14.55 A clinical trial may only be undertaken if the following conditions are fulfilled:[111]

(a) the foreseeable risks and inconveniences have been weighed against the anticipated benefit for the individual trial subject and other present and future patients. A clinical trial may be initiated only if the Ethics Committee and/or the competent authority comes to the conclusion that the anticipated therapeutic and public health benefits justify the risks and may be continued only if compliance with this requirement is permanently monitored;

(b) the trial subject or, when the person is not able to give informed consent, his legal representative has had the opportunity, in a prior interview with the investigator or a member of the investigating team, to understand the objectives, risks and inconveniences of the trial, and the conditions under which it is to be conducted and has also been informed of his right to withdraw from the trial at any time;

(c) the rights of the subject to physical and mental integrity, to privacy and to the protection of the data concerning him in accordance with Directive 95/46/EC are safeguarded;

(d) the trial subject or, when the person is not able to give informed consent, his legal representative has given his written consent after being informed of the nature, significance, implications and risks of the clinical trial; if the individual is unable to write, oral consent in the presence of at least one witness may be given in exceptional cases, as provided for in national legislation;

(e) the subject may without any resulting detriment withdraw from the clinical trial at any time by revoking his informed consent;

(f) provision has been made for insurance or indemnity to cover the liability of the investigator and sponsor;

(g) the medical care given to, and medical decisions made on behalf of, subjects shall be the responsibility of an appropriately qualified doctor or, where appropriate, of a qualified dentist;

(h) the subject shall be provided with a contact point where he may obtain further information.

14.56 The involvement of an ethics committee is a feature unique in product regulation to research on medicinal products and medical devices. Directive (EC) 2001/20 defines an ethics committee as:

an independent body in a Member State, consisting of healthcare professionals and non-medical members, whose responsibility it is to protect the rights, safety and well-being of human subjects involved in a trial and to provide public assurance of

---

[109] ibid, Art 12.
[110] ibid, Arts 11 and recital 9.
[111] ibid Art 3(2).

that protection, by, among other things, expressing an opinion on the trial protocol, the suitability of the investigators and the adequacy of facilities, and on the
methods and documents to be used to inform trial subjects and obtain their informed consent.[112]

Member States are required to take the measures necessary for the establishment   **14.57**
and operation of ethics committees, whose function is to give their opinion, before a clinical trial commences, on any issue requested.[113] In preparing its opinion
the ethics committee shall consider, in particular:[114]

(a) the relevance of the clinical trial and the trial design;
(b) whether the evaluation of the anticipated benefits and risks as required under
    Article 3(2)(a) is satisfactory and whether the conclusions are justified;
(c) the protocol;
(d) the suitability of the investigator and supporting staff;
(e) the investigator's brochure;
(f) the quality of the facilities;
(g) the adequacy and completeness of the written information to be given and the
    procedure to be followed for the purpose of obtaining informed consent and
    the justification for the research on persons incapable of giving informed con-
    sent as regards the specific restrictions laid down in Article 3;
(h) provision for indemnity or compensation in the event of injury or death attrib-
    utable to a clinical trial;
(i) any insurance of indemnity to cover the liability of the investigator and spon-
    sor;
(j) the amounts and, where appropriate, the arrangements for rewarding or com-
    pensating investigators and trial subjects and the relevant aspects of any agree-
    ment between the sponsor and the site;
(k) the arrangements for the recruitment of subjects.[115]

(viii) UK Arrangements Regarding Clinical Research and Ethics Committees

It is prohibited[116] to sell, supply or manufacture a medicinal product for the purposes   **14.58**
of a clinical trial unless this is authorised under a product licence, a clinical trial certificate (CTC) or where the conditions for exemption from a clinical trial licence
(CTX) apply.[117] The holder of a clinical trial certificate is subject to various conditions, including the reporting of specified information to the licensing authority.[118]

---

[112] ibid, Art 2(k).
[113] ibid, Art 6(1) and 6(2).
[114] ibid, Art 6(3).
[115] A Member State may decide that a competent authority shall consider and give an opinion on
items (h), (i) and (j) in this list: Directive (EC) 2001/20, Art 6(4).
[116] Medicines Act 1968, ss 31 and 35: there are certain exemptions for doctors, dentists and pharmacists (DDX).
[117] The Medicines (Exemption from Licences) (Clinical Trials) Order 1995, SI 1995/2808; the
Medicines (Exemption from Licences and Certificates) (Clinical Trials) Order 1995, SI 1995/2809.
[118] The Medicines (Standard Provisions for Licences and Certificates) Regulations 1971, SI
1971/972, Sch 1, Pt II.

The national provisions relating to ethics committees are discussed in Chapter 13.[119]

5. Manufacturing Authorisation

14.59   The manufacture of medicinal products is subject to the holding of an authorisation.[120] The authorisation may be granted upon application to a competent authority, although there is some lack of clarity over the criteria. In order to obtain the authorisation the applicant 'must meet at least the following requirements' and provide particulars in support of these requirements:[121]

  (i)   specify the medicinal products and pharmaceutical forms to be manufactured or imported and the place where they are to be manufactured or controlled;

  (ii)   have at his disposal for the manufacture or import suitable and sufficient premises, technical equipment and control facilities complying with the legal requirements which the Member State concerned lays down as regards both manufacture and control and the storage of products;[122]

  (iii) have permanently and continuously at his disposal the services of at least one qualified person who is responsible for securing[123] that the manufacturer or importer is able to carry out manufacture in accordance with the particulars supplied pursuant to the application for marketing authorisation[124] and/or to carry out controls according to the methods described in the particulars accompanying the application.[125]

14.60   The qualified person must fulfil specified minimum conditions of qualification, including a four year university course, or its equivalent, in one of the scientific disciplines of pharmacy, medicine, veterinary medicine, chemistry, pharmaceutical chemistry and technology or biology, plus at least two years practical experience, in one or more undertakings which are authorised to manufacture medicines, in qualitative and quantitative analysis of and quality testing and checking of medicinal products.[126]

---

[119] See in particular Department of Health, *Governance Arrangements for NHS Research Ethics Committees,* Central Office for Research Ethics Committees (COREC), 2001.

[120] Directive (EC) 2001/83, Art 40, first introduced by Directive (EEC) 75/319, Art 16; Medicines Act 1968, s 8(2). There are exceptions in relation to certain activities of doctors, dentists and pharmacists, notably in relation to a product specially prepared by or to the order of a doctor or dentist for administration to a particular patient of his (Medicines Act 1968, s 9(1)), or in relation to preparing or dispensing a medicinal product in a registered pharmacy or a hospital or health centre in accordance with a prescription given by a practitioner, by or under the supervision of a pharmacist (Medicines Act 1968, s 10). For the national criteria, procedures and conditions, see Medicines Act 1968, ss 19(5) and 20–24, the Medicines (Applications for Manufacturer's and Wholesale Dealer's Licences) Regulations 1971, SI 1971/974, and the Medicines (Standard Provisions for Licences and Certificates) Regulations 1971, SI 1971/972, Sch 2.

[121] Directive (EC) 2001/83, Art 41.

[122] pursuant to ibid, Art 20.

[123] ibid, Art 20, which empowers an authority to permit certain variations.

[124] ibid, Art 8(3)(d).

[125] ibid, Art 8(3)(h).

[126] ibid, Art 49.

The scheme of the legislation thus involves a measure of delegation of regulatory responsibility from the competent authority to the qualified person in relation to ensuring the consistent quality, and hence safety, of the products concerned. The qualified person will usually be employed by the holder of the manufacturing authorisation but is relied on to exercise personal, professional responsibility independent of the manufacturer.   **14.61**

Principles and guidelines of good manufacturing practice are to be applied by a manufacturer in the manufacture of medicinal products.[127]   **14.62**

6. Distribution and Sale

(i) Wholesale Distribution Authorisation

The wholesale distribution of medicinal products is subject to the possession of an authorisation granted by a competent authority, and subject to checks on their persons and establishments and inspection of premises.[128] Wholesalers are required in particular to:[129]   **14.63**

(i) have suitable and adequate premises, installations and equipment, so as to ensure proper conservation or distribution of medicinal products;

(ii) have a responsible, designated qualified person and other staff;

(iii) keep records of products received or dispatched, with dates, quantities, and names and addresses of suppliers and consignees;

(iv) have an emergency plan which ensures effective implementation of any recall from the market;

(v) comply with the principles and guidelines of good distribution practice for medicinal products (GDP) published by the Commission.[130]

(ii) Prescription Only Products

When a marketing authorisation is granted, the competent authority must specify the classification of the medicinal product as one that is, or is not, subject to   **14.64**

---

[127] ibid, Art 47: these principles and guidelines are set out in Commission Directive (EEC) 91/356.

[128] ibid, Art 77, first introduced by Directive (EEC) 92/25, Art 3; Medicines Act 1968, s 8(3). There are exemptions for certain activities of doctors and dentists, notably in relation to products specially prepared for administration to a particular patient of theirs: Medicines Act 1968, s 9(1). See also the Medicines for Human Use (Marketing Authorisations Etc) Regulations 1994, SI 1994/3144, reg 3.

[129] ibid, Arts 79–80; for the national criteria, procedures and conditions see Medicines Act 1968, ss 19(6) and 20–24. the Medicines (Applications for Manufacturer's and Wholesale Dealer's Licences) Regulations 1971 and the Medicines (Standard Provisions for Licences and Certificates) Regulations 1971, Sch 3.

[130] See European Commission, *Guidelines on Good Distribution Practice of Medicinal Products for Human Use* 94/C 63/03 [1994] OJ C63/4.

medical prescription.[131] Medicinal products shall be subject to medical prescription where they:

(i)   are likely to present a danger either directly or indirectly, even when used correctly, if utilised without medical supervision, or

(ii) are frequently and to a very wide extent used incorrectly, and as a result are likely to present a direct or indirect danger to human health, or

(iii) contain substances or preparations thereof the activity and/or side effects of which require further investigation, or

(iv) are normally prescribed by a doctor to be administered parenterally.[132]

14.65   Conversely, medicinal products that do not meet the above criteria shall not be subject to prescription.[133] Certain sub-categories may be fixed in relation to availability on renewable or non-renewable prescriptions, or subject to special medical prescription, or restricted prescription reserved for use in certain specialised areas.[134] The authorities have some discretion to waive the classification provisions[135] and products can have different status in different Member States.

14.66   The authorities must draw up a list of products subject to prescription in their territory, update it annually, and must examine and amend the classification on the five-yearly renewal of the marketing authorisation or when new facts are brought to their notice.[136]

(iii) Retail Sale

14.67   National provisions not harmonised by Community law, control pharmacies and the retail sale or supply of medicines to patients. Various matters are covered by English legislation. There are, for example, requirements covering the registration, licensing and inspection of pharmacy premises;[137] a requirement for retail sale and supply of medicines not on the general sale list to be made in registered pharmacy premises by or under the supervision of a pharmacist.[138]

---

[131] Directive (EC) 2001/83, Art 70, first included in Directive (EEC) 92/26.

[132] ibid, Art 71(1).

[133] ibid, Art 72.

[134] ibid, Art 70.2.

[135] ibid, Art 71.4.

[136] ibid, Arts 73 and 74; Medicines Act 1968, s 58: it is an offence to sell or supply a medicinal product that is listed within the 'prescription only' category except in accordance with a prescription given by an appropriate practitioner, save subject to specified exceptions. The list is drawn up under the Prescription Only Medicines (Human Use) Order 1997, SI 1997/1830.

[137] Medicines Act 1968, ss 69–83.

[138] Medicines Act 1968, s 52. This is subject to certain exemptions for doctors, dentists, hospitals and health centres: Medicines Act 1968, s 55.

7. Information and Promotion

(i) General Points

There are specific and detailed requirements and limitations on both the information provided with medicinal products[139] and on the advertising of medicinal products.[140]   **14.68**

Information provided with products covers the labelling of product packaging and package leaflets provided to users with products. One or more specimens or mock-ups of the outer packaging and the immediate packaging of a medicinal product, together with the draft package leaflet, shall be submitted to the authorities competent for authorising marketing when the authorisation for placing the medicinal product on the market is requested.[141]   **14.69**

The competent authorities shall refuse the authorisation for placing the medicinal product on the market if the labelling or the package leaflet do not comply with the provisions of Directive (EEC) 92/27 or if they are not in accordance with the particulars listed in the summary of product characteristics referred to in Article 4b of Directive (EEC) 65/65.[142] Where the labelling or leaflet provisions are not complied with, and a notice served on the person concerned has remained without effect, the competent authorities of the Member States may suspend the authorisation to place the medicinal product on the market, until the labelling and the package leaflet of the medicinal product in question have been made to comply with the requirements.[143]   **14.70**

The authorities may exempt labels and package leaflets for specific medicinal products from the obligation that certain particulars appear or that the leaflet must be in an official language, when the product is not intended to be delivered to the patient for self-administration.[144]   **14.71**

The Commission is required to publish guidelines on various aspects of labelling.[145]   **14.72**

The outer packaging and the package leaflet may include symbols or pictograms designed to clarify information and information compatible with the summary of   **14.73**

---

[139] These were first introduced by Directive (EEC) 92/27.
[140] First introduced by Directive (EEC) 92/28. A national prohibition on advertising which applies solely to foreign medicinal products not authorised in the Member State concerned is contrary to Art 30 of the EC Treaty: Case C-320/93 *Lucien Ortscheit GmbH v Eurim-Pharm Arznemittel GmbH* [1995] 2 CMLR 242.
[141] Directive (EC) 2001/83, Art 8(3)(j).
[142] ibid, Art 61(2).
[143] ibid, Art 64.
[144] ibid, Art 63(3).
[145] ibid, Art 65.

the product characteristics which is useful for health education, to the exclusion of any element of a promotional nature.[146]

(ii) Summary of Product Characteristics

14.74   An application for a marketing authorisation must contain a summary of the product characteristics (SmPC),[147] which is approved by the authorities and is issued with the product. The SmPC fulfils the dual function of a public, transparent rationale for the grant of an authorisation and an official, uniform, approved statement of those product characteristics which are thought to be important prescribing information for users. The SmPC must contain the information specified in table 2.

Table 2: Information to be specified in summary of product characteristics

1. Name of the proprietary product.
2. Qualitative and quantitative composition in terms of the active ingredients and constituents of the excipient, knowledge of which is essential for proper administration of the medicinal product; the international non-proprietary names recommended by the World Health Organisation shall be used, where such names exist, or failing this, the usual common name or chemical description.
3. Pharmaceutical form.
4. Pharmacological properties and, in so far as this information is useful for therapeutic purposes, pharmacokinetic particulars.
5. Clinical particulars:
   5.1   therapeutic indications,
   5.2   contra-indications,
   5.3   undesirable effects (frequency and seriousness),
   5.4   special precautions for use,
   5.5   use during pregnancy and lactation,
   5.6   interaction with other medicaments and other forms of interaction,
   5.7   posology and method of administration for adults and, where necessary, for children,
   5.8   overdose (symptoms, emergency procedures, antidotes),
   5.9   special warnings,
   5.10 effects on ability to drive and to use machines.
6. Pharmaceutical particulars:
   6.1   incompatibilities (major),
   6.2   shelf life, when necessary after reconstitution of the product or when the container is opened for the first time,
   6.3. special precautions for storage,
   6.4   nature and contents of container,
   6.5   name or style and permanent address or registered place of business of the holder of the marketing authorisation,

---

[146] ibid, Art 62.
[147] ibid, Art 8(2)(j).

6.6 special precautions for disposal of unused products or waste materials derived from such products, if appropriate.

(iii) Labelling

The following particulars are required to appear on the outer packaging of medi-cinal products or, where there is no outer packaging, on the immediate packag-ing:[148]   **14.75**

(i)   the name of the medicinal product followed by the common name where the product contains only one active ingredient and if its name is an in-vented name; where a medicinal product is available in several pharmaceu-tical forms and/or several strengths, the pharmaceutical form and/or the strength (baby, child or adult as appropriate) must be included in the name of the medicinal product;

(ii)   a statement of the active substances expressed qualitatively and quanti-tavely per dosage unit or according to the form of administration for a given volume or weight, using their common names;

(iii) the pharmaceutical form and the contents by weight, by volume or by number of doses of the product;

(iv)   a list of those excipients known to have a recognised action or effect and in-cluded in the guidelines published pursuant to Article 65. However, if the product is injectable, or a topical or eye preparation, all excipients must be stated;

(v)   the method and, if necessary, the route of administration;

(vi)   a special warning that the medicinal product must be stored out of reach of children;

(vii) a special warning, if this is necessary for the medicinal product concerned;

(viii) the expiry date in clear terms (month/year);

(ix)   special storage precautions, if any;

(x)   special precautions for disposal of unused medicinal products or waste ma-terials derived from such products, if appropriate;

(xi)   the name and address of the holder of the authorisation for placing the med-icinal product on the market;

(xii) the number of the authorisation for placing the medicinal product on the market;

(xiii) the manufacturer's batch number;

(xiv) in the case of self-medication, instructions on the use of the medicinal prod-ucts.

---

[148] ibid, Art 54; Medicines Act 1968, s 85.; the Medicines for Human Use (Marketing Authorisations Etc) Regulations 1994, Sch 5.

14.76 The particulars of Article 54 quoted above must appear on immediate packagings other than blister packs or small immediate packaging units. The Article 54 particulars shall appear in the official language or languages of the Member State where the product is placed on the market. This provision shall not prevent these particulars from being indicated in several languages, provided that the same particulars appear in all the languages used.[149]

14.77 The following particulars at least shall appear on immediate packaging that takes the form of blister packs and are placed in an outer packaging that complies with the requirements laid down in Article 54:

(i) the name of the medicinal product as laid down in Article 2(a),

(ii) the name of the holder of the authorisation for placing the product on the market,

(iii) the expiry date,

(iv) the batch number.[150]

14.78 The following particulars at least shall appear on small immediate packaging units on which the particulars laid down in Article 54 cannot be displayed:

(i) the name of the medicinal product and, if necessary, the strength and the route of administration;

(ii) the method of administration;

(iii) the expiry date,

(iv) the batch number,

(v) the contents by weight, by volume or by unit.[151]

14.79 All the labelling particulars shall be easily legible, clearly comprehensible and indelible.[152]

(iv) Package Leaflets

14.80 The inclusion in the packaging of all medicinal products of a package leaflet for the information of users is obligatory unless all the specified information required by Articles 59 and 62 of Directive (EC) 2001/83 is directly conveyed on the outer packaging or on the immediate packaging.[153]

14.81 The package leaflet must be drawn up in accordance with the summary of the product characteristics,[154] and include, in the following order:

---

[149] ibid, Art 63.

[150] ibid, Art 55(2).

[151] ibid, Art 55(3).

[152] ibid, Art 56.

[153] ibid, Art 58; Medicines Act 1968, s 86, the Medicines (Labelling) Regulations 1976, SI 1976/1726.

[154] See above.

(i) for the identification of the medicinal product:

—the name of the medicinal product, followed by the common name if the product contains only one active ingredient and if its name is an invented name; where a medicinal product is available in several pharmaceutical forms and/or several strengths, the pharmaceutical form and/or the strength (for example, baby, child, adult) must be included in the name of the medicinal product,

—a full statement of the active ingredients and excipients expressed qualitatively and a statement of the active substances expressed quantitatively, using their common names, in the case of each presentation of the product,

—the pharmaceutical form and the contents by weight, by volume or by number of doses of the product, in the case of each presentation of the product,

—the pharmaco-therapeutic group, or type of activity in terms easily comprehensible for the patient,

—the name and address of the holder of the authorisation for placing the medicinal product on the market and of the manufacturer;

(ii) the therapeutic indications;[155]

(iii) a list of information which is necessary before taking the medicinal product:

—contra-indications,

—appropriate precautions for use,

—forms of interaction with other medicinal products and other forms of interaction (for example, alcohol, tobacco, foodstuffs) which may affect the action of the medicinal product,

—special warnings;

this list must:

—take into account the particular condition of certain categories of users (eg, children, pregnant or breastfeeding women, the elderly, persons with specific pathological conditions),

—mention, if appropriate, potential effects on the ability to drive vehicles or to operate machinery,

—detail those excipients, knowledge of which is important for the sale and effective use of the medicinal product and included in the guidelinespublished pursuant to Article 65;

(iv) the necessary and usual instructions for proper use, in particular:

---

[155] The competent authorities may decide that certain therapeutic indications shall not be mentioned in the package leaflet, where the dissemination of such information might have serious disadvantages for the patient: Directive (EC) 2001/83, Art 59(2).

—the dosage,

—the method and, if necessary, route of administration,

—the frequency of administration, specifying if necessary the appropriate time at which the medicinal product may or must be administered, and, as appropriate, depending on the nature of the product:

—the duration of treatment, where it should be limited,

—the action to be taken in the case of an overdose (for example, symptoms, emergency procedures),

—the course of action to take when one or more doses have not been taken,

—indication, if necessary, of the risk of withdrawal effects;

(v) a description of the undesirable effects which can occur under normal use of the medicinal product and, if necessary, the action to be taken in such a case; the patient should be expressly invited to communicate any undesirable effect which is not mentioned in the leaflet to his doctor or to his pharmacist;

(vi) a reference to the expiry date indicated on the label, with:

—a warning against using the product after this date,

—where appropriate, special storage precautions,

—if necessary, a warning against certain visible signs of deterioration;

(vii) the date on which the package leaflet was last revised.

14.82 The package leaflet must be written in clear and understandable terms for the patient and be clearly legible in the official language or languages of the Member State where the medicinal product is placed on the market. This provision does not prevent the package leaflet being printed in several languages, provided that the same information is given in all the languages used.[156]

(v) Advertising

(a) Definition of advertising

14.83 Advertising of medicinal products is defined for regulatory purposes[157] as any form of door-to-door information, canvassing activity or inducement designed to promote the prescription, supply, sale or consumption of medicinal products; it shall include in particular:

(i) the advertising of medicinal products to the general public,

(ii) advertising of medicinal products to persons qualified to prescribe or supply them,

(iii) visits by medical sales representatives to persons qualified to prescribe medicinal products,

---

[156] ibid, Art 63.
[157] ibid, Art 86(1).

(iv)   the supply of samples,

(v)   the provision of inducements to prescribe or supply medicinal products by the gift, offer or promise of any benefit or bonus, whether in money or in kind, except when their intrinsic value is minimal,

(vi)   sponsorship of promotional meetings attended by persons qualified or supply medicinal products,

(vii)   sponsorship of scientific congresses attended by persons qualified to prescribe or supply medicinal products and in particular payment of their travelling and accommodation expenses in connection therewith.

(b) General provisions

Member States are to prohibit any advertising of a medicinal product in respect of which a marketing authorisation has not been granted in accordance with Community law.[158] All parts of the advertising of a medicinal product must comply with the particulars listed in the summary of product characteristics.[159] There is a positive obligation that the advertising of a medicinal product: **14.84**

(i)   shall encourage the rational use of the medicinal product, by presenting it objectively and without exaggerating its properties;

(ii)   shall not be misleading.[160]

Different rules apply to advertising of medicinal products to the general public and to health professionals, as discussed below.   **14.85**

(c) Advertising to the general public[161]

Medicinal products which are available on prescription only may not be advertised to the general public. Medicinal products may be advertised to the general public only if, by virtue of their composition and purpose, they are intended and designed for use without the intervention of a medical practitioner for diagnostic purposes or for the prescription or monitoring of treatment, with the advice of the pharmacist, if necessary.[162] Certain therapeutic indications may not be mentioned in advertising to the general public, including serious infectious diseases, cancer and diabetes.[163] Medicinal products may not be distributed direct to the public for promotional purposes save in special cases.[164]   **14.86**

---

[158]   ibid, Art 87(1); Medicines Act 1968, ss 92–97; the Medicines (Advertising) Regulations 1994, SI 1994/1932, reg 3.

[159]   ibid, Art 87(2): for the summary of product characteristics, see above.

[160]   ibid, Art 87(3).

[161]   See the Medicines (Advertising) Regulations 1994, Pt III.

[162]   Directive (EC) 2001/83, Art 88.

[163]   ibid, Art 88(2).

[164]   ibid, Art 88(6).

14.87   All advertising to the general public of a medicinal product shall:[165]

   (i)   be set out in such a way that it is clear that the message is an advertisement and that the product is clearly identified as a medicinal product;

   (ii)   include the following minimum information:

   —the name of the medicinal product, as well as the common name if the medicinal product contains only one active ingredient;

   —the information necessary for correct use of the medicinal product;

   —an express, legible invitation to read carefully the instructions on the package leaflet or on the outer packaging, according to the case

14.88   The advertising of a medicinal product to the general public shall not contain any material which:[166]

   (i)   gives the impression that a medical consultation or surgical operation is unnecessary, in particular by offering a diagnosis or by suggesting treatment by mail;

   (ii)   suggests that the effects of taking the medicine are guaranteed, are unaccompanied by side effects or are better than, or equivalent to, those of another treatment or medicinal product;

   (iii)   suggests that the health of the subject can be enhanced by taking the medicine;

   (iv)   suggests that the health of the subject could be affected by not taking the medicine; (this prohibition shall not apply to specified vaccination campaigns);

   (v)   is directed exclusively or principally at children;

   (vi)   refers to a recommendation by scientists, health professionals or persons who are neither of the foregoing but who, because of their celebrity, could encourage the consumption of medicinal products;

   (vii)   suggests that the medicinal product is a foodstuff, cosmetic or other consumer product;

   (viii) suggests that the safety or efficacy of the medicinal product is due to the fact that it is natural;

   (ix)   could, by a description or detailed representation of a case history, lead to erroneous self diagnosis;

   (x)   refers, in improper, alarming or misleading terms, to claims of recovery;

   (xi)   uses, in improper, alarming or misleading terms, pictorial representations of changes in the human body caused by disease or injury, or of the action of a medicinal product on the human body or parts thereof;

---

[165] Directive 2001/83/EC, Article 89.1: Member States may decide that only the name of the product may be included if it is intended solely as a reminder.
[166] Directive 2001/83/EC, Article 90.

(xii) mentions that the medicinal product has been granted a marketing authorisation.

(d) Advertising to health professionals[167]

Any advertising of a medicinal product to persons qualified to prescribe or supply   **14.89**
such products shall include:

(i) essential information compatible with the summary of product characteristics;
(ii) the supply classification of the medicinal product.[168]

Any documentation which is transmitted as part of the promotion of a product to   **14.90**
a person qualified to prescribe or supply it must include the above essential information and supply classification, and must state the date on which it was drawn
up or last revised.[169] All this information must be accurate, up-to-date, verifiable
and sufficiently complete to enable the recipient to form his or her own opinion
of the therapeutic value of the product.[170] Quotations, tables and other illustrative
matter taken from medical journals or other scientific works and included in this
documentation shall be faithfully reproduced and the precise sources indicated.[171]

Medical sales representatives must have adequate training and scientific knowl-   **14.91**
edge to be able to provide precise and complete information about the medicinal
products they promote.[172] They must give the persons visited, or have available to
them, summaries of the product characteristics of each medicinal product they
present.[173] There are restrictions on promotional activities.[174]

(e) Monitoring of advertising

Member States are required to ensure that there are adequate and effective methods   **14.92**
to monitor the advertising of medicinal products, optionally including a prior vet-
ting system or by self-regulatory bodies.[175] In the United Kingdom, the legal
scheme and requirements[176] exist as a backdrop but is very rarely invoked, since two
self-regulatory schemes are operated in practice. Manufacturers of prescription

---

[167] See the Medicines (Advertising) Regulations 1994, SI 1994 No 1932, Pt IV.
[168] Directive 2001/83/EC, Article 91.1: Member states may decide that only the name of the
product may be included if it is intended solely as a reminder: Article 91.2.
[169] Directive 2001/83/EC, Article 92.1.
[170] Directive 2001/83/EC, Article 92.2.
[171] Directive 2001/83/EC, Article 92.3.
[172] Directive 2001/83/EC, Article 93.1.
[173] Directive 2001/83/EC, Article 93.2.
[174] Directive 2001/83/EC, Articles 94 to 96.
[175] Directive 2001/83/EC, Article 97.
[176] The Medicines (Advertising) Requirements 1994, SI 1994 No 1932; the Medicines
(Monitoring of Advertising) Regulations 1994, SI 1994 No 1933; the Control of Misleading
Advertisement Regulations 1988, SI 1988 No 915.

products who are members of the Association of the British Pharmaceutical Industry observe its *Code of Practice for the Pharmaceutical Industry*, which is administered by the Prescription Medicines Code of Practice Authority. Manufacturers of over-the-counter products who are members of the Proprietary Association of Great Britain observe its *Code of Standards of Advertising Practice for Over-the-Counter Medicines*. There are also the more generalised *British Code of Advertising Practice* of the Committee of Advertising Practice, *The Code of Advertising Standards and Practice* of the Independent Television Commission, and *The Code of Advertising Practice and Programme Sponsorship* of the Radio Authority.

(f) Scientific information service

14.93 A marketing authorisation holder is required to establish within his undertaking a scientific service in charge of information about the medicinal products that he places on the market.[177]

14.94 The person responsible for placing the product on the market shall:[178]

(i) keep available for, or communicate to, the authorities or bodies responsible for monitoring advertising of medicinal products a sample of all advertisements emanating from his undertaking together with a statement indicating the persons to whom it is addressed, the method of dissemination and the date of first dissemination,

(ii) ensure that advertising of medicinal products by his undertaking conforms to the requirements of Title VIII of Directive (EC) 2001/83,

(iii) verify that medical sales representatives employed by his undertaking have been adequately trained and fulfil the obligations imposed upon them referred to above,

(iv) supply the authorities or bodies responsible for monitoring advertising of medicinal products with the information and assistance they require to carry out their responsibilities,

(v) ensure that the decisions taken by the authorities or bodies responsible for monitoring advertising of medicinal products are immediately and fully complied with.

8. Post-Marketing Requirements for Safety

(i) Pharmacovigilance

14.95 It is recognised that the safe use of medicinal products is not simply a matter to be

---

[177] Directive 2001/83/EC, Article 98.1; the Medicines (Advertising) Regulations 1994, SI 1994 No 1932, Regulation 4.
[178] Directive 2001/83/EC, Article 98.2.

assessed at the time of marketing, but that there is a need for the continuous collection and re-evaluation of data relating to a product, throughout the time that its product type is marketed and/or remains on the market.[179] The legislation recognises the limitations on the understanding of the level of safety which are possible at the time of authorising its marketing that use of a product will present in normal, 'practical conditions of use'.[180]

A sophisticated, integrated pharmacovigilance system is established under the **14.96** Community legislation and a series of guidelines,[181] which relies on spontaneous reporting by health care professionals and others, and imposes (i) recording and reporting obligations on the commercial enterprises involved, and (ii) surveillance and other regulatory obligations on Member States, the Commission, the EMEA and the CPMP. Different post-marketing obligations for medicinal products apply to the holders of marketing authorisations, the holders of manufacturing authorisations[182] and the holders of wholesale distribution authorisations.

The principal provisions are: **14.97**

> In order to ensure the adoption of appropriate regulatory decisions concerning the medicinal products authorised within the Community, having regard to information obtained about adverse reactions to medicinal products under normal conditions of use, the Member States shall establish a pharmacovigilance system. This system shall be used to collect information useful in the surveillance of medicinal products, with particular reference to adverse reactions in human beings, and to evaluate such information scientifically.
>
> Such information shall be collated with data on consumption of medicinal products.
>
> This system shall also take into account any available information on misuse and abuse[183] of medicinal products which may have an impact on the evaluation of their benefits and risks.[184]

---

[179] See Roden, SM, 'An Introduction to Drug Safety Surveillance', in Glaxo Group Research, *Drug Safety: A Shared responsibility*, (Churchill Livingstone, 1991).

[180] This phrase appeared in Directive 93/39/EEC recital 7 which justified the initial introduction into Community legislation of the pharmacovigilance system but was not repeated in recital 54 to Directive 2001/83/EC. Recital 15 to Regulation (EEC) No 2309/93, only refers to the mechanistic 'intensive monitoring of adverse reactions'.

[181] See in particular Notice to Marketing Authorisation Holders: Pharmacovigilance Guidelines, CPMP/PhVWP/108/99 and Note for Guidance on Procedure for Competent Authorities on the Undertaking of Pharmacovigilance Activities, CPMP/PhVWP/175/95 Rev. 1.

[182] The Medicines for Human Use (Marketing Authorisations Etc) Regulations 1994, SI 1994 No 3144, Regulation 8.

[183] Defined in Directive 2001/83/EC, Article 1.16 as persistent or sporadic, intentional exercise use of medicinal products which is accompanied by harmful physical or psychological effects.

[184] Directive 2001/83/EC, Article 102, adapted from its first introduction in Directive 93/39/EEC, Article 3.3.

(a) Primary reporting

14.98 Neither the centralised nor mutual recognition systems refer specifically to reports emanating from patients, nor place any reporting requirements on patients. Both systems envisage reports emanating essentially from health care professionals.[185] The UK voluntary reporting system is known as the 'Yellow Card' scheme. Under the mutual recognition system:

> The Member States shall take all appropriate measures to encourage doctors and other health care professionals to report suspected adverse reactions to the competent authorities.

> The Member States may impose specific requirements on doctors and other health care professionals, in respect of the reporting of suspected serious or unexpected adverse reactions, in particular where such reporting is a condition of the authorisation.[186]

14.99 In contrast, the legislation on the centralised system curiously includes no provision on reporting by doctors or other health care professionals. Seemingly, therefore, Member States have no power to require any such reporting under the centralised system. The only reference to source data is to all suspected adverse reactions that are reported to the company that holds the marketing authorisation.[187]

(b) Obligations of marketing companies

14.100 A marketing authorisation holder is required to have permanently and continuously at his disposal a 'qualified person' responsible for pharmacovigilance, who has the following obligations:

(a) the establishment and maintenance of a system which ensures that information about all suspected adverse reactions which are reported to the personnel of the company, and to medical representatives is collected and collated in order to be accessible at least at one point within the Community;

(b) the preparation for the competent authorities of reports on specified adverse reactions;

(c) ensuring that any request from the competent authorities for the provision of additional information necessary for the evaluation of the benefits and risks afforded by a medicinal product is answered fully and promptly, including the provision of information about the volume of sales or prescriptions for the medicinal product concerned; . . .[188]

---

[185] Regulation (EEC) No 2309/93, Article 22; Directive 2001/83/EC, Article 29e.

[186] Directive 2001/83/EC, Article 101.

[187] Regulation (EEC) No. 2309/93, Article 21(a).

[188] Directive 2001/83/EC, Article 103; for the centralised procedure see Regulation (EEC) No 2309/93, Article 21, which is almost identical. These provisions are supplemented by guidance in the Notice to Applicants and specific guidance on pharmacovigilance.

Technical and scientific progress in relation to production and control of a medicinal product must be taken into account by the person responsible for placing it on the market, who must apply for approval of any necessary amendments.[189] Under the centralised system (curiously, this does not appear in the Code as applying under the mutual recognition system), the person just referred to must also forthwith inform the EMEA, the Commission and Member States of any new information which might entail the amendment of the particulars and documents that were supplied with the application for marketing approval, or amendment of the summary of product characteristics.[190] He shall, in particular, inform them of any prohibition or restriction imposed by the competent authorities of any country in which the product is marketed and of any other new information that might influence the evaluation of the benefits and risks of the product.[191] Under the centralised system, if the person responsible for placing a medicinal product on the market proposes to make any alteration to the information and particulars submitted to support the grant of the marketing authorisation, he must submit an application to the EMEA:[192] under the Code applying to the mutual recognition procedure, a marketing authorisation holder must apply for the variation of the authorisation.[193]

14.101

The following definitions are specified:[194]

14.102

(i) 'adverse reaction' means a response to a medicinal product which is noxious and unintended and which occurs at doses normally used in man for the prophylaxis, diagnosis or therapy of disease or for the restoration, correction or modification of physiological function,

(ii) 'serious adverse reaction' means an adverse reaction which results in death, is life-threatening, requires inpatient hospitalisation or prolongation of existing hospitalisation, results in persistent or significant disability or incapacity, or is a congenital anomaly/birth defect;

(iii) 'unexpected adverse reaction' means an adverse reaction, the nature, severity or outcome of which is not consistent with the summary of product characteristics.

All *suspected serious* adverse reactions occurring within the Community to a medicinal product which are brought to the attention of the person responsible for pharmacovigilance by a health care professional must be recorded and reported immediately to the Member States in whose territory the incident occurred, and

14.103

---

[189] Regulation (EEC) No 2309/93, Article 15.1; Directive 2001/83/EC, Article 23.
[190] Regulation (EEC) No 2309/93, Article 15.2.
[191] Regulation (EEC) No 2309/93, Article 15.3.
[192] ibid.
[193] Directive 2001/83/EC, Article 35.
[194] Directive 2001/83/EC, Article 1: also adopted in Regulation (EEC) No. 2309/93, Article 19.

in no case later than 15 days following the receipt of the information.[195] There are further obligations in relation to maintaining detailed records of all *suspected* adverse reactions occurring within or outside the Community that are reported by a health care professional.[196] If a *serious unexpected* adverse reaction to a centrally licensed product occurs in a non-Community country, a report must be made both to all Member States and to the Agency. Commission Guidance covers the collection, verification and presentation of adverse reaction reports, including technical requirements for electronic exchange of pharmacovigilance information.[197]

14.104 Under the centralised system, arrangements for the reporting of suspected unexpected *non serious* adverse reactions shall be adopted by the procedure laid down by Article 72 of the Regulation, involving measures originating between the Commission and the Standing Committee. However, it is also stated:

> In addition, the person responsible for placing the medicinal product on the market shall be required to maintain detailed records of all suspected adverse reactions occurring within or outside the Community which are reported to him by a health care professional. Unless other requirements have been laid as a condition of the granting of the marketing authorisation by the Community, these records shall be submitted to the Agency and Member States immediately upon request or at least every six months during the first two years following authorisation and once a year for the following three years. Thereafter, the records shall be submitted at five-yearly intervals together with the application of renewal of the authorisation, or immediately upon request. These records shall be accompanied by a scientific evaluation.[198]

14.105 The main reporting requirements under the mutual recognition system[199] are shown in table 3.

14.106 The holder of a manufacturing authorisation must, inter alia, have qualifying staff, give prior notice to the competent authority of any changes he may wish to make in his approved particulars on facilities and the product, permit the authority access to his premises at any time, and comply with the principles and guidelines of good manufacturing practice for medicinal products.[200]

---

[195] Under the centralised procedure, Regulation (EEC) No 2309/93, Article 22: under the Code, Directive 2001/83/EC, Article 104, which adds that this applies to reactions brought to his attention by a healthcare professional and that separate guidance applies to other suspected serious adverse reactions.

[196] ibid, and Regulation (EEC) No 2309/93, Article 23.

[197] Directive 2001/83/EC, Article 106. The suspension or revocation of a marketing authorisation may only be decided on the grounds laid down in the Community provisions: Case C-83/92 *Pierrel SpA v Ministerio della Sanita* [1993] ECRI-06419.

[196] Regulation (EEC) No. 2309/93, Article 22.2.

[199] Directive 2001/83/EC, Article 104.

[200] Directive 2001/83/EC, Title IV.

Table 3: Reporting requirements under the Community Code

Type of adverse reaction	Where occurring	Report to competent authority in	Time limit
All suspected serious		Member State where occurred	Immediately: 15 days
All other suspected serious which meet the reporting criteria		Member State where occurred	Immediately: 15 days
All suspected serious and unexpected	In a non-EC country, reported by a health care professional	Accessible to the Agency and Member State where product is authorised	Immediately: 15 days
For high-technology or mutual recognition products, all suspected serious	In the Community	Accessible to the reference Member State	At intervals agreed with reference State
All		'To the competent authorities' in a periodic safety update report	Six monthly for the first two years after authorisation, annually for the subsequent two years, and at time of first renewal, then every five years.

(c) Obligations on Member States

Each Member State shall ensure that all *suspected serious* adverse reactions occur- **14.107**
ring within their territory to a medicinal product which are brought to their attention are recorded and reported immediately to the Agency and the person
responsible for placing the medicinal product on the market, and in no case later
than 15 days following the receipt of the information.[201] This provision is followed, under the centralised system but not the mutual recognition system, by
an obligation on the Agency to inform the national pharmacovigilance systems
of reports which it receives. Implicitly in this context such reports are received
only from Member States—the legislation seemingly does not contemplate that
the Agency will receive reports from any source other than Member States or

---

[201] Regulation (EEC) No. 2309/93, Article 23.

marketing authorisation holders, and it does not explicitly require the Agency to inform Member States of any reports which it receives other than those of suspected serious adverse reactions received from Member State authorities. Nevertheless, the legislation specifies a mechanism for the Commission in consultation with the Agency, Member States and interested parties, to draw up guidance on the collection, verification and presentation of adverse reaction reports.[202]

14.108   The legislation on the centralised system, but not on the mutual recognition system, states that the Agency, in consultation with the Member States and the Commission, shall set up a data-processing network for the rapid transmission of data between the competent Community authorities in the event of an alert relating to faulty manufacture, serious adverse reactions and other pharmacovigilance data regarding medicinal products marketed in the Community.[203] Further, the Agency shall collaborate with the World Health Organisation on international pharmacovigilance and shall take the necessary steps to submit promptly to the World Health Organisation appropriate and adequate information regarding the measures taken in the Community which may have a bearing on public health protection in third countries and shall send a copy thereof to the Commission and the Member States.[204]

14.109   Central co-ordination of pharmacovigilance in the Community is provided for:

> The Agency, acting in close co-operation with the national pharmacovigilance systems established in accordance with Article 29a of Directive 75/319/EEC, shall receive all relevant information about suspected adverse reactions to medicinal products which have been authorised by the Community in accordance with this Regulation. If necessary the Committee may, in accordance with Article 5, formulate opinions on the measures necessary to ensure the safe and effective use of such medicinal products. These measures shall be adopted in accordance with the procedure laid down in Article 18.

> The person responsible for placing the medicinal product on the market and the competent authorities of the Member States shall ensure that all relevant information about suspected adverse reactions to medicinal products authorised in accordance with this Regulation are brought to the attention of the Agency in accordance with the provisions of this Regulation.[205]

14.110   The legislation therefore recognises that use of medicinal products under normal conditions will always involve adverse reactions. The purpose of the pharmacovigilance system is to monitor and evaluate all adverse reactions systematically so as constantly to review the recorded information on the level of safety of products and to review decisions as to the continuation of marketing authorisations or

---

[202] Regulation (EEC) No. 2309/93, Article 24; Directive 2001/83/EC, Article 106.
[203] Regulation (EEC) No. 2309/93, Article 24.
[204] Regulation (EEC) No. 2309/93, Article 25.
[205] Regulation (EEC) No 2309/93, Article 20.

conditions attaching to them. The advantage of a pharmacovigilance system which covers the whole of the EU Member States lies in the statistical power of a system of this size.

(ii) Withdrawal From the Market: Suspension or Revocation of a Marketing Authorisation

Under the mutual recognition system, Member States: **14.111**

> shall take all appropriate measures to ensure that the supply of the medicinal product shall be prohibited and the medicinal product withdrawn from the market if:
>
> (a) the medicinal product proves to be harmful under normal conditions of use;
> (b) it is lacking in therapeutic efficacy;
> (c) its qualitative and quantitative composition is not as declared;
> (d) the controls on the medicinal product and/or on the ingredients and the controls at an intermediate stage of the manufacturing process have not been carried out or if some other requirement or obligation relating to the grant of the manufacturing authorisation has not been fulfilled.
>
> The competent authority may limit the prohibition to supply the product, or its withdrawal from the market, to those batches which are the subject of dispute.[206]

Under the centralised system, where any of the above triggering provisions occur, **14.112** a Member State or the Commission may initiate a procedure involving a CPMP opinion and Commission Decision suspending or revoking the authorisation.[207] A Member State may nevertheless suspend the use of a product in its territory where urgent action is essential to protect human or animal health or the environment.[208]

It will be seen that the competent authority is required to suspend or revoke the **14.113** authorisation where the criteria are met. The principal test as regards safety is where the product proves to be harmful in the normal conditions of use.[209] As with the criteria for the grant of a marketing authorisation, these criteria are problematic. Any medicinal product may prove harmful, either in general use or when used by a particular patient, since it is intended to have pharmacological effect in treating a diseased state. The key issue of what level of harm is or is not acceptable, in the general or particular situation, is not addressed. Decisions on these issues

---

[206] Directive 2001/83/EC, Article 117. Member States are also required under Article 116 to suspend or revoke an authorization where one of situations (a) to (c) occur.

[207] Regulation (EEC) No 2309/93, Article 18.

[208] Regulation (EEC) No 2309/93, Article 18.4.

[209] It should be noted that the wording in s 28 (3) (g) of the Medicines Act differs from the Community provisions (medicinal products of any description to which the licence relates can no longer be regarded as products which can safely be administered for the purposes indicated in the licence, or can no longer be regarded as efficacious). However, the Community provisions are applied by the Medicines for Human Use (Marketing Authorisations Etc) Regulations 1994, SI 1994 No 3144, Regulation 6.

require complex assessments and the relevant Community authority enjoys a wide discretion, which is only subject to limited judicial review, in the course of which the Community judicature may not substitute its assessment of the facts for the assessment made by the authority concerned.[210]

14.114   The authorisation shall also be suspended or revoked where the composition of the product is not as declared or the particulars and documents are incorrect or have not been updated. The justification for these provisions is that authorisation is based on a product with a precise specification for which the pharmacological effects and side-effects are as anticipated. Any variation in the specification, failure to prepare or control the product by the prevailing scientific standards would not continue to promote safety.

(iii) Suspension or Revocation of a Manufacturing Authorisation

14.115   In relation to the manufacturing and quality control aspects of a product, the supervisory authority in the case of a medicine manufactured within the Community is the competent authority of the Member State(s) that has granted the manufacturing authorisation for the product.[211] Where a product is imported into the Community, the supervising authority is that of the Member State into which it is imported, where the required quality controls are to be carried out, unless the Community has made appropriate alternative arrangements with the exporting country.[212]

14.116   The competent authority of the relevant Member State *shall* suspend or revoke a manufacturing authorisation where any one of the requirements laid down in Article 41 of Directive (EC) 2001/83, for grant of a manufacturing authorisation (see above) is no longer met.[213] For products approved under the centralised system, where the supervisory authorities, or the competent authorities of any other Member State, are of the opinion that the manufacturer or importer from third countries is no longer fulfilling the obligations laid down, they shall forthwith inform the CPMP and the Commission, stating their reasons in detail and indicating the course of action proposed.[214] The Commission shall examine the reasons advanced, together with the Agency, and prepare a draft of the decision to be taken.[215] Where urgent action is essential to protect human or animal health or the

---

[210] Case C-120/97 *Upjohn Ltd v The Licensing Authority established by the Medicines Act 1968 and Others* [1999] ECR I-223; contrast other situations not involving complex assessments (such as in relation to labelling issues) where the above of judicial review is not so limited: Case T-179/00 *A Menarini-Industrie Farmaceutiche Riunite Srl and European Federation of Pharmaceutical Industries and Associations v Commission* [2002] ECR II-2879.

[211] Regulation (EEC) No. 2309/93, Article 16.
[212] ibid.
[213] Directive 2001/83/EC, Article 118; Medicines Act, s 28.
[214] Regulation (EEC) No. 2309/93, Article 18.
[215] ibid.

environment, a Member State may suspend the use of a medicinal product in its territory, and shall then inform the Commission and the other Member States, giving its reasons.[216]

C. Regulation of Medical Devices

1. Overview

The regulatory system for medical devices is quite different from that for phar- **14.117** maceuticals. It does not involve the pre-marketing assessment of a product by a medicines agency or the grant of a marketing authorisation by a competent authority. Instead, the onus of ensuring and declaring that a product conforms to the legal *essential requirements* is placed on the *manufacturer* himself, but in many instances this is subject to approval by an independent technical organisation (known as a *notified body*).

The manufacturer must apply an appropriate *conformity assessment* procedure to **14.118** his device in order to ensure that it complies with the essential requirements, after which he must certify this fact by completing a *declaration of conformity*. There is usually a choice of conformity assessment procedures open to a manufacturer, depending on a risk-based *classification* of the class into which his device falls. The two main approaches to conformity assessment are based either on an approved total quality management system audited to ISO 9000 series standard, as customised for medical devices with EN 46000 series standard, or individual product assessment.

The essential requirements relate to the *safety* in use of the device, including la- **14.119** belling requirements, but are principally expressed in terms of scientific and technical *performance* characteristics. Efficacy, as such, is not a criterion. Confirmation of conformity must include evaluation of clinical data for many devices, generated from either a compilation of scientific literature or the results of *clinical investigations* on the product, for which prior ethical and regulatory approval is required. Conformity of a device with the essential requirements is denoted by affixing *CE marking* to the device. CE marking acts in effect as the passport which authorises the device to be placed on the market and to circulate freely within the EEA and must be marked on the device.

The legal obligation is that a product must comply with the relevant essential re- **14.120** quirements but where the manufacturer chooses to apply a national standard which adopts a European *harmonised standard* (EN series) to an aspect of his product, conformity will be prima facie presumed in respect of the aspects of the

---

[216] ibid, Article 18.4.

essential requirements covered by that standard. Other national or international standards do not have this regulatory benefit. Compliance with the essential requirements at the time of placing the device on the market, or declaration of this fact, should mean that the device is safe but it may later transpire that this is not the case. Manufacturers therefore have some post-marketing *vigilance* requirements. If a marketed device is unsafe, the *competent authority* of a Member State has power under a *safeguard clause* in each Medical Device Directive to take regulatory action to effect the withdrawal of the product from the market in its jurisdiction: the matter is then referred to the Commission and all Member States who then co-ordinate their actions.

14.121   Before the Medical Devices Directives came into being, most medical devices were unregulated in most European states. In some states, some were regulated (illogically, but this was the only available mechanism) as if they were medicines. Examples of products formerly regulated as medicines in the United Kingdom include contact lens products, intra-uterine contraceptives and certain medicated dressings, surgical ligatures and sutures, absorbent or protective materials and dental filling substances.

2. Law on Specific Device Categories

14.122   The EEA law on the marketing of medical devices is governed by three principal Directives which each adopt the Community's scheme for product regulation known as the 'new approach'.[217] The new approach applies to many product sectors, such as machinery, personal protective equipment, low voltage equipment and electromagnetic compatibility requirements but not to pharmaceuticals or cosmetics. The three Medical Device Directives are:

(i)   Directive (EEC) 90/385 on Active Implantable Medical Devices ('AIMDD') came into force on 1 January 1993 and is mandatory from 1 January 1995. This covers all powered implants or partial implants which are left in the human body such as a heart pacemaker.

(ii)   Directive EEC 93/42 on medical devices (MDD) came into force on 1 January 1995 and became mandatory on 14 June 1998. This covers a wide range of devices ranging from first aid bandages, tongue depressors and blood collection bags to hip prostheses and active (powered) devices. Ths MDD was amended by Directive (EC) 2001/104 as of 13 June 2002, but subject to further five and seven year transition periods, in relation to devices containing stable medicinal substances derived from human blood and plasma.

---

[217] Council Resolution of May 7, 1985 on a new approach to technical harmonisation and standards, OJ 1985 No. C 136/1, 4.6.85.

(iii) Directive (EC) 98/79 on *in vitro* diagnostics ('IVDD') came into force on 7 June 2000 and is mandatory from 7 December 2003. This covers products such as pregnancy tests, blood glucose monitoring and tests for transmissible diseases.

The IVDD contained amendments to the two earlier Directives. All of these Directives are implemented into UK law as from 13 June 2002 by the Medical Devices Regulations 2002.[218]   **14.123**

A *transitional period* is provided under each of these Directives so that during the period from the coming into force of the Directive until it is mandatory, a manufacturer may choose whether to apply the Directive to his device or the national rules which were in force immediately prior to the date on which the Directive came into force. From the date a Directive becomes mandatory, a device which is covered by national law implementing that Directive must comply with it.   **14.124**

The basic structure, concepts and terminology of the three Directives on AIMDs, MDs and IVDs is identical: such differences as exist between them arise out of the different nature of these products. The following discussion will therefore focus on the MDD, since this is the central Directive and covers most products. Short sections follow on AIMDs and IVDs. Detailed analysis of the relevant provisions would fill a large book: what is intended here is to highlight the important aspects which should be considered.   **14.125**

The intention behind the legislative scheme is that a product should essentially be regulated under a single product-specific regime as a medicinal product,[219] AIMD, MD, IVD, cosmetic,[220] blood or blood product,[221] or personal protective equipment.[222] However, certain other directives might apply to particular medical devices, including: **14.126**

(i) Directive (EEC) 89/336 on electromagnetic compatibility (the EMC Directive): EMC requirements are included within the essential requirements of the Medical Device Directives so the EMC Directive only applies to medical devices before the relevant Medical Device Directive is applicable.

---

[218] SI 2002 No 618 ('the Regulations'), replacing earlier provisions including the Medical Devices Regulations 1994, SI 1994 N0 3017. The Regulations deal with introductory provisions relating to all medical devices (Pt I), general medical devices (Pt II), active implantable medical devices (Pt III), in vitro diagnostic medical devices (Pt IV), notified bodies, conformity assessment bodies and marking of products (Pt V), fees charged by the Secretary of State (Pt VI) and general, enforcement and miscellaneous matters (Pt VII). For reasons of space, the following discussion is largely limited to an overview of and references to the provisions that apply to general medical devices.

[219] Directive 2001/83/EC, replacing Directive 65/65/EEC as amended and related Directives.

[220] Directive 76/768/EEC as amended.

[221] a Directive or Directives will be forthcoming on these products.

[222] Directive 89/686/EEC as amended.

(ii) Directive (EEC) 92/59 (from January 2004 replaced by (EC) 2001/95) on general product safety: this applies to all consumer products, some of its obligations apply to medical devices used by consumers (see below).

3. Resolution of Uncertainties

14.127 Since this legislation is extensive, complex, frequently written in generalised terms and seeks to create an entirely new regulatory system for products which were formerly largely unregulated, difficulties of interpretation or application are bound to arise. Since the Directives constitute a legal system, ultimate authority for interpretation rests with the courts, fundamentally with the Court of Justice of the European Communities in Luxembourg, to which questions of interpretation of Community law may be referred by national courts. A mechanism however, exists under the Medical Devices Directives by which measures and interpretations may be formally adopted: in the case of the MDD this is the Article 7 Committee, which is a committee of representatives of Member States chaired by the Commission. Under the Article 7 procedure, the Commission may submit to the Committee a draft of measures to be taken, on which the Committee delivers its opinion based on a weighted majority of representatives. The Commission shall adopt the measures envisaged if they are in accordance with the opinion of the Committee. If there is divergence, the Commission shall permit a proposal to the Council of members, which shall act by a qualified majority of votes.

14.128 Less formal, non-binding procedures also exist. There are frequent meetings between representatives of the Commission, Member States and notified bodies. The Commission is also assisted by a Working Group of Experts. A sequence of guidance notes have been issued by the Commission (MEDDEV series), by certain competent authorities (for example, the UK Medical Devices Agency's Bulletins), arising out of the meeting of notified bodies, by trade associations and others.

4. Competent Authorities and Notified Bodies

14.129 Each Member State has designated a competent authority, which is the governmental authority responsible for implementing the Directive in that Member State. In the case of the United Kingdom, the competent authority is the Medicines and Healthcare Products Regulatory Agency,[223] an executive agency of the Department of Health. The principal function of a competent authority in practice is to ensure the safety and health of patients and users of medical devices.

14.130 A competent authority is not involved in the assessment or authorisation for placing on the market of a medical device. As stated above, the legal responsibility in

---

[223] This Agency was created in 2003 on the merger of the Medicines Control Agency and the Medical Devices Agency.

each case rests with the individual manufacturer. However, in many cases the manufacturer is required to obtain independent certification from a third party testing house, called a notified body. Such testing houses are private, commercial enterprises who may apply for and be approved for the purposes of the legislation by the competent authority in their Member State and are then notified within the Community by their approval being published in the Official Journal. Notified bodies may be approved for all devices or only for specific classes of devices. Criteria which they must satisfy in order to be approved are set out in an Annex to the relevant Directive (Annex XI for the MDD). In effect, therefore, notified bodies, although private entities, perform certain delegated regulatory functions. A manufacturer who is required by law to utilise the services of a notified body may choose any notified body within the Community who has the appropriate certification, irrespective of where either of them is located. The relationship between manufacturer and notified body is based on contract even though certain actions of the notified body have regulatory authority.

5. *Definition of a Medical Device*

A medical device is defined as   **14.131**

> any instrument, apparatus, appliance, material or other article, whether used alone or in combination, including the software necessary for its proper application intended by the manufacturer to be used for human beings for the purpose of:[224]
>
> —diagnosis, prevention, monitoring, treatment or alleviation of disease,
> —diagnosis, monitoring, treatment, alleviation or compensation for an injury or handicap,
> —investigation, replacement or modification of the anatomy or of a physiological process,
> —control of conception,
>
> and which does not achieve its principal intended action in or on the human body by pharmacological, immunological or metabolic means, but which may be assisted in its function by such means.[225]

An accessory is also considered to be a medical device. An accessory is defined as: **14.132**

> an article which whilst not being a device is intended specifically by its manufacturer to be used together with a device to enable it to be used in accordance with the use of the device intended by the manufacturer of the device.[226]

---

[224] The important consideration is not the effect but the intended purpose: *Optident Limited and Another v Secretary of State for Trade and Industry and Another* [2001] UKHL 32, 28 June 2001, para 35, per Lord Slynn of Hadley.
[225] Directive 93/42/EEC, Article 1.2(a); Directive 90/385/EEC, Article 1.2(a); the Regulations, Regulation 2 (1).
[226] Directive 93/42/EEC, Article 1.2(b); the Regulations, Regularion 5 (1)

6. The Drug and Device Borderline

14.133 Difficult borderline questions arise in relation to a significant number of products,[227] particularly whether they are to be classified as medicinal products or as medical devices. As a general rule, a relevant product is regulated either under the Medical Devices Directives or by the Medicinal Products Directives (MPDs). Normally, the procedures of both Directives do not apply cumulatively. The Commission has issued Guidelines on this drug-device borderline issue[228] and also on what constitutes medical devices, AIMDs and accessories. In order to decide which regime applies, the relevant criteria are:

(i) The intended purpose of the product, taking into account the way the product is presented (this is likely to establish if either the MDD or MPD apply, rather than distinguish between the two regimes).

(ii) The method by which the principal intended action is achieved. This is crucial in the definition of a medical device. Typically, the medical device function is fulfilled by physical means (including mechanical action, physical barrier, replacement of or support to organs or body functions). The action of a medicinal product is achieved by pharmacological or immunological means or by metabolism.

14.134 The principal intended action of a product may be deduced from:

(i) the manufacturer's labelling and claims,

(ii) scientific data regarding mechanism of action.

14.135 Although the manufacturer's claims are important, it is not possible to place the product in one or other category in contradiction with current scientific data. Manufacturers may be required to justify scientifically their rationale for classification of borderline products.

14.136 Medical devices may be assisted in their function by pharmacological, immunological or metabolic means, but as soon as these means are no longer ancillary with respect to the principal purpose of a product, the product becomes a medicinal product. The claims made for a product, in accordance with its method of action

---

[227] The two regimes of regulation of medical device and cosmetics have been described as not only different but intended to be separate and distinct. The decision on whether a product is a cosmetic product or a medical device is to be decided by the competent authorities of a Member State and in the last resort by the courts, irrespective of whether a product bears CE marking. *Optident Limited and Another v Secretary of State for Trade and Industry and Another* [2001] UKHL 32, 28 June 2001, [27] and [29], *per* Lord Slynn of Hadley.

[228] *Guidelines relating to the Application of: The Council Directive 90/385/EEC on Active Implantable Medical Devices [and] The Council Directive 93/42/EEC on Medical Devices* 'Demarcation between: Directive 90/385/EEC on Active Implantable Medical Devices, Directive 93/42/EEC on Medical Devices, and Directive 65/65/EEC relating to Medicinal Products, and Related Directives', European Commission. MEDDEV. 2.1/3 rev. 2, July 2001.

may, in this context, represent an important factor for its classification as medical device or medicinal product. Examples of medical devices incorporating a medicinal substance with ancillary action include catheters coated with heparin or an antibiotic, bone cements containing antibiotic and blood bags containing anticoagulant.[229]

7. Products Comprising Both a Drug and a Device

For so called drug-device combinations, the MDD specifies the following approach:[230]   **14.137**

(i)   A device which is intended to administer a medicinal product (such as an unfilled syringe) is a medical device. The medicinal product itself remains regulated as a medicine.

(ii) If the device and the medicinal product form a single integral product which is intended exclusively for use in the given combination and which is not reusable (such as a pre-filled syringe), that single product is regulated as a medicine. An application for a marketing authorisation must be made under Directive (EC) 2001/83. However, the safety and performance of the device features of the integral product are assessed in accordance with the essential requirements of Annex I of the MDD.

(iii) Where a device incorporates, as an integral part, a substance which, if used separately, may be considered to be a medicinal product and which is liable to act upon the body with action ancillary to that of the device (such as a heparin-coated catheter), the product is classed as a medical device. However, the medicinal product is to be assessed in accordance with the requirements of Directive (EEC) 75/318 (replaced by (EC) 2001/83). A notified body undertaking conformity assessment on a medical device which incorporates a medicinal substance having ancillary action has a responsibility to consult a national medicines agency about the medicinal substance, to verify its safety, quality and usefulness by analogy with the appropriate methods specified in Directive (EEC) 75/318.

These provisions are explained further in Guidelines issued by the European   **14.138**
Commission.[231]

---

[229] ibid.

[230] Directive 93/42/EEC, Recital 6 and Article 1.3 and 1.4; these provisions are not repeated in this form in the Regulations, which provide in Regulations 12 (4) and 5 (1) for the second of the three situations, namely single-use combination products, and in Regulation 9 (8) that the medical device component of a single-use combination product need only comply with those essential requirements that relate to safety and performance, unless the medicinal product which forms part of that product is liabile to act on the human body with action ancillary to that of the medical device (I e the third situation), in which case the single-use combination product must comply with all the relevant essential requirements which apply to it.

[231] See the Guidelines referred to at footnote 228 above.

8. Classification

14.139 The purpose of classification of devices is simply so as to provide options for conformity assessment methods. Under the MDD Directive, medical devices are categorised into four classes, generally according to the degree of risk which they represent. In summary, Class I covers those which do not enter or interact with the body, Classes IIa and IIb are invasive or implantable devices or those which do interact with the body, Class III is for devices which affect the functions of vital organs. Implantables with an energy source are covered by the AIMDD. The detailed classification rules[232] are lengthy and are set out in Annex IX of Directive (EEC) 93/42. A sequence of rules must be worked through: charts and software are available to assist this.

14.140 The classification system uses three basic criteria, in various combinations: duration of contact with the body, degree of invasiveness and the anatomy affected by the use of the device. Duration is based on continuous use (ie, uninterrupted actual use) and categorised as transient (<60 minutes), short term (±30 days) and long term (>30 days). Invasive devices penetrate wholly or partly inside the body by way of an orifice or via the surface of the body. A body orifice is a natural opening in the body and includes the external surface of the eyeball and any permanent artificial opening, such as a stoma. Surgically invasive devices penetrate via the surface to the inside of the body by surgical intervention. Implantable devices are surgically invasive devices intended to be totally introduced to the body, to replace an epithelial surface or the surface of the eye and intended to remain in place after the procedure and also includes those partially introduced surgically invasive devices remaining in place for at least 30 days. The central circulatory system is defined by the following vessels: *arteriae pulmonales, aorta ascendens, arteriae coronarieae, arteria carotis communis, arteria carotis externa, arteria carotis interna, arteriae cerebrales, truncus brachicephalicus, venae cordis, venae pulmonales, vena cava superior, vena cava inferior.* The central nervous system consists of the brain, meninges and spinal cord. Active medical devices depend on a power source such as electricity for its operation, but not sources of power generated by the human body or gravity.

14.141 Non-invasive devices are covered by rules 1 to 4 and include the following classes:

Class I   eg, ostomy pouches, wheelchairs, eye glasses, incontinence pads, cups and spoons for administering medicines, wound dressings such as cotton wool and wound strips.

Class IIa eg, transfusion equipment, storage and transport of donor organs, polymer film dressings, hydrogel dressings.

Class IIb eg, haemodialyzers, dressings for chronic extensive ulcerated wounds.

---

[232] Applied by the Regulations, Regulation 7.

Invasive devices are covered by rules 5 to 8 and include following classes: **14.142**

Class I eg, dressings for nose bleeds, hand-held dentistry mirrors, enema devices, reusable surgical instruments.

Class IIa eg, contact lenses, urinary catheters, tracheal tubes connected to a ventilator, needles used for suturing, infusion cannulae, dental bridges and crowns.

Class IIb eg, urethral stents, insulin pens, devices supplying ionizing radiation, prosthetic joint replacements. intra-ocular lenses, maxillo-facial implants.

Class III eg, prosthetic heart valves, rechargeable non-active drug delivery systems, absorbable sutures, spinal stents, neurological catheters, temporary pacemaker leads.

Active devices, whilst covered under the above rules, are largely covered by rules 9 **14.143**
to 12 and including the following classes:

Class I eg, examination lights, surgical microscopes, wheelchairs, thermography devices, recording, processing or viewing of diagnostic images.

Class IIa eg, suction equipment, feeding pumps, anaesthesia machines, ventilators, hearing aids.

Class IIb eg, lung ventilators, incubators for babies, surgical lasers, X-ray sources,

Special rules 13 to 18 govern several hazardous characteristics that may be found **14.144**
in certain devices and require a certain level of control and conformity assessment.
Rule 13 deals with devices incorporating a medicinal substance whose action is
ancillary to that of the device—Class III, eg, antibiotic bone cements, condoms
with spermicides, heparin coated catheters.

Rule 14 deals with devices used for contraception or the prevention of transmis- **14.145**
sion of sexually transmitted diseases—Class IIb eg condoms, contraceptive di-
aphragms and if they are implantable or long term invasive—Class III, eg,
intra-uterine devices.

Rule 15 deals with devices for specific disinfecting, cleaning and rinsing and in- **14.146**
cludes contact lens disinfecting, cleaning, rinsing and hydrating—Class IIb, eg,
contact lens solutions, comfort solutions and devices specifically intended for disinfecting medical devices—Class IIa, eg, disinfectants for use with endoscopes.

Rule 16 classifies non-active devices specifically intended for recording X-ray di- **14.147**
agnostic images as Class IIa, eg, X-ray films.

Rule 17 classifies all devices utilising animal tissues or derivatives rendered non- **14.148**
viable and coming into contact with breached skin as Class III, eg, biological heart
valves, porcine xenograft dressings, catgut sutures, collagen implants and dressings.

14.149 Rule 18 puts blood bags into Class IIb. If several rules apply to a device, the strictest rule resulting in the higher classification applies.

14.150 It must be reiterated that classification is based on the manufacturer's intended use and thus the listing of devices into classes must be taken as guidance only. No classification system can be perfect and thus the aim is to capture the majority of products whilst recognising that there will always be products that are borderline either between classes or with other product types such as drugs and cosmetics and also new innovative products that do not fit the criteria laid down.

9. Conformity Assessment Procedures and CE Marking

14.151 Depending on the class of the device a manufacturer may be able to choose between a number of alternative conformity assessment procedures in the assessment of whether a medical device conforms to the essential requirements. Although the rules should be considered in detail in each case,[233] the basic options can be summarised as follows:

(i) For all products in classes IIa, IIb and III and AIMDs, a *full quality assurance* system, audited periodically by a notified body (Annex II of the MDD) *which includes* examination and certification by the notified body of the design dossier of each product covered. The manufacturer must keep documentation on the quality system and the design dossier of each product plus other documentation. The quality system obligations include post-marketing and vigilance aspects. Compliance with Annex II may be achieved (this is not mandatory but is invariably adopted voluntarily) by compliance with the EN 29000 and 46000 series standards, which apply the ISO 9000 series.

(ii) For products in classes IIa, IIb and III and AIMDs, examination and certification by a notified body of a specimen product (*type examination*: Annex III of the MDD) coupled with a varying degree (partially restricted by product class) of product or production quality assurance (MDD Annexes IV, V and VI) which ensures that the manufacturing process produces products which conform to the certified type and might involve a quality system for manufacture and final inspection (Annex V) or a quality system for final inspection and testing (Annex VI).

(iii) For products in class I, the manufacturer must have specified technical documentation on the design of the product showing that it conforms to the essential requirements: manufacturing aspects are not covered and a notified body is not involved unless there is a measuring function and/or the product is sterilised. (Annex VII: *EC declaration of conformity*).

---

[233] Directive 93/42/EEC, Article 11; the Regulations, Regulation 13.

In all cases, the specified documentation must be kept for five years after the last **14.152** product has been manufactured. The Annex VII procedure is also available for class IIa devices if coupled with the Annex IV or V or VI procedure.

10. Registration

The manufacturer of a class I device or of a custom-made device or a person who **14.153** markets a system or procedure pack must inform his competent authority of his registered place of business and the description of the devices concerned.[234] Such manufacturers who are located outside the EEA must designate persons established with the Community who are responsible for such registration.

11. Harmonised Standards

A manufacturer may voluntarily decide to apply any standard to his product or **14.154** business. Devices which are in conformity with a national standard adopted pursuant to a harmonised EC standard published in the Official Journal of the European Communities shall be presumed by Member States to comply with those aspects of the essential requirements which are covered by the standard.[235] Harmonised standards are those adopted by the EC standards bodies pursuant to a mandate issued by the Commission,[236] in this case the European Committee for Standardisation (CEN) and the European Committee for Electrotechnical Standardisation (CENELEC). A large number of standards are contemplated but may take time to be written and adopted. Standards may be horizontal (covering aspects common to all or a number of product types) or vertical (dealing only with a specific aspect or specific product type). Important harmonised standards exist on the following:

> EN 29000 and EN 46000 series quality systems for medical devices
> EN 1041 information and labelling for medical devices
> EN 980 graphical symbols
> EN 10993 series biological evaluation of medical devices
> EN 540 clinical investigation of devices
> EN 60601 series medical electrical equipment
> EN 1441 risk analysis
> EN 1174 sterilisation

12. Custom-Made Devices

A new device which is specifically made in accordance with a duly qualified med- **14.155** ical practitioner's written prescription and which gives, under his responsibility,

---

[234] Directive 93/42/EEC, Article 14; the Regulations, Regulation 19.
[235] The Regulations, Regulation 9 (4).
[236] See the definition of a harmonised standard in the Regulations, Regulation 2 (1).

specific design characteristics and is intended for the sole use of a particular patient is permitted to be marketed without CE marking under provisions referring to custom-made devices.[237] The prescription may be made by any person authorised by virtue of his professional qualifications to do so. Mass-produced devices which need to be adapted to meet the specific requirements of the medical practitioner or any other professional user are not considered to be custom-made devices.[238]

14.156 The manufacturer must undertake to keep available for the competent authorities documentation on the design, manufacture and performance of the product so as to allow assessment of conformity with the essential requirements.[239] He must also draw up a statement containing the following information:[240]

(i) data allowing identification of the device in question,

(ii) a statement that the device is intended for exclusive use by a particular patient, together with the name of the patient,

(iii) the name of the medical practitioner or other authorised person who made out the prescription and, where applicable, the name of the clinic concerned,

(iv) the particular features of the device as specified in the relevant medical prescription,

(v) a statement that the device in question conforms to the essential requirements set out in Annex I of the Directive and, where applicable, indicating which essential requirements have not been fully met, together with the grounds. The manufacturer must inform the competent authorities of his registered place of business and the description of the devices concerned.

13. Systems and Procedure Packs

14.157 It sometimes occurs that a number of items are assembled and marketed together as a particular system or to be used with a particular medical procedure. The individual items might or might not already bear CE marking.

14.158 Where all the devices bear CE marking and are put together within the intended purposes specified by their manufacturers, a person who puts them together shall draw up a declaration stating that:[241]

(i) He has verified the mutual compatibility of the devices in accordance with the manufacturers' instructions and has carried out his operations in accordance with these instructions; and

---

[237] Directive 93/42/EEC, Articles 1.2(d), 12.6 and Annex VIII; the Regulations, Regulations 15 and 5.
[238] ibid.
[239] ibid, see also Regulations 9 (5) and 12 (2).
[240] ibid.
[241] Directive 93/42/EEC, Article 12; the Regulations, regulations 14 and 5.

(ii) He has packaged the system or procedure pack and supplied relevant information to users incorporating relevant instructions from the manufacturers; and

(iii) The whole activity is subjected to appropriate methods of internal control and inspection.

14.159 The system or procedure pack must not bear additional CE marking and must be accompanied by the original manufacturers' information. The declaration must be kept for five years.

14.160 Where the above conditions are not met, as in cases where the system or procedure pack incorporates devices which do not bear CE marking or where the chosen combination of devices is not compatible in view of their original intended use, the system or procedure pack shall be treated as a device in its own right and the appropriate conformity assessment procedure must be followed.

14. Essential Requirements

14.161 The essential requirements contained in Annex I of each new approach directive specify the aspects of safety and performance which must be satisfied at the time at which a relevant product is placed on the market.[242] Essential requirements are stated as principles or as generalised aspects and exclude detailed technical requirements. The scheme of the Community's new approach is that detailed technical aspects are not required as legal obligations but, if they are generally accepted, may be applied voluntarily by manufacturers through being included in official standards.[243] The essential requirements are intended to be comprehensive and all must be satisfied save for those requirements which do not apply to a particular product as a matter of common sense.

14.162 The essential requirements in the MDD fall under two headings: general requirements and requirements regarding design and construction.[244] The general requirements include the following provisions:

(i) The devices must be designed and manufactured in such a way that, when used under the conditions and for the purposes intended, they will not compromise the clinical condition or the safety of patients, or the safety and health of users or, where applicable, other persons, provided that any risks which may be associated with their use constitute acceptable risks when weighed against the benefits to the patient and are compatible with a high level of protection of health and safety.

---

[242] The Regulations, Regulation 8.
[243] Council Resolution of December 21, 1989 on a global approach to conformity assessment, OJ 1989 No. C10/1, 16.1.90.
[244] The following paragraphs are taken from Directive 93/42?EEC, Annex I.

(ii) The solutions adopted by the manufacturer for the design and construction of the devices must conform to safety principles, taking account of the generally acknowledged state of the art. In selecting the most appropriate solutions, the manufacturer must apply the following principles in the following order:

—eliminate or reduce risks as far as possible (inherently safe design and construction),

—where appropriate take adequate protection measures including alarms if necessary, in relation to risks that cannot be eliminated,

—inform users of the residual risks due to any shortcomings of the protection measures adopted.

(iii) The devices must achieve the performances intended by the manufacturer and be designed, manufactured and packaged in such a way that they are suitable for one or more of the functions as specified by the manufacturer.

(iv) The characteristics and performances referred to in sections (i)–(iii) above must not be adversely affected to such a degree that the clinical conditions and safety of the patients and, where applicable, of other persons are compromised during the lifetime of the device as indicated by the manufacturer, when the device is subjected to the stresses which can occur during normal conditions of use.

(v) The devices must be designed, manufactured and packed in such a way that their characteristics and performances during their intended use will not be adversely affected during transport and storage taking account of the instructions and information provided by the manufacturer.

(vi) Any undesirable side-effect must constitute an acceptable risk when weighed against the performances intended.

14.163 Section (ii) above implies that a manufacturer must carry out a risk analysis. A harmonised standard is available on this topic, EN 1441, which amplifies the methodology for risk analysis, elimination or reduction required by section (ii).

14.164 The essential requirements regarding design and construction are too extensive to be summarised here. They cover the following headings:

(i) Clinical, physical and biological properties.

(ii) Infection and microbial contamination.

(iii) Construction and environmental properties.

(iv) Devices with a measuring function.

(v) Protection against radiation.

(iv) Requirements for medical devices connected to or equipped with an energy source.

(vii) Information supplied by the manufacturer (this is discussed further below).

15. Information Supplied by the Manufacturer

The general principle is that each device must be accompanied by the information **14.165** needed to use it safely and to identify the manufacturer, taking account of the training and knowledge of the potential users. This information comprises the details on the label and the data in the instructions for use. A series of 13 particular requirements are specified for inclusion in the label and the same 13 requirements plus a further 15 categories of information must be included in the instructions for use.

As far as practicable and appropriate, the information needed to use the device **14.166** safely must be set out on the device itself and/or on the packaging for each unit or, where appropriate, on the sales packaging. If individual packaging of each unit is not practicable, the information must be set out in the leaflet supplied with one or more devices. Instructions for use must be included in the packaging for every device. By way of exception, no such instructions for use are needed for devices in Class I or IIa if they can be used safely without any such instructions.

Where appropriate, this information should take the form of symbols. Any sym- **14.167** bol or identification colour used must conform to the harmonised standards. In areas for which no standards exist, the symbols and colours must be described in the documentation supplied with the device.

It will be noted that in the above three paragraphs, which are quoted verbatim **14.168** from Annex I, certain flexibility is permitted through use of the words 'where appropriate': this is a feature of many of the other essential requirements. The manufacturer is permitted some discretion over compliance with the essential requirements, based on an application of common sense to the circumstances of his particular product.

16. Definition of Manufacturer

A manufacturer is defined as the natural or legal person with responsibility for the **14.169** design, manufacture, packaging and labelling of a device before it is placed on the EU market under his own name, regardless of whether these operations are carried out by that person himself or on his behalf by a third party.[245] The Directives also apply to those who assemble, package, process, fully refurbish or label a product and in certain other situations.[246]

The intention is that the person (more normally, the company) who assumes the **14.170** legal responsibility of 'manufacturer' need not be the person who assembles the product. One or more of the activities of design, manufacture, packaging or

---

[245] Directive 93/42/EEC, Article 1.2(f); the Regulations, Regulation 2 (1).
[246] ibid.

labelling may be subcontracted by the legal manufacturer. The name or trade-name and address of the legal manufacturer must appear on the label and instructions for use.[247] In addition, for devices imported into the Community, the label, or the outer packaging, or instructions for use, must contain the name and address of either the authorised representative of the manufacturer established within the Community, or of the importer established in the Community (this is in effect for devices whose importation is not authorised by the manufacturer), or for the person who has the responsibility to register with the competent authorities in the case of class I or custom-made devices.[248]

14.171   The Regulations require a manufacturer or, where applicable, his authorised representative to observe the manufacturer's obligations set out in the relevant conformity assessment procedure,[249] and to take account of the results of any assessment or verification operations which have been carried out in accordance with the legislation at an intermediate stage of manufacture.[250]

14.172   A manufacturer located outside the EEA may place a Class I or custom-made medical device or a system or procedure pack on the EU market under his own name provided it has undergone a relevant conformity assessment procedure and bears CE marking and the competent authorities in the relevant Member State have been informed either of (i) his registered place of business in that Member State, if he has one, and the description of the device, or (ii) the registered place of business in that Member State of a person he has designated responsible for marketing the device in the European Union, and the category of the device.[251]

14.173   In relation to devices in Classes II, IIa and IIb, the manufacturer must certify conformity personally under the Annex II procedure but his authorised representative established in the European Union may do this in place of the manufacturer under the Annex III and IV procedures.

14.174   The functions of an authorised representative are not precisely defined in the Directives save for the IVD Directive but he is a person explicitly designated by the manufacturer and acts and may be addressed by authorities and bodies in the Community instead of the manufacturer with regard to the latter's obligations.[252] It would be good practice for the manufacturer and authorised representative to have a written contract recording their relationship.

---

[247] Directive 93/42/EEC, Annex I, paragraph 13.1.
[248] ibid.
[249] The Regulations, Regulation 17 (1).
[250] ibid, Regulation 17 (2).
[251] Directive 93/42/EEC, Article 14; the Regulations, Regulation 19.
[252] Directive 98/79/EC, Article 1.2(g).

17. CE Marking: Placing on the Market and Putting into Service

Medical devices may only be placed on the market and put into service if they **14.175** comply with the requirements laid down in the Directive when duly supplied and properly installed, maintained and used in accordance with their intended purpose.[253] Devices, other than devices which are custom-made or intended for clinical investigations, which are considered to meet the essential requirements set out in Annex I of the relevant Directive must bear the CE marking of conformity when they are placed on the market.[254]

The CE marking of conformity, as specified in MDD Annex XII, must appear in **14.176** a visible, legible and indelible form on the device or its sterile pack, where practicable and appropriate, and on the instructions for use.[255] Where applicable, the CE marking must also appear on the sales packaging.[256] It shall be accompanied by the identification number of the notified body responsible for implementation of the relevant conformity assessment procedure. It is prohibited to affix marks or inscriptions which are likely to mislead third parties with regard to the meaning or the graphics of the CE marking.[257] Any other mark may be affixed to the device, to the packaging or to the instruction leaflet accompanying the device provided that the visibility and legibility of the CE marking is not thereby reduced.

The concepts of 'placing on the market' and 'putting into service' are standard in **14.177** Community 'new approach' directives. For the purposes of the MDD, they are defined as follows:

'placing on the market' means the first making available in return for payment or free of charge of a device other than a device intended for clinical investigation, with a view to distribution and/or use on the Community market, regardless of whether it is new or fully refurbished;

'putting into service' means the stage at which a device has been made available to the final user as being ready for use on the Community market for the first time for its intended purpose.[258]

The European Commission has issued guidance on these concepts in the context **14.178** of all 'new approach Directives'.[259] In essence, a device is placed on the market when it is first put into the stream of distribution or commerce by its manufacturer. A device which is fully refurbished is treated as if it were a new device and

---

[253] eg Directive 93/42/EEC, Article 2; the Regulations, Regulation 8.
[254] eg Directive 93/42/EEC, Articles 17 and 3; the Regulations, Regulation 10.
[255] ibid.
[256] ibid.
[257] The Regulations, Regulation 10 (5).
[258] Directive 93/42/EEC, Article 1.2(h) and (i) as amended by Article 21 of Directive 98/79/EC; the Regulations, Regulation 2 (1).
[259] *Guide to the Implementation of Directives Based on the New Approach and the Global Approach*, European Commission, 2000.

must be subject afresh to the requirements of the Directive. Difficulties arise over the definition of what constitutes refurbishment (simple servicing is clearly not included) and aspects such as upgrading.

18. *Clinical Investigation*

14.179   Confirmation of conformity with the essential requirements must be based on clinical data in the case of, as a general rule, implantable and long term invasive devices falling within Classes IIa and IIb and all Class III devices under the MDD;[260] and all active implantable devices under the AIMDD.[261]

14.180   The adequacy of such clinical data must be based on either[262] a compilation of the relevant scientific literature and, 'if appropriate', a written report containing a critical evaluation, or the results of all clinical investigations made.

14.181   Thus, *evaluation* of the clinical safety and performance is required for all devices, whereas a clinical *investigation* of each device may or may not be necessary (the term clinical trial is not used in relation to devices). The Directives give some latitude over the circumstances in which a clinical investigation of a non-CE marked device is required. Guidance issued by the Medical Devices Agency[263] states that an investigation would be required where:

(i)   there is the introduction of a completely new concept of device into clinical practice where components, features and/or methods of action, are previously unknown;

(ii)   an existing device is modified in such a way that it contains a novel feature particularly if such a feature has an important physiological effect; or where the modification might significantly affect the clinical performance and/or safety of the device;

(iii)   a device incorporates materials previously untested in humans, coming into contact with the human body or where existing materials are applied to a new location in the human body, in which case compatibility and biological safety will need to be considered;

(iv)   a device, either CE-marked or non-CE-marked, is proposed for a new purpose or function.

---

[260]   Directive 93/42/EEC, Annex X and Article 15; this somewhat imprecise wording from Annex X is not reproduced in the Regulations. Regulation 9 (2) states that 'Where confirmation of conformity with the essential requirements must be based on clinical data, such data must be established in accordance with the requirements set out in Annex X.' There is therefore a legal uncertainty about when and how much clinical investigation is required: the issue remains a matter of scientific and technical judgment.

[261]   Directive 90/385/EEC, Article 10 and Annex 7; see also Annex 2 para 4.1 and Annex 3 para 3.

[262]   Directive 93/42/EEC, Annex X, para 1.

[263]   *Guidance Notes for Manufacturers on Clinical Investigations to be carried out in the UK.* Medical Devices Agency. September 1996.

Clinical investigation will also be required where a CE-marked device is to be used for a new purpose.   **14.182**

The regime of the Directives is that if clinical evaluation is required, it must be subject to ethical approval in accordance with the principles of the Declaration of Helsinki.[264] The Directives provide[265] that the purpose of clinical investigation is to: **14.183**

—verify that, under normal conditions of use, the performance of the devices conform to [those intended by the manufacturer, namely the device should be designed and manufactured in such a way that it is suitable for the functions specified by the manufacturer],

—determine any undesirable side effects, under normal conditions of use, and assess whether they are acceptable risks having regard to the intended performance of the device.

The Directives also specify the methodology to be adopted in clinical investigations. Adverse incidents occurring in the investigation must be reported to the competent authority. A general requirement in the MDD is: **14.184**

Clinical investigations must be performed on the basis of an appropriate plan of investigation reflecting the latest scientific and technical knowledge and defined in such a way as to confirm or refute the manufacturer's claims for the device; these investigations must include an adequate number of observations to guarantee the scientific validity of the conclusions.[266]

The primary consideration of a clinical investigation of a device is assessment verification of the manufacturer's claims for the technical performance of the device. Safety considerations are nevertheless relevant in that the clinical investigation should determine and assess any undesirable side effects, but the main thrust of the clinical evaluation, and in particular of the conformity assessment by a notified body or the manufacturer to permit marketing, is on technical performance rather than a complete evaluation of safety. It is an essential requirement for marketed devices that '[a]ny undesirable side-effect must constitute an acceptable risk when weighed against the performances intended'.[267]   **14.185**

Both the AIMDD[268] and the MDD[269] specify approval procedures for clinical investigations by the competent authority and relevant ethics committee(s). The manufacturer must submit to the competent authority of the Member State in which the investigation is to be conducted a statement in the specified form   **14.186**

---

[264] Directive 90/385/EEC, Annex 7, paragraph 2.2 and Directive 93/42/EEC, Annex X, paragraph 2.2.

[265] Directive 90/385/EEC, Annex 7 and Directive 93/42/EEC, Annex X.

[266] Directive 93/42/EEC, Annex X, Requirement 2.3.1.

[267] Directive 93/42/EEC, Annex I, Requirement 6.

[268] Directive 90/385/EEC, Article 10; the Regulations, Regulation 29.

[269] Directive 93/42/EEC, Article 15; the Regulation, Regulation 16.

(MDD Annex VIII) containing information as detailed as design drawings, manufacturing methods, descriptions and explanations and the results of calculations and technical tests. For Class II devices and implantable and long-term devices in Classes IIa and IIb the investigation may commence either after 60 days unless the authority has objected, or earlier if the authority so authorises, provided a favourable ethics committee opinion is available. For devices other than those just specified, the Member State may authorise immediate commencement after receipt of notification, provided a favourable ethics committee opinion has been issued. A device which is intended for clinical investigation must not bear CE marking.

14.187   Compliance with the requirements relating to clinical investigations (AIMDD Annex VII; MDD Annex X) is assisted by adoption of standard EN 540 on 'Clinical Investigation of Medical Devices for Human Subjects' which is very similar to pharmaceutical GCP.

14.188   Clinical investigation is not required for IVDs, for which the equivalent procedure is performance evaluation, discussed below.

19. In Vitro Diagnostic Medical Devices

(i) Definition of In Vitro Diagnostic Medical Device

14.189   An in vitro diagnostic medical device is defined as any medical device which is a reagent, reagent product, calibrator, control material, kit, instrument, apparatus, equipment or system whether used alone or in combination, intended by the manufacturer to be used in vitro for the examination of specimens including blood and tissue donations, derived from the human body, solely or principally for the purpose of providing information concerning a physiological or pathological state, or concerning a congenital abnormality, or to determine the safety and compatibility with potential recipients, or to monitor therapeutic measures.[270] For the purpose of this Directive, a specimen receptacle, whether evacuated or not, specifically intended by its manufacturer to contain a specimen for the purposes of in vitro diagnostic examination is considered to be a device. Products for general laboratory use are not devices unless such products, in view of their characteristics, are specifically intended by their manufacturer to be used for in vitro diagnostic examination.[271]

(ii) Classification

14.190   The IVD Directive follows the same general 'new approach' scheme as the other medical devices Directives with the following major differences. IVDs are divided

---

[270] Directive 98/79/EC, Article 1.2(b); the Regulations, Regulation 2(1).
[271] ibid.

into two classes: Annex II devices and everything else. Annex II devices are themselves divided into List A (high risk) and List B which include the following (each case also including calibrators and control materials):

List A
—Reagents and reagent products for determining the following blood groups: ABO system, Rhesus (C, c, D, E, e) anti-Kell.
—Reagents and reagent products for the detection, confirmation and quantification in human specimens of markers of HIV infection (HIV 1 and 2), HTLV I and II, and Hepatitus B, C and D.

List B
—Reagents and reagent products for determining the following blood groups: Anti-Duffy and Anti-Kidd.
—Reagents and reagent products for determining irregular anti-erythrocytic antibodies.
—Reagents and reagent products for the detection and quantification in human samples of the following congential infections: rubella, toxoplasmosis.
—Reagents and reagent products for diagnosing the following hereditary disease: phenylketonuria.
—Reagents and reagent products for determining the following human infections: cytomegalovirus, chlamydia.
—Reagents and reagent products for determining the following HLA tissue groups: DR, A, B.
—Reagents and reagent products for determining the following turmoral marker: PSA.
—Reagents and reagent products, including software, designed specifically for evaluating the risk of trisomy 21.
—The following device for self-diagnosis: device for the measurement of blood sugar.

(iii) Particular Provisions

One of two conformity assessment procedures may be followed for devices covered by Annex II:

14.191

(i) the EC Declaration of Conformity procedure (full quality assurance: Annex IV); or
(ii) the EC type examination procedure (Annex V) coupled with either the EC verification procedure (Annex VI) or the EC Declaration of Conformity (production quality assurance: Annex VII).

All devices other than those covered by Annex II are subject to the EC Declaration of Conformity procedure (Annex III), which does not involve the intervention of

14.192

a notified body, but which includes supplementary requirements for devices for self-testing, which does involve a notified body (Annex III).

14.193 Common Technical Specifications (CTS) are to be adopted by the Article 7.2 Committee (a working group of scientific experts appointed by the Member States) which will apply to devices in Annex II List A and, when required, devices in Annex II List B. There is some uncertainty about the circumstances in which the requirement might apply to List B devices. CTS establish appropriate performance evaluation and re-evaluation criteria, batch release criteria, reference methods and reference materials. If, for duly justified reasons, manufacturers do not comply with the CTS, they must adopt other solutions which are at least equivalent to these specifications. CTS are intended mainly for the evaluation of the safety of the blood supply and organ donations.

14.194 Manufacturers shall notify competent authorities:

(i) for reagents, reagent products, reference and control materials, of information concerning common technological characteristics and/or analytes, as well as any important and subsequent modification, including suspension of marketing authorisation;

(ii) for other IVDs, appropriate indications;

(iii) for devices in Annex II and devices for self-testing, all data allowing identification and the analytical parameters and, where applicable, for diagnostic products in Annex I.3, results of evaluation of performance in accordance with Annex VIII and certificates of notified bodies.

(iv) Performance Evaluation

14.195 Clinical evaluation is not appropriate for IVDs but a procedure is specified for performance evaluation studies in clinical laboratories or in other appropriate environments outside the manufacturer's premises (Annex VIII).[272] A manufacturer who places devices on the market under his own name must notify the competent authorities of the Member State in which he has his registered place of business of the address of that registered place of business, the categories of devices as defined in terms of common characteristics of technology and/or analytes and of any significant change thereto.

20. Adverse Event Reporting: Vigilance

14.196 All adverse events with medical devices of which the manufacturer becomes aware must be recorded. The detailed legal requirements in relation to recording and reporting are, curiously, more onerous in relation to MDs than AIMDs. However, the Commission's Guidance is that they should be treated the same in practice. In

---

[272] The Regulations, Regulation 43.

general,[273] a manufacturer of general medical devices should report, and a Member State record and evaluate:

(i) any malfunction or deterioration in the characteristics and performance of a device, or inadequacy in the labelling, which might lead to, or have led to, the death of a patient or user or to a serious deterioration in his state of health,

(ii) any technical or medical reason in relation to the characteristics or performance of a device for the reasons referred to in (i) above, leading to systematic recall of devices of the same type by the manufacturer.

Guidance is issued by the European Commission on medical device vigilance[274] which includes an explanation of the difficult concept of when a deterioration in state of health should be considered serious: **14.197**

(i) life-threatening illness or injury;

(ii) permanent impairment of a body function or permanent damage to a body structure;

(iii) a condition necessitating medical or surgical intervention to prevent permanent impairment of a body function or permanent damage to a body structure.

It is intended that regulatory data will be stored on a European database on medical devices accessible only to competent authorities. This will include data on registration, certificates issue or withdrawn and vigilance data.[275] **14.198**

21. Recall

A manufacturer may have a number of post-marketing obligations arising under either the medical devices legislation and/or the GPS legislation, and under product liability or negligence law. The precise legal provisions constitute a somewhat incomplete matrix, although the UK Medical Devices Agency has issued guidance on the subject of recall (defined to include the return, modification, exchange, destruction or retrofit of a device) which covers in general terms the circumstances in which a recall might be appropriate and how it should best be implemented.[276] **14.199**

22. Enforcement and Sanctions

The Medical Device Directives authorise Member States to take enforcement action against medical devices which prove to be unsafe. The specific powers, **14.200**

---

[273] See for example Directive 93/42/EEC, Annex II, para 3.1, seventh indent; these provisions match obligations imposed on member states by Article 12.

[274] *Guidelines on a Medical Devices Vigilance System,* European Commission, *MEDDEV 2.12-1 rev 4, April 2001.*

[275] Directive 93/42/EEC, Article 14a.

[276] Medical Devices Agency, *Guidance on the Recall of Medical Devices,* 2000.

offences, sanctions and penalties are subject to the discretion of Member States. Accordingly, these matters are provided for under national legislation and practice. It must be remembered that relevant national provisions may be found not only within national legislation implementing the relevant Medical Device Directive but also in other provisions such as general consumer protection, trade descriptions or criminal legislation. Where a Member State invokes the 'safeguard clause' under a Medical Device Directive, removing a product from the market on grounds of safety, a mechanism must be followed under which the Commission and other Member States are notified, the position discussed and a unified approach taken by the authorities.

14.201 Enforcement provisions are generally of two types: first, powers to investigate and take action against a product and, secondly, offences which may be committed by individuals for breach of which they may be prosecuted by the authorities and subject to criminal sanctions. In the United Kingdom, for example, the first category of provisions arise under the product-specific Regulations and Pt II of the Consumer Protection Act 1987. The offences are as specified in the product-specific Regulations. There is a considerable variation between Member States in the number and wording of criminal offences which may be committed and in the penalties which might be imposed.

14.202 Different national agencies have different practices on what action they may take when faced with dangerous products. The UK Medical Devices Agency, for example, operates a practice of issuing a sequence of three advisory notices to UK health services, for which the criteria for the various safety warning categories are as follows:[277]

14.203 Hazard Notices are issued:

(i)   in cases of actual death or serious injury, or where death or serious injury would have occurred but for fortuitous circumstances or the timely intervention of health care personnel (or a carer); and

(ii)   where the medical device is clearly implicated; and

(iii) where immediate action is necessary to prevent recurrence.

14.204 Device Alerts are issued:

(i)   in cases where there is the potential for death or serious injury, or there may be implications arising from the long term use of the medical device;

(ii)   where the medical device is likely to be implicated; and

(iii) where the recipient is expected to take immediate action on the advice.

14.205 Safety Notices are used to recommend or inform:

---

[277] Medical Devices Agency, *Safety Notices*, 2001.

(i)   where action by the recipient will improve safety;

(ii) where it is necessary to repeat warnings on long standing problems;

(iii) to support or follow up manufacturers' field modifications.

D. Impact of the General Consumer Product Safety Legislation

1. Complementarity between Community Rules

Directive (EEC) 92/59, implemented by the General Product Safety Regulations 1994,[278] and to be extended from January 2004 under Directive (EC) 2001/95, (referred to here as 'GPS' provisions) imposes general regulatory provisions on producers and distributors of consumer products.[279] These GPS provisions apply to producers and distributors of medicinal products or medical devices which are consumer products, to the extent that[280] there are no specific provisions with the same objective in other rules of Community law governing the safety of the products concerned. **14.206**

The extent to which the GPS provisions apply to medicinal products or medical devices is not entirely clear. The European Commission is to issue Guidelines which may clarify the position. It is clear that the GPS provisions will not apply to products which are not consumer products, and that certain medical devices may not fall within the definition of consumer products. **14.207**

In general, it would seem that medicinal products are totally excluded from the GPS provisions, since the sector-specific legislation ousts the latter. Much, if not all, of the GPS provisions are ousted by the sector-specific legislation on medical devices, with the exception that no device provisions govern distributors. For the sake of completeness, the GPS obligations on producers and distributors will now be summarised. This section omits discussion of the GPS obligations on Member States. **14.208**

2. GPS Obligations on Producers

(i) Definition of Producer

Several individuals or entities may qualify to be the producer of a consumer product at the same time. A producer is defined for GPS purposes as:[281] **14.209**

---

[278] SI 1994 No 2328.

[279] For the definition of consumer product see Directive 2001/95/EC Article 2(a). At the time of writing the 2001 Directive has not been implemented into United Kingdom law so this section does not quote references to the implementing Regulations.

[280] this quotes the revised provisions under Directive 2001/95/EC, Article 1.2.

[281] Directive 2001/95/EC, Article 2(e).

(i) the manufacturer of the product, when he is established in the Community, and any other person presenting himself as the manufacturer by affixing to the product his name, trade mark or other distinctive mark, or the person who re-conditions the product;

(ii) the manufacturer's representative, when the manufacturer is not established in the Community or, if there is no representative established in the Community, the importer of the product;

(iii) other professionals in the supply chain, insofar as their activities may affect the safety properties of a product;

(ii) Obligations on Producers

14.210 Under Directive (EC) 2001/95, producers of consumer products are subject to the following sequence of obligations. First, to place only safe products on the market.[282] A safe product is defined as[283] any product which, under normal or reasonably foreseeable conditions of use including duration and, where applicable, putting into service, installation and maintenance requirements, does not present any risk or only the minimum risks compatible with the product's use, considered to be acceptable and consistent with a high level of protection for the safety and health of persons, taking into account the following points in particular:

(i) the characteristics of the product, including its composition, packaging, instructions for assembly and, where applicable, for installation and maintenance;

(ii) the effect on other products, where it is reasonably foreseeable that it will be used with other products;

(iii) the presentation of the product, the labelling, any warnings and instructions for its use and disposal and any other indication or information regarding the product;

(iv) the categories of consumers at risk when using the product, in particular children and the elderly.

The feasibility of obtaining higher levels of safety or the availability of other products presenting a lesser degree of risk shall not constitute grounds for considering a product to be 'dangerous'.

14.211 Secondly, within the limits of their respective activities, producers shall provide consumers with the relevant information to enable them to assess the risks inherent in a product throughout the normal or reasonably foreseeable period of its use, where such risks are not immediately obvious without adequate warnings, and to take precautions against those risks.[284] The presence of warnings does not exempt

---

[282] Directive 2001/95/EC, Article 3.1. There is a hierarchy of rules, standards and guidelines against which the safety of a product is to be presumed assessed: Article 3.
[283] Directive 2001/95/EC, Article 2(b).
[284] Directive 2001/95/EEC, Article 5.1, first paragraph.

any person from compliance with the other requirements laid down in this Directive.[285]

Thirdly, within the limits of their respective activities, producers shall adopt measures commensurate with the characteristics of the products which they supply, enabling them to:[286]   **14.212**

(i) be informed of risks which these products might pose;
(ii) choose to take appropriate action including, if necessary to avoid these risks, withdrawal from the market, adequately and effectively warning consumers, or recall from consumers.

The measures referred to above may include, for example: **14.213**

(i) indication, by means of the product or its packaging, of the identity and details of the producer and the product reference or, where applicable, the batch of products to which it belongs, except where the lack of such an indication is justified, and
(ii) in all cases where appropriate, the carrying out of sample testing of marketed products, investigating and, if necessary, keeping a register of complaints and keeping distributors informed of such monitoring.

Action such as that referred to in (ii) above shall be undertaken on a voluntary basis or at the request of the competent authorities. Recall shall take place as a last resort, where other measures would not suffice to prevent the risks involved, in instances where the producers consider it necessary or where they are obliged to do so further to a measure taken by the competent authority. It may be effected within the framework of codes of good practice on the matter in the Member State concerned, where such codes exist.   **14.214**

Fourthly, where producers and distributors know or ought to know, on the basis of the information in their possession and as professionals, that a product that they have placed on the market poses risks to the consumer that are incompatible with the general safety requirement, they must immediately inform the competent authorities of the Member States thereof under the conditions laid down in Annex 1 of the GPS Directive, giving details, in particular, of action taken to prevent risk to the consumer.[287]   **14.215**

Finally, producers and distributors shall, within the limits of their respective activities, co-operate with the competent authorities, at the request of the latter, on action taken to avoid the risks posed by products which they supply or have supplied. The procedures for such co-operation, including procedures for dialogue   **14.216**

---

[285] ibid, second paragraph.
[286] Directive 2001/95/EEC, Article 5.1, third paragraph.
[287] Directive 2001/95/EC, Article 5.3.

with the producers and distributors concerned on issues related to product safety, shall be established by the competent authorities.[288]

3. GPS Obligations on Distributors

(i) Definition of Distributor

14.217 A distributor of a consumer product for GPS purposes is defined as:

> any professional in the supply chain whose activity does not affect the safety properties of a product.

14.218 Comparison of this definition with the definition of a producer, at para 14.209 above, reveals that a person who distributes a product will be subject to the significantly more onerous obligations of a producer where his activities may affect the safety properties of a product. Examples of activities that would affect the safety properties of a product are transporting, storing or handling it in a manner that makes it less safe than intended by the manufacturer.

(ii) Obligations on Distributors

14.219 The principal obligation on a distributor is:[289]

> Distributors shall be required to act with due care to help to ensure compliance with the applicable safety requirements, in particular by not supplying products which they know or should have presumed, on the basis of the information in their possession and as professionals, do not comply with those requirements. Moreover, within the limits of their respective activities, they shall participate in monitoring the safety of products placed on the market, especially by passing on information on product risks, keeping and providing the documentation necessary for tracing the origin of products, and cooperating in the action taken by producers and competent authorities to avoid the risks. Within the limits of their respective activities they shall take measures enabling them to cooperate efficiently.

14.220 In addition, distributors are subject to the obligations to inform the authorities and to co-operate with the authorities noted at paras 14.213 and 14.216 above as for producers.

---

[288] Directive 2001/95/EC, Article 5.4.
[289] Directive 2001/95/EC, Article 5.2.

15

PRODUCTS LIABILITY

A. Introduction

'Products liability' may be broadly defined as the liability of manufacturers and **15.01** other suppliers of products for injury or loss caused by their defective condition.[1] Liability for medicinal products is thus a particular instance of liability for products

---

[1] *Cf* the 'civil liability of manufacturers and others where damage or loss is caused by products which fail to meet the standards claimed expressly or impliedly for them or which are defective or otherwise dangerous'. Miller, C and Lovell, P, *Product Liability* (London, 1977) 1. 'The term "products liability" is an American invention. It does not describe a distinct category of law in the United Kingdom'. Royal Commission on Civil Liability and Compensation for Personal Injury (the 'Pearson Commission') (Cmnd 7054, 1978) vol 1, para 1216.

which cause injury because of the way in which they have been designed, manu-factured, or marketed. In the 1960s an elaborate regulatory structure was estab-lished for medicines, in the wake of the thalidomide tragedy.[2] The protracted litigation over thalidomide proved to be a catalyst for proposals during the 1970s, both in the United Kingdom[3] and in Europe,[4] to introduce strict liability regimes for injuries caused by defective products. The culmination of this activity was the European Community Directive on Products Liability (1985),[5] as implemented in England by Pt I of the Consumer Protection Act 1987 (hereafter the CPA).[6]

15.02   Products liability may arise by virtue of contract, tort, or statute. In contract, re-flecting the development of implied warranties in the nineteenth century, the main focus has been on merchantability—the condition or *quality* of the product in the light of presumed consumer expectations. Tort law, on the other hand, has stressed the defendant's *conduct* and society's interest in product *safety*. The dis-tinction is somewhat superficial, since 'almost all defects in goods can at some level be more accurately described as attributable to human agency'.[7] Most im-portantly now, in the guise of strict liability, a new statutory framework for the protection of consumers has emerged in the CPA. The CPA appears to blur the tort/contract divide by defining product *safety* in terms of consumer expectations. Defectiveness under the Act depends on proof that 'the safety of the product is not such as persons generally are entitled to expect . . .'.[8] However, it would seem that the CPA's conception of 'defectiveness' is rooted in product safety, rather than merchantability.[9]

15.03   The different sources of civil liability do not blend into a single, coherent body of legal doctrine. Leaving to one side the questionable logic of differentiating between the provision of products and services,[10] the CPA provides only an alternative or

---

    [2] Medicines Act 1968.

    [3] The Law Commission and the Scottish Law Commission, *Liability for Defective Products* Cmnd 6831, 1977); Royal Commission on Civil Liability and Compensation for Personal Injury (n 1 above), ch 22.

    [4] EEC Draft Directive on products liability [1976] OJ C241 (first draft), [1979] OJ C271 (sec-ond draft); Strasbourg Convention on Products Liability in Regard to Personal Injury and Death, (1977).

    [5] Directive (EEC) 85/374 on the approximation of the laws, regulations and administrative pro-visions of the Member States concerning liability for defective products [1985] OJ L210/29.

    [6] As amended by the Consumer Protection 1987 (Product Liability)(Modification) Order 2000, SI 2000/2771. See further n 226 below. The CPA does not apply to damage caused by defects in products supplied before 1 March 1988: CPA, s 50(7); CPA (Commencement No 1) Order 1987, SI 1987/1680.

    [7] Stapleton, J, *Product Liability* (London, 1994) 329.

    [8] s 3(1).

    [9] Department of Trade and Industry, 'Implementation of the EC Directive on Product Liability. An Explanatory and Consultative Note' (London, 1985), para 55. *Cf* EEC Draft Directive (first draft) (n 4 above), Explanatory Memorandum, Art 4.

    [10] See generally, Stapleton, J, 'Three Problems with the New Product Liability', in Cane, P and Stapleton, J (eds), *Essays for Patrick Atiyah* (Oxford, 1991), ch 11.

additional basis for a cause of action in damages.[11] Actions in tort and contract remain available for situations either not covered or less adequately covered by the 1987 Act. In addition to providing these civil actions, the law endeavours to enhance consumer protection by means of regulatory measures which contain criminal penalties for failure to comply with specified standards.[12] In recent years, such provision has become more elaborate following a series of EEC initiatives.[13]

Effective medicines are seldom risk-free. Determining whether or not they have **15.04** caused harm can present difficulties which, in the case of other products, either do not arise or are typically less pronounced. Problems include the unpredictable long-term or delayed effects of certain drugs,[14] idiosyncratic or allergic reactions, the synergistic effects of some drug interactions with other drugs or foods, and the difficulty of distinguishing the effects of medication from the natural progression of illness.[15] A causal complication of a different kind may arise when vaccines and, increasingly, drugs are generically prescribed, with the result that their source of origin is not readily identifiable.[16]

The scope of products liability in the medical sphere may also be affected by the way **15.05** in which a particular substance is legally defined. For example, though the common law has resisted classifying human bodies as 'goods',[17] there are unresolved doubts over whether human organs can be so regarded, or whether supplying bodily fluids

---

[11] CPA, s 2(6). See *AB v South West Water Services Ltd* [1993] QB 507 (CA), where, as well as claiming under the CPA, s 2(1), the plaintiffs pleaded breach of statutory duty; *Rylands v Fletcher*, breach of contract, nuisance, and negligence.

[12] eg under the Medicines Act 1968. The provisions of this Act may not be construed as conferring a civil right of action in respect of contraventions of the Act or of any regulations or order made under it: s 133(2). By contrast, safety regulations made under the Consumer Protection Act 1961 and the Consumer Safety Act 1978 did entitle a person injured by certain goods, which included cosmetics and asbestos products, to bring an action for breach of statutory duty against any seller in the chain of supply. These two Acts (and the Consumer Safety (Amendment) Act 1986) were repealed by the CPA, which has extended the regulation-making powers and which does permit an individual injured by infringement of a safety regulation to bring an action for breach of statutory duty: CPA, s 41. See eg the Active Implantable Medical Devices Regulations 1992, SI 1992/3146, as amended by SI 1995/1671. However, 'licensed medicinal products' and tobacco are not subject to regulatory control under the CPA: CPA, s 10(7)(e) and s 10(7)(f), respectively. See also, Miller, C, 'Consumer Protection' in Guest *et al* (eds), *Benjamin's Sale of Goods* (6th edn, London, 2002), ch 14, and O'Grady, J *et al*, *Medicines, Medical Devices and the Law* (London, 1999).

[13] *Benjamin's Sale of Goods* (n 12 above), para 14–001. See esp Product Safety Directive (EEC) 92/59 [1992] OJ L228/24, as implemented by the General Product Safety Regulations 1994, SI 1994/2328. See generally Ch 14, above.

[14] See eg *Sindell v Abbott Laboratories* (1980) 26 Cal 3d 588 (DES).

[15] DHSS, *Product Liability: Special Features of the Medical Sector*, Medicines Division Consultation Paper (London, 1979); Newdick, C, 'Defective Medicines: Unavoidable Danger or Unacceptable Risk?' (1990) 1 *Intl J of Risk and Safety in Medicine*, 195.

[16] As in *Loveday v Renton and Wellcome Foundation Ltd* [1990] 1 Med LR 117 (pertussis). On generics, see *Mann and Close v Wellcome Foundation Ltd* (1989, QBD); *Sindell v Abbott Laboratories* (n 14 above).

[17] See further para 15.20 below.

could connote a sale of goods rather than a supply of services. Although it is unclear whether or not transplants and blood transfusions constitute a supply of 'goods' within the Supply of Goods and Services Act 1982,[18] it has been accepted that blood and blood products for transfusion are 'products' within the meaning of the CPA and Directive 85/374.[19] Similarly, the applicable legal principles will vary according to a product's statutory classification and the manner in which it has been supplied. It may have been sold as a 'medicinal product'[20] on the General Sale List (GSL) or as a pharmacy medicine (P). Alternatively, it may have been a Prescription Only Medicine (POM)[21] made available either under the legal regime for drug prescription under the National Health Service or on private prescription.[22] In some circumstances, it would have been directly administered by way of injection.

15.06   The term 'product(s) liability' is primarily associated with claims against manufacturers or producers. However, in attributing or apportioning responsibility for harm it may be necessary to consider other suppliers in the chain of distribution, including the retailer. In the case of medicinal products, liability may attach to retail or hospital pharmacists and to doctors. In principle, it would seem that an action could also be brought against a regulatory agency with a licensing function,

---

[18] Bell, AP, 'The Doctor and the Supply of Goods and Services Act 1982' (1984) 4 LS, 175, 178. See further para 15.21 below.

[19] The point was conceded in *A v National Blood Authority* [2001] 3 All ER 289, 307 (Hepatitis C). See para 15.56 below.

[20] Under the Medicines Act 1968, a 'medicinal product' is 'any substance or article (not being an instrument, apparatus or appliance) . . . for use wholly or mainly' for a 'medicinal purpose', that is, to treat, prevent, or diagnose disease; to ascertain the existence, degree, or extent of a physiological condition; for contraception; to induce anaesthesia, or otherwise prevent or interfere with the normal operation of a physiological function: s 130(1), (2). And see Codified Pharmaceutical Directive (EEC) 2001/83, Art 1. Some biological, surgical, dental, and ophthalmic materials which were medicinal products within the Act or its subordinate legislation are now controlled under the CPA. They include IUDs and contact lens fluids. See Council Directive (EEC) 93/42 and the Medical Devices Regulations 1994, SI 1994/3017. In vitro diagnostic medical devices are covered by Council Directive (EC) 98/79, given effect to by the In Vitro Diagnostic Medical Devices Regulations 2000, SI 2000/1315. The Medical Devices Regulations 1994, SI 1994/3017 are amended by the In Vitro Diagnostic Medical Devices Regulations 2000, Sch 1. Cosmetics may be defined by the Medicines Control Agency as 'medicinal products' by virtue of their remedial or curative functions. See Medicines Control Agency, *A Guide to What is a Medicinal Product* (London, 2002). On judicial review of classification, see *R v Medicines Control Agency, ex p Pharma Nord (UK) Ltd* [1998] 3 CMLR 109. And see Longley, D, 'Who is Calling the Piper? Is there a Tune? The New Regulatory Systems for Medical Devices in the United Kingdom and Canada' (1998) 3 Med L Int 319.

[21] See Medicines Act 1968, s 51 (General Sale list), and s 58 (Prescription Only medicinal products). See also the Medicines (Prescription Only, Pharmacy and General Sale) Amendment Order, SI 1989/1852, and the Medicines Act 1968, s 58A, inserted by the Medicines Act 1968 (Amendment)(No 2) Regulations 1992, SI 1992/3271, reg 2 (implementing Council Directive (EEC) 92/26 [1992] OJ L113/5). See generally Medicines Control Agency, *Towards Safe Medicines* (revised edn, London, 1997).

[22] For an overview of the licensing regime, see Scott, C and Black, J (eds), *Cranston's Consumers and the Law* (London, 2000) 469–503.

such as the Licensing Authority and its advisory bodies established under the Medicines Act 1968. Although such an action could not be for breach of statutory duty,[23] it might lie in negligence, a possibility contemplated by the Court of Appeal in respect of haemophiliacs injured by blood products contaminated with HIV.[24]

Though numerous claims of drug-induced injury have been settled, no UK court has yet held a pharmaceutical company liable in negligence for injuries caused by a medicinal product. There has been scant judicial analysis of what constitutes an absence of 'reasonable care' by pharmaceutical manufacturers and still only a handful of reported cases of any description involving Pt I of the CPA. However, substantive aspects of medical products liability were examined at length in the important first instance decision of *A v National Blood Authority*, where, significantly, the European Directive was the almost exclusive focus of analysis.[25] Meanwhile, a number of drug injury claims have highlighted the procedural complexity and funding difficulties commonly associated with group actions.[26]   **15.07**

B. Contractual Liability

Historically, the boundaries of liability for injurious products largely derive from the law on sales warranties. Since, under the doctrine of privity, the seller of a defective product is, at common law, contractually liable only to the buyer, in practice contract has limited relevance to claims for harm caused by medicinal products.[27] Pharmaceutical companies very rarely have a contractual relationship   **15.08**

---

[23] See n 12 above.

[24] *Re HIV Haemophiliac Litigation* (1998) 41 BMLR 171 (decided in 1990), where the Committee on Safety of Medicines, the Licensing Authority and the Department of Health were joined as defendants. See also *Brown v Alberta* [1994] 2 WWR 283 (Alta QB); cf *H v Royal Alexandra Hospital for Children* [1990] 1 Med LR 297 (SC of NSW). Arguably, however, the only duty (of care) is to the public at large: Barton, A, 'The Basis of Liability of the Licensing Authority and its Advisers under the Medicines Act 1968 to an Individual' in Goldberg, A and Dodds-Smith, I (eds), *Pharmaceutical Medicine and the Law* (London, 1991). See further para 15.46 below.

[25] [2001] 3 All ER 289. See Hodges, C, 'Compensating Patients' (2001) 117 LQR 528; Howells, G and Mildred, M, 'Infected Blood: Defect and Discoverability—A First Exposition of the EC Product Liability Directive' (2002) 65 MLR 95. See further paras 15.49, n 194, 15.58 and 15.67 below. Only one case on liability under the CPA has reached the Court of Appeal: *Iman Abouzaid v Mothercare (UK) Ltd*, The Times, 20 February 2001 (CA). And see *Worsley v Tambrands Ltd* [2000] PIQR P95; *Richardson v LRC Products Ltd* [2000] Lloyd's Med Rep 280, and *Foster v Biosil Ltd* (2000) 59 BMLR 178. See also *AB v South West Water Services Ltd* [1993] QB 507 (CA). For the ECJ ruling on the UK formulation of the 'development risks' defence in the CPA, s 4(1)(e), see paras 15.65–15.68. below. See also Mildred, M, 'The Impact of the Directive in the United Kingdom' in Goyens, M, *Directive 85/374/EEC on product liability: ten years after* (Louvain-la-Neuve, 1996) 37–57.

[26] See further para 15.71 and n 284 below.

[27] *Dunlop Pneumatic Tyre Co v Selfridge & Co Ltd* [1915] AC 847; *Daniels and Daniels v R White*

with consumers for the supply of goods, unless they are private patients buying medical equipment direct from the manufacturer. Patients injured by the more potent drugs will usually have obtained them through NHS prescription. In such circumstances there is no contract with the prescribing doctor, or with the pharmacist, who is statutorily obliged to dispense drugs on presentation of a prescription and payment of any fixed charge.[28] A pharmacist could however be liable in contract for injury caused by privately prescribed drugs or by non-prescription medicines sold over-the-counter. Equally, a doctor or hospital supplying drugs or other medical materials privately could be contractually liable.[29]

1. General Principles of Liability

15.09 Sales of medicinal products, being subject to the common law and statutory principles generally applicable to consumer sales, can give rise to liability for innocent misrepresentation[30] or breach of contract. In addition to grounding a claim for the breach of any express or implied terms at common law, such transactions are subject to the implied terms of the Sale of Goods Act 1979 (hereafter the SGA 1979), which in essence consolidates the Sale of Goods Act 1893. Thus the seller can be held liable if the goods sold do not correspond with their description,[31] or do not meet the 'quality conditions', either because they are not of 'satisfactory quality'[32] or not fit for their particular purpose.[33] Liability for breach of the implied terms is

---

& Sons Ltd and Tarbard [1938] 4 All ER 258; *Woodar Investment Development Ltd v Wimpey Construction UK Ltd* [1980] 1 WLR 277 (HL). The Contracts (Rights of Third Parties) Act 1999 has little or no application to claims for personal injury resulting from defective medicines, but could, on appropriate facts, apply where damage was caused by medical equipment made to order for a retailer by a manufacturer. Contrast the relaxation of the privity rule in the US Uniform Commercial Code s 2–318, extending the seller's liability for breach of warranty to other members of the purchaser's household (including guests); cf *Henningsen v Bloomfield Motors Inc* 161 A 2d 69 (1960), and most importantly, *Greenman v Yuba Power Products Inc* 377 P 2d 897 (1963), where 'strict' liability in tort heralded the widely adopted rule in s 402A of the Restatement (Second) of Torts (1965), making commercial sellers strictly liable to the ultimate user or consumer for physical harm caused by 'unreasonably dangerous' products. See now Restatement (Third) of Torts: Products Liability (1998), s 2, which restores a negligence standard for design and marketing defects, preserving strict liability only for manufacturing defects. See further Owen, D, 'Products Liability Law Restated' (1998) 6 Consumer LJ 161.

[28] *Pfizer Corporation v Ministry of Health* [1965] AC 512, 535–6, *per* Lord Reid; *Appleby v Sleep* [1968] 1 WLR 948, 954–5.

[29] In such cases, liability can in principle move back up the chain of supply via third-party proceedings and successive indemnities. See para 15.16 below.

[30] Misrepresentation Act 1967, s 2(1).

[31] s 13(1). 'Description' is construed broadly to include the purpose and use to which goods are put; cf *Holmes v Ashford* [1950] 2 All ER 76 (CA); *Kubach v Hollands* [1937] 3 All ER 907.

[32] Sale and Supply of Goods Act 1994, s 1. The term 'satisfactory quality' has replaced the long-established expression 'merchantable quality' (SGA 1979, s 14(2)), which had been criticised as outmoded and inappropriate for consumer transactions: Law Commission, *Sale and Supply of Goods* (London, 1987) paras 2.9 and 2.10.

[33] SGA 1979, s 14(3).

'strict', there being no need to prove fault or negligence on the part of the vendor.[34] There are comparable provisions regarding contracts for services in the course of which goods are 'supplied', in the Supply of Goods and Services Act 1982 (hereafter the SGSA).[35]

Where a medicinal product is defective because of a manufacturing fault there **15.10** may be a breach of the implied condition of satisfactory quality, namely, that the goods 'meet the standard that a reasonable person would regard as satisfactory'.[36] For such liability to arise, there is no need for the buyer to have relied on the seller's skill or judgment. In principle this provision could also ground liability for unforeseen side effects resulting from defective design. However, it might be deemed unreasonable to expect drugs not to present any such dangers, and it would often be difficult to demonstrate that unavoidable risks of a powerful drug are incompatible with 'satisfactory quality'.

As regards fitness for purpose, inability of the seller to detect an unforeseen side ef- **15.11** fect is not in principle a defence.[37] However, 'where the circumstances show that the buyer does not rely, or that it is unreasonable for him to rely, on the skill or judgment of the seller . . .', the implied condition is inapplicable.[38] The onus is on the seller to show that there was no such reliance. Thus a dispensing pharmacist might be able to show that the implied condition was negated by a private patient's reliance on the judgment of the prescribing doctor. In addition, no liability arises in respect of the buyer's unexpected sensitivity unless it has been expressly or impliedly made known to the seller.[39] A pharmacist would therefore not normally be liable if unaware of a customer's abnormal condition or allergy.[40]

Since both of the 'quality conditions' refer to 'the goods supplied under the con- **15.12** tract', liability can arise in respect of packaging, containers, and instructions which render goods of unsatisfactory quality and/or unfit for their particular purpose(s).[41] However, the mere fact that a drug is potentially harmful will not ground liability if it is safe when taken according to the instructions.

---

[34] *Frost v Aylesbury Dairy Co Ltd* [1905] 1 KB 608 (CA). See also *Kendall (Henry) and Sons (a firm) v William Lillico and Sons Ltd* [1969] 2 AC 31, 84, *per* Lord Reid; *Vacwell Engineering Co Ltd v BDH Chemicals Ltd* [1971] 1 QB 88.

[35] See paras 15.18 and 15.19 below.

[36] SGA 1979, s 14(2A) and (2B), as amended by the Sale and Supply of Goods Act 1994, s 1.

[37] *Aswan Engineering Establishment Co v Lupdine Ltd* [1987] 1 WLR 1 (CA); *Hill (Christopher) Ltd v Ashington Piggeries Ltd* [1972] AC 441, 498; *Frost v Aylesbury Dairy Co Ltd* [1905] 1 KB 608 (CA); *Kendall (Henry) and Sons (a firm) v William Lillico and Sons Ltd* [1969] 2 AC 31; cf 'it is well settled that the implied condition as to fitness extends to latent defects': *Young and Marten v McManus Childs Ltd* [1969] 1 AC 454, 479, *per* Lord Wilberforce.

[38] SGA 1979, s 14(3).

[39] *Griffiths v Conway (Peter) Ltd* [1939] 1 All ER 685 (CA) (sale); cf *Ingham v Eves* [1955] 2 QB 366 (CA) (work and materials).

[40] For constructive knowledge, see Atiyah, P, *Sale of Goods* (10th edn, Adams, J, London, 2001), 196.

[41] *Vacwell Engineering Co Ltd v BDH Chemicals Ltd* [1971] 1 QB 88; *Wormell v RHM Agricultural (East)* [1987] 1 WLR 1091 (CA); *Amstrad plc v Seagate Technology Inc* (1997) 86 BLR 34.

15.13 Unlike the condition as to description, the quality conditions apply only to goods sold 'in the course of a business'.[42] This expression would appear to cover transactions undertaken by a private hospital. The position with regard to NHS hospitals is less clear. A statutory provision making records relating to a 'business' admissible in criminal proceedings has been held not to apply to the medical records of an NHS hospital,[43] on the ground that its commercial functions were ancillary to its main purpose. However, under legislation concerned to promote consumer protection, which defines a 'business' to include a 'profession' and the activities of a 'public authority',[44] there is a strong case for regarding the commercial transactions of NHS hospitals (a fortiori as Trusts), as taking place 'in the course of a business'.[45]

2. Exclusion of Liability

15.14 The right of the parties to a contract to exclude or restrict the implied conditions of description, satisfactory quality and fitness for purpose in the SGA 1979 is subject to the provisions of the Unfair Contract Terms Act 1977 (hereafter the UCTA).[46] Consequently, as regards sales 'in the course of a business',[47] any such exclusion or restriction is unenforceable against a party who 'deals as a consumer',[48] and enforceable only if 'reasonable' in other transactions.[49] More generally, a party cannot by reference to a term of the contract exclude or restrict liability for death or bodily injury caused by negligence.[50]

3. Privity and Collateral Contracts

15.15 By virtue of the doctrine of privity,[51] the consumer-purchaser of a medicinal product will not normally have a contractual right of action against the manufacturer unless there is a collateral contract between them. Only rarely have the courts so construed agreements arising from manufacturers' representations about their products.[52] Although in *Carlill v Carbolic Smoke Ball Co*[53] the defendants were

---

[42] SGA 1979, s 14(2), (3).

[43] Criminal Evidence Act 1965, s 1(1)(4); *R v Crayden* [1978] 1 WLR 604, 609 (CA).

[44] SGA 1979, s 61(1).

[45] See *Davies v Sumner* [1984] 1 WLR 1301 (HL); *Roberts v Leonard* (1995) 14 Tr LR 536; *Benjamin's Sale of Goods* (n 12 above), 11–046; cf *E v Australian Red Cross Society* (1991) 105 ALR 53 (FC) (blood contaminated with HIV): public hospital marginally engaged in business activities a 'trading corporation' within the Commonwealth Trade Practices Act 1974. Cf CPA s 45(1) (n 223 below).

[46] SGA 1979, s 55(1).

[47] UCTA, s 1(3)(a).

[48] UCTA, s 6(2) and s 12.

[49] UCTA, s 6(3).

[50] UCTA, s 2(1).

[51] See para 15.08 above.

[52] eg *Wells (Merstham) Ltd v Buckland Sand and Silica Co Ltd* [1965] 2 QB 170: specific and personal assurance to buyer by manufacturer; cf *Shanklin Pier Ltd v Detel Products Ltd* [1951] 2 KB 854.

[53] [1893] 1 QB 256 (CA).

held liable on the basis of a very specific collateral warranty in their advertisement, even factual representations contained in promotional material are seldom construed as intended to have contractual effect.[54] A fortiori, English law has not followed those US decisions in which collateral contracts based on implied warranties of quality and fitness have been derived from the mere presence of goods on the market.[55]

However, the consumer-purchaser may in effect be compensated by the manufacturer via third-party proceedings and successive indemnities. Thus, harm caused by non-prescription products sold by retail pharmacists can result in contractual claims that move back up the chain of supply. Intermediaries may, of course, prove to be insolvent, uninsured, or unidentifiable. Suing them could also prove to be impracticable if they trade exclusively outside the jurisdiction.[56] In sales between non-consumers, the chain of liability may be broken by a 'reasonable' exemption clause.[57]   **15.16**

Though the seller of a defective product is liable in contract only to the purchaser, very occasionally purchasers have been treated as contracting agents for some other individual who has suffered injury.[58] In such situations, they may recover for their own resultant losses[59] or, arguably, as contracting expressly for the benefit of another.[60]   **15.17**

4. *Contracts Involving the Supply of Products: Supply or Services?*

Where a contract for private medical treatment is exclusively for the provision of services, at common law a doctor who has not been negligent will not normally be liable for injury.[61] Similarly, under the SGSA, there is an implied term that the supplier need do no more than carry out such services with 'reasonable care and skill'.[62] If, for example, an operation on a private patient for sterilisation has been unsuccessful, in the absence of negligence there will be no breach of contract   **15.18**

---

[54] *Lambert v Lewis* [1980] 2 WLR 299 (CA). Contrast the position in some US and Commonwealth jurisdictions: eg *Baxter v Ford Motor Co* 35 P 2d 1090 (1934); *Henningsen v Bloomfield Motors Inc* 161 A 2d 69 (1960); Rest. 2d para 402A (1965); *Murray v Sperry Rand Corporation* (1979) 96 DLR (3d) 113; *Leitz v Saskatoon Drug & Stationery Co Ltd* (1981) 112 DLR (3d) 106. And see Australia's Federal Trade Practices Act 1974 (Cth), s 76G. See also, Atiyah, *Sale of Goods* (n 40 above) 266–7.

[55] As in *Henningsen* (n 54 above); *cf* Miller and Lovell, *Product Liability* (n 1 above), 65 and Atiyah, *Sale of Goods* (n 40 above), 266–7. See also CPA, s 3(2)(a), para 15.57 and n 239 below.

[56] Though 'extended' jurisdiction over foreign manufacturers is provided for under RSC Ord 11: *Distillers Co (Biochemicals) Ltd v Thompson* [1971] AC 458.

[57] UCTA, ss 6(2) and 6(3). See *Lambert v Lewis* [1980] (n 54 above).

[58] See eg *Lockett v A & M Charles Ltd* [1938] 4 All ER 170.

[59] *Preist v Last* [1903] 2 KB 148 (CA).

[60] *Jackson v Horizon Holidays Ltd* [1975] 1 WLR 1468 (CA). See also *Woodar Investment Ltd v Wimpey UK Ltd* [1980] 1 All ER 571, 576–7, *per* Lord Wilberforce.

[61] Nathan, Lord, *Medical Negligence* (London, 1957), 10–11.

[62] SGSA, s 13.

unless the doctor has guaranteed a successful outcome.[63] When, however, a doctor supplies or administers drugs or other medical materials to a private patient, as when giving an injection or anaesthetic, or applying an ointment, it may not be clear whether the contract is primarily for the provision of services or for the supply of medicines. The same problem can arise when a private doctor (or hospital) supplies medical equipment, such as a prosthesis or other medical device. Even when such products are supplied, the doctor's professional role in diagnosis, advice and/or treatment will commonly be regarded as the dominant feature of the transaction, so that it is not viewed as comparable to a contract of sale.[64]

15.19   However, at common law, a contract which in substance is for the supply of work and materials may contain implied terms analogous to those applicable to sales.[65] More importantly, when goods are supplied (or administered) 'in the course of a business',[66] either by way of transfer, as in the case of drugs, prosthetics, dentures, and injections, or hire, as in the temporary use of splints or crutches, the contract would now be subject to the strict liability provisions of the SGSA. Essentially, as regards the quality and fitness for purpose of any such 'goods', these provisions replicate the SGA s 14(2) and s 14(3) in respect of goods 'transferred'[67] or 'hired'[68] to the patient. In practice, most medical contracts for work and materials involve transfer, as the patient becomes the owner of the materials used. In some instances of temporary use, however, the contract will be one of hire.[69]

5. Medical Products as 'Goods'

15.20   Most of the materials used in medicine are undoubtedly 'goods' which can be the subject of commerce, but the position regarding human body products has not been free from difficulty. Judicial abhorrence at the idea of defining human beings, alive or dead, as 'goods or materials'[70] raised doubts about the legal status of

---

[63]   *Eyre v Measday* [1986] 1 All ER 488 (CA); *Thake v Maurice* [1986] QB 644 (CA); cf *Grey v Webster* (1985) 14 DLR (4th) 706 (NBCQB).

[64]   *Benjamin's Sale of Goods* (n 12 above), para 1–046. And see Nathan *Medical Negligence* (n 61 above), 19. Cf case 353/85 *Commission v UK* [1988] STC 251. But note *Commissioners of Customs and Excise v Wellington Private Hospital Ltd* [1997] STC 445 (CA) (supply of drugs and prostheses to private hospital in-patients constitutes a separate supply of goods for the purposes of VAT).

[65]   *Samuels v Davis* [1943] KB 526 (CA); *Dodd v Wilson* [1946] 2 All ER 691. The more like sale the transaction, the stricter the implied obligations: *Young & Marten Ltd v McManus Childs Ltd* [1969] 1 AC 454, 476, *per* Lord Wilberforce. In many American jurisdictions, pharmacists, unlike other retailers, have been characterised as professionals providing a service and not subject to strict liability: eg *Murphy v ER Squibb and Sons Inc* 710 P 2d 247, 251–3 (1985).

[66]   SGSA, ss 4, 9 and 18(1); cf para 15.13 above.

[67]   SGSA, s 4.

[68]   SGSA, s 9.

[69]   See further Bell, A, 'The Doctor and the Supply of Goods and Services Act 1982' (n 18 above).

[70]   *Bourne (Inspector of Taxes) v Norwich Crematorium Ltd* [1967] 1 WLR 691, 695; *cf Williams v Williams* (1882) 20 Ch D 659, 662–3 and *Dobson v North Tyneside HA* [1997] 1 WLR 596 (CA). It is not certain that property rights could not exist in such materials at common law: *Benjamin's Sale of Goods* (n 12 above), 1-089; Skegg, P, 'Human Corpses, Medical Specimens and the Law of Property' (1976) 4 Anglo-American L Rev 412; *Doodeward v Spence* (1908) 6 CLR 406 (Aus).

transactions involving human organs and bodily fluids such as blood and semen; although, as noted, blood has been deemed a 'product' within the CPA and the European Directive.[71]

It is thus possible that organ transplantation and artificial insemination, as well as the transfusion of whole blood and blood-products, involve a supply of goods capable of giving rise to strict liability under the SGSA. The argument is most cogent where commercial supply of the substance in question is both long-established and socially accepted, as in the case of blood transfusion.[72] In the United States there has been widespread resistance to a strict liability approach, partly in recognition of the need for available and affordable transfusion. Nearly all American jurisdictions have followed *Perlmutter v Beth David Hospital*[73] in defining blood transfusion as a service which does not involve sale.[74] When *Perlmutter* was rejected in *Cunningham v MacNeal Memorial Hospital*,[75] many states enacted 'blood shield statutes' to the effect that supplying blood or blood products constituted a service 'for all purposes', so that neither the manufacturer nor anyone else in the supply chain would be subject to an implied warranty of merchantable quality.[76] Recent case law has made it clear that the blood shield statutes apply to blood infected with HIV.[77]

15.21

---

[71] See para 15.05 and n 19 above. See further Kennedy, I and Grubb, A, *Medical Law* (3rd edn, London, 2000) ch 15; Bell, AP, 'The Doctor and the Supply of Goods and Services Act' (n 18 above) 178; Atiyah, P, *Sale of Goods* (n 40 above), 25–6; Meyers, D, *The Human Body and the Law* (2nd edn, Edinburgh, 1990), ch 7.

[72] Trading in human organs is prohibited by the Human Organ Transplants Act 1989, s 1. See further Kennedy and Grubb, *Medical Law* (n 71 above)

[73] *Perlmutter v Beth David Hospital* 123 NE 2d 792 (1954).

[74] See eg *Coffee v Cutter Biological* 809 F 2d 191 (USCA) (1987).

[75] *Cunningham v MacNeal Memorial Hospital* 266 NE 2d 897 (SC of Ill) (1970).

[76] See eg *Miles Laboratories v Doe* 556 A 2d 1167 (Md CA) (1989). In *Belle Bonfils Memorial Blood Bank v Hansen* 579 P 2d 1158 (Colo Sup Ct) (1978), supply by a blood bank—as distinct from a hospital—was construed as a sale of goods permitting an action for strict liability and breach of warranty. However, in a subsequent hearing, blood and blood products were held to fall within Comment k of the Restatement (Second) of Torts, s 402A, which excluded the application of strict liability to 'unavoidably unsafe' products: *Belle Bonfils Memorial Blood Bank v Hansen* 665 P 2d 118 (Colo Sup Ct) (1983). Restatement (Third) of Torts (n 27 above) expressly excludes services, human blood and blood tissue: s 19, Comment c.

[77] *Hyland Therapeutics v Superior Court* 175 Cal App 3d 509, 220 Cal Rptr 590 (1985). See further Giesen, D, 'Liability for the transfusion of HIV-infected blood in comparative perspective' (1994) 10 PN 2. See also *E v Australian Red Cross Society* (1991) 105 ALR 53 (FC): blood transfused by hospital not an act 'in trade and commerce' where the defendants had not been paid for the blood as such. Cf *Pittman Estate v Bain* (1994) 112 DLR (4th) 257 (Ont Ct Gen Div); *ter Neuzen v Korn* (1995) 127 DLR (4th) 577 (SCC): no implied warranty of quality by doctor in contract to administer artificial insemination which included the supply of (infected) semen. And see Grubb, A and Pearl, D, *Blood Testing, AIDS and DNA Profiling* (Bristol, 1990) ch 5.

C. Tort: Negligence

1. The Duty of Care

15.22   The expression 'products liability' has most commonly been used to describe the liability in negligence of those who supply products in the course of a business. In practice, the primary target has been the manufacturer who by act or omission has failed to take reasonable care to avoid injury to the ultimate consumer. The classic formulation of the manufacturer's duty is the 'narrow rule' in *Donoghue v Stevenson*:

> A manufacturer of products which he sells in such a form as to show that he intends them to reach the ultimate consumer in the form in which they left him, with no reasonable possibility of intermediate examination, and with the knowledge that the absence of reasonable care in the preparation or putting up of the products will result in injury to the consumer's life or property, owes a duty to the consumer to take that reasonable care.[78]

(i) Who Owes The Duty?

15.23   The duty owed by manufacturers has been extended to cover anyone in the chain of distribution and supply.[79] Thus, in respect of drugs it could apply to the product licence holder, a subsequent distributor, the prescribing doctor or the dispensing pharmacist. Pharmacists, for example, may incur liability if they cause injury by negligently dispensing the wrong drug, or the wrong strength of drug.[80] Likewise, a doctor may be liable in negligence for injury attributable to a carelessly written prescription,[81] or which results from prescribing a drug without having taken reasonable steps to explore the risks of side effects, reactions with other drugs or contra-indications. In principle, it might also be possible to impose liability for negligence on the Licensing Authority and its expert committees.[82]

(ii) Products Sold

15.24   The 'narrow rule' in *Donoghue v Stevenson* represents no more than a particular instance of liability for negligence. There being no separate category of 'products liability' as such at common law, no need arises in cases based on negligence to define 'product'. Though Lord Atkin's dictum refers to 'products', the general principles of negligence liability have been interpreted as covering the whole range

---

[78] [1932] AC 562, 599, *per* Lord Atkin.
[79] eg *Watson v Buckley, Osborne, Garrett & Co* [1940] 1 All ER 174; *Fisher v Harrods Ltd* [1966] 1 Lloyd's Rep 500.
[80] eg *Prendergast v Sam & Dee Ltd* [1989] 1 Med LR 36 (CA) (doctor held 25 per cent liable; pharmacist 75 per cent). And see McKevitt, T, 'Doctors, Pharmacists and Prescriptions: The Standard of Care Owed to the Patient' (1988) 4 PN 185. See also Civil Liability (Contribution) Act 1978.
[81] ibid; *cf Dwyer v Roderick* (1983) 127 SJ 806 (CA).
[82] See paras 15.42–15.47 below.

of production-related negligent acts.[83] Similarly, there is no reason to confine liability to goods 'sold', as distinct, for example, from free samples distributed by a manufacturer.[84]

2. The Standard of Care

In general terms, manufacturers are under an obligation to exercise such care as is reasonable in all aspects of the production process under their control. Liability may arise from inadequate care in matters as diverse as research and design, manufacture, presentation, and instructions for use, including warnings about risks.[85] Determining the requisite standard has sometimes been described as an exercise in cost–benefit analysis,[86] centring on such well-established negligence criteria as magnitude of risk,[87] probability of harm,[88] the burden of taking adequate precautions,[89] and the social utility of the defendant's conduct.[90]

15.25

The attempt, in essence, to establish where the balance of social interest lies can be unusually difficult in the case of medicinal products, the full risks and benefits of which may not become apparent for many years, if at all. The anticipated utility of any given drug, and the advantages of its early availability, may or may not be outweighed by its potential for harm. The benefits of elaborate safety precautions may or may not outweigh the inhibiting effects on innovation of cost and delay.[91] A marginally more effective new drug may be inherently less safe than available alternatives.[92] Many otherwise valuable drugs present a significant risk to a minority of the public, and it has been suggested that a product which is safe for most people should be considered dangerous 'if it might affect other users who had a higher degree of sensitivity than normal, so long as they were not altogether exceptional'.[93]

15.26

---

[83] eg *Herschtal v Stewart and Arden Ltd* [1940] 1 KB 155; *Malfroot v Noxal Ltd* (1935) 51 TLR 551; *Howard v Furness Houlder Argentine Lines Ltd and A and R Brown Ltd* [1936] 2 All ER 781.

[84] *Hawkins v Coulsdon and Purley UDC* [1954] 1 QB 319, 333, *per* Denning LJ; cf *Griffiths v Arch Engineering Co Ltd* [1968] 3 All ER 217, 220. And see Miller and Lovell, *Product Liability* (n 1 above), 308–9.

[85] *Cartwright v GKN Sankey Ltd* [1972] 2 Lloyd's Rep 242, 259 (CA); *Devilez v Boots PP Pure Drug Co Ltd* (1962) 106 SJ 552.

[86] As notably articulated in American case law and literature. See *US v Carroll Towing* 159 F 2d 169, 173 (1947), *per* Judge Learned Hand. See further Posner, R, 'A Theory of Negligence' (1972) 1 J of Legal Studies 29, 33. And see Stapleton, *Product Liability* (n 7 above), chs 5 and 6.

[87] *Paris v Stepney Borough Council* [1951] AC 367; *Wright v Dunlop Rubber Co* (1972) 13 KIR 255.

[88] *Bolton v Stone* [1951] AC 850.

[89] *Latimer v AEC Ltd* [1953] AC 643. And see *PQ v Australian Red Cross Society* [1992] 1 VR 19.

[90] *Buchan v Ortho Pharmaceuticals (Canada) Ltd* (1986) 25 DLR (4th) 658, 668 (Ont CA).

[91] Newdick, C, 'The Impact of Licensing Authority Approval on Pharmaceutical Product Liability: A Survey of American and UK Law' (1992) 47 F & DLJ 41; Teff, H, 'Regulation under the Medicines Act 1968: A Continuing Prescription for Health' (1984) 47 MLR 303, 309–318.

[92] See *Nicholson v John Deere Ltd* (1986) 34 DLR (4th) 542, 549 (Ont HC).

[93] *Board v Thomas Hedley* [1951] 2 All ER 431, 432 (CA), *per* Denning LJ. See also *Griffiths v Conway (Peter) Ltd* [1939] 1 All ER 685; Miller and Lovell, *Product Liability* (n 1 above), 324–6. For the duty to warn, see paras 15.32 and 15.33 below.

(i) Common Practice

15.27 Whether or not the defendant's conduct is deemed negligent is judged by reference to the prevailing state of scientific and technical knowledge.[94] Conformity with industry standards or custom, though prima facie evidence of reasonable prudence on the part of a manufacturer,[95] is not dispositive.[96] A general indication of what constitutes appropriate pre-marketing research for pharmaceutical products is contained in the guidelines produced by the regulatory authorities (the Licensing Authority and its advisory bodies) and the industry (the Code of Practice for the Pharmaceutical Industry). However, compliance with recommended testing procedures, for example, is not ipso facto a defence in any given case. Non-compliance with accepted practice would be strong, though not conclusive, evidence of negligence.[97] Similarly, the views of expert official committees are relevant but not determinative.[98]

(ii) Compliance With Statutory Provisions

15.28 Even full compliance with statutory requirements does not conclusively preclude liability for negligence at common law.[99] Hence the issue of a product licence does not automatically constitute a defence to a claim.[100] However, the courts would be loath to impose a standard of care that effectively penalised compliance with specific, statutorily prescribed, standards,[101] and they would be reluctant to hold negligent a manufacturer who had been granted a product licence for a drug after having disclosed to the Licensing Authority all the information deemed relevant to its safety.[102]

---

[94] *Vacwell Engineering Co v BDH Chemicals* [1971] 1 QB 88; *Stokes v Guest, Keen and Nettlefold (Bolts & Nuts) Ltd* [1968] 1 WLR 1776, 1783; *cf Fuller v Baxenden Chemical Co Ltd* (1985, QBD): failure to update company literature in line with changed knowledge and practice of others; *Ogden v Airedale HA* [1996] 7 Med LR 153.

[95] *cf R v British Pharmaceutical Industry Association Code of Practice Committee* The Independent, 1 November 1990.

[96] *Morris v West Hartlepool Navigation Co* [1956] AC 552; *Cavanagh v Ulster Weaving Co Ltd* [1960] AC 145. Miller and Lovell, *Product Liability* (n 1 above), 264 *et seq.*

[97] *Chin Keow v Government of Malaysia* [1967] 1 WLR 813 (PC).

[98] *Thompson v Johnson and Johnson Pty Ltd* [1992] 3 Med LR 148, 171–2 (SC of Victoria, App Div).

[99] *Bux v Slough Metals Ltd* [1973] 1 WLR 1358 (CA); *Dickson v Flack* [1953] 2 QB 464; *Best v Wellcome Foundation Ltd* [1994] 5 Med LR 81 (Irish Sup Ct). As licence holders, pharmaceutical companies are subject to regulation under the Medicines Act 1968 and its subordinate legislation. See further Newdick, C, 'The Impact of Licensing Authority Approval on Pharmaceutical Product Liability: A Survey of American and UK Law' (n 91 above), 52.

[100] *cf* 65/65/EEC OJ 22, 9 Feb 1965, 369.

[101] *Budden v BP Oil and Shell Oil* (1980) 124 SJ 376 (CA); cf the defence under the CPA, s 4(1)(a) (paras 15.59 and 15.60 below).

[102] *cf R v Licensing Authority Established under Medicines Act 1968, ex p Smith, Kline & French Laboratories Ltd* [1989] 1 All ER 578, 590, *per* Lord Templeman.

(iii) Manufacturing Defects

Defects arising from error in the manufacturing process are relatively rare in the   **15.29**
pharmaceutical industry. Examples would include a failure to combine ingredients in the correct proportions, excessive potency and toxicity,[103] the presence of
some impurity or foreign body,[104] and deterioration of the product from contamination or faulty packaging.[105] Though the full burden of proof is formally on the
claimant,[106] once it has been proved that there is a defect in the product[107] which
probably did not occur after it had left the manufacturer's control,[108] there is an
'inference of negligence' akin to res ipsa loquitur, if not tantamount to automatic
liability.[109] In fact, the stronger the evidence that the defendant has a careful quality control system, the more likely is it that a particular defect will be attributed to
negligence in the production process.[110] In principle, if manufacturers have an appropriate system for ordering raw materials and components and adequate testing
and inspection procedures, they will not incur liability for the negligence of an independent contractor,[111] though occasionally the manufacturer's duty has been
treated as non-delegable.[112]

(iv) Design Defects

Manufacturers are liable for harm caused by their failure to take reasonable care to   **15.30**
ensure that a product has been safely designed.[113] Though they cannot, by definition, be liable in negligence for not knowing about undiscoverable defects, some
cases have suggested that a high standard of care is expected, especially in the research that goes into the design of intrinsically dangerous and novel products.[114]

---

[103] *Best v Wellcome Foundation Ltd* [1994] 5 Med L Rev 81 (Irish Sup Ct) (pertussis component in DTP vaccine).

[104] *cf Donoghue v Stevenson* [1932] AC 562; *Daniels and Daniels v R White & Sons Ltd and Tarbard* [1938] 4 All ER 258.

[105] eg *Fisher v Harrods Ltd* [1966] 1 Lloyd's Rep 500; *Adelaide Chemical & Fertilizer Co Ltd v Carlyle* (1940) 64 CLR 514; *Hill v James Crowe (Cases) Ltd* [1978] 1 All ER 812.

[106] eg *Mason v Williams and Williams Ltd* [1955] 1 All ER 808, relying on *Donoghue v Stevenson* [1932] AC 562, 622, *per* Lord MacMillan.

[107] *Grant v Australian Knitting Mills Ltd* [1936] AC 85; *cf Hill v James Crowe (Cases) Ltd* [1978] 1 All ER 812; *Shandloff v City Dairy Ltd* [1936] 4 DLR 712, 719 (Ont CA).

[108] *Mason v Williams and Williams Ltd* [1955] 1 All ER 808, *Evans v Triplex Glass* [1936] 1 All ER 283.

[109] *Lockhart v Barr* (1943) SC (HL) 1.

[110] *Grant v Australian Knitting Mills Ltd* [1936] AC 85, 101; *Hill v James Crowe (Cases) Ltd* [1978] 1 All ER 812, 816; *Carroll v Fearon* [1999] ECC 73.

[111] *Taylor v Rover Co* [1966] 1 WLR 1491.

[112] *Winward v TVR Engineering Ltd* [1986] BTLC 366 (CA); *Cynat Products Ltd v Landbuild (Investment and Property) Ltd* [1984] 3 All ER 513.

[113] *Hindustan Steam Shipping Co Ltd v Siemens Bros & Co* [1955] 1 Lloyd's Rep 167.

[114] eg *Vacwell Engineering Co Ltd v BDH Chemicals Ltd* [1971] QB 88, 109: liability imposed for failure 'to provide and maintain a system for carrying out adequate research into scientific literature to ascertain known hazards' and for failure to conduct such research. The defendants had based their

However, though the manufacturer is under a duty to keep abreast of medical and scientific discoveries,[115] proof that design defects are attributable to negligence is often elusive, and seldom more so than in the case of medical products.[116]

15.31 A major obstacle to proof of negligence in medical products litigation is that what counts as 'knowledge' can be both intrinsically problematic and complicated by the fact that scientists and medical researchers may legitimately hold conflicting views.[117] There will often be a grey area between speculation, hypothesis, or information, on the one hand, and 'hard' knowledge on the other,[118] and the courts are mindful of the need to guard against hindsight.[119] Also, though 'the law requires even pioneers to be prudent',[120] it recognises the importance attached to innovation. In determining the level of acceptable risk for new drugs, allowance will be made for the fact that they need to be potent to be useful and that there are practical limits on discovering risks at the stage of pre-market testing on relatively small populations in animal studies and clinical trials. By contrast with the approach of the courts towards manufacturing defects, a previous good design safety record is of distinct evidential value to the defendant.

(v) Marketing Defects

(a) Warnings and Instructions

15.32 An important aspect of due care in the supply of products is the provision of adequate instructions for their use and, where necessary, of warnings about risks of which the defendant has actual or constructive knowledge. 'Failure-to-warn claims are now the most common form of litigated product case in the US.'[121] Since the manufacturer is required to make available such information as will

---

research on several modern texts (including the standard work on the industrial hazards of chemicals) which did not mention the explosive hazard documented in earlier literature. *Cf Independent Broadcasting Authority v EMI Electronics Ltd and BICC Construction Ltd* [1981] 14 Build LR 1 (HL). And See Howells, G, *Comparative Product Liability* (Aldershot, 1993) 74–5; Newdick, C, 'The Future of Negligence in Product Liability' (1987) 103 LQR 288, 293–4.

[115] *Stokes v Guest, Keen & Nettlefold (Bolts & Nuts) Ltd* [1968] 1 WLR 1776, 1783; *Cartwright v GKN Sankey Ltd* [1972] 2 Lloyd's Rep 242, 259.

[116] See para 15.04 above.

[117] See Lee, R, 'Vaccine Damage: Adjudicating Scientific Dispute' in Howells, G (ed) *Product Liability Insurance and the Pharmaceutical Industry: An Anglo-American Comparison* (Manchester, 1991); Newdick, C, 'The Development Risk Defence of the Consumer Protection Act 1987' (1988) 47 CLJ 455, 462.

[118] See para 15.68 below.

[119] *Roe v Minister of Health* [1954] 2 QB 66, 86 (CA), *per* Denning LJ; cf *Thompson v Smiths Shiprepairers (North Shields) Ltd* [1984] 1 All ER 881, 894, *per* Mustill J; *Mann and Close v Wellcome Foundation Ltd* (1989), QBD.

[120] *Independent Broadcasting Authority v EMI Electronics Ltd and BICC Construction Ltd* (n 114 above), 28, *per* Lord Edmund-Davies.

[121] Stapleton, *Product Liability* (n 7 above), 252.

enable products to be used safely,[122] any warnings must be readily intelligible and commensurate with risks,[123] bearing in mind that informing the medical profession normally suffices in respect of prescription medicines. Risks, in turn, must not be minimised by promotional material.[124] The manufacturer would normally be expected to warn of a drug's inherent and irreducible risks, though there is no duty to warn of a danger which is either patent or a matter of common knowledge.[125] There can, however, be liability for injury resulting from reasonably foreseeable misuse which has not been warned against.[126] A warning or instructions may also be needed where the danger is known to the user, but not the means of avoiding the risk. At the same time, the manufacturer may have regard to such factors as the remoteness of any danger and the possibility of causing needless alarm.[127] Where there has been a total failure to warn there is little scope for defences such as contributory negligence[128] or volenti, since the user will normally have been unaware of any danger. In principle, there is some scope for them where an inadequate warning has been given.[129]

---

[122] *Kubach v Hollands* [1937] 3 All ER 907; *Holmes v Ashford* [1950] 2 All ER 76 (CA); *Devilez v Boots Pure Drug Co* (1962) 106 SJ 552.

[123] *Vacwell Engineering Ltd v BDH Chemicals Ltd* [1971] 1 QB 111 (CA) (varying [1971] 1 QB 88); cf *Ward v Hopkins* [1959] 3 All ER 225, 239 (CA).

[124] *Watson v Buckley, Osborne, Garrett & Co Ltd* [1940] 1 All ER 174; cf *Vacwell Engineering Ltd* (n 123 above); *Buchan v Ortho Pharmaceuticals (Canada) Ltd* (1986) 25 DLR (4th) 658, 678–9 (Ont CA); *Rothwell v Raes* (1989) 54 DLR (4th) 193, 341–2 (Ont CA); *R v Roussel Laboratories; R v Good* (1989) 88 Cr App R 140. By virtue of an EC Directive on labels and leaflets, the provision of package leaflets for human medicinal products is now obligatory, unless all the required information is on the pack or label: Council Directive (EEC) 92/27 [1992] OJ L113/8, as implemented by the Medicines (Labelling) Amendment Regulations 1992, SI 1992/3273, amends SI 1976/1726; and the Medicines (Leaflets) Amendment Regulations 1992, SI 1992/3274, amends SI 1977/1055; the Medicines (Labelling and Leaflets) Amendment Regulations 1994, SI 1994/104, further amends SI 1976/1726 and SI 1977/1055, by implementing in part Council Directive (EEC) 92/73 [1992] OJ L297/8.

An EC Directive on advertising medicinal products for human use provides a common framework for advertising and promotion within the Community. It prohibits misleading advertising and the advertisement to the public of prescription only medicines. It also requires all advertising to conform with the terms of market authorisation: Council Directive (EEC) 92/28 [1992] OJ L113/13, as implemented by the Medicines (Advertising) Regulations 1994, SI 1994/1932 and by the Medicines (Monitoring of Advertising) Regulations 1994, SI 1994/1933, both amended by the Medicines (Advertising and Monitoring of Advertising) Amendment Regulations 1999, SI 1999/267. See generally, Bogaert, P, *EC Pharmaceutical Law* (London, 1992); Medicines Control Agency, *Towards Safe Medicines* (n 21 above).

[125] *Farr v Butters Bros & Co* [1932] 2 KB 606 (CA); *Devilez v Boots Pure Drug Co* (1962) 106 SJ 552; cf *Deshane v Deere & Co* (1993) 106 DLR (4th) 385 (Ont CA). See also Miller and Lovell, *Product Liability* (n 1 above), 239. In the US there is some support for the view that manufacturers should provide a warning for any users whom they know or should reasonably expect to be less informed than themselves about the dangers associated with the product. See eg *Micallef v Miehle Co* 39 NY 2d 376 (1976). See also Restatement (Third) of Torts (1998) (n 27 above), s 2 Comment i.

[126] *Hill v James Crowe (Cases) Ltd* [1978] 1 All ER 812.

[127] *Thompson v Johnson & Johnson Pty Ltd* [1992] 3 Med LR 148 (SC of Victoria, App Div) (tampons and toxic shock syndrome).

[128] But see *Devilez v Boots Pure Drug Co* (1962) 106 SJ 552.

[129] See Miller and Lovell, *Product Liability* (n 1 above), 293–6. See also *Cippolone v Liggett Group Inc* 112 S Ct 2608 (1992) (tobacco).

(b) Allergic Reactions

15.33 Particular difficulties surround the issue of allergic reactions. If a manufacturer knows or ought to know of the danger, in appropriate circumstances a warning would be required for the benefit of a vulnerable minority.[130] In the United States, courts have often relied on the 'narrow formulaic requirement that a certain percentage of persons must suffer an allergic reaction from the product before the manufacturer will be held liable'.[131] However, in any given case, whether or not failure to warn is reasonable could involve consideration of such factors as the severity of the consequences, the social value of the product, the availability of substitutes, and the claimant's access to information about allergy.[132]

(c) Causation

15.34 Inadequate warning or failure to warn is normally easier to establish than defective design, and plainly is more easily rectified. It will not, of course, result in liability without proof of causation. The court must be satisfied that the claimant would not have used the product had a proper warning been given.[133]

(vi) Continuing Duty of Care

15.35 If, after its potential for harm had become apparent, a marketed product caused injury, there could be liability in negligence for not having modified it or made its availability subject to a suitable warning,[134] for not having removed it from the market and, it would seem, for not having warned previous purchasers.[135] As regards prescription drugs, it would be negligent not to take reasonable steps to warn prescribing doctors[136] and presumably in certain instances not to issue

---

[130] *Ingham v Eves* [1955] 2 QB 366 (CA); *Parker v Oxolo Ltd and Senior* [1937] 3 All ER 524; *Chin Keow v Government of Malaysia* [1967] 1 WLR 813 (PC). See Newdick, C, 'Strict Liability for Defective Drugs in the Pharmaceutical Industry' (1985) 101 LQR 405, 412.

[131] Rogerson, C and Trebilcock, M, 'Products Liability and the Allergic Consumer: A Study in the Problems of Framing an Efficient Liability Regime' (1986) 36 University of Toronto LJ 52, 57. Typically an 'appreciable number': *Crotty v Shartenberg's New Haven Inc* 162 A 2d 513 (Conn, 1960).

[132] See Miller and Lovell, *Product Liability* (n 1 above), 324–6.

[133] *Buchan v Ortho Pharmaceuticals (Canada) Ltd* (1986) 25 DLR (4th) 658 (Ont CA); *H v Royal Alexandra Hospital for Children* [1990] 1 Med LR 297 (SC of NSW); *Davidson v Connaught Laboratories* (1980) 14 CCLT 251 (Ont HC). In *Buchan*, as in English law, the test of causation was subjective. See also *Hollis v Dow Corning Corporation* (1996) 129 DLR (4th) 609 (SCC). Presumably, where causation depends on what the prescribing doctor would have done if adequately warned, the test would be subjective to that doctor: Jones, M, *Medical Negligence* (3rd edn, London, 2003), 652–6.

[134] *Wright v Dunlop Rubber Co Ltd* (1972) 13 KIR 255, 272 (CA).

[135] *Walton v British Leyland UK Ltd* (1978) QBD, *Hobbs (E) (Farms) Ltd v Baxenden Chemical Co Ltd* [1992] 1 Lloyds Rep 54, 65; *Carroll v Dunlop Ltd* (1996) *Product Liability Intl*, Apr 1996, 58–9. *Cf Rivtow Marine Ltd v Washington Iron Works* [1973] 40 DLR (3d) 530, 536 (SCC). See also Restatement (Third) of Torts (1998) (n 27 above), ss 10 and 11.

[136] *Hollis v Dow Corning Corporation* (1996) 129 DLR (4th) 609 (SCC).

public warnings.[137] To this end, manufacturers need proper procedures for monitoring adverse reactions and product recall.[138]

(vii) Intermediate Examination

Lord Atkin described the manufacturer's liability for a defective product as contin- **15.36**
gent on there being 'no reasonable possibility of intermediate examination' before it
reaches the ultimate consumer.[139] In effect this requirement is simply an aspect of reasonable foreseeability, there being no liability[140] unless the manufacturer could reasonably have anticipated that the examination conducted by the intermediary would
be of such a type as to reveal the defect.[141] It is now clear that there must be a reasonable 'probability' of such examination if the manufacturer is to avoid liability.[142]

Plainly patients cannot normally be expected to have conducted the kind of in- **15.37**
spection of medicinal products that would reveal their potential for harm, but the
position of doctors and pharmacists is less clear.[143] The manufacturer will normally be absolved from liability where the pharmacist has failed to observe manifest defects connected with the production or distribution process, such as
deterioration or lack of sterility of products that have not been properly packaged
or stored. In addition, the manufacturer may be able to invoke the 'learned intermediary' rule against either the doctor or the pharmacist.[144]

(viii) The 'Learned Intermediary' Rule

An important aspect of the pharmaceutical manufacturer's duty of care is to see **15.38**
that the ultimate user is adequately warned about risks.[145] However, it is not
usually necessary for the relevant information to be communicated directly to the

---

[137] *Buchan v Ortho Pharmaceuticals (Canada) Ltd* (n 133 above), 667, 678.

[138] *McCain Foods Ltd v Grand Falls Industries Ltd* (1991) 80 DLR (4th) 252 (NBCA). For pharmaceuticals, the existence of such procedures is a prerequisite for the grant of a product licence:
Medicines (Standard Provisions for Licences and Certificates) Regulations 1971, SI 1971/972, Sch
1, para 6, as amended. On the 'yellow card' scheme for reporting adverse reactions to the CSM see
Teff, H, 'Regulation under the Medicines Act 1968: A Continuing Prescription for Health' (n 91
above). In 1999, the scheme was extended to include nationwide reporting by community pharmacists: (1999) 319 BMJ 1322.

[139] *Donoghue v Stevenson* [1932] AC 562, 599. See para 15.22 above.

[140] Subject to any possibility of apportionment under the Civil Liability (Contribution) Act 1978,
or of contributory negligence by the consumer.

[141] *Herschtal v Stewart & Ardern Ltd* [1940] 1 KB 155; *Griffiths v Arch Engineering Co (Newport)
Ltd* [1968] 3 All ER 217; *Aswan Engineering Establishment Co v Lupdine Ltd* [1987] 1 All ER 135,
153 (CA), *per* Lloyd LJ.

[142] eg *Paine v Colne Valley Electricity Supply Co Ltd* [1938] 4 All ER 803, 808–9; *Griffiths v Arch
Engineering Co Ltd* (n 141 above).

[143] As is that of certain regulatory bodies in regard to design defects. See paras 15.42–15.47 below.

[144] See Ferguson, P, 'Liability for Pharmaceutical Products: a Critique of the "Learned
Intermediary" Rule' (1992) 12 OJLS 59.

[145] See paras 15.32 and 15.33 above; cf *Thompson v Johnson and Johnson Pty Ltd* [1992] 3 Med LR
148 (SC of Victoria, App Div).

consumer when a product is to be used under expert supervision; adequate warning to a responsible intermediary normally suffices.[146] As regards prescription drugs, in many jurisdictions it has been held sufficient for the manufacturer to warn the doctor as 'learned intermediary'.[147] There is no express authority on the rule in England, but its spirit is reflected in the applicable regulatory regime. Though the 'standard labelling particulars' on directions for use and precautions required for OTC products[148] do not apply to 'dispensed medicinal products', a drug may not be promoted to doctors unless, within the preceding 15 months, they have received a copy of the manufacturer's data sheet specifying any necessary warnings or contra-indications.[149] A drug manufacturer cannot assume that doctors will have read all the relevant scientific literature: 'They rely on the drug companies to supply them with the necessary data.'[150]

15.39 Nevertheless, in any given case, doctors are still required to use their independent judgment in prescribing, based on their knowledge of the individual patient and the drug. Under English law, they have traditionally had considerable leeway as to what information they needed to disclose. By virtue of the '*Bolam* principle' they could normally discharge their duty in this respect by acting in accordance with any standard of practice recognised as proper by a responsible body of medical opinion. It followed that, in England, adherence to the 'learned intermediary' rule could in practice result in patients having less effective legal protection against failure to warn in respect of prescription drugs than in the case of the typically less powerful over-the-counter products.[151] There are however signs in recent case law, as well as in medical practice, of a more patient-oriented view of disclosure.[152]

---

[146] cf *Holmes v Ashford* [1950] 2 All ER 76 (CA).

[147] A term first used in *Sterling Drug, Inc v Cornish* 370 F 2d 82 (8th Cir) (1966). See eg *Reyes v Wyeth Laboratories* 498 F 2d 1264, 1276 (5th Cir) (1974); *Buchan v Ortho Pharmaceuticals (Canada) Ltd* (1986) 25 DLR (4th) 658, 680–1 (Ont CA) *per* Robins JA. Cf *H v Royal Alexandra Hospital for Children* [1990] 1 Med LR 297 (SC of NSW); *McKee v Moore* 648 P 2d 21 (Okla) (1982). See also Restatement (Third) of Torts (1998) (n 27 above), s 6 and Ferguson, 'Liability for Pharmaceutical Products: a Critique of the "Learned Intermediary" Rule' (n 144 above), 61.

[148] Medicines Act 1968, s 85(1) and the Medicines (Labelling) Regulations 1976, SI 1976/1726, as amended (see n 124 above).

[149] Medicines Act 1968, s 96 and the Medicines (Data Sheet) Regulations 1972, SI 1972/2076, as amended (see n 124 above).

[150] *Davidson v Connaught Laboratories* (1980) 14 CCLT 251, 276 *per* Linden J (Ont HC). Awareness that a report of an official advisory committee has been circulated to medical practitioners does not absolve the manufacturer from a common law duty to inform them: *Buchan v Ortho Pharmaceuticals (Canada) Ltd* (n 147 above), 680–1 *per* Robins JA. See also *Hollis v Dow Corning Corporation* (1996) 129 DLR (4th) 600 (SCC), (1993) 103 DLR (4th) 520 (BCCA), and Stapleton, *Product Liability* (n 7 above), 252–5.

[151] *Bolam v Friern Hospital Management Committee* [1957] 1 WLR 582; *Sidaway v Board of Governors of the Bethlem Royal Hospital and the Maudsley Hospital* [1985] AC 871. See Ferguson (n 144 above), 72.

[152] See especially *Pearce v United Bristol Healthcare NHS Trust* (1998) 48 BMLR 118, 124–5, *per* Lord Woolf MR. Cf *Bolitho v City and Hackney HA* [1998] AC 232. See Brazier, M and Miola, J, 'Bye-Bye Bolam: A Medical Litigation Revolution?' (2000) 8 Med L Rev 85.

Considerations of policy may argue against applying the 'learned intermediary' **15.40**
rule to certain medical procedures. For example, in the United States it has not always been applied to mass immunisation.[153] Some courts have stressed that voluntary participants in a procedure which benefits society at large should not be
deprived of a remedy against the manufacturer; that the injections are not necessarily administered by someone who is indisputably a 'learned intermediary', and
that, even when they are, there may be no 'individualized assessment' of risks and
benefits.[154] Nor does the rule invariably hold for the prescription of oral contraceptives, when the case for insisting on communication to the user is underlined
by the typically 'heightened participation' of patients in the decision; the danger
of doctors giving inadequate information about risks and allowing unmonitored
long-term and repeat prescriptions, and the elective, non-therapeutic nature of
the treatment.[155] American courts have, however, generally retained the 'learned
intermediary' rule for contraceptive devices.[156]

3. Proving Causation

In determining whether or not a medicinal product is responsible for harm, the **15.41**
problems of extrapolating from biochemical findings, animal studies and relatively small-scale tests on humans are frequently compounded by competing scientific views on evidence and the 'mismatch of legal and scientific notions of
causation'.[157] As a result, proof that on the balance of probabilities a given product caused or materially contributed to the claimant's injuries[158] is often elusive.[159]
Any suggestion that, following the decision in *McGhee v National Coal Board*,[160]

---

[153] *Davis v Wyeth Laboratories Inc* 399 F 2d 121 (9th Cir) (1968); *Reyes v Wyeth Laboratories* 498 F
2d 1264 (5th Cir) (1974).

[154] *Givens v Lederle* 566 F 2d 1341 (5th Cir) (1974).

[155] eg *Seley v GD Searle & Co* 423 NE 2d 831 (1981); *Lukaszewicz v Ortho Pharmaceutical
Corporation* 510 F Supp 961 (Wis) (1981); *Stephens v GD Searle & Co* 602 F Supp 379 (Mich)
(1985); *MacDonald v Ortho Pharmaceutical Corporation* 475 NE 2d 65 (Mass) (1985); *Odgers v
Ortho Pharmaceutical Corporation* 609 F Supp 867 (DC Mich) (1985). Cf *Buchan v Ortho
Pharmaceuticals (Canada) Ltd* (1986) 25 DLR (4th) 658, 670, 688–9 (Ont CA).

[156] *McKee v Moore* 648 P 2d 21 (Okla) (1982); contra *Hill v Searle Laboratories* 884 F 2d 1064 (8th
Cir) (1989).

[157] Lee, R, 'Vaccine Damage: Adjudicating Scientific Dispute'. See n 117 and para 15.31 above;
cf *Brock v Merrell Dow Pharmaceuticals Inc* 874 F 2d 307 (5th Cir) (1989). See also Goldberg, R,
'Scientific Evidence, Causation and the Law—Lessons of Bendectin (Debendox) Litigation' (1996)
4 Med L Rev 32.

[158] *Bonnington Castings Ltd v Wardlaw* [1956] AC 613.

[159] See eg *Kay v Ayrshire and Arran Health Board* [1987] 2 All ER 417 (HL) (penicillin and deafness). On pertussis, see eg *Loveday v Renton* [1990] 1 Med LR 117; *Rothwell v Raes* (1988) 54 DLR
(4th) 193, aff'd (1990) 76 DLR (4th) 280 (Ont CA). But see also *Best v Wellcome Foundation Ltd*
[1994] 5 Med LR 81 (Irish Sup Ct). And see Jones, *Medical Negligence* (n 133 above), 383–405;
Newdick, C, 'Strict Liability for Defective Drugs in the Pharmaceutical Industry' (1985) 101 LQR
405, 420–30. And see *Vadera v Shaw* (1999) 45 BMLR 162 (CA). See further Goldberg, R, 'The
Contraceptive Pill, Negligence and Causation: Views on *Vadera v Shaw*' (2000) 8 Med L Rev 316.

[160] *McGhee v National Coal Board* [1973] 1 WLR 1 (HL).

negligent conduct which materially increased the risk of injury would suffice to ground liability unless the defendant could show that it was not the cause has been rejected by the House of Lords. The burden is on the claimant to prove that the defendant's negligence was more likely than not to have caused or materially contributed to the injury, or, in exceptional circumstances, that it materially increased the risk of injury, as recently held by the House of Lords in *Fairchild v Glenhaven Funeral Services Ltd*.[161] The limitations of orthodox causation theory are also apparent in cases where injury is attributable to generic drugs but the claimant is unable to identify the manufacturer in question.[162]

4. Claims Against Regulatory Authorities

15.42 Legal responsibility for harm caused by products is not necessarily limited to those directly engaged in their production and distribution. It is convenient at this point to outline the statutory framework for the control of safety, quality and efficacy of medicines, with a view to considering whether any actions might lie against the relevant regulatory bodies.

15.43 Under the Medicines Act 1968,[163] the manufacture and distribution of medicines is regulated by a Licensing Authority (LA), comprising the UK Ministers of Health and Agriculture.[164] Its executive responsibilities in respect of the pharmaceutical sector are now discharged by the Medicines and Healthcare Products Regulatory Agency (MHRA). Under the 1968 Act, the right to grant a product licence or market authorisation is vested in the LA,[165] which receives advice from the Medicines Commission and various specialist committees.[166] These include the Committee on the Safety of Medicines (CSM), whose advice the LA may seek on questions of safety, quality, and efficacy of new medicines for human use.[167] If

---

[161] *Wilsher v Essex AHA* [1988] AC 1074; *Pickford v Imperial Chemical Industries plc* [1998] 1 WLR 1189 (HL), and *Fairchild v Glenhaven Funeral Services Ltd* [2002] 3 WLR 89 (HL). Cf *Snell v Farrell* (1990) 72 DLR (4th) 289 (Can SC). And see cases cited at n 159 above.

[162] See eg *Mann v Wellcome Foundation Ltd* (1989, QBD). For a radical and controversial solution based on defendant companies being held liable in proportion to their share of the national market, see *Sindell v Abbott Laboratories* 607 P 2d 924 (1980). Cf *Hymowitz v Eli Lilly & Co* 73 NY 2d 487 (1989); *Doe v Cutter Biological Inc* 971 F 2d 375 (1992): applied to HIV-infected Factor VIII, despite the fact that the manufactured product is not uniformly dangerous.

[163] In force from 1 September 1971. And see the Medicines for Human Use (Marketing Authorisations etc) Regulations 1994, SI 1994/3144.

[164] Medicines Act 1968, ss 1 and 6(1).

[165] ibid, s 6(1).

[166] ibid, s 2 and s 4, respectively. See further Medicines Control Agency, *Towards Safe Medicines* (n 21 above). See also HC Select Committee on Public Accounts, *Safety, Quality, Efficacy—Regulating Medicines in the UK* (26th Report, Session 2002–03). In April 2003, the MCA and the Medical Devices Agency combined to form a single executive agency, the Medicines and Healthcare products Regulatory Agency.

[167] ibid, ss 19–20. In respect of the safety, quality, and efficacy of products on the market before the Medicines Act 1968 took effect, the LA was advised by the Committee on the Review of Medicines. The Committee was disbanded in 1992.

the CSM provisionally advises against granting a licence, the applicant has a right to a hearing before it and, thereafter, a right of appeal to the Medicines Commission. Products to be marketed only in the United Kingdom continue to be validated by this national procedure. In addition, there has been a series of EC initiatives aimed at achieving a single European market in pharmaceuticals.[168] In 1995, following the establishment of the European Medicines Evaluation Agency (EMEA), a new dual EC licensing system was introduced. There is a centralised procedure, mandatory for most biotechnological medicines and optional for other high-technology medicines and those which contain a new active substance.[169] Applications are submitted to the EMEA and marketing authorisation is valid for all Member States. There is also a mutual recognition (decentralised) procedure for all other human medicines, compulsory since 1 January 1998, where it is sought to have an existing marketing authorisation recognised by one or more other Member States.[170]

Where injury is attributable to the defective design of medicinal products, it is unclear whether or not an action lies against the LA, which authorises their sale or supply, and against the other statutory bodies which advise on their safety, quality and efficacy, or where appropriate, against the Department of Health. No such right is conferred under the Medicines Act 1968, but neither does the Act purport to derogate from any pre-existing rights of claimants.[171] Bodies which license or advise on products do not attract liability under the CPA, as they are providers of services, not suppliers of products. Though the licensing authority and the CSM have occasionally been joined as defendants in negligence actions,[172] there has been no definitive ruling. The issue turns primarily on how far regulatory bodies enjoy immunity from suit in discharging their statutory duties. In accordance with the distinction adopted by Lord Wilberforce in *Anns v Merton*, discretionary policy decisions have been deemed non-justiciable and operational ones subject to a common law duty of care,[173] though the dividing line can be elusive.

15.44

---

[168] See Council Directive (EEC) 65/65 OJ No L 22, 9.2, as amended.

[169] See Council Regulation (EEC) 2309/93, as amended.

[170] Council Directive (EEC) 65/65 as amended, and Medicines for Human Use (Marketing Authorisations etc) Regulations 1994.

[171] Medicines Act 1968, s 133(2).

[172] See *Davies v Eli Lilly & Co* [1987] 3 All ER 94 (CA) (Opren), and *Re HIV Haemophiliac Litigation* (998) 41 BMLR 171 (decided in 1990) (contaminated blood), where the Court of Appeal considered that the plaintiffs had 'made out at least a good arguable claim in law based upon common law negligence' against, inter alia, the LA, the CSM and the Department of Health. See also *Brown v Alberta* [1994] 2 WWR 283 (Alta QB).

[173] See *Anns v Merton London Borough Council* [1978] AC 728, 754, *per* Lord Wilberforce; *Rowling v Takaro Properties* [1988] AC 473 (PC); *Home Office v Dorset Yacht Co Ltd* [1970] AC 1004, 1067–8, *per* Lord Diplock; *Sutherland Shire Council v Heyman* (1985) 157 CLR 424, 469, *per* Mason J. *Cf* on drug licensing: *R v Licensing Authority Established under Medicines Act 1968, ex p Smith, Kline & French* [1989] 1 All ER 578, 590 (HL); *Gray v US and Eli Lilly & Co* 445 F Supp 337 (DC Tex) (1978).

Promoting childhood vaccination has been treated as a non-justiciable exercise of statutory discretion, whereas claims that the DHSS had provided inadequate advice on contra-indications have been allowed to proceed, as have claims against the Department of Health in respect of Creutzfeldt-Jakob disease contracted following growth hormone treatment.[174]

15.45   It is uncertain, however, whether, or to what extent, the policy/operational distinction still obtains. Lord Wilberforce's speech in *Anns v Merton* was subjected to considerable criticism and subsequent appellate decisions tended to favour extensive immunity for regulatory bodies in the performance of their statutory functions.[175] Dicta to the effect that, in the context of consumer protection, it was perhaps 'best left to the legislature' to state the extent and limits of any such liability[176] seemed to reflect a general retreat from the expansion of liability for negligence. Regulatory agencies are only indirectly involved in the 'supply' of products, and the courts generally take a relatively strict approach to causation. In the context of prescribed drugs, they may be slow to find negligence against bodies which, in practice, exert only limited control over other potential defendants with more direct causal responsibility; though this argument seems less cogent when applied to those therapeutic categories for which NHS prescription is confined to drugs on the 'selected list'.[177]

15.46   Each case must now be considered in its context. There may be more scope for impugning the operational decisions of public bodies in respect of personal

---

[174] *Department of Health and Social Security v Kinnear* (1984) 134 NLJ 886 (the point was not ultimately pursued to judgment). cf *Rothwell v Raes* (1989) 54 DLR (4th) 193, 346 (Ont HC). But see *Bonthrone v Secretary of State for Scotland* 1987 SLT 34, where the nature and extent of such warnings was deemed a discretionary matter. Cf *Ross v Secretary of State for Scotland* [1990] 1 Med LR 235. Under the Vaccine Damage Payments Act 1979, as amended, anyone suffering at least 60 per cent disablement, who can establish that it was caused by vaccination against certain specified diseases, is entitled to no-fault compensation, up to a maximum of £100,000: Vaccine Damage Payments Act 1979 Statutory Sum Order 2000, SI 2000/1983 and Regulatory Reform (Vaccine Damage Payments Act 1979) Order, SI 2002/1592. S 6(4) of the Act provides for the deduction of such payment from any award based on negligence. For growth hormone treatment, see *N v UK Research Council: sub nom Creutzfeldt-Jakob Disease Litigation* [1996] 7 Med LR 309 and *Group B Plaintiffs v Medical Research Council* (1997) 41 BMLR 157.

[175] For criticism of *Anns v Merton* see eg *Yuen Kun-yeu v Attorney-General of Hong Kong* [1988] AC 175; *Murphy v Brentwood District Council* [1991] 1 AC 398. Cf *Hill v Chief Constable of West Yorkshire* [1989] AC 53; *X (Minors) v Bedfordshire County Council* [1995] 2 AC 633, and *Stovin v Wise, Norfolk County Council (Third Party)* [1996] AC 923, 951, *per* Lord Hoffmann. For the impact of the European Convention on Human Rights, see para 15.46, n 185 below.

[176] eg *Murphy v Brentwood District Council* [1991] 1 AC 398, 472, *per* Lord Keith; cf 491, *per* Lord Oliver, and *D and F Estates Ltd v Church Commissioners for England* [1989] AC 177, 193 and 210, *per* Lord Bridge.

[177] National Health Service (General Medical and Pharmaceutical Services) Amendment Regulations 1985, SI 1985/290, and ibid, Amendment No 2 Regulations 1985, SI 1985/540. For an example of a peripheral, causally remote defendant, see *Danns v Department of Health* [1998] PIQR P226 (CA). See further Grubb (1998) 6 Med L Rev 371. See also, *Smith v Secretary of State for Health* [2002] Lloyd's Rep Med 333—CSM not liable for failure to give post-marketing warning of risk to children from aspirin.

injury than for pure economic loss, the primary focus of judicial retrenchment. The courts have often laid much stress on 'statutory purpose' in determining whether or not a private right of action exists.[178] Traditionally, the role of statutory bodies has been to protect the general public interest rather than to confer rights on individuals,[179] though a duty to individuals is now more readily acknowledged where an agency has been established specifically to protect the public from dangerous practices.[180] Granted judicial disinclination to impugn discretionary decisions on the 'distribution of risks',[181] the public interest in early availability of valuable drugs must be set against the risks of allowing dangerous products onto the market, bearing in mind that protection of the public is the primary objective of the statutory bodies entrusted with the safety and licensing of medicinal products.[182] It has been suggested that 'a duty of care, by this test, would appear to be owed to the class of patients as a whole rather than individually'.[183] Equally, there may be 'cogent reasons of social policy'[184] for maintaining that such a 'statutory purpose' supports the case for granting a remedy to individual citizens.[185]

Assuming the existence of such a remedy, on whom would the duty lie and what standard of care would it entail? Though the LA is formally the ultimate decision-   **15.47**

---

[178] See eg *Governors of the Peabody Donation Fund v Sir Lindsay Parkinson & Co Ltd* [1985] AC 210.

[179] *Atkinson v Newcastle and Gateshead Waterworks Company* (1877) 2 Ex D 441 (CA).

[180] See *Swanson v The Queen in Right of Canada* (1991) 80 DLR (4th) 741 (Fed CA) *per* Linden J (commercial airlines).

[181] *Rowling v Takaro Properties Ltd* [1988] AC 473, 501 (PC), *per* Lord Keith. And see Craig, P, *Administrative Law* (4th edn, London 1999) 858–67.

[182] eg 'The principal task of the licensing authority is to protect the public . . . its duty [is] to safeguard the health of the nation . . . ': *R v Licensing Authority Established under Medicines Act 1968, ex p Smith Kline & French Laboratories* [1990] 1 AC 64, 103, *per* Lord Templeman. Cf Council Directive (EEC) 65/65 as amended: '. . . the primary purpose of any rules concerning the production and distribution of proprietary medicinal products must be to safeguard public health . . . '.

[183] Barton, A, 'The Basis of Liability of the Licensing Authority and its Advisers under the Medicines Act 1968 to an Individual' in Goldberg and Dodds-Smith (eds), *Pharmaceutical Medicine and the Law* (n 24 above), 99.

[184] *Murphy v Brentwood District Council* [1991] AC 398, 482, *per* Lord Bridge. Cf *Re HIV Haemophiliac Litigation* (n 172 above). And see Jones, *Medical Negligence* (n 133 above), 640, para 8-018.

[185] To strike out a negligence claim against a public authority on the ground that it did not owe the claimant a duty of care does not, however, infringe the claimant's right of access to a court under Art 6(1) of the ECHR, provided the striking out was not a procedural bar but resulted from the domestic court applying principles of substantive law: *Z v UK* (2002) 34 EHRR 3 and *TP and KH v UK* (2002) 34 EHRR 2, departing from *Osman v UK* (1998) 29 EHRR 245. Though the English courts have been very reluctant to strike out such claims since *Osman*—see *Phelps v Hillingdon London Borough Council* [2000] 3 WLR 776 (HL) and *Barrett v Enfield London Borough Council* [2002] AC 550—they can grant a defendant summary judgment when it is clear from the documentary evidence before them that the claimant has no real prospect of success: *S v Gloucestershire County Council* [2001] 2 WLR 90 (CA).

making body under the Medicines Act,[186] delegation of its advisory role to the CSM, as statutorily provided for,[187] should normally afford it protection against liability for negligence. It has also been argued that the CSM is, by the very nature of its composition, a 'responsible body of medical opinion' against which a finding of negligence is effectively precluded under the *Bolam* test.[188] It is not however self-evident that the *Bolam* principle, as pertaining to medicine, extends beyond the spheres of professional clinical practice and advice in the context of such practice.

D. Liability under the Consumer Protection Act 1987

1. The European Directive on Product Liability

15.48 The lengthy process of reassessing products liability law which began in the 1970s culminated in the European Directive on Product Liability of 1985,[189] on which Pt I of the Consumer Protection Act 1987 is substantially based.[190] The preamble to the Directive expressed concern that divergences between the laws of Member States could distort competition and result in differential protection of consumers. It also asserted that the imposition of liability without fault on producers was the fairest method of apportioning risk.[191] Accordingly, with a view to harmonising national laws, the Directive required all members of the European Community to introduce a strict liability regime for defective products.

15.49 Though Pt I of the CPA implements the EC Directive, there are some significant differences of wording, most notably on the 'development risks' defence.[192] English law subscribes to the doctrine of 'indirect effect', whereby any ambiguity in the domestic legislation which implements directives is, as far as possible, con-

---

[186] Medicines Act 1968, s 6.

[187] ibid, s 4.

[188] *Bolam v Friern HMC* [1957] 1 WLR 582. See Barton, A (n 183 above), 101. See also *AB v Tameside and Glossop HA* [1997] 8 Med L Rev 91, 98–9, *per* Brooke LJ, and Mildred, M, 'Responsibilities and Liabilities of Regulatory Agencies', in O'Grady, J *et al* (eds), *Medicines, Medical Devices and the Law* (London, 1999) 166–7.

[189] (EEC) 85/374. See generally Goyens, M (ed), *Directive 85/374/EEC on product liability: ten years after* (n 25 above).

[190] See Stapleton, *Product Liability* (n 7 above), ch 3. The Act's provisions extend to the whole of the UK. See Consumer Protection (Northern Ireland) Order 1987, SI 1987/2409. No liability arises under the Act in respect of goods put into circulation by the producer prior to 1 March 1988: CPA, s 50(7); SI 1987/1680.

[191] '. . . liability without fault on the part of the producer is the sole means of adequately solving the problem peculiar to our age of increasing technicality, of a fair apportionment of the risks inherent in modern technological production . . .'

[192] See paras 15.65–15.68 below. The term 'development risks' is normally used to refer to undiscoverable defects which come to light only after a product has been in use. It may be distinguished from 'state of the art', an expression which commonly signifies the most up-to-date technology and standards in a given industry. In both the Directive and the CPA, the defence actually refers to discoverability of the defect, not of a risk; Art 7(e) and s 4(1)(e), respectively.

strued so as to conform with Community law obligations.[193] In fact, the CPA itself states that Pt I of the Act 'shall have effect for the purpose of making such provision as is necessary in order to comply with the product liability Directive and shall be construed accordingly'.[194] This novel form of stipulation seemingly invites English courts to apply the Directive whenever the terms of the CPA appear to be incompatible with it. At the same time, assistance in construing ambiguous or obscure statutory wording may now be derived from clear Parliamentary statements of a Minister or other promoter of a Bill.[195] On the 'development risks' defence, in particular, several such statements suggest that the UK Government intended the Act to have a different meaning from that generally attributed to the Directive. The European Commission brought an action against the United Kingdom, under Article 169 of the EC Treaty, seeking a declaration of non-compliance. However, the European Court of Justice ruled that the UK formulation of the defence did not clearly conflict with the Directive.[196]

The European Court of Justice has held that non-discretionary provisions in a directive which are unconditional and sufficiently precise may be relied on directly by an individual against the state, if the state has failed to implement the directive correctly.[197] In addition, in certain circumstances, the state might be liable in damages.[198] In practice, the potential application of the doctrine of direct effect to products liability is severely limited. It could not apply to the 'development risks' defence, as the Directive permits derogation from it.[199] More generally, directives have direct effect only in so far as a state body is the defendant.[200] However, the doctrine could in principle apply to a health authority,[201] in the capacity, for example, of producer or supplier of pharmaceuticals, aids, appliances and blood products, or where equipment or products have been substantially modified by health authority employees.

15.50

---

[193] *Von Colson and Kamann v Land Nordrhein-Westfalen* [1986] CMLR 240; *Garland v British Railway Engineering Ltd* [1983] 2 AC 751, 771, *per* Lord Diplock; *Pickstone v Freeman plc* [1989] AC 66; *Litster v Forth Dry Dock & Engineering Co Ltd* [1990] 1 AC 456. And see Steiner, J, 'Coming to Terms with EEC Directives' (1990) 106 LQR 144.

[194] CPA, s 1(1). And see *A v National Blood Authority* [2001] 3 All ER 289, at [2]. Cf '[t]he judge in effect by-passed the wording of the Act and addressed himself to the Directive itself'. Howells, G and Mildred, M, 'Infected Blood: Defect and Discoverability—A First Exposition of the EC Product Liability Directive' (2002) 65 MLR 95.

[195] *Pepper (Inspector of Taxes) v Hart* [1993] AC 593.

[196] Case C-300/95 *European Commission v UK* [1997] All ER (EC) 481. See further paras 15.65–15.68 below.

[197] Case 103/88 *Fratelli Constanzo SpA v Commune di Milano* [1990] 3 CMLR 239, at [29]; Case 8/81 *Becker v Finanzamt Munster-Innenstadt* [1982] ECR 53. European Communities Act 1972, ss 2(1), (4).

[198] *Francovich v Italy* [1991] 1 ECR 5357, [1993] 2 CMLR 66.

[199] Art 15(1)(b). And see para 15.65 below.

[200] Case 152/84 *Marshall v Southampton and South-West Hampshire AHA,* [1986] 1 CMLR 688.

[201] ibid.

2. The Act

(i) The 'Strict Liability' Regime Under the CPA

15.51 A general principle of strict civil liability is contained in s 2(1) of the Act:

> Where any damage is caused wholly or partly by a defect in a product, every person to whom [s 2(2)] applies shall be liable for the damage.

The above wording points to the Act's stated focus on the condition of the product rather than on the conduct or state of mind of its producer. Once the claimant has proved that there is a 'defect' in the product and that the relevant damage was wholly or partly caused by it, the onus shifts to the defendant(s), for whom several specific defences are available under the Act.[202] Liability under Pt I of the Act may not be limited or excluded by any contract term, notice or other provision.[203]

(ii) Causation

15.52 Many of the more intractable problems associated with proving causation in drug-related claims based on negligence[204] remain under the Act. Moreover, its silence on causation and remoteness leaves a number of issues unresolved. For example, though, unlike negligence, the Act does not confine recovery to damage of a foreseeable kind,[205] the courts might still be disposed to treat 'cause' as importing foreseeability of consequences.[206] Medicinal products which cause injury through unforeseeable misuse would presumably not be deemed 'defective'. It should be noted that whereas, in negligence, intermediate examination is seen as breaking the chain of causation as regards defects existing when the manufacturer put a product into circulation, under the Act the manufacturer would be jointly and severally liable with any culpable intermediary.[207] Where damage is caused partly by a defect in the product and partly through the claimant's fault, contributory negligence may be invoked as a partial defence.[208] Any consequent reduction in the claimant's damages might be less than in negligence, given that, under the Act, the defendant's liability is not contingent on negligence.

---

[202] s 4. See paras 15.59–15.68, below.

[203] s 7.

[204] See paras 15.04 and 15.41 above. See *Richardson v LRC Products Ltd* [2000] Lloyd's Med Rep 280 (no recovery against a manufacturer under the CPA for the consequences of pregnancy following the failure of a condom because the claimant could reasonably have obtained the 'morning after pill' and thereby avoided the pregnancy).

[205] *Overseas Tankship (UK) Ltd v Morts Dock & Engineering Co Ltd, The Wagon Mound (No 1)* [1961] AC 388.

[206] See Whittaker, S, 'The EEC Directive on Product Liability' (1985), 5 *Yearbook of European Law* 233, 253–4.

[207] s 2(5); and see n 218 below.

[208] Law Reform (Contributory Negligence) Act 1945, s 6(4).

(iii) Who May Sue?

The Act confers a right of action on any person[209] who suffers damage from a de-   **15.53**
fective product. 'Damage' is defined so as to cover death, personal injury and loss
of or damage to property.[210] 'Personal injury', which includes 'any disease and any
other impairment of a person's physical or mental condition'[211] would seem broad
enough to cover claims for psychiatric damage.[212] No remedy is provided for loss
of or damage to the product itself,[213] or for pure economic loss.

(iv) Who May Be Strictly Liable?

Primary liability is imposed on the 'producer',[214] 'own brander',[215] and any person   **15.54**
who has imported a product into the EC in order to supply it to another in the course
of a business.[216] In addition, any persons in the chain of supply can be held strictly liable if they have failed, on request, to identify within a reasonable time either the 'producer' or their own supplier, where identification is not reasonably practicable for the
person who has suffered the damage.[217] Typically it is the manufacturer of the finished product who would incur liability, as 'producer'; but the manufacturer of a defective component part (or the producer of some raw materials) responsible for the
damage caused by the finished product is also liable as a 'producer',[218] as is a person
who has 'abstracted' a 'substance which has not been manufactured'.[219] So, too, is the
processor where the 'essential characteristics' of a product are attributable to an industrial or other process.[220] Depending on the circumstances, the assembly of products might fall within the definition, though presumably not mere packaging.[221]

---

[209] Including persons who have suffered ante-natal injury: CPA, s 6(3).

[210] s 5(1). Actionable damage to property is limited to property of a kind ordinarily intended for
private use, occupation or consumption and mainly so intended by the plaintiff, where the amount
to be awarded exceeds £275: s 5(3)(4). For a discussion of 'damage' under Art 9 of Council Directive
(EEC) 85/374, see Case C-203/99 *Veedfald v Arhus Amtskommune* [2001] ECRI 1-3569 (kidney intended for transplantation into claimant damaged and rendered unusable by defective flushing
agent produced by hospital within Danish health service).

[211] s 45(1).

[212] *Alcock v Chief Constable of the South Yorkshire Police* [1992] 1 AC 310; *Page v Smith* [1996] AC
155; *White v Chief Constable of South Yorkshire Police* [1999] 2 AC 455.

[213] CPA, s 5(2).

[214] ibid, s 1(2).

[215] ibid, s 2(2)(b).

[216] ibid, s 2(2)(c).

[217] ibid, s 2(3).

[218] ibid, s 1(2). Where two or more persons are liable for the same damage their liability is joint
and several: s 2(5), subject to any rights of contribution or indemnity. See s 2(6) and the Civil
Liability (Contribution) Act 1978.

[219] s 1(2)(b).

[220] s 1(2)(c).

[221] Except as regards defects in the packaging itself, ie qua product. See Dodds-Smith, I, 'The
Implications of Strict Liability for Medicinal Products under the Consumer Protection Act, 1987'
in Mann, R (ed) *Risk and Consent to Risk in Medicine* (Carnforth, 1989).

15.55   It is thus apparent that the application of the Act to the production and supply of medicinal products is, in principle, far-ranging. In addition to pharmaceutical companies, hospital and individual pharmacists manufacturing their own finished products, doctors, dentists, and any other health care staff who mix drugs for a prescription or an injection, or modify a piece of equipment, may be deemed producers.[222] The pharmacist, doctor or dentist dispensing drugs, and other health care personnel supplying medical equipment, could be held liable as suppliers if they were unable to identify the 'producer' or their own supplier.[223] There are, then, potentially draconian consequences for innocent intermediaries as a result of this legislative attempt to assist consumers in tracing producers and importers. All suppliers are now well advised to keep adequate records of their source of supply, and producers are similarly advised to label otherwise 'anonymous' products. Identification of source can pose acute problems in the distribution of pharmaceuticals, especially as, increasingly, generic drugs and blood products supplied in bulk originate from a variety of companies, and over fifty per cent of prescription items are dispensed generically.[224] In practice, suppliers would need to keep records for eleven years to avoid liability.[225]

(v)   The Meaning of 'Product'

15.56   'Product' is broadly defined under the Act, as 'any goods or electricity', including 'a product which is comprised in another product'.[226] Moreover 'goods' include 'substances', defined as 'any natural or artificial substance',[227] which, together with the still broader definition in the Directive—'electricity' and 'all movables'[228]— might be invoked in respect of problematic substances.[229] Now that it has been

---

[222] Under the Medicines (Labelling) Regulations 1976, the containers of all medicines prepared or dispensed must be labelled with the name and address of the supplying chemist. It seems unlikely that this of itself would amount to a holding out so as to make the chemist an 'own-brander', and hence a producer within the meaning of the CPA, s 2(2)(b). Aliter where the chemist's own brand name is attached to a product without indicating that it was manufactured by others. See also Directive (EEC) 92/27 [1992], OJ L113/10.

[223] 'Supplying goods' is, inter alia, defined as providing them 'in or in connection with the performance of any statutory function': s 46(1)(e). In the case of NHS employees, the effective 'producer' or 'supplier' will be the health authority. Pt I of the CPA binds the Crown: s 9. The activities of a 'public authority' are included within the definition of 'business' for the purpose of producer or supplier liability: s 45(1).

[224] 52% in 2001: Department of Health, *Prescriptions Dispensed in the Community Statistics for 1991 to 2001: England* (London, 2002), para 12.

[225] ie the limitation period of ten years after the product was put into circulation by the defendant: CPA, Sch 1; Limitation Act 1980, s 11A(3), plus a year for service of the claim form.

[226] s 1(2). Primary agricultural produce, originally excluded under the Act (s 2(4)), was made subject /2000/2771.

[227] s 45(1).

[228] Art 2. 'Movables' have elsewhere been defined by the ECJ as anything capable of money valuation and of being an object of commercial transactions: Case 7/68 *European Commission v Italy* [1968] ECR 423.

[229] ie under CPA, s 1(1). See para 15.49 above.

conceded that blood and blood products are covered by both the Act and the Directive,[230] it seems probable that the same would hold for human tissue and organs.[231] The inclusion of the term 'substances' strengthens the case for regarding them as 'products' within the Act, more especially when they have been abstracted,[232] for example by a surgeon. Equally, the processor of such products might be deemed a producer.[233] But, depending on the facts, any of these transactions might be more appropriately characterised as a provision of services. According to the Department of Trade and Industry, 'medicinal materials used in trials before marketing' would 'generally be exempt', not having been put into circulation in the normal course of business.[234] In fact, use for research purposes would seem to fall within the statutory definition of 'supply',[235] though, in any event, a product which is still being researched would rarely be deemed 'defective'.[236]

(vi) The Meaning of 'Defect'

Proof by the claimant that a product has a 'defect' is essential to liability under the Act. Under s 3(1), a product is deemed defective if 'its safety is not such as persons generally are entitled to expect . . .', an objective test, which has been construed as the 'expectations of the public at large, as determined by the Court'.[237] In determining the issue, 'all the circumstances shall be taken into account . . .'.[238] These include 'the manner in which, and purposes for which, the product has been marketed, its get-up, . . .' and any instructions or warnings concerning its use;[239] 'what might reasonably be expected to be done with or in relation to the product',[240] and 'the time when the product was supplied by its producer to another . . .'.[241] The choice of the date of supply as a factor in the evaluation of defectiveness means that, under the Act, no less than in negligence, the claimant has the burden of

15.57

---

[230] *A v National Blood Authority* (n 19 above).

[231] See paras 15.20 and 15.21 above. See further Grubb and Pearl (n 77 above), ch 5; Grubb, A (1993) 1 Med L Rev 259, and Stern, K, 'Strict Liability and the Supply of Donated Gametes' (1994) 2 Med L Rev 261.

[232] s 1(2)(b). See also the Pearson Commission (n 1 above), para 1276.

[233] s 1(2)(c).

[234] Department of Trade and Industry, *Implementation of EC Directive on Product Liability—An Explanatory and Consultative Note* (London, 1985) 14, para 56(a).

[235] s 46(1).

[236] See ss 3(1),(2), paras 15.57 and 15.58 below. See also s 4(1)(e) ('development risks' defence), paras 15.65–15.68 below.

[237] *Iman Abouzaid v Mothercare (UK) Ltd* The Times, 20 February 2001 (CA), *per* Pill LJ at [25]. See also the European Directive, Art 6 and Recital 6, and *A v National Blood Authority* (n 19 above) at [31]. And see *Scholten v Foundation Sanquin of Blood Supply* H/98.0896 (3 Feb 1999, County Court of Amsterdam).

[238] s 3(2). *Cf* Directive, Art 6(1).

[239] s 3(2)(a).

[240] s 3(2)(b). This subsection would permit liability for foreseeable misuse.

[241] s 3(2)(c).

establishing what safety standards were acceptable at some time in the past, perhaps many years previously in the case of drugs. The Act does not 'require' an inference of defectiveness to be drawn from the fact 'alone' that a product marketed at a later date is more safe,[242] though, where appropriate, liability could be imposed on the producer of the original product for its continued supply.

(vii) The 'Legitimate Expectation' Test

15.58   As the 'learned intermediary' principle implies, with many medicinal products there is a certain artificiality in trying to determine what 'persons generally are entitled to expect'. Section 3(2)'s formulation—that 'all the circumstances shall be taken into account', including how and why a product has been marketed and the nature of any instructions or warnings—had a familiar ring. It seemed to indicate that determinations on defectiveness of design and adequacy of warning would continue to revolve around issues of relative safety, reasonable care and foreseeability, thereby perpetuating the kind of balancing act characteristic of negligence and of American 'strict' products liability regimes alike.[243] However, the notable judgment of Burton J in *A v National Blood Authority*[244] marked a distinct shift towards the enhanced consumer protection to which the Directive aspires. Virtually confining himself to the wording of the Directive, he held that blood and blood products infected with Hepatitis C were defective within Article 6 because the public at large was entitled to expect that transfusions would be free of such infection.[245] The test, being the public's 'legitimate', not 'actual', expectation, public awareness of the remote but inevitable risk of a 'non-standard' or 'rogue' product did not preclude liability.[246] Nor did it matter that doctors giving transfusions were aware at the time of a 1 per cent to 3 per cent risk of Hepatitis C in the United Kingdom, since this risk had not been communicated to the public. In effect, the 'learned intermediary' rule was deemed inapplicable under the

---

[242] s 3(2).

[243] *Cf* . . . even where strict liability is ostensibly the chosen regime, doctrine is likely to reflect the long and enduring reach of negligence principles': Rogerson, C and Trebilcock, M, 'Products Liability and the Allergic Consumer: A Study in the Problems of Framing an Efficient Liability Regime' (n 131 above), 52. *Cf* Whittaker, S, 'The EEC Directive on Product Liability' (1985) (n 205 above), 233; Stapleton, J, 'Products Liability Reform—Real or Illusory?' (1986) 6 OJLS 392; Newdick, C, 'The Future of Negligence in Product Liability' (n 113 above); Stoppa, A, 'The Concept of Defectiveness in the Consumer Protection Act 1987: a Critical Analysis' (1992) 12 LS 210; Atiyah, *The Sale of Goods* (n 40 above), 275–9. See also Restatement (Third) of Torts: Products Liability (1998) (n 27 above), s 2.

[244] See n 19 above.

[245] See *A v National Blood Authority* (n 19 above) at [31]. And see n 194. See also *Richardson v LRC Products Ltd* (n 204 above).

[246] *A v National Blood Authority*, ibid, at [31 vi]. Burton J considered the terms 'standard' and 'non-standard' products more appropriate for construing the Directive than the categories of design and manufacturing defects as developed in US case law: ibid, at [36] and [39]. See also nn 243 and 27 above.

statutory regime.[247] Furthermore, 'taking all circumstances into account' meant all 'relevant' circumstances. These did not include unavoidability, for example the unavailability of a test to detect the presence of the virus; or impracticability, in terms of the cost or difficulty of preventing the defect, or the social benefits of the product.[248]

(viii) Defences

If the claimant can prove that damage has been caused by a 'defective product' (as defined above) for which the defendant is responsible under the Act, the burden shifts to the defence to establish any of six specific defences listed in s 4. **15.59**

(a) Section 4(1)(a)

That the defect 'is attributable to compliance with any requirement imposed by or under any enactment or with any Community obligation'.[249] **15.60**

Compliance with such a requirement is not in itself a defence. The defendant must show that the defect was caused by the compliance. Thus mere compliance with licensing regulations under the Medicines Act 1968 is not a defence, though it will often be strong evidence that the 'consumer expectation' test of safety has been met, and some indication that the producer has demonstrated the degree of scientific and technical knowledge needed to satisfy the 'development risks' defence.[250] The requirement relied upon must be mandatory.[251]

(b) Section 4(1)(b) and Section 46

That the defendant 'did not at any time supply the product to another'.[252] **15.61**

This defence derives from Article 7(a) of the Directive, under which a producer can avoid liability by proving that 'he did not put the product into circulation'. It could be relied on where, for example, damage has arisen from the theft of drugs or from the use of defective products, provided that they were not yet in the distribution chain.[253]

---

[247] See the criticism by Hodges, C, 'Compensating Patients' (2001) 117 LQR 528.

[248] See *A v National Blood Authority* (n 19 above) at [57], [58], [63] and [68]. For a critique which advocates combining consumer expectation with risk-utility analysis, see Goldberg, R, 'Paying for Bad Blood: Strict Product Liability after the Hepatitis C Litigation' (2002) 10 Med L Rev 165.

[249] s 4(1)(a).

[250] See paras 15.65–15.68 below.

[251] *Cf* 'mandatory regulations issued by the public authorities': European Directive (n 189 above), Art 7(d).

[252] ss 4(1)(b) and 46.

[253] In *Veedfald v Arhus Amtskommune* (n 210 above), the defective fluid, having been used in the provision of a specific medical service, was held to have been 'put into circulation' for the purposes of Art 7(a) of the Directive, even though it had never left the 'sphere of control' of the hospital. As regards products still under research, see para 15.56 above.

(c) Section 4(1)(c)

15.62   That the defendant did not supply the product 'in the course of a business' and, in the case of the producer, 'own-brander' or importer (ie a s 2(2) defendant), with a view to profit.[254]

(d) Section 4(1)(d) and Section 4(2)

15.63   That the defect 'did not exist in the product at the relevant time'.[255]

It is a defence for s 2(2) defendants to prove that the defect was not present when they supplied the product. A supplier[256] can succeed under the defence by showing that the defect did not exist when the product was last supplied by the producer, 'own-brander' or importer. The supplier is thus apparently not liable, under the Act, for introducing the defect into the product. The defence would be available to a pharmaceutical manufacturer where, for example, a product had deteriorated because of inadequate storage or poor handling by a wholesaler or pharmacist, or where injury was shown to have resulted from a pharmacist having removed a patient leaflet. It could also cover situations where a supplier had altered the original specifications of a product, as well as instances of criminal tampering.

(e) Section 4(1)(f)

15.64   That the defect in a component is wholly attributable to the design of the finished product in which it was comprised or to compliance with the instructions of that product's producer.[257]

Components manufacturers (and producers of raw materials) are not liable, under the Act, if their product is defective only as a consequence of the design of the finished product or of compliance with instructions given by its producer. In the European Directive, unlike the CPA, the defence that the defect was attributable to instructions is not confined to instructions given to the component manufacturer, and could cover instructions for use.[258]

---

[254] s 4(1)(c). 'Business' includes NHS provision: see para 15.55, n 223 above. The defence would not be available for promotional free samples. The equivalent defence under Art 7(c) of the Directive makes no reference to the product not being supplied 'with a view to profit' but applies where it was not made for an 'economic purpose' or in the course of a business. Art 7(c) has been held not to apply where the product had been manufactured and used in the course of a specific medical service financed entirely from public funds and for which the claimant did not pay directly: *Veedfald v Arhus Amtskommune* (n 210 above).
[255] s 4(1)(d), (2).
[256] s 2(3).
[257] s 4(1)(f).
[258] Art 7(f).

(f) Section 4(1)(e): The 'Development Risks' Defence[259]

That: . . . the state of scientific and technical knowledge at the relevant time was **15.65** not such that a producer of products of the same description as the product in question might be expected to have discovered the defect if it had existed in his products while they were under his control. . . .

This provision has been the most contentious feature of the legislation. The pharmaceutical industry was very prominent in the intensive lobbying to have a 'development risks' defence, emphasising concern about innovation and insurability. The availability of such a defence in the European Directive[260] was a key factor in obtaining the agreement of all Member States, especially the United Kingdom, to the introduction of a strict liability regime.[261] At the same time, there has been much criticism that it signified a reversion to negligence, was conceptually incompatible with strict liability and threatened to undermine the social and economic objectives of products liability reform.[262] These concerns were reflected in the Directive's requirement that, after ten years,[263] the European Commission would have to report on how 'consumer protection and the functioning of the common market' had been affected by court rulings of Member States based on the defence, to determine whether or not Article 7(e) should be repealed.[264]

(g) Section 4(1)(e) and Article 7(e)

The controversy was exacerbated by the difference in terminology between **15.66** s 4(1)(e) and Article 7(e).[265] Under the Act, manufacturers need only show that the state of knowledge when they supplied the product was not such that 'a producer of products of the same description . . . might be expected' to have discovered the defect.[266] The Directive requires the defendant to prove that the state of knowledge

---

[259] s 4(1)(e). See Newdick, C, 'The Development Risk Defence of the Consumer Protection Act 1987' (n 117 above), 455; Newdick, C, 'Risk, Uncertainty and "Knowledge" in the Development Risk Defence' (1991) Anglo-American L Rev 127; Stapleton, 'Products Liability Reform—Real or Illusory?' (n 248 above), 392; Stapleton, *Product Liability* (n 7 above), 236–42; Whittaker, S, 'The EEC Directive on Product Liability' (n 206, above), 233; Stoppa, A, (1992) 'The Concept of Defectiveness in the Consumer Protection Act 1987: A Critical Analysis' (n 248 above), 218–21.

[260] Art 7(e).

[261] Under Art 15(1)(b), Member States were given the option of adopting or derogating from the defence.

[262] See references at n 248 above.

[263] ie in 1995.

[264] Art 15(3). In its first report on the application of the Directive, the Commission did not propose any amendments to it. *First Report on the application of Council Directive on the approximation of laws, regulations and administrative provisions of the Member States concerning liability for defective products* (85/374/EEC): COM (95) 617 final, 13 December 1995, 2.

[265] See references at n 259 above.

[266] It is not entirely clear what is meant by 'a producer of products of the same description as the product in question'. In the pharmaceutical context, it could refer to drug manufacturers in general or might be limited to producers of drugs of the same therapeutic class, always assuming that they exist.

'was not such as to *enable* the existence of the defect to be discovered'.[267] The Directive is concerned with what is objectively discoverable; the CPA only with what might be expected of producers of a particular category of products.

15.67   Clearly this is a distinction which could have had major implications for the pharmaceutical industry in cases of defective design.[268] The imprecise wording of the CPA defence appeared to permit exactly the kind of balancing act which is familiar in negligence analysis. It seemed to leave the court free to consider what are appropriate standards within the industry, having regard to such factors as the resources of the producer and the feasibility of discovering a particular defect at the pre-marketing stage, in the light of the various financial and scientific constraints on investigative procedures. It has often been asserted that, by virtue of s 4(1)(e), the thalidomide victims might not have recovered damages under an Act which was in part prompted by their struggle. Certainly it is possible that Distillers could have shown that pharmaceutical manufacturers of comparable products might not have been expected to conduct the kind of tests that would have revealed the defect.[269] On the other hand, the reverse onus of proof and the expectations engendered by a strict liability regime would have made their task harder. In 1996, two experienced practitioners in the field observed:

> There is widespread expectation that any court would feel obliged to construe the defence in accordance with the Directive and thus in effect to override the literal words of the Act. Indeed, insurance is widely believed to be on this basis.[270]

The following year, in response to infringement proceedings brought by the European Commission, the European Court of Justice ruled that the test of scientific and technical knowledge under Article 7(e) is an objective one. It includes the most advanced level of such knowledge at the time when the product was put into circulation, provided that knowledge was accessible at that time. The Court found that s 4(1)(e) did not impose any restriction on the state of scientific and

---

[267] Emphasis added. Art 7(e) reads in full, 'that the state of scientific and technical knowledge at the time when he put the product into circulation was not such as to enable the existence of the defect to be discovered'.

[268] s 4(1)(e) would seem to have no application to the risk of manufacturing defects, which already effectively attract strict liability at common law. See *A v National Blood Authority* (n 19 above), where the existence of the generic defect was known. See Newdick, 'The Development Risk Defence of the Consumer Protection Act 1987' (n 117 above), 472–3. The comparable German provision under the *Produkthaftungsgesetz* (Product Liability Act 1990) has been held not to apply to unavoidable manufacturing defects: Bundesgerichtshof (VI ZR 158/94, 9 May 1995) NJW 1995, 2162. See further *A v National Blood Authority*, ibid, at [53(iii)]. Contrast *Graham Barclay Oysters Pty v Ryan* [2000] FCA 1099 (9 August 2000) (Aust Fed Ct), interpreting the Australian Trade Practices Act 1974, s 75AK(1)(c). See also Stapleton, J, 'Restatement (Third) of Torts: Products Liability, an Anglo-Australian Perspective' (2000) 39 Washburn LJ 363, 379–385.

[269] See generally Teff, H and Munro, C, *Thalidomide: The Legal Aftermath* (Farnborough, 1976).

[270] Mildred, M and Pannone, R, 'Liability in Tort: Class Actions' in Miller, *Product Liability and Safety Encyclopaedia* (n 268 above), Division IIIA, para 94 (1996).

technical knowledge to be taken into account and, more particularly, did not suggest that the availability of the defence depended on the subjective knowledge of a producer taking reasonable care in the light of standard precautions in the industrial sector in question. The Court further noted that s 1(1) of the Act expressly provided that relevant provisions be construed in conformity with the Directive. It therefore concluded that s 4(1)(e) did not clearly conflict with Article 7(e).[271] In *A v National Blood Authority*, Burton J invoked s 1(1) and the Court of Justice ruling to resolve the development risks issue in the case by reference to Article 7(e). Mindful that the Directive's purpose was to prevent injury and facilitate compensation for injury, he observed that 'Article 7(e) provides a very restricted escape route'.[272] Crucially, he held that when a product is known to be *generically* susceptible to a defect, the defendant cannot rely on Article 7(e) merely because of inability to detect the defect in an *individual* product. Put another way, once the risk of a defect occurring is known, it cannot be a development risk.

This is not to say that the wording of the Directive is free from ambiguity; there are practical difficulties in trying to apply it in a literal fashion. What does it mean to say that the state of scientific and technical knowledge enables the existence of a defect to be discovered? How reliable and beyond challenge must findings be, what level of recognition must they have achieved within the scientific community, before they can be said to constitute 'knowledge' at all, let alone 'the most advanced level of such knowledge'?[273] It has been forcefully argued that 'scientific and technical knowledge' cannot be said to exist merely because of what someone, somewhere knows, or may have published in an obscure journal. A court assessing the relevant state of scientific and technical knowledge would hardly 'require the defendant to prove . . . a worldwide absence of knowledge of the defect'.[274] The ruling by the European Court of Justice that the knowledge in question must have been 'accessible' indicates that, even under the Directive, only reasonably discoverable knowledge is in issue.[275]

15.68

---

[271] Case C-300/95 *European Commission v UK* [1997] All ER (EC) 481.

[272] *A v National Blood Authority* (n 19 above) at [64]. This restrictive view of the Art 7(e) defence has been criticised by Goldberg, R, 'Paying for Bad Blood: Strict Product Liability after the Hepatitis C Litigation' (n 248 above). For narrow interpretations of s 4(1)(e), see *Richardson v LRC Products Ltd* [2000] Lloyd's Rep Med 280, at 285, and *Iman Abouzaid v Mothercare (UK) Ltd*, The Times, 20 February 2001 (CA), *per* Pill LJ at [29].

[273] Newdick, 'Risk, Uncertainty and "Knowledge" in the Development Risk Defence' (n 259 above). *Cf* para 15.31 above.

[274] Newdick, 'The Development Risk Defence of the Consumer Protection Act 1987' (n 117 above), at 459, and see 461–7. *Cf* Atiyah, *Sale of Goods* (n 40 above), 279–81; Stapleton, *Product Liability* (n 7 above), 236–42.

[275] *European Commission v UK* (n 271 above), Opinion of AG Tesauro, paras 23–24. In *A v National Blood Authority* (n 19 above), Burton J, obiter, may have sought to restrict inaccessible knowledge to that contained in 'an unpublished document or unpublished research not available to the general public, retained within the laboratory or research department of a particular company' (at [49(i)]). In the US a number of jurisdictions permit a development risks defence along the lines

(ix) Limitation of Actions

15.69   The normal principles of limitation of actions apply under the Act, except in two respects.[276] First, the limitation period for damage to property is the same as for personal injury, namely three years from the date that the claimant became aware or should reasonably have become aware of the material facts relating to the damage.[277] Secondly, in no circumstances may an action be brought under the Act after ten years from when the defendant supplied the actual defective product which caused the damage.[278] This cut-off point is of particular significance in respect of drugs, since the latency period for adverse effects can be considerable,[279] but it does not preclude the possibility of a subsequent action in negligence (or breach of contract).

(x) Jurisdiction

15.70   For the purposes of jurisdiction, liability under Pt I of the Act is treated as liability in tort,[280] and the normal rules as to conflict of laws apply.[281] Generally speaking, and despite the scope for derogation under the Directive, there has not been such a degree of divergence in its implementation by Member States as to encourage widespread forum shopping. Nonetheless, apart from any extrinsic considerations as to choice of forum, several points merit attention. First, because the Directive applies only to products put into circulation once the domestic implementing law has come into force, liability for products supplied prior to that date is based on the applicable national law at the relevant time. Secondly, though nearly all Member States have implemented a 'development risks' defence, the United Kingdom's version is the one most open to a broad interpretation. However, specifically in respect of pharmaceutical products,

---

of the European Directive. Since the mid-1980s, the American courts have largely retreated from strict liability in cases based on defective design and failure to warn. Contrast *Beshada v Johns-Manville Products Corporation* 447 A 2d 539, 546 (1982) (Sup Ct of New Jersey) with the same court's holding in *Feldman v Lederle Laboratories* 479 A 2d 374, 387 (1984). In *Brown v Superior Court (Abbott Laboratories)* 751 P 2d 470, 480–2 (1988), the California Supreme Court held that the exemption from strict liability for 'unavoidably unsafe' products in Comment k to s 402A of the Restatement (Second) of Torts covered all prescription drugs in respect of failure to warn. Contrast *Shanks v Upjohn Co* 835 P 2d 1189 (Alaska 1992). See also Stapleton, J, *Product Liability* (n 7 above), ch 2. See now Restatement (Third) of Torts (1998), ss 2 and 6. And see n 27 above.

[276]   See s 6(6) and Sch 1, amending the Limitation Act 1980.
[277]   Limitation Act 1980, ss 11A(4) and 14(1A).
[278]   ibid, s 11A(3). On the scope for substituting a party after expiry of the ten-year period, see *Horne-Roberts v SmithKline Beecham plc* [2002] 1 WLR 1662 (CA).
[279]   See eg *Sindell v Abbott Laboratories* 607 P 2d 924 (Cal 1980).
[280]   s 6(7).
[281]   See Fawcett, J, 'Jurisdiction' in Howells, G (ed), *The Law of Product Liability* (London, 2000), ch 6, and Attree, R, 'Jurisdiction, Enforcement of Judgments and Conflicts of Laws' in Kelly, P and Attree, R (eds), *European Product Liability Law* (2nd edn, London, 1997), ch XVIII.

Germany has a statutory scheme under which manufacturers are subject to strict liability.[282]

E. Multi-Party Actions

Our substantive law, the rules of the Supreme Court and the legal aid system were all essentially designed to deal with individual claims. Because defective medical products and devices can cause injury on a large scale, they are liable to generate multi-party actions which may raise comparable, but often not identical, issues of liability[283] and pose intractable problems of procedure and case management.[284] In a legal system which does not provide for 'class actions',[285] and where it remains uncertain whether a representative action[286] can be maintained when damages are claimed for individuals,[287] the recently developed mechanism of Group Litigation Orders has been introduced in order to provide better management of multi-party litigation.[288]

15.71

---

[282] Drug Administration Act (*Arzneimittelgesetz*) 1976 BGBI, 1S 2445, amended 20 July 1988 BGBI, IS 1050.

[283] 'In the case of pharmaceutical products . . . patients of differing susceptibilities will have taken different quantities of the drug over differing periods of time and during different stages of the advancement of scientific knowledge, so that the issue of negligence or "defective product" will vary. Equally, patients taking the same drug may complain of different ill-effects, and so the issue of causation may vary.': Supreme Court Procedure Committee, *Guide for Use in Group Actions* (London, 1991), 6.

[284] See generally Hodges, C, *Multi-Party Actions* (Oxford, 2000), and Mildred, M, 'Group Actions' in Howells (ed), *The Law of Product Liability* (n 281 above). On cost-sharing, see CPR, Pt 48.6A; *Andrews v Secretary of State for Health* (1998) 54 BMLR 111 (CJD); *Sayers v Merck SmithKline Beecham plc* [2002] 1 WLR 2274 (CA) (MMR vaccine), and Mildred, M, 'Cost-sharing in Group Litigation: Preserving Access to Justice' (2002) 65 MLR 597. See also *Nash v Eli Lilly & Co* [1991] 2 Med L Rev 169 (Opren); *AB v John Wyeth & Brother Ltd* [1994] 5 Med L Rev 149, CA (benzodiazepine). And see Oliphant, K, 'Innovation in Procedure and Practice in Multi-Party Medical Cases' in Grubb, A (ed), *Choices and Decisions in Health Care* (Chichester, 1993); Legal Aid Board, *Issues arising for the Legal Aid Board and the Lord Chancellor's Department from Multi-Party Actions* (London, 1994).

[285] See eg *Davies v Eli Lilly & Co* [1987] 1 WLR 1136, 1139 (CA), *per* Lord Donaldson MR. Contrast the position in the US and certain Commonwealth jurisdictions which provide for numerous claimants with related claims against the same defendant to have them disposed of in a single action. See further Mildred and Pannone, 'Liability in Tort: Class Actions' (n 268 above), Division IIIA.

[286] RSC Ord 15, r 12.

[287] Contrast *Markt & Co Ltd v Knight Steamship Co Ltd* [1910] 2 KB 1021, 1040 (CA): 'absolutely inapplicable', *per* Fletcher Moulton LJ, with *Prudential Assurance Co Ltd v Newman Industries Ltd* [1979] 3 All ER 507 and *Irish Shipping Ltd v Commercial Union Assurance Co plc* [1991] 2 QB 206 (CA).

[288] See CPR, Pt 19.III and Hodges, C, *Multi-Party Actions* (n 284 above). And see eg *Chrzanowska v Glaxo Laboratories Ltd* [1990] 1 Med L Rev 385, 386 (Myodil); Supreme Court Procedure Committee, *Guide for Use in Group Actions* (n 283 above); Legal Aid Board, *Issues arising for the Legal Aid Board and the Lord Chancellor's Department from Multi-Party Actions* (n 284 above); Lord Woolf, *Access to Justice* (Final Report) (London, 1996), ch 17, *Access to Justice: Multi-Party Situations: Proposed New Procedure. A Consultation Paper.* (London, 1997), and *Multi-Party Situations: Draft rule and practice directions. A Lord Chancellor's Draft Consultation Paper* (London, 1999).

16

DONATION AND TRANSPLANTATION OF
ORGANS AND TISSUES

A. Introduction

1. The Scope of This Chapter

The list of materials in the human body that can be removed and transplanted **16.01**
into another person's body for therapeutic, cosmetic, reproductive or other purposes is growing.[1] Further, human cells outside the body can be cultured by

---

[1] See Nuffield Council on Bioethics, *Human Tissue: Ethical and Legal Issues* (London, 1995),
Appendix 3, 144. For a somewhat critical extended review of the report, see Matthews, P, 'The Man
of Property' (1995) 3 Med L Rev 251–274.

biotechnological processes and otherwise developed into commercially valuable products,[2] and surplus materials of human origin, such as placentas and umbilical cord blood that result from childbirth, can be of considerable therapeutic and industrial use.[3] Dead bodies, living persons and such products of human conception as foetal tissues can be sources of materials for transplantation, scientific research, industrial development and medical and related education.

16.02   The focus of this chapter is primarily donation of human organs and tissues for transplantation into patients.[4] Donations for purposes other than therapeutic transplantation, such as development of commercial products and therapeutic agents, are not the present concern. Transfers of materials including sperm, ova and pre-embryos for reproductive purposes are addressed directly in Chapter 10 and indirectly in Chapter 12, and research uses of human bodily materials used in treatments such as gene therapy and storing of materials in tissue or genetic data banks are addressed in Chapter 13. Further, plans are being elaborated to narrow the gap between the demand for human organs for transplantation and their supply, by employment of transgenically-prepared animal organs and tissues, such as from pigs and baboons.[5] Concerns with legal aspects of xenotransplantation, however, such as breeding of and care for selected animals and the legal status of their separated organs pending implantation, are touched on only from the narrow perspective of the intended human recipients. Despite the expanding range of transplantable human materials, this chapter will standardise its approach by citing primarily kidney transplantation as representative of organ transplantation, and bone marrow as representative of transplantable tissues, except when specific tissue raises special concerns, such as reproductive tissue. On the potential transplantation of animal tissue into humans by xenotransplantation, see: *Animal Tissues into Humans: A Report by the Advisory Group on the Ethics of Xenotransplantation* (1996) and *The Government Response to 'Animal Tissue into Humans'* (1997). For the regulatory scheme pertaining to xenotransplantation see the website of the UK Xenotransplantation Interim Regulatory Authority (*www.doh.gov.uk/ukxira.htm*).

---

[2] See *Moore v Regents of the University of California* (1990) 793 P 2d 479 (Cal Sup Ct), cert denied (1991) 111 S Ct 1388 (US Sup Ct), concerning a cell line with a potential market worth over $3 billion by 1990.

[3] See Royal Commission on New Reproductive Technologies, Final Report, *Proceed with Care* (Ottawa, 1993) ch 31, 981–5.

[4] For an international human rights framework, see Council of Europe, *Additional Protocol to the Convention on Human Rights and Biomedicine, on Transplantation of Organs and Tissues of Human Origin* (Strasbourg, 24 January 2002) Council of Europe ETS No 186.

[5] See Nuffield Council on Bioethics, *Animal-to-Human Transplants: The Ethics of Xenotransplantation* (London, 1996).

2. *Organs and Tissues*

The historical common law was more concerned with lost limbs and digits than   **16.03**
organs and tissues. Obtaining organs or tissues from living persons would usually
require that they be cut, but, particularly before the development of sterile practice in surgery, the law recognised that any breaking of the outer surface of the skin
endangered life itself, and was a wound that might constitute an unlawful maim
(or mayhem). The law also recognised the distinction between natural and induced separation of bodily materials from the person, such as in the contrast between release of waste products and the shedding of blood. The modern legal
distinction, however, between organs and tissues is based on legislation. In
Britain, the Human Tissue Act 1961,[6] dealing with cadaveric removal of materials, deals with them in an undifferentiated way, but the Human Organ
Transplants Act 1989,[7] addressing donations from living persons, provides that
the Act deals only with 'organs'. Section 7(2) of the Act provides that:

> 'organ' means any part of a human body consisting of a structured arrangement of
> tissues which, if wholly removed, cannot be replicated by the body.

Although unreplicable structured tissues are organs, 'tissue' remains the generic
description of bodily materials, so that the Human Tissue Act 1961 is appropriately titled in not distinguishing organs from unstructured tissues. Under the
1989 Act, the whole liver for instance is an organ, but a liver segment is not since,
following surgical removal of the segment, the liver remaining in the donor's body
spontaneously regenerates itself. The major purpose of the Act, as stated in its long
title, is 'to prohibit commercial dealings in human organs intended for transplanting', but its narrow definition of 'organ' leaves some objectionable commerce
in human tissues beyond its reach.

The legislation of each jurisdiction warrants particular attention, since statutory   **16.04**
language and definitions do not conform to any coherent pattern, although underlying purposes may be similar. In Ontario, for instance,[8] the legislation covering both inter vivos gifts for transplantation and post mortem gifts is the Human
Tissue Gift Act.[9] Section 1(c) provides that:

> 'tissue' includes an organ, but does not include any skin, bone, blood, blood con-
> stituent, or other tissue that is replaceable by natural processes of repair.

---

[6] 9 & 10 Eliz 2, c 54, as amended. For Recommendations for further amendment, see the Isaacs
Report by the Chief Medical Officer, 2003, at *www.doh.gov.uk/cmo/isaacsreport/index.htm.*
[7] Stats ch 31.
[8] Principal contrasts in this Chapter will be between the laws in England and Ontario.
[9] Human Tissue Gift Act, now renamed The Trillium Gift of Life Network Act, RSO 1990, c H-
20 as amended.

Accordingly, 'tissue' under this Act appears comparable to 'organ' under the British 1989 Act.[10] Blood is a tissue according to the 1989 Act, but not the Ontario Act. The former addresses only organs as defined, but leaves uncertainty regarding its application to important transplantable materials such as bone marrow. It is a matter of biology whether this is 'a structured arrangement of tissues', but if it is so considered it may be an 'organ' under the 1989 Act since it may not be replicated if 'wholly removed', although it regenerates in time if removed in limited and safe amounts. Since bone marrow is usually not considered to be structured tissue, however, it falls outside the 1989 Act and the prohibition, for instance, of commercial exchange.[11] In contrast, the prohibition of commerce in the Ontario Act applies to 'any tissue . . . or any body or part or parts thereof other than blood or a blood constituent',[12] which includes bone marrow.[13]

B. Issues Common to Living and Post Mortem Donation

1. Introduction

16.05 A functional distinction between tissues and organs is that the former tend to be donated primarily by live donors, whereas experience and policy favour the acquisition of organs primarily from cadaveric sources. This is largely self-evident where donations of vital organs such as hearts are concerned, but kidneys and organ segments from, for example, the liver and pancreas (which segments may be legally classified as tissues rather than organs)[14] may be donated by persons while living. Nevertheless, strong international endorsement supports the recovery of organs for transplantation from cadavers rather than from live donors, where local cultures, influenced by religious beliefs, are sympathetic to the practice.[15] The World Health Assembly has endorsed certain Guiding Principles for human organ transplantation proposed by the World Health Organisation that include the principle that:

> Organs for transplantation should be removed preferably from the bodies of deceased persons.[16]

---

[10] On uncertainties in the statutory language, see Kennedy, I and Grubb, A, *Medical Law* (3rd edn, London, 2000), 1763–5.

[11] Human Organ Transplants Act 1989, s 1(1)(a).

[12] Human Tissue Gift Act, s 10.

[13] On practical problems from the prohibition of commerce, and more generally, see Law Reform Commission of Canada, *Procurement and Transfer of Human Tissues and Organs* (Ottawa, 1992, Working Paper 66), 29 *et seq*.

[14] See para 16.03 above.

[15] For comparative international legislation and international institutional activity, see World Health Organisation, *Legislative Responses to Organ Transplantation* (Dordrecht, Boston, London, 1994).

[16] World Health Organisation, *Human Organ Transplantation: A Report on Developments under the Auspices of WHO (1987÷1991)* (Geneva, 1991), 8, Guiding Principle 3.

The Commentary on Guiding Principle 3 states that this provision:

> is intended to emphasize the importance of developing cadaveric donation pro-
> grammes ... and to discourage donations from living, genetically unrelated
> donors, except for transplantation of bone marrow and of other acceptable regener-
> ative tissues.[17]

The purpose is both to serve the humanitarian goal of sparing living persons from
the physical and emotional burdens of organ donation, and to reduce the incidence of donations that are inspired by material reward and the related commercialisation of inter vivos organ donation.

Cadaveric recovery of organs for transplantation depends in law[18] on appropriate   **16.06**
consents (see below at paras 16.28 *et seq*) and application of the legal criteria of
death.[19] Persons in a persistent vegetative state, including those it is legally permissible to let die by withdrawal of artificial means of life support or of nutrition
and hydration, are not dead because vital signs remain, notably spontaneous
brain-stem activity.[20] However, following death, respiration and cardiac action
may be artificially undertaken in order to preserve the tissue quality of organs for
purposes of transplantation. Since both patients receiving intensive care and the
bodies of deceased persons may be attached to medical devices that maintain
heartbeat and oxygenation of tissues, the process of distinguishing the former
from the latter is of legal significance.

The Human Tissue Act 1961 provides that death is determined when a regis-   **16.07**
tered medical practitioner is satisfied by personal examination of a body that life
is extinct.[21] In contrast, the legislation for instance in Ontario[22] provides in s 7
that:

(1) For the purposes of a *post mortem* transplant, the fact of death shall be deter-
    mined by at least two physicians in accordance with accepted medical practice.
(2) No physician who has had any association with the proposed recipient that
    might influence the physician's judgment shall take any part in the determina-
    tion of the fact of death of the donor.
(3) No physician who took any part in the determination of the fact of death of the
    donor shall participate in any way in the transplant procedures.

This provision recognises both that while the criteria of death are governed by law,
the law may defer to 'accepted medical practice', which is provable in judicial

---

[17] ibid, 10.
[18] The issue is not just legal, however; see Hazony, O, 'Increasing the Supply of Cadaver Organs
for Transplantation: Recognizing that the Real Problem is Psychological not Legal' (1993) 3 *Health
Matrix* 219–57.
[19] See Ch 19.
[20] *Airedale NHS Trust v Bland* [1993] 1 AC 789 (HL).
[21] Human Tissue Act 1961, s 1(4), (4A).
[22] The Human Tissue Gift Act.

proceedings by expert evidence, and that the legally set criteria of death are applied by physicians as a matter of judgment. This judgment determines the fact of death.

16.08   The Ontario legislation makes explicit what the Human Tissue Act 1961 leaves implicit, namely that a physician who determines death of a person must avoid any conflict of interest arising from any professional or personal association with the proposed recipient of that person's organ.[23] Management of such conflict is a matter both of law and of professional ethics. Physicians capable of determining death may be engaged in transplantation procedures in general. However, they are barred from making a determination when a potential donor may be the source of an organ of which one of their patients may be a recipient. The British Medical Association's ethical advice to the profession observes that:

> Awareness of a potential conflict of interest between donors and recipients has influenced the development of organ transplantation. The medical response to this in the conventional adult donor situation is to have two quite separate health care teams: one responsible for the care of the donor, the other responsible for the care of the recipient.[24]

Regarding dying patients who are potential donors, the advice is that '[n]o patient can be considered as a potential donor until all treatments for the benefit of that patient have been exhausted'.[25] As a patient, the dying potential donor may be expected to receive care from a health care team separate from that attending a potential recipient of that patient's posthumously donated organs. Departure from this principle may be excusable on grounds of unexpected emergency and necessity, but physicians would have to demonstrate that the welfare of the dying patient was not compromised and that they acted in good faith without advance knowledge of the likelihood of the recipient being a patient for whose care they become responsible.

16.09   Physicians and other health care professionals are legally accountable to their licensing or other disciplinary authorities, such as the General Medical Council, for unethical behaviour, such as failing satisfactorily to resolve conflicts of interest. Their duty to conduct themselves in accordance with professional ethics may be an implied term of contracts they enter, such as contracts for professional services. While Canadian courts are developing legal incidents of the fiduciary duties that physicians owe their patients,[26] this approach has been rejected in England and

---

[23] Shaw, BW Jr, 'Conflict of Interest in the Procurement of Organs from Cadavers Following Withdrawal of Life Support' (1993) 3 *Kennedy Institute of Ethics J* 179–87.

[24] British Medical Association, *Medical Ethics Today: Its Practice and Philosophy* (London, 1993), 26.

[25] ibid, 28.

[26] *Norberg v Wynrib* (1992), 92 DLR (4th) 449 (Sup Ct Can); *McInerney v MacDonald* (1992), 93 DLR (4th) 415 (Sup Ct Can).

other common law jurisdictions. However, whether as an incidence of a fiduciary duty or the common law duty of care, the duty to determine death competently, avoiding any conflict of interest, such as professional or personal commitments to potential recipients of organs that may be donated by or from patients whose deaths such physicians may be called on to determine, may be legally enforceable.

2. Anencephalic Neonates and Donors

Children born with the congenital absence of the cerebral cortex and of major **16.10** portions of the skull and scalp, described as anencephaly, may never achieve consciousness but nevertheless have a functioning brain stem, and so are not stillborn but born alive.[27] The condition is ordinarily incompatible with continuation of life beyond a few days, but measurement of the lifespan of anencephalic newborn children is compromised by the inability to apply brain death criteria to infants within the first few days after birth.[28] Claims that such infants are stillborn, however, or that they may be characterised if not as brain stem dead then as 'brain absent',[29] have no legal foundation. Because such children, born alive but dying, do not necessarily suffer genetic defects, their organs may be deemed appropriate for transplantation after death. Natural death, however, usually results in organ deterioration due to hypoxia and ischemia, so mechanical means may sometimes be used to maintain the quality of organs for posthumous transplantation. The acute shortage in the availability of infant-sized organs makes anencephalic sources particularly valuable to preserve the lives of newborn children suffering from organ failure. However, the Royal Medical Colleges take the view that:

> organs for transplantation can be removed from anencephalic infants when two doctors who are not members of the transplant team agree that spontaneous respiration has ceased.[30]

Any removal may be legally authorised by a parent of the deceased infant[31] but it is doubtful whether a parent has legal power to consent to the use of mechanical means before death to preserve organs for posthumous recovery.[32]

---

[27] See *In the Matter of Baby K* (1993) 832 F Supp 1022 (ED Va), affirmed (1994) 16 F3d 590 (4th Cir), certiorari denied (1994) 115 S Ct 95 (US Sup Ct); and Ch 19.

[28] See criteria for the diagnosis of brain stem death, (1995) 29 *J Royal College of Physicians* 381, para (e), and *A Code of Practice for the Diagnosis of Brain Stem Death*. See also Furrow, BR, Johnson, SH, Jost, TS and Schwartz, RL, *Health Law: Cases, Materials and Problems* (2nd edn, St Paul, Minn: 1991), 1049.

[29] McCullagh, P, *Brain Dead, Brain Absent, Brain Donors: Human Subjects or Human Objects?* (Chichester, 1993).

[30] Report of the Working Party of the Conference of Royal Medical Colleges and their Faculties in the United Kingdom on Organ Transplantation in Neonates, 1988.

[31] See para 16.33 below.

[32] See Ch 19.

3. Foetal Tissue Donation

16.11 Foetal tissues include not only organs and cells from foetuses aborted spontaneously and electively, but also placentas and umbilical cord blood[33] available following childbirth. They have a variety of uses in research and increasingly in therapy, such as the employment of placental tissues in the manufacture of therapeutic pharmaceutical products and the treatment of burn victims, and the transplantation of foetal cells into patients suffering for instance from diabetes and such neurological disorders as Parkinson's disease.[34] Foetal tissue possesses four qualities that make it valuable for transplantation to overcome a range of medical problems. It can proliferate when implanted, undergo cell and tissue differentiation, produce growth factors, and, in contrast to adult tissue, not always provoke a significant immune response from the host tissue.[35] Products of spontaneous abortion may be valuable in types of research,[36] but their utility for therapeutically intended transplantation will remain very limited due to the high incidence of genetic abnormalities in foetuses that are spontaneously aborted. If miscarriage occurs late in pregnancy due to a traumatic event or comparable misfortune, however, foetal organs may become available and be suitable for transplantation into infants suffering organ failure. For purposes of gathering vital statistics, abortions may be distinguished from stillbirths, the latter being marked by such criteria as delivery of a dead foetus after 20 weeks of pregnancy or of foetal weight of 500 grams or more.[37] However, the terms 'abortion' and 'miscarriage', whether spontaneous or induced, may be regarded as synonymous.[38]

16.12 Most contentious in foetal tissue transplantation, although minor in current practice, is recovery of such tissues as foetal neural cells that can stimulate dopamine production when transplanted into patients suffering from Parkinson's disease,[39]

---

[33] Marshall, E, 'Clinical Promise, Ethical Quandry' (1996) 271 *Science* 586–8 (transplanting umbilical cord blood as an alternative to bone marrow to treat a variety of life-threatening diseases).

[34] Because it is still novel and unproven, foetal neural cell transplantation into patients with Parkinson's disease tends to be classified as experimental, although it is therapeutic research, designed to benefit the patients, rather than pure research, designed to achieve generalisable knowledge for its own sake: see Goddard, JE, 'The NIH Revitalization Act of 1993 Washed Away Many Legal Problems with Fetal Tissue Transplantation Research But a Stain Remains' (1996) 49 Southern Methodist Univ L Rev 375–99, 378, and Gelfand, G and Levin, TR, 'Fetal Tissue Research: Legal Regulation of Human Fetal Tissue Transplantation' (1993) 50 Washington and Lee L Rev 647–94.

[35] Morgan, B, 'The Regulation of Fetal Tissue Transplantation' (1991) 14 U of New South Wales LJ 283–301, 284.

[36] The UK Medical Research Council has maintained a centralised foetal tissue bank in London since 1957, which distributes between four and five thousand tissue samples each year, derived from some 800 foetal specimens: see Royal Commission (n 3 above), 983.

[37] See eg The [Ontario] Vital Statistics Act, RSO 1990, ch V-4, s 1.

[38] See Keown, IJ, 'Miscarriage: a Medico-Legal Analysis' (1984) Crim LR 604–14.

[39] See Gelfand and Levin (n 34 above) 652.

and recovery of foetal islet cells from the pancreas for treatment of diabetes.[40] Recovery of such foetal tissues is controversial because it depends on elective abortions scheduled, for instance, before nine weeks of gestation in the case of treatment of Parkinson's disease, and during the fourteenth week for treatment of diabetes.[41] Further, the type of abortion procedure employed will affect the quality of the tissue and its utility for transplantation. A hysterotomy, similar to a caesarian section delivery, provides superior tissue because the foetus is damaged least, so that tissues can more easily be differentiated and recovered, but it presents the greatest risk of an adverse outcome to the health and future childbearing of the pregnant patient. In contrast, when appropriate to the stage of gestation, dilation and curettage procedures affect the patient the least, but are most destructive to foetal tissues.[42]

Recovery of foetal tissues for purposes of transplantation or research raises central issues of patients' informed consent to abortion itself, its timing and its method, since decisions on these matters affect the utility of resulting tissues for these purposes. Use for transplantation is closely analogous to use in research, and before transplantation becomes a therapeutic treatment of choice its procedures constitute clinical research. The Committee to Review the Guidance on the Research Use of Foetuses and Fetal Material (the Polkinghorne Committee) recommended that 'great care should be taken to separate the decisions relating to abortion and to the subsequent use of fetal material. The prior decision to carry out an abortion should be reached without consideration of the benefits of subsequent use.'[43] The Code of Practice the Committee recommended includes the provisions, among others, that:

16.13

> The decision to carry out an abortion must be reached without consideration of the benefit of subsequent use.[44]

> The written consent of the mother must be obtained before any research or therapy involving the fetus or fetal tissue takes place.[45]

> Consent to the termination of pregnancy must be reached before consent is sought to the use of fetal tissue, and without reference to the possibility of that use. Provided the question of use is not introduced until consent to the termination of pregnancy has been obtained, it is permissible to deal with the two issues on the same occasion.[46]

---

[40] ibid.

[41] ibid.

[42] ibid.

[43] *Review of the Guidance on the Research Use of Fetuses and Fetal Material* (Cm 762, 1989, para 4.1; see also Royal Commission (n 3 above), Recommendation 281 (b) at 998, and Recommendation 283, at 999, on separation of decisions on timing and methods of abortion from subsequent use of tissues. For a critique of the Royal Commission's approach, see Dickens, BM,'The Ethics of Fetal-Tissue Donation: Consensus and Contradiction' (editorial) (1994) 151 *Canadian Medical Association J*, 285–9.

[44] Review (n 43 above) 22; Code of Practice, para 3.1.

[45] ibid, 23; Code of Practice, para 4.1.

[46] Code of Practice para 4.2.

The Committee required that the question of subsequent use of the foetus not be raised with a patient by counsellors until she had made the decision to terminate pregnancy, but recognised that it is impossible to prevent her putting questions about the method and timing of abortion in relation to subsequent use. The Committee considered, however, that 'since it will not be permissible to give any indication of the use to which any particular foetus might be put, or even if it will be used at all, it will not be possible to give advice of this kind'.[47]

16.14   General concerns regarding the legality of elective abortion[48] frame the legal issue of control of foetal tissues that could become available thereby for transplantation. Assuming that the pregnant woman will survive the procedure, which, under medical management, is now almost invariably the case,[49] the issue is whether, (i) she may give consent as a living donor of her own tissues; (ii) she and/or the biological father or husband may give consent as for tissues of a deceased infant; or (iii) she is precluded from participation in the consent process on the analogy that a person who kills another is usually unable to donate the victim's tissues. The Code of Practice recommended by the Polkinghorne Committee requires the mother's consent, and observes that:

> It may be desirable to consult the father since, for example, tests on fetal tissue may reveal a finding of potential significance to him, and because he may have knowledge of a transmissible or hereditary disease, but his consent shall not be a requirement nor should he have the power to forbid research or therapy making use of fetal tissue.[50]

16.15   In the United States, the Uniform Anatomical Gift Act, adopted by all states, generally with some modification, defines a 'decedent' as a 'deceased individual and includes a stillborn infant or foetus'.[51] This leaves some ambivalence regarding donation of foetal tissues, since either parent may consent to donation of tissues from a deceased infant. The Uniform Anatomical Gift Act permits the 'parents' of a decedent to donate the body or its parts,[52] but does not define 'parent'. This failure leaves open the issues of whether 'parent' includes a biological unmarried father, and whether paternity presumptions apply to the husbands of married women. The distinction has been proposed that:

---

[47] Review (n 43 above) 14, para 6.6.
[48] See Ch 11.
[49] Between 1984 and 1988, six women died from abortion in the UK, while 1,044,099 abortions were performed, including on women from outside the UK. The death rate of under one in 100,000 procedures makes abortion about 20 times as safe as pregnancy and childbirth; Lloyd, L, 'Abortion and Health Care Ethics III' in Gillon, R and Lloyd, A (eds), *Principles of Health Care Ethics* (Chichester, 1994), 559–76 at 566–7.
[50] Review (n 43 above) 23, para 4.3.
[51] Uniform Anatomical Gift Act, ss 1(2), 8A, Uniform Laws Annotated (ULA) 9 (1987).
[52] ibid, ss 3, 8A ULA 17.

once the fetus is removed from the woman's body, it is no longer accurate to call it 'her' tissue in the same way that her liver or spleen would be called her tissue. The fetus is genetically distinct from her. It is a whole entity, not a functional part of an entity as is a woman's spleen, liver or kidney.[53]

This is not persuasive of a father's rights of disposition, however, since an intact dead foetus falls within the definition of an 'organ', which is controlled by the living source, under the Human Organ Transplants Act 1989,[54] and, like the foetus, the placenta is also genetically distinct from the mother, but it has never been suggested that it is at the biological father's disposal.[55]

Legal approaches to foetuses and foetal tissues are also conditioned by judicial assertions that foetuses are not to be equated to persons. In *R v Tait*,[56] the Court of Appeal (Criminal Division) quashed the conviction of a man who threatened to kill a foetus in utero. He had been convicted of the offence against s 16 of the Offences against the Person Act, 1861, as amended,[57] of making a threat to kill another 'or a third person'. The trial judge had directed the jury that 'Parliament . . . has not put any restriction on the definition of a third party',[58] and left members of the jury to decide whether the unborn baby was such a person. The Criminal Division held this to be a misdirection, since 'the foetus in utero was not, in the ordinary sense, "another person", distinct from its mother'.[59] Similarly, the Supreme Court of Canada considered itself to be expressing the long-standing common law in *R v Sullivan*[60] in observing that the expressions 'human being' and 'person' are synonymous, and that a foetus in the birth canal is not a person, so that negligence resulting in the pregnant woman suffering stillbirth is not convictable as manslaughter or criminal negligence causing death.[61]

16.16

Recipients of tissues from elective abortions, and of products developed from such tissues, who oppose such procedures in principle and consider any participants in or beneficiaries of their use to be complicit in immoral behaviour[62] may claim a legal right to know if any medical procedures or products proposed for them are tainted by this association.[63] The claim may be based on battery, alleging

16.17

---

[53] Bell, NMC, 'Regulating Transfer and Use of Fetal Tissue in Transplantation Procedures: The Ethical Dimensions' (1994) 20 American J Law and Medicine 277–94, 287.

[54] See text at n 7 above.

[55] See the Royal Commission (n 3 above), Recommendation 276 at 983: 'Hospitals obtain consent from women, by means of written consent forms, regarding the disposal of placentas.'

[56] [1989] 3 WLR 891 (CA).

[57] 24 & 25 Vict ch 100 s 16, as substituted by the Criminal Law Act 1977 (s 65, Sch 12).

[58] N 56 above, 895.

[59] ibid, 899. See also *Attorney-General's Reference (No 3 of 1994)* [1998] AC 245 (HL).

[60] (1991) 63 CCC (3d) 97 (Sup Ct Can).

[61] ibid, 106.

[62] See para 16.69 below.

[63] Finnis, J, 'Abortion and Health Care Ethics II' in Gillon and Lloyd, *Principles of Health Care Ethics* (n 49 above), 547–57, 554.

that consent to conduct of the transplant was vitiated by omission of information material to the patient's choice, or negligence in giving information, although in the latter, damage may be difficult to establish. Physicians proposing foetal neural cell transplants will usually inform patients, perhaps in naming the procedure. However, products developed from use of foetal tissues, such as vaccines against polio, measles, rubella and other diseases and diagnostic tests for viral diseases including hepatitis, influenza and human immunodeficiency virus (HIV), tend not to disclose their development from foetal tissues, including from elective abortions, in information to the public. Patients with strong sensitivities may ask about the origins of products proposed for their use, of course, and must be honestly answered[64] with specific regard to their concerns. Fee-paying patients may so claim under contractual law on misrepresentation. Others' claims for negligent non-disclosure are buttressed where no 'therapeutic privilege' of non-disclosure is recognised,[65] but they still have to establish damage. Patients are entitled to decline use of products for their own purposes to which they have moral objections but, on analogy to Jehovah's Witness parents and blood transfusions, are not legally entitled to violate the legal duties they owe their children to supply them with medically indicated health care including preventive health services.[66]

4. The Legal Status of Tissues Outside the Body

16.18 Dead bodies have long been governed by the 'no property' rule of the common law, despite its insecure historical foundations,[67] and, since abolition of slavery, living persons have not been considered the subject of property.[68] This raises the issue of the legal status of tissues that have come from persons while they are living[69] or following death.[70] A highly visible modern case in the Supreme Court of California, *Moore v Regents of the University of California*,[71] concerned a man from whose tissues, acquired without his understanding the purpose for which they were requested, a valuable cell-line was developed and patented for commercial exploitation. He sued on 13 causes of action, but was finally allowed to proceed

---

[64] See Lord Bridge, obiter in *Sidaway v Board of Governors of the Bethlem Royal Hospital* [1985] AC 871 (HL), 898.

[65] English law affords 'therapeutic privilege' only very limited recognition; see Kennedy and Grubb (n 10 above), 701–4.

[66] See *In re B (A Minor) (Wardship; Sterilisation)*, [1988] 1 AC 199 (HL) and para 16.21 below.

[67] Matthews, P, 'Whose Body? People as Property' (1983) 36 CLP 193–239.

[68] For a pre-abolition case of property in slaves, see *Gregson v Gilbert* (1783) 3 Dougl 232, 99 ER 629 (KB).

[69] For background, see Dickens, BM, 'The Control of Living Body Materials', (1977) 27 U of Toronto LJ 142–198.

[70] For a modern analysis, see Dworkin, G and Kennedy, I, 'Human Tissue: Rights in the Body and Its Parts' (1993) 1 Med L Rev 291–319. See also the Department of Health Code of Practice on the import and export of human body parts and tissue for non-therapeutic uses (*www.doh.gov.uk/tissue/imports.htm*).

[71] N 2 above.

only on his claims for lack of his informed consent to non-therapeutic tissue donation, which in essence was a claim in negligence,[72] and for breach of fiduciary duty.[73] His claim for violation of alleged property rights in his tissue, based on the tort of conversion, was rejected.[74] The Court found that, because Moore had voluntarily surrendered his tissues to his physicians, he clearly did not expect to retain possession of them, and no precedents supported his claim of ownership, either directly or indirectly.[75] The narrower ground on which the property claim was rejected was California's Health and Safety Code, which required human tissues, following conclusion of scientific use, to be disposed of by interment, incineration, or any other specified method to protect public health and safety.[76] The Court concluded that:

> the statute's practical effect is to limit, drastically, a patient's control over excised cells . . . the statute eliminates so many of the rights ordinarily attached to property that one cannot simply assume that what is left amounts to 'property' or 'ownership' for purposes of conversion law.[77]

The broader ground on which the Court refused to extend the tort of conversion to protect Moore's interest in the tissues which were removed, was the chilling effect this would have on biotechnological development, since conversion of property is a tort of strict liability[78] that would create legal liability in even innocent and bona fide holders of the property. The Court observed that:

> Research on human cells plays a critical role in medical research. This is so because researchers are increasingly able to isolate naturally occurring, medically useful biological substances and to produce useful quantities of such substances through genetic engineering . . . Products developed through biotechnology . . . include treatments and tests for leukaemia, cancer, diabetes, dwarfism, hepatitis-B, kidney transplant rejection, emphysema, osteoporosis, ulcers, anaemia, infertility and gynaecological tumours to name but a few.
>
> The extension of conversion law into this area will hinder research by restricting access to the necessary raw materials.[79]

In expressing the pragmatic basis of its conclusion, however, the Court left open the issue of principle. It declared that:

---

[72] *Cobbs v Grant* (1972) 501 P 2d 1 (Cal Sup Ct); in Canada, compare *Reibl v Hughes* (1980) 114 DLR (3d) 1 (Sup Ct Can).

[73] N 2 above, 485.

[74] ibid, 493–97.

[75] In *R v Stillman* (1997) 113 CCC (3d) 321 at 348, the Supreme Court of Canada indicated that when a person voluntarily surrenders or abandons bodily tissues, others may acquire and use them without the person's consent. For an argument in favour of a person's inchoate right of ownership in tissues involuntarily severed from the person's body, see Dickens, BM (n 69 above), 180–3.

[76] California Health and Safety Code, para 7054.4 (West Supp 1992).

[77] N 2 above, 492.

[78] See eg *Byer v Canadian Bank of Commerce* (1937) 65 P 2d 67 (Cal Sup Ct).

[79] N 2 above, 494 (citations omitted).

> We do not purport to hold that excised cells can never be property for any purpose whatsoever . . .[80]

and emphasized that its concern was the protection of:

> innocent parties who are engaged in socially useful activities, such as researchers who have no reason to believe that their use of a particular cell sample is, or may be, against a donor's wishes.[81]

16.19 Accordingly, a living source of tissue outside the body who made clear that he or she had no intention of abandoning or donating it in general, or in an unrestricted way, could in principle assert a property interest in it.[82] This might be particularly so if he or she, like those the Supreme Court of California was concerned to protect, was 'engaged in socially useful activities', such as being an altruistic tissue donor to a designated recipient like a family member affected by organ failure.[83] The pragmatism that protects a medical or scientific researcher's property interest in abandoned human cells over that of the source's would also operate to protect the source's property interest in tissue the source intended for a comparably valuable social interest such as organ donation, for instance to a family member.[84]

16.20 A reason to resist recognition of human tissues as property, whether from living or deceased sources,[85] is the way recognition might open to objectionable commerce.[86] However, legislation and judicial policy, for instance on contracts held to be void as being contrary to public policy, may offer adequate safeguards against commercialisation of human organs and other tissues.[87] Indeed, the legislative prohibition of commercial traffic in human tissue[88] may confirm its legal status as

---

[80] ibid, 493.

[81] ibid, 494

[82] See the differing views of Weisman, I, 'Organs as Assets' (1994) 27 Israel L Rev 610–23; Tedeschi, G, 'Ownership of Organs Taken from a Living Person', ibid, 624–51, and Weisman, I, ' "Ownership", "Assets" and "Transferability of Property Rights" ', ibid, 652–60.

[83] Where A donates an organ for the benefit of B, but the organ is transferred to C, claims of A and B against the transferor and C would be governed by principles of property law on transfer between A and B, but the transferor and perhaps C might be convicted on prosecution for theft or conspiracy if they acted knowingly.

[84] See Dickens, BM, 'Living Tissue and Organ Donors and Property Law: More on *Moore*' (1992) 8 J of Contemporary Health Law and Policy 73–93.

[85] On non-proprietary remedies for improper removal of cadaveric material, see Skegg, PDG, 'Liability for the Unauthorised Removal of Cadaveric Transplant Material' (1974) 14 *Medicine, Science and Law* 53–7; Kennedy, I, 'Further Thoughts on Liability for Non-observance of the Provisions of the Human Tissue Act 1961' (1976) 16 *Medicine, Science and Law* 49–55; Skegg, PDG, 'Liability for the Unauthorized Removal of Cadaveric Transplant Material: Some Further Thoughts' (1977) 17 *Medicine, Science and Law* 123–6.

[86] See Wagner, DM, 'Property Rights in the Human Body: The Commercialization of Organ Transplantation and Biotechnology' (1995) 33 Duquesne L Rev 931–59.

[87] See discussion of the Human Organ Transplants Act 1989, para 16.36 below.

[88] Influenced by the *Moore* case (n 2 above), for instance, the California State Legislature enacted a law that prohibits donors from receiving any 'valuable consideration' for donation. California Health and Safety Code, para 7155(a) (West Supp 1992).

property.[89] Status as property also provides protection against theft. In *R v Kelly*,[90] the Court of Appeal reaffirmed the rule that there is 'no property' in a corpse or parts of a corpse. The Court, nevertheless, upheld the defendant's conviction for theft of anatomical specimens on the basis that they became 'property' within s 4 of the Theft Act 1968 when they 'acquired different attributes by virtue of the application of skill, such as dissection or preservation techniques, for exhibition or teaching purposes'.[91] In *US v Arora*,[92] it was held that a cell-line was a chattel. Thus, an action in conversion lay against a researcher who tampered with, and destroyed, a cell-line stored in a research laboratory. In the Western Australian case of *Roche v Douglas as Administrator of the Estate of Rowan (Deceased)*[93] it was held that tissue specimens removed during surgery and subsequently preserved in paraffin wax were 'property' subject to the court's jurisdiction to make an order that they undergo DNA testing for the purposes of determining who inherited under a will.[94]

Tissue banking is increasingly common, including eye banks, blood banks, breast milk banks and, for instance, cord blood stem cell banks.[95] Operators of banks require legal security in their control of the materials they gather and preserve. Particularly sensitive are reproductive tissues and pre-embryos.[96] Beyond objections to treating a pre-embryo as property based on concepts of ensoulment are Kantian objections to treating people as objects, or only as means to ends, and to treating potential people as objects. Nevertheless, in *York v Jones*,[97] the US District Court for the Eastern District of Virginia found a bailor-bailee relationship to arise from the contract between a couple whose pre-embryo was preserved in the freezing facility of an infertility clinic, and the clinic,[98] creating the implication that the pre-embryo was property. In 1992, the Tennessee Supreme Court rejected the implication that frozen pre-embryos are subject to property rights,

16.21

---

[89] The Nuffield Council (n 1 above), made further recommendations for elimination of commerce, including the use of non-commercial agencies and payments for expenses only: see ch 6, 49–53.

[90] [1998] 3 All ER 741 (CA).

[91] See further discussion in para 19.44 below. See also *Buchanan v Milton* (1999) 53 BMLR 176 (Hale J).

[92] (1994) 860 F Supp 1091 (US Dist Ct My).

[93] [2000] WASC 146 (Sanderson M).

[94] See Grubb, A, 'I, Me, Mine: Bodies, Parts and Property' (1998) 3 *Medical Law International* 299. For a discussion of the legal status of human tissue see: *The Interim Report of the Inquiry into the Management of Care of Children Receiving Complex Heart Surgery at the Bristol Royal Infirmary: Removal and Retention of Human Material* (May 2000), especially Annexes A and B. See also para 19.39 below.

[95] On tissue banks see: *A Code of Practice for Tissue Banks: Providing Tissues of Human Origin for Therapeutic Purposes* (DoH, 2001).

[96] Meaning embryos prior to implantation in utero; see McCormick, RA, 'Who or What is the Preembryo?' (1991) 1 *Kennedy Institute of Ethics J* 1–15.

[97] (1989) 717 F Supp 421 (EDVa).

[98] ibid, 425.

however, and held them to be neither property nor living beings, but *sui generis*.[99] The Court observed that:

> pre-embryos are not strictly speaking either 'persons' or 'property', but occupy an interim category that entitles them to special respect because of their potential for human life.[100]

Nevertheless the Court, while stating that the formerly married couple did not have a 'true property interest' in the pre-embryos, held that:

> they do have an interest in the nature of ownership to the extent that they have decision-making authority concerning disposition of the pre-embryos, within the scope of policy set by law.[101]

Despite declaring the pre-embryos' entitlement to special respect because of their potential for life as human persons, the Court permitted the ex-husband's right not to procreate to outweigh his ex-wife's interest in donating them to a childless couple, while suggesting obiter that only the ex-wife's interest in using the pre-embryos herself could outweigh the ex-husband's right, and then only if she could not become pregnant with her own genetic child by any other means.[102]

16.22   In *Hecht v Superior Court*,[103] the California Court of Appeals, reversing the trial court, held that a man who died, by suicide, could bequeath to his girlfriend an interest in sperm he had previously deposited in a sperm bank, just as he could bequeath an interest in stock. However, under Sch 3 to the Human Fertilisation and Embryology Act 1990,[104] s 2(2)(b) requires that a consent to the storage of any gametes or any embryo must 'state what is to be done with the gametes or embryo if the person who gave the consent dies'. In *R v Human Fertilisation and Embryology Authority, ex p Blood*,[105] sperm samples were taken from a comatose man at his wife's request shortly before his death. He gave no consent or directions as to their posthumous use. The Court of Appeal upheld a ruling that storage of the sperm did not comply with legal requirements under the Act, and that the Authority was entitled to refuse to allow the wife exceptional use of the sperm without the donor's written consent. The Court also held, however, that since the donor's wife was entitled to receive medical treatment in the European Community where the Act did not apply, under Articles 59 and 60 of the EC Treaty,[106] and the HFEA is entitled under s 24(4) of the Act to authorise the sending of gametes outside the United Kingdom, the Authority's refusal to allow the sperm to be sent abroad

---

[99]   *Davis v Davis* (1992) 842 SW 2d 588 (Tenn Sup Ct).
[100] ibid, 597.
[101] ibid.
[102] ibid, 604.
[103] (1993) 20 Cal Rptr 2d 275 (Cal Ct App).
[104] 1990 ch 37.
[105] [1997] 2 WLR 806 (CA).
[106] [1992] OJ C224/6.

would be set aside and the Authority be invited to reconsider whether to authorise release of the stored sperm in another Member State.[107] This is consistent with the European Court of Human Rights limiting state restriction of individuals' intimate consensual conduct.[108]

16.23

The operation of sperm, ova and embryo storage facilities in the United Kingdom must comply with the terms of licences granted by the Human Fertilisation and Embryology Authority under the 1990 Act.[109] At the private level, sperm banks properly treat sperm as property of the donors,[110] and third party holders of ova and pre-embryos might be advised to act on the same basis. Nevertheless, in order not to violate legal prohibitions on sales of human tissues and to avoid breach of warranty provisions, sperm donation is usually treated as a service[111] rather than a commodity transaction,[112] and ova and pre-embryo donation may be approached similarly. A service can include an incidental transfer of property, maintaining the status of gametes and pre-embryos as legal property. Interests in preserving availability of such materials for scientific research and education may be protected in terms of the agreements under which possession of them may lawfully be transferred and managed. Donors' property rights protect their interests against uses they do not authorise. However, compensation for property loss or damage alone is usually set at its fair market value, but in the case of gametes and embryos legislation or judicial policy may preclude a market evaluation.[113]

C. Post Mortem Use

1. Introduction

Recovery of transplantable organs from cadavers raises fewer legal issues than their donation by living persons, but issues that arise are nevertheless profound and at times complex. Development of the concept of brain-stem death or neurological death permits recovery of materials for transplantation from bodies of persons

16.24

---

[107] See Ch 10.

[108] See for instance, *Dudgeon v UK* Series A No 45 (1981) 4 EHRR 149.

[109] See n 104 above, and Ch 10.

[110] See Collins, JL, '*Hecht v Superior Court:* Recognizing a Property Right in Reproductive Material' (1994–95) 33 J Family Law 661–84, 669, 675.

[111] By directions made in Britain by the Human Fertilisation and Embryology Authority (HFEA Directions, as amended Feb 1996; see HFEA *Fifth Annual Report 1996*, 18) individual donors of gametes may be paid a maximum of £15 for each donation plus reasonable expenses incurred. See also *HFEA Directions* Ref D 1998/1.

[112] See Dickens, BM, 'Reproduction Law and Medical Consent' (1985) 35 U of Toronto LJ 255–86, 284, and Hodgson, AM, 'Note: The Warranty of Sperm: A Modest Proposal to Increase the Accountability of Sperm Banks and Physicians in the Performance of Artificial Insemination Procedures' (1993) 26 Indiana L Rev 357–386, 367.

[113] For an alternative basis of assessment of loss, see Collins (n 110 above), 682–3.

who are diagnosed to be dead, although their hearts continue to beat, by artificial means that have been used for their care, and their organs thereby remain transfused and viable for transplantation.[114] Where a distinction is drawn between organs and tissues, turning on the potential for spontaneous regeneration,[115] it remains relevant notwithstanding the death of the source, since the distinction is generic to the materials themselves and not specific to the individual human source.

16.25   The historical management of bodies of dead persons under provisions of ecclesiastical law, the common law's so-called 'no property' rule which affected testamentary gifts and intestate succession,[116] and the emergence of medical transplantation only in the last few decades, denied the common law system opportunities to develop long standing principles on removal of materials for therapeutic purposes. Modern laws on post mortem recovery of organs and tissues for transplantation rest on legislation, historically founded on removal of corneas.[117] Legislation may govern post mortem availability of the whole body for educational, research or therapeutic purposes, and therapy would involve transplantation of particular organs or tissues.

16.26   The terms of the consent would govern the availability of individual organs or tissues for transplantation, and the range of users and recipients. Most donations are in general terms, but a consent may be limited to recipients in specified disease categories, or for instance to users in a particular institution such as a named hospital or university medical centre, perhaps as a response to an institutional drive to increase donations or a publicised case. Individuals making donations in anticipation of their death, and persons in lawful possession of bodies after death who are permitted under the terms of legislation to authorise acquisition of materials for transplantation, may specify the extent of the donation or authorisation they are willing to approve. In principle this is a private discretion, although circumstances may arise in which the person lawfully in possession of a body is a public or quasi-public officer, such as when a person dies in a public facility like a prison, public shelter or hospital and no family member claims the body for burial or cremation. A concern for potential recipient institutions is whether they may lawfully accept a donation or authorisation that draws an invidious distinction, for instance among members of racial groups for whose therapeutic care materials may be used. A positive selection, such as to favour residents of a specified area, a hospital with an affinity with a religious denomination or recipients in given age categories may be more acceptable than a negative selection, such as to deny

---

[114] See paras 19.05–19.10 below on Development of Criteria of Brain Stem Death.
[115] See para 16.03 above.
[116] See para 19.41 below.
[117] See the Corneal Grafting Act 1952.

transplantation to members of a given race or religion, but each form of expression must be critically assessed to determine whether the purpose is to exclude identified persons as recipients on an offensive ground. Acceptance of donations made on discriminatory terms may violate international and national human rights principles enforceable by law, and, more immediately, an institution's own by-laws.

2. *Legislation on Post Mortem Use for Transplantation*

In Britain, the Human Tissue Act 1961[118] provides in s 1 that: **16.27**

(1) If any person, either in writing at any time or orally in the presence of two or more witnesses during his last illness, has expressed a request that his body or any specified part of his body be used after his death for therapeutic purposes or for purposes of medical education or research, the person lawfully in possession of his body after his death may, unless he has reason to believe that the request was subsequently withdrawn, authorise the removal from the body of any part or, as the case may be, the specified part, for use in accordance with the request.

(2) Without prejudice to the foregoing subsection, the person lawfully in possession of the body of a deceased person may authorise the removal of any part from the body for use for the said purposes if, having made such reasonable enquiry as may be practicable, he has not reason to believe

   (a) that the deceased had expressed an objection to his body being so dealt with after his death, and had not withdrawn it; or

   (b) that the surviving spouse or any surviving relative of the deceased objects to the body being so dealt with.

(3) Subject to subsections (4) and (5) of this section, the removal and use of any part of a body in accordance with an authority given in pursuance of this section shall be lawful.

(4) No such removal shall be effected except by a fully registered medical practitioner, who must have satisfied himself by personal examination of the body that life is extinct.

(4A) No such removal of an eye or part of an eye shall be effected except[119] by

   (a) a registered medical practitioner who must have satisfied himself by personal examination of the body that life is extinct; or

   (b) a person in the employment of a health authority, Primary Care Trust[120] or NHS trust acting on the instructions of a registered medical practitioner who must, before giving those instructions, be satisfied that the person in question is sufficiently qualified and trained to perform the removal competently and must also either

      (i) have satisfied himself by personal examination of the body that life is extinct, or

---

[118] N 6 above.

[119] s 4A was added, with related adjustments, by the Corneal Tissue Act 1986, s 1.

[120] Amendment introduced by the Health Act 1999 (Supplementary, Consequential etc Provisions) Order 2000, SI 2000/90, Sch 1, art 4.

(ii) be satisfied that life is extinct on the basis of a statement to that effect by a registered medical practitioner who has satisfied himself by personal examination of the body that life is extinct.

(5) Where a person has reason to believe that an inquest may be required to be held on any body or that a post-mortem examination of any body may be required by the coroner, he shall not, except with the consent of the coroner,

(a) give an authority under this section in respect of the body; or
(b) act on such authority given by any other person.

(6) No authority shall be given under this section in respect of any body by a person entrusted with the body for the purpose only of its interment or cremation.

(7) In the case of a body lying in a hospital, nursing home or other institution, any authority under this section may be given on behalf of the person having the control and management thereof by any officer or person designated for that purpose by the first-mentioned person.

(8) Nothing in this section shall be construed as rendering unlawful any dealing with, or with any part of, the body of a deceased person which is lawful apart from the Act.

(9) In the application of this section to Scotland, for subsection (5) there shall be substituted the following subsection

(5) Nothing in this section shall authorise the removal of any part from a body in any case where the procurator fiscal has objected to such removal.

(i) Consent: The Deceased Donor

16.28 A person who wishes to express a request that the person lawfully in possession of his or her body or parts of it authorise use of tissues following death for transplantation may do so in one of two forms. The more usual is in writing. No specified form has been established for this purpose by legislation or regulation, and the form attached for instance to a motor vehicle driving licence has no special legal status. Donation post mortem in writing need not be witnessed and no confirmation of capacity is required. If the purported donor lacks relevant capacity,[121] or if capacity is questionable, the person lawfully in possession of the body may nevertheless authorise removal of any part from the body for transplantation under s 1(2), unless there is reason to believe that the deceased had expressed an objection and not withdrawn it.[122] If doubt exists about a donor's competence to give the consent that was expressed, the person in possession of the body may underwrite that consent through that person's authority under s 1(2). However, if there is doubt about the capacity of a person who expressed an objection to donation, the person in possession might be advised not to consent in his or her own capacity. Incapacity on the part of the deceased may be a separate ground for caution in use of material for transplantation, of course, if the condition has a genetic origin or may be due, for instance, to AIDS-related dementia.

---

[121] See generally Ch 4.
[122] See s 1(2)(a).

The alternative to written consent is oral consent expressed in the presence of two **16.29** or more witnesses during the donor's last illness. What constitutes a last illness is a matter of medical evidence of the cause of death and of the natural pathology of the disorder. An oral statement by a sick person who shortly afterwards suffers death from a cause unrelated to the illness, such as a road traffic accident, might not be considered adequate for purposes of s 1(1) of the Act, although evidence of the statement may reinforce consent given by the person lawfully in possession of the body under s 1(2). However, the donor's suicide in the course of that illness may be considered to be pathologically related to it, although a coroner's jury's verdict of suicide while the balance of the mind was disturbed may cast doubt on contemporaneous capacity. In the case of testamentary documents, witnesses attest only to the freedom of the testator's signature, not that the testator competently intends the consequences of the will. Under the 1961 Act, however, witnesses have to recognise the nature of the donor's oral expression, and be satisfied that the donor intends to make the request and any limitations or conditions that accompany it. Further, unlike witnesses to a will, they are apparently not precluded from subsequently becoming beneficiaries under the donation. The Act contains no requirement that witnesses be adults, but the younger a witness is, or the less capacity a witness possesses for a reason unrelated to age, the less reliable the oral statement may appear.

The Act similarly sets no minimum age to request donation. Section 8(1) of the **16.30** Family Law Reform Act 1969[123] provides that the consent to medical treatment of a minor of 16 or above 'shall be as effective as it would be if he were of full age'. Although a request for donation is not 'treatment',[124] this may be applied by analogy to posthumous donation. However, the oral expression of a person younger than 16 may serve only as reinforcement of consent given under s 1(2). Equally problematic is whether the written donation request of a minor would be effective under s 1(1). Posthumous donation is not the type of medical procedure to which s 8(1) of the 1969 Act applies, but the Act may embody the common law mature minor rule in this regard despite the Act's general purpose to reform the law. Again, if a donor younger than 18, or 16, cannot make an effective written posthumous donation request, willingness to donate may be the basis of a s 1(2) consent given by the person in possession of the young person's body.

It must be noted, however, that the donation of even an adult of unquestioned ca- **16.31** pacity in anticipation of death does not compel the person in subsequent possession of the donor's body to make it available for recovery of transplantable materials. Section 1(1) of the Human Tissue Act 1961 describes a donation only as 'a request', and provides that the person lawfully in possession of the body after

---

[123] 1969, ch 46.
[124] *Re W (A Minor) (Medical Treatment)* [1992] 4 All ER 627, 647 *per* Nolan LJ.

death 'may . . . authorise the removal from the body of any part or, as the case may be, the specified part, for use in accordance with the request'. The request is not simply for medical assessment of the body's suitability for recovery of transplantable materials, but for favourable exercise of discretion by the person in lawful possession. The request may be frustrated not simply because, at death, the body is unsuitable for use of its materials, for example due to organ damage, genetic defect, or infection of tissue, but also because the person in lawful possession of the body declines to respect the request, for whatever reason.[125] It is doubtful that a potential recipient person or institution has standing to compel that person's exercise of discretion in favour of compliance with the deceased person's request,[126] or that a request for posthumous donation constitutes an enforceable trust binding the person subsequently in possession of the body.[127] If the 'person' lawfully in possession of the body is a public body such as a hospital trust, its exercise of discretion might be amenable to judicial review to determine whether it had been lawfully exercised but, unless its decision is patently unreasonable, courts will be slow to interfere.[128]

16.32   By s 1(2), the person in possession of a body may not authorise recovery of materials for transplantation if, 'having made such reasonable enquiry as may be practicable', which the person is obliged to make, he or she has reason to believe that the deceased objected to such dealing with the body, or 'that the surviving spouse or any surviving relative of the deceased objects to the body being so dealt with'.[129] The Act sets no limits on proximity of relatives who are empowered to veto the deceased person's request, or on the relative's age or capacity.[130] Accordingly, remote relatives identified after the reasonable enquiry that it is practicable for the person in lawful possession of the body to make, may veto the deceased person's request, and apparently the concurring request of that person's spouse and of a more proximate relative. A remote relative who takes an initiative to notify the person in lawful possession of the body of his or her objection will not depend on the person's

---

[125] A Code of Practice on cadaveric organ donation is included in *A Code of Practice for the Diagnosis of Brain Stem Death* (March 1998) DoH (HSC 1998/999). See para 19.39 below.

[126] Difficulties in potential recipients' enforcement are recognised in Jardine, DG, 'Liability Issues Arising Out of Hospitals' and Organ Procurement Organizations' Rejection of Valid Anatomical Gifts' (1990) Wisconsin L Rev 1655–94, 1680–6.

[127] On whether the deceased may impose conditions, including discriminatory conditions, see *An Investigation into Conditional Organ Donation: The Report of a Panel* (DoH, 2000). In ch 5, the Panel rejected the possibility of any conditional donation under the 1961 Act.

[128] See *R v Human Fertilisation and Embryology Authority, ex p Blood* (n 105 above), 821, and *R v Sheffield HA, ex p Seale* [1996] 3 Med L Rev 326 and accompanying Commentary.

[129] s 1(2)(b).

[130] Skegg, PDG, argues that 'relative' is limited to genetic or blood relatives, as opposed to a relative by marriage, since the Act contrasts the spouse with 'any surviving relative'; see 'Human Tissue Act 1961' (1976) 16 *Medicine, Science and Law* 193–9, 197.

reasonable enquiry[131] for the veto to have effect. The Act seems to afford the person in possession of the body no power to follow a near relative's consent to removal of materials over a more distance relative's objection. The veto may be open to legal challenge, however, if, for instance, the deceased had failed to express a request in conformity with s 1(1) but could be shown to have wished for posthumous donation to assist survival of a more proximate relative than the objector, such as a child, brother or sister of the deceased. By contrast to the Human Tissue Act, legislation may explicitly favour the deceased person's preference of donation over the interest of an objecting relative, including a spouse. For instance, Ontario's Human Tissue Gift Act[132] permits the donor's consent to posthumous use of body materials to prevail over family members' opposition. Section 4(3) provides that:

> Upon the death of a person who has given a consent under this section, the consent is binding and is full authority for the use of the body or the removal and use of the specified part of parts for the purpose specified, except that no person shall act upon a consent . . . if the person has reason to believe that it was subsequently withdrawn.

(ii) Consent: The Person in Lawful Possession of the Body

It has been held that executors of a deceased person's estate have a right to lawful possession of the body.[133] Burial or cremation expenses are a charge on the deceased's assets, and those responsible for their administration possess legal power to direct disposition of the deceased's mortal remains. Since recovery of materials for transplantation may affect plans for disposition, the 1961 Act gives those in possession of the body power to authorise removal of such materials. However, without affecting the financial responsibility for disposal of remains, s 1(7) of the 1961 Act provides that when a body is lying in such an institution as a hospital or nursing home, power to authorise removal of any part of the body for purposes of the Act may be given by the institution through someone designated by the person having control and management of the institution.[134]

16.33

This is a matter on which details of legislation vary. For instance, in contrast to the 1961 Act, Ontario's Human Tissue Gift Act[135] establishes a hierarchy of persons entitled to consent to removal of transplantable material from the body of a person who, when living, neither expressed consent nor demonstrated objection. The spouse, child, parent, brother or sister and other next of kin are ranked in that

16.34

---

131 On 'reasonable enquiry', see Skegg, PDG, ibid, and Dworkin, G, 'The Law Relating to Organ Transplantation in England' (1970) 33 MLR 353–377, 364–365. Kennedy and Grubb (n 10 above), 1843 favour the latter's interpretation.

132 N 9 above.

133 *Williams v Williams* (1882) 20 Ch D 659.

134 N 125 above.

135 N 9 above.

order, one higher in rank who is readily available displacing all lower in rank. A peer in rank who objects might negate another's consent, since:

> no person shall act on a consent given under this section if the person has actual knowledge of an objection thereto by the person in respect of whom the consent was given or by a person of the same or closer relationship to the person in respect of whom the consent was given than the person who gave the consent.[136]

In the absence of a ranked family member and of other next of kin, consent may be given by 'the person lawfully in possession of the body other than, where the person died in hospital, the administrative head of the hospital'.[137] The 'person lawfully in possession of the body' further excludes the Chief Coroner and a coroner in possession of the body under provincial legislation governing coroners, the Public Guardian and Trustee in possession for purposes of burial or cremation, an embalmer or funeral director and the superintendent of a crematorium.[138] Canadian case law[139] recognises a general right to possession of the body of a deceased person in the surviving spouse or next of kin. It is not clear that a similar right is recognised under the British 1961 Act, or that that Act excludes coroners as such, since s 1(8) provides that nothing in s 1 renders unlawful any dealing with a body or part of a body that is lawful apart from the Act. A coroner's consent is necessary for removal of material from a body where an inquest or post mortem examination may be required, in addition to that of any other person,[140] and in Scotland no removal is authorised where the procurator fiscal has objected.[141] Further, in no case shall authority be given to remove materials from any body 'by a person entrusted with the body for the purpose only of its interment or cremation'.[142]

16.35   An addition to the Ontario legislation, designed to enhance the utility of recovered materials, is that, in advance of the imminent death of a person incapable of giving consent to posthumous donation, a family member may approve such donation. Section 5(2) provides that:

> Where a person who has not given or cannot give a consent . . . dies, or in the opinion of a physician is incapable of giving a consent by reason of injury or disease and the person's death is imminent,
>
> (a) the person's spouse; or
> (b) if none or if the spouse is not readily available, any of the person's children . . .
>
> may consent . . .

---

[136] ibid, s 5(4).
[137] ibid, s 5(2)(f).
[138] ibid, s 5(5).
[139] *Edmonds v Armstrong Funeral Home Ltd* [1931] 1 DLR 676 (Alta SC).
[140] Human Tissue Act 1961, s 1(5).
[141] ibid, s 1(9).
[142] ibid, s 1(6).

(g) in a writing signed by the spouse, relative or other person; or

(h) orally by the spouse, relative or other person in the presence of at least two witnesses; or

(i) by a telegraphic, recorded telephonic, or other recorded message of the spouse, relative or other person,

to the body or the part of parts thereof specified in the consent being used after death for therapeutic purposes, medical education or scientific research.

The section repeats the hierarchy of relatives and others empowered to consent, and is subject to the condition that no person may give consent who has reason to believe that the person whose death is imminent would have objected. The provision anticipates, for instance, a sudden trauma such as a road traffic injury, and a relative rushing to a hospital emergency department or being reached by telephone. Further, although a coroner normally has jurisdiction only over dead bodies, s 6 of the Act provides that where, in the opinion of the physician, the death of a person is imminent by reason of injury or disease and the physician has reason to believe an inquest or post mortem examination will be held but that consent has been given to posthumous donation, the physician may obtain the coroner's directions in advance of death to remove relevant materials after death. This places the coroner on notice of intended donation, and permits the coroner to give such directions as will optimise recovery of materials after death for transplantation.

(iii) Payment: Legislation

The Human Organ Transplants Act 1989[143] provides in s 1 that: **16.36**

(1) A person is guilty of an offence if in Great Britain he

  (a) makes or receives any payment for the supply of, or for an offer to supply, an organ which has been or is to be removed from a dead or living person and is intended to be transplanted into another person whether in Great Britain or elsewhere;

  (b) seeks to find a person willing to supply for payment such an organ . . . or offers to supply such an organ for payment;

  (c) initiates or negotiates any arrangement involving the making of any payment for the supply of, or for an offer to supply, such an organ; or

  (d) takes part in the management or control of a body of persons corporate or unincorporate whose activities consist of or include the initiation or negotiation of such arrangements.

(2) Without prejudice to paragraph (b) of subsection (1) above, a person is guilty of an offence if he causes to be published or distributed, or knowingly publishes or distributes, in Great Britain an advertisement

---

[143] N 7 above.

(a) inviting persons to supply for payment any such organs as are mentioned in paragraph (a) of that subsection or offering to supply any such organs for payment; or

(b) indicating that the advertiser is willing to initiate or negotiate any such arrangement as is mentioned in paragraph (c) of that subsection.

(3) In this section 'payment' means payment in money or money's worth but does not include any payment for defraying or reimbursing

(a) the cost of removing, transporting or preserving the organ to be supplied; or

(b) any expenses or loss of earnings incurred by a person so far as reasonably and directly attributable to his supplying an organ from his body.

(4) In this section 'advertisement' includes any form of advertising whether to the public generally, to any section of the public or individually to selected persons.

Section 4 of the Act provides that:

(1) Where an offence under this Act committed by a body corporate is proved to have been committed with the consent or connivance of, or to be attributable to any neglect on the part of, any director, manager, secretary or other similar officer of the body corporate or any person who was purporting to act in any such capacity, he as well as the body corporate is guilty of the offence and is liable to be proceeded against and punished accordingly.

(2) Where the affairs of a body corporate are managed by its members, subsection (1) above shall apply to the acts and defaults of a member in connection with his functions of management as if he were a director of the body corporate.

(iv) Payment: Commodities and Services

16.37 The distinction between organs and tissues is significant to the prohibitions and punishments of the Human Organ Transplants Act 1989, since they apply only to organs. Section 7(2) provides that:

In this Act, 'organ' means any part of a human body consisting of a structured arrangement of tissues which, if wholly removed, cannot be replicated by the body.

Accordingly, payments for naturally replicable materials such as blood and bone marrow would not violate the Act.[144] In contrast, the Ontario legislation,[145] for instance, provides in s 10 that:

No person shall buy, sell or otherwise deal in, directly or indirectly, for a valuable consideration, any tissue for a transplant, or any body or part or parts thereof other than blood or a blood constituent, for therapeutic purposes, medical education or scientific research, and any such dealing is invalid as being contrary to public policy.

The extension of the prohibition to a body and its parts is significant, since the Act defines 'tissue' much as the British 1989 Act defines 'organ', and it 'does not

---

[144] But see the following section on contracts that are void as contrary to public policy.
[145] Human Tissue Gift Act.

include . . . tissue that is replaceable by natural processes of repair'.[146] It has been seen that sperm donors receive payment not for the sperm themselves but for the time and inconvenience, including for instance repeated HIV testing, of making them available.[147] Payment for service is consistent with s 1(3) of the 1989 Act, which permits payment for costs and expenses involved in organ donation. Clause (b) of the section, permitting recovery of expenses which a person incurs that are attributable 'to his supplying an organ from his body', clearly relates only to donations made by living persons, but clause (a) allows reimbursement of 'the cost of removing, transporting or preserving the organ to be supplied', which would allow repayment of costs to executors and others responsible for deceased persons' assets when organ recovery increases costs of management of the body. Where physicians who remove materials for transplantation are paid on a fee-for-service basis, for instance, the estate may be charged, since costs may not be directly transferable to a recipient patient or institution, particularly when organs are transferable to distant locations and countries. Accordingly, donors' estates may pay these costs directly, and be entitled to appropriate reimbursement.

The legislation in Ontario that renders commercial dealings 'invalid as contrary to public policy' may reflect the position at common law that results from the criminalisation of commercial dealings achieved by the 1989 Act. Common law provisions on entitlement to money or other consideration actually exchanged under an illegal agreement will apply, as will provisions on recovery of money and its equivalent, and the illegal agreement will not be enforceable by any court. It must be asked, however, how common law principles apply to commerce in tissues, the exchange of which for reward is not prohibited under the terms of the 1989 Act. Courts may apply the spirit of the Ontario legislation, and conclude that these agreements are void as being contrary to public policy. Recipients of money, and of tissues, under such void agreements may nevertheless be recognised to have obtained legal title to them. Lawyers who draft agreements that are merely unenforceable face no professional disciplinary charges. Many agreements for personal services, such as in the conduct of the entertainment and sports industries, are valid though not enforceable by order of a court. However, where agreements not criminal in themselves are unenforceable and invalid as contrary to public policy, lawyers who draft them and physicians and other health care professionals who give effect to their terms may become liable to professional disciplinary sanctions for offending the public interest. **16.38**

The effect of public policy considerations is relevant to proposals[148] that people **16.39**

---

[146] ibid, s 1.

[147] See the payment limits set by the Human Fertilisation and Embryology Authority (n 111 above), and the Nuffield Council review of principles of payment (n 1 above) at 130.

[148] Explored, for instance, by the US National Kidney Foundation and United Network for Organ Sharing; see Dejong, W, Drachman, J, Gortmaker, SL *et al*, 'Options for Increasing Organ

may be induced to request posthumous use of their organs and tissues by the prospect of payments going to others they name at the time of donation if, after death, the person's organs or tissues are available for transplantation. The 1989 Act makes it an offence to offer, make or receive any payment,[149] and payment to a person other than a donor appears to be covered by the scope of the Act. The Act intends that donation be altruistic, and directing an intended payment to a person other than the donor, whether at the time the request for donation is made or later, appears to violate that intention no less than giving money directly to the donor. However, the definition of 'payment' excludes the cost of removing an organ,[150] and a donor's agreement that such costs be paid to the estate on removal of an organ would not violate the Act.

16.40   More speculatively, an agreement made at donation that, on posthumous recovery of an organ, a specified payment be made to a charity designated by the donor or, for instance, by a family member, might not violate the purpose of the 1989 Act to bar commercial dealings.[151] An arrangement of this nature would not seem to offend public policy, and would preserve the altruism the Act is designed to protect. Instead of the donor's altruism being directed to an unknown recipient, however, it would be directed to a charitable cause which the donor would identify, or to one approved for instance by a family member. The strategy to promote donation and recovery of transplantable organs post mortem by agreeing to make payments to charities on organs being recoverable might accordingly not be invalid as against public policy, nor offend the terms of the Act, and lawyers', physicians' and others' involvement in such agreements might not be offences or causes of disciplinary sanctions. Payments offered by prospective private recipients, whether individuals or institutions, might indicate the self-interest characteristic of commerce, but payments offered by public agencies might be compatible with the public interest and not legally or otherwise objectionable. A public health service authority intending to spare itself the expense, and patients the mounting health hazards, of dialysis might want to add an incentive to donation for posthumous recovery, and allocate organs in its customary way according to patients' needs, not recipients' means to pay. The unlinking of donating from receipt of a material reward might take the arrangement outside the purpose of the 1989 Act. Nevertheless, agreements of this nature appear contrary to the language of clauses

Donation: The Potential Role of Financial Incentives, Standardized Hospital Procedures, and Public Education to Promote Family Discussion' (1995) 73 *Milbank Quarterly* 463–79.

[149] Human Organ Transplants Act 1989, s 1(1).

[150] ibid, s 1(3).

[151] This is different from creating organ 'futures', by which a person receives payment for promising that, following death, organs will be made available; see Spurr, SJ, 'The Shortage of Transplantable Organs: An Analysis and a Proposal' (1993) 15 *Law and Policy* 355–95, 373–4, and Cohen, LR, 'Increasing the Supply of Transplant Organs: The Virtues of a Futures Market' (1989) 58 George Washington L Rev 1–51.

1(1)(a) and 1(1)(c) of the Act. Any progress towards such agreements might require action in court for a favourable declaratory judgment, or a favourable opinion of the Attorney-General, or perhaps of the Director of Public Prosecutions, without whose consent no proceedings for an offence under s 1 may be instituted.[152]

(v) The Removal of Organs and Tissues[153]

The common law respects the integrity of corpses by apparently recognising an offence of causing indignity to a dead body[154] and of violating public decency by improper handling.[155] The Human Tissue Act 1961[156] provides qualified relief in s 1(3), which states that '[s]ubject to subsection (4),(4A) and (5) of this section, the removal and use of any part of a body in accordance with an authority given in pursuance of this section shall be lawful'. The fact that the provision renders conduct in compliance with it lawful indicates that, in the absence of this provision, removing and using part of a body would be unlawful.[157] Although the provision refers only to 'any part of a body', s 1(1) allows donation of an entire body or any specified part or parts of it, so that s 1(3) may be read accordingly. Section 1(4) limits implementation of any authorisation to obtain materials from a dead body by providing that:

> no such removal, except of eyes or parts of eyes, shall be effected except by a registered medical practitioner, who must have satisfied himself by personal examination of the body that life is extinct.

16.41

---

[152] Human Organ Transplants Act 1989, s 5.

[153] For the reports concerned with the events at Alder Hey Hospital, Liverpool, see: *The Report of the Royal Liverpool Children's Inquiry* (January 2001) (*www.rlcinquiry.org.uk/index.htm*). For the interim and final reports of the Bristol Royal Infirmary Inquiry, see: *The Interim Report of the Inquiry into the Management of Care of Children Receiving Complex Heart Surgery at the Bristol Royal Infirmary: Removal and Retention of Human Material* (May 2000) and *Learning from Bristol: The Report Of The Public Inquiry Into Children's Heart Surgery at the Bristol Royal Infirmary 1984–1995* (Cm 5207, 2001) (*www.bristol-inquiry.org.uk/index.htm*). For professional guidance on tissue removal and retention, see *Interim BMA Guidelines on Retention of Human Tissue at Post-Mortem Examination for the Purposes of Medical Education and Research* (October 2000); The Royal College of Pathologists, *Transitional Guidelines to Facilitate Changes in Procedures for Handling 'Surplus' and Archival Material from Human Biological Samples* (June 2001) and *Human Tissue and Biological Samples for Use in Research* (MRC, April 2001). For the Chief Medical Officer's census of retained organs, see: *Report of a Census of Organs & Tissues Retained by Pathology Services in England Conducted in 2000 by the Chief Medical Officer* (January 2000) (*www.doh.gov.uk/organcensus*).

[154] *Foster v Dodd* (1866) LR 1 QB 475, 485 *per* Blackburn J.

[155] See *R v Gibson* [1991] 1 All ER 439 (CA) and Skegg, PDG, 'Medical Uses of Corpses and the 'No Property' Rule' (1992) 32 *Medicine, Science, and Law* 311–8.

[156] N 6 above.

[157] By s 1(8), see para 16.43 below, the section does not make unlawful actions that are lawful apart from the 1961 Act, indicating that the section makes lawful what is otherwise unlawful.

16.42   Organ removal requires the skills of a surgeon, who would have to be suitably registered as a medical practitioner,[158] but various tissues may be recoverable by the skills of health care practitioners who are not so registered. It appears that a medical practitioner who is registered would usually have to be satisfied by personal examination of the body that life is extinct,[159] but may then authorise the removal of tissues by an unregistered person. This appears so from analogy with the law on abortion. Although only registered medical practitioners are authorised to perform abortions under the Abortion Act 1967,[160] it was held in *Royal College of Nursing of the UK v Department of Health and Social Security*[161] that, provided that a physician remains in charge of a procedure and bears responsibility throughout, particular acts may lawfully be undertaken by others acting along extended lines of authority. The purpose of the 1967 Act was to widen access to the procedures it governs, and the same expansive purpose appears applicable to the 1961 Act, which may be understood similarly.

16.43   Acquisition of materials intended for transplantation from a dead body other than in accordance with the 1961 Act would risk prosecution for a common law or other offence,[162] although the Act itself contains no sanction for noncompliance.[163] Further, s 1 of the Act imposes no new legal liabilities, since s 1(8) provides that '[n]othing in this section shall be construed as rendering unlawful any dealing . . . which is lawful apart from this Act'. A registered physician whose only non-compliance with the Act was the removal of organs without the consent, prior to death, of the deceased or of the person lawfully in possession of the body might be guilty of offending public decency, but a charge of causing indignity to a dead body might not be made out if the procedure of removal was identical to that which would have been performed had due authorisation been granted. Further, the defence of necessity might be invoked to excuse any failure to comply with the terms of the Act where materials were intended for a life-preserving transplantation.[164] The same defence might resist any charge, for non-conformity with s 1(5) of the 1961 Act, which requires a person who has reason to believe that an inquest or post mortem examination may be required to have consent of the

---

[158] See the Medical Act 1983, s 56, Sch 6, paras 11, 20.

[159] Personal examination by a registered medical practitioner might not be necessary where death is self-evident, such as in cases of decapitation or other conditions incompatible with life; for earlier law concerning survival and inheritance rather than transplantation, however, see *Gugel's Administrator v Orth's Executors* (1950) 236 SW 2d 460 (Kentucky CA) (a decapitated woman held to have survived her husband whose heart and respiration had ceased, because blood gushed from her severed neck, evidencing heartbeat).

[160] s 1(1).

[161] [1981] 1 All ER 545 (HL); applied in *R (on the application of Quintavalle) v Human Fertilisation and Embryology Authority* [2003] EWCA Civ 667, [2003] 3 All ER 257 (CA).

[162] See *R v Lennox-Wright* [1973] Crim LR 529 (Cent Crim Ct).

[163] See Kennedy and Grubb (n 10 above), Ch15, 1845–9.

[164] See *R v Bourne* [1939] 1 KB 687 (Cent Crim Ct).

relevant coroner before giving or acting on authority to remove materials from a body, and any charge of breach of statutory duty.[165]

Section 1(4A) was added to the 1961 Act by the Corneal Tissue Act 1986,[166] s 1.   **16.44**
It provides that no removal of an eye or part of an eye shall be effected from a body except by a registered medical practitioner who by personal examination of the body is satisfied that life is extinct, or by a person in the employment of a health authority, NHS trust,[167] or Primary Care Trust[168] acting on the instructions of a registered medical practitioner who, before giving such instructions, is satisfied that the person in question is sufficiently qualified and trained to perform the removal competently, and who is satisfied by his or her own examination of the body or by confirmation of another such medical practitioner who has so examined the body that life is extinct. In light of the judgment in the *Royal College of Nursing* case,[169] this addition may have added little of substance, but it avoids doubt and the need for the type of litigation resulting in that judgment that afforded non-physicians the confidence to act under a physician's instructions.

(vi) Retention of Organs and Tissues

The retention and storage of human tissue and organs previously removed is reg-   **16.45**
ulated by the Retained Organs Commission, a Special Health Authority.[170] The Commission advises the Government on (i) how organs and tissue samples whose return is not requested should be dealt with; (ii) what system of regulation should apply to collections and archives of retained organs and tissue samples; (iii) future policy and legislation relating to the removal, storage, retention, and return of human organs and tissue samples, and that this takes full account of the needs of relatives and partners, the lessons and experience gained from Alder Hey,[171] and the needs of science and medicine.

(vii) The Duty to Supply Information

By s 3(1) of the Human Organ Transplants Act 1989,[172] the Secretary of State for   **16.46**

---

[165] See Kennedy and Grubb (n 10 above), 1847, doubting that this common law offence applies to the 1961 Act.

[166] 1986 ch 18.

[167] The Act above added s 1(10) to the 1961 Act, defining a 'health authority' in relation to England and Wales according to the meaning given by the National Health Service Act 1977, s 128(1).

[168] See n 120 above.

[169] See n 161 above.

[170] The Retained Organs Commission (Establishment and Constitution) Order 2001, SI 2001/743 (as amended by SI 2001/1813) and the Retained Organs Commission Regulations 2001, SI 2001/748 (*www.nhs.uk/retainedorgans* and *www.doh.gov.uk/tissue*).

[171] See n 153 above.

[172] N 7 above.

Health is empowered to make regulations requiring specified persons to supply particular information to a given authority 'with respect to transplants that have been or are proposed to be carried out in Great Britain using organs removed from dead or living persons'. The authority shall keep a record of such information.[173] Any person who without reasonable excuse fails to comply with the regulations is liable to summary conviction and fine, as is any person who, in purported compliance with the regulations, knowingly or recklessly supplies information that is false or misleading in a material respect.[174] The Human Organ Transplants (Supply of Information) Regulations 1989[175] came into force on 1 April 1990. The Regulations define a 'relevant organ' to which they apply as any kidney, heart, lung, pancreas or liver.[176]

D. Donation From Living Donors

1. Consent

16.47   The legal power of persons to donate materials from their bodies while they are alive, for transplantation into others, exists at common law, and is implicit rather than explicit in legislation. The Human Organ Transplants Act 1989[177] rests on the foundation that people may give organs from their bodies while alive within the general framework of the law. The Act does not address donation of non-organic materials such as blood and, probably, bone marrow, which therefore fall outside the Act's prohibition of commercial dealings.[178] Similarly, such legislation as the Human Fertilisation and Embryology Act 1990[179] regulates, but is not the origin of, the right to transfer human reproductive materials including pre-embryos. The common law on 'maim' places limits on what bodily invasions people can consent to for the purpose of donation,[180] and they cannot give legally effective consent to have death inflicted on them[181] by donation of vital organs such as

---

[173] ibid, s 3(2).

[174] ibid, s 3(3). S 4 further provides that any director, manager, secretary or other similar officer of a body corporate or any person purporting to act in such a capacity who consents to, connives in or otherwise contributes to an offence by a body corporate is also liable to conviction and punishment, as are members of an offending body corporate who manage its affairs.

[175] SI 1989/2108, as amended by SI 1991/1645.

[176] SI 1989/2108, reg 1(2).

[177] N 7 above.

[178] See para 16.03 above.

[179] 1990 ch 37.

[180] *R v Wright* (1603) Co Lit f 127 a-b (cutting off a beggar's hand with his approval to increase sympathetic responses was held convictable); see also *State of North Carolina v Bass* (1961) 120 SE 2d 580 (NC Sup Ct). In *R v Brown* [1994] 1 AC 212, on limits to sado-masochistic practices, the House of Lords addressed the modern relevance of the historical law of maim.

[181] The Criminal Code of Canada, RSC 1985, ch C-46, for instance, codifies the common law in providing in s 14 that '[n]o person is entitled to consent to have death inflicted on him, and such consent does not affect the criminal responsibility of any person by whom death may be inflicted on the person by whom consent is given'.

the heart.[182] In many circumstances, however, people have the legal power to risk inadvertent death or injury, and civil liability for death or injury may be reduced or excluded by the donor's assumption of risk, expressed in the doctrine *volenti non fit injuria*. Within this general framework, people in principle may lawfully consent to donate certain organs and other tissues while living, for transplantation into others.

Blood donation has almost invariably been undertaken anonymously for the benefit of strangers, and donation for instance of gametes, bone marrow[183] and breast milk may be similar. Designated donation of blood has gained some attention due to awareness of risk of contamination of donated blood, particularly by HIV. However, organs as defined in the 1989 Act[184] are almost invariably donated only to specifically identified recipients.[185] Indeed, the intention to assist survival of the person identified, as opposed to anyone else, is the motivating factor in donation. This alone explains the donor's willingness to give consent.[186]   **16.48**

The legal requirement that consent to a proposed medical intervention be appropriately informed, express and freely given applies to altruistic donation of body materials no less than to therapeutic procedures.[187] No laws compel individuals to render the resources of their bodies to sustain the lives of other human beings.[188] Parents have no legal duty to make, for instance, medically-indicated blood or bone marrow donations from their own bodies to sustain their children's lives, although it is arguable that a woman who declines to breastfeed her newborn child without medical reason when there is no accessible alternative source of nutrition for the infant might be convictable, for instance, for denying her child a necessity of life[189] or for a comparable offence of child neglect.[190] The legal basis of   **16.49**

---

[182] For an argument that respect for autonomy requires accepting a person's decision to die in order to donate organs to others, see Rakowski, E, 'Taking and Saving Lives' (1993) 93 Columbia L Rev 1063–1156, 1107–9.

[183] See Anderson, MA, 'Encouraging Bone Marrow Transplants from Unrelated Donors: Some Proposed Solutions to a Pressing Social Problem' (1993) 54 U of Pittsburgh L Rev 477–530, and Hartman, RQ, 'The Privacy Implications of Professor Anderson's Proposed Mandatory Registry for Bone Marrow Donation: A Reply', ibid, 531–51.

[184] See para 16.03 above.

[185] Considerable controversy exists in the scholarly literature regarding the propriety of permitting, and of prohibiting, designation of recipients of foetal tissues from induced abortion. On the so-called 'designer foetus' concern, see Robertson, JA, *Children of Choice: Freedom and the New Reproductive Technologies* (Princeton, NJ, 1994), 207–19.

[186] See Jones, MA and Keywood, K, 'Assessing the Patient's Competence to Consent to Medical Treatment' (1996) 2 *Medical Law International* 107–47.

[187] See *Sidaway* (n 64 above); contrast *Reibl v Hughes* (1980) 114 DLR (3d) 1 (Sup Ct Can), and *Rogers v Whitaker* (1992), 67 ALJR 47 (High Ct Aus).

[188] See *McFall v Shimp* (1978) 10 Pa D & C 3d 90 (Allegheny County Ct); see also Grey, TC, *The Legal Enforcement of Morality* (New York, 1983), 187–97.

[189] See *R v Instan* [1893] 1 QB 450 (CCCR), citing *Rex v Friend*, R & R 20 on the indictable offence at common law of refusing or neglecting to provide sufficient food to an infant of tender years.

[190] In *R v Brooks* (1902) 5 CCC 372 (Sup Ct BC), it was held that the duty of parents to provide

removing an organ or other tissue from a living person's body in order to transplant it into that of another person is freely given, express and appropriately informed consent.

16.50   Donors who are admitted to hospital for the purpose of donation, particularly donation of an organ removed through surgery, are likely to be admitted and cared for under the description that they are 'patients'. Surgery will clearly require that they be prepared, operated on and given aftercare in this capacity. They differ from other patients, however, in that they tend not to be sick or in need of medical treatment as the condition of admission to hospital. There is no concern for their therapeutic advantage that would justify or excuse physicians withholding countertherapeutic information relevant to their management, and, for instance, they would not be acting contrary to medical advice if they decided to discharge themselves, were they to decide not to undertake the procedures for which they were admitted. They are entitled to be told all of the implications that donation would have for them, such as preparation by drugs or diet, hospital admission and otherwise, including the risk of nosocomial infection, the actual process of organ or tissue removal, including anaesthesia, the risk of surgical error and accident,[191] including iatrogenic injury, the process of medical recovery from the procedure and of physical rehabilitation, and the level of restoration of their capacity to function which they could reasonably expect following removal of the organ or other tissue in question. Failure to offer them appropriate information would be liable to be pursued in law in an action for negligence, although actual surgery competently conducted within the scope that the patient authorised would probably not sustain a successful claim for battery.[192] Excessively graphic information given to a potential donor of the intended recipient's decline and process of death if transplantation is not undertaken may give rise to liability in negligence if it induces or pressures donation that results in injury to the donor, even if the injury itself, such as in surgery, is not caused by negligence.[193] Similarly, presenting too optimistic a prognosis of success of a transplant may leave a donor ill-prepared for the sense of loss and bereavement that follows its failure. In the United States, for example, a separate claim has been recognised for negligent infliction of emotional harm or distress,[194] such as regret that a donation was made, or remorse and guilt when a loved one died following donation refusal, or devastation when transplantation following donation fails.[195]

'necessaries of life', under s 215(1)(a) of the Criminal Code of Canada (n 181 above), includes the duty to provide medical aid, although breast-feeding may be considered the supply of nutrition and liquids rather than of medical treatment.

[191] See *Whitehouse v Jordan* [1981] 1 All ER 267 (HL).
[192] See *Hills v Potter* [1983] 3 All ER 716 (QBD) and *Reibl v Hughes* (n 187 above).
[193] See *Whitehouse v Jordan* (n 191 above).
[194] See Furrow, *et al* (n 28 above), 164–71.
[195] For development of the law on recovery of damages for nervous shock, see *Page v Smith* [1995] 2 All ER 736 (HL).

(i) Capacity of Adult Donor[196]

Adults must be legally competent to give consent.[197] People of adult years enjoy **16.51** the general presumption in law that they are competent to undertake the routine activities and risks of daily living, including acceptance of medical procedures, but the implications that are inherent in organ donation, and perhaps donation of other tissues such as bone marrow, take it beyond the nature of a routine activity. Competence in law is specific to particular functions;[198] for instance, a person proposing to execute a will must give satisfactory evidence of possessing testamentary capacity, and is liable to be questioned for establishment of such capacity, whereas a person may revoke a will in relatively informal ways, and without a prior need to show competence. Similarly in medical care, it has been observed that 'the common law test of competence to consent to medical treatment is functional and the threshold currently set for competence is low'.[199] The law seeks to minimize conditions and obstacles to a patient adhering to the conscientious advice offered by a disinterested physician discharging the duty to care for the patients' well-being.[200]

In contrast, organ and other tissue donation is not an indicated physical therapy **16.52** for a donor, and may be a source of physical harm, however much the donor considers the risk of harm to be justified or overborne by benefit to the recipient and satisfaction to the donor. If the transplant fails, however, and the recipient succumbs to disease and death, the donor's grief may be aggravated by a sense that the donation was ill-advised or futile. Accordingly, since donation is not intended for the donor's advantage and may be a source of physical and emotional detriment, a higher level of competency may be required. An analogy may be drawn with participation in medical experimentation or research, which is entered altruistically with no intention of personal benefit. Not every person legally competent to consent to indicated medical therapy is competent to consent to participation in research,[201] and the same is true of organ and tissue donation. Capacity to consent is related to the nature of the donation proposed, organ donation and bone marrow donation requiring greater capacity, for instance, than blood donation.

---

[196] 'Capacity' here refers primarily to mental or intellectual capacity. Legal capacity of live donors distinguishes between donors related and donors unrelated to intended recipients. The latter are considered at para 16.66 below.

[197] See Jones and Keywood (n 186 above).

[198] See Gunn, M, 'The Meaning of Incapacity' (1994) 2 Med L Rev 8–29, 13.

[199] Brazier, M and Bridge, C, 'Coercion or caring; analysing adolescent autonomy', (1996) 16 LS 84–109, 90.

[200] See *Chatterton v Gerson* [1981] 1 QB 432 (QBD); *Re C (adult; refusal of medical treatment)* [1994] 1 All ER 819 (Fam D).

[201] See Ch 13.

16.53   Capacity involves intellectual ability to appreciate the range of implications of the decision on donation, but also the ability to resist undue pressures, perhaps from close family members, and undue inducements. Pressures and inducements are inherent in the decision when donation is motivated by the urgent need of a close family member or friend. The pressure to act to relieve a loved one from the threat of organ-failure and disease is natural,[202] and inescapable. Undue pressure may be brought to bear, however, such as by family members' threats of ostracism, that compromises a potential donor's legal capacity to act voluntarily. The inducement of achieving a loved one's survival may appear irresistible and sufficient for acceptance of the known risks of donation. However, when the trusted informant significantly downplays chances of transplantation failure or factors likely to compromise the recipient's survival, the inducement to donate may become undue, and vitiate a potential donor's capacity to exercise choice voluntarily. Coercion negates consent, and non-consensual removal of tissues may constitute battery or criminal assault to which those who use pressure or deception are parties.

16.54   Physicians and other health care professionals responsible for informing and counselling prospective donors must be alert not only to intellectual obstacles to choice but also to donors' vulnerability to forces that compromise their freedom of choice. Findings that prospective donors are unsuitable to donate organs or tissues may afford such people relief from improper persuasion to donate,[203] though perhaps at a cost to needful potential recipients' well-being or very survival. Physicians bear legal obligations to those on whom they propose to undertake medical procedures, particularly procedures that are major, irreversible and non-therapeutic, to be reasonably assured that they are competent to give, and do actually give, adequately understood and voluntary consent. Physicians addressing prospective donors bear no corresponding duty to protect the interests and well-being of potential recipients of materials that may be donated. They must satisfy themselves that potential donors are acting voluntarily by questioning them, by seeking opinions from other physicians, psychologists or, for instance, social workers or chaplains, or by seeking legal advice.

16.55   The strongest safeguard in cases of doubt might be to seek a judicial declaration of the prospective donor's legal capacity to consent, but in many cases this would be impracticable, disruptive, or even destructive of relationships which the potential donor wants to preserve. Physicians may have to bear the burden, therefore, of acting with good sense and conscience to decide if they have received the quality

---

[202] *Urbanski v Patel* (1978) 84 DLR (3d) 650 (Manitoba QB) (father successfully sued doctor who negligently removed daughter's only kidney, causing father to donate a kidney). See also Spencer, J, 'Tissue Donors: Are They Rescuers, or Merely Volunteers?' (1979) CLJ 45–7.

[203] Fox, RC and Swazey, JP, *Spare Parts: Organ Replacement in American Society* (New York, 1992), 43–72.

of consent they require to give effect to a person's request to donate an organ or other tissue for transplantation. It may be of little comfort for physicians to know that Staughton L.J. has observed that:

> I cannot find authority that the decision of a doctor as to the existence or refusal of consent is sufficient protection, if the law subsequently finds otherwise. So the medical profession . . . must bear the responsibility unless it is possible to obtain a decision from the courts.[204]

(ii) Capacity of Adolescent Donors

There is doubt that the power of minors of 16 and above to consent to medical treatment on their own behalf, under s 8(1) of the Family Law Reform Act 1969,[205] applies to organ donation,[206] although they may be able to give their own consent to blood and perhaps bone marrow donation that serves a special interest of theirs. There is therefore related doubt that the general law on adolescent therapy applies to donation. For instance the 'mature minor' rule recognized in the *Gillick* case[207] regarding adolescents aged under 16 may be inapplicable. Although a court may find that, for instance, bone marrow donation from a person incapable of providing legally effective consent may be of emotional, psychological and social benefit and in that person's best interests,[208] it may be doubted that a person aged under 16 may make the decision to donate independently of judicial or at least adult concurrence. The power of parents to consent to donation by their adolescent children over the children's objection may similarly not be governed by legal principles regarding parental power to consent to therapeutically indicated procedures.[209] In this case, the 'strong predilection to give effect to the child's wishes'[210] will prevail. Further, the likelihood that parents may influence dependent children to express wishes favourable to their own[211] may require that a parental proposal for organ donation and perhaps bone marrow donation from an adolescent child with the child's agreement receive judicial or other independent scrutiny.[212] Any proposed removal of an organ for transplantation to a genetically unrelated recipient would be subject to review by the Unrelated Live Transplant Regulatory Authority.[213]

16.56

---

[204] *Re T (Adult) (Refusal of Medical Treatment)* [1992] 4 All ER 649 (CA), 670.
[205] See n 123 above and related text.
[206] See *Re W* (n 124 above).
[207] *Gillick v West Norfolk and Wisbech AHA* [1986] AC 112 (HL). See further Ch 4.
[208] See *In re Y (Mental Patient: Bone Marrow Donation)* [1997] 2 WLR 556 (Fam Div).
[209] See *Re W* (n 124 above), *per* Lord Donaldson, 635.
[210] ibid, *per* Balcombe LJ, 643.
[211] See *Re T* (n 204 above).
[212] See generally Ch 4.
[213] See para 16.64 below.

(iii) Capacity of Young Children as Donors

16.57 The strict proposition that parents may use their legal powers to consent to medical treatment on their young, dependent children only for the therapeutic benefit of the children[214] may be interpreted more widely to allow their consent to non-beneficial treatments provided that they risk no more than the harms naturally arising in everyday life.[215] Both common law and legislation permit parents to submit young children to bloodtesting for paternity claims,[216] for instance, and the use of reasonable constraints to compel compliance,[217] even though the benefit for the child is speculative, dependent in some measure on what the test result discloses.[218] It may be questioned whether kidney or similar organ donation can ever be legally authorised by a parent from the body of a young child,[219] and whether even bone marrow or blood donation is within the limits of permissible parental authority. An analogous case decided in Kentucky in 1969 demonstrates the vulnerability of dependent people to the judgment of their guardians on becoming sources of transplantable materials, and has been a basis of reaction. In *Strunk v Strunk*[220] the court approved kidney removal from an incompetent adult for transplantation to his twin brother, on the ground that, had his brother died, the loss would have caused him psychological and emotional injury. The incompetent adult had a mental age of six years.

16.58 Similarly in *Hart v Brown*,[221] the court accepted that the psychological benefit to the child that a sibling would survive and be a continuing companion considerably outweighed the risks of donation and justified removal of an organ for transplantation. A more remarkable and no less controversial incident received public attention when a couple in the US planned and conceived a child, and continued the pregnancy only on receiving evidence from foetal diagnosis of tissue compatibility, in order that, following birth, the child would serve as a source of bone marrow for transplantation to a teenage daughter suffering from leukemia. The transplantation took place in June 1991 when the child so conceived, a girl, had

---

[214] See Kennedy and Grubb (n 10 above), 1727, citing Dworkin, G.

[215] Brazier, M finds authority for parental consent for non-therapeutic procedures on children as long as they are not 'perceived as against the interests' of the children; *Medicine, Patients and the Law* (3rd edn, London, 2003), 408.

[216] *S v McC, W v W* [1972] AC 24 (HL).

[217] ibid.

[218] The Court reasoned (ibid) that paternity testing was of sufficient benefit to the child to be justifiable as legitimate pursuit of benefit; see also *In re H (A Minor) (Blood Tests: Parental Rights)* [1996] 4 All ER 28 (CA).

[219] See Skegg, PDG, *Law, Ethics and Medicine* (Oxford, 1984), 61; see also Mason, K, McCall Smith, RA, and Laurie, GT, *Law and Medical Ethics* (6th edn, London, Dublin, Edinburgh, 2002), 429–33.

[220] (1969) 445 SW 2d 145 (Ky CA).

[221] (1972) 289 A 2d 386 (Conn Sup Ct).

reached the age of 14 months.[222] Public and academic discussion centred on the ethics rather than on the legality of executing this plan.[223]

Several jurisdictions in the common law and civil law traditions have reacted to the prospect of parentally authorised acquisitions of organs from younger children by legislatively enacted prohibitions,[224] and similar controls on acquisition of tissues.[225] In jurisdictions where the defence of necessity is recognised, however, breach of prohibitive legislation may be excused on the ground that the urgency of the circumstances, the imminence of the recipient's death and the relatively minor comparative risk to the child from whom materials were removed rendered the violation defensible by objective risk-to-benefit criteria.[226] Removal of bone marrow or other regenerative tissue might be more easily defensible on this basis than removal of a kidney or lung. Nevertheless, because conduct excused by necessity is not lawful, even though not punishable, lawyers risk liability for professional misconduct in positively advising that it be undertaken. They may only advise that it may be judicially excused.

16.59

The claim that parents can necessarily identify the best interests of a potential donor child has been questioned. It has been observed that:

16.60

> it is increasingly suggested that the family may express interests which may not always adequately represent the best interests of the incompetent, especially with regard to non-therapeutic interventions. While family interests must be outweighed only by compelling interests, the proper forum for deciding must objectively weigh all considerations with predominant emphasis on the best interests of the incompetent individual.[227]

When it is intended to provide an organ or tissue such as bone marrow from a child incapable of understanding or resistance, for transplantation to another on the basis of parental consent, consideration will have to be given to a wide range of factors. These include the risks during surgical removal of the material, the risks of the child's immediate adverse reaction to removal, the child's longer-term prospects of physical and emotional dysfunction due to the loss, the child's prevailing and prospective emotional proximity to the intended recipient, the likelihood of the transplant succeeding in restoring or achieving the recipient's well-being, the effect on the child on learning of the donation on reaching an age

---

[222] 'Teen Gets Baby Sister's Marrow', New York Times, 5 June 1991, A-23.

[223] See Rachels, J, 'When Philosophers Shoot From the Hip' (1991) 5 *Bioethics* 67–71.

[224] See Giesen, D, *International Medical Malpractice Law* (Tübingen, Dordrecht, Boston, London, 1988) 611, n 72.

[225] ibid, 611–12, nn 63–9.

[226] On necessity, see *R v Bourne* (n 164 above), and the discussion in *Perka v The Queen* (1984) 14 CCC (3d) 385 (Sup Ct Can). See also Wilson, W and Smith, KJM, 'The Doctors' Dilemma: Necessity and the Legality of Medical Intervention' (1995) 1 Medical Law International 387–410.

[227] Law Reform Commission of Canada, *Medical Treatment and the Criminal Law* (Ottawa, Working Paper 26, 1980), 69.

of understanding, the effect on parent–child relations and attitudes if the child serves, and if the child does not serve, as a donor, the effect on the child if the intended recipient does, and does not, survive and, for instance, consequences for the child–parent relationship if the recipient survives and does not survive, with and without the transplantation procedure.[228]

16.61 Parents' natural anxieties concerning the child in need of the transplant, and their hopes for that child's well-being if the other provides an organ or tissue, present a classic conflict of interest in their management of the potential donor child's care. They may be liable to project their own fears, hopes and perception of benefit onto the potential donor child, and claim that its best interests, as well as their own, would be served by donation. The depth of detached consideration that needs to be given to parental assertions, the range of professional disciplines and expertise that would have to be applied to make the assessments called for, and the improbability of any generally agreed outcome being reached, persuade some analysts that prohibition, particularly of organ removals for transplantation, is the only appropriate legal policy. For instance, Professor Dieter Giesen wrote that:

> It is submitted that in the case of mentally incompetent persons who do not understand what removal of organs or tissue may entail, such a procedure is never permissible. It is likewise submitted that the same line should generally be taken with regard to minors. No exception should be allowed with regard to *non*-regenerative tissue or organs in the case of minors who are not yet of an age at which they can properly understand what is at stake with regard to their own health . . .
>
> A less rigid approach has been recommended with reference to isotransplantations, which, especially in the case of kidney transplantation between histo-compatible siblings, are said to have shown such exceptionally good results as to justify the procedure, provided that parents and minors have given their consent based on full and detailed information. We do not share this view. The vulnerability of minors to exploitation and manipulation is particularly problematic here, and exceptions to the general rule in this field will impose unacceptable pressures upon siblings or other relatives that are avoided only if the law prohibits the removal of non-regenerative organs in every case.[229]

Removals of regenerative tissues such as bone marrow from young children may be acceptable, however, subject to the objective and detached assessments indicated above. Because parents responsible for protecting the well-being of adequately healthy prospective donor children are almost invariably also responsible for the well-being of the intended recipients whose health and very survival are in jeopardy, parents alone cannot necessarily be relied on to exercise the required objectivity of assessment. Before acting on parents' volunteering of their children as sources of transplantable materials, hospitals should receive favourable

---

[228] See the factors weighed in the balance in *In re Y* (n 208 above).
[229] N 224 above, 611, emphasis in original, footnotes omitted.

assessments of the children's interests from paediatricians, psychologists, social workers or similar experts whose testimony courts would require to establish the children's psychological benefit and minor risk from donation. With this type of screening and assessment, young children may be accepted as donors of bone marrow and similar materials.

2. Relationships Between Donors and Recipients

In order to deter commerce in human organs and tissues that has arisen from impersonal, market-oriented dealings between suppliers and recipients, the Human Organ Transplants Act 1989[230] not only prohibits payments for organs, and advertising for and of organs,[231] but also regulates transplants between living persons not genetically related to each other. The purpose is to limit live persons' donations to strangers, while accommodating donations by relatives presumably moved to unrewarded altruism and self-sacrifice by sympathy for and affinity with their family members. The requirement of a genetic link both confirms the family relationship and increases the likelihood of transplantation success, although developments in immuno-therapy reduce recipients' dependency on the genetic compatibility of tissues. A limitation of this policy is that in itself it excludes transplants between spouses and members of unmarried unions. They may have the strongest incentives to be donors based on affection, but may also come under the greatest pressure due to such factors as economic and other dependency. A system that screens transplantations to ensure genetic links between donors and recipients must also accommodate exceptions for sympathetic cases of adequately voluntary donations where no genetic links to recipients exist.

16.62

Section 2 of the Human Organ Transplants Act 1989 provides that:

(1) Subject to subsection (3) below, a person is guilty of an offence if in Great Britain he—

   (a) removes from a living person an organ intended to be transplanted into another person; or

   (b) transplants an organ removed from a living person into another person, unless the person into whom the organ is to be or, as the case may be, is transplanted is genetically related to the person from whom the organ is removed.

(2) For the purposes of this section a person is genetically related to—

   (a) his natural parents and children;

   (b) his brothers and sisters of the whole or half blood;

   (c) the brothers and sisters of the whole or half blood of either of his natural parents; and

   (d) the natural children of his brothers and sisters of the whole or half blood or

---

[230] N 7 above.
[231] See para 16.36 above.

of the brothers and sisters of the whole or half blood of either of his natural parents;

but persons shall not in any particular case be treated as related in any of those ways unless the fact of the relationship has been established by such means as are specified by regulations made by the Secretary of State.

(3) The Secretary of State may by regulations provide that the prohibition in sub-section (1) above shall not apply in cases where—

(a) such authority as is specified in or constituted by the regulations is satis-fied—

(i) that no payment has been or is to be made in contravention of S 1 above;[232] and

(ii) that such other conditions as are specified in the regulations are satis-fied; and

(b) such other requirements as may be specified in the regulations are com-plied with.

16.63 With effect from April 1990, the Human Organ Transplants (Establishments of Relationship) Regulations 1989[233] came into effect under authority of s 2(2) of the 1989 Act. The Regulations provide:

1.—(1) These Regulations may be cited as the Human Organ Transplants (Establishment of Relationship) Regulations 1989 and shall come into force on 1st April 1990.

(2) In these Regulations—

'donor' means a living person from whom an organ is proposed to be re-moved which is intended to be transplanted;

'tester' means a person approved by the Secretary of State to carry out the tests described in regulation 2 of these Regulations.

The Establishment of the Genetic Relationship

2.—(1) The means by which the fact of a genetic relationship is to be established for the purposes of s 2 of the Human Organ Transplants Act 1989 are the carrying out by a tester of the appropriate tests described in paragraph (2) of this regulation.

(2) The tester shall carry out on the donor and the recipient and on such rel-atives of each as appear to the tester to be necessary—

(a) tests for the antigenic products of the Human Major Histocompatibility system HLA-A, HLA-B, HLA-DR, using con-ventional serological techniques, and

(b) tests to establish HLA-DR beta and HLA-DQ beta gene restriction fragment length polymorphisms, and

(c) where the tests in the preceding sub-paragraphs do not establish a ge-netic relationship between the donor and the recipient, tests to estab-lish DNA polymorphisms, using at least 2 multi-locus gene probes, and

---

[232] ibid.
[233] SI 1989/2107.

    (d) where the tests in the preceding sub-paragraphs do not establish a genetic relationship between the donor and the recipient, further tests to establish DNA polymorphisms, using at least 5 single locus polymorphic probes.

The need to accommodate donations by persons not genetically related to intended recipients is met through creation of the Unrelated Live Transplant Regulatory Authority,[234] under s 2(3) of the 1989 Act. The Human Organ Transplants (Unrelated Persons) Regulations 1989[235] provide in reg 3 that: **16.64**

(1) The prohibition in s 2(1) of the [Human Organ Transplants] Act (restriction on transplants between persons not genetically related) shall not apply in cases where a registered medical practitioner has caused the matter to be referred to the [Unrelated Live Transplant Regulatory] Authority and where the Authority is satisfied:—

    (a) that no payment has been, or is to be, made in contravention of s 1 of the Act;

    (b) that the registered medical practitioner who has caused the matter to be referred to the Authority has clinical responsibility for the donor; and

    (c) except in a case where the primary purpose of removal of an organ from a donor is the medical treatment of that donor, that the conditions specified in paragraph (2) of this regulation are satisfied.

(2) The conditions referred to in paragraph (1)(c) of this regulation are:—

    (a) that a registered medical practitioner has given the donor an explanation of the nature of the medical procedure for, and the risk involved in, the removal of the organ in question;

    (b) that the donor understands the nature of the medical procedure and the risks, as explained by the registered medical practitioner, and consents to the removal of the organ in question;

    (c) that the donor's consent to the removal of the organ in question was not obtained by coercion or the offer of an inducement;

    (d) that the donor understands that he is entitled to withdraw his consent if he wishes, but has not done so;

    (e) that the donor and the recipient have both been interviewed by a person who appears to the Authority to have been suitably qualified to conduct such interviews and who has reported to the Authority on the conditions contained in sub-paragraphs (a) to (d) above and has included in his report an account of any difficulties of communication with the donor or the recipient and an explanation of how those difficulties were overcome.

Although not expressed in the terms of regulations, it seems that in operation they are likely to bar organ donations by young children, and by adolescents vulnerable to coercion or undue inducement. It must be remembered, however, that the 1989 Act defines 'organ' as any part of a human body consisting of a structured

---

[234] Established by the Human Organ Transplants (Unrelated Persons) Regulations 1989, SI 1989/2480, reg 2.
[235] See Kennedy and Grubb (n 10 above), 1766–8.

arrangement of tissues which, if wholly removed, cannot be replicated by the body,[236] and therefore does not govern such replicable tissues as blood, or probably, bone marrow.

3. Payment and the Supply of Information

16.65 Developments in organ transplantation techniques and immunosuppressive pharmacology fuelled early speculation that people might in time come to sell their organs. The speculation quickly proved true with revelation that markets in organs from living donors[237] had indeed emerged.[238] The reality was given an identifiable human face in 1989 when it was discovered that impoverished Turkish visitors had come to England in order to sell their kidneys to unrelated recipients.[239] A prompt legislative reaction was the enactment of the Human Organ Transplants Act 1989,[240] the primary purpose of which was to eliminate commerce in human organs and any associated advertisements and the involvement of health professionals. The Act requires that donation be gratuitous and altruistic, but permits commercial services to attend the recovery, preparation and transport of donated organs, and donors themselves to recover their reasonable expenses. In defining the prohibition of payment, s 1(3) of the Act provides that:

> 'payment' means payment in money or money's worth but does not include any payment for defraying or reimbursing—
>
> (a) the cost of removing, transporting or preserving the organ to be supplied; or
> (b) any expenses or loss of earnings incurred by a person so far as reasonably and directly attributable to his supplying of an organ from his body.

16.66 The cost of removing and transporting an organ may reasonably be taken to extend to the cost of implanting it on a fee-for-service basis, unless, as is unlikely, the Act limits implantation surgery to physicians remunerated on a salaried basis by publicly maintained hospitals or clinics. Implantation fees may be considered 'expenses . . . incurred by a person . . . attributable to his supplying an organ', even if the person is not expected to meet those expenses thereby incurred, or 'the cost of . . . preserving the organ'. Expenses attributable to supplying an organ include not just surgical fees, but preliminary testing of prospective donors to minimise the risk of organ donations transmitting genetic hazards or infections such as sexually transmitted diseases or HIV. Some materials from a human source may be stored

---

[236] Human Organ Transplant Act 1989, s 7(2).

[237] It has been observed that 'donors' are voluntary givers, not sellers, and that even for voluntary giving a better description should be explored; see Gerrand, N, 'The Notion of Gift-Giving and Organ Donation' (1994) 8 *Bioethics* 126–50.

[238] Dorozynski, A, 'European Kidney Market', (1989) 299 *BMJ*, 1182; and Roscam Abbing, HDC, 'Transplantation of Organs: A European Perspective', (1993) 21 J of Law, Medicine and Ethics, 54–8.

[239] Mason, McCall Smith and Laurie (n 219 above), 434.

[240] N 7 above.

so that donors tested immediately before donation can be recalled for instance six or more months later for re-testing. If the later test shows no infection, the tissue given earlier may be removed from storage and transplanted. Fresh tissue is better not used if its liability to transmit infection cannot be detected. In particular, the AIDS virus is undetectable during its incubation period, but transmissible. However, solid organs are currently not preservable for transplantation for any length of time, and, although donors will be tested before donation to reduce the risk that transplantation will transmit infection, the risk cannot be eliminated, and is part of the disclosure that must be made to prospective recipients.[241]

A cultural issue affected by the 1989 Act is gift-exchange. Cultures attuned primarily to dealings among strangers and to the identification of monetary exchanges with materialism and self-interest, including the mutual self-interest of bargained trade, consider a monetary payment in exchange for donation of an organ, whether immediate or following death, as commerce.[242] Cultures based on mutuality or reciprocity might require, however, that a spontaneous act of altruism be reciprocated in some appropriate way, thereby ritualising and personalising gift-exchange that is culturally distinguishable from commerce. To the former, so-called 'rewarded gifting'[243] is a shallow euphemism for buying and selling. To the latter, however, failing appropriately to reciprocate organ donation would be an outrage to cultural values, discrediting the recipient of the gifted organ. Giving a reciprocal gift 'in money or money's worth'[244] would appear to be in breach of the 1989 Act. However, since the Act is also concerned with confining live donations to those between persons genetically related to each other, they are likely to have shared cultural values, so that a donor would be aware of the likelihood of the gift being appropriately reciprocated and the recipient would be similarly familiar with the expectation. One response may be that, in light of probable family links and the continuing association of donor and recipient, the reciprocal gesture might not be immediate, but made in due course. It might be so postponed as to escape scrutiny through United Kingdom Transplant,[245] which receives information, inter alia, of a kidney, lung, pancreas or liver removed for transplantation from a living donor.[246] A commercial payment centres on negotiation and prearrangement, including of the times within which obligations must be

16.67

---

[241] See para 16.73 below.

[242] The view that commerce is dysfunctional in the supply of tissues remains strongly influenced by Titmus, R, *The Gift Relationship: From Human Blood to Social Policy* (London, 1970).

[243] Daar, AS, 'Rewarded Gifting' (1992) 24 *Transplantation Proceedings* 2207–11.

[244] Human Organ Transplants Act 1989, s 1(3).

[245] See para 16.79 below.

[246] United Kingdom Transplant Support Service Authority (now United Kingdom Transplant) Regulations 1991, SI 1991/408: see amendments (n 289 below). The requirement to supply information of removal and implantation of a 'liver' may not include the supply of information of liver segment removal. This is consistent with a liver segment constituting only tissue, as opposed to an organ as defined in the 1989 Act.

discharged, whereas the operation of the culture of reciprocity is neither negotiated nor dependent on explicit arrangement and mutual performance at or by an agreed time. Accordingly, rewarded gifting may not amount to 'payment' as defined under the 1989 Act, nor, if it falls within the Act, be easily detected and proven beyond reasonable doubt.[247]

16.68 Special duties to supply information are created under the Human Organ Transplants (Supply of Information) Regulations 1989.[248] The Schedule to the Regulations, containing details of information to be supplied to UK Transplant, includes an identically worded provision in Pt I on organs removed and Pt II on organs that have been or are proposed to be transplanted. Section 5 of the former and s 6 of the latter require disclosure of:

> If the donor was living at the time of the removal of the organ—
>
> (a) whether or not, for the purposes of s 2(2) of the [1989] Act, a genetic relationship to the recipient has been established by the means specified in the Human Organ Transplants (Establishment of Relationship) Regulations 1989,[249]
> (b) if such a genetic relationship to the recipient has been established, the name of the person who carried out the test to establish that relationship,
> (c) where no such genetic relationship to the recipient has been established, the reference number if any in respect of the proposed transplant allocated by the authority specified in or constituted by regulations made under s 2(3) of the Act.

The Unrelated Live Transplant Regulatory Authority[250] may approve transplantation in a case referred to it as an exception to the restriction on unrelated donation if it is satisfied that no payment has been, or is to be, made in contravention of s 1 of the 1989 Act.[251] The regulations establishing the Authority may provide no appeal against its decisions, but they appear judicially reviewable by prerogative order.[252]

4. Transplant Recipients

(i) Informed Choice

16.69 Transplant recipients would appear to be the principal beneficiaries of the advances in surgical, pharmacological and related techniques that have made

---

[247] The Nuffield Council (n 1 above) considered that rewarded gifting arrangements should be viewed as commercial transactions; at 52, para 6.36.

[248] N 175 above.

[249] SI 1989/2107.

[250] N 234 above.

[251] ibid, reg 3(1)(a).

[252] Principles of administrative law that authorities such as the Unrelated Live Transplant Regulatory Authority must observe, and liability to judicial review, are helpfully summarised and explained, with regard to the Human Fertilisation and Embryology Authority but with application to comparable authorities, in Morgan, D and Lee, RG, *Blackstone's Guide to the Human Fertilisation and Embryology Act 1990* (London, 1991), 105–9.

transplantation the treatment of choice in routine cases, such as those involving kidney and bone marrow transplantation and such a mundane matter as blood transfusion, and an option when more complicated treatments are indicated such as cardiac and multiple-organ transplantation. Recipients are patients in the same way as others, however, and have basic legal entitlements to receive material information and exercise voluntary choice.[253] Their choice may be implicit rather than explicit, for instance when a sudden life threatening crisis requires a life preserving initiative to treat a patient who is unconscious or otherwise incapacitated,[254] but prospective transplant recipients who have achieved mental capacity for choice are free outside unanticipated conditions of emergency explicitly to decline the possibility of implantation, including refusing unwanted blood transfusion.[255] Patients are increasingly encouraged to complete advance medical directives[256] to express their preferences, and those declining indicated care tend to carry more weight, than those requiring care that is not considered medically appropriate.[257]

The ordinary rules of the common law[258] require that prospective recipients must be informed of such general matters as their health diagnosis and prognosis, options for their management including not seeking transplantation, preparation necessary for transplantation if that is to be pursued, their prospects of transplantation success and their predictable capacity to function under the range of likely outcomes of the procedure. Current English law probably does not stipulate, however, that prospective transplant recipients must be informed of their likely advance to the top of any waiting list, alternative reasonably accessible waiting lists and means of entry to them, including any priorisation criteria applied by list managers.[259] One reason may be that these factors are beyond the power of the treating doctor to control. Another is that a court still operating the *Bolam*[260] approach may not regard these matters as pertaining to the doctor–patient relationship. **16.70**

Although recommendations for patient management may appear to be a matter of professional judgment for which medical personnel bear legal responsibility,[261] patients may have an interest in knowing how medical options are priorised, and **16.71**

---

[253] See Ch 3.

[254] See the doctrine of necessity, *R v Bourne* and *Perka v The Queen* (n 226 above), and Ch 4.

[256] See *Walker (Litigation Guardian of) v Region 2 Hospital Corporation* (1994) 116 DLR (4th) 477 (New Brunswick CA).

[256] See Stern, K, 'Advance Directives' (1994) 2 Med L Rev, 57–76, and *Re C (Adult: Refusal of treatment)* [1994] 1 WLR 290 (Fam D).

[257] See Stern, K (n 256 above), 66.

[258] Reflected in legislation in some jurisdictions, such as in Ontario's Health Care Consent Act, Stats Ont, 1996, c 2, Sch A.

[259] See para 16.79 below.

[260] *Bolam v Friern HMC* [1957] 2 All ER 118 (QBD), applied in *Sidaway* (n 64 above).

[261] See *Whitehouse v Jordan* (n 191 above).

in contributing to the decision-making process. For instance, some medical practitioners may consider transplantation to be the option of last resort, and will recommend the range of alternatives other than transplantation before addressing its possibility and prospects. Others may consider transplantation to be an option competing equally with others, however, to advance a patient's interests in restoration or maintenance of health or capacity. The different approaches have different implications for a patient. If transplantation is considered the last resort, its prospects of success may be compromised by delay in seeking an organ or other tissue necessary for transplantation, and by the physical effects of the alternative treatments such as by use of drugs that are undertaken before that option is pursued. That is, earlier treatments may reduce the likelihood that transplantation will succeed. As against this, turning to transplantation sooner rather than later in the patient's plan of management may preserve the patient's subsequent options for care should transplantation fail, but at the cost of exposing the patient to the risks of subjection to a major procedure and its complications when a less invasive and less drastic procedure might have been no less or even more effective to preserve the patient's life and capacity. Patients might want to be engaged in deciding how such competing options for care are exercised.

16.72 It was thought that one of the effects of the House of Lords' decision in *Sidaway* was that patients who ask questions about treatment strategies, or about alternatives to what their physicians or surgeons recommend, must be given the information they request.[262] The decision of the Court of Appeal in *Blyth v Bloomsbury HA*,[263] however, casts doubt on the existence of such a duty. Moreover, how forthcoming physicians must be at their own initiative is governed by the general law on patients' consent.[264] Physicians cannot be certain to meet the legal standard of disclosure by giving patients voluminous data, because that may be overwhelming to them or confusing, preventing patients' adequate understanding of choices.[265]

16.73 Care must be exercised in the selection of organs and tissues for transplantation.[266] In the case of cadaveric tissue, the cause of death must be reliably known, and even if it was traumatic rather than pathological, any reasonably detectable diseases affecting the deceased person including harmful genetic conditions should be diagnosed. Patients should be informed, however, that a risk remains that some diseases will be undiagnosable. When live donors offer organs or tissues, family histories should be taken, and genetic and other protective tests conducted before materials are removed. However, when cadaveric materials such as organs remain

---

[262] See n 64 above.

[263] [1993] Med LR 151 (CA).

[264] See n 64 above and Ch 3.

[265] For discussion of negligence by excessive disclosure, see *Natanson v Kline* (1960) 350 P 2d 1093 (Kan SC).

[266] See Ch 5 on negligence.

transplantable for only a short time, before full testing can be completed, transmission of infection remains an irreducible risk of their use. Further, some tissue tests bear an irreducible risk of producing a false negative result, which means that organs or tissues may become eligible to be transplanted when they actually bear the harmful infection for which they were tested. The test result is not due to negligence,[267] but disclosure that materials for transplantation from donors carry some degree of risk of bearing adverse properties notwithstanding due testing reinforces physicians' positions in the event of suit.[268]

If it appears following transplantation or transfusion that the procedure had inadvertently, whether negligently or not, exposed the recipient to transmission of infection, it may be considered that the recipient is legally entitled to be informed.[269] The duty may be binding on tissue management agencies, hospitals, attending and family physicians, depending on the source of detection of the infection risk and the extent of subsequent communication. Family physicians undertaking continuing care of patients have no legal duty to take independent measures to verify the safety for instance of transplanted organs or bone marrow or that transfused blood was uncontaminated, but when they are given notice of a patient's past exposure they must ensure the patient's knowledge.[270] Information of exposure to even an apparently incurable condition such as HIV infection may allow the patient to limit the risk of spreading the infection, and to make social, business and other plans, lifestyle adjustments and, for instance, relevant advance medical directives in light of that information. Where the transmitted risk is of susceptibility to harm rather than of harm itself, care may need to be taken to offer the patient appropriate counselling, in order to limit the patient's liability to overreact and take unnecessary protections or seek unnecessary and unproven remedies that could cause injury.

16.74

Informed patients for whom transplantation is proposed are free to reject the option. They may prefer not to take the risks of surgery or infection, not want relatives to take the risks of live donation, not want dead persons' materials in their bodies or, for instance, not want to receive transgenically prepared animals' organs. They may enquire, if they are not informed, whether organs they may receive come from members of races different from their own, from other countries, or from involuntary 'donors', and may be aware of organ recovery, for instance,

16.75

---

[267] See *Whitehouse v Jordan* (n 191 above).
[268] On a possible product liability claim, see Ch 15 and Kennedy and Grubb (n 10 above), 1594–1664.
[269] See *Pittman Estate v Bain* (1994) 112 DLR (4th) 257 (Ont Ct Gen Div). English law may be less clear, particularly since the decision of the Court of Appeal in *Powell v Boladz* (1997) 39 BMLR 35 (CCA).
[270] *Pittman Estate v Bain* (n 269 above).

from executed prisoners.[271] Their decisions on whether or not to accept transplantation at all or from particular sources can give expression to their philosophical, social, religious, cultural or other convictions. Those with parental responsibility are not necessarily free, however, to make decisions on children's welfare on the same basis as they make decisions for themselves. It is trite law that while they may martyr themselves for their convictions, they cannot martyr their children who depend on them for protection and care.[272] Parents may balance such risks as transmission of infection against prospective benefits of transplantation for their children, and will not casually be contradicted by courts on procedures as invasive as organ transplantation.[273] However, courts are frequently willing to reverse refusals of blood transfusion for children incapable of making their own decisions that parents make on principles of the parents' religious faith.[274] The basis of the common law's intervention is the limited risk and overwhelming benefit when transfusion is medically indicated to sustain life.[275] Advances in organ and other tissue transplantation proposed for children may in time reach comparable levels of safety and efficacy. Courts may react similarly to parents' refusals of foetal tissues on the ground that their newborn children should not benefit from induced abortions.

(ii) Selection Criteria[276]

16.76 The gap between the demand for organs for transplantation and the supply may be self-perpetuating, since the availability of organs provides an incentive for physicians to advise patients to consider the option, and to place them on waiting lists. Scarcity of organs, and of personnel and other resources for transplantation, compels selection among candidate recipients, and development of principles for this purpose.[277] Public agencies must ensure that the selection criteria they invoke in principle and apply in practice are lawful. Principles and practices must not be

---

[271] See Owen, AK, 'Death Row Inmates or Organ Donors: China's Source of Body Organs for Medical Transplantation' (1995) 5 Indiana International & Comparative L Rev 495–517; and Patton, L-H M, 'A Call for Common Sense: Organ Donation and the Executed Prisoner' (1996) 3 *Virginia Journal of Social Policy and Law* 387–434; Hinkle, W, 'Giving Until It Hurts: Prisoners are not the Answer to the National Organ Shortage' (2002) 35 Indiana L Rev 593–619.

[272] *Prince v Massachusetts* (1944) 321 US 158, 166 (US Sup Ct).

[273] See *In re T (A Minor) (Wardship: Medical Treatment)*, [1997] 1 All ER 906 (CA) and Moore, DA, 'Challenging Parental Decisions to Overtreat Children' (1995) 5 *Health Matrix* 311–23.

[274] See Mason, McCall Smith and Laurie (n 219 above), 315–16 and Giesen (n 224 above), 468–75.

[275] See generally Ch 4 on court-ordered blood transfusion for children and pregnant women, and Arch, RR, 'The Maternal-Fetal Rights Dilemma: Honoring a Woman's Choice of Medical Care During Pregnancy' (1996) 12 J of Contemporary Health Law and Policy 637–73, 661–7.

[276] For a description of the selection and allocation of organs, see: *An Investigation into Conditional Organ Donation: The Report of a Panel* (DoH, 2000), ch 3.

[277] See Dickens, BM, 'Ethics Committees, Organ Transplantation and Public Policy' (1992) 20 *Law, Medicine and Health Care* 300–6.

discriminatory, for instance, on the basis of race or sex, or perhaps of age, and unreasonable criteria will be amenable to judicial review.[278] Some centres equate reformed alcoholic patients with non-alcoholic patients, but disfavour liver transplantation of unreformed alcoholic patients, for instance, on the ground that it would afford them only a brief respite from their affliction, but if alcoholism is seen as a physical or mental health dysfunction rather than a moral failing, it may seem perverse to deny patients respite from suffering on the ground that they are sick.[279] Medical futility, if adequately defined,[280] is a legitimate basis to withhold non-indicated treatment,[281] and patients may be stratified into those whose conditions render forms of management appropriate, or inappropriate for them and of no potential benefit. However, to refuse organ transplantation to a patient on a medically unrelated ground such as low intelligence may expose the decision-maker to judicial review.

It is understandable that courts will be disinclined to contradict how health authorities determine the allocation of resources to serve an individual patient's best interests and the authority's obligation reasonably to provide effective treatment for the population of patients for whose health care services it is responsible.[282] It has been observed that '[d]ifficult and agonizing judgments have to be made as to how a limited budget is best allocated to the maximum advantage of the maximum number of patients. That is not a judgment which the court can make.'[283] Considering a particular patient's circumstances and wishes and declining to accommodate them on grounds of economy may be distinguishable from declining to consider them on an impersonal ground of the patient's race, sex, age, intelligence or other status. **16.77**

US courts may consider whether denials of medical care offend the Americans with Disabilities Act of 1990.[284] Canadian courts may similarly review alleged discrimination in access to health services on grounds, for instance, of disability or age, under federal constitutional human rights provisions.[285] The European Convention on Human Rights, although addressing individuals' rights to require just treatment from public authorities, does not express a right to health services, **16.78**

---

[278] See *R v Sheffield HA* (n 128 above).

[279] Coehn, C, and Benjamin, M, 'Alcoholics and Liver Transplantation' (1991) 265 J of the American Medical Association 1299–1301.

[280] See generally Symposium on Medical Futility, (1995) 25 Seton Hall L Rev 873–1073 and Smith, GP, 'Utility and the Principle of Medical Futility' (1995) 12 J of Contemporary Health Law and Policy 1–39.

[281] See also Stern, K (n 256 above).

[282] See *R v Cambridge HA, ex p B* [1995] 2 All ER 129 (CA).

[283] ibid, *per* Sir Thomas Bingham MR, 137.

[284] Public Law, 101–336, 104 Stat 327 (1990).

[285] *Eldridge v British Columbia (Attorney-General)* (1997) 151 DLR (4th) 577 (Sup Ct Can) on the Canadian Charter of Rights and Freedoms.

and covers discrimination in health care only by implication of Article 14, which provides that:

> The enjoyment of the rights and freedoms set forth in this Convention shall be secured without discrimination on any ground such as sex, race, colour . . . birth or other status.

The absence of explicit reference to such criteria as age or physical or mental disability is not conclusive that these are not so-called 'non-enumerated' grounds of prohibited discrimination, but places a heavy burden on those who argue that the Convention or its implementation in national law bars discrimination on these grounds in the allocation of health care services such as transplantation. Dissatisfied patients may have greater prospects of resisting apparently discriminatory policies and practices by referring to the codes of ethics of health professionals and institutions rather than broadly based international declarations of aspirations to equality for all.[286]

(iii) United Kingdom Transplant

16.79 In exercise of powers conferred by various sections and Sch 5 to the National Health Service Act 1977[287] and s 3(1) of the Human Organ Transplants Act 1989,[288] this authority, previously named the United Kingdom Transplant Support Service Authority, was established by Regulations in 1991.[289] The Regulations empower UK Transplant to provide instruction and services, such as for diagnosis and treatment, relevant to transplantation, to conduct research into causes and prevention of illnesses that result in demands for transplantation, and to collaborate with others for these purposes.[290] UK Transplant may also, within limits, make available supplies of human blood and other bodily materials, and supplies of other substances and preparations not otherwise readily obtainable, and make appropriate charges, in order to assist, facilitate and promote services for organ transplantation. UK Transplant records information about donors and recipients of organs and of available organs, identifies potential recipients, notifies transplant centres accordingly and may arrange transport of organs. Its concerns extend to practices in respect of storage, transport and use of organs. An important function is provision of an organ matching and tissue-typing service. UK Transplant reports to the Secretary of State for Health as required and at least annually, and furnishes such information from time to time as the Secretary requires in connection with its functions.

---

[286] For a helpful bibliography, see McCarrick, PM, 'Organ Transplant Allocation' (1995) 5 Kennedy Institute of Ethics J 365–83.

[287] 1977 ch 49 as amended; see SI 1991/408 note (a) for relevant amendments.

[288] N 7 above.

[289] SI 1991/408, as amended by SI 1991/1645 and SI 2000/1621. For a description of the role of UK Transplant, see the Panel report (n 276 above), esp ch 3.

[290] See *The Review of the United Kingdom Transplant Support Service Authority (UKTSSA)*

E. Anonymity

Neither the Human Tissue Act 1961[291] nor the Human Organ Transplants Act **16.80** 1989[292] addresses anonymity between recipients and donors of transplanted materials. In contrast, Ontario's Human Tissue Gift Act[293] provides in s 11 that:

(1) Except where legally required, no person shall disclose or give to any other person any information or document whereby the identity of any person,

(a) who has given or refused to give a consent;
(b) with respect to whom a consent has been given; or
(c) into whose body tissue has been, is being or may be transplanted, may become known publicly.

(2) Where the information or document disclosed or given pertains only to the person who disclosed or gave the information or document, subsection (1) does not apply.

Anonymity prevents a living donor and family member of a deceased person from whose body materials were recovered and transplanted from approaching the recipient to request payment or other recognition of indebtedness, and prevents a recipient from acknowledging an obligation in a personalised way. There may be no need for provisions concerning anonymity in Britain, since live donors are confined primarily to genetic relations of recipients, both of whom will probably know the other's identity, and the 1989 Act is intended to preclude and punish transactions of a commercial nature.[294] Blood donation is conventionally anonymous, but has been the subject of litigation in some jurisdictions. Recipients who have contracted HIV infection from contaminated blood transfusions have sought to discover donors' identities to establish negligent donor recruitment and testing by blood supply agencies.[295] Some courts have given priority to donors' anonymity on the ground that disclosure of identity would prejudice the public interest in donation[296] and risk publicising a donor suffering from AIDS, but courts that have granted disclosure have set limits confining plaintiffs' access to essential information, and precluding any wider release, for instance to news media. Courts attempt to balance public interest in donation against plaintiffs' interests in obtaining compensation for negligent infliction of devastating infections, and hope to reconcile the interests.[297]

1998/1999 (DoH, March 2000), proposing organisational changes and increased responsibilities for the Authority.

[291] N 6 above.

[292] N 7 above.

[293] N 9 above.

[294] In practice, cadaveric donation is almost invariably anonymous: see Fox and Swazey (n 203 above), 37.

[295] See *PD v Australian Red Cross Society (NSW Division)* (1993) 30 NSWLR 376 (NSW CA), and US cases discussed in the case commentary by Grubb, A, 'Discovery: Identity of Blood Donor' (1994) 2 Med L Rev 111–13.

[296] See *AB v Scottish Blood Transfusion Service* [1990] SCLR. 263 (CS, OH).

[297] See Kennedy and Grubb (n 10 above), 1821–6.

17

PATENTING AND THE HUMAN BODY

A. Introduction

Access to medical treatments and medicinal products, the availability of new diagnostic tools, and the future direction of biomedical research are all profoundly influenced by the existence and exercise of intellectual property rights (IPRs). The philosophy of the intellectual property regime is disarmingly simple: the promise of a private property right to control the exploitation of a new creation—be it a drug, an artistic work or the design of a new article of commerce—encourages others to create and make their creations available to the community, all in the name of the public good. The reward to the innovator is a monopoly right, limited in time, to exclude competitors from the marketplace. The strength of the monopoly varies depending on the particular intellectual property right in question. Thus, for example, copyright only prevents direct copying of the work that is protected, whereas patent protection confers an absolute monopoly of the market making it possible to exclude even the innocent infringer who has independently and unknowingly invented the same product. Compensation for this uneven breadth of protection between these IPRs is reflected in the duration of the respective rights. Strong patent protection lasts a maximum of 20 years,[1] while

17.01

---

* I am indebted, as is so often the case, to my colleague Ken Mason for his comments on an earlier draft of this contribution. The usual disclaimer applies to my own efforts.

[1] Supplementary Protection Certificates are available in various jurisdictions for pharmaceuticals and agrochemicals to extend the protection period by up to five years. The rationale is that such

weaker copyright in original works subsists for the life of the author and 70 years *post mortem auctoris*. It is clear from this that intellectual property law is about seeking a balance between a range of potentially competing interests. A host of tensions abound. On the one hand, there is the need to regulate competing private interests between property rights holders and other entrepreneurs who may, as a result, be excluded from the market. This in turn has consequences for the public interest lest excessive monopolistic control reduces consumer choice and services. Relatedly, there is the perennial problem of striking an acceptable balance between the offer of attractive and effective IPRs and the restriction on the grant and exercise of those rights when protection of them no longer serves the public good. Nowhere is the tension felt more acutely than in the realm of patent law, and it is this area of intellectual property law that impacts most directly on the provision of health care and the carrying out of medical research.

17.02   This Chapter considers the current state of play regarding the influence on medical law of patent law and patent rights. Much recent debate has focused on the patentability of biotechnological inventions, most notably genes and gene fragments, and on the impact of aggressive patenting policies on research and the availability of diagnostic tests and therapies. Objections to patenting in the medical sphere have been directed to both (i) *absolute* grounds of objection, ie arguing that certain inventions should not be patentable at all, and (ii) *relative* grounds of objection, ie arguing that medical patents should not be exploited in a particular manner—the objection to the latter being that the exercise of the monopoly is unacceptable relative to other social values, such as access to medicines and health care. The structure of this chapter reflects these themes. Consideration is also given to the role and rights of research subjects or patients when their active participation in research has led to a patentable invention.

B. Obtaining and Exploiting a Patent

17.03   Although a range of IPRs is relevant to many aspects of a health service,[2] patents

---

inventions are delayed in reaching the market because of stringent safety regulations and so the actual time afforded to patentees to exploit their inventions is reduced. In Europe, see Council Regulations 1768/92 of 18 June 1992 (pharmaceuticals) and 1610/96 of 23 July 1996 (agrochemicals).

[2] For example, copyright subsists in all notes, records, photographs, x-rays, prescriptions and charts because these are protected as literary or artistic works under the Copyright, Designs and Patents Act 1988, ss 3–4. Similarly, the design of many instruments or other pieces of equipment might be the subject of design rights under the Registered Designs Act 1949 or the Copyright, Designs and Patents Act 1998, Pt III, while the Trade Marks Act 1994 is the legal basis for the grant of UK trade mark rights, the existence of which is responsible for the maintenance of high prices on drugs to which a successful mark is attached. Indeed, it is a universal intellectual property policy of pharmaceutical companies to ensure that drugs are marketed under a distinctive trade mark long

undoubtedly have the most direct and enduring effect on the provision of health care and the enterprise of medical research.

1. Patentability Criteria

Patents protect inventions. *Invention* is not defined in the law;[3] rather a patent will **17.04** be granted if a prospective patentee can overcome three significant hurdles. First, the putative invention must not be excluded from protection according to a defined list of non-patentable entities; most particularly the invention must not be a mere discovery.[4] Second, a patent shall not be granted 'for an invention the commercial exploitation of which would be contrary to public policy or morality'.[5] Finally, the invention must meet a stringent set of positive criteria for patentability, namely, that the invention must be *new* (in the sense of never before having been made available to the public),[6] it must involve an *inventive step* (ie, that the invention does not merely represent an obvious technical development to an expert in the relevant field),[7] and it should be capable of *industrial application* (ie, it can be made or used in any kind of industry).[8]

2. Exclusions of Methods of Medical Treatment or Diagnosis

Writ large in these provisions is the role of public policy. In essence, patents should **17.05** only be granted to worthy inventions that are not already available, which add substantial value to the sum total of human knowledge, and which do not offend public sensibilities. The letter of the law pays particular attention to policy concerns surrounding equitable access to health care. For example, s 4(2) of the Patents Act 1977 provides that:

> An invention of a method of treatment of the human or animal body by surgery or therapy or of diagnosis practised on the human or animal body shall not be taken to be capable of industrial application.

Various practices have been denied patent protection on these grounds, including a method for operating and monitoring heart pacemakers,[9] improved dosage

---

before any patent protection runs out. Once this occurs, after 20 years, the market share is defended by the enduring appeal of the trade mark, even although the drug itself is now available for any competitor to produce in the generics market. Further trade mark disputes affect the pricing and availability of drugs through regulation of the practice of parallel importing, see for example, Case C-143/00 *Boehringer Ingleheim KG v Swingward Ltd (joined actions); Glaxo Group Ltd v Dowelhurst Ltd* [2002] 3 WLR 1697, 65 BMLR 177.

[3] Patents Act 1977.
[4] ibid, s 1(2)(a).
[5] ibid, s 1(3).
[6] ibid, s 1(1)(a).
[7] ibid, s 1(1)(b).
[8] ibid, s 1(1)(c).
[9] *Tectronics/Pacemaker* [1996] OJ EPO 274.

regimes of established treatments,[10] and a method for vaccination against disease.[11] The rationale is that those who practise the public good of medicine should not be hindered in their art because of the potential inaccessibility of new and improved treatment methods through the obduracy of a patent holder.[12] This rationale, however, does not extend as broadly as logic might suggest. It should be noted, for example, that the exclusion only extends to *methods* of treatment *of* the human or animal body. Thus, anything done to, or created from, samples *derived from* the body is patentable, so long as the substances are not to be returned to the same body.[13] Likewise, if the method does not involve *treatment* of the human or animal body—in the sense of having a curative or prophylactic effect on a disease or malfunctioning of the body—then it is patentable. An example would be the administration of a chemical product for purely cosmetic reasons.[14] It has also been established, inter alia, that pregnancy[15] and infestation by lice[16] are not diseases as such, and methods for their treatment have accordingly been patented. As the Court of Appeal has confirmed: '[t]he section has the limited purpose of ensuring that the actual use, by practitioners, of methods of medical treatment when treating patients should not be subject to restraint or restriction by patent monopolies. The difficulty is to decide whether the restraint concerns a method of treatment as opposed to what is available for treatment.'[17]

17.06   Section 4(3) of the 1977 Act ensures that 'what is available for treatment' can also be protected:

> Subsection (2) . . . shall not prevent a product consisting of a substance or composition being treated as capable of industrial application merely because it is invented for use in any such method.

Pharmaceuticals are the most obvious and important example of such patentable products. The inclusion of this provision is entirely due to the lobbying power of the pharmaceutical industry and its insistence on the need for strong patent protection to maintain the incentive to develop an ever-burgeoning range of drugs. The threat that innovation will dry up if patent protection is not available is a powerful argument which is used across a range of industries that avail themselves

---

[10] *Bristol-Myers Squibb v Baker Norton* [2001] RPC 1 and *Instituo Gentili SpA v Teva Pharaceutical Industries Ltd* [2003] EWCA Civ 1545.

[11] *Unilever's (Davis') Application* [1983] RPC 219.

[12] See Thums, D, 'Patent Protection for Medical Treatment: A Distinction between Patent and Medical Law' (1996) 27 IIC 423.

[13] European Patent Office Guidelines Pt C, ch 4.3.

[14] Case T-144/83 *Du Pont/Appetite Suppressant* [1987] EPOR 6. Note, however, the European Patent Office guidelines define 'surgery' to include plastic surgery, so such methods would also be excluded from protection.

[15] *Schering's Application* [1971] RPC 337.

[16] *Stafford-Miller's Application* [1984] FSR 258.

[17] *Bristol-Myers Squibb v Baker Norton Pharmaceuticals* [2001] RPC 1, 17.

of the benefits of the patent system, but nowhere is that threat more effective than in the realm of pharmaceuticals. Although there is precious little empirical evidence that the denial of a patent has a disproportionately negative effect on innovation, the cost is thought to be too great to challenge the fixity of the pharmaceutical sector.

Some European countries such as Spain and Italy traditionally denied patent protection to pharmaceuticals for reasons similar to those that underpin the exclusion of methods of treatment. Eventually, however, these states bowed to international pressure and commitments to the European Union and brought their laws in line with other western states. And, while a number of developing and least developed countries continue to exclude patent protection in this field, their membership of the World Trade Organisation (WTO) and attendant obligations under the international TRIPS Agreement (1994) mean that this will soon change. In particular, TRIPS requires that: '. . . patents shall be available for any inventions, whether products or processes, in all fields of technology . . .'.[18] Least developed Countries have until 2016 to provide patent protection for pharmaceutical inventions.

17.07

Further restriction on the impact of s 4(2) of the 1977 Act comes in the form of s 2(6) of the Act. This provides:

17.08

> In the case of an invention consisting of a substance or composition for use in a method of treatment of the human or animal body by surgery or therapy or of diagnosis practised on the human or animal body, the fact that the substance or composition forms part of the state of the art shall not prevent the invention from being taken to be new if the use of the substance or composition in any such method does not form part of the state of the art.

Put simply, this provision ensures the patentability of a second, or even subsequent, medical use of a substance already employed in treatment or diagnosis. While the new use must be previously unknown for it to be patentable, it is irrelevant that a method of treatment is involved, or that the substance is already known and is being used (albeit to a different end), or indeed that the substance is manufactured in precisely the same way for the old and new uses.[19] An example is *Wyeth's Application*[20] in which the use of pharmaceutical compounds known as guanidines, which had been primarily used to lower blood pressure, was held to be patentable when employed in the manufacture of anti-diarrhoeal agents. The

---

[18] Agreement on Trade Related Aspects of Intellectual Property Rights 1994, Art 27(1). Note that Art 27(3) allows signatory states to exclude from patentability 'diagnostic, therapeutic and surgical methods for the treatment of humans and animals', while Art 27(2) permits exclusions from patentability of inventions '. . . the commercial exploitation of which is necessary to protect *ordre public* or morality, including to protect human, animal or plant life or health . . .'.
[19] *Eisai/Second Medical Indication* Decision G 0005/83 [1985] OJ EPO 64.
[20] *Wyeth's Application; Schering's Application* [1985] RPC 545.

important qualification on claims to second or subsequent medical use is that these must be drafted in such a way as to be limited to the *manufacture* of the medicament to be used in human treatment. Thus, it was not possible in *Wyeth* to claim 'the use of guanidine in treating diarrhoea' because this was tantamount to a claim to a method of treatment. Rather, the successful wording of the claim was to 'the use of a guanidine in the preparation of an anti-diarrhoeal agent for treating or preventing diarrhoea'. The distinction, albeit very fine, is carefully drawn by the courts in their interpretation of patent claims. For example, the Court of Appeal recently rejected a claim for the use of taxol in cancer treatment whereby the claimants had discovered that a change of treatment regime by controlled infusion of taxol in three-hour rather than 24-hour periods could produce a similar therapeutic benefit with less suppression of the white cells of the blood. The inclusion of a claim '. . . for manufacturing a medicamentation for simultaneous, separate, or sequential application . . .' did not change the essential feature of the invention; it was merely a method of treatment of the human body.[21]

17.09   This example aside, the general trend in contemporary patent law is to interpret patentability exclusions very restrictively. Indeed, the exclusion of methods of treatment and diagnosis in European patent law is now something of an anomaly. Not only has its scope been progressively reduced over the years, but its underlying logic is difficult to reconcile with other patenting practices around the globe. For example, there is no such exclusion in the United States and other jurisdictions have abandoned the provision as being no longer defensible.[22] That having been said, there are no current plans to do away with the exclusion in Europe, but its impact remains marginal in the patenting of new medical technologies.

C. Biotechnological Inventions

17.10   The most controversial field of patenting in recent years is that relating to biotechnological inventions. These are inventions involving biological material, that is, 'any material containing genetic information and capable of reproducing itself or being reproduced in a biological system'.[23] Put another way, these inventions embody, or are derived from, material taken from living organisms, be these from the plant, animal or human kingdoms. A number of objections have been raised to the application of patent law in this realm. These have often been confused and conflated under the emotive term 'patenting life', the use of which is unhelpful

---

[21]   *Bristol-Myers Squibb v Baker Norton Pharmaceuticals* [2001] RPC 1.
[22]   See, eg, *Anaesthetic Supplies Pty Ltd v Rescare Ltd* (1994) 122 ALR 141 (Aus) and Cuthbert, D, 'Patent Law Reform in New Zealand: Should Methods of Medical Treatment be Patentable?' (1997) *Patent World* May 32.
[23]   Directive (EC) 98/44 of 6 July 1998 on the legal protection of biotechnological inventions [1998] OJ L213/13, Art 2(1)(a).

and, for the most part, has served only to muddy the waters. Rather, the objections should be treated and assessed according to their aims, of which there are broadly two. First, *absolute* grounds of objection have been raised to exclude these inventions from patent protection because it is argued either (i) they do not meet the criteria for patentability and/or (ii) they are prohibited by the exceptions in patent law itself. Second, *relative* grounds of objection have been raised challenging the effects of a biotechnological patent either because of (i) the breadth of the monopoly that has been granted, and/or (ii) the ways in which the invention is exploited under patent law. We shall consider each of these objections in turn.

1. Absolute Grounds for Objection

(i) Discoveries

As has been already stated, the philosophy of the patent system requires that an invention is *new*, which means that it should not already be part of the state of the art (ie, available to the public by any means).[24] Furthermore, every patent system excludes *discoveries* from patentable subject matter.[25] The reasoning is self-evident: why should one party enjoy the reward of a powerful monopoly for something which she did not invent and which, in theory at least, is available to all? How, then, it is frequently asked, can naturally-occurring entities such as genes or partial gene sequences form part of a patentable invention? Why is this not merely discovery rather than invention? The answer emerges from the interpretation of patent terminology.

17.11

A *discovery* is the simple uncovering of a previously unrecognised substance or of a new property of a known substance. An *invention* is the production of a technical solution to a previously unsolved technical problem. It is of crucial importance to appreciate that the prohibition on discoveries relates only to discoveries *as such*.[26] This means that, while the mere discovery itself—for example, the discovery of the base pair sequence of a gene—cannot be the subject of a patent, applications or uses of the discovery may be patentable. And, because patent exclusions are interpreted restrictively, a discovery that can be put to use to solve a technical problem will overcome the prohibition and may itself be patentable.[27] Thus, locating a previously unknown gene, determining its function and making it accessible for further exploitation is an example of a technical solution to the pre-existing problem of the inaccessibility of the genetic product.[28] The

17.12

---

[24] Patents Act 1977, s 1(1)(a).
[25] In the UK, see ibid, s 1(2)(a).
[26] ibid, s 1(2).
[27] European Patent Office Guidelines Pt C, ch IV, 2a.
[28] See eg *Icos Decision* OJ EPO 6/2002 293 in which it was held that the production of a purified and isolated nucleic acid having a sequence that does not exist in nature is not a discovery (although note this patent failed on other grounds including lack of inventive step and lack of industrial applicability).

inventiveness that is rewarded is the making available of something that was previously beyond our reach. However, any patent granted only allows control of the invention in a commercial context. It does not extend to copies of the genetic material in a natural environment, for example, within human beings.

17.13 The essential character of the invention is irrelevant so long as it produces a technical effect in solving a problem. Indeed, the European Patent Office Guidelines direct examiners to consider the invention as a whole and 'to identify the real contribution which the subject-matter . . . adds to the known art'.[29]

17.14 The European Directive on the protection of biotechnological inventions confirms that while patents are not available for 'the human body or its parts in their natural state or for the simple discovery of one of its elements' (Article 5(1)), patents are available for 'elements that are isolated from the human body or otherwise produced by means of a technical process, including the sequence or partial sequence of a gene, even if the structure of that element is identical to that of a natural element' (Article 5(2)).[30] These fine distinctions have not proved uncontroversial. The French Government, for example, has refused to implement the full terms of the Directive arguing that Article 5(1) and 5(2) contradict each other. The Government is still negotiating with the European Commission over implementation. It is not alone in its concerns. By December 2002 only six Member States had implemented the Directive, some two and a half years after the deadline. The Commission formally requested the remaining nine States to implement the law or face the prospect of being taken to the European Court of Justice;[31] this occurred in July 2003 when eight States were so referred for non-implementation.[32] A Group of Experts has been established to monitor and to advise on biotechnology and patenting in Europe, as was required by the Directive itself.[33] A Europe-wide public consultation[34] has shown that numerous points of conflict remain over the application of patent law in this field and many respondents are uneasy about the practice. Of most concern are the levels of protection given to patents of sequences or partial sequences of human genes and the patentability of human stem cells and cell lines derived from them. The Expert

---

[29] European Patent Office Guidelines Pt C, ch IV, 2.

[30] N 23 above, Art 5.

[31] European Commission Communication, 'Legal Protection of Biotechnological Inventions: Commission Discusses Progress with Member States and Establishes Expert Group', 28 January 2003, IP/03/127.

[32] IP/03/911, 10 July 2003.

[33] This Group reported for the first time in October 2002. In essence, the Group reiterated the need, as it saw it, to maintain competitiveness through full and proper implementation of the Directive, lest Europe lose out on the enormous potential of the biotechnology market (*http://europa.eu.int/comm/internal_market/en/indprop/invent/com02-2en.pdf*).

[34] For the results of the public consultation see *http://europa.eu.int/comm/biotechnology/pdf/results_en.pdf*.

Group's first tasks are to examine these areas. The European Parliament, for its part, issued a resolution on the Commission's communication in November 2002 in which it stressed its support for greater public engagement with the issues surrounding biotechnology, including its protection by legal means.[35] In particular, the Parliament urged the Commission to revisit the text of the Directive, and especially Article 5(2), so as to exclude the total or partial sequence of a gene isolated from the body from patentability. The debate, therefore, is far from over. However, the response is monotonously repetitive from the economic perspective. It is argued that the proposed exclusions will not promote research and development activity in Europe and will put European biotechnology businesses at a competitive disadvantage because other jurisdictions, such as the United States and Japan, do not have these exclusions in their patent law.[36]

(ii) Morality

(a) In General

In contrast to the approach adopted in the United States and in many other jurisdictions, European patent law has long contemplated a role for moral considerations in the decision-making process on the grant of patents.[37] The European Patent Convention embodies the common fundamentals of patent law in 27 European states, including the United Kingdom.[38] Article 53 provides that:

17.15

> European patents shall not be granted in respect of:
>
> (a) inventions the publication or exploitation of which would be contrary to *ordre public* or morality, provided that the exploitation shall not be deemed to be so contrary merely because it is prohibited by law or regulation in some or all of the Contracting States;

These provisions lay more or less dormant in the Convention until the advent of biotechnological patents whereupon objectors seized the opportunity to challenge the patentability of these inventions. Without exception, their efforts have been fruitless. The first problem was to persuade the patent examiners in the European Patent Office that considerations of morality were within their sphere of responsibility and competence. The issue first arose in *Harvard/Oncomouse*[39] in

---

[35] For the provisional edition of the text see *www3.europarl.eu.int/omk/omnsapir.so/calendar? APP=PDF&TYPE=PV2&FILE=p0021121EN. pdf&LANGUE=EN.*

[36] Report from the Commission to the European Parliament and the Council, *Development and Implications of Patent Law in the Field of Biotechnology and Genetic Engineering,* COM (2002) 545 final, 7 October 2002.

[37] See also Art 27(2) of the TRIPS Agreement (1994) which permits, but does not require, signatory countries to include morality exceptions in their patent law in similar terms to those found in the EPC. In the UK s 1(3) of the Patents Act 1977 provides that: 'A patent shall not be granted for an invention the commercial exploitation of which would be contrary to public policy or morality'.

[38] Membership as at November 2003.

[39] *HARVARD/Oncomouse* [1991] EPOR 525.

which the European Patent Office upheld a patent on a transgenic mouse bred to develop cancer as a research tool. The European Patent Office relied on the strictly utilitarian analysis that the potential benefit to mankind outweighed the suffering of the animal, and accordingly there was no bar to patent protection. Proceedings were immediately instituted against the ruling which remained unresolved for a decade, during which time the patent remained in force. A solution was eventually found in 2001 when the scope of the patent was restricted to 'transgenic rodents containing an additional cancer gene' rather than 'any non-human transgenic mammal'.[40]

Harvard/Oncomouse is significant because it established the precedent for future challenges on grounds of morality. Its crude felicific calculus has been adopted and refined in other cases, and always in the vein of interpreting the morality exclusion narrowly. Thus, for example, in *Plant Genetic Systems/Glutamine Synthetase Inhibitors*,[41] the European Patent Office stated that it was only prepared to entertain challenges on grounds of morality if actual evidence of harm to society could be demonstrated. Moreover, survey evidence and opinion polls indicating distaste for patents over genetically modified organisms were insufficient evidence by which to judge the overall European moral tone. In *Howard Florey/H2 Relaxin*[42] the Office declared that the morality measure should be applied to prevent the grant of patents only in the case of inventions which would universally be regarded as outrageous. Accordingly, it upheld the grant of a patent over a genetically engineered human protein, H2 relaxin, which is produced by women during childbirth to soften the pelvis. The patent had been objected to on a number of grounds. First, that the granting of the patent was tantamount to slavery of women because it involved the 'dismemberment of women and the sale of their parts'; second, that it was offensive to human dignity to use pregnant women for profit; and finally that, because DNA was life itself, patenting of human DNA was intrinsically immoral.[43] The Office rejected each of these claims on a narrow construction of the morality exclusion. DNA, it said, is not life, nor was the taking and modification of samples anything approximating to slavery. Importantly, the European Patent Office placed considerable store in the fact that consent had been obtained from the women to take the samples from which the patentable subject matter was derived. This, in itself, was thought to be enough to accord respect to human dignity. Interestingly, however, it is not clear what the women consented to, and in

---

[40] By way of contrast the Supreme Court of Canada revoked the Harvard patent over Oncomouse itself (but not the process to manufacture it) in December 2002, claiming that, '[a] higher life form is not patentable because it is not a "manufacture" or "composition of matter" ': see *Harvard College v Canada (Commissioner of Patents)* [2002] SCJ No 77. This ruling cannot now be changed except by express legislation.

[41] *Plant Genetic Systems/Glutamine Synthetase Inhibitors* [1995] EPOR 357.

[42] *Howard Florey/Relaxin* [1995] EPOR 541.

[43] ibid.

particular whether they were ever told of the prospect of patents being granted over material derived from them and the consequent economic potential.[44]

(b) Consent to Patenting

This issue of consent also arose in the negotiations on the draft of the Biotechnology Directive. Initial proposals required that specific consent to patenting be obtained from individuals who provided samples that might lead to the manufacture of patentable products, but, after much lobbying from industry and the research community, no such measure appears in the body of the Directive. However, recitals in the preamble to a Directive exist as aids to interpretation of the Articles contained therein and Recital 26 of the Biotechnology Directive provides: **17.16**

> Whereas if an invention is based on biological material of human origin or if it uses such material, where a patent application is filed, the person from whose body the material is taken must have had an opportunity of expressing free and informed consent thereto, in accordance with national law . . .

While the legal status of recitals is unclear,[45] as is, in particular, whether they have the force of law in Member States, the UK implementing regulations contain nothing on this requirement for consent.[46] Moreover, the recital itself is opaque as to what consent should relate to: is it the taking of the material or the filing of the patent application? The former is merely a reflection of sound ethical research practice, while the latter is a potentially more onerous requirement, not only for the researcher who obtains consent, but also for the patentee (who will not necessarily be the same person). Indeed, the patent office itself could feel the weight of such a provision—upon whom should the onus lie to ensure the provision is complied with, and what sanction, if any, will apply if it is not? The Directive is silent on the matter, but the burden of examination for patent offices could be considerable if this became a ground on which to challenge the validity of a patent. None the less, it is the opinion of the European Group of Advisors on the Ethical Implications of Biotechnology that, when someone contributes a biological element that might later be included in an invention, then information disclosure must be 'complete and specific' for the consent to be valid. In particular, there must be information 'on the potential patent application on the invention which could be made from the use of this element'.[47] The Group further opines that a

---

[44] See further *Moore v Regents of the University of California* (n 49 below).

[45] Case C-162/97 *Criminal proceedings against Nilsson, Hagelgren and Arrborn* [1998] ECR I-07477.

[46] The Patents Regulations 2000, SI 2000/2037.

[47] European Group of Advisors on the Ethical Implications of Biotechnology, *Ethical Aspects of Patenting Inventions Involving Elements of Human Origin*, Opinion No 8, 25 September 1996, para 2.4. This body was succeed by the European Group on Ethics in Science and New Technologies which reiterated this position in its Opinion No 16 of 17 May 2002 on *Ethical Aspects of Patenting Inventions Involving Human Stem Cells*, para 2.6.

patent should be refused if there is evidence of disrespect for individual rights or human dignity.[48] At the time of writing the Danish Government is contemplating making consent to patenting a requirement of their law and its efforts will doubtless be keenly observed around the Union.

17.17   Consent and patenting have been considered together in one other famous instance, this time from across the Atlantic. In *Moore v Regents of the University of California*[49] the plaintiff failed in his attempt to claim property rights in his excised spleen cells from which his doctor and other researchers had profited after developing and patenting a cell-line using those cells. The court pointed to the hindrance to research that recognition of property rights in such material could create, and preferred instead to grant Moore remedies for lack of informed consent and breach of fiduciary duty. The court concluded that: '(1) a physician must disclose personal interests unrelated to the patient's health, whether research or economic, that may affect the physician's professional judgment; and (2) a physician's failure to disclose such interests may give rise to a cause of action for performing medical procedures without informed consent or breach of fiduciary duty'.[50] While this is not tantamount to requiring a disclosure of an intent to patent per se, the reference to economic interests indicates that it would be sound practice to alert patients at least to the prospect. This is particularly so when '[t]he scope of the physician's communication to the patient . . . must be measured by the patient's need, and that need is whatever information is material to the decision'.[51] It is important to note, too, that there was no question of the court in *Moore* revoking the patent over the cell-line. It was held to be both 'legally and factually distinct' from the cells taken from the plaintiff's body and the resultant financial gain was a valid reward for the inventive effort of the researchers. Thus, not only was Moore denied the recognition of property rights in his own cells but he was also deprived of the opportunity to ensure that other forms of property right did not pass to other parties.

17.18   Similar arguments have arisen more recently in *Greenberg v Miami Children's Hospital Research Institute Inc.* This was a class action by families of sufferers of Canavan's disease, a rare genetic disorder, brought against the researchers and the hospital who patented the Canavan disease gene after carrying out extensive research on samples and information provided by the families. Inter alia, arguments were advanced in conversion, lack of informed consent and breach of fiduciary duty. A motion at the behest of the defendants to strike out the action was refused, but the grounds for complaint were reduced to the unjust enrichment of the

---

[48] ibid, para 2.1.
[49] *Moore v Regents of the University of California* (1990) 51 Cal 3d 120.
[50] ibid, 129.
[51] *Cobbs v Grant* (1972) 8 Cal 3d 229, 245.

defendants at the expense of the plaintiffs,[52] and the case subsequently settled out of court. Nonetheless, the overarching aim throughout the proceedings had been to obtain an injunction to prevent the defendants relying on the patent. It is to be regretted that a full judicial hearing did not materialise because there were always are at least two reasons to suspect that the case would not blindly follow the precedent in Moore. First, the suit was being heard in Florida, whereas Moore is only binding authority in California. The tendency to assume that Moore encapsulates a universal precedent is, of course, erroneous. Second, the policy arguments are not as clear-cut as the Supreme Court of California suggested over a decade ago. Its concern, then, was to avoid erecting barriers to research and to ensure the development of, and on-going access to, medicines. The Greenberg case was representative of a groundswell of opinion against the use of patents in the medical sphere when these are used to block research by others or to limit access to health care. The owners of the Canavan patent, for example, charged a fixed royalty of $12.50 per test and placed a limit on the number of tests that could be carried out annually by any licensee. Research uses were also tightly controlled through licensing. The plaintiffs in Greenberg were challenging the patent precisely because of these practices and not for personal profit. They did so to ensure that further research is carried out and, in this sense, the policy arguments in Moore are turned on their heads.

(c) The European Directive

The European Directive imposes certain limitations on patenting, namely that '[i]nventions shall be considered unpatentable where their commercial exploitation would be contrary to *ordre public* or morality'.[53] While morality is left undefined, specific exclusions are applied to the patenting of processes for cloning human beings or modifying the human germ-line, to uses of human embryos for industrial or commercial purposes, and to any processes for modifying the genetic identity of animals which are likely to cause them suffering without any substantial medical benefit to man or animal. The last example is a modification of the test laid down in *Harvard/Oncomouse*. The list is non-exhaustive and represents the few, most contentious, issues that all concerned could agree upon at the time of the adoption of the Directive. In so doing, it was hoped that the moral objectors would be placated while, at the same time, legislation would be passed that permitted patenting in all but a few narrowly defined realms.

17.19

The debate about the scope of the morality provisions nonetheless rumbles on. Although Article 6 excludes uses of human embryos from patenting, it says nothing about cells derived from embryos. Nor is it clear whether the prohibition on

17.20

---

[52] Gorner, P, 'Court Allows Suit on Use of Dead Kids' DNA for Patent', The Chicago Tribune, 8 June 2003, (*www.chicagotribune.com*).
[53] N 23 above, Art 6(1).

processes for cloning human beings relates only to reproductive cloning techniques or extends to cloning to produce stem cells for therapeutic purposes. The European Group on Ethics in Science and New Technologies reported that by 2002 over 2000 patent applications had been lodged around the world involving both human and non-human stem cells; a quarter of which related to embryonic stem cells. Over a third of all stem cell applications had been granted, as had a quarter of those related to embryonic stem cells.[54] One of the most controversial of these applications was the so-called 'Edinburgh Patent' which was originally granted by the European Patent Office over 'animal transgenic stem cells'. However, this raised considerable concern when it was suggested that this might lead to human cloning. In opposition proceedings before the Office in July 2002, however, the patent was amended to exclude human or animal embryonic cells, although it still covers modified human and animal stem cells, and the patent was upheld on this basis. The European Parliament has pointed to the decision and requested Member States to recognise that this demonstrates that the Office can, and does, show due concern and respect for the ethical dimensions of patenting.[55] The European Group on Ethics, for its part, has urged a cautious approach and recommended 'excluding the patentability of the process of creation of a human embryo by cloning for stem cells'.[56]

17.21 It is clear, then, that despite the adoption of the Directive and the favourable rulings of the European Patent Office, the presence of a morality clause in European patent law has remained problematic for the biotechnology industry. Objections to the Directive based on moral grounds were primarily responsible for the delay in adopting the legislation, a process that took ten years. Even after its eventual adoption in July 1998, the Directive was challenged by the Netherlands, Italy and Norway before the European Court of Justice. The court took until October 2001 to uphold the validity of the law,[57] but as has been stated, a number of Member States have still to implement the Directive, some on the basis that moral objections remain.

17.22 The irony is that many of these objections are misguided in their aims and can never achieve what they seek. It must be borne in mind that the sole purpose of the patent system is to grant private rights to facilitate the public exploitation of inventions through monopoly control of the market. That is, a patent only gives the

---

[54] European Group on Ethics in Science and New Technologies, *Ethical Aspects of Patenting Inventions Involving Human Stem Cells*, Opinion No 16, 17 May 2002, para 1.16.

[55] European Parliament resolution on the Commission communication on life sciences and biotechnology—A strategy for Europe, 21 November 2002, 68/PE 325.104, para 3.9.

[56] N 54 above, para 2.5. For further discussion of patenting practices relating to stem cells see Laurie, G, 'Patenting Stem Cells of Human Origin' [2004] EIPR 59.

[57] Case C-377/98 *Netherlands v Council of the European Union and the European Parliament* [2002] All ER (EC) 97.

right to exclude others from the marketplace. The only effect of a successful challenge to a patent is the denial of this market advantage. Anyone is then at liberty to produce and exploit the invention. Those who object to patenting because they object to the invention itself therefore cannot hope to prevent the creative or exploitative process by this means. The only hope is that the absence of patent protection might act as a disincentive to invent, but there are many examples of industrial developments that never qualify for patent protection and yet are not hindered by this fact. The problem stems from a misguided desire to use the patent system as a tool for the regulation of science, industry and medicine.[58] To say that the system is ill-equipped for the task is an understatement of considerable proportions.[59]

(iii) Interpretation

The most effective measures to reduce the impact of biotechnological patents **17.23** have arisen in the interpretation of the criteria for patentability themselves, ie, in the need to show that an invention is new, involves an inventive step and is capable of industrial application. We have already considered the meaning of novelty in the biotechnology context and noted the vulnerability of a patent at any time in its life to challenge on the grounds of lack of novelty. The requirement of an inventive step ensures that protection is only granted when the invention represents a sufficiently significant advance in the field. The test asks whether the invention would be obvious to an expert who is apprised of the current state of the art and who compares what was already known to what has been invented. Thus, in *Genentech Inc's Patent*[60] the Court of Appeal considered the validity of Genentech's patent for human tissue plasminogen activator (t-PA)—a naturally occurring human protein that plays a role in the dissolution of blood clots. Genentech applied relatively standard genetic engineering techniques to reproduce sufficiently pure amounts of t-PA to develop a therapeutic agent. However, at least five other teams had embarked on the same task applying more or less the same techniques and the patent was subsequently challenged for lack of the inventive step. The Court revoked the patent holding that it was obvious to a person skilled in the art to set out to produce human t-PA by these means. The court was at pains to point out that being first, or expending considerable sums in the process of development, were not necessarily indications of inventiveness. The industry later showed concern that the decision might have raised the standard for

---

[58] European Group of Advisors on the Ethical Implications of Biotechnology, *Opinion on Ethical Questions Arising from the Commission Proposal for a Council Directive on Legal Protection for Biotechnological Inventions*, Opinion No 3, 30 September 1993.

[59] In *LELAND STANFORD/Modified Animal* [2002] EPOR 2 the European Patent Office confirmed the validity of a patent for an immuno-compromised chimera mouse on the grounds that the controversial nature of the technology was insufficient on its own to deny a patent.

[60] [1989] RPC 147 (CA).

inventiveness in the realm of biotechnological inventions. This was because the Court considered that the expert who assesses inventiveness in such industries can possess a degree of imagination and ingenuity, and that collaborative efforts within a team can also be used to assess the criterion. Normally the notional expert test contemplates an ordinarily skilled but unimaginative person. This having been said, there is no significant evidence that subsequent biotechnological patents have been subjected to a higher threshold.

2. Relative Grounds of Objection

(i) Morality of Monopoly

17.24   While it is possible to challenge the grant of a patent per se, an equally credible option is to challenge the grant of a market monopoly over inventions. The basis of this objection is that the abusive exercise of the private property right would undermine certain valued public interests. Access to medicines and diagnostic tools and the pursuit of medical research are undeniable public goods, while the control of drug and therapeutics markets and the impact on research are equally axiomatic concerns that are raised by the grant of pharmaceutical and biotechnological patents. The scene is set, then, for a classic conflict scenario. No example illustrates the problem better than the case of Myriad Genetics which owns patents worldwide over the breast cancer genes BRCA1 and BRCA2 and which are the subject of opposition proceedings before the European Patent Office. As the Nuffield Council on Bioethics states:

> The opposition is aimed at curtailing any possible deleterious consequences which might stem from sanctioning the monopoly conferred on Myriad Genetics, including the possible threat to the development of research and the identification of new tests and diagnostic methods. It has also been argued that the patent will have a serious impact on equitable access to testing. It is suggested that the monopoly is antithetical to an approach to public health that is based on a commitment to the comprehensive care of patients at high-risk.[61]

17.25   Moreover, and as the Council goes on to point out, because of the way in which Myriad Genetics has used its patent monopolies world-wide, 'there are currently no other methods of diagnosing the presence of the breast cancer susceptibility gene BRCA1 that can be used without infringing the patents'.[62]

17.26   A European Parliament resolution from October 2001 called upon the European Patent Office to reconsider the grant of patents and for amendment to the European Patent Convention which would allow the Office to revoke patents on

---

[61] Nuffield Council on Bioethics, *The Ethics of Patenting DNA*, 2002, para 4.6.
[62] ibid, para 5.4.

its own initiative.[63] The Office replied by pointing to the role of opposition proceedings, which in Europe can be invoked by any party with a valid concern about a patent. It also stressed that its policy was not to make a special case of biotechnological inventions.[64] Certainly, the concern over monopolistic control is not restricted to these kinds of invention, and pharmaceutical patents are open to precisely the same grounds of objection. The dilemma for the Patent Office and the state in whose name patents are granted is to strike a balance between encouraging sufficient investment and research through the availability of patent protection while not being seen to prejudice, and so dissuade, patentees by setting the qualifying criteria too high. An additional problem is that wholesale challenges that go to the heart of the patent only offer an all or nothing option: either the patent stands or it does not. Other strategies are, however, available which leave more scope for balance.

(a) Balanced Court Rulings

The ruling of the House of Lords in *Biogen v Medeva*[65] is a good example of a **17.27** search for the middle ground. This case confirmed that there is no need to prove an 'invention' in the biotechnology sphere beyond satisfying the criteria of novelty, inventive step and industrial applicability. This additional criterion had been suggested in *Genentech*, but the House of Lords stated categorically that to meet the basic patentability criteria *is* to define a patentable invention. Indeed, the general tenor of this decision is to the effect that no special case should be made of biotechnological patents, thus sharing the clear policy position of the European Patent Office. However, the court did strike down the patent on a number of technical grounds, inter alia, because the claimed monopoly was far in excess of what the invention actually contributed to the state of the art. Essentially, the House of Lords took a very measured approach in *Biogen* and sent the clear message that the criterion of inventiveness should only reward actual technical contributions to human knowledge—no more and no less. It is a frequent problem with new and emerging technologies that initial grants are pleaded broadly before the patent offices and it is left to the courts to get to grips with the true nature of the technology. *Biogen* was an early attempt to keep the United Kingdom on a straight and narrow path.

Most recently, the Court of Appeal upheld the validity of a patent over genetically **17.28** engineered Erythropoietin (EPO)—a protein found in minute levels in the body which regulates the production of red blood cells—while at the same time ruling

---

[63] European Parliament resolution on the patenting of BRCA1 and BRCA2 ('breast cancer') genes, 4 October 2001, B5-0633, 0641, 0651 and 0663/2001.
[64] European Patent Office Declaration of 17 October 2001, AC/145/01.
[65] *Biogen v Medeva* [1997] RPC 1.

out the infringement claim of the patent holders.[66] The Court allowed a broad claim to the DNA sequence for EPO as well as to variants that performed the same function on the basis that the defendants could not show that the variants did not work. By the same token, the Court adopted a less abstracted interpretation of how the defendants' invention worked compared to the court of first instance and found sufficient differences with the patent in suit to hold that there had been no infringement. In many respects the decision is a good example of the balance of interests that is so crucial to the operation of a sound and socially useful patent system. It is, however, due for appeal to the House of Lords at the time of writing.

17.29   The careful policing of the boundaries of the tests for patentability is now a clear policy objective advocated in many quarters. The Nuffield Council on Bioethics, for example, has called for more stringent assessments of all criteria, and most especially the need to demonstrate inventive step.[67] The Council suspects that significant numbers of patents have been granted over biotechnological inventions that do not meet the full rigours of the test. The Council also draws attention to subtle, yet significant, differences in interpretation between the patent offices of Europe and the United States which lead to the conclusion that a lower threshold is applied in the United States, thus making biotechnology patenting easier. In both economic areas, however, revised guidance has been produced on the third criterion for patentability with special reference to genetic inventions. A biotechnological invention in the United States must now demonstrate a 'specific and substantial and credible utility', ie, it must have a clear function, although this can include a sufficiently defined theoretical use.[68] The European Directive of 1998 states that full or partial gene sequences with no known function will not be patentable,[69] and this has been confirmed by the European Court of Justice[70] and the European Patent Office which has held that the mere speculative function for a genetically engineered gene sequence is no demonstration that the product is capable of industrial application.[71] Such a restrictive policy is perfectly sensible and clear: when one considers the plethora of such inventions that occur; a corresponding number of indistinct and unknowable monopolies is clearly not in the public interest.

(b) Further Limits on Monopolies

17.30   A recent report from the European Commission points to a possible role for

---

[66] *Kirin Amgen Inc v Transkaryotic Therapies Inc.* [2003] RPC 3.

[67] N 61 above.

[68] While European law requires that an invention be capable of industrial application, US law focuses on the need for *utility*.

[69] N 23 above, Art 5(3) read in conjunction with Recitals 23 and 24.

[70] N 57 above, point 74 of the judgment.

[71] *Ibos Decision* OJ EPO 6/2002 293.

compulsory licences in the biotechnological sector.[72] A compulsory licence can be sought by an outside party if a patent holder refuses to grant licences for use on reasonable terms and when the patentee is not exploiting the invention herself. Compulsory licences exist, in theory at least, to ensure public availability of new inventions and they are granted when the patentee is not upholding her side of the bargain with the state. At the domestic level, the relevant patent office will decide the terms of the licence in negotiation with the parties and the patentee is entitled to 'reasonable remuneration'.[73] The Commission also stresses the importance of the principle of exempting prior use whereby anyone already using an invention prior to the patent application, or who had made 'effective and serious preparations for such use', can continue in that use.[74] What the report does not highlight is the considerable antipathy with which compulsory licensing is viewed, both by patentees and patent offices alike. Also, the prior use exemption only allows ongoing *private*, ie non-commercial, use and does not in that sense assist competitors.

It is also worth noting the role of research exemptions in patent law worldwide, as a result of which things done on, or to, an invention for purely experimental purposes are not considered to be an infringement of the patent. There is, for example, a long history of antipathy in the United States towards any attempt to limit the private rights of the patent holder. The so-called Bolar exemption provides protection for 'uses reasonably related to the development and submission of information under a Federal law which regulates the manufacture, use, or sale of drugs or veterinary biological products',[75] but this only extends to measures aimed at obtaining regulatory approval for the rapid release of generics onto the market at the expiry of any existing patent. Furthermore, the scope of the common law research exemption—which as its name suggests allows research to be carried out on a patented invention without fear of an infringement suit—has been interpreted progressively more restrictively over the years. It received its strictest interpretation to date in the Federal Circuit decision on *Madey v Duke University*[76] where the court limited the scope of the exemption 'strictly to philosophical enquiry only'. In particular, the exemption does not apply where the use 'furthers the researcher's legitimate business'; a concept that the court interpreted widely to

17.31

---

[72] Report from the Commission to the European Parliament and the Council, *Development and Implications of Patent Law in the Field of Biotechnology and Genetic Engineering*, COM (2002) 545 final, 7 October 2002, para 4.1.3.

[73] Patents Act 1977, s 48. Compulsory licences can also be granted for Crown use or as a result of a report from the Competition Commission which has found unacceptable monopolistic practices, ibid, ss 51–58.

[74] Commission Report (n 72 above), 21.

[75] *Cf Roche Products, Inc v Bolar Pharmaceutical Co* (1984) 733 F2d 858 (CA Fed.) and the Act which overturned the ruling to create the 'Bolar exemption': the Drug Price Competition and Patent Term Restoration Act 1984 (Waxman-Hatch Act) 21 USC ss301 *et seq.*

[76] *Madey v Duke University*, 307 F 3d 1351 (Fed Cir 2002).

exclude any use if it has the 'slightest commercial implication'.[77] In this particular instance, the court held that the status of the defendant as a non-profit educational institution was not determinative—the research work was lucrative for the University in terms of increasing prestige and attracting further research monies and future students.

17.32 There is little clarity and no consistency of approach in Europe regarding these possible limits to patent monopolies. Bolar exemptions exist in some national systems and these are accepted as valuable in principle by the European Commission, but a harmonised way forward eludes the Union.[78] A research exemption also operates across a number of European jurisdictions but in an equally disharmonious fashion.[79] In particular, and as the Nuffield Council has observed: '. . . it is not clear whether the research exemption extends to clinical trials. Case law in some countries suggests that it does, in other countries, the contrary is suggested.'[80] Whatever the position in Europe, however, the exemption, where it exists, is invariably interpreted more generously than is its US counterpart.

A combination of these, and other, approaches is required to ensure a balanced and equitable way forward in the future as a host of bodies, reviews and reports has concluded.[81] Additional factors to be considered include the vigilance of patent offices in carrying out thorough searches of the prior art, an on-going review of the role for imaginative licensing options, and, as we have seen above, careful application of the criteria for patentability. The OECD has indicated the difficulty of finding common solutions because of the complexity of the area, but it has nevertheless recommended that a multi-strategy approach should be considered at governmental level requiring, inter alia, review of the policies within the IP system itself, the manner by which patents are administered, and changing the behaviour of patentees in the way they exploit their monopolies.[82] The Organisation notes in particular that the role of compulsory licences, although not popular to date, should be revisited.[83]

---

[77] Citing *Embrex Inc v Service Engineering Corp*, 216 F3d 1343 (Fed Cir 2000) at 1353.

[78] See, Proposal for a Regulation of the European Parliament and Council laying down Community procedures for the authorisation and supervision of medicinal products for human and veterinary use and establishing a European Agency for Evaluation of Medicinal Products, COM (2001) 404 final, 26 November 2001 and Amended Proposal for a Directive of the European Parliament and Council amending Directive 2001/83/EC on the Community Code relating to medicinal products for human use, COM (2003) 163 final, 3 April 2003.

[79] See, eg, s60(5)(a) of the UK Patents Act 1977,

[80] Nuffield Council on Bioethics (n 61 above), para 5.44, note 26.

[81] For a good account, see Nuffield Council on Bioethics (n 61 above).

[82] Organisation for Economic Co-operation and Development, *Genetic Inventions, Intellectual Property Rights and Licensing Practices: Evidence and Policies* (2002), 80.

[83] ibid, 81.

D. Access to Medicines: The International Dimension

It has already been suggested that the impact of compulsory licensing schemes has **17.33** been marginal in the health sector. Nonetheless, there is growing support for their use as a fair and reasonable restriction on the effects of patent monopoly control. Arguments in this respect are most advanced, although as yet not especially effective, at the international level.

The DOHA Declaration of November 2001, issued by the Council of Ministers of the World Trade Organisation, is designed to address some of the issues arising from the existence and exercise of IPRs as these relate to public health. The Declaration stresses the importance of interpreting and implementing the TRIPS Agreement[84] in ways that both promote access to existing medicines and encourage the creation of new medicines.[85] The primary effects of the Declaration, and a separate Declaration on public health,[86] make it incumbent on the TRIPS Council to address the use of compulsory licences by developing countries in the pharmaceutical realm, and to extend the deadline for least-developed countries to provide pharmaceutical patent protection under the TRIPS Agreement until 1 January 2016.[87] DOHA reiterates the underlying principle of Article 8 of TRIPS that 'members may . . . adopt measures *necessary* to protect public health and nutrition . . .'. Thus, para 4 of the Declaration on the TRIPS Agreement and Public Health provides that:

> We agree that the TRIPS Agreement does not and should not prevent members from taking measures to protect public health. Accordingly, while reiterating our commitment to the TRIPS Agreement, we affirm that the Agreement can and should be interpreted and implemented in a manner supportive of WTO members' right to protect public health and, in particular, to promote access to medicines for all.

Such measures include restricting patentability or imposing conditions on the use of a patent, for example, by permitting compulsory licences to be granted. However, attempts to rely on these provisions[88] have met with vigorous opposition

---

[84] N 18 above.

[85] For an account of the history of DOHA and its future direction, see World Trade Organisation, *The Road to DOHA and Beyond* (2002).

[86] Declaration on the TRIPS Agreement and Public Health, November 2001.

[87] This, of course, does not deal with the problem of individual (western) countries finding other means to ensure that developing countries provide the sort of protection they would wish, for example, by forcing the issue of bilateral treaties, linked perhaps to aid or other trade incentives, in return for 'adequate' patent protection.

[88] eg, the South African Medicines and Related Substances Control Amendment Act 1997 sought to improve access to medicines, and in particular treatments for HIV/AIDS, by authorising parallel imports of drugs from other countries where they are available more cheaply and by restricting the rights exercisable under a patent in respect of designated medicines. In Brazil Art 68 of the Industrial Property Law, Law No 9.279 of 14 May 1996 introduced an obligation on drug

from pharmaceutical companies in some states, and most notably in the United States. This in turn led to a further round of negotiations between members of the World Trade Organisation as to the precise meaning of Article 8 TRIPS and para 4 of DOHA. When, for example, are measures *necessary* to protect public health? Who should decide this? And, how far can a state go to *promote* access to medicines for all?

17.34   The problem is particularly acute for developing and least developed countries, as is recognised by para 6 of the Declaration on Public Health:

> We recognize that WTO members with insufficient or no manufacturing capacities in the pharmaceutical sector could face difficulties in making effective use of compulsory licensing under the TRIPS Agreement.

The stumbling block in this regard has been Article 31(f) of the TRIPS Agreement which provides that production under compulsory licence must be predominantly for the domestic market. How, then, can drugs be produced in developing countries—even with the exemption of compulsory licence protection—if those countries do not possess the infrastructure to manufacture such drugs? Moreover, how can other states assist if their own generics production should be limited to their own market?

17.35   The TRIPS Council was given the difficult task of finding an equitable solution to this problem before the end of 2002. This did not happen. Negotiations reached stalemate when the United States emerged as the sole country to reject an EU proposal to amend TRIPS so as to allow members to grant compulsory licences for the export of medicines to countries that do not have any substantial manufacturing capacity of their own.[89] The United States objected to the fact that developing countries could declare for themselves when measures were necessary, and sought to limit the regime only to medicines for the treatment of HIV/AIDS, malaria and tuberculosis. A further suggestion from the European Union that an extended list of 22 diseases should be introduced, subject to review and extension on the advice of the World Health Organisation, was also rejected.[90] The debacle demonstrates only too well the range of political agenda that influence and shape intellectual property law and policy at all levels, from the global through the

---

patentees to produce the patented drug in the country or face a compulsory licensing scheme, except where production was economically 'unfeasible'. This was challenged by the US as an abuse of TRIPS, the resolution being agreed negotiations between the countries should Brazil seek to invoke the licensing scheme against a US company.

[89]   Currently the TRIPS Agreement, Art 31(f) restricts the legitimate use of compulsory licences to the supply of a domestic market.

[90]   A Declaration from the Second Least Developed Country Trade Ministers meeting in Dhaka, Bangladesh, 31 May–2 June 2003 contains proposals advocating, inter alia, that public health problems and the terms of compulsory licences should be the prerogative of least developed countries so long as they retain that status.

regional to the local. It highlights too the serious incongruities that arise in the search for a fair balance of the interests at stake: economic and moral agenda rarely make good bedfellows. Add to the equation a political unwillingness to compromise and the prospects for change look bleak.

This having been said, a compromise was eventually reached on 30 August 2003. **17.36** This takes the form of a decision to waive countries' obligations under Article 31(f) of TRIPS and to allow countries producing generics under compulsory licence to export to eligible importing countries. This is subject to the caveat that it is done in good faith and in the name of public health. Notably, there is no longer a need to show an emergency nor is there a list of qualifying diseases. It should also be pointed out, however, that 23 countries immediately declared that they would not allow importation under the waiver in what is little more than a thinly veiled act of protectionism. These include the United States, Canada, Europe, Australia and Japan. The measure has been hailed as an equitable solution to the global problem of access to medicines, but in other ways it merely widens the gap between the West and the Rest. While western companies continue to tighten their grip over their domestic markets, new markets are simultaneously opened up to them with no means to influence or control the prices of their products. In the absence of measures to ensure that generic production takes place, developing countries will have precious little option but to trade on terms driven by the intellectual property owners, thereby merely accentuating the power imbalance endemic in this area.

18

ENDING LIFE

A. The Law and the Protection of Human Life

Human life is unquestionably the most important value which the law sets out to **18.01** protect. In the criminal law context, any action which is calculated to endanger, or which is reckless in relation to, human life may be the subject of criminal prosecution, and acts which are intended to destroy human life are particularly severely punished by the law of homicide. In this respect, the criminal law is doing no more than reflect the intense attachment of most ethical systems to the preservation of human life as the supreme moral value.[1] Moral consensus on death, however, has been considerably undermined by a fundamental questioning of the basic premise that death is to be avoided at all costs. The notion that there are certain persons for whom death is preferable, whether as a result of their own choice or of the paternalistically-motivated choice of others, now commands fairly wide acceptance: to describe death as a right might have seemed counter-intuitive in the past, but sounds less inappropriate in an era of right to die societies and right to die legislation. The sanctity of life doctrine, previously widely-accepted, is now routinely described by moral philosophers as unreflective and vague.[2] Defences of a strict doctrine of the sanctity of life are now the exception, and, when they are

---

[1] For a philosophical discussion of this fundamental moral question, see Kamm, FM, *Morality, Mortality*, Vol 1 (Oxford: OUP, 1993).
[2] See, for example, Kuhse, H, *The Sanctity-of-Life Doctrine in Medicine*, (Oxford: Clarendon Press, 1987).

made, encounter the additional hurdle of objections based on moral pluralism.[3] This change in moral climate is profound, and has inevitably affected the nature of the legal discussion of death.

18.02 The protection of human life which the law has traditionally provided, is not absolute; there are recognised exceptions to the prohibition of killing. Certain forms of human life (such as the human embryo and the foetus) are protected only to a limited degree against destruction, and the law also recognises the legitimacy of the intentional taking of human life in circumstance of self defence and, in some jurisdictions, coercion.[4] The circumstances in which the deliberate killing of another will be legally permissible are, however, very limited; in English law, for example, although few would hold one who killed under threat of death to be morally culpable, the taking of life under duress has been explicitly disapproved of in a decision of the House of Lords[5] and courts have occasionally stressed that even the last few moments of life are of very considerable value for the individual and not be treated as disposable.[6]

18.03 The century old prohibition on taking someone's life on grounds of necessity; to save the life of another,[7] was circumscribed in *Re A (children) (conjoined twins)*.[8] Here the Court of Appeal determined that it would be lawful to operate to separate twins, whose continued conjoined existence would have meant certain death for both of them, in order to save the life of the stronger, although it would necessitate the death of the weaker twin. The defence of necessity is almost indistinguishable from that of duress of circumstances and so it was incumbent on the court to distinguish the House of Lords' prohibition on permitting a defence of duress to a charge of murder. It did so on the grounds that the type of sacrificial operation with which the Court of Appeal was dealing had not been within the contemplation of their Lordships. Ward LJ was also prepared to see the killing of one twin as rendered lawful by application of a modification of the rule of self defence; viewing the weaker twin's slow killing of the stronger as justifying the surgeons actions, being within 'quasi self defence'. That the court was prepared to declare the killing of the weaker twin to be lawful, notwithstanding that it involved a positive act, is important because it breached for the first time the distinction between acts and omissions which courts have routinely drawn in cases where they have sanctioned medical treatment, or non-treatment, the outcome of

---

[3] For a pluralistic vision of the ethics of euthanasia (and other issues) see Charlesworth, M, *Bioethics in a Liberal Society* (Cambridge: CUP, 1993).

[4] See discussion in Devine, PE, *The Ethics of Homicide* (Ithaca: Cornell University Press, 1978).

[5] *R v Howe* [1987] AC 417.

[6] For example, Mars-Jones J in *R v Carr*, Sunday Times, 30 December 1986, 1: 'However gravely ill a man may be . . . he is entitled in our law to every hour . . .'

[7] *R v Dudley and Stevens* (1884) 14 QBD 273.

[8] (2000) 57 BMLR 1.

which was the near certainty of the patient's death or indeed where death was the very purpose of the proposed treatment or non-treatment.[9]

Even if moral attitudes have changed, it is against a background of respect for the value of human life that the reaction of the law to the medical treatment of the dying must be considered. The basic legal value—that of the protection of human life—may be unambiguous, but the requirements of patients for whom prospects are poor have necessitated a delicate dialogue between the law and medicine, the aim of which has been to allow doctors to treat dying patients within the law but with room for the exercise of discretion. In English law this has been achieved without recourse to legislation, and indeed legislation on the central issue of euthanasia is not currently contemplated.[10]

18.04

1. Euthanasia: Active and Passive

Euthanasia is the process whereby human life is ended by another in order to avoid the distressing effects of an illness. It may be voluntary, in the sense that the person killed either requests death or agrees to it, or it may be involuntary, in that the person killed either objects or is incapable of expressing an opinion either way and has not given consent in the past. The term 'euthanasia' is not restricted to acts performed within a medical context; any taking of life for this reason is euthanasia.

18.05

The distinction between 'active' and 'passive' euthanasia is one which has bedevilled the discussion of this issue, at least from the point of view of the ethics of euthanasia. The distinction is of such significance—even if for many it is wholly misleading—that no analysis of the subject can avoid it, and indeed it continues to underpin the legal response to the issue. In spite of philosophical criticism, the law appears reluctant to abandon the notion that there is a significant difference between bringing about a desired result through active intervention and merely allowing that same result to occur through inaction.[11]

18.06

The term 'active euthanasia' is used in ethical discussion to refer to the process whereby death is brought about by a specific act directed towards the causing of death. The act must be accompanied by an intention on the part of the actor that death result, and this intention must be the predominant one rather than a secondary, or oblique intention. This means that if the principal intention of the actor is to relieve immediate pain, any act directed towards that end will not amount to the intentional ending of the patient's life if, as a consequence, the life of the patient is shortened. Passive euthanasia, by contrast, occurs where the

18.07

---

[9] As in *Airedale NHS Trust v Bland* [1993] AC 789, and *NHS Trust v M* (2000) 58 BMLR 87.

[10] Government Response to the Report of the Select Committee on Medical Ethics, (London: HMSO, 1994) (Cmnd 2553).

[11] Discussed below, in the context of the omission/commission distinction.

doctor, or other person caring for the patient, refrains from performing a particular act, with the specific intention that the patient should die as a result. It would be an act of passive euthanasia, for example, to refrain from treating a simple infection in a terminally ill person in the hope that the infection will lead to the patient's death and thereby bring to an end current or future suffering.

18.08   Arguments over the moral distinction between active and passive euthanasia are generally indistinguishable from the broader argument as to the moral difference between acts and omissions. Many moral philosophers now discount any such difference, pointing out that omissions are as causally potent as actions and are therefore capable of bearing the same consequences for responsibility.[12] In this view, there is no moral distinction between the administration of a fatal injection to a patient and refraining from offering a treatment if, in each case, the intention is that the patient should die as a result. Indeed, it is sometimes argued that the course of ending suffering quickly–by positive intervention–is morally preferable to standing by while death occurs slowly.[13]

18.09   Whether or not the distinction between active and passive euthanasia is of any moral weight, the criminal law nonetheless reflects a stark discrimination between act and omission. As a general rule, the law is slow to impose liability for omissions, and will generally only do so where there is a close relationship between persons or where there has been previous conduct which gives rise to a duty to act. In view of this attitude to omissions, it is not surprising that the law on euthanasia should itself embody this distinction between acting and refraining to act. In general, active euthanasia attracts legal attention; passive euthanasia, being an omission, will attract legal attention only in very unusual circumstances.

2. The Prohibition of Euthanasia

18.10   In criminal law, the motive with which an act is committed is, in general, irrelevant to the question of criminal guilt. Thus an accused person's concern to end the victim's pain will have no effect on liability for an intentional act of homicide, even if it may incline the court to accept in an appropriate case a mitigating plea of diminished responsibility. Euthanasia, even if voluntary and resorted to for the highest motives, is therefore a legally hazardous undertaking. It may be charged as murder, on the grounds that the mens rea of murder is present. There is intention to kill and an act is committed which brings about death. In murder cases not involving doctors, the appellate courts have repeatedly held that a result, although

---

[12] There is a considerable literature on this point. See, in particular, Steinbock, B, (ed), *Killing and Letting Die* (New Jersey, Prentice-Hall, 1980); Harris, J, *The Value of Life* (Routledge and Kegan Paul, 1985); Kuhse, H, *The Sanctity-of-Life Doctrine in Medicine* (Oxford: Clarendon Press, 1987), 58–81.

[13] For a contrary view see: Gillet, 'Euthanasia, Letting Die and the Pause' (1988) 14 J of Medical Ethics 61, in turn criticised by Parker, 'Moral Institution, Good Deaths and Ordinary Medical Practitioners' (1990) 16 J of Medical Ethics 28.

not the purpose, aim, or desire of the actor, may nevertheless be said to be intended by him if a jury is satisfied that he foresaw that result as 'virtually certain' to result from his actions[14] Thus the administration of strong pain-killing drugs as palliative care, in the knowledge that they are virtually certain to shorten the patient's life, puts the administrator of those drugs at risk of being charged with murder (see para 18.13 below). Consequently, unless there are grounds for the reduction of the offence to manslaughter, the person who performs an act of euthanasia faces the mandatory sentence of life imprisonment.

In spite of the legal prohibition, doctors and others do resort to active euthanasia, **18.11** both consensual and otherwise. Where this is done medically, it may well go undetected; where the act of euthanasia is committed by a relative or friend of the patient it is more likely to be brought to the attention of the authorities. The exercise of prosecutorial discretion—where this is possible—may result in a decision not to proceed with charges, not necessarily on the grounds of inadequate evidence but out of sympathy for the accused.[15] As research on the plea of diminished responsibility has disclosed, where a charge is brought in such cases it will more likely be one of manslaughter rather than murder,[16] although there are noted cases in which the charge has been that of murder. The bringing of the lesser charge may be justified legally on the grounds that the evidence does not support the inference of the mens rea of murder, or, more commonly, a plea of diminished responsibility is readily accepted by the prosecution. This requires medical evidence, but the readiness of doctors to diagnose a reactive depression in these circumstances is unlikely to be challenged by the court in a case which engages sympathies.[17] Even if a charge of manslaughter is brought, juries may be unwilling to convict out of sympathy for the accused, and, even if there is a conviction, the sentence is likely to be light. Mercy killing not uncommonly attracts a sentence of probation,[18] or even conditional discharge.[19] If a term of imprisonment is imposed, it is unlikely to be lengthy, and even where a mandatory life sentence is imposed on a conviction for murder, the actual time spent in prison may be short.[20]

---

[14] *R v Woollin* [1999] AC 82 (HL).

[15] See Otlowski, M, 'Mercy killing cases in the Australian Criminal Justice System' (1993) Crim LJ 10, 16. In this study of 19 cases over a period of 30 years, the author identified a number of cases where sympathy on the part of state prosecutors resulted in the discontinuation of proceedings.

[16] Dell, S, *Murder into Manslaughter* (Oxford: OUP, 1984), 35–6.

[17] For example, *R v Johnson, The Times*, 2 July 1960: diminished responsibility accepted in the case of a father who killed his three month old Down's syndrome child having decided that it was not in the best interests of the child to survive, a decision which appears to have been based on a rational assessment of the child's prospects. See comment by Leng, R, 'Mercy killing and the CLRC' 1982 NLJ 76.

[18] *R v Taylor* [1980] CLY 510; 12 months' probation for the killing by a father of his nine year old autistic son with a mental age of around two years.

[19] *R v Jones*, The Guardian, 4 December 1979.

[20] Otlowski (n 15 above) refers to the South Australian case of *Johnstone* (21 January 1987, S Ct of South Australia), in which the non-parole period of a life sentence imposed on a man convicted

18.12 Whatever the actual response of prosecutors, juries, and judges may be, in theory the taking of any step directly intended to bring to an end the life of a terminally-ill patient constitutes the crime of murder. (Omissions constitute a distinct problem, which is dealt with below.) There are relatively few reported English cases on the subject, although prosecutions of this sort, especially those involving a medically qualified accused, attract considerable attention. *R v Adams*,[21] a case in which the accused doctor was acquitted of the murder of a patient to whom he had given large doses of morphine, posed the question of the legitimacy of the administration of pain-killing drugs in such doses as to shorten the patient's life. In *R v Carr*[22] a doctor was charged with the attempted murder of a terminally ill patient into whom he had injected a very large dose of phenobarbitone; he too was acquitted. Other cases in which fatal injections were administered include *R v Lodwig*,[23] in which the prosecution was abandoned after the Crown offered no evidence in respect of the administration of a fatal dose of potassium chloride and lignocaine, and the Scottish case of *HM Advocate v Watson*.[24] In the latter case, the accused had administered ten times the normal dose of diamorphine to a patient suffering from intractable pain. He was unable to explain why he administered such a dose, but was none the less acquitted of culpable homicide. Doctor Moor, a GP, was prosecuted for the murder of one of his patients after admitting in a public forum that he had used drugs to ensure an easy death for some of his patients. The charge alleged he had injected a patient with a fatal dose of diamorphine. A jury took under an hour to find him not guilty; no doubt influenced by the trial judge's observation that it was 'a great irony' that Dr Moor who had assiduously cared for the deceased was now facing a charge of murder.[25]

18.13 In *R v Cox*,[26] by contrast, a conviction was achieved, in this case for attempted murder. Dr Cox, a rheumatologist, was charged with attempted murder after he had injected a fatal dose of potassium chloride into a patient suffering from pain which was not otherwise relievable. Two aspects of the case are noteworthy: firstly, the drug employed was not one which has generally-recognised pain-killing properties and Dr Cox was therefore unable to establish that his action had been intended to have a therapeutic effect; secondly, the charge was one of attempted murder, rather than murder, although the patient had died. The first of these factors made it difficult for the prosecution authorities not to act, without implicitly

---

of the murder of his mentally ill wife (who had asked for his assistance in dying) was fixed by the court at ten days.

[21] 1957. Palmer, H, 'Dr Adams' Trial for Murder' [1957] Crim LR 365. See the full treatment of the case by the presiding judge, Devlin, P, *Easing the Passing* (1985).

[22] The Times, 30 Dec 1986.

[23] The Times, 16 March 1990, 3.

[24] The Scotsman, 11 June 1990, 8; 12 June 1990, 3.

[25] See Dyer, 'British GP cleared of murder charge' (1999) 318 BMJ 1306.

[26] (1992) 12 BMLR 38.

accepting the legitimacy of active euthanasia; had Dr Cox been in a position to employ an accepted pain-killer, then prosecution may well have been unlikely. The second factor–that of the charge of attempted murder–is explicable by the Crown's doubts as to its ability to prove causation (the body had been cremated), although another explanation might be the unwillingness of the Crown to risk acquittal by a jury which would quite simply not be prepared to contemplate a life-sentence being imposed on a man with whose motives individual jurors might well be expected to be in some degree of sympathy. The sentence imposed was non-custodial, although Dr Cox was admonished by the General Medical Council and suffered some professional restriction in his employment.[27]

Cases of this sort are, from the legal point of view, relatively uncomplicated, even if juries may be unwilling to convict members of the medical profession accused of such a serious crime as murder or attempted murder. Where considerable difficulty may arise, however, is in those cases where the drug administered to the patient is one which has a recognised analgesic effect, as is the case with morphine or other pain-killing agents. Such drugs may be administered with a view to controlling pain, but may have the additional effect of precipitating death. Morphine, for example, administered in sufficient quantities will suppress respiration and lead to cardio-respiratory failure. The use of this drug therefore requires a balancing of the pain-killing effect with the possible consequence of the shortening of the patient's life. **18.14**

A programme of treatment with a pain-killing drug, in the knowledge that the drug will shorten life, will not be criminal provided that the aim of the treatment is to control pain rather than to bring life to a premature end. As Devlin J said in his instructions to the jury in the trial of Dr Adams: **18.15**

> If the first purpose of medicine, the restoration of health, can no longer be achieved, there is still much for a doctor to do, and he is entitled to do all that is proper and necessary to relieve pain and suffering, even if the measures he takes may incidentally shorten life.[28]

In *Airedale NHS Trust v Bland*[29] this principle is described by Lord Goff, in obiter remarks, as the 'established rule that a doctor may, when caring for a patient who is, for example, dying of cancer, lawfully administer painkilling drugs despite the fact that he knows that an effect of that application will be to abbreviate the patient's life.' Such a decision, he observes, may be made as part of the care of the living patient, in his best interests; and on this basis, the treatment will be lawful. This principle is based simply on the issue of intention; where the predominant intention is to relieve pain, the existence of an unavoidable side-effect

---

[27] Dyer, C, 'GMC tempers Justice with Mercy in Cox Case' (1992) 305 *BMJ 1311*.
[28] 'Easing the Passing' (n 21 above), 171.
[29] [1993] 1 All ER 821.

will not necessarily make the act illegal. This is the doctrine of double-effect, which recognises that acts may have more than one effect. Where there is more than one effect, or consequence, the status of the act may be determined according to the nature of that consequence which is selected–according to objectively defensible moral (or legal) criteria–as being of adequate weight to justify the act. The doctrine of double effect was held to be inapplicable in the previously referred to case involving the separation of conjoined twins. This was because the evil to be avoided (the death of the weaker) was a prerequisite to the good to be achieved (saving the life of the stronger). An alternative approach in such a case would have been to apply a 'destined for death' analysis, in which the weaker twin, who survived solely by virtue of her parasitic attachment to the stronger and who lacked vital organs of her own, was demonstrably destined to die. Analogously, the mountaineer who is at risk of being dragged to his death because a fellow climer, lower on the mountain, to whom he is attached has lost his footing, can surely sever the rope joining them. The fellow climber will fall to a certain death, but was, buy virtue of events, destined to die anyway. In a case in which a doctor realises that the control of pain will have the additional effect of the shortening of life, the control of pain may clearly be a consequence of such weight that it obscures, in moral terms, the additional consequence, namely, the shortening of life. Obviously this principle is subject to limitations; it would be unacceptable to use such extreme measures in a case where there is an effective, safe alternative to the drug in question, and it might not be appropriate where the illness is not terminal. The mere fact of intractable pain alone may not justify the use of a drug which will radically shorten life; it is questionable, for example, whether the use of a life-shortening drug would be legally permissible in a case where the patient, although in considerable pain, is not dying.

18.16   The legal history of this worryingly opaque area of a routine medical practice now has to be re-evaluated in the light of the Human Rights Act 1998, which brought the articles of the European Convention on Human Rights into domestic law. Article 2's protection of an individual from being intentionally deprived of his life has generated difficulties for the courts and is likely to continue to do so. The obvious problem created by the wide scope of 'intention', to include consequences foreseen as virtually certain to occur, although not desired, has been sidelined by a simple expedient. The Court of Appeal has ruled that the articles of the Convention are to be interpreted as an autonomous text, in accordance with European jurisprudence and not as per domestic law.[30] Thus 'intention' is to be given its narrower, 'natural and ordinary' meaning and so excludes that which was not the actor's purpose. However, the Court of Appeal subsequently specifically

---

[30] *Re A (children) (conjoined twins)* [2000] 2 WLR 480 at 589, *per* Robert Walker LJ, affirmed in *NHS Trust A v M*—see below.

declined to say whether a doctor who gave palliative care drugs to a terminally ill patient in the knowledge that they would shorten his life, would thereby violate the patient's Article 2 rights.[31]

B. The Intentional Ending of Life

1. Defining the Boundaries

While the criminal law is unambiguous in its prohibition of any act intended to end the life of another, considerable difficulties attend the issue of what constitutes such an act. We have already seen that acts intended to relieve pain may be permissible even if they have the effect of shortening life; in other cases attention may be focused on inaction or refraining from treatment, or the cessation of treatment which is already being provided. Legal discussion of this issue is intricately linked with the ethical debate. In essence the issue is one of the duty to act and of the circumstances in which the existence of this duty will make an omission criminal. **18.17**

The criminal law of England and Wales in general is reluctant to impose liability in respect of omissions; hence the absence in the common law of a general duty to rescue.[32] Thus, at its most extreme, a doctor who fails to render assistance to a person in distress commits no criminal offence, provided that he has no contractual or other legally-relevant relationship with that person, and provided that past actings on his part do not lead to a duty to act. It is under these concepts of relationship and past actings that the courts have succeeded in imposing liability for omissions. **18.18**

The distinction which the law has traditionally made between omissions and acts of commission has long bedevilled the discussion of the law relating to euthanasia. Much confusion stems from the rigidity with which this distinction has been advanced, with the suggestion that the fact that death is caused by an omission rather than a positive act is sufficient defence to any inference of responsibility for the death. This line of defence was advanced, for example, in the case of *R v Arthur*.[33] As a result of this lingering reluctance to convict on the basis of omissions, much effort has been devoted to the elucidation of the distinction, and to the classification of some forms of conduct as omissions rather than acts of **18.19**

---

[31] *NHS Trust A v M* (2000) 58 BMLR 87, at [31].

[32] In *R v Miller* [1983] 2 AC 161 the House of Lords created a novel legal duty based on one's inadvertent antecedent conduct, in which the actor, on becoming aware of the danger that he has inadvertently created comes under a duty to take such reasonable steps as are open to him to ameliorate or remove the danger. While the case concerned criminal damage, the logic of their Lordships' reasoning may be equally applicable to the causing of harm to human beings.

[33] (1981) 12 BMLR 1.

commission. The distinction, however, can sometimes seem to be no more than semantic. For example, a failure to administer a particular form of treatment can be seen as an omission–the doctor omits to take steps to provide the treatment–or it can be seen as a positive act–the doctor makes a decision not to provide the treatment. Alternatively, it can be seen as a *particular form* of positive action–the treating of the patient in such a way as to exclude a particular form of treatment.

18.20 The making of an act/omission distinction depends to an extent on the isolation of events within a course of action. There are certainly circumstances in which there occurs what might be termed a 'pure omission'; as, for example, where a person sees a crime being committed and does not report the matter. This is an omission in the pure sense because the failure to act occurs in isolation from any factors such as relationship or past actings. By contrast, the non-provision of a particular form of treatment will occur in the context of previous care and, even more significantly, in the context of an existing duty to the patient. The non-provision of treatment is therefore more readily viewed as potentially a form of conduct involving fault.

18.21 The act/omission distinction may therefore be viewed as confusing, and, in any event, is of controversial moral weight; yet it continues to play an important role in criminal jurisprudence and whether conduct is classified as an act or an omission may determine the question of criminal liability. In *Airedale NHS Trust v Bland*[34] the issue of the withdrawal of artificial nutrition and hydration was portrayed by the Official Solicitor as an act of commission which could amount to murder. This argument was rejected by Lord Goff, who took the view that 'the mere failure to continue to do what you have previously done is not, in any ordinary sense, to do anything positive; on the contrary it is by definition an omission to what you have previously done'.

18.22 Omissions may be criminal in the presence of some factor which makes them exceptional. This factor is readily identified as a duty to act; in the absence of such a duty the omission is legally irrelevant. The duty is inferred on the basis of the relationship between the parties, and the reasonable expectations that the patient may have of the doctor. If a patient is entitled to expect a particular course of action of the doctor, then the doctor's failure to do what is expected of him becomes legally relevant.

18.23 The difficult issue is not when the duty of care arises but setting its extent, and it is this issue which dominates the topic of selective non-treatment. The essential question is whether a duty to care for another, once it has come into existence, involves a duty to do everything possible to preserve life. If this is the case, any omission to act potentially constitutes a culpable failure. In so far as there is consensus

---

[34] [1993] 1 All ER 821.

on this issue, contemporary medical ethics recognises that limits should be placed on the provision of treatment and endorses the view that heroic efforts for the preservation of life at all costs are not only unnecessary, but may also be an affront to the dignity of the patient. The fact that modern medicine is capable of sustaining life well beyond what are widely seen as 'natural limits' has led to the rise in North America of the 'natural death' movement, which has sought to protect patients in the face of this medical onslaught at the end of life.[35] Continuing treatment is therefore potentially as bad as stopping it prematurely; what must be sought is a position where patients are protected against premature cessation of treatment (in the interests of convenience, or as a form of involuntary euthanasia), and where the patient's interests are taken into account in determining whether a course of treatment is futile and will only lead to an undue prolongation of life.

The actual formulation of such a policy has proved to be difficult. Various approaches have been suggested, many of which are mere linguistic reworkings of earlier formulae. The distinction between 'ordinary' and 'extraordinary' means played an important part in the earlier debate. Ordinary means were taken to be those treatments which were not scientifically novel, and which were part of the everyday range of treatments available to the doctor. Antibiotics and common operations fell into this category. Extraordinary means were those which involved an element of scientific novelty, entailed a considerable degree of medical effort and expense, or which might lead to considerable discomfort to the patient. This distinction was evidently helpful, but it tended to focus on the status or classification of the medical procedure rather than on the situation of the individual patient.   **18.24**

An alternative approach is to ask whether the procedure in question was 'appropriate' or 'inappropriate' for the patient. This at least focuses on the circumstances of the individual, and appears to allow greater flexibility. Thus it might be considered inappropriate to embark on a course of antibiotic treatment of a respiratory infection in a ninety-year-old patient with a very poor quality of life and a very poor prognosis. Antibiotic treatment in itself is an ordinary treatment, but there may be little point in providing it in such a case. The terms 'appropriate' and 'inappropriate', however, do little to illuminate the real nature of the decision being taken, although they are useful in emphasising the subjective and consequentialist nature of such decisions. In an attempt to address this issue, reference might be made to the *interest* of the patient, which should draw attention to the issues of suffering, dignity, and autonomy which are crucial factors in this context.   **18.25**

Two cases in which the courts sanctioned the withdrawal of life-sustaining treatment from patients who were not in PVS give rise to concern that we may be   **18.26**

---

[35] Berger, AS, *Dying and Death in the Law and Medicine* (Praeger, 1993). An argument for the need for restraint in the face of high technology medicine is made by Callahan, D, *Setting Limits* (Simon and Schuster, 1987).

approaching a 'slippery slope' in which those who are not dying but whose lives are deemed not worthwhile are sacrificed under a variation of the convenient cloak of best interests. In *Re R (adult: medical treatment)*[36] a 23 year old male, who had a serious malformation of the brain and suffered from cerebral palsy, existed in a low awareness state. Sir Stephen Brown, P granted a declaration that it would be lawful not to subject him to cardio-pulmonary resuscitation and further, that antibiotics could lawfully be withheld were he to develop a life-threatening infection. The court applied the test first identified in *Re J (a minor) (wardship: medical treatment)*[37] that the patient's life, were he to survive, would be 'intolerable'. In the second case, *Re G (adult incompetent: withdrawal of treatment)*[38] Dame Butler-Sloss P granted a declaration that the withdrawal of artificial feeding would be lawful in respect of a 45 year old woman who suffered extremely severe anoxic damage to her brain. Although her prospects of recovery were nil she had a life expectancy of four to five years—if fed. Somewhat ironically the court's decision was motivated by the patient's right to be treated with respect and that right was not diminished by virtue of the fact that she was unable to express her views. Any incompatibility in dying from starvation and the death with dignity to which the court said she was entitled, appears not to have troubled the judge.

18.27   By virtue of *Practice Note (Official Solicitor: Vegetative State)* of 26 July 1996, the withdrawal of nutrition and hydration will require the prior sanction of a High Court judge in virtually all cases for the foreseeable future, which seems to represent some protection for patients against the worst possible excesses of medical paternalism. Faced with the applications to withdraw treatment, without which the patient will die, the courts adamantly maintain that the question is not whether it is in the patient's best interests to be dead. (There may be sound theological reasons for this.) Rather they insist the issue is whether the continuation of the treatment, which it is being proposed to withdraw, would be in the patient's best interests. It is difficult not to see this as sophistry for the inevitable and most often the desired outcome of the withdrawal will be the death of the patient. In the case of Tony Bland and in others the courts emphasise the futility of the treatment, but where that treatment is artificial feeding it is far from futile, since the purpose of such feeding is to maintain the recipient's life and if it is administered it will in all probability do precisely that. A more honest approach would be to say that the patient's continued existence is futile and (if total honesty can be tolerated) expensive to maintain. However, in effect to establish an enquiry into whether an individual's existence is worthless is, perhaps not surprisingly, one which the judges prefer not to confront. Notwithstanding doubts as to the accuracy of diagnoses of PVS, the condition does have defined parameters: we know that the

---

[36] (1996) 31 BMLR 127.
[37] (1990) 6 BMLR 25.
[38] (2001) 65 BMLR 6.

sufferer is insensate and that recovery is impossible. Sanctity of life arguments apart, we can reasonably conclude that there is no benefit derived from living in such an existence. When the courts, as they have done, embark on deciding to withdraw life-sustaining treatment from persons not in PVS and not dying, they are entering morally murky and deep waters.

2. The 'Switching Off' Issue[39]

18.28 The removal of artificial ventilation is perhaps the starkest of the forms of cessation of treatment in that it normally, although not always, involves the fairly rapid death of the patient. For this reason it tends to be seen as a significant intervention in which death follows upon an act of the doctor. If the cessation of artificial ventilation is to be treated as legitimate, it must be distinguished from acts such as the administration of a lethal injection, which amounts to homicide. In one view, what distinguishes the two situations is the fact that the removal of the ventilator merely allows death to follow on from an already existing cause (damage to the capacity to breathe spontaneously), whereas the act of administering a lethal injection is a more self-sufficient cause of death, for which the doctor bears responsibility as the *initiator* of what follows. In causal terms, it might be argued that the two acts are qualitatively different. Analyses of causation are notoriously contentious, and such an analysis as this is no exception. The causal significance attributed to a particular act depends on the perspective from which it is approached and on the moral weighting given to particular events in a sequence. The actual (or immediate) cause of death in the ventilator case is surely the withdrawal. Similarly, the lethal injection occurs in the context of other causes, namely the patient's underlying condition. Ultimately, causal arguments may stand as cyphers for more general moral decisions and it is therefore unprofitable to rely on causation to provide any real key solution to the moral dilemmas involved in such cases.

18.29 Once the patient has become reliant on the respirator, not every withdrawal will be appropriate. The following possibilities should be considered here:

(i) Where the Patient's General Condition May Be Expected to Improve, and Where the Capacity For Spontaneous Respiration May Develop

18.30 In such a case the withdrawal of mechanical assistance might amount to a wrongful act, actionable at civil law and possibly even attracting criminal liability for criminal negligence. A difficulty in such a case will be deciding the boundaries between this stage and those stages in which the prognosis is sufficiently poor to merit withdrawal. This is a matter which would require to be resolved by expert evidence. A refusal to switch off a ventilator, upon which the patient was

---

[39] For an extended discussion of treatment-limiting decisions in relation to competent patients, see Ch 3 above, and in relation to incompetent patients, see Ch 4 above.

dependent, (largely because those whose responsibility it was to do so did not want to see their patient die unnecessarily) led to a court holding their employer NHS Trust liable in trespass for unlawfully continuing to subject the patient to the ventilation process, after she had competently refused her consent to further ventilation.[40]

(ii) Where the Patient's Ability to Breathe Spontaneously is Temporarily Compromised, but Where the Patient is Likely to be Severely Brain-Damaged Should He Survive Removal From the Respirator

18.31 Here the decision to remove the patient from ventilation may be prompted in part by the desire to avoid the patient's survival in a badly damaged state. The conclusion might be reached that the quality of life which the patient would enjoy would be so poor that his survival is not in his own best interests. This decision is one which doctors may properly make, and is covered by the principle that treatment need not be given if its effect will be to prolong inappropriately a life which is marred to an unacceptable degree by factors such as pain, gross disability, or very limited awareness of self and surroundings.

(iii) Where the Patient has Suffered Such a Degree of Brain Damage as to be Incapable of Surviving Disconnection From the Respirator

18.32 Patients in this position might have suffered such damage to the brain-stem as to be unlikely to survive for very long even if connected to the respirator. In other cases, the damage to the brain-stem may not be so great as to amount to brain-stem death, but assistance with breathing will still be necessary. Where there is brain-stem death, some commentators have argued that since such persons can be considered dead from a legal and moral point of view their disconnection from the respirator gives rise to no ethical or legal difficulty. In practice, however, the disconnection of patients in this category would be covered by the proposition in (ii) above in that it would amount to a proper treatment decision made in the light of the poor prognosis.

18.33 The courts have considered the question of the cessation of artificial ventilation in a number of cases where it has arisen as a causation issue in homicide trials. One of the earlier cases was a Scottish one, *Finlayson v HM Advocate*[41] in which the appellant had caused the deceased to go into a coma after he injected him—consensually—with Temazepam. He was convicted of culpable homicide, and appealed on the grounds that the act of doctors in withdrawing the victim from the respirator actually constituted a *novus actus interveniens*. The Court of Criminal Appeals rejected this argument and treated the act of withdrawal, after proper

---

[40] *Re B (adult: refusal of treatment)* [2002] EWHC 429 (Fam); 65 BMLR 149.
[41] 1979 JC 33.

medical consideration and consultation, as being a normal incident of the deceased's medical treatment. A similar conclusion was later reached by the Court of Appeal in England in *R v Malcherek, R v Steel*,[42] where cessation of artificial ventilation was held not to interrupt the causal link between the original assault and the death of the victim.

The decision in *Re A*[43] provides a clear statement as to the lawfulness of withdrawing respiratory support in cases where there is clear medical evidence that brain-stem death has occurred and where there is no medical purpose served in continuing to ventilate the patient. The parents of the patient opposed–for medico-legal reasons–the decision to discontinue ventilation, but the court ruled that the respirator could be withdrawn. In his judgment, the judge ruled that the child was in fact dead, and that 'it would be wholly contrary to the interests of the child, as they may now be, for his body to be subjected to what would seem to me to be the continuing indignity to which it is subject'. It was also, he said, 'quite unfair to the nursing and medical staff' that ventilation should continue in these circumstances. This is a significant decision, in that it amounts to an explicit judicial recognition of brain death criteria of death, although the actual circumstances–those of disagreement between doctors and parents as to continued ventilation–are unlikely to rise with any frequency.   **18.34**

In *Auckland Area Health Board v Attorney-General*[44] a declaratory judgment was successfully sought from the court to the effect that no criminal offence would be committed if a patient suffering from Guillian-Barré syndrome were to be removed from the respirator upon which he relied. Under New Zealand legislation, the court is technically empowered to make such a declaration as to the criminal law, and the court took the view that this was an appropriate case in which to exercise this power.[45] In his judgment Thomas J said: **18.35**

> I have come to accept that the doctors' request for guidance is wholly reasonable. I do not consider that the doctors should be required to pursue their 'healing vocation inhibited in making their independent medical judgments for the well-being of their dying patients' under the threat of a nightmarish criminal prosecution if they, or their advisers, prove to be in error in their evaluation of the law or the legal process. In such circumstances I consider that it is appropriate for the court to respond by clarifying the law.

The judgment turns on the wording of the relevant section of the New Zealand Crimes Act, which creates a duty–in specified circumstances–to provide the   **18.36**

---

[42] [1981] 2 All ER 422.
[43] [1992] 3 Med L Rev 303.
[44] [1993] 4 Med L Rev 239.
[45] On the status of pronouncements by civil courts on criminal matters, see *Imperial Tobacco Ltd v Attorney-General* [1980] 1 All ER 866; *cf R v Sloan* [1990] 1 NZLR 474; *Sankey v Whitlam* (1978) 21 ALR 505.

necessities of life to the vulnerable and provides for criminal conviction if this duty is not discharged and death is caused by such an omission. The questions for resolution by the court were therefore: (i) whether the patient's death could be regarded as being caused by the withdrawal of the respirator; and (ii) whether the provision of ventilation was a necessity of life.

18.37   On the issue of causation, the court considered the argument that in circumstances of this sort the cause of death would not be the withdrawal of artificial ventilation in itself but the underlying disease. This issue, it was felt, could only be determined if the prior question of the lawfulness of the withdrawal was settled. An unlawful withdrawal of ventilation would be the *legal cause* of death; a lawful withdrawal—one made *with lawful excuse*—would not be the cause of death in these terms. The important issue, then, becomes that of whether artificial ventilation is a necessity of life which has to be provided by those caring for the patient. On this issue, Thomas J said:

> . . . the provision of artificial respiration may be regarded as a necessary of life where it is required to prevent, cure or alleviate a disease that endangers the health or life of the patient. If, however, the patient is only surviving by virtue of the mechanical means which induces heartbeat and breathing and is beyond recovery, I do not consider that the provision of a ventilator can properly be construed as a necessary of life. It is repugnant that a doctor who has in good faith and with complete medical propriety undertaken treatment which has failed should be held responsible to continue that treatment on the basis that it is, or continues to be, a necessary of life.

18.38   This approach still requires a medical decision as to whether the point has been reached at which treatment serves no further therapeutic purpose. The court held that this decision must be made in accordance with 'good medical practice', a standard which the court stipulated includes taking into the account the patient's best interests, the views of the recognised bodies concerned with medical ethics, and close consultation with the patient's family.

18.39   A decision to withhold medical treatment, which it is known will result in the death of the patient, prima facie represents the mens rea sufficient for conviction of murder. Therefore, only if the withholding can be viewed as an omission, as opposed to an act, and the omission is itself not a breach of the duty owed to the patient, is there likely to be no risk of liability for murder.

18.40   *Bland* type applications, whereby a patient is to be deprived of medical treatment without which he will die, were always liable to challenge under Article 2 of the European Convention on Human Rights since manifestly they result in the patient being intentionally deprived of his life. The first case post the coming into force of the Human Rights Act 1998, was *NHS Trust A v M and NHS Trust B v H*.[46] Both

---

[46] (2000) 58 BMLR 87.

patients were, on substantial medical evidence, in PVS. Dame Butler-Sloss affirmed[47] that since the purpose of withdrawing nutrition was to bring about death, there was no distinction to be drawn between intention and purpose, but held that the omission to provide a life-sustaining treatment was not an intentional deprivation. She decided that the phrase 'deprivation of life' imported a deliberate act, as opposed to an omission and the the deprivation of the patients' lives would result from their pre-existing medical condition, and not from the withdrawal of food.

The court went on to consider whether Article 2 imposed a positive obligation on states to take adequate steps to safeguard life which could require patients in PVS to be artificially fed. It held that, where a responsible clinical decision to withhold artificial feeding on the grounds that it was not in the best interests of the patient, had been made and was supported by a responsible body of medical opinion, the state's positive obligation had been discharged. Thus, remarkably, the *Bolam* test trumped Strasbourg jurisprudence as far as Dame Butler-Sloss was concerned. Indeed she went further, declaring that because the domestic best interests test required consideration of the patient's overall best interests and is not confined to medical best interests, it provided greater protection than she perceived set by the European Court. She based her views on the decision in *Widmer v Switzerland*[48] in which the Commission rejected the idea that the state was obliged to take all reasonable steps to save life, and in *Osman v UK*[49] where the Court stated that Article 2 had to be interpreted in a manner which did not impose disproportionate obligations on states.

18.41

Whilst it is clear that the state could not be under an obligation to ensure that in every instance the zenith of medical expertise was applied in order to ensure the last possible hours of every patient's life, it is far from clear that something as elementary but essential as feeding should not be part of a state's positive obligation under Article 2. Clearly the costs of treatment could legitimately be part of a 'disproportionate' argument, but they would appear to have little relevance in the matter of artificial feeding. That said, the enduring costs of looking after and caring long term for patients in PVS may be considerable.

18.42

3. Assisted Suicide

Assisted suicide is a central issue in the debate on euthanasia because it provides a possible middle-ground between the apparently irreconcilable positions of the legalisation of euthanasia and the preservation of the existing criminal law prohibition. The proponents of euthanasia argue that if legislatures feel disinclined to

18.43

---

[47] Lord Browne-Wilkinson had so opined in *Airedale NHS Trust v Bland* [1993] AC 789, 881.
[48] *Widmer v Switzerland* (1993) Application No 20527/92.
[49] (1997) 29 EHRR 245.

legalise euthanasia outright, then allowing physician-assisted suicide would at least make the process of dying easier for those who wish to end their life in these circumstances. It is perhaps for this reason that opponents of the legalisation of euthanasia see such measures as a mere semantic device under which euthanasia itself will rapidly be subsumed. This difference requires the initial question to be addressed: is there any moral difference between helping another to kill himself and taking that life oneself? If there is no such morally-significant distinction, then any justification that the law might have for embodying that distinction is itself weakened.

(a) Defining Suicide

18.44 The moral assessment of suicide requires a satisfactory definition of the act itself. To commit suicide is to bring one's life to an end intentionally. Death must be wanted for itself. Suicide requires that death be sought not as a means to an end, but as an end in itself. The person who proposes to take a fatal dose of a drug in order to escape from insupportable pain or mental distress might argue that death is not wanted in itself; what is wanted is relief from pain, and this, in the particular circumstances, can only come about through death. His death, then, should be classified as an act intended to achieve a goal other than mere death.

18.45 This argument, however, has obvious flaws. Firstly, this interpretation deprives the concept of suicide of virtually all meaning, and possibly leaves it only with those acts in which death is sought for frivolous reasons or for no reasons at all. Secondly, it ignores the point that what the suicide actually desires is death, whatever the motive may be; the achievement of death is the dominant reason for acting; in order to achieve the absence of the pain of being alive.[50]

(b) The Morality of Assisted Suicide

18.46 The moral status of suicide has in the past had an important bearing on its legal status, and, in an important sense, it is still a relevant matter in discussions of the legal response to the issue of assisting another to commit suicide. If suicide is considered to be a wrong, then there are grounds for criminalising attempts to commit suicide. Suicide is no longer widely considered to be a morally wrongful act, however, and the grounds for its criminalisation have consequently disappeared. There may still be respects in which suicide causes harm to others, of course, but

---

[50] In the case of *Re B (adult: refusal of treatment)* (2002) 65 BMLR 149, the patient, who was a former health worker, although troubled by the fact that to determine that she would die was at variance with tenets of the Christian faith which she held, nevertheless viewed death as preferable to living life as a tetraplegic, paralysed from the neck down. Giving evidence to the court, specially convened in the ICU where she was resident, she persuaded Dame Butler-Sloss of her competence to make the decision to have the ventilator, upon she was dependent, switched off.

such harm (distress or financial hardship, for example) is not considered to be sufficiently weighty to justify punishing the attempted suicide. Added to this, of course, is the general objection to punishing those whose acts speak to inner distress.

If suicide is not wrongful, then a person has the right to commit suicide. This **18.47** means that if a person chooses to kill himself, attempts to interfere with the exercise of this right are themselves wrong, unless they are made for the legitimate protection of others. Furthermore, if a person has the right not to be interfered with in the exercise of a right, then this prohibition of interference should extend to attempts to stop his being assisted in the exercise of his right. This leads to the proposition that if it is lawful to do x, then it should be lawful to assist a person to do x. Consequently, if suicide is not a crime, then it should not be a crime to assist another to commit suicide. The logic of this is recognised in both German and French criminal law where it is acknowledged that since suicide is not a criminal offence it cannot be an offence to help another to commit suicide. Many legal systems, however, including English law, reject this reasoning and continue to punish as a criminal offence any act which is intended to assist another to take his life. This continued penalisation requires justification, in the light of the substantial rights-based critique to which it has been subjected.

(c) Justifying the Illegality of Assisted Suicide

The justification of the continued prohibition of aiding and abetting suicide may **18.48** be based on pragmatic grounds or on principle and was explored by the Divisional Court, the House of Lords and the European Court of Human Rights in the case of Dianne Pretty (see para 18.51 below). The consequentialist argument for the existing law is that to allow someone to assist another to commit suicide raises the possibility that the would-be suicide may be subjected to external pressure in the making of the decision. The ready provision of assistance may serve to encourage those who might otherwise be reluctant to act and brings others into the penumbra of a decision which should be uninfluenced by others. The issue of voluntariness gives rise to some concern.[51] It is a matter of intellectual as well as psychological regret that those who advance this argument consistently appear to fail to recognise that precisely the same pressures might be applied to persuade or coerce someone who was dependent upon medication or therapy for continued life to reject that medication or therapy; yet providing a court is satisfied that such a person is competent to refuse the treatment it will not stand in the way of someone determined to die as a result of such a refusal.[52] A request for assistance in

---

[51] For discussion of the voluntariness issue, see Drickamer, MA, Lee, MA and Ganzini, L, 'Practical Issues in Physician-Assisted Suicide' 1995 (126) *Annals of Internal Medicine* 146.
[52] *Re B (adult: refusal of treatment)* [2002] EWHC 429 (Fam); 65 BMLR 149.

suicide may be made in response to a feeling of guilt over financial and physical dependence; it may also be associated with depression, possibly caused by the illness. To deny help in suicide in some cases may be to thwart a considered and long-held desire to die and may therefore involve a substantial restriction on individual autonomy, but it is also to prevent a situation where a person might wish to live, but feels that dying compliantly is expected of them. It may be difficult to resolve this conflict of values, which is essentially a moral rather than a legal issue.

18.49 The principled objection to allowing assisted suicide focuses on the proposition that competence to perform a particular act may properly be restricted to the actor himself. This is a privacy-related argument; suicide is a private matter in which no person other than the suicide has any *locus*. To assist another in suicide, then, is to intrude into the private sphere of another, and such intrusions may legitimately be prohibited by the criminal law. An obvious objection to this view is that it ignores the plight of those who are incapable, through physical disability, of performing the act in question. If they are denied assistance, then they may claim to be at a considerable disadvantage as compared with those who do have the ability to act within this private sphere. The issue then is whether society is to redress this disadvantage by allowing assistance in such cases, or whether the value of protecting the privacy of such acts precludes the making of any exceptions.

18.50 A further argument of principle holds that life is the supreme value endorsed by the law. The weakening of this endorsement, by any recognition of the legitimacy of taking life, threatens the value itself. If a life is seen as disposable, even if only at the instance of the holder of that life, then the moral awe with which life is viewed is compromised. The direct response to this view, of course, is that there is nothing valuable in life itself; what gives value to life is the capacity for enjoyment of and engagement in the world. If this is destroyed, then life itself becomes a burden which there should be no need to endure. The decision to commit suicide then becomes a legitimate exercise of the autonomous right vested in every person to shape and control his existence.

18.51 Dianne Pretty suffered from motor neurone disease. She was aware of the painful trajectory of her terminal condition and wished to be able to end her life at the time of her choosing. As a result of the already very developed nature of her illness she would require assistance from her husband, who was also her principal carer, to achieve this. She sought to secure an assurance of proleptic immunity from the Director of Public Prosecutions that he would not bring charges against her husband under s 2 of the Suicide Act 1961; an assurance which he declined to give, arguing that it was beyond his statutory powers. She sought, unsuccessfully, to persuade the Divisional Court, the House of Lords[53] and then the European

---

[53] *R (on the application of Pretty) v Director of Public Prosecutions* [2001] UKHL 61; 63 BMLR 1.

Court of Human Rights[54] that the denial of assistance which s 2 effectively represented to her constituted a violation of her Convention rights in that it breached Articles 2, 3, 8, 9 and 14.

At all levels the courts denied that Article 2 could be interpreted to constitute a **18.52** right to self determination: a right to die; for such would be diametrically opposite the right to life protected by the article. The European Court of Human Rights expressly rejected the argument that Article 2 was concerned with issues to do an individual's quality of living or what an individual did with his or her life. This appears to be a pessimistically narrow view of Article 2's scope in which 'life' is interpreted to mean essentially one's biological existence. Yet the value of life, the recognition of which surely underpins the article's *raison d'etre*, lies in its worth to the person living it and for Dianne Pretty it was soon to become not merely worthless, but less than worthless.

She fared no better in her contention that the suffering which she would experi **18.53** ence as a result of not being legally able to end her life represented a violation of Article 3's protection from inhuman or degrading treatment. The House of Lords, whilst recognising that she would suffer as a consequence of being denied assistance to commit suicide, found that such suffering was caused by her disease and not by the Director of Public Prosecutions' refusal to grant immunity to her husband. The European Court rejected the argument that Article 3 called upon the state to take positive action to permit her to end her life so as to avoid the claimant suffering prohibited treatment. Both courts were heavily influenced by the belief that the prohibition on assistance to die in s 2 of the 1961 Act was to avoid the abuse which might put the lives of weak and vulnerable persons at risk. However the European Court recognised that there was no obligation on a state to have such a prohibition in its laws.

Clearly how and indeed whether one lives one's life must be thought to come **18.54** within the ambit of Article 8 of the Convention's protection of autonomy and psychological integrity. Surprisingly, then, their Lordships found the article not to be engaged. Whilst determining that Article 8 protected the way that Dianne Pretty sought to live the remainder of her life, they rejected the idea that it could create a positive obligation to give effect to her wish to end her life. Any interference with her autonomy—in depriving her of suicide—could be justified by the need to protect others from their vulnerability were s 2 not in place. The morality, or indeed the logic, of requiring some individuals (like Ms Pretty) to suffer agonising deaths in order to safeguard against the possibility of others being persuaded to endure painless deaths, seems not to have disturbed their Lordships. The European Court, although acknowledging that the effect of s 2 could

---

[54] *Pretty v UK* (Application No 2346/02) 66 BMLR 146.

constitute an interference with the claimant's right to respect for private life, concluded that the blanket ban on assisted suicide was not disproportionate and could be justified as necessary in a democratic society.

(d) Means of Assisting Suicide

18.55   The legal prohibition of direct acts of euthanasia may lead to a request to medical or nursing personnel to provide assistance to a patient who wishes to end his own life. The provision to such a patient of the means of committing suicide or advice as to an appropriate technique may amount to a criminal offence, although the patient's own act of suicide is not criminal. Suicide has not been a crime in English law since the Suicide Act 1961 decriminalised the act of attempted suicide. The offence of aiding and abetting a suicide was retained under s 2 of this Act. The mens rea of aiding and abetting suicide is an intention to assist another to take his own life. That does not mean that the person assisting positively wants the other to end his life, rather that he intentionally gives assistance, which he knows may facilitate the other to end his life. By analogy with murder, the accomplice probably need not be proven to know that the person assisted would end his life pursuant to the assistance rendered. If the accomplice contemplates as a real possibility that the other might intend to end his life, that would likely be sufficient mens rea.[55] For example, it could be aiding and abetting suicide to give a bottle of potentially lethal pills to a person whom one knows to be depressed and who has talked of committing suicide.

18.56   The provision of advice as to means of ending life was considered in *Attorney-General v Able*.[56] In this case the question arose as to whether the publication or circulation of a booklet setting out suicide techniques could amount to aiding and abetting suicide. The case was a civil one, the Attorney General seeking a declaration to this effect. The court declined to issue the declaration, but it also declined to say that the supply of the booklet was lawful. The judge did say, however, that a supplier of such advice could be guilty of the offence of aiding and abetting suicide if he intended to encourage the suicide of the recipient and if the recipient was, in fact, encouraged or assisted to commit suicide. This suggests that the link between the act of the accused and the deceased's act of suicide must be a close one. The *Able* case is unsatisfactory authority on the scope of criminal liability for aiding suicide, but it is significant that the supply of books detailing methods of suicide now appears to have been officially tolerated, with such books even being made available in book shops rather than to members of voluntary euthanasia societies.

---

[55] *R v Powell* [1999] AC 1. The analogy is not complete since in murder the person assisting is genuinely an accomplice to the principal offender, whereas under s 2 of the Suicide Act 1961 the person assisting is the only offender.
[56] [1984] 1 All ER 277.

(e) Homicide

As an alternative to the statutory offence, in an appropriate case it is possible that **18.57** a prosecution might be brought for homicide. Theoretically, the charge could be murder or manslaughter, depending on whether the intention necessary for murder could be established—it is certainly possible to envisage a situation where an accused has provided a drug to another with the full intention that the other person should use it. The only reason why this should not be homicide is that the act of the victim amounts to a *novus actus interveniens* breaking the chain of causation between the accused's act and the result (the death).

The English courts have not pronounced on this point, but similar questions of **18.58** causation have arisen in other contexts. The nearest analogy is provided by those cases in which there has been an initial unlawful act on the part of the accused, followed by a response by a self-harming response by the victim. The applicability of the analogy depends on whether the act of assistance is in itself unlawful. This would depend on whether it is considered an unlawful act to give to another the means of harming himself or herself, in the knowledge that the means might be used.

In a number of cases, a suicidal or self-endangering act of the victim has not been **18.59** considered to be a *novus actus*. In a series of cases involving a self-injuring escape attempted in the face of a threat which the accused has made, the courts have held that the victim's act does not necessarily constitute a *novus actus*. This was so in *Williams*,[57] where the court stressed that the victim's act must be proportionate to the threat and not so unreasonable as to make it a voluntary act that breaks the chain of causation. Other escape cases reach a similar conclusion.[58] The test, then, would appear to be whether the act of the deceased was an unforseeable one, something that a reasonable person would not have expected to happen. As Brennan J says in the leading Australian case on this point, *Royall v R*:[59]

> The question whether an accused whose conduct has led to a death is criminally responsible for the death when the death has been caused by a final fatal step taken by the victim thus depends on the reasonableness (or proportionality) of the victim's attempt at self-preservation and the accused's foresight, or the reasonable foreseeability of the possibility that a fatal final step might be taken by the victim in response to the accused's conduct.[60]

R v Dalby[61] involved an appeal against a conviction of manslaughter in a case **18.60** where the appellant had illegally supplied a drug of abuse to the victim, who had

---

[57] [1992] 2 All ER 183.
[58] For example, *Roberts* (1971) 56 Crim App 95; *DPP v Daley* [1980] AC 237.
[59] (1991) 65 ALJR 451.
[60] ibid, 460.
[61] [1982] 1 All ER 916.

then injected it in excessive quantities and died as a result. The appellant's conviction of manslaughter was set aside by the Court of Appeal on the grounds that the act of supplying the drugs to the victim was not one 'directed against the victim'. It was held that manslaughter requires an act of this nature, and that the provision of drugs could not be so interpreted because it would 'itself have caused no harm unless the deceased had subsequently used the drugs in a form and quantity which was dangerous'. Waller LJ concluded:

> In the judgment of this court, where the charge of manslaughter is based on an unlawful and dangerous act, it must be an act directed at the victim and likely to cause immediate injury, however slight.[62]

18.61 This approach to the unlawful and dangerous act basis of manslaughter has led to confusion, which was clarified, to an extent, in *Goodfellow*[63] in which a conviction of manslaughter was upheld where the accused, having set fire to a house, caused the death of two persons when the fire spread. Even if he had not directed his act against his victims, it was still an objectively dangerous act which caused death and therefore an unlawful and dangerous act. The decision in *Dalby*, it was said, was only intended to stress that there must not be a novus actus interveniens to break the causal link. *Dalby*, however, is capable of constituting a hurdle for any attempted manslaughter or murder prosecution in a case where a drug has been supplied to a prospective suicide. The difficulty may be overcome by distinguishing *Dalby* on its facts. It is one thing to give a drug to a drug abuser who might be expected to use it in normal quantities; it is another to pass on such a drug to one whom one knows is going to take a fatal dose. In the former case, it might be accepted that the act is not 'directed against' the victim, whereas in the latter, in view of the foreseen consequence (death), the act may clearly be described as being so directed.

4. Assisted Suicide in Other Jurisdictions

(a) United States

18.62 The paucity of English case law authority on this matter lends particular interest to the experience of other jurisdictions. In the United States, where in many states there is legislation prohibiting the aiding and abetting of suicide, challenges have been made to the constitutionality of such measures.[64] In *Vacco v Quill*[65] the matter eventually came before the US Supreme Court, which ruled in favour of the constitutionality of such provisions. In the case of New York the legislation in

---

[62] ibid, 919.
[63] (1986) 83 Crim App R 23.
[64] Legal attitudes vary within the US: in Texas the courts have held that since there suicide is not a crime it cannot be a crime to assist another to take his own life: *Aven v State* 277 SW 1080 (1925).
[65] (1997) 50 BMLR 119 (US Sup Ct).

question was the New York Penal Law, s 12.15, which provides: 'A person is guilty of manslaughter in the second degree when . . . (3) he intentionally causes or aids another person to commit suicide'. Section 12.30 of the same legislation states: 'A person is guilty of promoting a suicide attempt when he intentionally causes or aids another person to attempt suicide'.

The appellants in *Vacco* argued that this law infringed the Fourteenth   **18.63**
Amendment of the United States' Constitution in that it treated different classes of dying patients unequally. The Court of Appeals agreed, observing:

> New York law does not treat equally all competent persons who are in the final stages of fatal illness and who wish to hasten their deaths . . . [T]hose in the final stages of terminal illness who are on life support systems are allowed to hasten their deaths by directing the removal of such systems; but those who are similarly situated, except for the previous attachment of life sustaining equipment, are not allowed to hasten death by self administering prescribed drugs.

The Supreme Court reversed this decision, holding that there was a distinction, widely recognised and endorsed in the medical profession, between suicide and withdrawing life sustaining treatment. This distinction, the court said, was a rational one; a person who commits suicide with the assistance of a doctor has a specific intention to end his own life, while one who refuses or discontinues treatment might not have such an intention. There were other grounds too; Chief Justice Rehnquist identified the State's motives in the following terms:

> New York's reasons for recognising and acting on this distinction–including prohibiting intentional killing and preserving life; preventing suicide; maintaining physicians' role as their patients' healers; protecting vulnerable people from indifference, prejudice, and psychological and financial pressure to end their lives; and avoiding a possible slide towards euthanasia . . . these valid and important public interests easily satisfy the constitutional requirement that a legislative classification bear a rational relation to some legitimate end.[66]

(b) Scotland

In Scotland, where there is no counterpart of the Suicide Act 1961, and where sui-   **18.64**
cide has not been a criminal offence in modern times,[67] diverging views have been expressed as to the legality of assisting a person to take his own life. In one view, it could be the common law offence of 'recklessly endangering life' to supply information on suicide to one who is likely to put it into effect; and, if death results, this could possibly amount to culpable homicide. The grounds of a culpable homicide prosecution would be that death resulted from the illegal act of the accused (that is, from the reckless endangerment). This is open, however, to the challenge that

---

[66] ibid, 128.
[67] See Ferguson, 'Killing "Without Getting into Trouble?" Assisted Suicide and Scots Criminal Law' (1998) 2 Edinburgh L Rev 288.

the act of the deceased in taking his life amounted to a *novus actus interveniens*, relieving the accused of responsibility for the death. It is not clear how a Scottish court would respond to this argument, although in *Ulaqh v HM Advocate*[68] a case involving the supply of solvents for purposes of ingestion, the court declined to regard the act of the recipients in using the solvents as amounting to a *novus actus*. Similarly, in *Lord Advocate's Reference (No 1 of 1994)*[69] the High Court ruled that a culpable homicide conviction was competent where the supplier of illicit recreational drugs gives drugs to another who then administers them himself, with fatal results.

(c) Canada and New Zealand

18.65 Patients suffering from progressive and severe neurological conditions have been involved in litigation in Canada and New Zealand in a series of cases which have attracted considerable attention. In *Nancy B v Hôtel-Dieu de Quebec*,[70] the plaintiff, who suffered from Guillain-Barré syndrome (which entails the development of the 'locked-in' syndrome, in which the mind becomes trapped in a totally immobile body), had lost almost all her capacity to move and was dependent on a respirator; her mental faculties, however, remained unaffected. She sought an injunction against the hospital in which she was a patient to the effect that she could lawfully be removed from the respirator even if this inevitably resulted in her death. This was granted on the grounds that artificial respiration constituted treatment and that every patient is entitled to reject treatment if he or she so desires.[71] The court cited with approval the opinion expressed in the US case, *Re Conroy*,[72] in which it was pointed out that: '. . . declining life-sustaining medical treatment may not properly be viewed as an attempt to commit suicide. Refusing medical treatment merely allows the disease to take its natural course; if death were eventually to occur, it would be the result, primarily, of the underlying disease, and not the result of a self-inflicted injury.' As far as possible criminal liability was concerned, the court also observed that in removing the respirator, the doctors would not be committing an offence under the law of homicide.[73]

18.66 In treating the issue as one of cessation of treatment, the court in *Nancy B* did not need to pronounce on the question of assisted suicide, although the decision provides clear support for the right of the individual to determine the point at which

---

[68] 1990 SCCR 593.

[68] 1995 SLT 248.

[70] 86 DLR 4th 385; (1992) 15 BMLR 95.

[71] A principle recognised in Canada in *Malette v Shulman* (1990) 67 DLR (4th) 321.

[72] 486 A 2d 1209, 1224.

[73] This was on two grounds: (i) s 45 of the Criminal Code states that surgical operations do not give rise to criminal liability if they are *reasonable*; and (ii) such conduct would not manifest a wanton or reckless disregard for the life of another.

his or her life comes to a 'natural end'. In *Rodriguez and Attorney General of British Columbia et al*[74] the Supreme Court of Canada was confronted with a direct challenge to the legality of the section in the Criminal Code which makes it an offence to aid or abet another to commit suicide. The plaintiff in this case was afflicted by a motor neurone disease from which she would not recover and which would, in time, deprive her of movement and therefore of any ability to take her own life. She sought a declaration to the effect that she was entitled to assistance in ending her life, a course of action which would otherwise result in criminal liability under s 241 of the Criminal Code (which punishes the aiding and abetting of suicide). The Supreme Court determined, by a narrow majority, that the validity of s 241 should be upheld in face of the challenge that it infringed the provision of the Charter of Rights and Freedoms which recognises and protects the right of individual autonomy.[75] The majority judgment rejects at the outset the argument that a terminally ill person who takes his own life is merely determining the time and manner of death rather than actively 'choosing death'. Even so, it accepts that to prevent a person seeking assistance to commit suicide does, in fact, impinge upon the security of the person, and may cause distress and discomfort. This does not mean the principles of fundamental justice, protected by s 7 of the Charter are thereby compromised; the relationship between the state interest in the preservation of life and the individual's interest in autonomy has to be considered. This, the court said, involves a balancing process which, in the end results in a victory for the state interest. As Sopinka J pointed out:

> The issue here . . . can be characterised as being whether the blanket prohibition on assisted suicide is arbitrary or unfair in that it is unrelated to the state's interest in protecting the vulnerable, and that it lacks a foundation in the legal tradition and societal beliefs which are said to be represented by the prohibition.[76]

It is clear that in preferring the state interest the majority was swayed by the fact that the blanket prohibition of assistance in suicide was endorsed in the overwhelming majority of legal systems and that to adopt a contrary approach would be to invite abuse.[77] There is, thus, a strong policy flavour to this decision.

C. Euthanasia: Legislative Reform

Euthanasia, in the sense of a positive act intended to bring about death, remains universally a criminal offence, even if permissible in certain circumstances in the   **18.67**

---

[74] 107 DLR (4th) 342, (1993) 50 BMLR 1 (Can Sup Ct).
[75] s 7 of the Charter states: 'Everyone has the right to life, liberty and security of the person and the right not to be deprived thereof except in accordance with the principles of fundamental justice'.
[76] N 73 above, 396.
[77] See the majority judgment, ibid at 410 g–h.

Netherlands. In the common law homicide liability is determined by intention, and there is therefore no distinct category of 'mercy killing'. Consequently it is only if a mitigating defence such as diminished responsibility is applied, or prosecutorial discretion is shown in charging with the lesser offence of manslaughter, that the courts are free to recognise the considerably lower level of moral guilt entailed in euthanasia. Other jurisdictions typically recognise more categories of gravity in homicide, with the result that the courts may have considerable sentencing discretion in relation to the punishment of acts of euthanasia. Swiss criminal law allows for the reduction of punishment where a homicide is committed 'for honourable motives';[78] German law similarly recognises a broad concept of extenuating circumstances. In Norway, there is explicit recognition of mercy killing, with a lesser punishment being provided for in such cases.[79]

18.68 Punishing acts of euthanasia leniently does not meet many of the objections of those who favour a fundamental change in the criminal law. Pro-euthanasia campaigns claim widespread support for the principle of voluntary euthanasia, and to a great extent this is borne out by public attitude surveys.[80] There would also appear to be a measure of support in the medical profession for a change in the law, although many doctors are uneasy about the legalisation of euthanasia.[81] In spite of this evidence of considerable support for legal change, no attempt to introduce a parliamentary measure has ever succeeded in the United Kingdom and only three jurisdictions, the Netherlands, Belgium[82] and, briefly, the Northern Territory in Australia, have taken substantial steps in the direction of legalising the practice of voluntary euthanasia.

1. The Experience of the Netherlands

18.69 Euthanasia is widely and openly practised in the Netherlands. Estimates of the incidence of the practice differ, and a degree of caution should be exercised over the statistics, particularly in the light of concerns over under-notification. Most

---

[78] Penal Code, s 155.

[79] Penal Code, s 235.

[80] There are numerous surveys on this issue. For examples, see Wise, J, 'Public supports euthanasia for most desperate cases', 1996 (313) BMJ 1423, discussing a survey which revealed public support for the permissibility of euthanasia—in some circumstances—at 86 per cent. Emanuel, EJ, Fairclough, DL, Daniels, ER, and Clarridge, BR, 'Euthanasia and physician-assisted suicide: attitudes and experiences of oncology patients, oncologists, and the public' (1996) 347 *The Lancet*, 1805: two thirds of the patient group and the public expressed support for euthanasia and physician-assisted suicide for those afflicted with unremitting pain.

[81] Coulson, J, 'Doctors oppose legal mercy killing for dying', *BMA News Review*, March 1995, 15: revealing 57 per cent of the sample of doctors as being opposed to the legalisation of assisted suicide. See also: Bachman, JG, *et al*, 'Attitudes of Michigan physicians and public toward legalizing physician-assisted suicide and voluntary euthanasia' 1996 (334) NEJ Med, 303.

[82] For a discussion of the new Belgium Law (Euthanasia Act) which came into force on 23 September 2003 see Adams, M, and Nys, H, 'Euthanasia in the Low Countries' (2003) 11 Med L Rev 353–376. In November 2003, the Belgian Federal Ministry for Public Health published figures showing 203 euthanasic deaths in the first year of the operation of the new law.

studies, however, reveal a rise in incidence since the practice became legally tolerated.[83] In theory, all homicide is illegal in the Netherlands: Article 293 of the Penal Code makes it an offence to cause another's death at his request, and this article remains in force.[84] However, in a series of decisions the Dutch courts have allowed a defence of necessity to doctors who have taken the lives of patients in order to protect them from undue suffering. The effect of such decisions was to hold that where there is a conflict between the duty to preserve life and the duty to alleviate suffering, opting for the latter may be the right choice. The defence of necessity was therefore available to doctors reaching a decision to take life in such cases, but there was anxiety in the medical profession that it would still be possible to face prosecution. In 1990 an agreement was reached between the Ministry of Justice and the Royal Dutch Medical Association whereby a doctor would not face prosecution if he complied with the agreed notification procedure and this agreement was subsequently given formal legal status.

The working of the Netherlands provisions are of considerable interest in the light **18.70** of pressure for change in other countries. It is a common warning that tolerance of euthanasia under limited conditions will lead to its application in an increasingly wide range of cases. To an extent, the Netherlands experience bears this out; certainly the courts have applied the necessity principle in cases which would not have met earlier criteria. In its decision in the *Chabot* case in 1994,[85] the Supreme Court held that the euthanasia of a patient suffering from psychological as opposed to physical distress was admissible as a case of necessity, even if in the case in question the doctor could not claim the defence because of his failure to seek an independent opinion. In December 2002, the Supreme Court upheld the conviction of Doctor Sutorios for assisting the suicide of a man who, although not suffering from any serious clinical or terminal condition, was 'tired of life'. The Court held that the absence of a disease or serious illness rendered the physician incompetent to determine the intensity of the patient's suffering, as the law required.[86] Other cases have involved the euthanasia of infants, which offends the voluntary principle.[87] There is also evidence that the procedural safeguards set out are not always observed, and this is taken as supporting the argument that it may be difficult to control the practice of euthanasia once it is admitted.[88]

---

[83] For a general survey, see van der Maas, PJ, van Delden, JJM, and Pijnebourg, L, *Euthanasia and Other Medical Decisions Concerning the End of life* (New York: Elsevier, 1992); also, Hendin, H, *Seduced by Death* (Norton, 1997).

[84] The former legal position in the Netherlands is discussed by Keown, J, 'The law and practice of euthanasia in the Netherlands' (1992) 108 LQR 51; Griffiths, J, 'The Regulation of Euthanasia and Related Medical Procedures that Shorten Life in the Netherlands' (1994) 1 Med L Int, 137.

[85] This case is discussed at length by Hendin (n 82 above), 60.

[86] BBC News: World Edition, 24 December 2002.

[87] Sheldon, T, 'Dutch appeal court dismisses case against doctor' 1995 (311) BMJ 1322.

[88] See, for example, Keown, J, 'Euthanasia in the Netherlands: Sliding down the Slippery Slope?' in Keown J (ed), *Euthansia Examined: Ethical, Legal and Clinical Perspectives* (Cambridge: CUP, 1995), 269.

18.71   The position has more recently been put on a clearer statutory footing. The Termination of Life on Request and Assisted Suicide (Review Procedures) Act amends Article 293 of the Penal Code of the Netherlands, so that a physician who terminates another's life is not punishable if he has met the requirements of due care specified in the Act and has informed the municipal autopist. The requirements of due care require the physician to be satisfied that the patient's request for euthanasia is voluntary and well considered and to have consulted an independent doctor who, having seen the patient, supports the case for physician assisted death. The patient, whose condition must be unbearable, must have been informed about, and rejected, any alternatives. The law also permits minors over the age of 12 to be subject to such a death.[89]

18.72   In the United States, Oregon introduced the Death with Dignity Act in 1994, but this is confined to assisted suicide only. Under the Act a physician may supply a lethal drug to a patient who, if able to administer it, may do so to end his life. The Act does not grant the physician any immunity in respect of the administration of the drug, only its supply. The patient must be competent, have made repeated requests for death and suffer from a terminal illness. Clearly such legislative provision suffers from the significant defect that those who may be in most need of a drug to ensure an easy death will be, like Dianne Pretty, too ill to self administer it. As such the Act seems manifestly discriminatory.

---

[89]   See discussion in de Haan, J, 'The New Dutch Law on Euthanasia' (2002) 10 Med L Rev 57.

19

DEATH

A. Introduction: The Historical Criteria of Death

The historic common law regarded death as an event rather than a process. The **19.01** determination of death was addressed more as a matter of common observation than of medical science. The ecclesiastical courts dealt with many of the spiritual and social incidents of death, and the royal courts were interested in fines and forfeitures to the Crown when deaths were caused by crimes. The criminal law provided that if a victim's death occurred at a time later than a year and a day from an offence such as the infliction of a wound, the offence was not convictable as culpable homicide.[1] The common law evolved to address death as an indication for other events to occur, notably burial, distribution of estates and payments under life insurance policies. In contrast, increasingly sophisticated medical concepts

---

[1] The Law Commission recommended abolition of this historic rule; see Law Commission, *Legislating the Criminal Code: The Year and a Day Rule in Homicide* (Law Com No 230, 1995) and it was abolished by the Law Reform (Year and a Day Rule) Act 1996.

evolved to regard death primarily as a process.[2] In 1979, the Conference of Royal Colleges and their Faculties (UK) published a report that observed that:

> Exceptionally, as a result of massive trauma, death occurs instantaneously or near-instantaneously. Far more commonly, death is not an event, it is a process, the various organs and systems supporting the continuation of life failing and eventually ceasing altogether to function, successively and at different times.[3]

Nevertheless, death is considered a matter of legal status, medicine serving to determine whether or not the legal criteria of death have been satisfied.[4]

19.02   The utility of organs and tissues from recently deceased persons for transplantation has created some modern urgency to determine whether or not deaths have occurred. Before this development, death was usually established only relatively to the time of death of another. In the absence of evidence of which of two or more persons died first, the common law presumption as to commorientes (people who die together) applies. The presumption reflects nature in deeming older persons to have died before younger persons. When spouses had made common wills, each leaving the bulk of the estate to the other in the event of surviving the testator, and they perished in a common disaster, the families of the two spouses might seek evidence of their family member's survival of the partner. In an Ontario case in 1936,[5] a husband was found to have survived his wife in a common drowning accident because the volume of water in his lungs was greater than the volume in hers, assessed proportionately to lung size. Respiration was taken as evidence of life, and the greater volume of water in his lungs indicated that he was breathing after his wife ceased to breathe. Similarly, in a macabre Kentucky case in 1950,[6] a couple died in a railway level-crossing tragedy. The wife was decapitated, and was found with blood surging from her trunk. The husband's body was observed at the same time motionless and not bleeding. The court concluded that, since the husband was neither breathing nor bleeding when his wife's body was gushing blood, she had survived him. Heart-beat or respiration were legal evidence of life, and her bleeding provided evidence that her heart was beating.

---

[2] See Kennedy, I, and Grubb, A, *Medical Law* (3rd edn, London, 2000) ch18, 2191–263; and Morison, RS, 'Death: Process or Event?' (1971) 173 *Science* 694–8.

[3] 'Memorandum on the Diagnosis of Death', (1979) 1 BMJ, 332, para 2.

[4] For criticism of legal involvement in medical decision-making at the end of life, see Flick, MR, 'The Due Process of Dying' (1991) 79 California L Rev 1121–67.

[5] *Re Warwicker, McLeod et al v Toronto General Trust Co* (1936) 3 DLR 368 (Sup Ct Ont).

[6] *Gugel's Administrator v Orth's Executors* (1950) 236 SW 2nd 460 (Kentucky, CA).

B. Brain Stem Death

1. Introduction

The development of artificial means to preserve patients' vital functions, such as **19.03** by mechanical ventilators to maintain patients' oxygen supply and heartbeat, affords patients an opportunity to survive when they are incapable of breathing spontaneously and maintaining heart function. In response to this development, the law preserved its focus on respiration and pulsation as evidence of life, but accepted the artificial source of energy sustaining vital functions as the equivalent of a person's spontaneous maintenance of such functions. A patient dependent for survival on artificial life support equipment is clearly alive. It became increasingly clear, however, that heartbeat and respiration alone are not necessarily sufficient to preserve human life. Although the heart retains its conventional status as the source of human sentiment, it has become progressively recognised that the seat of human personality and character is the brain, the location of human intellect. Accordingly, the neurological status and prognosis of a human being assumed increasing legal significance, eventually paving the way to concurrent legal recognition of death due to failure of heartbeat and respiration, and of so-called 'brain death', now medically described as brain stem death.[7]

In March 1998 the Department of Health published *A Code of Practice for the* **19.04** *Diagnosis of Brain Stem Death*.[8] This publication includes *Guidelines for the Identification and Management of Potential Organ and Tissue Donors*, and replaces the earlier code, *Cadaveric Organs for Transplantation: A Code of Practice including the Diagnosis of Brain Death* (1983). The 1998 Code of Practice, reinforcing the earlier publications, recognises the concept of 'brain stem death' and provides criteria for its diagnosis. The Code reflects the definition set out in the 1995 Report of the Royal College of Physicians of 'irreversible loss of capacity for consciousness, combined with irreversible loss of the capacity to breathe'.[9]

2. Development of Criteria of Brain Stem Death

The first case in a common law jurisdiction to recognise the concept of basing **19.05** death on neurological criteria appears to have been one decided in 1967 in Kansas.[10] A husband whose wife was suffering from terminal cancer fired five revolver shots into her head and then shot himself with the same weapon. Evidence showed that she had bled profusely, whereas he appeared not to have bled at all. By conventional tests of evidence of heart-beat, she would have been considered to

---

[7] 'Criteria for the diagnosis of brain stem death', (1995) 29 J Royal College of Physicians 381–2.
[8] HSC 1998/1999 (*www.doh.gov.uk/pdfs/brainstemdeath.pdf*).
[9] N 7 above.
[10] *United Trust Co v Pyke* (1967) 427 P 2d 67 (Sup Ct Kansas).

have survived him,[11] if only for a brief time. The court accepted, however, not only that the severe brain damage suffered by the wife was incompatible with survival, but that it had caused an immediate and irreversible end to her vital functions, and that she had died before her husband killed himself. The court did not address refined explanations of brain structure and function nor the process of neocortical death, but applied a common sense, if crude, approach to the facts. Without addressing the decisive function of the brain stem, the court responded to an intuitive perception that the permanent loss of brain capacity would quickly lead to organ failure and satisfaction of physiological criteria of death.

19.06 Although the classical tests of death, amounting to the irreversible loss of cardiopulmonary function, were widely accepted, due perhaps to their relatively easy application and the absence of an accessible, easily operable alternative, they were not fully satisfactory. The tests did not always produce true results, even advanced mechanical methods sometimes failing to detect faint pulse and shallow breathing associated for instance with the taking of drugs, and afforded continuing currency to popular superstitious fears of being buried alive.

19.07 The tests were also frustrated by the fact that mechanical means could appear to satisfy them. Patients on mechanical life support systems appeared permanently incapable of resuming consciousness and yet continued to maintain a pulse and breathe. Use of mechanical means that were pioneered to maintain patients for the different purpose of preserving tissue quality in organs destined for transplantation[12] aggravated medical dissatisfaction with the legal criteria of death, and confounded legal decision-making on matters of public concern. Medical acceptance that the best way to preserve an organ until transplantation was in the body in which it had grown, transfused by its own blood, led to increasing employment of mechanical organ support in bodies of recently deceased persons. Because conventional legal criteria of death might record death in persons capable of medical revival, and life in persons treated medically as having died, pressures arose to develop more satisfactory criteria of death that the law could accept.

19.08 The first well accepted definition of death to include what then was described as brain death was developed in 1968 by the Ad Hoc Committee of the Harvard Medical School to Examine the Definition of Brain Death.[13] The Ad Hoc Committee used the term 'irreversible coma' to define what is now generally called brain stem death, and described two reasons why a new definition of death was needed. The first was the need to provide a basis for withdrawal of resuscitative and supportive measures applied in the hope of saving desperately injured

---

[11] See *Gugel's Administrator* (n 6 above).
[12] See the discussion of *Potter* (n 71 below), para 19.28.
[13] Report of the Ad Hoc Committee of the Harvard Medical School, 'A Definition of Irreversible Coma', (1968) 205 *J of the American Medical Association*, 337–40.

patients, when their comatose state could not be relieved although their hearts could be induced to continue beating. The second reason was that obsolete criteria for the definition of death can lead to controversy in obtaining organs for transplantation. The Ad Hoc Committee observed that no change in the law would be necessary to adopt its criteria, since 'the law treats this question [the establishment of death] essentially as one of fact to be determined by physicians'.[14] This observation was unduly optimistic in light both of legal caution in identifying what fact physicians are called on to determine, and of continuing controversy among physicians themselves.

The Ad Hoc Committee presented the first authoritative statement of medical criteria of death under modern conditions of medical care, but it proved to be far from the last word. The 1976 Report of the Conference of Medical Royal Colleges and their Faculties in the United Kingdom,[15] supplemented in 1979 to address brain death,[16] which now appears to be given legal effect in UK courts,[17] is one of several authoritative but slightly differing formulations developed by medical professional bodies in the English-speaking world. **19.09**

The widely discussed case of Karen Quinlan,[18] decided by the New Jersey courts in the mid-1970s, alerted public attention in many countries to the medico-legal need to distinguish not just between the living and the dead but between those affected by cortical or higher-brain death, brain-stem death and whole brain death, and to issues in legal management of patients in a persistent vegetative state. It was primarily for neurologists and related medical specialists to distinguish patients whose higher-brain had suffered irreversible damage, such as Karen Quinlan, from others, such as those whose higher-brains were substantially intact but whose brain-stem functions were severely compromised,[19] and to distinguish both categories of patients from those whose brain-stem had irreversibly ceased to function, and who were therefore dead. Issues were raised that attracted professional attention,[20] and to which several jurisdictions proposed legislative responses. **19.10**

3. *Legislative Approaches to Criteria of Death*[21]

Historically, the criteria and processes for the determination of death were governed by common law, but the pressures that led the Ad Hoc Committee at **19.11**

---

[14] ibid, 338.
[15] 'Diagnosis of Brain Death' (1976) 2 BMJ 1187–8.
[16] 'Memorandum on the Diagnosis of Death' (1979) 1 BMJ 332, para 2; see also n 7 above.
[17] See *Re A (A Minor)* [1992] 3 Med LR 303 (Fam Div).
[18] *In re Quinlan* (1976) 355 A 2d 647, 664 (Sup Ct NJ).
[19] See Pearce, JMS, 'The Locked In Syndrome' (1987) 294 BMJ 1989; Allan, CMC, 'Conscious but Paralysed: Releasing the Locked-in' (1993) 17 *Lancet* 130–2.
[20] See nn 7 and 8 above.
[21] For valuable references to international legislation, see Giesen, D, *International Medical Malpractice Law* (Tübingen, Dordrecht, Boston, London, 1988) 612, n 73.

Harvard to propose criteria appropriate in modern circumstances of medical care also persuaded legislatures in North America and beyond to take action. Their incentives were partially to resolve legal uncertainties, but also partially to quell public disquiet at the appearance of a collection of physicians settling among themselves the criteria according to which patients could be declared dead and their organs taken for medical transplantation.[22] The tendency of legislation was to incorporate medical criteria into a framework of legislative overview.

19.12 The first North American jurisdiction to enact a statute incorporating brain death was Kansas.[23] The Kansas legislation of 1970 addressed both cardiopulmonary and brain death as equally available alternatives by providing that:

> A person will be considered medically and legally dead if, in the opinion of a physician, based on ordinary standards of medical practice, there is the absence of spontaneous respiratory and cardiac function and ... attempts at resuscitation are considered hopeless; and, in this event, death will have occurred at the time these functions ceased; or A person will be considered medically and legally dead if ... there is the absence of spontaneous brain function; and if based on ordinary standards of medical practice, during reasonable attempts to either maintain or restore spontaneous circulatory or respiratory function in the absence of aforesaid brain function, it appears that further attempts at resuscitation or supportive maintenance will not succeed, death will have occurred at the time when these conditions first coincide.

The statute was quickly copied in several other states, but it was also subjected to criticism on a variety of grounds,[24] not least that its references to when a person was considered 'medically and legally dead' perpetuated the very notion of medical death and legal death being different in principle which the legislation was designed to end. To meet this criticism, some legislatures adopted brain death as the only legal criterion. For instance, Manitoba amended its Vital Statistics Act in 1975 to provide that:

> For all purposes within the legislative competence of the Legislature of Manitoba the death of a person takes place at the time at which irreversible cessation of all of that person's brain function occurs.[25]

19.13 This brought together legal and medical criteria of death, but for constitutional reasons had to leave open whether Canadian federal law, governing, for instance, criminal law, would take the same approach.[26] Other legislatures codified

---

[22] Capron, AM and Kass, L, 'A Statutory Definition of the Standards for Determining Human Death' (1972) 121 U of Pennsylvania Law Rev 87–118.

[23] Kan Stat Ann ch 77–202.

[24] See Kennedy, IM, 'The Kansas Statute on Death: An Appraisal' (1971) 285 New England J of Medicine 946–50, and Capron and Kass (n 22 above).

[25] See now R Stats Man 1987, cV60, s 2.

[26] In the criminal case of *R v Kitching and Adams* (1976) 32 CCC (2d) 159 (Man CA) a brain stem death criterion was applied; organ removal, prior to death certification, was found not to have broken the chain of criminal causation between an injury and the victim's death: see paras 19.27 *et seq* below.

cardiopulmonary criteria of death, but added a brain death test for application only when artificial life support precludes the use of such criteria, some requiring the opinion of a specialist in neurology, neurosurgery or electroencephalography as a condition of use of the brain death criterion.[27]

In many jurisdictions there is no legislation defining death for general purposes, but legislation on cadaveric organ donation for transplantation specifies how death is to be determined before organ recovery.[28] This necessarily covers brain death, since organ recovery frequently depends on artificial ventilation or other means being applied to a body at death to preserve the suitability of organs for transplantation. Such legislation usually contains no criteria of death, but requires that usual medical practice be observed. Typical is the Human Tissue Gift Act of Ontario,[29] s 7(1) of which provides that:

> For the purposes of a post mortem transplant, the fact of death shall be determined by at least two physicians in accordance with accepted medical practice.

19.14

In the event of litigation or other need of clarification, expert medical opinion will be obtained to establish accepted medical practice, by reference to prevailing literature, codes of practice and their application. This approach may not resolve philosophical, spiritual or similar uncertainties, but it affords physicians the security of knowing that their demonstrable conformity to the practice of their profession will be respected by the courts.

4. Judicial Approaches to Brain Stem Death

In England, as in many other jurisdictions in the English-speaking world, no legislation establishes criteria of death. However, modern judgments now confirm that criteria of what may generically be called brain death[30] developed among leaders of the medical profession are incorporated into the law. A Family Division judgment confirming that a young child was dead (see below), and a House of Lords judgment finding that an adult in a persistent vegetative state was not (see below), showed that the English courts have subscribed to the brain stem criterion of brain death. This may be distinguished from the so-called 'whole brain death' test adopted, for instance, by the Manitoba legislature[31] and which may be

19.15

---

[27] In 1978, the US National Conference of Commissioners on Uniform State Laws adopted a Uniform Brain Death Act, which in 1980 was superseded by the Uniform Determination of Death Act. This provides alternative definitions of death, but presents death as a phenomenon that can be tested by alternative criteria: see Furrow, BR, Johnson, SH, Jost, TS and Schwartz, RL, *Health Law: Cases, Materials and Problems* (2nd edn, St Paul, Minn, 1991) 1046.

[28] See Jones, D, 'Retrospective on the Future: Brain Death and Evolving Legal Regimes for Tissue Replacement Technology' (1993) 38 McGill LJ 394–415.

[29] RSO 1990, c H-20 as amended; now named the Trillium Gift of Life Network Act.

[30] But see the growing medical use of 'brain stem death' (nn 7 and 8 above).

[31] N 25 above.

favoured by courts elsewhere.[32] Simply put, the brain stem controls reflexive functions of the body including breathing and heartbeat, while the higher-brain controls consciousness and interaction with surroundings, that is, sensation and
cognition. Brain stem function is necessary to sustain higher-brain function, but
a functioning brain stem will keep alive a person, such as Karen Quinlan (see para
19.10 above), whose higher-brain no longer allows recovery of consciousness.

(i) *Re A (A Minor)*

19.16   *Re A (A Minor)*[33] concerned a child aged under two years who was found to have
no heartbeat on admission to a hospital's accident and emergency department.
Extensive resuscitation attempts were unsuccessful, and he was transferred into
another hospital for intensive care and assessment, and placed on a ventilator.
When briefly removed from the ventilator to test whether he could breathe independently, he made slight gasping noises, indicating to the consultant that he was
not brain stem dead. The next day, however, when tests were conducted, the consultant was satisfied that A was brain-stem dead. A consultant paediatric neurolo-
gist repeated the tests the following day, which confirmed the earlier finding. Both
physicians made efforts to determine whether A's state could have been explained
on other grounds before reaching the conclusion of brain stem death.

19.17   The boy was kept on ventilation and fed intravenously, and the proceedings were
brought to clarify the legality of the consultant's proposal to withdraw ventilation.
The consultant explained to the judge that she was aware of recommendations on
the definition of death made by the Royal College of Surgeons, the Royal College
of Physicians and a working party of the British Paediatric Association, and had
applied the criteria laid down by her profession. The judge expressed no hesitation
in holding that A had been dead, according to the medical procedures that had
been followed to reach the conclusion of brain stem death, since the consultant
made her initial determination. The judge also found, inter alia, that he had jurisdiction to declare that it would not be unlawful to disconnect A from the ventilator.[34] The date of death determined in *Re A* as no later than the time at which the
first tests were completed is followed in the Department of Health's 1998 Code of
Practice, at para 3.3.[35]

(ii) *Airedale NHS Trust v Bland*

19.18   The criterion of brain stem death was incorporated into English law more explicitly

---

[32] See Furrow *et al* (n 27 above), 1046.
[33] [1992] 3 Med LR 303 (Fam D).
[34] For a somewhat critical commentary on the judge's rulings on his finding of A's earlier death,
see Kennedy, I, 'Commentary' (1993) 1 Med L Rev 99–100.
[35] N 8 above.

by the House of Lords in *Airedale National Health Service Trust v Bland*.[36] A patient diagnosed as being in a persistent vegetative state was maintained in a hospital that proposed withdrawal of artificial nutrition and hydration, with the forseeable consequence of his death through dehydration. He breathed unaided, but could not swallow, and was fed by a nasogastric tube.

In proceedings to determine the legality of this proposed course of conduct, an issue central to the courts' jurisdiction in the case was whether the patient was currently alive, since, if he were not, the approach to the courts and their jurisdiction would be quite different. Their Lordships were aware through judgments of the courts below of medical criteria relevant both to brain stem death and to the persistent vegetative state. They accepted the medical conclusion that, by this test, the patient was not dead, and accordingly accepted their jurisdiction in the case. Lord Keith observed that: **19.19**

> [i]n the eyes of the medical world and of the law a person is not clinically dead so long as the brain stem retains its function.[37]

Lord Goff similarly stated that:

> as a result of developments in modern medical technology, doctors no longer associate death exclusively with breathing and heart beat, and it has come to be accepted that death occurs when the brain, and in particular the brain stem, has been destroyed. . . . The evidence is that Anthony's brain stem is still alive and functioning and it follows that, in the present state of medical science, he is still alive and should be so regarded as a matter of law.[38]

Lord Browne-Wilkinson went so far as to describe a ventilator-assisted being whose heart was beating 'even though the brain stem, and therefore in medical terms the patient, is dead', as 'the ventilated corpse',[39] but was careful to exclude the patient Anthony Bland from that category. Having located him among the living, however, their Lordships accepted the medical evidence that he was persistently vegetative and would never regain consciousness. Specifying the conditions under which courts could so act,[40] their Lordships approved withdrawal of artificial nutrition and hydration. The Court found that the resulting death would not leave those responsible for his medical care liable in law.   **19.20**

(iii) Jurisdictional Difficulties

The problem that a judicial finding of death poses to a court's jurisdiction   **19.21**

---

[36] [1993] 1 AC 789 (HL).
[37] ibid, 856.
[38] ibid, 863.
[39] ibid, 878.
[40] See *Practice Note* [1994] 2 All ER 413.

warrants brief attention. In *Re TC (A Minor)*,[41] the Family Division of the High Court of Justice in Northern Ireland accepted the diagnosis of brain stem death in a child on a ventilator who was a ward of court, but nevertheless granted declarations that the application for a declaration should have been brought before the court because a wardship was involved, and that the body could be removed from ventilation when the hospital's medical staff considered removal appropriate. It has reasonably been objected that, in view of the finding of the ward's death, the court had no further wardship jurisdiction to determine her legal status, nor to provide for subsequent ventilation of her dead body at the discretion of the hospital's medical staff except under very special conditions.[42] As against this, however, to deny the court its general supervisory jurisdiction because of the ward's death would paradoxically make answering the question whether the ward was alive or dead a precondition to asking it. Courts may have to be afforded some jurisdictional latitude to try cases from which a legal finding of death may result.

(iv) The US Approach

19.22 Homicide cases in the United States have occasionally been defended, although never successfully,[43] on the ground that physicians' motives to acquire organs for transplantation caused them to terminate the lives of injured ventilated patients who otherwise could have survived, and that those responsible for their injuries were not responsible for their deaths. Rejection of the defence motivated two states to accept the brain death criterion for homicide cases only,[44] and others to recognize brain death for more general and perhaps civil purposes.[45] The particular form of brain death that these cases accept is whole brain rather than brain stem death, although it has been doubted that the distinction merits emphasis except in very unusual circumstances.[46]

5. Persistent Vegetative State (PVS) and Anencephaly

(i) Introduction

19.23 The most recent endorsement of the 'brain stem death' criteria is in the Department of Health's publication, *A Code of Practice for the Diagnosis of Brain Stem Death*.[47] For the position of children, see the Department of Health's Code

---

[41] Reported and discussed in (1994) 2 Med L Rev 376–377.

[42] ibid.

[43] See Furrow, *et al*, (n 27 above), 1052.

[44] See *Commonwealth v Golston* (1977) 366 NE 2d 744 (Mass Sup Jud Ct); *State v Meints* (1982) 322 NW 2d 809 (Sup Ct Neb).

[45] See *People v Eulo* (1984) 472 NE 2d 286 (NYCA), *State v Matthews* (1986) 353 SE 2d 444 (Sup Ct SC) and *State v Velarde* (1986) 734 P2d 449 (Sup Ct Utah).

[46] See Mason, K , McCall Smith, RA, and Laurie, GT, *Law and Medical Ethics* (6th edn, London, Dublin, Edinburgh, 2002) 413–4.

[47] N 8 above.

of Practice at para 3.2 referring to *A Working Party of the Conference of Colleges on Organ Transplantation in Neonates*[48] and a 1991 Working Party of the British Paediatric Association, *Diagnosis of Brain Stem Death in Infants and Children*. Problems relating to the diagnosis and management of the persistent vegetative state must not be confused, however, with those relating to brain stem death. Similar confusion has concerned anencephalic newborn children, who some want to consider dead or 'brain absent', although they have functioning brain stems. By prevailing legal criteria, both PVS patients and anencephalic newborn children are alive.[49]

(ii) Persistent Vegetative State

In *Airedale NHS Trust v Bland*, the House of Lords, addressing the issue of letting die patients diagnosed to be in a persistent vegetative state, specified measures to be adopted as a precondition to legality. These included attempting rehabilitation such as by coma arousal programmes,[50] and are now amplified in a Practice Note.[51] Although current methods of diagnosing PVS are not infallible,[52] their Lordships unanimously accepted, as did all judges below, that Anthony Bland's brain stem functioned, and that he was therefore not dead.[53]

19.24

(iii) Anencephaly

Anencephaly is a condition in which children suffer a congenital disorder resulting in the absence of major portions of the brain, skull and scalp.[54] Lacking the higher-brain, the cerebral cortex, they will never achieve consciousness, and it is highly doubtful that they feel sensations such as pain and discomfort. The large majority of anencephalic fetuses are stillborn or aborted when detected prenatally,[55] since the condition is incompatible with consciousness and survival. However, they have at least rudimentary brain stems, and some are born alive and survive for a few days, although rarely exceeding ten.[56] Because anencephalic

19.25

---

[48] DHSS 1988.

[49] See Kennedy and Grubb (n 2 above), 2225–2233, and Furrow, *et al* (n 27 above), 1049–1051.

[50] N 36 above, *per* Lord Goff, 870–871.

[51] N 40 above.

[52] ibid, para 2, referring to the Medical Ethics Committee of the British Medical Association guidelines on treatment decisions for PVS patients, of July 1993; for discussion of the diagnosis and of other conditions with which PVS is sometimes confused, see Appendix 4 and paras 156–162 and 251–258 of the *Report of the House of Lords Select Committee on Medical Ethics* (HL Paper (1993–94) 21-I), and text at n 48 above.

[53] See also *Frenchay Healthcare NHS Trust v S* [1994] 2 All ER 403 (CA), applying the *Bland* judgment (n 36 above).

[54] See Medical Task Force on Anencephaly, 'The Infant with Anencephaly' (1990) 322 New England J of Medicine 669–74.

[55] Medearis, DN and Holmes, LB, 'On the Use of Anencephalic Infants as Organ Donors' (1989) 321 New England J of Medicine 391–3.

[56] See Furrow *et al* (n 27 above), 1049.

children show some brain stem activity, they are neither brain stem dead, nor whole brain dead, but must be considered to have been born alive as human beings.[57] The 1995 review of criteria for brain stem death by the Royal College of Physicians suggested that, in children over the age of two months, brain stem death criteria should be the same as those in adults. It found, however, that '[t]here is insufficient information on children under the age of two months and on premature babies to define guidelines.'[58] In the normal course of events, anencephalic children born alive are given only comfort measures until death,[59] since aggressive care is futile. In the exceptional *Baby K* case in Virginia,[60] however, the US laws on emergency medical treatment and disability were held to compel a hospital to give ventilation and other care to such a child at its mother's request, made on religious grounds,[61] resulting in its survival for two and a half years.[62]

19.26   A medical incentive to ventilate and otherwise care for such children is to preserve their organs for transplantation on death. Anencephaly is not a genetic condition, and normal organs would be transplantable if tissue quality can be preserved in vivo. Deterioration of organs would almost invariably occur in the course of the child's natural death, due to hypoxia and ischemia. Recovery of organs following natural death is unlikely to provide any suitable for transplantation. Invasive mechanical support for the organ systems of a living anencephalic child on the parents' consent could maintain tissue quality in organs, but raises legal and ethical concerns. Such treatments would not be intended for the child's benefit,[63] but for that of prospective transplant recipients. Usually, parents have at best restricted legal capacity to consent to non-therapeutic medical care for their children.[64] Mechanical support might be considered acceptable, however, since it would not

---

[57] *In re TACP* (1992) 609 So 2d 588 (Sup Ct Florida). In *Montreal Tramways v Léveillé* [1933] SCR 456, the Supreme Court of Canada held that the status of being a human being is dependent on being born alive and viable, but the viability condition has not been pursued in later jurisprudence: See *R v Sullivan* (1991) 63 CCC (3d) 97 (Sup Ct Can).

[58] N 7 above, 381, para (e), and n 8 above.

[59] Death is determined on physiological indications, in the absence of brain stem death indications: see Furrow *et al* (n 27 above), 1049.

[60] *In the Matter of Baby K* (1993) 832 F Supp 1022 (ED Va) affirmed (1994) 16 F 3d 590 (4th Cir), certiorari denied (1994) 115 S Ct 95 (US Sup Ct).

[61] The US legislation invoked included the Emergency Medical Treatment and Active Labor Act, 42 USC ch 1395 and the Americans with Disability Act, 42, USC ch12112. See Flannery, EJ, 'One Advocate's Viewpoint: Conflicts and Tensions in the *Baby K* Case' (1995) 23 J Law Medicine and Ethics 7–12; Clayton, EW, 'Commentary: What is Really at Stake in Baby K? A Response to Eileen Flannery', ibid, 13–14; and Bonanno, MA, 'The Case of Baby K: Exploring the Concept of Medical Futility' (1995) 4 *Annals of Health Law* 151–72.

[62] The cost of infant care, covered by a private insurance carrier, was reported to be $1464 each day; Knepper, K, 'Withholding Medical Treatment from Infants: When is it Child Neglect?' (1994–95) 33 U of Louisville J Fam Law 1–53, n 265.

[63] The *Baby K* case (n 60 above) may offer a basis for an argument that active care is in the child's interests.

[64] See Giesen (n 21 above), 440, and Dickens, BM, 'The Modern Function and Limits of Parental Rights' (1981) 97 LQR 462–485.

be counter to the child's interests. Treatment administered with parental consent that postpones death may escape legal condemnation, for instance for constituting child abuse, because the child is incapable of experiencing distress, and it cannot be considered to have any interest in early as opposed to slightly later death.

According to the brain stem criteria approved in *Bland*,[65] anencephalic children are not dead, and describing them as 'brain absent' is a euphemism the law does not accommodate.[66] Similarly, arguments that they be registered at birth as stillborn cannot stand, for reasons both of the same law and of medical practice; some children living longer than expected have been shown on further examination to be microcephalic or otherwise to be misdiagnosed, and not anencephalic.[67] Nevertheless, the *Bland* preconditions to withdrawal and denial of care such as nutrition, hydration and ventilation appear not to apply, since anencephalic newborn children do not have comparable interests in the exercise of due caution.[68] Taking a proposal for non-active treatment to court for approval is possible, but does not seem mandatory, since, unlike Anthony Bland, such children are in the process of natural death. Further, for physicians to meet the condition of 12 months of patient insentience[69] before they request a judicial declaration on the legality of withdrawing care seems not to serve any patient's interest, and to contradict good husbanding of scarce health care resources. Unless legislation is interpreted to require application of any procedures, anencephalic newborn children may be given only basic comfort measures while they are allowed to die, although use of mechanical supports until death is determined by physiological tests seems permissible.[70]

19.27

6. *Termination of Mechanical Life Support Systems and Legal Liability*

When human life can be sustained by use of an artificial life support system, a legal concern is whether withdrawal is in law a culpable cause of the death that follows. Recognition of different uses of life supports arose in consideration of the advice of the Director of Public Prosecutions to lay a charge only of common assault in the 1963 case of *R v Potter*.[71] The accused inflicted a severe head injury on the victim during a fight. The victim stopped spontaneous breathing 14 hours after admission to hospital, and was then placed on an artificial ventilator for 24 hours.

19.28

---

[65] N 56 above.

[66] McCullagh, P, *Brain Dead, Brain Absent, Brain Donors: Human Subjects or Human Objects?* (Chichester, 1993).

[67] McDowell, DT, 'Death of An Idea: The Anencephalic as an Organ Donor' (1994) 72 Texas L Rev, 893–930, 929.

[68] See Steinbock, B, *Life Before Birth* (New York; Oxford: 1992), 35.

[69] *Practice Note* (n 40 above) para 2.

[70] See Ch 16 on Donation and Transplantation of Organs and Tissue.

[71] The Times, 26 July 1963; discussed in (1963) 4 Med Sci & Law 59–64: (1964) Medico-Legal J 31–37, 195 and Myers, D, *The Human Body and the Law* (2nd edn, Edinburgh, 1990), 196.

After this time, with the consent of his wife and a coroner, a kidney was removed for transplantation. The ventilator was then shut off and, lacking spontaneous respiration and circulation, the victim was pronounced dead. A coroner's inquest led to a decision to charge the accused for his offence that resulted in the death. By traditional criteria of death, the victim was alive when the kidney was removed, because he had both respiration and heartbeat, although by mechanical means. The accused claimed that physicians' actions in removing the kidney and shutting off the ventilator broke the chain of causation between the assault and death, and that he accordingly could not be convicted of a crime based on causing death.

19.29   The Director of Public Prosecutions appears to have been responsive to this conventional interpretation of the law in advising a charge of assault rather than of manslaughter, which requires proof that the accused caused the death. Nevertheless, both the surgeon who removed the kidney on the wife's consent, and the coroner, whose jurisdiction is primarily over dead bodies, appear to have treated the victim as dead, and the ventilator as preserving tissue quality of the organ to be removed for transplantation rather than the life of the victim. Inconsistently, however, death was not pronounced until the ventilator was shut off. Death might have been pronounced before initiation of ventilation on the basis of a neurological or 'brain death' criterion, had the law at that time clearly so permitted.

19.30   In a civil case in Virginia in 1972,[72] a person suffered serious cranial injuries in a fall, and was placed on a ventilator in a hospital. When an electroencephalogram showed a total absence of neocortical activity, physicians stopped ventilation, pronounced him dead and immediately removed his heart for transplantation. His brother sued them, claiming that at the time of heart removal he was alive, since the traditional signs of life, heartbeat and respiration, were still present. The judge directed the jury members that they could establish the time of death by either the classical cardio-vascular tests or the new, neurological criteria the defendant physicians explained they had applied. The jury found the defendants not liable.

19.31   Courts have been uniformly resistant to claims that physicians incur legal liability when, in the course of conscientious and competent management of patients, they terminate life support systems and patients' deaths follow.[73] *R* v *Malcherek, R v Steel* [74] involved victims of separate attacks who were placed on life support systems that were eventually withdrawn, whereupon they died. The defendants, who were convicted of causing their deaths, claimed that the physicians attending their

---

[72] *Tucker* v *Lower*, May 1972, Richmond VA no 2831; discussed in Converse, R, 'But When Did He Die?: *Tucker* v *Lower* and the Brain Death Concept' (1975) 12 San Diego L Rev 424–35.

[73] See, eg, *Finlayson* v *HM Advocate* 1978 SLT (Notes) 60 (Scotland); *R* v *Kitching and Adams* (n 26 above); *R* v *Kinash* [1982] Qld R 648 (Queensland CCA); *Nancy B* v *Hôtel-Dieu de Québec* (1992) 86 DLR (4th) 385 (Quebec Superior Ct). If care is not competent, however, physicians may be convictable: See *People* v *Eulo* (n 45 above), 297, and *R* v *Prentice* [1993] 4 All ER 935 (CA).

[74] [1981] 2 All ER 422 (CA).

victims failed, in different ways, to conform to the Code of Practice for the diagnosis of brain death established in 1976 in the Report of the Conference of Medical Royal Colleges and their Faculties.[75] The failures were alleged to have broken the chain of causation between the attacks and the deaths. In each case, the trial judge withdrew from the jury the question of whether the defendant's attack had caused the victim's death, since there was no evidence that might permit the jury any doubt that they had. Although juries determine facts, they must do so on evidence, and whether or not there is any evidence is a matter of law to be determined by the judge. In the Court of Appeal, Lord Lane CJ stated that:

> [t]he way in which the [defendants'] submissions are put . . . is as follows: the doctors, by switching off the ventilator and the life support machine, were the cause of death or, to put it more accurately, there was evidence which the jury should have been allowed to consider that the doctors, and not the assailant, in each case may have been the cause of death.[76]

Lord Lane upheld the trial judge's direction that the defendants had caused their victims' deaths, and observed that:

> [w]here a medical practitioner adopting methods which are generally accepted comes bona fide and conscientiously to the conclusion that the patient is for practical purposes dead, and that such vital functions as exist (for example, circulation) are being maintained solely by mechanical means, and therefore discontinues treatment, that does not prevent the person who inflicted the initial injury from being responsible for the victim's death. Putting it in another way, the discontinuance of treatment in those circumstances does not break the chain of causation between the initial injury and the death.[77]

19.32 There can be more than a single cause of death,[78] but the physicians are not considered to have any part in such causation. Indeed, Lord Lane added, *obiter*, that:

> [w]hatever the strict logic of the matter may be, it is perhaps somewhat bizarre to suggest, as counsel have impliedly done, that where a doctor tries his conscientious best to save the life of a patient brought to hospital in extremis, skilfully using sophisticated methods, drugs and machinery to do so, but fails in his attempt and therefore discontinues treatment, he can be said to have caused the death of the patient.[79]

19.33 Nevertheless, where organs are proposed to be recovered for transplantation or other use is intended for the body,[80] prudence suggests that death should be

---

[75] N 15 above, and addendum, (n 16 above).

[76] N 74 above, 427.

[77] ibid, 429.

[78] See *R v Kitching and Adams* (n 26 above), 175.

[79] N 74 above, 429.

[80] See eg Hayes, GJ, 'Issues of Consent: The Use of the Recently Deceased for Endotracheal Intubation Training' (1994) 5 J Clinical Ethics 211–216. For discussion of a controversial incident in Germany, see Tuffs, A, 'Keeping a Brain-dead Pregnant Woman "Alive"' (1992) 340 *Lancet* 1029–30.

pronounced and certified beforehand. Lord Lane's apparent endorsement of a physician's power to discontinue life support methods on reaching a conscientious assessment that a patient is 'for practical purposes dead'[81] begs a number of legal questions concerning more abstract or speculative purposes,[82] and falls short of legal acceptance of the concept of brain stem death reviewed, for instance, by the Royal College of Physicians and endorsed by the Conference of Medical Royal Colleges.[83] Lord Lane observed that '[i]t is no part of the task of this court to inquire whether the criteria, the Royal Medical College confirmatory tests, are a satisfactory code of practice',[84] but it is doubtful whether courts will permit physicians who establish death for removal of organs for transplantation to apply less rigorous criteria of brain stem death than their profession expects of them.

C. After Death

1. Coroners' Powers

(i) Procedure

19.34 The Coroners Act 1988[85] consolidates the English Coroners Acts 1887 to 1980, but regulations made under the repealed legislation continue in force unless legislation or regulations provide otherwise.[86] A doctor who has attended someone during the last illness must report the cause of death to the local registrar of births and deaths.[87] Although there is no statutory duty to report a death to the coroner, it is usual practice for a doctor to do so in the event of doubt or suspicion. Upon receipt of information that the body of a person is lying within the coroner's district, even though death may have occurred elsewhere,[88] and there is reasonable cause to suspect that the deceased (i) died a violent or unnatural death;[89] (ii) died a sudden death of unknown cause; or (iii) died in prison or in such a place or circumstances as to require an inquest under other legislation,[90] the coroner shall hold an inquest into the death as soon as practicable.[91]

---

[81] N 74 above, 429.
[82] See Hayes (n 80 above).
[83] N 7 above.
[84] See n 74 above, 427.
[85] Stats 1988, ch13.
[86] Interpretation Act 1978, s 17(2)(b).
[87] Births and Deaths Registration Act 1953, s 22(1), and Registration of Births and Deaths Regulations 1987, SI 1987/2088, reg. 40(1)(a), Sch 2, Form 14.
[88] *R v West Yorkshire Coroner, ex p Smith* [1982] 3 All ER 1098 (CA).
[89] See *R v Poplar Coroner, ex p Thomas* [1993] QB 610 (CA).
[90] Coroners Act 1988, s 8(1).
[91] In *Re Hull* (1882) 9 QBD 689 it was held that an interval of five days between receipt of information and the holding of the inquest was too long.

Whether sitting with or without a jury,[92] the inquest shall consider how, when and   **19.35**
where the deceased died. The evidence before the inquest is not limited to what is
admissible at a criminal trial,[93] but is limited to evidence that establishes facts. The
inquest is further limited to finding only proven particulars.[94] The inquest may
identify a person found to have caused death by criminal means, except that a
coroner's inquest cannot present a finding of murder, manslaughter or infanticide,
and accordingly cannot charge a person on inquisition with any of these offences.[95] A verdict should be framed in a way that does not appear to determine
any question of criminal or civil liability on the part of a named person.[96] A finding of a cause of death should be construed narrowly, to refer to the means of death
rather than the broad circumstances that resulted in death.[97]

It is usual for a coroner's inquest to consider results of an examination of the body   **19.36**
of the deceased person conducted by a physician or a forensic pathologist. Where
a coroner has reason to believe that an inquest ought to be held but that, owing to
the destruction of the body by fire or otherwise, or because the body is lying in a
place from which it cannot be recovered, no examination of the body is possible,
the coroner may report the facts to the Secretary of State for the Home
Department.[98] The Home Secretary may then direct a coroner's inquest into the
death if that is considered desirable, and the provisions of the Coroners Act and
additional relevant law shall apply with any necessary modifications.[99]

(ii) Post Mortem Examinations

When informed that a body is lying within the coroner's district and there is rea-   **19.37**
sonable cause to suspect that the person died a sudden death of unknown cause,
the coroner may, if of the opinion that a post mortem examination may prove an
inquest unnecessary, direct a legally qualified medical practitioner to conduct a
post mortem examination of the body and provide the coroner with a written report.[100] The coroner is not authorised to dispense with an inquest, however, when
there is reasonable cause to suspect that the deceased died a violent or unnatural
death, died in prison or in such other circumstances as require an inquest under
other legislation.[101] A coroner may request that examination of a body be

---

[92] Coroners Act 1988, s 8. Procedures for summoning a jury prescribed by this Act and by the
Coroners Rules 1984, SI 1984/552 are mandatory; *R v Merseyside Coroner, ex p Carr* [1993] 4 All
ER 65 (QBD).
[93] See *The Times*, 18 March 1890, Will J in charge to a grand jury.
[94] *R v Huntbach, ex p Lockley* [1944] KB 606.
[95] Coroners Act 1988, s 11(6).
[96] Coroners Rules 1984, SI 1984/552, r 42; see *R v Surrey Coroner, ex p Campbell* [1982] QB 661.
[97] *R. v North Humberside Coroner, ex p Jamieson* [1994] 3 All ER 972 (CA).
[98] Coroners Act 1988, s 15(1).
[99] ibid, s 15(2), (3).
[100] ibid, s 19(1).
[101] ibid, s 19(4).

conducted by a person considered to possess special qualifications for conducting a special examination,[102] and if summoned as a witness at an inquest such person may give evidence of any matter arising out of the examination, and express an opinion as to how the deceased died.[103] In requesting a post mortem or special examination under s 20 of the Coroners Act 1988, the coroner does not require the consent of the deceased person's relatives; their entitlement is to be notified of the fact and of the date and time of the proposed post mortem.[104]

(iii) Medical Witnesses

19.38   At an inquest into death, the coroner may summon as a witness any medical practitioner who appears to have attended at the death or during the last illness of the deceased, or, where there appears to have been no such practitioner, any medical practitioner in actual practice in or near the place where the death occurred. Any medical witness summoned to appear may be asked to express an opinion as to how the deceased died.[105] In the summons for attendance of a medical witness, or at any time after its issue and before the end of the inquest, the coroner may also direct the medical witness to conduct a post mortem examination of the body of the deceased.[106] This does not apply where a person has stated to the coroner on oath a belief that death was caused entirely or in part by the medical practitioner's improper or negligent treatment of the deceased.[107] A medical practitioner who fails to obey a coroner's summons to attend an inquest shall, unless able to show good and sufficient cause for such failure, be liable on summary conviction to a fine not exceeding £1,000.[108] Prosecution can be brought by the coroner or by any two members of the coroner's jury.[109] Scheduled fees are payable to medical witnesses and to those who conduct required post-mortem examinations.[110]

(iv) Retention of Tissue and Organs

19.39   On the removal and retention of tissue and organs following a coroner's post-mortem see: *The Interim Report of the Inquiry into the Management of Care of Children Receiving Complex Heart Surgery at the Bristol Royal Infirmary: Removal and Retention of Human Material* (May 2000) and *Guidelines for the Retention of*

---

[102]   ibid, s 20(1)(b).

[103]   ibid, s 20(2).

[104]   Coroners Rules 1984, r 7; see *R v HM Coroner for Northumberland, ex p Jacobs* (1999) 53 BMLR 21 (CA).

[105]   Coroners Act 1988, s 21(1).

[106]   ibid, s 21(2). An interested party, such as the deceased's spouse, may compel a coroner to order a post mortem examination unless there are good grounds for refusal; see *R v Greater London Coroner, ex p Ridley* [1986] 1 All ER 37 (QBD).

[107]   Criminal Justice Act 1991, s 17(3)(a), Sch 4, Pt 1.

[108]   ibid, s 21(3), as amended.

[109]   Coroners Act 1988, s 21(5).

[110]   ibid, s 24; see Home Office Circulars detailing fees, which are circulated to all local authorities.

Tissues and Organs at Post-Mortem Examination (Royal College of Pathologists) (March 2000). See also, *Interim BMA Guidelines on Retention of Human Tissue at Post-Mortem Examination for the Purposes of Medical Education and Research* (October 2000), The Royal College of Pathologists, *Transitional Guidelines to Facilitate Changes in Procedures for Handling 'Surplus' and Archival Material from Human Biological Samples* (June 2001), and the advice and recommendations for reform of the Chief Medical Officer in *The Removal, Retention and Use of Human Organs and Tissue from Post-Mortem Examination* (Department of Health, 2001). In England see also the role of the Retained Organs Commission, established in 2001.[111]

(v) Exhumation

Under s 23 of the Coroners Act 1988, a coroner may by warrant order the exhumation of the body of a person buried within the coroner's district when this appears necessary for its examination for an inquest or for discharge of any other of the coroner's functions in relation to the body or the death. The same powers exist for the purposes of any criminal proceedings instituted or contemplated in respect of the death of the person whose body is to be exhumed for examination, or of some other person who died in circumstances connected with the death of that person.[112]   **19.40**

2. Legal Status and Medical Uses of Corpses

(i) Legal Status

On a person's death, the corpse does not constitute part of the estate for purposes of testate or intestate succession.[113] Questions therefore arise as to who may lawfully deal with the body. The executor of the estate is usually empowered to direct disposition of the body because the costs of burial, cremation or other lawful disposal are a charge on the estate. English legislation on organ and tissue recovery from cadavers for transplantation and other uses permits legally effective consent to be given for such recovery by 'the person lawfully in possession of the body' except when the deceased person when alive gave consent to posthumous recovery, or had expressed an objection.[114] A surviving spouse or any surviving relative of   **19.41**

---

[111] See the Retained Organs Commission (Establishment and Constitution) Order 2001, SI 2001/743, as amended in SI 2001/1813, and the Retained Organs Commission Regulations 2001, SI 2001/748. In April 2003, the Department of Health collected relevant guidance at *www.doh.gov.uk/tissue*. Further reform recommendations were made in the Isaacs Report (*www.doh.gov.uk/cmo/isaacsreport/index.htm*).

[112] Coroners Act 1988, s 23(1)(b).

[113] See Skegg, PDG, 'Medical Uses of Corpses and the "No Property" Rule' (1992) 32 Med Sci & Law 311–18; Matthews, P, 'Whose Body? People as Property' (1983) 36 CLP 193–239.

[114] Human Tissue Act 1961, s 1(2)(a).

the deceased may also object to recovery,[115] preventing such use by those having charge of the body. It has been held that executors have a right to possession of a corpse, until its burial or other lawful disposition.[116] In 1931, a Canadian appeal court found that a right to possession of a body was held by the surviving spouse or next of kin,[117] whose rights of burial were described as a 'quasi-property' interest.

19.42 For cases concerned with disputes over the disposal of the deceased's remains see: *Holtham v Arnold*[118] (estranged wife as administrator entitled to corpse in order to dispose of it); *Grandison v Nembhard*[119] (executor entitled to corpse to dispose of it and the court would only interfere with his discretion as to where and how it would be disposed if he acted unreasonably); *Fessi v Whitmore*[120] (inappropriate to divide the ashes of dead son between two places where his divorced parents lived separately. The ashes should be scattered near the home of the mother where the family lived, apart from his father who had recently moved); *Buchanan v Milton*[121] (the adoptive family of the deceased who was of Australian aboriginal descent were entitled to arrange cremation and burial in England given his close bonds with the family here including his own daughter).

(ii) Medical and Other Uses

19.43 The Human Tissue Act 1961 and comparable legislation in other jurisdictions addresses recovery of cadaveric materials for therapeutic purposes, meaning transplantation, and for research and medical education. On the removal and retention of tissue and organs following a hospital post mortem under s 2(2) of the Human Tissue Act 1961, see para 19.39, including the role of the Retained Organs Commission. Recovery for other purposes may find legal justification elsewhere. Cosmetic purposes might fall inside or outside therapy, depending on their nature, but, for instance, where 'tissue' includes hair recovery for manufacture of wigs, appears commercial. The legislative reference to 'research'[122] does not appear limited to medical or academic research, so that commercial research and development might be included, but use of human (including fetal) materials for purposes of routine manufacturing processes of pharmaceutical or other products

---

[115] ibid, s 1(2)(b). The Isaacs Report (n 111 above), recommended reform of the 1961 Act to require family members' positive consent.

[116] *Williams v Williams* (1882) 20 Ch D 659; see generally Kennedy and Grubb (n 2 above), 1837–1839.

[117] *Edmonds v Armstrong Funeral Home Ltd* [1931] 1 DLR 676 (Alberta CA); see also *Burney v Children's Hospital in Boston* (1897) 47 NE 401 (Sup Ct Mass).

[118] (1986) 2 BMLR 123 (Hoffmann J).

[119] (1989) 4 BMLR 140 (Vinelott J).

[120] [1999] 1 FLR 767 (Ch D).

[121] (1999) 53 BMLR 176 (Hale J).

[122] Human Tissue Act 1961, s 1(1).

would appear to fall outside the legislation. On the common law principle that whatever is not prohibited is permitted, and in the absence of generally recognised property rights in dead bodies,[123] recovery of materials appears lawful provided that it does not offend the law on public decency[124] or against causing indignity to a dead body.[125] Medical removal of materials by routine surgical or other medical procedures that do not cause indignity when conducted with consent would appear not to cause indignity even when undertaken in the absence of consent.

The Anatomy Act 1984[126] provides for removal of cadaveric materials for examination, and for use of a body in 'the course of teaching or studying or researching'.[127] The Act provides a scheme for retention of body materials through licensing by the Secretary of State, licensees being entitled to use the body and its tissues for instruction, and to retain them. Licensee's interests in possession may be described as proprietary, although whether courts would, for instance, uphold the so-called 'no property' rule in dead bodies, deliberately reject or modify the rule, or deny that it ever possessed the influence attributed to it, has been unclear.[128] In *Dobson v North Tyneside HA*[129] the Court of Appeal dismissed a claim by next of kin to a property interest in brain tissue of a deceased person left following an autopsy, which the next of kin wanted for development of forensic evidence in litigation. In *R v Kelly*,[130] however, it was held that anatomical specimens were 'property' within s 4 of the Theft Act 1968[131] and capable of being stolen. The court approved *Doodeward v Spence*[132] and *Dobson v North Tyneside HA*.[133] The defendant, an artist, obtained human body parts held by the Royal College of Surgeons in London as anatomical specimens. The specimens were all preserved, fixed or dissected. The defendant was convicted of theft of the body parts. The Court of Appeal upheld his conviction:

19.44

(i) however questionable the historical origins of the rule, at common law a corpse or part of a corpse was not property;

(ii) there was an exception where the corpse (or part) acquired different attributes by virtue of the application of skill, such as dissection or preservation techniques for exhibition or teaching purposes;

---

[123] See Skegg (n 113 above), and *Dobson v North Tyneside HA* [1996] 4 All ER 474 (CA).
[124] In *R v Gibson* [1991] 1 All ER 439 (CA), the display of freeze-dried aborted foetuses as earrings was held convictable as outraging public decency.
[125] See *Foster v Dodd* (1866), LR 1 QB 475, 485, *per* Blackburn J.
[126] Stats 1984, ch14.
[127] ibid, s 3(3).
[128] See Skegg (n 113 above).
[129] *Dobson v North Tyneside HA* (n 123 above).
[130] [1998] 3 All ER 741 (CA).
[131] 16 & 17 Eliz 2, ch 60.
[132] (1908) 6 CLR 406 (HC Aus), suggesting that in special circumstances a corpse may become the subject of property.
[133] N 123 above, 479 *per* Peter Gibson LJ.

(iii) it may be that in the future the courts will hold that human body parts are capable of being property even without the acquisition of different attributes, if they have a use or significance beyond their mere existence, for example if they are intended for use in an organ transplant operation or as an exhibit in a trial;

(iv) on the facts, the body parts fell within the exception and were, at all relevant times, in the possession of the Royal College of Surgeons.[134]

19.45 In the Californian *Moore* case,[135] involving the status of tissue from a living person, the court rejected property-based claims on grounds both of history and of modern benefits of third parties being able to use such tissues for therapeutic and other purposes unrestrained by the need to obtain consent from the human source. This approach to tissues, from both living and cadaveric sources, does not preclude comparably instrumental reasoning leading to recognition of property interests.[136] The court specifically left open this possibility, observing that 'we do not purport to hold that excised cells can never be property for any purposes whatsoever'.[137]

19.46 Management of tissues from the dead is accordingly at an historic point of transition from the sacred to, if not the profane, at least the commercial. Proprietary claims in products from human tissues and tissues themselves are likely to grow under the impact of developments in biotechnology and advancing understanding of human genetics. Control and protection of human tissue banks that not only preserve cadaveric tissues but 'immortalise' them will become a growing legal concern. Patented cell lines developed from human, including cadaveric, tissues have immense commercial potential. The value of the cell line in the *Moore* case was assessed to be $3 billion in 1990. Legal regimes will influence the direction of commercial, and social, reactions to possibilities opened up by biotechnology and new knowledge of the human genome, and those possibilities and new realities will influence developments and proposals for development in the law.[138]

---

[134] For further discussion see Grubb, A, (1998) 6 Med L Rev 247 (Commentary).

[135] *Moore v Regents of the University of California* (1990) 793 P 2d 479 (Sup Ct Cal), certiorari denied (1991) 111 S Ct 1388 (US Sup Ct).

[136] Dickens, BM, 'Living Tissue and Organ Donors and Property Law: More on *Moore*' (1992) 8 J of Contemporary Health Law and Policy 73–93.

[137] N 135 above, 493.

[138] See recommendations of the Nuffield Council on Bioethics, in *Human Tissue: Ethical and Legal Issues* (London, 1995), and Ch 16 above.

INDEX